14
GREAT
PLAYS

Heinemann/Octopus

This collection first published
in 1977 jointly by

William Heinemann Limited
15–16 Queen Street
London W1

Martin Secker & Warburg Limited
14 Carlisle Street
London W1

and

Octopus Books Limited
59 Grosvenor Street
London W1

ISBN 0 905712 20 X

Printed in Great Britain by
Jarrold & Sons Limited, Norwich

CONTENTS

A
DOLL'S
HOUSE
HENRIK
IBSEN

A DOLL'S HOUSE

First published in Great Britain in 1906
by William Heinemann Limited

A DOLL'S HOUSE

(1879)

Translated by William Archer

CHARACTERS

TORVALD HELMER
NORA (*his Wife*)
DOCTOR RANK
MRS LINDEN (1)
NILS KROGSTAD
THE HELMERS' THREE CHILDREN
ANNA (2) (*their Nurse*)
A MAID-SERVANT (ELLEN)
A PORTER

The action passes in Helmer's house (a flat) in Christiania.

(1) In the original 'Fru Linde'.
(2) In the original 'Anne-Marie'.

ACT ONE

A room, comfortably and tastefully, but not expensively, furnished. In the back, on the right, a door leads to the hall; on the left another door leads to HELMER's study. Between the two doors a pianoforte. In the middle of the left wall a door, and nearer the front a window. Near the window a round table with arm-chairs and a small sofa. In the right wall, somewhat to the back, a door, and against the same wall, further forward, a porcelain stove; in front of it a couple of arm-chairs and a rocking-chair. Between the stove and the side-door a small table. Engravings on the walls. A what-not with china and bric-à-brac. A small bookcase filled with handsomely bound books. Carpet. A fire in the stove. It is a winter day.

> *A bell rings in the hall outside. Presently the outer door of the flat is heard to open. Then* NORA *enters, humming gaily. She is in outdoor dress, and carries several parcels, which she lays on the right-hand table. She leaves the door into the hall open, and a* PORTER *is seen outside, carrying a Christmas-tree and a basket, which he gives to the* MAID-SERVANT *who has opened the door.*

NORA: Hide the Christmas-tree carefully, Ellen; the children must on no account see it before this evening, when it's lighted up. [*To the* PORTER, *taking out her purse.*] How much?
PORTER: Fifty öre.[1]
NORA: There is a crown. No, keep the change.

> *The* PORTER *thanks her and goes.* NORA *shuts the door. She continues smiling in quiet glee as she takes off her outdoor things. Taking from her pocket a bag of macaroons, she eats one or two. Then she goes on tip-toe to her husband's door and listens.*

Yes; he is at home. [*She begins humming again, crossing to the table on the right.*]
HELMER [*in his room*]: Is that my lark twittering there?
NORA [*busy opening some of her parcels*]: Yes, it is.
HELMER: Is it the squirrel frisking around?
NORA: Yes!
HELMER: When did the squirrel get home?
NORA: Just this minute. [*Hides the bag of macaroons in her pocket and wipes her mouth.*] Come here, Torvald, and see what I've been buying.
HELMER: Don't interrupt me. [*A little later he opens the door and looks in, pen in hand.*] Buying, did you say? What! All that? Has my little spend-thrift been making the money fly again?

---

[1] There are 100 öre in a Norwegian krone or crown.

NORA: Why, Torvald, surely we can afford to launch out a little now. It's the first Christmas we haven't had to pinch.

HELMER: Come come; we can't afford to squander money.

NORA: Oh yes, Torvald, do let us squander a little now—just the least little bit! You know you'll soon be earning heaps of money.

HELMER: Yes, from New Year's Day. But there's a whole quarter before my first salary is due.

NORA: Never mind; we can borrow in the meantime.

HELMER: Nora! [*He goes up to her and takes her playfully by the ear.*] Still my little featherbrain! Supposing I borrowed a thousand crowns to-day, and you made ducks and drakes of them during Christmas week, and then on New Year's Eve a tile blew off the roof and knocked my brains out—

NORA [*laying her hand on his mouth*]: Hush! How can you talk so horridly?

HELMER: But supposing it were to happen—what then?

NORA: If anything so dreadful happened, it would be all the same to me whether I was in debt or not.

HELMER: But what about the creditors?

NORA: They! Who cares for them? They're only strangers.

HELMER: Nora, Nora! What a woman you are! But seriously, Nora, you know my principles on these points. No debts! No borrowing! Home life ceases to be free and beautiful as soon as it is founded on borrowing and debt. We two have held out bravely till now, and we are not going to give in at the last.

NORA [*going to the fireplace*]: Very well—as you please, Torvald.

HELMER [*following her*]: Come come; my little lark mustn't droop her wings like that. What? Is my squirrel in the sulks? [*Takes out his purse.*] Nora, what do you think I have here?

NORA [*turning round quickly*]: Money!

HELMER: There! [*Gives her some notes.*] Of course I know all sorts of things are wanted at Christmas.

NORA: [*counting*]: Ten, twenty, thirty, forty. Oh, thank you, thank you, Torvald! This will go a long way.

HELMER: I should hope so.

NORA: Yes, indeed; a long way! But come here, and let me show you all I've been buying. And so cheap! Look, here's a new suit for Ivar, and a little sword. Here are a horse and a trumpet for Bob. And here are a doll and a cradle for Emmy. They're only common; but they're good enough for her to pull to pieces. And dress-stuffs and kerchiefs for the servants. I ought to have got something better for old Anna.

HELMER: And what's in that other parcel?

NORA [*crying out*]: No, Torvald, you're not to see that until this evening!

HELMER: Oh! Ah! But now tell me, you little spend-thrift, have you thought of anything for yourself?

NORA: For myself! Oh, I don't want anything.

HELMER: Nonsense! Just tell me something sensible you would like to have.

NORA: No, really I don't know of anything— Well, listen, Torvald—

HELMER: Well?

NORA [*playing with his coat-buttons, without looking him in the face*]: If you really want to give me something, you might, you know—you might—

HELMER: Well? Out with it!

NORA [*quickly*]: You might give me money, Torvald. Only just what you think you can spare; then I can buy something with it later on.

HELMER: But, Nora—

NORA: Oh, please do, dear Torvald, please do! I should hang the money in lovely gilt paper on the Christmas-tree. Wouldn't that be fun?

HELMER: What do they call the birds that are always making the money fly?

NORA: Yes, I know—spendthrifts,[1] of course. But please do as I ask you, Torvald. Then I shall have time to think what I want most. Isn't that very sensible, now?

HELMER [*smiling*]: Certainly; that is to say, if you really kept the money I gave you, and really spent it on something for yourself. But it all goes in housekeeping, and for all manner of useless things, and then I have to pay up again.

NORA: But, Torvald—

HELMER: Can you deny it, Nora dear? [*He puts his arm round her.*] It's a sweet little lark, but it gets through a lot of money. No one would believe how much it costs a man to keep such a little bird as you.

NORA: For shame! How can you say so? Why, I save as much as ever I can.

HELMER [*laughing*]: Very true—as much as you can—but that's precisely nothing.

NORA [*hums and smiles with covert glee*]: H'm! If you only knew, Torvald, what expenses we larks and squirrels have.

HELMER: You're a strange little being! Just like your father—always on the look-out for all the money you can lay your hands on; but the moment you have it, it seems to slip through your fingers; you never know what becomes of it. Well, one must take you as you are. It's in the blood. Yes, Nora, that sort of thing is hereditary.

NORA: I wish I had inherited many of papa's qualities.

HELMER: And I don't wish you anything but just what you are—my own, sweet little song-bird. But I say—it strikes me you look so—so—what shall I call it?—so suspicious to-day—

NORA: Do I?

HELMER: You do, indeed. Look me full in the face.

NORA [*looking at him*]: Well?

HELMER [*threatening with his finger*]: Hasn't the little sweet-tooth been playing pranks to-day?

NORA: No; how can you think such a thing!

HELMER: Didn't she just look in at the confectioner's?

NORA: No, Torvald; really—

HELMER: Not to sip a little jelly?

NORA: No; certainly not.

HELMER: Hasn't she even nibbled a macaroon or two?

NORA: No, Torvald, indeed, indeed!

HELMER: Well, well, well; of course I'm only joking.

NORA [*goes to the table on the right*]: I shouldn't think of doing what you disapprove of.

HELMER: No, I'm sure of that; and, besides, you've given me your word—[*Going towards her.*] Well, keep your little Christmas secrets to yourself, Nora darling. The Christmas-tree will bring them all to light, I daresay.

NORA: Have you remembered to invite Doctor Rank?

HELMER: No. But it's not necessary; he'll come as a matter of course. Besides, I

---

[1] 'Spillefugl', literally 'playbird', means a gambler.

shall ask him when he looks in to-day. I've ordered some capital wine. Nora, you can't think how I look forward to this evening.

NORA: And I too. How the children will enjoy themselves, Torvald!

HELMER: Ah, it's glorious to feel that one has an assured position and ample means. Isn't it delightful to think of?

NORA: Oh, it's wonderful!

HELMER: Do you remember last Christmas? For three whole weeks beforehand you shut yourself up every evening till long past midnight to make flowers for the Christmas-tree, and all sorts of other marvels that were to have astonished us. I was never so bored in my life.

NORA: I didn't bore myself at all.

HELMER [*smiling*]: But it came to little enough in the end, Nora.

NORA: Oh, are you going to tease me about that again? How could I help that cat getting in and pulling it all to pieces?

HELMER: To be sure you couldn't, my poor little Nora. You did your best to give us all pleasure, and that's the main point. But, all the same, it's a good thing the hard times are over.

NORA: Oh, isn't it wonderful?

HELMER: Now I needn't sit here boring myself all alone; and you needn't tire your blessed eyes and your delicate little fingers—

NORA [*clapping her hands*]: No, I needn't, need I, Torvald? Oh, how wonderful it is to think of? [*Takes his arm.*] And now I'll tell you how I think we ought to manage, Torvald. As soon as Christmas is over—

The hall-door bell rings.

Oh, there's a ring! [*Arranging the room.*] That's somebody come to call. How tiresome!

HELMER: I'm 'not at home' to callers; remember that.

ELLEN [*in the doorway*]: A lady to see you, ma'am.

NORA: Show her in.

ELLEN [*to* HELMER]: And the doctor has just come, sir.

HELMER: Has he gone into my study?

ELLEN: Yes, sir.

HELMER *goes into his study.* ELLEN *ushers in* MRS LINDEN, *in travelling costume, and goes out, closing the door.*

MRS LINDEN [*embarrassed and hesitating*]: How do you do, Nora?

NORA [*doubtfully*]: How do you do?

MRS LINDEN: I see you don't recognise me.

NORA: No, I don't think—oh yes!—I believe— [*Suddenly brightening.*] What, Christina! Is it really you?

MRS LINDEN: Yes; really I!

NORA: Christina! And to think I didn't know you! But how could I— [*More softly.*] How changed you are, Christina!

MRS LINDEN: Yes, no doubt. In nine or ten years—

NORA: Is it really so long since we met? Yes, so it is. Oh, the last eight years have been a happy time, I can tell you. And now you have come to town? All that long journey in mid-winter! How brave of you!

MRS LINDEN: I arrived by this morning's steamer.

NORA: To have a merry Christmas, of course. Oh, how delightful! Yes, we will have a merry Christmas. Do take your things off. Aren't you frozen? [*Helping her.*] There; now we'll sit cosily by the fire. No, you take the arm-chair; I shall sit in this rocking-chair. [*Seizes her hands.*] Yes, now I can see the dear old face again. It was only at the first glance— But you're a little paler, Christina—and perhaps a little thinner.

MRS LINDEN: And much, much older, Nora.

NORA: Yes, perhaps a little older—not much—ever so little. [*She suddenly checks herself; seriously.*] Oh, what a thoughtless wretch I am! Here I sit chattering on, and— Dear, dear Christina, can you forgive me!

MRS LINDEN: What do you mean, Nora?

NORA [*softly*]: Poor Christina! I forgot: you are a widow.

MRS LINDEN: Yes; my husband died three years ago.

NORA: I know, I know; I saw it in the papers. Oh, believe me, Christina, I did mean to write to you; but I kept putting it off, and something always came in the way.

MRS LINDEN: I can quite understand that, Nora dear.

NORA: No, Christina; it was horrid of me. Oh, you poor darling! how much you must have gone through!—And he left you nothing?

MRS LINDEN: Nothing.

NORA: And no children?

MRS LINDEN: None.

NORA: Nothing, nothing at all?

MRS LINDEN: Not even a sorrow or a longing to dwell upon.

NORA [*looking at her incredulously*]: My dear Christina, how is that possible?

MRS LINDEN [*smiling sadly and stroking her hair*]: Oh, it happens so sometimes, Nora.

NORA: So utterly alone! How dreadful that must be! I have three of the loveliest children. I can't show them to you just now; they're out with their nurse. But now you must tell me everything.

MRS LINDEN: No, no; I want you to tell me—

NORA: No, you must begin; I won't be egotistical to-day. To-day I'll think only of you. Oh! but I must tell you one thing—perhaps you've heard of our great stroke of fortune?

MRS LINDEN: No. What is it?

NORA: Only think! my husband has been made manager of the Joint Stock Bank.

MRS LINDEN: Your husband! Oh, how fortunate!

NORA: Yes; isn't it? A lawyer's position is so uncertain, you see, especially when he won't touch any business that's the least bit—shady, as of course Torvald never would; and there I quite agree with him. Oh! you can imagine how glad we are. He is to enter on his new position at the New Year, and then he'll have a large salary, and percentages. In future we shall be able to live quite differently—just as we please, in fact. Oh, Christina, I feel so lighthearted and happy! It's delightful to have lots of money, and no need to worry about things, isn't it?

MRS LINDEN: Yes; at any rate it must be delightful to have what you need.

NORA: No, not only what you need, but heaps of money—*heaps!*

MRS LINDEN [*smiling*]: Nora, Nora, haven't you learnt reason yet? In our schooldays you were a shocking little spendthrift.

NORA [*quietly smiling*]: Yes; that's what Torvald says I am still. [*Holding up her forefinger*.] But 'Nora, Nora' is not so silly as you all think. Oh! I haven't had the chance to be much of a spendthrift. We have both had to work.

MRS LINDEN: You too?

NORA: Yes, light fancy work: crochet, and embroidery, and things of that sort; [*Carelessly*] and other work too. You know, of course, that Torvald left the Government service when we were married. He had little chance of promotion, and of course he required to make more money. But in the first year after our marriage he overworked himself terribly. He had to undertake all sorts of extra work, you know, and to slave early and late. He couldn't stand it, and fell dangerously ill. Then the doctors declared he must go to the South.

MRS LINDEN: You spent a whole year in Italy, didn't you?

NORA: Yes, we did. It wasn't easy to manage, I can tell you. It was just after Ivar's birth. But of course we had to go. Oh, it was a wonderful, delicious journey! And it saved Torvald's life. But it cost a frightful lot of money, Christina.

MRS LINDEN: So I should think.

NORA: Twelve hundred dollars! Four thousand eight hundred crowns![1] Isn't that a lot of money?

MRS LINDEN: How lucky you had the money to spend!

NORA: We got it from father, you must know.

MRS LINDEN: Ah, I see. He died just about that time, didn't he?

NORA: Yes, Christina, just then. And only think! I couldn't go and nurse him! I was expecting little Ivar's birth daily; and then I had my poor sick Torvald to attend to. Dear, kind old father! I never saw him again, Christina. Oh! that's the hardest thing I have had to bear since my marriage.

MRS LINDEN: I know how fond you were of him. But then you went to Italy?

NORA: Yes; you see, we had the money, and the doctors said we must lose no time. We started a month later.

MRS LINDEN: And your husband came back completely cured.

NORA: Sound as a bell.

MRS LINDEN: But—the doctor?

NORA: What do you mean?

MRS LINDEN: I thought as I came in your servant announced the doctor—

NORA: Oh, yes; Doctor Rank. But he doesn't come professionally. He is our best friend, and never lets a day pass without looking in. No, Torvald hasn't had an hour's illness since that time. And the children are so healthy and well, and so am I. [*Jumps up and claps her hands*.] Oh, Christina, Christina, what a wonderful thing it is to live and to be happy!—Oh, but it's really too horrid of me! Here am I talking about nothing but my own concerns. [*Seats herself upon a footstool close to* CHRISTINA. *and lays her arms on her friend's lap*.] Oh, don't be angry with me! Now tell me, is it really true that you didn't love your husband? What made you marry him, then?

MRS LINDEN: My mother was still alive, you see, bedridden and helpless; and then I had my two younger brothers to think of. I didn't think it would be right for me to refuse him.

NORA: Perhaps it wouldn't have been. I suppose he was rich then?

MRS LINDEN: Very well off, I believe. But his business was uncertain. It fell to

---

[1] The dollar was the old unit of currency in Norway. The crown was substituted for it shortly before the date of this play.

pieces at his death, and there was nothing left.

NORA: And then—?

MRS LINDEN: Then I had to fight my way by keeping a shop, a little school, anything I could turn my hand to. The last three years have been one long struggle for me. But now it is over, Nora. My poor mother no longer needs me; she is at rest. And the boys are in business, and can look after themselves.

NORA: How free your life must feel!

MRS LINDEN: No, Nora; only inexpressibly empty. No one to live for! [*Stands up restlessly.*] That's why I could not bear to stay any longer in that out-of-the-way corner. Here it must be easier to find something to take one up–to occupy one's thoughts. If I could only get some settled employment–some office work.

NORA: But, Christina, that's such drudgery, and you look worn out already. It would be ever so much better for you to go to some watering-place and rest.

MRS LINDEN [*going to the window*]: I have no father to give me the money, Nora.

NORA [*rising*]: Oh, don't be vexed with me.

MRS LINDEN [*going to her*]: My dear Nora, don't you be vexed with me. The worst of a position like mine is that it makes one so bitter. You have no one to work for, yet you have to be always on the strain. You must live; and so you become selfish. When I heard of the happy change in your fortunes–can you believe it?–I was glad for my own sake more than for yours.

NORA: How do you mean? Ah, I see! You think Torvald can perhaps do something for you.

MRS LINDEN: Yes; I thought so.

NORA: And so he shall, Christina. Just you leave it all to me. I shall lead up to it beautifully!–I shall think of some delightful plan put him in a good humour! Oh, I should so love to help you.

MRS LINDEN: How good of you, Nora, to stand by me so warmly! Doubly good in you, who know so little of the troubles and burdens of life.

NORA: I? I know so little of—?

MRS LINDEN [*smiling*]: Oh, well–a little fancy-work, and so forth.–You're a child, Nora.

NORA [*tosses her head and paces the room*]: Oh, come, you mustn't be so patronising!

MRS LINDEN: No?

NORA: You're like the rest. You all think I'm fit for nothing really serious—

MRS LINDEN: Well, well—

NORA: You think I've had no troubles in this weary world.

MRS LINDEN: My dear Nora, you've just told me all your troubles.

NORA: Pooh–those trifles! [*Softly.*] I haven't told you the great thing.

MRS LINDEN: The great thing? What do you mean?

NORA: I know you look down upon me, Christina; but you have no right to. You are proud of having worked so hard and so long for your mother.

MRS LINDEN: I am sure I don't look down upon any one; but it's true I am both proud and glad when I remember that I was able to keep my mother's last days free from care.

NORA: And you're proud to think of what you have done for your brothers, too.

MRS LINDEN: Have I not the right to be?

NORA: Yes indeed. But now let me tell you, Christina–I, too, have something to be proud and glad of.

MRS LINDEN: I don't doubt it. But what do you mean?

NORA: Hush! Not so loud. Only think, if Torvald were to hear! He mustn't—not for worlds! No one must know about it, Christina—no one but you.

MRS LINDEN: Why, what can it be?

NORA: Come over here. [*Draws her down beside her on the sofa.*] Yes, Christina—I, too, have something to be proud and glad of. I saved Torvald's life.

MRS LINDEN: Saved his life? How?

NORA: I told you about our going to Italy. Torvald would have died but for that.

MRS LINDEN: Well—and your father gave you the money.

NORA [*smiling*]: Yes, so Torvald and every one believes; but—

MRS LINDEN: But—?

NORA: Papa didn't give us one penny. It was *I* that found the money.

MRS LINDEN: You? All that money?

NORA: Twelve hundred dollars. Four thousand eight hundred crowns. What do you say to that?

MRS LINDEN: My dear Nora, how did you manage it? Did you win it in the lottery?

NORA [*contemptuously*]: In the lottery? Pooh! Any one could have done *that*!

MRS LINDEN: Then wherever did you get it from?

NORA [*hums and smiles mysteriously*]: H'm; tra-la-la-la!

MRS LINDEN: Of course you couldn't borrow it.

NORA: No? Why not?

MRS LINDEN: Why, a wife can't borrow without her husband's consent.

NORA [*tossing her head*]: Oh! when the wife has some idea of business, and knows how to set about things—

MRS LINDEN: But, Nora, I don't understand—

NORA: Well, you needn't. I never said I borrowed the money. There are many ways I may have got it. [*Throws herself back on the sofa.*] I may have got it from some admirer. When one is so—attractive as I am—

MRS LINDEN: You're too silly, Nora.

NORA: Now I'm sure you're dying of curiosity, Christina—

MRS LINDEN: Listen to me, Nora dear: haven't you been a little rash?

NORA [*sitting upright again*]: Is it rash to save one's husband's life?

MRS LINDEN: I think it was rash of you, without his knowledge—

NORA: But it would have been fatal for him to know! Can't you understand that? He wasn't even to suspect how ill he was. The doctors came to me privately and told me his life was in danger—that nothing could save him but a winter in the south. Do you think I didn't try diplomacy first? I told him how I longed to have a trip abroad, like other young wives; I wept and prayed; I said he ought to think of my condition, and not to thwart me; and then I hinted that he could borrow the money. But then, Christina, he got almost angry. He said I was frivolous, and that it was his duty as a husband not to yield to my whims and fancies—so he called them. Very well, thought I, but saved you must be; and then I found the way to do it.

MRS LINDEN: And did your husband never learn from your father that the money was not from him?

NORA: No; never. Papa died at that very time. I meant to have told him all about it, and begged him to say nothing. But he was so ill—unhappily, it wasn't necessary.

MRS LINDEN: And you have never confessed to your husband?

NORA: Good heavens! What can you be thinking of? Tell him, when he has such a loathing of debt! And besides—how painful and humiliating it would be for Torvald, with his manly self-respect, to know that he owed anything to me! It would utterly upset the relation between us; our beautiful, happy home would never again be what it is.

MRS LINDEN: Will you never tell him?

NORA [*thoughtfully, half-smiling*]: Yes, some time perhaps—many, many years hence, when I'm—not so pretty. You mustn't laugh at me! Of course I mean when Torvald is not so much in love with me as he is now; when it doesn't amuse him any longer to see me dancing about, and dressing up and acting. Then it might be well to have something in reserve. [*Breaking off.*] Nonsense! nonsense! That time will never come. Now, what do you say to my grand secret, Christina? Am I fit for nothing now? You may believe it has cost me a lot of anxiety. It has been no joke to meet my engagements punctually. You must know, Christina, that in business there are things called instalments, and quarterly interest, that are terribly hard to provide for. So I've had to pinch a little here and there, wherever I could. I couldn't save much out of the housekeeping, for of course Torvald had to live well. And I couldn't let the children go about badly dressed; all I got for them, I spent on them, the blessed darlings!

MRS LINDEN: Poor Nora! So it had to come out of your own pocket-money.

NORA: Yes, of course. After all, the whole thing was my doing. When Torvald gave me money for clothes, and so on, I never spent more than half of it; I always bought the simplest and cheapest things. It's a mercy that everything suits me so well—Torvald never had any suspicions. But it was often very hard, Christina dear. For it's nice to be beautifully dressed—now, isn't it?

MRS LINDEN: Indeed it is.

NORA: Well, and besides that, I made money in other ways. Last winter I was so lucky—I got a heap of copying to do. I shut myself up every evening and wrote far into the night. Oh, sometimes I was so tired, so tired. And yet it was splendid to work in that way and earn money. I almost felt as if I was a man.

MRS LINDEN: Then how much have you been able to pay off?

NORA: Well, I can't precisely say. It's difficult to keep that sort of business clear. I only know that I've paid everything I could scrape together. Sometimes I really didn't know where to turn. [*Smiles.*] Then I used to sit here and pretend that a rich old gentleman was in love with me—

MRS LINDEN: What! What gentleman?

NORA: Oh, nobody!—that he was dead now, and that when his will was opened, there stood in large letters: 'Pay over at once everything of which I die possessed to that charming person, Mrs Nora Helmer.'

MRS LINDEN: But, my dear Nora—what gentleman do you mean?

NORA: Oh dear, can't you understand? There wasn't any old gentleman: it was only what I used to dream and dream when I was at my wits' end for money. But it doesn't matter now—the tiresome old creature may stay where he is for me. I care nothing for him or his will; for now my troubles are over. [*Springing up.*] Oh, Christina, how glorious it is to think of! Free from all anxiety! Free, quite free. To be able to play and romp about with the children; to have things tasteful and pretty in the house, exactly as Torvald likes it! And then the spring will soon be here, with the great blue sky. Perhaps then we shall have a little holiday. Perhaps I shall see the sea again. Oh, what a wonderful thing it is to live and to be happy!

The hall-door bell rings.

MRS LINDEN [*rising*]: There's a ring. Perhaps I had better go.

NORA: No; do stay. No one will come here. It's sure to be some one for Torvald.

ELLEN [*in the doorway*]: If you please, ma'am, there's a gentleman to speak to Mr Helmer.

NORA: Who is the gentleman?

KROGSTAD [*in the doorway*]: It is I, Mrs Helmer.

MRS LINDEN *starts and turns away to the window.*

NORA [*goes a step towards him, anxiously, speaking low*]: You? What is it? What do you want with my husband?

KROGSTAD: Bank business—in a way. I hold a small post in the Joint Stock Bank, and your husband is to be our new chief, I hear.

NORA: Then it is—?

KROGSTAD: Only tiresome business, Mrs Helmer; nothing more.

NORA: Then will you please go to his study.

KROGSTAD *goes. She bows indifferently while she closes the door into the hall. Then she goes to the stove and looks to the fire.*

MRS LINDEN: Nora—who was that man?

NORA: A Mr Krogstad—a lawyer.

MRS LINDEN: Then it was really he?

NORA: Do you know him?

MRS LINDEN: I used to know him—many years ago. He was in a lawyer's office in our town.

NORA: Yes, so he was.

MRS LINDEN: How he has changed!

NORA: I believe his marriage was unhappy.

MRS LINDEN: And he is a widower now?

NORA: With a lot of children. There! Now it will burn up. [*She closes the stove, and pushes the rocking-chair a little aside.*]

MRS LINDEN: His business is not of the most creditable, they say?

NORA: Isn't it? I daresay not. I don't know. But don't let us think of business—it's so tiresome.

DR RANK *comes out of* HELMER'S *room.*

RANK [*still in the doorway*]: No, no; I'm in your way. I shall go and have a chat with your wife. [*Shuts the door and sees* MRS LINDEN.] Oh, I beg your pardon. I'm in the way here too.

NORA: No, not in the least. [*Introduces them.*] Doctor Rank—Mrs Linden.

RANK: Oh, indeed; I've often heard Mrs Linden's name; I think I passed you on the stairs as I came up.

MRS LINDEN: Yes; I go so very slowly. Stairs try me so much.

RANK: Ah—you are not very strong?

MRS LINDEN: Only overworked.

RANK: Nothing more? Then no doubt you've come to find rest in a round of dissipation?

MRS LINDEN: I have come to look for employment.

RANK: Is that an approved remedy for overwork?

MRS LINDEN: One must live, Doctor Rank.

RANK: Yes, that seems to be the general opinion.

NORA: Come, Doctor Rank–you want to live yourself.

RANK: To be sure I do. However wretched I may be, I want to drag on as long as possible. All my patients, too, have the same mania. And it's the same with people whose complaint is moral. At this very moment Helmer is talking to just such a moral incurable—

MRS LINDEN [*softly*]: Ah!

NORA: Whom do you mean?

RANK: Oh, a fellow named Krogstad, a man you know nothing about–corrupt to the very core of his character. But even he began by announcing, as a matter of vast importance, that he must live.

NORA: Indeed? And what did he want with Torvald?

RANK: I haven't an idea; I only gathered that it was some bank business.

NORA: I didn't know that Krog–that this Mr Krogstad had anything to do with the Bank?

RANK: Yes. He has got some sort of place there. [*To* MRS LINDEN.] I don't know whether, in your part of the country, you have people who go grubbing and sniffing around in search of moral rottenness–and then, when they have found a 'case', don't rest till they have got their man into some good position, where they can keep a watch upon him. Men with a clean bill of health they leave out in the cold.

MRS LINDEN: Well, I suppose the–delicate characters require most care.

RANK [*shrugs his shoulders*]: There we have it! It's that notion that makes society a hospital.

NORA, *deep in her own thoughts, breaks into half-stifled laughter and claps her hands.*

Why do you laugh at that? Have you any idea what 'society' is?

NORA: What do I care for your tiresome society? I was laughing at something else–something excessively amusing. Tell me, Doctor Rank, are all the employees at the Bank dependent on Torvald now?

RANK: Is that what strikes you as excessively amusing?

NORA [*smiles and hums*]: Never mind, never mind! [*Walks about the room.*] Yes, it is funny to think that we–that Torvald has such power over so many people. [*Takes the bag from her pocket.*] Doctor Rank, will you have a macaroon?

RANK: What!–macaroons! I thought they were contraband here.

NORA: Yes; but Christina brought me these.

MRS LINDEN: What! I—?

NORA: Oh, well! Don't be frightened. You couldn't possibly know that Torvald had forbidden them. The fact is, he's afraid of me spoiling my teeth. But, oh bother, just for once!–That's for you, Doctor Rank! [*Puts a macaroon into his mouth.*] And you too, Christina. And I'll have one while we're about it–only a tiny one, or at most two. [*Walks about again.*] Oh dear, I am happy! There's only one thing in the world I really want.

RANK: Well; what's that?

NORA: There's something I should so like to say–in Torvald's hearing.

RANK: Then why don't you say it?

NORA: Because I daren't, it's so ugly.

MRS LINDEN: Ugly?

RANK: In that case you'd better not. But to us you might— What is it you would so like to say in Helmer's hearing?

NORA: I should so love to say 'Damn it all!'*

* 'Död og pine', literally 'death and torture'; but by usage a comparatively mild oath.

RANK: Are you out of your mind?

MRS LINDEN: Good gracious, Nora—!

RANK: Say it–there he is!

NORA [*hides the macaroons*]: Hush–sh–sh

HELMER *comes out of his room, hat in hand, with his overcoat on his arm.*

NORA [*going to him*]: Well, Torvald dear, have you got rid of him?

HELMER: Yes; he has just gone.

NORA: Let me introduce you–this is Christina, who has come to town—

HELMER: Christina? Pardon me, I don't know—

NORA: Mrs Linden, Torvald dear–Christina Linden.

HELMER [*to* MRS LINDEN]: Indeed! A school-friend of my wife's, no doubt?

MRS LINDEN: Yes; we knew each other as girls.

NORA: And only think! she has taken this long journey on purpose to speak to you.

HELMER: To speak to me!

MRS LINDEN: Well, not quite—

NORA: You see, Christina is tremendously clever at office-work, and she's so anxious to work under a first-rate man of business in order to learn still more—

HELMER [*to* MRS LINDEN]: Very sensible indeed.

NORA: And when she heard you were appointed manager–it was telegraphed, you know–she started off at once, and— Torvald, dear, for my sake, you must do something for Christina. Now can't you?

HELMER: It's not impossible. I presume Mrs Linden is a widow?

MRS LINDEN: Yes.

HELMER: And you have already had some experience of business?

MRS LINDEN: A good deal.

HELMER: Well, then, it's very likely I may be able to find a place for you.

NORA [*clapping her hands*]: There now! There now!

HELMER: You have come at a fortunate moment, Mrs Linden.

MRS LINDEN: Oh, how can I thank you—?

HELMER [*smiling*]: There is no occasion. [*Puts on his overcoat.*] But for the present you must excuse me—

RANK: Wait; I am going with you. [*Fetches his fur coat from the hall and warms it at the fire.*]

NORA: Don't be long, Torvald dear.

HELMER: Only an hour; not more.

NORA: Are you going too, Christina?

MRS LINDEN [*putting on her walking things*]: Yes; I must set about looking for lodgings.

HELMER: Then perhaps we can go together?

NORA [*helping her*]: What a pity we haven't a spare room for you; but it's impossible—

MRS LINDEN: I shouldn't think of troubling you. Good-bye, dear Nora, and thank you for all your kindness.

NORA: Good-bye for the present. Of course you'll come back this evening. And you, too, Doctor Rank. What! If you're well enough? Of course you'll be well enough. Only wrap up warmly.

They go out, talking, into the hall. Outside on the stairs are heard children's voices.

There they are! There they are!

She runs to the outer door and opens it. The nurse, ANNA, enters the hall with the children.

Come in! Come in! [*Stoops down and kisses the children.*] Oh, my sweet darlings! Do you see them, Christina? Aren't they lovely?

RANK: Don't let us stand here chattering in the draught.

HELMER: Come, Mrs Linden; only mothers can stand such a temperature.

DR RANK, HELMER, and MRS LINDEN go down the stairs; ANNA enters the room with the children; NORA also, shutting the door.

NORA: How fresh and bright you look! And what red cheeks you've got! Like apples and roses.

The children chatter to her during what follows.

Have you had great fun? That's splendid! Oh, really! You've been giving Emmy and Bob a ride on your sledge!—both at once, only think! Why, you're quite a man, Ivar. Oh, give her to me a little, Anna. My sweet little dolly! [*Takes the smallest from the nurse and dances with her.*] Yes, yes; mother will dance with Bob too. What! Did you have a game of snowballs? Oh, I wish I'd been there. No; leave them, Anna; I'll take their things off. Oh, yes, let me do it; it's such fun. Go to the nursery; you look frozen. You'll find some hot coffee on the stove.

The NURSE goes into the room on the left. NORA takes off the children's things and throws them down anywhere, while the children talk all together.

Really! A big dog ran after you? But he didn't bite you? No; dogs don't bite dear little dolly children. Don't peep into those parcels, Ivar. What is it? Wouldn't you like to know? Take care—it'll bite! What? Shall we have a game? What shall we play at? Hide-and-seek? Yes, let's play hide-and-seek. Bob shall hide first. Am I to? Yes, let me hide first.

She and the children play, with laughter and shouting, in the room and the adjacent one to the right. At last NORA hides under the table; the children come rushing in, look for her, but cannot find her, hear her half-choked laughter,

*rush to the table, lift up the cover and see her. Loud shouts. She creeps out, as
though to frighten them. Fresh shouts. Meanwhile there has been a knock at
the door leading into the hall. No one has heard it. Now the door is half opened
and* KROGSTAD *appears. He waits a little; the game is renewed.*

KROGSTAD: I beg your pardon, Mrs Helmer—

NORA [*with a suppressed cry, turns round and half jumps up*]: Ah! What do you
want?

KROGSTAD: Excuse me; the outer door was ajar—somebody must have forgotten
to shut it—

NORA [*standing up*]: My husband is not at home, Mr Krogstad.

KROGSTAD: I know it.

NORA: Then what do you want here?

KROGSTAD: To say a few words to you.

NORA: To me? [*To the children, softly.*] Go in to Anna. What? No, the strange
man won't hurt mamma. When he's gone we'll go on playing. [*She leads the
children into the left-hand room, and shuts the door behind them. Uneasy, in
suspense.*] It is to me you wish to speak?

KROGSTAD: Yes, to you.

NORA: To-day? But it's not the first yet—

KROGSTAD: No, to-day is Christmas Eve. It will depend upon yourself whether
you have a merry Christmas.

NORA: What do you want? I'm not ready to-day—

KROGSTAD: Never mind that just now. I have come about another matter. You
have a minute to spare?

NORA: Oh, yes, I suppose so; although—

KROGSTAD: Good. I was sitting in the restaurant opposite, and I saw your
husband go down the street—

NORA: Well?

KROGSTAD: —with a lady

NORA: What then?

KROGSTAD: May I ask if the lady was a Mrs Linden?

NORA: Yes.

KROGSTAD: Who has just come to town?

NORA: Yes. To-day.

KROGSTAD: I believe she is an intimate friend of yours?

NORA: Certainly. But I don't understand—

KROGSTAD: I used to know her too.

NORA: I know you did.

KROGSTAD: Ah! You know all about it. I thought as much. Now, frankly, is Mrs
Linden to have a place in the Bank?

NORA: How dare you catechise me in this way, Mr Krogstad—you, a
subordinate of my husband's? But since you ask, you shall know. Yes, Mrs
Linden is to be employed. And it is I who recommended her, Mr Krogstad.
Now you know.

KROGSTAD: Then my guess was right.

NORA [*walking up and down*]: You see one has a wee bit of influence, after all. It
doesn't follow because one's only a woman— When people are in a
subordinate position, Mr Krogstad, they ought really to be careful how they
offend anybody who—h'm—

KROGSTAD: —who has influence?

NORA: Exactly!

KROGSTAD [*taking another tone*]: Mrs Helmer, will you have the kindness to employ your influence on my behalf?

NORA: What? How do you mean?

KROGSTAD: Will you be so good as to see that I retain my subordinate position in the Bank?

NORA: What do you mean? Who wants to take it from you?

KROGSTAD: Oh, you needn't pretend ignorance. I can very well understand that it cannot be pleasant for your friend to meet me; and I can also understand now for whose sake I am to be hounded out.

NORA: But I assure you—

KROGSTAD: Come come now, once for all: there is time yet, and I advise you to use your influence to prevent it.

NORA: But, Mr Krogstad, I have no influence—absolutely none.

KROGSTAD: None? I thought you said a moment ago—

NORA: Of course not in that sense. I! How can you imagine that I should have any such influence over my husband?

KROGSTAD: Oh, I know your husband from our college days. I don't think he is any more inflexible than other husbands.

NORA: If you talk disrespectfully of my husband, I must request you to leave the house.

KROGSTAD: You are bold, madam.

NORA: I am afraid of you no longer. When New Year's Day is over, I shall soon be out of the whole business.

KROGSTAD [*controlling himself*]: Listen to me, Mrs Helmer. If need be, I shall fight as though for my life to keep my little place in the Bank.

NORA: Yes, so it seems.

KROGSTAD: It's not only for the salary: that is what I care least about. It's something else— Well, I had better make a clean breast of it. Of course you know, like every one else, that some years ago I—got into trouble.

NORA: I think I've heard something of the sort.

KROGSTAD: The matter never came into court; but from that moment all paths were barred to me. Then I took up the business you know about. I had to turn my hand to something; and I don't think I've been one of the worst. But now I must get clear of it all. My sons are growing up; for their sake I must try to recover my character as well as I can. This place in the Bank was the first step; and now your husband wants to kick me off the ladder, back into the mire.

NORA: But I assure you, Mr Krogstad, I haven't the least power to help you.

KROGSTAD: That is because you have not the will; but I can compel you.

NORA: You won't tell my husband that I owe you money?

KROGSTAD: H'm; suppose I were to?

NORA: It would be shameful of you. [*With tears in her voice.*] The secret that is my joy and my pride—that he should learn it in such an ugly, coarse way—and from you. It would involve me in all sorts of unpleasantness—

KROGSTAD: Only unpleasantness?

NORA [*hotly*]: But just do it. It's you that will come off worst, for then my husband will see what a bad man you are, and then you certainly won't keep your place.

KROGSTAD: I asked whether it was only domestic unpleasantness you feared?

NORA: If my husband gets to know about it, he will of course pay you off at once, and then we shall have nothing more to do with you.

KROGSTAD [*coming a pace nearer*]: Listen, Mrs Helmer: either your memory is defective, or you don't know much about business. I must make the position a little clearer to you.

NORA: How so?

KROGSTAD: When your husband was ill, you came to me to borrow twelve hundred dollars.

NORA: I knew of nobody else.

KROGSTAD: I promised to find you the money—

NORA: And you did find it.

KROGSTAD: I promised to find you the money, on certain conditions. You were so much taken up at the time about your husband's illness, and so eager to have the wherewithal for your journey, that you probably did not give much thought to the details. Allow me to remind you of them. I promised to find you the amount in exchange for a note of hand, which I drew up.

NORA: Yes, and I signed it.

KROGSTAD: Quite right. But then I added a few lines, making your father security for the debt. Your father was to sign this.

NORA: Was to—? He did sign it!

KROGSTAD: I had left the date blank. That is to say, your father was himself to date his signature. Do you recollect that?

NORA: Yes, I believe—

KROGSTAD: Then I gave you the paper to send to your father, by post. Is not that so?

NORA: Yes.

KROGSTAD: And of course you did so at once; for within five or six days you brought me back the document with your father's signature; and I handed you the money.

NORA: Well? Have I not made my payments punctually?

KROGSTAD: Fairly–yes. But to return to the point: You were in great trouble at the time, Mrs Helmer.

NORA: I was indeed!

KROGSTAD: Your father was very ill, I believe?

NORA: He was on his death-bed.

KROGSTAD: And died soon after?

NORA: Yes.

KROGSTAD: Tell me, Mrs Helmer: do you happen to recollect the day of his death? The day of the month, I mean?

NORA: Father died on the 29th of September.

KROGSTAD: Quite correct. I have made inquiries. And here comes in the remarkable point–[*produces a paper*] which I cannot explain.

NORA: What remarkable point? I don't know—

KROGSTAD: The remarkable point, madam, that your father signed this paper three days after his death!

NORA: What! I don't understand—

KROGSTAD: Your father died on the 29th of September. But look here: he has dated his signature October 2nd! Is not that remarkable, Mrs Helmer?

NORA *is silent*.

Can you explain it?

NORA *continues silent.*

It is noteworthy, too, that the words 'October 2nd' and the year are not in your father's handwriting, but in one which I believe I know. Well, this may be explained; your father may have forgotten to date his signature, and somebody may have added the date at random, before the fact of your father's death was known. There is nothing wrong in that. Everything depends on the signature. Of course it is genuine, Mrs Helmer? It was really your father himself who wrote his name here?

NORA [*after a short silence, throws her head back and looks defiantly at him*]: No, it was not. *I* wrote father's name.

KROGSTAD: Ah!—Are you aware, madam, that that is a dangerous admission?

NORA: How so? You will soon get your money.

KROGSTAD: May I ask you one more question? Why did you not send the paper to your father?

NORA: It was impossible. Father was ill. If I had asked him for his signature, I should have had to tell him why I wanted the money; but he was so ill I really could not tell him that my husband's life was in danger. It was impossible.

KROGSTAD: Then it would have been better to have given up your tour.

NORA: No, I couldn't do that; my husband's life depended on that journey. I couldn't give it up.

KROGSTAD: And did it never occur to you that you were playing me false?

NORA: That was nothing to me. I didn't care in the least about you. I couldn't endure you for all the cruel difficulties you made, although you knew how ill my husband was.

KROGSTAD: Mrs Helmer, you evidently do not realise what you have been guilty of. But I can assure you it was nothing more and nothing worse that made me an outcast from society.

NORA: You! You want me to believe that you did a brave thing to save your wife's life?

KROGSTAD: The law takes no account of motives.

NORA: Then it must be a very bad law.

KROGSTAD: Bad or not, if I produce this document in court, you will be condemned according to law.

NORA: I don't believe that. Do you mean to tell me that a daughter has no right to spare her dying father trouble and anxiety?—that a wife has no right to save her husband's life? I don't know much about the law, but I'm sure you'll find, somewhere or another, that that is allowed. And you don't know that—you, a lawyer! You must be a bad one, Mr Krogstad.

KROGSTAD: Possibly. But business—such business as ours—I do understand. You believe that? Very well; now do as you please. But this I may tell you, that if I am flung into the gutter a second time, you shall keep me company. [*Bows and goes out through hall.*]

NORA: [*stands a while thinking, then tosses her head*]: Oh nonsense! He wants to frighten me. I'm not so foolish as that. [*Begins folding the children's clothes. Pauses.*] But—? No, it's impossible! Why, I did it for love!

CHILDREN [*at the door, left*]: Mamma, the strange man has gone now.

NORA: Yes, yes, I know. But don't tell any one about the strange man. Do you hear? Not even papa!

CHILDREN: No, mamma; and now will you play with us again?

NORA: No, no; not now.

CHILDREN: Oh, do, mamma; you know you promised.

NORA: Yes, but I can't just now. Run to the nursery; I have so much to do. Run along, run along, and be good, my darlings! [*She pushes them gently into the inner room, and closes the door behind them. Sits on the sofa, embroiders a few stitches, but soon pauses.*] No! [*Throws down the work, rises, goes to the hall door and calls out.*] Ellen, bring in the Christmas-tree! [*Goes to table, left, and opens the drawer; again pauses.*] No, it's quite impossible!

ELLEN [*with Christmas-tree*]: Where shall I stand it, ma'am?

NORA: There, in the middle of the room.

ELLEN: Shall I bring in anything else?

NORA: No, thank you, I have all I want.

ELLEN, *having put down the tree, goes out.*

NORA [*busy dressing the tree*]: There must be a candle here—and flowers there.—That horrible man! Nonsense, nonsense! there's nothing to be afraid of. The Christmas-tree shall be beautiful. I'll do everything to please you, Torvald; I'll sing and dance, and—

Enter HELMER *by the hall door, with a bundle of documents.*

Oh! You're back already?

HELMER: Yes. Has anybody been here?

NORA: Here? No.

HELMER: That's odd. I saw Krogstad come out of the house.

NORA: Did you? Oh, yes, by-the-bye, he was here for a minute.

HELMER: Nora, I can see by your manner that he has been begging you to put in a good word for him?

NORA: Yes.

HELMER: And you were to do it as if of your own accord? You were to say nothing to me of his having been here. Didn't he suggest that too?

NORA: Yes, Torvald; but—

HELMER: Nora, Nora! And you could condescend to that! To speak to such a man, to make him a promise! And then to tell me an untruth about it!

NORA: An untruth!

HELMER: Didn't you say that nobody had been here? [*Threatens with his finger.*] My little bird must never do that again! A song-bird must sing clear and true; no false notes. [*Puts his arm round her.*] That's so, isn't it? Yes, I was sure of it. [*Lets her go.*] And now we'll say no more about it. [*Sits down before the fire.*] Oh, how cosy and quiet it is here! [*Glances into his documents.*]

NORA [*busy with the tree, after a short silence*]: Torvald!

HELMER: Yes.

NORA: I'm looking forward so much to the Stenborgs' fancy ball the day after to-morrow.

HELMER: And I'm on tenterhooks to see what surprise you have in store for me.

NORA: Oh, it's too tiresome!

HELMER: What is?

NORA: I can't think of anything good. Everything seems so foolish and meaningless.

HELMER: Has little Nora made that discovery?

NORA [*behind his chair, with her arms on the back*]: Are you very busy, Torvald?

HELMER: Well—

NORA: What papers are those?

HELMER: Bank business.

NORA: Already!

HELMER: I have got the retiring manager to let me make some necessary changes in the staff and the organization. I can do this during Christmas week. I want to have everything straight by the New Year.

NORA: Then that's why that poor Krogstad—

HELMER: H'm.

NORA: [*still leaning over the chair-back and slowly stroking his hair*]: If you hadn't been so very busy, I should have asked you a great, great favour, Torvald.

HELMER: What can it be? Out with it.

NORA: Nobody has such perfect taste as you; and I should so love to look well at the fancy ball. Torvald, dear, couldn't you take me in hand, and settle what I'm to be, and arrange my costume for me?

HELMER: Aha! So my wilful little woman is at a loss, and making signals of distress.

NORA: Yes, please, Torvald. I can't get on without your help.

HELMER: Well, well, I'll think it over, and we'll soon hit upon something.

NORA: Oh, how good that is of you! [*Goes to the tree again; pause.*] How well the red flowers show.—Tell me, was it anything so very dreadful this Krogstad got into trouble about?

HELMER: Forgery, that's all. Don't you know what that means?

NORA: Mayn't he have been driven to it by need?

HELMER: Yes; or, like so many others, he may have done it in pure heedlessness. I am not so hard-hearted as to condemn a man absolutely for a single fault.

NORA: No, surely not, Torvald!

HELMER: Many a man can retrieve his character, if he owns his crime and takes the punishment.

NORA: Punishment—?

HELMER: But Krogstad didn't do that. He evaded the law by means of tricks and subterfuges; and that is what has morally ruined him.

NORA: Do you think that—?

HELMER: Just think how a man with a thing of that sort on his conscience must be always lying and canting and shamming. Think of the mask he must wear even towards those who stand nearest him—towards his own wife and children. The effect on the children—that's the most terrible part of it, Nora.

NORA: Why?

HELMER: Because in such an atmosphere of lies home life is poisoned and contaminated in every fibre. Every breath the children draw contains some germ of evil.

NORA [*closer behind him*]: Are you sure of that?

HELMER: As a lawyer, my dear, I have seen it often enough. Nearly all cases of early corruption may be traced to lying mothers.

NORA: Why—mothers?

HELMER: It generally comes from the mother's side; but of course the father's influence may act in the same way. Every lawyer knows it too well. And here has this Krogstad been poisoning his own children for years past by a life of lies and hypocrisy—that is why I call him morally ruined. [*Holds out both hands to her.*] So my sweet little Nora must promise not to plead his cause. Shake hands upon it. Come, come, what's this? Give me your hand. That's right. Then it's a bargain. I assure you it would have been impossible for me to work with him. It gives me a positive sense of physical discomfort to come in contact with such people.

NORA *draws her hand away, and moves to the other side of the Christmas-tree.*

NORA: How warm it is here. And I have so much to do.

HELMER [*rises and gathers up his papers*]: Yes, and I must try to get some of these papers looked through before dinner. And I shall think over your costume too. Perhaps I may even find something to hang in gilt paper on the Christmas-tree. [*Lays his hand on her head.*] My precious little song-bird! [*He goes into his room and shuts the door.*]

NORA [*softly, after a pause*]: It can't be. It's impossible. It must be impossible!

ANNA [*at the door, left*]: The little ones are begging so prettily to come to mamma.

NORA: No, no, no; don't let them come to me! Keep them with you, Anna.

ANNA: Very well, ma'am. [*Shuts the door.*]

NORA [*pale with terror*]: Corrupt my children!—Poison my home! [*Short pause. She throws back her head.*] It's not true! It can never, never be true!

ACT TWO

The same room. In the corner, beside the piano, stands the Christmas-tree, stripped, and with the candles burnt out. NORA's outdoor things lie on the sofa.

> NORA, *alone, is walking about restlessly. At last she stops by the sofa, and takes up her cloak.*

NORA [*dropping the cloak*]: There's somebody coming! [*Goes to the hall door and listens.*] Nobody; of course nobody will come to-day, Christmas-day; nor to-morrow either. But perhaps— [*Opens the door and looks out.*]No, nothing in the letter-box; quite empty. [*Comes forward.*] Stuff and nonsense! Of course he won't really do anything. Such a thing couldn't happen. It's impossible! Why, I have three little children.

> ANNA *enters from the left, with a large cardboard box.*

ANNA: I've found the box with the fancy dress at last.

NORA: Thanks; put it down on the table.

ANNA [*does so*]: But I'm afraid it's very much out of order.

NORA: Oh, I wish I could tear it into a hundred thousand pieces!

ANNA: Oh, no. It can easily be put to rights—just a little patience.

NORA: I shall go and get Mrs Linden to help me.

ANNA: Going out again? In such weather as this! You'll catch cold, ma'am, and be ill.

NORA: Worse things might happen.—What are the children doing?

ANNA: They're playing with their Christmas presents, poor little dears; but—

NORA: Do they often ask for me?

ANNA: You see they've been so used to having their mamma with them.

NORA: Yes; but, Anna, I can't have them so much with me in future.

ANNA: Well, little children get used to anything.

NORA: Do you think they do? Do you believe they would forget their mother if she went quite away?

ANNA: Gracious me! Quite away?

NORA: Tell me, Anna—I've so often wondered about it—how could you bring yourself to give your child up to strangers?

ANNA: I had to when I came to nurse my little Miss Nora.

NORA: But how could you make up your mind to it?

ANNA: When I had the chance of such a good place? A poor girl who's been in trouble must take what comes. That wicked man did nothing for me.

NORA: But your daughter must have forgotten you.

ANNA: Oh, no, ma'am, that she hasn't. She wrote to me both when she was confirmed and when she was married.

NORA [*embracing her*]: Dear old Anna—you were a good mother to me when I was little.

ANNA: My poor little Nora had no mother but me.

NORA: And if my little ones had nobody else, I'm sure you would— Nonsense, nonsense! [*Opens the box.*] Go in to the children. Now I must— You'll see how lovely I shall be to-morrow.

ANNA: I'm sure there will be no one at the ball so lovely as my Miss Nora. [*She goes into the room on the left.*]

NORA [*takes the costume out of the box, but soon throws it down again*]: Oh, if I dared go out. If only nobody would come. If only nothing would happen here in the meantime. Rubbish; nobody is coming. Only not to think. What a delicious muff! Beautiful gloves, beautiful gloves! To forget–to forget! One, two, three, four, five, six— [*With a scream.*] Ah, there they come. [*Goes towards the door, then stands irresolute.*]

MRS LINDEN *enters from the hall, where she has taken off her things.*

Oh, it's you, Christina. There's nobody else there? I'm so glad you have come.

MRS LINDEN: I hear you called at my lodgings.

NORA: Yes, I was just passing. There's something you must help me with. Let us sit here on the sofa–so. To-morrow evening there's to be a fancy ball at Consul Stenborg's overhead, and Torvald want me to appear as a Neapolitan fisher-girl, and dance the tarantella; I learned it at Capri.

MRS LINDEN: I see–quite a performance.

NORA: Yes, Torvald wishes it. Look, this is the costume; Torvald had it made for me in Italy. But now it's all so torn, I don't know—

MRS LINDEN: Oh, we shall soon set that to rights. It's only the trimming that has come loose here and there. Have you a needle and thread? Ah, here's the very thing.

NORA: Oh, how kind of you.

MRS LINDEN [*sewing*]: So you're to be in costume to-morrow, Nora? I'll tell you what–I shall come in for a moment to see you in all your glory. But I've quite forgotten to thank you for the pleasant evening yesterday.

NORA [*rises and walks across the room*]: Oh, yesterday, it didn't seem so pleasant as usual.–You should have come to town a little sooner, Christina.–Torvald has certainly the art of making home bright and beautiful.

MRS LINDEN: You too, I should think, or you wouldn't be your father's daughter. But tell me–is Doctor Rank always so depressed as he was last evening?

NORA: No, yesterday it was particularly noticeable. You see, he suffers from a dreadful illness. He has spinal consumption, poor fellow. They say his father was a horrible man, who kept mistresses and all sorts of things–so the son has been sickly from his childhood, you understand.

MRS LINDEN [*lets her sewing fall into her lap*]: Why, my darling Nora, how do you come to know such things?

NORA [*moving about the room*]: Oh, when one has three children, one sometimes has visits from women who are half–half doctors–and they talk of one thing and another.

MRS LINDEN [*going on sewing; a short pause*]: Does Doctor Rank come here every day?

NORA: Every day of his life. He has been Torvald's most intimate friend from boyhood, and he's a good friend of mine too. Doctor Rank is quite one of the family.

MRS LINDEN: But tell me—is he quite sincere? I mean, isn't he rather given to flattering people?

NORA: No, quite the contrary. Why should you think so?

MRS LINDEN: When you introduced us yesterday he said he had often heard my name; but I noticed afterwards that your husband had no notion who I was. How could Doctor Rank—?

NORA: He was quite right, Christina. You see, Torvald loves me so indescribably, he wants to have me all to himself, as he says. When we were first married he was almost jealous if I even mentioned any of my old friends at home; so naturally I gave up doing it. But I often talk of the old times to Doctor Rank, for he likes to hear about them.

MRS LINDEN: Listen to me, Nora! You are still a child in many ways. I am older than you, and have had more experience. I'll tell you something? You ought to get clear of all this with Dr Rank.

NORA: Get clear of what?

MRS LINDEN: The whole affair, I should say. You were talking yesterday of a rich admirer who was to find you money—

NORA: Yes, one who never existed, worse luck. What then?

MRS LINDEN: Has Doctor Rank money?

NORA: Yes, he has.

MRS LINDEN: And nobody to provide for?

NORA: Nobody. But—?

MRS LINDEN: And he comes here every day?

NORA: Yes, I told you so.

MRS LINDEN: I should have thought he would have had better taste.

NORA: I don't understand you a bit.

MRS LINDEN: Don't pretend, Nora. Do you suppose I can't guess who lent you the twelve hundred dollars?

NORA: Are you out of your senses? How can you think such a thing? A friend who comes here every day! Why, the position would be unbearable!

MRS LINDEN: Then it really is not he?

NORA: No, I assure you. It never for a moment occurred to me— Besides, at that time he had nothing to lend; he came into his property afterwards.

MRS LINDEN: Well, I believe that was lucky for you, Nora dear.

NORA: No, really, it would never have struck me to ask Dr Rank— And yet, I'm certain that if I did—

MRS LINDEN: But of course you never would.

NORA: Of course not. It's inconceivable that it should ever be necessary. But I'm quite sure that if I spoke to Doctor Rank—

MRS LINDEN: Behind your husband's back?

NORA: I must get clear of the other thing; that's behind his back too. I *must* get clear of that.

MRS LINDEN: Yes, yes, I told you so yesterday; but—

NORA: [*walking up and down*]: A man can manage these things much better than a woman.

MRS LINDEN: One's own husband, yes.

NORA: Nonsense. [*Stands still.*] When everything is paid, one gets back the paper.

MRS LINDEN: Of course.

NORA: And can tear it into a hundred thousand pieces, and burn it up, the nasty, filthy thing!

MRS LINDEN [*looks at her fixedly, lays down her work, and rises slowly*]: Nora, you are hiding something from me.

NORA: Can you see it in my face?

MRS LINDEN: Something has happened since yesterday morning. Nora, what is it?

NORA [*going towards her*]: Christina—! [*Listens.*] Hush! There's Torvald coming home. Do you mind going into the nursery for the present? Torvald can't bear to see dressmaking going on. Get Anna to help you.

MRS LINDEN [*gathers some of the things together*]: Very well; but I shan't go away until you have told me all about it.

She goes out to the left, as HELMER *enters from the hall.*

NORA [*runs to meet him*]: Oh, how I've been longing for you to come, Torvald dear!

HELMER: Was that the dressmaker—?

NORA: No, Christina. She's helping me with my costume. You'll see how nice I shall look.

HELMER: Yes, wasn't that a happy thought of mine?

NORA: Splendid! But isn't it good of me, too, to have given in to you about the tarantella?

HELMER [*takes her under the chin*]: Good of you! To give in to your own husband? Well well, you little madcap, I know you don't mean it. But I won't disturb you. I daresay you want to be 'trying on'.

NORA: And you are going to work, I suppose?

HELMER: Yes. [*Shows her a bundle of papers.*] Look here. I've just come from the Bank— [*Goes towards his room.*]

NORA: Torvald.

HELMER [*stopping*]: Yes?

NORA: If your little squirrel were to beg you for something so prettily—

HELMER: Well?

NORA: Would you do it?

HELMER: I must know first what it is.

NORA: The squirrel would skip about and play all sorts of tricks if you would only be nice and kind.

HELMER: Come, then, out with it.

NORA: Your lark would twitter from morning till night—

HELMER: Oh, that she does in any case.

NORA: I'll be an elf and dance in the moonlight for you, Torvald.

HELMER: Nora—you can't mean what you were hinting at this morning?

NORA [*coming nearer*]: Yes, Torvald, I beg and implore you!

HELMER: Have you really the courage to begin that again?

NORA: Yes, yes; for my sake, you must let Krogstad keep his place in the Bank.

HELMER: My dear Nora, it's his place I intend for Mrs Linden.

NORA: Yes, that's so good of you. But instead of Krogstad, you could dismiss some other clerk.

HELMER: Why, this is incredible obstinacy! Because you have thoughtlessly promised to put in a word for him, I am to—!

NORA: It's not that, Torvald. It's for your own sake. This man writes for the most scurrilous newspapers; you said so yourself. He can do you no end of harm. I'm so terribly afraid of him—

HELMER: Ah, I understand; it's old recollections that are frightening you.

NORA: What do you mean?

HELMER: Of course you're thinking of your father.

NORA: Yes–yes, of course. Only think of the shameful slanders wicked people used to write about father. I believe they would have got him dismissed if you hadn't been sent to look into the thing, and been kind to him, and helped him.

HELMER: My little Nora, between your father and me there is all the difference in the world. Your father was not altogether unimpeachable. I am; and I hope to remain so.

NORA: Oh, no one knows what wicked men may hit upon. We could live so quietly and happily now, in our cosy, peaceful home, you and I and the children, Torvald! That's why I beg and implore you—

HELMER: And it is just by pleading his cause that you make it impossible for me to keep him. It's already known at the Bank that I intend to dismiss Krogstad. If it were now reported that the new manager let himself be turned round his wife's little finger—

NORA: What then?

HELMER: Oh, nothing, so long as a wilful woman can have her way—! I am to make myself a laughing-stock to the whole staff, and set people saying that I am open to all sorts of outside influence? Take my word for it, I should soon feel the consequences. And besides–there is one thing that makes Krogstad impossible for me to work with—

NORA: What thing?

HELMER: I could perhaps have overlooked his moral failings at a pinch—

NORA: Yes, couldn't you, Torvald?

HELMER: And I hear he is good at his work. But the fact is, he was a college chum of mine–there was one of those rash friendships between us that one so often repents of later. I may as well confess it at once–he calls me by my Christian name;[1] and he is tactless enough to do it even when others are present. He delights in putting on airs of familiarity–Torvald here, Torvald there! I assure you it's most painful to me. He would make my position at the Bank perfectly unendurable.

NORA: Torvald, surely you're not serious?

HELMER: No? Why not?

NORA: That's such a petty reason.

HELMER: What! Petty! Do you consider me petty!

NORA: No, on the contrary, Torvald dear; and that's just why—

HELMER: Never mind; you call my motives petty; then I must be petty too. Petty! Very well!–Now we'll put an end to this, once for all. [*Goes to the door into the hall and calls.*] Ellen!

NORA: What do you want?

HELMER [*searching among his papers*]: To settle the thing. [ELLEN *enters.*] Here; take this letter; give it to a messenger. See that he takes it at once. The address is on it. Here's the money.

ELLEN: Very well, sir. [*Goes with the letter.*]

[1] In the original, 'We say "thou" to each other'.

HELMER [*putting his papers together*]: There, Madam Obstinacy.

NORA [*breathless*]: Torvald—what was in the letter?

HELMER: Krogstad's dismissal.

NORA: Call it back again, Torvald! There's still time. Oh, Torvald, call it back again! For my sake, for your own, for the children's sake! Do you hear, Torvald? Do it! You don't know what that letter may bring upon us all.

HELMER: Too late.

NORA: Yes, too late.

HELMER: My dear Nora, I forgive your anxiety, though it's anything but flattering to me. Why should you suppose that *I* would be afraid of a wretched scribbler's spite? But I forgive you all the same, for it's a proof of your great love for me. [*Takes her in his arms.*] That's as it should be, my own dear Nora. Let what will happen—when it comes to the pinch, I shall have strength and courage enough. You shall see: my shoulders are broad enough to bear the whole burden.

NORA [*terror-struck*]: What do you mean by that?

HELMER: The whole burden, I say—

NORA [*with decision*]: That you shall never, never do!

HELMER: Very well; then we'll share it, Nora, as man and wife. That is how it should be. [*Petting her.*] Are you satisfied now? Come, come, come, don't look like a scared dove. It's all nothing—foolish fancies.—Now you ought to play the tarantella through and practise with the tambourine. I shall sit in my inner room and shut both doors, so that I shall hear nothing. You can make as much noise as you please. [*Turns round in doorway.*] And when Rank comes, just tell him where I'm to be found. [*He nods to her, and goes with his papers into his room, closing the door.*]

NORA [*bewildered with terror, stands as though rooted to the ground, and whispers*]: He would do it. Yes, he would do it. He would do it, in spite of all the world.—No, never that, never, never! Anything rather than that! Oh, for some way of escape! What shall I do—!

Hall bell rings.

Doctor Rank—!—Anything, anything, rather than—!

NORA *draws her hands over her face, pulls herself together, goes to the door and opens it.* RANK *stands outside hanging up his fur coat. During what follows it begins to grow dark.*

Good afternoon, Doctor Rank. I knew you by your ring. But you mustn't go to Torvald now. I believe he's busy.

RANK: And you? [*Enters and closes the door.*]

NORA: Oh, you know very well, I have always time for you.

RANK: Thank you. I shall avail myself of your kindness as long as I can.

NORA: What do you mean? As long as you can?

RANK: Yes. Does that frighten you?

NORA: I think it's an odd expression. Do you expect anything to happen?

RANK: Something I have long been prepared for; but I didn't think it would come so soon.

NORA [*catching at his arm*]: What have you discovered? Doctor Rank, you must tell me!

RANK [*sitting down by the stove*]: I am running down hill. There's no help for it.

NORA [*draws a long breath of relief*]: It's *you*—?

RANK: Who else should it be?—Why lie to one's self? I am the most wretched of all my patients, Mrs Helmer. In these last days I have been auditing my life-account—bankrupt! Perhaps before a month is over, I shall lie rotting in the churchyard.

NORA: Oh! What an ugly way to talk.

RANK: The thing itself is so confoundedly ugly, you see. But the worst of it is, so many other ugly things have to be gone through first. There is only one last investigation to be made, and when that is over I shall know pretty certainly when the break-up will begin. There's one thing I want to say to you: Helmer's delicate nature shrinks so from all that is horrible: I will not have him in my sick-room—

NORA: But, Doctor Rank—

RANK: I won't have him, I say—not on any account! I shall lock my door against him.—As soon as I am quite certain of the worst, I shall send you my visiting-card with a black cross on it; and then you will know that the final horror has begun.

NORA: Why, you're perfectly unreasonable to-day; and I did so want you to be in a really good humour.

RANK: With death staring me in the face?—And to suffer thus for another's sin! Where's the justice of it? And in one way or another you can trace in every family some such inexorable retribution—

NORA [*stopping her ears*]: Nonsense, nonsense! Now cheer up!

RANK: Well, after all, the whole thing's only worth laughing at. My poor innocent spine must do penance for my father's wild oats.

NORA [*at table, left*]: I suppose he was too fond of asparagus and Strasbourg pâté, wasn't he?

RANK: Yes; and truffles.

NORA: Yes, truffles, to be sure. And oysters, I believe?

RANK: Yes, oysters; oysters, of course.

NORA: And then all the port and champagne! It's sad that all these good things should attack the spine.

RANK: Especially when the luckless spine attacked never had any good of them.

NORA: Ah, yes, that's the worst of it.

RANK [*looks at her searchingly*]: H'm—

NORA [*a moment later*]: Why did you smile?

RANK: No; it was you that laughed.

NORA: No; it was you that smiled, Doctor Rank.

RANK [*standing up*]: I see you're deeper than I thought.

NORA: I'm in such a crazy mood to-day.

RANK: So it seems.

NORA [*with her hands on his shoulders*]: Dear, dear Doctor Rank, death shall not take you away from Torvald and me.

RANK: Oh, you'll easily get over the loss. The absent are soon forgotten.

NORA [*looks at him anxiously*]: Do you think so?

RANK: People make fresh ties, and then—

NORA: Who make fresh ties?

RANK: You and Helmer will, when I am gone. You yourself are taking time by the forelock, it seems to me. What was that Mrs Linden doing here yesterday?

NORA: Oh!—you're surely not jealous of poor Christina?

RANK: Yes, I am. She will be my successor in this house. When I am out of the way, this woman will perhaps—

NORA: Hush! Not so loud! She's in there.

RANK: To-day as well? You see!

NORA: Only to put my costume in order—dear me, how unreasonable you are! [*Sits on sofa.*] Now do be good, Doctor Rank! To-morrow you shall see how beautifully I shall dance; and then you may fancy that I'm doing it all to please you—and of course Torvald as well. [*Takes various things out of box.*] Doctor Rank, sit down here, and I'll show you something.

RANK [*sitting*]: What is it?

NORA: Look here. Look!

RANK: Silk stockings.

NORA: Flesh-coloured. Aren't they lovely? It's so dark here now; but to-morrow— No, no, no; you must only look at the feet. Oh, well, I suppose you may look at the rest too.

RANK: H'm—

NORA: What are you looking so critical about? Do you think they won't fit me?

RANK: I can't possibly give any competent opinion on that point.

NORA [*looking at him a moment*]: For shame! [*Hits him lightly on the ear with the stockings.*] Take that. [*Rolls them up again.*]

RANK: And what other wonders am I to see?

NORA: You sha'n't see anything more; for you don't behave nicely. [*She hums a little and searches among the things.*]

RANK [*after a short silence*]: When I sit here gossiping with you, I can't imagine—I simply cannot conceive—what would have become of me if I had never entered this house.

NORA [*smiling*]: Yes, I think you do feel at home with us.

RANK [*more softly—looking straight before him*]: And now to have to leave it all—

NORA: Nonsense. You sha'n't leave us.

RANK [*in the same tone*]: And not to be able to leave behind the slightest token of gratitude; scarcely even a passing regret—nothing but an empty place, that can be filled by the first comer.

NORA: And if I were to ask you for—? No—

RANK: For what?

NORA: For a great proof of your friendship.

RANK: Yes—yes?

NORA: I mean—for a very, very great service—

RANK: Would you really, for once, make me so happy?

NORA: Oh, you don't know what it is.

RANK: Then tell me.

NORA: No, I really can't, Doctor Rank. It's far, far too much—not only a service, but help and advice besides—

RANK: So much the better. I can't think what you can mean. But go on. Don't you trust me?

NORA: As I trust no one else. I know you are my best and truest friend. So I will tell you. Well then, Doctor Rank, there is something you must help me to prevent. You know how deeply, how wonderfully Torvald loves me; he wouldn't hesitate a moment to give his very life for my sake.

RANK [*bending towards her*]: Nora—do you think he is the only one who—?

NORA [*with a slight start*]: Who—?

RANK: Who would gladly give his life for you?

NORA [*sadly*]: Oh!

RANK: I have sworn that you shall know it before I–go. I shall never find a better opportunity.–Yes, Nora, now I have told you; and now you know that you can trust me as you can no one else.

NORA [*standing up; simply and calmly*]: Let me pass, please.

RANK [*makes way for her, but remains sitting*]: Nora—

NORA [*in the doorway*]: Ellen, bring the lamp. [*Crosses to the stove.*] Oh dear, Doctor Rank, that was too bad of you.

RANK [*rising*]: That I have loved you as deeply as–any one else? Was that too bad of me?

NORA: No, but that you should have told me so. It was so unnecessary—

RANK: What do you mean? Did you know—?

ELLEN *enters with the lamp; sets it on the table and goes out again.*

Nora–Mrs Helmer–I ask you, did you know?

NORA: Oh, how can I tell what I knew or didn't know? I really can't say— How could you be so clumsy, Doctor Rank? It was all so nice!

RANK: Well, at any rate, you know now that I am at your service, body and soul. And now, go on.

NORA [*looking at him*]: Go on–now?

RANK: I beg you to tell me what you want.

NORA: I can tell you nothing now.

RANK: Yes, yes! You mustn't punish me in that way. Let me do for you whatever a man can.

NORA: You can do nothing for me now.–Besides, I really want no help. You shall see it was only my fancy. Yes, it must be so. Of course! [*Sits in the rocking-chair, looks at him and smiles.*] You are a nice person, Doctor Rank! Aren't you ashamed of yourself, now that the lamp is on the table?

RANK: No; not exactly. But perhaps I ought to go–for ever.

NORA: No, indeed you mustn't. Of course you must come and go as you've always done. You know very well that Torvald can't do without you.

RANK: Yes, but you?

NORA: Oh, you know I always like to have you here.

RANK: That is just what led me astray. You are a riddle to me. It has often seemed to me as if you liked being with me almost as much as being with Helmer.

NORA: Yes; don't you see? There are people one loves, and others one likes to talk to.

RANK: Yes–there's something in that.

NORA: When I was a girl, of course I loved papa best. But it always delighted me to steal into the servants' room. In the first place they never lectured me, and in the second it was such fun to hear them talk.

RANK: Ah, I see; then it's their place I have taken?

NORA [*jumps up and hurries towards him*]: Oh, my dear Doctor Rank, I don't mean that. But you understand, with Torvald it's the same as with papa—

ELLEN *enters from the hall.*

ELLEN: Please, ma'am— [*Whispers to* NORA, *and gives her a card.*]

NORA [*glancing at card*]: Ah! [*Puts it in her pocket.*]

RANK: Anything wrong?

NORA: No, no, not in the least. It's only–it's my new costume—

RANK: Your costume! Why, it's there.

NORA: Oh, that one, yes. But this is another that–I have ordered it–Torvald mustn't know—

RANK: Aha! So that's the great secret.

NORA: Yes, of course. Please go to him; he's in the inner room. Do keep him while I—

RANK: Don't be alarmed; he sha'n't escape. [*Goes into* HELMER'*s room.*]

NORA [*to* ELLEN]: Is he waiting in the kitchen?

ELLEN: Yes, he came up the back stair—

NORA: Didn't you tell him I was engaged?

ELLEN: Yes, but it was no use.

NORA: He won't go away?

ELLEN: No, ma'am, not until he has spoken to you.

NORA: Then let him come in; but quietly. And, Ellen–say nothing about it; it's a surprise for my husband.

ELLEN: Oh, yes, ma'am, I understand. [*She goes out.*]

NORA: It is coming! The dreadful thing is coming, after all. No, no, no, it can never be; it shall not!

> *She goes to* HELMER'*s door and slips the bolt.* ELLEN *opens the hall door for* KROGSTAD, *and shuts it after him. He wears a travelling-coat, high boots, and a fur cap.*

NORA [*goes towards him*]: Speak softly; my husband is at home.

KROGSTAD: All right. That's nothing to me.

NORA: What do you want?

KROGSTAD: A little information.

NORA: Be quick, then. What is it?

KROGSTAD: You know I have got my dismissal.

NORA: I couldn't prevent it, Mr Krogstad. I fought for you to the last, but it was of no use.

KROGSTAD: Does your husband care for you so little? He knows what I can bring upon you, and yet he dares—

NORA: How could you think I should tell him?

KROGSTAD: Well, as a matter of fact, I didn't think it. It wasn't like my friend Torvald Helmer to show so much courage—

NORA: Mr Krogstad, be good enough to speak respectfully of my husband.

KROGSTAD: Certainly, with all due respect. But since you are so anxious to keep the matter secret, I suppose you are a little clearer than yesterday as to what you have done.

NORA: Clearer than you could ever make me.

KROGSTAD: Yes, such a bad lawyer as I—

NORA: What is it you want?

KROGSTAD: Only to see how you are getting on, Mrs Helmer. I've been thinking about you all day. Even a mere money-lender, a gutter-journalist, a–in short, a creature like me–has a little bit of what people call feeling.

NORA: Then show it; think of my little children.

KROGSTAD: Did you and your husband think of mine? But enough of that. I only wanted to tell you that you needn't take this matter too seriously. I shall not lodge any information, for the present.

NORA: No, surely not. I knew you wouldn't.

KROGSTAD: The whole thing can be settled quite amicably. Nobody need know. It can remain among us three.

NORA: My husband must never know.

KROGSTAD: How can you prevent it? Can you pay off the balance?

NORA: No, not at once.

KROGSTAD: Or have you any means of raising the money in the next few days?

NORA: None—that I will make use of.

KROGSTAD: And if you had, it would not help you now. If you offered me ever so much money down, you should not get back your I.O.U.

NORA: Tell me what you want to do with it.

KROGSTAD: I only want to keep it—to have it in my possession. No outsider shall hear anything of it. So, if you have any desperate scheme in your head—

NORA: What if I have?

KROGSTAD: If you should think of leaving your husband and children—

NORA: What if I do?

KROGSTAD: Or if you should think of—something worse—

NORA: How do you know that?

KROGSTAD: Put all that out of your head.

NORA: How did you know what I had in my mind?

KROGSTAD: Most of us think of that at first. I thought of it, too; but I hadn't the courage—

NORA [*tonelessly*]: Nor I.

KROGSTAD [*relieved*]: No, one hasn't. You haven't the courage either, have you?

NORA: I haven't, I haven't.

KROGSTAD: Besides, it would be very foolish.—Just one domestic storm, and it's all over. I have a letter in my pocket for your husband—

NORA: Telling him everything?

KROGSTAD: Sparing you as much as possible.

NORA [*quickly*]: He must never read that letter. Tear it up. I will manage to get the money somehow—

KROGSTAD: Pardon me, Mrs Helmer, but I believe I told you—

NORA: Oh, I'm not talking about the money I owe you. Tell me how much you demand from my husband—I will get it.

KROGSTAD: I demand no money from your husband.

NORA: What do you demand then?

KROGSTAD: I will tell you. I want to regain my footing in the world. I want to rise; and your husband shall help me to do it. For the last eighteen months my record has been spotless; I have been in bitter need all the time; but I was content to fight my way up, step by step. Now, I've been thrust down again, and I will not be satisfied with merely being reinstated as a matter of grace. I want to rise, I tell you. I must get into the Bank again, in a higher position than before. Your husband shall create a place on purpose for me—

NORA: He will never do that!

KROGSTAD: He will do it; I know him—he won't dare to show fight! And when he and I are together there, you shall soon see! Before a year is out I shall be the manager's right hand. It won't be Torvald Helmer, but Nils Krogstad, that manages the Joint Stock Bank.

NORA: That shall never be.

KROGSTAD: Perhaps you will—?

NORA: Now I have the courage for it.

KROGSTAD: Oh, you don't frighten me! A sensitive, petted creature like you—

NORA: You shall see, you shall see!

KROGSTAD: Under the ice, perhaps? Down into the cold, black water? And next spring to come up again, ugly, hairless, unrecognisable—

NORA: You can't terrify me.

KROGSTAD: Nor you me. People don't do that sort of thing, Mrs Helmer. And, after all, what would be the use of it? I have your husband in my pocket, all the same.

NORA: Afterwards? When I am no longer—?

KROGSTAD: You forget, your reputation remains in my hands!

> NORA *stands speechless and looks at him.*

Well, now you are prepared. Do nothing foolish. As soon as Helmer has received my letter, I shall expect to hear from him. And remember that it is your husband himself who has forced me back again into such paths. That I will never forgive him. Good-bye, Mrs Helmer.

> *Goes out through the hall.* NORA *hurries to the door, opens it a little, and listens.*

NORA: He's going. He's not putting the letter into the box. No, no, it would be impossible! [*Opens the door further and further.*] What's that. He's standing still; not going down stairs. Has he changed his mind? Is he—?

> *A letter falls into the box.* KROGSTAD's *footsteps are heard gradually receding down the stair.* NORA *utters a suppressed shriek, and rushes forward towards the sofa-table; pause.*

In the letter-box! [*Slips shrinkingly up to the hall door.*] There it lies.—Torvald, Torvald—now we are lost!

> MRS LINDEN *enters from the left with the costume.*

MRS LINDEN: There, I think it's all right now. Shall we just try it on?

NORA [*hoarsely and softly*]: Christina, come here.

MRS LINDEN [*throws down the dress on the sofa*]: What's the matter? You look quite distracted.

NORA: Come here. Do you see that letter? There, see—through the glass of the letter-box.

MRS LINDEN: Yes, yes, I see it.

NORA: That letter is from Krogstad—

MRS LINDEN: Nora—it was Krogstad who lent you the money.

NORA: Yes; and now Torvald will know everything.

MRS LINDEN: Believe me, Nora, it's the best thing for both of you.

NORA: You don't know all yet. I have forged a name—

MRS LINDEN: Good heavens!

NORA: Now, listen to me, Christina; you shall bear me witness—

MRS LINDEN: How 'witness'? What am I to—?

NORA: If I should go out of my mind—it might easily happen—

MRS LINDEN: Nora!

NORA: Or if anything else should happen to me—so that I couldn't be here—!

MRS LINDEN: Nora, Nora, you're quite beside yourself!

NORA: In case any one wanted to take it all upon himself—the whole blame—you understand—

MRS LINDEN: Yes, yes; but how can you think—?

NORA: You shall bear witness that it's not true, Christina. I'm not out of my mind at all; I know quite well what I'm saying; and I tell you nobody else knew anything about it; I did the whole thing, I myself. Remember that.

MRS LINDEN: I shall remember. But I don't understand what you mean—

NORA: Oh, how should you? It's the miracle coming to pass.

MRS LINDEN: The miracle?

NORA: Yes, the miracle. But it's so terrible, Christina; it mustn't happen for all the world.

MRS LINDEN: I shall go straight to Krogstad and talk to him.

NORA: Don't; he'll do you some harm.

MRS LINDEN: Once he would have done anything for me.

NORA: He?

MRS LINDEN: Where does he live?

NORA: Oh, how can I tell—? Yes— [*Feels in her pocket.*] Here's his card. But the letter, the letter—!

HELMER [*knocking outside*]: Nora!

NORA [*shrieks in terror*]: Oh, what is it? What do you want?

HELMER: Well, well, don't be frightened. We're not coming in; you've bolted the door. Are you trying on your dress?

NORA: Yes, yes, I'm trying it on. It suits me so well, Torvald.

MRS LINDEN [*who has read the card*]: Why, he lives close by here.

NORA: Yes, but it's no use now. We are lost. The letter is there in the box.

MRS LINDEN: And your husband has the key?

NORA: Always.

MRS LINDEN: Krogstad must demand his letter back, unread. He must find some pretext—

NORA: But this is the very time when Torvald generally—

MRS LINDEN: Prevent him. Keep him occupied. I shall come back as quickly as I can. [*She goes out hastily by the hall door.*]

NORA [*opens* HELMER's *door and peeps in*]: Torvald!

HELMER: Well, may one come into one's own room again at last? Come, Rank, we'll have a look— [*In the doorway.*] But how's this?

NORA: What, Torvald dear?

HELMER: Rank led me to expect a grand transformation.

RANK [*in the doorway*]: So I understand. I suppose I was mistaken.

NORA: No, no one shall see me in my glory till to-morrow evening.

HELMER: Why, Nora dear, you look so tired. Have you been practising too hard?

NORA: No, I haven't practised at all yet.

HELMER: But you'll have to—

NORA: Oh yes, I must, I must! But, Torvald, I can't get on at all without your help. I've forgotten everything.

HELMER: Oh, we shall soon freshen it up again.

NORA: Yes, do help me, Torvald. You must promise me— Oh, I'm so nervous about it. Before so many people— This evening you must give yourself up entirely to me. You mustn't do a stroke of work; you mustn't even touch a pen. Do promise, Torvald dear!

HELMER: I promise. All this evening I shall be your slave. Little helpless thing—! But, by-the-bye, I must just— [*Going to hall door.*]

NORA: What do you want there?

HELMER: Only to see if there are any letters.

NORA: No, no, don't do that, Torvald.

HELMER: Why not?

NORA: Torvald, I beg you not to. There are none there.

HELMER: Let me just see. [*Is going.*]

NORA, *at the piano, plays the first bars of the tarantella.*

HELMER [*at the door, stops*]: Aha!

NORA: I can't dance to-morrow if I don't rehearse with you first.

HELMER [*going to her*]: Are you really so nervous, dear Nora?

NORA: Yes, dreadfully! Let me rehearse at once. We have time before dinner. Oh, do sit down and play for me, Torvald dear; direct me and put me right, as you used to do.

HELMER: With all the pleasure in life, since you wish it. [*Sits at piano.*]

NORA *snatches the tambourine out of the box, and hurriedly drapes herself in a long parti-coloured shawl; then, with a bound, stands in the middle of the floor.*

NORA: Now play for me! Now I'll dance!

HELMER *plays and* NORA *dances.* RANK *stands at the piano behind* HELMER *and looks on.*

HELMER [*playing*]: Slower! Slower!

NORA: Can't do it slower!

HELMER: Not so violently, Nora.

NORA: I must! I must!

HELMER [*stops*]: No, no, Nora–that will never do.

NORA [*laughs and swings her tambourine*]: Didn't I tell you so!

RANK: Let me play for her.

HELMER [*rising*]: Yes, do–then I can direct her better.

RANK *sits down to the piano and plays;* NORA *dances more and more wildly.* HELMER *stands by the stove and addresses frequent corrections to her; she seems not to hear. Her hair breaks loose, and falls over her shoulders. She does not notice it, but goes on dancing.* MRS LINDEN *enters and stands spellbound in the doorway.*

MRS LINDEN: Ah—!

NORA [*dancing*]: We're having such fun here Christina!

HELMER: Why, Nora dear, you're dancing as if it were a matter of life and death.

NORA: So it is.

HELMER: Rank, stop! This is the merest madness. Stop, I say!

RANK *stops playing, and* NORA *comes to a sudden standstill.*

HELMER [*going towards her*]: I couldn't have believed it. You've positively
. forgotten all I taught you.
NORA [*throws the tambourine away*]: You see for yourself.
HELMER: You really do want teaching.
NORA: Yes, you see how much I need it. You must practise with me up to the last
moment. Will you promise me, Torvald?
HELMER: Certainly, certainly.
NORA: Neither to-day nor to-morrow must you think of anything but me. You
mustn't open a single letter—mustn't look at the letter-box!
HELMER: Ah, you're still afraid of that man—
NORA: Oh yes, yes, I am.
HELMER: Nora, I can see it in your face—there's a letter from him in the box.
NORA: I don't know, I believe so. But you're not to read anything now; nothing
ugly must come between us until all is over.
RANK [*softly, to* HELMER]: You mustn't contradict her.
HELMER [*putting his arm around her*]: The child shall have her own way. But to-
morrow night, when the dance is over—
NORA: Then you shall be free.

ELLEN *appears in the doorway, right.*

ELLEN: Dinner is on the table, ma'am.
NORA: We'll have some champagne, Ellen.
ELLEN: Yes, ma'am. [*Goes out.*]
HELMER: Dear me! Quite a banquet.
NORA: Yes, and we'll keep it up till morning. [*Calling out.*] And macaroons,
Ellen—plenty—just this once.
HELMER [*seizing her hand*]: Come, come, don't let us have this wild excitement!
Be my own little lark again.
NORA: Oh yes, I will. But now go into the dining-room; and you too, Doctor
Rank. Christina, you must help me to do up my hair.
RANK [*softly, as they go*]: There's nothing in the wind? Nothing—I mean—?
HELMER: Oh no, nothing of the kind. It's merely this babyish anxiety I was
telling you about.

They go out to the right.

NORA: Well?
MRS LINDEN: He's gone out of town.
NORA: I saw it in your face.
MRS LINDEN: He comes back to-morrow evening. I left a note for him.
NORA: You shouldn't have done that. Things must take their course. After all,
there's something glorious in waiting for the miracle.
MRS LINDEN: What is it you're waiting for?
NORA: Oh, you can't understand. Go to them in the dining-room; I shall come
in a moment.

MRS LINDEN *goes into the dining-room.* NORA *stands for a moment as though
collecting her thoughts; then looks at her watch.*

Five. Seven hours till midnight. Then twenty-four hours till the next midnight. Then the tarantella will be over. Twenty-four and seven? Thirty-one hours to live.

HELMER *appears at the door, right.*

HELMER: What has become of my little lark?
NORA [*runs to him with open arms*]: Here she is!

ACT THREE

The same room. The table, with the chairs around it, in the middle. A lighted lamp on the table. The door to the hall stands open. Dance music is heard from the floor above.

> MRS LINDEN *sits by the table and absently turns the pages of a book. She tries to read, but seems unable to fix her attention; she frequently listens and looks anxiously towards the hall door.*

MRS LINDEN [*looks at her watch*]: Not here yet; and the time is nearly up. If only he hasn't— [*Listens again.*] Ah, there he is. [*She goes into the hall and cautiously opens the outer door; soft footsteps are heard on the stairs; she whispers.*] Come in; there is no one here.

KROGSTAD [*In the doorway*]: I found a note from you at my house. What does it mean?

MRS LINDEN: I *must* speak to you.

KROGSTAD: Indeed? And in this house?

MRS LINDEN: I could not see you at my rooms. They have no separate entrance. Come in; we are quite alone. The servants are asleep, and the Helmers are at the ball upstairs.

KROGSTAD [*coming into the room*]: Ah! So the Helmers are dancing this evening? Really?

MRS LINDEN: Yes. Why not?

KROGSTAD: Quite right. Why not?

MRS LINDEN: And now let us talk a little.

KROGSTAD: Have we two anything to say to each other?

MRS LINDEN: A great deal.

KROGSTAD: I should not have thought so.

MRS LINDEN: Because you have never really understood me.

KROGSTAD: What was there to understand? The most natural thing in the world—a heartless woman throws a man over when a better match offers.

MRS LINDEN: Do you really think me so heartless? Do you think I broke with you lightly?

KROGSTAD: Did you not?

MRS LINDEN: Do you really think so?

KROGSTAD: If not, why did you write me that letter?

MRS LINDEN: Was it not best? Since I had to break with you, was it not right that I should try to put an end to all that you felt for me?

KROGSTAD [*clenching his hands together*]: So that was it? And all this—for the sake of money!

MRS LINDEN: You ought not to forget that I had a helpless mother and two little brothers. We could not wait for you, Nils, as your prospects then stood.

KROGSTAD: Perhaps not; but you had no right to cast me off for the sake of others, whoever the others might be.

MRS LINDEN: I don't know. I have often asked myself whether I had the right.

KROGSTAD [*more softly*]: When I had lost you, I seemed to have no firm ground left under my feet. Look at me now. I am a shipwrecked man clinging to a spar.

MRS LINDEN: Rescue may be at hand.

KROGSTAD: It was at hand; but then you came and stood in the way.

MRS LINDEN: Without my knowledge, Nils. I did not know till to-day that it was you I was to replace in the Bank.

KROGSTAD: Well, I take your word for it. But now that you do know, do you mean to give way?

MRS LINDEN: No, for that would not help you in the least.

KROGSTAD: Oh, help, help—! I should do it whether or no.

MRS LINDEN: I have learnt prudence. Life and bitter necessity have schooled me.

KROGSTAD: And life has taught me not to trust fine speeches.

MRS LINDEN: Then life has taught you a very sensible thing. But deeds you will trust?

KROGSTAD: What do you mean?

MRS LINDEN: You said you were a shipwrecked man, clinging to a spar.

KROGSTAD: I have good reason to say so.

MRS LINDEN: I too am shipwrecked, and clinging to a spar. I have no one to mourn for, no one to care for.

KROGSTAD: You made your own choice.

MRS LINDEN: No choice was left me.

KROGSTAD: Well, what then?

MRS LINDEN: Nils, how if we two shipwrecked people could join hands?

KROGSTAD: What!

MRS LINDEN: Two on a raft have a better chance than if each clings to a separate spar.

KROGSTAD: Christina!

MRS LINDEN: What do you think brought me to town?

KROGSTAD: Had you any thought of me?

MRS LINDEN: I must have work or I can't bear to live. All my life, as long as I can remember, I have worked; work has been my one great joy. Now I stand quite alone in the world, aimless and forlorn. There is no happiness in working for one's self. Nils, give me somebody and something to work for.

KROGSTAD: I cannot believe in all this. It is simply a woman's romantic craving for self-sacrifice.

MRS LINDEN: Have you ever found me romantic?

KROGSTAD: Would you really—? Tell me: do you know all my past?

MRS LINDEN: Yes.

KROGSTAD: And do you know what people say of me?

MRS LINDEN: Did you not say just now that with me you could have been another man?

KROGSTAD: I am sure of it.

MRS LINDEN: Is it too late?

KROGSTAD: Christina, do you know what you are doing? Yes, you do; I see it in your face. Have you the courage then—?

MRS LINDEN: I need some one to be a mother to, and your children need a mother. You need me, and I–I need you. Nils, I believe in your better self.

With you I fear nothing.

KROGSTAD [*seizing her hands*]: Thank you—thank you, Christina. Now I shall make others see me as you do.—Ah, I forgot—

MRS LINDEN [*listening*]: Hush! The tarantella! Go! go!

KROGSTAD: Why? What is it?

MRS LINDEN: Don't you hear the dancing overhead? As soon as that is over they will be here.

KROGSTAD: Oh yes, I shall go. Nothing will come of this, after all. Of course, you don't know the step I have taken against the Helmers.

MRS LINDEN: Yes, Nils, I do know.

KROGSTAD: And yet you have the courage to—?

MRS LINDEN: I know to what lengths despair can drive a man.

KROGSTAD: Oh, if I could only undo it!

MRS LINDEN: You could. Your letter is still in the box.

KROGSTAD: Are you sure?

MRS LINDEN: Yes; but—

KROGSTAD [*looking to her searchingly*]: Is that what it all means? You want to save your friend at any price. Say it out—is that your idea?

MRS LINDEN: Nils, a woman who has once sold herself for the sake of others, does not do so again.

KROGSTAD: I shall demand my letter back again.

MRS LINDEN: No, no.

KROGSTAD: Yes, of course. I shall wait till Helmer comes; I shall tell him to give it back to me—that it's only about my dismissal—that I don't want it read—

MRS LINDEN: No, Nils, you must not recall the letter.

KROGSTAD: But tell me, wasn't that just why you got me to come here?

MRS LINDEN: Yes, in my first alarm. But a day has passed since then, and in that day I have seen incredible things in this house. Helmer must know everything; there must be an end to this unhappy secret. These two must come to a full understanding. They must have done with all these shifts and subterfuges.

KROGSTAD: Very well, if you like to risk it. But *one* thing I can do, and at once—

MRS LINDEN [*listening*]: Make haste! Go, go! The dance is over; we're not safe another moment.

KROGSTAD: I shall wait for you in the street.

MRS LINDEN: Yes, do; you must see me home.

KROGSTAD: I never was so happy in all my life! [KROGSTAD *goes out by the outer door. The door between the room and the hall remains open.*]

MRS LINDEN [*arranging the room and getting her outdoor things together*]: What a change! What a change! To have some one to work for, to live for; a home to make happy! Well, it shall not be my fault if I fail.—I wish they would come.— [*Listens.*] Ah, here they are! I must get my things on.

> *Takes bonnet and cloak.* HELMER'*s and* NORA'*s voices are heard outside, a key is turned in the lock, and* HELMER *drags* NORA *almost by force into the hall. She wears the Italian costume with a large black shawl over it. He is in evening dress and wears a black domino, open.*

NORA [*struggling with him in the doorway*]: No, no, no! I won't go in! I want to go upstairs again; I don't want to leave so early!

HELMER: But, my dearest girl—!

NORA: Oh, please, please, Torvald, I beseech you—only one hour more!

HELMER: Not one minute more, Nora dear; you know what we agreed. Come, come in; you're catching cold here. [*He leads her gently into the room in spite of her resistance.*]

MRS LINDEN: Good-evening.

NORA: Christina!

HELMER: What, Mrs Linden! You here so late?

MRS LINDEN: Yes, I ought to apologise. I did so want to see Nora in her costume.

NORA: Have you been sitting here waiting for me?

MRS LINDEN: Yes; unfortunately I came too late. You had gone upstairs already, and I felt I couldn't go away without seeing you.

HELMER [*taking* NORA*'s shawl off*]: Well then, just look at her! I assure you she's worth it. Isn't she lovely, Mrs Linden?

MRS LINDEN: Yes, I must say—

HELMER: Isn't she exquisite? Every one said so. But she's dreadfully obstinate, dear little creature. What's to be done with her? Just think, I had almost to force her away.

NORA: Oh, Torvald, you'll be sorry some day that you didn't let me stay, if only for one half-hour more.

HELMER: There! You hear her, Mrs Linden? She dances her tarantella with wild applause, and well she deserved it, I must say—though there was, perhaps, a little too much nature in her rendering of the idea—more than was, strictly speaking, artistic. But never mind—the point is, she made a great success, a tremendous success. Was I to let her remain after that—to weaken the impression? Not if I know it. I took my sweet little Capri girl—my capricious little Capri girl, I might say—under my arm; a rapid turn round the room, curtsey to all sides, and—as they say in novels—the lovely apparition vanished! And exit should always be effective, Mrs Linden; but I can't get Nora to see it. By Jove! it's warm here. [*Throws his domino on a chair and opens the door to his room.*] What! No light there? Oh, of course. Excuse me—[*Goes in and lights candles.*]

NORA [*whispers breathlessly*]: Well?

MRS LINDEN [*softly*]: I've spoken to him.

NORA: And—?

MRS LINDEN: Nora—you must tell your husband everything—

NORA [*tonelessly*]: I knew it!

MRS LINDEN: You have nothing to fear from Krogstad; but you must speak out.

NORA: I shall not speak?

MRS LINDEN: Then the letter will.

NORA: Thank you, Christina. Now I know what I have to do. Hush—!

HELMER [*coming back*]: Well, Mrs Linden, have you admired her?

MRS LINDEN: Yes; and now I must say good-night.

HELMER: What, already? Does this knitting belong to you?

MRS LINDEN [*takes it*]: Yes, thanks; I was nearly forgetting it.

HELMER: Then you do knit?

MRS LINDEN: Yes.

HELMER: Do you know, you ought to embroider instead?

MRS LINDEN: Indeed! Why?

HELMER: Because it's so much prettier. Look now! You hold the embroidery in the left hand, so, and then work the needle with the right hand, in a long, graceful curve—don't you?

MRS LINDEN: Yes, I suppose so.

HELMER: But knitting is always ugly. Just look—your arms close to your sides, and the needles going up and down—there's something Chinese about it.—They really gave us splendid champagne to-night.

MRS LINDEN: Well, good-night, Nora, and don't be obstinate any more.

HELMER: Well said, Mrs Linden!

MRS LINDEN: Good-night, Mr Helmer.

HELMER [*accompanying her to the door*]: Good-night, good-night; I hope you'll get safely home. I should be glad to—but you have such a short way to go. Good-night, good-night. [*She goes;* HELMER *shuts the door after her and comes forward again.*] At last we've got rid of her: she's a terrible bore.

NORA: Aren't you very tired, Torvald?

HELMER: No, not in the least.

NORA: Nor sleepy?

HELMER: Not a bit. I feel particularly lively. But you? You do look tired and sleepy.

NORA: Yes, very tired. I shall soon sleep now.

HELMER: There, you see. I was right after all not to let you stay longer.

NORA: Oh, everything you do is right.

HELMER [*kissing her forehead*]: Now my lark is speaking like a reasonable being. Did you notice how jolly Rank was this evening?

NORA: Indeed? Was he? I had no chance of speaking to him.

HELMER: Nor I, much; but I haven't seen him in such good spirits for a long time. [*Looks at* NORA *a little, then comes nearer her.*] It's splendid to be back in our own home, to be quite alone together!—Oh, you enchanting creature!

NORA: Don't look at me in that way, Torvald.

HELMER: I am not to look at my dearest treasure?—at all the loveliness that is mine, mine only, wholly and entirely mine?

NORA [*goes to the other side of the table*]: You mustn't say these things to me this evening.

HELMER [*following*]: I see you have the tarantella still in your blood—and that makes you all the more enticing. Listen! the other people are going now. [*More softly.*] Nora—soon the whole house will be still.

NORA: Yes, I hope so.

HELMER: Yes, don't you, Nora darling? When we are among strangers, so you know why I speak so little to you, and keep so far away, and only steal a glance at you now and then—do you know why I do it? Because I am fancying that we love each other in secret, that I am secretly betrothed to you, and that no one dreams that there is anything between us.

NORA: Yes, yes, yes. I know all your thoughts are with me.

HELMER: And then, when the time comes to go, and I put the shawl about your smooth, soft shoulders, and this glorious neck of yours, I imagine you are my bride, that our marriage is just over, that I am bringing you for the first time to my home—that I am alone with you for the first time—quite alone with you, in your trembling loveliness! All this evening I have been longing for you, and you only. When I watched you swaying and whirling in the tarantella—my blood boiled—I could endure it no longer; and that's why I made you come home with me so early—

NORA: Go now, Torvald! Go away from me. I won't have all this.

HELMER: What do you mean? Ah, I see you're teasing me, little Nora! Won't—won't! Am I not your husband—?

A knock at the outer door.

NORA [*starts*]: Did you hear—?

HELMER [*going towards the hall*]: Who's there?

RANK [*outside*]: It is I; may I come in for a moment?

HELMER [*in a low tone, annoyed*]: Oh! what can he want just now? [*Aloud.*] Wait a moment. [*Opens door.*] Come, it's nice of you to look in.

RANK: I thought I heard your voice, and that put it into my head. [*Looks round.*] Ah, this dear old place! How cosy you two are here!

HELMER: You seemed to find it pleasant enough upstairs, too.

RANK: Exceedingly. Why not? Why shouldn't one take one's share of everything in this world? All one can, at least, and as long as one can. The wine was splendid—

HELMER: Especially the champagne.

RANK: Did you notice it? It's incredible the quantity I contrived to get down.

NORA: Torvald drank plenty of champagne, too.

RANK: Did he?

NORA: Yes, and it always puts him in such spirits.

RANK: Well, why shouldn't one have a jolly evening after a well-spent day?

HELMER: Well-spent! Well, I haven't much to boast of in that respect.

RANK [*slapping him on the shoulder*]: But I *have*, don't you see?

NORA: I suppose you have been engaged in a scientific investigation, Doctor Rank?

RANK: Quite right.

HELMER: Bless me! Little Nora talking about scientific investigations!

NORA: Am I to congratulate you on the result?

RANK: By all means.

NORA: It was good then?

RANK: The best possible, both for doctor and patient–certainty.

NORA [*quickly and searchingly*]: Certainty?

RANK: Absolute certainty. Wasn't I right to enjoy myself after that?

NORA: Yes, quite right, Doctor Rank.

HELMER: And so say I, provided you don't have to pay for it to-morrow.

RANK: Well, in this life nothing is to be had for nothing.

NORA: Doctor Rank–I'm sure you are very fond of masquerades?

RANK: Yes, when there are plenty of amusing disguises—

NORA: Tell me, what shall we two be at our next masquerade?

HELMER: Little featherbrain! Thinking of your next already!

RANK: We two? I'll tell you. You must go as a good fairy.

HELMER: Ah, but what costume would indicate that?

RANK: She has simply to wear her everyday dress.

HELMER: Capital! But don't you know what you will be yourself?

RANK: Yes, my dear friend, I am perfectly clear upon that point.

HELMER: Well?

RANK: At the next masquerade I shall be invisible.

HELMER: What a comical idea!

RANK: There's a big black hat–haven't you heard of the invisible hat? It comes down all over you, and then no one can see you.

HELMER [*with a suppressed smile*]: No, you're right there.

RANK: But I'm quite forgetting what I came for. Helmer, give me a cigar–one of the dark Havanas.

HELMER: With the greatest pleasure. [*Hands cigar-case.*]

RANK [*takes one and cuts the end off*]: Thank you.

NORA [*striking a wax match*]: Let me give you a light.

RANK: A thousand thanks.

She holds the match. He lights his cigar at it.

And now, good-bye!

HELMER: Good-bye, good-bye, my dear fellow.

NORA: Sleep well, Doctor Rank.

RANK: Thanks for the wish.

NORA: Wish me the same.

RANK: You? Very well, since you ask me – Sleep well. And thanks for the light. [*He nods to them both and goes out.*]

HELMER [*in an undertone*]: He's been drinking a good deal.

NORA [*absently*]: I daresay.

HELMER *takes his bunch of keys from his pocket and goes into the hall.*

Torvald, what are you doing there?

HELMER: I must empty the letter-box; it's quite full; there will be no room for the newspapers to-morrow morning.

NORA: Are you going to work to-night?

HELMER: You know very well I am not. – Why, how is this? Some one has been at the lock.

NORA: The lock—?

HELMER: I'm sure of it. What does it mean? I can't think that the servants—? Here's a broken hair-pin. Nora, it's one of yours.

NORA [*quickly*]: It must have been the children—

HELMER: Then you must break them of such tricks. – There! At last I've got it open. [*Takes contents out and calls into the kitchen.*] Ellen! – Ellen, just put the hall door lamp out. [*He returns with letters in his hand, and shuts the inner door.*] Just see how they've accumulated. [*Turning them over.*] Why, what's this?

NORA [*at the window*]: The letter! Oh no, no, Torvald!

HELMER: Two visiting-cards – from Rank.

NORA: From Doctor Rank?

HELMER [*looking at them*]: Doctor Rank. They were on the top. He must just have put them in.

NORA: Is there anything on them?

HELMER: There's a black cross over the name. Look at it. What an unpleasant idea! It looks just as if he were announcing his own death.

NORA: So he is.

HELMER: What! Do you know anything? Has he told you anything?

NORA: Yes. These cards mean that he has taken his last leave of us. He is going to shut himself up and die.

HELMER: Poor fellow! Of course I knew we couldn't hope to keep him long. But so soon—! And to go and creep into his lair like a wounded animal—

NORA: When we *must* go, it is best to go silently. Don't you think so, Torvald?

HELMER [*walking up and down*]: He had so grown into our lives, I can't realise that he is gone. He and his sufferings and his loneliness formed a sort of cloudy background to the sunshine of our happiness.—Well, perhaps it's best as it is—at any rate for him. [*Stands still.*] And perhaps for us too, Nora. Now we two are thrown entirely upon each other. [*Takes her in his arms.*] My darling wife! I feel as if I could never hold you close enough. Do you know, Nora, I often wish some danger might threaten you, that I might risk body and soul, and everything, everything, for your dear sake.

NORA [*tears herself from him and says firmly*]: Now you shall read your letters, Torvald.

HELMER: No, no; not to-night. I want to be with you, my sweet wife.

NORA: With the thought of your dying friend—?

HELMER: You are right. This has shaken us both. Unloveliness has come between us—thoughts of death and decay. We must seek to cast them off. Till then—we will remain apart.

NORA [*her arms round his neck.*] Torvald! Good-night! good-night!

HELMER [*kissing her forehead*]: Good-night, my little song-bird. Sleep well, Nora. Now I shall go and read my letters. [*He goes with the letters in his hand into his room and shuts the door.*]

NORA [*with wild eyes, gropes about her, seizes* HELMER'*s domino, throws it round her, and whispers quickly, hoarsely, and brokenly*]: Never to see him again. Never, never, never. [*Throws her shawl over her head.*] Never to see the children again. Never, never.—Oh that black, icy water! Oh that bottomless—! If it were only over! Now he has it; he's reading it. Oh, no, no, no, not yet. Torvald, good-bye—! Good-bye, my little ones—!

She is rushing out by the hall; at the same moment HELMER *flings his door open, and stands there with an open letter in his hand.*

HELMER: Nora!

NORA [*shrieks*]: Ah—!

HELMER: What is this? Do you know what is in this letter?

NORA: Yes, I know. Let me go! Let me pass!

HELMER [*holds her back*]: Where do you want to go?

NORA [*tries to break away from him*]: You shall not save me, Torvald.

HELMER [*falling back*]: True! Is what he writes true? No, no, it is impossible that this can be true.

NORA: It is true. I have loved you beyond all else in the world.

HELMER: Pshaw—no silly evasions!

NORA [*a step nearer him.*] Torvald—!

HELMER: Wretched woman—what have you done?

NORA: Let me go—you shall not save me! You shall not take my guilt upon yourself!

HELMER: I don't want any melodramatic airs. [*Locks the outer door.*] Here you shall stay and give an account of yourself. Do you understand what you have done? Answer! Do you understand it?

NORA [*looks at him fixedly, and says with a stiffening expression*]: Yes; now I begin fully to understand it.

HELMER [*walking up and down*]: Oh! what an awful awakening! During all these eight years—she who was my pride and my joy—a hypocrite, a liar—worse, worse—a criminal. Oh, the unfathomable hideousness of it all! Ugh! Ugh!

NORA *says nothing, and continues to look fixedly at him.*

I ought to have known how it would be. I ought to have foreseen it. All your father's want of principle–be silent!–all your father's want of principle you have inherited–no religion, no morality, no sense of duty. Now I am punished for screening him! I did it for your sake; and you reward me like this.

NORA: Yes–like this.

HELMER: You have destroyed my whole happiness. You have ruined my future. Oh, it's frightful to think of! I am in the power of a scoundrel; he can do whatever he pleases with me, demand whatever he chooses; he can domineer over me as much as he likes, and I must submit. And all this disaster and ruin is brought upon me by an unprincipled woman!

NORA: When I am out of the world, you will be free.

HELMER: Oh, no fine phrases. Your father, too, was always ready with them. What good would it do me, if you were 'out of the world', as you say? No good whatever! He can publish the story all the same; I might even be suspected of collusion. People will think I was at the bottom of it all and egged you on. And for all this I have you to thank–you whom I have done nothing but pet and spoil during our whole married life. Do you understand now what you have done to me?

NORA [*with cold calmness*]: Yes.

HELMER: The thing is so incredible, I can't grasp it. But we must come to an understanding. Take that shawl off. Take it off, I say! I must try to pacify him in one way or another–the matter must be hushed up, cost what it may.–As for you and me, we must make no outward change in our way of life–no *outward* change, you understand. Of course, you will continue to live here. But the children cannot be left in your care. I dare not trust them to you.–Oh, to have to say this to one I have loved so tenderly–whom I still—! But that must be a thing of the past. Henceforward there can be no question of happiness, but merely of saving the ruins, the shreds, the show—

A ring; HELMER *starts.*

What's that? So late! Can it be the worst? Can he—? Hide yourself, Nora; say you are ill.

NORA *stands motionless.* HELMER *goes to the door and opens it.*

ELLEN [*half dressed, in the hall*]: Here is a letter for you, ma'am.

HELMER: Give it to me. [*Seizes the letter and shuts the door.*] Yes, from him. You shall not have it. I shall read it.

NORA: Read it!

HELMER [*by the lamp*]: I have hardly the courage to. We may both be lost, both you and I. Ah! I *must* know. [*Hastily tears the letter open; reads a few lines, looks at an enclosure; with a cry of joy.*] Nora!

NORA *looks inquiringly at him.*

HELMER: Nora!–Oh! I must read it again.–Yes, yes, it is so. I am saved! Nora, I am saved!

NORA: And I?

HELMER: You too, of course; we are both saved, both of us. Look here–he sends you back your promissory note. He writes that he regrets and apologises that a happy turn in his life— Oh, what matter what he writes. We are saved, Nora! No one can harm you. Oh, Nora, Nora—; but first to get rid of this hateful thing. I'll just see— [*Glances at the I.O.U.*] No, I will not look at it; the whole thing shall be nothing but a dream to me. [*Tears the I.O.U. and both letters in pieces. Throws them into the fire and watches them burn.*] There! it's gone–He said that ever since Christmas Eve— Oh, Nora, they must have been three terrible days for you!

NORA: I have fought a hard fight for the last three days.

HELMER: And in your agony you saw no other outlet but— No; we won't think of that horror. We will only rejoice and repeat–it's over, all over! Don't you hear, Nora? You don't seem able to grasp it. Yes, it's over. What is this set look on your face? Oh, my poor Nora, I understand; you cannot believe that I have forgiven you. But I have, Nora; I swear it. I have forgiven everything. I know that what you did was all for love of me.

NORA: That is true.

HELMER: You loved me as a wife should love her husband. It was only the means that, in your inexperience, you misjudged. But do you think I love you the less because you cannot do without guidance? No, no. Only lean on me; I will counsel you, and guide you. I should be no true man if this very womanly helplessness did not make you doubly dear in my eyes. You mustn't dwell upon the hard things I said in my first moment of terror, when the world seemed to be tumbling about my ears. I have forgiven you, Nora–I swear I have forgiven you.

NORA: I thank you for your forgiveness. [*Goes out, to the right.*]

HELMER: No, stay—! [*Looking through the doorway.*] What are you going to do?

NORA [*inside*]: To take off my masquerade dress.

HELMER [*in the doorway*]: Yes, do, dear. Try to calm down, and recover your balance, my scared little song-bird. You may rest secure. I have broad wings to shield you. [*Walking up and down near the door.*] Oh, how lovely–how cosy out home is, Nora! Here you are safe; here I can shelter you like a hunted dove whom I have saved from the claws of the hawk. I shall soon bring your poor beating heart to rest; believe me, Nora, very soon. To-morrow all this will seem quite different–everything will be as before. I shall not need to tell you again that I forgive you; you will feel for yourself that it is true. How could you think I could find it in my heart to drive you away, or even so much as to reproach you? Oh, you don't know a true man's heart, Nora. There is something indescribably sweet and soothing to a man in having forgiven his wife–honestly forgiven her, from the bottom of his heart. She becomes his property in a double sense. She is as though born again; she has become, so to speak, at once his wife and his child. That is what you shall henceforth be to me, my bewildered, helpless darling. Don't be troubled about anything, Nora; only open your heart to me, and I will be both will and conscience to you.

NORA *enters in everyday dress.*

Why, what's this? Not gone to bed? You have changed your dress?

NORA: Yes, Torvald; now I have changed my dress.

HELMER: But why now, so late—?

NORA: I shall not sleep to-night.

HELMER: But, Nora dear—

NORA [*looking at her watch*]: It's not so late yet. Sit down, Torvald; you and I have much to say to each other. [*She sits at one side of the table.*]

HELMER: Nora—what does this mean? Your cold, set face—

NORA: Sit down. It will take some time. I have much to talk over with you.

HELMER *sits at the other side of the table.*

HELMER: You alarm me, Nora. I don't understand you.

NORA: No, that is just it. You don't understand me; and I have never understood you—till to-night. No, don't interrupt. Only listen to what I say.—We must come to a final settlement, Torvald.

HELMER: How do you mean?

NORA [*after a short silence*]: Does not one thing strike you as we sit here?

HELMER: What should strike me?

NORA: We have been married eight years. Does it not strike you that this is the first time we two, you and I, man and wife, have talked together seriously?

HELMER: Seriously! What do you call seriously?

NORA: During eight whole years, and more—ever since the day we first met—we have never exchanged one serious word about serious things.

HELMER: Was I always to trouble you with the cares you could not help me to bear?

NORA: I am not talking of cares. I say that we have never yet set ourselves seriously to get to the bottom of anything.

HELMER: Why, my dearest Nora, what have you to do with serious things?

NORA: There we have it! You have never understood me.—I have had great injustice done me, Torvald; first by father, and then by you.

HELMER: What! By your father and me?—By us, who have loved you more than all the world?

NORA [*shaking her head*]: You have never loved me. You only thought it amusing to be in love with me.

HELMER: Why, Nora, what a thing to say!

NORA: Yes, it is so, Torvald. While I was at home with father, he used to tell me all his opinions, and I held the same opinions. If I had others I said nothing about them, because he wouldn't have liked it. He used to call me his doll-child, and played with me as I played with my dolls. Then I came to live in your house—

HELMER: What an expression to use about our marriage!

NORA [*undisturbed*]: I mean I passed from father's hands into yours. You arranged everything according to your taste; and I got the same tastes as you; or I pretended to—I don't know which—both ways, perhaps; sometimes one and sometimes the other. When I look back on it now, I seem to have been living here like a beggar, from hand to mouth. I lived by performing tricks for you, Torvald. But you would have it so. You and father have done me a great wrong. It is your fault that my life has come to nothing.

HELMER: Why, Nora, how unreasonable and ungrateful you are! Have you not been happy here?

NORA: No, never. I thought I was; but I never was.

HELMER: Not—not happy!

NORA: No; only merry. And you have always been so kind to me. But our house has been nothing but a play-room. Here I have been your doll-wife, just as at home I used to be papa's doll-child. And the children, in their turn, have been my dolls. I thought it fun when you played with me, just as the children did when I played with them. That has been our marriage, Torvald.

HELMER: There is some truth in what you say, exaggerated and overstrained though it be. But henceforth it shall be different. Play-time is over; now comes the time for education.

NORA: Whose education? Mine, or the children's?

HELMER: Both, my dear Nora.

NORA: Oh, Torvald, you are not the man to teach me to be a fit wife for you.

HELMER: And you can say that?

NORA: And I—how have I prepared myself to educate the children?

HELMER: Nora!

NORA: Did you not say yourself, a few minutes ago, you dared not trust them to me?

HELMER: In the excitement of the moment! Why should you dwell upon that?

NORA: No—you were perfectly right. That problem is beyond me. There is another to be solved first—I must try to educate myself. You are not the man to help me in that. I must set about it alone. And that is why I am leaving you.

HELMER [*jumping up*]: What—do you mean to say—?

NORA: I must stand quite alone if I am ever to know myself and my surroundings; so I cannot stay with you.

HELMER: Nora! Nora!

NORA: I am going at once. I daresay Christina will take me in for to-night—

HELMER: You are mad! I shall not allow it! I forbid it!

NORA: It is of no use your forbidding me anything now. I shall take with me what belongs to me. From you I will accept nothing, either now or afterwards.

HELMER: What madness this is!

NORA: To-morrow I shall go home—I mean to what was my home. It will be easier for me to find some opening there.

HELMER: Oh, in your blind inexperience—

NORA: I must try to gain experience, Torvald.

HELMER: To forsake your home, your husband, and your children! And you don't consider what the world will say.

NORA: I can pay no heed to that. I only know that I must do it.

HELMER: This is monstrous! Can you forsake your holiest duties in this way?

NORA: What do you consider my holiest duties?

HELMER: Do I need to tell you that? Your duties to your husband and your children.

NORA: I have other duties equally sacred.

HELMER: Impossible! What duties do you mean?

NORA: My duties towards myself.

HELMER: Before all else you are a wife and a mother.

NORA: That I no longer believe. I believe that before all else I am a human being, just as much as you are—or at least that I should try to become one. I know that most people agree with you, Torvald, and that they say so in books. But henceforth I can't be satisfied with what most people say, and what is in books. I must think things out for myself, and try to get clear about them.

HELMER: Are you not clear about your place in your own home? Have you not an infallible guide in questions like these? Have you not religion?

NORA: Oh, Torvald, I don't really know what religion is.

HELMER: What do you mean?

NORA: I know nothing but what Pastor Hansen told me when I was confirmed. He explained that religion was this and that. When I get away from all this and stand alone, I will look into that matter too. I will see whether what he taught me is right, or, at any rate, whether it is right for me.

HELMER: Oh, this is unheard of! And from so young a woman! But if religion cannot keep you right, let me appeal to your conscience–for I suppose you have some moral feeling? Or, answer me: perhaps you have none?

NORA: Well, Torvald, it's not easy to say. I really don't know–I am all at sea about these things. I only know that I think quite differently from you about them. I hear, too, that the laws are different from what I thought; but I can't believe that they can be right. It appears that a woman has no right to spare her dying father, or to save her husband's life! I don't believe that.

HELMER: You talk like a child. You don't understand the society in which you live.

NORA: No, I do not. But now I shall try to learn. I must make up my mind which is right–society or I.

HELMER: Nora, you are ill; you are feverish; I almost think you are out of your senses.

NORA: I have never felt so much clearness and certainty as to-night.

HELMER: You are clear and certain enough to forsake husband and children?

NORA: Yes, I am.

HELMER: Then there is only one explanation possible.

NORA: What is that?

HELMER: You no longer love me.

NORA: No; that is just it.

HELMER: Nora!–Can you say so!

NORA: Oh, I'm so sorry, Torvald; for you've always been so kind to me. But I can't help it. I do not love you any longer.

HELMER [*mastering himself with difficulty*]: Are you clear and certain on this point too?

NORA: Yes, quite. That is why I will not stay here any longer.

HELMER: And can you also make clear to me how I have forfeited your love?

NORA: Yes, I can. It was this evening, when the miracle did not happen; for then I saw you were not the man I had imagined.

HELMER: Explain yourself more clearly; I don't understand.

NORA: I have waited so patiently all these eight years; for of course I saw clearly enough that miracles don't happen every day. When this crushing blow threatened me, I said to myself so confidently, 'Now comes the miracle!' When Krogstad's letter lay in the box, it never for a moment occurred to me that you would think of submitting to that man's conditions. I was convinced that you would say to him, 'Make it known to all the world'; and that then—

HELMER: Well? When I had given my own wife's name up to disgrace and shame—?

NORA: Then I firmly believed that you would come forward, take everything upon yourself, and say, 'I am the guilty one.'

HELMER: Nora—!

NORA: You mean I would never have accepted such a sacrifice? No, certainly not. But what would my assertions have been worth in opposition to yours?–*That* was the miracle that I hoped for and dreaded. And it was to hinder *that* that I wanted to die.

HELMER: I would gladly work for you day and night, Nora—bear sorrow and want for your sake. But no man sacrifices his honour, even for one he loves.

NORA: Millions of women have done so.

HELMER: Oh, you think and talk like a silly child.

NORA: Very likely. But you neither think nor talk like the man I can share my life with. When your terror was over—not for what threatened me, but for yourself—when there was nothing more to fear—then it seemed to you as though nothing had happened. I was your lark again, your doll, just as before—whom you would take twice as much care of in future, because she was so weak and fragile. [*Stands up.*] Torvald—in that moment it burst upon me that I had been living here these eight years with a strange man, and had borne him three children.—Oh, I can't bear to think of it! I could tear myself to pieces!

HELMER [*sadly*]: I see it, I see it; an abyss has opened between us.—But, Nora, can it never be filled up?

NORA: As I now am, I am no wife for you.

HELMER: I have strength to become another man.

NORA: Perhaps—when your doll is taken away from you.

HELMER: To part—to part from you! No, Nora, no; I can't grasp the thought.

NORA [*going into room on the right*]: The more reason for the thing to happen. [*She comes back with out-door things and a small travelling-bag, which she places on a chair.*]

HELMER: Nora, Nora, not now! Wait till to-morrow.

NORA [*putting on cloak*]: I can't spend the night in a strange man's house.

HELMER: But can we not live here, as brother and sister—?

NORA [*fastening her hat*]: You know very well that wouldn't last long. [*Puts on the shawl.*] Good-bye, Torvald. No, I won't go to the children. I know they are in better hands than mine. As I now am, I can be nothing to them.

HELMER: But some time, Nora—some time—?

NORA: How can I tell? I have no idea what will become of me.

HELMER: But you are my wife, now and always!

NORA: Listen, Torvald—when a wife leaves her husband's house, as I am doing, I have heard that in the eyes of the law he is free from all duties towards her. At any rate, I release you from all duties. You must not feel yourself bound, any more than I shall. There must be perfect freedom on both sides. There, I give you back your ring. Give me mine.

HELMER: That too?

NORA: That too.

HELMER: Here it is.

NORA: Very well. Now it is all over. I lay the keys here. The servants know about everything in the house—better than I do. To-morrow, when I have started, Christina will come to pack up the things I brought with me from home. I will have them sent after me.

HELMER: All over! all over! Nora, will you never think of me again?

NORA: Oh, I shall often think of you, and the children, and this house.

HELMER: May I write to you, Nora?

NORA: No—never. You must not.

HELMER: But I must send you—

NORA: Nothing, nothing.

HELMER: I must help you if you need it.

NORA: No, I say. I take nothing from strangers.

HELMER: Nora–can I never be more than a stranger to you?

NORA [*taking her travelling-bag*]: Oh, Torvald, then the miracle of miracles would have to happen—

HELMER: What is the miracle of miracles?

NORA: Both of us would have to change so that— Oh, Torvald, I no longer believe in miracles.

HELMER: But *I* will believe. Tell me! We must so change that—?

NORA: That communion between us shall be a marriage. Good-bye. [*She goes out by the hall door.*]

HELMER [*sinks into a chair by the door with his face in his hands*]: Nora! Nora! [*He looks round and rises.*] Empty. She is gone. [*A hope springs up in him.*] Ah! The miracle of miracles—?!

From below is heard the reverberation of a heavy door closing.

THE END

THE
FATHER
AUGUST
STRINDBERG

THE FATHER

This translation first published in England in 1964 by
Martin Secker & Warburg Limited, 14 Carlisle Street,
London W1

English translation © 1964 by Michael Meyer

THE FATHER

A Tragedy in Three Acts
(1887)

Translated from the Swedish by

MICHAEL MEYER

CHARACTERS

THE CAPTAIN
LAURA (*his Wife*)
BERTHA (*their Daughter*)
DR ÖSTERMARK
THE PASTOR
THE NURSE
NÖJD (*a Servant*)
THE CAPTAIN'S BATMAN

This translation of *The Father* was first performed on 14 January 1964 at the Piccadilly Theatre, London. The cast was:

THE CAPTAIN	*Trevor Howard*
LAURA	*Joyce Redman*
BERTHA	*Jo Maxwell-Muller*
DR ÖSTERMARK	*Nigel Stock*
THE PASTOR	*Alfred Burke*
THE NURSE	*Gwen Nelson*
NÖJD	*Trevor Peacock*
BATMAN	*Malcolm Tierney*

Designed by MALCOLM PRIDE
Produced by CASPER WREDE

ACT ONE

A room in the CAPTAIN's house. Upstage right, a door. In the centre of the room is a large round table, with newspapers and magazines. On the right, a leather sofa and a table. In the right-hand corner, a concealed door. On the left, a secretaire, with an ornamental clock on it, and a door which leads to the rest of the house. There are weapons on the wall; rifles and game-bags. By the door, clothes-hangers with military tunics on them. On the large table a lamp is burning.

SCENE I

The CAPTAIN *and the* PASTOR *on the leather sofa. The* CAPTAIN *is in undress uniform, with riding-boots and spurs. The* PASTOR *is in black, with a white stock, but without his clerical bands. He is smoking a pipe.*

The CAPTAIN *rings. The* BATMAN *enters.*

BATMAN: Sir?

CAPTAIN: Is Nöjd out there?

BATMAN: He's waiting for orders in the kitchen, sir.

CAPTAIN: In the kitchen again! Send him here at once!

BATMAN: Sir! [*Goes.*]

PASTOR: What's the matter now?

CAPTAIN: Oh, the blackguard's been mucking about with one of the girls again. Damned nuisance, that fellow!

PASTOR: Nöjd? Why, you had trouble with him last year too!

CAPTAIN: You remember? Perhaps you'd give him a friendly talking-to–that might have some effect. I've sworn at him, and given him a tanning, but it doesn't do any good.

PASTOR: So you want me to read him a sermon! Do you think the Word of God will have any effect on a cavalryman?

CAPTAIN: Well, brother-in-law, it doesn't have much effect on me, as you know—

PASTOR: Yes, I know!

CAPTAIN: But on him—? Try, anyway.

SCENE 2

The CAPTAIN. *The* PASTOR. NÖJD.

CAPTAIN: Well, Nöjd, what have you been up to now?

NÖJD: God bless you, Captain, I couldn't tell you before his Reverence.

PASTOR: Come, come, don't be bashful, my lad!

CAPTAIN: Own up, or you know what'll happen!

NÖJD: Well, sir, it was like this, you see. We was dancing up at Gabriel's, and then, yes, well, Louis said—

CAPTAIN: What's Louis got to do with it? Stick to the facts!

NÖJD: Well, Emma suggested we should go to the barn.

CAPTAIN: I see! So it was Emma who seduced you!

NÖJD: Not far off. And I'll say this—if a girl ain't willing, she don't run no danger.

CAPTAIN: Out with it! Are you the child's father or not?

NÖJD: How should I know?

CAPTAIN: What! You don't know!

NÖJD: Well, you can never be sure.

CAPTAIN: Weren't you the only one, then?

NÖJD: I was that time, but that don't mean to say I was the only one.

CAPTAIN: Are you saying Louis's to blame? Is that it?

NÖJD: It ain't easy to say who's to blame.

CAPTAIN: But you've told Emma you want to marry her.

NÖJD: Yes, well, you have to tell them that.

CAPTAIN [*to* PASTOR]: This is monstrous!

PASTOR: It's the old story. Now, look here, Nöjd, surely you're man enough to know whether you're the father!

NÖJD: Well, I did go with her, but, as your Reverence knows, that don't necessarily mean anything need happen.

PASTOR: Come, come, my lad, don't start trying to evade the issue! You surely don't want to leave the girl alone with the child! Of course we can't force you to marry her, but you must accept responsibility for the child. You must!

NÖJD: All right, but Louis must pay his share.

CAPTAIN: Oh, very well, it'll have to go to court. I can't unravel the rights and wrongs of this, and I don't feel inclined to try. Right, get out!

PASTOR: Nöjd! One moment. Hm! Don't you regard it as dishonourable to leave a girl high and dry like that with a child? Eh? Well? Don't you feel such behaviour would be—hm—?

NÖJD: Oh, yes, if I knew I was the child's father. But that's something a man can never be sure of, your Reverence. And it's no joke spending your whole life sweating for other men's children. I'm sure you and the Captain'll both appreciate that.

CAPTAIN: Get out!

NÖJD: Sir! [*Goes.*]

CAPTAIN: And keep out of the kitchen, damn you!

SCENE 3

CAPTAIN: Well, why didn't you lay into him?

PASTOR: What? I thought I spoke very strictly.

CAPTAIN: Oh, you just sat there mumbling to yourself.

PASTOR: To be honest, I don't know what one ought to say. It's bad luck on the girl, yes. But it's bad luck on the boy, too. Suppose he isn't the father? The girl can suckle the child for four months at the orphanage, and then she'll be shot of him, but the boy can't dodge his responsibility like that. She'll get a good job afterwards in some decent home, but if he gets thrown out of his regiment, he's finished.

CAPTAIN: Yes, I wouldn't like to be the magistrate who has to judge this case. I don't suppose the lad's completely innocent—one can't be sure. But one thing you can be sure of. The girl's guilty—if you can say anyone's guilty.

PASTOR: Yes, yes! I'm not condemning anyone! But what were we speaking about when this blessed business intervened? Bertha's confirmation, wasn't it?

CAPTAIN: It's not just her confirmation. It's the whole question of her upbringing. This house is stuffed with women every one of whom wants to bring up my child. My mother-in-law wants to make her a spiritualist, Laura wants her to be a painter, her governess wants her to be a Methodist, old Margaret wants her to be a Baptist, and the maids are trying to get her into the Salvation Army. Well, you can't patch a soul together like a damned quilt. I have the chief right to decide her future, and I'm obstructed whichever way I turn. I've got to get her out of this house.

PASTOR: You've too many women running your home.

CAPTAIN: You needn't tell me that. It's like a cage full of tigers—if I didn't keep a red-hot iron in front of their noses, they'd claw me to the ground the first chance they got. Yes, you can laugh, you old fox! It wasn't enough that I married your sister, you had to palm your old stepmother off on me too!

PASTOR: Well, good heavens, one can't have one's stepmother living under one's roof.

CAPTAIN: No, they're better off in rooms. Someone else's!

PASTOR: Well, well. We all have our cross to bear.

CAPTAIN: Yes, but I've a damned sight too many. I've got my old nurse too, and she treats me as though I was still in a bib! Oh, she's a dear old soul, heaven knows, but she doesn't belong here!

PASTOR: You should keep your women in their place, Adolf. You let them rule you.

CAPTAIN: My dear brother-in-law, will you kindly tell me how one keeps women in their place?

PASTOR: To speak frankly, Laura—I know she's my sister, but—well, she was always a little difficult.

CAPTAIN: Oh, Laura has her moods, but she's not too bad.

PASTOR: Ah, come on! I know her!

CAPTAIN: Well, she's had a romantic upbringing, and has a little difficulty in accepting life, but, after all, she is my wife—

PASTOR: And is therefore the best of women. No, Adolf, she's the biggest stone round your neck.

CAPTAIN: Yes, well, anyway, now the whole house has become impossible. Laura doesn't want to let Bertha out of her sight. But I can't let her stay in this asylum.

PASTOR: So? Laura won't—? Hm, then I'm afraid things aren't going to be easy. When she was a child, she used to lie absolutely still like a corpse until she'd got what she wanted. And when she'd got it, she'd give it back, explaining that it wasn't the *thing* she wanted, simply the fact of having her will.

CAPTAIN: I see, she was like that already, was she? Hm! She gets so emotional sometimes that I become frightened, and wonder if she isn't—well—sick.

PASTOR: But what is it you want for Bertha that she finds so unacceptable? Can't you meet each other halfway?

CAPTAIN: You mustn't imagine I want to build the child into a prodigy, or a copy of myself. But I don't want to play the pimp and educate her just simply for marriage—if I do that and she stays single, she'll become one of these embittered spinsters. On the other hand, I don't want to train her for some masculine vocation that'll need years of study and be completely wasted if she does get married.

PASTOR: What do you want, then?

CAPTAIN: I'd like her to become a teacher. Then, if she stays single she'll be able to look after herself, and won't be worse off than these wretched schoolmasters who have to support a family. And if she does marry, she can use the knowledge she's gained in bringing up her own children. That's logical, isn't it?

PASTOR: Perfectly. But hasn't she shown a great talent for painting? Wouldn't it be bad for her to repress that?

CAPTAIN: No, no. I've shown her efforts to a prominent artist, and he says it's only the kind of thing people learn to do at schools. But then some young ass came here last summer who knew more about such matters, and said she was a genius—and as far as Laura was concerned, that settled it.

PASTOR: Was he in love with the girl?

CAPTAIN: I presume so.

PASTOR: Then God help you, my dear fellow, for there'll be nothing you can do about that! But this is a sad business, and of course Laura has allies—in there.

CAPTAIN: Oh, yes, never you fear! The whole household is up in arms—and, between you and me, they're not fighting strictly according to the rules of chivalry.

PASTOR [*gets up*]: Do you think I haven't been through all this?

CAPTAIN: You too?

PASTOR: Are you surprised?

CAPTAIN: But the worst is, it seems to me Bertha's future is being decided in there from motives of hatred. They keep dropping hints that men will see that women can do this and do that. Man versus woman, that's their theme, all day long. Must you go now? No, stay for supper. I can't offer you much, but, did I tell you, I'm expecting the new doctor to pay a call? Have you seen him?

PASTOR: I caught a glimpse of him on my way here. He looks a pleasant, straightforward chap.

CAPTAIN: Does he? Good! Think he might be on my side?

PASTOR: Who knows? It depends how much he's had to do with women.

CAPTAIN: Oh, come on, do stay!

PASTOR: No thanks, my dear fellow. I've promised to be home for supper, and my old lady gets so worried if I'm late.

CAPTAIN: Worried? Angry, you mean! Well, as you wish. Let me give you a hand with your coat.

PASTOR: It's certainly very cold tonight. Thank you. You want to look after yourself, Adolf. You look nervy.

CAPTAIN: Do I?

PASTOR: You're not quite yourself, are you?

CAPTAIN: Has Laura given you that idea? She's been treating me like a budding corpse for twenty years.

PASTOR: Laura? No, no, I just wondered— Take care of yourself! That's my advice. Well, goodbye, old chap. But didn't you want to talk to me about confirmation?

CAPTAIN: No. Chalk that one up to society's conscience. I'm not an evangelist—and I don't intend to be a martyr! I'm past all that. Goodbye! Give my regards to your wife!

PASTOR: Goodbye, brother! Give mine to Laura!

SCENE 4

The CAPTAIN. *Then* LAURA.

CAPTAIN [*opens the secretaire, sits down at it and starts counting*]: Thirty-four—nine—forty-three—seven eights—fifty-six.

LAURA [*enters from the main part of the house*]: Would you mind—

CAPTAIN: In a moment. Sixty-six, seventy-one, eighty-four, eighty-nine, ninety-two, one hundred. What is it?

LAURA: Perhaps I'm disturbing you.

CAPTAIN: Not at all. The housekeeping money, I suppose?

LAURA: Yes. The housekeeping money.

CAPTAIN: Leave the bills there, and I'll go through them.

LAURA: Bills?

CAPTAIN: Yes.

LAURA: Oh, you want bills now?

CAPTAIN: Of course I want bills. We are financially embarrassed, and if things come to a head I've got to be able to produce accounts. Otherwise I can be punished as a negligent debtor.

LAURA: It isn't my fault if we're financially embarrassed.

CAPTAIN: That's just what the bills will establish.

LAURA: I'm not to blame if our tenant won't pay the lease of his farm.

CAPTAIN: Who recommended him? You. Why did you recommend such a—what shall we call him? Drone?

LAURA: If he's such a drone, why did you take him?

CAPTAIN: Because you wouldn't let me eat in peace, sleep in peace or work in peace until you'd got him here. You wanted to have him because your brother wanted to be rid of him, your mother wanted to have him because I didn't want to have him, the governess wanted to have him because he was a Methodist, and old Margaret wanted to have him because she'd known his grandmother since they were children. So we took him, and if I hadn't I should now be either sitting in an asylum or lying in the family vault. However, here is your household allowance, and some pin money. You can give me the bills later.

LAURA [*curtseys*]: Thank you, sir. Do you keep bills for your private expenses?

CAPTAIN: That's none of your business.

LAURA: True; no more than my child's upbringing. Have you gentlemen reached a decision now, after your evening session?

CAPTAIN: I had already made my decision. I merely wished to impart it to the only friend whom I and my family have in common. Bertha is to live in town. She will leave in a fortnight.

LAURA: And where is she to live, if I may be allowed to ask?

CAPTAIN: I have arranged for her to lodge with my lawyer, Mr Saevberg.

LAURA: That freethinker!

CAPTAIN: The law states that a child is to be brought up in her father's faith.

LAURA: And the mother has no say in the matter?

CAPTAIN: None. She has sold her birthright by legal contract, and has surrendered all her claims. In return, the husband supports her and her children.

LAURA: So she has no rights over her own child?

CAPTAIN: None whatever. Once you have sold something, you can't get it back and keep the money.

LAURA: But if the father and mother should agree on a compromise—?

CAPTAIN: How is that possible? I want her to live in town, you want her to stay at home. The arithmetical mean would be that she should live on the railway line, halfway between. This is a situation which cannot be resolved by compromise.

LAURA: Then it must be resolved by force. What did Nöjd want here?

CAPTAIN: That is my professional secret.

LAURA: The whole kitchen knows.

CAPTAIN: Then you should.

LAURA: I do.

CAPTAIN: And have passed judgment?

LAURA: The law is quite explicit on the matter.

CAPTAIN: The law is not explicit as to who is the child's father.

LAURA: No. But one usually knows.

CAPTAIN: Wise men say one can never be sure about such things.

LAURA: Not be sure who is a child's father?

CAPTAIN: They say not.

LAURA: How extraordinary! Then how can the father have all these rights over her child?

CAPTAIN: He only has them if he accepts responsibility for the child—or has the responsibility forced upon him. And in marriage, of course, the question of paternity does not arise.

LAURA: Never?

CAPTAIN: I should hope not.

LAURA: But if the wife has been unfaithful?

CAPTAIN: That is not relevant to our discussion. Are there any other questions you want to ask me?

LAURA: None whatever.

CAPTAIN: Then I shall go to my room. Please be so good as to inform me when the Doctor comes. [*Shuts the secretaire and rises.*]

LAURA: Very well.

CAPTAIN [*going through concealed door right*]: The moment he arrives! I don't wish to insult him. You understand? [*Goes.*]

LAURA: I understand.

SCENE 5

LAURA *alone. She looks at the banknotes she is holding in her hand.*

GRANDMOTHER [*offstage*]: Laura!

LAURA: Yes?

GRANDMOTHER: Is my tea ready?

LAURA [*in the doorway left*]: I'll bring it in a moment.

Goes towards the door upstage. Just before she reaches it, the BATMAN *opens it.*

BATMAN: Dr Östermark!

DOCTOR [*enters*]: Mrs Lassen?

LAURA [*goes to greet him, and stretches out her hand*]: How do you do, Doctor! Welcome to our home. The Captain is out, but he will be back shortly.

DOCTOR: Please forgive me for coming so late. I've already had to visit some patients.

LAURA: Won't you sit down?

DOCTOR: Thank you, Mrs Lassen, thank you.

LAURA: Yes, there's a lot of illness around here just now. However, I do hope you'll be happy here. We lead such a lonely life out here in the country, so it's important for us to have a doctor who takes an interest in his patients. And I've heard many flattering reports of you, so I hope we shall see a good deal of each other.

DOCTOR: You are too kind, Mrs Lassen. But I trust, for your sake, that my visits will not always have to be professional! Your family enjoys good health—?

LAURA: We've never had any serious illnesses, I am glad to say. But things aren't quite as they should be—

DOCTOR: Indeed?

LAURA: I'm afraid they are not at all as we could wish.

DOCTOR: Really? You alarm me!

LAURA: There are certain domestic matters which a woman's honour and conscience require her to conceal from the world—

DOCTOR: But not from her doctor.

LAURA: Precisely. So I feel it is my painful duty to be quite open with you from the start.

DOCTOR: Could we not postpone this conversation until I have had the pleasure of making the Captain's acquaintance?

LAURA: No. You must hear what I have to say before you see him.

DOCTOR: It concerns him, then?

LAURA: Yes—my poor, beloved husband!

DOCTOR: You alarm me, Mrs Lassen. Believe me, I am deeply touched by your distress.

LAURA [*takes out her handkerchief*]: My husband is mentally unbalanced. Now you know. You will be able to judge for yourself later.

DOCTOR: What! But I have read with admiration the Captain's excellent dissertations on mineralogy, and have always received the impression of a powerful and lucid intelligence.

LAURA: Indeed? I should be most happy if it could be proved that we have all been mistaken.

DOCTOR: It is of course possible that his judgment may be disturbed where other matters are concerned. Pray proceed.

LAURA: That is what we fear. You see, sometimes he has the most extraordinary ideas, which we would gladly indulge if they didn't threaten the existence of his whole family. For example, he has a mania for buying things.

DOCTOR: That is unfortunate. But what does he buy?

LAURA: Whole crates of books, which he never reads.

DOCTOR: Well, it isn't so unusual for a scholar to buy books.

LAURA: You don't believe me?

DOCTOR: Yes, Mrs Lassen, I am sure that what you say is true.

LAURA: But is it reasonable for a man to claim that he can see in a microscope what is happening on another planet?

DOCTOR: Does he say that?

LAURA: Yes.

DOCTOR: In a microscope?

LAURA: Yes, in a microscope.

DOCTOR: If that is so, it is indeed unfortunate—

LAURA: *If* it is so! You don't believe me, Doctor. And I sit here telling you all our family secrets—

DOCTOR: Now listen, Mrs Lassen. I am honoured that you should confide in me. But as a doctor, I must investigate the matter thoroughly before I can make a diagnosis. Has the Captain shown any symptoms of capriciousness or vacillation?

LAURA: Any symptoms! We've been married for twenty years, and he has never yet taken a decision without reversing it.

DOCTOR: Is he stubborn?

LAURA: He always insists on having his own way, but once he has got it he loses interest and begs me to decide.

DOCTOR: This is serious. I must observe him closely. You see, my dear Mrs Lassen, will is the backbone of the mind. If the will is impaired, the mind crumbles.

LAURA: God knows I've done my best to meet his wishes during all these long years of trial. Oh, if you knew the things I have had to put up with! If you knew!

DOCTOR: Mrs Lassen, your distress moves me deeply, and I promise you I will see what can be done. But after what you have told me, I must ask you one thing. Avoid touching on any subject that might excite your husband. In a sick brain, fancies grow like weeds, and can easily develop into obsessions or even monomania. You understand?

LAURA: You mean I must take care not to make him suspicious?

DOCTOR: Exactly. A sick man is receptive to the slightest impression, and can therefore be made to imagine anything.

LAURA: Really? I understand. Yes. Yes.

A bell rings within the house.

Excuse me, my mother wishes to speak with me. Wait a moment—this must be Adolf!

SCENE 6

The DOCTOR. *The* CAPTAIN *enters through the concealed door.*

CAPTAIN: Ah, you here already, Doctor? Delighted to meet you!

DOCTOR: Good evening, Captain. It is a great honour for me to make the acquaintance of so distinguished a scientist.

CAPTAIN: Oh, nonsense. My military duties don't allow me much time for research. All the same, I think I'm on to a new discovery.

DOCTOR: Indeed?

CAPTAIN: Yes, I've been submitting meteorites to spectral analysis, and I've discovered carbon! Evidence of organic life! What do you say to that?

DOCTOR: You can see that in the microscope?

CAPTAIN: Microscope? Good God, no—spectroscope!

DOCTOR: Spectroscope? Ah—forgive me! Well, then, you'll soon be able to tell us what is happening on Jupiter.

CAPTAIN: Not what *is* happening, but what *has* happened. If only that damned shop in Paris would send those books! I really believe all the booksellers in the world have entered into a conspiracy against me. Would you believe it, for two months I haven't had a reply to a single order, letter or even telegram! It's driving me mad. I just don't understand it.

DOCTOR: Oh, that's just common laziness. You mustn't take it too seriously.

CAPTAIN: Yes, but, damn it, I won't be able to get my thesis ready in time—I know there's a fellow in Berlin working on the same lines. Still, we haven't met to talk about that, but about you. If you'd care to live here, we have a small apartment in the wing—or would you rather take over your predecessor's lodgings?

DOCTOR: Just as you please.

CAPTAIN: No, as *you* please. Say, now.

DOCTOR: You must decide, Captain.

CAPTAIN: No, no, I can't decide. You must say what you want. I've no feelings in the matter, no feelings at all.

DOCTOR: Yes, but I can't decide—

CAPTAIN: For God's sake, man, say what you want! I've no inclinations in the matter, I couldn't care less what you do! Are you such a nitwit that you don't know what you want? Answer, or I'll get angry!

DOCTOR: If I must decide, then I'll live here!

CAPTAIN: Good! Thank you. Oh—! Forgive me, Doctor, but nothing annoys me so much as to hear people say it's all the same to them!

He rings. The NURSE *enters.*

Oh, is it you, Margaret? Tell me, old dear, do you know if the wing is ready for the doctor?

NURSE: Yes, sir, it's all ready.

CAPTAIN: Good. Then I won't keep you, Doctor—I expect you're tired. Good night. I'll look forward to seeing you again tomorrow.

DOCTOR: Good night, Captain.

CAPTAIN: I suppose my wife told you a few things about conditions here, to put you in the picture?

DOCTOR: She did mention one or two details she thought it might be useful for a stranger to know. Good night, Captain.

SCENE 7

The CAPTAIN. *The* NURSE.

CAPTAIN: What do you want, old darling? Is something the matter?

NURSE: Now, listen, Mr Adolf, pet.

CAPTAIN: What is it, Margaret? Speak out, my dear. You're the only one I can listen to without getting spasms.

NURSE: Now, listen, Mr Adolf. Why don't you go halfway to meet madam about the child? Remember, she's a mother.

CAPTAIN: Remember I'm a father, Margaret.

NURSE: Now, now, now! A father has other things beside his child, but a mother has nothing. She's only got her child.

CAPTAIN: Exactly. She has only one burden, but I have three, including hers. Do you think I'd have stayed a soldier all my life if I hadn't been saddled with her and her child?

NURSE: Oh, I didn't mean that.

CAPTAIN: No, I'm sure you didn't. You're trying to put me in the wrong.

NURSE: Surely you think I want what's best for you, Mr Adolf?

CAPTAIN: Yes, yes, my dear, I'm sure you do. But you don't know what's best for me. You see, it isn't enough for me to have given the child life. I want to give it my soul too.

NURSE: Well, I don't understand that. But I still think you ought to be able to come to some agreement.

CAPTAIN: You are not my friend, Margaret.

NURSE: I? Why, Mr Adolf, how can you say such a thing? Do you think I can forget you were my baby when you were little?

CAPTAIN: Have *I* ever forgotten it, my dear? You've been like a mother to me—you've supported me, up to now, when everyone's been against me—but now, when I need you most, now you betray me and go over to the enemy.

NURSE: Enemy!

CAPTAIN: Yes, enemy! You know how things are in this house. You've seen it all, from the beginning.

NURSE: Yes, I've seen enough. Blessed Jesus, why must two human beings torment the life out of each other? You're both so good and kind—madam's never like that to me or anyone else.

CAPTAIN: Only to me. Yes, I know. But I'm telling you, Margaret—if you betray me now, you are committing a sin. A web is being spun around me here, and that doctor is not my friend.

NURSE: Oh, Mr Adolf, you think bad of everyone. But that's because you don't follow the true faith. That's the cause of it.

CAPTAIN: And you've found the only true faith, you and your Baptists. Aren't you lucky!

NURSE: Well, I'm luckier than you, Mr Adolf. Humble your heart, and you'll see. God will make you happy, and you'll love your neighbour.

CAPTAIN: It's extraordinary—as soon as you start talking about God and love, your voice becomes hard and your eyes fill with hatred. No, Margaret, you haven't found the true faith.

NURSE: Ah, you're proud. All your learning won't get you far at the Day of Judgment.

CAPTAIN: How arrogantly thou speakest, O humble heart! Yes, I know learning means nothing to animals like you.

NURSE: Shame on you! Never mind. Old Margaret loves her big, big boy best of all, and when the storm comes he'll creep back to her like the good little child he is.

CAPTAIN: Margaret! Forgive me, but—believe me, there's no one here who loves me except you. Help me. I feel something is going to happen here—I don't know what, but there's something evil threatening—

There is a scream from within the house.

What's that? Who's screaming?

SCENE 8

The CAPTAIN. *The* NURSE. BERTHA *enters.*

BERTHA: Father, father! Help me! Save me!

CAPTAIN: What is it, my beloved child? Tell me.

BERTHA: Help me! I think she wants to hurt me!

CAPTAIN: Who wants to hurt you? Tell me. Tell me.

BERTHA: Grandmamma. But it was my fault. I played a trick on her.

CAPTAIN: Tell me about it.

BERTHA: But you mustn't say anything! Promise you won't!

CAPTAIN: Very well. But tell me what it is.

The NURSE *goes.*

BERTHA: Well—in the evenings, she turns down the lamp and sits me down at the table with a pen and paper. And then she says that the spirits are going to write.

CAPTAIN: What! Why haven't you told me about this before?

BERTHA: Forgive me—I didn't dare. Grandmamma says the spirits take their revenge if anyone talks about them. And then the pen writes, but I don't know if it's me. And sometimes it goes all right, but sometimes it won't move at all. And when I'm tired, nothing comes—but its *got* to come! And tonight I thought I was writing well, but then grandmamma said I was copying from some old poem and playing a trick on her—and then she became so horribly angry!

CAPTAIN: Do you believe that spirits exist?

BERTHA: I don't know.

CAPTAIN: But I know they do not!

BERTHA: But grandmamma says you don't understand, and that you have much worse things, that can see what's happening on other planets.

CAPTAIN: She says that, does she? What else does she say?

BERTHA: She says you can't work magic.

CAPTAIN: I haven't said I can. You know what meteorites are? Yes, stones that fall from other heavenly bodies. I can study them and say whether they contain the same elements as our earth. That's all I can see.

BERTHA: But grandmamma says there are things that she can see but you can't.

CAPTAIN: Well, she's lying.

BERTHA: Grandmamma doesn't tell lies.

CAPTAIN: How do you know?

BERTHA: Then mother would be lying too.

CAPTAIN: Hm!

BERTHA: If you say mother's lying, I'll never believe you again!

CAPTAIN: I haven't said that, and you must believe me when I tell you that your happiness and your whole future depend on your leaving this house. Would you like that? Would you like to go and live in town, and learn something new?

BERTHA: Oh, I'd so love to live in town and get away from here! As long as I can see you sometimes—often! In there everything's so gloomy, so horrible, like a winter night—but when you come, father, it's like throwing open the window on a spring morning!

CAPTAIN: My child! My child!

BERTHA: But, father, you must be nice to mother, do you hear? She cries so often.

CAPTAIN: Hm! So you want to go and live in town?

BERTHA: Yes! Yes!

CAPTAIN: But if your mother doesn't want you to?

BERTHA: But she must!

CAPTAIN: But if she doesn't?

BERTHA: Well, then—I don't know. But she must! She must!

CAPTAIN: Will you ask her?

BERTHA: You must ask her, nicely. She doesn't pay any attention to me.

CAPTAIN: Hm! Well, if you want it and I want it, and she doesn't want it, what shall we do then?

BERTHA: Oh, then everything'll be difficult again. Why can't you both—?

SCENE 9

The CAPTAIN. BERTHA. LAURA.

LAURA: Oh, she's here. Now perhaps we can hear her opinion, since her fate is about to be decided.

CAPTAIN: The child can hardly be expected to hold an informed opinion on what a young girl ought to do with her life. We are at least partly qualified to judge, since we have seen a good many young girls grow up.

LAURA: But since we differ, let Bertha decide.

CAPTAIN: No! I permit no one to usurp my rights—neither woman nor child. Bertha, leave us.

BERTHA *goes.*

LAURA: You were afraid to let her speak, because you knew she'd agree with me.

CAPTAIN: I happen to know she wants to leave home. But I also know that you have the power to alter her will at your pleasure.

LAURA: Oh, am I so powerful?

CAPTAIN: Yes. You have a satanic genius for getting what you want. But that's always the way with people who aren't scrupulous about what means they use. How, for example, did you get rid of Dr Norling, and find this new man?

LAURA: Well, how did I?

CAPTAIN: You insulted Norling, so that he went, and got your brother to fix this fellow's appointment.

LAURA: Well, that was very simple, wasn't it? And quite legal. Is Bertha to leave at once?

CAPTAIN: In a fortnight.

LAURA: Is that final?

CAPTAIN: Yes.

LAURA: Have you spoken to Bertha?

CAPTAIN: Yes.

LAURA: Then I shall have to stop it.

CAPTAIN: You can't.

LAURA: Can't? You think I'm prepared to let my daughter live with people who'll tell her that everything I taught her is nonsense, so that she'll despise her mother for the rest of her life?

CAPTAIN: Do you think I am prepared to allow ignorant and conceited women to teach my daughter that her father is a charlatan?

LAURA: That should matter less to you.

CAPTAIN: Why?

LAURA: Because a mother is closer to her child. It has recently been proved that no one can be sure who is a child's father.

CAPTAIN: What has that to do with us?

LAURA: You can't be sure that you are Bertha's father.

CAPTAIN: I–can't be sure—!

LAURA: No. No one can be sure, so you can't.

CAPTAIN: Are you trying to be funny?

LAURA: I'm only repeating what you've said to me. Anyway, how do you know I haven't been unfaithful to you?

CAPTAIN: I could believe almost anything of you, but not that. Besides, if it were true you wouldn't talk about it.

LAURA: Suppose I were prepared for anything–to be driven out, despised, anything–rather than lose my child? Suppose I am telling you the truth now, when I say to you: 'Bertha is my child, but not yours!' Suppose—!

CAPTAIN: Stop!

LAURA: Just suppose. Your power over her would be ended.

CAPTAIN: If you could prove I was not the father.

LAURA: That wouldn't be difficult. Would you like me to?

CAPTAIN: Stop it! At once!

LAURA: I'd only need to name the true father, and tell you the time and place. When was Bertha born? Three years after our marriage—

CAPTAIN: Stop it, or—!

LAURA: Or what? All right, I'll stop. But think carefully before you take any decision. And, above all, don't make yourself ridiculous.

CAPTAIN: God–I could almost weep—!

LAURA: Then you *will* be ridiculous.

CAPTAIN: But not you!

LAURA: No. Things have been arranged more wisely for us.

CAPTAIN: That is why one cannot fight with you.

LAURA: Why try to fight with an enemy who is so much stronger?

CAPTAIN: Stronger?

LAURA: Yes. It's strange, but I've never been able to look at a man without feeling that I am stronger than him.

CAPTAIN: Well, for once you're going to meet your match. And I'll see you never forget it.

LAURA: That'll be interesting.

NURSE [*enters*]: Dinner's ready. Will you come and eat?

LAURA: Thank you.

The CAPTAIN *hesitates, then sits in a chair by the table, next to the sofa.*

Aren't you going to eat?

CAPTAIN: No, thank you. I don't want anything.

LAURA: Are you sulking?

CAPTAIN: No. I'm not hungry.

LAURA: Come along, or there'll be questions asked. Be sensible, now. Oh, very well. If you won't, you'd better go on sitting there. [*Goes.*]

NURSE: Mr Adolf! What is all this?

CAPTAIN: I don't know. Can you explain to me how it is that you women can treat an old man as though he was a child?

NURSE: Don't ask me. I suppose it's because, whether you're little boys or grown men, you're all born of woman.

CAPTAIN: But no woman is born of man. Yes, but I *am* Bertha's father! Tell me, Margaret! You do believe that? Don't you?

NURSE: Lord, what a child you are! Of course you're your own daughter's father. Come and eat now, and don't sit there sulking. There! There now, come along!

CAPTAIN [*gets up*]: Get out, woman! Back to hell, you witches! [*Goes to the door leading to the hall.*] Svaerd! Svaerd!

BATMAN [*enters*]: Sir?

CAPTAIN: Harness the sleigh! At once!

NURSE: Captain! Now, listen—!

CAPTAIN: Out, woman! At once!

NURSE: Lord help us, what's going to happen now?

CAPTAIN [*puts on his hat and makes ready to go out*]: Don't expect me home before midnight! [*Goes.*]

NURSE: Blessed Jesus preserve us, how's all this going to end?

ACT TWO

As in Act One. The lamp is burning on the table. It is night.

SCENE I

The DOCTOR. LAURA.

DOCTOR: After my conversation with your husband, I am by no means convinced that your fears are justified. You made a mistake when you told me he had reached these surprising conclusions about other heavenly bodies by the use of a microscope. Now that I hear it was a spectroscope, he must not only be acquitted of any suspicion of derangement, but appears to have made a genuine contribution to science.

LAURA: But I never said that.

DOCTOR: Madam, I took notes of our conversation, and I remember I questioned you on this very point, because I thought I must have misheard you. One must be most meticulous in such accusations, for they could result in a man being certified as incapable of managing his affairs.

LAURA: Certified as incapable—?

DOCTOR: Yes. Surely you know that a person who is *non compos* loses all his civic and family rights?

LAURA: No, I didn't know that.

DOCTOR: There is one further point on which I feel uneasy. He told me that his letters to booksellers had remained unanswered. Permit me to ask whether you, no doubt from the best of motives, perhaps intercepted them?

LAURA: Yes, I did. I had to protect my family. I couldn't let him ruin us all without doing something.

DOCTOR: Forgive me, but I don't think you can have realised the consequences of such an action. If he finds that you have been secretly interfering in his affairs, his suspicions will be confirmed, and they will grow like an avalanche. Besides, by doing this you have fettered his will and further inflamed his impatience. You must have felt yourself how agonising it is when one's most fervent wishes are obstructed, and one's wings are clipped.

LAURA: Yes, I have.

DOCTOR: Well, then, judge how he must feel.

LAURA [*rises*]: It's midnight, and he hasn't come home. We must be ready for the worst.

DOCTOR: But, tell me, Mrs Lassen, what happened this evening after I left? I must know everything.

LAURA: Oh, he raved and said the most extraordinary things. Can you imagine—he asked if he really was the father of his child!

DOCTOR: How very strange! Where did he get that idea?

LAURA: I can't imagine. Unless—well, he'd been questioning one of the servants

about who was the father to some baby, and when I took the girl's side he
became furious and said no one could know for sure who was any child's
father. God knows I tried my best to calm him, but now I don't see that
there's anything more we can do. [*Weeps.*]

DOCTOR: This mustn't be allowed to continue. Something must be done. But we
mustn't arouse his suspicions. Tell me, has the Captain had such
hallucinations before?

LAURA: It was the same six years ago. Then he actually admitted in a letter to the
doctor that he feared for his own sanity.

DOCTOR: Dear me! This obviously springs from something very deep-rooted. I
mustn't enquire into the sacred secrets of family life, etcetera; I must con-
fine myself to visible symptoms. What is done cannot, alas, be undone; but
some steps should have been taken earlier. Where do you suppose he is
now?

LAURA: I can't imagine. He gets such crazy ideas nowadays.

DOCTOR: Would you like me to wait till he comes back? I could say that your
mother has been feeling poorly, and that I have been attending her. That
would lull his suspicions.

LAURA: Yes, do that. Oh, please don't leave us! If you knew how worried I am!
But wouldn't it be better to tell him straight out what you think about his
condition?

DOCTOR: No, one must never do that with people who are mentally sick.
Certainly not until they raise the subject themselves, and then only under
certain circumstances. It all depends how things develop. But we mustn't sit
in here. Perhaps I should go next door? Then he won't suspect anything.

LAURA: Yes, that's a good idea. Margaret can sit in here. She always stays up
when he goes out, and she's the only one who can do anything with him.
[*Goes to the door, left.*] Margaret! Margaret!

NURSE: What is it, madam? Is the master home?

LAURA: No, but I want you to sit here and wait for him. When he comes, tell him
that my mother is ill and the doctor has come to visit her.

NURSE: Very well. You leave it to me.

LAURA [*opens the door, left*]: Will you come in here, Doctor?

DOCTOR: Thank you.

SCENE 2

NURSE [*at the table; picks up a prayerbook and her spectacles*]: Yes, yes! Yes, yes!
[*Reads half to herself.*]

> A wretched and a grievous thing
> Is life, this vale of suffering.
> Death's angel hovers ever near,
> And whispers into each man's ear:
> 'All's vanity! All's vanity!'
>   Yes, yes! Yes, yes!
>
> All things that live upon the earth
> Fall to the ground before his wrath;
> And only sorrow's ghost survives
> To carve above the green-dug grave:

> 'All's vanity! All's vanity!'
> Yes, yes! Yes, yes!

BERTHA [*enters with a tray of coffee and a piece of embroidery. She whispers*]: Margaret, can I sit with you? It's so horrid up there.

NURSE: Heaven preserve us! Are you still up?

BERTHA: I've got to finish father's Christmas present, you see. And, look! I've something for you!

NURSE: But, my dear Miss Bertha, you can't do this. You've got to get up in the morning, and it's past midnight.

BERTHA: Well, what of it? I daren't sit up there alone. I'm sure there are ghosts about.

NURSE: You see! What did I say? Yes, mark my word, there's no good angel guarding this house. What kind of thing did you hear?

BERTHA: Oh, do you know – I heard someone singing in the attic!

NURSE: In the attic! At this time of night!

BERTHA: Yes. It was a sad song – so sad – I've never heard anything like it before. And it sounded as if it came from the cupboard where the cradle is – you know, on the left—

NURSE: Oi, oi, oi! And with such a storm blowing tonight! I'm frightened it'll bring the chimney-pots down. 'What is this life but toil and care? A moment's hope, then long despair!' Well, my dear child, may God grant us a happy Christmas!

BERTHA: Margaret, is it true father is ill?

NURSE: I'm afraid so.

BERTHA: Then we won't be able to have Christmas. But how can he be up, if he's ill?

NURSE: Well, my child, with his kind of illness you can stay up. Ssh! There's someone on the steps. Go to bed, now, and hide this [*indicates the coffee tray*], or the master'll be angry.

BERTHA [*goes out with the tray*]: Good night, Margaret.

NURSE: Good night, my child. God bless you.

SCENE 3

The NURSE. *The* CAPTAIN.

CAPTAIN [*takes off his greatcoat*]: Are you still up? Go to bed!

NURSE: I only wanted to wait till you—

> *The* CAPTAIN *lights a candle, opens the secretaire, sits down at it immediately and takes from his pocket letters and newspapers.*

Mr Adolf!

CAPTAIN: What do you want?

NURSE: The old lady's sick. And the doctor's here.

CAPTAIN: Is it dangerous?

NURSE: No, I don't think so. Just a chill.

CAPTAIN [*gets up*]: Who was the father of your child, Margaret?

NURSE: Oh, I've told you so many times. That good-for-nothing Johansson.

CAPTAIN: Are you sure it was he?

NURSE: Don't be silly. Of course I'm sure. He was the only one.

CAPTAIN: Yes, but was *he* sure he was the only one? No, he couldn't be. But you could be. There's a difference, you see.

NURSE: I can't see the difference.

CAPTAIN: No, you can't see it, but the difference is there. [*Turns the pages of a photograph album on the table.*] Do you think Bertha is like me? [*Looks at a portrait in the album.*]

NURSE: You're as alike as two berries on a bough.

CAPTAIN: Did Johansson admit he was the father?

NURSE: He had to.

CAPTAIN: It's horrible—! There's the doctor.

SCENE 4

The CAPTAIN. *The* NURSE. *The* DOCTOR.

CAPTAIN: Good evening, Doctor. How is my mother-in-law?

DOCTOR: Oh, it's nothing serious. She's just sprained her left foot slightly.

CAPTAIN: I thought Margaret said she had a chill. There seem to be two rival diagnoses. Go to bed, Margaret.

The NURSE *goes. Pause.*

Please sit down, Doctor.

DOCTOR [*sits*]: Thank you.

CAPTAIN: Is it true that if you cross a zebra with a horse, you get striped foals?

DOCTOR [*surprised*]: That is perfectly correct.

CAPTAIN: Is it also true that if you cross the same mare with an ordinary stallion, the foals may continue to be striped?

DOCTOR: Yes, that is also true.

CAPTAIN: Then, in certain circumstances a brown stallion can sire a striped foal, and vice versa?

DOCTOR: Apparently.

CAPTAIN: *Ergo*, the resemblance that a child bears to its father means nothing?

DOCTOR: Oh—

CAPTAIN: *Ergo*, it can never be proved who is a child's father?

DOCTOR: Er–hm—!

CAPTAIN: You are a widower and have had children?

DOCTOR: Er–yes—

CAPTAIN: Didn't you sometimes feel that your position was ridiculous? I know nothing so ludicrous as to see a father walking with his child on the street, or hear a father talking about his children. 'My wife's children', he should say. Did you never feel the falseness of your position, had you never any pinpricks of doubt? I don't use the word suspicion, for as a gentleman I assume that your wife was above suspicion.

DOCTOR: Indeed I did not! Has not Goethe written: 'A man must take his children on trust'?

CAPTAIN: Trust, where a woman's concerned? That's risky!

DOCTOR: But there are so many kinds of women.

CAPTAIN: Recent research has proved that there is only one kind. When I was young, I was strong and, I flatter myself, handsome. Let me quote you just two incidents which subsequently caused me to ponder. Once I was travelling on a steamer. I was sitting with some friends in the lounge. The young waitress came and sat herself opposite me in tears, and told me that her fiancé had been drowned. We pitied her, and I ordered some champagne. After the second glass, I touched her foot; after the fourth, her knee; and before morning, I had consoled her.

DOCTOR: That was just a fly in winter.

CAPTAIN: Now to my second; and this was a fly in summer. I was at Lysekil. There was a young wife there, with her children—but her husband was in town. She was religious, had very strict principles, read me moral lectures, preached sermons at me—was completely honourable, I still believe. I lent her a book, two books. When the time came for her to leave, strange to relate, she returned them. Three months later, I found in one of these books a visiting card bearing a pretty explicit declaration of love. It was innocent, as innocent as a declaration of love can be from a married woman to a stranger who has never made an advance to her. The moral? Never trust anyone too much!

DOCTOR: Or too little!

CAPTAIN: Exactly; just so far and no further. But, you see, Doctor, that woman was so unconsciously mischievous that she told her husband she had developed a passion for me. That's just the danger, they don't realise their instinctive capacity for creating mischief. It's an extenuating circumstance, but it doesn't nullify their guilt, it merely lessens it.

DOCTOR: Captain, these are unhealthy thoughts. You should keep a watch on yourself—

CAPTAIN: You mustn't use that word, unhealthy. You see, all boilers explode when the manometer reaches breaking-point; but they don't all have the same breaking-point—you understand? Still, you're here to keep an eye on me. If I were not a man I would have the right to accuse—or, as the polite phrase is, to lay a complaint. Then I might perhaps be able to give you a complete diagnosis of my illness, and, what is more, its history. But unfortunately, I am a man, and so I can only, like a Roman, fold my arms across my breast and hold my breath until I die. Good night.

DOCTOR: Captain! If you are ill, it cannot be any reflection on your honour as a man to tell me the truth. I must hear both sides.

CAPTAIN: I should have thought you'd had enough listening to one.

DOCTOR: No, Captain. Do you know, when I sat in the theatre the other evening and heard Mrs Alving orating over her dead husband, I thought to myself: 'What a damned shame the fellow's dead and can't defend himself!'

CAPTAIN: If he'd been alive, do you think he'd have dared to open his mouth? If any dead man rose from his grave, do you think he'd be believed? Good night, Doctor. As you can hear, I am perfectly calm, so you can sleep in peace.

DOCTOR: Good night, then, Captain. I cannot take any further part in this matter.

CAPTAIN: Are we enemies?

DOCTOR: By no means. The pity is that we cannot be friends. Good night. [*Goes.*]

CAPTAIN [*accompanies the* DOCTOR *to the door upstage. Then he goes to the door left, and opens it slightly*]: Come in. I heard you listening.

SCENE 5

LAURA *enters embarrassed. The* CAPTAIN *sits down at the secretaire.*

CAPTAIN: It's late, but we must talk this matter out. Sit down! [*Pause.*] This evening I went to the post office and collected my letters. It is evident from them that you have been intercepting both my outgoing and my incoming correspondence. The resultant waste of time has virtually destroyed the value of my researches.

LAURA: I was acting from kindness. You were neglecting your duties for this work.

CAPTAIN: You were not acting from kindness. You feared that some day I might win more honour through these researches than through my military career, and you were determined that I should not win any honour, because that would throw into relief your insignificance. Now I have confiscated some letters addressed to you.

LAURA: How noble of you.

CAPTAIN: I'm glad you appreciate my qualities. It is clear from these letters that for some time you have been turning all my former friends against me by spreading a rumour concerning my sanity. And you've succeeded, for now hardly one of them, from my commanding officer to my cook, regards me as sane. The situation regarding my mental condition is as follows. My brain is, as you know, unaffected, since I can perform both my professional duties and my duties as a father. I still have my emotions more or less under control, and my will is, to date, fairly unimpaired, but you have been chipping and chafing at it so that soon the cogs will disengage and the wheels will start whirling backwards. I shall not appeal to your feelings, for you have none – that is your strength. But I appeal to your self-interest.

LAURA: Go on.

CAPTAIN: By your behaviour you have succeeded in filling my mind with doubt, so that soon my judgment will be clouded and my thoughts begin to wander. This is the approaching dementia for which you have been waiting, and which may come at any time. Now you must ask yourself the question: is it not more to your interest that I should be well rather than ill? Think carefully? If I break down, I shall lose my job, and you will be without support. If I die, you will receive the insurance on my life; but if I kill myself, you will get nothing. So it is to your own interest that I should go on living.

LAURA: Is this a trap?

CAPTAIN: Yes. It is up to you whether you go round it or stick your neck in it.

LAURA: You say you'll kill yourself. You won't.

CAPTAIN: Are you sure? Do you think a man can live when he has nothing and no one to live for?

LAURA: Then you capitulate?

CAPTAIN: No. I propose an armistice.

LAURA: And your conditions?

CAPTAIN: That I retain my sanity. Free me from my doubts, and I will abandon the battle.

LAURA: What doubts?

CAPTAIN: About Bertha's parentage.

LAURA: Are there any doubts about that?

CAPTAIN: In my mind there are. You have awoken them.

LAURA: I?

CAPTAIN: Yes. You have dripped them into my ear like poison, and events have fostered their growth. Free me from my uncertainty, tell me straight out: 'It is so!' and already I forgive you.

LAURA: How can I confess to a crime I have not committed?

CAPTAIN: What does it matter? You know I shan't reveal it. Do you think a man goes around trumpeting his shame?

LAURA: If I say it isn't true, you won't be sure; but if I say it is, you will be. So you would rather it was true.

CAPTAIN: Yes. It's strange, but I suppose it's because the one cannot be proved, whereas the other can.

LAURA: Have you any grounds for your suspicions?

CAPTAIN: Yes and no.

LAURA: I suppose you'd like me to be guilty so that you could throw me out and keep the child to yourself. But you won't catch me with a trick like that.

CAPTAIN: Do you think I'd want to keep some other man's child if I knew you were guilty?

LAURA: I'm sure you wouldn't. And that's why I realise you were lying just now when you said you already forgave me.

CAPTAIN [gets up]: Laura, save me and my sanity. You don't understand what I'm saying. If the child is not mine, I have no rights over her, and want none—and that is all that *you* want. Isn't it? Or do you want something else too? Do you want to retain your power over the child, but to keep me here as the breadwinner?

LAURA: Power? Yes. What has this life-and-death struggle been for if not for power?

CAPTAIN: I do not believe in resurrection, and to me this child was my life hereafter. She was my idea of immortality—perhaps the only one that has any roots in reality. If you take her away, you cut short my life.

LAURA: Why didn't we part while there was still time?

CAPTAIN: Because the child bound us together. But the bond became a chain. How did it become that? How? I've never thought about it, but now memories return, accusing, condemning. We had been married for two years, and had no children, you know why. I fell ill, and lay near to death. In a lucid moment I hear voices from the drawing-room. It is you and the lawyer, talking about my money—I still had some then. He is explaining that you cannot inherit anything because we have no children, and he asks if you are pregnant. I didn't hear your reply. I got better, and we had a child. Who is the father?

LAURA: You!

CAPTAIN: No, it is not I! A crime lies buried here, and it's beginning to come to light. And what a hellish crime! You women were soft-hearted enough to free your black slaves, but you keep your white ones! I have worked and slaved for you, for your child, your mother, your servants. I have sacrificed my life and my career, I have undergone torture, scourging, sleeplessness, every kind of torment for you, my hair has turned grey, all so that you might live free from care and, when you grow old, enjoy new life through your child. All this I have borne without complaint, because I believed I was the father to this child. This is the most arrant form of theft, the most brutal slavery. I have served seventeen years of hard labour for a crime I did not commit. What can you give me in return?

LAURA: Now you really *are* mad.

CAPTAIN [*sits*]: So you hope. And I have seen how you worked to hide your crime. I pitied you, because I didn't understand why you were sad. I often calmed your evil conscience, supposing that I was driving away some sick thought. I heard you cry aloud in your sleep, though I didn't want to listen. Now I remember—the night before last! It was Bertha's birthday. It was between two and three o'clock in the morning, and I was sitting up, reading. You screamed as though someone was trying to strangle you: 'Don't come, don't come!' I banged on the wall because—because I didn't want to hear any more. I have had my suspicions for a long time, but I didn't dare to hear them confirmed. I have suffered all this for you. What will you do for me?

LAURA: What can I do? I will swear by God and all that is sacred that you are Bertha's father.

CAPTAIN: What good will that do, when you have already said that a mother can and should commit any crime for the sake of her child? I entreat you, by the memory of the past—I beg you, as a wounded man begs for mercy—tell me everything! Don't you see that I am as helpless as a child, can't you hear me crying for pity like a child crying to its mother, can't you forget that I am a man, a soldier who with a word can tame men and beasts? I ask only for the pity you would extend to a sick man, I lay down the insignia of my power and cry for mercy—for my life.

LAURA [*has approached him and lays her hand on his forehead*]: What! Man, you're crying!

CAPTAIN: Yes, I am crying, although I am a man. But has not a man eyes? Has not a man hands, limbs, heart, thoughts, passions? Does he not live by the same food, is he not wounded by the same weapons, warmed and cooled by the same summer and winter as a woman? If you prick us, do we not bleed? If you tickle us, do we not laugh? If you poison us, do we not die? Why should a man be forbidden to complain, or a soldier to weep? Because it is unmanly? Why is it unmanly?

LAURA: Weep, my child. Your mother is here to comfort you. Do you remember, it was as your second mother that I first entered into your life? Your big, strong body was afraid. You were a great child who had come too late into the world, or had come unwanted.

CAPTAIN: Yes, I suppose it was that. Father and mother had me against their will, and so I was born without a will. When you and I became one, I thought I was making myself whole; so I let you rule; and I who, in the barracks, among the soldiers, issued commands, was, with you, the one who obeyed. I grew up at your side, looked up to you as though to a superior being, listened to you as though I was your innocent child.

LAURA: Yes. That's how it was, and I loved you as my child. But, do you know—I suppose you noticed it—every time your feelings towards me changed, and you approached me as my lover, I felt bashful, and your embrace was an ecstasy followed by pangs of conscience, as though my blood was ashamed. The mother became the mistress—ugh!

CAPTAIN: Yes. I saw it, but I didn't understand. I thought you despised my lack of masculinity, and I wanted to win you as a woman by being a man.

LAURA: That was where you made your mistake. The mother was your friend, you see, but the woman was your enemy. Love between man and woman is

war. And don't think I gave myself. I didn't give, I took–what I wanted
to have. But you had the upper hand. I felt it, and I wanted to make you
feel it.

CAPTAIN: No, you were always the one who had the upper hand. You could
hypnotise me so that I neither saw nor heard, but only obeyed. You could
give me a raw potato and make me think it was a peach, you could force me to
admire your stupid whims as strokes of genius, you could have driven me to
crime, yes, even to vice. For you lacked intelligence, and instead of following
my advice you did as *you* wanted. But when, later, I awoke and looked about
me and saw that my honour had been sullied, I wanted to wipe out the stain
through a noble action, a brave deed, a discovery, or an honourable suicide. I
wanted to go to war, but I couldn't. It was then that I turned to science. Now,
when I should stretch out my hand to receive the fruits of my labour, you
chop off my arm. Now I am without honour, and I cannot go on living, for a
man cannot live without honour.

LAURA: But a woman—

CAPTAIN: She has her children, but he has none. Yet you and I and all the other
men and women in the world have gone on living, as innocently as children,
living on fancies, ideals and illusions. And then we awoke. Yes, we awoke,
but with our feet on the pillow, and He Who woke us was Himself a
sleepwalker. When women grow old and cease to be women, they get beards
on their chins. I wonder what men get when they grow old and cease to be
men? We who greeted the dawn were no longer cocks but capons, and the
hens answered our false call, so that when the sun should have risen we found
ourselves sitting in moonlight among ruins, just like in the good old days. It
had only been a fretful slumber, a mad dream. It was no awakening.

LAURA: You know, you ought to have been a poet.

CAPTAIN: Perhaps I ought.

LAURA: Well, I'm sleepy. If you've any more fantasies, keep them until
morning.

CAPTAIN: One word more–and this isn't a fantasy. Do you hate me?

LAURA: Sometimes. When you are a man.

CAPTAIN: It's like racial hatred. If it is true that we are descended from the ape,
it must have been from two different species. We aren't of the same blood, are
we?

LAURA: What do you mean by all that?

CAPTAIN: I feel that, in this war, one of us must go under.

LAURA: Which one?

CAPTAIN: The weaker, of course.

LAURA: And the stronger is in the right?

CAPTAIN: Always. Because he is the one with power.

LAURA: Then I am in the right.

CAPTAIN: You think you have the power?

LAURA: Yes. And tomorrow I shall have it legally, when I have you certified.

CAPTAIN: Certified—?

LAURA: Yes. And then I shall bring up the child myself, without having to listen
to your visions.

CAPTAIN: And who will pay for the child's upbringing, when I am gone?

LAURA: Your pension.

CAPTAIN [*goes towards her threateningly*]: How can you have me certified?

LAURA [*takes out a letter*]: By this letter, an attested copy of which I have deposited with the authorities.

CAPTAIN: What letter?

LAURA [*moves backwards towards the door*]: Yours! The one you wrote to the doctor telling him you were mad.

The CAPTAIN *looks at her dumbly.*

You have done your job as a father and a breadwinner. Now you are no longer needed, and you can go. You realise that my intelligence is equal to my will, and since you are not prepared to stay and admit it, you can go!

The CAPTAIN *goes to the table, takes the burning lamp and throws it at* LAURA, *who has retreated through the door.*

ACT THREE

As in Act Two. But another lamp. The concealed door is barricaded with a chair.

SCENE I

LAURA. *The* NURSE.

LAURA: Did he give you the keys?
NURSE: Give them to me? No, God forgive me, I took them out of his pocket. He'd left them in the coat he'd given Nöjd to brush.
LAURA: So Nöjd's on duty today, is he?
NURSE: Yes.
LAURA: Give them to me.
NURSE: But that's like stealing! Very well. Oh, listen to him up there, madam! To and fro, to and fro.
LAURA: Is the door safely locked?
NURSE: Yes. It's locked all right.
LAURA [*opens the secretaire and sits down to it*]: You must try to control your feelings, Margaret. Our only hope is to remain calm.

There is a knock on the door.

Who's that?
NURSE [*opens the door to the hall*]: It's Nöjd.
LAURA: Tell him to come in.
NÖJD [*enters*]: A despatch from the Colonel!
LAURA: Give it to me. [*Reads.*] Nöjd, have you removed all the cartridges from the rifles and pouches?
NÖJD: As you ordered, ma'am.
LAURA: Then wait outside, while I answer the Colonel's letter.

NÖJD *goes.* LAURA *writes.*

NURSE: Madam, listen! Whatever can he be doing up there?
LAURA: Be quiet while I'm writing.

The sound of sawing is heard.

NURSE [*half to herself*]: Merciful Jesus preserve us all! Where's this going to end?
LAURA: There. Give this to Nöjd. My mother must know nothing of this. You hear!

The NURSE *goes to the door.* LAURA *opens the drawers of the secretaire and takes out some papers.*

SCENE 2

LAURA. *The* PASTOR *takes a chair and sits beside* LAURA *at the secretaire.*

PASTOR: Good evening, sister. I've been away all day, as you know, so I couldn't come before. Well, this is a sad story.

LAURA: Yes, brother. It's the worst twenty-four hours I have ever experienced.

PASTOR: At all events I see no harm has come to you.

LAURA: No, thank God. But think what could have happened.

PASTOR: But tell me one thing. How did it begin? I've heard so many different versions.

LAURA: Well, it started with him talking some nonsense about not being Bertha's father, and ended with him throwing the burning lamp in my face.

PASTOR: But this is terrible! This is real madness. What are we to do?

LAURA: Try to prevent any further violence. The doctor has sent to the asylum for a straitjacket. I've written to the Colonel, and am trying to get these accounts into some kind of order. It's really disgraceful the way he's neglected them.

PASTOR: What a tragedy! Mind you, I've always feared something like this might happen! Fire and water, you know–they're bound to end in an explosion. What have you got in that drawer?

LAURA [*has pulled a drawer out of the desk*]: Look. This is where he's been hiding everything.

PASTOR [*looks in the drawer*]: Great heavens! Why, there's your doll! And your christening-cap–and Bertha's rattle–and your letters–and that locket—! [*Touches his eyes with his handkerchief.*] He must have loved you very much, Laura, in spite of everything. I haven't kept things like that.

LAURA: I think he used to love me once. But time–time changes so many things.

PASTOR: What's that big paper? Why, it's a receipt for–for a grave! Well, better a grave than the asylum. Laura! Tell me–have you no share of the blame for all this?

LAURA: I? How could I be to blame for a man going mad?

PASTOR: Well, well. I shan't say anything. After all, blood is thicker than water.

LAURA: What do you mean by that?

PASTOR [*looks at her*]: Now, listen, Laura.

LAURA: Yes?

PASTOR: Listen to me. You cannot deny that this fits in very nicely with your wish that you should bring up the child yourself.

LAURA: I don't understand.

PASTOR: I can't help but admire you!

LAURA: Me! Hm!

PASTOR: And I am to become the guardian of that freethinker! Do you know, I have always regarded him as a tare among our wheat.

LAURA [*gives a short, stifled laugh. Then, suddenly serious*]: And you dare say that to me–his wife?

PASTOR: You are too strong for me, Laura. Incredibly strong! Like a fox in a trap; you'd rather bite off your own leg than let yourself be caught. Like a master-thief; you scorn any accomplice, even your own conscience. Look at yourself in the mirror! You daren't!

LAURA: I never use mirrors.

PASTOR: No, you daren't. May I look at your hand? Not one spot of blood to betray you, no trace of the poison that lies hidden there! A little innocent murder, that the law cannot touch; an unconscious crime–unconscious? Brilliant, my dear, brilliant! But do you hear how he's working away up there? Take care? If that man breaks loose, he'll cut you to pieces!

LAURA: You talk too much. Have you a bad conscience? Accuse me; if you can.

PASTOR: I cannot.

LAURA: You see! You can't; I am innocent. You do your duty, and I'll do mine. Here comes the Doctor.

SCENE 3

LAURA. *The* PASTOR. *The* DOCTOR.

LAURA [*rises*]: Good evening, Doctor. At least you'll help me, won't you? Though I'm afraid there's not much anyone can do. You hear how he's carrying on up there? Are you convinced now?

DOCTOR: I am convinced that an act of violence has been committed. The question is whether it was an outbreak of anger or of madness.

PASTOR: Even if one ignores the actual assault, you must surely admit that he suffers from fixed ideas.

DOCTOR: I think your ideas are even more fixed, Pastor.

PASTOR: If you are referring to my spiritual convictions—

DOCTOR: I wasn't. Madam, it is up to you whether you choose to condemn your husband to imprisonment and a fine, or the asylum. How would you describe the Captain's conduct?

LAURA: I can't answer that now.

DOCTOR: You mean you are not certain which course would best serve the interests of your family? Well, Pastor, what do you say?

PASTOR: There'll be a terrible scandal either way. I really don't know—

LAURA: If he only has to pay a fine, he may commit violence again.

DOCTOR: And if he goes to prison he will soon be released. Then I suppose we must regard it as best for all concerned that he be treated as insane. Where is the nurse?

LAURA: Why do you ask?

DOCTOR: She must put the straitjacket on him, after I have talked with him and given her the signal. But not before! I have the thing outside. [*Goes into the hall and returns with a large package.*] Please ask the nurse to come in.

LAURA *rings*.

PASTOR: Dreadful, dreadful!

The NURSE *enters.*

DOCTOR [*unpacks the straitjacket*]: You see this? When I decide that the moment has come, you must approach the Captain from behind and put this coat on him, to prevent any further outbreaks. As you see, it has unusually long sleeves, to limit his movements. You must fasten these behind his back. These two straps go through these buckles here, and you can then tie them to the back of the chair, or the sofa, whichever is more convenient. Will you do this?

NURSE: No, Doctor, I can't. I can't!

LAURA: Why don't you do it yourself, Doctor?

DOCTOR: Because the patient mistrusts me. You, madam, would be the most proper person to do it; but I fear he mistrusts you too?

LAURA *does not reply*.

Perhaps you, Pastor—?

PASTOR: No, no! I couldn't possibly!

SCENE 4

LAURA. *The* PASTOR. *The* DOCTOR. *The* NURSE. NÖJD.

LAURA: Have you delivered the letter already?

NÖJD: Yes, madam.

DOCTOR: Ah, it's you, Nöjd. Now you know what's happened, don't you? The Captain is—ill. You must help us to take care of him.

NÖJD: If there's anything I can do for the Captain, he knows I'll do it.

DOCTOR: Good. Now you must put this jacket on him—

NURSE: No, he mustn't touch him! He'd hurt him. No, I'll do it myself—so gently, gently. Let him wait outside, to help me if need be. He can do that.

There is a banging on the concealed door.

DOCTOR: There he is! Hide this under the shawl—yes, on that chair—and go outside, all of you. The Pastor and I will wait in here. That door won't hold for long. Get outside, now, all of you!

NURSE [*goes out left*]: Blessed Jesus, help us!

LAURA *closes the secretaire and goes out.* NÖJD *exits upstage.*

SCENE 5

The lock snaps, the chair crashes to the floor and the concealed door is flung open. The CAPTAIN *enters with a pile of books under his arm. The* DOCTOR. *The* PASTOR.

CAPTAIN [*puts the books on the table*]: It's all here. I wasn't mad, you see. For example—*The Odyssey*, Book 1, line 215, page 6 in the Upsala translation. Telemachus speaking to Athene. 'Truly my mother asserts that he whom men call Odysseus is my father. But of this I cannot be sure, for no man knows for sure from whom he springs.' And he says this of Penelope, the chastest of women! Pretty, eh? And here we have the prophet Ezekiel. 'The fool saith: "See, here is my father!" But who can tell whose loins have begotten him?' That's clear enough. Now, what have we here? Mersläkow's

History of Russian Literature. 'Alexander Pushkin, Russia's greatest poet, died more of grief at the widespread rumours of his wife's infidelity than of the bullet he received in the breast in a duel. On his deathbed, he swore that she was innocent.' Idiot! Idiot! How could he swear to *that*? You see! I read my books! Hullo, Jonas, you here? And the Doctor—yes, of course! Have they told you what I once said to an Englishwoman who complained that the Irish throw burning lamps in their wives' faces? 'God, what women!' I said. 'Women?' she lisped. 'Yes!' I replied. 'When things have reached the pitch that a man who has loved and worshipped a woman takes a burning lamp and throws it in her face, then you know—!'

PASTOR: Then you know what?

CAPTAIN: Nothing! One never knows—one only believes—eh, Jonas? One believes, and is saved. Yes, saved! But I know that belief can damn a man! I know that.

DOCTOR: Captain!

CAPTAIN: Oh, shut up. I don't want to talk to you. I don't want to hear you relay everything they say in there like one of these damned telephones! Yes, you know what I mean! Tell me, Jonas, do you believe that you are your children's father? I remember you used to have a tutor living with you whom people talked about. Such beautiful eyes, they said he had.

PASTOR: Adolf! Take care, now—!

CAPTAIN: Put your hand under your hair and see if you can't feel a couple of bumps there! I'm blessed if he hasn't gone pale! Yes, yes, it was only talk—but, my God, how they talked! But we're all objects of ridicule, we husbands. Isn't that true, Doctor? How about your marriage couch? Didn't you have a lieutenant billeted on you? Wait, now, let me guess—wasn't he called—? [*Whispers in the* DOCTOR'*s ear.*] You see, he's gone pale too! Don't cry, now. She's dead and buried, and what's done can't be done again! I knew him, though—now he's a—look at me, Doctor!—no, in the eyes!—a major in the Dragoons. By God, I believe he's grown horns too!

DOCTOR: Captain, can we please discuss something else?

CAPTAIN: You see! As soon as I mention the word horns, he wants to talk about something else!

PASTOR: My poor brother, don't you realise you are mad?

CAPTAIN: Yes, I know. But if I had the care of your antlered heads for a week or two, I'd have you all behind bars too! I am mad, but how did I become mad? You don't care. Nobody cares. Let's talk about something else. [*Takes the photograph album from the table.*] Dear God—there is my child! Mine? How can we tell? Do you know what we have to do to be sure? First, marry to become socially respectable; then, soon afterwards, get divorced; and become lovers; and adopt the child. Then at least you can be sure it's your own adopted child. That's right, isn't it? But what good is all this to me? What good is anything to me now that you have taken away my hope of immortality, what good is my science and my philosophy now that I have nothing to live for, what use is my life to me now that I have no honour left? I grafted my right arm, half my brain, half my spinal cord on to another stem, because I believed they would unite into a single, more perfect tree, and then someone comes with a knife and cuts beneath the graft, so that now I am only half a tree—but the other tree goes on growing with my arm and half my brain, while I wither and die, for I gave the best parts of myself. Now I want to die! Do what you will with me! I no longer exist!

The DOCTOR *whispers to the* PASTOR. *They go into the room on the left. A few moments later,* BERTHA *enters.*

SCENE 6

The CAPTAIN. BERTHA.

The CAPTAIN *sits huddled at the table.* BERTHA *goes over to him.*

BERTHA: Are you ill, father?

CAPTAIN [*looks up dully*]: I?

BERTHA: Do you know what you've done? Do you know you threw a burning lamp at mother?

CAPTAIN: Did I?

BERTHA: Yes, you did! Think if you'd hurt her!

CAPTAIN: What would that have mattered?

BERTHA: You aren't my father if you can talk like that!

CAPTAIN: What's that you say? I'm not your father? How do you know? Who has told you that? Who is your father, then? Who?

BERTHA: Well, not you, anyway.

CAPTAIN: Still not me! Who, then? Who? You seem well informed. Who's been priming you? Must I endure this, that my child comes and tells me to my face that I am not her father? But do you realise you're insulting your mother by saying that? Don't you understand that, if this is true, she is the one who has sinned?

BERTHA: Don't say anything against Mother, do you hear?

CAPTAIN: No, you stick together, you're all against me! And you've done so all the time!

BERTHA: Father!

CAPTAIN: Don't use that word again!

BERTHA: Father, father!

CAPTAIN [*draws her to him*]: Bertha, my darling, my beloved child, of course you are my child! Yes, yes–it must be so–it *is* so. Those were just sick thoughts that came with the wind like pestilence and fever. Look at me, let me see my soul in your eyes! But I see her soul too! You have two souls, and you love me with one and hate me with the other! You must only love me! You must only have one soul, or you will never find peace, nor shall I. You must have only one thought, the child of my thought, and you shall have only one will, mine.

BERTHA: I don't want that! I want to be myself!

CAPTAIN: I won't let you do that! You see, I'm a cannibal, and I want to eat you. Your mother wanted to eat me, but she couldn't. I am Saturn, who ate his children because it had been prophesied that otherwise they would eat him. To eat or be eaten! That is the question. If I don't eat you, you will eat me, and you have already shown me your teeth. But don't be afraid, my beloved child. I won't hurt you. [*Goes to where the guns are on the wall and takes a revolver.*]

BERTHA [*tries to escape*]: Help, mother, help! He wants to murder me!

NURSE [*enters*]: Mr Adolf, what is it?

CAPTAIN [*looks at the revolver*]: Have you taken the cartridges?

NURSE: Yes, I've hidden them away. But sit down and calm yourself, and I'll bring them back to you.

She takes the CAPTAIN *by the arm and coaxes him down into the chair, where he remains sitting dully. Then she takes the straitjacket and goes behind his chair.* BERTHA *tiptoes out left.*

Do you remember, Mr Adolf, when you were my dear little baby, how I used to tuck you up at night and say your prayers with you? And do you remember how I used to get up in the night to fetch you a drink? Do you remember how I lit the candle and told you pretty stories when you had bad dreams and couldn't sleep? Do you remember?

CAPTAIN: Go on talking, Margaret. It soothes my head so. Go on talking.

NURSE: All right, but you must listen, then. Do you remember how once you took the big carving knife and wanted to make boats, and I came in and had to get the knife away from you by telling you a story? You were such a silly baby, so we had to tell you stories, because you thought we all wanted to hurt you. Give me that snake, I said, otherwise he'll bite you. And you let go of the knife. [*Takes the gun from the* CAPTAIN'*s hand.*] And then, when you had to get dressed and you didn't want to. Then I had to coax you and say I'd give you a gold coat and dress you like a prince. And I took your little body-garment, which was only of green wool, and held it in front of you and said: 'Put your arms in', and then I said: 'Sit still, now, and be a good boy while I button up the back!' [*She has got the straitjacket on him.*] And then I said: 'Stand up now, and walk nicely, so I can see how you look.' [*She leads him to the sofa.*] And then I said: 'Now it's time to go to bed.'

CAPTAIN: What's that, Nanny? Must I go to bed when I'm dressed? Damnation! What have you done to me? [*Tries to free himself.*] Oh, you damned cunning woman! Who would have believed you were so crafty? [*Lies down on the sofa.*] Caught, cropped, and cozened! And not to be allowed to die!

NURSE: Forgive me, Mr Adolf, forgive me! But I wanted to stop you from killing the child!

CAPTAIN: Why didn't you let me kill the child? Life is a hell, and death a heaven, and the child belongs to heaven.

NURSE: What do you know about what comes after death?

CAPTAIN: That is all one does know. About life, one knows nothing. Oh, if one had only known from the beginning!

NURSE: Mr Adolf! Humble your proud heart and pray to God for mercy. It still isn't too late. It wasn't too late for the robber on the cross, when our Saviour said to him: 'Today shalt thou be with me in Paradise.'

CAPTAIN: Are you croaking for carrion already, you old crow?

The NURSE *takes a prayer-book from her pocket. The* CAPTAIN *roars.*

Nöjd! Is Nöjd there?

NÖJD *enters.*

Throw this woman out! She wants to choke me to death with her prayer-book! Throw her out through the window, or up the chimney! Anywhere!

NÖJD [*looks at the* NURSE.] God bless you, Captain, I can't do that! I just can't! If there were six men, yes, but a woman—

CAPTAIN: Aren't you stronger than a woman?

NÖJD: Of course I'm stronger, but there's something special about a woman that stops a man raising his hand against her.

CAPTAIN: What's special about them? Haven't they raised their hands against me?

NÖJD: Yes, but I can't, Captain! It's just as though you was to ask me to strike the Pastor. It's something that's in a man's blood, like religion. I can't!

SCENE 7

As before. LAURA *gestures to* NÖJD *to go.*

CAPTAIN: Omphale! Omphale! Now you play with the club while Hercules winds your wool!

LAURA [*comes over to the sofa*]: Adolf! Look at me! Do you think I am your enemy?

CAPTAIN: Yes, I do. I think you are all my enemies. My mother was my enemy. She didn't want to bring me into the world because my birth would cause her pain. She robbed my first embryo of its nourishment, so that I was born half-crippled. My sister was my enemy, when she taught me that I was her inferior. The first woman I kissed was my enemy—she gave me ten years of disease in return for the love I gave her. My daughter became my enemy, when you forced her to choose between you and me. And you, my wife, you were my mortal enemy, for you didn't let go of me until you had throttled the life out of me.

LAURA: I don't know that I ever planned, or intended, what you think I have done. I may have felt a vague desire to be rid of you, because you were an obstacle in my path; but if you see a plan in the way I have acted, then perhaps there was one, though I wasn't aware of it. I didn't plot any of this—it just glided forward on rails which you laid yourself—and before God and my conscience, I feel that I am innocent, even if I am not. Your presence has been like a stone on my heart, pressing and pressing until my heart rebelled against its suffocating weight. This is the truth, and if I have unintentionally hurt you, I ask your forgiveness.

CAPTAIN: That all sounds plausible. But how does it help me? And who is to blame? Perhaps the idea of marriage is to blame. In the old days, one married a wife; now one forms a company with a female partner, or moves in to live with a friend. And then one seduces the partner, or defiles the friend. What became of love—healthy, sensuous love? It died, starved. And what is the offspring of this broker's-love, a blank cheque drawn on a bankrupt account? Who will honour it when the crash comes? Who is the bodily father to the spiritual child?

LAURA: Those suspicions of yours about the child are completely unfounded.

CAPTAIN: That's just what's so horrible. If they were real, at least one would have something to grip on, something to cling to. Now there are only shadows, hiding in the bushes and poking out their heads to laugh—it's like fighting with air, a mock battle with blank cartridges. A real betrayal would have acted as a challenge, roused my soul to action. But now my thoughts dissolve in twilight, my brain grinds emptiness until it catches fire! Give me a pillow under my head! And put something over me, I'm cold. I'm so terribly cold!

> LAURA *takes her shawl and spreads it over him. The* NURSE *goes out to fetch a pillow.*

LAURA: Give me your hand, friend.

CAPTAIN: My hand! Which you have tied behind my back? Omphale! Omphale! But I feel your soft shawl against my mouth. It's warm and smooth like your arm, and it smells of vanilla, as your hair did when you were young. Laura—when you were young—and we walked in the birch woods among the primroses—and thrushes sang! Beautiful, beautiful! How beautiful life was! And now it has become like this. You didn't want it to be like this, I didn't want it, and yet it happened. Who rules our lives?

LAURA: God alone rules—

CAPTAIN: The God of battle, then! Or the goddess, nowadays! Take away this cat that's lying on me! Take it away!

> *The* NURSE *enters with the pillow and removes the shawl.*

Give me my tunic. Put it over me!

> *The* NURSE *takes his military tunic from the clothes-hanger and drapes it over him.*

Ah, my brave lion's skin, that you would take from me! Omphale! Omphale! O cunning woman, who so loved peace that you discovered the art of disarming men! Awake, Hercules, before they take your club from you! You would rob us of our armour and have us believe that it is only tinsel. No, it was iron before it became tinsel. In the old days it was the smith who forged the soldier's tunic; now it is the seamstress. Omphale! Omphale! Strength has been vanquished by craft and weakness! Curse you, damned woman, and all your sex! [*Raises himself to spit, but falls back on the couch.*] What kind of a pillow have you given me, Margaret? It's so hard, and so cold, so cold! Come and sit beside me here, on the chair. That's right. May I rest my head in your lap? So. That's warm! Bend over so that I can feel your breast. Oh, it is sweet to sleep at a woman's breast, whether a mother's or a mistress's, but sweetest at a mother's!

LAURA: Do you want to see your child, Adolf? Speak!

CAPTAIN: My child? A man has no children. Only women have children, and so the future belongs to them, while we die childless. Gentle Jesus, meek and mild, look upon this little child—!

NURSE: Listen! He's praying to God!

CAPTAIN: No, to you, to send me to sleep. I'm so tired, so tired. Good night, Margaret. Blessed be thou amongst women— [*He raises himself, but falls with a cry in the* NURSE'*s lap.*]

SCENE 8

LAURA *goes left, and calls the* DOCTOR, *who enters with the* PASTOR.

LAURA: Help us, Doctor, if it isn't too late. Look, he's stopped breathing!

DOCTOR [*takes the* CAPTAIN*'s pulse*]: He has had a stroke.

PASTOR: Is he dead?

DOCTOR: No. He may still awake, and live. But to what he will awake, we do not know.

PASTOR: 'Once to die, but after this the judgment—'

DOCTOR: We must not judge or accuse him. You, who believe that there is a God who rules men's destinies, must plead this man's cause before the bar of Heaven.

NURSE: Oh, Pastor, he prayed to God in his last moment!

PASTOR [*to* LAURA]: Is this true?

LAURA: It is true.

DOCTOR: Then my art is useless. Now you must try yours, Pastor.

LAURA: Is that all you have to say at this death-bed, Doctor?

DOCTOR: That is all. My knowledge ends here. He who knows more, let him speak.

BERTHA [*enters left and runs to her mother*]: Mother, mother!

LAURA: My child! *My* child!

PASTOR: Amen!

THE
SEAGULL
ANTON
CHEKHOV

THE SEAGULL

First published in 1923 by
Chatto & Windus, London

THE SEAGULL

A Comedy in Four Acts
(1896)

Translated from the Russian by

CONSTANCE GARNETT

CHARACTERS

IRINA NIKOLAYEVNA ARKADIN
  (MADAME TREPLEV) (*an Actress*)
KONSTANTIN GAVRILOVITCH TREPLEV
  (*her Son, a young man*)
PYOTR NIKOLAYEVITCH SORIN (*her Brother*)
NINA MIHAILOVNA ZARETCHNY
  (*a young Girl, the daughter of a wealthy Landowner*)
ILYA AFANASYEVITCH SHAMRAEV
  (*a retired Lieutenant,* SORIN'*s Steward*)
POLINA ANDREYEVNA (*his Wife*)
MASHA (*his Daughter*)
BORIS ALEXEYEVITCH TRIGORIN
  (*a Literary Man*)
YEVGENY SERGEYEVITCH DORN (*a Doctor*)
SEMYON SEMYONOVITCH MEDVEDENKO
  (*a Schoolmaster*)
YAKOV (*a Labourer*)
A MAN COOK
A HOUSEMAID

The action takes place in Sorin's house and garden.
Between the Third and the Fourth Acts there is an
interval of two years.

First performed at St Petersburg,
17 October 1896

ACT ONE

Part of the park on SORIN's estate. Wide avenue leading away from the spectators into the depths of the park towards the lake is blocked up by a platform roughly put together for private theatricals, so that the lake is not visible. To right and left of the platform, bushes. A few chairs, a little table.

The sun has just set. YAKOV *and other labourers are at work on the platform behind the curtain; there is the sound of coughing and hammering.* MASHA *and* MEDVEDENKO *enter on the left, returning from a walk.*

MEDVEDENKO: Why do you always wear black?

MASHA: I am in mourning for my life. I am unhappy.

MEDVEDENKO: Why? [*Pondering.*] I don't understand. . . . You are in good health; though your father is not very well off, he has got enough. My life is much harder than yours. I only get twenty-three roubles a month, and from that they deduct something for the pension fund, and yet I don't wear mourning.

They sit down.

MASHA: It isn't money that matters. A poor man may be happy.

MEDVEDENKO: Theoretically, yes; but in practice it's like this: there are my two sisters and my mother and my little brother and I, and my salary is only twenty-three roubles. We must eat and drink, mustn't we? One must have tea and sugar. One must have tobacco. It's a tight fit.

MASHA [*looking round at the platform*]: The play will soon begin.

MEDVEDENKO: Yes. Miss Zaretchny will act: it is Konstantin Gavrilitch's play. They are in love with each other and to-day their souls will be united in the effort to realise the same artistic effect. But your soul and mine have not a common point of contact. I love you. I am so wretched I can't stay at home. Every day I walk four miles here and four miles back and I meet with nothing but indifference from you. I can quite understand it. I am without means and have a big family to keep. . . . Who would care to marry a man who hasn't a penny to bless himself with?

MASHA: Oh, nonsense! [*Takes a pinch of snuff.*] Your love touches me, but I can't reciprocate it—that's all. [*Holding out the snuff-box to him.*] Help yourself.

MEDVEDENKO: I don't feel like it [*a pause*].

MASHA: How stifling it is! There must be a storm coming. . . . You're always discussing theories or talking about money. You think there is no greater misfortune than poverty, but to my mind it is a thousand times better to go in rags and be a beggar than . . . But you wouldn't understand that, though. . . .

SORIN *and* TREPLEV *enter on the right.*

SORIN [*leaning on his walking-stick*]: I am never quite myself in the country, my boy, and, naturally enough, I shall never get used to it. Last night I went to bed at ten and woke up this morning at nine feeling as though my brain were glued to my skull, through sleeping so long [*laughs*]. And after dinner I accidentally dropped off again, and now I am utterly shattered and feel as though I were in a nightmare, in fact. . . .

TREPLEV: Yes, you really ought to live in town. [*Catches sight of* MASHA *and* MEDVEDENKO.] When the show begins, my friends, you will be summoned, but you mustn't be here now. You must please go away.

SORIN [*to* MASHA]: Marya Ilyinishna, will you be so good as to ask your papa to tell them to take the dog off the chain?—it howls. My sister could not sleep again last night.

MASHA: Speak to my father yourself; I am not going to. Please don't ask me. [*To* MEDVEDENKO.] Come along!

MEDVEDENKO [*to* TREPLEV]: So you will send and let us know before it begins.

Both go out.

SORIN: So I suppose the dog will be howling all night again. What a business it is! I have never done as I liked in the country. In old days I used to get leave for twenty-eight days and come here for a rest and so on, but they worried me so with all sorts of trifles that before I had been here two days I was longing to be off again [*laughs*]. I've always been glad to get away from here. . . . But now I am on the retired list, and I have nowhere else to go, as a matter of fact. I've got to live here whether I like it or not. . . .

YAKOV [*to* TREPLEV]: We are going to have a bathe, Konstantin Gavrilitch.

TREPLEV: Very well; but don't be more than ten minutes [*looks at his watch*]. It will soon begin.

YAKOV: Yes, sir [*goes out*].

TREPLEV [*looking round the stage*]: Here is our theatre. The curtain, then the first wing, then the second, and beyond that—open space. No scenery of any sort. there is an open view of the lake and the horizon. We shall raise the curtain at exactly half-past eight, when the moon rises.

SORIN: Magnificent.

TREPLEV: If Nina is late it will spoil the whole effect. It is time she was here. Her father and her stepmother keep a sharp eye on her, and it is as hard for her to get out of the house as to escape from prison [*puts his uncle's cravat straight*]. Your hair and your beard are very untidy. They want clipping or something. . . .

SORIN [*combing out his beard*]: It's the tragedy of my life. Even as a young man I looked as though I had been drinking for days or something of the sort. I was never a favourite with the ladies [*sitting down*]. Why is your mother out of humour?

TREPLEV: Why? Because she is bored [*sitting down beside him*]. She is jealous. She is set against me, and against the performance, and against my play because Nina is acting in it, and she is not. She does not know my play, but she hates it.

SORIN [*laughs*]: What an idea!

TREPLEV: She is annoyed to think that even on this little stage Nina will have a triumph and not she [*looks at his watch*]. My mother is a psychological freak. Unmistakably talented, intelligent, capable of sobbing over a book, she will reel off all Nekrassov by heart; as a sick nurse she is an angel; but just try praising Duse in her presence! O-ho! You must praise no one but herself, you must write about her, make a fuss over her, be in raptures over her extraordinary acting in 'La Dame aux Camélias' or the 'Ferment of Life'; but she has none of this narcotic in the country, she is bored and cross, and we are all her enemies–we are all in fault. Then she is superstitious–she is afraid of three candles, of the number thirteen. She is stingy. She has got seventy thousand roubles in a bank at Odessa–I know that for a fact–but ask her to lend you some money, and she will burst into tears.

SORIN: You imagine your mother does not like your play, and you are already upset and all that. Don't worry; your mother adores you.

TREPLEV [*pulling the petals off a flower*]: Loves me, loves me not; loves me, loves me not; loves me, loves me not [*laughs*]. You see, my mother does not love me. I should think not! She wants to live, to love, to wear light blouses; and I am twenty-five, and I am a continual reminder that she is no longer young. When I am not there she is only thirty-two, but when I am there she is forty-three, and for that she hates me. She knows, too, that I have no belief in the theatre. She loves the stage, she fancies she is working for humanity, for the holy cause of art, while to my mind the modern theatre is nothing but tradition and conventionality. When the curtain goes up, and by artificial light, in a room with three walls, these great geniuses, the devotees of holy art, represent how people eat, drink, love, move about, and wear their jackets; when from these commonplace sentences and pictures they try to draw a moral–a petty moral, easy of comprehension and convenient for domestic use; when in a thousand variations I am offered the same thing over and over again–I run away as Maupassant ran away from the Eiffel Tower which weighed upon his brain with its vulgarity.

SORIN: You can't do without the stage.

TREPLEV: We need new forms of expression. We need new forms, and if we can't have them we had better have nothing [*looks at his watch*]. I love my mother–I love her very much–but she leads a senseless sort of life, always taken up with this literary gentleman, her name is always trotted out in the papers–and that wearies me. And sometimes the simple egoism of an ordinary mortal makes me feel sorry that my mother is a celebrated actress, and I fancy that if she were an ordinary woman I should be happier. Uncle, what could be more hopeless and stupid than my position? She used to have visitors, all celebrities–artists and authors–and among them all I was the only one who was nothing, and they only put up with me because I was her son. Who am I? What am I? I left the University in my third year–owing to circumstances 'for which we accept no responsibility,' as the editors say; I have no talents, I haven't a penny of my own, and on my passport I am described as an artisan of Kiev. You know my father was an artisan of Kiev, though he too was a well-known actor. So, when in her drawing-room all these artists and authors graciously noticed me, I always fancied from their faces that they were taking the measure of my insignificance–I guessed their thoughts and suffered from the humiliation. . . .

SORIN: And, by the way, can you tell me, please, what sort of man this literary gentleman is? There's no making him out. He never says anything.

TREPLEV: He is an intelligent man, good-natured and rather melancholy, you know. A very decent fellow. He is still a good distance off forty, but he is already celebrated and has enough and to spare of everything. As for his writings . . . what shall I say? They are charming, full of talent, but . . . after Tolstoy or Zola you do not care to read Trigorin.

SORIN: Well, I am fond of authors, my boy. At one time I had a passionate desire for two things: I wanted to get married, and I wanted to become an author; but I did not succeed in doing either. Yes, it is pleasant to be even a small author, as a matter of fact.

TREPLEV [*listens*]: I hear steps . . . [*embraces his uncle*]. I cannot live without her. . . . The very sound of her footsteps is lovely. . . . I am wildly happy.

    Goes quickly to meet NINA ZARETCHNY *as she enters.*

My enchantress—my dream. . . .

NINA [*in agitation*]: I am not late. . . . Of course I am not late. . . .

TREPLEV [*kissing her hands*]: No, no, no!

NINA: I have been uneasy all day. I was so frightened. I was afraid father would not let me come. . . . But he has just gone out with my stepmother. The sky is red, the moon is just rising, and I kept urging on the horse [*laughs*]. But I am glad [*shakes* SORIN's *hand warmly*].

SORIN [*laughs*]: Your eyes look as though you have been crying. . . . Fie, fie! That's not right!

NINA: Oh, it was nothing. . . . You see how out of breath I am. I have to go in half an hour. We must make haste. I can't stay, I can't! For God's sake don't keep me! My father doesn't know I am here.

TREPLEV: It really is time to begin. We must go and call the others.

SORIN: I'll go this minute. [*Goes to the right, singing* 'To France two grenadiers.' *Looks round.*] Once I sang like that, and a deputy prosecutor said to me, 'You have a powerful voice, your Excellency'; then he thought a little and added, 'but not a pleasant one' [*laughs and goes off*].

NINA: My father and his wife won't let me come here. They say it is so Bohemian here . . . they are afraid I shall go on the stage. . . . But I feel drawn to the lake here like a sea-gull. . . . My heart is full of you [*looks round*].

TREPLEV: We are alone.

NINA: I fancy there is someone there.

TREPLEV: There's nobody.

    They kiss.

NINA: What tree is this?

TREPLEV: An elm.

NINA: Why is it so dark?

TREPLEV: It's evening; everything is getting dark. Don't go away early, I entreat you!

NINA: I must.

TREPLEV: And if I come to you, Nina, I'll stand in the garden all night, watching your window.

NINA: You can't; the watchman would notice you. Trésor is not used to you, and he would bark.

TREPLEV: I love you!

NINA: Sh-h. . . .

TREPLEV [*hearing footsteps*]: Who is there? You, Yakov?

YAKOV [*behind the stage*]: Yes, sir.

TREPLEV: Take your places. It's time to begin. Is the moon rising?

YAKOV: Yes, sir.

TREPLEV: Have you got the methylated spirit? Have you got the sulphur? When the red eyes appear there must be a smell of sulphur. [*To* NINA.] Go, it's all ready. Are you nervous?

NINA: Yes, awfully! Your mother is all right—I am not afraid of her—but there's Trigorin . . . I feel frightened and ashamed of acting before him . . . a celebrated author. . . . Is he young?

TREPLEV: Yes.

NINA: How wonderful his stories are.

TREPLEV [*coldly*]: I don't know. I haven't read them.

NINA: It is difficult to act in your play. There are no living characters in it.

TREPLEV: Living characters! One must depict life not as it is, and not as it ought to be, but as we see it in our dreams.

NINA: There is very little action in your play—nothing but speeches. And to my mind there ought to be love in a play.

Both go behind the stage. Enter POLINA ANDREYEVNA *and* DORN.

POLINA: It is getting damp. Go back and put on your goloshes.

DORN: I am hot.

POLINA: You don't take care of yourself. It's obstinacy. You are a doctor, and you know perfectly well that damp air is bad for you, but you want to make me miserable; you sat out on the verandah all yesterday evening on purpose. . . .

DORN [*hums*]: 'Do not say that youth is ruined.'

POLINA: You were so absorbed in conversation with Irina Nikolayevna . . . you did not notice the cold. Own up . . . you are attracted by her.

DORN: I am fifty-five.

POLINA: Nonsense! That's not old for a man. You look very young for your age, and are still attractive to women.

DORN: Well, what would you have?

POLINA: All you men are ready to fall down and worship an actress, all of you!

DORN [*hums*]: 'Before thee once again I stand.' If artists are liked in society and treated differently from merchants, for example, that's only in the nature of things. It's idealism.

POLINA: Women have always fallen in love with you and thrown themselves on your neck. Is that idealism too?

DORN [*shrugs his shoulders*]: Well, in the attitude of women to me there has been a great deal that was good. What they principally loved in me was a first-rate doctor. You remember that ten or fifteen years ago I was the only decent accoucheur in the district. Then, too, I have always been an honest man.

POLINA [*seizes him by the hand*]: Dearest!

DORN: Sh-h! They are coming.

Enter MADAME ARKADIN *arm in arm with* SORIN, TRIGORIN, SHAMRAEV, MEDVEDENKO *and* MASHA.

SHAMRAEV: In the year 1873 she acted marvellously at the fair at Poltava. It was a delight! She acted exquisitely! Do you happen to know, madam, where Pavel Semyonitch Tchadin, a comic actor, is now? His Rasplyuev was inimitable, even finer than Sadovsky's, I assure you, honoured lady. Where is he now?

MADAME ARKADIN: You keep asking me about antediluvians. How should I know? [*Sits down.*]

SHAMRAEV [*with a sigh*]: Pashka Tchadin! There are no such actors now. The stage has gone down, Irina Nikolayevna! In old days there were mighty oaks, but now we see nothing but stumps.

DORN: There are few actors of brilliant talents nowadays, that's true; but the average level of acting is far higher than it was.

SHAMRAEV: I can't agree with you. But, of course, it's a matter of taste. *De gustibus aut bene aut nihil.*

TREPLEV *comes out from behind the stage.*

MADAME ARKADIN [*to her son*]: My dear son, when is it going to begin?

TREPLEV: In a minute. I beg you to be patient.

MADAME ARKADIN [*recites from* 'Hamlet']:

> 'Oh, Hamlet, speak no more!
> Thou turn'st mine eyes into my very soul;
> And there I see such black and grained spots
> As will not leave their tinct.'

TREPLEV [*from* 'Hamlet']:

> 'And let me wring your heart, for so I shall,
> If it be made of penetrable stuff.'

A horn is sounded behind the stage.

Ladies and gentlemen, we begin! I beg you to attend [*a pause*]. I begin [*taps with a stick and recites aloud*]. Oh, you venerable old shadows that float at night-time over this lake, lull us to sleep and let us dream of what will be in two hundred thousand years!

SORIN: There will be nothing in two hundred thousand years.

TREPLEV: Then let them present that nothing to us.

MADAME ARKADIN: Let them. We are asleep.

The curtain rises; the view of the lake is revealed; the moon is above the horizon, its reflection in the water; NINA ZARETCHNY, *all in white, is sitting on a big stone.*

NINA: Men, lions, eagles and partridges, horned deer, geese, spiders, silent fish that dwell in the water, starfishes and creatures which cannot be seen by the eye—all living things, all living things, all living things, having completed their cycle of sorrow, are extinct. . . . For thousands of years the earth has borne no living creature on its surface, and this poor moon lights its lamp in vain. On the meadow the cranes no longer waken with a cry, and there is no sound of the May beetles in the lime trees. It is cold, cold, cold! Empty,

empty, empty! Dreadful, dreadful, dreadful! [*a pause*]. The bodies of living creatures have vanished into dust, and eternal matter has transformed them into rocks, into water, into clouds, while the souls of all have melted into one. That world-soul I am–I. . . . In me is the soul of Alexander the Great, of Cæsar, of Shakespeare and of Napoleon, and of the lowest leech. In me the consciousness of men is blended with the instincts of the animals, and I remember all, all, all! And I live through every life over again in myself!

Will-of-the-wisps appear.

MADAME ARKADIN [*softly*]: It's something decadent.

TREPLEV [*in an imploring and reproachful voice*]: Mother!

NINA: I am alone. Once in a hundred years I open my lips to speak, and my voice echoes mournfully in the void, and no one hears. . . . You too, pale lights, hear me not. . . . The stagnant marsh begets you before daybreak and you wander until dawn, but without thought, without will, without the tremor of life. For fear that life should spring up in you the father of eternal matter, the devil, keeps the atoms in you, as in the stones and in the water, in continual flux, and you are changing perpetually. For in all the universe nothing remains permanent and unchanged but the spirit [*a pause*]. Like a prisoner cast into a deep, empty well I know not where I am and what awaits me. All is hidden from me but that in the cruel, persistent struggle with the devil–the principle of the forces of matter–I am destined to conquer, and, after that, matter and spirit will be blended in glorious harmony and the Kingdom of the Cosmic Will will come. But that will come only little by little, through long, long thousands of years when the moon and the bright Sirius and the earth are changed to dust. . . . Till then–terror, terror . . .

A pause; two red spots appear upon the background of the lake.

Here my powerful foe, the devil, is approaching. I see his dreadful crimson eyes. . . .

MADAME ARKADIN: There's a smell of sulphur. Is that as it should be?

TREPLEV: Yes.

MADAME ARKADIN [*laughs*]: Oh, it's a stage effect!

TREPLEV: Mother!

NINA: He is dreary without man—

POLINA [*to* DORN]: You have taken your hat off. Put it on or you will catch cold.

MADAME ARKADIN: The doctor has taken his hat off to the devil, the father of eternal matter.

TREPLEV [*firing up, aloud*]: The play is over! Enough! Curtain!

MADAME ARKADIN: What are you cross about?

TREPLEV: Enough! The curtain! Let down the curtain! [*Stamping.*] Curtain! [*The curtain falls.*] I am sorry! I lost sight of the fact that only a few of the elect may write plays and act in them. I have infringed the monopoly. I . . . I . . . [*tries to say something more, but with a wave of his hand goes out on left*].

MADAME ARKADIN: What's the matter with him?

SORIN: Irina, you really must have more consideration for youthful vanity, my dear.

MADAME ARKADIN: What did I say to him?

SORIN: You hurt his feelings.

MADAME ARKADIN: He told us beforehand that it was a joke, and I regarded his play as a joke.

SORIN: All the same . . .

MADAME ARKADIN: Now it appears that he has written a great work. What next! So he has got up this performance and smothered us with sulphur not as a joke but as a protest. . . . He wanted to show us how to write and what to act. This is getting tiresome! These continual sallies at my expense—these continual pin-pricks would put anyone out of patience, say what you like. He is a vain, whimsical boy!

SORIN: He meant to give you pleasure.

MADAME ARKADIN: Really? He did not choose an ordinary play, however, but made us listen to this decadent delirium. For the sake of a joke I am ready to listen to delirium, but here we have pretensions to new forms and a new view of art. To my thinking it's no question of new forms at all, but simply bad temper.

TRIGORIN: Everyone writes as he likes and as he can.

MADAME ARKADIN: Let him write as he likes and as he can, only let him leave me in peace.

DORN: Jupiter! you are angry. . . .

MADAME ARKADIN: I am not Jupiter—I am a woman [*lights a cigarette*]. I am not angry—I am only vexed that a young man should spend his time so drearily. I did not mean to hurt his feelings.

MEDVEDENKO: No one has any grounds to separate spirit from matter, seeing that spirit itself may be a combination of material atoms. [*With animation, to* TRIGORIN.] But you know someone ought to write a play on how we poor teachers live, and get it acted. We have a hard, hard life.

MADAME ARKADIN: That's true, but don't let us talk either of plays or of atoms. It is such a glorious evening! Do you hear? There is singing! [*Listens.*] How nice it is!

POLINA: It's on the other side of the lake [*a pause*].

MADAME ARKADIN [*to* TRIGORIN]: Sit down beside me. Ten or fifteen years ago there were sounds of music and singing on that lake continually almost every night. There are six country houses on the shores of the lake. I remember laughter, noise, shooting, and love affairs without end. . . . The *jeune premier* and the idol of all those six households was in those days our friend here, the doctor [*motions with her head towards* DORN], Yevgeny Sergeitch. He is fascinating still, but in those days he was irresistible. But my conscience is beginning to trouble me. Why did I hurt my poor boy's feelings? I feel worried. [*Aloud.*] Kostya! Son! Kostya!

MASHA: I'll go and look for him.

MADAME ARKADIN: Please do, my dear.

MASHA [*going to the left*]: Aa-oo! Konstantin Gavrilitch! Aa-oo! [*goes off*].

NINA [*coming out from behind the stage*]: Apparently there will be no going on, and I may come out. Good evening! [*Kisses* MADAME ARKADIN *and* POLINA ANDREYEVNA.]

SORIN: Bravo! Bravo!

MADAME ARKADIN: Bravo! Bravo! We admired you. With such an appearance, with such a lovely voice, you really cannot stay in the country; it is a sin. You must have talent. Do you hear? It's your duty to go on the stage.

NINA: Oh, that's my dream! [*sighing*]. But it will never be realised.

MADAME ARKADIN: Who knows? Here, let me introduce Boris Alexeyevitch Trigorin.

NINA: Oh, I am so glad . . . [*overcome with embarrassment*]. I am always reading your . . .

MADAME ARKADIN [*making her sit down beside them*]: Don't be shy, my dear. He is a celebrity, but he has a simple heart. You see, he is shy himself.

DORN: I suppose we may raise the curtain; it's rather uncanny.

SHAMRAEV [*aloud*]: Yakov, pull up the curtain, my lad.

The curtain goes up.

NINA [*to* TRIGORIN]: It is a queer play, isn't it?

TRIGORIN: I did not understand it at all. But I enjoyed it. You acted so genuinely. And the scenery was delightful [*a pause*]. There must be a lot of fish in that lake.

NINA: Yes.

TRIGORIN: I love angling. There is nothing I enjoy so much as sitting on the bank of a river in the evening and watching the float.

NINA: But I should have thought that for anyone who has known the enjoyment of creation, no other enjoyment can exist.

MADAME ARKADIN [*laughing*]: Don't talk like that. When people say nice things to him he is utterly floored.

SHAMRAEV: I remember one evening in the opera theatre in Moscow the celebrated Silva took the lower *C!* As it happened, there was sitting in the gallery the bass of our church choir, and all at once—imagine our intense astonishment—we heard from the gallery 'Bravo, Silva!' a whole octave lower—like this: [*in a deep bass*] 'Bravo, Silva!' The audience sat spellbound [*a pause*].

DORN: The angel of silence has flown over us.

NINA: It's time for me to go. Good-bye.

MADAME ARKADIN: Where are you off to? Why so early? We won't let you go.

NINA: My father expects me.

MADAME ARKADIN: What a man, really . . . [*kisses her*]. Well, there is no help for it. I am sorry—I am sorry to let you go.

NINA: If you knew how grieved I am to go.

MADAME ARKADIN: Someone ought to see you home, my little dear.

NINA [*frightened*]: Oh, no, no!

SORIN [*to her, in an imploring voice*]: Do stay!

NINA: I can't, Pyotr Nikolayevitch.

SORIN: Stay for an hour. What is there in that?

NINA [*thinking a minute, tearfully*]: I can't! [*Shakes hands and hurriedly goes off.*]

MADAME ARKADIN: Unfortunate girl she is, really. They say her mother left her father all her immense property—every farthing of it—and now the girl has got nothing, as her father has already made a will leaving everything to his second wife. It's monstrous!

DORN: Yes, her father is a pretty thorough scoundrel, one must do him the justice to say so.

SORIN [*rubbing his cold hands*]: Let us go too, it's getting damp. My legs ache.

MADAME ARKADIN: They seem like wooden legs, you can hardly walk. Let us go, unlucky old man! [*Takes his arm.*]

SHAMRAEV [*offering his arm to his wife*]: Madame?

SORIN: I hear that dog howling again. [*To* SHAMRAEV] Be so kind, Ilya Afanasyitch, as to tell them to let it off the chain.

SHAMRAEV: It's impossible, Pyotr Nikolayevitch, I am afraid of thieves getting into the barn. Our millet is there. [*To* MEDVEDENKO *who is walking beside him.*] Yes, a whole octave lower: 'Bravo, Silva!' And he not a singer—simply a church chorister!

MEDVEDENKO: And what salary does a chorister get?

All go out except DORN.

DORN [*alone*]: I don't know, perhaps I know nothing about it, or have gone off my head, but I liked the play. There is something in it. When that girl talked about loneliness and afterwards when the devil's eyes appeared, I was so excited that my hands trembled. It is fresh, naïve. . . . Here he comes, I believe. I want to say all the nice things I can to him.

TREPLEV [*enters*]: They have all gone.

DORN: I am here.

TREPLEV: Mashenka is looking for me all over the park. Insufferable creature she is!

DORN: Konstantin Gavrilitch, I liked your play extremely. It's a strange thing, and I haven't heard the end, and yet it made a strong impression! You are a gifted man—you must persevere.

TREPLEV *presses his hand warmly and embraces him impulsively.*

Fie, what an hysterical fellow! There are tears in his eyes! What I mean is this. You have taken a subject from the realm of abstract ideas. So it should be, for a work of art ought to express a great idea. A thing is only fine when it is serious. How pale you are!

TREPLEV: So you tell me to persevere?

DORN: Yes. . . . But write only of what is important and eternal. You know, I have had varied experiences of life, and have enjoyed it; I am satisfied, but if it had been my lot to know the spiritual heights which artists reach at the moment of creation, I should, I believe, have despised my bodily self and all that appertains to it and left all things earthly as far behind as possible.

TREPLEV: Excuse me, where is Nina?

DORN: And another thing. In a work of art there ought to be a clear definite idea. You ought to know what is your aim in writing, for if you go along that picturesque route without a definite goal you will be lost and your talent will be your ruin.

TREPLEV [*impatiently*]: Where is Nina?

DORN: She has gone home.

TREPLEV [*in despair*]: What am I to do? I want to see her . . . I must see her. . . . I must go. . . .

Enter MASHA.

DORN [*to* TREPLEV]: Calm yourself, my boy.

TREPLEV: But I am going all the same. I must go.

MASHA: Come indoors, Konstantin Gavrilitch. Your mother wants you. She is worried.

TREPLEV: Tell her that I have gone away. And I beg you—all of you—leave me in peace! Let me alone! Don't follow me about!

DORN: Come, come, come, dear boy. . . . You can't go on like that. . . . That's not the thing.

TREPLEV [*in tears*]: Good-bye, doctor. Thank you . . . [*goes off*].

DORN [*with a sigh*]: Youth! youth!

MASHA: When people have nothing better to say, they say, 'Youth! youth!' . . . [*Takes a pinch of snuff.*]

DORN [*takes her snuff-box from her and flings it into the bushes*]: That's disgusting! [*a pause*]. I believe they are playing the piano indoors. We must go in.

MASHA: Wait a little.

DORN: What is it?

MASHA: I want to tell you once more. I have a longing to talk . . . [*growing agitated*]. I don't care for my father . . . but I feel drawn to you. For some reason I feel with all my heart that you are very near me. . . . Help me. Help me, or I shall do something silly, I shall make a mock of my life and ruin it. . . . I can't go on. . . .

DORN: What is it? Help you in what?

MASHA: I am miserable. No one, no one knows how miserable I am! [*Laying her head on his breast, softly.*] I love Konstantin!

DORN: How hysterical they all are! How hysterical! And what a lot of love. . . . Oh, the sorcery of the lake! [*Tenderly.*] But what can I do, my child? What? What?

CURTAIN

ACT TWO

A croquet lawn. The house with a big verandah in the background on the right, on the left is seen the lake with the blazing sun reflected in it.
Flower beds. Midday. Hot. MADAME ARKADIN, DORN *and* MASHA *are sitting on a garden seat in the shade of an old lime tree on one side of the croquet lawn.* DORN *has an open book on his knee.*

MADAME ARKADIN [*to* MASHA]: Come, let us stand up.

They both get up.

Let us stand side by side. You are twenty-two and I am nearly twice as old. Yevgeny Sergeitch, which of us looks the younger?
DORN: You, of course.
MADAME ARKADIN: There! And why is it? Because I work, I feel I am always on the go, while you stay always in the same place and have no life at all. . . . And it is my rule never to look into the future. I never think about old age or death. What is to be, will be.
MASHA: And I feel as though I had been born long, long ago; I trail my life along like an endless train. . . . And often I have not the slightest desire to go on living [*sits down*]. Of course, that's all nonsense. I must shake myself and throw it all off.
DORN [*hums quietly*]: 'Tell her, my flowers.'
MADAME ARKADIN: Then I am as particular as an Englishman. I keep myself in hand, as they say, my dear, and am always dressed and have my hair done *comme il faut*. Do I allow myself to go out of the house even into the garden in a dressing-gown, or without my hair being done? Never! What has preserved me, is that I have never been a dowdy, I have never let myself go, as some women do . . . [*walks about the lawn with her arms akimbo*]. Here I am, as brisk as a bird. I could take the part of a girl of fifteen.
DORN: Nevertheless, I shall go on [*takes up the book*]. We stopped at the corn merchant and the rats. . . .
MADAME ARKADIN: And the rats. Read [*sits down*]. But give it to me, I'll read. It is my turn [*takes the book and looks in it*]. And rats. . . . Here it is. . . . [*Reads.*] 'And of course for society people to spoil novelists and to attract them to themselves is as dangerous as for a corn merchant to rear rats in his granaries. And yet they love them. And so, when a woman has picked out an author whom she desires to captivate, she lays siege to him by means of compliments, flattery and favours . . .' Well, that may be so with the French, but there is nothing like that with us, we have no set rules. Among us, before a woman sets to work to captivate an author, she is generally head over ears in love herself, if you please. To go no further, take Trigorin and me. . . .

Enter SORIN, *leaning on his stick and with him* NINA; MEDVEDENKO *wheels an empty bath-chair in after them.*

SORIN [*in a caressing tone, as to a child*]: Yes? We are delighted, aren't we? We are happy to-day at last? [*To his sister.*] We are delighted! Our father and stepmother have gone off to Tver, and we are free now for three whole days.

NINA [*sits down beside* MADAME ARKADIN *and embraces her*]: I am happy! Now I belong to you.

SORIN [*sits down in his bath-chair*]: She looks quite a beauty to-day.

MADAME ARKADIN: Nicely dressed and interesting. . . . That's a good girl [*kisses* NINA]. But we mustn't praise you too much for fear of ill-luck. Where is Boris Alexeyevitch?

NINA: He is in the bathing-house, fishing.

MADAME ARKADIN: I wonder he doesn't get sick of it! [*Is about to go on reading.*]

NINA: What is that?

MADAME ARKADIN: Maupassant's 'Sur l'eau,' my dear [*reads a few lines to herself*]. Well, the rest isn't interesting or true [*shuts the book*]. I feel uneasy. Tell me, what's wrong with my son? Why is he so depressed and ill-humoured? He spends whole days on the lake and I hardly ever see him.

MASHA: His heart is troubled. [*To* NINA, *timidly.*] Please, do read us something out of his play!

NINA [*shrugging her shoulders*]: Would you like it? It's so uninteresting.

MASHA [*restraining her enthusiasm*]: When he reads anything himself his eyes glow and his face turns pale. He has a fine mournful voice, and the gestures of a poet.

There is a sound of SORIN *snoring.*

DORN: Good-night!

MADAME ARKADIN: Petrusha!

SORIN: Ah?

MADAME ARKADIN: Are you asleep?

SORIN: Not a bit of it [*a pause*].

MADAME ARKADIN: You do nothing for your health, brother, and that's not right.

SORIN: I should like to take something, but the doctor won't give me anything.

DORN: Take medicine at sixty!

SORIN: Even at sixty one wants to live!

DORN [*with vexation*]: Oh, very well, take valerian drops!

MADAME ARKADIN: It seems to me it would do him good to go to some mineral springs.

DORN: Well, he might go. And he might not.

MADAME ARKADIN: What is one to make of that?

DORN: There's nothing to make of it. It's quite clear [*a pause*].

MEDVEDENKO: Pyotr Nikolayevitch ought to give up smoking.

SORIN: Nonsense!

DORN: No, it's not nonsense. Wine and tobacco destroy the personality. After a cigar or a glass of vodka, you are not Pyotr Nikolayevitch any more but Pyotr Nikolayevitch plus somebody else; your ego is diffused and you feel towards yourself as to a third person.

SORIN [*laughs*]: It's all very well for you to argue! You've lived your life, but what about me? I have served in the Department of Justice for twenty-eight years, but I haven't lived yet, I've seen and done nothing as a matter of fact, and very naturally I want to live very much. You've had enough and you don't care, and so you are inclined to be philosophical, but I want to live, and so I drink sherry at dinner and smoke cigars and so on. That's all it comes to.

DORN: One must look at life seriously, but to go in for cures at sixty and to regret that one hasn't enjoyed oneself enough in one's youth is frivolous, if you will forgive my saying so.

MASHA [*gets up*]: It must be lunch-time [*walks with a lazy, lagging step*]. My leg is gone to sleep [*goes off*].

DORN: She will go and have a couple of glasses before lunch.

SORIN: She has no personal happiness, poor thing.

DORN: Nonsense, your Excellency.

SORIN: You argue like a man who has had all he wants.

MADAME ARKADIN: Oh, what can be more boring than this sweet country boredom! Hot, still, no one ever doing anything, everyone airing their theories. . . . It's nice being with you, my friends, charming to listen to you, but . . . to sit in a hotel room somewhere and learn one's part is ever so much better.

NINA [*enthusiastically*]: Delightful! I understand you.

SORIN: Of course, it's better in town. You sit in your study, the footman lets no one in unannounced, there's a telephone . . . in the streets there are cabs and everything. . . .

DORN [*hums*]: 'Tell her, my flowers.'

Enter SHAMRAEV, *and after him* POLINA ANDREYEVNA.

SHAMRAEV: Here they are! Good morning! [*Kisses* MADAME ARKADIN's *hand and then* NINA's.] Delighted to see you in good health. [*To* MADAME ARKADIN.] My wife tells me that you are proposing to drive into town with her to-day. Is that so?

MADAME ARKADIN: Yes, we are thinking of it.

SHAMRAEV: Hm! that's splendid, but how are you going, honoured lady? They are carting the rye to-day; all the men are at work. What horses are you to have, allow me to ask?

MADAME ARKADIN: What horses? How can I tell which?

SORIN: We've got carriage horses.

SHAMRAEV [*growing excited*]: Carriage horses! But where am I to get collars for them? Where am I to get collars? It's a strange thing! It passes my understanding! Honoured lady! forgive me, I am full of reverence for your talent. I would give ten years of my life for you, but I cannot let you have the horses!

MADAME ARKADIN: But if I have to go! It's a queer thing!

SHAMRAEV: Honoured lady! you don't know what farming means.

MADAME ARKADIN [*flaring up*]: That's the old story! If that's so, I go back to Moscow to-day. Give orders for horses to be hired for me at the village, or I'll walk to the station.

SHAMRAEV [*flaring up*]: In that case I resign my position! You must look for another steward [*goes off*].

MADAME ARKADIN: It's like this every summer; every summer I am insulted here! I won't set my foot in the place again.

Goes off at left where the bathing shed is supposed to be; a minute later she can be seen entering the house. TRIGORIN *follows her, carrying fishing rods and tackle, and a pail.*

SORIN [*flaring up*]: This is insolence! It's beyond everything. I am thoroughly sick of it. Send all the horses here this minute!

NINA [*to* POLINA ANDREYEVNA]: To refuse Irina Nikolayevna, the famous actress! Any wish of hers, any whim even, is of more consequence than all your farming. It's positively incredible!

POLINA [*in despair*]: What can I do? Put yourself in my position: what can I do?

SORIN [*to* NINA]: Let us go to my sister. We will all entreat her not to go away. Won't we? [*Looking in the direction in which* SHAMRAEV *has gone.*] Insufferable man! Despot!

NINA [*preventing him from getting up*]: Sit still, sit still. We will wheel you in.

She and MEDVEDENKO *push the bath-chair.*

Oh, how awful it is!

SORIN: Yes, yes, it's awful. But he won't leave, I'll speak to him directly.

They go out; DORN *and* POLINA ANDREYEVNA *are left alone on the stage.*

DORN: People are tiresome. Your husband ought to be simply kicked out, but it will end in that old woman Pyotr Nikolayevitch and his sister begging the man's pardon. You will see!

POLINA: He has sent the carriage horses into the fields too! And there are misunderstandings like this every day. If you only knew how it upsets me! It makes me ill; see how I am trembling. . . . I can't endure his rudeness. [*In an imploring voice.*] Yevgeny, dearest, light of my eyes, my darling, let me come to you. . . . Our time is passing, we are no longer young, and if only we could lay aside concealment and lying for the end of our lives, anyway . . . [*a pause*].

DORN: I am fifty-five; it's too late to change my life.

POLINA: I know you refuse me because there are other women too who are as near to you. You can't take them all to live with you. I understand. Forgive me, you are tired of me.

NINA *appears near the house; she is picking flowers.*

DORN: No, it's all right.

POLINA: I am wretched from jealousy. Of course you are a doctor, you can't avoid women. I understand.

DORN [*to* NINA, *who comes up to them*]: How are things going?

NINA: Irina Nikolayevna is crying and Pyotr Nikolayevitch has an attack of asthma.

DORN [*gets up*]: I'd better go and give them both valerian drops.

NINA [*gives him the flowers*]: Please take these.

DORN: *Merci bien* [*goes towards the house*].

POLINA [*going with him*]: What charming flowers! [*Near the house, in a smothered voice.*] Give me those flowers! Give me those flowers!

On receiving them tears the flowers to pieces and throws them away; both go into the house.

NINA [*alone*]: How strange it is to see a famous actress cry, and about such a trivial thing! And isn't it strange? A famous author, adored by the public, written about in all the papers, his photographs for sale, his works translated into foreign languages–and he spends the whole day fishing and is delighted that he has caught two gudgeon. I thought famous people were proud, unapproachable, that they despised the crowd, and by their fame and the glory of their name, as it were, revenged themselves on the vulgar herd for putting rank and wealth above everything. But here they cry and fish, play cards, laugh and get cross like everyone else!

TREPLEV [*comes in without a hat on, with a gun and a dead sea-gull*]: Are you alone here?

NINA: Yes.

TREPLEV *lays the sea-gull at her feet.*

What does that mean?

TREPLEV: I was so mean as to kill this bird to-day. I lay it at your feet.

NINA: What is the matter with you? [*Picks up the bird and looks at it.*]

TREPLEV [*after a pause*]: Soon I shall kill myself in the same way.

NINA: You have so changed, I hardly know you.

TREPLEV: Yes, ever since the day when I hardly knew you. You have changed to me, your eyes are cold, you feel me in the way.

NINA: You have become irritable of late, you express yourself so incomprehensibly, as it were in symbols. This bird is a symbol too, I suppose, but forgive me, I don't understand it [*lays the sea-gull on the seat*]. I am too simple to understand you.

TREPLEV: This began from that evening when my play came to grief so stupidly. Women never forgive failure. I have burnt it all; every scrap of it. If only you knew how miserable I am! Your growing cold to me is awful, incredible, as though I had woken up and found this lake had suddenly dried up or sunk into the earth. You have just said that you are too simple to understand me. Oh, what is there to understand? My play was not liked, you despise my inspiration, you already consider me commonplace, insignificant, like so many others . . . [*stamping*]. How well I understand it all, how I understand it! I feel as though I had a nail in my brain, damnation take it together with my vanity which is sucking away my life, sucking it like a snake . . .

Sees TRIGORIN, *who comes in reading a book.*

Here comes the real genius, walking like Hamlet and with a book too. [*Mimics.*] 'Words, words, words.' . . . The sun has scarcely reached you and you are smiling already, your eyes are melting in its rays. I won't be in your way [*goes off quickly*].

TRIGORIN [*making notes in his book*]. Takes snuff and drinks vodka. Always in black. The schoolmaster is in love with her. . . .

NINA: Good morning, Boris Alexeyevitch!

TRIGORIN: Good morning. Circumstances have turned out so unexpectedly that it seems we are setting off to-day. We are hardly likely to meet again. I am sorry. I don't often have the chance of meeting young girls, youthful and charming; I have forgotten how one feels at eighteen or nineteen and can't picture it to myself, and so the young girls in my stories and novels are usually false. I should like to be in your shoes just for one hour to find out how you think, and altogether what sort of person you are.

NINA: And I should like to be in your shoes.

TRIGORIN: What for?

NINA: To know what it feels like to be a famous, gifted author. What does it feel like to be famous? How does it affect you, being famous?

TRIGORIN: How? Nohow, I believe. I have never thought about it. [*After a moment's thought.*] It's one of two things: either you exaggerate my fame, or it never is felt at all.

NINA: But if you read about yourself in the newspapers?

TRIGORIN: When they praise me I am pleased, and when they abuse me I feel out of humour for a day or two.

NINA: What a wonderful world! If only you knew how I envy you! How different people's lots in life are! Some can scarcely get through their dull, obscure existence, they are all just like one another, they are all unhappy; while others—you, for instance—you are one out of a million, have an interesting life full of brightness and significance. You are happy.

TRIGORIN: I? [*Shrugging his shoulders.*] Hm. . . . You talk of fame and happiness, of bright interesting life, but to me all those fine words, if you will forgive my saying so, are just like a sweetmeat which I never taste. You are very young and very good-natured.

NINA: Your life is splendid!

TRIGORIN: What is there particularly nice in it? [*Looks at his watch.*] I must go and write directly. Excuse me, I mustn't stay . . . [*laughs*]. You have stepped on my favourite corn, as the saying is, and here I am beginning to get excited and a little cross. Let us talk though. We will talk about my splendid bright life. . . . Well, where shall we begin? [*After thinking a little.*] There are such things as fixed ideas, when a man thinks day and night for instance, of nothing but the moon. And I have just such a moon. I am haunted day and night by one persistent thought: I ought to be writing, I ought to be writing, I ought . . . I have scarcely finished one novel when, for some reason, I must begin writing another, then a third, after the third a fourth. I write incessantly, post haste, and I can't write in any other way. What is there splendid and bright in that, I ask you? Oh, it's an absurd life! Here I am with you; I am excited, yet every moment I remember that my unfinished novel is waiting for me. Here I see a cloud that looks like a grand piano. I think that I must put into a story somewhere that a cloud sailed by that looked like a grand piano. There is a scent of heliotrope. I hurriedly make a note: a sickly smell, a widow's flower, to be mentioned in the description of a summer evening. I catch up myself and you at every sentence, every word, and make haste to put those sentences and words away into my literary treasure-house—it may come in useful! When I finish work I race off to the theatre or to fishing; if only I could rest in that and forget myself. But no, there's a new subject rolling about in my head like a heavy iron cannon ball, and I am drawn to my writing table and must make haste again to go on writing and writing. And it's always like that, always. And I have no rest from myself, and I feel that I am eating up my own life, and that for the sake of the honey. I give to someone in space I am stripping the pollen from my best flowers, tearing up the flowers themselves and trampling on their roots. Don't you think I am mad? Do my friends and acquaintances treat me as though I were sane? 'What are you writing? What are you giving us?' It's the same thing again and again, and it seems to me as though my friends' notice, their praises, their enthusiasm—that it's all a sham, that they are deceiving me as an invalid and I am somehow afraid that they will steal up to me from behind, snatch me and carry me off and put me in a mad-house. And in those years, the best years of my youth, when I was beginning, my writing was unmixed torture. A small writer, particularly when he is not successful, seems to himself clumsy, awkward, unnecessary; his nerves are strained and over-wrought. He can't resist hanging about people connected with literature and art, unrecognised and unnoticed by anyone, afraid to look anyone boldly in the face, like a passionate gambler without any money. I hadn't seen my reader, but for some reason I always imagined him hostile, and mistrustful. I was afraid of the public, it alarmed me, and when I had to produce my first play it always seemed to me that all the dark people felt hostile and all the fair ones were coldly indifferent. Oh, how awful it was! What agony it was!

NINA: But surely inspiration and the very process of creation give you moments of exalted happiness?

TRIGORIN: Yes. While I am writing I enjoy it. And I like reading my proofs, but . . . as soon as it is published I can't endure it, and I see that it is all wrong, a mistake, that it ought not to have been written at all, and I feel vexed and sick about it . . . [*laughing*]. And the public reads it and says: 'Yes, charming, clever. Charming, but very inferior to Tolstoy,' or, 'It's a fine thing, but Turgenev's "Fathers and Children" is finer.' And it will be the same to my dying day, only charming and clever, charming and clever—and nothing more. And when I die my friends, passing by my tomb, will say, 'Here lies Trigorin. He was a good writer, but inferior to Turgenev.'

NINA: Forgive me, but I refuse to understand you. You are simply spoiled by success.

TRIGORIN: What success? I have never liked myself; I dislike my own work. The worst of it is that I am in a sort of delirium, and often don't understand what I am writing. I love this water here, the trees, the sky. I feel nature, it arouses in me a passionate, irresistible desire to write. But I am not simply a landscape painter; I am also a citizen. I love my native country, my people; I feel that if I am a writer I am in duty bound to write of the people, of their sufferings, of their future, to talk about science and the rights of man and so on, and so on, and I write about everything. I am hurried and flustered, and on all sides they whip me up and are angry with me; I dash about from side to side like a fox beset by hounds. I see life and culture continually getting farther and farther away while I fall farther and farther behind like a peasant too late for the train; and what it comes to is that I feel I can only describe scenes and in everything else I am false to the marrow of my bones.

NINA: You are overworked and have not the leisure nor the desire to appreciate your own significance. You may be dissatisfied with yourself, but for others you are great and splendid! If I were a writer like you, I should give up my whole life to the common herd, but I should know that there could be no greater happiness for them than to rise to my level, and they would harness themselves to my chariot.

TRIGORIN: My chariot, what next! Am I an Agamemnon, or what?

Both smile.

NINA: For such happiness as being a writer or an artist I would be ready to endure poverty, disappointment, the dislike of those around me; I would live in a garret and eat nothing but rye bread, I would suffer from being dissatisfied with myself, from recognising my own imperfections, but I should ask in return for fame . . . real, resounding fame. . . . [*Covers her face with her hands.*] It makes me dizzy. . . . Ough!

The voice of MADAME ARKADIN *from the house.*

MADAME ARKADIN: Boris Alexeyevitch!

TRIGORIN: They are calling for me. I suppose it's to pack. But I don't want to leave here. [*Looks round at the lake.*] Just look how glorious it is! It's splendid!

NINA: Do you see the house and garden on the other side of the lake?

TRIGORIN: Yes.

NINA: That house was my dear mother's. I was born there. I have spent all my life beside this lake and I know every little islet on it.

TRIGORIN: It's very delightful here! [*Seeing the sea-gull.*] And what's this?

NINA: A sea-gull. Konstantin Gavrilitch shot it.

TRIGORIN: A beautiful bird. Really, I don't want to go away. Try and persuade Irina Nikolayevna to stay [*makes a note in his book*].

NINA: What are you writing?

TRIGORIN: Oh, I am only making a note. A subject struck me [*putting away the note-book*]. A subject for a short story: a young girl, such as you, has lived all her life beside a lake; she loves the lake like a sea-gull, and is as free and happy as a sea-gull. But a man comes by chance, sees her, and having nothing better to do, destroys her like that sea-gull here [*a pause*].

MADAME ARKADIN *appears at the window.*

MADAME ARKADIN: Boris Alexeyevitch, where are you?

TRIGORIN: I am coming. [*Goes and looks back at* NINA. *To* MADAME ARKADIN *at the window.*] What is it?

MADAME ARKADIN: We are staying.

TRIGORIN *goes into the house.*

NINA [*advances to the footlights; after a few moments' meditation*]: It's a dream!

CURTAIN

ACT THREE

The dining-room in SORIN's *house. Doors on right and on left. A sideboard. A medicine cupboard. A table in the middle of the room. A portmanteau and hat-boxes; signs of preparation for departure.* TRIGORIN *is having lunch;* MASHA *stands by the table.*

MASHA: I tell all this to you as a writer. You may make use of it. I am telling you the truth: if he had hurt himself seriously I would not have gone on living another minute. But I have pluck enough all the same. I just made up my mind that I would tear this love out of my heart, tear it out by the roots.

TRIGORIN: How are you going to do that?

MASHA: I am going to be married. To Medvedenko.

TRIGORIN: That's the schoolmaster?

MASHA: Yes.

TRIGORIN: I don't understand what's the object of it.

MASHA: To love without hope, to spend whole years waiting for something. . . . But when I marry, there will be no time left for love, new cares will smother all the old feelings. And, anyway, it will be a change, you know. Shall we have another?

TRIGORIN: Won't that be too much?

MASHA: Oh, come! [*Fills two glasses.*] Don't look at me like that! Women drink much oftener than you imagine. Only a small proportion drink openly as I do, the majority drink in secret. Yes. And it's always vodka or brandy. [*Clinks glasses.*] My best wishes! You are a good-hearted man; I am sorry to be parting from you.

They drink.

TRIGORIN: I don't want to go myself.

MASHA: You should beg her to stay.

TRIGORIN: No, she won't stay now. Her son is behaving very tactlessly. First he shoots himself, and now they say he is going to challenge me to a duel. And whatever for? He sulks, and snorts, and preaches new forms of art. . . . But there is room for all—new and old—why quarrel about it?

MASHA: Well, there's jealousy too. But it is nothing to do with me.

A pause. YAKOV *crosses from right to left with a portmanteau.* NINA *enters and stands by the window.*

My schoolmaster is not very brilliant, but he is a good-natured man, and poor, and he is very much in love with me. I am sorry for him. And I am sorry for his old mother. Well, let me wish you all happiness. Don't remember evil against me [*shakes hands with him warmly*]. I am very grateful for your friendly interest. Send me your books and be sure to put in an inscription. Only don't write, 'To my honoured friend,' but write simply, 'To Marya who belongs nowhere and has no object in life.' Good-bye! [*Goes out.*]

NINA [*stretching out her arm towards* TRIGORIN, *with her fist clenched*]: Odd or even?

TRIGORIN: Even.

NINA [*with a sigh*]: Wrong. I had only one pea in my hand. I was trying my fortune whether to go on the stage or not. I wish someone would advise me.

TRIGORIN: It's impossible to advise in such a matter [*a pause*].

NINA: We are parting and . . . perhaps we shall never meet again. Won't you please take this little medallion as a parting gift? I had your initials engraved on one side of it . . . and on the other the title of your book, 'Days and Nights.'

TRIGORIN: How exquisite! [*Kisses the medallion.*] A charming present!

NINA: Think of me sometimes.

TRIGORIN: I shall think of you. I shall think of you as you were on that sunny day—do you remember?—a week ago, when you were wearing a light dress . . . we were talking . . . there was a white sea-gull lying on the seat.

NINA [*pensively*]: Yes, a sea-gull . . . [*a pause*]. We can't talk any more, there's someone coming. . . . Let me have two minutes before you go, I entreat you. . . .

Goes out on the left. At the same instant MADAME ARKADIN, SORIN *in a dress coat with a star of some order on it, then* YAKOV, *occupied with the luggage, enter on the right.*

MADAME ARKADIN: Stay at home, old man. With your rheumatism you ought not to go gadding about. [*To* TRIGORIN.] Who was that went out? Nina?

TRIGORIN: Yes.

MADAME ARKADIN: *Pardon*, we interrupted you [*sits down*]. I believe I have packed everything. I am worn out.

TRIGORIN [*reads on the medallion*]: '"Days and Nights," page 121, lines 11 and 12.'

YAKOV [*clearing the table*]: Am I to pack your fishing things too, sir?

TRIGORIN: Yes, I shall want them again. You can give away the hooks.

YAKOV: Yes, sir.

TRIGORIN [*to himself*]: Page 121, lines 11 and 12. What is there in those lines? [*To* MADAME ARKADIN.] Are there copies of my books in the house?

MADAME ARKADIN: Yes, in my brother's study, in the corner bookcase.

TRIGORIN: Page 121 . . . [*goes out*].

MADAME ARKADIN: Really, Petrusha, you had better stay at home.

SORIN: You are going away; it will be dreary for me at home without you.

MADAME ARKADIN: And what is there in the town?

SORIN: Nothing particular, but still . . . [*laughs*]. There will be the laying of the foundation-stone of the Zemstvo hall, and all that sort of thing. One longs to shake oneself free from this stagnant existence, if only for an hour or two. I've been too long on the shelf like some old cigarette-holder. I have ordered the horses for one o'clock; we'll set off at the same time.

MADAME ARKADIN [*after a pause*]: Come, stay here, don't be bored and don't catch cold. Look after my son. Take care of him. Give him good advice [*a pause*]. Here I am going away and I shall never know why Konstantin tried to shoot himself. I fancy jealousy was the chief cause, and the sooner I get Trigorin away from here, the better.

SORIN: What can I say? There were other reasons too. It's easy to understand; he is young, intelligent, living in the country, in the wilds, with no money, no position and no future. He has nothing to do. He is ashamed of his idleness and afraid of it. I am very fond of him indeed, and he is attached to me, yet in spite of it all he feels he is superfluous in the house, that he is a dependant, a poor relation. It's easy to understand, it's *amour propre*. . . .

MADAME ARKADIN: He is a great anxiety to me! [*Pondering*.] He might go into the service, perhaps.

SORIN [*begins to whistle, then irresolutely*]: I think that quite the best thing would be if you were to . . . let him have a little money. In the first place he ought to be able to be dressed like other people and all that. Just look at him, he's been going about in the same wretched jacket for the last three years and he has no overcoat . . . [*laughs*]. It would do him no harm to have a little fun . . . to go abroad or something. . . . It wouldn't cost much.

MADAME ARKADIN: But all the same . . . I might manage the suit, perhaps, but as for going abroad . . . No, just at the moment I can't even manage the suit. [*Resolutely*.] I have no money!

SORIN *laughs*.

No!

SORIN [*begins to whistle*]: Quite so. Forgive me, my dear, don't be cross. I believe you. . . . You are a generous, noble-hearted woman.

MADAME ARKADIN [*weeping*]: I have no money.

SORIN: If I had money, of course I would give him some myself, but I have nothing, not a half-penny [*laughs*]. My steward takes all my pension and spends it all on the land and the cattle and the bees, and my money is all wasted. The bees die, and the cows die, they never let me have horses. . . .

MADAME ARKADIN: Yes, I have money, but you see I am an actress; my dresses alone are enough to ruin me.

SORIN: You are a kind, good creature . . . I respect you. . . . Yes . . . but there, I got a touch of it again . . . [*staggers*]. I feel dizzy [*clutches at the table*]. I feel ill and all that.

MADAME ARKADIN [*alarmed*]: Petrusha! [*Trying to support him.*] Petrusha, my dear! [*Calling.*] Help! help!

Enter TREPLEV *with a bandage round his head and* MEDVEDENKO.

He feels faint!

SORIN: It's all right, it's all right! [*Smiles and drinks some water.*] It's passed off . . . and all that.

TREPLEV [*to his mother*]: Don't be frightened, mother, it's not serious. Uncle often has these attacks now. [*To his uncle.*] You must lie down, uncle.

SORIN: For a little while, yes. . . . But I am going to the town all the same. . . . I'll lie down a little and then set off. . . . It's quite natural. [*Goes out leaning on his stick.*]

MEDVEDENKO [*gives him his arm*]: There's a riddle: in the morning on four legs, at noon on two, in the evening on three. . . .

SORIN [*laughs*]: Just so. And at night on the back. Thank you, I can manage alone. . . .

MEDVEDENKO: Oh come, why stand on ceremony! [*Goes out with* SORIN.]

MADAME ARKADIN: How he frightened me!

TREPLEV: It is not good for him to live in the country. He gets depressed. If you would be generous for once, mother, and lend him fifteen hundred or two thousand roubles, he could spend a whole year in town.

MADAME ARKADIN: I have no money. I am an actress, not a banker [*a pause*].

TREPLEV: Mother, change my bandage. You do it so well.

MADAME ARKADIN [*takes out of the medicine cupboard some iodoform and a box with bandaging material*]: The doctor is late.

TREPLEV: He promised to be here at ten, and it is midday already.

MADAME ARKADIN: Sit down [*takes the bandage off his head*]. It's like a turban. Yesterday a stranger asked in the kitchen what nationality you were. But you have almost completely healed. There is the merest trifle left [*kisses him on the head*]. You won't do anything naughty again while I am away, will you?

TREPLEV: No, mother. It was a moment of mad despair when I could not control myself. It won't happen again. [*Kisses her hand.*] You have such clever hands. I remember, long ago, when you were still acting at the Imperial Theatre— I was little then—there was a fight in our yard and a washerwoman, one of the tenants, was badly beaten. Do you remember? She was picked up senseless . . . you looked after her, took her remedies and washed her children in a tub. Don't you remember?

MADAME ARKADIN: No [*puts on a fresh bandage*].

TREPLEV: Two ballet dancers lived in the same house as we did at the time. . . . They used to come to you and have coffee. . . .

MADAME ARKADIN: I remember that.

TREPLEV: They were very pious [*a pause*]. Just lately, these last days, I have loved you as tenderly and completely as when I was a child. I have no one left now but you. Only why, why do you give yourself up to the influence of that man?

MADAME ARKADIN: You don't understand him, Konstantin. He is a very noble character. . . .

TREPLEV: And yet when he was told I was going to challenge him, the nobility of his character did not prevent him from funking it. He is going away. Ignominious flight!

MADAME ARKADIN: What nonsense! It is I who am asking him to go.

TREPLEV: A very noble character! Here you and I are almost quarrelling over him, and at this very moment he is somewhere in the drawing-room or the garden laughing at us . . . developing Nina, trying to convince her finally that he is a genius.

MADAME ARKADIN: You take a pleasure in saying unpleasant things to me. I respect that man and beg you not to speak ill of him before me.

TREPLEV: And I don't respect him. You want me to think him a genius too, but forgive me, I can't tell lies, his books make me sick.

MADAME ARKADIN: That's envy. There's nothing left for people who have pretension without talent but to attack real talent. Much comfort in that, I must say!

TREPLEV [*ironically*]: Real talent! [*Wrathfully.*] I have more talent than all of you put together if it comes to that! [*Tears the bandage off his head.*] You, with your hackneyed conventions, have usurped the supremacy in art and consider nothing real and legitimate but what you do yourselves; everything else you stifle and suppress. I don't believe in you! I don't believe in you or in him!

MADAME ARKADIN: Decadent!

TREPLEV: Get away to your charming theatre and act there in your paltry, stupid plays!

MADAME ARKADIN: I have never acted in such plays. Let me alone! You are not capable of writing even a wretched burlesque! You are nothing but a Kiev shopman! living on other people!

TREPLEV: You miser!

MADAME ARKADIN: You ragged beggar!

> TREPLEV *sits down and weeps quietly.*

Nonentity! [*Walking up and down in agitation.*] Don't cry. . . . You mustn't cry [*weeps*]. Don't . . . [*kisses him on the forehead, on the cheeks and on the head*]. My dear child, forgive me. . . . Forgive your sinful mother. Forgive me, you know I am wretched.

TREPLEV [*puts his arms round her*]: If only you knew! I have lost everything! She does not love me, and now I cannot write . . . all my hopes are gone. . . .

MADAME ARKADIN: Don't despair . . . Everything will come right. He is going away directly, she will love you again [*wipes away his tears*]. Give over. We have made it up now.

TREPLEV [*kisses her hands*]: Yes, mother.

MADAME ARKADIN [*tenderly*]: Make it up with him too. You don't want a duel, do you?

TREPLEV: Very well. Only, mother, do allow me not to meet him. It's painful to me–it's more than I can bear.

> *Enter* TRIGORIN.

Here he is . . . I am going . . . [*rapidly puts away the dressings in the cupboard*]. The doctor will do the bandaging now.

TRIGORIN [*looking in a book*]: Page 121 . . . lines 11 and 12. Here it is. [*Reads.*] 'If ever my life can be of use to you, come and take it.'

> TREPLEV *picks up the bandage from the floor and goes out.*

MADAME ARKADIN [*looking at her watch*]: The horses will soon be here.

TRIGORIN [*to himself*]: 'If ever my life can be of use to you, come and take it.'

MADAME ARKADIN: I hope all your things are packed?

TRIGORIN [*impatiently*]: Yes, yes. [*Musing.*] Why is it that I feel so much sorrow in that appeal from a pure soul and that it wrings my heart so painfully? 'If every my life can be of use to you, come and take it.' [*To* MADAME ARKADIN.] Let us stay one day longer.

> MADAME ARKADIN *shakes her head.*

Let us stay!

MADAME ARKADIN: Darling, I know what keeps you here. But have control over yourself. You are a little intoxicated, try to be sober.

TRIGORIN: You be sober too, be sensible and reasonable, I implore you; look at it all as a true friend should. [*Presses her hand.*] You are capable of sacrifice. Be a friend to me, let me be free!

MADAME ARKADIN [*in violent agitation*]: Are you so enthralled?

TRIGORIN: I am drawn to her! Perhaps it is just what I need.

MADAME ARKADIN: The love of a provincial girl? Oh, how little you know yourself!

TRIGORIN: Sometimes people sleep as they walk—that's how it is with me, I am talking to you and yet I am asleep and dreaming of her. . . . I am possessed by sweet, marvellous dreams. . . . Let me be free. . . .

MADAME ARKADIN [*trembling*]: No, no! I am an ordinary woman, you can't talk like that to me. Don't torture me, Boris. It terrifies me.

TRIGORIN: If you cared to, you could be not ordinary. Love—youthful, charming, poetical, lifting one into a world of dreams—that's the only thing in life that can give happiness! I have never yet known a love like that. . . . In my youth I never had time, I was always hanging about the editors' offices, struggling with want. Now it is here, that love, it has come, it beckons to me. What sense is there in running away from it?

MADAME ARKADIN [*wrathfully*]: You have gone mad!

TRIGORIN: Well, let me?

MADAME ARKADIN: You are all in a conspiracy together to torment me to-day! [*Weeps.*]

TRIGORIN [*clutching at his heart*]: She does not understand! She won't understand!

MADAME ARKADIN: Am I so old and ugly that you don't mind talking of other women to me? [*Puts her arms round him and kisses him.*] Oh, you are mad! My wonderful, splendid darling. . . . You are the last page of my life! [*Falls on her knees.*] My joy, my pride, my bliss! . . . [*Embraces his knees.*] If you forsake me even for one hour I shall not survive it, I shall go mad, my marvellous, magnificent one, my master. . . .

TRIGORIN: Someone may come in [*helps her to get up*].   .

MADAME ARKADIN: Let them, I am not ashamed of my love for you [*kisses his hands*]. My treasure, you desperate boy, you want to be mad, but I won't have it, I won't let you . . . [*laughs*]. You are mine . . . mine. . . . This forehead is mine, and these eyes, and this lovely silky hair is mine too . . . you are mine all over. You are so gifted, so clever, the best of all modern writers, you are the one hope of Russia. . . . You have so much truthfulness, simplicity, freshness, healthy humour. . . . In one touch you can give all the essential characteristics of a person or a landscape, your characters are living. One can't read you without delight! You think this is exaggerated? That I am flattering you? But look into my eyes . . . look. . . . Do I look like a liar? You see, I am the only one who can appreciate you; I am the only one who tells you the truth, my precious, wonderful darling. . . . Are you coming? Yes? You won't abandon me? . . .

TRIGORIN: I have no will of my own . . . I have never had a will of my own. . . . Flabby, feeble, always submissive—how can a woman care for such a man? Take me, carry me off, but don't let me move a step away from you. . . .

MADAME ARKADIN [*to herself*]: Now he is mine! [*In an easy tone as though nothing had happened.*] But, of course, if you like, you can stay. I'll go by myself and you can come afterwards, a week later. After all, why should you be in a hurry?

TRIGORIN: No, we may as well go together.

MADAME ARKADIN: As you please. Let us go together then.

A pause. TRIGORIN *makes a note.*

What are you writing?

TRIGORIN: I heard a good name this morning, 'The Maiden's Forest.' It may be of use [*stretches*]. So we are to go then? Again there will be railway carriages, stations, refreshment bars, mutton chops, conversations. . . .

SHAMRAEV [*enters*]: I have the honour to announce, with regret, that the horses are ready. It's time, honoured lady, to set off for the station; the train comes in at five minutes past two. So please do me a favour, Irina Nikolaevna, do not forget to inquire what has become of the actor Suzdaltsev. Is he alive and well? We used to drink together at one time. . . . In 'The Plundered Mail' he used to play incomparably . . . I remember the tragedian Izmaïlov, also a remarkable personality, acted with him in Elisavetograd. . . . Don't be in a hurry, honoured lady, you need not start for five minutes. Once they were acting conspirators in a melodrama and when they were suddenly discovered Izmaïlov had to say, 'We are caught in a trap,' but he said, 'We are caught in a tap!' [*Laughs.*] A tap!

While he is speaking YAKOV *is busy looking after the luggage. The maid brings* MADAME ARKADIN *her hat, her coat, her umbrella and her gloves; they all help* MADAME ARKADIN *to put on her things. The man-cook looks in at the door on left and after some hesitation comes in. Enter* POLINA ANDREYEVNA, *then* SORIN *and* MEDVEDENKO.

POLINA [*with a basket*]: Here are some plums for the journey. . . . Very sweet ones. You may be glad to have something nice. . . .

MADAME ARKADIN: You are very kind, Polina Andreyevna.

POLINA: Good-bye, my dear! If anything has not been to your liking, forgive it [*weeps*].

MADAME ARKADIN [*embraces her*]: Everything has been nice, everything! But you mustn't cry.

POLINA: The time flies so fast!

MADAME ARKADIN: There's no help for it.

SORIN [*in a great-coat with a cape to it, with his hat on and a stick in his hand, enters from door on left, crossing the stage*]: Sister, it's time to start, or you may be too late after all. I am going to get into the carriage [*goes out*].

MEDVEDENKO: And I shall walk to the station . . . to see you off. I'll be there in no time . . . [*goes out*].

MADAME ARKADIN: Good-bye, dear friends. . . . If we are all alive and well, we shall meet again next summer.

The maid, the cook and YAKOV *kiss her hand.*

Don't forget me. [*Gives the cook a rouble.*] Here's a rouble for the three of you.

THE COOK: We humbly thank you, madam! Good journey to you! We are very grateful for your kindness!

YAKOV: May God give you good luck!

SHAMRAEV: You might rejoice our hearts with a letter! Good-bye, Boris Alexeyevitch!

MADAME ARKADIN: Where is Konstantin? Tell him that I am starting; I must say good-bye. Well, don't remember evil against me. [*To* YAKOV.] I gave the cook a rouble. It's for the three of you.

All go out on right. The stage is empty. Behind the scenes the noise that is usual when people are being seen off. The maid comes back to fetch the basket of plums from the table and goes out again.

TRIGORIN [*coming back*]: I have forgotten my stick. I believe it is out there, on the verandah.

Goes and, at door on left, meets NINA *who is coming in.*

Is that you? We are going. . . .

NINA: I felt that we should see each other once more. [*Excitedly.*] Boris Alexeyevitch, I have come to a decision, the die is cast, I am going on the stage. I shall be gone from here to-morrow; I am leaving my father, I am abandoning everything, I am beginning a new life. Like you, I am going . . . to Moscow. We shall meet there.

TRIGORIN [*looking round*]: Stay at the 'Slavyansky Bazaar' . . . Let me know at once . . . Molchanovka, Groholsky House. . . . I am in a hurry . . . [*a pause*].

NINA: One minute more. . . .

TRIGORIN [*in an undertone*]: You are so lovely. . . . Oh, what happiness to think that we shall see each other soon!

She sinks on his breast.

I shall see again those wonderful eyes, that inexpressibly beautiful tender smile . . . those soft features, the expression of angelic purity. . . . My darling. . . .

A prolonged kiss.

CURTAIN

Between the Third and Fourth Acts there is an interval of two years.

ACT FOUR

One of the drawing-rooms in SORIN's *house, which has been turned into a study for* KONSTANTIN TREPLEV. *On the right and left, doors leading to inner apartments. In the middle, glass door leading on to the verandah. Besides the usual drawing-room furniture there is, in corner on right, a writing-table, near door on left, a sofa, a bookcase and books in windows and on the chairs. Evening. There is a single lamp alight with a shade on it. It is half dark. There is the sound of the trees rustling, and the wind howling in the chimney. A watchman is tapping. Enter* MEDVEDENKO *and* MASHA.

MASHA [*calling*]: Konstantin Gavrilitch! Konstantin Gavrilitch! [*Looking round.*] No, there is no one here. The old man keeps asking every minute, where is Kostya, where is Kostya? He cannot live without him. . . .

MEDVEDENKO: He is afraid of being alone. [*Listening.*] What awful weather! This is the second day of it.

MASHA [*turns up the lamp*]: There are waves on the lake. Great big ones.

MEDVEDENKO: How dark it is in the garden! We ought to have told them to break up that stage in the garden. It stands as bare and ugly as a skeleton, and the curtain flaps in the wind. When I passed it yesterday evening, it seemed as though someone were crying in it.

MASHA: What next . . . [*a pause*].

MEDVEDENKO: Let us go home, Masha.

MASHA [*shakes her head*]: I shall stay here for the night.

MEDVEDENKO [*in an imploring voice*]: Masha, do come! Our baby must be hungry.

MASHA: Nonsense. Matryona will feed him [*a pause*].

MEDVEDENKO: I am sorry for him. He has been three nights now without his mother.

MASHA: You are a bore. In old days you used at least to discuss general subjects, but now it is only home, baby, home, baby—that's all one can get out of you.

MEDVEDENKO: Come along, Masha!

MASHA: Go by yourself.

MEDVEDENKO: Your father won't let me have a horse.

MASHA: Yes, he will. You ask, and he will.

MEDVEDENKO: Very well, I'll ask. Then you will come to-morrow?

MASHA [*taking a pinch of snuff*]: Very well, to-morrow. How you pester me.

Enter TREPLEV *and* POLINA ANDREYEVNA; TREPLEV *brings in pillows and a quilt, and* POLINA ANDREYEVNA *sheets and pillow-cases; they lay them on the sofa, then* TREPLEV *goes to his table and sits down.*

What's this for, mother?

POLINA: Pyotr Nikolayevitch asked us to make a bed for him in Kostya's room.

MASHA: Let me do it [*makes the bed*].

POLINA [*sighing*]: Old people are like children [*goes up to the writing-table, and leaning on her elbow, looks at the manuscript; a pause*].

MEDVEDENKO: Well, I am going then. Good-bye, Masha [*kisses his wife's hand*]. Good-bye, mother [*tries to kiss his mother-in-law's hand*].

POLINA [*with vexation*]: Come, if you are going, go.

MEDVEDENKO: Good-bye, Konstantin Gavrilitch.

TREPLEV *gives him his hand without speaking;* MEDVEDENKO *goes out.*

POLINA [*looking at the MS.*]: No one would have guessed or thought that you would have become a real author, Kostya. And now, thank God, they send you money from the magazines. [*Passes her hand over his hair.*] And you have grown good-looking too. . . . Dear, good Kostya, do be a little kinder to my Mashenka!

MASHA [*as she makes the bed*]. Leave him alone, mother.

POLINA [*to* TREPLEV]: She is a nice little thing [*a pause*]. A woman wants nothing, you know, Kostya, so long as you give her a kind look. I know from myself.

TREPLEV *gets up from the table and walks away without speaking.*

MASHA: Now you have made him angry. What induced you to pester him?

POLINA: I feel so sorry for you, Mashenka.

MASHA: Much use that is!

POLINA: My heart aches for you. I see it all, you know, I understand it all.

MASHA: It's all foolishness. There is no such thing as hopeless love except in novels. It's of no consequence. The only thing is one mustn't let oneself go and keep expecting something, waiting for the tide to turn. . . . When love gets into the heart there is nothing to be done but to clear it out. Here they promised to transfer my husband to another district. As soon as I am there, I shall forget it all . . . I shall tear it out of my heart.

Two rooms away a melancholy waltz is played.

POLINA: That's Kostya playing. He must be depressed.

MASHA [*noiselessly dances a few waltz steps*]: The great thing, mother, is not to have him before one's eyes. If they only give my Semyon his transfer, trust me, I shall get over it in a month. It's all nonsense.

Door on left opens. DORN *and* MEDVEDENKO *wheel in* SORIN *in his chair.*

MEDVEDENKO: I have six of them at home now. And flour is two kopeks per pound.

DORN: You've got to look sharp to make both ends meet.

MEDVEDENKO: It's all very well for you to laugh. You've got more money than you know what to do with.

DORN: Money? After thirty years of practice, my boy, troublesome work during which I could not call my soul my own by day or by night, I only succeeded in saving two thousand roubles, and that I spent not long ago abroad. I have nothing.

MASHA [*to her husband*]: You have not gone?

MEDVEDENKO [*guiltily*]: Well, how can I when they won't let me have a horse?

MASHA [*with bitter vexation in an undertone*]: I can't bear the sight of you.

The wheel-chair remains in the left half of the room; POLINA ANDREYEVNA, MASHA *and* DORN *sit down beside it,* MEDVEDENKO *moves mournfully to one side.*

DORN: What changes there have been here! The drawing-room has been turned into a study.

MASHA: It is more convenient for Konstantin Gavrilitch to work here. Whenever he likes, he can walk out into the garden and think there.

A watchman taps.

SORIN: Where is my sister?

DORN: She has gone to the station to meet Trigorin. She will be back directly.

SORIN: Since you thought it necessary to send for my sister, I must be dangerously ill. [*After a silence.*] It's a queer thing, I am dangerously ill and here they don't give me any medicines.

DORN: Well, what would you like to have? Valerian drops? Soda? Quinine?

SORIN: Ah, he is at his moralising again! What an infliction it is! [*With a motion of his head towards the sofa.*] Is that bed for me?

POLINA: Yes, it's for you, Pyotr Nikolayevitch.

SORIN: Thank you.

DORN [*hums*]: 'The moon is floating in the midnight sky.'

SORIN: I want to give Kostya a subject for a story. It ought to be called 'The Man who Wished'—*L'homme qui a voulu*. In my youth I wanted to become a literary man—and didn't; I wanted to speak well—and I spoke horribly badly [*mimicking himself*], 'and all the rest of it, and all that, and so on, and so forth' . . . and I would go plodding on and on, trying to sum up till I was in a regular perspiration; I wanted to get married—and I didn't; I always wanted to live in town and here I am ending my life in the country—and so on.

DORN: I wanted to become an actual civil councillor—and I have.

SORIN [*laughs*]: That I had no hankerings after. That happened of itself.

DORN: To be expressing dissatisfaction with life at sixty-two is really ungracious, you know.

SORIN: What a persistent fellow he is! You might understand that one wants to live!

DORN: That's just frivolity. It's the law of nature that every life must have an end.

SORIN: You argue like a man who has had enough. You are satisfied and so you are indifferent to life, nothing matters to you. But even you will be afraid to die.

DORN: The dread of death is an animal fear. One must overcome it. A rational fear of death is only possible for those who believe in eternal life and are conscious of their sins. And you, in the first place, don't believe, and, in the second, what sins have you to worry about? You have served in the courts of justice for twenty-five years–that's all.

SORIN [*laughs*]: Twenty-eight. . . .

TREPLEV *comes in and sits down on a stool at* SORIN'*s feet.* MASHA *never takes her eyes off him.*

DORN: We are hindering Konstantin Gavrilitch from working.

TREPLEV: Oh no, it doesn't matter [*a pause*].

MEDVEDENKO: Allow me to ask you, doctor, what town did you like best abroad?

DORN: Genoa.

TREPLEV: Why Genoa?

DORN: The life in the streets is so wonderful there. When you go out of the hotel in the evening, the whole street is packed with people. You wander aimlessly zigzagging about among the crowd, backwards and forwards; you live with it, are psychologically at one with it and begin almost to believe that a world-soul is really possible, such as was acted by Nina Zaretchny in your play. And, by the way, where is she now? How is she getting on?

TREPLEV: I expect she is quite well.

DORN: I was told that she was leading a rather peculiar life. How was that?

TREPLEV: That's a long story, doctor.

DORN: Well, tell it us shortly [*a pause*].

TREPLEV: She ran away from home and had an affair with Trigorin. You know that?

DORN: I know.

TREPLEV: She had a child. The child died. Trigorin got tired of her and went back to his old ties, as might have been expected. Though, indeed, he had never abandoned them, but in his weak-willed way contrived to keep both going. As far as I can make out from what I have heard, Nina's private life was a complete failure.

DORN: And the stage?

TREPLEV: I fancy that was worse still. She made her début at some holiday place near Moscow, then went to the provinces. All that time I did not lose sight of her, and wherever she went I followed her. She always took big parts, but she acted crudely, without taste, screamingly, with violent gestures. There were moments when she uttered a cry successfully or died successfully, but they were only moments.

DORN: Then she really has some talent?

TREPLEV: It was difficult to make it out. I suppose she has. I saw her but she would not see me, and the servants would not admit me at the hotel. I understood her state of mind and did not insist on seeing her [*a pause*]. What more can I tell you? Afterwards, when I was back at home, I had some letters from her–warm, intelligent, interesting letters. She did not complain, but I felt that she was profoundly unhappy; every line betrayed sick overstrained nerves. And her imagination is a little unhinged. She signed herself the Sea-gull. In Pushkin's 'Mermaid' the miller says that he is a raven, and in the same way in her letters she kept repeating that she was a sea-gull. Now she is here.

DORN: Here? How do you mean?

TREPLEV: In the town, staying at an inn. She has been there for five days. I did go to see her, and Marya Ilyinishna here went too, but she won't see anyone. Semyon Semyonitch declares he saw her yesterday afternoon in the fields a mile and a half from here.

MEDVEDENKO: Yes, I saw her. She went in that direction, towards the town. I bowed to her and asked her why she did not come to see us. She said she would come.

TREPLEV: She won't come [*a pause*]. Her father and stepmother refuse to recognise her. They have put watchmen about so that she may not even go near the house [*walks away with the doctor towards the writing table*]. How easy it is to be a philosopher on paper, doctor, and how difficult it is in life!

SORIN: She was a charming girl.

DORN: What?

SORIN: She was a charming girl, I say. Actual Civil Councillor Sorin was positively in love with her for a time.

DORN: The old Lovelace.

SHAMRAEV'*s laugh is heard.*

POLINA: I fancy our people have come back from the station. . . .

TREPLEV: Yes, I hear mother.

Enter MADAME ARKADIN, TRIGORIN *and with them* SHAMRAEV.

SHAMRAEV [*as he enters*]: We all grow old and dilapidated under the influence of the elements, while you, honoured lady, are still young . . . a light blouse, sprightliness, grace. . . .

MADAME ARKADIN: You want to bring me ill-luck again, you tiresome man!

TRIGORIN: How do you do, Pyotr Nikolayevitch! So you are still poorly? That's bad! [*Seeing* MASHA, *joyfully.*] Marya Ilyinishna!

MASHA: You know me, do you? [*shakes hands*].

TRIGORIN: Married?

MASHA: Long ago.

TRIGORIN: Are you happy? [*Bows to* DORN *and* MEDVEDENKO, *then hesitatingly approaches* TREPLEV.] Irina Nikolayevna has told me that you have forgotten the past and are no longer angry.

TREPLEV *holds out his hand.*

MADAME ARKADIN [*to her son*]: Boris Alexeyevitch has brought the magazine with your new story in it.

TREPLEV [*taking the magazine, to* TRIGORIN]: Thank you, you are very kind.

They sit down.

TRIGORIN: Your admirers send their greetings to you. . . . In Petersburg and Moscow there is great interest in your work and I am continually being asked questions about you. People ask what you are like, how old you are, whether you are dark or fair. Everyone imagines, for some reason, that you are no longer young. And no one knows you real name, as you always publish under a pseudonym. You are as mysterious as the Iron Mask.

TREPLEV: Will you be able to make a long stay?

TRIGORIN: No, I think I must go back to Moscow to-morrow. I am obliged to. I am in a hurry to finish my novel, and besides, I have promised something for a collection of tales that is being published. It's the old story, in fact.

While they are talking MADAME ARKADIN *and* POLINA ANDREYEVNA *put a card-table in the middle of the room and open it out.* SHAMRAEV *lights candles and sets chairs. A game of loto is brought out of the cupboard.*

The weather has not given me a friendly welcome. There is a cruel wind. If it has dropped by to-morrow morning I shall go to the lake to fish. And I must have a look at the garden and that place where—you remember?—your play was acted. I've got a subject for a story, I only want to revive my recollections of the scene in which it is laid.

MASHA [*to her father*]: Father, let my husband have a horse! He must get home.

SHAMRAEV [*mimicking*]: Must get home—a horse! [*Sternly.*] You can see for yourself: they have just been to the station. I can't send them out again.

MASHA: But there are other horses. [*Seeing that her father says nothing, waves her hand.*] There's no doing anything with you.

MEDVEDENKO: I can walk, Masha. Really. . . .

POLINA [*with a sigh*]: Walk in such weather . . . [*sits down to the card-table*]. Come, friends.

MEDVEDENKO: It is only four miles. Good-bye [*kisses his wife's hand*]. Good-bye, mother.

His mother-in-law reluctantly holds out her hand for him to kiss.

I wouldn't trouble anyone, but the baby . . . [*bows to the company*]. Good-bye . . . [*goes out with a guilty step*].

SHAMRAEV: He can walk right enough. He's not a general.

POLINA [*tapping on the table*]: Come, friends. Don't let us waste time, we shall soon be called to supper.

SHAMRAEV, MASHA *and* DORN *sit down at the table.*

MADAME ARKADIN [*to* TRIGORIN]: When the long autumn evenings come on, they play loto here. Look, it's the same old loto that we had when our mother used to play with us, when we were children. Won't you have a game before supper? [*Sits down to the table with* TRIGORIN.] It's a dull game, but it is not so bad when you are used to it [*deals three cards to everyone*].

TREPLEV [*turning the pages of the magazine*]: He has read his own story, but he has not even cut mine. [*Puts the magazine down on the writing-table, then goes towards door on left; as he passes his mother he kisses her on the head.*]

MADAME ARKADIN: And you, Kostya?

TREPLEV: Excuse me, I would rather not . . . I am going out [*goes out*].

MADAME ARKADIN: The stake is ten kopeks. Put it down for me, doctor, will you?

DORN: Right.

MASHA: Has everyone put down their stakes? I begin . . . Twenty-two.

MADAME ARKADIN: Yes.

MASHA: Three!

DORN: Right!

MASHA: Did you play three? Eight! Eighty-one! Ten!

SHAMRAEV: Don't be in a hurry!

MADAME ARKADIN: What a reception I had in Harkov! My goodness! I feel dizzy with it still.

MASHA: Thirty-four!

A melancholy waltz is played behind the scenes.

MADAME ARKADIN: The students gave me an ovation. . . . Three baskets of flowers . . . two wreaths and this, see [*unfastens a brooch on her throat and lays it on the table*].

SHAMRAEV: Yes, that is a thing. . . .

MASHA: Fifty!

DORN: Exactly fifty?

MADAME ARKADIN: I had a wonderful dress. . . . Whatever I don't know, I do know how to dress.

POLINA: Kostya is playing the piano; he is depressed, poor fellow.

SHAMRAEV: He is awfully abused in the newspapers.

MASHA: Seventy-seven!

MADAME ARKADIN: As though that mattered!

TRIGORIN: He never quite comes off. He has not yet hit upon his own medium. There is always something queer and vague, at times almost like delirium. Not a single living character.

MASHA: Eleven!

MADAME ARKADIN [*looking round at* SORIN]: Petrusha, are you bored? [*a pause*]. He is asleep.

DORN: The actual civil councillor is asleep.

MASHA: Seven! Ninety!

TRIGORIN: If I lived in such a place, beside a lake, do you suppose I should write? I should overcome this passion and should do nothing but fish.

MASHA: Twenty-eight!

TRIGORIN: Catching perch is so delightful!

DORN: Well, I believe in Konstantin Gavrilitch. There is something in him! There is something in him! He thinks in images; his stories are vivid, full of colour and they affect me strongly. The only pity is that he has not got definite aims. He produces an impression and that's all, but you can't get far with nothing but an impression. Irina Nikolayevna, are you glad that your son is a writer?

MADAME ARKADIN: Only fancy, I have not read anything of his yet. I never have time.

MASHA: Twenty-six!

TREPLEV *comes in quietly and sits down at his table.*

SHAMRAEV [*to* TRIGORIN]: We have still got something here belonging to you, Boris Alexeyevitch.

TRIGORIN: What's that?

SHAMRAEV: Konstantin Gavrilitch shot a sea-gull and you asked me to get it stuffed for you.

TRIGORIN: I don't remember! [*Pondering*]. I don't remember!

MASHA: Sixty-six! One!

TREPLEV [*flinging open the window, listens*]: How dark it is! I don't know why I feel so uneasy.

MADAME ARKADIN: Kostya, shut the window, there's a draught.

TREPLEV *shuts the window.*

MASHA: Eighty-eight!

TRIGORIN: The game is mine!

MADAME ARKADIN [*gaily*]: Bravo, bravo!

SHAMRAEV: Bravo!

MADAME ARKADIN: That man always has luck in everything [*gets up*]. And now let us go and have something to eat. Our great man has not dined to-day. We will go on again after supper. [*To her son.*] Kostya, leave your manuscripts and come to supper.

TREPLEV: I don't want any, mother, I am not hungry.

MADAME ARKADIN: As you like. [*Wakes* SORIN.] Petrusha, supper! [*Takes* SHAMRAEV'*s arm.*] I'll tell you about my reception in Harkov.

POLINA ANDREYEVNA *puts out the candles on the table. Then she and* DORN *wheel the chair. All go out by door on left; only* TREPLEV, *sitting at the writing-table, is left on the stage.*

TREPLEV [*settling himself to write; runs through what he has written already*]: I have talked so much about new forms and now I feel that little by little I am falling into a convention myself. [*Reads*] 'The placard on the wall proclaimed. . . . The pale face in its setting of dark hair.' Proclaimed, setting. That's stupid [*scratches out*]. I will begin where the hero is awakened by the patter of the rain, and throw out all the rest. The description of the moonlight evening is long and over elaborate. Trigorin has worked out methods for himself, it's easy for him now. . . . With him the broken bottle neck glitters on the dam and the mill-wheel casts a black shadow—and there you have the moonlight night, while I have the tremulous light, and the soft twinkling of the stars, and the far-away strains of the piano dying away in the still fragrant air. . . . It's agonising [*a pause*]. I come more and more to the conviction that it is not a question of new and old forms, but that what matters is that a man should write without thinking about forms at all, write because it springs freely from his soul.

There is a tap at the window nearest to the table.

What is that? [*Looks out of window*]. There is nothing to be seen . . . [*opens the glass door and looks out into the garden*]. Someone ran down the steps. [*Calls.*] Who is there?

Goes out and can be heard walking rapidly along the verandah; returns half a minute later with NINA ZARETCHNY.

Nina, Nina!

NINA *lays her head on his breast and weeps with subdued sobs.*

TREPLEV [*moved*]: Nina! Nina! It's you . . . you. . . . It's as though I had foreseen it, all day long my heart has been aching and restless [*takes off her hat and cape*]. Oh, my sweet, my precious, she has come at last! Don't let us cry, don't let us!

NINA: There is someone here.

TREPLEV: No one.

NINA: Lock the doors, someone may come in.

TREPLEV: No one will come in.

NINA: I know Irina Nikolayevna is here. Lock the doors.

TREPLEV [*locks the door on right, goes to door on left*]: There is no lock on this one, I'll put a chair against it [*puts an armchair against the door*]. Don't be afraid, no one will come.

NINA [*looking intently into his face*]: Let me look at you. [*Looking round.*] It's warm, it's nice. . . . In old days this was the drawing-room. Am I very much changed?

TREPLEV: Yes. . . . You are thinner and your eyes are bigger. Nina, how strange it is that I should be seeing you. Why would not you let me see you? Why haven't you come all this time? I know you have been here almost a week. . . . I have been to you several times every day; I stood under your window like a beggar.

NINA: I was afraid that you might hate me. I dream every night that you look at me and don't know me. If only you knew! Ever since I came I have been walking here . . . by the lake. I have been near your house many times and could not bring myself to enter it. Let us sit down.

They sit down.

Let us sit down and talk and talk. It's nice here, it's warm and snug. Do you hear the wind? There's a passage in Turgenev, 'Well for the man on such a night who sits under the shelter of home, who has a warm corner in safety.' I am a sea-gull. . . . No, that's not it [*rubs her forehead*]. What was I saying? Yes . . . Turgenev . . . 'And the Lord help all homeless wanderers!' . . . It doesn't matter [*sobs*].

TREPLEV: Nina, you are crying again. . . . Nina!

NINA: Never mind, it does me good . . . I haven't cried for two years. Yesterday, late in the evening, I came into the garden to see whether our stage was still there. It is still standing. I cried for the first time after two years and it eased the weight on my heart and made it lighter. You see, I am not crying now [*takes him by the hand*]. And so now you are an author. . . . You are an author, I am an actress. . . . We too have been drawn into the whirlpool. I lived joyously, like a child—I woke up singing in the morning; I loved you and dreamed of fame, and now? Early to-morrow morning I must go to Yelets third-class . . . with peasants, and at Yelets the cultured tradesmen will pester me with attentions. Life is a coarse business!

TREPLEV: Why to Yelets?

NINA: I have taken an engagement for the whole winter. It is time to go.

TREPLEV: Nina, I cursed you, I hated you, I tore up your letters and photographs, but I was conscious every minute that my soul is bound to yours for ever. It's not in my power to leave off loving you, Nina. Ever since I lost you and began to get my work published my life has been unbearable–I am wretched. . . . My youth was, as it were, torn away all at once and it seems to me as though I have lived for ninety years already. I call upon you, I kiss the earth on which you have walked; wherever I look I see your face, that tender smile that lighted up the best days of my life. . . .

NINA [*distractedly*]: Why does he talk like this, why does he talk like this?

TREPLEV: I am alone in the world, warmed by no affection. I am as cold as though I were in a cellar, and everything I write is dry, hard and gloomy. Stay here, Nina, I entreat you, or let me go with you!

NINA *rapidly puts on her hat and cape.*

Nina, why is this? For God's sake, Nina! [*Looks at her as she puts her things on; a pause.*]

NINA: My horses are waiting at the gate. Don't see me off, I'll go alone. . . . [*Through her tears.*] Give me some water. . . .

TREPLEV [*gives her some water*]: Where are you going now?

NINA: To the town [*a pause*]. Is Irina Nikolayevna here?

TREPLEV: Yes. . . . Uncle was taken worse on Thursday and we telegraphed for her.

NINA: Why do you say that you kissed the earth on which I walked? I ought to be killed. [*Bends over the table.*] I am so tired! If I could rest . . . if I could rest! [*Raising her head.*] I am a sea-gull. . . . No, that's not it. I am an actress. Oh, well! [*Hearing* MADAME ARKADIN *and* TRIGORIN *laughing, she listens, then runs to door on left and looks through the keyhole.*] He is here too. . . . [*Turning back to* TREPLEV.] Oh, well . . . it doesn't matter . . . no. . . . He did not believe in the stage, he always laughed at my dreams and little by little I left off believing in it too, and lost heart. . . . And then I was fretted by love and jealousy, and continually anxious over my little one. . . . I grew petty and trivial, I acted stupidly. . . . I did not know what to do with my arms, I did not know how to stand on the stage, could not control my voice. You can't understand what it feels like when one knows one is acting disgracefully. I am a sea-gull. No, that's not it. . . . Do you remember you shot a sea-gull? A man came by chance, saw it and, just to pass the time, destroyed it. . . . A subject for a short story. . . . That's not it, though [*rubs her forehead*]. What was I saying? . . . I am talking of the stage. Now I am not like that. I am a real actress, I act with enjoyment, with enthusiasm, I am intoxicated when I am on the stage and feel that I am splendid. And since I have been here, I keep walking about and thinking, thinking and feeling that my soul is getting stronger every day. Now I know, I understand, Kostya, that in our work–in acting or writing–what matters is not fame, not glory, not what I dreamed of, but knowing how to be patient. To bear one's cross and have faith. I have faith and it all doesn't hurt so much, and when I think of my vocation I am not afraid of life.

TREPLEV [*mournfully*]: You have found your path, you know which way you are going, but I am still floating in a chaos of dreams and images, not knowing what use it is to anyone. I have no faith and don't know what my vocation is.

NINA [*listening*]: 'Sh-sh . . . I am going. Good-bye. When I become a great actress, come and look at me. Will you promise? But now ... [*presses his hand*] it's late. I can hardly stand on my feet. ... I am worn out and hungry.. . .

TREPLEV: Stay, I'll give you some supper.

NINA: No, no. . . . Don't see me off, I will go by myself. My horses are close by. . . . So she brought him with her? Well, it doesn't matter. When you see Trigorin, don't say anything to him. . . . I love him! I love him even more than before. . . . A subject for a short story ... I love him, I love him passionately, I love him to despair. It was nice in old days, Kostya! Do you remember? How clear, warm, joyous and pure life was, what feelings we had—feelings like tender, exquisite flowers. . . . Do you remember? [*Recites.*] 'Men, lions, eagles, and partridges, horned deer, geese, spiders, silent fish that dwell in the water, starfishes, and creatures which cannot be seen by the eye—all living things, all living things, all living things, have completed their cycle of sorrow, are extinct. . . . For thousands of years the earth has borne no living creature on its surface, and this poor moon lights its lamp in vain. On the meadow the cranes no longer waken with a cry and there is no sound of the May beetles in the lime trees . . .' [*impulsively embraces* TREPLEV *and runs out of the glass door*].

TREPLEV [*after a pause*]: It will be a pity if someone meets her in the garden and tells mother. It may upset mother. . . . [*He spends two minutes in tearing up all his manuscripts and throwing them under the table; then unlocks the door on right and goes out.*]

DORN [*trying to open the door on left*]: Strange. The door seems to be locked . . . [*comes in and puts the armchair in its place*]. An obstacle race.

Enter MADAME ARKADIN *and* POLINA ANDREYEVNA, *behind them* YAKOV *carrying a tray with bottles;* MASHA; *then* SHAMRAEV *and* TRIGORIN.

MADAME ARKADIN: Put the claret and the beer for Boris Alexeyevitch here on the table. We will play as we drink it. Let us sit down, friends.

POLINA [*to* YAKOV]: Bring tea too at the same time [*lights the candles and sits down to the card table*].

SHAMRAEV [*leads* TRIGORIN *to the cupboard*]: Here's the thing I was speaking about just now [*takes the stuffed sea-gull from the cupboard*]. This is what you ordered.

TRIGORIN [*looking at the sea-gull*]: I don't remember it. [*Musing.*] I don't remember.

The sound of a shot coming from right of stage; everyone starts.

MADAME ARKADIN [*frightened*]: What's that?

DORN: That's nothing. It must be something in my medicine-chest that has gone off. Don't be anxious [*goes out at door on right, comes back in half a minute*]. That's what it is. A bottle of ether has exploded. [*Hums.*] 'I stand before thee enchanted again. . . .'

MADAME ARKADIN [*sitting down to the table*]: Ough, how frightened I was. It reminded me of how ... [*hides her face in her hands*]. It made me quite dizzy. . . .

DORN [*turning over the leaves of the magazine, to* TRIGORIN]: There was an article in this two months ago—a letter from America—and I wanted to ask you, among other things [*puts his arm round* TRIGORIN's *waist and leads him to the footlights*] as I am very much interested in the question. . . . [*In a lower tone, dropping his voice.*] Get Irina Nikolayevna away somehow. The fact is, Konstantin Gavrilitch has shot himself. . . .

CURTAIN

THE PLAYBOY OF THE WESTERN WORLD

J. M. SYNGE

THE PLAYBOY OF THE WESTERN WORLD

First published in 1907

PREFACE

In writing *The Playboy of the Western World*, as in my other plays, I have used one or two words only that I have not heard among the country people of Ireland, or spoken in my own nursery before I could read the newspapers. A certain number of the phrases I employ I have heard also from herds and fishermen along the coast from Kerry to Mayo or from beggar-women and ballad-singers nearer Dublin; and I am glad to acknowledge how much I owe to the folk-imagination of these fine people. Anyone who has lived in real intimacy with the Irish peasantry will know that the wildest sayings and ideas in this play are tame indeed, compared with the fancies one may hear in any little hillside cabin in Geesala, or Carraroe, or Dingle Bay. All art is a collaboration; and there is little doubt that in the happy ages of literature, striking and beautiful phrases were as ready to the story-teller's or the playwright's hand, as the rich cloaks and dresses of his time. It is probable that when the Elizabethan dramatist took his ink-horn and sat down to his work he used many phrases that he had just heard, as he sat at dinner, from his mother or his children. In Ireland, those of us who know the people have the same privilege. When I was writing *The Shadow of the Glen*, some years ago, I got more aid than any learning could have given me from a chink in the floor of the old Wicklow house where I was staying, that let me hear what was being said by the servant girls in the kitchen. This matter, I think, is of importance, for in countries where the imagination of the people, and the language they use, is rich and living, it is possible for a writer to be rich and copious in his words, and at the same time to give the reality, which is the root of all poetry, in a comprehensive and natural form. In the modern literature of towns, however, richness is found only in sonnets, or prose poems, or in one or two elaborate books that are far away from the profound and common interests of life. One has, on one side, Mallarmé and Huysmans producing this literature; and on the other, Ibsen and Zola dealing with the reality of life in joyless and pallid words. On the stage one must have reality, and one must have joy; and that is why the intellectual modern drama has failed, and people have grown sick of the false joy of the musical comedy, that has been given them in place of the rich joy found only in what is superb and wild in reality. In a good play every speech should be as fully flavoured as a nut or apple, and such speeches cannot be written by anyone who works among people who have shut their lips on poetry. In Ireland, for a few years more, we have a popular imagination that is fiery, and magnificent, and tender; so that those of us who wish to write start with a chance that is not given to writers in places where the spring-time of the local life has been forgotten, and the harvest is a memory only, and the straw has been turned into bricks.

21 January 1907   J.M.S.

CHARACTERS

CHRISTOPHER MAHON
OLD MAHON (*his Father, a Squatter*)
MICHAEL JAMES FLAHERTY (MICHAEL
  JAMES) (*a Publican*)
MARGARET FLAHERTY (PEGEEN MIKE)
  (*his Daughter*)
SHAWN KEOGH (*her Cousin, a young Farmer*)
WIDOW QUIN (*a Woman of about thirty*)
PHILLY CULLEN and JIMMY FARRELL
  (*small Farmers*)
SARA TANSEY, SUSAN BRADY, HONOR
  BLAKE, and NELL McLAUGHLIN (*Village Girls*)
A BELLMAN
SOME PEASANTS

The action takes place near a village, on a wild coast of
Mayo. The First Act passes on an evening of autumn,
the other two Acts on the following day.

ACT ONE

Country public-house or shebeen, very rough and untidy. There is a sort of counter on the right with shelves, holding many bottles and jugs, just seen above it. Empty barrels stand near the counter. At back, a little to left of counter, there is a door into the open air, then, more to the left, there is a settle with shelves above it, with more jugs, and a table beneath a window. At the left there is a large open fire-place, with turf fire, and a small door into inner room. PEGEEN, a wild-looking but fine girl, of about twenty, is writing at table. She is dressed in the usual peasant dress.

PEGEEN [*slowly as she writes*]: Six yards of stuff for to make a yellow gown. A pair of lace boots with lengthy heels on them and brassy eyes. A hat is suited for a wedding-day. A fine-tooth comb. To be sent with three barrels of porter in Jimmy Farrell's creel cart on the evening of the coming Fair to Mister Michael James Flaherty. With the best compliments of this season. Margaret Flaherty.

> SHAWN KEOGH, *a fat and fair young man comes in as she signs, looks round awkwardly, when he sees she is alone.*

SHAWN: Where's himself?
PEGEEN [*without looking at him*]: He's coming. [*She directs letter.*] To Mister Sheamus Mulroy, Wine and Spirit Dealer, Castlebar.
SHAWN [*uneasily*]: I didn't see him on the road.
PEGEEN: How would you see him [*licks stamp and puts it on letter*] and it dark night this half-hour gone by?
SHAWN [*turning towards door again*]: I stood a while outside wondering would I have a right to pass on or to walk in and see you, Pegeen Mike [*comes to fire*], and I could hear the cows breathing and sighing in the stillness of the air, and not a step moving any place from this gate to the bridge.
PEGEEN [*putting letter in envelope*]: It's above at the cross-roads he is, meeting Philly Cullen and a couple more are going along with him to Kate Cassidy's wake.
SHAWN [*looking at her blankly*]: And he's going that length in the dark night.
PEGEEN [*impatiently*]: He is surely, and leaving me lonesome on the scruff of the hill. [*She gets up and puts envelope on dresser, then winds clock.*] Isn't it long the nights are now, Shawn Keogh, to be leaving a poor girl with her own self counting the hours to the dawn of day?
SHAWN [*with awkward humour*]: If it is, when we're wedded in a short while you'll have no call to complain, for I've little will to be walking off to wakes or weddings in the darkness of the night.
PEGEEN [*with rather scornful good-humour*]: You're making mighty certain, Shaneen, that I'll wed you now.

SHAWN: Aren't we after making a good bargain, the way we're only waiting these days on Father Reilly's dispensation from the bishops, or the Court of Rome.

PEGEEN [*looking at him teasingly, washing up at dresser*]: It's a wonder, Shaneen, the Holy Father'd be taking notice of the likes of you; for if I was him I wouldn't bother with this place where you'll meet none but Red Linahan, has a squint in his eye, and Patcheen is lame in his heel, or the mad Mulrannies were driven from California and they lost in their wits. We're a queer lot these times to go troubling the Holy Father on his sacred seat.

SHAWN [*scandalized*]: If we are, we're as good this place as another, maybe, and as good these times as we were for ever.

PEGEEN [*with scorn*]: As good, is it? Where now will you meet the like of Daneen Sullivan knocked the eye from a peeler; or Marcus Quin, God rest him, got six months for maiming ewes, and he a great warrant to tell stories of holy Ireland till he'd have the old women shedding down tears about their feet. Where will you find the like of them, I'm saying?

SHAWN [*timidly*]: If you don't, it's a good job, maybe; for [*with peculiar emphasis on the words*] Father Reilly has small conceit to have that kind walking around and talking to the girls.

PEGEEN [*impatiently throwing water from basin out of the door*]: Stop tormenting me with Father Reilly [*imitating his voice*] when I'm asking only what way I'll pass these twelve hours of dark, and not take my death with the fear. [*Looking out of door.*]

SHAWN [*timidly*]: Would I fetch you the Widow Quin, maybe?

PEGEEN: Is it the like of that murderer? You'll not, surely.

SHAWN [*going to her, soothingly*]: Then I'm thinking himself will stop along with you when he sees you taking on; for it'll be a long night-time with great darkness, and I'm after feeling a kind of fellow above in the furzy ditch, groaning wicked like a maddening dog, the way it's good cause you have, maybe, to be fearing now.

PEGEEN [*turning on him sharply*]: What's that? Is it a man you seen?

SHAWN [*retreating*]: I couldn't see him at all; but I heard him groaning out, and breaking his heart. It should have been a young man from his words speaking.

PEGEEN [*going after him*]: And you never went near to see was he hurted or what ailed him at all?

SHAWN: I did not, Pegeen Mike. It was a dark, lonesome place to be hearing the like of him.

PEGEEN: Well, you're a daring fellow, and if they find his corpse stretched above in the dews of dawn, what'll you say then to the peelers, or the Justice of the Peace?

SHAWN [*thunderstruck*]: I wasn't thinking of that. For the love of God, Pegeen Mike, don't let on I was speaking of him. Don't tell your father and the men is coming above; for if they heard that story they'd have great blabbing this night at the wake.

PEGEEN: I'll maybe tell them, and I'll maybe not.

SHAWN: They are coming at the door. Will you whisht, I'm saying?

PEGEEN: Whisht yourself.

She goes behind counter. MICHAEL JAMES, *fat jovial publican, comes in followed by* PHILLY CULLEN, *who is thin and mistrusting, and* JIMMY FARRELL, *who is fat and amorous, about forty-five.*

MEN [*together*]: God bless you! The blessing of God on this place!

PEGEEN: God bless you kindly.

MICHAEL [*to men, who go to the counter*]: Sit down now, and take your rest. [*Crosses to* SHAWN *at the fire.*] And how is it you are, Shawn Keogh? Are you coming over the sands to Kate Cassidy's wake?

SHAWN: I am not, Michael James. I'm going home the short cut to my bed.

PEGEEN [*speaking across the counter*]: He's right, too, and have you no shame, Michael James, to be quitting off for the whole night, and leaving myself lonesome in the shop?

MICHAEL [*good-humouredly*]: Isn't it the same whether I go for the whole night or a part only? and I'm thinking it's a queer daughter you are if you'd have me crossing backward through the Stooks of the Dead Women, with a drop taken.

PEGEEN: If I am a queer daughter, it's a queer father'd be leaving me lonesome these twelve hours of dark, and I piling the turf with the dogs barking, and the calves mooing, and my own teeth rattling with the fear.

JIMMY [*flatteringly*]: What is there to hurt you, and you a fine, hardy girl would knock the head of any two men in the place?

PEGEEN [*working herself up*]: Isn't there the harvest boys with their tongues red for drink, and the ten tinkers is camped in the east glen, and the thousand militia—bad cess to them!—walking idle through the land. There's lots surely to hurt me, and I won't stop alone in it, let himself do what he will.

MICHAEL: If you're that afeard, let Shawn Keogh stop along with you. It's the will of God, I'm thinking, himself should be seeing to you now.

They all turn on SHAWN.

SHAWN [*in horrified confusion*]: I would and welcome, Michael James, but I'm afeard of Father Reilly; and what at all would the Holy Father and the Cardinals of Rome be saying if they heard I did the like of that?

MICHAEL [*with contempt*]: God help you! Can't you sit by the hearth with the light lit and herself beyond in the room? You'll do that surely, for I've heard tell there's a queer fellow above, going mad or getting his death, maybe, in the gripe of the ditch, so she'd be safer this night with a person here.

SHAWN [*with plaintive despair*]: I'm afeard of Father Reilly, I'm saying. Let you not be tempting me, and we near married itself.

PHILLY [*with cold contempt*]: Lock him in the west room. He'll stay then and have no sin to be telling to the priest.

MICHAEL [*to* SHAWN, *getting between him and the door*]: Go up now.

SHAWN [*at the top of his voice*]: Don't stop me, Michael James. Let me out of the door, I'm saying, for the love of the Almighty God. Let me out [*trying to dodge past him*]. Let me out of it, and may God grant you His indulgence in the hour of need.

MICHAEL [*loudly*]: Stop your noising, and sit down by the hearth. [*Gives him a push and goes to counter laughing.*]

SHAWN [*turning back, wringing his hands*]: Oh, Father Reilly, and the saints of God, where will I hide myself to-day? Oh, St Joseph and St Patrick and St Brigid and St James, have mercy on me now! [*He turns round, sees door clear, and makes a rush for it.*]

MICHAEL [*catching him by the coat-tail*]: You'd be going, is it?

SHAWN [*screaming*]: Leave me go, Michael James, leave me go, you old Pagan, leave me go, or I'll get the curse of the priests on you, and of the scarlet-coated bishops of the Courts of Rome. [*With a sudden movement he pulls himself out of his coat, and disappears out of the door, leaving his coat in* MICHAEL's *hands.*]

MICHAEL [*turning round, and holding up coat*]: Well, there's the coat of a Christian man. Oh, there's sainted glory this day in the lonesome west; and by the will of God I've got you a decent man, Pegeen, you'll have no call to be spying after if you've a score of young girls, maybe, weeding in your fields.

PEGEEN [*taking up the defence of her property*]: What right have you to be making game of a poor fellow for minding the priest, when it's your own the fault is, not paying a penny pot-boy to stand along with me and give me courage in the doing of my work? [*She snaps the coat away from him, and goes behind counter with it.*]

MICHAEL [*taken aback*]: Where would I get a pot-boy? Would you have me send the bell-man screaming in the streets of Castlebar?

SHAWN [*opening the door a chink and putting in his head, in a small voice*]: Michael James!

MICHAEL [*imitating him*]: What ails you?

SHAWN: The queer dying fellow's beyond looking over the ditch. He's come up, I'm thinking, stealing your hens. [*Looks over his shoulder.*] God help me, he's following me now [*he runs into room*], and if he's heard what I said, he'll be having my life, and I going home lonesome in the darkness of the night.

For a perceptible moment they watch the door with curiosity. Some one coughs outside. Then CHRISTY MAHON, *a slight young man, comes in very tired and frightened and dirty.*

CHRISTY [*in a small voice*]: God save all here!

MEN: God save you kindly!

CHRISTY [*going to the counter*]: I'd trouble you for a glass of porter, woman of the house. [*He puts down coin.*]

PEGEEN [*serving him*]. You're one of the tinkers, young fellow, is beyond camped in the glen?

CHRISTY: I am not; but I'm destroyed walking.

MICHAEL [*patronizingly*]: Let you come up then to the fire. You're looking famished with the cold.

CHRISTY: God reward you. [*He takes up his glass and goes a little way across to the left, then stops and looks about him.*] It is often the polis do be coming into this place, master of the house?

MICHAEL: If you'd come in better hours, you'd have seen 'Licensed for the Sale of Beer and Spirits, to be Consumed on the Premises,' written in white letters above the door, and what would the polis want spying on me, and not a decent house within four miles, the way every living Christian is a bona fide, saving one widow alone?

CHRISTY [*with relief*]: It's a safe house, so. [*He goes over to the fire, sighing and moaning. Then he sits down, putting his glass beside him, and begins gnawing a turnip, too miserable to feel the others staring at him with curiosity.*]

MICHAEL [*going after him*]: Is it yourself is fearing the polis? You're wanting, maybe?

CHRISTY: There's many wanting.

MICHAEL: Many, surely, with the broken harvest and the ended wars. [*He picks up some stockings, etc., that are near the fire, and carries them away furtively.*] It should be larceny, I'm thinking?

CHRISTY [*dolefully*]: I had it in my mind it was a different word and a bigger.

PEGEEN: There's a queer lad. Were you never slapped in school, young fellow, that you don't know the name of your deed?

CHRISTY [*bashfully*]: I'm slow at learning, a middling scholar only.

MICHAEL: If you're a dunce itself, you'd have a right to know that larceny's robbing and stealing. Is it for the like of that you're wanting?

CHRISTY [*with a flash of family pride*]: And I the son of a strong farmer [*with a sudden qualm*], God rest his soul, could have bought up the whole of your old house a while since, from the butt of his tail-pocket, and not have missed the weight of it gone.

MICHAEL [*impressed*]: If it's not stealing, it's maybe something big.

CHRISTY [*flattered*]: Aye; it's maybe something big.

JIMMY: He's a wicked-looking young fellow. Maybe he followed after a young woman on a lonesome night.

CHRISTY [*shocked*]: Oh, the saints forbid, mister; I was all times a decent lad.

PHILLY [*turning on* JIMMY]: You're a silly man, Jimmy Farrell. He said his father was a farmer a while since, and there's himself now in a poor state. Maybe the land was grabbed from him, and he did what any decent man would do.

MICHAEL [*to* CHRISTY, *mysteriously*]: Was it bailiffs?

CHRISTY: The divil a one.

MICHAEL: Agents?

CHRISTY: The divil a one.

MICHAEL: Landlords?

CHRISTY [*peevishly*]: Ah, not at all, I'm saying. You'd see the like of them stories on any little paper of a Munster town. But I'm not calling to mind any person, gentle, simple, judge or jury, did the like of me.

They all draw nearer with delighted curiosity.

PHILLY: Well, that lad's a puzzle-the-world.

JIMMY: He'd beat Dan Davies' circus, or the holy missioners making sermons on the villainy of man. Try him again, Philly.

PHILLY: Did you strike golden guineas out of solder, young fellow, or shilling coins itself?

CHRISTY: I did not, mister, not sixpence nor a farthing coin.

JIMMY: Did you marry three wives maybe? I'm told there's a sprinkling have done that among the holy Luthers of the preaching north.

CHRISTY [*shyly*]: I never married with one, let alone with a couple or three.

PHILLY: Maybe he went fighting for the Boers, the like of the man beyond, was judged to be hanged, quartered, and drawn. Were you off east, young fellow, fighting bloody wars for Kruger and the freedom of the Boers?

CHRISTY: I never left my own parish till Tuesday was a week.

PEGEEN [*coming from counter*]: He's done nothing, so. [*To* CHRISTY.] If you didn't commit murder or a bad, nasty thing; or false coining, or robbery, or butchery, or the like of them, there isn't anything that would be worth your troubling for to run from now. You did nothing at all.

CHRISTY [*his feelings hurt*]: That's an unkindly thing to be saying to a poor orphaned traveller, has a prison behind him, and hanging before, and hell's gap gaping below.

PEGEEN [*with a sigh to the men to be quiet*]. You're only saying it. You did nothing at all. A soft lad the like of you wouldn't slit the windpipe of a screeching sow.

CHRISTY [*offended*]: You're not speaking the truth.

PEGEEN [*in mock rage*]: Not speaking the truth, is it? Would you have me knock the head of you with the butt of the broom?

CHRISTY [*twisting round on her with a sharp cry of horror*]: Don't strike me. I killed my poor father, Tuesday was a week, for doing the like of that.

PEGEEN [*with blank amazement*]: Is it killed your father?

CHRISTY [*subsiding*]: With the help of God I did, surely, and that the Holy Immaculate Mother may intercede for his soul.

PHILLY [*retreating with* JIMMY]: There's a daring fellow.

JIMMY: Oh, glory be to God!

MICHAEL [*with great respect*]: That was a hanging crime, mister honey. You should have had good reason for doing the like of that.

iCHRISTY [*in a very reasonable tone*]: He was a dirty man, God forgive him, and he getting old and crusty, the way I couldn't put up with him at all.

PEGEEN: And you shot him dead?

CHRISTY [*shaking his head*]: I never used weapons. I've no licence, and I'm a law-fearing man.

MICHAEL: It was with a hilted knife maybe? I'm told, in the big world, it's bloody knives they use.

CHRISTY [*loudly, scandalized*]: Do you take me for a slaughter-boy?

PEGEEN: You never hanged him, the way Jimmy Farrell hanged his dog from the licence, and had it screeching and wriggling three hours at the butt of a string, and himself swearing it was a dead dog, and the peelers swearing it had life?

CHRISTY: I did not, then. I just riz the loy and let fall the edge of it on the ridge of his skull, and he went down at my feet like an empty sack, and never let a grunt or groan from him at all.

MICHAEL [*making a sign to* PEGEEN *to fill* CHRISTY'*s glass*]: And what way weren't you hanged, mister? Did you bury him then?

CHRISTY [*considering*]: Aye. I buried him then. Wasn't I digging spuds in the field?

MICHAEL: And the peelers never followed after you the eleven days that you're out?

CHRISTY [*shaking his head*]: Never a one of them, and I walking forward facing hog, dog, or divil on the highway of the road.

PHILLY [*nodding wisely*]: It's only with a common week-day kind of a murderer them lads would be trusting their carcase, and that man should be a great terror when his temper's roused.

MICHAEL: He should then. [*To* CHRISTY.] And where was it, mister honey, that you did the deed?

CHRISTY [*looking at him with suspicion*]: Oh, a distant place, master of the house, a windy corner of high, distant hills.

PHILLY [*nodding with approval*]: He's a close man, and he's right, surely.

PEGEEN: That'd be a lad with the sense of Solomon to have for a pot-boy, Michael James, if it's the truth you're seeking one at all.

PHILLY: The peelers is fearing him, and if you'd that lad in the house there isn't one of them would come smelling around if the dogs itself were lapping poteen from the dung-pit of the yard.

JIMMY: Bravery's a treasure in a lonesome place, and a lad would kill his father, I'm thinking, would face a foxy divil with a pitchpike on the flags of hell.

PEGEEN: It's the truth they're saying, and if I'd that lad in the house, I wouldn't be fearing the looséd kharki cut-throats, or the walking dead.

CHRISTY [*swelling with surprise and triumph*]: Well, glory be to God!

MICHAEL [*with deference*]: Would you think well to stop here and be pot-boy, mister honey, if we gave you good wages, and didn't destroy you with the weight of work.

SHAWN [*coming forward uneasily*]: That'd be a queer kind to bring into a decent, quiet household with the like of Pegeen Mike.

PEGEEN [*very sharply*]: Will you whisht? Who's speak'ng to you?

SHAWN [*retreating*]: A bloody-handed murderer the like of . . .

PEGEEN [*snapping at him*]: Whisht, I am saying; we'll take no fooling from your like at all. [*To* CHRISTY *with a honeyed voice.*] And you, young fellow, you'd have a right to stop, I'm thinking, for we'd do our all and utmost to content your needs.

CHRISTY [*overcome with wonder*]: And I'd be safe this place from the searching law?

MICHAEL: You would, surely. If they're not fearing you, itself, the peelers in this place is decent, drouthy poor fellows, wouldn't touch a cur dog and not give warning in the dead of night.

PEGEEN [*very kindly and persuasively*]: Let you stop a short while anyhow. Aren't you destroyed walking with your feet in bleeding blisters, and your whole skin needing washing like a Wicklow sheep.

CHRISTY [*looking round with satisfaction*]: It's a nice room, and if it's not humbugging me you are, I'm thinking that I'll surely stay.

JIMMY [*jumps up*]: Now, by the grace of God, herself will be safe this night, with a man killed his father holding danger from the door, and let you come on, Michael James, or they'll have the best stuff drunk at the wake.

MICHAEL [*going to the door with men*]: And begging your pardon, mister, what name will we call you, for we'd like to know?

CHRISTY: Christopher Mahon.

MICHAEL: Well, God bless you, Christy, and a good rest till we meet again when the sun'll be rising to the noon of day.

CHRISTY: God bless you all.

MEN: God bless you.

They go out, except SHAWN, *who lingers at the door.*

SHAWN [*to* PEGEEN]: Are you wanting me to stop along with you and keep you from harm?

PEGEEN [*gruffly*]: Didn't you say you were fearing Father Reilly?

SHAWN: There'd be no harm staying now, I'm thinking, and himself in it too.

PEGEEN: You wouldn't stay when there was need for you, and let you step off nimble this time when there's none.

SHAWN: Didn't I say it was Father Reilly . . .

PEGEEN: Go on, then, to Father Reilly [*in a jeering tone*], and let him put you in the holy brotherhoods, and leave that lad to me.

SHAWN: If I meet the Widow Quin . . .

PEGEEN: Go on, I'm saying, and don't be waking this place with your noise. [*She hustles him out and bolts door.*] That lad would wear the spirits from the saints of peace.

> *Bustles about, then takes off her apron and pins it up in the window as a blind,* CHRISTY *watching her timidly. Then she comes to him and speaks with bland good-humour.*

Let you stretch out now by the fire, young fellow. You should be destroyed travelling.

CHRISTY [*shyly again, drawing off his boots*]: I'm tired surely, walking wild eleven days, and waking fearful in the night. [*He holds up one of his feet, feeling his blisters, and looking at them with compassion.*]

PEGEEN [*standing beside him, watching him with delight*]: You should have had great people in your family, I'm thinking, with the little, small feet you have, and you with a kind of a quality name, the like of what you'd find on the great powers and potentates of France and Spain.

CHRISTY [*with pride*]: We were great, surely, with wide and windy acres of rich Munster land.

PEGEEN: Wasn't I telling you, and you a fine, handsome young fellow with a noble brow?

CHRISTY [*with a flash of delighted surprise*]: Is it me?

PEGEEN: Aye. Did you never hear that from the young girls where you come from in the west or south?

CHRISTY [*with venom*]: I did not, then. Oh, they're bloody liars in the naked parish where I grew a man.

PEGEEN: If they are itself, you've heard it these days, I'm thinking, and you walking the world telling out your story to young girls or old.

CHRISTY: I've told my story no place till this night, Pegeen Mike, and it's foolish I was here, maybe, to be talking free; but you're decent people, I'm thinking, and yourself a kindly woman, the way I wasn't fearing you at all.

PEGEEN [*filling a sack with straw*]: You've said the like of that, maybe, in every cot and cabin where you've met a young girl on your way.

CHRISTY [*going over to her, gradually raising his voice*]: I've said it nowhere till this night, I'm telling you; for I've seen none the like of you the eleven long days I am walking the world, looking over a low ditch or a high ditch on my north or south, into stony, scattered fields, or scribes of bog, where you'd see young, limber girls, and fine, prancing women making laughter with the men.

PEGEEN: If you weren't destroyed travelling, you'd have as much talk and streeleen, I'm thinking, as Owen Roe O'Sullivan or the poets of the Dingle Bay; and I've heard all times it's the poets are your like—fine, fiery fellows with great rages when their temper's roused.

CHRISTY [*drawing a little nearer to her*]: You've a power of rings, God bless you, and would there be any offence if I was asking are you single now?

PEGEEN: What would I want wedding so young?

CHRISTY [*with relief*]: We're alike, so.

PEGEEN [*she puts sack on settle and beats it up*]: I never killed my father. I'd be afeard to do that, except I was the like of yourself with blind rages tearing me within, for I'm thinking you should have had great tussling when the end was come.

CHRISTY [*expanding with delight at the first confidential talk he has ever had with a woman*]: We had not then. It was a hard woman was come over the hill; and if he was always a crusty kind when he'd a hard woman setting him on, not the divil himself or his four fathers could put up with him at all.

PEGEEN [*with curiosity*]: And isn't it a great wonder that one wasn't fearing you?

CHRISTY [*very confidentially*]: Up to the day I killed my father, there wasn't a person in Ireland knew the kind I was, and I there drinking, waking, eating, sleeping, a quiet, simple poor fellow with no man giving me heed.

PEGEEN [*getting a quilt out of cupboard and putting it on the sack*]: It was the girls were giving you heed, maybe, and I'm thinking it's most conceit you'd have to be gaming with their like.

CHRISTY [*shaking his head, with simplicity*]: Not the girls itself, and I won't tell you a lie. There wasn't anyone heeding me in that place saving only the dumb beasts of the field. [*He sits down at fire.*]

PEGEEN [*with disappointment*]: And I thinking you should have been living the like of a king of Norway or the eastern world. [*She comes and sits beside him after placing bread and mug of milk on the table.*]

CHRISTY [*laughing piteously*]: The like of a king, is it? And I after toiling, moiling, digging, dodging from the dawn till dusk; with never a sight of joy or sport saving only when I'd be abroad in the dark night poaching rabbits on hills, for I was a divil to poach, God forgive me [*very naïvely*], and I near got six months for going with a dung fork and stabbing a fish.

PEGEEN: And it's that you'd call sport, is it, to be abroad in the darkness with yourself alone?

CHRISTY: I did, God help me, and there I'd be as happy as the sunshine of St Martin's Day, watching the light passing the north or the patches of fog, till I'd hear a rabbit starting to screech and I'd go running in the furze. Then, when I'd my full share, I'd come walking down where you'd see the ducks and geese stretched sleeping on the highway of the road, and before I'd pass the dunghill, I'd hear himself snoring out—a loud, lonesome snore he'd be making all times, the while he was sleeping; and he a man'd be raging all times, the while he was waking, like a gaudy officer you'd hear cursing and damning and swearing oaths.

PEGEEN: Providence and Mercy, spare us all!

CHRISTY: It's that you'd say surely if you seen him and he after drinking for weeks, rising up in the red dawn, or before it maybe, and going out into the yard as naked as an ash-tree in the moon of May, and shying clods against the visage of the stars he'd till put the fear of death into the banbhs and the screeching sows.

PEGEEN: I'd be well-nigh afeard of that lad myself, I'm thinking. And there was no one in it but the two of you alone?

CHRISTY: The divil a one, though he'd sons and daughters walking all great states and territories of the world, and not a one of them, to this day, but would say their seven curses on him, and they rousing up to let a cough or sneeze, maybe, in the deadness of the night.

PEGEEN [*nodding her head*]: Well, you should have been a queer lot. I never cursed my father the like of that, though I'm twenty and more years of age.

CHRISTY: Then you'd have cursed mine, I'm telling you, and he a man never gave peace to any, saving when he'd get two months or three, or be locked in the asylums for battering peelers or assaulting men [*with depression*], the way it was a bitter life he led me till I did up a Tuesday and halve his skull.

PEGEEN [*putting her hand on his shoulder*]: Well, you'll have peace in this place, Christy Mahon, and none to trouble you, and it's near time a fine lad like you should have your good share of the earth.

CHRISTY: It's time surely, and I a seemly fellow with great strength in me and bravery of . . .

Someone knocks.

CHRISTY [*clinging to* PEGEEN]: Oh, glory! it's late for knocking, and this last while I'm in terror of the peelers, and the walking dead.

Knocking again.

PEGEEN: Who's there?
VOICE [*outside*]: Me.
PEGEEN: Who's me?
VOICE: The Widow Quin.
PEGEEN [*jumping up and giving him the bread and milk*]: Go on now with your supper, and let on to be sleepy, for if she found you were such a warrant to talk, she'd be stringing gabble till the dawn of day.

He takes bread and sits shyly with his back to the door.

PEGEEN [*opening door, with temper*]: What ails you, or what is it you're wanting at this hour of the night?

WIDOW QUIN [*coming in a step and peering at* CHRISTY]: I'm after meeting Shawn Keogh and Father Reilly below, who told me of your curiosity man, and they fearing by this time he was maybe roaring, romping on your hands with drink.

PEGEEN [*pointing to* CHRISTY]: Look now is he roaring, and he stretched out drowsy with his supper and his mug of milk. Walk down and tell that to Father Reilly and to Shaneen Keogh.

WIDOW QUIN [*coming forward*]: I'll not see them again, for I've their word to lead that lad forward for to lodge with me.

PEGEEN [*in blank amazement*]: This night is it?

WIDOW QUIN [*going over*]: This night. 'It isn't fitting,' says the priesteen, 'to have his likeness lodging with an orphaned girl.' [*To* CHRISTY.] God save you, mister!

CHRISTY [*shyly*]: God save you kindly!

WIDOW QUIN [*looking at him with half-amused curiosity*]: Well, aren't you a little smiling fellow? It should have been great and bitter torments did rouse your spirits to a deed of blood.

CHRISTY [*doubtfully*]: It should, maybe.

WIDOW QUIN: It's more than 'maybe' I'm saying, and it'd soften my heart to see you sitting so simple with your cup and cake, and you fitter to be saying your catechism than slaying your da.

PEGEEN [*at counter, washing glasses*]: There's talking when any'd see he'd fit to be holding his head high with the wonders of the world. Walk on from this, for I'll not have him tormented, and he destroyed travelling since Tuesday was a week.

WIDOW QUIN [*peaceably*]: We'll be walking surely when his supper's done, and you'll find we're great company, young fellow, when it's of the like of you and me you'd hear the penny poets singing in an August Fair.

CHRISTY [*innocently*]: Did you kill your father?

PEGEEN [*contemptuously*]: She did not. She hit himself with a worn pick, and the rusted poison did corrode his blood the way he never overed it, and died after. That was a sneaky kind of murder did win small glory with the boys itself. [*She crosses to* CHRISTY'*s left.*]

WIDOW QUIN [*with good-humour*]: If it didn't, maybe all knows a widow woman has buried her children and destroyed her man is a wiser comrade for a young lad than a girl, the like of you, who'd go helter-skeltering after any man would let you a wink upon the road.

PEGEEN [*breaking out into wild rage*]. And you'll say that, Widow Quin, and you gasping with the rage you had racing the hill beyond to look on his face.

WIDOW QUIN [*laughing derisively*]: Me, is it? Well, Father Reilly has cuteness to divide you now. [*She pulls* CHRISTY *up.*] There's great temptation in a man did slay his da, and we'd best be going, young fellow; so rise up and come with me.

PEGEEN [*seizing his arm*]: He'll not stir. He's pot-boy in this place, and I'll not have him stolen off and kidnapped while himself's abroad.

WIDOW QUIN: It'd be a crazy pot-boy'd lodge him in the shebeen where he works by day, so you'd have a right to come on, young fellow, till you see my little houseen, a perch off on the rising hill.

PEGEEN: Wait till morning, Christy Mahon. Wait till you lay eyes on her leaky thatch is growing more pasture for her buck goat than her square of fields, and she without a tramp itself to keep in order her place at all.

WIDOW QUIN: When you see me contriving in my little gardens, Christy Mahon, you'll swear the Lord God formed me to be living lone, and that there isn't my match in Mayo for thatching, or mowing, or shearing a sheep.

PEGEEN [*with noisy scorn*]: It's true the Lord God formed you to contrive indeed. Doesn't the world know you reared a black ram at your own breast, so that the Lord Bishop of Connaught felt the elements of a Christian, and he eating it after in a kidney stew? Doesn't the world know you've been seen shaving the foxy skipper from France for a three-penny-bit and a sop of grass tobacco would wring the liver from a mountain goat you'd meet leaping the hills?

WIDOW QUIN [*with amusement*]: Do you hear her now, young fellow? Do you hear the way she'll be rating at your own self when a week is by?

PEGEEN [*to* CHRISTY]: Don't heed her. Tell her to go on into her pigsty and not plague us here.

WIDOW QUIN: I'm going; but he'll come with me.

PEGEEN [*shaking him*]: Are you dumb, young fellow?

CHRISTY [*timidly to* WIDOW QUIN]: God increase you; but I'm pot-boy in this place, and it's here I liefer stay.

PEGEEN [*triumphantly*]: Now you have heard him, and go on from this.

WIDOW QUIN [*looking round the room*]: It's lonesome this hour crossing the hill, and if he won't come along with me, I'd have a right maybe to stop this night with yourselves. Let me stretch out on the settle, Pegeen Mike; and himself can lie by the hearth.

PEGEEN [*short and fiercely*]: Faith, I won't. Quit off or I will send you now.

WIDOW QUIN [*gathering her shawl up*]: Well, it's a terror to be aged a score. [*To* CHRISTY.] God bless you now, young fellow, and let you be wary, or there's right torment will await you here if you go romancing with her like, and she waiting only, as they bade me say, on a sheepskin parchment to be wed with Shawn Keogh of Killakeen.

CHRISTY [*going to* PEGEEN *as she bolts door*]: What's that she's after saying?

PEGEEN: Lies and blather, you've no call to mind. Well, isn't Shawn Keogh an impudent fellow to send up spying on me? Wait till I lay hands on him. Let him wait, I'm saying.

CHRISTY: And you're not wedding him at all?

PEGEEN: I wouldn't wed him if a bishop came walking for to join us here.

CHRISTY: That God in glory may be thanked for that.

PEGEEN: There's your bed now. I've put a quilt upon you I'm after quilting a while since with my own two hands, and you'd best stretch out now for your sleep, and may God give you a good rest till I call you in the morning when the cocks will crow.

CHRISTY [*as she goes to inner room*]: May God and Mary and St Patrick bless you and reward you for your kindly talk.

> *She shuts the door behind her. He settles his bed slowly, feeling the quilt with immense satisfaction.*

Well, it's a clean bed and soft with it, and it's great luck and company I've won me in the end of time–two fine women fighting for the likes of me–till I'm thinking this night wasn't I a foolish fellow not to kill my father in the years gone by.

CURTAIN

ACT TWO

Scene as before. Brilliant morning light. CHRISTY, *looking bright and cheerful, is cleaning a girl's boots.*

CHRISTY [*to himself, counting jugs on dresser*]: Half a hundred beyond. Ten there. A score that's above. Eighty jugs. Six cups and a broken one. Two plates. A power of glasses. Bottles, a school-master'd be hard set to count, and enough in them, I'm thinking, to drunken all the wealth and wisdom of the county Clare. [*He puts down the boot carefully.*] There's her boots now, nice and decent for her evening use, and isn't it grand brushes she has? [*He puts them down and goes by degrees to the looking-glass.*] Well, this'd be a fine place to be my whole life talking out with swearing Christians, in place of my old dogs and cat; and I stalking around, smoking my pipe and drinking my fill, and never a day's work but drawing a cork an odd time, or wiping a glass, or rinsing out a shiny tumbler for a decent man. [*He takes the looking-glass from the wall and puts it on the back of a chair; then sits down in front of it and begins washing his face.*] Didn't I know rightly, I was handsome, though it was the divil's own mirror we had beyond, would twist a squint across an angel's brow; and I'll be growing fine from this day, the way I'll have a soft lovely skin on me and won't be the like of the clumsy young fellows do be ploughing all times in the earth and dung. [*He starts.*] Is she coming again? [*He looks out.*] Stranger girls. God help me, where'll I hide myself away and my long neck naked to the world? [*He looks out.*] I'd best go to the room maybe till I'm dressed again.

He gathers up his coat and the looking-glass, and runs into the inner room. The door is pushed open, and SUSAN BRADY *looks in, and knocks on door.*

SUSAN: There's nobody in it. [*Knocks again.*]

NELLY [*pushing her in and following her, with* HONOR BLAKE *and* SARA TANSEY]: It'd be early for them both to be out walking the hill.

SUSAN: I'm thinking Shawn Keogh was making game of us, and there's no such man in it at all.

HONOR [*pointing to straw and quilt*]: Look at that. He's been sleeping there in the night. Well, it'll be a hard case if he's gone off now, the way we'll never set our eyes on a man killed his father, and we after rising early and destroying ourselves running fast on the hill.

NELLY: Are you thinking them's his boots?

SARA [*taking them up*]: If they are, there should be his father's track on them. Did you never read in the papers the way murdered men do bleed and drip?

SUSAN: Is that blood there, Sara Tansey?

SARA [*smelling it*]: That's bog water, I'm thinking; but it's his own they are, surely, for I never seen the like of them for whitey mud, and red mud, and turf on them, and the fine sands of the sea. That man's been walking, I'm telling you. [*She goes down right, putting on one of his boots.*]

SUSAN [*going to window*]: Maybe he's stolen off to Belmullet with the boots of Michael James, and you'd have a right so to follow after him, Sara Tansey, and you the one yoked the ass cart and drove ten miles to set your eyes on the man bit the yellow lady's nostril on the northern shore. [*She looks out.*]

SARA [*running to window, with one boot on*]: Don't be talking, and we fooled to-day. [*Putting on the other boot.*] There's a pair do fit me well and I'll be keeping them for walking to the priest, when you'd be ashamed this place, going up winter and summer with nothing worth while to confess at all.

HONOR [*who has been listening at door*]: Whisht! there's some one inside the room. [*She pushes door a chink open.*] It's a man.

> SARA *kicks off boots and puts them where they were. They all stand in a line looking through chink.*

SARA: I'll call him. Mister! Mister!

> *He puts in his head.*

Is Pegeen within?

CHRISTY [*coming in as meek as a mouse, with the looking-glass held behind his back*]: She's above on the cnuceen, seeking the nanny goats, the way she'd have a sup of goats' milk for to colour my tea.

SARA: And asking your pardon, is it you's the man killed his father?

CHRISTY [*sidling toward the nail where the glass was hanging*]: I am, God help me!

SARA [*taking eggs she has brought*]: Then my thousand welcomes to you, and I've run up with a brace of duck's eggs for your food to-day. Pegeen's ducks is no use, but these are the real rich sort. Hold out your hand and you'll see it's no lie I'm telling you.

CHRISTY [*coming forward shyly, and holding out his left hand*]: They're a great and weighty size.

SUSAN: And I run up with a pat of butter, for it'd be a poor thing to have you eating your spuds dry, and you after running a great way since you did destroy your da.

CHRISTY: Thank you kindly.

HONOR: And I brought you a little cut of a cake, for you should have a thin stomach on you, and you that length walking the world.

NELLY: And I brought you a little laying pullet—boiled and all she is—was crushed at the fall of night by the curate's car. Feel the fat of that breast, mister.

CHRISTY: It's bursting, surely. [*He feels with the back of his hand, in which he holds the presents.*]

SARA: Will you pinch it? Is your right hand too sacred for to use at all? [*She slips round behind him.*] It's a glass he has. Well, I never seen to this day a man with a looking-glass held to his back. Them that kills their fathers is a vain lot surely.

> GIRLS *giggle.*

CHRISTY [*smiling innocently and piling presents on glass*]: I'm very thankful to you all to-day. . . .

WIDOW QUIN [*coming in quickly, at door*]: Sara Tansey, Susan Brady, Honor Blake! What in glory has you here at this hour of day?

GIRLS [*giggling*]: That's the man killed his father.

WIDOW QUIN [*coming to them*]: I know well it's the man; and I'm after putting him down in the sports below for racing, leaping, pitching, and the Lord knows what.

SARA [*exuberantly*]: That's right, Widow Quin. I'll bet my dowry that he'll lick the world.

WIDOW QUIN: If you will, you'd have a right to have him fresh and nourished in place of nursing a feast. [*Taking presents.*] Are you fasting or fed, young fellow?

CHRISTY: Fasting, if you please.

WIDOW QUIN [*loudly*]: Well, you're the lot. Stir up now and give him his breakfast. [*To* CHRISTY.] Come here to me [*she puts him on bench beside her while the* GIRLS *make tea and get his breakfast*], and let you tell us your story before Pegeen will come, in place of grinning your ears off like the moon of May.

CHRISTY [*beginning to be pleased*]: It's a long story; you'd be destroyed listening.

WIDOW QUIN: Don't be letting on to be shy, a fine, gamey, treacherous lad the like of you. Was it in your house beyond you cracked his skull?

CHRISTY [*shy but flattered*]: It was not. We were digging spuds in his cold, sloping, stony, divil's patch of a field.

WIDOW QUIN: And you went asking money of him, or making talk of getting a wife would drive him from his farm?

CHRISTY: I did not, then; but there I was, digging and digging, and 'You squinting idiot,' says he, 'let you walk down now and tell the priest you'll wed the Widow Casey in a score of days.'

WIDOW QUIN: And what kind was she?

CHRISTY [*with horror*]: A walking terror from beyond the hills, and she two score and five years, and two hundredweights and five pounds in the weighing scales, with a limping leg on her, and a blinded eye, and she a woman of noted misbehaviour with the old and young.

GIRLS [*clustering round him, serving him*]: Glory be.

WIDOW QUIN: And what did he want driving you to wed with her? [*She takes a bit of the chicken.*]

CHRISTY [*eating with growing satisfaction*]: He was letting on I was wanting a protector from the harshness of the world, and he without a thought the whole while but how he'd have her hut to live in and her gold to drink.

WIDOW QUIN: There's maybe worse than a dry hearth and a widow woman and your glass at night. So you hit him then?

CHRISTY [*getting almost excited*]: I did not. 'I won't wed her,' says I, 'when all know she did suckle me for six weeks when I came into the world, and she a hag this day with a tongue on her has the crows and seabirds scattered, the way they wouldn't cast a shadow on her garden with the dread of her curse.'

WIDOW QUIN [*teasingly*]: That one should be right company.

SARA [*eagerly*]: Don't mind her. Did you kill him then?

CHRISTY: 'She's too good for the like of you,' says he, 'and go on now or I'll flatten you out like a crawling beast has passed under a dray.' 'You will not if

I can help it,' says I. 'Go on,' says he, 'or I'll have the divil making garters of your limbs to-night.' 'You will not if I can help it,' says I. [*He sits up brandishing his mug.*]

SARA: You were right surely.

CHRISTY [*impressively*]: With that the sun came out between the cloud and the hill, and it shining green in my face. 'God have mercy on your soul,' says he, lifting a scythe. 'Or on your own,' says I, raising the loy.

SUSAN: That's a grand story.

HONOR: He tells it lovely.

CHRISTY [*flattered and confident, waving bone*]: He gave a drive with the scythe, and I gave a lep to the east. Then I turned around with my back to the north, and I hit a blow on the ridge of his skull, laid him stretched out, and he split to the knob of his gullet. [*He raises the chicken bone to his Adam's apple.*]

GIRLS [*together*]: Well, you're a marvel! Oh, God bless you! You're the lad, surely!

SUSAN: I'm thinking the Lord God sent him this road to make a second husband to the Widow Quin, and she with a great yearning to be wedded, though all dread her here. Lift him on her knee, Sara Tansey.

WIDOW QUIN: Don't tease him.

SARA [*going over to dresser and counter very quickly, and getting two glasses and porter*]: You're heroes, surely, and let you drink a supeen with your arms linked like the outlandish lovers in the sailor's song. [*She links their arms and gives them the glasses.*] There now. Drink a health to the wonders of the western world, the pirates, preachers, poteen-makers, with the jobbing jockies; parching peelers, and the juries fill their stomachs selling judgments of the English law. [*Brandishing the bottle.*]

WIDOW QUIN: That's a right toast, Sara Tansey. Now, Christy.

They drink with their arms linked, he drinking with his left hand, she with her right. As they are drinking, PEGEEN MIKE comes in with a milk-can and stands aghast. They all spring away from CHRISTY. He goes down left. WIDOW QUIN remains seated.

PEGEEN [*angrily, to* SARA]: What is it you're wanting?

SARA [*twisting her apron*]: An ounce of tobacco.

PEGEEN: Have you tuppence?

SARA: I've forgotten my purse.

PEGEEN: Then you'd best be getting it and not be fooling us here. [*To the* WIDOW QUIN, *with more elaborate scorn.*] And what is it you're wanting, Widow Quin?

WIDOW QUIN [*insolently*]: A penn'orth of starch.

PEGEEN [*breaking out*]: And you without a white shift or a shirt in your whole family since the drying of the flood. I've no starch for the like of you, and let you walk on now to Killamuck.

WIDOW QUIN [*turning to* CHRISTY, *as she goes out with the* GIRLS]: Well, you're mighty huffy this day, Pegeen Mike, and you, young fellow, let you not forget the sports and racing when the noon is by.

They go out.

PEGEEN [*imperiously*]: Fling out that rubbish and put them cups away.

CHRISTY *tidies away in great haste.*

Shove in the bench by the wall.

He does so.

And hang that glass on the nail. What disturbed it at all?

CHRISTY [*very meekly*]: I was making myself decent only, and this a fine country for young lovely girls.

PEGEEN [*sharply*]: Whisht your talking of girls. [*Goes to counter on right.*]

CHRISTY: Wouldn't any wish to be decent in a place . . .

PEGEEN. Whisht, I'm saying.

CHRISTY [*looks at her face for a moment with great misgivings, then as a last effort takes up a loy, and goes towards her, with feigned assurance*]. It was with a loy the like of that I killed my father.

PEGEEN [*still sharply*]: You've told me that story six times since the dawn of day.

CHRISTY [*reproachfully*]: It's a queer thing you wouldn't care to be hearing it and them girls after walking four miles to be listening to me now.

PEGEEN [*turning round astonished*]: Four miles?

CHRISTY [*apologetically*]: Didn't himself say there were only bona fides living in the place?

PEGEEN: It's bona fides by the road they are, but that lot came over the river lepping the stones. It's not three perches when you go like that, and I was down this morning looking on the papers the post-boy does have in his bag. [*With meaning and emphasis.*] For there was great news this day, Christopher Mahon [*She goes into room on left.*]

CHRISTY [*suspiciously*]: Is it news of my murder?

PEGEEN [*inside*]: Murder, indeed.

CHRISTY [*loudly*]: A murdered da?

PEGEEN [*coming in again and crossing right*]: There was not, but a story filled half a page of the hanging of a man. Ah, that should be a fearful end, young fellow, and it worst of all for a man destroyed his da; for the like of him would get small mercies, and when it's dead he is they'd put him in a narrow grave, with cheap sacking wrapping him round, and pour down quicklime on his head, the way you'd see a woman pouring any frish-frash from a cup.

CHRISTY [*very miserably*]: Oh, God help me. Are you thinking I'm safe? You were saying at the fall of night I was shut of jeopardy and I here with yourselves.

PEGEEN [*severely*]: You'll be shut of jeopardy no place if you go talking with a pack of wild girls the like of them do be walking abroad with the peelers, talking whispers at the fall of night.

CHRISTY [*with terror*]: And you're thinking they'd tell?

PEGEEN [*with mock sympathy*]: Who knows, God help you?

CHRISTY [*loudly*]: What joy would they have to bring hanging to the likes of me?

PEGEEN: It's queer joys they have, and who knows the thing they'd do, if it'd make the green stones cry itself to think of you swaying and swiggling at the butt of a rope, and you with a fine, stout neck, God bless you! the way you'd be a half an hour, in great anguish, getting your death.

CHRISTY [*getting his boots and putting them on*]: If there's that terror of them, it'd be best, maybe, I went on wandering like Esau or Cain and Abel on the sides of Neifin or the Erris plain.

PEGEEN [*beginning to play with him*]: It would, maybe, for I've heard the Circuit Judges this place is a heartless crew.

CHRISTY [*bitterly*]: It's more than Judges this place is a heartless crew. [*Looking up at her.*] And isn't it a poor thing to be starting again, and I a lonesome fellow will be looking out on women and girls the way the needy fallen spirits do be looking on the Lord?

PEGEEN: What call have you to be that lonesome when there's poor girls walking Mayo in their thousands now?

CHRISTY [*grimly*]: It's well you know what call I have. It's well you know it's a lonesome thing to be passing small towns with the lights shining sideways when the night is down, or going in strange places with a dog noising before you and a dog noising behind, or drawn to the cities where you'd hear a voice kissing and talking deep love in every shadow of the ditch, and you passing on with an empty, hungry stomach failing from your heart.

PEGEEN: I'm thinking you're an odd man, Christy Mahon. The oddest walking fellow I ever set my eyes on to this hour to-day.

CHRISTY: What would any be but odd men and they living lonesome in the world?

PEGEEN: I'm not odd, and I'm my whole life with my father only.

CHRISTY [*with infinite admiration*]: How would a lovely, handsome woman the like of you be lonesome when all men should be thronging around to hear the sweetness of your voice, and the little infant children should be pestering your steps, I'm thinking, and you walking the roads.

PEGEEN: I'm hard set to know what way a coaxing fellow the like of yourself should be lonesome either.

CHRISTY: Coaxing.

PEGEEN: Would you have me think a man never talked with the girls would have the words you've spoken to-day? It's only letting on you are to be lonesome, the way you'd get around me now.

CHRISTY: I wish to God I was letting on; but I was lonesome all times, and born lonesome, I'm thinking, as the moon of dawn. [*Going to door.*]

PEGEEN [*puzzled by his talk*]: Well, it's a story I'm not understanding at all why you'd be worse than another, Christy Mahon, and you a fine lad with the great savagery to destroy your da.

CHRISTY: It's little I'm understanding myself, saving only that my heart's scalded this day, and I going off stretching out the earth between us, the way I'll not be waking near you another dawn of the year till the two of us do arise to hope or judgment with the saints of God, and now I'd best be going with my wattle in my hand, for hanging is a poor thing [*turning to go*], and it's little welcome only is left me in this house to-day.

PEGEEN [*sharply*]: Christy.

He turns round.

Come here to me.

He goes towards her.

Lay down that switch and throw some sods on the fire. You're pot-boy in this place, and I'll not have you mitch off from us now.

CHRISTY: You were saying I'd be hanged if I stay.

PEGEEN [*quite kindly at last*]: I'm after going down and reading the fearful crimes of Ireland for two weeks or three, and there wasn't a word of your murder. [*Getting up and going over to the counter.*] They've likely not found the body. You're safe so with ourselves.

CHRISTY [*astonished, slowly*]: It's making game of me you were [*following her with fearful joy*], and I can stay so, working at your side, and I not lonesome from this mortal day.

PEGEEN: What's to hinder you staying, except the widow woman or the young girls would inveigle you off?

CHRISTY [*with rapture*]: And I'll have your words from this day filling my ears, and that look is come upon you meeting my two eyes, and I watching you loafing around in the warm sun, or rinsing your ankles when the night is come.

PEGEEN [*kindly, but a little embarrassed*]: I'm thinking you'll be a loyal young lad to have working around, and if you vexed me a while since with your leaguing with the girls, I wouldn't give a thraneen for a lad hadn't a mighty spirit in him and a gamey heart.

SHAWN KEOGH *runs in carrying a cleeve on his back, followed by the* WIDOW QUIN.

SHAWN [*to* PEGEEN]: I was passing below, and I seen your mountainy sheep eating cabbages in Jimmy's field. Run up or they'll be bursting, surely.

PEGEEN: Oh, God mend them! [*She puts a shawl over her head and runs out.*]

CHRISTY [*looking from one to the other. Still in high spirits*]: I'd best go to her aid maybe. I'm handy with ewes.

WIDOW QUIN [*closing the door*]: She can do that much, and there is Shaneen has long speeches for to tell you now. [*She sits down with an amused smile.*]

SHAWN [*taking something from his pocket and offering it to* CHRISTY]: Do you see that, mister?

CHRISTY [*looking at it*]: The half of a ticket to the Western States!

SHAWN [*trembling with anxiety*]: I'll give it to you and my new hat [*pulling it out of hamper*]; and my breeches with the double seat [*pulling it out*]; and my new coat is woven from the blackest shearings for three miles around [*giving him the coat*]; I'll give you the whole of them, and my blessing, and the blessing of Father Reilly itself, maybe, if you'll quit from this and leave us in the peace we had till last night at the fall of dark.

CHRISTY [*with a new arrogance*]: And for what is it you're wanting to get shut of me?

SHAWN [*looking to the* WIDOW *for help*]: I'm a poor scholar with middling faculties to coin a lie, so I'll tell you the truth, Christy Mahon. I'm wedding with Pegeen beyond, and I don't think well of having a clever, fearless man the like of you dwelling in her house.

CHRISTY [*almost pugnaciously*]: And you'd be using bribery for to banish me?

SHAWN [*in an imploring voice*]: Let you not take it badly, mister honey; isn't beyond the best place for you, where you'll have golden chains and shiny coats and you riding upon hunters with the ladies of the land. [*He makes an eager sign to the* WIDOW QUIN *to come to help him.*]

WIDOW QUIN [*coming over*]: It's true for him, and you'd best quit off and not have that poor girl setting her mind on you, for there's Shaneen thinks she wouldn't suit you, though all is saying that she'll wed you now.

CHRISTY *beams with delight.*

SHAWN [*in terrified earnest*]: She wouldn't suit you, and she with the divil's own temper the way you'd be strangling one another in a score of days. [*He makes the movement of strangling with his hands.*] It's the like of me only that she's fit for; a quiet simple fellow wouldn't raise a hand upon her if she scratched itself.

WIDOW QUIN [*putting* SHAWN'*s hat on* CHRISTY]: Fit them clothes on you anyhow, young fellow, and he'd maybe loan them to you for the sports. [*Pushing him towards inner door.*] Fit them on and you can give your answer when you have them tried.

CHRISTY [*beaming, delighted with the clothes*]: I will then. I'd like herself to see me in them tweeds and hat. [*He goes into room and shuts the door.*]

SHAWN [*in great anxiety*]: He'd like herself to see them. He'll not leave us, Widow Quin. He's a score of divils in him the way it's well-nigh certain he will wed Pegeen.

WIDOW QUIN [*jeeringly*]: It's true all girls are fond of courage and do hate the like of you.

SHAWN [*walking about in desperation*]: Oh, Widow Quin, what'll I be doing now? I'd inform again him, but he'd burst from Kilmainham and he'd be sure and certain to destroy me. If I wasn't so God-fearing, I'd near have courage to come behind him and run a pike into his side. Oh, it's a hard case to be an orphan and not to have your father that you're used to, and you'd easy kill and make yourself a hero in the sight of all. [*Coming up to her.*] Oh, Widow Quin, will you find me some contrivance when I've promised you a ewe?

WIDOW QUIN: A ewe's a small thing, but what would you give me if I did wed him and did save you so?

SHAWN [*with astonishment*]: You?

WIDOW QUIN: Aye. Would you give me the red cow you have and the mountainy ram, and the right of way cross your rye path, and a load of dung at Michaelmas, and turbary upon the western hill?

SHAWN [*radiant with hope*]: I would, surely, and I'd give you the wedding-ring I have, and the loan of a new suit, the way you'd have him decent on the wedding-day. I'd give you two kids for your dinner, and a gallon of poteen, and I'd call the piper on the long car to your wedding from Crossmolina or from Ballina. I'd give you . . .

WIDOW QUIN: That'll do, so, and let you whisht, for he's coming now again.

CHRISTY *comes in very natty in the new clothes.* WIDOW QUIN *goes to him admiringly.*

If you seen yourself now, I'm thinking you'd be too proud to speak to at all, and it'd be a pity surely to have your like sailing from Mayo to the western world.

CHRISTY [*as proud as a peacock*]: I'm not going. If this is a poor place itself, I'll make myself contented to be lodging here.

WIDOW QUIN *makes a sign to* SHAWN *to leave them.*

SHAWN: Well, I'm going measuring the racecourse while the tide is low, so I'll leave you the garments and my blessing for the sports to-day. God bless you! [*He wriggles out.*]

WIDOW QUIN [*admiring* CHRISTY]: Well, you're mighty spruce, young fellow. Sit down now while you're quiet till you talk with me.

CHRISTY [*swaggering*]: I'm going abroad on the hillside for to seek Pegeen.

WIDOW QUIN: You'll have time and plenty for to seek Pegeen, and you heard me saying at the fall of night the two of us should be great company.

CHRISTY: From this out I'll have no want of company when all sorts is bringing me their food and clothing [*he swaggers to the door, tightening his belt*], the way they'd set their eyes upon a gallant orphan cleft his father with one blow to the breeches belt. [*He opens door, then staggers back.*] Saints of glory! Holy angels from the throne of light!

WIDOW QUIN [*going over*]: What ails you?

CHRISTY: It's the walking spirit of my murdered da!

WIDOW QUIN [*looking out*]: Is it that tramper?

CHRISTY [*wildly*]: Where'll I hide my poor body from that ghost of hell?

The door is pushed open, and old MAHON *appears on threshold.* CHRISTY *darts in behind door.*

WIDOW QUIN [*in great amusement*]: God save you, my poor man.

MAHON [*gruffly*]: Did you see a young lad passing this way in the early morning or the fall of night?

WIDOW QUIN: You're a queer kind to walk in not saluting at all.

MAHON: Did you see the young lad?

WIDOW QUIN [*stiffly*]: What kind was he?

MAHON: An ugly young streeler with a murderous gob on him, and a little switch in his hand. I met a tramper seen him coming this way at the fall of night.

WIDOW QUIN: There's harvest hundreds do be passing these days for the Sligo boat. For what is it you're wanting him, my poor man?

MAHON: I want to destroy him for breaking the head on me with the clout of a loy. [*He takes off a big hat, and shows his head in a mass of bandages and plaster, with some pride.*] It was he did that, and amn't I a great wonder to think I've traced him ten days with that rent in my crown?

WIDOW QUIN [*taking his head in both hands and examining it with extreme delight*]: That was a great blow. And who hit you? A robber maybe?

MAHON: It was my own son hit me, and he the divil a robber, or anything else, but a dirty, stuttering lout.

WIDOW QUIN [*letting go his skull and wiping her hands in her apron*]: You'd best be wary of a mortified scalp, I think they call it, lepping around with that wound in the splendour of the sun. It was a bad blow, surely, and you should have vexed him fearful to make him strike that gash in his da.

MAHON: Is it me?

WIDOW QUIN [*amusing herself*]: Aye. And isn't it a great shame when the old and hardened do torment the young?

MAHON [*raging*]: Torment him is it? And I after holding out with the patience of a martyred saint till there's nothing but destruction on, and I'm driven out in my old age with none to aid me.

WIDOW QUIN [*greatly amused*]: It's a sacred wonder the way that wickedness will spoil a man.

MAHON: My wickedness, is it? Amn't I after saying it is himself has me destroyed, and he a lier on walls, a talker of folly, a man you'd see stretched the half of the day in the brown ferns with his belly to the sun.

WIDOW QUIN: Not working at all?

MAHON: The divil a work, or if he did itself, you'd see him raising up a haystack like the stalk of a rush, or driving our last cow till he broke her leg at the hip, and when he wasn't at that he'd be fooling over little birds he had—finches and felts—or making mugs at his own self in the bit of a glass we had hung on the wall.

WIDOW QUIN [*looking at* CHRISTY]: What way was he so foolish? It was running wild after the girls maybe?

MAHON [*with a shout of derision*]: Running wild, is it? If he seen a red petticoat coming swinging over the hill, he'd be off to hide in the sticks, and you'd see him shooting out his sheep's eyes between the little twigs and the leaves, and his two ears rising like a hare looking out through a gap. Girls, indeed!

WIDOW QUIN: It was drink maybe?

MAHON: And he a poor fellow would get drunk on the smell of a pint. He'd a queer rotten stomach, I'm telling you, and when I gave him three pulls from my pipe a while since, he was taken with contortions till I had to send him in the ass-cart to the females' nurse.

WIDOW QUIN [*clasping her hands*]: Well, I never, till this day, heard tell of a man the like of that!

MAHON: I'd take a mighty oath you didn't, surely, and wasn't he the laughing joke of every female woman where four baronies meet, the way the girls would stop their weeding if they seen him coming the road to let a roar at him, and call him the looney of Mahon's.

WIDOW QUIN: I'd give the world and all to see the like of him. What kind was he?

MAHON: A small, low fellow.

WIDOW QUIN: And dark?

MAHON: Dark and dirty.

WIDOW QUIN [*considering*]: I'm thinking I seen him.

MAHON [*eagerly*]: An ugly young blackguard.

WIDOW QUIN: A hideous, fearful villain, and the spit of you.

MAHON: What way is he fled?

WIDOW QUIN: Gone over the hills to catch a coasting steamer to the north or south

MAHON: Could I pull up on him now?

WIDOW QUIN: If you'll cross the sands below where the tide is out, you'll be in it as soon as himself, for he had to go round ten miles by the top of the bay. [*She points to the door.*] Strike down by the head beyond and then follow on the roadway to the north and east.

　　　MAHON *goes abruptly.*

WIDOW QUIN [*shouting after him*]: Let you give him a good vengeance when you come up with him, but don't put yourself in the power of the law, for it'd be a poor thing to see a judge in his black cap reading out his sentence on a civil warrior the like of you.

　　　She swings the door to and looks at CHRISTY, *who is cowering in terror, for a moment, then she bursts into a laugh.*

Well, you're the walking Playboy of the Western World, and that's the poor man you had divided to his breeches belt.

CHRISTY [*looking out; then, to her*]: What'll Pegeen say when she hears that story? What'll she be saying to me now?

WIDOW QUIN: She'll knock the head of you, I'm thinking, and drive you from the door. God help her to be taking you for a wonder, and you a little schemer making up a story you destroyed your da.

CHRISTY [*turning to the door, nearly speechless with rage, half to himself*]: To be letting on he was dead, and coming back to his life, and following after me like an old weasel tracing a rat, and coming in here laying desolation between my own self and the fine women of Ireland, and he a kind of carcase that you'd fling upon the sea. . . .

WIDOW QUIN [*more soberly*]: There's talking for a man's one only son.

CHRISTY [*breaking out*]: His one son, is it? May I meet him with one tooth and it aching, and one eye to be seeing seven and seventy divils in the twists of the road, and one old timber leg on him to limp into the scalding grave. [*Looking out.*] There he is now crossing the strands, and that the Lord God would send a high wave to wash him from the world.

WIDOW QUIN [*scandalized*]: Have you no shame? [*putting her hand on his shoulder and turning him round*]. What ails you? Near crying, is it?

CHRISTY [*in despair and grief*]: Amn't I after seeing the love-light of the star of knowledge shining from her brow, and hearing words would put you thinking on the holy Brigid speaking to the infant saints, and now she'll be turning again, and speaking hard words to me, like an old woman with a spavindy ass she'd have, urging on a hill.

WIDOW QUIN: There's poetry talk for a girl you'd see itching and scratching, and she with a stale stink of poteen on her from selling in the shop.

CHRISTY [*impatiently*]: It's her like is fitted to be handling merchandise in the heavens above, and what'll I be doing now, I ask you, and I a kind of wonder was jilted by the heavens when a day was by.

There is a distant noise of GIRLS' *voices.* WIDOW QUIN *looks from window and comes to him, hurriedly.*

WIDOW QUIN: You'll be doing like myself, I'm thinking, when I did destroy my man, for I'm above many's the day, odd times in great spirits, abroad in the sunshine, darning a stocking or stitching a shift; and odd times again looking out on the schooners, hookers, trawlers is sailing the sea, and I thinking on the gallant hairy fellows are drifting beyond, and myself long years living alone.

CHRISTY [*interested*]: You're like me, so.

WIDOW QUIN: I am your like, and it's for that I'm taking a fancy to you, and I with my little houseen above where there'd be myself to tend you, and none to ask were you a murderer or what at all.

CHRISTY: And what would I be doing if I left Pegeen?

WIDOW QUIN: I've nice jobs you could be doing—gathering shells to make a white-wash for our hut within, building up a little goose-house, or stretching a new skin on an old curagh I have, and if my hut is far from all sides, it's there you'll meet the wisest old men, I tell you, at the corner of my wheel, and it's there yourself and me will have great times whispering and hugging. . . .

VOICES [*outside, calling far away*]: Christy! Christy Mahon! Christy!

CHRISTY: Is it Pegeen Mike?

WIDOW QUIN: It's the young girls, I'm thinking, coming to bring you to the sports below, and what is it you'll have me to tell them now?

CHRISTY: Aid me for to win Pegeen. It's herself only that I'm seeking now.

   WIDOW QUIN *gets up and goes to window.*

Aid me for to win her, and I'll be asking God to stretch a hand to you in the hour of death, and lead you short cuts through the Meadows of Ease, and up the floor of Heaven to the Footstool of the Virgin's Son.

WIDOW QUIN: There's praying!

VOICES [*nearer*]: Christy! Christy Mahon!

CHRISTY [*with agitation*]: They're coming. Will you swear to aid and save me, for the love of Christ?

WIDOW QUIN [*looks at him for a moment*]: If I aid you, will you swear to give me a right of way I want, and a mountainy ram, and a load of dung at Michaelmas, the time that you'll be master here?

CHRISTY: I will, by the elements and stars of night.

WIDOW QUIN: Then we'll not say a word of the old fellow, the way Pegeen won't know your story till the end of time.

CHRISTY: And if he chances to return again?

WIDOW QUIN: We'll swear he's a maniac and not your da. I could take an oath I seen him raving on the sands to-day.

   GIRLS *run in.*

SUSAN: Come on to the sports below. Pegeen says you're to come.

SARA TANSEY: The lepping's beginning, and we've a jockey's suit to fit upon you for the mule race on the sands below.

HONOR: Come on, will you?

CHRISTY: I will then if Pegeen's beyond.

SARA: She's in the boreen making game of Shaneen Keogh.

CHRISTY: Then I'll be going to her now. [*He runs out, followed by the* GIRLS.]

WIDOW QUIN: Well, if the worst comes in the end of all, it'll be great game to see there's none to pity him but a widow woman, the like of me, has buried her children and destroyed her man. [*She goes out.*]

                          CURTAIN

ACT THREE

Scene as before. Later in the day. JIMMY *comes in, slightly drunk.*

JIMMY [*calls*]: Pegeen! [*Crosses to inner door.*] Pegeen Mike! [*Comes back again into the room.*] Pegeen!

PHILLY *comes in in the same state.*

JIMMY [*to* PHILLY]: Did you see herself?

PHILLY: I did not; but I sent Shawn Keogh with the ass-cart for to bear him home. [*Trying cupboards, which are locked.*] Well, isn't he a nasty man to get into such staggers at a morning wake; and isn't herself the divil's daughter for locking, and she so fussy after that young gaffer, you might take your death with drouth and none to heed you?

JIMMY: It's little wonder she'd be fussy, and he after bringing bankrupt ruin on the roulette man, and the trick-o'-the-loop man, and breaking the nose of the cockshot-man, and winning all in the sports below, racing, lepping, dancing, and the Lord knows what! He's right luck, I'm telling you.

PHILLY: If he has, he'll be rightly hobbled yet, and he not able to say ten words without making a brag of the way he killed his father, and the great blow he hit with the loy.

JIMMY: A man can't hang by his own informing, and his father should be rotten by now.

OLD MAHON *passes window slowly.*

PHILLY: Supposing a man's digging spuds in that field with a long spade, and supposing he flings up the two halves of that skull, what'll be said then in the papers and the courts of law?

JIMMY: They'd say it was an old Dane, maybe, was drowned in the flood.

OLD MAHON *comes in and sits down near door listening.*

Did you never hear tell of the skulls they have in the city of Dublin, ranged out like blue jugs in a cabin of Connaught?

PHILLY: And you believe that?

JIMMY [*pugnaciously*]: Didn't a lad see them and he after coming from harvesting in the Liverpool boat? 'They have them there,' says he, 'making a show of the great people there was one time walking the world. White skulls and black skulls and yellow skulls, and some with full teeth, and some haven't only but one.'

PHILLY: It was no lie, maybe, for when I was a young lad there was a graveyard beyond the house with the remnants of a man who had thighs as long as your arm. He was a horrid man, I'm telling you, and there was many a fine Sunday I'd put him together for fun, and he with shiny bones, you wouldn't meet the like of these days in the cities of the world.

MAHON [*getting up*]: You wouldn't, is it? Lay your eyes on that skull, and tell me where and when there was another the like of it, is splintered only from the blow of a loy.

PHILLY: Glory be to God! And who hit you at all?

MAHON [*triumphantly*]: It was my own son hit me. Would you believe that?

JIMMY: Well, there's wonders hidden in the heart of man!

PHILLY [*suspiciously*]: And what way was it done?

MAHON [*wandering about the room*]: I'm after walking hundreds and long scores of miles, winning clean beds and the fill of my belly four times in the day, and I doing nothing but telling stories of that naked truth. [*He comes to them a little aggressively.*] Give me a supeen and I'll tell you now.

> *Widow Quin comes in and stands aghast behind him. He is facing* JIMMY *and* PHILLY, *who are on the left.*

JIMMY: Ask herself beyond. She's the stuff hidden in her shawl.

WIDOW QUIN [*coming to* MAHON *quickly*]: You here, is it? You didn't go far at all?

MAHON: I seen the coasting steamer passing, and I got a drouth upon me and a cramping leg, so I said, 'The divil go along with him,' and turned again. [*Looking under her shawl.*] And let you give me a supeen, for I'm destroyed travelling since Tuesday was a week.

WIDOW QUIN [*getting a glass, in a cajoling tone*]: Sit down then by the fire and take your ease for a space. You've a right to be destroyed indeed, with your walking, and fighting, and facing the sun. [*Giving him poteen from a stone jar she has brought in.*] There now is a drink for you, and may it be to your happiness and length of life.

MAHON [*taking glass greedily, and sitting down by fire*]: God increase you!

WIDOW QUIN [*taking men to the right stealthily*]: Do you know what? That man's raving from his wound to-day, for I met him a while since telling a rambling tale of a tinker had him destroyed. Then he heard of Christy's deed, and he up and says it was his son had cracked his skull. Oh, isn't madness a fright, for he'll go killing some one yet, and he thinking it's the man has struck him so?

JIMMY [*entirely convinced*]: It's a fright surely. I knew a party was kicked in the head by a red mare, and he went killing horses a great while, till he eat the insides of a clock and died after.

PHILLY [*with suspicion*]: Did he see Christy?

WIDOW QUIN: He didn't. [*With a warning gesture.*] Let you not be putting him in mind of him, or you'll be likely summoned if there's murder done. [*Looking round at* MAHON.] Whisht! He's listening. Wait now till you hear me taking him easy and unravelling all. [*She goes to* MAHON.] And what way are you feeling, mister? Are you in contentment now?

MAHON [*slightly emotional from his drink*]: I'm poorly only, for it's a hard story the way I'm left to-day, when it was I did tend him from his hour of birth, and he a dunce never reached his second book, the way he'd come from school, many's the day, with his legs lamed under him, and he blackened with his beatings like a tinker's ass. It's a hard story, I'm saying, the way some do have their next and nighest raising up a hand of murder on them, and some is lonesome getting their death with lamentation in the dead of night.

WIDOW QUIN [*not knowing what to say*]: To hear you talking so quiet, who'd know you were the same fellow we seen pass to-day?

MAHON: I'm the same surely. The wrack and ruin of three-score years; and it's a terror to live that length, I tell you, and to have your sons going to the dogs against you, and you wore out scolding them, and skelping them, and God knows what.

PHILLY [*to* JIMMY]: He's not raving. [*To* WIDOW QUIN.] Will you ask him what kind was his son?

WIDOW QUIN [*to* MAHON, *with a peculiar look*]: Was your son that hit you a lad of one year and a score maybe, a great hand at racing and lepping and licking the world?

MAHON [*turning on her with a roar of rage*]: Didn't you hear me say he was the fool of men, the way from this out he'll know the orphan's lot, with old and young making game of him, and they swearing, raging, kicking at him like a mangy cur.

A great burst of cheering outside, some way off.

MAHON [*putting his hands to his ears*]: What in the name of God do they want roaring below?

WIDOW QUIN [*with the shade of a smile*]: They're cheering a young lad, the champion Playboy of the Western World.

More cheering.

MAHON [*going to window*]: It's split my heart to hear them, and I with pulses in my brain-pan for a week gone by. Is it racing they are?

JIMMY [*looking from door*]: It is, then. They are mounting him for the mule race will be run upon the sands. That's the playboy on the winkered mule.

MAHON [*puzzled*]: That lad, is it? If you said it was a fool he was, I'd have laid a mighty oath he was the likeness of my wandering son. [*Uneasily, putting his hand to his head.*] Faith, I'm thinking I'll go walking for to view the race.

WIDOW QUIN [*stopping him, sharply*]: You will not. You'd best take the road to Belmullet, and not be dilly-dallying in this place where there isn't a spot you could sleep.

PHILLY [*coming forward*]: Don't mind her. Mount there on the bench and you'll have a view of the whole. They're hurrying before the tide will rise, and it'd be near over if you went down the pathway through the crags below.

MAHON [*mounts on bench*, WIDOW QUIN *beside him*]: That's a right view again the edge of the sea. They're coming now from the point. He's leading. Who is he at all?

WIDOW QUIN: He's the champion of the world, I tell you, and there isn't a hap'orth isn't falling lucky to his hands to-day.

PHILLY [*looking out, interested in the race*]: Look at that. They're pressing him now.

JIMMY: He'll win it yet.

PHILLY: Take your time, Jimmy Farrell. It's too soon to say.

WIDOW QUIN [*shouting*]: Watch him taking the gate. There's riding.

JIMMY [*cheering*]: More power to the young lad!

MAHON: He's passing the third.

JIMMY: He'll lick them yet.

WIDOW QUIN: He'd lick them if he was running races with a score itself.

MAHON: Look at the mule he has, kicking the stars.

WIDOW QUIN: There was a lep! [*Catching hold of* MAHON *in her excitement.*] He's fallen? He's mounted again! Faith, he's passing them all!

JIMMY: Look at him skelping her!

PHILLY: And the mountain girls hooshing him on!

JIMMY: It's the last turn! The post's cleared for them now!

MAHON: Look at the narrow place. He'll be into the bogs! [*With a yell.*] Good rider! He's through it again!

JIMMY: He neck and neck!

MAHON: Good boy to him! Flames, but he's in!

Great cheering, in which all join.

MAHON [*with hesitation*]: What's that? They're raising him up. They're coming this way. [*With a roar of rage and astonishment.*] It's Christy, by the stars of God! I'd know his way of spitting and he astride the moon.

He jumps down and makes a run for the door, but WIDOW QUIN *catches him and pulls him back.*

WIDOW QUIN: Stay quiet, will you? That's not your son. [*To* JIMMY.] Stop him, or you'll get a month for the abetting of manslaughter and be fined as well.

JIMMY: I'll hold him.

MAHON [*struggling*]: Let me out! Let me out, the lot of you, till I have my vengeance on his head to-day.

WIDOW QUIN [*shaking him, vehemently*]: That's not your son. That's a man is going to make a marriage with the daughter of this house, a place with fine trade, with a licence, and with poteen too.

MAHON [*amazed*]: That man marrying a decent and a moneyed girl! Is it mad yous are? Is it in a crazy-house for females that I'm landed now?

WIDOW QUIN: It's mad yourself is with the blow upon your head. That lad is the wonder of the western world.

MAHON: I seen it's my son.

WIDOW QUIN: You seen that you're mad.

Cheering outside.

Do you hear them cheering him in the zig-zags of the road? Aren't you after saying that your son's a fool, and how would they be cheering a true idiot born?

MAHON [*getting distressed*]: It's maybe out of reason that that man's himself.

Cheering again.

There's none surely will go cheering him. Oh, I'm raving with a madness that would fright the world! [*He sits down with his hand to his head.*] There was one time I seen ten scarlet divils letting on they'd cork my spirit in a gallon can; and one time I seen rats as big as badgers sucking the lifeblood from the butt of my lug; but I never till this day confused that dribbling idiot with a likely man. I'm destroyed surely.

WIDOW QUIN: And who'd wonder when it's your brain-pan that is gaping now?

MAHON: Then the blight of the sacred drouth upon myself and him, for I never went mad to this day, and I not three weeks with the Limerick girls drinking myself silly and parlatic from the dusk to dawn. [*To* WIDOW QUIN, *suddenly.*] Is my visage astray?

WIDOW QUIN: It is, then. You're a sniggering maniac, a child could see.

MAHON [*getting up more cheerfully*]: Then I'd best be going to the union beyond, and there'll be a welcome before me, I tell you [*with great pride*], and I a terrible and fearful case, the way that there I was one time, screeching in a straightened waistcoat, with seven doctors writing out my sayings in a printed book. Would you believe that?

WIDOW QUIN: If you're a wonder itself, you'd best be hasty, for them lads caught a maniac one time and pelted the poor creature till he ran out, raving and foaming, and was drowned in the sea.

MAHON [*with philosophy*]: It's true mankind is the divil when your head's astray. Let me out now and I'll slip down the boreen, and not see them so.

WIDOW QUIN [*showing him out*]: That's it. Run to the right, and not a one will see.

He runs off.

PHILLY [*wisely*]: You're at some gaming, Widow Quin; but I'll walk after him and give him his dinner and a time to rest, and I'll see then if he's raving or as sane as you.

WIDOW QUIN [*annoyed*]: If you go near that lad, let you be wary of your head, I'm saying. Didn't you hear him telling he was crazed at times?

PHILLY: I heard him telling a power; and I'm thinking we'll have right sport before night will fall. [*He goes out.*]

JIMMY: Well, Philly's a conceited and foolish man. How could that madman have his senses and his brain-pan slit? I'll go after them and see him turn on Philly now.

He goes; WIDOW QUIN *hides poteen behind counter. Then hubbub outside.*

VOICES: There you are! Good jumper! Grand lepper! Darlint boy! He's the racer! Bear him on, will you!

CHRISTY *comes in, in jockey's dress, with* PEGEEN MIKE, SARA, *and other* GIRLS *and* MEN.

PEGEEN [*to crowd*]: Go on now and don't destroy him and he drenching with sweat. Go along, I'm saying, and have your tug-of-warring till he's dried his skin.

CROWD: Here's his prizes! A bagpipes! A fiddle was played by a poet in the years gone by! A flat and three-thorned blackthorn would lick the scholars out of Dublin town!

CHRISTY [*taking prizes from the* MEN]: Thank you kindly, the lot of you. But you'd say it was little only I did this day if you'd seen me a while since striking my one single blow.

TOWN CRIER [*outside ringing a bell*]: Take notice, last event of this day! Tug-of-warring on the green below! Come on, the lot of you! Great achievements for all Mayo men!

PEGEEN: Go on and leave him for to rest and dry. Go on, I tell you, for he'll do no more.

She hustles crowd out; WIDOW QUIN *following them.*

MEN [*going*]: Come on, then. Good luck for the while!

PEGEEN [*radiantly, wiping his face with her shawl*]: Well, you're the lad, and you'll have great times from this out when you could win that wealth of prizes, and you sweating in the heat of noon!

CHRISTY [*looking at her with delight*]: I'll have great times if I win the crowning prize I'm seeking now, and that's your promise that you'll wed me in a fortnight, when our banns is called.

PEGEEN [*backing away from him*]: You've right daring to go ask me that, when all knows you'll be starting to some girl in your own townland, when your father's rotten in four months, or five.

CHRISTY [*indignantly*]: Starting from you, is it? [*He follows her.*] I will not, then, and when the airs is warming, in four months or five, it's then yourself and me should be pacing Neifin in the dews of night, the times sweet smells do be rising, and you'd see a little, shiny new moon, maybe, sinking on the hills.

PEGEEN [*looking at him playfully*]: And it's that kind of a poacher's love you'd make, Christy Mahon, on the sides of Neifin, when the night is down?

CHRISTY: It's little you'll think if my love's a poacher's, or an earl's itself, when you'll feel my two hands stretched around you, and I squeezing kisses on your puckered lips, till I'd feel a kind of pity for the Lord God is all ages sitting lonesome in His golden chair.

PEGEEN: That'll be right fun, Christy Mahon, and any girl would walk her heart out before she'd meet a young man was your like for eloquence, or talk at all.

CHRISTY [*encouraged*]: Let you wait, to hear me talking, till we're astray in Erris, when Good Friday's by, drinking a sup from a well, and making mighty kisses with our wetted mouths, or gaming in a gap of sunshine, with yourself stretched back unto your necklace, in the flowers of the earth.

PEGEEN [*in a low voice, moved by his tone*]: I'd be nice so, is it?

CHRISTY [*with rapture*]: If the mitred bishops seen you that time, they'd be the like of the holy prophets, I'm thinking, do be straining the bars of Paradise to lay eyes on the Lady Helen of Troy, and she abroad, pacing back and forward, with a nosegay in her golden shawl.

PEGEEN [*with real tenderness*]: And what is it I have, Christy Mahon, to make me fitting entertainment for the like of you, that has such poet's talking, and such bravery of heart.

CHRISTY [*in a low voice*]: Isn't there the light of seven heavens in your heart alone, the way you'll be an angel's lamp to me from this out, and I abroad in the darkness, spearing salmons in the Owen or the Carrowmore?

PEGEEN: If I was your wife I'd be along with you those nights, Christy Mahon, the way you'd see I was a great hand at coaxing bailiffs, or coining funny nicknames for the stars of night.

CHRISTY: You, is it? Taking your death in the hailstones, or in the fogs of dawn.

PEGEEN: Yourself and me would shelter easy in a narrow bush [*with a qualm of dread*]; but we're only talking, maybe, for this would be a poor, thatched place to hold a fine lad is the like of you.

CHRISTY [*putting his arm round her*]: If I wasn't a good Christian, it's on my naked knees I'd be saying my prayers and paters to every jackstraw you have roofing your head, and every stony pebble is paving the laneway to your door.

PEGEEN [*radiantly*]: If that's the truth I'll be burning candles from this out to the miracles of God that have brought you from the south to-day, and I with my gowns bought ready, the way that I can wed you, and not wait at all.

CHRISTY: It's miracles, and that's the truth. Me there toiling a long while, and walking a long while, not knowing at all I was drawing all times nearer to this holy day.

PEGEEN: And myself, a girl, was tempted often to go sailing the seas till I'd marry a Jew-man, with ten kegs of gold, and I not knowing at all there was the like of you drawing nearer, like the stars of God.

CHRISTY: And to think I'm long years hearing women talking that talk, to all bloody fools, and this the first time I've heard the like of your voice talking sweetly for my own delight.

PEGEEN: And to think it's me is talking sweetly, Christy Mahon, and I the fright of seven townlands for my biting tongue. Well, the heart's a wonder; and, I'm thinking, there won't be our like in Mayo, for gallant lovers, from this hour to-day.

Drunken singing is heard outside.

There's my father coming from the wake, and when he's had his sleep we'll tell him, for he's peaceful then.

They separate.

MICHAEL [*singing outside*]:

> The jailer and the turnkey
> They quickly ran us down,
> And brought us back as prisoners
> Once more to Cavan town.

He comes in supported by SHAWN.

> There we lay bewailing
> All in a prison bound. . . .

He sees CHRISTY. *Goes and shakes him drunkenly by the hand, while* PEGEEN *and* SHAWN *talk on the left.*

MICHAEL [*to* CHRISTY]: The blessing of God and the holy angels on your head, young fellow. I hear tell you're after winning all in the sports below; and wasn't it a shame I didn't bear you along with me to Kate Cassidy's wake, a fine, stout lad, the like of you, for you'd never see the match of it for flows of drink, the way when we sunk her bones at noonday in her narrow grave, there were five men, aye, and six men, stretched out retching speechless on the holy stones.

CHRISTY [*uneasily, watching* PEGEEN]: Is that the truth?

MICHAEL: It is, then; and aren't you a louty schemer to go burying your poor father unbeknownst when you'd a right to throw him on the crupper of a Kerry mule and drive him westwards, like holy Joseph in the days gone by, the way we could have given him a decent burial, and not have him rotting beyond, and not a Christian drinking a smart drop to the glory of his soul?

CHRISTY [*gruffly*]: It's well enough he's lying, for the likes of him.

MICHAEL [*slapping him on the back*]: Well, aren't you a hardened slayer? It'll be a poor thing for the household man where you go sniffing for a female wife; and [*pointing to* SHAWN] look beyond at that shy and decent Christian I have chosen for my daughter's hand, and I after getting the gilded dispensation this day for to wed them now.

CHRISTY: And you'll be wedding them this day, is it?

MICHAEL [*drawing himself up*]: Aye. Are you thinking, if I'm drunk itself, I'd leave my daughter living single with a little frisky rascal is the like of you?

PEGEEN [*breaking away from* SHAWN]: Is it the truth the dispensation's come?

MICHAEL [*triumphantly*]: Father Reilly's after reading it in gallous Latin, and 'It's come in the nick of time,' says he; 'so I'll wed them in a hurry, dreading that young gaffer who'd capsize the stars.'

PEGEEN [*fiercely*]: He's missed his nick of time, for it's that lad, Christy Mahon, that I'm wedding now.

MICHAEL [*loudly, with horror*]: You'd be making him a son to me, and he wet and crusted with his father's blood?

PEGEEN: Aye. Wouldn't it be a bitter thing for a girl to go marrying the like of Shaneen, and he a middling kind of a scarecrow, with no savagery or fine words in him at all?

MICHAEL [*gasping and sinking on a chair*]: Oh, aren't you a heathen daughter to go shaking the fat of my heart, and I swamped and drownded with the weight of drink? Would you have them turning on me the way that I'd be roaring to the dawn of day with the wind upon my heart? Have you not a word to aid me, Shaneen? Are you not jealous at all?

SHAWN [*in great misery*]: I'd be afeard to be jealous of a man did slay his da?

PEGEEN: Well, it'd be a poor thing to go marrying your like. I'm seeing there's a world of peril for an orphan girl, and isn't it a great blessing I didn't wed you before himself came walking from the west or south?

SHAWN: It's a queer story you'd go picking a dirty tramp up from the highways of the world.

PEGEEN [*playfully*]: And you think you're a likely beau to go straying along with the shiny Sundays of the opening year, when it's sooner on a bullock's liver you'd put a poor girl thinking than on the lily or the rose?

SHAWN: And have you no mind of my weight of passion, and the holy dispensation, and the drift of heifers I'm giving, and the golden ring?

PEGEEN: I'm thinking you're too fine for the like of me, Shawn Keogh of Killakeen, and let you go off till you'd find a radiant lady with droves of bullocks on the plains of Meath, and herself bedizened in the diamond jewelleries of Pharaoh's ma. That'd be your match, Shaneen. So God save you now! [*She retreats behind* CHRISTY.]

SHAWN: Won't you hear me telling you . . .?

CHRISTY [*with ferocity*]: Take yourself from this, young fellow, or I'll maybe add a murder to my deed to-day.

MICHAEL [*springing up with a shriek*]: Murder is it? Is it mad yous are? Would you go making murder in this place, and it piled with poteen for our drink tonight? Go on to the foreshore if it's fighting you want, where the rising tide will wash all traces from the memory of man. [*Pushing* SHAWN *towards* CHRISTY.]

SHAWN [*shaking himself free, and getting behind* MICHAEL]: I'll not fight him, Michael James. I'd liefer live a bachelor, simmering in passions to the end of time, than face a lepping savage the like of him has descended from the Lord knows where. Strike him yourself, Michael James, or you'll lose my drift of heifers and my blue bull from Sneem.

MICHAEL: Is it me fight him, when it's father-slaying he's bred to now? [*Pushing* SHAWN.] Go on, you fool, and fight him now.

SHAWN [*coming forward a little*]: Will I strike him with my hand?

MICHAEL: Take the loy is on your western side.

SHAWN: I'd be afeard of the gallows if I struck with that.

CHRISTY [*taking up the loy*]: Then I'll make you face the gallows or quit off from this.

SHAWN *flies out of the door.*

Well, fine weather be after him [*going to* MICHAEL, *coaxingly*], and I'm thinking you wouldn't wish to have that quaking blackguard in your house at all. Let you give us your blessing and hear her swear her faith to me, for I'm mounted on the spring-tide of the stars of luck, the way it'll be good for any to have me in the house.

PEGEEN [*at the other side of* MICHAEL]: Bless us now, for I swear to God I'll wed him, and I'll not renege.

MICHAEL [*standing up in the centre, holding on to both of them*]: It's the will of God, I'm thinking, that all should win an easy or a cruel end, and it's the will of God that all should rear up lengthy families for the nurture of the earth. What's a single man, I ask you, eating a bit in one house and drinking a sup in another, and he with no place of his own, like an old braying jackass strayed upon the rocks? [*To* CHRISTY.] It's many would be in dread to bring your like into their house for to end them, maybe, with a sudden end; but I'm a decent man of Ireland, and I liefer face the grave untimely and I seeing a score of grandsons growing up little gallant swearers by the name of God, than go peopling my bedside with puny weeds the like of what you'd breed, I'm thinking, out of Shaneen Keogh. [*He joins their hands.*] A daring fellow is the jewel of the world, and a man did split his father's middle with a single clout should have the bravery of ten, so may God and Mary and St Patrick bless you, and increase you from this mortal day.

CHRISTY AND PEGEEN: Amen, O Lord!

Hubbub outside. OLD MAHON *rushes in, followed by all the crowd, and* WIDOW QUIN. *He makes a rush at* CHRISTY, *knocks him down, and begins to beat him.*

PEGEEN [*dragging back his arm*]: Stop that, will you? Who are you at all?

MAHON: His father, God forgive me!

PEGEEN [*drawing back*]: Is it rose from the dead?

MAHON: Do you think I look so easy quenched with the tap of a loy? [*Beats* CHRISTY *again.*]

PEGEEN [*glaring at* CHRISTY]. And it's lies you told, letting on you had him slitted, and you nothing at all.

CHRISTY [*catching* MAHON*'s stick*]: He's not my father. He's a raving maniac would scare the world. [*Pointing to* WIDOW QUIN.] Herself knows it is true.

CROWD: You're fooling Pegeen! The Widow Quin seen him this day, and you likely knew! You're a liar!

CHRISTY [*dumbfounded*]: It's himself was a liar, lying stretched out with an open head on him, letting on he was dead.

MAHON: Weren't you off racing the hills before I got my breath with the start I had seeing you turn on me at all?

PEGEEN: And to think of the coaxing glory we had given him, and he after doing nothing but hitting a soft blow and chasing northward in a sweat of fear. Quit off from this.

CHRISTY [*piteously*]: You've seen my doings this day, and let you save me from the old man; for why would you be in such a scorch of haste to spur me to destruction now?

PEGEEN: It's there your treachery is spurring me, till I'm hard set to think you're the one I'm after lacing in my heart-strings half an hour gone by. [*To* MAHON.] Take him on from this, for I think bad the world should see me raging for a Munster liar, and the fool of men.

MAHON: Rise up now to retribution, and come on with me.

CROWD [*jeeringly*]: There's the playboy! There's the lad thought he'd rule the roost in Mayo! Slate him now, mister.

CHRISTY [*getting up in shy terror*]: What is it drives you to torment me here, when I'd asked the thunders of the might of God to blast me if I ever did hurt to any saving only that one single blow.

MAHON [*loudly*]: If you didn't, you're a poor good-for-nothing, and isn't it by the like of you the sins of the whole world are committed?

CHRISTY [*raising his hands*]: In the name of the Almighty God . . .

MAHON: Leave troubling the Lord God. Would you have Him sending down droughts, and fevers, and the old hen and the cholera morbus?

CHRISTY [*to* WIDOW QUIN]: Will you come between us and protect me now?

WIDOW QUIN: I've tried a lot, God help me, and my share is done.

CHRISTY [*looking round in desperation*]: And I must go back into my torment is it, or run off like a vagabond straying through the unions with the dust of August making mudstains in the gullet of my throat; or the winds of March blowing on me till I'd take an oath I felt them making whistles of my ribs within?

SARA: Ask Pegeen to aid you. Her like does often change.

CHRISTY: I will not, then, for there's torment in the splendour of her like, and she a girl any moon of midnight would take pride to meet, facing southwards on the heaths of Keel. But what did I want crawling forward to scorch my understanding at her flaming brow?

PEGEEN [*to* MAHON, *vehemently, fearing she will break into tears*]. Take him on from this or I'll set the young lads to destroy him here.

MAHON [*going to him, shaking his stick*]: Come on now if you wouldn't have the company to see you skelped.

PEGEEN [*half-laughing, through her tears*]: That's it, now the world will see him pandied, and he an ugly liar was playing off the hero, and the fright of men.

CHRISTY [*to* MAHON, *very sharply*]: Leave me go!

CROWD: That's it. Now, Christy. If them two set fighting, it will lick the world.

MAHON [*making a grab at* CHRISTY]: Come here to me.

CHRISTY [*more threateningly*]: Leave me go, I'm saying.

MAHON: I will, maybe, when your legs is limping, and your back is blue.

CROWD: Keep it up, the two of you. I'll back the old one. Now the playboy.

CHRISTY [*in low and intense voice*]: Shut your yelling, for if you're after making a mighty man of me this day by the power of a lie, you're setting me now to think if it's a poor thing to be lonesome it's worse, maybe, go mixing with the fools of earth.

MAHON *makes a movement towards him.*

CHRISTY [*almost shouting*]: Keep off . . . lest I do show a blow unto the lot of you would set the guardian angels winking in the clouds above. [*He swings round with a sudden rapid movement and picks up a loy.*]

CROWD [*half-frightened, half-amused*]: He's going mad! Mind yourselves! Run from the idiot!

CHRISTY: If I am an idiot, I'm after hearing my voice this day saying words would raise the top-knot on a poet in a merchant's town. I've won your racing, and your lepping, and . . .

MAHON: Shut your gullet and come on with me.

CHRISTY: I'm going, but I'll stretch you first.

He runs at OLD MAHON *with the loy, chases him out of the door, followed by crowd and* WIDOW QUIN. *There is a great noise outside, then a yell, and dead silence for a moment.* CHRISTY *comes in, half-dazed, and goes to fire.*

WIDOW QUIN [*coming in hurriedly, and going to him*]: They're turning again you. Come on, or you'll be hanged, indeed.

CHRISTY: I'm thinking, from this out, Pegeen'll be giving me praises, the same as in the hours gone by.

WIDOW QUIN [*impatiently*]: Come by the back door. I'd think bad to have you stifled on the gallows tree.

CHRISTY [*indignantly*]: I will not, then. What good'd be my lifetime if I left Pegeen?

WIDOW QUIN: Come on, and you'll be no worse than you were last night; and you with a double murder this time to be telling to the girls.

CHRISTY: I'll not leave Pegeen Mike.

WIDOW QUIN [*impatiently*]: Isn't there the match of her in every parish public, from Binghamstown unto the plain of Meath? Come on, I tell you, and I'll find you finer sweethearts at each waning moon.

CHRISTY: It's Pegeen I'm seeking only, and what'd I care if you brought me a drift of chosen females, standing in their shifts itself, maybe, from this place to the eastern world?

SARA [*runs in, pulling off one of her petticoats*]: They're going to hang him. [*Holding out petticoat and shawl.*] Fit these upon him, and let him run off to the east.

WIDOW QUIN: He's raving now; but we'll fit them on him, and I'll take him in the ferry to the Achill boat.

CHRISTY [*struggling feebly*]: Leave me go, will you? when I'm thinking of my luck to-day, for she will wed me surely, and I a proven hero in the end of all.

They try to fasten petticoat round him.

WIDOW QUIN: Take his left hand, and we'll pull him now. Come on, young fellow.

CHRISTY [*suddenly starting up*]: You'll be taking me from her? You're jealous, is it, of her wedding me? Go on from this. [*He snatches up a stool, and threatens them with it.*]

WIDOW QUIN [*going*]: It's in the madhouse they should put him, not in jail, at all. We'll go by the back-door to call the doctor, and we'll save him so.

She goes out, with SARA, *through inner room.* MEN *crowd in the doorway.* CHRISTY *sits down again by the fire.*

MICHAEL [*in a terrified whisper*]: Is the old lad killed surely?

PHILLY: I'm after feeling the last gasps quitting his heart. [*They peer in at* CHRISTY.]

MICHAEL [*with a rope*]: Look at the way he is. Twist a hangman's knot on it, and slip it over his head, while he's not minding at all.

PHILLY: Let you take it, Shaneen. You're the soberest of all that's here.

SHAWN: Is it me to go near him, and he the wickedest and worst with me? Let you take it, Pegeen Mike.

PEGEEN: Come on, so. [*She goes forward with the others, and they drop the double hitch over his head.*]

CHRISTY: What ails you?

SHAWN [*triumphantly, as they pull the rope tight on his arms*]. Come on to the peelers, till they stretch you now.

CHRISTY: Me!

MICHAEL: If we took pity on you the Lord God would, maybe, bring us ruin from the law to-day, so you'd best come easy, for hanging is an easy and a speedy end.

CHRISTY: I'll not stir. [*To* PEGEEN.] And what is it you'll say to me, and I after doing it this time in the face of all?

PEGEEN: I'll say, a strange man is a marvel, with his mighty talk; but what's a squabble in your backyard, and the blow of a loy, have taught me that there's a great gap between a gallous story and a dirty deed. [*To* MEN.] Take him on from this, or the lot of us will be likely put on trial for his deed to-day.

CHRISTY [*with horror in his voice*]: And it's yourself will send me off, to have a horny-fingered hangman hitching his bloody slipknots at the butt of my ear.

MEN [*pulling rope*]: Come on, will you?

He is pulled down on the floor.

CHRISTY [*twisting his legs round the table*]: Cut the rope, Pegeen, and I'll quit the lot of you, and live from this out, like the madmen of Keel, eating muck and green weeds on the faces of the cliffs.

PEGEEN: And leave us to hang, is it, for a saucy liar the like of you? [*To* MEN.] Take him on, out from this.

SHAWN: Pull a twist on his neck, and squeeze him so.

PHILLY: Twist yourself. Sure he cannot hurt you, if you keep your distance from his teeth alone.

SHAWN: I'm afeard of him. [*To* PEGEEN.] Lift a lighted sod, will you, and scorch his leg.

PEGEEN [*blowing the fire with a bellows*]: Leave go now, young fellow, or I'll scorch your shins.

CHRISTY: You're blowing for to torture me. [*His voice rising and growing stronger.*] That's your kind, is it? Then let the lot of you be wary, for, if I've to face the gallows, I'll have a gay march down, I tell you, and shed the blood of some of you before I die.

SHAWN [*in terror*]: Keep a good hold, Philly. Be wary, for the love of God. For I'm thinking he would liefest wreak his pains on me.

CHRISTY [*almost gaily*]: If I do lay my hands on you, it's the way you'll be at the fall of night, hanging as a scarecrow for the fowls of hell. Ah, you'll have a gallous jaunt, I'm saying, coaching out through Limbo with my father's ghost.

SHAWN [*to* PEGEEN]: Make haste, will you? Oh, isn't he a holy terror, and isn't it true for Father Reilly, that all drink's a curse that has the lot of you so shaky and uncertain now?

CHRISTY: If I can wring a neck among you, I'll have a royal judgment looking on the trembling jury in the courts of law. And won't there be crying out in Mayo the day I'm stretched upon the rope, with ladies in their silks and satins snivelling in their lacy kerchiefs, and they rhyming songs and ballads on the terror of my fate? [*He squirms round on the floor and bites* SHAWN'*s leg.*]

SHAWN [*shrieking*]: My leg's bit on me. He's the like of a mad dog, I'm thinking, the way that I will surely die.

CHRISTY [*delighted with himself*]: You will, then, the way you can shake out hell's flags of welcome for my coming in two weeks or three, for I'm thinking Satan hasn't many have killed their da in Kerry, and in Mayo too.

OLD MAHON *comes in behind on all fours and looks on unnoticed.*

MEN [*to* PEGEEN]: Bring the sod, will you?

PEGEEN [*coming over*]: God help him so. [*Burns his leg.*]

CHRISTY [*kicking and screaming*]: Oh, glory be to God!

He kicks loose from the table, and they all drag him towards the door.

JIMMY [*seeing* OLD MAHON]: Will you look what's come in?

They all drop CHRISTY *and run left.*

CHRISTY [*scrambling on his knees face to face with* OLD MAHON]: Are you coming to be killed a third time, or what ails you now?

MAHON: For what is it they have you tied?

CHRISTY: They're taking me to the peelers to have me hanged for slaying you.

MICHAEL [*apologetically*]: It is the will of God that all should guard their little cabins from the treachery of law, and what would my daughter be doing if I was ruined or was hanged itself?

MAHON [*grimly, loosening* CHRISTY]: It's little I care if you put a bag on her back, and went picking cockles till the hour of death; but my son and myself will be going our own way, and we'll have great times from this out telling stories of the villainy of Mayo, and the fools is here. [*To* CHRISTY, *who is freed.*] Come on now.

CHRISTY: Go with you, is it? I will then, like a gallant captain with his heathen slave. Go on now and I'll see you from this day stewing my oatmeal and washing my spuds, for I'm master of all fights from now. [*Pushing* MAHON.] Go on, I'm saying.

MAHON: Is it me?

CHRISTY: Not a word out of you. Go on from this.

MAHON [*walking out and looking back at* CHRISTY *over his shoulder*]: Glory be to God! [*With a broad smile.*] I am crazy again. [*Goes.*]

CHRISTY: Ten thousand blessings upon all that's here, for you've turned me a likely gaffer in the end of all, the way I'll go romancing through a romping lifetime from this hour to the dawning of the judgment day. [*He goes out.*]

MICHAEL: By the will of God, we'll have peace now for our drinks. Will you draw the porter, Pegeen?

SHAWN [*going up to her*]. It's a miracle Father Reilly can wed us in the end of all, and we'll have none to trouble us when his vicious bite is healed.

PEGEEN [*hitting him a box on the ear*]: Quit my sight. [*Putting her shawl over her head and breaking out into wild lamentations.*] Oh, my grief, I've lost him surely. I've lost the only Playboy of the Western World.

CURTAIN

HEARTBREAK HOUSE
BERNARD SHAW

HEARTBREAK HOUSE

First published 1919

HEARTBREAK HOUSE

A fantasia in the Russian
Manner on English Themes

CONTENTS

HEARTBREAK HOUSE
AND
HORSEBACK HALL

WHERE HEARTBREAK HOUSE STANDS

Heartbreak House is not merely the name of the play which
follows this preface. It is cultured, leisured Europe before the
war. When the play was begun not a shot had been fired; and only
the professional diplomatists and the very few amateurs whose
hobby is foreign policy even knew that the guns were loaded. A
Russian playwright, Tchekov, had produced four fascinating
dramatic studies of Heartbreak House, of which three, The
Cherry Orchard, Uncle Vanya, and The Seagull, had been
performed in England. Tolstoy, in his Fruits of Enlightenment,
had shewn us through it in his most ferociously contemptuous
manner. Tolstoy did not waste any sympathy on it: it was to him
the house in which Europe was stifling its soul; and he knew that
our utter enervation and futilization in that overheated drawing-
room atmosphere was delivering the world over to the control of
ignorant and soulless cunning and energy, with the frightful
consequences which have now overtaken it. Tolstoy was no
pessimist: he was not disposed to leave the house standing if he
could bring it down about the ears of its pretty and amiable
voluptuaries; and he wielded the pickaxe with a will. He treated
the case of the inmates as one of opium poisoning, to be dealt with
by seizing the patients roughly and exercising them violently
until they were broad awake. Tchekov, more of a fatalist, had no
faith in these charming people extricating themselves. They
would, he thought, be sold up and sent adrift by the bailiffs;
therefore he had no scruple in exploiting and even flattering their
charm.

THE INHABITANTS

Tchekov's plays, being less lucrative than swings and roundabouts, got no further in England, where theatres are only
ordinary commercial affairs, than a couple of performances by
the Stage Society. We stared and said, 'How Russian!' They did
not strike me in that way. Just as Ibsen's intensely Norwegian
plays exactly fitted every middle and professional class suburb in
Europe, these intensely Russian plays fitted all the country

houses in Europe in which the pleasures of music, art, literature, and the theatre had supplanted hunting, shooting, fishing, flirting, eating and drinking. The same nice people, the same utter futility. The nice people could read; some of them could write; and they were the only repositories of culture who had social opportunities of contact with our politicians, administrators, and newspaper proprietors, or any chance of sharing or influencing their activities. But they shrank from that contact. They hated politics. They did not wish to realize Utopia for the common people: they wished to realize their favourite fictions and poems in their own lives; and, when they could, they lived without scruple on incomes which they did nothing to earn. The women in their girlhood made themselves look like variety theatre stars, and settled down later into the types of beauty imagined by the previous generation of painters. They took the only part of our society in which there was leisure for high culture, and made it an economic, political, and, as far as practicable, a moral vacuum; and as Nature, abhorring the vacuum, immediately filled it up with sex and with all sorts of refined pleasures, it was a very delightful place at its best for moments of relaxation. In other moments it was disastrous. For prime ministers and their like, it was a veritable Capua.

HORSEBACK HALL

But where were our front benchers to nest if not here? The alternative to Heartbreak House was Horseback Hall, consisting of a prison for horses with an annex for the ladies and gentlemen who rode them, hunted them, talked about them, bought them and sold them, and gave nine-tenths of their lives to them, dividing the other tenth between charity, churchgoing (as a substitute for religion), and conservative electioneering (as a substitute for politics). It is true that the two establishments got mixed at the edges. Exiles from the library, the music room, and the picture gallery would be found languishing among the stables, miserably discontented; and hardy horsewomen who slept at the first chord of Schumann were born, horribly misplaced, into the garden of Klingsor; but sometimes one came upon horsebreakers and heartbreakers who could make the best of both worlds. As a rule, however, the two were apart and knew little of one another; so the prime minister folk had to choose between barbarism and Capua. And of the two atmospheres it is hard to say which was the more fatal to statesmanship.

REVOLUTION ON THE SHELF

Heartbreak House was quite familiar with revolutionary ideas on paper. It aimed at being advanced and freethinking, and hardly ever went to church or kept the Sabbath except by a little extra fun at week-ends. When you spent a Friday to Tuesday in it you found on the shelf in your bedroom not only the books of poets and novelists, but of revolutionary biologists and even economists. Without at least a few plays by myself and Mr Granville Barker, and a few stories by Mr H.G.Wells, Mr Arnold Bennett, and Mr John Galsworthy, the house would have been out of the movement. You would find Blake among the poets, and beside him Bergson, Butler, Scott Haldane, the poems of Meredith and Thomas Hardy, and, generally speaking, all the literary implements for forming the mind of the perfect modern Socialist and Creative Evolutionist. It was a curious experience to spend Sunday in dipping into these books, and on Monday morning to read in the daily paper that the country had just been brought to the verge of anarchy because a new Home Secretary or chief of police, without an idea in his head that his great-grandmother might not have had to apologize for, had refused to 'recognize' some powerful Trade Union, just as a gondola might refuse to recognize a 20,000-ton liner.

In short, power and culture were in separate compartments. The barbarians were not only literally in the saddle, but on the front bench in the House of Commons, with nobody to correct their incredible ignorance of modern thought and political science but upstarts from the counting-house, who had spent their lives furnishing their pockets instead of their minds. Both, however, were practised in dealing with money and with men, as far as acquiring the one and exploiting the other went; and although this is as undesirable an expertness as that of the medieval robber baron, it qualifies men to keep an estate or a business going in its old routine without necessarily understanding it, just as Bond Street tradesmen and domestic servants keep fashionable society going without any instruction in sociology.

THE CHERRY ORCHARD

The Heartbreak people neither could nor would do anything of the sort. With their heads as full of the Anticipations of Mr H.G.Wells as the heads of our actual rulers were empty even of the anticipations of Erasmus or Sir Thomas More, they refused the drudgery of politics, and would have made a very poor job of it if they had changed their minds. Not that they would have been allowed to meddle anyhow, as only through the accident of being a hereditary peer can anyone in these days of Votes for Everybody get into parliament if handicapped by a serious modern cultural equipment; but if they had, their habit of living in a vacuum would have left them helpless and ineffective in public affairs. Even in private life they were often helpless wasters of their inheritance, like the people in Tchekov's Cherry Orchard. Even those who lived within their incomes were really kept going by their solicitors and agents, being unable to manage an estate or run a business without continual prompting from those who have to learn how to do such things or starve.

From what is called Democracy no corrective to this state of things could be hoped. It is said that every people has the Government it deserves. It is more to the point that every Government has the electorate it deserves; for the orators of the front bench can edify or debauch an ignorant electorate at will. Thus our democracy moves in a vicious circle of reciprocal worthiness and unworthiness.

NATURE'S LONG CREDITS

Nature's way of dealing with unhealthy conditions is unfortunately not one that compels us to conduct a solvent hygiene on a cash basis. She demoralizes us with long credits and reckless overdrafts, and then pulls us up cruelly with catastrophic bankruptcies. Take, for example, common domestic sanitation. A whole city generation may neglect it utterly and scandalously, if not with absolute impunity, yet without any evil consequences that anyone thinks of tracing to it. In a hospital two generations of medical students may tolerate dirt and carelessness, and then go out into general practice to spread the doctrine that fresh air is a fad, and sanitation an imposture set up to make profits for plumbers. Then suddenly Nature takes her revenge. She strikes at the city with a pestilence and at the hospital with an epidemic of hospital gangrene, slaughtering right and left until the innocent young have paid for the guilty old, and the account is balanced. And then she goes to sleep again and gives another period of credit, with the same result.

This is what has just happened in our political hygiene. Political science has been as recklessly neglected by Governments and electorates during my lifetime as sanitary science was in the days of Charles the Second. In international relations diplomacy has been a boyishly lawless affair of family intrigues, commercial and territorial brigandage, torpors of pseudo-goodnature produced by laziness, and spasms of ferocious activity produced by terror. But in these islands we muddled through. Nature gave us a longer credit than she gave to France or Germany or Russia. To British centenarians who died in their beds in 1914, any dread of having to hide underground in London from the shells of an enemy seemed more remote and fantastic than a dread of the appearance of a colony of cobras and rattlesnakes in Kensington Gardens. In the prophetic works of Charles Dickens we were warned against many evils which have since come to pass; but of the evil of being slaughtered by a foreign foe on our own doorsteps there was no shadow. Nature gave us a very long credit; and we abused it to the utmost. But when she struck at last she struck with a vengeance. For four years she smote our firstborn and heaped on us plagues of which Egypt never dreamed. They were all as preventible as the great Plague of London, and came solely because they had not been prevented. They were not undone by winning the war. The earth is still bursting with the dead bodies of the victors.

THE WICKED HALF CENTURY

It is difficult to say whether indifference and neglect are worse than false doctrine; but Heartbreak House and Horseback Hall unfortunately suffered from both. For half a century before the war civilization had been going to the devil very precipitately under the influence of a pseudo-science as disastrous as the blackest Calvinism. Calvinism taught that as we are predestinately saved or damned, nothing that we do can alter our destiny. Still, as Calvinism gave the individual no clue as to whether he had drawn a lucky number or an unlucky one, it left him a fairly strong interest in encouraging his hopes of salvation and allaying his fear of damnation by behaving as one of the elect might be expected to behave rather than as one of the reprobate. But in the middle of the nineteenth century naturalists and physicists assured the world, in the name of Science, that salvation and damnation are all nonsense, and that predestination is the central truth of religion, inasmuch as human beings are produced by their environment, their sins and good deeds being only a series of chemical and mechanical reactions over which they have no control. Such figments as mind, choice, purpose, conscience, will, and so forth, are, they taught, mere illusions, produced because they are useful in the continual struggle of the human machine to maintain its environment in a favourable condition, a process incidentally involving the ruthless destruction or subjection of its competitors for the supply (assumed to be limited) of subsistence available. We taught Prussia this religion; and Prussia bettered our instruction so effectively that we presently found ourselves confronted with the necessity of destroying Prussia to prevent Prussia destroying us. And that has just ended in each destroying the other to an extent doubtfully reparable in our time.

It may be asked how so imbecile and dangerous a creed ever came to be accepted by intelligent beings. I will answer that question more fully in my next volume of plays, which will be entirely devoted to the subject. For the present I will only say that there were better reasons than the obvious one that such sham science as this opened a scientific career to very stupid men, and all the other careers to shameless rascals, provided they were industrious enough. It is true that this motive operated very powerfully; but when the new departure in scientific doctrine which is associated with the name of the great naturalist Charles Darwin began, it was not only a reaction against a barbarous pseudo-evangelical teleology intolerably obstructive to all scientific progress, but was accompanied, as it happened, by discoveries of extraordinary interest in physics, chemistry, and that lifeless method of evolution which its investigators called Natural Selection. Howbeit, there was only one result possible in the ethical sphere, and that was the banishment of conscience from human affairs, or, as Samuel Butler vehemently put it, 'of mind from the universe.'

HYPOCHONDRIA

Now Heartbreak House, with Butler and Bergson and Scott Haldane alongside Blake and the other major poets on its shelves (to say nothing of Wagner and the tone poets), was not so completely blinded by the doltish materialism of the laboratories as the uncultured world outside. But being an idle house it was a hypochondriacal house, always running after cures. It would stop eating meat, not on valid Shelleyan grounds, but in order to get rid of a bogey called Uric Acid; and it would actually let you pull all its teeth out to exorcize another demon named Pyorrhea. It was superstitious, and addicted to table-rapping, materialization séances, clairvoyance, palmistry, crystal-gazing and the like to such an extent that it may be doubted whether ever before in the history of the world did soothsayers, astrologers, and unregistered therapeutic specialists of all sorts flourish as they did during this half century of the drift to the abyss. The registered doctors and surgeons were hard put to it to compete with the unregistered. They were not clever enough to appeal to the imagination and sociability of the Heartbreakers by the arts of the actor, the orator, the poet, the winning conversationalist. They had to fall back coarsely on the terror of infection and death. They prescribed inoculations and operations. Whatever part of a human being could be cut out without necessarily killing him they cut out; and he often died (unnecessarily of course) in consequence. From such trifles as uvulas and tonsils they went on to ovaries and appendices until at last no one's inside was safe. They explained that the human intestine was too long, and that nothing could make a child of Adam healthy except short circuiting the pylorus by cutting a length out of the lower intestine and fastening it directly to the stomach. As their mechanist theory taught them that medicine was the business of the chemist's laboratory, and surgery of the carpenter's shop, and also that Science (by which they meant their practices) was so important that no consideration for the interests of any individual creature, whether frog or philosopher, much less the vulgar commonplaces of sentimental ethics, could weigh for a moment against the remotest off-chance of an addition to the body of scientific knowledge, they operated and vivisected and inoculated and lied on a stupendous scale, clamoring for and actually acquiring such legal powers over the bodies of their fellow-citizens as neither king, pope, nor parliament dare ever have claimed. The Inquisition itself was a Liberal institution compared to the General Medical Council.

THOSE WHO DO NOT KNOW HOW TO LIVE MUST MAKE A MERIT OF DYING

Heartbreak House was far too lazy and shallow to extricate itself from this palace of evil enchantment. It rhapsodized about love; but it believed in cruelty. It was afraid of the cruel people; and it saw that cruelty was at least effective. Cruelty did things that made money, whereas Love did nothing but prove the soundness of Larochefoucauld's saying that very few people would fall in love if they had never read about it. Heartbreak House, in short, did not know how to live, at which point all that was left to it was the boast that at least it knew how to die: a melancholy accomplishment which the outbreak of war presently gave it practically unlimited opportunities of displaying. Thus were the firstborn of Heartbreak House smitten; and the young, the innocent, the hopeful expiated the folly and worthlessness of their elders.

WAR DELIRIUM

Only those who have lived through a first-rate war, not in the field, but at home, and kept their heads, can possibly understand the bitterness of Shakespear and Swift, who both went through this experience. The horror of Peer Gynt in the madhouse, when the lunatics, exalted by illusions of splendid talent and visions of a dawning millennium, crowned him as their emperor, was tame in comparison. I do not know whether anyone really kept his head completely except those who had to keep it because they had to conduct the war at first hand. I should not have kept my own (as far as I did keep it) if I had not at once understood that as a scribe and speaker I too was under the most serious public obligation to keep my grip on realities; but this did not save me from a considerable degree of hyperaesthesia. There were of course some happy people to whom the war meant nothing: all political and general matters lying outside their little circle of interest. But the ordinary war-conscious civilian went mad, the main symptom being a conviction that the whole order of nature had been reversed. All foods, he felt, must now be adulterated.

All schools must be closed. No advertisements must be sent to the newspapers, of which new editions must appear and be bought up every ten minutes. Travelling must be stopped, or, that being impossible, greatly hindered. All pretences about fine art and culture and the like must be flung off as an intolerable affectation; and the picture galleries and museums and schools at once occupied by war workers. The British Museum itself was saved only by a hairsbreadth. The sincerity of all this, and of much more which would not be believed if I chronicled it, may be established by one conclusive instance of the general craziness. Men were seized with the illusion that they could win the war by giving away money. And they not only subscribed millions to Funds of all sorts with no discoverable object, and to ridiculous voluntary organizations for doing what was plainly the business of the civil and military authorities, but actually handed out money to any thief in the street who had the presence of mind to pretend that he (or she) was 'collecting' it for the annihilation of the enemy. Swindlers were emboldened to take offices; label themselves Anti-Enemy Leagues; and simply pocket the money that was heaped on them. Attractively dressed young women found that they had nothing to do but parade the streets, collecting-box in hand, and live gloriously on the profits. Many months elapsed before, as a first sign of returning sanity, the police swept an Anti-Enemy secretary into prison *pour encourager les autres*, and the passionate penny collecting of the Flag Days was brought under some sort of regulation.

MADNESS IN COURT

The demoralization did not spare the Law Courts. Soldiers were acquitted, even on fully proved indictments for wilful murder, until at last the judges and magistrates had to announce that what was called the Unwritten Law, which meant simply that a soldier could do what he liked with impunity in civil life, was not the law of the land, and that a Victoria Cross did not carry with it a perpetual plenary indulgence. Unfortunately the insanity of the juries and magistrates did not always manifest itself in indulgence. No person unlucky enough to be charged with any sort of conduct, however reasonable and salutary, that did not smack of war delirium had the slightest chance of acquittal. There were in the country, too, a certain number of people who had conscientious objections to war as criminal or unchristian. The Act of Parliament introducing Compulsory Military Service thoughtlessly exempted these persons, merely requiring them to prove the genuineness of their convictions. Those who did so were very ill-advised from the point of view of their own personal interest; for they were persecuted with savage logicality in spite of the law; whilst those who made no pretence of having any objection to war at all, and had not only had military training in

Officers' Training Corps, but had proclaimed on public occasions that they were perfectly ready to engage in civil war on behalf of their political opinions, were allowed the benefit of the Act on the ground that they did not approve of this particular war. For the Christians there was no mercy. In cases where the evidence as to their being killed by ill treatment was so unequivocal that the verdict would certainly have been one of wilful murder had the prejudice of the coroner's jury been on the other side, their tormentors were gratuitously declared to be blameless. There was only one virtue, pugnacity: only one vice, pacifism. That is an essential condition of war; but the Government had not the courage to legislate accordingly; and its law was set aside for Lynch law.

The climax of legal lawlessness was reached in France. The greatest Socialist statesman in Europe, Jaurès, was shot and killed by a gentleman who resented his efforts to avert the war. M. Clemenceau was shot by another gentleman of less popular opinions, and happily came off no worse than having to spend a precautionary couple of days in bed. The slayer of Jaurès was recklessly acquitted: the would-be slayer of M. Clemenceau was carefully found guilty. There is no reason to doubt that the same thing would have happened in England if the war had begun with a successful attempt to assassinate Keir Hardie, and ended with an unsuccessful one to assassinate Mr Lloyd George.

THE LONG ARM OF WAR

The pestilence which is the usual accompaniment of war was called influenza. Whether it was really a war pestilence or not was made doubtful by the fact that it did its worst in places remote from the battle-fields, notably on the west coast of North Africa and in India. But the moral pestilence, which was un- questionably a war pestilence, reproduced this phenomenon. One would have supposed that the war fever would have raged most furiously in the countries actually under fire, and that the others would be more reasonable. Belgium and Flanders, where over large districts literally not one stone was left upon another as the opposed armies drove each other back and forward over it after terrific preliminary bombardments, might have been pardoned for relieving their feelings more emphatically than by shrugging their shoulders and saying '*C'est la guerre.*' England, inviolate for so many centuries that the swoop of war on her homesteads had long ceased to be more credible than a return of the Flood, could hardly be expected to keep her temper sweet when she knew at last what it was to hide in cellars and underground railway stations, or lie quaking in bed, whilst bombs crashed, houses crumbled, and aircraft guns distributed shrapnel on friend and foe alike until certain shop windows in London, formerly full of fashionable hats, were filled with steel

helmets. Slain and mutilated women and children, and burnt and
wrecked dwellings, excuse a good deal of violent language, and
produce a wrath on which many suns go down before it is
appeased. Yet it was in the United States of America, where
nobody slept the worse for the war, that the war fever went
beyond all sense and reason. In European Courts there was
vindictive illegality: in American Courts there was raving
lunacy. It is not for me to chronicle the extravagances of an Ally:
let some candid American do that. I can only say that to us sitting
in our gardens in England, with the guns in France making
themselves felt by a throb in the air as unmistakable as an audible
sound, or with tightening hearts studying the phases of the moon
in London in their bearing on the chances whether our houses
would be standing or ourselves alive next morning, the
newspaper accounts of the sentences American Courts were
passing on young girls and old men alike for the expression of
opinions which were being uttered amid thundering applause
before huge audiences in England, and the more private records
of the methods by which the American War Loans were raised,
were so amazing that they would put the guns and the
possibilities of a raid clean out of our heads for the moment.

THE RABID WATCHDOGS OF LIBERTY

Not content with these rancorous abuses of the existing law, the
war maniacs made a frantic rush to abolish all constitutional
guarantees of liberty and well-being. The ordinary law was
superseded by Acts under which newspapers were seized and
their printing machinery destroyed by simple police raids *à la
Russe*, and persons arrested and shot without any pretence of trial
by jury or publicity of procedure or evidence. Though it was
urgently necessary that production should be increased by the
most scientific organization and economy of labor, and though
no fact was better established than that excessive duration and
intensity of toil reduces production heavily instead of increasing
it, the factory laws were suspended, and men and women
recklessly overworked until the loss of their efficiency became too
glaring to be ignored. Remonstrances and warnings were met
either with an accusation of pro-Germanism or the formula,
'Remember that we are at war now.' I have said that men
assumed that war had reversed the order of nature, and that all
was lost unless we did the exact opposite of everything we had
found necessary and beneficial in peace. But the truth was worse
than that. The war did not change men's minds in any such
impossible way. What really happened was that the impact of
physical death and destruction, the one reality that every fool can
understand, tore off the masks of education, art, science, and
religion from our ignorance and barbarism, and left us glorifying
grotesquely in the licence suddenly accorded to our vilest

passions and most abject terrors. Ever since Thucydides wrote
his history, it has been on record that when the angel of death
sounds his trumpet the pretences of civilization are blown from
men's heads into the mud like hats in a gust of wind. But when
this scripture was fulfilled among us, the shock was not the less
appalling because a few students of Greek history were not
surprised by it. Indeed these students threw themselves into the
orgy as shamelessly as the illiterate. The Christian priest joining
in the war dance without even throwing off his cassock first, and
the respectable school governor expelling the German professor
with insult and bodily violence, and declaring that no English
child should ever again be taught the language of Luther and
Goethe, were kept in countenance by the most impudent
repudiations of every decency of civilization and every lesson of
political experience on the part of the very persons who, as
university professors, historians, philosophers, and men of
science, were the accredited custodians of culture. It was crudely
natural, and perhaps necessary for recruiting purposes, that
German militarism and German dynastic ambition should be
painted by journalists and recruiters in black and red as
European dangers (as in fact they are), leaving it to be inferred
that out own militarism and our own political constitution are
millennially democratic (which they certainly are not); but when
it came to frantic denunciations of German chemistry, German
biology, German poetry, German music, German literature,
German philosophy, and even German engineering, as
malignant abominations standing towards British and French
chemistry and so forth in the relation of heaven to hell, it was
clear that the utterers of such barbarous ravings had never really
understood or cared for the arts and sciences they professed and
were profaning, and were only the appallingly degenerate
descendants of the men of the seventeenth and eighteenth
centuries who, recognizing no national frontiers in the great
realm of the human mind, kept the European comity of that
realm loftily and even ostentatiously above the rancors of the
battle-field. Tearing the Garter from the Kaiser's leg, striking
the German dukes from the roll of our peerage, changing the
King's illustrious and historically appropriate surname for that
of a traditionless locality, was not a very dignified business; but
the erasure of German names from the British rolls of science and
learning was a confession that in England the little respect paid to
science and learning is only an affectation which hides a savage
contempt for both. One felt that the figure of St George and the
Dragon on our coinage should be replaced by that of the soldier
driving his spear through Archimedes. But by that time there
was no coinage: only paper money in which ten shillings called
itself a pound as confidently as the people who were disgracing
their country called themselves patriots.

THE SUFFERINGS OF THE SANE

The mental distress of living amid the obscene din of all these carmagnoles and corobberies was not the only burden that lay on sane people during the war. There was also the emotional strain, complicated by the offended economic sense, produced by the casualty lists. The stupid, the selfish, the narrow-minded, the callous and unimaginative were spared a great deal. 'Blood and destruction shall be so in use that mothers shall but smile when they behold their infants quartered by the hands of war,' was a Shakespearean prophecy that very nearly came true; for when nearly every house had a slaughtered son to mourn, we should all have gone quite out of our senses if we had taken our own and our friends' bereavements at their peace value. It became necessary to give them a false value; to proclaim the young life worthily and gloriously sacrificed to redeem the liberty of mankind, instead of to expiate the heedlessness and folly of their fathers, and expiate it in vain. We had even to assume that the parents and not the children had made the sacrifice, until at last the comic papers were driven to satirize fat old men, sitting comfortably in club chairs, and boasting of the sons they had 'given' to their country.

No one grudged these anodynes to acute personal grief; but they only embittered those who knew that the young men were having their teeth set on edge because their parents had eaten sour political grapes. Then think of the young men themselves! Many of them had no illusions about the policy that led to the war: they went clear-sighted to a horribly repugnant duty. Men essentially gentle and essentially wise, with really valuable work in hand, laid it down voluntarily and spent months forming fours in the barrack yard, and stabbing sacks of straw in the public eye, so that they might go out to kill and maim men as gentle as themselves. These men, who were perhaps, as a class, our most efficient soldiers (Frederick Keeling, for example), were not duped for a moment by the hypocritical melodrama that consoled and stimulated the others. They left their creative work to drudge at destruction, exactly as they would have left it to take their turn at the pumps in a sinking ship. They did not, like some of the conscientious objectors, hold back because the ship had been neglected by its officers and scuttled by its wreckers. The ship had to be saved, even if Newton had to leave his fluxions and Michael Angelo his marbles to save it; so they threw away the tools of their beneficent and ennobling trades, and took up the bloodstained bayonet and the murderous bomb, forcing themselves to pervert their divine instinct for perfect artistic execution to the effective handling of these diabolical things, and their economic faculty for organization to the contriving of ruin and slaughter. For it gave an ironic edge to their tragedy that the very talents they were forced to prostitute made the prostitution not only effective, but even interesting; so that some of them were rapidly promoted, and found themselves actually becoming artists in war, with a growing relish for it, like Napoleon and all the other scourges of mankind, in spite of themselves. For many of them there was not even this consolation. They 'stuck it,' and hated it, to the end.

EVIL IN THE THRONE OF GOOD

This distress of the gentle was so acute that those who shared it in civil life, without having to shed blood with their own hands, or witness destruction with their own eyes, hardly cared to obtrude their own woes. Nevertheless, even when sitting at home in safety, it was not easy for those who had to write and speak about the war to throw away their highest conscience, and deliberately work to a standard of inevitable evil instead of to the ideal of life more abundant. I can answer for at least one person who found the change from the wisdom of Jesus and St Francis to the morals of Richard III and the madness of Don Quixote extremely irksome. But that change had to be made; and we are all the worse for it, except those for whom it was not really a change at all, but only a relief from hypocrisy.

Think, too, of those who, though they had neither to write nor to fight, and had no children of their own to lose, yet knew the inestimable loss to the world of four years of the life of a generation wasted on destruction. Hardly one of the epoch-making works of the human mind might not have been aborted or destroyed by taking their authors away from their natural work for four critical years. Not only were Shakespears and Platos being killed outright; but many of the best harvests of the survivors had to be sown in the barren soil of the trenches. And this was no mere British consideration. To the truly civilized man, to the good European, the slaughter of the German youth was as disastrous as the slaughter of the English. Fools exulted in 'German losses.' They were our losses as well. Imagine exulting in the death of Beethoven because Bill Sykes dealt him his death blow!

STRAINING AT THE GNAT AND SWALLOWING THE CAMEL

But most people could not comprehend these sorrows. There was a frivolous exultation in death for its own sake, which was at bottom an inability to realize that the deaths were real deaths and not stage ones. Again and again, when an air raider dropped a bomb which tore a child and its mother limb from limb, the people who saw it, though they had been reading with great cheerfulness of thousands of such happenings day after day in their newspapers, suddenly burst into furious imprecations on 'the Huns' as murderers, and shrieked for savage and satisfying vengeance. At such moments it became clear that the deaths they had not seen meant no more to them than the mimic deaths of the cinema screen. Sometimes it was not necessary that death should be actually witnessed: it had only to take place under circumstances of sufficient novelty and proximity to bring it home almost as sensationally and effectively as if it had been actually visible.

For example, in the spring of 1915 there was an appalling slaughter of our young soldiers at Neuve Chapelle and at the Gallipoli landing. I will not go so far as to say that our civilians were delighted to have such exciting news to read at breakfast. But I cannot pretend that I noticed either in the papers, or in general intercourse, any feeling beyond the usual one that the cinema show at the front was going splendidly, and that our boys were the bravest of the brave. Suddenly there came the news that an Atlantic liner, the Lusitania, had been torpedoed, and that several well-known first class passengers, including a famous theatrical manager and the author of a popular farc/, had been drowned, among others. The others included Sir Hugh Lane; but as he had only laid the country under great obligations in the sphere of the fine arts, no great stress was laid on that loss.

Immediately an amazing frenzy swept through the country. Men who up to that time had kept their heads now lost them utterly. 'Killing saloon passengers! What next?' was the essence of the whole agitation; but it is far too trivial a phrase to convey the faintest notion of the rage which possessed us. To me, with my mind full of the hideous cost of Neuve Chapelle, Ypres, and the Gallipoli landing, the fuss about the Lusitania seemed almost a heartless impertinence, though I was well acquainted personally with the three best-known victims, and understood, better perhaps than most people, the misfortune of the death of Lane. I even found a grim satisfaction, very intelligible to all soldiers, in the fact that the civilians who found the war such splendid British sport should get a sharp taste of what it was to the actual combatants. I expressed my impatience very freely, and found that my very straightforward and natural feeling in the matter was received as a monstrous and heartless paradox. When I asked those who gaped at me whether they had anything to say about the holocaust of Festubert, they gaped wider than before, having totally forgotten it, or rather, having never realized it. They were not heartless any more than I was; but the big catastrophe was too big for them to grasp, and the little one had been just the right size for them. I was not surprised. Have I not seen a public body for just the same reason pass a vote for £30,000 without a word, and then spend three special meetings, prolonged into the night, over an item of seven shillings for refreshments?

LITTLE MINDS AND BIG BATTLES

Nobody will be able to understand the vagaries of public feeling during the war unless they bear constantly in mind that the war in its entire magnitude did not exist for the average civilian. He could not conceive even a battle, much less a campaign. To the suburbs the war was nothing but a suburban squabble. To the miner and navvy it was only a series of bayonet fights between German champions and English ones. The enormity of it was quite beyond most of us. Its episodes had to be reduced to the dimensions of a railway accident or a shipwreck before it could produce any effect on our minds at all. To us the ridiculous bombardments of Scarborough and Ramsgate were colossal tragedies, and the battle of Jutland a mere ballad. The words 'after thorough artillery preparation' in the news from the front meant nothing to us; but when our seaside trippers learned that an elderly gentleman at breakfast in a week-end marine hotel had been interrupted by a bomb dropping into his egg-cup, their wrath and horror knew no bounds. They declared that this would put a new spirit into the army, and had no suspicion that the soldiers in the trenches roared with laughter over it for days, and told each other that it would do the blighters at home good to have a taste of what the army was up against. Sometimes the smallness of view was pathetic. A man would work at home regardless of the call 'to make the world safe for democracy.' His brother would be killed at the front. Immediately he would throw up his work and take up the war as a family blood feud against the Germans. Sometimes it was comic. A wounded man, entitled to his discharge, would return to the trenches with a grim determination to find the Hun who had wounded him and pay him out for it.

It is impossible to estimate what proportion of us, in khaki or out of it, grasped the war and its political antecedents as a whole in the light of any philosophy of history or knowledge of what war is. I doubt whether it was as high as our proportion of higher mathematicians. But there can be no doubt that it was prodigiously outnumbered by the comparatively ignorant and childish. Remember that these people had to be stimulated to make the sacrifices demanded by the war, and that this could not be done by appeals to a knowledge which they did not possess, and a comprehension of which they were incapable. When the armistice at last set me free to tell the truth about the war at the following general election, a soldier said to a candidate whom I was supporting 'If I had known all that in 1914, they would never have got me into khaki.' And that, of course, was precisely why it had been necessary to stuff him with a romance that any diplomatist would have laughed at. Thus the natural confusion of ignorance was increased by a deliberately propagated confusion of nursery bogey stories and melodramatic nonsense, which at last overreached itself and made it impossible to stop the war before we had not only achieved the triumph of vanquishing

the German army and thereby overthrowing its militarist
monarchy, but made the very serious mistake of ruining the
centre of Europe, a thing that no sane European State could
afford to do.

THE DUMB CAPABLES AND THE NOISY
INCAPABLES

Confronted with this picture of insensate delusion and folly, the
critical reader will immediately counterplead that England all
this time was conducting a war which involved the organization
of several millions of fighting men and of the workers who were
supplying them with provisions, munitions, and transport, and
that this could not have been done by a mob of hysterical ranters.
This is fortunately true. To pass from the newspaper offices and
political platforms and club fenders and suburban drawing-
rooms to the Army and the munition factories was to pass from
Bedlam to the busiest and sanest of workaday worlds. It was to
rediscover England, and find solid ground for the faith of those
who still believed in her. But a necessary condition of this
efficiency was that those who were efficient should give all their
time to their business and leave the rabble raving to its heart's
content. Indeed the raving was useful to the efficient, because, as
it was always wide of the mark, it often distracted attention very
conveniently from operations that would have been defeated or
hindered by publicity. A precept which I endeavored vainly to
popularize early in the war, 'If you have anything to do go and do
it: if not, for heaven's sake get out of the way,' was only half
carried out. Certainly the capable people went and did it; but the
incapables would by no means get out of the way: they fussed and
bawled and were only prevented from getting very seriously into
the way by the blessed fact that they never knew where the way
was. Thus whilst all the efficiency of England was silent and
invisible, all its imbecility was deafening the heavens with its
clamor and blotting out the sun with its dust. It was also
unfortunately intimidating the Government by its blusterings
into using the irresistible powers of the State to intimidate the
sensible people, thus enabling a despicable minority of would-be
lynchers to set up a reign of terror which could at any time have
been broken by a single stern word from a responsible minister.
But our ministers had not that sort of courage: neither
Heartbreak House nor Horseback Hall had bred it, much less the
suburbs. When matters at last came to the looting of shops by
criminals under patriotic pretexts, it was the police force and not
the Government that put its foot down. There was even one
deplorable moment, during the submarine scare, in which the
Government yielded to a childish cry for the maltreatment of
naval prisoners of war, and, to our great disgrace, was forced by
the enemy to behave itself. And yet behind all this public

blundering and misconduct and futile mischief, the effective England was carrying on with the most formidable capacity and activity. The ostensible England was making the empire sick with its incontinences, its ignorances, its ferocities, its panics, and its endless and intolerable blarings of Allied national anthems in season and out. The esoteric England was proceeding irresistibly to the conquest of Europe.

THE PRACTICAL BUSINESS MEN

From the beginning the useless people set up a shriek for 'practical business men.' By this they meant men who had become rich by placing their personal interests before those of the country, and measuring the success of every activity by the pecuniary profit it brought to them and to those on whom they depended for their supplies of capital. The pitiable failure of some conspicuous samples from the first batch we tried of these poor devils helped to give the whole public side of the war an air of monstrous and hopeless farce. They proved not only that they were useless for public work, but that in a well-ordered nation they would never have been allowed to control private enterprise.

HOW THE FOOLS SHOUTED THE WISE MEN DOWN

Thus, like a fertile country flooded with mud, England shewed no sign of her greatness in the days when she was putting forth all her strength to save herself from the worst consequences of her littleness. Most of the men of action, occupied to the last hour of their time with urgent practical work, had to leave to idler people, or to professional rhetoricians, the presentation of the war to the reason and imagination of the country and the world in speeches, poems, manifestos, picture posters, and newspaper articles. I have had the privilege of hearing some of our ablest commanders talking about their work; and I have shared the common lot of reading the accounts of that work given to the world by the newspapers. No two experiences could be more different. But in the end the talkers obtained a dangerous ascendancy over the rank and file of the men of action; for though the great men of action are always inveterate talkers and often very clever writers, and therefore cannot have their minds formed for them by others, the average man of action, like the average fighter with the bayonet, can give no account of himself in words even to himself, and is apt to pick up and accept what he reads about himself and other people in the papers, except when the writer is rash enough to commit himself on technical points.

It was not uncommon during the war to hear a soldier, or a civilian engaged on war work, describing events within his own experience that reduced to utter absurdity the ravings and maunderings of his daily paper, and yet echo the opinions of that paper like a parrot. Thus, to escape from the prevailing confusion and folly, it was not enough to seek the company of the ordinary man of action: one had to get into contact with the master spirits. This was a privilege which only a handful of people could enjoy. For the unprivileged citizen there was no escape. To him the whole country seemed mad, futile, silly, incompetent, with no hope of victory except the hope that the enemy might be just as mad. Only by very resolute reflection and reasoning could he reassure himself that if there was nothing more solid beneath these appalling appearances the war could not possibly have gone on for a single day without a total breakdown of its organization.

THE MAD ELECTION

Happy were the fools and the thoughtless men of action in those days. The worst of it was that the fools were very strongly represented in parliament, as fools not only elect fools, but can persuade men of action to elect them too. The election that immediately followed the armistice was perhaps the maddest that has ever taken place. Soldiers who had done voluntary and heroic service in the field were defeated by persons who had apparently never run a risk or spent a farthing that they could avoid, and who even had in the course of the election to apologize publicly for bawling Pacifist or Pro-German at their opponent. Party leaders seek such followers, who can always be depended on to walk tamely into the lobby at the party whip's orders, provided the leader will make their seats safe for them by the process which was called, in derisive reference to the war rationing system, 'giving them the coupon.' Other incidents were so grotesque that I cannot mention them without enabling the reader to identify the parties, which would not be fair, as they were no more to blame than thousands of others who must necessarily be nameless. The general result was patently absurd; and the electorate, disgusted at its own work, instantly recoiled to the opposite extreme, and cast out all the coupon candidates at the earliest bye-elections by equally silly majorities. But the mischief of the general election could not be undone; and the Government had not only to pretend to abuse its European victory as it had promised, but actually to do it by starving the enemies who had thrown down their arms. It had, in short, won the election by pledging itself to be thriftlessly wicked, cruel, and vindictive; and it did not find it as easy to escape from this pledge as it had from nobler ones. The end, as I write, is not yet; but it is clear that this thoughtless savagery will recoil on the heads of the

Allies so severely that we shall be forced by the sternest necessity to take up our share of healing the Europe we have wounded almost to death instead of attempting to complete her destruction.

THE YAHOO AND THE ANGRY APE

Contemplating this picture of a state of mankind so recent that no denial of its truth is possible, one understands Shakespear comparing Man to an angry ape, Swift describing him as a Yahoo rebuked by the superior virtue of the horse, and Wellington declaring that the British can behave themselves neither in victory nor defeat. Yet none of the three had seen war as we have seen it. Shakespear blamed great men, saying that 'Could great men thunder as Jove himself does Jove would ne'er be quiet; for every pelting petty officer would use his heaven for thunder: nothing but thunder.' What would Shakespear have said if he had seen something far more destructive than thunder in the hand of every village laborer, and found on the Messines Ridge the craters of the nineteen volcanoes that were let loose there at the touch of a finger that might have been a child's finger without the result being a whit less ruinous? Shakespear may have seen a Stratford cottage struck by one of Jove's thunderbolts, and have helped to extinguish the lighted thatch and clear away the bits of the broken chimney. What would he have said if he had seen Ypres as it is now, or returned to Stratford, as French peasants are returning to their homes today, to find the old familiar signpost inscribed 'To Stratford, 1 mile,' and at the end of the mile nothing but some holes in the ground and a fragment of a broken churn here and there? Would not the spectacle of the angry ape endowed with powers of destruction that Jove never pretended to, have beggared even his command of words?

And yet, what is there to say except that war puts a strain on human nature that breaks down the better half of it, and makes the worse half a diabolical virtue? Better for us if it broke it down altogether; for then the warlike way out of our difficulties would be barred to us, and we should take greater care not to get into them. In truth, it is, as Byron said, 'not difficult to die,' and enormously difficult to live: that explains why, at bottom, peace is not only better than war, but infinitely more arduous. Did any hero of the war face the glorious risk of death more bravely than the traitor Bolo faced the ignominious certainty of it? Bolo taught us all how to die: can we say that he taught us all how to live? Hardly a week passes now without some soldier who braved death in the field so recklessly that he was decorated or specially commended for it, being haled before our magistrates for having failed to resist the paltriest temptations of peace, with no better excuse than the old one that 'a man must live.' Strange that one who, sooner than do honest work, will sell his honor for a bottle of wine, a visit to the theatre, and an hour with a strange woman, all obtained by passing a worthless cheque, could yet stake his life on the most desperate chances of the battle-field! Does it not seem as if, after all, the glory of death were cheaper than the glory of life? If it is not easier to attain, why do so many more men attain it? At all events it is clear that the kingdom of the Prince of Peace has not yet become the kingdom of this world. His attempts at invasion have been resisted far more fiercely than the Kaiser's. Successful as that resistance has been, it has piled up a sort of National Debt that is not the less oppressive because we have no figures for it and do not intend to pay it. A blockade that cuts off 'the grace of our Lord' is in the long run less bearable than the blockades which merely cut off raw materials; and against that blockade our Armada is impotent. In the blockader's house, he has assured us, there are many mansions; but I am afraid they do not include either Heartbreak House or Horseback Hall.

PLAGUE ON BOTH YOUR HOUSES!

Meanwhile the Bolshevist picks and petards are at work on the foundations of both buildings; and though the Bolshevists may be buried in the ruins, their deaths will not save the edifices. Unfortunately they can be built again. Like Doubting Castle, they have been demolished many times by successive Great-hearts, and rebuilt by Simple, Sloth, and Presumption, by Feeble Mind and Much Afraid, and by all the jurymen of Vanity Fair. Another generation of 'secondary education' at our ancient public schools and the cheaper institutions that ape them will be quite sufficient to keep the two going until the next war.

For the instruction of that generation I leave these pages as a record of what civilian life was during the war: a matter on which history is usually silent. Fortunately it was a very short war. It is true that the people who thought it could not last more than six months were very signally refuted by the event. As Sir Douglas Haig has pointed out, its Waterloos lasted months instead of hours. But there would have been nothing surprising in its lasting thirty years. If it had not been for the fact that the blockade achieved the amazing feat of starving out Europe, which it could not possibly have done had Europe been properly organized for war, or even for peace, the war would have lasted until the belligerents were so tired of it that they could no longer be compelled to compel themselves to go on with it. Considering its magnitude, the war of 1914–18 will certainly be classed as the shortest in history. The end came so suddenly that the combatants literally stumbled over it; and yet it came a full year later than it should have come if the belligerents had not been far too afraid of one another to face the situation sensibly. Germany, having failed to provide for the war she began, failed again to surrender before she was dangerously exhausted. Her opponents, equally improvident, went as much too close to bankruptcy as Germany to starvation. It was a bluff at which both were bluffed. And, with the usual irony of war, it remains doubtful whether Germany and Russia, the defeated, will not be the gainers; for the victors are already busy fastening on themselves the chains they have struck from the limbs of the vanquished.

HOW THE THEATRE FARED

Let us now contract our view rather violently from the European theatre of war to the theatre in which the fights are sham fights, and the slain, rising the moment the curtain has fallen, go comfortably home to supper after washing off their rosepink wounds. It is nearly twenty years since I was last obliged to introduce a play in the form of a book for lack of an opportunity of presenting it in its proper mode by a performance in a theatre. The war has thrown me back on this expedient. Heartbreak House has not yet reached the stage. I have withheld it because the war has completely upset the economic conditions which formerly enabled serious drama to pay its way in London. The change is not in the theatres nor in the management of them, nor in the authors and actors, but in the audiences. For four years the London theatres were crowded every night with thousands of soldiers on leave from the front. These soldiers were not seasoned London playgoers. A childish experience of my own gave me a clue to their condition. When I was a small boy I was taken to the opera. I did not then know what an opera was, though I could whistle a good deal of opera music. I had seen in my mother's album photographs of all the great opera singers, mostly in evening dress. In the theatre I found myself before a gilded balcony filled with persons in evening dress whom I took to be the opera singers. I picked out one massive dark lady as Alboni, and wondered how soon she would stand up and sing. I was puzzled by the fact that I was made to sit with my back to the singers instead of facing them. When the curtain went up, my astonishment and delight were unbounded.

THE SOLDIER AT THE THEATRE FRONT

In 1915 I saw in the theatres men in khaki in just the same predicament. To everyone who had my clue to their state of mind it was evident that they had never been in a theatre before and did not know what it was. At one of our great variety theatres I sat beside a young officer, not at all a rough specimen, who, even when the curtain rose and enlightened him as to the place where he had to look for his entertainment, found the dramatic part of it utterly incomprehensible. He did not know how to play his part of the game. He could understand the people on the stage singing and dancing and performing gymnastic feats. He not only understood but intensely enjoyed an artist who imitated cocks crowing and pigs squeaking. But the people who pretended that they were somebody else, and that the painted picture behind them was real, bewildered him. In his presence I realized how very sophisticated the natural man has to become before the conventions of the theatre can be easily acceptable, or the purpose of the drama obvious to him.

Well, from the moment when the routine of leave for our soldiers was established, such novices, accompanied by damsels (called flappers) often as innocent as themselves, crowded the theatres to the doors. It was hardly possible at first to find stuff crude enough to nurse them on. The best music-hall comedians ransacked their memories for the oldest quips and the most childish antics to avoid carrying the military spectators out of their depth. I believe that this was a mistake as far as the novices were concerned. Shakespear, or the dramatized histories of George Barnwell, Maria Martin, or the Demon Barber of Fleet Street, would probably have been quite popular with them. But the novices were only a minority after all. The cultivated soldier, who in time of peace would look at nothing theatrical except the most advanced post-Ibsen plays in the most artistic settings, found himself, to his own astonishment, thirsting for silly jokes, dances, and brainlessly sensuous exhibitions of pretty girls. The author of some of the most grimly serious plays of our time told me that after enduring the trenches for months without a glimpse of the female of his species, it gave him an entirely innocent but delightful pleasure merely to see a flapper. The reaction from the battle-field produced a condition of hyperaesthesia in which all the theatrical values were altered. Trivial things gained intensity and stale things novelty. The actor, instead of having to coax his audiences out of the boredom which had driven them to the theatre in an ill humor to seek some sort of distraction, had only to exploit the bliss of smiling men who were no longer under fire and under military discipline, but actually clean and comfortable and in a mood to be pleased with anything and everything that a bevy of pretty girls and a funny man, or even a bevy of girls pretending to be pretty and a man pretending to by funny, could do for them.

Then could be seen every night in the theatres old-fashioned farcical comedies, in which a bedroom, with four doors on each side and a practicable window in the middle, was understood to resemble exactly the bedroom in the flats beneath and above, all three inhabited by couples consumed with jealousy. When these people came home drunk at night; mistook their neighbors' flats for their own; and in due course got into the wrong beds, it was not only the novices who found the resulting complications and scandals exquisitely ingenious and amusing, nor their equally verdant flappers who could not help squealing in a manner that astonished the oldest performers when the gentleman who had just come in drunk through the window pretended to undress, and allowed glimpses of his naked person to be descried from time to time. Men who had just read the news that Charles Wyndham was dying, and were thereby sadly reminded of Pink Dominos and the torrent of farcical comedies that followed it in his heyday until every trick of that trade had become so stale that the laughter they provoked turned to loathing: these veterans also, when they returned from the field, were as much pleased by what they knew to be stale and foolish as the novices by what they thought fresh and clever.

COMMERCE IN THE THEATRE

Wellington said that an army moves on its belly. So does a London theatre. Before a man acts he must eat. Before he performs plays he must pay rent. In London we have no theatres for the welfare of the people: they are all for the sole purpose of producing the utmost obtainable rent for the proprietor. If the twin flats and twin beds produce a guinea more than Shakespear, out goes Shakespear, and in come the twin flats and the twin beds. If the brainless bevy of pretty girls and the funny man outbid Mozart, out goes Mozart.

UNSER SHAKESPEAR

Before the war an effort was made to remedy this by establishing a national theatre in celebration of the tercentenary of the death of Shakespear. A committee was formed; and all sorts of illustrious and influential persons lent their names to a grand appeal to our national culture. My play, The Dark Lady of The Sonnets, was one of the incidents of that appeal. After some years of effort the result was a single handsome subscription from a German gentleman. Like the celebrated swearer in the anecdote when the cart containing all his household goods lost its tailboard at the top of the hill and let its contents roll in ruin to the bottom, I can only say, 'I cannot do justice to this situation,' and let it pass without another word.

THE HIGHER DRAMA PUT OUT OF ACTION

The effect of the war on the London theatres may now be imagined. The beds and the bevies drove every higher form of art out of it. Rents went up to an unprecedented figure. At the same time prices doubled everywhere except at the theatre pay-boxes, and raised the expenses of management to such a degree that unless the houses were quite full every night, profit was impossible. Even bare solvency could not be attained without a very wide popularity. Now what had made serious drama possible to a limited extent before the war was that a play could pay its way even if the theatre were only half full until Saturday and three-quarters full then. A manager who was an enthusiast and a desperately hard worker, with an occasional grant-in-aid from an artistically disposed millionaire, and a due proportion of those rare and happy accidents by which plays of the higher sort turn out to be potboilers as well, could hold out for some years, by which time a relay might arrive in the person of another enthusiast. Thus and not otherwise occurred that remarkable revival of the British drama at the beginning of the century which made my own career as a playwright possible in England. In America I had already established myself, not as part of the ordinary theatre system, but in association with the exceptional genius of Richard Mansfield. In Germany and Austria I had no difficulty: the system of publicly aided theatres there, Court and Municipal, kept drama of the kind I dealt in alive; so that I was indebted to the Emperor of Austria for magnificent productions of my works at a time when the sole official attention paid me by the British Court was the announcement to the English-speaking world that certain plays of mine were unfit for public performance, a substantial set-off against this being that the British Court, in the course of its private playgoing, paid no regard to the bad character given me by the chief officer of its household.

Howbeit, the fact that my plays effected a lodgment on the London stage, and were presently followed by the plays of Granville Barker, Gilbert Murray, John Masefield, St John Hankin, Laurence Housman, Arnold Bennett, John Galsworthy, John Drinkwater, and others which would in the nineteenth century have stood rather less chance of production at a London theatre than the Dialogues of Plato, not to mention revivals of the ancient Athenian drama, and a restoration to the stage of Shakespear's plays as he wrote them, was made economically possible solely by a supply of theatres which could hold nearly twice as much money as it cost to rent and maintain them. In such theatres work appealing to a relatively small class of cultivated persons, and therefore attracting only from half to three-quarters as many spectators as the more popular pastimes, could nevertheless keep going in the hands of young adventurers who were doing it for its own sake, and had not yet been forced by advancing age and responsibilities to consider the commercial value of their time and energy too closely. The war struck this foundation away in the manner I have just described. The expenses of running the cheapest west-end theatres rose to a sum which exceeded by twenty-five per cent the utmost that the higher drama can, as an ascertained matter of fact, be depended on to draw. Thus the higher drama, which has never really been a commercially sound speculation, now became an impossible one. Accordingly, attempts are being made to provide a refuge for it in suburban theatres in London and repertory theatres in the provinces. But at the moment when the army had at last disgorged the survivors of the gallant band of dramatic pioneers whom it swallowed, they find that the economic conditions which formerly made their work no worse than precarious now put it out of the question altogether, as far as the west end of London is concerned.

CHURCH AND THEATRE

I do not suppose many people care particularly. We are not brought up to care; and a sense of the national importance of the theatre is not born in mankind: the natural man, like so many of the soldiers at the beginning of the war, does not know what a theatre is. But please note that all these soldiers who did not know what a theatre was, knew what a church was. And they had been taught to respect churches. Nobody had ever warned them against a church as a place where frivolous women paraded in their best clothes; where stories of improper females like Potiphar's wife, and erotic poetry like the Song of Songs, were read aloud; where the sensuous and sentimental music of Schubert, Mendelssohn, Gounod, and Brahms was more popular than severe music by greater composers; where the prettiest sort of pretty pictures of pretty saints assailed the imagination and senses through stained-glass windows; and where sculpture and architecture came to the help of painting. Nobody ever reminded them that these things had sometimes produced such developments of erotic idolatry that men who were not only enthusiastic amateurs of literature, painting, and music, but famous practitioners of them, had actually exulted when mobs and even regular troops under express command had mutilated church statues, smashed church windows, wrecked church organs, and torn up the sheets from which the church music was read and sung. When they saw broken statues in churches, they were told that this was the work of wicked godless rioters, instead of, as it was, the work partly of zealots bent on driving the world, the flesh, and the devil out of the temple, and partly of insurgent men who had become intolerably poor because the temple had become a den of thieves. But all the sins and perversions that were so carefully hidden from them in the history of the Church were laid on the shoulders of the Theatre: that stuffy, uncomfortable place of penance in which we suffer so much inconvenience on the slenderest chance of gaining a scrap of food for our starving souls. When the Germans bombed the Cathedral of Rheims the world rang with the horror of the sacrilege. When they bombed the Little Theatre in the Adelphi, and narrowly missed bombing two writers of plays who lived within a few yards of it, the fact was not even mentioned in the papers. In point of appeal to the senses no theatre ever built could touch the fane at Rheims: no actress could rival its Virgin in beauty, nor any operatic tenor look otherwise than a fool beside its David. Its picture glass was glorious even to those who had seen the glass of Chartres. It was wonderful in its very grotesques: who would look at the Blondin Donkey after seeing its leviathans? In spite of the Adam-Adelphian decoration on which Miss Kingston had lavished so much taste and care, the Little Theatre was in comparison with Rheims the gloomiest of little conventicles: indeed the cathedral must, from the Puritan point of view, have debauched a million voluptuaries for every one whom the Little Theatre had sent home thoughtful to a chaste bed after Mr Chesterton's Magic or Brieux's *Les Avariés*. Perhaps that is the real reason why the Church is lauded and the Theatre reviled. Whether or no, the fact remains that the lady to whose public spirit and sense of the national value of the theatre I owed the first regular public performance of a play of mine had to conceal her action as if it had been a crime, whereas if she had given the money to the Church she would have worn a halo for it. And I admit, as I have always done, that this state of things may have been a very sensible one. I have asked Londoners again and again why they pay half a guinea to go to a theatre when they can go to St Paul's or Westminster Abbey for nothing. Their only possible reply is that they want to see something new and possibly something wicked; but the theatres mostly disappoint both hopes. If ever a revolution makes me Dictator, I shall establish a heavy charge for admission to our churches. But everyone who pays at the church door shall receive a ticket entitling him or her to free admission to one performance at any theatre he or she prefers. Thus shall the sensuous charms of the church service be made to subsidize the sterner virtue of the drama.

THE NEXT PHASE

The present situation will not last. Although the newspaper I read at breakfast this morning before writing these words contains a calculation that no less than twenty-three wars are at present being waged to confirm the peace, England is no longer in khaki; and a violent reaction is setting in against the crude theatrical fare of the four terrible years. Soon the rents of theatres will once more be fixed on the assumption that they cannot always be full, nor even on the average half full week in and week out. Prices will change. The higher drama will be at no greater disadvantage than it was before the war; and it may benefit, first, by the fact that many of us have been torn from the fools' para-dise in which the theatre formerly traded, and thrust upon the sternest realities and necessities until we have lost both faith in and patience with the theatrical pretences that had no root either in reality or necessity; second, by the startling change made by the war in the distribution of income. It seems only the other day that a millionaire was a man with £50,000 a year. Today, when he has paid his income tax and super tax, and insured his life for the amount of his death duties, he is lucky if his net income is £10,000, though his nominal property remains the same. And this is the result of a Budget which is called 'a respite for the rich.' At the other end of the scale millions of persons have had regular incomes for the first time in their lives; and their men have been regularly clothed, fed, lodged, and taught to make up their minds that certain things have to be done, also for the first time in their lives. Hundreds of thousands of women have been taken out of their domestic cages and tasted both discipline and independence. The thoughtless and snobbish middle classes have been pulled up short by the very unpleasant experience of being ruined to an unprecedented extent. We have all had a tremendous jolt; and although the widespread notion that the shock of the war would automatically make a new heaven and a new earth, and that the dog would never go back to his vomit nor the sow to her wallowing in the mire, is already seen to be a delusion, yet we are far more conscious of our condition than we were, and far less disposed to submit to it. Revolution, lately only a sensational chapter in history or a demagogic claptrap, is now a possibility so imminent that hardly by trying to suppress it in other countries by arms and defamation, and calling the process anti-Bolshevism, can our Government stave it off at home.

Perhaps the most tragic figure of the day is the American President who was once a historian. In those days it became his task to tell us how, after that great war in America which was more clearly than any other war of our time a war for an idea, the conquerors, confronted with a heroic task of reconstruction, turned recreant, and spent fifteen years in abusing their victory under cover of pretending to accomplish the task they were doing what they could to make impossible. Alas! Hegel was right when he said that we learn from history that men never learn anything from history. With what anguish of mind the President sees that we, the new conquerors, forgetting everything we professed to fight for, are sitting down with watering mouths to a good square meal of ten years revenge upon the humiliation of our prostrate foe, can only be guessed by those who know, as he does, how hopeless is remonstrance, and how happy Lincoln was in perishing from the earth before his inspired messages became scraps of paper. He knows well that from the Peace Conference will come, in spite of his utmost, no edict on which he will be able, like Lincoln, to invoke 'the considerate judgment of mankind, and the gracious favor of Almighty God.' He led his people to destroy the militarism of Zabern; and the army they rescued is busy in Cologne imprisoning every German who does not salute a British officer; whilst the Government at home, asked whether it approves, replies that it does not propose even to discontinue this Zabernism when the Peace is concluded, but in effect looks forward to making Germans salute British officers until the end of the world. That is what war makes of men and women. It will wear off; and the worst it threatens is already proving impracticable; but before the humble and contrite heart ceases to be despised, the President and I, being of the same age, will be dotards. In the meantime there is, for him, another history to write; for me, another comedy to stage. Perhaps, after all, that is what wars are for, and what historians and playwrights are for. If men will not learn until their lessons are written in blood, why, blood they must have, their own for preference.

THE EPHEMERAL THRONES AND THE ETERNAL THEATRE

To the theatre it will not matter. Whatever Bastilles fall, the theatre will stand. Apostolic Hapsburg has collapsed; All Highest Hohenzollern languishes in Holland, threatened with trial on a capital charge of fighting for his country against England; Imperial Romanoff, said to have perished miserably by a more summary method of murder, is perhaps alive or perhaps dead: nobody cares more than if he had been a peasant; the lord of Hellas is level with his lackeys in republican Switzerland; Prime Ministers and Commanders-in-Chief have passed from a brief glory as Solons and Caesars into failure and obscurity as closely on one another's heels as the descendants of Banquo; but Euripides and Aristophanes, Shakespear and Molière, Goethe and Ibsen remain fixed in their everlasting seats.

HOW WAR MUZZLES THE DRAMATIC POET

As for myself, why, it may be asked, did I not write two plays about the war instead of two pamphlets on it? The answer is significant. You cannot make war on war and on your neighbor at the same time. War cannot bear the terrible castigation of comedy, the ruthless light of laughter that glares on the stage. When men are heroically dying for their country, it is not the time to shew their lovers and wives and fathers and mothers how they are being sacrificed to the blunders of boobies, the cupidity of capitalists, the ambition of conquerors, the electioneering of demagogues, the Pharisaism of patriots, the lusts and lies and rancors and bloodthirsts that love war because it opens their prison doors, and sets them in the thrones of power and popularity. For unless these things are mercilessly exposed they will hide under the mantle of the ideals on the stage just as they do in real life.

And though there may be better things to reveal, it may not, and indeed cannot, be militarily expedient to reveal them whilst the issue is still in the balance. Truth telling is not compatible with the defence of the realm. We are just now reading the revelations of our generals and admirals, unmuzzled at last by the armistice. During the war, General A, in his moving despatches from the field, told how General B had covered himself with deathless glory in such and such a battle. He now tells us that General B came within an ace of losing us the war by disobeying his orders on that occasion, and fighting instead of running away as he ought to have done. An excellent subject for comedy now that the war is over, no doubt; but if General A had let this out at the time, what would have been the effect on General B's soldiers? And had the stage made known what the Prime Minister and the Secretary of State for War who overruled General A thought of him, and what he thought of them, as now revealed in raging controversy, what would have been the effect on the nation? That is why comedy, though sorely tempted, had to be loyally silent; for the art of the dramatic poet knows no patriotism; recognizes no obligation but truth to natural history; cares not whether Germany or England perish; is ready to cry with Brynhild, *'Lass' uns verderben, lachend zu Grunde geh'n'* sooner than deceive or be deceived; and thus becomes in time of war a greater military danger than poison, steel, or tri-nitrotoluene. That is why I had to withhold Heartbreak House from the footlights during the war; for the Germans might on any night have turned the last act from play into earnest, and even then might not have waited for their cues.

June 1919

ACT ONE

The hilly country in the middle of the north edge of Sussex, looking very pleasant on a fine evening at the end of September, is seen through the windows of a room which has been built so as to resemble the after part of an old-fashioned high-pooped ship with a stern gallery; for the windows are ship built with heavy timbering, and run right across the room as continuously as the stability of the wall allows. A row of lockers under the windows provides an unupholstered window-seat interrupted by twin glass doors, respectively halfway between the stern post and the sides. Another door strains the illusion a little by being apparently in the ship's port side, and yet leading, not to the open sea, but to the entrance hall of the house. Between this door and the stern gallery are bookshelves. There are electric light switches beside the door leading to the hall and the glass doors in the stern gallery. Against the starboard wall is a carpenter's bench. The vice has a board in its jaws; and the floor is littered with shavings, overflowing from a waste-paper basket. A couple of planes and a centrebit are on the bench. In the same wall, between the bench and the windows, is a narrow doorway with a half door, above which a glimpse of the room beyond shews that it is a shelved pantry with bottles and kitchen crockery.

On the starboard side, but close to the middle, is a plain oak drawing-table with drawing-board, T-square, straightedges, set squares, mathematical instruments, saucers of water color, a tumbler of discolored water, Indian ink, pencils, and brushes on it. The drawing-board is set so that the draughtsman's chair has the window on its left hand. On the floor at the end of the table, on his right, is a ship's fire bucket. On the port side of the room, near the bookshelves, is a sofa with its back to the windows. It is a sturdy mahogany article, oddly upholstered in sailcloth, including the bolster, with a couple of blankets hanging over the back. Between the sofa and the drawing-table is a big wicker chair, with broad arms and a low sloping back, with its back to the light. A small but stout table of teak, with a round top and gate legs, stands against the port wall between the door and the bookcase. It is the only article in the room that suggests (not at all convincingly) a woman's hand in the furnishing. The uncarpeted floor of narrow boards is caulked and holystoned like a deck.

The garden to which the glass doors lead dips to the south before the landscape rises again to the hills. Emerging from the hollow is the cupola of an observatory. Between the observatory and the house is a flagstaff on a little esplanade, with a hammock on the east side and a long garden seat on the west.

A YOUNG LADY, *gloved and hatted, with a dust coat on, is sitting in the window-seat with her body twisted to enable her to look out at the view. One hand props her chin: the other hangs down with a volume of the Temple Shakespear in it, and her finger stuck in the page she has been reading.*
A clock strikes six.

THE YOUNG LADY *turns and looks at her watch. She rises with an air of one who waits and is almost at the end of her patience. She is a pretty girl, slender, fair, and intelligent looking, nicely but not expensively dressed, evidently not a smart idler.*

With a sigh of weary resignation she comes to the draughtsman's chair; sits down; and begins to read Shakespear. Presently the book sinks to her lap; her eyes close; and she dozes into a slumber.

An elderly WOMANSERVANT *comes in from the hall with three unopened bottles of rum on a tray. She passes through and disappears in the pantry without noticing* THE YOUNG LADY. *She places the bottles on the shelf and fills her tray with empty bottles. As she returns with these,* THE YOUNG LADY *lets her book drop, awakening herself, and startling* THE WOMANSERVANT *so that she all but lets the tray fall.*

THE WOMANSERVANT: God bless us!

THE YOUNG LADY *picks up the book and places it on the table.*

Sorry to wake you, miss, I'm sure; but you are a stranger to me. What might you be waiting here for now?

THE YOUNG LADY: Waiting for somebody to shew some signs of knowing that I have been invited here.

THE WOMANSERVANT: Oh, youre invited, are you? And has nobody come? Dear! dear!

THE YOUNG LADY: A wild-looking old gentleman came and looked in at the window; and I heard him calling out 'Nurse: there is a young and attractive female waiting in the poop. Go and see what she wants.' Are you the nurse?

THE WOMANSERVANT: Yes, miss: I'm Nurse Guinness. That was old Captain Shotover, Mrs Hushabye's father. I heard him roaring; but I thought it was for something else. I suppose it was Mrs Hushabye that invited you, ducky?

THE YOUNG LADY: I understood her to do so. But really I think I'd better go.

NURSE GUINNESS: Oh, dont think of such a thing, miss. If Mrs Hushabye has forgotten all about it, it will be a pleasant surprise for her to see you, wont it?

THE YOUNG LADY: It has been a very unpleasant surprise to me to find that nobody expects me.

NURSE GUINNESS: Youll get used to it, miss: this house is full of surprises for them that dont know our ways.

CAPTAIN SHOTOVER [*looking in from the hall suddenly: an ancient but still hardy man with an immense white beard, in a reefer jacket with a whistle hanging from his neck*]: Nurse: there is a hold-all and a handbag on the front steps for everybody to fall over. Also a tennis racquet. Who the devil left them there?

THE YOUNG LADY: They are mine, I'm afraid.

THE CAPTAIN [*advancing to the drawing-table*]: Nurse: who is this misguided and unfortunate young lady?

NURSE GUINNESS: She says Miss Hessy invited her, sir.

THE CAPTAIN: And had she no friend, no parents, to warn her against my daughter's invitations? This is a pretty sort of house, by heavens! A young and attractive lady is invited here. Her luggage is left on the steps for hours; and she herself is deposited in the poop and abandoned, tired and starving. This is our hospitality. These are our manners. No room ready. No hot water. No welcoming hostess. Our visitor is to sleep in the toolshed, and to wash in the duckpond.

NURSE GUINNESS: Now it's all right, Captain: I'll get the lady some tea; and her room shall be ready before she has finished it. [*To* THE YOUNG LADY] Take off your hat, ducky; and make yourself at home [*she goes to the door leading to the hall*].

THE CAPTAIN [*as she passes him*]: Ducky! Do you suppose, woman, that because this young lady has been insulted and neglected, you have the right to address her as you address my wretched children, whom you have brought up in ignorance of the commonest decencies of social intercourse?

NURSE GUINNESS: Never mind him, doty. [*Quite unconcerned, she goes out into the hall on her way to the kitchen*].

THE CAPTAIN: Madam: will you favor me with your name? [*He sits down in the big wicker chair*].

THE YOUNG LADY: My name is Ellie Dunn.

THE CAPTAIN: Dunn! I had a boatswain whose name was Dunn. He was originally a pirate in China. He set up as a ship's chandler with stores which I have every reason to believe he stole from me. No doubt he became rich. Are you his daughter?

ELLIE [*indignant*]: No: certainly not. I am proud to be able to say that though my father has not been a successful man, nobody has ever had one word to say against him. I think my father is the best man I have ever known.

THE CAPTAIN: He must be greatly changed. Has he attained the seventh degree of concentration?

ELLIE: I dont understand.

THE CAPTAIN: But how could he, with a daughter! I, madam, have two daughters. One of them is Hesione Hushabye, who invited you here. I keep this house: she upsets it. I desire to attain the seventh degree of concentration: she invites visitors and leaves me to entertain them.

> NURSE GUINNESS *returns with the tea-tray, which she places on the teak table.*

I have a second daughter who is, thank God, in a remote part of the Empire with her numskull of a husband. As a child she thought the figure-head of my ship, the Dauntless, the most beautiful thing on earth. He resembled it. He had the same expression: wooden yet enterprising. She married him, and will never set foot in this house again.

NURSE GUINNESS [*carrying the table, with the tea-things on it, to* ELLIE*'s side*]: Indeed you never were more mistaken. She is in England this very moment. You have been told three times this week that she is coming home for a year for her health. And very glad you should be to see your own daughter again after all these years.

THE CAPTAIN: I am not glad. The natural term of the affection of the human animal for its offspring is six years. My daughter Ariadne was born when I was forty-six. I am now eighty-eight. If she comes, I am not at home. If she wants anything, let her take it. If she asks for me, let her be informed that I am extremely old, and have totally forgotten her.

NURSE GUINNESS: Thats no talk to offer to a young lady. Here, ducky, have some tea; and dont listen to him [*she pours out a cup of tea*].

THE CAPTAIN [*rising wrathfully*]: Now before high heaven they have given this innocent child Indian tea: the stuff they tan their own leather insides with.

[*He seizes the cup and the tea-pot and empties both into the leathern bucket*].

ELLIE [*almost in tears*]: Oh, please! I am so tired. I should have been glad of anything.

NURSE GUINNESS: Oh, what a thing to do! The poor lamb is ready to drop.

THE CAPTAIN: You shall have some of my tea. Do not touch that fly-blown cake: nobody eats it here except the dogs. [*He disappears into the pantry*].

NURSE GUINNESS: Theres a man for you! They say he sold himself to the devil in Zanzibar before he was a captain; and the older he grows the more I believe them.

A WOMAN'S VOICE [*in the hall*]: Is anyone at home? Hesione! Nurse! Papa! Do come, somebody; and take in my luggage.

Thumping heard, as of an umbrella, on the wainscot.

NURSE GUINNESS: My gracious! It's Miss Addie, Lady Utterword, Mrs Hushabye's sister: the one I told the Captain about. [*Calling*] Coming, Miss, coming.

She carries the table back to its place by the door, and is hurrying out when she is intercepted by LADY UTTERWORD, *who bursts in much flustered.* LADY UTTERWORD, *a blonde, is very handsome, very well dressed, and so precipitate in speech and action that the first impression (erroneous) is one of comic silliness.*

LADY UTTERWORD: Oh, is that you, Nurse? How are you? You dont look a day older. Is nobody at home? Where is Hesione? Doesnt she expect me? Where are the servants? Whose luggage is that on the steps? Where's Papa? Is everybody asleep? [*Seeing* ELLIE] Oh! I beg your pardon. I suppose you are one of my nieces. [*Approaching her with out-stretched arms*] Come and kiss your aunt, darling.

ELLIE: I'm only a visitor. It is my luggage on the steps.

NURSE GUINNESS: I'll go get you some fresh tea, ducky. [*She takes up the tray*].

ELLIE: But the old gentleman said he would make some himself.

NURSE GUINNESS: Bless you! he's forgotten what he went for already. His mind wanders from one thing to another.

LADY UTTERWORD: Papa, I suppose?

NURSE GUINNESS: Yes, Miss.

LADY UTTERWORD [*vehemently*]: Dont be silly, nurse. Dont call me Miss.

NURSE GUINNESS [*placidly*]: No, lovey [*she goes out with the tea-tray*].

LADY UTTERWORD [*sitting down with a flounce on the sofa*]: I know what you must feel. Oh, this house, this house! I come back to it after twenty-three years; and it is just the same: the luggage lying on the steps, the servants spoilt and impossible, nobody at home to receive anybody, no regular meals, nobody ever hungry because they are always gnawing bread and butter or munching apples, and, what is worse, the same disorder in ideas, in talk, in feeling. When I was a child I was used to it: I had never known anything better, though I was unhappy, and longed all the time—oh, how I longed!—to be respectable, to be a lady, to live as others did, not to have to think of everything for myself. I married at nineteen to escape from it. My husband is Sir Hastings Utterword, who has been governor of all the crown colonies in

succession. I have always been the mistress of Government House. I have
been so happy: I had forgotten that people could live like this. I wanted to see
my father, my sister, my nephews and nieces (one ought to, you know), and I
was looking forward to it. And now the state of the house! the way I'm
received! the casual impudence of that woman Guinness, our old nurse!
really Hesione might at least have been here: some preparation might have
been made for me. You must excuse my going on in this way; but I am really
very much hurt and annoyed and disillusioned: and if I had realized it was to
be like this, I wouldnt have come. I have a great mind to go away without
another word [*she is on the point of weeping*].

ELLIE [*also very miserable*]: Nobody has been here to receive me either. I
thought I ought to go away too. But how can I, Lady Utterword? My luggage
is on the steps; and the station fly has gone.

> THE CAPTAIN *emerges from the pantry with a tray of Chinese lacquer and
> a very fine tea-set on it. He rests it provisionally on the end of the table;
> snatches away the drawing-board, which he stands on the floor against the
> table legs; and puts the tray in the space thus cleared.* ELLIE *pours out a cup
> greedily.*

THE CAPTAIN: Your tea, young lady. What! another lady! I must fetch another
cup [*he makes for the pantry*].

LADY UTTERWORD [*rising from the sofa, suffused with emotion*]: Papa! Dont you
know me? I'm your daughter.

THE CAPTAIN: Nonsense! my daughter's upstairs asleep.

> *He vanishes through the half door.* LADY UTTERWORD *retires to the window to
> conceal her tears.*

ELLIE [*going to her with the cup*]: Dont be so distressed. Have this cup of tea. He
is very old and very strange: he has been just like that to me. I know how
dreadful it must be: my own father is all the world to me. Oh, I'm sure he
didnt mean it.

> THE CAPTAIN *returns with another cup.*

THE CAPTAIN: Now we are complete. [*He places it on the tray*].

LADY UTTERWORD [*hysterically*]: Papa: you cant have forgotten me. I am
Ariadne. I'm little Paddy Patkins. Wont you kiss me? [*She goes to him and
throws her arms round his neck*].

THE CAPTAIN [*woodenly enduring her embrace*]: How can you be Ariadne? You
are a middle-aged woman: well preserved, madam, but no longer young.

LADY UTTERWORD: But think of all the years and years I have been away, Papa. I
have had to grow old, like other people.

THE CAPTAIN [*disengaging himself*]: You should grow out of kissing strange men:
they may be striving to attain the seventh degree of concentration.

LADY UTTERWORD: But I'm your daughter. You havnt seen me for years.

THE CAPTAIN: So much the worse! When our relatives are at home, we have to
think of all their good points or it would be impossible to endure them. But
when they are away, we console ourselves for their absence by dwelling on
their vices. That is how I have come to think my absent daughter Ariadne a

perfect fiend; so do not try to ingratiate yourself here by impersonating her [*he walks firmly away to the other side of the room*].

LADY UTTERWORD: Ingratiating myself indeed! [*With dignity*] Very well, papa. [*She sits down at the drawing-table and pours out tea for herself*].

THE CAPTAIN: I am neglecting my social duties. You remember Dunn? Billy Dunn?

LADY UTTERWORD: Do you mean that villainous sailor who robbed you?

THE CAPTAIN [*introducing* ELLIE]: His daughter. [*He sits down on the sofa*].

ELLIE [*protesting*]: No—

NURSE GUINNESS *returns with fresh tea.*

THE CAPTAIN: Take that hogwash away. Do you hear?

NURSE: Youve actually remembered about the tea! [*To* ELLIE] O, miss, he didnt forget you after all! You have made an impression.

THE CAPTAIN [*gloomily*]: Youth! beauty! novelty! They are badly wanted in this house. I am excessively old. Hesione is only moderately young. Her children are not youthful.

LADY UTTERWORD: How can children be expected to be youthful in this house? Almost before we could speak we were filled with notions that might have been all very well for pagan philosophers of fifty, but were certainly quite unfit for respectable people of any age.

NURSE: You were always for respectability, Miss Addy.

LADY UTTERWORD: Nurse: will you please remember that I am Lady Utterword, and not Miss Addy, nor lovey, nor darling, nor doty? Do you hear?

NURSE: Yes, ducky: all right. I'll tell them all they must call you my lady. [*She takes her tray out with undisturbed placidity*].

LADY UTTERWORD: What comfort? what sense is there in having servants with no manners?

ELLIE [*rising and coming to the table to put down her empty cup*]: Lady Utterword: do you think Mrs Hushabye really expects me?

LADY UTTERWORD: Oh, dont ask me. You can see for yourself that Ive just arrived; her only sister, after twenty-three years absence! and it seems that *I* am not expected.

THE CAPTAIN: What does it matter whether the young lady is expected or not? She is welcome. There are beds: there is food. I'll find a room for her myself [*he makes for the door*].

ELLIE [*following him to stop him*]: Oh please–[*he goes out*]. Lady Utterword: I dont know what to do. Your father persists in believing that my father is some sailor who robbed him.

LADY UTTERWORD: You had better pretend not to notice it. My father is a very clever man; but he always forgot things; and now that he is old, of course he is worse. And I must warn you that it is sometimes very hard to feel quite sure that he really forgets.

MRS HUSHABYE *bursts into the room tempestuously, and embraces* ELLIE. *She is a couple of years older than* LADY UTTERWORD *and even better looking. She has magnificent black hair, eyes like the fishpools of Heshbon, and a nobly modelled neck, short at the back and low between her shoulders in front. Unlike her sister she is uncorseted and dressed anyhow in a rich robe of black pile that shews off her white skin and statuesque contour.*

MRS HUSHABYE: Ellie, my darling, my pettikins [*kissing her*]: how long have you been here? Ive been at home all the time: I was putting flowers and things in your room; and when I just sat down for a moment to try how comfortable the armchair was I went off to sleep. Papa woke me and told me you were here. Fancy your finding no one, and being neglected and abandoned. [*Kissing her again*]. My poor love!

> She deposits ELLIE *on the sofa. Meanwhile* ADRIADNE *has left the table and come over to claim her share of attention.*

Oh! youve brought someone with you. Introduce me.

LADY UTTERWORD: Hesione: is it possible that you dont know me?

MRS HUSHABYE [*conventionally*]: Of course I remember your face quite well. Where have we met?

LADY UTTERWORD: Didnt Papa tell you I was here? Oh! this is really too much. [*She throws herself sulkily into the big chair*].

MRS HUSHABYE: Papa!

LADY UTTERWORD: Yes: Papa. Our papa, you unfeeling wretch [*Rising angrily*] I'll go straight to a hotel.

MRS HUSHABYE [*seizing her by the shoulders*]: My goodness gracious goodness, you dont mean to say that youre Addy!

LADY UTTERWORD: I certainly am Addy; and I dont think I can be so changed that you would not have recognized me if you had any real affection for me. And Papa didnt think me even worth mentioning!

MRS HUSHABYE: What a lark! Sit down [*she pushes her back into the chair instead of kissing her, and posts herself behind it*]. You do look a swell. Youre much handsomer than you used to be. Youve made the acquaintance of Ellie, of course. She is going to marry a perfect hog of a millionaire for the sake of her father, who is as poor as a church mouse; and you must help me to stop her.

ELLIE: Oh please, Hesione.

MRS HUSHABYE: My pettikins, the man's coming here today with your father to begin persecuting you; and everybody will see the state of the case in ten minutes; so whats the use of making a secret of it?

ELLIE: He is not a hog, Hesione. You dont know how wonderfully good he was to my father, and how deeply grateful I am to him.

MRS HUSHABYE [*to* LADY UTTERWORD]: Her father is a very remarkable man, Addy. His name is Mazzini Dunn. Mazzini was a celebrity of some kind who knew Ellie's grandparents. They were both poets, like the Brownings; and when her father came into the world Mazzini said 'Another soldier born for freedom!' So they christened him Mazzini; and he has been fighting for freedom in his quiet way ever since. Thats why he is so poor.

ELLIE: I am proud of his poverty.

MRS HUSHABYE: Of course you are, pettikins. Why not leave him in it, and marry someone you love?

LADY UTTERWORD [*rising suddenly and explosively*]: Hesione: are you going to kiss me or are you not?

MRS HUSHABYE: What do you want to be kissed for?

LADY UTTERWORD: I don't want to be kissed; but I do want you to behave properly and decently. We are sisters. We have been separated for twenty-three years. You ought to kiss me.

MRS HUSHABYE: Tomorrow morning, dear, before you make up. I hate the smell of powder.

LADY UTTERWORD: Oh! you unfeeling—[*she is interrupted by the return of* THE CAPTAIN].

THE CAPTAIN [*to* ELLIE]: Your room is ready.

ELLIE *rises*

The sheets were damp; but I have changed them [*he makes for the garden door on the port side*].

LADY UTTERWORD: Oh! What about my sheets?

THE CAPTAIN [*halting at the door*]: Take my advice: air them; or take them off and sleep in blankets. You shall sleep in Ariadne's old room.

LADY UTTERWORD: Indeed I shall do nothing of the sort. That little hole! I am entitled to the best spare room.

THE CAPTAIN [*continuing unmoved*]: She married a numskull. She told me she would marry anyone to get away from home.

LADY UTTERWORD: You are pretending not to know me on purpose. I will leave the house.

MAZZINI DUNN *enters from the hall. He is a little elderly man with bulging credulous eyes and earnest manners. He is dressed in a blue serge jacket suit with an unbuttoned mackintosh over it, and carries a soft black hat of clerical cut.*

ELLIE: At last! Captain Shotover: here is my father.

THE CAPTAIN: This! Nonsense! not a bit like him [*he goes away through the garden, shutting the door sharply behind him*].

LADY UTTERWORD: I will not be ignored and pretended to be somebody else. I will have it out with papa now, this instant. [*To* MAZZINI] Excuse me. [*She follows* THE CAPTAIN *out, making a hasty bow to* MAZZINI, *who returns it*].

MRS HUSHABYE [*hospitably, shaking hands*]: How good of you to come, Mr Dunn! You don't mind papa, do you? He is as mad as a hatter, you know, but quite harmless, and extremely clever. You will have some delightful talks with him.

MAZZINI: I hope so. [*To* ELLIE] So here you are, Ellie, dear. [*He draws her arm affectionately through his*]. I must thank you, Mrs Hushabye, for your kindness to my daughter. I'm afraid she would have had no holiday if you had not invited her.

MRS HUSHABYE: Not at all. Very nice of her to come and attract young people to the house for us.

MAZZINI [*smiling*]: I'm afraid Ellie is not interested in young men, Mrs Hushabye. Her taste is on the graver, solider side.

MRS HUSHABYE [*with a sudden rather hard brightness in her manner*]: Wont you take off your overcoat, Mr Dunn? You will find a cupboard for coats and hats and things in the corner of the hall.

MAZZINI [*hastily releasing* ELLIE]: Yes—thank you—I had better—[*he goes out*].

MRS HUSHABYE [*emphatically*]: The old brute!

ELLIE: Who?

MRS HUSHABYE: Who! Him. He. It [*pointing after* MAZZINI]. 'Graver, solider tastes,' indeed!

ELLIE [*aghast*]: You dont mean that you were speaking like that of my father!

MRS HUSHABYE: I was. You know I was.

ELLIE [*with dignity*]: I will leave your house at once. [*She turns to the door*].

MRS HUSHABYE: If you attempt it, I'll tell your father why.

ELLIE [*turning again*]: Oh! How can you treat a visitor like this, Mrs Hushabye?

MRS HUSHABYE: I thought you were going to call me Hesione.

ELLIE: Certainly not now?

MRS HUSHABYE: Very well: I'll tell your father.

ELLIE [*distressed*]: Oh!

MRS HUSHABYE: If you turn a hair—if you take his part against me and against your own heart for a moment, I'll give that born soldier of freedom a piece of my mind that will stand him on his selfish old head for a week.

ELLIE: Hesione! My father selfish! How little you know—

She is interrupted by MAZZINI, *who returns, excited and perspiring.*

MAZZINI: Ellie: Mangan has come: I thought youd like to know. Excuse me, Mrs Hushabye: the strange old gentleman—

MRS HUSHABYE: Papa. Quite so.

MAZZINI: Oh, I beg your pardon: of course: I was a little confused by his manner. He is making Mangan help him with something in the garden; and he wants me too—

A powerful whistle is heard.

THE CAPTAIN'S VOICE: Bosun ahoy!

The whistle is repeated.

MAZZINI [*flustered*]: Oh dear! I believe he is whistling for me. [*He hurries out*].

MRS HUSHABYE: Now my father is a wonderful man if you like.

ELLIE: Hesione: listen to me. You dont understand. My father and Mr Mangan were boys together. Mr Ma—

MRS HUSHABYE: I dont care what they were: we must sit down if you are going to begin as far back as that [*She snatches at* ELLIE's *waist, and makes her sit down on the sofa beside her*]. Now, pettikins: tell me all about Mr Mangan. They call him Boss Mangan, dont they? He is a Napoleon of industry and disgustingly rich, isn't he? Why isnt your father rich?

ELLIE: My poor father should never have been in business. His parents were poets; and they gave him the noblest ideas; but they could not afford to give him a profession.

MRS HUSHABYE: Fancy your grandparents, with their eyes in fine frenzy rolling! And so your poor father had to go into business. Hasnt he succeeded in it?

ELLIE: He always used to say he could succeed if he only had some capital. He fought his way along, to keep a roof over our heads and bring us up well; but it was always a struggle: always the same difficulty of not having capital enough. I dont know how to describe it to you.

MRS HUSHABYE: Poor Ellie! I know. Pulling the devil by the tail.

ELLIE [*hurt*]: Oh no. Not like that. It was at least dignified.

MRS HUSHABYE: That made it all the harder, didnt it? *I* shouldnt have pulled the devil by the tail with dignity. I should have pulled hard—[*between her teeth*] hard. Well? Go on.

ELLIE: At last it seemed that all our troubles were at an end. Mr Mangan did an extraordinary noble thing out of pure friendship for my father and respect for his character. He asked him how much capital he wanted, and gave it to him. I dont mean that he lent it to him, or that he invested it in his business. He just simply made him a present of it. Wasnt that splendid of him?

MRS HUSHABYE: On condition that you married him?

ELLIE: Oh no, no, no. This was when I was a child. He had never even seen me: he never came to our house. It was absolutely disinterested. Pure generosity.

MRS HUSHABYE: Oh! I beg the gentleman's pardon. Well, what became of the money?

ELLIE: We all got new clothes and moved into another house. And I went to another school for two years.

MRS HUSHABYE: Only two years?

ELLIE: That was all; for at the end of two years my father was utterly ruined.

MRS HUSHABYE: How?

ELLIE: I dont know. I never could understand. But it was dreadful. When we were poor my father had never been in debt. But when he launched out into business on a large scale, he had to incur liabilities. When the business went into liquidation he owed more money than Mr Mangan had given him.

MRS HUSHABYE: Bit off more than he could chew, I suppose.

ELLIE: I think you are a little unfeeling about it.

MRS HUSHABYE: My pettikins: you mustnt mind my way of talking. I was quite as sensitive and particular as you once; but I have picked up so much slang from the children that I am really hardly presentable. I suppose your father had no head for business, and made a mess of it.

ELLIE: Oh, that just shews how entirely you are mistaken about him. The business turned out a great success. It now pays forty-four per cent after deducting the excess profits tax.

MRS HUSHABYE: Then why arnt you rolling in money?

ELLIE: I dont know. It seems very unfair to me. You see, my father was made bankrupt. It nearly broke his heart, because he had persuaded several of his friends to put money into the business. He was sure it would succeed; and events proved that he was quite right. But they all lost their money. It was dreadful. I dont know what we should have done but for Mr Mangan.

MRS HUSHABYE: What! Did the Boss come to the rescue again, after all his money being thrown away?

ELLIE: He did indeed, and never uttered a reproach to my father. He bought what was left of the business—the buildings and the machinery and things—from the official trustee for enough money to enable my father to pay six and eightpence in the pound and get his discharge. Everyone pitied papa so much, and saw so plainly that he was an honorable man, that they let him off at six-and-eightpence instead of ten shillings. Then Mr Mangan started a company to take up the business, and made my father a manager in it to save us from starvation; for I wasnt earning anything then.

MRS HUSHABYE: Quite a romance. And when did the Boss develop the tender passion?

ELLIE: Oh, that was years after, quite lately. He took the chair one night at a sort of people's concert. I was singing there. As an amateur, you know: half a guinea for expenses and three songs with three encores. He was so pleased with my singing that he asked might he walk home with me. I never saw anyone so taken aback as he was when I took him home and introduced him to my father: his own manager. It was then that my father told me how nobly he had behaved. Of course it was considered a great chance for me, as he is so rich. And—and—we drifted into a sort of understanding—I suppose I should call it an engagement—[*she is distressed and cannot go on*].

MRS HUSHABYE [*rising and marching about*]: You may have drifted into it; but you will bounce out of it, my pettikins, if I am to have anything to do with it.

ELLIE [*hopelessly*]: No: it's no use. I am bound in honor and gratitude. I will go through with it.

MRS HUSHABYE [*behind the sofa, scolding down at her*]: You know, of course, that its not honorable or grateful to marry a man you dont love. Do you love this Mangan man?

ELLIE: Yes. At least—

MRS HUSHABYE: I dont want to know about 'the least': I want to know the worst. Girls of your age fall in love with all sorts of impossible people, especially old people.

ELLIE: I like Mr Mangan very much; and I shall always be—

MRS HUSHABYE [*impatiently completing the sentence and prancing away intolerantly to starboard*]:—grateful to him for his kindness to dear father. I know. Anybody else?

ELLIE: What do you mean?

MRS HUSHABYE: Anybody else? Are you in love with anybody else?

ELLIE: Of course not.

MRS HUSHABYE: Humph! [*The book on the drawing-table catches her eye. She picks it up, and evidently finds the title very unexpected. She looks at* ELLIE, *and asks, quaintly*]. Quite sure youre not in love with an actor?

ELLIE: No, no. Why? What put such a thing into your head?

MRS HUSHABYE: This is yours, isnt it? Why else should you be reading Othello?

ELLIE: My father taught me to love Shakespear.

MRS HUSHABYE [*flinging the book down on the table*]: Really! your father does seem to be about the limit.

ELLIE [*naïvely*]: Do you never read Shakespear, Hesione? That seems to me so extraordinary. I like Othello.

MRS HUSHABYE: Do you indeed? He was jealous, wasn't he?

ELLIE: Oh, not that. I think all the part about jealousy is horrible. But dont you think it must have been a wonderful experience for Desdemona, brought up so quietly at home, to meet a man who had been out in the world doing all sorts of brave things and having terrible adventures, and yet finding something in her that made him love to sit and talk with her and tell her about them?

MRS HUSHABYE: Thats your idea of romance, is it?

ELLIE: Not romance, exactly. It might really happen.

> ELLIE's *eyes shew that she is not arguing, but in a daydream.* MRS HUSHABYE, *watching her inquisitively, goes deliberately back to the sofa and resumes her seat beside her.*

MRS HUSHABYE: Ellie darling: have you noticed that some of those stories that Othello told Desdemona couldnt have happened?

ELLIE: Oh no. Shakespear thought they could have happened.

MRS HUSHABYE: Hm! Desdemona thought they could have happened. But they didnt.

ELLIE: Why do you look so enigmatic about it? You are such a sphinx: I never know what you mean.

MRS HUSHABYE: Desdemona would have found him out if she had lived, you know. I wonder was that why he strangled her!

ELLIE: Othello was not telling lies.

MRS HUSHABYE: How do you know?

ELLIE: Shakespear would have said if he was. Hesione: there are men who have done wonderful things: men like Othello, only, of course, white, and very handsome, and—

MRS HUSHABYE: Ah! Now we're coming to it. Tell me all about him. I knew there must be somebody, or youd never have been so miserable about Mangan: youd have thought it quite a lark to marry him.

ELLIE [*blushing vividly*]: Hesione: you are dreadful. But I dont want to make a secret of it, though of course I dont tell everybody. Besides, I dont know him.

MRS HUSHABYE: Dont know him! What does that mean?

ELLIE: Well, of course I know him to speak to.

MRS HUSHABYE: But you want to know him ever so much more intimately, eh?

ELLIE: No no: I know him quite–almost intimately.

MRS HUSHABYE: You dont know him; and you know him almost intimately. How lucid!

ELLIE: I mean that he does not call on us. I–I got into conversation with him by chance at a concert.

MRS HUSHABYE: You seem to have rather a gay time at your concerts, Ellie.

ELLIE: Not at all: we talk to everyone in the green-room waiting for our turns. I though he was one of the artists: he looked so splendid. But he was only one of the committee. I happened to tell him that I was copying a picture at the National Gallery. I make a little money that way. I cant paint much; but as it's always the same picture I can do it pretty quickly and get two or three pounds for it. It happened that he came to the National Gallery one day.

MRS HUSHABYE: One student's day. Paid sixpence to stumble about through a crowd of easels, when he might have come in next day for nothing and found the floor clear! Quite by accident?

ELLIE [*triumphantly*]: No. On purpose. He liked talking to me. He knows lots of the most splendid people. Fashionable women who are all in love with him. But he ran away from them to see me at the National Gallery and persuade me to come with him for a drive round Richmond Park in a taxi.

MRS HUSHABYE: My pettikins, you have been going it. It's wonderful what you good girls can do without anyone saying a word.

ELLIE: I am not in society, Hesione. If I didnt make acquaintances in that way I shouldnt have any at all.

MRS HUSHABYE: Well, no harm if you know how to take care of yourself. May I ask his name?

ELLIE [*slowly and musically*]: Marcus Darnley.

MRS HUSHABYE [*echoing the music*]: Marcus Darnley! What a splendid name!

ELLIE: Oh, I'm so glad you think so. I think so too; but I was afraid it was only a silly fancy of my own.

MRS HUSHABYE: Hm! Is he one of the Aberdeen Darnleys?

ELLIE: Nobody knows. Just fancy! He was found in an antique chest—

MRS HUSHABYE: A what?

ELLIE: An antique chest, one summer morning in a rose garden, after a night of the most terrible thunderstorm.

MRS HUSHABYE: What on earth was he doing in the chest? Did he get into it because he was afraid of the lightning?

ELLIE: Oh no, no: he was a baby. The name Marcus Darnley was embroidered on his babyclothes. And five hundred pounds in gold.

MRS HUSHABYE [*looking hard at her*]: Ellie!

ELLIE: The garden of the Viscount—

MRS HUSHABYE:—de Rougemont?

ELLIE [*innocently*]: No: de Larochejaquelin. A French family. A vicomte. His life has been one long romance. A tiger—

MRS HUSHABYE: Slain by his own hand?

ELLIE: Oh no: nothing vulgar like that. He saved the life of the tiger from a hunting party: one of King Edward's hunting parties in India. The King was furious: that was why he never had his military services properly recognized. But he doesnt care. He is a Socialist and despises rank, and has been in three revolutions fighting on the barricades.

MRS HUSHABYE: How can you sit there telling me such lies? You, Ellie, of all people! And I thought you were a perfectly simple, straightforward, good girl.

ELLIE [*rising, dignified but very angry*]: Do you mean to say you dont believe me?

MRS HUSHABYE: Of course I dont believe you. Youre inventing every word of it. Do you take me for a fool?

ELLIE *stares at her. Her candor is so obvious that* MRS HUSHABYE *is puzzled.*

ELLIE: Goodbye, Hesione. I'm very sorry. I see now that it sounds very improbable as I tell it. But I cant stay if you think that way about me.

MRS HUSHABYE [*catching her dress*]: You shant go. I couldnt be so mistaken: I know too well what liars are like. Somebody has really told you all this.

ELLIE [*flushing*]: Hesione: dont say that you dont believe him. I couldnt bear that.

MRS HUSHABYE [*soothing her*]: Of course I believe him, dearest. But you should have broken it to me by degrees. [*Drawing her back to the seat*] Now tell me all about him. Are you in love with him?

ELLIE: Oh no, I'm not so foolish. I dont fall in love with people. I'm not so silly as you think.

MRS HUSHABYE: I see. Only something to think about—to give some interest and pleasure to life.

ELLIE: Just so. Thats all, really.

MRS HUSHABYE: It makes the hours go fast, doesnt it? No tedious waiting to go to sleep at nights and wondering whether you will have a bad night. How delightful it makes waking up in the morning! How much better than the happiest dream! All life transfigured! No more wishing one had an interesting book to read, because life is so much happier than any book! No desire but to be alone and not to have to talk to anyone: to be alone and just think about it.

ELLIE [*embracing her*]: Hesione: you are a witch. How do you know? Oh, you are the most sympathetic woman in the world.

MRS HUSHABYE [*caressing her*]: Pettikins, my pettikins: how I envy you! and how I pity you!

ELLIE: Pity me! Oh, why?

A very handsome man of fifty, with mousquetaire moustaches, wearing a rather dandified curly brimmed hat, and carrying an elaborate walking-stick, comes into the room from the hall, and stops short at sight of the women on the sofa.

ELLIE [*seeing him and rising in glad surprise*]: Oh! Hesione: this is Mr Marcus Darnley.

MRS HUSHABYE [*rising*]: What a lark! He is my husband.

ELLIE: But how–[*she stops suddenly; then turns pale and sways*].

MRS HUSHABYE [*catching her and sitting down with her on the sofa*]: Steady, my pettikins.

THE MAN [*with a mixture of confusion and effrontery, depositing his hat and stick on the teak table*]: My real name, Miss Dunn, is Hector Hushabye. I leave you to judge whether that is a name any sensitive man would care to confess to. I never use it when I can possibly help it. I have been away for nearly a month; and I had no idea you knew my wife, or that you were coming here. I am none the less delighted to find you in our little house.

ELLIE [*in great distress*]: I dont know what to do. Please, may I speak to papa? Do leave me. I cant bear it.

MRS HUSHABYE: Be off, Hector.

HECTOR: I—

MRS HUSHABYE: Quick, quick. Get out.

HECTOR: If you think it better—[*he goes out, taking his hat with him but leaving the stick on the table*].

MRS HUSHABYE [*laying* ELLIE *down at the end of the sofa*]: Now, pettikins, he is gone. Theres nobody but me. You can let yourself go. Dont try to control yourself. Have a good cry.

ELLIE [*raising her head*]: Damn!

MRS HUSHABYE: Splendid! Oh, what a relief! I thought you were going to be broken-hearted. Never mind me. Damn him again.

ELLIE: I am not damning him: I am damning myself for being such a fool. [*Rising*] How could I let myself be taken in so? [*She begins prowling to and fro, her bloom gone, looking curiously older and harder*].

MRS HUSHABYE [*cheerfully*]: Why not, pettikins? Very few young women can resist Hector. I couldnt when I was your age. He is really rather splendid, you know.

ELLIE [*turning on her*]: Splendid! Yes: splendid looking, of course. But how can you love a liar?

MRS HUSHABYE: I dont know. But you can, fortunately. Otherwise there wouldnt be much love in the world.

ELLIE: But to lie like that! To be a boaster! a coward!

MRS HUSHABYE [*rising in alarm*]: Pettikins: none of that, if you please. If you hint the slightest doubt of Hector's courage, he will go straight off and do the most horribly dangerous things to convince himself that he isnt a coward. He has a dreadful trick of getting out of one third-floor window and coming in at another, just to test his nerve. He has a whole drawerful of Albert Medals for saving people's lives.

ELLIE: He never told me that.

MRS HUSHABYE: He never boasts of anything he really did: he cant bear it; and it makes him shy if anyone else does. All his stories are made-up stories.

ELLIE [*coming to her*]: Do you mean that he is really brave, and really has adventures, and yet tells lies about things that he never did and that never happened?

MRS HUSHABYE: Yes, pettikins, I do. People dont have their virtues and vices in sets: they have them anyhow: all mixed.

ELLIE [*staring at her thoughtfully*]: Theres something odd about this house, Hesione, and even about you. I dont know why I'm talking to you so calmly. I have a horrible fear that my heart is broken, but that heartbreak is not like what I thought it must be.

MRS HUSHABYE [*fondling her*]: It's only life educating you, pettikins. How do you feel about Boss Mangan now?

ELLIE [*disengaging herself with an expression of distaste*]: Oh, how can you remind me of him, Hesione?

MRS HUSHABYE: Sorry, dear. I think I hear Hector coming back. You dont mind now, do you, dear?

ELLIE: Not in the least. I am quite cured.

MAZZINI DUNN *and* HECTOR *come in from the hall.*

HECTOR [*as he opens the door and allows* MAZZINI *to pass in*]: One second more, and she would have been a dead woman!

MAZZINI: Dear! dear! what an escape! Ellie, my love: Mr Hushabye has just been telling me the most extraordinary—

ELLIE: Yes: Ive heard it [*She crosses to the other side of the room*].

HECTOR [*following her*]: Not this one: I'll tell it to you after dinner. I think youll like it. The truth is, I made it up for you, and I was looking forward to the pleasure of telling it to you. But in a moment of impatience at being turned out of the room, I threw it away on your father.

ELLIE [*turning at bay with her back to the carpenter's bench, scornfully self-possessed*]: It was not thrown away. He believes it. I should not have believed it.

MAZZINI [*benevolently*]: Ellie is very naughty, Mr Hushabye. Of course she does not really think that.

He goes to the bookshelves, and inspects the titles of the volumes. Boss MANGAN *comes in from the hall, followed by the* CAPTAIN. MANGAN, *carefully frock-coated as for church or for a directors' meeting, is about fiftyfive, with a careworn, mistrustful expression, standing a little on an entirely imaginary dignity, with a dull complexion, straight, lustreless hair, and features so entirely commonplace that it is impossible to describe them.*

CAPTAIN SHOTOVER [*to* MRS HUSHABYE, *introducing the newcomer*]: Says his name is Mangan. Not ablebodied.

MRS HUSHABYE [*graciously*]: How do you do, Mr Mangan?

MANGAN [*shaking hands*]: Very pleased.

CAPTAIN SHOTOVER: Dunn's lost his muscle, but recovered his nerve. Men seldom do after three attacks of delirium tremens [*he goes into the pantry*].

MRS HUSHABYE: I congratulate you, Mr Dunn.

MAZZINI [*dazed*]: I am a lifelong teetotaler.

MRS HUSHABYE: You will find it far less trouble to let papa have his own way than try to explain.

MAZZINI: But three attacks of delirium tremens, really!

MRS HUSHABYE [*to* MANGAN]: Do you know my husband, Mr Mangan [*she indicates* HECTOR].

MANGAN [*going to* HECTOR, *who meets him with outstretched hand*]: Very pleased. [*Turning to* ELLIE] I hope, Miss Ellie, you have not found the journey down too fatiguing. [*They shake hands*].

MRS HUSHABYE: Hector: shew Mr Dunn his room.

HECTOR: Certainly. Come along, Mr Dunn. [*He takes* MAZZINI *out*].

ELLIE: You havnt shewn me my room yet, Hesione.

MRS HUSHABYE: How stupid of me! Come along. Make yourself quite at home, Mr Mangan. Papa will entertain you. [*She calls to the* CAPTAIN *in the pantry*] Papa: come and explain the house to Mr Mangan.

She goes out with ELLIE. *The* CAPTAIN *comes from the pantry.*

CAPTAIN SHOTOVER: Youre going to marry Dunn's daughter. Dont. Youre too old.

MANGAN [*staggered*]: Well! Thats fairly blunt, Captain.

CAPTAIN SHOTOVER: It's true.

MANGAN: She doesnt think so.

CAPTAIN SHOTOVER: She does.

MANGAN: Older men than I have—

CAPTAIN SHOTOVER [*finishing the sentence for him*]:—made fools of themselves. That, also, is true.

MANGAN [*asserting himself*]: I dont see that this is any business of yours.

CAPTAIN SHOTOVER: It is everybody's business. The stars in their courses are shaken when such things happen.

MANGAN: I'm going to marry her all the same.

CAPTAIN SHOTOVER: How do you know?

MANGAN [*playing the strong man*]: I intend to. I mean to. See? I never made up my mind to do a thing yet that I didnt bring it off. Thats the sort of man I am; and there will be a better understanding between us when you make up your mind to that, Captain.

CAPTAIN SHOTOVER: You frequent picture palaces.

MANGAN: Perhaps I do. Who told you?

CAPTAIN SHOTOVER: Talk like a man, not like a movy. You mean that you make a hundred thousand a year.

MANGAN: I dont boast. But when I meet a man that makes a hundred thousand a year, I take off my hat to that man, and stretch out my hand to him and call him brother.

CAPTAIN SHOTOVER: Then you also make a hundred thousand a year, hey?

MANGAN: No. I cant say that. Fifty thousand, perhaps.

CAPTAIN SHOTOVER: His half brother only [*he turns away from* MANGAN *with his usual abruptness, and collects the empty tea-cups on the Chinese tray*].

MANGAN [*irritated*]: See here, Captain Shotover. I dont quite understand my position here. I came here on your daughter's invitation. Am I in her house or in yours?

CAPTAIN SHOTOVER: You are beneath the dome of heaven, in the house of God. What is true within these walls is true outside them. Go out on the seas; climb the mountains; wander through the valleys. She is still too young.

MANGAN [*weakening*]: But I'm very little over fifty.

CAPTAIN SHOTOVER: You are still less under sixty. Boss Mangan: you will not marry the pirate's child [*he carries the tray away into the pantry*].

MANGAN [*following him to the half door*]: What pirate's child? What are you talking about?

CAPTAIN SHOTOVER [*in the pantry*]: Ellie Dunn. You will not marry her.

MANGAN: Who will stop me?

CAPTAIN SHOTOVER [*emerging*]: My daughter [*he makes for the door leading to the hall*].

MANGAN [*following him*]: Mrs Hushabye! Do you mean to say she brought me down here to break it off?

CAPTAIN SHOTOVER [*stopping and turning on him*]: I know nothing more than I have seen in her eye. She will break it off. Take my advice: marry a West Indian negress: they make excellent wives. I was married to one myself for two years.

MANGAN: Well, I am damned!

CAPTAIN SHOTOVER: I thought so. I was, too, for many years. The negress redeemed me.

MANGAN [*feebly*]: This is queer. I ought to walk out of this house.

CAPTAIN SHOTOVER: Why?

MANGAN: Well, many men would be offended by your style of talking.

CAPTAIN SHOTOVER: Nonsense! It's the other sort of talking that makes quarrels. Nobody ever quarrels with me.

A GENTLEMAN, *whose firstrate tailoring and frictionless manners proclaim the wellbred West Ender, comes in from the hall. He has an engaging air of being young and unmarried, but on close inspection is found to be at least over forty.*

THE GENTLEMAN. Excuse my intruding in this fashion; but there is no knocker on the door; and the bell does not seem to ring.

CAPTAIN SHOTOVER: Why should there be a knocker? Why should the bell ring? The door is open.

THE GENTLEMAN: Precisely. So I ventured to come in.

CAPTAIN SHOTOVER: Quite right. I will see about a room for you [*he makes for the door*].

THE GENTLEMAN [*stopping him*]: But I'm afraid you don't know who I am.

CAPTAIN SHOTOVER: Do you suppose that at my age I make distinctions between one fellowcreature and another?

He goes out. MANGAN *and the newcomer stare at one another.*

MANGAN: Strange character, Captain Shotover, sir.

THE GENTLEMAN: Very.

CAPTAIN SHOTOVER [*shouting outside*]: Hesione: another person has arrived and wants a room. Man about town, well dressed, fifty.

THE GENTLEMAN: Fancy Hesione's feelings! May I ask are you a member of the family?

MANGAN: No.

THE GENTLEMAN: I am. At least a connexion.

MRS HUSHABYE *comes back.*

MRS HUSHABYE: How do you do? How good of you to come!

THE GENTLEMAN: I am very glad indeed to make your acquaintance, Hesione.

Instead of taking her hand he kisses her. At the same moment the CAPTAIN *appears in the doorway.*

You will excuse my kissing your daughter, Captain, when I tell you that—

CAPTAIN SHOTOVER: Stuff! Everyone kisses my daughter. Kiss her as much as you like [*he makes for the pantry*].

THE GENTLEMAN: Thank you. One moment. Captain.

The CAPTAIN *halts and turns.* THE GENTLEMAN *goes to him affably.*

Do you happen to remember—but probably you dont, as it occurred many years ago—that your younger daughter married a numskull.

CAPTAIN SHOTOVER: Yes. She said she'd marry anybody to get away from this house. I should not have recognized you: your head is no longer like a walnut. Your aspect is softened. You have been boiled in bread and milk for years and years, like other married men. Poor devil! [*He disappears into the pantry*].

MRS HUSHABYE [*going past* MANGAN *to the* GENTLEMAN *and scrutinizing him*]: I dont believe you are Hastings Utterword.

THE GENTLEMAN: I am not.

MRS HUSHABYE: Then what business had you to kiss me?

THE GENTLEMAN: I thought I would like to. The fact is, I am Randall Utterword, the unworthy younger brother of Hastings. I was abroad diplomatizing when he was married.

LADY UTTERWORD [*dashing in*]: Hesione: where is the key of the wardrobe in my room? My diamonds are in my dressing-bag: I must lock it up—[*recognizing the stranger with a shock*] Randall: how dare you?

She marches at him past MRS HUSHABYE, *who retreats and joins* MANGAN *near the sofa.*

RANDALL: How dare I what? I am not doing anything.

LADY UTTERWORD: Who told you I was here?

RANDALL: Hastings. You had just left when I called on you at Claridge's; so I followed you down here. You are looking extremely well.

LADY UTTERWORD: Dont presume to tell me so.

MRS HUSHABYE: What is wrong with Mr Randall, Addy?

LADY UTTERWORD [*recollecting herself*]: Oh, nothing. But he has no right to come bothering you and papa without being invited.

She goes to the window-seat and sits down, turning away from them ill-humoredly and looking into the garden, where HECTOR *and* ELLIE *are now seen strolling together.*

MRS HUSHABYE: I think you have not met Mr Mangan, Addy.

LADY UTTERWORD [*turning her head and nodding coldly to* MANGAN]: I beg your pardon. Randall: you have flustered me so: I made a perfect fool of myself.

MRS HUSHABYE: Lady Utterword. My sister. My younger sister.

MANGAN [*bowing*]: Pleased to meet you, Lady Utterword.

LADY UTTERWORD [*with marked interest*]: Who is that gentleman walking in the garden with Miss Dunn?

MRS HUSHABYE: I don't know. She quarrelled mortally with my husband only ten minutes ago; and I didn't know anyone else had come. It must be a visitor. [*She goes to the window to look*]. Oh, it is Hector. Theyve made it up.

LADY UTTERWORD: Your husband! That handsome man?

MRS HUSHABYE: Well, why shouldnt my husband be a handsome man?

RANDALL [*joining them at the window*]: One's husband never is, Ariadne [*he sits by* LADY UTTERWORD, *on her right*].

MRS HUSHABYE: One's sister's husband always is, Mr Randall.

LADY UTTERWORD: Dont be vulgar, Randall. And you, Hesione, are just as bad.

> ELLIE *and* HECTOR *come in from the garden by the starboard door.* RANDALL *rises.* ELLIE *retires into the corner near the pantry.* HECTOR *comes forward; and* LADY UTTERWORD *rises looking her very best.*

MRS HUSHABYE: Hector: this is Addy.

HECTOR [*apparently surprised*]: Not this lady.

LADY UTTERWORD [*smiling*]: Why not?

HECTOR [*looking at her with a piercing glance of deep but respectful admiration, his moustache bristling*]: I thought—[*pulling himself together*] I beg your pardon, Lady Utterword. I am extremely glad to welcome you at last under our roof [*he offers his hand with grave courtesy*].

MRS HUSHABYE: She wants to be kissed, Hector.

LADY UTTERWORD: Hesione! [*but she still smiles*].

MRS HUSHABYE: Call her Addy; and kiss her like a good brother-in-law; and have done with it. [*She leaves them to themselves*].

HECTOR: Behave yourself, Hesione. Lady Utterword is entitled not only to hospitality but to civilization.

LADY UTTERWORD [*gratefully*]: Thank you, Hector.

> *They shake hands cordially.* MAZZINI DUNN *is seen crossing the garden from the starboard to port.*

CAPTAIN SHOTOVER [*coming from the pantry and addressing* ELLIE]: Your father has washed himself.

ELLIE [*quite self-possessed*]: He often does, Captain Shotover.

CAPTAIN SHOTOVER: A strange conversion! I saw him through the pantry window.

> MAZZINI DUNN *enters through the port window door, newly washed and brushed, and stops, smiling benevolently, between* MANGAN *and* MRS HUSHABYE.

MRS HUSHABYE [*introducing*]: Mr Mazzini Dunn, Lady Ut— oh, I forgot: youve met. [*Indicating* ELLIE] Miss Dunn.

MAZZINI [*walking across the room to take* ELLIE'*s hand, and beaming at his own naughty irony*]: I have met Miss Dunn also. She is my daughter. [*He draws her arm through his caressingly*].

MRS HUSHABYE: Of course: how stupid! Mr Utterword, my sister's–er—

RANDALL [*shaking hands agreeably*]: Her brother-in-law, Mr Dunn. How do you do?

MRS HUSHABYE: This is my husband.

HECTOR: We have met, dear. Dont introduce us any more. [*He moves away to the big chair, and adds*] Wont you sit down, Lady Utterword?

She does so very graciously

MRS HUSHABYE: Sorry. I hate it: it's like making people shew their tickets.

MAZZINI [*sententiously*]: How little it tells us, after all! The great question is, not who we are, but what we are.

CAPTAIN SHOTOVER: Ha! What are you?

MAZZINI [*taken aback*]: What am I?

CAPTAIN SHOTOVER: A thief, a pirate, and a murderer.

MAZZINI: I assure you you are mistaken.

CAPTAIN SHOTOVER: An adventurous life; but what does it end in? Respectability. A ladylike daughter. The language and appearance of a city missionary. Let it be a warning to all of you [*he goes out through the garden*].

DUNN: I hope nobody here believes that I am a thief, a pirate, or a murderer. Mrs Hushabye: will you excuse me a moment? I must really go and explain. [*He follows the* CAPTAIN].

MRS HUSHABYE [*as he goes*]: It's no use. Youd really better–[*but* DUNN *has vanished*]. We had better all go out and look for some tea. We never have regular tea; but you can always get some when you want: the servants keep it stewing all day. The kitchen veranda is the best place to ask. May I shew you? [*She goes to the starboard door*].

RANDALL [*going with her*]: Thank you, I dont think I'll take any tea this afternoon. But if you will shew me the garden—?

MRS HUSHABYE: Theres nothing to see in the garden except papa's observatory, and a gravel pit with a cave where he keeps dynamite and things of that sort. However, it's pleasanter out of doors; so come along.

RANDALL: Dynamite! Isnt that rather risky?

MRS HUSHABYE: Well, we dont sit in the gravel pit when theres a thunderstorm.

LADY UTTERWORD: Thats something new. What is the dynamite for?

HECTOR: To blow up the human race if it goes too far. He is trying to discover a psychic ray that will explode all the explosives at the will of a Mahatma.

ELLIE: The Captain's tea is delicious, Mr Utterwood.

MRS HUSHABYE [*stopping in the doorway*]: Do you mean to say that youve had some of my father's tea? that you got round him before you were ten minutes in the house?

ELLIE: I did.

MRS HUSHABYE: You little devil! [*She goes out with* RANDALL].

MANGAN: Wont you come, Miss Ellie?

ELLIE: I'm too tired. I'll take a book up to my room and rest a little. [*She goes to the bookshelf*].

MANGAN: Right. You cant do better. But I'm disappointed.

He follows RANDALL *and* MRS HUSHABYE. ELLIE, HECTOR, *and* LADY UTTERWORD *are left.* HECTOR *is close to* LADY UTTERWORD. *They look at* ELLIE, *waiting for her to go.*

ELLIE [*looking at the title of a book*]: Do you like stories of adventure, Lady Utterword?

LADY UTTERWORD [*patronizingly*]: Of course, dear.

ELLIE: Then I'll leave you to Mr Hushabye. [*She goes out through the hall*].

HECTOR: That girl is mad about tales of adventure. The lies I have to tell her!

LADY UTTERWORD [*not interested in* ELLIE]: When you saw me what did you mean by saying that you thought, and then stopping short? What did you think?

HECTOR [*folding his arms and looking down at her magnetically*]: May I tell you?

LADY UTTERWORD: Of course.

HECTOR: It will not sound very civil. I was on the point of saying 'I thought you were a plain woman.'

LADY UTTERWORD: Oh for shame, Hector! What right had you to notice whether I am plain or not?

HECTOR: Listen to me, Ariadne. Until today I have seen only photographs of you; and no photograph can give the strange fascination of the daughters of that supernatural old man. There is some damnable quality in them that destroys men's moral sense, and carries them beyond honor and dishonor. You know that, dont you?

LADY UTTERWORD: Perhaps I do, Hector. But let me warn you once for all that I am rigidly conventional woman. You may think because I'm a Shotover that I'm a Bohemian, because we are all so horribly Bohemian. But I'm not. I hate and loathe Bohemianism. No child brought up in a strict Puritan household ever suffered from Puritanism as I suffered from our Bohemianism.

HECTOR: Our children are like that. They spend their holidays in the houses of their respectable schoolfellows.

LADY UTTERWORD: I shall invite them for Christmas.

HECTOR: Their absence leaves us both without our natural chaperons.

LADY UTTERWORD: Children are certainly very inconvenient sometimes. But intelligent people can always manage, unless they are Bohemians.

HECTOR: You are no Bohemian; but you are no Puritan either: your attraction is alive and powerful. What sort of woman do you count yourself?

LADY UTTERWORD: I am a woman of the world, Hector; and I can assure you that if you will only take the trouble always to do the perfectly correct thing, and to say the perfectly correct thing, you can do just what you like. An ill-conducted, careless woman gets simply no chance. An ill-conducted, careless man is never allowed within arm's length of any woman worth knowing.

HECTOR: I see. You are neither a Bohemian woman nor a Puritan woman. You are a dangerous woman.

LADY UTTERWORD: On the contrary, I am a safe woman.

HECTOR: You are a most accursedly attractive woman. Mind: I am not making love to you. I do not like being attracted. But you had better know how I feel if you are going to stay here.

LADY UTTERWORD: You are an exceedingly clever lady-killer, Hector. And terribly handsome. I am quite a good player, myself, at that game. Is it quite understood that we are only playing?

HECTOR: Quite. I am deliberately playing the fool, out of sheer worthlessness.

LADY UTTERWORD [*rising brightly*]: Well, you are my brother-in-law. Hesione asked you to kiss me.

He seizes her in his arms, and kisses her strenuously.

Oh! that was a little more than play, brother-in-law. [*She pushes him suddenly away*]. You shall not do that again.

HECTOR: In effect, you got your claws deeper into me than I intended.

MRS HUSHABYE [*coming in from the garden*]: Dont let me disturb you: I only want a cap to put on daddiest. The sun is setting; and he'll catch cold [*she makes for the door leading to the hall*].

LADY UTTERWORD: Your husband is quite charming, darling. He has actually condescended to kiss me at last. I shall go into the garden: it's cooler now [*she goes out by the port door*].

MRS HUSHABYE: Take care, dear child. I dont believe any man can kiss Addy without falling in love with her. [*She goes into the hall*].

HECTOR [*striking himself on the chest*]: Fool! Goat!

MRS HUSHABYE *comes back with the* CAPTAIN's *cap*

Your sister is an extremely enterprising old girl. Wheres Miss Dunn!

MRS HUSHABYE: Mangan says she has gone up to her room for a nap. Addy wont let you talk to Ellie: she has marked you for her own.

HECTOR: She has the diabolical family fascination. I began making love to her automatically. What am I to do? I cant fall in love; and I cant hurt a woman's feelings by telling her so when she falls in love with me. And as women are always falling in love with my moustache I get landed in all sorts of tedious and terrifying flirtations in which I'm not a bit in earnest.

MRS HUSHABYE: Oh, neither is Addy. She has never been in love in her life, though she has always been trying to fall in head over ears. She is worse than you, because you had one real go at least, with me.

HECTOR: That was a confounded madness. I cant believe that such an amazing experience is common. It has left its mark on me. I believe that is why I have never been able to repeat it.

MRS HUSHABYE [*laughing and caressing his arm*]: We were frightfully in love with one another, Hector. It was such an enchanting dream that I have never been able to grudge it to you or anyone else since. I have invited all sorts of pretty women to the house on the chance of giving you another turn. But it has never come off.

HECTOR: I dont know that I want it to come off. It was damned dangerous. You fascinated me; but I loved you; so it was heaven. This sister of yours fascinates me; but I hate her; so it is hell. I shall kill her if she persists.

MRS HUSHABYE: Nothing will kill Addy: she is as strong as a horse. [*Releasing him*] Now *I* am going off to fascinate somebody.

HECTOR: The Foreign Office toff? Randall?

MRS HUSHABYE: Goodness gracious, no! Why should I fascinate him?

HECTOR: I presume you dont mean the bloated capitalist, Mangan?

MRS HUSHABYE: Hm! I think he had better be fascinated by me than by Ellie.

She is going into the garden when the CAPTAIN *comes in from it with some sticks in his hand.*

What have you got there, daddiest?

CAPTAIN SHOTOVER: Dynamite.

MRS HUSHABYE: Youve been to the gravel pit. Dont drop it about the house: theres a dear. [*She goes into the garden, where the evening light is now very red*].

HECTOR: Listen, O sage. How long dare you concentrate on a feeling without risking having it fixed in your consciousness all the rest of your life?

CAPTAIN SHOTOVER: Ninety minutes. An hour and a half.

> *He goes into the pantry.* HECTOR, *left alone, contracts his brows, and falls into a daydream. He does not move for some time. Then he folds his arms. Then, throwing his hands behind him, and gripping one with the other, he strides tragically once to and fro. Suddenly he snatches his walking-stick from the teak table, and draws it; for it is a sword-stick. He fights a desperate duel with an imaginary antagonist, and after many vicissitudes runs him through the body up to the hilt. He sheathes his sword and throws it on the sofa, falling into another reverie as he does so. He looks straight into the eyes of an imaginary woman; seizes her by the arms; and says in a deep and thrilling tone* 'Do you love me!' *The* CAPTAIN *comes out of the pantry at this moment; and* HECTOR, *caught with his arms stretched out and his fists clenched, has to account for his attitude by going through a series of gymnastic exercises.*

That sort of strength is no good. You will never be as strong as a gorilla.

HECTOR: What is the dynamite for?

CAPTAIN SHOTOVER: To kill fellows like Mangan.

HECTOR: No use. They will always be able to buy more dynamite than you.

CAPTAIN SHOTOVER: I will make a dynamite that he cannot explode.

HECTOR: And that you can, eh?

CAPTAIN SHOTOVER: Yes: when I have attained the seventh degree of concentration.

HECTOR: Whats the use of that? You never do attain it.

CAPTAIN SHOTOVER: What then is to be done? Are we to be kept for ever in the mud by these hogs to whom the universe is nothing but a machine for greasing their bristles and filling their snouts?

HECTOR: Are Mangan's bristles worse than Randall's lovelocks?

CAPTAIN SHOTOVER: We must win powers of life and death over them both. I refuse to die until I have invented the means.

HECTOR: Who are we that we should judge them?

CAPTAIN SHOTOVER: What are they that they should judge us? Yet they do, unhesitatingly. There is enmity between our seed and their seed. They know it and act on it, strangling our souls. They believe in themselves. When we believe in ourselves, we shall kill them.

HECTOR: It is the same seed. You forget that your pirate has a very nice daughter. Mangan's son may be a Plato: Randall's a Shelley. What was my father?

CAPTAIN SHOTOVER: The damndest scoundrel I ever met. [*He replaces the drawing-board; sits down at the table; and begins to mix a wash of color*].

HECTOR: Precisely. Well, dare you kill his innocent grandchildren?

CAPTAIN SHOTOVER: They are mine also.

HECTOR: Just so. We are members one of another. [*He throws himself carelessly on the sofa*]. I tell you I have often thought of this killing of human vermin. Many men have thought of it. Decent men are like Daniel in the lion's den:

their survival is a miracle; and they do not always survive. We live among the Mangans and Randalls and Billie Dunns as they, poor devils, live among the disease germs and the doctors and the lawyers and the parsons and the restaurant chefs and the tradesmen and the servants and all the rest of the parasites and blackmailers. What are our terrors to theirs? Give me the power to kill them; and I'll spare them in sheer—

CAPTAIN SHOTOVER [*cutting in sharply*]: Fellow feeling?

HECTOR: No. I should kill myself if I believed that. I must believe that my spark, small as it is, is divine, and that the red light over their doors is hell fire. I should spare them in simple magnanimous pity.

CAPTAIN SHOTOVER: You cant spare them until you have the power to kill them. At present they have the power to kill you. There are millions of blacks over the water for them to train and let loose on us. Theyre going to do it. Theyre doing it already.

HECTOR: They are too stupid to use their power.

CAPTAIN SHOTOVER [*throwing down his brush and coming to the end of the sofa*]: Do not deceive yourself: they do use it. We kill the better half of ourselves every day to propitiate them. The knowledge that these people are there to render all our aspirations barren prevents us having the aspirations. And when we are tempted to seek their destruction they bring forth demons to delude us, disguised as pretty daughters, and singers and poets and the like, for whose sake we spare them.

HECTOR [*sitting up and leaning towards him*]: May not Hesione be such a demon, brought forth by you lest I should slay you?

CAPTAIN SHOTOVER: That is possible. She has used you up, and left you nothing but dreams, as some women do.

HECTOR: Vampire women, demon women.

CAPTAIN SHOTOVER: Men think the world well lost for them, and lose it accordingly. Who are the men that do things? The husbands of the shrew and of the drunkard, the men with the thorn in the flesh. [*Walking distractedly away towards the pantry*] I must think these things out. [*Turning suddenly*] But I go on with the dynamite none the less. I will discover a ray mightier than any X-ray: a mind ray that will explode the ammunition in the belt of my adversary before he can point his gun at me. And I must hurry. I am old: I have no time to waste in talk.

He is about to go into the pantry, and HECTOR *is making for the hall, when* HESIONE *comes back.*

MRS HUSHABYE: Daddiest: you and Hector must come and help me to entertain all these people. What on earth were you shouting about?

HECTOR [*stopping in the act of turning the doorhandle*]: He is madder than usual.

MRS HUSHABYE: We all are.

HECTOR: I must change [*he resumes his door opening*].

MRS HUSHABYE: Stop, stop. Come back, both of you. Come back.

They return, reluctantly.

Money is running short.

HECTOR: Money! Where are my April dividends?

MRS HUSHABYE: Where is the snow that fell last year?

CAPTAIN SHOTOVER: Where is all the money you had for that patent lifeboat I invented?

MRS HUSHABYE: Five hundred pounds; and I have made it last since Easter!

CAPTAIN SHOTOVER: Since Easter! Barely four months! Monstrous extravagance! I could live for seven years on £500.

MRS HUSHABYE: Not keeping open house as we do here, daddiest.

CAPTAIN SHOTOVER: Only £500 for that lifeboat! I got twelve thousand for the invention before that.

MRS HUSHABYE: Yes, dear; but that was for the ship with the magnetic keel that sucked up submarines. Living at the rate we do, you cannot afford life-saving inventions. Cant you think of something that will murder half Europe at one bang?

CAPTAIN SHOTOVER: No. I am ageing fast. My mind does not dwell on slaughter as it did when I was a boy. Why doesnt your husband invent something? He does nothing but tell lies to women.

HECTOR: Well, that is a form of invention, is it not? However, you are right: I ought to support my wife.

MRS HUSHABYE: Indeed you shall do nothing of the sort: I should never see you from breakfast to dinner. I want my husband.

HECTOR [*bitterly*]: I might as well be your lapdog.

MRS HUSHABYE: Do you want to be my breadwinner, like the other poor husbands?

HECTOR: No, by thunder! What a damned creature a husband is anyhow!

MRS HUSHABYE [*to the* CAPTAIN]: What about that harpoon cannon?

CAPTAIN SHOTOVER: No use. It kills whales, not men.

MRS HUSHABYE: Why not? You fire the harpoon out of a cannon. It sticks in the enemy's general; you wind him in; and there you are.

HECTOR: You are your father's daughter, Hesione.

CAPTAIN SHOTOVER: There is something in it. Not to wind in generals: they are not dangerous. But one could fire a grapnel and wind in a machine gun or even a tank. I will think it out.

MRS HUSHABYE [*squeezing the* CAPTAIN'*s arm affectionately*]: Saved! You are a darling, daddiest. Now we must go back to these dreadful people and entertain them.

CAPTAIN SHOTOVER: They have had no dinner. Dont forget that.

HECTOR: Neither have I. And it is dark: it must be all hours.

MRS HUSHABYE: Oh, Guinness will produce some sort of dinner for them. The servants always take jolly good care that there is food in the house.

CAPTAIN SHOTOVER [*raising a strange wail in the darkness*]: What a house! What a daughter!

MRS HUSHABYE [*raving*]: What a father!

HECTOR [*following suit*]: What a husband!

CAPTAIN SHOTOVER: Is there no thunder in heaven?

HECTOR: Is there no beauty, no bravery, on earth?

MRS HUSHABYE: What do men want? They have their food, their firesides, their clothes mended, and our love at the end of the day. Why are they not satisfied? Why do they envy us the pain with which we bring them into the world, and make strange dangers and torments for themselves to be even with us?

CAPTAIN SHOTOVER [*weirdly chanting*]:

　　I built a house for my daughters, and opened the doors thereof,

That men might come for their choosing, and their betters spring from
    their love;
But one of them married a numskull;

HECTOR [*taking up the rhythm*]:
The other a liar wed;

MRS HUSHABYE [*completing the stanza*]:
And now must she lie beside him, even as she made her bed.

LADY UTTERWORD [*calling from the garden*]: Hesione! Hesione! Where are you?

HECTOR: The cat is on the tiles.

MRS HUSHABYE: Coming, darling, coming.

She goes quickly into the garden. The CAPTAIN *goes back to his place at the
table.*

HECTOR [*going into the hall*]: Shall I turn up the lights for you?

CAPTAIN SHOTOVER: No. Give me deeper darkness. Money is not made in the
    light.

ACT TWO

The same room, with the lights turned up and the curtains drawn. ELLIE *comes in, followed by* MANGAN. *Both are dressed for dinner. She strolls to the drawing-table. He comes between the table and the wicker chair.*

MANGAN: What a dinner! I dont call it a dinner: I call it a meal.

ELLIE: I am accustomed to meals, Mr Mangan, and very lucky to get them. Besides, the captain cooked some macaroni for me.

MANGAN [*shuddering liverishly*]: Too rich: I cant each such things. I suppose it's because I have to work so much with my brain. Thats the worst of being a man of business: you are always thinking, thinking. By the way, now that we are alone, may I take the opportunity to come to a little understanding with you?

ELLIE [*settling into the draughtsman's seat*]: Certainly. I should like to.

MANGAN [*taken aback*]: Should you? That surprises me; for I thought I noticed this afternoon that you avoided me all you could. Not for the first time either.

ELLIE: I was very tired and upset. I wasnt used to the ways of this extraordinary house. Please forgive me.

MANGAN: Oh, thats all right: I dont mind. But Captain Shotover has been talking to me about you. You and me, you know.

ELLIE [*interested*]: The Captain! What did he say?

MANGAN: Well, he noticed the difference between our ages.

ELLIE: He notices everything.

MANGAN: You dont mind, then?

ELLIE: Of course I know quite well that our engagement—

MANGAN: Oh! you call it an engagement.

ELLIE: Well, isnt it?

MANGAN: Oh, yes, yes: no doubt it is if you hold to it. This is the first time youve used the word; and I didnt quite know where we stood: thats all. [*He sits down in the wicker chair; and resigns himself to allow her to lead the conversation*]. You were saying—?

ELLIE: Was I? I forget. Tell me. Do you like this part of the country? I heard you ask Mr Hushabye at dinner whether there are any nice houses to let down here.

MANGAN: I like the place. The air suits me. I shouldnt be surprised if I settled down here.

ELLIE: Nothing would please me better. The air suits me too. And I want to be near Hesione.

MANGAN [*with growing uneasiness*]: The air may suit us; but the question is, should we suit one another? Have you thought about that?

ELLIE: Mr Mangan: we must be sensible, mustnt we? It's no use pretending that we are Romeo and Juliet. But we can get on very well together if we choose to make the best of it. Your kindness of heart will make it easy for me.

MANGAN [*leaning forward, with the beginning of something like deliberate unpleasantness in his voice*]: Kindness of heart, eh? I ruined your father, didnt I?

ELLIE: Oh, not intentionally.

MANGAN: Yes I did. Ruined him on purpose.

ELLIE: On purpose!

MANGAN: Not out of ill-nature, you know. And youll admit that I kept a job for him when I had finished with him. But business is business; and I ruined him as a matter of business.

ELLIE: I dont understand how that can be. Are you trying to make me feel that I need not be grateful to you, so that I may choose freely?

MANGAN [*rising aggressively*]: No. I mean what I say.

ELLIE: But how could it possibly do you any good to ruin my father? The money he lost was yours.

MANGAN [*with a sour laugh*]: Was mine! It is mine, Miss Ellie, and all the money the other fellows lost too. [*He shoves his hands into his pockets and shews his teeth*]. I just smoked them out like a hive of bees. What do you say to that? A bit of a shock, eh?

ELLIE: It would have been, this morning. Now! you cant think how little it matters. But it's quite interesting. Only you must explain it to me. I dont understand it. [*Propping her elbows on the drawing-board and her chin on her hands, she composes herself to listen with a combination of conscious curiosity with unconscious contempt which provokes him to more and more unpleasantness, and an attempt at patronage of her ignorance*].

MANGAN: Of course you dont understand: what do you know about business? You just listen and learn. Your father's business was a new business; and I dont start new businesses: I let other fellows start them. They put all their money and their friends' money into starting them. They wear out their souls and bodies trying to make a success of them. Theyre what you call enthusiasts. But the first dead lift of the thing is too much for them; and they havnt enough financial experience. In a year or so they have either to let the whole show go bust, or sell out to a new lot of fellows for a few deferred ordinary shares: that is, if theyre lucky enough to get anything at all. As likely as not the very same thing happens to the new lot. They put in more money and a couple of years more work; and then perhaps they have to sell out to a third lot. If it's really a big thing the third lot will have to sell out too, and leave their work and their money behind them. And thats where the real business man comes in: where I come in. But I'm cleverer than some: I dont mind dropping a little money to start the process. I took your father's measure. I saw that he had a sound idea, and that he would work himself silly for it if he got the chance. I saw that he was a child in business, and was dead certain to outrun his expenses and be in too great a hurry to wait for his market. I knew that the surest way to ruin a man who doesnt know how to handle money is to give him some. I explained my idea to some friends in the city, and they found the money; for I take no risks in ideas, even when theyre my own. Your father and the friends that ventured their money with him were no more to me than a heap of squeezed lemons. Youve been wasting your gratitude: my kind heart is all rot. I'm sick of it. When I see your father beaming at me with his moist, grateful eyes, regularly wallowing in gratitude, I sometimes feel I must tell him the truth or burst. What stops me is that I know he wouldnt believe me. He'd think it was my modesty, as you

did just now. He'd think anything rather than the truth, which is that he's a
blamed fool, and I am a man that knows how to take care of himself. [*He
throws himself back into the big chair with large self-approval*]. Now what do
you think of me, Miss Ellie?

ELLIE [*dropping her hands*]: How strange! that my mother, who knew nothing at
all about business, should have been quite right about you! She always
said—not before papa, of course, but to us children—that you were just that
sort of man.

MANGAN [*sitting up, much hurt*]: Oh! did she? And yet she'd have let you marry
me.

ELLIE: Well, you see, Mr Mangan, my mother married a very good man—for
whatever you may think of my father as a man of business, he is the soul of
goodness—and she is not at all keen on my doing the same.

MANGAN: Anyhow, you dont want to marry me now, do you?

ELLIE [*very calmly*]: Oh, I think so. Why not?

MANGAN [*rising aghast*]: Why not!

ELLIE: I dont see why we shouldnt get on very well together.

MANGAN: Well, but look here, you know—[*he stops, quite at a loss*].

ELLIE [*patiently*]: Well?

MANGAN: Well, I thought you were rather particular about people's characters.

ELLIE: If we women were particular about men's characters, we should never
get married at all, Mr Mangan.

MANGAN: A child like you talking of 'we women'! What next! Youre not in
earnest?

ELLIE: Yes I am. Arnt you?

MANGAN: You mean to hold me to it?

ELLIE: Do you wish to back out of it?

MANGAN: Oh no. Not exactly back out of it.

ELLIE: Well?

> *He has nothing to say. With a long whispered whistle, he drops into the wicker
> chair and stares before him like a beggared gambler. But a cunning look soon
> comes into his face. He leans over towards her on his right elbow, and speaks in
> a low steady voice.*

MANGAN: Suppose I told you I was in love with another woman!

ELLIE [*echoing him*]: Suppose I told you I was in love with another man!

MANGAN [*bouncing angrily out of his chair*]: I'm not joking.

ELLIE: Who told you *I* was?

MANGAN: I tell you I'm serious. Youre too young to be serious; but youll have to
believe me. I want to be near your friend Mrs Hushabye. I'm in love with
her. Now the murder's out.

ELLIE: I want to be near your friend Mr Hushabye. I'm in love with him. [*She
rises and adds with a frank air*] Now we are in one another's confidence, we
shall be real friends. Thank you for telling me.

MANGAN [*almost beside himself*]: Do you think I'll be made a convenience of like
this?

ELLIE: Come, Mr Mangan! you made a business convenience of my father.
Well, a woman's business is marriage. Why shouldnt I make a domestic
convenience of you?

MANGAN: Because I dont choose, see? Because I'm not a silly gull like your father. Thats why.

ELLIE [*with serene contempt*]: You are not good enough to clean my father's boots, Mr Mangan; and I am paying you a great compliment in condescending to make a convenience of you, as you call it. Of course you are free to throw over our engagement if you like; but, if you do, youll never enter Hesione's house again: I will take care of that.

MANGAN [*gasping*]: You little devil, youve done me [*On the point of collapsing into the big chair again he recovers himself*] Wait a bit, though: youre not so cute as you think. You cant beat Boss Mangan as easy as that. Suppose I go straight to Mrs Hushabye and tell her that youre in love with her husband.

ELLIE: She knows it.

MANGAN: You told her!!!

ELLIE: She told me.

MANGAN [*clutching at his bursting temples*]: Oh, this is a crazy house. Or else I'm going clean off my chump. Is she making a swop with you—she to have your husband and you to have hers?

ELLIE: Well, you dont want us both, do you?

MANGAN [*throwing himself into the chair distractedly*]: My brain wont stand it. My head's going to split. Help! Help me to hold it. Quick: hold it: squeeze it. Save me.

ELLIE *comes behind his chair; clasps his head hard for a moment; then begins to draw her hands from his forehead back to his ears.*

Thank you. [*Drowsily*] Thats very refreshing. [*Waking a little*] Dont you hypnotize me, though. Ive seen men made fools of by hypnotism.

ELLIE [*steadily*]: Be quiet. Ive see men made fools of without hypnotism.

MANGAN [*humbly*]: You dont dislike touching me, I hope. You never touched me before, I noticed.

ELLIE: Not since you fell in love naturally with a grown-up nice woman, who will never expect you to make love to her. And I will never expect him to make love to me.

MANGAN: He may, though.

ELLIE [*making her passes rhythmically*]: Hush. Go to sleep. Do you hear? You are to go to sleep, go to sleep, go to sleep; be quiet, deeply deeply quiet; sleep, sleep, sleep, sleep, sleep.

He falls asleep. ELLIE *steals away; turns the light out; and goes into the garden.* NURSE GUINNESS *opens the door and is seen in the light which comes in from the hall.*

GUINNESS [*speaking to someone outside*]: Mr Mangan's not here, ducky: theres no one here. It's all dark.

MRS HUSHABYE [*without*]: Try the garden. Mr Dunn and I will be in my boudoir. Shew him the way.

GUINNESS: Yes, ducky. [*She makes for the garden door in the dark; stumbles over the sleeping Mangan; and screams*] Ahoo! Oh Lord, sir! I beg your pardon, I'm sure: I didnt see you in the dark. Who is it? [*She goes back to the door and turns on the light*]. Oh, Mr Mangan, sir, I hope I havnt hurt you plumping into your lap like that. [*Coming to him*] I was looking for you, sir. Mrs Hushabye says will you please—[*noticing that he remains quite insensible*] Oh, my good Lord, I hope I havnt killed him. Sir! Mr Mangan! Sir! [*She shakes him; and he is rolling inertly off the chair on the floor when she holds him up and props him against the cushion*]. Miss Hessy! Miss Hessy! Quick, doty darling. Miss Hessy!

MRS HUSHABYE *comes in from the hall, followed by* MAZZINI DUNN

Oh, Miss Hessy, Ive been and killed him.

MAZZINI *runs round the back of the chair to* MANGAN'*s right hand, and sees that the nurse's words are apparently only too true.*

MAZZINI: What tempted you to commit such a crime, woman?

MRS HUSHABYE [*trying not to laugh*]: Do you mean you did it on purpose?

GUINNESS: Now is it likely I'd kill any man on purpose. I fell over him in the dark; and I'm a pretty tidy weight. He never spoke nor moved until I shook him; and then he would have dropped dead on the floor. Isnt it tiresome?

MRS HUSHABYE [*going past the nurse to* MANGAN'*s side, and inspecting him less credulously than* MAZZINI]: Nonsense! he is not dead: he is only asleep. I can see him breathing.

GUINNESS: But why wont he wake?

MAZZINI [*speaking very politely into* MANGAN'*s ear*]: Mangan! My dear Mangan! [*he blows into* MANGAN'*s ear*].

MRS HUSHABYE: Thats no good [*she shakes him vigorously*]. Mr Mangan: wake up. Do you hear?

He begins to roll over.

Oh! Nurse, nurse: he's falling: help me.

NURSE GUINNESS *rushes to the rescue. With* MAZZINI'*s assistance,* MANGAN *is propped safely up again.*

GUINNESS [*behind the chair; bending over to test the case with her nose*]: Would he be drunk, do you think, pet?

MRS HUSHABYE: Had he any of papa's rum?

MAZZINI: It cant be that: he is most abstemious. I am afraid he drank too much formerly, and has to drink too little now. You know, Mrs Hushabye, I really think he has been hypnotized.

GUINNESS: Hip no what, sir?

MAZZINI: One evening at home, after we had seen a hypnotizing performance, the children began playing at it; and Ellie stroked my head. I assure you I went off dead asleep; and they had to send for a professional to wake me up after I had slept eighteen hours. They had to carry me upstairs; and as the poor children were not very strong, they let me slip; and I rolled right down the whole flight and never woke up.

MRS HUSHABYE *splutters.*

Oh, you may laugh, Mrs Hushabye; but I might have been killed.

MRS HUSHABYE: I couldnt have helped laughing even if you had been, Mr Dunn.

So Ellie has hypnotized him. What fun!

MAZZINI: Oh no, no, no. It was such a terrible lesson to her: nothing would induce her to try such a thing again.

MRS HUSHABYE: Then who did it? *I* didn't.

MAZZINI: I thought perhaps the Captain might have done it unintentionally. He is so fearfully magnetic: I feel vibrations whenever he comes close to me.

GUINNESS: The Captain will get him out of it anyhow, sir: I'll back him for that. I'll go fetch him [*she makes for the pantry*].

MRS HUSHABYE: Wait a bit. [*To* MAZZINI] You say he is all right for eighteen hours?

MAZZINI: Well, *I* was asleep for eighteen hours.

MRS HUSHABYE: Were you any the worse for it?

MAZZINI: I dont quite remember. They had poured brandy down my throat, you see; and—

MRS HUSHABYE: Quite. Anyhow, you survived. Nurse, darling: go and ask Miss Dunn to come to us here. Say I want to speak to her particularly. You will find her with Mr Hushabye probably.

GUINNESS: I think not, ducky: Miss Addy is with him. But I'll find her and send her to you. [*She goes out into the garden*].

MRS HUSHABYE [*calling* MAZZINI'*s attention to the figure on the chair*]: Now, Mr Dunn, look. Just look. Look hard. Do you still intend to sacrifice your daughter to that thing?

MAZZINI [*troubled*]: You have completely upset me, Mrs Hushabye, by all you have said to me. That anyone could imagine that I—*I*, a consecrated soldier of freedom, if I may say so—could sacrifice Ellie to anybody or anyone, or that I should ever have dreamed of forcing her inclinations in any way, is a most painful blow to my—well, I suppose you would say to my good opinion of myself.

MRS HUSHABYE [*rather stolidly*]: Sorry.

MAZZINI [*looking forlornly at the body*]: What is your objection to poor Mangan, Mrs Hushabye? He looks all right to me. But then I am so accustomed to him.

MRS HUSHABYE: Have you no heart? Have you no sense? Look at the brute! Think of poor weak innocent Ellie in the clutches of this slavedriver, who spends his life making thousands of rough violent workmen bend to his will and sweat for him: a man accustomed to have great masses of iron beaten into shape for him by steam-hammers! to fight with women and girls over a halfpenny an hour ruthlessly! a captain of industry, I think you call him, dont you? Are you going to fling your delicate, sweet, helpless child into such a beast's claws just because he will keep her in an expensive house and make her wear diamonds to shew how rich he is?

MAZZINI [*staring at her in wide-eyed amazement*]: Bless you, dear Mrs Hushabye, what romantic ideas of business you have! Poor dear Mangan isnt a bit like that.

MRS HUSHABYE [*scornfully*]: Poor dear Mangan indeed!

MAZZINI: But he doesnt know anything about machinery. He never goes near the men: he couldnt manage them: he is afraid of them. I never can get him to take the least interest in the works: he hardly knows more about them than you do. People are cruelly unjust to Mangan: they think he is all rugged strength just because his manners are bad.

MRS HUSHABYE: Do you mean to tell me he isnt strong enough to crush poor little Ellie?

MAZZINI: Of course it's very hard to say how any marriage will turn out; but speaking for myself, I should say that he wont have a dog's chance against Ellie. You know, Ellie has remarkable strength of character. I think it is because I taught her to like Shakespear when she was very young.

MRS HUSHABYE [*contemptuously*]: Shakespear! The next thing you will tell me is that you could have made a great deal more money than Mangan. [*She retires to the sofa, and sits down at the port end of it in the worst of humors*].

MAZZINI [*following her and taking the other end*]: No: I'm no good at making money. I dont care enough for it, somehow. I'm not ambitious! that must be it. Mangan is wonderful about money: he thinks of nothing else. He is so dreadfully afraid of being poor. I am always thinking of other things: even at the works I think of the things we are doing and not of what they cost. And the worst of it is, poor Mangan doesnt know what to do with his money when he gets it. He is such a baby that he doesnt know even what to eat and drink: he has ruined his liver eating and drinking the wrong things; and now he can hardly eat at all. Ellie will diet him splendidly. You will be surprised when you come to know him better: he is really the most helpless of mortals. You get quite a protective feeling towards him.

MRS HUSHABYE: Then who manages his business, pray?

MAZZINI: I do. And of course other people like me.

MRS HUSHABYE: Footling people, you mean.

MAZZINI: I suppose youd think us so.

MRS HUSHABYE: And pray why dont you do without him if youre all so much cleverer?

MAZZINI: Oh, we couldnt: we should ruin the business in a year. I've tried; and I know. We should spend too much on everything. We should improve the quality of the goods and make them too dear. We should be sentimental about the hard cases among the workpeople. But Mangan keeps us in order. He is down on us about every extra halfpenny. We could never do without him. You see, he will sit up all night thinking of how to save sixpence. Wont Ellie make him jump, though, when she takes his house in hand!

MRS HUSHABYE: Then the creature is a fraud even as a captain of industry!

MAZZINI: I am afraid all the captains of industry are what you call frauds, Mrs Hushabye. Of course there are some manufacturers who really do understand their own works; but they dont make as high a rate of profit as Mangan does. I assure you Mangan is quite a good fellow in his way. He means well.

MRS HUSHABYE: He doesnt look well. He is not in his first youth, is he?

MAZZINI: After all, no husband is in his first youth for very long, Mrs Hushabye. And men cant afford to marry in their first youth nowadays.

MRS HUSHABYE: Now if *I* said that, it would sound witty. Why cant you say it wittily? What on earth is the matter with you? Why dont you inspire everybody with confidence? with respect?

MAZZINI [*humbly*]: I think that what is the matter with me is that I am poor. You dont know what that means at home. Mind: I dont say they have ever complained. Theyve all been wonderful: theyve been proud of my poverty. Theyve even joked about it quite often. But my wife has had a very poor time of it. She has been quite resigned—

MRS HUSHABYE [*shuddering involuntarily*]!!

MAZZINI: There! You see, Mrs Hushabye. I dont want Ellie to live on resignation.

MRS HUSHABYE: Do you want her to have to resign herself to living with a man she doesnt love?

MAZZINI [*wistfully*]: Are you sure that would be worse than living with a man she did love, if he was a footling person?

MRS HUSHABYE [*relaxing her contemptuous attitude, quite interested in* MAZZINI *now*]: You know, I really think you must love Ellie very much; for you become quite clever when you talk about her.

MAZZINI: I didnt know I was so very stupid on other subjects.

MRS HUSHABYE: You are, sometimes.

MAZZINI [*turning his head away; for his eyes are wet*]: I have learnt a good deal about myself from you, Mrs Hushabye; and I'm afraid I shall not be the happier for your plain speaking. But if you thought I needed it to make me think of Ellie's happiness you were very much mistaken.

MRS HUSHABYE [*leaning towards him kindly*]: Have I been a beast?

MAZZINI [*pulling himself together*]: It doesnt matter about me, Mrs Hushabye. I think you like Ellie; and that is enough for me.

MRS HUSHABYE: I'm beginning to like you a little. I perfectly loathed you at first. I thought you the most odious, self-satisfied, boresome elderly prig I ever met.

MAZZINI [*resigned, and now quite cheerful*]: I daresay I am all that. I never have been a favorite with gorgeous women like you. They always frighten me.

MRS HUSHABYE [*pleased*]: Am I a gorgeous woman, Mazzini? I shall fall in love with you presently.

MAZZINI [*with placid gallantry*]: No you wont, Hesione. But you would be quite safe. Would you believe it that quite a lot of women have flirted with me because I am quite safe? But they get tired of me for the same reason.

MRS HUSHABYE [*mischievously*]: Take care. You may not be so safe as you think.

MAZZINI: Oh yes, quite safe. You see, I have been in love really: the sort of love that only happens once. [*Softly*] Thats why Ellie is such a lovely girl.

MRS HUSHABYE: Well, really, you are coming out. Are you quite sure you wont let me tempt you into a second grand passion?

MAZZINI: Quite. It wouldnt be natural. The fact is, you dont strike on my box, Mrs Hushabye; and I certainly dont strike on yours.

MRS HUSHABYE: I see. Your marriage was a safety match.

MAZZINI: What a very witty application of the expression I used! I should never have thought of it.

ELLIE *comes in from the garden, looking anything but happy.*

MRS HUSHABYE [*rising*]: Oh! here is Ellie at last. [*She goes behind the sofa*].

ELLIE [*on the threshold of the starboard door*]: Guinness said you wanted me: you and papa.

MRS HUSHABYE: You have kept us waiting so long that it almost came to—well, never mind. Your father is a very wonderful man [*she ruffles his hair affectionately*]: the only one I ever met who could resist me when I made myself really agreeable. [*She comes to the big chair, on* MANGAN'*s left*]. Come here. I have something to shew you.

ELLIE *strolls listlessly to the other side of the chair.*

Look.

ELLIE [*contemplating* MANGAN *without interest*]: I know. He is only asleep. We had a talk after dinner; and he fell asleep in the middle of it.

MRS HUSHABYE: You did it, Ellie. You put him asleep.

MAZZINI [*rising quickly and coming to the back of the chair*]: Oh, I hope not. Did you, Ellie?

ELLIE [*wearily*]: He asked me to.

MAZZINI: But its dangerous. You know what happened to me.

ELLIE [*utterly indifferent*]: Oh, I daresay I can wake him. If not, somebody else can.

MRS HUSHABYE: It doesnt matter, anyhow, because I have at last persuaded your father that you dont want to marry him.

ELLIE [*suddenly coming out of her listlessness, much vexed*]: But why did you do that, Hesione? I do want to marry him. I fully intend to marry him.

MAZZINI: Are you quite sure, Ellie? Mrs Hushabye has made me feel that I may have been thoughtless and selfish about it.

ELLIE [*very clearly and steadily*]: Papa. When Mrs Hushabye takes it on herself to explain to you what I think or dont think, shut your ears tight; and shut your eyes too. Hesione knows nothing about me: she hasnt the least notion of the sort of person I am, and never will. I promise you I wont do anything I dont want to do and mean to do for my own sake.

MAZZINI: You are quite, quite sure?

ELLIE: Quite, quite sure. Now you must go away and leave me to talk to Mrs Hushabye.

MAZZINI: But I should like to hear. Shall I be in the way?

ELLIE [*inexorable*]: I had rather talk to her alone.

MAZZINI [*affectionately*]: Oh, well, I know what a nuisance parents are, dear. I will be good and go. [*He goes to the garden door*]. By the way, do you remember the address of that professional who woke me up? Dont you think I had better telegraph to him.

MRS HUSHABYE [*moving towards the sofa*]: It's too late to telegraph tonight.

MAZZINI: I suppose so. I do hope he'll wake up in the course of the night. [*He goes out into the garden*].

ELLIE [*turning vigorously on* HESIONE *the moment her father is out of the room*]: Hesione: what the devil do you mean by making mischief with my father about Mangan?

MRS HUSHABYE [*promptly losing her temper*]: Dont you dare speak to me like that, you little minx. Remember that you are in my house.

ELLIE: Stuff! Why dont you mind your own business? What is it to you whether I choose to marry Mangan or not?

MRS HUSHABYE: Do you suppose you can bully me, you miserable little matrimonial adventurer?

ELLIE: Every woman who hasnt any money is a matrimonial adventurer. It's easy for you to talk: you have never known what it is to want money; and you can pick up men as if they were daisies. I am poor and respectable—

MRS HUSHABYE [*interrupting*]: Ho! respectable! How did you pick up Mangan? How did you pick up my husband? You have the audacity to tell me that I am a—a—a—

ELLIE: A siren. So you are. You were born to lead men by the nose: if you werent, Marcus would have waited for me, perhaps.

MRS HUSHABYE [*suddenly melting and half laughing*]: Oh, my poor Ellie, my pettikins, my unhappy darling! I am so sorry about Hector. But what can I do? It's not my fault: I'd give him to you if I could.

ELLIE: I dont blame you for that.

MRS HUSHABYE: What a brute I was to quarrel with you and call you names! Do kiss me and say youre not angry with me.

ELLIE [*fiercely*]: Oh, dont slop and gush and be sentimental. Dont you see that unless I can be hard—as hard as nails—I shall go mad. I dont care a damn about your calling me names: do you think a woman in my situation can feel a few hard words?

MRS HUSHABYE: Poor little woman! Poor little situation!

ELLIE: I suppose you think youre being sympathetic. You are just foolish and stupid and selfish. You see me getting a smasher right in the face that kills a whole part of my life: the best part that can never come again; and you think you can help me over it by a little coaxing and kissing. When I want all the strength I can get to lean on: something iron, something stony, I dont care how cruel it is, you go all mushy and want to slobber over me. I'm not angry; I'm not unfriendly; but for God's sake do pull yourself together; and dont think that because youre on velvet and always have been, women who are in hell can take it as easily as you.

MRS HUSHABYE [*shrugging her shoulders*]: Very well. [*She sits down on the sofa in her old place*]. But I warn you that when I am neither coaxing and kissing nor laughing, I am just wondering how much longer I can stand living in this cruel, damnable world. You object to the siren: well, I drop the siren. You want to rest your wounded bosom against a grindstone. Well [*folding her arms*], here is the grindstone.

ELLIE [*sitting down beside her, appeased*]: Thats better: you really have the trick of falling in with everyone's mood; but you dont understand, because you are not the sort of woman for whom there is only one man and only one chance.

MRS HUSHABYE: I certainly dont understand how your marrying that object [*indicating* MANGAN] will console you for not being able to marry Hector.

ELLIE: Perhaps you dont understand why I was quite a nice girl this morning, and am now neither a girl nor particularly nice.

MRS HUSHABYE: Oh yes I do. It's because you have made up your mind to do something despicable and wicked.

ELLIE: I dont think so, Hesione. I must make the best of my ruined house.

MRS HUSHABYE: Pooh! Youll get over it. Your house isnt ruined.

ELLIE: Of course I shall get over it. You dont suppose I'm going to sit down and die of a broken heart, I hope, or be an old maid living on a pittance from the Sick and Indigent Roomkeepers' Association. But my heart is broken, all the same. What I mean by that is that I know that what has happened to me with Marcus will not happen to me ever again. In the world for me there is Marcus and a lot of other men of whom one is just the same as another. Well, if I cant have love, thats no reason why I should have poverty. If Mangan has nothing else, he has money.

MRS HUSHABYE: And are there no young men with money?

ELLIE: Not within my reach. Besides, a young man would have the right to expect love from me, and would perhaps leave me when he found I could not give it to him. Rich young men can get rid of their wives, you know, pretty cheaply. But this object, as you call him, can expect nothing more from me than I am prepared to give him.

MRS HUSHABYE: He will be your owner, remember. If he buys you, he will make the bargain pay him and not you. Ask your father.

ELLIE [*rising and strolling to the chair to contemplate their subject*]: You need not trouble on that score, Hesione. I have more to give Boss Mangan than he has to give me: it is I who am buying him, and at a pretty good price too, I think. Women are better at that sort of bargain than men. I have taken the Boss's measure; and ten Boss Mangans shall not prevent me doing far more as I please as his wife than I have ever been able to do as a poor girl. [*Stooping to the recumbent figure*] Shall they, Boss? I think not. [*She passes on to the drawing-table, and leans against the end of it, facing the windows*]. I shall not have to spend most of my time wondering how long my gloves will last, anyhow.

MRS HUSHABYE [*rising superbly*]: Ellie: you are a wicked sordid little beast. And to think that I actually condescended to fascinate that creature there to save you from him! Well, let me tell you this: if you make this disgusting match, you will never see Hector again if I can help it.

ELLIE [*unmoved*]: I nailed Mangan by telling him that if he did not marry me he should never see you again [*she lifts herself on her wrists and seats herself on the end of the table*].

MRS HUSHABYE [*recoiling*]: Oh!

ELLIE: So you see I am not unprepared for your playing that trump against me. Well, you just try it: thats all. I should have made a man of Marcus, not a household pet.

MRS HUSHABYE [*flaming*]: You dare!

ELLIE [*looking almost dangerous*]: Set him thinking about me if you dare.

MRS HUSHABYE: Well, of all the impudent little fiends I ever met! Hector says there is a certain point at which the only answer you can give to a man who breaks all the rules is to knock him down. What would you say if I were to box your ears?

ELLIE [*calmly*]: I should pull your hair.

MRS HUSHABYE [*mischievously*]: That wouldnt hurt me. Perhaps it comes off at night.

ELLIE [*so taken aback that she drops off the table and runs to her*]: Oh, you dont mean to say, Hesione, that your beautiful black hair is false?

MRS HUSHABYE [*patting it*]: Dont tell Hector. He believes in it.

ELLIE [*groaning*]: Oh! Even the hair that ensnared him false! Everything false!

MRS HUSHABYE: Pull it and try. Other women can snare men in their hair; but I can swing a baby on mine. Aha! you cant do that, Goldylocks.

ELLIE [*heartbroken*]: No. You have stolen my babies.

MRS HUSHABYE: Pettikins: dont make cry. You know, what you said about my making a household pet of him is a little true. Perhaps he ought to have waited for you. Would any other woman on earth forgive you?

ELLIE: Oh, what right had you to take him all for yourself! [*Pulling herself together*] There! You couldn't help it: neither of us could help it. He couldnt help it. No: dont say anything more: I cant bear it. Let us wake the object. [*She begins stroking* MANGAN*'s head, reversing the movement with which she put him to sleep*]. Wake up, do you hear? You are to wake up at once. Wake up, wake up, wake—

MANGAN [*bouncing out of the chair in a fury and turning on them*]: Wake up! So you think Ive been asleep, do you? [*He kicks the chair violently out of his way, and gets between them*]. You throw me into a trance so that I cant move hand or foot–I might have been buried alive! it's a mercy I wasnt–and then you think I was only asleep. If youd let me drop the two times you rolled me about, my nose would have been flattened for life against the floor. But Ive found you all out, anyhow. I know the sort of people I'm among now. Ive heard every word youve said, you and your precious father, and [*to* MRS HUSHABYE] you too. So I'm an object, am I? I'm a thing, am I? I'm a fool that hasnt sense enough to feed myself properly, am I? I'm afraid of the men that would starve if it werent for the wages I give them, am I? I'm nothing but a disgusting old skinflint to be made a convenience of by designing women and fool managers of my works, am I? I'm—

MRS HUSHABYE [*with the most elegant aplomb*]: Sh-sh-sh-sh-sh! Mr Mangan: you are bound in honor to obliterate from your mind all you heard while you were pretending to be asleep. It was not meant for you to hear.

MANGAN: Pretending to be asleep! Do you think if I was only pretending that I'd have sprawled there helpless, and listened to such unfairness, such lies, such injustice and plotting and backbiting and slandering of me, if I could have up and told you what I thought of you! I wonder I didnt burst.

MRS HUSHABYE [*sweetly*]: You dreamt it all, Mr Mangan. We were only saying how beautifully peaceful you looked in your sleep. That was all, wasnt it, Ellie? Believe me, Mr Mangan, all those unpleasant things came into your mind in the last half second before you woke. Ellie rubbed your hair the wrong way; and the disagreeable sensation suggested a disagreeable dream.

MANGAN [*doggedly*]: I believe in dreams.

MRS HUSHABYE: So do I. But they go by contraries, dont they?

MANGAN [*depths of emotion suddenly welling up in him*]: I shant forget, to my dying day, that when you gave me the glad eye that time in the garden, you were making a fool of me. That was a dirty low mean thing to do. You had no right to let me come near you if I disgusted you. It isnt my fault if I'm old and havnt a moustache like a bronze candlestick as your husband has. There are things no decent woman would do to a man–like a man hitting a woman in the breast.

> HESIONE, *utterly shamed, sits down on the sofa and covers her face with her hands.* MANGAN *sits down also on his chair and begins to cry like a child.* ELLIE *stares at them.* MRS HUSHABYE, *at the distressing sound he makes, takes down her hands and looks at him. She rises and runs to him.*

MRS HUSHABYE: Dont cry: I cant bear it. Have I broken your heart? I didnt know you had one. How could I?

MANGAN: I'm a man aint I?

MRS HUSHABYE [*half coaxing, half rallying, altogether tenderly*]: Oh no: not what I call a man. Only a Boss: just that and nothing else. What business has a Boss with a heart?

MANGAN: Then youre not a bit sorry for what you did, nor ashamed?

MRS HUSHABYE: I was ashamed for the first time in my life when you said that about hitting a woman in the breast, and I found out what I'd done. My very bones blushed red. Youve had your revenge, Boss. Arnt you satisfied?

MANGAN: Serve you right! Do you hear? Serve you right! Youre just cruel. Cruel.

MRS HUSHABYE: Yes: cruelty would be delicious if one could only find some sort of cruelty that didnt really hurt. By the way [*sitting down beside him on the arm of the chair*], whats your name? It's not really Boss, is it?

MANGAN [*shortly*]: If you want to know, my name's Alfred

MRS HUSHABYE [*springing up*]: Alfred!! Ellie: he was christened after Tennyson!!!

MANGAN [*rising*]: I was christened after my uncle, and never had a penny from him, damn him! What of it?

MRS HUSHABYE: It comes to me suddenly that you are a real person: that you had a mother, like anyone else. [*Putting her hands on his shoulder and surveying him*] Little Alf!

MANGAN: Well, you have a nerve.

MRS HUSHABYE: And you have a heart, Alfy, a whimpering little heart, but a real one. [*Releasing him suddenly*] Now run and make it up with Ellie. She has had time to think what to say to you, which is more than I had [*she goes out quickly into the garden by the port door*].

MANGAN: That woman has a pair of hands that go right through you.

ELLIE: Still in love with her, in spite of all we said about you?

MANGAN: Are all women like you two? Do they never think of anything about a man except what they can get out of him? You werent even thinking that about me. You were only thinking whether your gloves would last.

ELLIE: I shall not have to think about that when we are married.

MANGAN: And you think I am going to marry you after what I heard there!

ELLIE: You heard nothing from me that I did not tell you before.

MANGAN: Perhaps you think I cant do without you.

ELLIE: I think you would feel lonely without us all now, after coming to know us so well.

MANGAN [*with something like a yell of despair*]: Am I never to have the last word?

CAPTAIN SHOTOVER [*appearing at the starboard garden door*]: There is a soul in torment here. What is the matter?

MANGAN: This girl doesnt want to spend her life wondering how long her gloves will last.

CAPTAIN SHOTOVER [*passing through*]: Dont wear any. I never do [*he goes into the pantry*].

LADY UTTERWORD [*appearing at the port garden door, in a handsome dinner dress*]: Is anything the matter?

ELLIE: This gentleman wants to know is he never to have the last word?

LADY UTTERWORD [*coming forward to the sofa*]: I should let him have it, my dear. The important thing is not to have the last word, but to have your own way.

MANGAN: She wants both.

LADY UTTERWORD: She wont get them, Mr Mangan. Providence always has the last word.

MANGAN [*desperately*]: Now you are going to come religion over me. In this house a man's mind might as well be a football. I'm going.

He makes for the hall, but is stopped by a hail from the CAPTAIN, *who has just emerged from his pantry.*

CAPTAIN SHOTOVER: Whither away, Boss Mangan?

MANGAN: To hell out of this house: let that be enough for you and all here.

CAPTAIN SHOTOVER: You were welcome to come: you are free to go. The wide earth, the high seas, the spacious skies are waiting for you outside.

LADY UTTERWORD: But your things, Mr Mangan. Your bags, your comb and brushes, your pyjamas—

HECTOR [*who has just appeared in the port doorway in a handsome Arab costume*]: Why should the escaping slave take his chains with him?

MANGAN: Thats right, Hushabye. Keep the pyjamas, my lady; and much good may they do you.

HECTOR [*advancing to* LADY UTTERWORD'*s left hand*]: Let us all go out into the night and leave everything behind us.

MANGAN: You stay where you are, the lot of you. I want no company, especially female company.

ELLIE: Let him go. He is unhappy here. He is angry with us.

CAPTAIN SHOTOVER: Go, Boss Mangan; and when you have found the land where there is happiness and where there are no women, send me its latitude and longitude; and I will join you there.

LADY UTTERWORD: You will certainly not be comfortable without your luggage, Mr Mangan.

ELLIE [*impatient*]: Go, go: why dont you go? It is a heavenly night: you can sleep on the heath. Take my waterproof to lie on: it is hanging up in the hall.

HECTOR: Breakfast at nine, unless you prefer to breakfast with the Captain at six.

ELLIE: Good night, Alfred.

HECTOR: Alfred! [*He runs back to the door and calls into the garden*] Randall: Mangan's Christian name is Alfred.

RANDALL [*appearing in the starboard doorway in evening dress*]: Then Hesione wins her bet.

MRS HUSHABYE *appears in the port doorway. She throws her left arm round* HECTOR'*s neck; draws him with her to the back of the sofa; and throws her right arm round* LADY UTTERWORD'*s neck.*

MRS HUSHABYE: They wouldnt believe me, Alf.

They contemplate him.

MANGAN: Is there any more of you coming in to look at me, as if I was the latest thing in a menagerie.

MRS HUSHABYE: You are the latest thing in this menagerie.

Before MANGAN *can retort, a fall of furniture is heard from upstairs; then a pistol shot, and a yell of pain. The staring group breaks up in consternation.*

MAZZINI'S VOICE [*from above*]: Help! A burglar! Help!

HECTOR [*his eyes blazing*]: A burglar!!!

MRS HUSHABYE: No, Hector, youll be shot.

But it is too late: he has dashed out past MANGAN, *who hastily moves towards the bookshelves out of his way.*

CAPTAIN SHOTOVER [*blowing his whistle*]: All hands aloft! [*He strides out after* HECTOR].

LADY UTTERWORD: My diamonds! [*She follows the* CAPTAIN].

RANDALL [*rushing after her*]: No, Ariadne. Let me.

ELLIE: Oh, is papa shot? [*she runs out*].

MRS HUSHABYE: Are you frightened, Alf?

MANGAN: No. It aint my house, thank God.

MRS HUSHABYE: If they catch a burglar, shall we have to go into court as witnesses, and be asked all sorts of questions about our private lives?

MANGAN: You wont be believed if you tell the truth.

> MAZZINI, *terribly upset, with a duelling pistol in his hand, comes from the hall, and makes his way to the drawing-table.*

MAZZINI: Oh, my dear Mrs Hushabye, I might have killed him [*He throws the pistol on the table and staggers round to the chair*]. I hope you wont believe I really intended to.

> HECTOR *comes in, marching an old and villainous looking man before him by the collar. He plants him in the middle of the room and releases him.* ELLIE *follows, and immediately runs across to the back of her father's chair, and pats his shoulders.*

RANDALL [*entering with a poker*]: Keep your eye on this door, Mangan. I'll look after the other.

> *He goes to the starboard door and stands on guard there.* LADY UTTERWORD *comes in after* RANDALL, *and goes between* MRS HUSHABYE *and* MANGAN. NURSE GUINNESS *brings up the rear, and waits near the door, on* MANGAN's *left.*

MRS HUSHABYE: What has happened?

MAZZINI: Your housekeeper told me there was somebody upstairs, and gave me a pistol that Mr Hushabye had been practising with. I thought it would frighten him; but it went off at a touch.

THE BURGLAR: Yes, and took the skin off my ear. Precious near took the top off my head. Why dont you have a proper revolver instead of a thing like that, that goes off if you as much as blow on it?

HECTOR: One of my duelling pistols. Sorry.

MAZZINI: He put his hands up and said it was a fair cop.

THE BURGLAR: So it was. Send for the police.

HECTOR: No, by thunder! It was not a fair cop. We were four to one.

MRS HUSHABYE: What will they do to him?

THE BURGLAR: Ten years. Beginning with solitary. Ten years off my life. I shant serve it all: I'm too old. It will see me out.

LADY UTTERWORD: You should have thought of that before you stole my diamonds.

THE BURGLAR: Well, youve got them back, lady: havnt you? Can you give me back the years of my life you are going to take from me?

MRS HUSHABYE: Oh, we cant bury a man alive for ten years for a few diamonds.

THE BURGLAR: Ten little shining diamonds! Ten long black years!

LADY UTTERWORD: Think of what it is for us to be dragged through the horrors of a criminal court, and have all our family affairs in the papers! If you were a native, and Hastings could order you a good beating and send you away, I shouldnt mind; but here in England there is no real protection for any respectable person.

THE BURGLAR: I'm too old to be giv a hiding, lady. Send for the police and have done with it. It's only just and right you should.

RANDALL [*who has relaxed his vigilance on seeing the burglar so pacifically disposed, and comes forward swinging the poker between his fingers like a well-folded umbrella*]: It is neither just nor right that we should be put to a lot of inconvenience to gratify your moral enthusiasm, my friend. You had better get out, while you have the chance.

THE BURGLAR [*inexorably*]: No. I must work my sin off my conscience. This has come as a sort of call to me. Let me spend the rest of my life repenting in a cell. I shall have my reward above.

MANGAN [*exasperated*]: The very burglars cant behave naturally in this house.

HECTOR: My good sir: you must work out your salvation at somebody else's expense. Nobody here is going to charge you.

THE BURGLAR: Oh, you wont charge me, wont you?

HECTOR: No. I'm sorry to be inhospitable; but will you kindly leave the house?

THE BURGLAR: Right. I'll go the the police station and give myself up.

He turns resolutely to the door; but HECTOR *stops him.*

HECTOR:		Oh no. You mustnt do that.
RANDALL:	}	No, no. Clear out, man, cant you; and dont be a fool.
MRS HUSHABYE:		Dont be so silly. Cant you repent at home?

LADY UTTERWORD: You will have to do as you are told.

THE BURGLAR: It's compounding a felony, you know.

MRS HUSHABYE: This is utterly ridiculous. Are we to be forced to prosecute this man when we dont want to?

THE BURGLAR: Am I to be robbed of my salvation to save you the trouble of spending a day at the sessions? Is that justice? Is it right? Is it fair to me?

MAZZINI [*rising and leaning across the table persuasively as if it were a pulpit desk or a shop counter*]: Come, come! let me shew you how you can turn your crimes to account. Why not set up as a locksmith? You must know more about locks than most honest men?

THE BURGLAR: Thats true, sir. But I couldnt set up as a locksmith under twenty pounds.

RANDALL: Well, you can easily steal twenty pounds. You will find it in the nearest bank.

THE BURGLAR [*horrified*]: Oh what a thing for a gentleman to put into the head of a poor criminal scrambling out of the bottomless pit as it were! Oh, shame on you, sir! Oh, God forgive you! [*He throws himself into the big chair and covers his face as if in prayer*].

LADY UTTERWORD: Really, Randall!

HECTOR: It seems to me that we shall have to take up a collection for this inopportunely contrite sinner.

LADY UTTERWORD: But twenty pounds is ridiculous.

THE BURGLAR [*looking up quickly*]: I shall have to buy a lot of tools, lady.

LADY UTTERWORD: Nonsense: you have your burgling kit.

THE BURGLAR: Whats a jemmy and a centrebit and an acetylene welding plant and a bunch of skeleton keys? I shall want a forge, and a smithy, and a shop, and fittings. I cant hardly do it for twenty.

HECTOR: My worthy friend, we havnt got twenty pounds.

THE BURGLAR [*now master of the situation*]: You can raise it among you, cant you?

MRS HUSHABYE: Give him a sovereign, Hector; and get rid of him.

HECTOR [*giving him a pound*]: There! Off with you.

THE BURGLAR [*rising and taking the money very ungratefully*]: I wont promise nothing. You have more on you than a quid: all the lot of you, I mean.

LADY UTTERWORD [*vigorously*]: Oh, let us prosecute him and have done with it. I have a conscience too, I hope; and I do not feel at all sure that we have any right to let him go, especially if he is going to be greedy and impertinent.

THE BURGLAR [*quickly*]: All right, lady, all right. I've no wish to be anything but agreeable. Good evening, ladies and gentlemen; and thank you kindly.

> *He is hurrying out when he is confronted in the doorway by* CAPTAIN SHOTOVER.

CAPTAIN SHOTOVER [*fixing the burglar with a piercing regard*]: What's this? Are there two of you?

THE BURGLAR [*falling on his knees before the* CAPTAIN *in abject terror*]: Oh my good Lord, what have I done? Dont tell me it's your house Ive broken into, Captain Shotover.

> *The* CAPTAIN *seizes him by the collar; drags him to his feet; and leads him to the middle of the group,* HECTOR *falling back beside his wife to make way for them.*

CAPTAIN SHOTOVER [*turning him towards* ELLIE]: Is that your daughter? [*He releases him*].

THE BURGLAR: Well, how do I know, Captain? You know the sort of life you and me has led. Any young lady of that age might be my daughter anywhere in the wide world, as you might say.

CAPTAIN SHOTOVER [*to* MAZZINI]: You are not Billy Dunn. This is Billy Dunn. Why have you imposed on me?

THE BURGLAR [*indignantly to* MAZZINI]: Have you been giving yourself out to be me? You, that nigh blew my head off! Shooting yourself, in a manner of speaking!

MAZZINI: My dear Captain Shotover, ever since I came into this house I have done hardly anything else but assure you that I am not Mr William Dunn, but Mazzini Dunn, a very different person.

THE BURGLAR: He dont belong to my branch, Captain. Theres two sets in the family: the thinking Dunns and the drinking Dunns, each going their own ways. I'm a drinking Dunn: he's a thinking Dunn. But that didnt give him any right to shoot me.

CAPTAIN SHOTOVER: So youve turned burglar, have you?

THE BURGLAR: No, Captain: I wouldnt disgrace our old sea calling by such a thing. I am no burglar.

LADY UTTERWORD: What were you doing with my diamonds?

GUINNESS: What did you break into the house for if youre no burglar?

RANDALL: Mistook the house for your own and came in by the wrong window, eh?

THE BURGLAR: Well, it's no use my telling you a lie: I can take in most captains, but not Captain Shotover, because he sold himself to the devil in Zanzibar, and can divine water, spot gold, explode a cartridge in your pocket with a glance of his eye, and see the truth hidden in the heart of man. But I'm no burglar.

CAPTAIN SHOTOVER: Are you an honest man?

THE BURGLAR: I dont set up to be better than my fellow-creatures, and never did, as you well know, Captain. But what I do is innocent and pious. I enquire about for houses where the right sort of people live. I work it on them same as I worked it here. I break into the house; put a few spoons or diamonds in my pocket; make a noise; get caught; and take up a collection. And you wouldnt believe how hard it is to get caught when youre actually trying to. I have knocked over all the chairs in a room without a soul paying any attention to me. In the end I have had to walk out and leave the job.

RANDALL: When that happens, do you put back the spoons and diamonds?

THE BURGLAR: Well, I dont fly in the face of Providence, if thats what you want to know.

CAPTAIN SHOTOVER: Guinness: you remember this man?

GUINNESS: I should think I do, seeing I was married to him, the blackguard!

HESIONE: ⎱ *exclaiming* ⎰ Married to him!
LADY UTTERWORD: ⎰ *together* ⎱ Guinness!!

THE BURGLAR: It wasnt legal. Ive been married to no end of women. No use coming that over me.

CAPTAIN SHOTOVER: Take him to the forecastle [*he flings him to the door with a strength beyond his years*].

GUINNESS: I suppose you mean the kitchen. They wont have him there. Do you expect servants to keep company with thieves and all sorts?

CAPTAIN SHOTOVER: Land-thieves and water-thieves are the same flesh and blood. I'll have no boatswain on my quarter-deck. Off with you both.

THE BURGLAR: Yes, Captain. [*He goes out humbly*].

MAZZINI: Will it be safe to have him in the house like that?

GUINNESS: Why didnt you shoot him, sir? If I'd known who he was, I'd have shot him myself. [*She goes out*].

MRS HUSHABYE: Do sit down, everybody.

She sits down on the sofa. They all move except ELLIE. MAZZINI *resumes his seat.* RANDALL *sits down in the window seat near the starboard door, again making a pendulum of his poker, and studying it as Galileo might have done.* HECTOR *sits on his left, in the middle.* MANGAN, *forgotten, sits in the port corner.* LADY UTTERWORD *takes the big chair.* CAPTAIN SHOTOVER *goes into the pantry in deep abstraction. They all look after him; and* LADY UTTERWORD *coughs unconsciously.*

So Billy Dunn was poor nurse's little romance. I knew there had been somebody.

RANDALL: They will fight their battles over again and enjoy themselves immensely.

LADY UTTERWORD [*irritably*]: You are not married; and you know nothing about it, Randall. Hold your tongue.

RANDALL: Tyrant!

MRS HUSHABYE: Well, we have had a very exciting evening. Everything will be an anticlimax after it. We'd better all go to bed.

RANDALL: Another burglar may turn up.

MAZZINI: Oh, impossible! I hope not.

RANDALL: Why not? There is more than one burglar in England.

MRS HUSHABYE: What do you say, Alf?

MANGAN [*huffily*]: Oh, I dont matter. I'm forgotten. The burglar has put my nose out of joint. Shove me into a corner and have done with me.

MRS HUSHABYE [*jumping up mischievously, and going to him*]: Would you like a walk on the heath, Alfred? With me?

ELLIE: Go, Mr Mangan. It will do you good. Hesione will soothe you.

MRS HUSHABYE [*slipping her arm under his and pulling him upright*]: Come, Alfred. There is a moon: it's like the night in Tristan and Isolde. [*She caresses his arm and draws him to the port garden door*].

MANGAN [*writhing but yielding*]: How you can have the face—the heart—[*he breaks down and is heard sobbing as she takes him out.*]

LADY UTTERWORD: What an extraordinary way to behave! What is the matter with the man?

ELLIE [*in a strangely calm voice, staring into an imaginary distance*]: His heart is breaking: that is all.

> *The* CAPTAIN *appears at the pantry door, listening*

It is a curious sensation: the sort of pain that goes mercifully beyond our powers of feeling. When your heart is broken, your boats are burned: nothing matters any more. It is the end of happiness and the beginning of peace.

LADY UTTERWORD [*suddenly rising in a rage, to the astonishment of the rest*]: How dare you?

HECTOR: Good heavens! Whats the matter?

RANDALL [*in a warning whisper*]: Tch—tch—tch! Steady!

ELLIE [*surprised and haughty*]: I was not addressing you particularly, Lady Utterword. And I am not accustomed to be asked how dare I.

LADY UTTERWORD: Of course not. Anyone can see how badly you have been brought up.

MAZZINI: Oh, I hope not, Lady Utterword. Really!

LADY UTTERWORD: I know very well what you meant. The impudence!

ELLIE: What on earth do you mean?

CAPTAIN SHOTOVER [*advancing to the table*]: She means that her heart will not break. She has been longing all her life for someone to break it. At last she has become afraid she has none to break.

LADY UTTERWORD [*flinging herself on her knees and throwing her arms round him*]: Papa: dont say you think Ive no heart.

CAPTAIN SHOTOVER [*raising her with grim tenderness*]: If you had no heart how could you want to have it broken, child?

HECTOR [*rising with a bound*]: Lady Utterword: you are not to be trusted. You have made a scene [*he runs out into the garden through the starboard door*].

LADY UTTERWORD: Oh! Hector, Hector! [*she runs out after him*].

RANDALL: Only nerves, I assure you. [*He rises and follows her, waving the poker in his agitation*] Ariadne! Ariadne! For God's sake be careful. You will—[*he is gone*].

MAZZINI [*rising*]: How distressing! Can I do anything, I wonder?

CAPTAIN SHOTOVER [*promptly taking his chair and setting to work at the drawing-board*]: No. Go to bed. Goodnight.

MAZZINI [*bewildered*]: Oh! Perhaps you are right.

ELLIE: Goodnight, dearest. [*She kisses him*].

MAZZINI: Goodnight, love. [*He makes for the door, but turns aside to the bookshelves*]. I'll just take a book [*he takes one*]. Goodnight.

He goes out, leaving ELLIE *alone with the* CAPTAIN. *The* CAPTAIN *is intent on his drawing.* ELLIE, *standing sentry over his chair, contemplates him for a moment.*

ELLIE: Does nothing ever disturb you, Captain Shotover?

CAPTAIN SHOTOVER: Ive stood on the bridge for eighteen hours in a typhoon. Life here is stormier; but I can stand it.

ELLIE: Do you think I ought to marry Mr Mangan?

CAPTAIN SHOTOVER [*never looking up*]: One rock is as good as another to be wrecked on.

ELLIE: I am not in love with him.

CAPTAIN SHOTOVER: Who said you were?

ELLIE: You are not surprised?

CAPTAIN SHOTOVER: Surprised! At my age!

ELLIE: It seems to me quite fair. He wants me for one thing: I want him for another.

CAPTAIN SHOTOVER: Money?

ELLIE [*wearily, leaving him and beginning to wander restlessly about the room*]: I'm sorry, Captain Shotover; but it's no use talking like that to me. Old-fashioned people are no use to me. Old-fashioned people think you can have a soul without money. They think the less money you have, the more soul you have. Young people nowadays know better. A soul is a very expensive thing to keep: much more so than a motor car.

CAPTAIN SHOTOVER: Is it? How much does your soul eat?

ELLIE: Oh, a lot. It eats music and pictures and books and mountains and lakes and beautiful things to wear and nice people to be with. In this country you cant have them without lots of money: that is why our souls are so horribly starved.

CAPTAIN SHOTOVER: Mangan's soul lives on pigs' food.

ELLIE: Yes: money is thrown away on him. I suppose his soul was starved when he was young. But it will not be thrown away on me. It is just because I want to save my soul that I am marrying for money. All the women who are not fools do.

CAPTAIN SHOTOVER: There are other ways of getting money. Why dont you steal it?

ELLIE: Because I dont want to go to prison.

CAPTAIN SHOTOVER: Is that the only reason? Are you quite sure honesty has nothing to do with it?

ELLIE: Oh, you are very old-fashioned, Captain. Does any modern girl believe that the legal and illegal ways of getting money are the honest and dishonest ways? Mangan robbed my father and my father's friends. I should rob all the money back from Mangan if the police would let me. As they wont, I must get it back by marrying him.

CAPTAIN SHOTOVER: I cant argue: I'm too old: my mind is made up and finished. All I can tell you is that, old-fashioned or new-fashioned, if you sell yourself, you deal your soul a blow that all the books and pictures and concerts and scenery in the world wont heal [*he gets up suddenly and makes for the pantry*].

ELLIE [*running after him and seizing him by the sleeve*]: Then why did you sell yourself to the devil in Zanzibar?

CAPTAIN SHOTOVER [*stopping, startled*]: What?

ELLIE: You shall not run away before you answer. I have found out that trick of yours. If you sold yourself, why shouldnt I?

CAPTAIN SHOTOVER: I had to deal with men so degraded that they wouldnt obey me unless I swore at them and kicked them and beat them with my fists. Foolish people took young thieves off the streets; flung them into a training ship where they were taught to fear the cane instead of fearing God; and thought theyd make men and sailors of them by private subscription. I tricked these thieves into believing I'd sold myself to the devil. It saved my soul from the kicking and swearing that was damning me by inches.

ELLIE [*releasing him*]: I shall pretend to sell myself to Boss Mangan to save my soul from the poverty that is damning me by inches.

CAPTAIN SHOTOVER: Riches will damn you ten times deeper. Riches wont save even your body.

ELLIE: Old-fashioned again. We know now that the soul is the body, and the body the soul. They tell us they are different because they want to persuade us that we can keep our souls if we let them make slaves of our bodies. I am afraid you are no use to me, Captain.

CAPTAIN SHOTOVER: What did you expect? A Savior, eh? Are you old-fashioned enough to believe in that?

ELLIE: No. But I thought you were very wise, and might help me. Now I have found you out. You pretend to be busy, and think of fine things to say, and run in and out to surprise people by saying them, and get away before they can answer you.

CAPTAIN SHOTOVER: It confuses me to be answered. It discourages me. I cannot bear men and women. I have to run away. I must run away now [*he tries to*].

ELLIE [*again seizing his arm*]: You shall not run away from me. I can hypnotize you. You are the only person in the house I can say what I like to. I know you are fond of me. Sit down. [*She draws him to the sofa*].

CAPTAIN SHOTOVER [*yielding*]: Take care: I am in my dotage. Old men are dangerous: it doesnt matter to them what is going to happen to the world.

They sit side by side on the sofa. She leans affectionately against him with her head on his shoulder and her eyes half closed.

ELLIE [*dreamily*]: I should have thought nothing else mattered to old men. They cant be very interested in what is going to happen to themselves.

CAPTAIN SHOTOVER: A man's interest in the world is only the overflow from his interest in himself. When you are a child your vessel is not yet full; so you care for nothing but your own affairs. When you grow up, your vessel overflows; and you are a politician, a philosopher, or an explorer and adventurer. In old age the vessel dries up: there is no overflow: you are a child again. I can give you the memories of my ancient wisdom: mere scraps and leavings; but I no longer really care for anything but my own little wants and hobbies. I sit here working out my old ideas of destroying my fellow-creatures. I see my daughters and their men living foolish lives of romance and sentiment and snobbery. I see you, the younger generation, turning from their romance and sentiment and snobbery to money and comfort and hard common sense. I was ten times happier on the bridge in the typhoon, or frozen into Arctic ice for months in darkness, than you or they have ever been. You are looking for a rich husband. At your age I looked for hardship, danger, horror, and death, that I might feel the life in me more intensely. I did not let the fear of death govern my life; and my reward was, I had my life. You are going to let the fear of poverty govern your life; and your reward will be that you will eat, but you will not live.

ELLIE [*sitting up impatiently*]: But what can I do? I am not a sea captain: I cant stand on bridges in typhoons, or go slaughtering seals and whales in Greenland's icy mountains. They wont let women be captains. Do you want me to be a stewardess?

CAPTAIN SHOTOVER: There are worse lives. The stewardesses could come ashore if they liked; but they sail and sail and sail.

ELLIE: What could they do ashore but marry for money? I dont want to be a stewardess: I am too bad a sailor. Think of something else for me.

CAPTAIN SHOTOVER: I cant think so long and continuously. I am too old. I must go in and out. [*He tries to rise*].

ELLIE [*pulling him back*]: You shall not. You are happy here, arnt you?

CAPTAIN SHOTOVER: I tell you it's dangerous to keep me. I cant keep awake and alert.

ELLIE: What do you run away for? To sleep?

CAPTAIN SHOTOVER: No. To get a glass of rum.

ELLIE [*frightfully disillusioned*]: Is that it? How disgusting! Do you like being drunk?

CAPTAIN SHOTOVER: No: I dread being drunk more than anything in the world. To be drunk means to have dreams; to go soft; to be easily pleased and deceived; to fall into the clutches of women. Drink does that for you when you are young. But when you are old: very very old, like me, the dreams come by themselves. You dont know how terrible that is: you are young: you sleep at night only, and sleep soundly. But later on you will sleep in the afternoon. Later still you will sleep even in the morning; and you will awake tired, tired of life. You will never be free from dozing and dreams: the dreams will steal upon your work every ten minutes unless you can awaken yourself with rum. I drink now to keep sober; but the dreams are conquering: rum is not what it was: I have had ten glasses since you came; and it might be so much water. Go get me another: Guinness knows where it is. You had better see for yourself the horror of an old man drinking.

ELLIE: You shall not drink. Dream. I like you to dream. You must never be in the real world when we talk together.

CAPTAIN SHOTOVER: I am too weary to resist or too weak. I am in my second childhood. I do not see you as you really are. I cant remember what I really am. I feel nothing but the accursed happiness I have dreaded all my life long: the happiness that comes as life goes, the happiness of yielding and dreaming instead of resisting and doing, the sweetness of the fruit that is going rotten.

ELLIE: You dread it almost as much as I used to dread losing my dreams and having to fight and do things. But that is all over for me: my dreams are dashed to pieces. I should like to marry a very old, very rich man. I should like to marry you. I had much rather marry you than marry Mangan. Are you very rich?

CAPTAIN SHOTOVER: No. Living from hand to mouth. And I have a wife somewhere in Jamaica: a black one. My first wife. Unless she's dead.

ELLIE: What a pity! I feel so happy with you. [*She takes his hand, almost unconsciously, and pats it*]. I thought I should never feel happy again.

CAPTAIN SHOTOVER: Why?

ELLIE: Dont you know?

CAPTAIN SHOTOVER: No.

ELLIE: Heartbreak. I fell in love with Hector, and didnt know he was married.

CAPTAIN SHOTOVER: Heartbreak? Are you one of those who are so sufficient to themselves that they are only happy when they are stripped of everything, even of hope?

ELLIE [*gripping the hand*]: It seems so; for I feel now as if there was nothing I could not do, because I want nothing.

CAPTAIN SHOTOVER: Thats the only real strength. Thats genius. Thats better than rum.

ELLIE [*throwing away his hand*]: Rum! Why did you spoil it?

> HECTOR *and* RANDALL *come in from the garden through the starboard door.*

HECTOR: I beg your pardon. We did not know there was anyone here.

ELLIE [*rising*]: That means that you want to tell Mr Randall the story about the tiger. Come, Captain: I want to talk to my father; and you had better come with me.

CAPTAIN SHOTOVER [*rising*]: Nonsense! the man is in bed.

ELLIE: Aha! Ive caught you. My real father has gone to bed; but the father you gave me is in the kitchen. You knew quite well all along. Come. [*She draws him out into the garden with her through the port door*].

HECTOR: Thats an extraordinary girl. She has the Ancient Mariner on a string like a Pekinese dog.

RANDALL: Now that they have gone, shall we have a friendly chat?

HECTOR: You are in what is supposed to be my house. I am at your disposal.

> HECTOR *sits down in the draughtsman's chair, turning it to face* RANDALL, *who remains standing, leaning at his ease against the carpenter's bench.*

RANDALL: I take it that we may be quite frank. I mean about Lady Utterword.

HECTOR: You may. I have nothing to be frank about. I never met her until this afternoon.

RANDALL [*straightening up*]: What! But you are her sister's husband.

HECTOR: Well, if you come to that, you are her husband's brother.

RANDALL: But you seem to be on intimate terms with her.

HECTOR: So do you.

RANDALL: Yes; but I am on intimate terms with her. I have known her for years.

HECTOR: It took her years to get to the same point with you that she got to with me in five minutes, it seems.

RANDALL [*vexed*]: Really, Ariadne is the limit [*he moves away huffishly towards the windows*].

HECTOR [*coolly*]: She is, as I remarked to Hesione, a very enterprising woman.

RANDALL [*returning, much troubled*]: You see, Hushabye, you are what women consider a good-looking man.

HECTOR: I cultivated that appearance in the days of my vanity; and Hesione insists on my keeping it up. She makes me wear these ridiculous things [*indicating his Arab costume*] because she thinks me absurd in evening dress.

RANDALL: Still, you do keep it up, old chap. Now, I assure you I have not an atom of jealousy in my disposition—

HECTOR: The question would seem to be rather whether your brother has any touch of that sort.

RANDALL: What! Hastings! Oh, dont trouble about Hastings. He has the gift of being able to work sixteen hours a day at the dullest detail, and actually likes it. That gets him to the top wherever he goes. As long as Ariadne takes care that he is fed regularly, he is only too thankful to anyone who will keep her in good humour for him.

HECTOR: And as she has all the Shotover fascination, there is plenty of competition for the job, eh?

RANDALL [*angrily*]: She encourages them. Her conduct is perfectly scandalous. I assure you, my dear fellow, I havnt an atom of jealousy in my composition; but she makes herself the talk of every place she goes to by her thoughtlessness. It's nothing more: she doesn't really care for the men she keeps hanging about her; but how is the world to know that? It's not fair to Hastings. It's not fair to me.

HECTOR: Her theory is that her conduct is so correct—

RANDALL: Correct! She does nothing but make scenes from morning til night. You be careful, old chap. She will get you into trouble: that is, she would if she really cared for you.

HECTOR: Doesn't she?

RANDALL: Not a scrap. She may want your scalp to add to her collection; but her true affection has been engaged years ago. You had really better be careful.

HECTOR: Do you suffer much from this jealousy?

RANDALL: Jealousy! I jealous! My dear fellow, havnt I told you that there is not an atom of—

HECTOR: Yes. And Lady Utterword told me she never made scenes. Well, dont waste your jealousy on my moustache. Never waste jealousy on a real man: it is the imaginary hero that supplants us all in the long run. Besides, jealousy does not belong to your easy man-of-the-world pose, which you carry so well in other respects.

RANDALL: Really, Hushabye, I think a man may be allowed to be a gentleman without being accused of posing.

HECTOR: It is a pose like any other. In this house we know all the poses: our game is to find out the man under the pose. The man under your pose is apparently Ellie's favorite, Othello.

RANDALL: Some of your games in this house are damned annoying, let me tell you.

HECTOR: Yes: I have been their victim for many years. I used to writhe under them at first; but I became accustomed to them. At last I learned to play them.

RANDALL: If it's all the same to you, I had rather you didnt play them on me. You evidently dont quite understand my character, or my notions of good form.

HECTOR: Is it your notion of good form to give away Lady Utterword?

RANDALL [*a childishly plaintive note breaking into his huff*]: I have not said a word against Lady Utterword. This is just the conspiracy over again.

HECTOR: What conspiracy?

RANDALL: You know very well, sir. A conspiracy to make me out to be pettish and jealous and childish and everything I am not. Everyone knows I am just the opposite.

HECTOR [*rising*]: Something in the air of the house has upset you. It often does have that effect. [*He goes to the garden door and calls* LADY UTTERWORD *with commanding emphasis*] Ariadne!

LADY UTTERWORD [*at some distance*]: Yes.

RANDALL: What are you calling her for? I want to speak—

LADY UTTERWORD [*arriving breathless*]: Yes. You really are a terribly commanding person. Whats the matter?

HECTOR: I do not know how to manage your friend Randall. No doubt you do.

LADY UTTERWORD: Randall: have you been making yourself ridiculous, as usual? I can see it in your face. Really, you are the most pettish creature.

RANDALL: You know quite well, Ariadne, that I have not an ounce of pettishness in my disposition. I have made myself perfectly pleasant here. I have remained absolutely cool and imperturbable in the face of a burglar. Imperturbability is almost too strong a point of mine. But [*putting his foot down with a stamp, and walking angrily up and down the room*] I insist on being treated with a certain consideration. I will not allow Hushabye to take liberties with me. I will not stand your encouraging people as you do.

HECTOR: The man has a rooted delusion that he is your husband.

LADY UTTERWORD: I know. He is jealous. As if he had any right to be! He compromises me everywhere. He makes scenes all over the place. Randall: I will not allow it. I simply will not allow it. You had no right to discuss me with Hector. I will not be discussed by men.

HECTOR: Be reasonable, Ariadne. Your fatal gift of beauty forces men to discuss you.

LADY UTTERWORD: Oh indeed! what about your fatal gift of beauty?

HECTOR: How can I help it?

LADY UTTERWORD: You could cut off your moustache: I cant cut off my nose. I get my whole life messed up with people falling in love with me. And then Randall says I run after men.

RANDALL: I—

LADY UTTERWORD: Yes you do: you said it just now. Why cant you think of something else than women? Napoleon was quite right when he said that women are the occupation of the idle man. Well, if ever there was an idle man on earth, his name is Randall Utterword.

RANDALL: Ariad—

LADY UTTERWORD [*overwhelming him with a torrent of words*]: Oh yes you are: it's no use denying it. What have you ever done? What good are you? You are as much trouble in the house as a child of three. You couldnt live without your valet.

RANDALL: This is—

LADY UTTERWORD: Laziness! You are laziness incarnate. You are selfishness itself. You are the most uninteresting man on earth. You cant even gossip about anything but yourself and your grievances and your ailments and the people who have offended you. [*Turning to* HECTOR] Do you know what they call him, Hector?

HECTOR: ⎱[*speaking* ⎰Please dont tell me.
RANDALL: ⎰*together*] ⎱I'll not stand it—

LADY UTTERWORD: Randall the Rotter: that is his name in good society.

RANDALL [*shouting*]: I'll not bear it, I tell you. Will you listen to me, you infernal—[*he chokes*].

LADY UTTERWORD: Well: go on. What were you going to call me? An infernal what? Which unpleasant animal is it to be this time?

RANDALL [*foaming*]: There is no animal in the world so hateful as a woman can be. You are a maddening devil. Hushabye: you will not believe me when I tell you that I have loved this demon all my life; but God knows I have paid for it [*he sits down in the draughtsman's chair, weeping*].

LADY UTTERWORD [*standing over him with triumphant contempt*]: Cry-baby!

HECTOR [*gravely, coming to him*]: My friend: the Shotover sisters have two strange powers over men. They can make them love; and they can make them cry. Thank your stars that you are not married to one of them.

LADY UTTERWORD [*haughtily*]: And pray, Hector—

HECTOR [*suddenly catching her round the shoulders; swinging her right round him and away from* RANDALL; *and gripping her throat with the other hand*]: Ariadne: if you attempt to start on me, I'll choke you: do you hear? The cat-and-mouse game with the other sex is a good game; but I can play your head off at it. [*He throws her, not at all gently, into the big chair, and proceeds, less fiercely but firmly*] It is true that Napoleon said that woman is the occupation of the idle man. But he added that she is the relaxation of the warrior. Well, *I* am the warrior. So take care.

LADY UTTERWORD [*not in the least put out, and rather pleased by his violence*]: My dear Hector: I have only done what you asked me to do.

HECTOR: How do you make that out, pray?

LADY UTTERWORD: You called me in to manage Randall, didnt you? You said you couldnt manage him yourself.

HECTOR: Well, what if I did? I did not ask you to drive the man mad.

LADY UTTERWORD: He isnt mad. Thats the way to manage him. If you were a mother, youd understand.

HECTOR: Mother! What are you up to now?

LADY UTTERWORD: It's quite simple. When the children got nerves and were naughty, I smacked them just enough to give them a good cry and a healthy nervous shock. They went to sleep and were quite good afterwards. Well, I cant smack Randall: he is too big; so when he gets nerves and is naughty, I just rag him til he cries. He will be all right now. Look: he is half asleep already [*which is quite true*].

RANDALL [*waking up indignantly*]: I'm not. You are most cruel, Ariadne. [*Sentimentally*] But I suppose I must forgive you, as usual [*he checks himself in the act of yawning*].

LADY UTTERWORD [*to* HECTOR]: Is the explanation satisfactory, dread warrior?

HECTOR: Some day I shall kill you, if you go too far. I thought you were a fool.

LADY UTTERWORD [*laughing*]: Everybody does, at first. But I am not such a fool as I look. [*She rises complacently*]. Now, Randall: go to bed. You will be a good boy in the morning.

RANDALL [*only very faintly rebellious*]: I'll go to bed when I like. It isnt ten yet.

LADY UTTERWORD: It is long past ten. See that he goes to bed at once, Hector. [*She goes into the garden*].

HECTOR: Is there any slavery on earth viler than this slavery of men to women?

RANDALL [*rising resolutely*]: I'll not speak to her tomorrow. I'll not speak to her for another week. I'll give her such a lesson. I'll go straight to bed without bidding her goodnight. [*He makes for the door leading to the hall*].

HECTOR: You are under a spell, man. Old Shotover sold himself to the devil in

Zanzibar. The devil gave him a black witch for a wife; and these two demon daughters are their mystical progeny. I am tied to Hesione's apron-string; but I'm her husband; and if I did go stark staring mad about her, at least we became man and wife. But why should you let yourself be dragged about and beaten by Ariadne as a toy donkey is dragged about and beaten by a child? What do you get by it? Are you her lover?

RANDALL: You must not misunderstand me. In a higher sense—in a Platonic sense—

HECTOR: Psha! Platonic sense! She makes you her servant; and when pay-day comes round, she bilks you: that is what you mean.

RANDALL [*feebly*]: Well, if I dont mind, I dont see what business it is of yours. Besides, I tell you I am going to punish her. You shall see: *I* know how to deal with women. I'm really very sleepy. Say goodnight to Mrs Hushabye for me, will you, like a good chap. Goodnight. [*He hurries out*].

HECTOR: Poor wretch! Oh women! women! women! [*He lifts his fists in invocation to heaven*] Fall. Fall and crush. [*He goes out into the garden*].

ACT THREE

In the garden, HECTOR, *as he comes out through the glass door of the poop, finds* LADY UTTERWORD *lying voluptuously in the hammock on the east side of the flagstaff, in the circle of light cast by the electric arc, which is like a moon in its opal globe. Beneath the head of the hammock, a campstool. On the other side of the flagstaff, on the long garden seat,* CAPTAIN SHOTOVER *is asleep, with* ELLIE *beside him, leaning affectionately against him on his right hand. On his left is a deck chair. Behind them in the gloom,* HESIONE *is strolling about with* MANGAN. *It is a fine still night, moonless.*

LADY UTTERWORD: What a lovely night! It seems made for us.

HECTOR: The night takes no interest in us. What are we to the night? [*He sits down moodily in the deck chair*].

ELLIE [*dreamily, nestling against the* CAPTAIN]: Its beauty soaks into my nerves. In the night there is peace for the old and hope for the young.

HECTOR: Is that remark your own?

ELLIE: No. Only the last thing the Captain said before he went to sleep.

CAPTAIN SHOTOVER: I'm not asleep.

HECTOR: Randall is. Also Mr Mazzini Dunn. Mangan too, probably.

MANGAN: No.

HECTOR: Oh, you are there. I thought Hesione would have sent you to bed by this time.

MRS HUSHABYE [*coming to the back of the garden seat, into the light, with* MANGAN]: I think I shall. He keeps telling me he had a presentiment that he is going to die. I never met a man so greedy for sympathy.

MANGAN [*plaintively*]: But I have a presentiment. I really have. And you wouldnt listen.

MRS HUSHABYE: I was listening for something else. There was a sort of splendid drumming in the sky. Did none of you hear it? It came from a distance and then died away.

MANGAN: I tell you it was a train.

MRS HUSHABYE: And *I* tell you, Alf, there is no train at this hour. The last is nine fortyfive.

MANGAN: But a goods train.

MRS HUSHABYE: Not on our little line. They tack a truck on to the passenger train. What can it have been, Hector?

HECTOR: Heaven's threatening growl of disgust at us useless futile creatures. [*Fiercely*] I tell you, one of two things must happen. Either out of that darkness some new creation will come to supplant us as we have supplanted the animals, or the heavens will fall in thunder and destroy us.

LADY UTTERWORD [*in a cool instructive manner, wallowing comfortably in her hammock*]: We have not supplanted the animals, Hector. Why do you ask heaven to destroy this house, which could be made quite comfortable if

Hesione had any notion of how to live? Dont you know what is wrong with
it?

HECTOR: We are wrong with it. There is no sense in us. We are useless,
dangerous, and ought to be abolished.

LADY UTTERWORD: Nonsense! Hastings told me the very first day he came here,
nearly twentyfour years ago, what is wrong with the house.

CAPTAIN SHOTOVER: What! The numskull said there was something wrong with
my house!

LADY UTTERWORD: I said Hastings said it; and he is not in the least a numskull.

CAPTAIN SHOTOVER: Whats wrong with my house?

LADY UTTERWORD: Just what is wrong with a ship, papa. Wasnt it clever of
Hastings to see that?

CAPTAIN SHOTOVER: The man's a fool. Theres nothing wrong with a ship.

LADY UTTERWORD: Yes there is.

MRS HUSHABYE: But what is it? Dont be aggravating, Addy.

LADY UTTERWORD: Guess.

HECTOR: Demons. Daughters of the witch of Zanzibar. Demons.

LADY UTTERWORD: Not a bit. I assure you, all this house needs to make it a
sensible, healthy, pleasant house, with good appetites and sound sleep in it, is
horses.

MRS HUSHABYE: Horses! What rubbish!

LADY UTTERWORD: Yes: horses. Why have we never been able to let this house?
Because there are no proper stables. Go anywhere in England where there
are natural, wholesome, contented, and really nice English people; and what
do you always find? That the stables are the real centre of the household; and
that if any visitor wants to play the piano the whole room has to be upset
before it can be opened, there are so many things piled on it. I never lived
until I learned to ride; and I shall never ride really well because I didnt begin
as a child. There are only two classes in good society in England: the
equestrian classes and the neurotic classes. It isnt mere convention:
everybody can see that the people who hunt are the right people and the
people who dont are the wrong ones.

CAPTAIN SHOTOVER: There is some truth in this. My ship made a man of me; and
a ship is the horse of the sea.

LADY UTTERWORD: Exactly how Hastings explained your being a gentleman.

CAPTAIN SHOTOVER: Not bad for a numskull. Bring the man here with you next
time: I must talk to him.

LADY UTTERWORD: Why is Randall such an obvious rotter? He is well bred; he
has been at a public school and a university; he has been in the Foreign
Office; he knows the best people and has lived all his life among them. Why is
he so unsatisfactory, so contemptible? Why cant he get a valet to stay with
him longer than a few months? Just because he is too lazy and pleasure-
loving to hunt and shoot. He strums the piano, and sketches, and runs after
married women, and reads literary books and poems. He actually plays the
flute; but I never let him bring it into my house. If he would only--[*she is
interrupted by the melancholy strains of a flute coming from an open window
above. She raises herself indignantly in the hammock*]. Randall: you have not
gone to bed. Have you been listening?

The flute replies pertly:

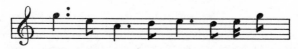

How vulgar! Go to bed instantly, Randall: how dare you?

The window is slammed down. She subsides.

How can anyone care for such a creature!

MRS HUSHABYE: Addy: do you think Ellie ought to marry poor Alfred merely for his money?

MANGAN [*much alarmed*]: Whats that? Mrs Hushabye: are my affairs to be discussed like this before everybody?

LADY UTTERWORD: I dont think Randall is listening now.

MANGAN: Everybody is listening. It isnt right.

MRS HUSHABYE: But in the dark, what does it matter? Ellie doesnt mind. Do you, Ellie?

ELLIE: Not in the least. What is your opinion, Lady Utterword? You have so much good sense.

MANGAN: But it isnt right. It—

MRS HUSHABYE *puts her hand on his mouth.*

Oh, very well.

LADY UTTERWORD: How much money have you, Mr Mangan?

MANGAN: Really–No: I cant stand this.

LADY UTTERWORD: Nonsense, Mr Mangan! It all turns on your income, doesnt it?

MANGAN: Well, if you come to that, how much money has she?

ELLIE: None.

LADY UTTERWORD: You are answered, Mr Mangan. And now, as you have made Miss Dunn throw her cards on the table, you cannot refuse to shew your own.

MRS HUSHABYE: Come, Alf! out with it! How much?

MANGAN [*baited out of all prudence*]: Well, if you want to know, I have no money and never had any.

MRS HUSHABYE: Alfred: you mustnt tell naughty stories.

MANGAN: I'm not telling you stories. I'm telling you the raw truth.

LADY UTTERWORD: Then what do you live on, Mr Mangan?

MANGAN: Travelling expenses. And a trifle of commission.

CAPTAIN SHOTOVER: What more have any of us but travelling expenses for our life's journey?

MRS HUSHABYE: But you have factories and capital and things?

MANGAN: People think I have. People think I'm an industrial Napoleon. Thats why Miss Ellie wants to marry me. But I tell you I have nothing.

ELLIE: Do you mean that the factories are like Marcus's tigers? That they dont exist?

MANGAN: They exist all right enough. But theyre not mine. They belong to syndicates and shareholders and all sorts of lazy good-for-nothing capitalists. I get money from such people to start the factories. I find people like Miss Dunn's father to work them, and keep a tight hand so as to make them pay. Of course I make them keep me going pretty well; but it's a dog's life; and I dont own anything.

MRS HUSHABYE: Alfred, Alfred: you are making a poor mouth of it to get out of marrying Ellie.

MANGAN: I'm telling the truth about my money for the first time in my life; and it's the first time my word has ever been doubted.

LADY UTTERWORD: How sad! Why dont you go in for politics, Mr Mangan?

MANGAN: Go in for politics! Where have you been living? I am in politics.

LADY UTTERWORD: I'm sure I beg your pardon. I never heard of you.

MANGAN: Let me tell you, Lady Utterword, that the Prime Minister of this country asked me to join the Government without even going through the nonsense of an election, as the dictator of a great public department.

LADY UTTERWORD: As a Conservative or a Liberal?

MANGAN: No such nonsense. As a practical business man.

They all burst out laughing.

What are you all laughing at?

MRS HUSHABYE: Oh, Alfred, Alfred!

ELLIE: You! who have to get my father to do everything for you!

MRS HUSHABYE: You! who are afraid of your own workmen!

HECTOR: You! with whom three women have been playing cat and mouse all the evening!

LADY UTTERWORD: You must have given an immense sum to the party funds, Mr Mangan.

MANGAN: Not a penny out of my own pocket. The syndicate found the money: they knew how useful I should be to them in the Government.

LADY UTTERWORD: This is most interesting and unexpected, Mr Mangan. And what have your administrative achievements been, so far?

MANGAN: Achievements? Well, I dont know what you call achievements; but Ive jolly well put a stop to the games of the other fellows in the other departments. Every man of them thought he was going to save the country all by himself, and do me out of the credit and out of my chance of a title. I took good care that if they wouldnt let me do it they shouldnt do it themselves either. I may not know anything about my own machinery; but I know how to stick a ramrod into the other fellow's. And now they all look the biggest fools going.

HECTOR: And in heaven's name, what do you look like?

MANGAN: I look like the fellow that was too clever for all the others, dont I? If that isnt a triumph of practical business, what is?

HECTOR: Is this England, or is it a madhouse?

LADY UTTERWORD: Do you expect to save the country, Mr Mangan?

MANGAN: Well, who else will? Will your Mr Randall save it?

LADY UTTERWORD: Randall the Rotter! Certainly not.

MANGAN: Will your brother-in-law save it with his moustache and his fine talk.

HECTOR: Yes, if they will let me.

MANGAN [*sneering*]: Ah! Will they let you?

HECTOR: No. They prefer you.

MANGAN: Very well then, as youre in a world where I'm appreciated and youre not, youd best be civil to me, hadnt you? Who else is there but me?

LADY UTTERWORD: There is Hastings. Get rid of your ridiculous sham democracy; and give Hastings the necessary powers, and a good supply of bamboo to bring the British native to his senses: he will save the country with the greatest ease.

CAPTAIN SHOTOVER: It had better be lost. Any fool can govern with a stick in his hand. *I* could govern that way. It is not God's way. The man is a numskull.

LADY UTTERWORD: The man is worth all of you rolled into one. What do you say, Miss Dunn?

ELLIE: I think my father would do very well if people did not put upon him and cheat him and despise him because he is so good.

MANGAN [*contemptuously*]: I think I see Mazzini Dunn getting into parliament or pushing his way into the Government. Weve not come to that, yet, thank God! What do you say, Mrs Hushabye?

MRS HUSHABYE: Oh, *I* say it matters very little which of you governs the country so long as we govern you.

HECTOR: We? Who is we, pray?

MRS HUSHABYE: The devil's granddaughters, dear. The lovely women.

HECTOR [*raising his hands as before*]: Fall, I say; and deliver us from the lures of Satan!

ELLIE: There seems to be nothing real in the world except my father and Shakespear. Marcus's tigers are false; Mr Mangan's millions are false; there is nothing really strong and true about Hesione but her beautiful black hair; and Lady Utterword's is too pretty to be real. The one thing that was left to me was the Captain's seventh degree of concentration; and that turns out to be—

CAPTAIN SHOTOVER: Rum.

LADY UTTERWORD [*placidly*]: A good deal of my hair is quite genuine. The Duchess of Dithering offered me fifty guineas for this [*touching her forehead*] under the impression that it was a transformation; but it is all natural except the color.

MANGAN [*wildly*]: Look here: I'm going to take off all my clothes [*he begins tearing off his coat*].

LADY UTTERWORD:		Mr Mangan!
CAPTAIN SHOTOVER:	[*in	Whats that?
HECTOR:	consternation*]	Ha! ha! Do. Do.
ELLIE:		Please dont.

MRS HUSHABYE [*catching his arm and stopping him*]: Alfred: for shame! Are you mad?

MANGAN: Shame! What shame is there in this house? Let's all strip stark naked. We may as well do the thing thoroughly when we're about it. Weve stripped ourselves morally naked: well, let us strip ourselves physically naked as well, and see how we like it. I tell you I cant bear this. I was brought up to be respectable. I dont mind the women dyeing their hair and the men drinking: it's human nature. But it's not human nature to tell everybody about it. Every time one of you opens your mouth I go like this [*he cowers as if to avoid a missile*] afraid of what will come next. How are we to have any self-respect if we dont keep it up that we're better than we really are?

LADY UTTERWORD: I quite sympathize with you, Mr Mangan. I have been through it all; and I know by experience that men and women are delicate plants and must be cultivated under glass. Our family habit of throwing stones in all directions and letting the air in is not only unbearably rude, but positively dangerous. Still, there is no use catching physical colds as well as moral ones; so please keep your clothes on.

MANGAN: I'll do as I like: not what you tell me. Am I a child or a grown man? I wont stand this mothering tyranny. I'll go back to the city, where I'm respected and made much of.

MRS HUSHABYE: Goodbye, Alf. Think of us sometimes in the city. Think of Ellie's youth!

ELLIE: Think of Hesione's eyes and hair!

CAPTAIN SHOTOVER: Think of this garden in which you are not a dog barking to keep the truth out!

HECTOR: Think of Lady Utterword's beauty! her good sense! her style!

LADY UTTERWORD: Flatterer. Think, Mr Mangan, whether you can really do any better for yourself elsewhere: that is the essential point, isnt it?

MANGAN [*surrendering*]: All right: all right. I'm done. Have it your own way. Only let me alone. I dont know whether I'm on my head or my heels when you all start on me like this. I'll stay. I'll marry her. I'll do anything for a quiet life. Are you satisfied now?

ELLIE: No. I never really intended to make you marry me, Mr Mangan. Never in the depths of my soul. I only wanted to feel my strength: to know that you could not escape if I chose to take you.

MANGAN [*indignantly*]: What! Do you mean to say you are going to throw me over after my acting so handsome?

LADY UTTERWORD: I should not be too hasty, Miss Dunn. You can throw Mr Mangan over at any time up to the last moment. Very few men in his position go bankrupt. You can live very comfortably on his reputation for immense wealth.

ELLIE: I cannot commit bigamy, Lady Utterword.

MRS HUSHABYE:		Bigamy! Whatever on earth are you talking about, Ellie?
LADY UTTERWORD:	[*exclaiming all together*]	Bigamy! What do you mean, Miss Dunn?
MANGAN:		Bigamy! Do you mean to say youre married already?
HECTOR:		Bigamy! This is some enigma.

ELLIE: Only half an hour ago I became Captain Shotover's white wife.

MRS HUSHABYE: Ellie! What nonsense! Where?

ELLIE: In heaven, where all true marriages are made.

LADY UTTERWORD: Really, Miss Dunn! Really, papa!

MANGAN: He told me *I* was too old! And him a mummy!

HECTOR [*quoting Shelley*]:
> Their altar the grassy earth outspread,
> And their priest the muttering wind.

ELLIE: Yes: I, Ellie Dunn, give my broken heart and my strong sound soul to its natural captain, my spiritual husband and second father.

She draws the CAPTAIN'S *arm through hers, and pats his hand. The* CAPTAIN *remains fast asleep.*

MRS HUSHABYE: Oh, thats very clever of you, pettikins. Very clever. Alfred: you could never have lived up to Ellie. You must be content with a little share of me.

MANGAN [*sniffing and wiping his eyes*]: It isnt kind—[*his emotion chokes him*].

LADY UTTERWORD: You are well out of it, Mr Mangan. Miss Dunn is the most conceited young woman I have met since I came back to England.

MRS HUSHABYE: Oh, Ellie isnt conceited. Are you, pettikins?

ELLIE: I know my strength now, Hesione.

MANGAN: Brazen, I call you. Brazen.

MRS HUSHABYE: Tut tut, Alfred: dont be rude. Dont you feel how lovely this marriage night is, made in heaven? Arnt you happy, you and Hector? Open your eyes: Addy and Ellie look beautiful enough to please the most fastidious man: we live and love and have not a care in the world. We women have managed all that for you. Why in the name of common sense do you go on as if you were two miserable wretches?

CAPTAIN SHOTOVER: I tell you happiness is no good. You can be happy when you are only half alive. I am happier now I am half dead than ever I was in my prime. But there is no blessing on my happiness.

ELLIE [*her face lighting up*]: Life with a blessing! that is what I want. Now I know the real reason why I couldnt marry Mr Mangan: there would be no blessing on our marriage. There is a blessing on my broken heart. There is a blessing on your beauty, Hesione. There is a blessing on your father's spirit. Even on the lies of Marcus there is a blessing; but on Mr Mangan's money there is none.

MANGAN: I dont understand a word of that.

ELLIE: Neither do I. But I know it means something.

MANGAN: Dont say there was any difficulty about the blessing. I was ready to get a bishop to marry us.

MRS HUSHABYE: Isnt he a fool, pettikins?

HECTOR [*fiercely*]: Do not scorn the man. We are all fools.

MAZZINI, *in pyjamas and a richly colored silk dressing-gown, comes from the house, on* LADY UTTERWORD's *side.*

MRS HUSHABYE: Oh! here comes the only man who ever resisted me. Whats the matter, Mr Dunn? Is the house on fire?

MAZZINI: Oh no: nothing's the matter; but really it's impossible to go to sleep with such an interesting conversation going on under one's window, and on such a beautiful night too. I just had to come down and join you all. What has it all been about?

MRS HUSHABYE: Oh, wonderful things, soldier of freedom.

HECTOR: For example, Mangan, as a practical business man, has tried to undress himself and has failed ignominiously; whilst you, as an idealist, have succeeded brilliantly.

MAZZINI: I hope you dont mind my being like this, Mrs Hushabye. [*He sits down on the campstool*].

MRS HUSHABYE: On the contrary, I could wish you always like that.

LADY UTTERWORD: Your daughter's match is off, Mr Dunn. It seems that Mr Mangan, whom we all supposed to be a man of property, owns absolutely nothing.

MAZZINI: Well of course I knew that, Lady Utterword. But if people believe in him and are always giving him money, whereas they dont believe in me and never give me any, how can I ask poor Ellie to depend on what I can do for her?

MANGAN: Dont you run away with this idea that I have nothing. I—

HECTOR: Oh, dont explain. We understand. You have a couple of thousand pounds in exchequer bills, 50,000 shares worth tenpence a dozen, and half a dozen tabloids of cyanide of potassium to poison yourself with when you are found out. Thats the reality of your millions.

MAZZINI: Oh no, no, no. He is quite honest: the businesses are genuine and perfectly legal.

HECTOR [*disgusted*]: Yah! Not even a great swindler!

MANGAN: So you think. But Ive been too many for some honest men, for all that.

LADY UTTERWORD: There is no pleasing you, Mr Mangan. You are determined to be neither rich nor poor, honest nor dishonest.

MANGAN: There you go again. Ever since I came into this silly house I have been made to look a fool, though I'm as good a man in this house as in the city.

ELLIE [*musically*]: Yes: this silly house, this strangely happy house, this agonizing house, this house without foundations. I shall call it Heartbreak House.

MRS HUSHABYE: Stop, Ellie; or I shall howl like an animal.

MANGAN [*breaks into a low snivelling*] !!!

MRS HUSHABYE: There! you have set Alfred off.

ELLIE: I like him best when he is howling.

CAPTAIN SHOTOVER: Silence!

MANGAN *subsides into silence.*

I say, let the heart break in silence.

HECTOR: Do you accept that name for your house?

CAPTAIN SHOTOVER: It is not my house: it is only my kennel.

HECTOR: We have been too long here. We do not live in this house: we haunt it.

LADY UTTERWORD [*heart torn*]: It is dreadful to think how you have been here all these years while I have gone round the world. I escaped young; but it has drawn me back. It wants to break my heart too. But it shant. I have left you and it behind. It was silly of me to come back. I felt sentimental about papa and Hesione and the old place. I felt them calling to me.

MAZZINI: But what a very natural and kindly and charming human feeling, Lady Utterword!

LADY UTTERWORD: So I thought, Mr Dunn. But I know now that it was only the last of my influenza. I found that I was not remembered and not wanted.

CAPTAIN SHOTOVER: You left because you did not want us. Was there no heartbreak in that for your father? You tore yourself up by the roots; and the ground healed up and brought forth fresh plants and forgot you. What right had you to come back and probe old wounds?

MRS HUSHABYE: You were a complete stranger to me at first, Addy; but now I feel as if you had never been away.

LADY UTTERWORD: Thank you, Hesione; but the influenza is quite cured. The place may be Heartbreak House to you, Miss Dunn, and to this gentleman from the city who seems to have so little self-control; but to me it is only a very ill-regulated and rather untidy villa without any stables.

HECTOR: Inhabited by—?

ELLIE: A crazy old sea captain and a young singer who adores him.

MRS HUSHABYE: A sluttish female, trying to stave off a double chin and an elderly spread, vainly wooing a born soldier of freedom.

MAZZINI: Oh, really, Mrs Hushabye—

MANGAN: A member of His Majesty's Government that everybody sets down as a nincompoop: dont forget him, Lady Utterword.

LADY UTTERWORD: And a very fascinating gentleman whose chief occupation is to be married to my sister.

HECTOR: All heartbroken imbeciles.

MAZZINI: Oh no. Surely, if I may say so, rather a favorable specimen of what is best in our English culture. You are very charming people, most advanced, unprejudiced, frank, humane, unconventional, democratic, free-thinking, and everything that is delightful to thoughtful people.

MRS HUSHABYE: You do us proud, Mazzini.

MAZZINI: I am not flattering, really. Where else could I feel perfectly at ease in my pyjamas? I sometimes dream that I am in very distinguished society, and suddenly I have nothing on but my pyjamas! Sometimes I havnt even pyjamas. And I always feel overwhelmed with confusion. But here, I dont mind in the least: it seems quite natural.

LADY UTTERWORD: An infallible sign that you are not now in really distinguished society, Mr Dunn. If you were in my house, you would feel embarrassed.

MAZZINI: I shall take particular care to keep out of your house, Lady Utterwood.

LADY UTTERWORD: You will be quite wrong, Mr Dunn. I should make you very comfortable; and you would not have the trouble and anxiety of wondering whether you should wear your purple and gold or your green and crimson dressing-gown at dinner. You complicate life instead of simplifying it by doing these ridiculous things.

ELLIE: Your house is not Heartbreak House: is it, Lady Utterword?

HECTOR: Yet she breaks hearts, easy as her house is. That poor devil upstairs with his flute howls when she twists his heart, just as Mangan howls when my wife twists his.

LADY UTTERWORD: That is because Randall has nothing to do but have his heart broken. It is a change from having his head shampooed. Catch anyone breaking Hastings' heart!

CAPTAIN SHOTOVER: The numskull wins, after all.

LADY UTTERWORD: I shall go back to my numskull with the greatest satisfaction when I am tired of you all, clever as you are.

MANGAN [*huffily*]: I never set up to be clever.

LADY UTTERWORD: I forgot you, Mr Mangan.

MANGAN: Well, I dont see that quite, either.

LADY UTTERWORD: You may not be clever, Mr Mangan; but you are successful.

MANGAN: But I dont want to be regarded merely as a successful man. I have an imagination like anyone else. I have a presentiment—

MRS HUSHABYE: Oh, you are impossible, Alfred. Here I am devoting myself to you; and you think of nothing but your ridiculous presentiment. You bore me. Come and talk poetry to me under the stars. [*She drags him away into the darkness*].

MANGAN [*tearfully, as he disappears*]: Yes: it's all very well to make fun of me; but if you only knew—

HECTOR [*impatiently*]: How is all this going to end?

MAZZINI: It wont end, Mr Hushabye. Life doesnt end: it goes on.

ELLIE: Oh, it cant go on for ever. I'm always expecting something. I dont know what it is; but life must come to a point sometime.

LADY UTTERWORD: The point for a young woman of your age is a baby.

HECTOR: Yes, but damn it, I have the same feeling; and *I* cant have a baby.

LADY UTTERWORD: By deputy, Hector.

HECTOR: But I have children. All that is over and done with for me: and yet I too feel that this cant last. We sit here talking, and leave everything to Mangan and to chance and to the devil. Think of the powers of destruction that Mangan and his mutual admiration gang wield! It's madness: it's like giving a torpedo to a badly brought up child to play at earthquakes with.

MAZZINI: I know I used often to think about that when I was young.

HECTOR: Think! Whats the good of thinking about it? Why didnt you do something?

MAZZINI: But I did. I joined societies and made speeches and wrote pamphlets. That was all I could do. But, you know, though the people in the societies thought they knew more than Mangan, most of them wouldnt have joined if they had known as much. You see they had never had any money to handle or any men to manage. Every year I expected a revolution, or some frightful smash-up: it seemed impossible that we could blunder and muddle on any longer. But nothing happened, except, of course, the usual poverty and crime and drink that we are used to. Nothing ever does happen. It's amazing how well we get along, all things considered.

LADY UTTERWORD: Perhaps, somebody cleverer than you and Mr Mangan was at work all the time.

MAZZINI: Perhaps so. Though I was brought up not to believe in anything, I often feel that there is a great deal to be said for the theory of an overruling Providence, after all.

LADY UTTERWORD: Providence! I meant Hastings.

MAZZINI: Oh, I beg your pardon, Lady Utterword.

CAPTAIN SHOTOVER: Every drunken skipper trusts to Providence. But one of the ways of Providence with drunken skippers is to run them on the rocks.

MAZZINI: Very true, no doubt, at sea. But in politics, I assure you, they only run into jellyfish. Nothing happens.

CAPTAIN SHOTOVER: At sea nothing happens to the sea. Nothing happens to the sky. The sun comes up from the east and goes down to the west. The moon grows from a sickle to an arc lamp, and comes later and later until she is lost in the light as other things are lost in the darkness. After the typhoon, the flying-fish glitter in the sunshine like birds. It's amazing how they get along, all things considered. Nothing happens, except something not worth mentioning.

ELLIE: What is that, O Captain, my captain?

CAPTAIN SHOTOVER [*savagely*]: Nothing but the smash of the drunken skipper's ship on the rocks, the splintering of her rotten timbers, the tearing of her rusty plates, the drowning of the crew like rats in a trap.

ELLIE: Moral: dont take rum.

CAPTAIN SHOTOVER [*vehemently*]: That is a lie, child. Let a man drink ten barrels of rum a day, he is not a drunken skipper until he is a drifting skipper. Whilst he can lay his course and stand on his bridge and steer it, he is no drunkard. It is the man who lies drinking in his bunk and trusts to Providence that I call the drunken skipper, though he drank nothing but the waters of the River Jordan.

ELLIE: Splendid! And you havnt had a drop for an hour. You see you dont need it: your own spirit is not dead.

CAPTAIN SHOTOVER: Echoes: nothing but echoes. The last shot was fired years ago.

HECTOR: And this ship we are all in? This soul's prison we call England?

CAPTAIN SHOTOVER: The captain is in his bunk, drinking bottled ditch-water; and the crew is gambling in the forecastle. She will strike and sink and split. Do you think the laws of God will be suspended in favor of England because you were born in it?

HECTOR: Well, I dont mean to be drowned like a rat in a trap. I still have the will to live. What am I to do?

CAPTAIN SHOTOVER: Do? Nothing simpler. Learn your business as an Englishman.

HECTOR: And what may my business as an Englishman be, pray?

CAPTAIN SHOTOVER: Navigation. Learn it and live; or leave it and be damned.

ELLIE: Quiet, quiet; youll tire yourself.

MAZZINI: I thought all that once, Captain; but I assure you nothing will happen.

A dull distant explosion is heard.

HECTOR [*starting up*]: What was that?

CAPTAIN SHOTOVER: Something happening [*he blows his whistle*]. Breakers ahead!

The light goes out.

HECTOR [*furiously*]: Who put that light out? Who dared put that light out?

NURSE GUINNESS [*running in from the house to the middle of the esplanade*]: I did, sir. The police have telephoned to say we'll be summoned if we dont put that light out: it can be seen for miles.

HECTOR: It shall be seen for a hundred miles [*he dashes into the house*].

NURSE GUINNESS: The rectory is nothing but a heap of bricks, they say. Unless we can give the rector a bed he has nowhere to lay his head this night.

CAPTAIN SHOTOVER: The Church is on the rocks, breaking up. I told him it would unless it headed for God's open sea.

NURSE GUINNESS: And you are all to go down to the cellars.

CAPTAIN SHOTOVER: Go there yourself, you and all the crew. Batten down the hatches.

NURSE GUINNESS: And hide beside the coward I married! I'll go on the roof first.

The lamp lights up again.

There! Mr Hushabye's turned it on again.

THE BURGLAR [*hurrying in and appealing to Nurse Guinness*]: Here: wheres the way to that gravel pit? The boot-boy says theres a cave in the gravel pit. Them cellars is no use. Wheres the gravel pit, Captain?

NURSE GUINNESS: Go straight on past the flagstaff until you fall into it and break your dirty neck.

She pushes him contemptuously towards the flagstaff, and herself goes to the foot of the hammock and waits there, as it were by Ariadne's cradle. Another and louder explosion is heard. THE BURGLAR *stops and stands trembling.*

ELLIE [*rising*]: That was nearer.

CAPTAIN SHOTOVER: The next one will get us. [*He rises*]. Stand by, all hands, for judgment.

THE BURGLAR: Oh my Lordy God! [*He rushes away frantically past the flagstaff into the gloom*].

MRS HUSHABYE [*emerging panting from the darkness*]: Who was that running away? [*She comes to* ELLIE]. Did you hear the explosions? And the sound in the sky: it's splendid: it's like an orchestra: it's like Beethoven.

ELLIE: By thunder, Hesione: it is Beethoven.

She and HESIONE *throw themselves into one another's arms in wild excitement. The light increases.*

MAZZINI [*anxiously*]: The light is getting brighter.

NURSE GUINNESS [*looking up at the house*]: It's Mr Hushabye turning on all the lights in the house and tearing down the curtains.

RANDALL [*rushing in in his pyjamas, distractedly waving a flute*]: Ariadne: my soul, my precious, go down to the cellars: I beg and implore you, go down to the cellars!

LADY UTTERWORD [*quite composed in her hammock*]: The governor's wife in the cellars with the servants! Really, Randall!

RANDALL: But what shall I do if you are killed?

LADY UTTERWORD: You will probably be killed, too, Randall. Now play your flute to shew that you are not afraid; and be good. Play us Keep the home fires burning.

NURSE GUINNESS [*grimly*]: Theyll keep the home fires burning for us: them up there.

RANDALL [*having tried to play*]: My lips are trembling. I cant get a sound.

MAZZINI: I hope poor Mangan is safe.

MRS HUSHABYE: He is hiding in the cave in the gravel pit.

CAPTAIN SHOTOVER: My dynamite drew him there. It is the hand of God.

HECTOR [*returning from the house and striding across to his former place*]: There is not half light enough. We should be blazing to the skies.

ELLIE [*tense with excitement*]: Set fire to the house, Marcus.

MRS HUSHABYE: My house! No.

HECTOR: I thought of that; but it would not be ready in time.

CAPTAIN SHOTOVER: The judgment has come. Courage will not save you; but it will shew that your souls are still alive.

MRS HUSHABYE: Sh-sh! Listen: do you hear it now? It's magnificent.

They all turn away from the house and look up, listening.

HECTOR [*gravely*]: Miss Dunn: you can do no good here. We of this house are only moths flying into the candle. You had better go down to the cellar.

ELLIE [*scornfully*]: I dont think.

MAZZINI: Ellie, dear, there is no disgrace in going to the cellar. An officer would order his soldiers to take cover. Mr Hushabye is behaving like an amateur. Mangan and the burglar are acting very sensibly; and it is they who will survive.

ELLIE: Let them. I shall behave like an amateur. But why should you run any risk?

MAZZINI: Think of the risk those poor fellows up there are running!

NURSE GUINNESS: Think of them, indeed, the murdering blackguards! What next?

A terrific explosion shakes the earth. They reel back into their seats, or clutch the nearest support. They hear the falling of the shattered glass from the windows.

MAZZINI: Is anyone hurt?

HECTOR: Where did it fall?

NURSE GUINNESS [*in hideous triumph*]: Right in the gravel pit: I seen it. Serve un right! I seen it [*she runs away towards the gravel pit, laughing harshly*].

HECTOR: One husband gone.

CAPTAIN SHOTOVER: Thirty pounds of good dynamite wasted.

MAZZINI: Oh, poor Mangan!

HECTOR: Are you immortal that you need pity him? Our turn next.

They wait in silence and intense expectation. HESIONE *and* ELLIE *hold each other's hand tight.*
A distant explosion is heard.

MRS HUSHABYE [*relaxing her grip*]: Oh! they have passed us.

LADY UTTERWORD: The danger is over, Randall. Go to bed.

CAPTAIN SHOTOVER: Turn in, all hands. The ship is safe. [*He sits down and goes asleep*].

ELLIE [*disappointedly*]: Safe!

HECTOR [*disgustedly*]: Yes, safe. And how damnably dull the world has become again suddenly! [*He sits down*].

MAZZINI [*sitting down*]: I was quite wrong, after all. It is we who have survived; and Mangan and the burglar—

HECTOR:—the two burglars—

LADY UTTERWORD:—the two practical men of business—

MAZZINI:—both gone. And the poor clergyman will have to get a new house.

MRS HUSHABYE: But what a glorious experience! I hope theyll come again tomorrow night.

ELLIE [*radiant at the prospect*]: Oh, I hope so.

RANDALL *at last succeeds in keeping the home fires burning on his flute.*

PRIVATE LIVES
NOEL COWARD

PRIVATE LIVES

First published in Great Britain in 1930
by William Heinemann Limited

CAUTION
Application for professional rights in this play should be referred to
Curtis Brown Ltd, 1 Craven Hill, London W2. Application for
amateur rights in this play should be referred to Samuel French
Ltd, 26 Southampton Street, Strand, London WC2E 7JE.

PRIVATE LIVES

(1930)

CHARACTERS

AMANDA PRYNNE
VICTOR PRYNNE (*her Husband*)
LOUISE (*a Maid*)
SIBYL CHASE
ELYOT CHASE (*her Husband*)

ACT ONE
The Terrace of a Hotel in France.
Summer evening.

ACT TWO
Amanda's flat in Paris.
A few days later.
Evening.

ACT THREE
The same.
The next morning.

Time: The Present.

ACT ONE

The scene is the terrace of a hotel in France. There are two French windows at the back opening on to two separate suites. The terrace space is divided by a line of small trees in tubs, and, down-stage, running parallel with the footlights, there is a low stone balustrade. Upon each side of the line of tree tubs is a set of suitable terrace furniture, a swinging seat, two or three chairs, and a table. There are orange and white awnings shading the windows, as it is summer.

When the curtain rises it is about eight o'clock in the evening. There is an orchestra playing not very far off. SIBYL CHASE *opens the windows on the right, and steps out on to the terrace. She is very pretty and blonde, and smartly dressed in travelling clothes. She comes down stage, stretches her arms wide with a little sigh of satisfaction, and regards the view with an ecstatic expression.*

SIBYL [*calling*]: Elli, Elli dear, do come out. It's so lovely.
ELYOT [*inside*]: Just a minute.

After a pause ELYOT *comes out. He is about thirty, quite slim and pleasant looking, and also in travelling clothes. He walks right down to the balustrade and looks thoughtfully at the view.* SIBYL *stands beside him, and slips her arm through his.*

ELYOT: Not so bad.
SIBYL: It's heavenly. Look at the lights of that yacht reflected in the water. Oh dear, I'm so happy.
ELYOT [*smiling*]: Are you?
SIBYL: Aren't you?
ELYOT: Of course I am. Tremendously happy.
SIBYL: Just to think, here we are, you and I, married!
ELYOT: Yes, things have come to a pretty pass.
SIBYL: Don't laugh at me, you mustn't be *blasé* about honeymoons just because this is your second.
ELYOT [*frowning*]: That's silly.
SIBYL: Have I annoyed you by saying that?
ELYOT: Just a little.
SIBYL: Oh, darling, I'm so sorry. [*She holds her face up to his.*] Kiss me.
ELYOT [*doing so*]: There.
SIBYL: Ummm, not so very enthusiastic.
ELYOT [*kissing her again*]: That better?
SIBYL: Three times, please, I'm superstitious.
ELYOT [*kissing her*]: You really are very sweet.
SIBYL: Are you glad you married me?

ELYOT: Of course I am.

SIBYL: How glad?

ELYOT: Incredibly, magnificently glad.

SIBYL: How lovely.

ELYOT: We ought to go in and dress.

SIBYL: Gladder than before?

ELYOT: Why do you keep harping on that?

SIBYL: It's in my mind, and yours too, I expect.

ELYOT: It isn't anything of the sort.

SIBYL: She was pretty, wasn't she? Amanda?

ELYOT: Very pretty.

SIBYL: Prettier than I am?

ELYOT: Much.

SIBYL: Elyot!

ELYOT: She was pretty and sleek, and her hands were long and slim, and her legs were long and slim, and she danced like an angel. You dance very poorly, by the way.

SIBYL: Could she play the piano as well as I can?

ELYOT: She couldn't play the piano at all.

SIBYL [*triumphantly*]: Aha! Had she my talent for organisation?

ELYOT: No, but she hadn't your mother either.

SIBYL: I don't believe you like mother.

ELYOT: Like her! I can't bear her.

SIBYL: Elyot! She's a darling, underneath.

ELYOT: I never got underneath.

SIBYL: It makes me unhappy to think you don't like mother.

ELYOT: Nonsense. I believe the only reason you married me was to get away from her.

SIBYL: I married you because I loved you.

ELYOT: Oh dear, oh dear, oh dear, oh dear!

SIBYL: I love you far more than Amanda loved you. I'd never make you miserable like she did.

ELYOT: We made each other miserable.

SIBYL: It was all her fault, you know it was.

ELYOT [*with vehemence*]: Yes, it was. Entirely her fault.

SIBYL: She was a fool to lose you.

ELYOT: We lost each other.

SIBYL: She lost you, with her violent tempers and carryings on.

ELYOT: Will you stop talking about Amanda?

SIBYL: But I'm very glad, because if she hadn't been uncontrolled, and wicked, and unfaithful, we shouldn't be here now.

ELYOT: She wasn't unfaithful.

SIBYL: How do you know? I bet she was. I bet she was unfaithful every five minutes.

ELYOT: It would take a far more concentrated woman than Amanda to be unfaithful every five minutes.

SIBYL [*anxiously*]: You do hate her, don't you?

ELYOT: No, I don't hate her. I think I despise her.

SIBYL [*with satisfaction*]: That's much worse.

ELYOT: And yet I'm sorry for her.

SIBYL: Why?

ELYOT: Because she's marked for tragedy; she's bound to make a mess of everything.

SIBYL: If it's all her fault, I don't see that it matters much.

ELYOT: She has some very good qualities.

SIBYL: Considering what a hell she made of your life, I think you are very nice about her. Most men would be vindictive.

ELYOT: What's the use of that? It's all over now, such a long time ago.

SIBYL: Five years isn't very long.

ELYOT [*seriously*]: Yes it is.

SIBYL: Do you think you could ever love her again?

ELYOT: Now then, Sibyl.

SIBYL: But could you?

ELYOT: Of course not, I love you.

SIBYL: Yes, but you love me differently; I know that.

ELYOT: More wisely perhaps.

SIBYL: I'm glad. I'd rather have that sort of love.

ELYOT: You're right. Love is no use unless it's wise, and kind, and undramatic. Something steady and sweet, to smooth out your nerves when you're tired. Something tremendously cosy; and unflurried by scenes and jealousies. That's what I want, what I've always wanted really. Oh my dear, I do hope it's not going to be dull for you.

SIBYL: Sweetheart, as tho' you could ever be dull.

ELYOT: I'm much older than you.

SIBYL: Not so very much.

ELYOT: Seven years.

SIBYL [*snuggling up to him*]: The music has stopped now and you can hear the sea.

ELYOT: We'll bathe to-morrow morning.

SIBYL: I mustn't get sunburnt.

ELYOT: Why not?

SIBYL: I hate it on women.

ELYOT: Very well, you shan't then. I hope you don't hate it on men.

SIBYL: Of course I don't. It's suitable to men.

ELYOT: You're a completely feminine little creature aren't you?

SIBYL: Why do you say that?

ELYOT: Everything in its place.

SIBYL: What do you mean?

ELYOT: If you feel you'd like me to smoke a pipe, I'll try and master it.

SIBYL: I like a man to be a man, if that's what you mean.

ELYOT: Are you going to understand me, and manage me?

SIBYL: I'm going to try to understand you.

ELYOT: Run me without my knowing it?

SIBYL [*withdrawing slightly*]: I think you're being a little unkind.

ELYOT: No, I don't mean to be. I was only wondering.

SIBYL: Well?

ELYOT: I was wondering what was going on inside your mind, what your plans are really?

SIBYL: Plans; Oh, Elli!

ELYOT: Apart from loving me and all that, you must have plans.

SIBYL: I haven't the faintest idea what you're talking about.

ELYOT: Perhaps it's subconscious then, age old instincts working away deep

down, mincing up little bits of experience for future use, watching me
carefully like a little sharp-eyed, blonde kitten.

SIBYL: How can you be so horrid.

ELYOT: I said Kitten, not Cat.

SIBYL: Kittens grow into cats.

ELYOT: Let that be a warning to you.

SIBYL [*slipping her arm through his again*]: What's the matter, darling; are you
hungry?

ELYOT: Not a bit.

SIBYL: You're very strange all of a sudden, and rather cruel. Just because I'm
feminine. It doesn't mean that I'm crafty and calculating.

ELYOT: I didn't say you were either of those things.

SIBYL: I hate these half masculine women who go banging about.

ELYOT: I hate anybody who goes banging about.

SIBYL: I should think you needed a little quiet womanliness after
Amanda.

ELYOT: Why will you keep on talking about her?

SIBYL: It's natural enough isn't it?

ELYOT: What do you want to find out?

SIBYL: Why did you really let her divorce you?

ELYOT: She divorced me for cruelty, and flagrant infidelity. I spent a whole
week-end at Brighton with a lady called Vera Williams. She had the nastiest
looking hair brush I have ever seen.

SIBYL: Misplaced chivalry, I call it. Why didn't you divorce her?

ELYOT: It would not have been the action of a gentleman, whatever that may
mean.

SIBYL: I think she got off very lightly.

ELYOT: Once and for all will you stop talking about her.

SIBYL: Yes, Elli dear.

ELYOT: I don't wish to see her again or hear her name mentioned.

SIBYL: Very well, darling.

ELYOT: Is that understood?

SIBYL: Yes, darling. Where did you spend your honeymoon?

ELYOT: St. Moritz. Be quiet.

SIBYL: I hate St Moritz.

ELYOT: So do I, bitterly.

SIBYL: Was she good on skis?

ELYOT: Do you want to dine donwstairs here, or at the Casino?

SIBYL: I love you, I love you, I love you.

ELYOT: Good, let's go in and dress.

SIBYL: Kiss me first.

ELYOT [*kissing her*]: Casino?

SIBYL: Yes. Are you a gambler? You never told me.

ELYOT: Every now and then.

SIBYL: I shall come and sit just behind your chair and bring you luck.

ELYOT: That will be fatal.

> *They go off into their suite. There is a slight pause and then* VICTOR PRYNNE
> *enters from the left suite. He is quite nice looking, about thirty or thirty-five.
> He is dressed in a light travelling suit. He sniffs the air, looks at the view, and
> then turns back to the window.*

VICTOR [*calling*]: Mandy.

AMANDA [*inside*]: What?

VICTOR: Come outside, the view is wonderful.

AMANDA: I'm still damp from the bath. Wait a minute—

> VICTOR *lights a cigarette. Presently* AMANDA *comes out on to the terrace. She is quite exquisite with a gay face and a perfect figure. At the moment she is wearing a negligee.*

I shall catch pneumonia, that's what I shall catch.

VICTOR [*looking at her*]: God!

AMANDA: I beg your pardon?

VICTOR: You look wonderful.

AMANDA: Thank you, darling.

VICTOR: Like a beautiful advertisement for something.

AMANDA: Nothing peculiar, I hope.

VICTOR: I can hardly believe it's true. You and I, here alone together, married!

AMANDA [*rubbing her face on his shoulder*]: That stuff's very rough.

VICTOR: Don't you like it?

AMANDA: A bit hearty, isn't it?

VICTOR: Do you love me?

AMANDA: Of course, that's why I'm here.

VICTOR: More than—

AMANDA: Now then, none of that.

VICTOR: No, but do you love me more than you loved Elyot?

AMANDA: I don't remember, it's such a long time ago.

VICTOR: Not so very long.

AMANDA [*flinging out her arms*]: All my life ago.

VICTOR: I'd like to break his damned neck.

AMANDA [*laughing*]: Why?

VICTOR: For making you unhappy.

AMANDA: It was mutual.

VICTOR: Rubbish! It was all his fault, you know it was.

AMANDA: Yes, it was, now I come to think about it.

VICTOR: Swine!

AMANDA: Don't be so vehement, darling.

VICTOR: I'll never treat you like that.

AMANDA: That's right.

VICTOR: I love you too much.

AMANDA: So did he.

VICTOR: Fine sort of love that is. He struck you once, didn't he?

AMANDA: More than once.

VICTOR: Where?

AMANDA: Several places.

VICTOR: What a cad.

AMANDA: I struck him too. Once I broke four gramophone records over his head. It was very satisfying.

VICTOR: You must have been driven to distraction.

AMANDA: Yes, I was, but don't let's talk about it, please. After all, it's a dreary subject for our honeymoon night.

VICTOR: He didn't know when he was well off.

AMANDA: Look at the lights of that yacht reflected in the water. I wonder whose it is.

VICTOR: We must bathe to-morrow.

AMANDA: Yes. I want to get a nice sunburn.

VICTOR [*reproachfully*]: Mandy!

AMANDA: Why, what's the matter?

VICTOR: I hate sunburnt women.

AMANDA: Why?

VICTOR: It's somehow, well, unsuitable.

AMANDA: It's awfully suitable to me, darling.

VICTOR: Of course if you really want to.

AMANDA: I'm absolutely determined. I've got masses of lovely oil to rub all over myself.

VICTOR: Your skin is so beautiful as it is.

AMANDA: Wait and see. When I'm done a nice crisp brown, you'll fall in love with me all over again.

VICTOR: I couldn't love you more than I do now.

AMANDA: Oh, dear. I did so hope our honeymoon was going to be progressive.

VICTOR: Where did you spend the last one?

AMANDA [*warningly*]: Victor.

VICTOR: I want to know.

AMANDA: St Moritz. It was very attractive.

VICTOR: I hate St Moritz.

AMANDA: So do I.

VICTOR: Did he start quarrelling with you right away?

AMANDA: Within the first few days. I put it down to the high altitudes.

VICTOR: And you loved him?

AMANDA: Yes, Victor.

VICTOR: You poor child.

AMANDA: You must try not to be pompous, dear. [*She turns away.*]

VICTOR [*hurt*]: Mandy!

AMANDA: I don't believe I'm a bit like what you think I am.

VICTOR: How do you mean?

AMANDA: I was never a poor child.

VICTOR: Figure of speech, dear, that's all.

AMANDA: I suffered a good deal, and had my heart broken. But it wasn't an innocent girlish heart. It was jagged with sophistication. I've always been sophisticated, far too knowing. That caused many of my rows with Elyot. I irritated him because he knew I could see through him.

VICTOR: I don't mind how much you see through me.

AMANDA: Sweet. [*She kisses him.*]

VICTOR: I'm going to make you happy.

AMANDA: Are you?

VICTOR: Just by looking after you, and seeing that you're all right, you know.

AMANDA [*a trifle wistfully*]: No, I don't know.

VICTOR: I think you love me quite differently from the way you loved Elyot.

AMANDA: Do stop harping on Elyot.

VICTOR: It's true, though, isn't it?

AMANDA: I love you much more calmly, if that's what you mean.

VICTOR: More lastingly?

AMANDA: I expect so.

VICTOR: Do you remember when I first met you?

AMANDA: Yes. Distinctly.

VICTOR: At Marion Vale's party.

AMANDA: Yes.

VICTOR: Wasn't it wonderful?

AMANDA: Not really, dear, It was only redeemed from the completely commonplace by the fact of my having hiccoughs.

VICTOR: I never noticed them.

AMANDA: Love at first sight.

VICTOR: Where did you first meet Elyot?

AMANDA: To hell with Elyot.

VICTOR: Mandy!

AMANDA: I forbid you to mention his name again. I'm sick of the sound of it. You must be raving mad. Here we are on the first night of our honeymoon, with the moon coming up, and the music playing, and all you can do is to talk about my first husband. It's downright sacrilegious.

VICTOR: Don't be angry.

AMANDA: Well, it's very annoying.

VICTOR: Will you forgive me?

AMANDA: Yes; only don't do it again.

VICTOR: I promise.

AMANDA: You'd better go and dress now, you haven't bathed yet.

VICTOR: Where shall we dine, downstairs here, or at the Casino?

AMANDA: The Casino is more fun, I think.

VICTOR: We can play Boule afterwards.

AMANDA: No, we can't, dear.

VICTOR: Don't you like dear old Boule?

AMANDA: No, I hate dear old Boule. We'll play a nice game of Chemin de fer.

VICTOR [*apprehensively*]: Not at the big table?

AMANDA: Maybe at the biggest table.

VICTOR: You're not a terrible gambler, are you?

AMANDA: Inveterate. Chance rules my life.

VICTOR: What nonsense.

AMANDA: How can you say it's nonsense. It was chance meeting you. It was chancing falling in love; it's chance that we're here, particularly after your driving. Everything that happens is chance.

VICTOR: You know I feel rather scared of you at close quarters.

AMANDA: That promises to be very embarrassing.

VICTOR: You're somehow different now, wilder than I thought you were, more strained.

AMANDA: Wilder! Oh Victor, I've never felt less wild in my life. A little strained, I grant you, but that's the newly married atmosphere; you can't expect anything else. Honeymooning is a very overrated amusement.

VICTOR: You say that because you had a ghastly experience before.

AMANDA: There you go again.

VICTOR: It couldn't fail to embitter you a little.

AMANDA: The honeymoon wasn't such a ghastly experience really; it was afterwards that was so awful.

VICTOR: I intend to make you forget it all entirely.

AMANDA: You won't succeed by making constant references to it.

VICTOR: I wish I knew you better.

AMANDA: It's just as well you don't. The 'woman'–in italics–should always retain a certain amount of alluring feminine mystery for the 'man'–also in italics.

VICTOR: What about the man? Isn't he allowed to have any mystery?

AMANDA: Absolutely none. Transparent as glass.

VICTOR: Oh, I see.

AMANDA: Never mind, darling; it doesn't necessarily work out like that; it's only supposed to.

VICTOR: I'm glad I'm normal.

AMANDA: What an odd thing to be glad about. Why?

VICTOR: Well, aren't you?

AMANDA: I'm not so sure I'm normal.

VICTOR: Oh, Mandy, of course you are, sweetly, divinely normal.

AMANDA: I haven't any peculiar cravings for Chinamen or old boots, if that's what you mean.

VICTOR [*scandalised*]: Mandy!

AMANDA: I think very few people are completely normal really, deep down in their private lives. It all depends on a combination of circumstances. If all the various cosmic thingummys fuse at the same moment, and the right spark is struck, there's no knowing what one mightn't do. That was the trouble with Elyot and me, we were like two violent acids bubbling about in a nasty little matrimonial bottle.

VICTOR: I don't believe you're nearly as complex as you think you are.

AMANDA: I don't think I'm particularly complex, but I know I'm unreliable.

VICTOR: You're frightening me horribly. In what way unreliable?

AMANDA: I'm so apt to see things the wrong way round.

VICTOR: What sort of things?

AMANDA: Morals. What one should do and what one shouldn't.

VICTOR [*fondly*]: Darling, you're so sweet.

AMANDA: Thank you, Victor, that's most encouraging. You really must have your bath now. Come along.

VICTOR: Kiss me.

AMANDA [*doing so*]: There, dear, hurry now; I've only got to slip my dress on and then I shall be ready.

VICTOR: Give me ten minutes.

AMANDA: I'll bring the cocktails out here when they come.

VICTOR: All right.

AMANDA: Go along now, hurry.

They both disappear into their suite. After a moment's pause ELYOT *steps carefully on to the terrace carrying a tray upon which are two champagne cocktails. He puts the tray down on the table.*

ELYOT [*calling*]: Sibyl.

SIBYL [*inside*]: Yes.

ELYOT: I've brought the cocktails out here, hurry up.

SIBYL: I can't find my lipstick.

ELYOT: Never mind, send down to the kitchen for some cochineal.

SIBYL: Don't be so silly.

ELYOT: Hurry.

Elyot saunters down to the balustrade. He looks casually over on to the next terrace, and then out at the view. He looks up at the moon and sighs, then he sits down in a chair with his back towards the line of tubs, and lights a cigarette. AMANDA *steps gingerly on to her terrace carrying a tray with two champagne cocktails on it. She is wearing a charmingly simple evening gown, her cloak is flung over her right shoulder. She places the tray carefully on the table, puts her cloak over the back of a chair, and sits down with her back towards* ELYOT. *She takes a small mirror from her handbag, and scrutinizes her face in it. The orchestra downstairs strikes up a new melody. Both* ELYOT *and* AMANDA *give a little start. After a moment,* ELYOT *pensively begins to hum the tune the band is playing. It is a sentimental, romantic little tune.* AMANDA *hears him, and clutches at her throat suddenly as though she were suffocating. Then she jumps up noiselessly, and peers over the line of tubs.* ELYOT, *with his back to her, continues to sing obliviously. She sits down again, relaxing with a gesture almost of despair. Then she looks anxiously over her shoulder at the window in case* VICTOR *should be listening, and then, with a little smile, she takes up the melody herself, clearly.* ELYOT *stops dead and gives a gasp, then he jumps up, and stands looking at her. She continues to sing, pretending not to know that he is there. At the end of the song, she turns slowly, and faces him.*

AMANDA: Thoughtful of them to play that, wasn't it?
ELYOT [*in a stifled voice*]: What are you doing here?
AMANDA: I'm on honeymoon.
ELYOT: How interesting, so am I.
AMANDA: I hope you're enjoying it.
ELYOT: It hasn't started yet.
AMANDA: Neither has mine.
ELYOT: Oh, my God!
AMANDA: I can't help feeling that this is a little unfortunate.
ELYOT: Are you happy?
AMANDA: Perfectly.
ELYOT: Good. That's all right, then, isn't it?
AMANDA: Are you?
ELYOT: Ecstatically.
AMANDA: I'm delighted to hear it. We shall probably meet again sometime. Au revoir! [*She turns.*]
ELYOT [*firmly*]: Good-bye.

She goes indoors without looking back. He stands gazing after her with an expression of horror on his face. SIBYL *comes brightly on to the terrace in a very pretty evening frock.*

SIBYL: Cocktail please.

ELYOT *doesn't answer.*

Elli, what's the matter?
ELYOT: I feel very odd.
SIBYL: Odd, what do you mean, Ill?
ELYOT: Yes, ill.
SIBYL [*alarmed*]: What sort of

ELYOT: We must leave at once.

SIBYL: Leave!

ELYOT: Yes, dear. Leave immediately.

SIBYL: Elli!

ELYOT: I have a strange foreboding.

SIBYL: You must be mad.

ELYOT: Listen, darling. I want you to be very sweet, and patient, and understanding, and not be upset, or ask any questions, or anything. I have an absolute conviction that our whole future happiness depends upon our leaving here instantly.

SIBYL: Why?

ELYOT: I can't tell you why.

SIBYL: But we've only just come.

ELYOT: I know that, but it can't be helped.

SIBYL: What's happened, what has happened?

ELYOT: Nothing has happened.

SIBYL: You've gone out of your mind.

ELYOT: I haven't gone out of my mind, but I shall if we stay here another hour.

SIBYL: You're not drunk, are you?

ELYOT: Of course I'm not drunk. What time have I had to get drunk?

SIBYL: Come down and have some dinner, darling, and then you'll feel ever so much better.

ELYOT: It's no use trying to humour me. I'm serious.

SIBYL: But darling, please be reasonable. We've only just arrived; everything's unpacked. It's our first night together. We can't go away now.

ELYOT: We can have our first night together in Paris.

SIBYL: We shouldn't get there until the small hours.

ELYOT [*with a great effort at calmness*]: Now please, Sibyl, I know it sounds crazy to you, and utterly lacking in reason and sense, but I've got second sight over certain things. I'm almost psychic. I've got the most extraordinary sensation of impending disaster. If we stay here something appalling will happen. I know it.

SIBYL [*firmly*]: Hysterical nonsense.

ELYOT: It isn't hysterical nonsense. Presentiments are far from being nonsense. Look at the woman who cancelled her passage on the *Titanic*. All because of a presentiment.

SIBYL: I don't see what that has to do with it.

ELYOT: It has everything to do with it. She obeyed her instincts, that's what she did, and saved her life. All I ask is to be allowed to obey my instincts.

SIBYL: Do you mean that there's going to be an earthquake or something?

ELYOT: Very possibly, very possibly indeed, or perhaps a violent explosion.

SIBYL: They don't have earthquakes in France.

ELYOT: On the contrary, only the other day they felt a distinct shock at Toulon.

SIBYL: Yes, but that's in the South where it's hot.

ELYOT: Don't quibble, Sibyl.

SIBYL: And as for explosions, there's nothing here that can explode.

ELYOT: Oho, isn't there.

SIBYL: Yes, but Elli—

ELYOT: Darling, be sweet. Bear with me. I beseech you to bear with me.

SIBYL: I don't understand. It's horrid of you to do this.

ELYOT: I'm not doing anything. I'm only asking you, imploring you to come away from this place.

SIBYL: But I love it here.

ELYOT: There are thousands of other places far nicer.

SIBYL: It's a pity we didn't go to one of them.

ELYOT: Now, listen, Sibyl—

SIBYL: Yes, but why are you behaving like this, why, why, why?

ELYOT: Don't ask why. Just give in to me. I swear I'll never ask you to give into me over anything again.

SIBYL [*with complete decision*]: I won't think of going to-night. It's utterly ridiculous. I've done quite enough travelling for one day, and I'm tired.

ELYOT: You're as obstinate as a mule.

SIBYL: I like that, I must say.

ELYOT [*hotly*]: You've got your nasty little feet dug into the ground, and you don't intend to budge an inch, do you?

SIBYL [*with spirit*]: No, I do not.

ELYOT: If there's one thing in the world that infuriates me, it's sheer wanton stubbornness. I should like to cut off your head with a meat axe.

SIBYL: How dare you talk to me like that, on our honeymoon night.

ELYOT: Damn our honeymoon night. Damn it, damn it, damn it!

SIBYL [*bursting into tears*]: Oh, Elli, Elli—

ELYOT: Stop crying. Will you or will you not come away with me to Paris?

SIBYL: I've never been so miserable in my life. You're hateful and beastly. Mother was perfectly right. She said you had shifty eyes.

ELYOT: Well, she can't talk. Her's are so close together, you couldn't put a needle between them.

SIBYL: You don't love me a little bit. I wish I were dead.

ELYOT: Will you or will you not come to Paris?

SIBYL: No, no I won't.

ELYOT: Oh, my God! [*He stamps indoors.*]

SIBYL [*following him, wailing*]: Oh, Elli, Elli, Elli—

VICTOR *comes stamping out of the French windows on the left, followed by* AMANDA.

VICTOR: You were certainly right when you said you weren't normal. You're behaving like a lunatic.

AMANDA: Not at all. All I have done is to ask you a little favour.

VICTOR: Little favour indeed.

AMANDA: If we left now we could be in Paris in a few hours.

VICTOR: If we crossed Siberia by train we could be in China in a fortnight, but I don't see any reason to do it.

AMANDA: Oh, Victor darling—please, please—be sensible, just for my sake.

VICTOR: Sensible!

AMANDA: Yes, sensible. I shall be absolutely miserable if we stay here. You don't want me to be absolutely miserable all through my honeymoon, do you?

VICTOR: But why on earth didn't you think of your sister's tragedy before?

AMANDA: I forgot.

VICTOR: You couldn't forget a thing like that.

AMANDA: I got the places muddled. Then when I saw the Casino there in the moonlight, it all came back to me.

VICTOR: When did all this happen?

AMANDA: Years ago, but it might just as well have been yesterday. I can see her now lying dead, with that dreadful expression on her face. Then all that awful business of taking the body home to England. It was perfectly horrible.

VICTOR: I never knew you had a sister.

AMANDA: I haven't any more.

VICTOR: There's something behind all this.

AMANDA: Don't be silly. What could there be behind it?

VICTOR: Well, for one thing, I know you're lying.

AMANDA: Victor!

VICTOR: Be honest. Aren't you?

AMANDA: I can't think how you can be so mean and suspicious.

VICTOR [*patiently*]: You're lying, Amanda. Aren't you?

AMANDA: Yes, Victor.

VICTOR: You never had a sister, dead or alive?

AMANDA: I believe there was a stillborn one in 1902.

VICTOR: What is your reason for all this?

AMANDA: I told you I was unreliable.

VICTOR: Why do you want to leave so badly?

AMANDA: You'll be angry if I tell you the truth.

VICTOR: What is it?

AMANDA: I warn you.

VICTOR: Tell me. Please tell me.

AMANDA: Elyot's here.

VICTOR: What!

AMANDA: I saw him.

VICTOR: When?

AMANDA: Just now, when you were in the bath.

VICTOR: Where was he?

AMANDA [*hesitatingly*]: Down there, in a white suit. [*She points over the balustrade.*]

VICTOR [*sceptically*]: White suit?

AMANDA: Why not? It's summer, isn't it?

VICTOR: You're lying again.

AMANDA: I'm not. He's here. I swear he is.

VICTOR: Well, what of it?

AMANDA: I can't enjoy a honeymoon with you, with Elyot liable to bounce in at any moment.

VICTOR: Really, Mandy.

AMANDA: Can't you see how awful it is? It's the most embarrassing thing that ever happened to me in my whole life.

VICTOR: Did he see you?

AMANDA: No, he was running.

VICTOR: What was he running for?

AMANDA: How on earth do I know. Don't be so annoying.

VICTOR: Well, as long as he didn't see you it's all right, isn't it?

AMANDA: It isn't all right at all. We must leave immediately.

VICTOR: But why?

AMANDA: How can you be so appallingly obstinate.

VICTOR: I'm not afraid of him.

AMANDA: Neither am I. It isn't a question of being afraid. It's just a horrible awkward situation.

VICTOR: I'm damned if I can see why our whole honeymoon should be upset by Elyot.

AMANDA: My last one was.

VICTOR: I don't believe he's here at all.

AMANDA: He is I tell you. I saw him.

VICTOR: It was probably an optical illusion. This half light is very deceptive.

AMANDA: It was no such thing.

VICTOR: I absolutely refuse to change all our plans at the last moment, just because you think you've seen Elyot. It's unreasonable and ridiculous of you to demand it. Even if he is here I can't see that it matters. He'll probably feel much more embarrassed than you, and a damned good job too; and if he annoys you in any way I'll knock him down.

AMANDA: That would be charming.

VICTOR: Now don't let's talk about it any more.

AMANDA: Do you mean to stand there seriously and imagine that the whole thing can be glossed over as easily as that?

VICTOR: I'm not going to leave, Mandy. If I start giving into you as early as this, our lives will be unbearable.

AMANDA [*outraged*]: Victor!

VICTOR [*calmly*]: You've worked yourself up into a state over a situation which really only exists in your mind.

AMANDA [*controlling herself with an effort*]: Please, Victor, please, for this last time I implore you. Let's go to Paris now, to-night. I mean it with all my heart—please—

VICTOR [*with gentle firmness*]: No, Mandy!

AMANDA: I see quite clearly that I have been foolish enough to marry a fat old gentleman in a club armchair.

VICTOR: It's no use being cross.

AMANDA: You're a pompous ass.

VICTOR [*horrified*]: Mandy!

AMANDA [*enraged*]: Pompous ass, that's what I said, and that's what I meant. Blown out with your own importance.

VICTOR: Mandy, control yourself.

AMANDA: Get away from me. I can't bear to think I'm married to such rugged grandeur.

VICTOR [*with great dignity*]: I shall be in the bar. When you are ready to come down and dine, let me know.

AMANDA [*flinging herself into a chair*]: Go away, go away.

VICTOR *stalks off, at the same moment that* ELYOT *stamps on, on the other side, followed by* SIBYL *in tears.*

ELYOT: If you don't stop screaming, I'll murder you.

SIBYL: I wish to heaven I'd never seen you in my life, let alone married you. I don't wonder Amanda left you, if you behaved to her as you've behaved to me. I'm going down to have dinner by myself and you can just do what you like about it.

ELYOT: Do, and I hope it chokes you.

SIBYL: Oh Elli, Elli—

She goes wailing indoors. ELYOT *stamps down to the balustrade and lights a cigarette, obviously trying to control his nerves.* AMANDA *sees him, and comes down too.*

AMANDA: Give me one for God's sake.
ELYOT [*hands her his case laconically*]: Here.
AMANDA [*taking a cigarette*]: I'm in such a rage.
ELYOT [*lighting up*]: So am I.
AMANDA: What are we to do?
ELYOT: I don't know.
AMANDA: Whose yacht is that?
ELYOT: The Duke of Westminster's I expect. It always is.
AMANDA: I wish I were on it.
ELYOT: I wish you were too.
AMANDA: There's no need to be nasty.
ELYOT: Yes there is, every need. I've never in my life felt a greater urge to be nasty.
AMANDA: And you've had some urges in your time, haven't you?
ELYOT: If you start bickering with me, Amanda, I swear I'll throw you over the edge.
AMANDA: Try it, that's all, just try it.
ELYOT: You've upset everything, as usual.
AMANDA: I've upset everything! What about you?
ELYOT: Ever since the first moment I was unlucky enough to set eyes on you, my life has been insupportable.
AMANDA: Oh do shut up, there's no sense in going on like that.
ELYOT: Nothing's any use. There's no escape, ever.
AMANDA: Don't be melodramatic.
ELYOT: Do you want a cocktail? There are two here.
AMANDA: There are two over here as well.
ELYOT: We'll have my two first.

AMANDA *crosses over into* ELYOT's *part of the terrace. He gives her one, and keeps one himself.*

AMANDA: Shall we get roaring screaming drunk?
ELYOT: I don't think that would help, we did it once before and it was a dismal failure.
AMANDA: It was lovely at the beginning.
ELYOT: You have an immoral memory Amanda. Here's to you.

They raise their glasses solemnly and drink.

AMANDA: I tried to get away the moment after I'd seen you, but he wouldn't budge.
ELYOT: What's his name.
AMANDA: Victor, Victor Prynne.
ELYOT [*toasting*]: Mr and Mrs Victor Prynne. [*He drinks.*] Mine wouldn't budge either.
AMANDA: What's her name?
ELYOT: Sibyl.

AMANDA [*toasting*]: Mr and Mrs Elyot Chase. [*She drinks.*] God pity the poor girl.

ELYOT: Are you in love with him?

AMANDA: Of course.

ELYOT: How funny.

AMANDA: I don't see anything particularly funny about it, you're in love with yours aren't you?

ELYOT: Certainly.

AMANDA: There you are then.

ELYOT: There we both are then.

AMANDA: What's she like?

ELYOT: Fair, very pretty, plays the piano beautifully.

AMANDA: Very comforting.

ELYOT: How's yours?

AMANDA: I don't want to discuss him.

ELYOT: Well, it doesn't matter, he'll probably come popping out in a minute and I shall see for myself. Does he know I'm here?

AMANDA: Yes, I told him.

ELYOT [*with sarcasm*]: That's going to make things a whole lot easier.

AMANDA: You needn't be frightened, he won't hurt you.

ELYOT: If he comes near me I'll scream the place down.

AMANDA: Does Sibyl know I'm here?

ELYOT: No, I pretended I'd had a presentiment. I tried terribly hard to persuade her to leave for Paris.

AMANDA: I tried too, it's lucky we didn't both succeed, isn't it? Otherwise we should probably all have joined up in Rouen or somewhere.

ELYOT [*laughing*]: In some frowsy little hotel.

AMANDA [*laughing too*]: Oh dear, it would have been much, much worse.

ELYOT: I can see us all sailing down in the morning for an early start.

AMANDA [*weakly*]: Lovely, oh lovely.

ELYOT: Glorious! [*They both laugh helplessly.*]

AMANDA: What's happened to yours?

ELYOT: Didn't you hear her screaming? She's downstairs in the dining-room I think.

AMANDA: Mine is being grand, in the bar.

ELYOT: It really is awfully difficult.

AMANDA: Have you known her long?

ELYOT: About four months, we met in a house party in Norfolk.

AMANDA: Very flat, Norfolk.

ELYOT: How old is dear Victor?

AMANDA: Thirty-four, or five; and Sibyl?

ELYOT: I blush to tell you, only twenty-three.

AMANDA: You've gone a mucker alright.

ELYOT: I shall reserve my opinion of your choice until I've met dear Victor.

AMANDA: I wish you wouldn't go on calling him 'Dear Victor'. It's extremely irritating.

ELYOT: That's how I see him. Dumpy, and fair, and very considerate, with glasses. Dear Victor.

AMANDA: As I said before I would rather not discuss him. At least I have good taste enough to refrain from making cheap gibes at Sibyl.

ELYOT: You said Norfolk was flat.

AMANDA: That was no reflection on her, unless she made it flatter.
ELYOT: Your voice takes on an acid quality whenever you mention her name.
AMANDA: I'll never mention it again.
ELYOT: Good, and I'll keep off Victor.
AMANDA [*with dignity*]: Thank you.

There is silence for a moment. The orchestra starts playing the same tune that they were singing previously.

ELYOT: That orchestra has a remarkably small repertoire.
AMANDA: They don't seem to know anything but this, do they?

She sits down on the balustrade, and sings it, softly. Her eyes are looking out to sea, and her mind is far away. ELYOT *watches her while she sings. When she turns to him at the end, there are tears in her eyes. He looks away awkwardly and lights another cigarette.*

ELYOT: You have always had a sweet voice, Amanda.
AMANDA [*a littly huskily*]: Thank you.
ELYOT: I'm awfully sorry about all this, really I am. I wouldn't have had it happen for the world.
AMANDA: I know. I'm sorry too. It's just rotten luck.
ELYOT: I'll go away to-morrow whatever happens, so don't you worry.
AMANDA: That's nice of you.
ELYOT: I hope everything turns out splendidly for you, and that you'll be very happy.
AMANDA: I hope the same for you, too.

The music, which has been playing continually through this little scene, returns persistently to the refrain. They both look at one another and laugh.

ELYOT: Nasty insistent little tune.
AMANDA: Extraordinary how potent cheap music is.
ELYOT: What exactly were you remembering at that moment?
AMANDA: The Palace Hotel Skating Rink in the morning, bright strong sunlight, and everybody whirling round in vivid colours, and you kneeling down to put on my skates for me.
ELYOT: You'd fallen on your fanny a few moments before.
AMANDA: It was beastly of you to laugh like that, I felt so humiliated.
ELYOT: Poor darling.
AMANDA: Do you remember waking up in the morning, and standing on the balcony, looking out across the valley?
ELYOT: Blue shadows on white snow, cleanness beyond belief, high above everything in the world. How beautiful it was.
AMANDA: It's nice to think we had a few marvellous moments.
ELYOT: A few: We had heaps really, only they slip away into the background, and one only remembers the bad ones.
AMANDA: Yes. What fools we were to ruin it all. What utter, utter fools.
ELYOT: You feel like that too, do you?
AMANDA [*wearily*]: Of course.
ELYOT: Why did we?

AMANDA: The whole business was too much for us.

ELYOT: We were so ridiculously over in love.

AMANDA: Funny wasn't it?

ELYOT [*sadly*]: Horribly funny.

AMANDA: Selfishness, cruelty, hatred, possessiveness, petty jealousy. All those qualities came out in us just because we loved each other.

ELYOT: Perhaps they were there anyhow.

AMANDA: No, it's love that does it. To hell with love.

ELYOT: To hell with love.

AMANDA: And yet here we are starting afresh with two quite different people. In love all over again, aren't we? [ELYOT *doesn't answer.*] Aren't we?

ELYOT: No.

AMANDA: Elyot.

ELYOT: We're not in love all over again, and you know it. Good night, Amanda. [*He turns abruptly, and goes towards the French windows.*]

AMANDA: Elyot—don't be silly—come back.

ELYOT: I must go and find Sibyl.

AMANDA: I must go and find Victor.

ELYOT [*savagely*]: Well, why don't you?

AMANDA: I don't want to.

ELYOT: It's shameful, shameful of us.

AMANDA: Don't: I feel terrible. Don't leave me for a minute, I shall go mad if you do. We won't talk about ourselves any more, we'll talk about outside things, anything you like, only just don't leave me until I've pulled myself together.

ELYOT: Very well.

There is a dead silence.

AMANDA: What have you been doing lately? During these last years?

ELYOT: Travelling about. I went round the world you know after—

AMANDA [*hurriedly*]: Yes, yes, I know. How was it?

ELYOT: The world?

AMANDA: Yes.

ELYOT: Oh, highly enjoyable.

AMANDA: China must be very interesting.

ELYOT: Very big, China.

AMANDA: And Japan—

ELYOT: Very small.

AMANDA: Did you eat sharks' fins, and take your shoes off, and use chopsticks and everything?

ELYOT: Practically everything.

AMANDA: And India, the burning Ghars or Ghats, or whatever they are, and the Taj Mahal. How was the Taj Mahal?

ELYOT [*looking at her*]: Unbelievable, a sort of dream.

AMANDA: That was the moonlight I expect, you must have seen it in the moonlight.

ELYOT [*never taking his eyes off her face*]: Yes, moonlight is cruelly deceptive.

AMANDA: And it didn't look like a biscuit box did it? I've always felt that it might.

ELYOT [*quietly*]: Darling, darling, I love you so.

AMANDA: And I do hope you met a sacred Elephant. They're lint white I believe, and very, very sweet.

ELYOT: I've never loved anyone else for an instant.

AMANDA [*raising her hand feebly in protest*]: No, no, you mustn't—Elyot—stop.

ELYOT: You love me, too, don't you? There's no doubt about it anywhere, is there?

AMANDA: No, no doubt anywhere.

ELYOT: You're looking very lovely you know, in this damned moonlight. Your skin is clear and cool, and your eyes are shining, and you're growing lovelier and lovelier every second as I look at you. You don't hold any mystery for me, darling, do you mind? There isn't a particle of you that I don't know, remember, and want.

AMANDA [*softly*]: I'm glad, my sweet.

ELYOT: More than any desire anywhere, deep down in my deepest heart I want you back again—please—

AMANDA [*putting her hand over his mouth*]: Don't say any more, you're making me cry so dreadfully.

> *He pulls her gently into his arms and they stand silently, completely oblivious to everything but the moment, and each other. When finally, they separate, they sit down, rather breathlessly, on the balustrade.*

AMANDA: What now? Oh darling, what now?

ELYOT: I don't know, I'm lost, utterly.

AMANDA: We must think quickly, oh quickly—

ELYOT: Escape?

AMANDA: Together?

ELYOT: Yes, of course, now, now.

AMANDA: We can't, we can't, you know we can't.

ELYOT: We must.

AMANDA: It would break Victor's heart.

ELYOT: And Sibyl's too probably, but they're bound to suffer anyhow. Think of the hell we'd lead them into if we stayed. Infinitely worse than any cruelty in the world, pretending to love them, and loving each other, so desperately.

AMANDA: We must tell them.

ELYOT: What?

AMANDA: Call them, and tell them.

ELYOT: Oh no, no, that's impossible.

AMANDA: It's honest.

ELYOT: I can't help how honest it is, it's too horrible to think of. How should we start? What should we say?

AMANDA: We should have to trust to the inspiration of the moment.

ELYOT: It would be a moment completely devoid of inspiration. The most appalling moment imaginable. No, no, we can't, you must see that, we simply can't.

AMANDA: What do you propose to do then? As it is they might appear at any moment.

ELYOT: We've got to decide instantly one way or another. Go away together now, or stay with them, and never see one another again, ever.

AMANDA: Don't be silly, what choice is there?

ELYOT: No choice at all, come— [*He takes her hand.*]

AMANDA: No, wait. This is sheer raving madness, something's happened to us, we're not sane.

ELYOT: We never were.

AMANDA: Where can we go?

ELYOT: Paris first, my car's in the garage, all ready.

AMANDA: They'll follow us.

ELYOT: That doesn't matter, once the thing's done.

AMANDA: I've got a flat in Paris.

ELYOT: Good.

AMANDA: It's in the Avenue Montaigne. I let it to Freda Lawson, but she's in Biarritz, so it's empty.

ELYOT: Does Victor know?

AMANDA: No, he knows I have one but he hasn't the faintest idea where.

ELYOT: Better and better.

AMANDA: We're being so bad, so terribly bad, we'll suffer for this, I know we shall.

ELYOT: Can't be helped.

AMANDA: Starting all those awful rows all over again.

ELYOT: No, no, we're older and wiser now.

AMANDA: What difference does that make? The first moment either of us gets a bit nervy, off we'll go again.

ELYOT: Stop shilly-shallying, Amanda.

AMANDA: I'm trying to be sensible.

ELYOT: You're only succeeding in being completely idiotic.

AMANDA: Idiotic indeed! What about you?

ELYOT: Now look here Amanda—

AMANDA [*stricken*]: Oh my God!

ELYOT [*rushing to her and kissing her*]: Darling, darling, I didn't mean it—

AMANDA: I won't move from here unless we have a compact, a sacred, sacred compact never to quarrel again.

ELYOT: Easy to make but difficult to keep.

AMANDA: No, no, it's the bickering that always starts it. The moment we notice we're bickering, either of us, we must promise on our honour to stop dead. We'll invent some phrase or catchword, which when either of us says it, automatically cuts off all conversation for at least five minutes.

ELYOT: Two minutes dear, with an option of renewal.

AMANDA: Very well, what shall it be?

ELYOT [*hurriedly*]: Solomon Isaacs.

AMANDA: All right, that'll do.

ELYOT: Come on, come on.

AMANDA: What shall we do if we meet either of them on the way downstairs?

ELYOT: Run like stags.

AMANDA: What about clothes?

ELYOT: I've got a couple of bags I haven't unpacked yet.

AMANDA: I've got a small trunk.

ELYOT: Send the porter up for it.

AMANDA: Oh this is terrible–terrible—

ELYOT: Come on, come on, don't wast time.

AMANDA: Oughtn't we to leave notes or something?

ELYOT: No, no, no, we'll telegraph from somewhere on the road.

AMANDA: Darling, I daren't, it's too wicked of us, I simply daren't.

ELYOT [*seizing her in his arms and kissing her violently*]: Now will you behave?
AMANDA: Yes, but Elyot darling—
ELYOT: Solomon Isaacs!

They rush off together through ELYOT'*s suite. After a moment or so,* VICTOR *steps out on to the terrace and looks round anxiously. Then he goes back indoors again, and can be heard calling '*MANDY'. *Finally he again comes out on to the terrace and comes despondently down to the balustrade. He hears* SIBYL'*s voice calling '*ELLI' *and looks round as she comes out of the French windows. She jumps slightly upon seeing him.*

VICTOR: Good evening.
SIBYL [*rather flustered*]: Good-evening–I was–er–looking for my husband.
VICTOR: Really, that's funny. I was looking for my wife.
SIBYL: Quite a coincidence. [*She laughs nervously.*]
VICTOR [*after a pause*]: It's very nice here isn't it?
SIBYL: Lovely.
VICTOR: Have you been here long?
SIBYL: No, we only arrived to-day.
VICTOR: Another coincidence. So did we.
SIBYL: How awfully funny.
VICTOR: Would you care for a cocktail?
SIBYL: On no thank you–really—
VICTOR: There are two here on the table.

SIBYL *glances at the two empty glasses on the balustrade, and tosses her head defiantly.*

SIBYL: Thanks very much, I'd love one.
VICTOR: Good, here you are.

SIBYL *comes over to* VICTOR'*s side on the terrace. He hands her one and takes one himself.*

SIBYL: Thank you.
VICTOR [*with rather forced gaiety*]: To absent friends. [*He raises his glass.*]
SIBYL [*raising hers*]: To absent friends.

They both laugh rather mirthlessly and then sit down on the balustrade, pensively sipping their cocktails and looking at the view.

It's awfully pretty isn't it? The moonlight, and the lights of that yacht reflected in the water—
VICTOR: I wonder who it belongs to.

THE CURTAIN SLOWLY FALLS

ACT TWO

The scene is AMANDA's *flat in Paris. A few days have elapsed since Act I. The flat is charmingly furnished, its principal features being a Steinway Grand on the left, facing slightly up stage. Down stage centre, a very large comfortable sofa, behind which is a small table. There is also another sofa somewhere about, and one or two small tables, and a gramophone. The rest can be left to the discretion and taste of the decorator.*

When the curtain rises it is about ten o'clock in the evening. The windows are wide open, and the various street sounds of Paris can be heard but not very loudly as the apartment is high up.

AMANDA and ELYOT *are seated opposite one another at the table. They have finished dinner and dallying over coffee and liqueurs.* AMANDA *is wearing pyjamas, and* ELYOT *a comfortable dressing-gown.*

AMANDA: I'm glad we let Louise go. I am afraid she is going to have a cold.

ELYOT: Going to have a cold; she's been grunting and snorting all the evening like a whole herd of Bison.

AMANDA [*thoughtfully*]: Bison never sounds right to me somehow. I have a feeling it ought to be Bisons, a flock of Bisons.

ELYOT: You might say a covey of Bisons, or even a school of Bisons.

AMANDA: Yes, lovely. The Royal London School of Bisons. Do you think Louise is happy at home?

ELYOT: No, profoundly miserable.

AMANDA: Family beastly to her?

ELYOT [*with conviction*]: Absolutely vile. Knock her about dreadfully I expect, make her eat the most disgusting food, and pull her fringe.

AMANDA [*laughing*]: Oh, poor Louise.

ELYOT: Well, you know what the French are.

AMANDA: Oh yes, indeed. I know what the Hungarians are too.

ELYOT: What are they?

AMANDA: Very wistful. It's all those Pretzles I shouldn't wonder.

ELYOT: And the Poostza; I always felt the Poostza was far too big, Danube or no Danube.

AMANDA: Have you ever crossed the Sahara on a camel?

ELYOT: Frequently. When I was a boy we used to do it all the time. My Grandmother had a lovely seat on a camel.

AMANDA: There's no doubt about it, foreign travel's the thing.

ELYOT: Would you like some brandy?

AMANDA: Just a little. [*He pours some into her glass and some into his own.*]

ELYOT: I'm glad we didn't go out to-night.

AMANDA: Or last night.

ELYOT: Or the night before.

AMANDA: There's no reason to, really, when we're cosy here.

ELYOT: Exactly.

AMANDA: It's nice, isn't it?

ELYOT: Strangely peaceful. It's an awfully bad reflection on our characters. We ought to be absolutely tortured with conscience.

AMANDA: We are, every now and then.

ELYOT: Not nearly enough.

AMANDA: We sent Victor and Sibyl a nice note from wherever it was, what more can they want?

ELYOT: You're even more ruthless than I am.

AMANDA: I don't believe in crying over my bridge before I've eaten it.

ELYOT: Very sensible.

AMANDA: Personally I feel grateful for a miraculous escape. I know now that I should never have been happy with Victor. I was a fool ever to consider it.

ELYOT: You did a little more than consider it.

AMANDA: Well, you can't talk.

ELYOT: I wonder whether they met each other, or whether they've been suffering alone.

AMANDA: Oh dear, don't let's go on about it, it really does make one feel rather awful.

ELYOT: I suppose one or other or both of them will turn up here eventually.

AMANDA: Bound to; it won't be very nice, will it?

ELYOT [*cheerfully*]: Perfectly horrible.

AMANDA: Do you realise that we're living in sin?

ELYOT: Not according to the Catholics, Catholics don't recognise divorce. We're married as much as ever we were.

AMANDA: Yes, dear, but we're not Catholics.

ELYOT: Never mind, it's nice to think they'd sort of back us up. We were married in the eyes of heaven, and we still are.

AMANDA: We may be alright in the eyes of heaven, but we look like being in the hell of a mess socially.

ELYOT: Who cares?

AMANDA: Are we going to marry again, after Victor and Sibyl divorce us?

ELYOT: I suppose so. What do you think?

AMANDA: I feel rather scared of marriage really.

ELYOT: It is a frowsy business.

AMANDA: I believe it was just the fact of our being married, and clamped together publicly, that wrecked us before.

ELYOT: That, and not knowing how to manage each other.

AMANDA: Do you think we know how to manage each other now?

ELYOT: This week's been very successful. We've hardly used Solomon Isaacs at all.

AMANDA: Solomon Isaacs is so long, let's shorten it to Sollocks.

ELYOT: All right.

AMANDA: Darling, you do look awfully sweet in your little dressing-gown.

ELYOT: Yes, it's pretty ravishing, isn't it?

AMANDA: Do you mind if I come round and kiss you?

ELYOT: A pleasure, Lady Agatha.

AMANDA *comes round the table, kisses him, picks up the coffee pot, and returns to her chair.*

AMANDA: What fools we were to subject ourselves to five years' unnecessary suffering.

ELYOT: Perhaps it wasn't unnecessary, perhaps it mellowed and perfected us like beautiful ripe fruit.

AMANDA: When we were together, did you really think I was unfaithful to you?

ELYOT: Yes, practically every day.

AMANDA: I thought you were too; often I used to torture myself with visions of your bouncing about on divans with awful widows.

ELYOT: Why widows?

AMANDA: I was thinking of Claire Lavenham really.

ELYOT: Oh Claire.

AMANDA [*sharply*]: What did you say 'Oh Claire' like that for? It sounded far too careless to me.

ELYOT [*wistfully*]: What a lovely creature she was.

AMANDA: Lovely, lovely, lovely!

ELYOT [*blowing her a kiss*]: Darling!

AMANDA: Did you ever have an affair with her? Afterwards I mean?

ELYOT: Why do you want to know?

AMANDA: Curiosity, I suppose.

ELYOT: Dangerous.

AMANDA: Oh, not now, not dangerous now. I wouldn't expect you to have been celibate during those five years, any more than I was.

ELYOT [*jumping*]: What?

AMANDA: After all, Claire was undeniably attractive. A trifle over-vivacious I always thought, but that was probably because she was fundamentally stupid.

ELYOT: What do you mean about not being celibate during those five years?

AMANDA: What do you think I mean?

ELYOT: Oh God! [*He looks down miserably.*]

AMANDA: What's the matter?

ELYOT: You know perfectly well what's the matter.

AMANDA [*gently*]: You mustn't be unreasonable, I was only trying to stamp out the memory of you. I expect your affairs well outnumbered mine anyhow.

ELYOT: That is a little different. I'm a man.

AMANDA: Excuse me a moment while I get a caraway biscuit and change my crinoline.

ELYOT: It doesn't suit women to be promiscuous.

AMANDA: It doesn't suit men for women to be promiscuous.

ELYOT [*with sarcasm*]: Very modern dear; really your advanced views quite startle me.

AMANDA: Don't be cross, Elyot, I haven't been so dreadfully loose actually. Five years is a long time, and even if I did nip off with someone every now and again, they were none of them very serious.

ELYOT [*rising from the table and walking away*]: Oh, do stop it please—

AMANDA: Well, what about you?

ELYOT: Do you want me to tell you?

AMANDA: No, no, I don't–I take everything back–I don't.

ELYOT [*viciously*]: I was madly in love with a woman in South Africa.

AMANDA: Did she have a ring through her nose?

ELYOT: Don't be revolting.

AMANDA: We're tormenting one another. Sit down, sweet, I'm scared.

ELYOT [*slowly*]: Very well. [*He sits down thoughtfully.*]

AMANDA: We should have said Sollocks ages ago.

ELYOT: We're in love alright.

AMANDA: Don't say it so bitterly. Let's try to get the best out of it this time, instead of the worst.

ELYOT [*stretching his hand across the table*]: Hand please.

AMANDA [*clasping it*]: Here.

ELYOT: More comfortable?

AMANDA: Much more.

ELYOT [*after a slight pause*]: Are you engaged for this dance?

AMANDA: Funnily enough I was, but my partner was suddenly taken ill.

ELYOT [*rising and going to the gramophone*]: It's this damned smallpox epidemic.

AMANDA: No, as a matter of fact it was kidney trouble.

ELYOT: You'll dance it with me I hope?

AMANDA [*rising*]: I shall be charmed.

ELYOT [*as they dance*]: Quite a good floor, isn't it?

AMANDA: Yes, I think it needs a little Borax.

ELYOT: I love Borax.

AMANDA: Is that the Grand Duchess Olga lying under the piano?

ELYOT: Yes, her husband died a few weeks ago, you know, on his way back from Pulborough. So sad.

AMANDA: What on earth was he doing in Pulborough?

ELYOT: Nobody knows exactly, but there have been the usual stories.

AMANDA: I see.

ELYOT: Delightful parties Lady Bundle always gives, doesn't she?

AMANDA: Entrancing. Such a dear old lady.

ELYOT: And so gay: Did you notice her at supper blowing all those shrimps through her ear trumpet?

The tune comes to an end. AMANDA *sits on the edge of the sofa, pensively.*

ELYOT: What are you thinking about?

AMANDA: Nothing in particular.

ELYOT: Come on, I know that face.

AMANDA: Poor Sibyl.

ELYOT: Sibyl?

AMANDA: Yes, I suppose she loves you terribly.

ELYOT: Not as much as all that, she didn't have a chance to get really under way.

AMANDA: I expect she's dreadfully unhappy.

ELYOT: Oh, do shut up, Amanda, we've had all that out before.

AMANDA: We've certainly been pretty busy trying to justify ourselves.

ELYOT: It isn't a question of justifying ourselves, it's the true values of the situation that are really important. The moment we saw one another again we knew it was no use going on. We knew it instantly really, although we tried to pretend to ourselves that we didn't. What we've got to be thankful for is that we made the break straight away, and not later.

AMANDA: You think we should have done it anyhow?

ELYOT: Of course, and things would have been in a worse mess than they are now.

AMANDA: And what if we'd never happened to meet again. Would you have been quite happy with Sibyl?

ELYOT: I expect so.

AMANDA: Oh, Elyot!

ELYOT: You needn't look so stricken. It would have been the same with you and Victor. Life would have been smooth, and amicable, and quite charming, wouldn't it?

AMANDA: Poor dear Victor. He certainly did love me.

ELYOT: Splendid.

AMANDA: When I met him I was so lonely and depressed, I felt that I was getting old, and crumbling away unwanted.

ELYOT: It certainly is horrid when one begins to crumble.

AMANDA [*wistfully*]: He used to look at me hopelessly like a lovely spaniel, and I sort of melted like snow in the sunlight.

ELYOT: That must have been an edifying spectacle.

AMANDA: Victor really had a great charm.

ELYOT: You must tell me all about it.

AMANDA: He had a positive mania for looking after me, and protecting me.

ELYOT: That would have died down in time, dear.

AMANDA: You mustn't be rude, there's no necessity to be rude.

ELYOT: I wasn't in the least rude, I merely made a perfectly rational statement.

AMANDA: Your voice was decidedly bitter.

ELYOT: Victor had glorious legs, hadn't he? And fascinating ears.

AMANDA: Don't be silly.

ELYOT: He probably looked radiant in the morning, all flushed and tumbled on the pillow.

AMANDA: I never saw him on the pillow.

ELYOT: I'm surprised to hear it.

AMANDA [*angrily*]: Elyot!

ELYOT: There's no need to be cross.

AMANDA: What did you mean by that?

ELYOT: I'm sick of listening to you yap, yap, yap, yap, yap, yapping about Victor.

AMANDA: Now listen Elyot, once and for all—

ELYOT: Oh my dear, Sollocks! Sollocks!–two minutes–Sollocks.

AMANDA: But—

ELYOT [*firmly*]: Sollocks!

They sit in dead silence, looking at each other. AMANDA *makes a sign that she wants a cigarette.* ELYOT *gets up, hands her the box, and lights one for her and himself.* AMANDA *rises and walks over to the window, and stands there, looking out for a moment. Presently* ELYOT *joins her. She slips her arm through his, and they kiss lightly. They draw the curtains and then come down and sit side by side on the sofa.* ELYOT *looks at his watch.* AMANDA *raises her eyebrows at him and he nods, then they both sigh, audibly.*

That was a near thing.

AMANDA: It was my fault. I'm terribly sorry, darling.

ELYOT: I was very irritating, I know I was. I'm sure Victor was awfully nice, and you're perfectly right to be sweet about him.

AMANDA: That's downright handsome of you. Sweetheart! [*She kisses him.*]

ELYOT [*leaning back with her on the sofa*]: I think I love you more than ever before. Isn't it ridiculous? Put your feet up.

She puts her legs across his, and they snuggle back together in the corner of the sofa, his head resting on her shoulder.

AMANDA: Comfortable?

ELYOT: Almost, wait a minute. [*He struggles a bit and then settles down with a sigh.*]

AMANDA: How long, Oh Lord, how long?

ELYOT [*drowsily*]: What do you mean, 'How long, Oh Lord, how long?'

AMANDA: This is far too perfect to last.

ELYOT: You have no faith, that's what's wrong with you.

AMANDA: Absolutely none.

ELYOT: Don't you believe in——? [*He nods upwards.*]

AMANDA: No, do you?

ELYOT [*shaking his head*]: No. What about——? [*He points downwards.*]

AMANDA: Oh dear no.

ELYOT: Don't you believe in anything?

AMANDA: Oh yes, I believe in being kind to everyone, and giving money to old beggar women, and being as gay as possible.

ELYOT: What about after we're dead?

AMANDA: I think a rather gloomy merging into everything, don't you?

ELYOT: I hope not, I'm a bad merger.

AMANDA: You won't know a thing about it.

ELYOT: I hope for a glorious oblivion, like being under gas.

AMANDA: I always dream the most peculiar things under gas.

ELYOT: Would you be young always? If you could choose?

AMANDA: No, I don't think so, not if it meant having awful bull's glands popped into me.

ELYOT: Cows for you dear. Bulls for me.

AMANDA: We certainly live in a marvellous age.

ELYOT: Too marvellous. It's alright if you happen to be a specialist at something, then you're too concentrated to pay attention to all the other things going on. But, for the ordinary observer, it's too much.

AMANDA [*snuggling closer*]: Far, far too much.

ELYOT: Take the radio for instance.

AMANDA: Oh darling, don't let's take the radio.

ELYOT: Well, aeroplanes then, and Cosmic Atoms, and Television, and those gland injections we were talking about just now.

AMANDA: It must be so nasty for the poor animals, being experimented on.

ELYOT: Not when the experiments are successful. Why in Vienna I believe you can see whole lines of decrepit old rats carrying on like Tiller Girls.

AMANDA [*laughing*]: Oh, how very, very sweet.

ELYOT [*burying his face in her shoulder*]: I do love you so.

AMANDA: Don't blow, dear heart, it gives me the shivers.

ELYOT [*trying to kiss her*]: Swivel your face round a bit more.

AMANDA [*obliging*]: That better?

ELYOT [*kissing her lingeringly*]: Very nice, thank you kindly.

AMANDA [*twining her arms round his neck*]: Darling, you're so terribly, terribly dear, and sweet, and attractive. [*She pulls his head down to her again and they kiss lovingly.*]

ELYOT [*softly*]: We were raving mad, ever to part, even for an instant.

AMANDA: Utter imbeciles.

ELYOT: I realised it almost immediately, didn't you?

AMANDA: Long before we got our decree.

ELYOT: My heart broke on that damned trip round the world. I saw such beautiful things, darling. Moonlight shining on old Temples, strange barbaric dances in jungle villages, scarlet flamingoes flying over deep, deep blue water. Breathlessly lovely, and completely unexciting because you weren't there to see them with me.

AMANDA [*kissing him again*]: Take me please, take me at once, let's make up for lost time.

ELYOT: Next week?

AMANDA: To-morrow.

ELYOT: Done.

AMANDA: I must see those dear flamingoes. [*There is a pause.*] Eight years all told, we've loved each other. Three married and five divorced.

ELYOT: Angel. Angel. Angel. [*He kisses her passionately.*]

AMANDA [*struggling slightly*]: No, Elyot, stop now, stop—

ELYOT: Why should I stop? You know you adore being made love to.

AMANDA [*through his kisses*]: It's so soon after dinner.

ELYOT [*jumping up rather angrily*]: You really do say most awful things.

AMANDA [*tidying her hair*]: I don't see anything particularly awful about that.

ELYOT: No sense of glamour, no sense of glamour at all.

AMANDA: It's difficult to feel really glamorous with a crick in the neck.

ELYOT: Why didn't you say you had a crick in your neck?

AMANDA [*sweetly*]: It's gone now.

ELYOT: How convenient. [*He lights a cigarette.*]

AMANDA [*holding out her hand*]: I want one please.

ELYOT [*throwing her one*]: Here.

AMANDA: Match?

ELYOT [*impatiently*]: Wait a minute, can't you?

AMANDA: Chivalrous little love.

ELYOT [*throwing the matches at her*]: Here.

AMANDA [*coldly*]: Thank you very much indeed. [*There is a silence for a moment.*]

ELYOT: You really can be more irritating than anyone in the world.

AMANDA: I fail to see what I've done that's so terribly irritating.

ELYOT: You have no tact.

AMANDA: Tact. You have no consideration.

ELYOT [*walking up and down*]: Too soon after dinner indeed.

AMANDA: Yes, much too soon.

ELYOT: That sort of remark shows rather a common sort of mind I'm afraid.

AMANDA: Oh it does, does it?

ELYOT: Very unpleasant, makes me shudder.

AMANDA: Making all this fuss just because your silly vanity is a little upset.

ELYOT: Vanity: What do you mean, vanity?

AMANDA: You can't bear the thought that there are certain moments when our chemical, what d'you call 'ems, don't fuse properly.

ELYOT [*derisively*]: Chemical what d'you call 'ems: Please try to be more explicit.

AMANDA: You know perfectly well what I mean, and don't try to patronise me.

ELYOT [*loudly*]: Now look here, Amanda—

AMANDA [*suddenly*]: Darling Sollocks! Oh, for God's sake, Sollocks!

ELYOT: But listen—

AMANDA: Sollocks, Sollocks, Oh dear–triple Sollocks!

They stand looking at one another in silence for a moment, then AMANDA *flings herself down on the sofa and buries her face in the cushions.* ELYOT *looks at her, then goes over to the piano. He sits down and begins to play idly.* AMANDA *raises her head, screws herself round on the sofa, and lies there listening.* ELYOT *blows a kiss to her and goes on playing. He starts to sing softly to her, never taking his eyes off her. When he has finished the little refrain, whatever it was, he still continues to play it looking at her.*

AMANDA: Big romantic stuff, darling.
ELYOT [*smiling*]: Yes, big romantic stuff.

He wanders off into another tune. AMANDA *sits up crossed legged on the sofa, and begins to sing it, then, still singing, she comes over and perches on the piano. They sing several old refrains from dead and gone musical comedies finishing with the song that brought them together again in the first Act. Finally* AMANDA *comes down and sits next to him on the piano stool, they both therefore have their backs half turned to the audience. She rests her head on his shoulder, until finally his fingers drop off the keys, and they melt into one another's arms.*

ELYOT [*after a moment*]: You're the most thrilling, exciting woman that was ever born.
AMANDA [*standing up, and brushing her hand lightly over his mouth*]: Dearest, dearest heart—

He catches at her hand and kisses it, and then her arm, until he is standing up, embracing her ardently. She struggles a little, half laughing, and breaks away, but he catches her, and they finish up on the sofa again, clasped in each other's arms, both completely given up to the passion of the moment, until the telephone bell rings violently, and they both spring apart.

ELYOT: Good God!
AMANDA: Do you think it's them?
ELYOT: I wonder.
AMANDA: Nobody knows we're here except Freda, and she wouldn't ring up.
ELYOT: It must be them then.
AMANDA: What are we to do?
ELYOT [*suddenly*]: We're alright darling, aren't we—whatever happens?
AMANDA: Now and always, Sweet.
ELYOT: I don't care then.

He gets up and goes defiantly over to the telephone, which has been ringing incessantly during the little preceding scene.

AMANDA: It was bound to come sooner or later.
ELYOT [*at telephone*]: Hallo—hallo—what—comment? Madame, qui? 'allo—'allo—oui c'est ca. Oh, Madame Duvallon—Oui, oui, oui. [*He puts his hand over the mouthpiece.*] It's only somebody wanting to talk to the dear Madame Duvallon.
AMANDA: Who's she?
ELYOT: I haven't the faintest idea. [*At telephone.*] Je regrette beaucoup Monsieur, mais Madame Duvallon viens de partir—cette apres midi, pour

Madagascar. [*He hangs up the telephone.*] Whew; that gave me a fright.

AMANDA: It sent shivers up my spine.

ELYOT: What shall we do if they suddenly walk in on us?

AMANDA: Behave exquisitely.

ELYOT: With the most perfect poise?

AMANDA: Certainly, I shall probably do a Court Curtsey.

ELYOT [*sitting on the edge of the sofa*]: Things that ought to matter dreadfully, don't matter at all when one's happy, do they?

AMANDA: What is so horrible is that one can't stay happy.

ELYOT: Darling, don't say that.

AMANDA: It's true. The whole business is a very poor joke.

ELYOT: Meaning that sacred and beautiful thing, Love?

AMANDA: Yes, meaning just that.

ELYOT [*striding up and down the room dramatically*]: What does it all mean, that's what I ask myself in my ceaseless quest for ultimate truth. Dear God, what does it all mean?

AMANDA: Don't laugh at me, I'm serious.

ELYOT [*seriously*]: You mustn't be serious, my dear one, it's just what they want.

AMANDA: Who's they?

ELYOT: All the futile moralists who try to make life unbearable. Laugh at them. Be flippant. Laugh at everything, all their sacred shibboleths. Flippancy brings out the acid in their damned sweetness and light.

AMANDA: If I laugh at everything, I must laugh at us too.

ELYOT: Certainly you must. We're figures of fun alright.

AMANDA: How long will it last, this ludicrous, over-bearing love of ours?

ELYOT: Who knows?

AMANDA: Shall we always want to bicker and fight?

ELYOT: No, that desire will fade, along with our passion.

AMANDA: Oh dear, shall we like that?

ELYOT: It all depends on how well we've played.

AMANDA: What happens if one of us dies? Does the one that's left still laugh?

ELYOT: Yes, yes, with all his might.

AMANDA [*wistfully clutching his hand*]: That's serious enough, isn't it?

ELYOT: No, no, it isn't. Death's very laughable, such a cunning little mystery. All done with mirrors.

AMANDA: Darling, I believe you're talking nonsense.

ELYOT: So is everyone else in the long run. Let's be superficial and pity the poor Philosophers. Let's blow trumpets and squeakers, and enjoy the party as much as we can, like very small, quite idiotic school-children. Let's savour the delight of the moment. Come and kiss me darling, before your body rots, and worms pop in and out of your eye sockets.

AMANDA: Elyot, worms don't pop.

ELYOT [*kissing her*]: I don't mind what you do see? You can paint yourself bright green all over, and dance naked in the Place Vendome, and rush off madly with all the men in the world, and I shan't say a word, as long as you love me best.

AMANDA: Thank you, dear. The same applies to you, except that if I catch you so much as looking at another woman, I'll kill you.

ELYOT: Do you remember that awful scene we had in Venice?

AMANDA: Which particular one?

ELYOT: The one when you bought that little painted wooden snake on the

Piazza, and put it on my bed.

AMANDA: Oh Charles. That was his name, Charles. He did wriggle so beautifully.

ELYOT: Horrible thing, I hated it.

AMANDA: Yes, I know you did. You threw it out of the window into the Grand Canal. I don't think I'll ever forgive you for that.

ELYOT: How long did the row last?

AMANDA: It went on intermittently for days.

ELYOT: The worst one was in Cannes when your curling irons burnt a hole in my new dressing-gown. [*He laughs.*]

AMANDA: It burnt my comb too, and all the towels in the bathroom.

ELYOT: That was a rouser, wasn't it?

AMANDA: That was the first time you ever hit me.

ELYOT: I didn't hit you very hard.

AMANDA: The manager came in and found us rolling on the floor, biting and scratching like panthers. Oh dear, oh dear— [*She laughs helplessly.*]

ELYOT: I shall never forget his face.

> *They both collapse with laughter.*

AMANDA: How ridiculous, how utterly, utterly ridiculous.

ELYOT: We were very much younger then.

AMANDA: And very much sillier.

ELYOT: As a matter of fact the real cause of that row was Peter Burden.

AMANDA: You knew there was nothing in that.

ELYOT: I didn't know anything of the sort, you took presents from him.

AMANDA: Presents: only a trivial little brooch.

ELYOT: I remember it well, bristling with diamonds. In the worst possible taste.

AMANDA: Not at all, it was very pretty. I still have it, and I wear it often.

ELYOT: You went out of your way to torture me over Peter Burden.

AMANDA: No, I didn't, you worked the whole thing up in your jealous imagination.

ELYOT: You must admit that he was in love with you, wasn't he?

AMANDA: Just a little perhaps. Nothing serious.

ELYOT: You let him kiss you. You said you did.

AMANDA: Well, what of it?

ELYOT: What of it!

AMANDA: It gave him a lot of pleasure, and it didn't hurt me.

ELYOT: What about me?

AMANDA: If you hadn't been so suspicious and nosey you'd never have known a thing about it.

ELYOT: That's a nice point of view I must say.

AMANDA: Oh dear, I'm bored with this conversation.

ELYOT: So am I, bored stiff. [*He goes over to the table.*] Want some brandy?

AMANDA: No thanks.

ELYOT: I'll have a little, I think.

AMANDA: I don't see why you want it, you've already had two glasses.

ELYOT: No particular reason, anyhow they were very small ones.

AMANDA: It seems so silly to go on, and on, and on with a thing.

ELYOT [*pouring himself out a glassful*]: You can hardly call three liqueur glasses in a whole evening going on, and on, and on.

AMANDA: It's become a habit with you.

ELYOT: You needn't be so grand, just because you don't happen to want any yourself at the moment.

AMANDA: Don't be so stupid.

ELYOT [*irritably*]: Really Amanda—

AMANDA: What?

ELYOT: Nothing.

AMANDA *sits down on the sofa, and, taking a small mirror from her bag, gazes at her face critically, and then uses some lipstick and powder. A trifle nastily.*

Going out somewhere dear?

AMANDA: No, just making myself fascinating for you.

ELYOT: That reply has broken my heart.

AMANDA: The woman's job is to allure the man. Watch me a minute will you?

ELYOT: As a matter of fact that's perfectly true.

AMANDA: Oh, no, it isn't.

ELYOT: Yes it is.

AMANDA [*snappily*]: Oh be quiet.

ELYOT: It's a pity you did't have any more brandy; it might have made you a little less disagreeable.

AMANDA: It doesn't seem to have worked such wonders with you.

ELYOT: Snap, snap, snap; like a little adder.

AMANDA: Adders don't snap, they sting.

ELYOT: Nonsense, they have a little bag of venom behind their fangs and they snap.

AMANDA: They sting.

ELYOT: They snap.

AMANDA [*with exasperation*]: I don't care, do you understand? I don't care. I don't mind if they bark, and roll about like hoops.

ELYOT [*after a slight pause*]: Did you see much of Peter Burden after our divorce?

AMANDA: Yes, I did, quite a lot.

ELYOT: I suppose you let him kiss you a good deal more then.

AMANDA: Mind your own business.

ELYOT: You must have had a riotous time. [AMANDA *doesn't answer, so he stalks about the room.*] No restraint at all—very enjoyable—you never had much anyhow.

AMANDA: You're quite insufferable; I expect it's because you're drunk.

ELYOT: I'm not in the least drunk.

AMANDA: You always had a weak head.

ELYOT: I think I mentioned once before that I have only had three minute liqueur glasses of brandy the whole evening long. A child of two couldn't get drunk on that.

AMANDA: On the contrary, a child of two could get violently drunk on only one glass of brandy.

ELYOT: Very interesting. How about a child of four, and a child of six, and a child of nine?

AMANDA [*turning her head away*]: Oh do shut up.

ELYOT [*witheringly*]: We might get up a splendid little debate about that, you know, Intemperate Tots.

AMANDA: Not very funny, dear; you'd better have some more brandy.

ELYOT: Very good idea, I will. [*He pours out another glass and gulps it down defiantly.*]
AMANDA: Ridiculous ass.
ELYOT: I beg your pardon?
AMANDA: I said ridiculous ass!
ELYOT [*with great dignity*]: Thank you.

There is a silence. AMANDA *gets up, and turns the gramophone on.*

You'd better turn that off, I think.
AMANDA [*coldly*]: Why?
ELYOT: It's very late and it will annoy the people upstairs.
AMANDA: There aren't any people upstairs. It's a photographer's studio.
ELYOT: There are people downstairs, I suppose?
AMANDA: They're away in Tunis.
ELYOT: This is no time of the year for Tunis. [*He turns the gramophone off.*]
AMANDA [*icily*]: Turn it on again, please.
ELYOT: I'll do no such thing.
AMANDA: Very well, if you insist on being boorish and idiotic. [*She gets up and turns it on again.*]
ELYOT: Turn it off. It's driving me mad.
AMANDA: You're far too temperamental. Try to control yourself.
ELYOT: Turn it off.
AMANDA: I won't.

ELYOT *rushes at the gramophone.* AMANDA *tries to ward him off. They struggle silently for a moment then the needle screeches across the record.*

There now, you've ruined the record. [*She takes it off and scrutinises it.*]
ELYOT: Good job, too.
AMANDA: Disagreeable pig.
ELYOT [*suddenly stricken with remorse*]: Amanda darling–Sollocks.
AMANDA [*furiously*]: Sollocks yourself. [*She breaks the record over his head.*]
ELYOT [*staggering*]: You spiteful little beast.

He slaps her face. She screams loudly and hurls herself sobbing with rage on to the sofa, with her face buried in the cushions.

AMANDA [*wailing*]: Oh, oh, oh—
ELYOT: I'm sorry, I didn't mean it–I'm sorry, darling, I swear I didn't mean it.
AMANDA: Go away, go away, I hate you.

ELYOT *kneels on the sofa and tries to pull her round to look at him.*

ELYOT: Amanda–listen–listen—
AMANDA [*turning suddenly, and fetching him a welt across the face*]: Listen indeed; I'm sick and tired of listening to you, you damned sadistic bully.
ELYOT [*with great grandeur*]: Thank you.

He stalks towards the door, in stately silence. AMANDA *throws a cushion at him, which misses him and knocks down a lamp and a vase on the side table.* ELYOT *laughs falsely.*

A pretty display I must say.

AMANDA [*wildly*]: Stop laughing like that.

ELYOT [*continuing*]: Very amusing indeed.

AMANDA [*losing control*]: Stop–stop–stop—

She rushes at him, he grabs her hands and they sway about the room, until he manages to twist her round by the arms so that she faces him, closely, quivering with fury.

—I hate you–do you hear? You're conceited, and overbearing, and utterly impossible!

ELYOT [*shouting her down*]: You're a vile tempered loose-living wicked little beast, and I never want to see you again so long as I live.

He flings her away from him, she staggers, and falls against a chair. They stand gasping at one another in silence for a moment.

AMANDA [*very quietly*]: This is the end, do you understand? The end, finally and forever.

She goes to the door, which opens on to the landing, and wrenches it open. He rushes after her and clutches her wrist.

ELYOT: You're not going like this.

AMANDA: Oh yes I am.

ELYOT: You're not.

AMANDA: I am; let go of me—

He pulls her away from the door, and once more they struggle. This time a standard lamp crashes to the ground. AMANDA, *breathlessly, as they fight.*

You're a cruel fiend, and I hate and loathe you; thank God I've realised in time what you're really like; marry you again, never, never, never. .... I'd rather die in torment—

ELYOT [*at the same time*]: Shut up; shut up. I wouldn't marry you again if you came crawling to me on your bended knees, you're a mean, evil minded, little vampire–I hope to God I never set eyes on you again as long as I live—

At this point in the proceedings they trip over a piece of carpet, and fall on to the floor, rolling over and over in paroxysms of rage. VICTOR *and* SIBYL *enter quietly, through the open door, and stand staring at them in horror. Finally* AMANDA *breaks free and half gets up,* ELYOT *grabs her leg, and she falls against a table, knocking it completely over.*

AMANDA [*screaming*]: Beast; brute; swine; cad; beast; beast; brute; devil—

She rushes back at ELYOT *who is just rising to his feet, and gives him a stinging blow, which knocks him over again. She rushes blindly off left, and slams the door, at the same moment that he jumps up and rushes off right, also slamming the door.* VICTOR *and* SIBYL *advance apprehensively into the room, and sink on to the sofa—*

THE CURTAIN FALLS

ACT THREE

The scene is the same as Act Two. It is the next morning. The time is about eight-thirty. VICTOR *and* SIBYL *have drawn the two sofas across the doors right, and left, and are stretched on them, asleep.* VICTOR *is in front of* AMANDA's *door, and* SIBYL *in front of* ELYOT's.

The room is in chaos, as it was left the night before.

As the curtain rises, there is the rattling of a key in the lock of the front door, and LOUISE *enters. She is rather a frowsy looking girl, and carries a string bag with various bundles of eatables crammed into it, notably a long roll of bread, and a lettuce. She closes the door after her, and in the half light trips over the standard lamp lying on the floor. She puts her string bag down, and gropes her way over to the window. She draws the curtains, letting sunlight stream into the room. When she looks round, she gives a little cry of horror. Then she sees* VICTOR *and* SIBYL *sleeping peacefully, and comes over and scrutinises each of them with care, then she shakes* SIBYL *by the shoulder.*

SIBYL [*waking*]: Oh dear.
LOUISE: Bon jour, Madame.
SIBYL [*bewildered*]: What?–Oh–bon jour.
LOUISE: Qu'est-ce que vous faites ici, madame?
SIBYL: What–what?–Wait a moment, attendez un instant–oh dear—
VICTOR [*sleepily*]: What's happening? [*Jumping up.*] Of course, I remember now. [*He sees* LOUISE.] Oh!
LOUISE [*firmly*]: Bon jour, Monsieur:
VICTOR: Er–bon jour–What time is it?
LOUISE [*rather dully*]: Eh, Monsieur?
SIBYL [*sitting up on the sofa*]: Quelle heure est il s'il vous plait?
LOUISE: C'est neuf heure moins dix madame.
VICTOR: What did she say?
SIBYL: I think she said nearly ten o'clock.
VICTOR [*taking situation in hand*]: Er–voulez–er–wake–revillez Monsieur et Madame–er–toute suite?
LOUISE [*shaking her head*]: Non, Monsieur. Il m'est absolument defendu de les appeler jusqu'à ce qu'ils sonnent.

She takes her bag and goes off into the kitchen. VICTOR *and* SIBYL *look at each other helplessly.*

SIBYL: What are we to do?
VICTOR [*with determination*]: Wake them ourselves. [*He goes towards* AMANDA's *door.*]
SIBYL: No, no, wait a minute.
VICTOR: What's the matter?

SIBYL [*plaintively*]: I couldn't face them yet, really, I couldn't; I feel dreadful.
VICTOR: So do I. [*He wanders gloomily over to the window.*] It's a lovely morning.
SIBYL: Lovely. [*She bursts into tears.*]
VICTOR [*coming to her*]: I say, don't cry.
SIBYL: I can't help it.
VICTOR: Please don't, please—
SIBYL: It's all so squalid, I wish we hadn't stayed; what's the use?
VICTOR: We've got to see them before we go back to England, we must get things straightened out.
SIBYL [*sinking down on to the sofa*]: Oh dear, oh dear, oh dear, I wish I were dead.
VICTOR: Hush, now, hush. Remember your promise. We've got to see this through together and get it settled one way or another.
SIBYL [*sniffling*]: I'll try to control myself, only I'm so ... so tired, I haven't slept properly for ages.
VICTOR: Neither have I.
SIBYL: If we hadn't arrived when we did, they'd have killed one another.
VICTOR: They must have been drunk.
SIBYL: She hit him.
VICTOR: He'd probably hit her, too, earlier on.
SIBYL: I'd no idea anyone ever behaved like that; it's so disgusting, so degrading, Elli of all people–oh dear— [*She almost breaks down again, but controls herself.*]
VICTOR: What an escape you've had.
SIBYL: What an escape we've both had.

AMANDA *opens her door and looks out. She is wearing travelling clothes, and is carrying a small suitcase. She jumps, upon seeing* SIBYL *and* VICTOR.

AMANDA: Oh!–good morning.
VICTOR [*with infinite reproach in his voice*]: Oh, Amanda.
AMANDA: Will you please move this sofa, I can't get out.

VICTOR *moves the sofa, and she advances into the room and goes towards the door.*

VICTOR: Where are you going?
AMANDA: Away.
VICTOR: You can't.
AMANDA: Why not?
VICTOR: I want to talk to you.
AMANDA [*wearily*]: What on earth is the use of that?
VICTOR: I must talk to you.
AMANDA: Well, all I can say is, it's very inconsiderate. [*She plumps the bag down by the door and comes down to* VICTOR.]
VICTOR: Mandy, I—
AMANDA [*gracefully determined to rise above the situation*]: I suppose you're Sibyl; how do you do?

SIBYL *turns her back on her.*

Well, if you're going to take up that attitude, I fail to see the point of your coming here at all.

SIBYL: I came to see Elyot.

AMANDA: I've no wish to prevent you, he's in there, probably wallowing in an alcoholic stupor.

VICTOR: This is all very unpleasant, Amanda.

AMANDA: I quite agree, that's why I want to go away.

VICTOR: That would be shirking; this must be discussed at length.

AMANDA: Very well, if you insist, but not just now, I don't feel up to it. Has Louise come yet?

VICTOR: If Louise is the maid, she's in the kitchen.

AMANDA: Thank you. You'd probably like some coffee, excuse me a moment. [*She goes off into the kitchen.*]

SIBYL: Well! How dare she?

VICTOR [*irritably*]: How dare she what?

SIBYL: Behave so calmly, as though nothing had happened.

VICTOR: I don't see what else she could have done.

SIBYL: Insufferable I call it.

ELYOT *opens his door and looks out.*

ELYOT [*seeing them*]: Oh God. [*He shuts the door again quickly.*]

SIBYL: Elyot–Elyot— [*She rushes over to the door and bangs on it.*] Elyot–Elyot–Elyot—

ELYOT [*inside*]: Go away.

SIBYL [*falling on to the sofa*]: Oh, oh, oh. [*She bursts into tears again.*]

VICTOR: Do pull yourself together for heaven's sake.

SIBYL: I can't, I can't–oh, oh, oh—

AMANDA *re-enters.*

AMANDA: I've ordered some coffee and rolls, they'll be here soon. I must apologise for the room being so untidy.

She picks up a cushion, and pats it into place on the sofa. There is a silence except for SIBYL*'s sobs.* AMANDA *looks at her, and then at* VICTOR*; then she goes off into her room again, and shuts the door.*

VICTOR: It's no use crying like that, it doesn't do any good.

After a moment, during which SIBYL *makes renewed efforts to control her tears,* ELYOT *opens the door immediately behind her, pushes the sofa, with her on it, out of the way, and walks towards the front door. He is in travelling clothes, and carrying a small suitcase.*

SIBYL [*rushing after him*]: Elyot, where are you going?

ELYOT: Canada.

SIBYL: You can't go like this, you can't.

ELYOT: I see no point in staying.

VICTOR: You owe it to Sibyl to stay.

ELYOT: How do you do, I don't think we've met before.

SIBYL: You must stay, you've got to stay.

ELYOT: Very well, if you insist. [*He plumps his bag down.*] I'm afraid the room is in rather a mess. Have you seen the maid Louise?

VICTOR: She's in the kitchen.

ELYOT: Good. I'll order some coffee. [*He makes a movement towards the kitchen.*]

VICTOR [*stopping him*]: No, your–er–my–er–Amanda has already ordered it.

ELYOT: Oh, I'm glad the old girl's up and about.

VICTOR: We've got to get things straightened out, you know.

ELYOT [*looking around the room*]: Yes, it's pretty awful. We'll get the concierge up from downstairs.

VICTOR: You're being purposely flippant, but it's no good.

ELYOT: Sorry. [*He lapses into silence.*]

VICTOR [*after a pause*]: What's to be done?

ELYOT: I don't know.

SIBYL [*with spirit*]: It's all perfectly horrible. I feel smirched and unclean as though slimy things had been crawling all over me.

ELYOT: Maybe they have, that's a very old sofa.

VICTOR: If you don't stop your damned flippancy, I'll knock your head off.

ELYOT [*raising his eyebrows*]: Has it ever struck you that flippancy might cover a very real embarrassment?

VICTOR: In a situation such as this, it's in extremely bad taste.

ELYOT: No worse than bluster, and invective. As a matter of fact, as far as I know, this situation is entirely without precedent. We have no prescribed etiquette to fall back upon. I shall continue to be flippant.

SIBYL: Oh Elyot, how can you–how can you.

ELYOT: I'm awfully sorry, Sibyl.

VICTOR: It's easy enough to be sorry.

ELYOT: On the contrary. I find it exceedingly difficult. I seldom regret anything. This is a very rare and notable exception, a sort of red letter day. We must all make the most of it.

SIBYL: I'll never forgive you, never. I wouldn't have believed anyone could be so callous and cruel.

ELYOT: I absolutely see your point, and as I said before, I'm sorry.

There is silence for a moment. Then AMANDA *comes in again. She has obviously decided to carry everything off in a high handed manner.*

AMANDA [*in social tones*]: What! Breakfast not ready yet? Really, these French servants are too slow for words. [*She smiles gaily.*] What a glorious morning. [*She goes to the window.*] I do love Paris, it's so genuinely gay. Those lovely trees in the Champs Elysées, and the little roundabouts for the children to play on, and those shiny red taxis. You can see Sacre Cœur quite clearly to-day, sometimes it's a bit misty, particularly in August, all the heat rising up from the pavements you know.

ELYOT [*drily*]: Yes, dear, we know.

AMANDA [*ignoring him*]: And it's heavenly being so high up. I found this flat three years ago, quite by merest chance. I happened to be staying at the Plaza Athenee, just down the road—

ELYOT [*enthusiastically*]: Such a nice hotel, with the most enchanting courtyard with a fountain that goes plopplopplopplopplopplopplopplopplop—

VICTOR: This is ridiculous, Amanda.

ELYOT [*continuing*]: Plop plop plop plop plop plop plop plop plop plop—

AMANDA [*overriding him*]: Now, Victor, I refuse to discuss anything in the least important until after breakfast. I couldn't concentrate now, I know I couldn't.

ELYOT [*sarcastically*]: What manner. What poise. How I envy it. To be able to carry off the most embarrassing situation with such tact, and delicacy, and above all–such subtlety. Go on Amanda, you're making everything so much easier. We shall all be playing Hunt the Slipper in a minute.

AMANDA: Please don't address me, I don't wish to speak to you.

ELYOT: Splendid.

AMANDA: And what's more, I never shall again as long as I live.

ELYOT: I shall endeavour to rise above it.

AMANDA: I've been brought up to believe that it's beyond the pale, for a man to strike a woman.

ELYOT: A very poor tradition. Certain women should be struck regularly, like gongs.

AMANDA: You're an unmitigated cad, and a bully.

ELYOT: And you're an ill mannered, bad tempered slattern.

AMANDA [*loudly*]: Slattern indeed.

ELYOT: Yes, slattern, slattern, slattern, and fishwife.

VICTOR: Keep your mouth shut, you swine.

ELYOT: Mind your own damned business.

They are about to fight, when SIBYL *rushes between them.*

SIBYL: Stop, stop, it's no use going on like this. Stop, please. [*To* AMANDA.] Help me, do, do, do, help me—

AMANDA: I'm not going to interfere. Let them fight if they want to, it will probably clear the air anyhow.

SIBYL: Yes but—

AMANDA: Come into my room, perhaps you'd like to wash or something.

SIBYL: No, but—

AMANDA [*firmly*]: Come along.

SIBYL: Very well.

She tosses her head at ELYOT, *and* AMANDA *drags her off.*

VICTOR [*belligerently*]: Now then!

ELYOT: Now then what?

VICTOR: Are you going to take back those things you said to Amanda?

ELYOT: Certainly, I'll take back anything, if only you'll stop bellowing at me.

VICTOR [*contemptuously*]: You're a coward too.

ELYOT: They want us to fight, don't you see?

VICTOR: No, I don't, why should they?

ELYOT: Primitive feminine instincts–warring males–very enjoyable.

VICTOR: You think you're very clever, don't you?

ELYOT: I think I'm a bit cleverer than you, but apparently that's not saying much.

VICTOR [*violently*]: What?

ELYOT: Oh, do sit down.

VICTOR: I will not.

ELYOT: Well, if you'll excuse me, I will, I'm extremely tired. [*He sits down.*]

VICTOR: Oh, for God's sake, behave like a man.

ELYOT [*patiently*]: Listen a minute, all this belligerency is very right and proper and highly traditional, but if only you'll think for a moment, you'll see that it won't get us very far.

VICTOR: To hell with all that.

ELYOT: I should like to explain that if you hit me, I shall certainly hit you, probably equally hard, if not harder. I'm just as strong as you I should imagine. Then you'd hit me again, and I'd hit you again, and we'd go on until one or the other was knocked out. Now if you'll explain to me satisfactorily how all that can possibly improve the situation, I'll tear off my coat, and we'll go at one another hammer and tongs, immediately.

VICTOR: It would ease my mind.

ELYOT: Only if you won.

VICTOR: I should win alright.

ELYOT: Want to try?

VICTOR: Yes.

ELYOT [*jumping up*]: Here goes then— [*He tears off his coat.*]

VICTOR: Just a moment.

ELYOT: Well?

VICTOR: What did you mean about them wanting us to fight?

ELYOT: It would be balm to their vanity.

VICTOR: Do you love Amanda?

ELYOT: Is this a battle or a discussion? If it's the latter I shall put on my coat again, I don't want to catch a chill.

VICTOR: Answer my question, please.

ELYOT: Have a cigarette?

VICTOR [*stormily*]: Answer my question.

ELYOT: If you analyse it, it's rather a silly question.

VICTOR: Do you love Amanda?

ELYOT [*confidentially*]: Not very much this morning to be perfectly frank, I'd like to wring her neck. Do you love her?

VICTOR: That's beside the point.

ELYOT: On the contrary, it's the crux of the whole affair. If you do love her still, you can forgive her, and live with her in peace and harmony until you're ninety-eight.

VICTOR: You're apparently even more of a cad than I thought you were.

ELYOT: You are completely in the right over the whole business, don't imagine I'm not perfectly conscious of that.

VICTOR: I'm glad.

ELYOT: It's all very unfortunate.

VICTOR: Unfortunate: My God!

ELYOT: It might have been worse.

VICTOR: I'm glad you think so.

ELYOT: I do wish you'd stop about being so glad about everything.

VICTOR: What do you intend to do? That's what I want to know. What do you intend to do?

ELYOT [*suddenly serious*]: I don't know, I don't care.

VICTOR: I suppose you realise that you've broken that poor little woman's heart?

ELYOT: Which poor little woman?

VICTOR: Sibyl, of course.

ELYOT: Oh, come now, not as bad as that. She'll get over it, and forget all about me.

VICTOR: I sincerely hope so . . . for her sake.

ELYOT: Amanda will forget all about me too. Everybody will forget all about me. I might just as well lie down and die in fearful pain and suffering, nobody would care.

VICTOR: Don't talk such rot.

ELYOT: You must forgive me for taking rather a gloomy view of everything but the fact is, I suddenly feel slightly depressed.

VICTOR: I intend to divorce Amanda, naming you as co-respondent.

ELYOT: Very well.

VICTOR: And Sibyl will divorce you for Amanda. It would be foolish of either of you to attempt any defence.

ELYOT: Quite.

VICTOR: And the sooner you marry Amanda again, the better.

ELYOT: I'm not going to marry Amanda.

VICTOR: What?

ELYOT: She's a vile tempered wicked woman.

VICTOR: You should have thought of that before.

ELYOT: I did think of it before.

VICTOR [*firmly*]: You've got to marry her.

ELYOT: I'd rather marry a ravening leopard.

VICTOR [*angrily*]: Now look here. I'm sick of all this shilly-shallying. You're getting off a good deal more lightly than you deserve; you can consider yourself damned lucky I didn't shoot you.

ELYOT [*with sudden vehemence*]: Well, if you'd had a spark of manliness in you, you would have shot me. You're all fuss and fume, one of these cotton wool Englishmen. I despise you.

VICTOR [*through clenched teeth*]: You despise me?

ELYOT: Yes, utterly. You're nothing but a rampaging gas bag!

He goes off into his room and slams the door, leaving VICTOR *speechless with fury,* AMANDA *and* SIBYL *re-enter.*

AMANDA [*brightly*]: Well, what's happened?

VICTOR [*sullenly*]: Nothing's happened.

AMANDA: You ought to be ashamed to admit it.

SIBYL: Where's Elyot?

VICTOR: In there.

AMANDA: What's he doing?

VICTOR [*turning angrily away*]: How do I know what he's doing?

AMANDA: If you were half the man I thought you were, he'd be bandaging himself.

SIBYL [*with defiance*]: Elyot's just as strong as Victor.

AMANDA [*savagely*]: I should like it proved.

SIBYL: There's no need to be so vindictive.

AMANDA: You are abusing Elyot like a pick-pocket to me a little while ago, now you are standing up for him.

SIBYL: I'm beginning to suspect that he wasn't quite so much to blame as I thought.

AMANDA: Oh really?

SIBYL: You certainly have a very unpleasant temper.

AMANDA: It's a little difficult to keep up with your rapid changes of front, but you're young and inexperienced, so I forgive you freely.

SIBYL [*heatedly*]: Seeing the depths of degradation to which age and experience have brought you, I'm glad I'm as I am!

AMANDA [*with great grandeur*]: That was exceedingly rude. I think you'd better go away somewhere. [*She waves her hand vaguely.*]

SIBYL: After all, Elyot is my husband.

AMANDA: Take him with you, by all means.

SIBYL: If you're not very careful, I will! [*She goes over to* ELYOT's *door and bangs on it.*] Elyot—Elyot—

ELYOT [*inside*]: What is it?

SIBYL: Let me in. Please, please let me in; I want to speak to you!

AMANDA: Heaven preserve me from nice women!

SIBYL: Your own reputation ought to do that.

AMANDA [*irritably*]: Oh, go to hell!

ELYOT *opens the door, and* SIBYL *disappears inside,* AMANDA *looks at* VICTOR, *who is standing with his back turned, staring out of the window, then she wanders about the room, making rather inadequate little attempts to tidy up. She glances at* VICTOR *again.*

AMANDA: Victor.

VICTOR [*without turning*]: What?

AMANDA [*sadly*]: Nothing.

She begins to wrestle with one of the sofas in an effort to get it in place. VICTOR *turns, sees her, and comes down and helps her, in silence.*

VICTOR: Where does it go?

AMANDA: Over there. [*After they have placed it,* AMANDA *sits on the edge of it and gasps a little.*] Thank you, Victor.

VICTOR: Don't mention it.

AMANDA [*after a pause*]: What did you say to Elyot?

VICTOR: I told him he was beneath contempt.

AMANDA: Good.

VICTOR: I think you must be mad, Amanda.

AMANDA: I've often thought that myself.

VICTOR: I feel completely lost, completely bewildered.

AMANDA: I don't blame you. I don't feel any too cosy.

VICTOR: Had you been drinking last night?

AMANDA: Certainly not!

VICTOR: Had Elyot been drinking?

AMANDA: Yes—gallons.

VICTOR: Used he to drink before? When you were married to him?

AMANDA: Yes, terribly. Night after night he'd come home roaring and hiccoughing.

VICTOR: Disgusting!

AMANDA: Yes, wasn't it?

VICTOR: Did he really strike you last night?

AMANDA: Repeatedly. I'm bruised beyond recognition.

VICTOR [*suspecting slight exaggeration*]: Amanda!

AMANDA [*putting her hand on his arm*]: Oh, Victor, I'm most awfully sorry to have given you so much trouble, really I am! I've behaved badly, I know, but something strange happened to me. I can't explain it, there's no excuse, but I am ashamed of having made you unhappy.

VICTOR: I can't understand it at all. I've tried to, but I can't. It all seems so unlike you.

AMANDA: It isn't really unlike me, that's the trouble. I ought never to have married you; I'm a bad lot.

VICTOR: Amanda!

AMANDA: Don't contradict me. I know I'm a bad lot.

VICTOR: I wasn't going to contradict you.

AMANDA: Victor!

VICTOR: You appal me–absolutely!

AMANDA: Go on, go on, I deserve it.

VICTOR: I didn't come here to accuse you; there's no sense in that!

AMANDA: Why did you come?

VICTOR: To find out what you want me to do.

AMANDA: Divorce me, I suppose, as soon as possible. I won't make any difficulties. I'll go away, far away, Morocco, or Tunis, or somewhere. I shall probably catch some dreadful disease, and die out there, all alone–oh dear!

VICTOR: It's no use pitying yourself.

AMANDA: I seem to be the only one who does. I might just as well enjoy it. [*She sniffs.*] I'm thoroughly unprincipled; Sibyl was right!

VICTOR [*irritably*]: Sibyl's an ass.

AMANDA [*brightening slightly*]: Yes, she is rather, isn't she? I can't think why Elyot ever married her.

VICTOR: Do you love him?

AMANDA: She seems so insipid, somehow—

VICTOR: Do you love him?

AMANDA: Of course she's very pretty, I suppose, in rather a shallow way, but still—

VICTOR: Amanda!

AMANDA: Yes, Victor?

VICTOR: You haven't answered my question.

AMANDA: I've forgotten what it was.

VICTOR [*turning away*]: You're hopeless–hopeless.

AMANDA: Don't be angry, it's all much too serious to be angry about.

VICTOR: You're talking utter nonsense!

AMANDA: No, I'm not, I mean it. It's ridiculous for us all to stand round arguing with one another. You'd much better go back to England and let your lawyers deal with the whole thing.

VICTOR: But what about you?

AMANDA: I'll be all right.

VICTOR: I only want to know one thing, and you won't tell me.

AMANDA: What is it?

VICTOR: Do you love Elyot?

AMANDA: No, I hate him. When I saw him again suddenly at Deauville, it was an odd sort of shock. It swept me away completely. He attracted me; he always has attracted me, but only the worst part of me. I see that now.

VICTOR: I can't understand why? He's so terribly trivial and superficial.

AMANDA: That sort of attraction can't be explained, it's a sort of a chemical what d'you call 'em.

VICTOR: Yes; it must be!

AMANDA: I don't expect you to understand, and I'm not going to try to excuse myself in any way. Elyot was the first love affair of my life, and in spite of all the suffering he caused me before, there must have been a little spark left smouldering, which burst into flame when I came face to face with him again. I completely lost grip of myself and behaved like a fool, for which I shall pay all right, you needn't worry about that. But perhaps one day, when all this is dead and done with, you and I might meet and be friends. That's something to hope for, anyhow. Good-bye, Victor dear. [*She holds out her hand.*]

VICTOR [*shaking her hand mechanically*]: Do you want to marry him?

AMANDA: I'd rather marry a boa constrictor.

VICTOR: I can't go away and leave you with a man who drinks, and knocks you about.

AMANDA: You needn't worry about leaving me, as though I were a sort of parcel. I can look after myself.

VICTOR: You said just now you were going away to Tunis, to die.

AMANDA: I've changed my mind, it's the wrong time of the year for Tunis. I shall go somewhere quite different. I believe Brioni is very nice in the summer.

VICTOR: Why won't you be serious for just one moment?

AMANDA: I've told you, it's no use.

VICTOR: If it will make things any easier for you, I won't divorce you.

AMANDA: Victor!

VICTOR: We can live apart until Sibyl has got her decree against Elyot, then, some time after that, I'll let you divorce me.

AMANDA [*turning away*]: I see you're determined to make me serious, whether I like it or not.

VICTOR: I married you because I loved you.

AMANDA: Stop it, Victor! Stop it! I won't listen!

VICTOR: I expect I love you still; one doesn't change all in a minute. You never loved me. I see that now, of course, so perhaps everything has turned out for the best really.

AMANDA: I thought I loved you, honestly I did.

VICTOR: Yes, I know, that's all right.

AMANDA: What an escape you've had.

VICTOR: I've said that to myself often during the last few days.

AMANDA: There's no need to rub it in.

VICTOR: Do you agree about the divorce business?

AMANDA: Yes. It's very, very generous of you.

VICTOR: It will save you some of the mud-slinging. We might persuade Sibyl not to name you.

AMANDA [*ruefully*]: Yes, we might.

VICTOR: Perhaps she'll change her mind about divorcing him.

AMANDA: Perhaps. She certainly went into the bedroom with a predatory look in her eye.

VICTOR: Would you be pleased if that happened?

AMANDA: Delighted.

She laughs suddenly. VICTOR *looks at her, curiously.* SIBYL *and* ELYOT *come out of the bedroom. There is an awkward silence for a moment.*

SIBYL [*looking at* AMANDA *triumphantly*]: Elyot and I have come to a decision.

AMANDA: How very nice!

VICTOR: What is it?

AMANDA: Don't be silly, Victor. Look at their faces.

ELYOT: Feminine intuition, very difficult.

AMANDA [*looking at* SIBYL]: Feminine determination, very praiseworthy.

SIBYL: I am not going to divorce Elyot for a year.

AMANDA: I congratulate you.

ELYOT [*defiantly*]: Sibyl has behaved like an angel.

AMANDA: Well, it was certainly her big moment.

> LOUISE *comes staggering in with a large tray of coffee and rolls, etc.; she stands peering over the edge of it, not knowing where to put it.*

ELYOT: Il faut le met sur la petite table la bas.

LOUISE: Oui, monsieur.

> ELYOT *and* VICTOR *hurriedly clear the things off the side table, and* LOUISE *puts the tray down, and goes back into the kitchen.* AMANDA *and* SIBYL *eye one another.*

AMANDA: It all seems very amicable.

SIBYL: It is, thank you.

AMANDA: I don't wish to depress you, but Victor isn't going to divorce me either.

ELYOT [*looking up sharply*]: What!

AMANDA: I believe I asked you once before this morning, never to speak to me again.

ELYOT: I only said 'What.' It was a general exclamation denoting extreme satisfaction.

AMANDA [*politely to* SIBYL]: Do sit down, won't you?

SIBYL: I'm afraid I must be going now. I'm catching the Golden Arrow; it leaves at twelve.

ELYOT [*coaxingly*]: You have time for a little coffee surely?

SIBYL: No, I really must go!

ELYOT: I shan't be seeing you again for such a long time.

AMANDA [*brightly*]: Living apart? How wise!

ELYOT [*ignoring her*]: Please, Sibyl, do stay!

SIBYL [*looking at* AMANDA *with a glint in her eye*]: Very well, just for a little.

AMANDA: Sit down, Victor, darling.

> *They all sit down in silence.* AMANDA *smiles sweetly at* SIBYL *and holds up the coffee pot and milk jug.*

Half and half?

SIBYL: Yes, please.

AMANDA [*sociably*]: What would one do without one's morning coffee? That's what I often ask myself.

ELYOT: Is it?

AMANDA [*withering him with a look*]: Victor, sugar for Sibyl. [*To* SIBYL] It would be absurd for me to call you anything but Sibyl, wouldn't it?

SIBYL [*not to be outdone*]: Of course, I shall call you Mandy.

AMANDA *represses a shudder.*

ELYOT: Oh God! We're off again. What weather!

AMANDA *hands* SIBYL *her coffee.*

SIBYL: Thank you.
VICTOR: What's the time?
ELYOT: If the clock's still going after last night, it's ten fifteen.
AMANDA [*handing* VICTOR *cup of coffee*]: Here, Victor dear.
VICTOR: Thanks.
AMANDA: Sibyl, sugar for Victor.
ELYOT: I should like some coffee, please.

AMANDA *pours some out for him, and hands it to him in silence.*

AMANDA [*to* VICTOR]: Brioche?
VICTOR [*jumping*]: What?
AMANDA: Would you like a Brioche?
VICTOR: No thank you.
ELYOT: I would. And some butter, and some jam. [*He helps himself.*]
AMANDA [*to* SIBYL]: Have you ever been to Brioni?
SIBYL: No. It's in the Adriatic, isn't it?
VICTOR: The Baltic, I think.
SIBYL: I made sure it was in the Adriatic.
AMANDA: I had an aunt who went there once.
ELYOT [*with his mouth full*]: I once had an aunt who went to Tasmania.

AMANDA *looks at him stonily. He winks at her, and she looks away hurriedly.*

VICTOR: Funny how the South of France has become so fashionable in the
summer, isn't it?
SIBYL: Yes, awfully funny.
ELYOT: I've been laughing about it for months.
AMANDA: Personally, I think it's a bit too hot, although of course one can lie in
the water all day.
SIBYL: Yes, the bathing is really divine!
VICTOR: A friend of mine has a house right on the edge of Cape Ferrat.
SIBYL: Really?
VICTOR: Yes, right on the edge.
AMANDA: That must be marvellous!
VICTOR: Yes, he seems to like it very much.

The conversation languishes slightly.

AMANDA [*with great vivacity*]: Do you know, I really think I love travelling more
than anything else in the world! It always gives me such a tremendous feeling
of adventure. First of all, the excitement of packing, and getting your passport visa'd and everything, then the thrill of actually starting, and trundling

on trains and ships, and then the most thrilling thing of all, arriving
at strange places, and seeing strange people, and eating strange foods—
ELYOT: And making strange noises afterwards.

AMANDA *chokes violently.* VICTOR *jumps up and tries to offer assistance, but she*
waves him away, and continues to choke.

VICTOR [*to* ELYOT]: That was a damned fool thing to do.
ELYOT: How did I know she was going to choke?
VICTOR [*to* AMANDA]: Here, drink some coffee.
AMANDA [*breathlessly gasping*]: Leave me alone. I'll be all right in a minute.
VICTOR [*to* ELYOT]: You waste too much time trying to be funny.
SIBYL [*up in arms*]: It's no use talking to Elyot like that; it wasn't his fault.
VICTOR: Of course it was his fault entirely, making rotten stupid jokes—
SIBYL: I thought what Elyot said was funny.
VICTOR: Well, all I can say is, you must have a very warped sense of humour.
SIBYL: That's better than having none at all.
VICTOR: I fail to see what humour there is in incessant trivial flippancy.
SIBYL: You couldn't be flippant if you tried until you were blue in the face.
VICTOR: I shouldn't dream of trying.
SIBYL: It must be very sad not to be able to see any fun in anything.

AMANDA *stops choking, and looks at* ELYOT. *He winks at her again, and she*
smiles.

VICTOR: Fun! I should like you to tell me what fun there is in—
SIBYL: I pity you, I really do. I've been pitying you ever since we left Deauville.
VICTOR: I'm sure it's very nice of you, but quite unnecessary.
SIBYL: And I pity you more than ever now.
VICTOR: *Why* now particularly?
SIBYL: If you don't see why, I'm certainly not going to tell you.
VICTOR: I see no reason for you to try to pick a quarrel with me. I've tried my
best to be pleasant to you, and comfort you.
SIBYL: You weren't very comforting when I lost my trunk.
VICTOR: I have little patience with people who go about losing luggage.
SIBYL: I don't go about losing luggage. It's the first time I've lost anything in
my life.
VICTOR: I find that hard to believe.
SIBYL: Anyhow, if you'd tipped the porter enough, everything would have been
all right. Small economies never pay; it's absolutely no use—
VICTOR: Oh, for God's sake be quiet!

AMANDA *lifts her hand as though she were going to interfere, but* ELYOT *grabs*
her wrist. They look at each other for a moment, she lets her hand rest in his.

SIBYL [*rising from the table*]: How dare you speak to me like that!
VICTOR [*also rising*]: Because you've been irritating me for days.
SIBYL [*outraged*]: Oh!
VICTOR [*coming down to her*]: You're one of the most completely idiotic women
I've ever met.
SIBYL: And you're certainly the rudest man I've ever met!

VICTOR: Well then, we're quits, aren't we?

SIBYL [*shrilly*]: One thing, you'll get your deserts all right.

VICTOR: What do you mean by that?

SIBYL: You know perfectly well what I mean. And it'll serve you right for being weak-minded enough to allow that woman to get round you so easily.

VICTOR: What about you? Letting that unprincipled roué persuade you to take him back again!

AMANDA and ELYOT *are laughing silently.* ELYOT *blows her a lingering kiss across the table.*

SIBYL: He's nothing of the sort, he's just been victimized, as you were victimized.

VICTOR: Victimized! What damned nonsense!

SIBYL [*furiously*]: It isn't damned nonsense! You're very fond of swearing and blustering and threatening, but when it comes to the point you're as weak as water. Why, a blind cat could see what you've let yourself in for.

VICTOR [*equally furious*]: Stop making those insinuations.

SIBYL: I'm not insinuating anything. When I think of all the things you said about her, it makes me laugh, it does really; to see how completely she's got you again.

VICTOR: You can obviously speak with great authority, having had the intelligence to marry a drunkard.

SIBYL: So that's what she's been telling you. I might have known it! I suppose she said he struck her too!

VICTOR: Yes, she did, and I'm quite sure it's perfectly true.

SIBYL: I expect she omitted to tell you that she drank fourteen glasses of brandy last night straight off; and that the reason their first marriage was broken up was that she used to come home at all hours of the night, screaming and hiccoughing.

VICTOR: If he told you that, he's a filthy liar.

SIBYL: He isn't—he isn't!

VICTOR: And if you believe it, you're a silly scatter-brained little fool.

SIBYL [*screaming*]: How dare you speak to me like that! How dare you! I've never been so insulted in my life! How dare you!

AMANDA and ELYOT *rise quietly, and go, hand in hand, towards the front door.*

VICTOR [*completely giving way*]: It's a tremendous relief to me to have an excuse to insult you. I've had to listen to your weeping and wailings for days. You've clacked at me, and snivelled at me until you've nearly driven me insane, and I controlled my nerves and continued to try to help you and look after you, because I was sorry for you. I always thought you were stupid from the first, but I must say I never realised that you were a malicious little vixen as well!

SIBYL [*shrieking*]: Stop it! Stop it! You insufferable great brute!

She slaps his face hard, and he takes her by the shoulders and shakes her like a rat, as AMANDA *and* ELYOT *go smilingly out of the door, with their suitcases, and—*

THE CURTAIN FALLS.

THE
CIRCLE
W. SOMERSET
MAUGHAM

THE CIRCLE

THE CIRCLE

A Comedy
in Three Acts

CHARACTERS

CLIVE CHAMPION-CHENEY
ARNOLD CHAMPION-CHENEY, M.P.
LORD PORTEOUS
EDWARD LUTON
LADY CATHERINE CHAMPION-CHENEY
ELIZABETH
MRS SHENSTONE
A FOOTMAN AND A BUTLER

The action takes place at Aston-Adey, Arnold
Champion-Cheney's house in Dorset.

ACT ONE

The scene is a stately drawing-room at Aston-Adey, with fine pictures on the walls and Georgian furniture. Aston-Adey has been described, with many illustrations, in Country Life. *It is not a house, but a place. Its owner takes a great pride in it, and there is nothing in the room which is not of the period. Through the French windows at the back can be seen the beautiful gardens which are one of the features.*

It is a fine summer morning.

ARNOLD *comes in. He is a man of about thirty-five, tall and good-looking, fair, with a clean-cut, sensitive face. He has a look that is intellectual, but somewhat bloodless. He is very well dressed.*

ARNOLD [*calling*]: Elizabeth! [*He goes to the window and calls again.*] Elizabeth!

He rings the bell. While he is waiting he gives a look round the room. He slightly alters the position of one of the chairs. He takes an ornament from the chimney-piece and blows the dust from it. A FOOTMAN *comes in.*

Oh, George! See if you can find Mrs Cheney, and ask her if she'd be good enough to come here.
FOOTMAN: Very good, sir. [*He turns to go.*]
ARNOLD: Who is supposed to look after this room?
FOOTMAN: I don't know, sir.
ARNOLD: I wish when they dust they'd take care to replace the things exactly as they were before.
FOOTMAN: Yes, sir.
ARNOLD [*dismissing him*]: All right.

The FOOTMAN *goes out. He goes again to the window and calls.*

Elizabeth! [*He sees* MRS SHENSTONE.] Oh, Anna, do you know where Elizabeth is?

MRS SHENTONE *comes in from the garden. She is a woman of forty, pleasant and of elegant appearance.*

ANNA: Isn't she playing tennis?
ARNOLD: No, I've been down to the tennis court. Something very tiresome has happened.
ANNA: Oh?
ARNOLD: I wonder where the deuce she is.

ANNA: When do you expect Lord Porteous and Lady Kitty?

ARNOLD: They're motoring down in time for luncheon.

ANNA: Are you sure you want me to be here? It's not too late yet, you know. I can have my things packed and catch a train for somewhere or other.

ARNOLD: No, of course we want you. It'll make it so much easier if there are people here. It was exceedingly kind of you to come.

ANNA: Oh, nonsense!

ARNOLD: And I think it was a good thing to have Teddie Luton down.

ANNA: He is so breezy, isn't he?

ARNOLD: Yes, that's his great asset. I don't know that he's very intelligent, but, you know, there are occasions when you want a bull in a china shop. I sent one of the servants to find Elizabeth.

ANNA: I daresay she's putting on her shoes. She and Teddie were going to have a single.

ARNOLD: It can't take all this time to change one's shoes.

ANNA [*with a smile*]: One can't change one's shoes without powdering one's nose, you know.

> ELIZABETH *comes in. She is a very pretty creature in the early twenties. She wears a light summer frock.*

ARNOLD: My dear, I've been hunting for you everywhere. What *have* you been doing?

ELIZABETH: Nothing! I've been standing on my head.

ARNOLD: My father's here.

ELIZABETH [*startled*]: Where?

ARNOLD: At the cottage. He arrived last night.

ELIZABETH: Damn!

ARNOLD [*good-humouredly*]: I wish you wouldn't say that, Elizabeth.

ELIZABETH: If you're not going to say Damn when a thing's damnable, when are you going to say Damn?

ARNOLD: I should have thought you could say, Oh, bother! or something like that.

ELIZABETH: But that wouldn't express my sentiments. Besides, at that speech day when you were giving away the prizes you said there were no synonyms in the English language.

ANNA [*smiling*]: Oh, Elizabeth! It's very unfair to expect a politician to live in private up to the statements he makes in public.

ARNOLD: I'm always willing to stand by anything I've said. There *are* no synonyms in the English language.

ELIZABETH: In that case I shall be regretfully forced to continue to say Damn whenever I feel like it.

> EDWARD LUTON *shows himself at the window. He is an attractive youth in flannels.*

TEDDIE: I say, what about this tennis?

ELIZABETH: Come in. We're having a scene.

TEDDIE [*entering*]: How splendid! What about?

ELIZABETH: The English language.

TEDDIE: Don't tell me you've been splitting your infinitives.

ARNOLD [*with the shadow of a frown*]: I wish you'd be serious, Elizabeth. The situation is none too pleasant.

ANNA: I think Teddie and I had better make ourselves scarce.

ELIZABETH: Nonsense! You're both in it. If there's going to be any unpleasantness we want your moral support. That's why we asked you to come.

TEDDIE: And I thought I'd been asked for my blue eyes.

ELIZABETH: Vain beast! And they happen to be brown.

TEDDIE: Is anything up?

ELIZABETH: Arnold's father arrived last night.

TEDDIE: Did he, by Jove! I thought he was in Paris.

ARNOLD: So did we all. He told me he'd be there for the next month.

ANNA: Have you seen him?

ARNOLD: No! He rang me up. It's a mercy he had a telephone put in the cottage. It would have been a pretty kettle of fish if he'd just walked in.

ELIZABETH: Did you tell him Lady Catherine was coming?

ARNOLD: Of course not. I was flabbergasted to know he was here. And then I thought we'd better talk it over first.

ELIZABETH: Is he coming along here?

ARNOLD: Yes. He suggested it, and I couldn't think of any excuse to prevent him.

TEDDIE: Couldn't you put the other people off?

ARNOLD: They're coming by car. They may be here any minute. It's too late to do that.

ELIZABETH: Besides, it would be beastly.

ARNOLD: I knew it was silly to have them here. Elizabeth insisted.

ELIZABETH: After all, she *is* your mother, Arnold.

ARNOLD: That meant precious little to her when she—went away. You can't imagine it means very much to me now.

ELIZABETH: It's thirty years ago. It seems so absurd to bear malice after all that time.

ARNOLD: I don't bear malice, but the fact remains that she did me the most irreparable harm. I can find no excuse for her.

ELIZABETH: Have you ever tried to?

ARNOLD: My dear Elizabeth, it's no good going over all that again. The facts are lamentably simple. She had a husband who adored her, a wonderful position, all the money she could want, and a child of five. And she ran away with a married man.

ELIZABETH: Lady Porteous is not a very attractive woman, Arnold. [*To* ANNA.] Do you know her?

ANNA [*smiling*]: Forbidding is the word, I think.

ARNOLD: If you're going to make little jokes about it, I have nothing more to say.

ANNA: I'm sorry, Arnold.

ELIZABETH: Perhaps your mother couldn't help herself—if she was in love?

ARNOLD: And had no sense of honour, duty, or decency? Oh, yes, under those circumstances you can explain a great deal.

ELIZABETH: That's not a very pretty way to speak of your mother.

ARNOLD: I can't look on her as my mother.

ELIZABETH: What you can't get over is that she didn't think of you. Some of us are more mother and some of us more woman. It gives me a little thrill when I think that she loved that man so much. She sacrificed her name, her position and her child to him.

ARNOLD: You really can't expect the said child to have any great affection for the mother who treated him like that.

ELIZABETH: No, I don't think I do. But I think it's a pity after all these years that you shouldn't be friends.

ARNOLD: I wonder if you realise what it was to grow up under the shadow of that horrible scandal. Everywhere, at school, and at Oxford, and afterwards in London, I was always the son of Lady Kitty Cheney. Oh, it was cruel, cruel!

ELIZABETH: Yes, I know, Arnold. It was beastly for you.

ARNOLD: It would have been bad enough if it had been an ordinary case, but the position of the people made it ten times worse. My father was in the House then, and Porteous—he hadn't succeeded to the title—was in the House too; he was Under-Secretary for Foreign Affairs, and he was very much in the public eye.

ANNA: My father always used to say he was the ablest man in the party. Every one was expecting him to be Prime Minister.

ARNOLD: You can imagine what a boon it was to the British public. They hadn't had such a treat for a generation. The most popular song of the day was about my mother. Did you ever hear it? 'Naughty Lady Kitty. Thought it such a pity . . .'

ELIZABETH [*interrupting*]: Oh, Arnold, don't!

ARNOLD: And then they never let people forget them. If they'd lived quietly in Florence and not made a fuss the scandal would have died down. But those constant actions between Lord and Lady Porteous kept on reminding everyone.

TEDDIE: What were they having actions about?

ARNOLD: Of course my father divorced his wife, but Lady Porteous refused to divorce Porteous. He tried to force her by refusing to support her and turning her out of her house, and heaven knows what. They were constantly wrangling in the law courts.

ANNA: I think it was monstrous of Lady Porteous.

ARNOLD: She knew he wanted to marry my mother, and she hated my mother. You can't blame her.

ANNA: It must have been very difficult for them.

ARNOLD: That's why they've lived in Florence. Porteous has money. They found people there who were willing to accept the situation.

ELIZABETH: This is the first time they've ever come to England.

ARNOLD: My father will have to be told, Elizabeth.

ELIZABETH: Yes.

ANNA [*to* ELIZABETH]: Has he ever spoken to you about Lady Kitty?

ELIZABETH: Never.

ARNOLD: I don't think her name has passed his lips since she ran away from this house thirty years ago.

TEDDIE: Oh, they lived here?

ARNOLD: Naturally. There was a house-party, and one evening neither Porteous not my mother came down to dinner. The rest of them waited. They couldn't make it out. My father sent up to my mother's room, and a note was found on the pin-cushion.

ELIZABETH [*with a faint smile*]: That's what they did in the Dark Ages.

ARNOLD: I think he took a dislike to this house from that horrible night. He never lived here again, and when I married he handed the place over to me. He just has a cottage now on the estate that he comes to when he feels inclined.

ELIZABETH: It's been very nice for us.

ARNOLD: I owe everything to my father. I don't think he'll ever forgive me for asking these people to come here.

ELIZABETH: I'm going to take all the blame on myself, Arnold.

ARNOLD [*irritably*]: The situation was embarrassing enough anyhow. I don't know how I ought to treat them.

ELIZABETH: Don't you think that'll settle itself when you see them.

ARNOLD: After all, they're my guests. I shall try and behave like a gentleman.

ELIZABETH: I wouldn't. We haven't got central heating.

ARNOLD [*taking no notice*]: Will she expect me to kiss her?

ELIZABETH [*with a smile*]: Surely.

ARNOLD: It always makes me uncomfortable when people are effusive.

ANNA: But I can't understand why you never saw her before.

ARNOLD: I believe she tried to see me when I was little, but my father thought it better she shouldn't.

ANNA: Yes, but when you were grown up?

ARNOLD: She was always in Italy. I never went to Italy.

ELIZABETH: It seems to me so pathetic that if you saw one another in the street you wouldn't recognise each other.

ARNOLD: Is it my fault?

ELIZABETH: You've promised to be very gentle with her and very kind.

ARNOLD: The mistake was asking Porteous to come too. It looks as though we condoned the whole thing. And how am I to treat him? Am I to shake him by the hand and slap him on the back? He absolutely ruined my father's life.

ELIZABETH [*smiling*]: How much would you give for a nice motor accident that prevented them from coming?

ARNOLD: I let you persuade me against my better judgment, and I've regretted it ever since.

ELIZABETH [*good-humouredly*]: I think it's very lucky that Anna and Teddie are here. I don't foresee a very successful party.

ARNOLD: I'm going to do my best. I gave you my promise and I shall keep it. But I can't answer for my father.

ANNA: Here is your father.

MR CHAMPION-CHENEY *shows himself at one of the French windows.*

CHAMPION-CHENEY: May I come in through the window, or shall I have myself announced by a supercilious flunkey?

ELIZABETH: Come in. We've been expecting you.

CHAMPION-CHENEY: Impatiently, I hope, my dear child.

MR CHAMPION-CHENEY *is a tall man in the early sixties, spare, with a fine head of grey hair and an intelligent, somewhat ascetic face. He is very carefully dressed. He is a man who makes the most of himself. He bears his years jauntily. He kisses* ELIZABETH *and then holds out his hand to* ARNOLD.

ELIZABETH: We thought you'd be in Paris for another month.

CHAMPION-CHENEY: How are you, Arnold? I always reserve to myself the privilege of changing my mind. It's the only one elderly gentlemen share with pretty women.

ELIZABETH: You know Anna.

CHAMPION-CHENEY [*shaking hands with her*]: Of course I do. How very nice to see you here. Are you staying long?

ANNA: As long as I'm welcome.

ELIZABETH: And this is Mr Luton.

CHAMPION-CHENEY: How do you do? Do you play bridge?

LUTON: I do.

CHAMPION-CHENEY: Capital. Do you declare without top honours?

LUTON: Never.

CHAMPION-CHENEY: Of such is the kingdom of heaven. I see that you are a good young man.

LUTON: But, like the good in general, I am poor.

CHAMPION-CHENEY: Never mind; if your principles are right, you can play ten shillings a hundred without danger. I never play less, and I never play more.

ARNOLD: And you—are you going to stay long, father?

CHAMPION-CHENEY: To luncheon, if you'll have me.

ARNOLD *gives* ELIZABETH *a harassed look.*

ELIZABETH: That'll be jolly.

ARNOLD: I didn't mean that. Of course you're going to stay for luncheon. I meant, how long are you going to stay down here?

CHAMPION-CHENEY: A week.

There is a moment's pause. Everyone but CHAMPION-CHENEY *is slightly embarrassed.*

TEDDIE: I think we'd better chuck our tennis.

ELIZABETH: Yes. I want my father-in-law to tell me what they're wearing in Paris this week.

TEDDIE: I'll go and put the rackets away. [*He goes out.*]

ARNOLD: It's nearly one o'clock, Elizabeth.

ELIZABETH: I didn't know it was so late.

ANNA [*to* ARNOLD]: I wonder if I can persuade you to take a turn in the garden before luncheon.

ARNOLD [*jumping at the idea*]: I'd love it.

ANNA *goes out of the window, and as he follows her he stops irresolutely.*

I want you to look at this chair I've just got. I think it's rather good.

CHAMPION-CHENEY: Charming.

ARNOLD: About 1750, I should say. Good design, isn't it? It hasn't been restored or anything.

CHAMPION-CHENEY: Very pretty.

ARNOLD: I think it was a good buy, don't you?

CHAMPION-CHENEY: Oh, my dear boy, you know I'm entirely ignorant about these things.

ARNOLD: It's exactly my period . . . I shall see you at luncheon, then.

He follows ANNA *through the window.*

CHAMPION-CHENEY: Who is that young man?

ELIZABETH: Mr Luton. He's only just been demobilised. He's the manager of a rubber estate in the F.M.S.

CHAMPION-CHENEY: And what are the F.M.S. when they're at home?

ELIZABETH: The Federated Malay States. He joined up at the beginning of the war. He's just going back there.

CHAMPION-CHENEY: And why have we been left alone in this very marked manner?

ELIZABETH: Have we? I didn't notice it.

CHAMPION-CHENEY: I suppose it's difficult for the young to realise that one may be old without being a fool.

ELIZABETH: I never thought you that. Everyone knows you're very intelligent.

CHAMPION-CHENEY: They certainly ought to by now. I've told them often enough. Are you a little nervous?

ELIZABETH: Let me feel my pulse. [*She puts her finger on her wrist.*] It's perfectly regular.

CHAMPION-CHENEY: When I suggested staying to luncheon Arnold looked exactly like a dose of castor oil.

ELIZABETH: I wish you'd sit down.

CHAMPION-CHENEY: Will it make it easier for you? [*He takes a chair.*] You have evidently something very disagreeable to say to me.

ELIZABETH: You won't be cross with me?

CHAMPION-CHENEY: How old are you?

ELIZABETH: Twenty-five.

CHAMPION-CHENEY: I'm never cross with a woman under thirty.

ELIZABETH: Oh, then, I've got ten years.

CHAMPION-CHENEY: Mathematics?

ELIZABETH: No. Paint.

CHAMPION-CHENEY: Well?

ELIZABETH [*reflectively*]: I think it would be easier if I sat on your knees.

CHAMPION-CHENEY: That is a pleasing taste of yours, but you must take care not to put on weight.

She sits down on his knees.

ELIZABETH: Am I boney?

CHAMPION-CHENEY: On the contrary. . . . I'm listening.

ELIZABETH: Lady Catherine's coming here.

CHAMPION-CHENEY: Who's Lady Catherine?

ELIZABETH: Your—Arnold's mother.

CHAMPION-CHENEY: Is she?

He withdraws himself a little and ELIZABETH *gets up.*

ELIZABETH: You mustn't blame Arnold. It's my fault. I insisted. He was against it. I nagged him till he gave way. And then I wrote and asked her to come.

CHAMPION-CHENEY: I didn't know you knew her.

ELIZABETH: I don't. But I heard she was in London. She's staying at Claridge's. It seemed so heartless not to take the smallest notice of her.

CHAMPION-CHENEY: When is she coming?

ELIZABETH: We're expecting her in time for luncheon.

CHAMPION-CHENEY: As soon as that? I understand the embarrassment.

ELIZABETH: You see, we never expected you to be here. You said you'd be in Paris for another month.

CHAMPION-CHENEY: My dear child, this is your house. There's no reason why you shouldn't ask whom you please to stay with you.

ELIZABETH: After all, whatever her faults, she's Arnold's mother. It seemed so unnatural that they should never see one another. My heart ached for that poor lonely woman.

CHAMPION-CHENEY: I never heard that she was lonely, and she certainly isn't poor.

ELIZABETH: And there's something else. I couldn't ask her by herself. It would have been so—so insulting. I asked Lord Porteous, too.

CHAMPION-CHENEY: I see.

ELIZABETH: I daresay you'd rather not meet them.

CHAMPION-CHENEY: I daresay they'd rather not meet me. I shall get a capital luncheon at the cottage. I've noticed you always get the best food if you come in unexpectedly and have the same as they're having in the servants' hall.

ELIZABETH: No one's ever talked to me about Lady Kitty. It's always been a subject that everyone has avoided. I've never even seen a photograph of her.

CHAMPION-CHENEY: The house was full of them when she left. I think I told the butler to throw them in the dust-bin. She was very much photographed.

ELIZABETH: Won't you tell me what she was like?

CHAMPION-CHENEY: She was very like you, Elizabeth, only she had dark hair instead of red.

ELIZABETH: Poor dear! It must be quite white now.

CHAMPION-CHENEY: I daresay. She was a pretty little thing.

ELIZABETH: But she was one of the great beauties of her day. They say she was lovely.

CHAMPION-CHENEY: She had the most adorable little nose, like yours. . . .

ELIZABETH: D'you like my nose?

CHAMPION-CHENEY: And she was very dainty, with a beautiful little figure; very light on her feet. She was like a *marquise* in an old French comedy. Yes, she was lovely.

ELIZABETH: And I'm sure she's lovely still.

CHAMPION-CHENEY: She's no chicken, you know.

ELIZABETH: You can't expect me to look at it as you and Arnold do. When you've loved as she's loved you may grow old, but you grow old beautifully.

CHAMPION-CHENEY: You're very romantic.

ELIZABETH: If everyone hadn't made such a mystery of it I daresay I shouldn't feel as I do. I know she did a great wrong to you and a great wrong to Arnold. I'm willing to acknowledge that.

CHAMPION-CHENEY: I'm sure it's very kind of you.

ELIZABETH: But she loved and she dared. Romance is such an illusive thing. You read of it in books, but it's seldom you see it face to face. I can't help it if it thrills me.

CHAMPION-CHENEY: I am painfully aware that the husband in these cases is not a romantic object.

ELIZABETH: She had the world at her feet. You were rich. She was a figure in society. And she gave up everything for love.

CHAMPION-CHENEY [*dryly*]: I'm beginning to suspect it wasn't only for her sake and for Arnold's that you asked her to come here.

ELIZABETH: I seem to know her already. I think her face is a little sad, for a love like that doesn't leave you gay, it leaves you grave, but I think her pale face is unlined. It's like a child's.

CHAMPION-CHENEY: My dear, how you let your imagination run away with you!

ELIZABETH: I imagine her slight and frail.

CHAMPION-CHENEY: Frail, certainly.

ELIZABETH: With beautiful thin hands and white hair. I've pictured her so often in that Renaissance palace that they live in, with old masters on the walls and lovely carved things all round, sitting in a black silk dress with old lace round her neck and old-fashioned diamonds. You see, I never knew my mother; she died when I was a baby. You can't confide in aunts with huge families of their own. I want Arnold's mother to be a mother to me. I've got so much to say to her.

CHAMPION-CHENEY: Are you happy with Arnold?

ELIZABETH: Why shouldn't I be?

CHAMPION-CHENEY: Why haven't you got any babies?

ELIZABETH: Give us a little time. We've only been married three years.

CHAMPION-CHENEY: I wonder what Hughie is like now?

ELIZABETH: Lord Porteous?

CHAMPION-CHENEY: He wore his clothes better than any man in London. You know he'd have been Prime Minister if he'd remained in politics.

ELIZABETH: What was he like then?

CHAMPION-CHENEY: He was a nice-looking fellow. Fine horseman, I suppose there was something very fascinating about him. Yellow hair and blue eyes, you know. He had a very good figure. I liked him. I was his parliamentary secretary. He was Arnold's godfather.

ELIZABETH: I know.

CHAMPION-CHENEY: I wonder if he ever regrets.

ELIZABETH: I wouldn't.

CHAMPION-CHENEY: Well, I must be strolling back to my cottage.

ELIZABETH: You're not angry with me?

CHAMPION-CHENEY: Not a bit.

She puts up her face for him to kiss. He kisses her on both cheeks and then goes out. In a moment TEDDIE *is seen at the window.*

TEDDIE: I saw the old blighter go.

ELIZABETH: Come in.

TEDDIE: Everything all right?

ELIZABETH: Oh, quite, as far as he's concerned. He's going to keep out of the way.

TEDDIE: Was it beastly?

ELIZABETH: No, he made it very easy for me. He's a nice old thing.

TEDDIE: You were rather scared.

ELIZABETH: A little. I am still. I don't know why.

TEDDIE: I guessed you were. I thought I'd come and give you a little moral support. It's ripping here, isn't it?

ELIZABETH: It is rather nice.

TEDDIE: It'll be jolly to think of it when I'm back in the F.M.S.

ELIZABETH: Aren't you homesick sometimes?

TEDDIE: Oh, everyone is now and then, you know.

ELIZABETH: You could have got a job in England if you'd wanted to, couldn't you?

TEDDIE: Oh, but I love it out there. England's ripping to come back to, but I couldn't live here now. It's like a woman you're desperately in love with as long as you don't see her, but when you're with her she maddens you so that you can't bear her.

ELIZABETH [*smiling*]: What's wrong with England?

TEDDIE: I don't think anything's wrong with England. I expect something's wrong with me. I've been away too long. England seems to me full of people doing things they don't want to because other people expect it of them.

ELIZABETH: Isn't that what you call a high degree of civilisation?

TEDDIE: People seem to me so insincere. When you go to parties in London they're all babbling about art, and you feel that in their hearts they don't care twopence about it. The read the books that everybody is talking about because they don't want to be out of it. In the F.M.S. we don't get very many books, and we read those we have over and over again. They mean so much to us. I don't think the people over there are half so clever as the people at home, but one gets to know them better. You see, there are so few of us that we have to make the best of one another.

ELIZABETH: I imagine that frills are not much worn in the F.M.S. It must be a comfort.

TEDDIE: It's not much good being pretentious where everyone knows exactly who you are and what your income is.

ELIZABETH: I don't think you want too much sincerity in society. It would be like an iron girder in a house of cards.

TEDDIE: And then, you know, the place is ripping. You get used to a blue sky and you miss it in England.

ELIZABETH: What do you do with yourself all the time?

TEDDIE: Oh, one works like blazes. You have to be a pretty hefty fellow to be a planter. And then there's ripping bathing. You know, it's lovely, with palm trees all along the beach. And there's shooting. And now and then we have a little dance to a gramophone.

ELIZABETH [*pretending to tease him*]: I think you've got a young woman out there, Teddie.

TEDDIE [*vehemently*]: Oh, no!

She is a little taken aback by the earnestness of his disclaimer. There is a moment's silence, then she recovers herself.

ELIZABETH: But you'll have to marry and settle down one of these days, you know.

TEDDIE: I want to, but it's not a thing you can do lightly.

ELIZABETH: I don't know why there more than elsewhere.

TEDDIE: In England if people don't get on they go their own ways and jog along after a fashion. In a place like that you're thrown a great deal on your own resources.

ELIZABETH: Of course.

TEDDIE: Lots of girls come out because they think they're going to have a good time. But if they're empty-headed, then they're just faced with their own emptiness and they're done. If their husbands can afford it they go home and settle down as grass-widows.

ELIZABETH: I've met them. They seem to find it a very pleasant occupation.

TEDDIE: It's rotten for their husbands, though.

ELIZABETH: And if the husbands can't afford it?

TEDDIE: Oh, then they tipple.

ELIZABETH: It's not a very alluring prospect.

TEDDIE: But if the woman's the right sort she wouldn't exchange it for any life in the world. When all's said and done, it's we who've made the Empire.

ELIZABETH: What sort is the right sort?

TEDDIE: A woman of courage and endurance and sincerity. Of course, it's hopeless unless she's in love with her husband.

He is looking at her earnestly and she, raising her eyes, gives him a long look. There is silence between them.

TEDDIE: My house stands on the side of a hill, and the coconut trees wind down to the shore. Azaleas grow in my garden, and camellias, and all sorts of ripping flowers. And in front of me is the winding coast line, and then the blue sea.

A pause.

Do you know that I'm awfully in love with you?

ELIZABETH [*gravely*]: I wasn't quite sure. I wondered.

TEDDIE: And you?

She nods slowly.

I've never kissed you.

ELIZABETH: I don't want you to.

They look at one another steadily. They are both grave. ARNOLD *comes in hurriedly.*

ARNOLD: They're coming, Elizabeth.

ELIZABETH [*as though returning from a distant world*]: Who?

ARNOLD [*impatiently*]: My dear! My mother, of course. The car is just coming up the drive.

TEDDIE: Would you like me to clear out?

ARNOLD: No, no! For goodness' sake stay.

ELIZABETH: We'd better go and meet them, Arnold.

ARNOLD: No, no; I think they'd much better be shown in. I feel simply sick with nervousness.

ANNA *comes in from the garden.*

ANNA: Your guests have arrived.

ELIZABETH: Yes, I know.

ARNOLD: I've given orders that luncheon should be served at once.

ELIZABETH: Why? It's not half-past one already, is it?

ARNOLD: I thought it would help. When you don't know exactly what to say you can always eat.

The BUTLER *comes in and announces.*

BUTLER: Lady Catherine Champion-Cheney. Lord Porteous.

LADY KITTY *comes in followed by* PORTEOUS, *and the* BUTLER *goes out.* LADY KITTY *is a gay little lady, with dyed red hair and painted cheeks. She is somewhat outrageously dressed. She never forgets that she has been a pretty woman and she still behaves as if she were twenty-five.* LORD PORTEOUS *is a very bald, elderly gentleman in loose, rather eccentric clothes. He is snappy and gruff. This is not at all the couple that* ELIZABETH *expected, and for a moment she stares at them with round, startled eyes.* LADY KITTY *goes up to her with outstretched hands.*

LADY KITTY: Elizabeth! Elizabeth! [*She kisses her effusively.*] What an adorable creature! [*Turning to* PORTEOUS.] Hughie, isn't she adorable?
PORTEOUS [*with a grunt*]: Ugh!

ELIZABETH, *smiling now, turns to him and gives him her hand.*

ELIZABETH: How d'you do?
PORTEOUS: Damnable road you've got down here. How d'you do, my dear? Why d'you have such damnable roads in England?

LADY KITTY*'s eyes fall on* TEDDIE *and she goes up to him with her arms thrown back, prepared to throw them round him.*

LADY KITTY: My boy, my boy! I should have know you anywhere!
ELIZABETH [*hastily*]: That's Arnold.
LADY KITTY [*without a moment's hesitation*]: The image of his father! I should have known him anywhere! [*She throws her arms round his neck.*] My boy, my boy!
PORTEOUS [*with a grunt*]: Ugh!
LADY KITTY: Tell me, would you have known me again? Have I changed?
ARNOLD: I was only five, you know, when—when you . . .
LADY KITTY [*emotionally*]: I remember as if it was yesterday. I went up into your room. [*With a sudden change of manner.*] By the way, I always thought that nurse drank. Did you ever find out if she really did?
PORTEOUS: How the devil can you expect him to know that, Kitty?
LADY KITTY: You've never had a child, Hughie; how can you tell what they know and what they don't?
ELIZABETH [*coming to the rescue*]: This is Arnold, Lord Porteous.
PORTEOUS [*shaking hands with him*]: How d'you do? I knew your father.
ARNOLD: Yes.
PORTEOUS: Alive still?
ARNOLD: Yes.
PORTEOUS: He must be getting on. Is he well?
ARNOLD: Very.
PORTEOUS: Ugh! Takes care of himself, I suppose. I'm not at all well. This

damned climate doesn't agree with me.

ELIZABETH [*to* LADY KITTY]: This is Mrs Shenstone. And this is Mr Luton. I hope you don't mind a very small party.

LADY KITTY [*shaking hands with* ANNA *and* TEDDIE]: Oh, no, I shall enjoy it. I used to give enormous parties here. Political, you know. How nice you've made this room!

ELIZABETH: Oh, that's Arnold.

ARNOLD [*nervously*]: D'you like this chair? I've just bought it. It's exactly my period.

PORTEOUS [*bluntly*]: It's a fake.

ARNOLD [*indignantly*]: I don't think it is for a minute.

PORTEOUS: The legs are not right.

ARNOLD: I don't know how you can say that. If there is anything right about it, it's the legs.

LADY KITTY: I'm sure they're right.

PORTEOUS: You know nothing whatever about it, Kitty.

LADY KITTY: That's what you think. *I* think it's a beautiful chair. Hepplewhite?

ARNOLD: No, Sheraton.

LADY KITTY: Oh, I know. The School for Scandal.

PORTEOUS: Sheraton, my dear. Sheraton.

LADY KITTY: Yes, that's what I say. I acted the screen scene at some amateur theatricals in Florence, and Ermete Novelli, the great Italian tragedian, told me he'd never seen a Lady Teazle like me.

PORTEOUS: Ugh!

LADY KITTY [*to* ELIZABETH]: Do you act?

ELIZABETH: Oh, I couldn't. I should be too nervous.

LADY KITTY: I'm never nervous. I'm a born actress. Of course, if I had my time over again I'd go on the stage. You know, it's extraordinary how they keep young. Actresses, I mean. I think it's because they're always playing different parts. Hughie, do you think Arnold takes after me or after his father? Of course I think he's the very image of me. Arnold, I think I ought to tell you that I was received into the Catholic Church last winter. I'd been thinking about it for years, and last time we were at Monte Carlo I met such a nice monsignore. I told him what my difficulties were and he was too wonderful. I knew Hughie wouldn't approve, so I kept it a secret. [*To* ELIZABETH.] Are you interested in religion? I think it's too wonderful. We must have a long talk about it one of these days. [*Pointing to her frock.*] Callot?

ELIZABETH: No, Worth.

LADY KITTY: I knew it was either Worth or Callot. Of course, it's line that's the important thing. I go to Worth myself, and I always say to him, Line, my dear Worth, line. What *is* the matter, Hughie?

PORTEOUS: These new teeth of mine are so damned uncomfortable.

LADY KITTY: Men are extraordinary. They can't stand the smallest discomfort. Why, a woman's life is uncomfortable from the moment she gets up in the morning till the moment she goes to bed at night. And d'you think it's comfortable to sleep with a mask on your face.

PORTEOUS: They don't seem to hold up properly.

LADY KITTY: Well, that's not the fault of your teeth. That's the fault of your gums.

PORTEOUS: Damned rotten dentist. That's what's the matter.

LADY KITTY: I thought he was a very nice dentist. He told me *my* teeth would last till I was fifty. He has a Chinese room. It's so interesting; while he scrapes your teeth he tells you all about the dear Empress Dowager. Are you interested in China? I think it's too wonderful. You know they've cut off their pigtails. I think it's such a pity. They were so picturesque.

The BUTLER *comes in.*

BUTLER: Luncheon is served, sir.
ELIZABETH: Would you like to see your rooms?
PORTEOUS: We can see our rooms after luncheon.
LADY KITTY: I must powder my nose, Hughie.
PORTEOUS: Powder it down here.
LADY KITTY: I never saw any one so inconsiderate.
PORTEOUS: You'll keep us all waiting half an hour. I know you.
LADY KITTY [*fumbling in her bag*]: Oh, well, peace at any price, as Lord Beaconsfield said.
PORTEOUS: He said a lot of damned silly things, Kitty, but he never said that.

LADY KITTY'*s face changes. Perplexity is followed by dismay, and dismay by consternation.*

LADY KITTY: Oh!
ELIZABETH: What is the matter?
LADY KITTY [*with anguish*]: My lip-stick.
ELIZABETH: Can't you find it?
LADY KITTY: I had it in the car. Hughie, you remember that I had it in the car.
PORTEOUS: I don't remember anything about it.
LADY KITTY: Don't be so stupid, Hughie. Why, when we came through the gates I said: My home, my home! and I took it out and put some on my lips.
ELIZABETH: Perhaps you dropped it in the car.
LADY KITTY: For heaven's sake send someone to look for it.
ARNOLD: I'll ring.
LADY KITTY: I'm absolutely lost without my lip-stick. Lend me yours, darling, will you?
ELIZABETH: I'm awfully sorry. I'm afraid I haven't got one.
LADY KITTY: Do you mean to say you don't use a lip-stick?
ELIZABETH: Never.
PORTEOUS: Look at her lips. What the devil d'you think she wants muck like that for?
LADY KITTY: Oh, my dear, what a mistake you make! You *must* use a lip-stick. It's so good for the lips. Men like it, you know. I couldn't *live* without a lip-stick.

CHAMPION-CHENEY *appears at the window holding in his upstretched hand a little gold case.*

CHAMPION-CHENEY [*as he comes in*]: Has any one here lost a diminutive utensil containing, unless I am mistaken, a favourite preparation for the toilet?

ARNOLD *and* ELIZABETH *are thunderstruck at his appearance and even* TEDDIE *and* ANNA *are taken aback. But* LADY KITTY *is overjoyed.*

LADY KITTY: My lip-stick!

CHAMPION-CHENEY: I found it in the drive and I ventured to bring it in.

LADY KITTY: It's Saint Antony. I said a little prayer to him when I was hunting in my bag.

PORTEOUS: Saint Antony be blowed! It's Clive, by God!

LADY KITTY [*startled, her attention suddenly turning from the lip-stick*]: Clive!

CHAMPION-CHENEY: You didn't recognise me. It's many years since we met.

LADY KITTY: My poor Clive, your hair has gone quite white!

CHAMPION-CHENEY [*holding out his hand*]: I hope you had a pleasant journey down from London.

LADY KITTY [*offering him her cheek*]: You may kiss me, Clive.

CHAMPION-CHENEY [*kissing her*]: You don't mind, Hughie?

PORTEOUS [*with a grunt*]: Ugh!

CHAMPION-CHENEY [*going up to him cordially*]: And how are you, my dear Hughie?

PORTEOUS: Damned rheumatic if you want to know. Filthy climate you have in this country.

CHAMPION-CHENEY: Aren't you going to shake hands with me, Hughie?

PORTEOUS: I have no objection to shaking hands with you.

CHAMPION-CHENEY: You've aged, my poor Hughie.

PORTEOUS: Someone was asking me how old you were the other day.

CHAMPION-CHENEY: Were they surprised when you told them?

PORTEOUS: Surprised! They wondered you weren't dead.

The BUTLER *comes in.*

BUTLER: Did you ring, sir?

ARNOLD: No. Oh, yes, I did. It doesn't matter now.

CHAMPION-CHENEY [*as the* BUTLER *is going*]: One moment. My dear Elizabeth. I've come to throw myself on your mercy. My servants are busy with their own affairs. There's not a thing for me to eat in my cottage.

ELIZABETH: Oh, but we shall be delighted if you'll lunch with us.

CHAMPION-CHENEY: It either means that or my immediate death from starvation. You don't mind, Arnold?

ARNOLD: My dear father!

ELIZABETH [*to the* BUTLER]: Mr Cheney will lunch here.

BUTLER: Very good, ma'am.

CHAMPION-CHENEY [*to* LADY KITTY]: And what do you think of Arnold?

LADY KITTY: I adore him.

CHAMPION-CHENEY: He's grown, hasn't he? But then you'd expect him to do that in thirty years.

ARNOLD: For God's sake let's go in to lunch, Elizabeth!

END OF ACT ONE

ACT TWO

The scene is the same as in the preceding Act. It is afternoon. When the curtain rises PORTEOUS *and* LADY KITTY, ANNA *and* TEDDIE *are playing bridge.* ELIZABETH *and* CHAMPION-CHENEY *are watching.* PORTEOUS *and* LADY KITTY *are partners.*

CHAMPION-CHENEY: When will Arnold be back, Elizabeth?

ELIZABETH: Soon, I think.

CHAMPION-CHENEY: Is he addressing a meeting?

ELIZABETH: No, it's only a conference with his agent and one or two constituents.

PORTEOUS [*irritably*]: How any one can be expected to play bridge when people are shouting at the top of their voices all round them, I for one cannot understand.

ELIZABETH [*smiling*]: I'm so sorry.

ANNA: I can see your hand, Lord Porteous.

PORTEOUS: It may help you.

LADY KITTY: I've told you over and over again to hold your cards up. It ruins one's game when one can't help seeing one's opponent's hand.

PORTEOUS: One isn't obliged to look.

LADY KITTY: What was Arnold's majority at the last election?

ELIZABETH: Seven hundred and something.

CHAMPION-CHENEY: He'll have to fight for it if he wants to keep his seat next time.

PORTEOUS: Are we playing bridge, or talking politics?

LADY KITTY: I never find that conversation interferes with my game.

PORTEOUS: You certainly play no worse when you talk than when you hold your tongue.

LADY KITTY: I think that's a very offensive thing to say, Hughie. Just because I don't play the same game as you do you think I can't play.

PORTEOUS: I'm glad you acknowledge it's not the same game as I play. But why in God's name do you call it bridge?

CHAMPION-CHENEY: I agree with Kitty. I hate people who play bridge as though they were at a funeral and knew their feet were getting wet.

PORTEOUS: Of course you take Kitty's part.

LADY KITTY: That's the least he can do.

CHAMPION-CHENEY: I have a naturally cheerful disposition.

PORTEOUS: You've never had anything to sour it.

LADY KITTY: I don't know what you mean by that, Hughie.

PORTEOUS [*trying to contain himself*]: Must you trump my ace?

LADY KITTY [*innocently*]: Oh, was that your ace, darling?

PORTEOUS [*furiously*]: Yes, it was my ace.

LADY KITTY: Oh, well, it was the only trump I had. I shouldn't have made it anyway.

PORTEOUS: You needn't have told them that. Now she knows exactly what I've got.

LADY KITTY: She knew before.

PORTEOUS: How could she know?

LADY KITTY: She said she'd seen your hand.

ANNA: Oh, I didn't. I said I could see it.

LADY KITTY: Well, I naturally supposed that if she could see it she did.

PORTEOUS: Really, Kitty, you have the most extraordinary ideas.

CHAMPION-CHENEY: Not at all. If any one is such a fool as to show me his hand, of course I look at it.

PORTEOUS [*fuming*]: If you study the etiquette of bridge, you'll discover that onlookers are expected not to interfere with the game.

CHAMPION-CHENEY: My dear Hughie, this is a matter of ethics, not of bridge.

ANNA: Anyhow, I get the game. And rubber.

TEDDIE: I claim a revoke.

PORTEOUS: Who revoked?

TEDDIE: You did.

PORTEOUS: Nonsense. I've never revoked in my life.

TEDDIE: I'll show you. [*He turns over the tricks to show the faces of the cards.*] You threw away a club on the third heart trick and you had another heart.

PORTEOUS: I never had more than two hearts.

TEDDIE: Oh, yes, you had. Look here. That's the card you played on the last trick but one.

LADY KITTY [*delighted to catch him out*]: There's no doubt about it, Hughie. You revoked.

PORTEOUS: I tell you I did not revoke. I never revoke.

CHAMPION-CHENEY: You did, Hughie. I wondered what on earth you were doing.

PORTEOUS: I don't know how any one can be expected not to revoke when there's this confounded chatter going on all the time.

TEDDIE: Well, that's another hundred to us.

PORTEOUS [*to* CHAMPION-CHENEY]: I wish you wouldn't breathe down my neck. I never can play bridge when there's somebody breathing down my neck.

The party have risen from the bridge-table, and they scatter about the room.

ANNA: Well, I'm going to take a book and lie down in the hammock till it's time to dress.

TEDDIE [*who has been adding up*]: I'll put it down in the book, shall I?

PORTEOUS [*who has not moved, setting out the cards for a patience*]: Yes, yes, put it down. I never revoke.

ANNA goes out.

LADY KITTY: Would you like to come for a little stroll, Hughie?

PORTEOUS: What for?

LADY KITTY: Exercise.

PORTEOUS: I hate exercise.

CHAMPION-CHENEY [*looking at the patience*]: The seven goes on the eight.

PORTEOUS takes no notice.

LADY KITTY: The seven goes on the eight, Hughie.

PORTEOUS: I don't choose to put the seven on the eight.

CHAMPION-CHENEY: That knave goes on the queen.

PORTEOUS: I'm not blind, thank you.

LADY KITTY: The three goes on the four.

CHAMPION-CHENEY: All these go over.

PORTEOUS [*furiously*]: Am I playing this patience, or are you playing it?

LADY KITTY: But you're missing everything.

PORTEOUS: That's my business.

CHAMPION-CHENEY: It's no good losing your temper over it, Hughie.

PORTEOUS: Go away, both of you. You irritate me.

LADY KITTY: We were only trying to help you, Hughie.

PORTEOUS: I don't want to be helped. I want to do it by myself.

LADY KITTY: I think your manners are perfectly deplorable, Hughie.

PORTEOUS: It's simply maddening when you're playing patience and people won't leave you alone.

CHAMPION-CHENEY: We won't say another word.

PORTEOUS: That three goes. I believe it's coming out. If I'd been such a fool as to put that seven up I shouldn't have been able to bring these down.

He puts down several cards while they watch him silently.

LADY KITTY AND CHAMPION-CHENEY [*together*]: The four goes on the five.

PORTEOUS [*throwing down the cards violently*]: Damn you! Why don't you leave me alone? It's intolerable.

CHAMPION-CHENEY: It was coming out, my dear fellow.

PORTEOUS: I know it was coming out. Confound you!

LADY KITTY: How petty you are, Hughie!

PORTEOUS: Petty, be damned! I've told you over and over again that I will not be interfered with when I'm playing patience.

LADY KITTY: Don't talk to me like that, Hughie.

PORTEOUS: I shall talk to you as I please.

LADY KITTY [*beginning to cry*]: Oh, you brute! You brute! [*She flings out of the room.*]

PORTEOUS: Oh, damn! Now she's going to cry.

He shambles out into the garden. CHAMPION-CHENEY, ELIZABETH *and* TEDDIE *are left alone. There is a moment's pause.* CHAMPION-CHENEY *looks from* TEDDIE *to* ELIZABETH, *with an ironical smile.*

CHAMPION-CHENEY: Upon my soul, they might be married. They frip so much.

ELIZABETH [*frigidly*]: It's been nice of you to come here so often since they arrived. It's helped to make things easy.

CHAMPION-CHENEY: Irony? It's a rhetorical form not much favoured in this blessed plot, this earth, this realm, this England.

ELIZABETH: What exactly are you getting at?

CHAMPION-CHENEY: How slangy the young women of the present day are! I suppose the fact that Arnold is a purist leads you to the contrary extravagance.

ELIZABETH: Anyhow you know what I mean.

CHAMPION-CHENEY [*with a smile*]: I have a dim, groping suspicion.

ELIZABETH: You promised to keep away. Why did you come back the moment they arrived?

CHAMPION-CHENEY: Curiosity, my dear child. A surely pardonable curiosity.

ELIZABETH: And since then you've been here all the time. You don't generally favour us with so much of your company when you're down at your cottage.

CHAMPION-CHENEY: I've been excessively amused.

ELIZABETH: It has struck me that whenever they started fripping you took a malicious pleasure in goading them on.

CHAMPION-CHENEY: I don't think there's much love lost between them now, do you?

TEDDIE *is making as though to leave the room.*

ELIZABETH: Don't go, Teddie.

CHAMPION-CHENEY: No, please don't. I'm only staying a minute. We were talking about Lady Kitty just before she arrived. [*To* ELIZABETH.] Do you remember? The pale, frail lady in black satin and old lace.

ELIZABETH [*with a chuckle*]: You are a devil, you know.

CHAMPION-CHENEY: Ah, well, he's always had the reputation of being a humorist and a gentleman.

ELIZABETH: Did *you* expect her to be like that, poor dear?

CHAMPION-CHENEY: My dear child, I hadn't the vaguest idea. You were asking me the other day what she was like when she ran away. I didn't tell you half. She was so gay and so natural. Who would have thought that animation would turn into such frivolity, and that charming impulsiveness lead to such a ridiculous affectation?

ELIZABETH: It rather sets my nerves on edge to hear the way you talk of her.

CHAMPION-CHENEY: It's the truth that sets your nerves on edge, not I.

ELIZABETH: You loved her once. Have you no feeling for her at all?

CHAMPION-CHENEY: None. Why should I?

ELIZABETH: She's the mother of your son.

CHAMPION-CHENEY: My dear child, you have a charming nature, as simple, frank and artless as hers was. Don't let pure humbug obscure your common sense.

ELIZABETH: We have no right to judge. She's only been here two days. We know nothing about her.

CHAMPION-CHENEY: My dear, her soul is as thickly rouged as her face. She hasn't an emotion that's sincere. She's tinsel. You think I'm a cruel, cynical old man. Why, when I think of what she was, if I didn't laugh at what she has become I should cry.

ELIZABETH: How do you know she wouldn't be just the same now if she'd remained your wife? Do you think your influence would have had such a salutary effect on her?

CHAMPION-CHENEY [*good-humouredly*]: I like you when you're bitter and rather insolent.

ELIZABETH: D'you like me enough to answer my question?

CHAMPION-CHENEY: She was only twenty-seven when she went away. She might have become anything. She might have become the woman you expected her to be. There are very few of us who are strong enough to make circumstances serve us. We are the creatures of our environment. She's a silly worthless woman because she's led a silly worthless life.

ELIZABETH [*disturbed*]: You're horrible to-day.

CHAMPION-CHENEY: I don't say it's I who could have prevented her from becoming this ridiculous caricature of a pretty woman grown old. But life could. Here she would have had the friends fit to her station, and a decent activity, and worthy interests. Ask her what her life has been all these years among divorced women and kept women and the men who consort with them. There is no more lamentable pursuit than a life of pleasure.

ELIZABETH: At all events she loved and she loved greatly. I have only pity and affection for her.

CHAMPION-CHENEY: And if she loved what d'you think she felt when she saw that she had ruined Hughie? Look at him. He was tight last night after dinner and tight the night before.

ELIZABETH: I know.

CHAMPION-CHENEY: And she took it as a matter of course. How long do you suppose he's been getting tight every night? Do you think he was like that thirty years ago? Can you imagine that that was a brilliant young man, whom every one expected to be Prime Minister? Look at him now. A grumpy sodden old fellow with false teeth.

ELIZABETH: You have false teeth, too.

CHAMPION-CHENEY: Yes, but damn it all, they fit. She's ruined him and she knows she's ruined him.

ELIZABETH [*looking at him suspiciously*]: Why are you saying all this to me?

CHAMPION-CHENEY: Am I hurting your feelings?

ELIZABETH: I think I've had enough for the present.

CHAMPION-CHENEY: I'll go and have a look at the gold-fish. I want to see Arnold when he comes in. [*Politely.*] I'm afraid we've been boring Mr Luton.

TEDDIE: Not at all.

CHAMPION-CHENEY: When are you going back to the F.M.S.?

TEDDIE: In about a month.

CHAMPION-CHENEY: I see. [*He goes out.*]

ELIZABETH: I wonder what he has at the back of his head.

TEDDIE: D'you think he was talking *at* you?

ELIZABETH: He's as clever as a bagful of monkeys.

There is a moment's pause. TEDDIE *hesitates a little, and when he speaks it is in a different tone. He is grave and somewhat nervous.*

TEDDIE: It seems very difficult to get a few minutes alone with you. I wonder if you've been making it difficult?

ELIZABETH: I wanted to think.

TEDDIE: I've made up my mind to go away to-morrow.

ELIZABETH: Why?

TEDDIE: I want you altogether or not at all.

ELIZABETH: You're so arbitrary.

TEDDIE: You said you—you said you cared for me.

ELIZABETH: I do.

TEDDIE: Do you mind if we talk it over now?

ELIZABETH: No.

TEDDIE [*frowning*]: It makes me feel rather shy and awkward. I've repeated to myself over and over again exactly what I want to say to you, and now all I'd prepared seems rather footling.

ELIZABETH: I'm so afraid I'm going to cry.

TEDDIE: I feel it's all so tremendously serious and I think we ought to keep emotion out of it. You're rather emotional, aren't you?

ELIZABETH [*half smiling and half in tears*]: So are you for the matter of that.

TEDDIE: That's why I wanted to have everything I meant to say to you cut and dried. I think it would be awfully unfair if I made love to you and all that sort of thing, and you were carried away. I wrote it all down and thought I'd send it you as a letter.

ELIZABETH: Why didn't you?

TEDDIE: I got the wind up. A letter seems so—so cold. You see, I love you so awfully.

ELIZABETH: For goodness' sake don't say that.

TEDDIE: You mustn't cry. Please don't, or I shall go all to pieces.

ELIZABETH [*trying to smile*]: I'm sorry. It doesn't mean anything really. It's only tears running out of my eyes.

TEDDIE: Our only chance is to be awfully matter-of-fact. [*He stops for a moment. He finds it quite difficult to control himself. He clears his throat. He frowns with annoyance at himself.*]

ELIZABETH: What's the matter?

TEDDIE: I've got a sort of lump in my throat. It is idiotic. I think I'll have a cigarette.

She watches him in silence while he lights a cigarette.

You see, I've never been in love with anyone before, not really. It's knocked me endways. I don't know how I can live without you now. . . . Does that old fool know I'm in love with you?

ELIZABETH: I think so.

TEDDIE: When he was talking about Lady Kitty smashing up Lord Porteous' career I thought there was something at the back of it.

ELIZABETH: I think he was trying to persuade me not to smash up yours.

TEDDIE: I'm sure that's very considerate of him, but I don't happen to have one to smash. I wish I had. It's the only time in my life I've wished I were a hell of a swell so that I could chuck it all and show you how much more you are to me than anything else in the world.

ELIZABETH [*affectionately*]: You're a dear old thing, Teddie.

TEDDIE: You know, I don't really know how to make love, but if I did I couldn't do it now because I just want to be absolutely practical.

ELIZABETH [*chaffing him*]: I'm glad you don't know how to make love. It would be almost more than I could bear.

TEDDIE: You see, I'm not at all romantic and that sort of thing. I'm just a common or garden business man. All this is so dreadfully serious and I think we ought to be sensible.

ELIZABETH [*with a break in her voice*]: You owl!

TEDDIE: No, Elizabeth, don't say things like that to me. I want you to consider all the *pros* and *cons*, and my heart's thumping against my chest, and you know I love you, I love you, I love you.

ELIZABETH [*in a sigh of passion*]: Oh, my precious.

TEDDIE [*impatiently, but with himself, rather than with* ELIZABETH]: Don't be idiotic, Elizabeth. I'm not going to tell you that I can't live without you and a lot of muck like that. You know that you mean everything in the world to me.

[*Almost giving it up as a bad job.*] Oh, my God!

ELIZABETH [*her voice faltering*]: D'you think there's anything you can say to me that I don't know already?

TEDDIE [*desperately*]: But I haven't said a single thing I wanted to. I'm a business man and I want to put it all in a business way, if you understand what I mean.

ELIZABETH [*smiling*]: I don't believe you're a very good business man.

TEDDIE [*sharply*]: You don't know what you're talking about. I'm a first-rate business man, but somehow this is different. [*Hopelessly.*] I don't know why it won't go right.

ELIZABETH: What are we going to do about it?

TEDDIE: You see, it's not just because you're awfully pretty that I love you. I'd love you just as much if you were old and ugly. It's you I love, not what you look like. And it's not only love; love be blowed! It's that I *like* you so tremendously. I think you're such a ripping good sort. I just want to be with you. I feel so jolly and happy just to think you're there. I'm so awfully *fond* of you.

ELIZABETH [*laughing through her tears*]: I don't know if this is your idea of introducing a business proposition.

TEDDIE: Damn you, you won't let me.

ELIZABETH: You said, Damn you.

TEDDIE: I meant it.

ELIZABETH: Your voice sounded as if you meant, you perfect duck.

TEDDIE: Really, Elizabeth, you're intolerable.

ELIZABETH: I'm doing nothing.

TEDDIE: Yes, you are, you're putting me off my blow. What I want to say is perfectly simple. I'm a very ordinary business man.

ELIZABETH: You've said that before.

TEDDIE [*angrily*]: Shut up. I haven't got a bob besides what I earn. I've got no position. I'm nothing. You're rich and you're a big pot and you've got everything that anyone can want. It's awful cheek my saying anything to you at all. But after all there's only one thing that really matters in the world, and that's love. I love you. Chuck all this, Elizabeth, and come to me.

ELIZABETH: Are you cross with me?

TEDDIE: Furious.

ELIZABETH: Darling!

TEDDIE: If you don't want me tell me so at once and let me get out quickly.

ELIZABETH: Teddie, nothing in the world matters anything to me but you. I'll go wherever you take me. I love you.

TEDDIE [*all to pieces*]: Oh, my God!

ELIZABETH: Does it mean as much to you as that? Oh, Teddie!

TEDDIE [*trying to control himself*]: Don't be a fool, Elizabeth.

ELIZABETH: It's you're the fool. You're making me cry.

TEDDIE: You're so damned emotional.

ELIZABETH: Damned emotional yourself. I'm sure you're a rotten business man.

TEDDIE: I don't care what you think. You've made me so awfully happy. I say, what a lark life's going to be.

ELIZABETH: Teddie, you are an angel.

TEDDIE: Let's get out quick. It's no good wasting time. Elizabeth.

ELIZABETH: What?

TEDDIE: Nothing. I just like to say Elizabeth.

ELIZABETH: You fool.

TEDDIE: I say, can you shoot?

ELIZABETH: No.

TEDDIE: I'll teach you. You don't know how ripping it is to start out from your camp at dawn and travel through the jungle. And you're so tired at night and the sky's all starry. It's a fair treat. Of course I didn't want to say anything about all that till you'd decided. I'd made up my mind to be absolutely practical.

ELIZABETH [*chaffing him*]: The only practical thing you said was that love is the only thing that really matters.

TEDDIE [*happily*]: Pull the other leg next time, will you? I should hate to have one longer than the other.

ELIZABETH: Isn't it fun being in love with someone who's in love with you?

TEDDIE: I say, I think I'd better clear out at once, don't you? It seems rather rotten to stay on in—in this house.

ELIZABETH: You can't go to-night. There's no train.

TEDDIE: I'll go to-morrow. I'll wait in London till you're ready to join me.

ELIZABETH: I'm not going to leave a note on the pincushion like Lady Kitty, you know. I'm going to tell Arnold.

TEDDIE: Are you? Don't you think there'll be an awful bother?

ELIZABETH: I must face it. I should hate to be sly and deceitful.

TEDDIE: Well, then, let's face it together.

ELIZABETH: No, I'll talk to Arnold by myself.

TEDDIE: You won't let anyone influence you?

ELIZABETH: No.

He holds out his hand and she takes it. They look into one another's eyes with grave, almost solemn affection. There is the sound outside of a car driving up.

ELIZABETH: There's the car. Arnold's come back. I must go and bathe my eyes. I don't want them to see I've been crying.

TEDDIE: All right. [*As she is going.*] Elizabeth.

ELIZABETH [*stopping*]: What?

TEDDIE: Bless you.

ELIZABETH [*affectionately*]: Idiot!

She goes out of the door and TEDDIE *through the French window into the garden. For an instant the room is empty.* ARNOLD *comes in. He sits down and takes some papers out of his dispatch-case.* LADY KITTY *enters. He gets up.*

LADY KITTY: I saw you come in. Oh, my dear, don't get up. There's no reason why you should be so dreadfully polite to me.

ARNOLD: I've just rung for a cup of tea.

LADY KITTY: Perhaps we shall have the chance of a little talk. We don't seem to have had five minutes by ourselves. I want to make your acquaintance, you know.

ARNOLD: I should like you to know that it's not by my wish that my father is here.

LADY KITTY: But I'm so interested to see him.

ARNOLD: I was afraid that you and Lord Porteous must find it embarrassing.

LADY KITTY: Oh, no. Hughie was his greatest friend. They were at Eton and

Oxford together. I think your father has improved so much since I saw him last. He wasn't good-looking as a young man, but now he's quite handsome.

The FOOTMAN *brings in a tray on which are tea-things.*

LADY KITTY: Shall I pour it out for you?

ARNOLD: Thank you very much.

LADY KITTY: Do you take sugar?

ARNOLD: No. I gave it up during the war.

LADY KITTY: So wise of you. It's so bad for the figure. Besides being patriotic, of course. Isn't it absurd that I should ask my son if he takes sugar or not? Life is really very quaint. Sad, of course, but oh, so quaint! Often I lie in bed at night and have a good laugh to myself as I think how quaint life is.

ARNOLD: I'm afraid I'm a very serious person.

LADY KITTY: How old are you now, Arnold?

ARNOLD: Thirty-five.

LADY KITTY: Are you really? Of course, I was a child when I married your father.

ARNOLD: Really. He always told me you were twenty-two.

LADY KITTY: Oh, what nonsense! Why, I was married out of the nursery. I put my hair up for the first time on my wedding-day.

ARNOLD: Where is Lord Porteous?

LADY KITTY: My dear, it sounds too absurd to hear you call him Lord Porteous. Why don't you call him—Uncle Hughie?

ARNOLD: He doesn't happen to be my uncle.

LADY KITTY: No, but he's your godfather. You know, I'm sure you'll like him when you know him better. I'm so hoping that you and Elizabeth will come and stay with us in Florence. I simply adore Elizabeth. She's too beautiful.

ARNOLD: Her hair is very pretty.

LADY KITTY: It's not touched up, is it?

ARNOLD: Oh, no.

LADY KITTY: I just wondered. It's rather a coincidence that her hair should be the same colour as mine. I suppose it shows that your father and you are attracted by just the same thing. So interesting, heredity, isn't it?

ARNOLD: Very.

LADY KITTY: Of course, since I joined the Catholic Church I don't believe in it any more. Darwin and all that sort of thing. Too dreadful. Wicked, you know. Besides, it's not very good form, is it?

CHAMPION-CHENEY *comes in from the garden.*

CHAMPION-CHENEY: Do I intrude?

LADY KITTY: Come in, Clive. Arnold and I have been having such a wonderful heart-to-heart talk.

CHAMPION-CHENEY: Very nice.

ARNOLD: Father, I stepped in for a moment at the Harveys' on my way back. It's simply criminal what they're doing with that house.

CHAMPION-CHENEY: What are they doing?

ARNOLD: It's an almost perfect Georgian house and they've got a lot of dreadful Victorian furniture. I gave them my ideas on the subject, but it's quite hopeless. They said they were attached to their furniture.

CHAMPION-CHENEY: Arnold should have been an interior decorator.

LADY KITTY: He has wonderful taste. He gets that from me.

ARNOLD: I suppose I have a certain *flair*. I have a passion for decorating houses.

LADY KITTY: You've made this one charming.

CHAMPION-CHENEY: D'you remember, we just had chintzes and comfortable chairs when we lived here, Kitty.

LADY KITTY: Perfectly hideous, wasn't it?

CHAMPION-CHENEY: In those days gentlemen and ladies were not expected to have taste.

ARNOLD: You know, I've been looking at this chair again. Since Lord Porteous said the legs weren't right I've been very uneasy.

LADY KITTY: He only said that because he was in a bad temper.

CHAMPION-CHENEY: His temper seems to me very short these days, Kitty.

LADY KITTY: Oh, it is.

ARNOLD: You feel he knows what he's talking about. I gave seventy-five pounds for that chair. I'm very seldom taken in. I always think if a thing's right you feel it.

CHAMPION-CHENEY: Well, don't let it disturb your night's rest.

ARNOLD: But, my dear father, that's just what it does. I had a most horrible dream about it last night.

LADY KITTY: Here is Hughie.

ARNOLD: I'm going to fetch a book I have on Old English furniture. There's an illustration of a chair which is almost identical with this one.

PORTEOUS *comes in.*

PORTEOUS: Quite a family gathering, by George!

CHAMPION-CHENEY: I was thinking just now we'd make a very pleasing picture of a typical English home.

ARNOLD: I'll be back in five minutes. There's something I want to show you, Lord Porteous. [*He goes out.*]

CHAMPION-CHENEY: Would you like to play piquet with me, Hughie?

PORTEOUS: Not particularly.

CHAMPION-CHENEY: You were never much of a piquet player, were you?

PORTEOUS: My dear Clive, you people don't know what piquet is in England.

CHAMPION-CHENEY: Let's have a game then. You may make money.

PORTEOUS: I don't want to play with you.

LADY KITTY: I don't know why not, Hughie.

PORTEOUS: Let me tell you that I don't like your manner.

CHAMPION-CHENEY: I'm sorry for that. I'm afraid I can't offer to change it at my age.

PORTEOUS: I don't know what you want to be hanging around here for.

CHAMPION-CHENEY: A natural attachment to my home.

PORTEOUS: If you'd had any tact you'd have kept out of the way while we were here.

CHAMPION-CHENEY: My dear Hughie, I don't understand your attitude at all. If I'm willing to let bygones be bygones why should you object?

PORTEOUS: Damn it all, they're not bygones.

CHAMPION-CHENEY: After all, I am the injured party.

PORTEOUS: How the devil are you the injured party?

CHAMPION-CHENEY: Well, you did run away with my wife, didn't you?

LADY KITTY: Now, don't let's go into ancient history. I can't see why we shouldn't all be friends.

PORTEOUS: I beg you not to interfere, Kitty.

LADY KITTY: I'm very fond of Clive.

PORTEOUS: You never cared two straws for Clive. You only say that to irritate me.

LADY KITTY: Not at all. I don't see why he shouldn't come and stay with us.

CHAMPION-CHENEY: I'd love to. I think Florence in spring-time is delightful. Have you central heating?

PORTEOUS: I never liked you, I don't like you now, and I never shall like you.

CHAMPION-CHENEY: How very unfortunate! Because I liked you, I like you now, and I shall continue to like you.

LADY KITTY: There's something very nice about you, Clive.

PORTEOUS: If you think that, why the devil did you leave him?

LADY KITTY: Are you going to reproach me because I loved you? How utterly, utterly, utterly detestable you are!

CHAMPION-CHENEY: Now, now, don't quarrel with one another.

LADY KITTY: It's all his fault. I'm the easiest person in the world to live with. But really he'd try the patience of a saint.

CHAMPION-CHENEY: Come, come, don't get upset, Kitty. When two people live together there must be a certain amount of give and take.

PORTEOUS: I don't know what the devil you're talking about.

CHAMPION-CHENEY: It hasn't escaped my observation that you are a little inclined to frip. Many couples are. I think it's a pity.

PORTEOUS: Would you have the very great kindness to mind your own business?

LADY KITTY: It is his business. He naturally wants me to be happy.

CHAMPION-CHENEY: I have the very greatest affection for Kitty.

PORTEOUS: Then why the devil didn't you look after her properly?

CHAMPION-CHENEY: My dear Hughie, you were my greatest friend. I trusted you. It may have been rash.

PORTEOUS: It was inexcusable.

LADY KITTY: I don't know what you mean by that, Hughie.

PORTEOUS: Don't, don't, don't try and bully me, Kitty.

LADY KITTY: Oh, I know what you mean.

PORTEOUS: Then why the devil did you say you didn't?

LADY KITTY: When I think that I sacrificed everything for that man! And for thirty years I've had to live in a filthy marble palace with no sanitary conveniences.

CHAMPION-CHENEY: D'you mean to say you haven't got a bathroom?

LADY KITTY: I've had to wash in a tub.

CHAMPION-CHENEY: My poor Kitty, how you've suffered!

PORTEOUS: Really, Kitty, I'm sick of hearing of the sacrifices you made. I suppose you think I sacrificed nothing. I should have been Prime Minister by now if it hadn't been for you.

LADY KITTY: Nonsense!

PORTEOUS: What do you mean by that? Every one said I should be Prime Minister. Shouldn't I have been Prime Minister, Clive?

CHAMPION-CHENEY: It was certainly the general expectation.

PORTEOUS: I was the most promising young man of my day. I was bound to get a seat in the Cabinet at the next election.

LADY KITTY: They'd have found you out just as I've found you out. I'm sick of hearing that I ruined your career. You never had a career to ruin. Prime Minister! You haven't the brain. You haven't the character.

CHAMPION-CHENEY: Cheek, push, and a gift of the gab will serve very well instead, you know.

LADY KITTY: Besides, in politics it's not the men that matter. It's the women at the back of them. I could have made Clive a Cabinet Minister if I'd wanted to.

PORTEOUS: Clive?

LADY KITTY: With my beauty, my charm, my force of character, my wit, I could have done anything.

PORTEOUS: Clive was nothing but my political secretary. When I was Prime Minister I might have made him Governor of some Colony or other. Western Australia, say. Out of pure kindliness.

LADY KITTY [*with flashing eyes*]: D'you think I would have buried myself in Western Australia? With my beauty? My charm?

PORTEOUS: Or Barbados, perhaps.

LADY KITTY [*furiously*]: Barbados! Barbados can go to–Barbados.

PORTEOUS: That's all you'd have got.

LADY KITTY: Nonsense! I'd have India.

PORTEOUS: I would never have given you India.

LADY KITTY: You would have given me India.

PORTEOUS: I tell you I wouldn't.

LADY KITTY: The King would have given me India. The nation would have insisted on my having India. I would have been a vicereine or nothing.

PORTEOUS: I tell you that as long as the interests of the British Empire–Damn it all, my teeth are coming out! [*He hurries from the room.*]

LADY KITTY: It's too much. I can't bear it any more. I've put up with him for thirty years and now I'm at the end of my tether.

CHAMPION-CHENEY: Calm yourself, my dear Kitty.

LADY KITTY: I won't listen to a word. I've quite made up my mind. It's finished, finished, finished. [*With a change of tone.*] I was so touched when I heard that you never lived in this house again after I left it.

CHAMPION-CHENEY: The cuckoos have always been very plentiful. Their note has a personal application which, I must say, I have found extremely offensive.

LADY KITTY: When I saw that you didn't marry again I couldn't help thinking that you still loved me.

CHAMPION-CHENEY: I am one of the few men I know who is able to profit by experience.

LADY KITTY: In the eyes of the Church I am still your wife. The Church is so wise. It knows that in the end a woman always comes back to her first love. Clive, I am willing to return to you.

CHAMPION-CHENEY: My dear Kitty, I couldn't take advantage of your momentary vexation with Hughie to let you take a step which I know you would bitterly regret.

LADY KITTY: You've waited for me a long time. For Arnold's sake.

CHAMPION-CHENEY: Do you think we really need bother about Arnold? In the last thirty years he's had time to grow used to the situation.

LADY KITTY [*with a little smile*]: I think I've sown my wild oats, Clive.

CHAMPION-CHENEY: I haven't. I was a good young man, Kitty.

LADY KITTY: I know.

CHAMPION-CHENEY: And I'm very glad, because it has enabled me to be a wicked old one.

LADY KITTY: I beg your pardon.

ARNOLD *comes in with a large book in his hand.*

ARNOLD: I say, I've found the book I was hunting for. Oh, isn't Lord Porteous here?

LADY KITTY: One moment, Arnold. Your father and I are busy.

ARNOLD: I'm so sorry.

He goes out into the garden.

LADY KITTY: Explain yourself, Clive.

CHAMPION-CHENEY: When you ran away from me, Kitty, I was sore and angry and miserable. But above all I felt a fool.

LADY KITTY: Men are so vain.

CHAMPION-CHENEY: But I was a student of history, and presently I reflected that I shared my misfortune with very nearly all the greatest men.

LADY KITTY: I'm a great reader myself. It has always struck me as peculiar.

CHAMPION-CHENEY: The explanation is very simple. Women dislike intelligence, and when they find it in their husbands they revenge themselves on them in the only way they can, by making them—well, what you made me.

LADY KITTY: It's ingenious. It may be true.

CHAMPION-CHENEY: I felt I had done my duty by society and I determined to devote the rest of my life to my own entertainment. The House of Commons had always bored me excessively and the scandal of our divorce gave me an opportunity to resign my seat. I have been relieved to find that the country got on perfectly well without me.

LADY KITTY: But has love never entered your life?

CHAMPION-CHENEY: Tell me frankly, Kitty, don't you think people make a lot of unnecessary fuss about love?

LADY KITTY: It's the most wonderful thing in the world.

CHAMPION-CHENEY: You're incorrigible. Do you really think it was worth sacrificing so much for?

LADY KITTY: My dear Clive, I don't mind telling you that if I had my time over again I should be unfaithful to you, but I should not leave you.

CHAMPION-CHENEY: For some years I was notoriously the prey of a secret sorrow. But I found so many charming creatures who were anxious to console that in the end it grew rather fatiguing. Out of regard to my health I ceased to frequent the drawing-rooms of Mayfair.

LADY KITTY: And since then?

CHAMPION-CHENEY: Since then I have allowed myself the luxury of assisting financially a succession of dear little things, in a somewhat humble sphere, between the ages of twenty and twenty-five.

LADY KITTY: I cannot understand the infatuation of men for young girls. I think they're so dull.

CHAMPION-CHENEY: It's a matter of taste. I love old wine, old friends and old books, but I like young women. On their twenty-fifth birthday I give them a diamond ring and tell them they must no longer waste their youth and beauty on an old fogey like me. We have a most affecting scene, my technique on these occasions is perfect, and then I start all over again.

LADY KITTY: You're a wicked old man, Clive.

CHAMPION-CHENEY: That's what I told you. But, by George! I'm a happy one.

LADY KITTY: There's only one course open to me now.

CHAMPION-CHENEY: What is that!

LADY KITTY [*with a flashing smile*]: To go and dress for dinner.

CHAMPION-CHENEY: Capital. I will follow your example.

As LADY KITTY *goes out* ELIZABETH *comes in.*

ELIZABETH: Where is Arnold?

CHAMPION-CHENEY: He's on the terrace. I'll call him.

ELIZABETH: Don't bother.

CHAMPION-CHENEY: I was just strolling along to my cottage to put on a dinner jacket. [*As he goes out.*] Arnold. [*Exit* CHAMPION-CHENEY.]

ARNOLD: Hulloa! [*He comes in.*] Oh, Elizabeth, I've found an illustration here of a chair which is almost identical with mine. It's dated 1750. Look!

ELIZABETH: That's very interesting.

ARNOLD: I want to show it to Porteous. [*Moving a chair which has been misplaced.*] You know, it does exasperate me the way people will not leave things alone. I no sooner put a thing in its place than somebody moves it.

ELIZABETH: It must be maddening for you.

ARNOLD: It is. You are the worst offender. I can't think why you don't take the pride that I do in the house. After all, it's one of the show places in the county.

ELIZABETH: I'm afraid you find me very unsatisfactory.

ARNOLD [*good-humouredly*]: I don't know about that. But my two subjects are politics and decoration. I should be a perfect fool if I didn't see that you don't care two straws about either.

ELIZABETH: We haven't very much in common, Arnold, have we?

ARNOLD: I don't think you can blame me for that.

ELIZABETH: I don't. I blame you for nothing. I have no fault to find with you.

ARNOLD [*surprised at her significant tone*]: Good gracious me, what's the meaning of all this?

ELIZABETH: Well, I don't think there's any object in beating about the bush. I want you to let me go.

ARNOLD: Go where?

ELIZABETH: Away. For always.

ARNOLD: My dear child, what *are* you talking about?

ELIZABETH: I want to be free.

ARNOLD [*amused rather than disconcerted*]: Don't be ridiculous, darling. I daresay you're run down and want a change. I'll take you over to Paris for a fortnight if you like.

ELIZABETH: I shouldn't have spoken to you if I hadn't quite made up my mind. We've been married for three years and I don't think it's been a great success. I'm frankly bored by the life you want me to lead.

ARNOLD: Well, if you'll allow me to say so, the fault is yours. We lead a very distinguished, useful life. We know a lot of extremely nice people.

ELIZABETH: I'm quite willing to allow that the fault is mine. But how does that make it any better? I'm only twenty-five. If I've made a mistake I have time to correct it.

ARNOLD: I can't bring myself to take you very seriously.

ELIZABETH: You see, I don't love you.

ARNOLD: Well, I'm awfully sorry. But you weren't obliged to marry me. You've made your bed and I'm afraid you must lie on it.

ELIZABETH: That's one of the falsest proverbs in the English language. Why should you lie on the bed you've made if you don't want to? There's always the floor.

ARNOLD: For goodness' sake don't be funny, Elizabeth.

ELIZABETH: I've quite made up my mind to leave you, Arnold.

ARNOLD: Come, come, Elizabeth, you must be sensible. You haven't any reason to leave me.

ELIZABETH: Why should you wish to keep a woman tied to you who wants to be free?

ARNOLD: I happen to be in love with you.

ELIZABETH: You might have said that before.

ARNOLD: I thought you'd take it for granted. You can't expect a man to go on making love to his wife after three years. I'm very busy. I'm awfully keen on politics and I've worked like a dog to make this house a thing of beauty. After all, a man marries to have a home, but also because he doesn't want to be bothered with sex and all that sort of thing. I fell in love with you the first time I saw you and I've been in love ever since.

ELIZABETH: I'm sorry, but if you're not in love with a man his love doesn't mean very much to you.

ARNOLD: It's so ungrateful. I've done everything in the world for you.

ELIZABETH: You've been very kind to me. But you've asked me to lead a life I don't like and that I'm not suited for. I'm awfully sorry to cause you pain, but now you must let me go.

ARNOLD: Nonsense! I'm a good deal older than you are and I think I have a little more sense. In your interest as well as in mine I'm not going to do anything of the sort.

ELIZABETH [*with a smile*]: How can you prevent me? You can't keep me under lock and key.

ARNOLD: Please don't talk to me as if I were a foolish child. You're my wife and you're going to remain my wife.

ELIZABETH: What sort of a life do you think we should lead? Do you think there'd be any more happiness for you than for me?

ARNOLD: But what is it precisely that you suggest?

ELIZABETH: Well, I want you to let me divorce you.

ARNOLD [*astounded*]: Me? Thank you very much. Are you under the impression I'm going to sacrifice my career for a whim of yours?

ELIZABETH: How will it do that?

ARNOLD: My seat's wobbly enough as it is. Do you think I'd be able to hold it if I were in a divorce case? Even if it were a put-up job, as most divorces are nowadays, it would damn me.

ELIZABETH: It's rather hard on a woman to be divorced.

ARNOLD [*with sudden suspicion*]: What do you mean by that? Are you in love with someone?

ELIZABETH: Yes.

ARNOLD: Who?

ELIZABETH: Teddie Luton.

He is astonished for a moment, then bursts into a laugh.

ARNOLD: My poor child, how can you be so ridiculous? Why, he hasn't a bob. He's a perfectly commonplace young man. It's so absurd I can't even be angry with you.

ELIZABETH: I've fallen desperately in love with him, Arnold.

ARNOLD: Well, you'd better fall desperately out.

ELIZABETH: He wants to marry me.

ARNOLD: I daresay he does. He can go to hell.

ELIZABETH: It's no good talking like that.

ARNOLD: Is he your lover?

ELIZABETH: No, certainly not.

ARNOLD: It shows that he's a mean skunk to take advantage of my hospitality to make love to you.

ELIZABETH: He's never even kissed me.

ARNOLD: I'd try telling that to the horse marines if I were you.

ELIZABETH: It's because I wanted to do nothing shabby that I told you straight out how things were.

ARNOLD: How long have you been thinking of this?

ELIZABETH: I've been in love with Teddie ever since I knew him.

ARNOLD: And you never thought of me at all, I suppose.

ELIZABETH: Oh, yes, I did. I was miserable. But I can't help myself. I wish I loved you, but I don't.

ARNOLD: I recommend you to think very carefully before you do anything foolish.

ELIZABETH: I have thought very carefully.

ARNOLD: By God, I don't know why I don't give you a sound hiding. I'm not sure if that wouldn't be the best thing to bring you to your senses.

ELIZABETH: Oh, Arnold, don't take it like that.

ARNOLD: How do you expect me to take it? You come to me quite calmly and say: 'I've had enough of you. We've been married three years and I think I'd like to marry somebody else now. Shall I break up your home? What a bore for you! Do you mind my divorcing you? It'll smash up your career, will it? What a pity!' Oh, no, my girl, I may be a fool, but I'm not a damned fool.

ELIZABETH: Teddie is leaving here by the first train tomorrow. I warn you that I mean to join him as soon as he can make the necessary arrangements.

ARNOLD: Where is he?

ELIZABETH: I don't know. I suppose he's in his room.

ARNOLD goes to the door and calls.

ARNOLD: George!

For a moment he walks up and down the room impatiently. ELIZABETH *watches him. The* FOOTMAN *comes in.*

FOOTMAN: Yes, sir.

ARNOLD: Tell Mr Luton to come here at once.

ELIZABETH: Ask Mr Luton if he wouldn't mind coming here for a moment.

FOOTMAN: Very good, madam. [*Exit* FOOTMAN.]

ELIZABETH: What are you going to say to him?

ARNOLD: That's my business.

ELIZABETH: I wouldn't make a scene if I were you.

ARNOLD: I'm not going to make a scene.

They wait in silence.

Why did you insist on my mother coming here?

ELIZABETH: It seemed to me rather absurd to take up the attitude that I should be contaminated by her when . . .

ARNOLD [*interrupting*]: When you were proposing to do exactly the same thing. Well, now you've seen her what do you think of her? Do you think it's been a success? Is that the sort of woman a man would like his mother to be?

ELIZABETH: I've been ashamed. I've been so sorry. It all seemed dreadful and horrible. This morning I happened to notice a rose in the garden. It was all overblown and bedraggled. It looked like a painted old woman. And I remembered that I'd looked at it a day or two ago. It was lovely then, fresh and blooming and fragrant. It may be hideous now, but that doesn't take away from the beauty it had once. That was real.

ARNOLD: Poetry, by God! As if this were the moment for poetry!

TEDDIE *comes in. He has changed into a dinner jacket.*

TEDDIE [*to* ELIZABETH]: Did you want me?

ARNOLD: *I* sent for you.

TEDDIE *looks from* ARNOLD *to* ELIZABETH. *He sees that something has happened.*

When would it be convenient for you to leave this house?

TEDDIE: I was proposing to go to-morrow morning. But I can very well go at once if you like.

ARNOLD: I do like.

TEDDIE: Very well. Is there anything else you wish to say to me?

ARNOLD: Do you think it was a very honourable thing to come down here and make love to my wife?

TEDDIE: No, I don't. I haven't been very happy about it. That's why I wanted to go away.

ARNOLD: Upon my word you're cool.

TEDDIE: I'm afraid it's no good saying I'm sorry and that sort of thing. You know what the situation is.

ARNOLD: Is it true that you want to marry Elizabeth?

TEDDIE: Yes. I should like to marry her as soon as ever I can.

ARNOLD: Have you thought of me at all? Has it struck you that you're destroying my home and breaking up my happiness?

TEDDIE: I don't see how there could be much happiness for you if Elizabeth doesn't care for you.

ARNOLD: Let me tell you that I refuse to have my home broken up by a twopenny-halfpenny adventurer who takes advantage of a foolish woman. I refuse to allow myself to be divorced. I can't prevent my wife from going off with you if she's determined to make a damned fool of herself, but this I tell you: nothing will induce me to divorce her.

ELIZABETH: Arnold, that would be monstrous.

TEDDIE: We could force you.

ARNOLD: How?

TEDDIE: If we went away together openly you'd have to bring an action.

ARNOLD: Twenty-four hours after you leave this house I shall go down to Brighton with a chorus-girl. And neither you nor I will be able to get a divorce. We've had enough divorces in our family. And now get out, get out, get out!

TEDDIE *looks uncertainly at* ELIZABETH.

ELIZABETH [*with a little smile*]: Don't bother about me. I shall be all right.

ARNOLD: Get out! Get out!

END OF ACT TWO

ACT THREE

The scene is the same. It is the night of the same day as that on which takes place the action of the second Act. CHAMPION-CHENEY *and* ARNOLD, *both in dinner jackets, are discovered.* CHAMPION-CHENEY *is seated.* ARNOLD *walks restlessly up and down the room.*

CHAMPION-CHENEY: I think, if you'll follow my advice to the letter, you'll probably work the trick.

ARNOLD: I don't like it, you know. It's against all my principles.

CHAMPION-CHENEY: My dear Arnold, we all hope that you have before you a distinguished political career. You can't learn too soon that the most useful thing about a principle is that it can always be sacrificed to expediency.

ARNOLD: But supposing it doesn't come off? Women are incalculable.

CHAMPION-CHENEY: Nonsense! Men are romantic. A woman will always sacrifice herself if you give her the opportunity. It is her favourite form of self-indulgence.

ARNOLD: I never know whether you're a humorist or a cynic, father.

CHAMPION-CHENEY: I'm neither, my dear boy; I'm merely a very truthful man. But people are so unused to the truth that they're apt to mistake it for a joke or a sneer.

ARNOLD [*irritably*]: It seems so unfair that this should happen to me.

CHAMPION-CHENEY: Keep your head, my boy, and do what I tell you.

LADY KITTY *and* ELIZABETH *come in.* LADY KITTY *is in a gorgeous evening gown.*

ELIZABETH: Where is Lord Porteous?

CHAMPION-CHENEY: He's on the terrace. He's smoking a cigar. [*Going to window.*] Hughie!

PORTEOUS *comes in.*

PORTEOUS [*with a grunt*]: Yes? Where's Mrs Shenstone?

ELIZABETH: Oh, she had a headache. She's gone to bed.

When PORTEOUS *comes in* LADY KITTY *with a very haughty air purses her lips and takes up an illustrated paper.* PORTEOUS *gives her an irritated look, takes another illustrated paper and sits himself down at the other end of the room. They are not on speaking terms.*

CHAMPION-CHENEY: Arnold and I have just been down to my cottage.

ELIZABETH: I wondered where you'd gone.

CHAMPION-CHENEY: I came across an old photograph album this afternoon. I meant to bring it along before dinner, but I forgot, so we went and fetched it.

ELIZABETH: Oh, do let me see it. I love old photographs.

He gives her the album, and she, sitting down, puts it on her knees and begins to turn over the pages. He stands over her. LADY KITTY *and* PORTEOUS *take surreptitious glances at one another.*

CHAMPION-CHENEY: I thought it might amuse you to see what pretty women looked like five-and-thirty years ago. That was the day of beautiful women.

ELIZABETH: Do you think they were more beautiful then than they are now?

CHAMPION-CHENEY: Oh, much. Now you see lots of pretty little things, but very few beautiful women.

ELIZABETH: Aren't their clothes funny?

CHAMPION-CHENEY [*pointing to a photograph*]: That's Mrs Langtry.

ELIZABETH: She has a lovely nose.

CHAMPION-CHENEY: She was the most wonderful thing you every saw. Dowagers used to jump on chairs in order to get a good look at her when she came into a drawing-room. I was riding with her once, and we had to have the gates of the livery stable closed when she was getting on her horse because the crowd was so great.

ELIZABETH: And who's that?

CHAMPION-CHENEY: Lady Lonsdale. That's Lady Dudley.

ELIZABETH: This is an actress, isn't it?

CHAMPION-CHENEY: It is, indeed. Ellen Terry. By George, how I loved that woman!

ELIZABETH [*with a smile*]: Dear Ellen Terry!

CHAMPION-CHENEY: That's Bwabs. I never saw a smarter man in my life. And Oliver Montagu. Henry Manners with his eye-glass.

ELIZABETH: Nice-looking, isn't he? And this?

CHAMPION-CHENEY: That's Mary Anderson. I wish you could have seen her in A Winter's Tale. Her beauty just took your breath away. And look! There's Lady Randolph. Bernal Osborne—the wittiest man I ever knew.

ELIZABETH: I think it's too sweet. I love their absurd bustles and those tight sleeves.

CHAMPION-CHENEY: What figures they had! In those days a woman wasn't supposed to be as thin as a rail and as flat as a pancake.

ELIZABETH: Oh, but aren't they laced in? How could they bear it?

CHAMPION-CHENEY: They didn't play golf then, and nonsense like that, you know. They hunted, in a tall hat and a long black habit, and they were very gracious and charitable to the poor in the village.

ELIZABETH: Did the poor like it?

CHAMPION-CHENEY: They had a very thin time if they didn't. When they were in London they drove in the Park every afternoon, and they went to ten-course dinners, where they never met anybody they didn't know. And they had their box at the opera when Patti was singing or Madame Albani.

ELIZABETH: Oh, what a lovely little thing! Who on earth is that?

CHAMPION-CHENEY: That?

ELIZABETH: She looks so fragile, like a piece of exquisite china, with all those furs on and her face up against her muff, and the snow falling.

CHAMPION-CHENEY: Yes, there was quite a rage at that time for being taken in an artificial snowstorm.

ELIZABETH: What a sweet smile, so roguish and frank, and debonair! Oh, I wish I looked like that. Do tell me who it is.

CHAMPION-CHENEY: Don't you know?

ELIZABETH: No.

CHAMPION-CHENEY: Why—it's Kitty.

ELIZABETH: Lady Kitty! [*To* LADY KITTY.] Oh, my dear, do look. It's too ravishing. [*She takes the album over to her impulsively.*] Why didn't you tell me you looked like that? Everybody must have been in love with you.

> LADY KITTY *takes the album and looks at it. Then she lets it slip from her hands and covers her face with her hands. She is crying.*

ELIZABETH [*in consternation*]: My dear, what's the matter? Oh, what have I done? I'm so sorry.

LADY KITTY: Don't, don't talk to me. Leave me alone. It's stupid of me.

> ELIZABETH *looks at her for a moment perplexed, then, turning round, slips her arm in* CHAMPION-CHENEY's *and leads him out on to the terrace.*

ELIZABETH [*as they are going, in a whisper*]: Did you do that on purpose?

> PORTEOUS *gets up and goes over to* LADY KITTY. *He puts his hand on her shoulder. They remain thus for a little while.*

PORTEOUS: I'm afraid I was very rude to you before dinner, Kitty.

LADY KITTY [*taking his hand which is on her shoulder*]: It doesn't matter. I'm sure I was very exasperating.

PORTEOUS: I didn't mean what I said, you know.

LADY KITTY: Neither did I.

PORTEOUS: Of course I know that I'd never have been Prime Minister.

LADY KITTY: How can you talk such nonsense, Hughie? No one would have had a chance if you'd remained in politics.

PORTEOUS: I haven't the character.

LADY KITTY: You have more character than anyone I've ever met.

PORTEOUS: Besides, I don't know that I much wanted to be Prime Minister.

LADY KITTY: Oh, but I should have been so proud of you. Of course you'd have been Prime Minister.

PORTEOUS: I'd have given you India, you know. I think it would have been a very popular appointment.

LADY KITTY: I don't care twopence about India. I'd have been quite content with Western Australia.

PORTEOUS: My dear, you don't think I'd have let you bury yourself in Western Australia?

LADY KITTY: Or Barbados.

PORTEOUS: Never. It sounds like a cure for flat feet. I'd have kept you in London.

> *He picks up the album and is about to look at the photograph of Lady Kitty. She puts her hand over it.*

LADY KITTY: No, don't look.

He takes her hand away.

PORTEOUS: Don't be so silly.

LADY KITTY: Isn't it hateful to grow old?

PORTEOUS: You know, you haven't changed much.

LADY KITTY [*enchanted*]: Oh, Hughie, how can you talk such nonsense?

PORTEOUS: Of course you're a little more mature, but that's all. A woman's all the better for being rather mature.

LADY KITTY: Do you really think that?

PORTEOUS: Upon my soul I do.

LADY KITTY: You're not saying it just to please me?

PORTEOUS: No, no.

LADY KITTY: Let me look at the photograph again. [*She takes the album and looks at the photograph complacently.*] The fact is, if your bones are good, age doesn't really matter. You'll always be beautiful.

PORTEOUS [*with a little smile, almost as if he were talking to a child*]: It was silly of you to cry.

LADY KITTY: It hasn't made my eyelashes run, has it?

PORTEOUS: Not a bit.

LADY KITTY: It's very good stuff I use now. They don't stick together either.

PORTEOUS: Look here, Kitty, how much longer do you want to stay here?

LADY KITTY: Oh, I'm quite ready to go whenever you like.

PORTEOUS: Clive gets on my nerves. I don't like the way he keeps hanging about you.

LADY KITTY [*surprised, rather amused, and delighted*]: Hughie, you don't mean to say you're jealous of poor Clive?

PORTEOUS: Of course I'm not jealous of him, but he does look at you in a way that I can't help thinking rather objectionable.

LADY KITTY: Hughie, you may throw me downstairs like Amy Robsart; you may drag me about the floor by the hair of my head; I don't care, you're jealous. I shall never grow old.

PORTEOUS: Damn it all, the man was your husband.

LADY KITTY: My dear Hughie, he never had your style. Why, the moment you come into a room everyone looks and says, Who the devil is that?

PORTEOUS: What? You think that, do you? Well, I daresay there's something in what you say. These damned Radicals can say what they like, but, by God, Kitty, when a man's a gentleman—well, damn it all, you know what I mean.

LADY KITTY: I think Clive has degenerated dreadfully since we left him.

PORTEOUS: What do you say to making a bee-line for Italy and going to San Michele?

LADY KITTY: Oh, Hughie! It's years since we were there.

PORTEOUS: Wouldn't you like to see it again—just once more?

LADY KITTY: Do you remember the first time we went? It was the most heavenly place I'd ever seen. We'd only left England a month, and I said I'd like to spend all my life there.

PORTEOUS: Of course, I remember. And in a fortnight it was yours, lock, stock and barrel.

LADY KITTY: We were very happy there, Hughie.

PORTEOUS: Let's go back once more.

LADY KITTY: I daren't. It must be all peopled with the ghosts of our past. One should never go again to a place where one has been happy. It would break my heart.

PORTEOUS: Do you remember how we used to sit on the terrace of the old castle and look at the Adriatic? We might have been the only people in the world, you and I, Kitty.

LADY KITTY [*tragically*]: And we thought our love would last for ever.

[*Enter* CHAMPION-CHENEY.]

PORTEOUS: Is there any chance of bridge this evening?

CHAMPION-CHENEY: I don't think we can make up a four.

PORTEOUS: What a nuisance that boy went away like that! He wasn't a bad player.

CHAMPION-CHENEY: Teddie Luton?

LADY KITTY: I think it was very funny his going without saying good-bye to anyone.

CHAMPION-CHENEY: The young men of the present day are very casual.

PORTEOUS: I thought there was no train in the evening.

CHAMPION-CHENEY: There isn't. The last train leaves at 5.45.

PORTEOUS: How did he go then?

CHAMPION-CHENEY: He went.

PORTEOUS: Damned selfish I call it.

LADY KITTY [*intrigued*]: Why did he go, Clive?

CHAMPION-CHENEY *looks at her for a moment reflectively.*

CHAMPION-CHENEY: I have something very grave to say to you. Elizabeth wants to leave Arnold.

LADY KITTY: Clive! What on earth for?

CHAMPION-CHENEY: She's in love with Teddie Luton. That's why he went. The men of my family are really very unfortunate.

PORTEOUS: Does she want to run away with him.

LADY KITTY [*with consternation*]: My dear, what's to be done?

CHAMPION-CHENEY: I think you can do a great deal.

LADY KITTY: I? What?

CHAMPION-CHENEY: Tell her, tell her what it means.

He looks at her fixedly. She stares at him.

LADY KITTY: Oh, no, no!

CHAMPION-CHENEY: She's a child. Not for Arnold's sake. For her sake. You must.

LADY KITTY: You don't know what you're asking.

CHAMPION-CHENEY: Yes, I do.

LADY KITTY: Hughie, what shall I do?

PORTEOUS: Do what you like. I shall never blame you for anything.

The FOOTMAN *comes in with a letter on a salver. He hesitates on seeing that* ELIZABETH *is not in the room.*

CHAMPION-CHENEY: What is it?

FOOTMAN: I was looking for Mrs Champion-Cheney, sir.
CHAMPION-CHENEY: She's not here. Is that a letter?
FOOTMAN: Yes, sir. It's just been sent up from The Champion Arms.
CHAMPION-CHENEY: Leave it. I'll give it to Mrs Cheney.
FOOTMAN: Very good, sir.

He brings the tray to CLIVE, *who takes the letter. The* FOOTMAN *goes out.*

PORTEOUS: Is The Champion Arms the local pub?
CHAMPION-CHENEY [*looking at the letter*]: It's by way of being an hotel, but I never heard of anyone staying there.
LADY KITTY: If there was no train I suppose he had to go there.
CHAMPION-CHENEY: Great minds. I wonder what he has to write about. [*He goes to the door leading on to the garden.*] Elizabeth.
ELIZABETH [*outside*]: Yes.
CHAMPION-CHENEY: Here's a note for you.

There is silence. They wait for ELIZABETH *to come. She enters.*

ELIZABETH: It's lovely in the garden to-night.
CHAMPION-CHENEY: They've just sent this up from The Champion Arms.
ELIZABETH: Thank you. [*Without embarrassment she opens the letter. They watch her while she reads it. It covers three pages. She puts it away in her bag.*]
LADY KITTY: Hughie, I wish you'd fetch me a cloak. I'd like to take a little stroll in the garden, but after thirty years in Italy I find these English summers rather chilly.

Without a word PORTEOUS *goes out.* ELIZABETH *is lost in thought.*

I want to talk to Elizabeth, Clive.
CHAMPION-CHENEY: I'll leave you.

He goes out.

LADY KITTY: What does he say?
ELIZABETH: Who?
LADY KITTY: Mr Luton.
ELIZABETH [*gives a little start. Then she looks at* LADY KITTY]: They've told you?
LADY KITTY: Yes. And now they have I think I knew it all along.
ELIZABETH: I don't expect you to have much sympathy for me. Arnold is your son.
LADY KITTY: So pitifully little.
ELIZABETH: I'm not suited for this sort of existence. Arnold wants me to take what he calls my place in Society. Oh, I get so bored with those parties in London. All those middle-aged painted women, in beautiful clothes, lolloping round ball-rooms with rather old young men. And the endless luncheons where they gossip about so-and-so's love affairs.
LADY KITTY: Are you very much in love with Mr Luton?
ELIZABETH: I love him with all my heart.
LADY KITTY: And he?

ELIZABETH: He's never cared for anyone but me. He never will.

LADY KITTY: Will Arnold let you divorce him?

ELIZABETH: No, he won't hear of it. He refuses even to divorce me.

LADY KITTY: Why?

ELIZABETH: He thinks a scandal will revive all the old gossip.

LADY KITTY: Oh, my poor child.

ELIZABETH: It can't be helped. I'm quite willing to accept the consequences.

LADY KITTY: You don't know what it is to have a man tied to you only by his honour. When married people don't get on they can separate, but if they're not married it's impossible. It's a tie that only death can sever.

ELIZABETH: If Teddie stopped caring for me I shouldn't want him to stay with me for five minutes.

LADY KITTY: One says that when one's sure of a man's love, but when one isn't any more–oh, it's so different. In those circumstances one's got to keep a man's love. It's the only thing one has.

ELIZABETH: I'm a human being. I can stand on my own feet.

LADY KITTY: Have you any money of your own?

ELIZABETH: None.

LADY KITTY: Then how can you stand on your own feet? You think I'm a silly, frivolous woman, but I've learnt something in a bitter school. They can make what laws they like, they can give us the suffrage, but when you come down to bedrock it's the man who pays the piper who calls the tune. Woman will only be the equal of man when she earns her living in the same way that he does.

ELIZABETH [*smiling*]: It sounds rather funny to hear you talk like that.

LADY KITTY: A cook who marries a butler can snap her fingers in his face because she can earn just as much as he can. But a woman in your position and a woman in mine will always be dependent on the men who keep them.

ELIZABETH: I don't want luxury. You don't know how sick I am of all this beautiful furniture. These over-decorated houses are like a prison in which I can't breathe. When I drive about in a Callot frock and a Rolls-Royce I envy the shop-girl in a coat and skirt whom I see jumping on the tailboard of a bus.

LADY KITTY: You mean that if need be you could earn your own living?

ELIZABETH: Yes.

LADY KITTY: What could you be? A nurse or a typist. It's nonsense. Luxury saps a woman's nerve. And when she's known it once it becomes a necessity.

ELIZABETH: That depends on the woman.

LADY KITTY: When we're young we think we're different from everyone else, but when we grow a little older we discover we're all very much of a muchness.

ELIZABETH: You're very kind to take so much trouble about me.

LADY KITTY: It breaks my heart to think that you're going to make the same pitiful mistake that I made.

ELIZABETH: Oh, don't say it was that, don't, don't.

LADY KITTY: Look at me, Elizabeth, and look at Hughie. Do you think it's been a success? If I had my time over again do you think I'd do it again? Do you think he would?

ELIZABETH: You see, you don't know how much I love Teddie.

LADY KITTY: And do you think I didn't love Hughie? Do you think he didn't love me?

ELIZABETH: I'm sure he did.

LADY KITTY: Oh, of course in the beginning it was heavenly. We felt so brave and adventurous and we were so much in love. The first two years were wonderful. People cut me, you know, but I didn't mind. I thought love was everything. It *is* a little uncomfortable when you come upon an old friend and go towards her eagerly, so glad to see her, and are met with an icy stare.

ELIZABETH: Do you think friends like that are worth having?

LADY KITTY: Perhaps they're not very sure of themselves. Perhaps they're honestly shocked. It's a test one had better not put one's friends to if one can help it. It's rather bitter to find how few one has.

ELIZABETH: But one has some.

LADY KITTY: Yes, they ask you to come and see them when they're quite certain no one will be there who might object to meeting you. Or else they say to you, My dear, you know I'm devoted to you, and I wouldn't mind at all, but my girl's growing up—I'm sure you understand; you won't think it unkind of me if I don't ask you to the house?

ELIZABETH [*smiling*]: That doesn't seem to me very serious.

LADY KITTY: At first I thought it rather a relief, because it threw Hughie and me together more. But you know, men are very funny. Even when they are in love they're not in love all day long. They want change and recreation.

ELIZABETH: I'm not inclined to blame them for that, poor dears.

LADY KITTY: Then we settled in Florence. And because we couldn't get the society we'd been used to, we became used to the society we could get. Loose women and vicious men. Snobs who liked to patronise people with a handle to their names. Vague Italian princes who were glad to borrow a few francs from Hughie and seedy countesses who liked to drive with me in the Cascine. And then Hughie began to hanker after his old life. He wanted to go big game shooting, but I dared not let him go. I was afraid he'd never come back.

ELIZABETH: But you knew he loved you.

LADY KITTY: Oh, my dear, what a blessed institution marriage is—for women, and what fools they are to meddle with it! The Church is so wise to take its stand on the indi—indi—

ELIZABETH: Solu—

LADY KITTY: Bility of marriage. Believe me, it's no joke when you have to rely only on yourself to keep a man. I could never afford to grow old. My dear, I'll tell you a secret that I've never told a living soul.

ELIZABETH: What is that?

LADY KITTY: My hair is not naturally this colour.

ELIZABETH: Really.

LADY KITTY: I touch it up. You would never have guessed, would you?

ELIZABETH: Never.

LADY KITTY: Nobody does. My dear, it's white, prematurely of course, but white. I always think it's a symbol of my life. Are you interested in symbolism? I think it's too wonderful.

ELIZABETH: I don't think I know very much about it.

LADY KITTY: However tired I've been I've had to be brilliant and gay. I've never let Hughie see the aching heart behind my smiling eyes.

ELIZABETH [*amused and touched*]: You poor dear.

LADY KITTY: And when I saw he was attracted by someone else the fear and the jealousy that seized me! You see, I didn't dare make a scene as I should have done if I'd been married. I had to pretend not to notice.

ELIZABETH [*taken aback*]: But do you mean to say he fell in love with anyone else?

LADY KITTY: Of course he did eventually.

ELIZABETH [*hardly knowing what to say*]: You must have been very unhappy.

LADY KITTY: Oh, I was, dreadfully. Night after night I sobbed my heart out when Hughie told me he was going to play cards at the club and I knew he was with that odious woman. Of course, it wasn't as if there weren't plenty of men who were only too anxious to console me. Men have always been attracted by me, you know.

ELIZABETH: Oh, of course, I can quite understand it.

LADY KITTY: But I had my self-respect to think of. I felt that whatever Hughie did I would do nothing that I should regret.

ELIZABETH: You must be very glad now.

LADY KITTY: Oh, yes. Notwithstanding all my temptations I've been absolutely faithful to Hughie in spirit.

ELIZABETH: I don't think I quite understand what you mean.

LADY KITTY: Well, there was a poor Italian boy, young Count Castel Giovanni, who was so desperately in love with me that his mother begged me not to be too cruel. She was afraid he'd go into a consumption. What could I do? And then, oh, years later, there was Antonio Melita. He said he'd shoot himself unless I—well, you understand I couldn't let the poor boy shoot himself.

ELIZABETH: D'you think he really would have shot himself?

LADY KITTY: Oh, one never knows, you know. Those Italians are so passionate. He was really rather a lamb. He had such beautiful eyes.

ELIZABETH *looks at her for a long time and a certain horror seizes her of this dissolute, painted old woman.*

ELIZABETH [*hoarsely*]: Oh, but I think that's—dreadful.

LADY KITTY: Are you shocked? One sacrifices one's life for love and then one finds that love doesn't last. The tragedy of love isn't death or separation. One gets over them. The tragedy of love is indifference.

ARNOLD *comes in.*

ARNOLD: Can I have a little talk with you, Elizabeth?

ELIZABETH: Of course.

ARNOLD: Shall we go for a stroll in the garden?

ELIZABETH: If you like.

LADY KITTY: No, stay here. I'm going out anyway. [*Exit* LADY KITTY.]

ARNOLD: I want you to listen to me for a few minutes, Elizabeth. I was so taken aback by what you told me just now that I lost my head. I was rather absurd and I beg your pardon. I said things I regret.

ELIZABETH: Oh, don't blame yourself. I'm sorry that I should have given you occasion to say them.

ARNOLD: I want to ask you if you've quite made up your mind to go.

ELIZABETH: Quite.

ARNOLD: Just now I seem to have said all that I didn't want to say and nothing that I did. I'm stupid and tongue-tied. I never told you how deeply I loved you.

ELIZABETH: Oh, Arnold.

ARNOLD: Please let me speak now. It's so very difficult. If I seemed absorbed in politics and the house, and so on, to the exclusion of my interest in you, I'm dreadfully sorry. I suppose it was absurd of me to think you would take my great love for granted.

ELIZABETH: But, Arnold, I'm not reproaching you.

ARNOLD: I'm reproaching myself. I've been tactless and neglectful. But I do ask you to believe that it hasn't been because I didn't love you. Can you forgive me?

ELIZABETH: I don't think that there's anything to forgive.

ARNOLD: It wasn't till to-day when you talked of leaving me that I realised how desperately in love with you I was.

ELIZABETH: After three years?

ARNOLD: I'm so proud of you. I admire you so much. When I see you at a party, so fresh and lovely, and everybody wondering at you, I have a sort of little thrill because you're mine, and afterwards I shall take you home.

ELIZABETH: Oh, Arnold, you're exaggerating.

ARNOLD: I can't imagine this house without you. Life seems on a sudden all empty and meaningless. Oh, Elizabeth, don't you love me at all?

ELIZABETH: It's much better to be honest. No.

ARNOLD: Doesn't my love mean anything to you?

ELIZABETH: I'm very grateful to you. I'm sorry to cause you pain. What would be the good of my staying with you when I should be wretched all the time?

ARNOLD: Do you love that man as much as all that? Does my unhappiness mean nothing to you?

ELIZABETH: Of course it does. It breaks my heart. You see, I never knew I meant so much to you. I'm so touched. And I'm so sorry, Arnold, really sorry. But I can't help myself.

ARNOLD: Poor child, it's cruel of me to torture you.

ELIZABETH: Oh, Arnold, believe me, I have tried to make the best of it. I've tried to love you, but I can't. After all, one either loves or one doesn't. Trying is no help. And now I'm at the end of my tether. I can't help the consequences—I must do what my whole self yearns for.

ARNOLD: My poor child, I'm so afraid you'll be unhappy. I'm so afraid you'll regret.

ELIZABETH: You must leave me to my fate. I hope you'll forget me and all the unhappiness I've caused you.

ARNOLD [*there is a pause.* ARNOLD *walks up and down the room reflectively. He stops and faces her*]: If you love this man and want to go to him I'll do nothing to prevent you. My only wish is to do what is best for you.

ELIZABETH: Arnold, that's awfully kind of you. If I'm treating you badly at least I want you to know that I'm grateful for all your kindness to me.

ARNOLD: But there's one favour I should like you to do me. Will you?

ELIZABETH: Oh, Arnold, of course I'll do anything I can.

ARNOLD: Teddie hasn't very much money. You've been used to a certain amount of luxury, and I can't bear to think that you should do without anything you've had. It would kill me to think that you were suffering any hardship or privation.

ELIZABETH: Oh, but Teddie can earn enough for our needs. After all, we don't want much money.

ARNOLD: I'm afraid my mother's life hasn't been very easy, but it's obvious that the only thing that's made it possible is that Porteous was rich. I want you to let me make you an allowance of two thousand a year.

ELIZABETH: Oh, no, I couldn't think of it. It's absurd.

ARNOLD: I beg you to accept it. You don't know what a difference it will make.

ELIZABETH: It's awfully kind of you, Arnold. It humiliates me to speak about it. Nothing would induce me to take a penny from you.

ARNOLD: Well, you can't prevent me from opening an account at my bank in your name. The money shall be paid in every quarter whether you touch it or not, and if you happen to want it, it will be there waiting for you.

ELIZABETH: You overwhelm me, Arnold. There's only one thing I want you to do for me. I should be very grateful if you would divorce me as soon as you possibly can.

ARNOLD: No, I won't do that. But I'll give you cause to divorce me.

ELIZABETH: You!

ARNOLD: Yes. But of course you'll have to be very careful for a bit. I'll put it through as quickly as possible, but I'm afraid you can't hope to be free for over six months.

ELIZABETH: But, Arnold, your seat and your political career!

ARNOLD: Oh, well, my father gave up his seat under similar circumstances. He's got along very comfortably without politics.

ELIZABETH: But they're your whole life.

ARNOLD: After all one can't have it both ways. You can't serve God and Mammon. If you want to do the decent thing you have to be prepared to suffer for it.

ELIZABETH: But I don't want you to suffer for it.

ARNOLD: At first I rather hesitated at the scandal. But I daresay that was only weakness on my part. In the circumstances I should have liked to keep out of the Divorce Court if I could.

ELIZABETH: Arnold, you're making me absolutely miserable.

ARNOLD: What you said before dinner was quite right. It's nothing for a man, but it makes so much difference to a woman. Naturally I must think of you first.

ELIZABETH: That's absurd. It's out of the question. Whatever there's to pay I must pay it.

ARNOLD: It's not very much I'm asking for, Elizabeth.

ELIZABETH: I'm taking everything from you.

ARNOLD: It's the only condition I make. My mind is absolutely made up. I will never divorce you, but I will enable you to divorce me.

ELIZABETH: Oh, Arnold, it's cruel to be so generous.

ARNOLD: It's not generous at all. It's the only way I have of showing you how deep and passionate and sincere my love is for you.

There is a silence. He holds out his hand.

Good-night. I have a great deal of work to do before I go to bed.

ELIZABETH: Good-night.

ARNOLD: Do you mind if I kiss you?

ELIZABETH [*with agony*]: Oh, Arnold!

He gravely kisses her on the forehead and then goes out. ELIZABETH *stands lost in thought. She is shattered.* LADY KITTY *and* PORTEOUS *come in.* LADY KITTY *wears a cloak.*

LADY KITTY: You're alone, Elizabeth?

ELIZABETH: That note you asked me about, Lady Kitty, from Teddie . . .

LADY KITTY: Yes?

ELIZABETH: He wanted to have a talk with me before he went away. He's waiting for me in the summer house by the tennis court. Would Lord Porteous mind going down and asking him to come here?

PORTEOUS: Certainly. Certainly.

ELIZABETH: Forgive me for troubling you. But it's very important.

PORTEOUS: No trouble at all. [*He goes out.*]

LADY KITTY: Hughie and I will leave you alone.

ELIZABETH: But I don't want to be left alone. I want you to stay.

LADY KITTY: What are you going to say to him?

ELIZABETH [*desperately*]: Please don't ask me questions. I'm so frightfully unhappy.

LADY KITTY: My poor child.

ELIZABETH: Oh, isn't life rotten? Why can't one be happy without making other people unhappy?

LADY KITTY: I wish I knew how to help you. I'm simply devoted to you. [*She hunts about in her mind for something to do or say.*] Would you like my lipstick?

ELIZABETH [*smiling through her tears*]: Thanks. I never use one.

LADY KITTY: Oh, but just try. It's such a comfort when you're in trouble.

Enter PORTEOUS *and* TEDDIE.

PORTEOUS: I brought him. He said he'd be damned if he'd come.

LADY KITTY: When a lady sent for him? Are these the manners of the young men of to-day?

TEDDIE: When you've been solemnly kicked out of a house once I think it seems rather pushing to come back again as though nothing had happened.

ELIZABETH: Teddie, I want you to be serious.

TEDDIE: Darling, I had such a rotten dinner at that pub. If you ask me to be serious on the top of that I shall cry.

ELIZABETH: Don't be idiotic, Teddie. [*Her voice faltering.*] I'm so utterly wretched.

He looks at her for a moment gravely.

TEDDIE: What is it?

ELIZABETH: I can't come away with you, Teddie.

TEDDIE: Why not?

ELIZABETH [*looking away in embarrassment*]: I don't love you enough.

TEDDIE: Fiddle!

ELIZABETH [*with a flash of anger*]: Don't say Fiddle to me.

TEDDIE: I shall say exactly what I like to you.

ELIZABETH: I won't be bullied.

TEDDIE: Now look here, Elizabeth, you know perfectly well that I'm in love with you, and I know perfectly well that you're in love with me. So what are you talking nonsense for?

ELIZABETH [*her voice breaking*]: I can't say it if you're cross with me.

TEDDIE [*smiling very tenderly*]: I'm not cross with you, silly.

ELIZABETH: It's harder still when you're being rather an owl.

TEDDIE [*with a chuckle*]: Am I mistaken in thinking you're not very easy to please?

ELIZABETH: Oh, it's monstrous. I was all wrought up and ready to do anything, and now you've thoroughly put me out. I feel like a great big fat balloon that some one has put a long pin into. [*With a sudden look at him.*] Have you done it on purpose?

TEDDIE: Upon my soul I don't know what you're talking about.

ELIZABETH: I wonder if you're really much cleverer than I think you are.

TEDDIE [*taking her hands and making her sit down*]: Now tell me exactly what you want to say. By the way, do you want Lady Kitty and Lord Porteous to be here?

ELIZABETH: Yes.

LADY KITTY: Elizabeth asked us to stay.

TEDDIE: Oh, I don't mind, bless you. I only thought you might feel rather in the way.

LADY KITTY [*frigidly*]: A gentlewoman never feels in the way, Mr Luton.

TEDDIE: Won't you call me Teddie? Everybody does, you know.

> LADY KITTY *tries to give him a withering look, but she finds it very difficult to prevent herself from smiling.* TEDDIE *strokes* ELIZABETH'*s hands. She draws them away.*

ELIZABETH: No, don't do that. Teddie, it wasn't true when I said I didn't love you. Of course I love you. But Arnold loves me, too. I didn't know how much.

TEDDIE: What has he been saying to you?

ELIZABETH: He's been very good to me, and so kind. I didn't know he could be so kind. He offered to let me divorce him.

TEDDIE: That's very decent of him.

ELIZABETH: But don't you see, it ties my hands. How can I accept such a sacrifice? I should never forgive myself if I profited by his generosity.

TEDDIE: If another man and I were devilish hungry and there was only one mutton chop between us, and he said, You eat it, I wouldn't waste a lot of time arguing. I'd wolf it before he changed his mind.

ELIZABETH: Don't talk like that. It maddens me. I'm trying to do the right thing.

TEDDIE: You're not in love with Arnold; you're in love with me. It's idiotic to sacrifice your life for a slushy sentiment.

ELIZABETH: After all, I did marry him.

TEDDIE: Well, you made a mistake. A marriage without love is no marriage at all.

ELIZABETH: *I* made the mistake. Why should he suffer for it? If anyone has to suffer it's only right that I should.

TEDDIE: What sort of a life do you think it would be with him? When two people are married it's very difficult for one of them to be unhappy without making the other unhappy too.

ELIZABETH: I can't take advantage of his generosity.

TEDDIE: I daresay he'll get a lot of satisfaction out of it.

ELIZABETH: You're being beastly, Teddie. He was simply wonderful. I never knew he had it in him. He was really noble.

TEDDIE: You are talking rot, Elizabeth.

ELIZABETH: I wonder if you'd be capable of acting like that.

TEDDIE: Acting like what?

ELIZABETH: What would you do if I were married to you and came and told you I loved somebody else and wanted to leave you?

TEDDIE: You have very pretty blue eyes, Elizabeth. I'd black first one and then the other. And after that we'd see.

ELIZABETH: You damned brute!

TEDDIE: I've often thought I wasn't quite a gentleman. Had it never struck you?

They look at one another for a while.

ELIZABETH: You know, you are taking an unfair advantage of me. I feel as if I came to you quite unsuspectingly and when I wasn't looking you kicked me on the shins.

TEDDIE: Don't you think we'd get on rather well together?

PORTEOUS: Elizabeth's a fool if she don't stick to her husband. It's bad enough for the man, but for the woman – it's damnable. I hold no brief for Arnold. He plays bridge like a foot. Saving your presence, Kitty, I think he's a prig.

LADY KITTY: Poor dear, his father was at his age. I daresay he'll grow out of it.

PORTEOUS: But you stick to him, Elizabeth, stick to him. Man is a gregarious animal. We're members of a herd. If we break the herd's laws we suffer for it. And we suffer damnably.

LADY KITTY: Oh, Elizabeth, my dear child, don't go. It's not worth it. It's not worth it. I tell you that, and I've sacrificed everything to love.

A pause.

ELIZABETH: I'm afraid.

TEDDIE [*in a whisper*]: Elizabeth.

ELIZABETH: I can't face it. It's asking too much of me. Let's say good-bye to one another, Teddie. It's the only thing to do. And have pity on me. I'm giving up all my hope of happiness.

He goes up to her and looks into her eyes.

TEDDIE: But I wasn't offering you happiness. I don't think my sort of love tends to happiness. I'm jealous. I'm not a very easy man to get on with. I'm often out of temper and irritable. I should be fed to the teeth with you sometimes, and so would you be with me. I daresay we'd fight like cat and dog, and sometimes we'd hate each other. Often you'd be wretched and bored stiff and lonely, and often you'd be frightfully homesick, and then you'd regret all you'd lost. Stupid women would be rude to you because we'd run away together. And some of them would cut you. I don't offer you peace and quietness. I offer you unrest and anxiety. I don't offer you happiness. I offer you love.

ELIZABETH [*stretching out her arms*]: You hateful creature, I absolutely adore you.

He throws his arms round her and kisses her passionately on the lips.

LADY KITTY: Of course the moment he said he'd give her a black eye I knew it was finished.

PORTEOUS [*good-humouredly*]: You are a fool, Kitty.

LADY KITTY: I know I am, but I can't help it.

TEDDIE: Let's make a bolt for it now.

ELIZABETH: Shall we?

TEDDIE: This minute.

PORTEOUS: You're damned fools, both of you, damned fools. If you like you can have my car.

TEDDIE: That's awfully kind of you. As a matter of fact, I got it out of the garage. It's just along the drive.

PORTEOUS [*indignantly*]: How do you mean, you got it out of the garage?

TEDDIE: Well, I thought there'd be a lot of bother, and it seemed to me the best thing would be for Elizabeth and me not to stand upon the order of our going, you know. Do it now. An excellent motto for a business man.

PORTEOUS: Do you mean to say you were going to steal my car.

TEDDIE: Not exactly. I was only going to bolshevise it, so to speak.

PORTEOUS: I'm speechless. I'm absolutely speechless.

TEDDIE: Hang it all, I couldn't carry Elizabeth all the way to London. She's so damned plump.

ELIZABETH: You dirty dog!

PORTEOUS [*spluttering*]: Well, well, well! . . . [*Helplessly.*] I like him, Kitty, it's no good pretending I don't. I like him.

TEDDIE: The moon's shining, Elizabeth. We'll drive all through the night.

PORTEOUS: They'd better go to San Michele. I'll wire to have it got ready for them.

LADY KITTY: That's where we went when Hughie and I . . . [*Faltering.*] Oh, you dear things, how I envy you.

PORTEOUS [*mopping his eyes*]: Now don't cry, Kitty. Confound you, don't cry.

TEDDIE: Come, darling.

ELIZABETH: But I can't go like this.

TEDDIE: Nonsense! Lady Kitty will lend you her cloak. Won't you?

LADY KITTY [*taking it off*]: You're capable of tearing it off my back if I don't.

TEDDIE [*putting the cloak on* ELIZABETH]: And we'll buy you a tooth-brush in London in the morning.

LADY KITTY: She must write a note for Arnold, I'll put it on her pincushion.

TEDDIE: Pincushion be blowed. Come, darling. We'll drive through the dawn and through the sunrise.

ELIZABETH [*kissing* LADY KITTY *and* PORTEOUS]: Good-bye. Good-bye.

TEDDIE *stretches out his hand and she takes it. Hand in hand they go out into the night.*

LADY KITTY: Oh, Hughie, how it all comes back to me. Will they suffer all we suffered? And have we suffered all in vain?

PORTEOUS: My dear, I don't know that in life it matters so much what you do as what you are. No one can learn by the experience of another because no circumstances are quite the same. If we made rather a hash of things perhaps it was because we were rather trivial people. You can do anything in this world if you're prepared to take the consequences, and consequences depend on character.

Enter CHAMPION-CHENEY, *rubbing his hands. He is as pleased as Punch.*

CHAMPION-CHENEY: Well, I think I've settled the hash of that young man.

LADY KITTY: Oh?

CHAMPION-CHENEY: You have to get up very early in the morning to get the better of your humble servant.

There is the sound of a car starting.

LADY KITTY: What is that?

CHAMPION-CHENEY: It sounds like a car. I expect it's your chauffeur taking one of the maids for a joy-ride.

PORTEOUS: Whose hash are you talking about?

CHAMPION-CHENEY: Mr Edward Luton's, my dear Hughie. I told Arnold exactly what to do and he's done it. What makes a prison? Why, bars and bolts. Remove them and a prisoner won't want to escape. Clever, I flatter myself.

PORTEOUS: You were always that, Clive, but at the moment you're obscure.

CHAMPION-CHENEY: I told Arnold to go to Elizabeth and tell her she could have her freedom. I told him to sacrifice himself all along the line. I know what women are. The moment every obstacle was removed to her marriage with Teddie Luton, half the allurement was gone.

LADY KITTY: Arnold did that?

CHAMPION-CHENEY: He followed my instructions to the letter. I've just seen him. She's shaken. I'm willing to bet five hundred pounds to a penny that she won't bolt. A downy old bird, eh? Downy's the word. Downy.

He begins to laugh. They laugh too. Presently they are all three in fits of laughter.

THE END

BLOOD WEDDING

FEDERICO GARCIA LORCA

BLOOD WEDDING

First published in England in 1959

BLOOD WEDDING

Tragedy in Three Acts
and Seven Scenes
(1933)

Translated by

JAMES GRAHAM-LUJÁN and
RICHARD L. O'CONNELL

CHARACTERS

THE MOTHER
THE BRIDE
THE MOTHER-IN-LAW
LEONARDO'S WIFE
THE SERVANT WOMAN
THE NEIGHBOUR WOMAN
YOUNG GIRLS
LEONARDO
THE BRIDEGROOM
THE BRIDE'S FATHER
THE MOON
DEATH (*as a Beggar Woman*)
WOODCUTTERS
YOUNG MEN

NOTICE

This edition of *Blood Wedding* has been printed with
the proper authorization. It was scrupulously revised
in accordance with the original manuscript of Federico
García Lorca which I have in my possession, and it
contains his very latest revisions.

Buenos Aires, July 1938   MARGARITA XIRGU

ACT ONE

SCENE I

A room painted yellow.

BRIDEGROOM [*entering*]: Mother.
MOTHER: What?
BRIDEGROOM: I'm going.
MOTHER: Where?
BRIDEGROOM: To the vineyard. [*He starts to go.*]
MOTHER: Wait.
BRIDEGROOM: You want something?
MOTHER: Your breakfast, son.
BRIDEGROOM: Forget it. I'll eat grapes. Give me the knife.
MOTHER: What for?
BRIDEGROOM [*laughing*]: To cut the grapes with.
MOTHER [*muttering as she looks for the knife*]: Knives, knives. Cursed be all knives, and the scoundrel who invented them.
BRIDEGROOM: Let's talk about something else.
MOTHER: And guns and pistols and the smallest little knife—and even hoes and pitchforks.
BRIDEGROOM: All right.
MOTHER: Everything that can slice a man's body. A handsome man, full of young life, who goes out to the vineyards or to his own olive groves—his own because he's inherited them . . .
BRIDEGROOM [*lowering his head*]: Be quiet.
MOTHER: . . . and then that man doesn't come back. Or if he does come back it's only for someone to cover him over with a palm leaf or a plate of rock salt so he won't bloat. I don't know how you dare carry a knife on your body—or how I let this serpent [*she takes a knife from a kitchen chest*] stay in the chest.
BRIDEGROOM: Have you had your say?
MOTHER: If I lived to be a hundred I'd talk of nothing else. First your father; to me he smelled like a carnation and I had him for barely three years. Then your brother. Oh, is it right—how can it be—that a small thing like a knife or a pistol can finish off a man—a bull of a man? No, I'll never be quiet. The months pass and the hopelessness of it stings in my eyes and even to the roots of my hair.
BRIDEGROOM [*forcefully*]: Let's quit this talk!
MOTHER: No. No. Let's not quit this talk. Can anyone bring me your father back? Or your brother? Then there's the jail. What do they mean, jail? They eat there, smoke there, play music there! My dead men choking with weeds, silent, turning to dust. Two men like two beautiful flowers. The killers in jail, carefree, looking at the mountains.

BRIDEGROOM: Do you want me to go kill them?

MOTHER: No . . . If I talk about it it's because . . . Oh, how can I help talking about it, seeing you go out that door? It's . . . I don't like you to carry a knife. It's just that . . . that I wish you wouldn't go out to the fields.

BRIDEGROOM [*laughing*]: Oh, come now!

MOTHER: I'd like it if you were a woman. Then you wouldn't be going out to the arroyo now and we'd both of us embroider flounces and little woolly dogs.

BRIDEGROOM [*he puts his arm around his* MOTHER *and laughs*]: Mother, what if I should take you with me to the vineyards?

MOTHER: What would an old lady do in the vineyards? Were you going to put me down under the young vines?

BRIDEGROOM [*lifting her in his arms*]: Old lady, old lady—you little old, little old lady!

MOTHER: Your father, he used to take me. That's the way with men of good stock; good blood. Your grandfather left a son on every corner. That's what I like. Men, men; wheat, wheat.

BRIDEGROOM: And I, Mother?

MOTHER: You, what?

BRIDEGROOM: Do I need to tell you again?

MOTHER [*seriously*]: Oh!

BRIDEGROOM: Do you think it's bad?

MOTHER: No.

BRIDEGROOM: Well, then?

MOTHER: I don't really know. Like this, suddenly, it always surprises me. I know the girl is good. Isn't she? Well behaved. Hard working. Kneads her bread, sews her skirts, but even so when I say her name I feel as though someone had hit me on the forehead with a rock.

BRIDEGROOM: Foolishness.

MOTHER: More than foolishness. I'll be left alone. Now only you are left me—I hate to see you go.

BRIDEGROOM: But you'll come with us.

MOTHER: No. I can't leave your father and brother here alone. I have to go to them every morning and if I go away it's possible one of the Félix family, one of the killers, might die—and they'd bury him next to ours. And that'll never happen! Oh, no! That'll never happen! Because I'd dig them out with my nails and, all by myself, crush them against the wall.

BRIDEGROOM [*sternly*]: There you go again.

MOTHER: Forgive me.

Pause.

How long have you known her?

BRIDEGROOM: Three years. I've been able to buy the vineyard.

MOTHER: Three years. She used to have another sweetheart, didn't she?

BRIDEGROOM: I don't know. I don't think so. Girls have to look at what they'll marry.

MOTHER: Yes: Yes. I looked at nobody. I looked at your father, and when they killed him I looked at the wall in front of me. One woman with one man, and that's all.

BRIDEGROOM: You know my girl's good.

MOTHER: I don't doubt it. All the same, I'm sorry not to have known what her mother was like.

BRIDEGROOM: What difference does it make now?

MOTHER [*looking at him*]: Son.

BRIDEGROOM: What is it?

MOTHER: That's true! You're right! When do you want me to ask for her?

BRIDEGROOM [*happily*]: Does Sunday seem all right to you?

MOTHER [*seriously*]: I'll take her bronze earrings, they're very old–and you buy her . . .

BRIDEGROOM: You know more about that . . .

MOTHER: . . . you buy her some open-work stockings–and for you, two suits–three! I have no one but you now!

BRIDEGROOM: I'm going. Tomorrow I'll go see her.

MOTHER: Yes, yes–and see if you can make me happy with six grandchildren–or as many as you want, since your father didn't live to give them to me.

BRIDEGROOM: The first-born for you!

MOTHER: Yes, but have some girls. I want to embroider and make lace, and be at peace.

BRIDEGROOM: I'm sure you'll love my wife.

MOTHER: I'll love her. [*She starts to kiss him but changes her mind.*] Go on. You're too big now for kisses. Give them to your wife. [*Pause. To herself.*] When she is your wife.

BRIDEGROOM: I'm going.

MOTHER: And that land around the little mill–work it over. You've not taken good care of it.

BRIDEGROOM: You're right. I will.

MOTHER: God keep you.

The SON *goes out. The* MOTHER *remains seated–her back to the door. A* NEIGHBOUR WOMAN *with a 'kerchief on her head appears in the door.*

Come in.

NEIGHBOUR: How are you?

MOTHER: Just as you see me.

NEIGHBOUR: I came down to the store and stopped in to see you. We live so far away!

MOTHER: It's twenty years since I've been up to the top of the street.

NEIGHBOUR: You're looking well.

MOTHER: You think so?

NEIGHBOUR: Things happen. Two days ago they brought in my neighbour's son with both arms sliced off by the machine. [*She sits down*].

MOTHER: Rafael?

NEIGHBOUR: Yes. And there you have him. Many times I've thought your son and mine are better off where they are–sleeping, resting–not running the risk of being left helpless.

MOTHER: Hush. That's all just something thought up–but no consolation.

NEIGHBOUR [*sighing*]: Ay!

MOTHER [*sighing*]: Ay!

Pause.

NEIGHBOUR [*sadly*]: Where's your son?

MOTHER: He went out.

NEIGHBOUR: He finally bought the vineyard!

MOTHER: He was lucky.

NEIGHBOUR: Now he'll get married.

MOTHER [*as though reminded of something, she draws her chair near the* NEIGHBOUR]: Listen.

NEIGHBOUR [*in a confidential manner*]: Yes. What is it?

MOTHER: You know my son's sweetheart?

NEIGHBOUR: A good girl!

MOTHER: Yes, but . . .

NEIGHBOUR: But who knows her really well? There's nobody. She lives out there alone with her father—so far away—fifteen miles from the nearest house. But she's a good girl. Used to being alone.

MOTHER: And her mother?

NEIGHBOUR: Her mother I *did* know. Beautiful. Her face glowed like a saint's—but *I* never liked her. She didn't love her husband.

MOTHER [*sternly*]: Well, what a lot of things certain people know!

NEIGHBOUR: I'm sorry. I didn't mean to offend—but it's true. Now, whether she was decent or not nobody said. That wasn't discussed. She was haughty.

MOTHER: There you go again!

NEIGHBOUR: You asked me.

MOTHER: I wish no one knew anything about them—either the live one or the dead one—that they were like two thistles no one even names but cuts off at the right moment.

NEIGHBOUR: You're right. Your son is worth a lot.

MOTHER: Yes—a lot. That's why I look after him. They told me the girl had a sweetheart some time ago.

NEIGHBOUR: She was about fifteen. He's been married two years now—to a cousin of hers, as a matter of fact. But nobody remembers about their engagement.

MOTHER: How do you remember it?

NEIGHBOUR: Oh, what questions you ask!

MOTHER: We like to know all about the things that hurt us. Who was the boy?

NEIGHBOUR: Leonardo.

MOTHER: What Leonardo?

NEIGHBOUR: Leonardo Félix.

MOTHER: Félix!

NEIGHBOUR: Yes, but—how is Leonardo to blame for anything? He was eight years old when those things happened.

MOTHER: That's true. But I hear that name—Félix—and it's all the same. [*Muttering.*] Félix, a slimy mouthful. [*She spits.*] It makes me spit—spit so I won't kill!

NEIGHBOUR: Control yourself. What good will it do?

MOTHER: No good. But you see how it is.

NEIGHBOUR: Don't get in the way of your son's happiness. Don't say anything to him. You're old. So am I. It's time for you and me to keep quiet.

MOTHER: I'll say nothing to him.

NEIGHBOUR [*kissing her*]: Nothing.

MOTHER [*calmly*]: Such things . . .!

NEIGHBOUR: I'm going. My men will soon be coming in from the fields.

MOTHER: Have you ever known such a hot sun?

NEIGHBOUR: The children carrying water out to the reapers are black with it. Good-bye, woman.

MOTHER: Good-bye. [*She starts toward the door at the left. Half-way there she stops and slowly crosses herself.*]

SCENE 2

A room painted rose with copperware and wreaths of common flowers. In the centre of the room is a table with a tablecloth. It is morning.

> LEONARDO'S MOTHER-IN-LAW *sits in one corner holding a child in her arms and rocking it. His* WIFE *is in the other corner mending stockings.*

MOTHER-IN-LAW:

> Lullaby, my baby
> once there was a big horse
> who didn't like water.
> The water was black there
> under the branches.
> When it reached the bridge
> it stopped and it sang.
> Who can say, my baby,
> what the stream holds
> with its long tail
> in its green parlour?

WIFE [*softly*]:

> Carnation, sleep and dream,
> the horse won't drink from the stream.

MOTHER-IN-LAW:

> My rose, asleep now lie,
> the horse is starting to cry.
> His poor hooves were bleeding,
> his long mane was frozen,
> and deep in his eyes
> stuck a silvery dagger.
> Down he went to the river,
> Oh, down he went down!
> And his blood was running,
> Oh, more than the water.

WIFE:

> Carnation, sleep and dream,
> the horse won't drink from the stream.

MOTHER-IN-LAW:

> My rose, asleep now lie,
> the horse is starting to cry.

WIFE:

> He never did touch
> the dank river shore
> though his muzzle was warm
> and with silvery flies.

So, to the hard mountains
he could only whinny
just when the dead stream
covered his throat.
Ay-y-y, for the big horse
who didn't like water!
Ay-y-y, for the snow-wound
big horse of the dawn!

MOTHER-IN-LAW:
Don't come in! Stop him
and close up the window
with branches of dreams
and a dream of branches.

WIFE:
My baby is sleeping.

MOTHER-IN-LAW:
My baby is quiet.

WIFE:
Look, horse, my baby
has him a pillow.

MOTHER-IN-LAW:
His cradle is metal.

WIFE:
His quilt a fine fabric.

MOTHER-IN-LAW:
Lullaby, my baby.

WIFE:
Ay-y-y, for the big horse
who didn't like water!

MOTHER-IN-LAW:
Don't come near, don't come in!
Go away to the mountains
and through the grey valleys,
that's where your mare is.

WIFE [*looking at the baby*]:
My baby is sleeping.

MOTHER-IN-LAW:
My baby is resting.

WIFE [*softly*]:
Carnation, sleep and dream,
The horse won't drink from the stream.

MOTHER-IN-LAW [*getting up, very softly*]:
My rose, asleep now lie
for the horse is starting to cry.

She carries the child out. LEONARDO *enters.*

LEONARDO: Where's the baby?
WIFE: He's sleeping.
LEONARDO: Yesterday he wasn't well. He cried during the night.
WIFE: Today he's like a dahlia. And you? Were you at the blacksmith's?

LEONARDO: I've just come from there. Would you believe it? For more than two months he's been putting new shoes on the horse and they're always coming off. As far as I can see he pulls them off on the stones.

WIFE: Couldn't it just be that you use him so much?

LEONARDO: No. I almost never use him.

WIFE: Yesterday the neighbours told me they'd seen you on the far side of the plains.

LEONARDO: Who said that?

WIFE: The women who gather capers. It certainly surprised me. Was it you?

LEONARDO: No. What would I be doing there, in that wasteland?

WIFE: That's what I said. But the horse was streaming sweat.

LEONARDO: Did you see him?

WIFE: No. Mother did.

LEONARDO: Is she with the baby?

WIFE: Yes. Do you want some lemonade?

LEONARDO: With good cold water.

WIFE: And then you didn't come to eat!

LEONARDO: I was with the wheat weighers. They always hold me up.

WIFE [*very tenderly, while she makes the lemonade*]: Did they pay you a good price?

LEONARDO: Fair.

WIFE: I need a new dress and the baby a bonnet with ribbons.

LEONARDO [*getting up*]: I'm going to take a look at him.

WIFE: Be careful. He's asleep.

MOTHER-IN-LAW [*coming in*]: Well! Who's been racing the horse that way? He's down there, worn out, his eyes popping from their sockets as though he'd come from the ends of the earth.

LEONARDO [*acidly*]: I have.

MOTHER-IN-LAW: Oh, excuse me! He's your horse.

WIFE [*timidly*]: He was at the wheat buyers.

MOTHER-IN-LAW: He can burst for all of me!

She sits down. Pause.

WIFE: Your drink. Is it cold?

LEONARDO: Yes.

WIFE: Did you hear they're going to ask for my cousin?

LEONARDO: When?

WIFE: Tomorrow. The wedding will be within a month. I hope they're going to invite us.

LEONARDO [*gravely*]: I don't know.

MOTHER-IN-LAW: His mother, I think, wasn't very happy about the match.

LEONARDO: Well, she may be right. She's a girl to be careful with.

WIFE: I don't like to have you thinking bad things about a good girl.

MOTHER-IN-LAW [*meaningfully*]: If he does, it's because he knows her. Didn't you know he courted her for three years?

LEONARDO: But I left her.

To his WIFE.

Are you going to cry now? Quit that! [*He brusquely pulls her hands away from her face.*] Let's go see the baby.

> *They go in with their arms around each other. A* GIRL *appears. She is happy. She enters running.*

GIRL: Señora.

MOTHER-IN-LAW: What is it?

GIRL: The groom came to the store and he's bought the best of everything they had.

MOTHER-IN-LAW: Was he alone?

GIRL: No. With his mother. Stern, tall. [*She imitates her.*] And such extravagance!

MOTHER-IN-LAW: They have money.

GIRL: And they bought some open-work stockings! Oh, such stockings! A woman's dream of stockings! Look: a swallow here [*she points to her ankle*], a ship here [*she points to her calf*], and here [*she points to her thigh*] a rose!

MOTHER-IN-LAW: Child!

GIRL: A rose with the seeds and the stem! Oh! All in silk.

MOTHER-IN-LAW: Two rich families are being brought together.

> LEONARDO *and his* WIFE *appear.*

GIRL: I came to tell you what they're buying.

LEONARDO [*loudly*]: We don't care.

WIFE: Leave her alone.

MOTHER-IN-LAW: Leonardo, it's not that important.

GIRL: Please excuse me. [*She leaves, weeping.*]

MOTHER-IN-LAW: Why do you always have to make trouble with people?

LEONARDO: I didn't ask for your opinion. [*He sits down.*]

MOTHER-IN-LAW: Very well.

> *Pause.*

WIFE [*to* LEONARDO]: What's the matter with you? What idea've you got boiling there inside your head? Don't leave me like this, not knowing anything.

LEONARDO: Stop that.

WIFE: No. I want you to look at me and tell me.

LEONARDO: Let me alone. [*He rises.*]

WIFE: Where are you going, love?

LEONARDO [*sharply*]: Can't you shut up?

MOTHER-IN-LAW [*energetically, to her daughter*]: Be quiet!

> LEONARDO *goes out.*

The baby!

> *She goes into the bedroom and comes out again with the baby in her arms. The* WIFE *has remained standing, unmoving.*

MOTHER-IN-LAW:

His poor hooves were bleeding,

his long mane was frozen,
and deep in his eyes
stuck a silvery dagger.
Down he went to the river,
Oh, down he went down!
And his blood was running,
Oh, more than the water.

WIFE [*turning slowly, as though dreaming*]:
Carnation, sleep and dream,
the horse is drinking from the stream.

MOTHER-IN-LAW:
My rose, asleep now lie
the horse is starting to cry.

WIFE:
Lullaby, my baby.

MOTHER-IN-LAW:
Ay-y-y, for the big horse
who didn't like water!

WIFE [*dramatically*]:
Don't come near, don't come in!
Go away to the mountains!
Ay-y-y, for the snow-wound,
big horse of the dawn!

MOTHER-IN-LAW [*weeping*]:
My baby is sleeping . . .

WIFE [*weeping, as she slowly moves closer*]:
My baby is resting . . .

MOTHER-IN-LAW:
Carnation, sleep and dream,
the horse won't drink from the stream.

WIFE [*weeping, and leaning on the table*]:
My rose, asleep now lie,
the horse is starting to cry.

SCENE 3

Interior of the cave where the BRIDE lives. At the back is a cross of large rose-coloured flowers. The round doors have lace curtains with rose-coloured ties. Around the walls, which are of a white and hard material, are round fans, blue jars, and little mirrors.

SERVANT: Come right in . . .

She is very affable, full of humble hypocrisy. The BRIDEGROOM *and his* MOTHER *enter. The* MOTHER *is dressed in black satin and wears a lace mantilla; The* BRIDEGROOM *in black corduroy with a great golden chain.*

Won't you sit down? They'll be right here.

She leaves. The MOTHER *and* SON *are left sitting motionless as statues. Long pause.*

MOTHER: Did you wear the watch?
BRIDEGROOM: Yes. [*He takes it out and looks at it.*]
MOTHER: We have to be back on time. How far away these people live!
BRIDEGROOM: But this is good land.
MOTHER: Good; but much too lonesome. A four-hour trip and not one house, not one tree.
BRIDEGROOM: This is the wasteland.
MOTHER: Your father would have covered it with trees.
BRIDEGROOM: Without water?
MOTHER: He would have found some. In the three years we were married he planted ten cherry trees, [*remembering*] those three walnut trees by the mill, a whole vineyard and a plant called Jupiter which had scarlet flowers–but it dried up.

Pause.

BRIDEGROOM [*referring to the* BRIDE]: She must be dressing.

The Bride's FATHER *enters. He is very old, with shining white hair. His head is bowed. The* MOTHER *and the* BRIDEGROOM *rise. They shake hands in silence.*

FATHER: Was it a long trip?
MOTHER: Four hours.

They sit down.

FATHER: You must have come the longest way.
MOTHER: I'm too old to come along the cliffs by the river.
BRIDEGROOM: She gets dizzy.

Pause.

FATHER: A good hemp harvest.
BRIDEGROOM: A really good one.
FATHER: When I was young this land didn't even grow hemp. We've had to punish it, even weep over it, to make it give us anything useful.
MOTHER: But now it does. Don't complain. I'm not here to ask you for anything.
FATHER [*smiling*]: You're richer than I. Your vineyards are worth a fortune. Each young vine a silver coin. But–do you know?–what bothers me is that our lands are separated. I like to have everything together. One thorn I have in my heart, and that's the little orchard there, stuck in between my fields–and they won't sell it to me for all the gold in the world.
BRIDEGROOM: That's the way it always is.
FATHER: If we could just take twenty teams of oxen and move your vineyards over here, and put them down on that hillside, how happy I'd be!
MOTHER: But why?
FATHER: What's mine is hers and what's yours is his. That's why. Just to see it all together. How beautiful it is to bring things together!
BRIDEGROOM: And it would be less work.
MOTHER: When I die, you could sell ours and buy here, right alongside.
FATHER: Sell, sell? Bah! Buy, my friend, buy everything. If I had had sons I

would have bought all this mountainside right up to the part with the stream. It's not good land, but strong arms can make it good, and since no people pass by, they don't steal your fruit and you can sleep in peace.

Pause.

MOTHER: You know what I'm here for.
FATHER: Yes.
MOTHER: And?
FATHER: It seems all right to me. They have talked it over.
MOTHER: My son has money and knows how to manage it.
FATHER: My daughter, too.
MOTHER: My son is handsome. He's never known a woman. His good name cleaner than a sheet spread out in the sun.
FATHER: No need to tell you about my daughter. At three, when the morning star shines, she prepares the bread. She never talks: soft as wool, she embroiders all kinds of fancy work and she can cut a strong cord with her teeth.
MOTHER: God bless her house.
FATHER: May God bless it.

The SERVANT *appears with two trays. One with drinks and the other with sweets.*

MOTHER [*to the* SON]: When would you like the wedding?
BRIDEGROOM: Next Thursday.
FATHER: The day on which she'll be exactly twenty-two years old.
MOTHER: Twenty-two! My eldest son would be that age if he were alive. Warm and manly as he was, he'd be living now if men hadn't invented knives.
FATHER: One mustn't think about that.
MOTHER: Every minute. Always a hand on your breast.
FATHER: Thursday, then? Is that right?
BRIDEGROOM: That's right.
FATHER: You and I and the bridal couple will go in a carriage to the church which is very far from here; the wedding party on the carts and horses they'll bring with them.
MOTHER: Agreed.

The SERVANT *passes through.*

FATHER: Tell her she may come in now. [*To the* MOTHER.] I shall be much pleased if you like her.

The BRIDE *appears. Her hands fall in a modest pose and her head is bowed.*

MOTHER: Come here. Are you happy?
BRIDE: Yes, señora.
FATHER: You shouldn't be so solemn. After all, she's going to be your mother.
BRIDE: I'm happy. I've said 'yes' because I wanted to.
MOTHER: Naturally. [*She takes her by the chin.*] Look at me.
FATHER: She resembles my wife in every way.

MOTHER: Yes? What a beautiful glance! Do you know what it is to be married, child?

BRIDE [*seriously*]: I do.

MOTHER: A man, some children and a wall two yards thick for everything else.

BRIDEGROOM: Is anything else needed?

MOTHER: No. Just that you all live—that's it! Live long!

BRIDE: I'll know how to keep my word.

MOTHER: Here are some gifts for you.

BRIDE: Thank you.

FATHER: Shall we have something?

MOTHER: Nothing for me. [*To the* SON.] But you?

BRIDEGROOM: Yes, thank you.

> *He takes one sweet, the* BRIDE *another.*

FATHER [*to the* BRIDEGROOM]: Wine?

MOTHER: He doesn't touch it.

FATHER: All the better.

> *Pause. All are standing.*

BRIDEGROOM [*to the* BRIDE]: I'll come tomorrow.

BRIDE: What time?

BRIDEGROOM: Five.

BRIDE: I'll be waiting for you.

BRIDEGROOM: When I leave your side I feel a great emptiness, and something like a knot in my throat.

BRIDE: When you are my husband you won't have it any more.

BRIDEGROOM: That's what I tell myself.

MOTHER: Come. The sun doesn't wait. [*To the* FATHER.] Are we agreed on everything?

FATHER: Agreed.

MOTHER [*to the* SERVANT]: Good-bye, woman.

SERVANT: God go with you!

> *The* MOTHER *kisses the* BRIDE *and they begin to leave in silence.*

MOTHER [*at the door*]: Good-bye, daughter.

> *The* BRIDE *answers with her hand.*

FATHER: I'll go out with you.

> *They leave.*

SERVANT: I'm bursting to see the presents.

BRIDE [*sharply*]: Stop that!

SERVANT: Oh, child, show them to me.

BRIDE: I don't want to.

SERVANT: At least the stockings. They say they're all open work. Please!

BRIDE: I said no.

SERVANT: Well, my Lord. All right then. It looks as if you didn't want to get married.

BRIDE [*biting her hand in anger*]: Ay-y-y!

SERVANT: Child, child! What's the matter with you? Are you sorry to give up your queen's life? Don't think of bitter things. Have you any reason to? None. Let's look at the presents. [*She takes the box.*]

BRIDE [*holding her by the wrists*]: Let go.

SERVANT: Ay-y-y, girl!

BRIDE: Let go, I said.

SERVANT: You're stronger than a man.

BRIDE: Haven't I done a man's work? I wish I were.

SERVANT: Don't talk like that.

BRIDE: Quiet, I said. Let's talk about something else.

The light is fading from the stage. Long pause.

SERVANT: Did you hear a horse last night?

BRIDE: What time?

SERVANT: Three.

BRIDE: It might have been a stray horse–from the herd.

SERVANT: No. It carried a rider.

BRIDE: How do you know?

SERVANT: Because I saw him. He was standing by your window. It shocked me greatly.

BRIDE: Maybe it was my fiancé. Sometimes he comes by at that time.

SERVANT: No.

BRIDE: You saw him?

SERVANT: Yes.

BRIDE: Who was it?

SERVANT: It was Leonardo.

BRIDE [*strongly*]: Liar! You liar! Why should he come here?

SERVANT: He came.

BRIDE: Shut up! Shut your cursed mouth.

The sound of a horse is heard.

SERVANT [*at the window*]: Look. Lean out. Was it Leonardo?

BRIDE: It was!

QUICK CURTAIN

ACT TWO

SCENE I

The entrance hall of the BRIDE's house. A large door in the back. It is night. The BRIDE enters wearing ruffled white petticoats full of laces and embroidered bands, and a sleeveless white bodice. The SERVANT is dressed the same way.

SERVANT: I'll finish combing your hair out here.
BRIDE: It's too warm to stay in there.
SERVANT: In this country it doesn't even cool off at dawn.

> *The* BRIDE *sits on a low chair and looks into a little hand mirror. The* SERVANT *combs her hair.*

BRIDE: My mother came from a place with lots of trees—from a fertile country.
SERVANT: And she was so happy!
BRIDE: But she wasted away here.
SERVANT: Fate.
BRIDE: As we're all wasting away here. The very walls give off heat. Ay-y-y! Don't pull so hard.
SERVANT: I'm only trying to fix this wave better. I want it to fall over your forehead.

> *The* BRIDE *looks at herself in the mirror.*

How beautiful you are! Ay-y-y! [*She kisses her passionately.*]
BRIDE [*seriously*]: Keep right on combing.
SERVANT [*combing*]: Oh, lucky you—going to put your arms around a man; and kiss him; and feel his weight.
BRIDE: Hush.
SERVANT: And the best part will be when you'll wake up and you'll feel him at your side and when he caresses your shoulders with his breath, like a little nightingale's feather!
BRIDE [*sternly*]: Will you be quiet.
SERVANT: But, child! What *is* a wedding? A wedding is just that and nothing more. Is it the sweets—or the bouquets of flowers? No. It's a shining bed and a man and a woman.
BRIDE: But you shouldn't talk about it.
SERVANT: Oh, *that's* something else again. But fun enough too.
BRIDE: Or bitter enough.
SERVANT: I'm going to put the orange blossoms on from here to here, so the wreath will shine out on top of your hair. [*She tries on the sprigs of orange blossom.*]

BRIDE [*looking at herself in the mirror*]: Give it to me. [*She takes the wreath, looks at it and lets her head fall in discouragement.*]

SERVANT: Now what's the matter?

BRIDE: Leave me alone.

SERVANT: This is no time for you to start feeling sad. [*Encouragingly.*] Give me the wreath.

The BRIDE *takes the wreath and hurls it away.*

Child! You're just asking God to punish you, throwing the wreath on the floor like that. Raise your head! Don't you want to get married? Say it. You can still withdraw.

The BRIDE *rises.*

BRIDE: Storm clouds. A chill wind that cuts through my heart. Who hasn't felt it?

SERVANT: You love your sweetheart, don't you?

BRIDE: I love him.

SERVANT: Yes, yes. I'm sure you do.

BRIDE: But this is a very serious step.

SERVANT: You've got to take it.

BRIDE: I've already given my word.

SERVANT: I'll put on the wreath.

BRIDE [*she sits down*]: Hurry. They should be arriving by now.

SERVANT: They've already been at least two hours on the way.

BRIDE: How far is it from here to the church?

SERVANT: Five leagues by the stream, but twice that by the road.

The BRIDE *rises and the* SERVANT *grows excited as she looks at her.*

SERVANT:

> Awake, O Bride, awaken,
> On your wedding morning waken!
> The world's rivers may all
> Bear along your bridal Crown!

BRIDE [*smiling*]: Come now.

SERVANT [*enthusiastically kissing her and dancing around her*]:

> Awake,
> with the fresh bouquet
> of flowering laurel.
> Awake,
> by the trunk and branch
> of the laurels!

The banging of the front door latch is heard.

BRIDE: Open the door! That must be the first guests.

She leaves. The SERVANT *opens the door.*

SERVANT [*in astonishment*]: You!
LEONARDO: Yes, me. Good morning.
SERVANT: The first one!
LEONARDO: Wasn't I invited?
SERVANT: Yes.
LEONARDO: That's why I'm here.
SERVANT: Where's your wife?
LEONARDO: I came on my horse. She's coming by the road.
SERVANT: Didn't you meet anyone?
LEONARDO: I *passed* them on my horse.
SERVANT: You're going to kill that horse with so much racing.
LEONARDO: When he dies, he's dead!

Pause.

SERVANT: Sit down. Nobody's up yet.
LEONARDO: Where's the bride?
SERVANT: I'm just on my way to dress her.
LEONARDO: The bride! She ought to be happy!
SERVANT [*changing the subject*]: How's the baby?
LEONARDO: What baby?
SERVANT: Your son.
LEONARDO [*remembering, as though in a dream*]: Ah!
SERVANT: Are they bringing him?
LEONARDO: No.

Pause. VOICES *sing distantly.*

VOICES:

> Awake, O Bride, awaken,
> On your wedding morning waken!

LEONARDO:

> Awake, O Bride, awaken,
> On your wedding morning waken!

SERVANT: It's the guests. They're still quite a way off.
LEONARDO: The bride's going to wear a big wreath, isn't she? But it ought not to be so large. One a little smaller would look better on her. Has the groom already brought her the orange blossom that must be worn on the breast?
BRIDE [*appearing, still in petticoats and wearing the wreath*]: He brought it.
SERVANT [*sternly*]: Don't come out like that.
BRIDE: What does it matter? [*Seriously.*] Why do you ask if they brought the orange blossom? Do you have something in mind?
LEONARDO: Nothing. What would I have in mind? [*Drawing near her.*] You, you know me; you know I don't. Tell me so. What have I ever meant to you? Open your memory, refresh it. But two oxen and an ugly little hut are almost nothing. That's the thorn.
BRIDE: What have you come here to do?
LEONARDO: To see your wedding.
BRIDE: Just as I saw yours!
LEONARDO: Tied up by you, done with your two hands. Oh, they can kill me but

they can't spit on me. But even money, which shines so much, spits sometimes.

BRIDE: Liar!

LEONARDO: I don't want to talk. I'm hot-blooded and I don't want to shout so all these hills will hear me.

BRIDE: My shouts would be louder.

SERVANT: You'll have to stop talking like this. [*To the* BRIDE.] You don't have to talk about what's past. [*The* SERVANT *looks around uneasily at the doors.*]

BRIDE: She's right. I shouldn't even talk to you. But it offends me to the soul that you come here to watch me, and spy on my wedding, and ask about the orange blossom with something on your mind. Go and wait for your wife at the door.

LEONARDO: But, can't you and I even talk?

SERVANT [*with rage*]: No. No, you can't talk.

LEONARDO: Ever since I got married I've been thinking night and day about whose fault it was, and every time I think about it, out comes a new fault to eat up the old one; but always there's a fault left.

BRIDE: A man with a horse knows a lot of things and can do a lot to ride roughshod over a girl stuck out in the desert. But I have my pride. And that's why I'm getting married. I'll lock myself in with my husband and then I'll have to love him above everyone else.

LEONARDO: Pride won't help you a bit. [*He draws near to her.*]

BRIDE: Don't come near me!

LEONARDO: To burn with desire and keep quiet about it is the greatest punishment we can bring on ourselves. What good was pride to me—and not seeing you, and letting you lie awake night after night? No good! It only served to bring the fire down on me! You think that time heals and walls hide things, but it isn't true, it isn't true! When things get that deep inside you there isn't anybody can change them.

BRIDE [*trembling*]: I can't listen to you. I can't listen to your voice. It's as though I'd drunk a bottle of anise and fallen asleep wrapped in a quilt of roses. It pulls me along, and I know I'm drowning—but I go on down.

SERVANT [*seizing* LEONARDO *by the lapels*]: You've got to go right now!

LEONARDO: This is the last time I'll ever talk to her. Don't you be afraid of anything.

BRIDE: And I know I'm crazy and I know my breast rots with longing; but here I am—calmed by hearing him, by just seeing him move his arms.

LEONARDO: I'd never be at peace if I didn't tell you these things. I got married. Now you get married.

SERVANT: But she *is* getting married!

VOICES *are heard singing, nearer.*

VOICES:
> Awake, O Bride, awaken,
> On your wedding morning waken!

BRIDE:
> Awake, O Bride, awaken. [*She goes out, running toward her room.*]

SERVANT: The people are here now. [*To* LEONARDO.] Don't you come near her again.

LEONARDO: Don't worry.

He goes out to the left. Day begins to break.

FIRST GIRL [*entering*]:
> Awake, O Bride, awaken,
> the morning you're to marry;
> sing round and dance round;
> balconies a wreath must carry.

VOICES:
> Bride, awaken!

SERVANT [*creating enthusiasm*]:
> Awake,
> with the green bouquet
> of love in flower.
> Awake,
> by the trunk and the branch
> of the laurels!

SECOND GIRL [*entering*]:
> Awake,
> with her long hair,
> snowy sleeping gown,
> patent leather boots with silver—
> her forehead jasmines crown.

SERVANT:
> Oh, shepherdess,
> the moon begins to shine!

FIRST GIRL:
> Oh, gallant,
> leave your hat beneath the vine!

FIRST YOUNG MAN [*entering, holding his hat on high*]:
> Bride, awaken,
> for over the fields
> the wedding draws nigh
> with trays heaped with dahlias
> and cakes piled high.

VOICES:
> Bride, awaken!

SECOND GIRL:
> The bride
> has set her white wreath in place
> and the groom
> ties it on with a golden lace.

SERVANT:
> By the orange tree,
> sleepless the bride will be.

THIRD GIRL [*entering*]:
> By the citron vine,
> gifts from the groom will shine.

Three GUESTS *come in.*

FIRST YOUTH:
> Dove, awaken!
> In the dawn
> shadowy bells are shaken.

GUEST:
> The bride, the white bride
> today a maiden,
> tomorrow a wife.

FIRST GIRL:
> Dark one, come down
> trailing the train of your silken gown.

GUEST:
> Little dark one, come down,
> cold morning wears a dewy crown.

FIRST GUEST:
> Awaken, wife, awake,
> orange blossoms the breezes shake.

SERVANT:
> A tree I would embroider her
> with garnet sashes wound,
> And on each sash a cupid,
> with 'Long Live' all around.

VOICES:
> Bride, awaken.

FIRST YOUTH:
> The morning you're to marry!

GUEST:
> The morning you're to marry
> how elegant you'll seem;
> worthy, mountain flower,
> of a captain's dream.

FATHER [*entering*]:
> A captain's wife
> the groom will marry.
> He comes with his oxen the treasure to carry!

THIRD GIRL:
> The groom
> is like a flower of gold.
> When he walks,
> blossoms at his feet unfold.

SERVANT:
> Oh, my lucky girl!

SECOND YOUTH:
> Bride, awaken.

SERVANT:
> Oh, my elegant girl!

FIRST GIRL:
> Through the windows
> hear the wedding shout.

SECOND GIRL:
> Let the bride come out.

FIRST GIRL:
                    Come out, come out!
SERVANT:
                    Let the bells
                    ring and ring out clear!
FIRST YOUTH:
                    For here she comes!
                    For now she's near!
SERVANT:
                    Like a bull, the wedding
                    is arising here!

The BRIDE *appears. She wears a black dress in the style of 1900, with a bustle
and large train covered with pleated gauzes and heavy laces. Upon her hair,
brushed in a wave over her forehead, she wears an orange blossom wreath.
Guitars sound. The* GIRLS *kiss the* BRIDE.

THIRD GIRL: What scent did you put on your hair?
BRIDE [*laughing*]: None at all.
SECOND GIRL [*looking at her dress*]: This cloth is what you can't get.
FIRST YOUTH: Here's the groom!
BRIDEGROOM: Salud!
FIRST GIRL [*putting a flower behind his ear*]:
                    The groom
                    is like a flower of gold.
SECOND GIRL:
                    Quiet breezes
                    from his eyes unfold.

The GROOM *goes to the* BRIDE.

BRIDE: Why did you put on those shoes?
BRIDEGROOM: They're gayer than the black ones.
LEONARDO'S WIFE [*entering and kissing the* BRIDE]: Salud!

They all speak excitedly.

LEONARDO [*entering as one who performs a duty*]:
                    The morning you're to marry
                    We give you a wreath to wear.
LEONARDO'S WIFE:
                    So the fields may be made happy
                    with the dew dropped from your hair!
MOTHER [*to the* FATHER]: Are those people here, too?
FATHER: They're part of the family. Today is a day of forgiveness!
MOTHER: I'll put up with it, but I don't forgive.
BRIDEGROOM: With your wreath, it's a joy to look at you!
BRIDE: Let's go to the church quickly.
BRIDEGROOM: Are you in a hurry?
BRIDE: Yes. I want to be your wife right now so that I can be with you alone, not
    hearing any voice but yours.

BRIDEGROOM: That's what I want!

BRIDE: And not seeing any eyes but yours. And for you to hug me so hard, that even though my dead mother should call me, I wouldn't be able to draw away from you.

BRIDEGROOM: My arms are strong. I'll hug you for forty years without stopping.

BRIDE [*taking his arm, dramatically*]: For ever!

FATHER: Quick now! Round up the teams and carts! The sun's already out.

MOTHER: And go along carefully! Let's hope nothing goes wrong.

The great door in the background opens.

SERVANT [*weeping*]:
>   As you set out from your house,
>   oh, maiden white,
>   remember you leave shining
>   with a star's light.

FIRST GIRL:
>   Clean of body, clean of clothes
>   from her home to church she goes.

They start leaving.

SECOND GIRL:
>   Now you leave your home
>   for the church!

SERVANT:
>   The wind sets flowers
>   on the sands.

THIRD GIRL:
>   Ah, the white maid!

SERVANT:
>   Dark winds are the lace
>   of her mantilla.

They leave. Guitars, castanets and tambourines are heard. LEONARDO *and his* WIFE *are left alone.*

WIFE: Let's go.

LEONARDO: Where?

WIFE: To the church. But not on your horse. You're coming with me.

LEONARDO: In the cart?

WIFE: Is there anything else?

LEONARDO: I'm not the kind of man to ride in a cart.

WIFE: Nor I the wife to go to a wedding without her husband. I can't stand any more of this!

LEONARDO: Neither can I!

WIFE: And why do you look at me that way? With a thorn in each eye.

LEONARDO: Let's go!

WIFE: I don't know what's happening. But I think, and I don't want to think. One thing I do know. I'm already cast off by you. But I have a son. And another coming. And so it goes. My mother's fate was the same. Well, I'm not moving from here.

VOICES *outside*.

VOICES:
>   As you set out from your home
>   and to the church go
>   remember you leave shining
>   with a star's glow.

WIFE [*weeping*]:
>   Remember you leave shining
>   with a star's glow.

I left my house like that too. They could have stuffed the whole countryside in my mouth. I was that trusting.

LEONARDO [*rising*]: Let's go!

WIFE: But you with me!

LEONARDO: Yes. [*Pause.*] Start moving!

They leave.

VOICES:
>   As you set out from your home
>   and to the church go,
>   remember you leave shining
>   with a star's glow.

SCENE 2

The exterior of the BRIDE's Cave Home, in white, grey and cold blue tones. Large cactus trees. Shadowy and silver tones. Panoramas of light tan tablelands, everything hard like a landscape in popular ceramics.

SERVANT [*arranging glasses and trays on a table*]:
>   A-turning,
>   the wheel was a-turning
>   and the water was flowing,
>   for the wedding night comes.
>   May the branches part
>   and the moon be arrayed
>   at her white balcony rail.

[*In a loud voice.*] Set out the tablecloths!

[*In a pathetic voice.*]
>   A-singing,
>   bride and groom were singing
>   and the water was flowing
>   for their wedding night comes.
>   Oh, rime-frost, flash!—
>   and almonds bitter
>   fill with honey!

[*In a loud voice.*] Get the wine ready!

[*In a poetic tone.*]

Elegant girl,
most elegant in the world,
see the way the water is flowing,
for your wedding night comes.
Hold your skirts close in
under the bridegroom's wing
and never leave your house,
for the bridegroom is a dove
with his breast a firebrand
and the fields wait for the whisper
of spurting blood.
A-turning
the wheel was a-turning
and the water was flowing
and your wedding night comes.
Oh, water, sparkle!

MOTHER [*entering*]: At last!

FATHER: Are we the first ones?

SERVANT: No. Leonardo and his wife arrived a while ago. They drove like demons. His wife got here dead with fright. They made the trip as though they'd come on horseback.

FATHER: That one's looking for trouble. He's not of good blood.

MOTHER: What blood would you expect him to have? His whole family's blood. It comes down from his great grandfather, who started in killing, and it goes on down through the whole evil breed of knife wielding and false smiling men.

FATHER: Let's leave it at that!

SERVANT: But how can she leave it at that?

MOTHER: It hurts me to the tips of my veins. On the forehead of all of them I see only the hand with which they killed what was mine. Can you really see me? Don't I seem mad to you? Well, it's the madness of not having shrieked out all my breast needs to. Always in my breast there's a shriek standing tiptoe that I have to beat down and hold in under my shawl. But the dead are carried off and one has to keep still. And then, people find fault. [*She removes her shawl.*]

FATHER: Today's not the day for you to be remembering these things.

MOTHER: When the talk turns on it, I have to speak. And more so today. Because today I'm left alone in my house.

FATHER: But with the expectation of having someone with you.

MOTHER: That's my hope: grandchildren.

They sit down.

FATHER: I want them to have a lot of them. This land needs hands that aren't hired. There's a battle to be waged against weeds, the thistles, the big rocks that come from one doesn't know where. And those hands have to be the owner's, who chastises and dominates, who makes the seeds grow. Lots of sons are needed.

MOTHER: And some daughters! Men are like the wind! They're forced to handle weapons. Girls never go out into the street.

FATHER [*happily*]: I think they'll have both.

MOTHER: My son will cover her well. He's of good seed. His father could have had many sons with me.

FATHER: What I'd like is to have all this happen in a day. So that right away they'd have two or three boys.

MOTHER: But it's not like that. It takes a long time. That's why it's so terrible to see one's own blood spilled out on the ground. A fountain that spurts for a minute, but costs us years. When I got to my son, he lay fallen in the middle of the street. I wet my hands with his blood and licked them with my tongue—because it was my blood. You don't know what that's like. In a glass and topaz' shrine I'd put the earth moistened by his blood.

FATHER: Now you must hope. My daughter is wide-hipped and your son is strong.

MOTHER: That's why I'm hoping.

They rise.

FATHER: Get the wheat trays ready!

SERVANT: They're all ready.

LEONARDO'S WIFE [*entering*]: May it be for the best!

MOTHER: Thank you.

LEONARDO: Is there going to be a celebration?

FATHER: A small one. People can't stay long.

SERVANT: Here they are!

Guests begin entering in gay groups. The BRIDE *and* GROOM *come in arm-in-arm.* LEONARDO *leaves.*

BRIDEGROOM: There's never been a wedding with so many people!

BRIDE [*sullen*]: Never.

FATHER: It was brilliant.

MOTHER: Whole branches of families came.

BRIDEGROOM: People who never went out of the house.

MOTHER: Your father sowed well, and now you're reaping it.

BRIDEGROOM: There were cousins of mine whom I no longer knew.

MOTHER: All the people from the seacoast.

BRIDEGROOM [*happily*]: They were frightened of the horses.

They talk.

MOTHER [*to the* BRIDE]: What are you thinking about?

BRIDE: I'm not thinking about anything.

MOTHER: Your blessings weigh heavily.

Guitars are heard.

BRIDE: Like lead.

MOTHER [*stern*]: But they shouldn't weigh so. Happy as a dove you ought to be.

BRIDE: Are you staying here tonight?

MOTHER: No. My house is empty.

BRIDE: You ought to stay!

FATHER [*to the* MOTHER]: Look at the dance they're forming. Dances of the faraway seashore.

LEONARDO *enters and sits down. His* WIFE *stands rigidly behind him.*

MOTHER: They're my husband's cousins. Stiff as stones at dancing.
FATHER: It makes me happy to watch them. What a change for this house! [*He leaves.*]
BRIDEGROOM [*to the* BRIDE]: Did you like the orange blossom?
BRIDE [*looking at him fixedly*]: Yes.
BRIDEGROOM: It's all of wax. It will last for ever. I'd like you to have had them all over your dress.
BRIDE: No need of that.

LEONARDO *goes off to the right.*

FIRST GIRL: Let's go and take out your pins.
BRIDE [*to the* GROOM]: I'll be right back.
LEONARDO'S WIFE: I hope you'll be happy with my cousin!
BRIDEGROOM: I'm sure I will.
LEONARDO'S WIFE: The two of you here; never going out; building a home. I wish I could live far away like this, too!
BRIDEGROOM: Why don't you buy land? The mountainside is cheap and children grow up better.
LEONARDO'S WIFE: We don't have any money. And at the rate we're going . . .!
BRIDEGROOM: Your husband is a good worker.
LEONARDO'S WIFE: Yes, but he likes to fly around too much; from one thing to another. He's not a patient man.
SERVANT: Aren't you having anything? I'm going to wrap up some wine cakes for your mother. She likes them so much.
BRIDEGROOM: Put up three dozen for her.
LEONARDO'S WIFE: No, no. A half-dozen's enough for her!
BRIDEGROOM: But today's a day!
LEONARDO'S WIFE [*to the* SERVANT]: Where's Leonardo?
BRIDEGROOM: He must be with the guests.
LEONARDO'S WIFE: I'm going to go see. [*She leaves.*]
SERVANT [*looking off at the dance*]: That's beautiful there.
BRIDEGROOM: Aren't you dancing?
SERVANT: No one will ask me.

Two GIRLS *pass across the back of the stage; during this whole scene the background should be an animated crossing of figures.*

BRIDEGROOM [*happily*]: They just don't know anything. Lively old girls like you dance better than the young ones.
SERVANT: Well! Are you tossing me a compliment, boy? What a family yours is! Men among men! As a little girl I saw your grandfather's wedding. What a figure! It seemed as if a mountain were getting married.
BRIDEGROOM: I'm not as tall.
SERVANT: But there's the same twinkle in your eye. Where's the girl?
BRIDEGROOM: Taking off her wreath.
SERVANT: Ah! Look. For midnight, since you won't be sleeping, I have prepared ham for you, and some large glasses of old wine. On the lower shelf of the cupboard. In case you need it.

BRIDEGROOM [*smiling*]: I won't be eating at midnight.
SERVANT [*slyly*]: If not you, maybe the bride. [*She leaves.*]
FIRST YOUTH [*entering*]: You've got to come have a drink with us!
BRIDEGROOM: I'm waiting for the bride.
SECOND YOUTH: You'll have her at dawn!
FIRST YOUTH: That's when it's best!
SECOND YOUTH: Just for a minute.
BRIDEGROOM: Let's go.

> *They leave. Great excitement is heard. The* BRIDE *enters. From the opposite side two* GIRLS *come running to meet her.*

FIRST GIRL: To whom did you give the first pin; me or this one?
BRIDE: I don't remember.
FIRST GIRL: To me, you gave it to me here.
SECOND GIRL: To me, in front of the altar.
BRIDE [*uneasily, with a great inner struggle*]: I don't know anything about it.
FIRST GIRL: It's just that I wish you'd . . .
BRIDE [*interrupting*]: Nor do I care. I have a lot to think about.
SECOND GIRL: Your pardon.

> LEONARDO *crosses at the rear of the stage.*

BRIDE [*she sees* LEONARDO]: And this is an upsetting time.
FIRST GIRL: We wouldn't know anything about that!
BRIDE: You'll know about it when your time comes. This step is a very hard one to take.
FIRST GIRL: Has she offended you?
BRIDE: No. You must pardon me.
SECOND GIRL: What for? But *both* the pins are good for getting married, aren't they?
BRIDE: Both of them.
FIRST GIRL: Maybe now one will get married before the other.
BRIDE: Are you so eager?
SECOND GIRL [*shyly*]: Yes.
BRIDE: Why?
FIRST GIRL: Well . . .

> *She embraces the* SECOND GIRL. *Both go running off. The* GROOM *comes in very slowly and embraces the* BRIDE *from behind.*

BRIDE [*in sudden fright*]: Let go of me!
BRIDEGROOM: Are you frightened of me?
BRIDE: Ay-y-y! It's you?
BRIDEGROOM: Who else would it be?

> *Pause.*

Your father or me.
BRIDE: That's true!
BRIDEGROOM: Of course, your father would have hugged you more gently.

BRIDE [*darkly*]: Of course!

BRIDEGROOM [*embracing her strongly and a little bit brusquely*]: Because he's old.

BRIDE [*curtly*]: Let me go!

BRIDEGROOM: Why? [*He lets her go.*]

BRIDE: Well . . . the people. They can see us.

> *The* SERVANT *crosses at the back of the stage again without looking at the* BRIDE *and* BRIDEGROOM.

BRIDEGROOM: What of it? It's consecrated now.

BRIDE: Yes, but let me be . . . Later.

BRIDEGROOM: What's the matter with you? You look frightened!

BRIDE: I'm all right. Don't go.

> LEONARDO'S WIFE *enters.*

LEONARDO'S WIFE: I don't mean to intrude . . .

BRIDEGROOM: What is it?

LEONARDO'S WIFE: Did my husband come through here?

BRIDEGROOM: No.

LEONARDO'S WIFE: Because I can't find him, and his horse isn't in the stable either.

BRIDEGROOM [*happily*]: He must be out racing it.

> *The* WIFE *leaves, troubled. The* SERVANT *enters.*

SERVANT: Aren't you two proud and happy with so many good wishes?

BRIDEGROOM: I wish it were over with. The bride is a little tired.

SERVANT: That's no way to act, child.

BRIDE: It's as though I'd been struck on the head.

SERVANT: A bride from these mountains must be strong. [*To the* GROOM.] You're the only one who can cure her, because she's yours. [*She goes running off.*]

BRIDEGROOM [*embracing the* BRIDE]: Let's go dance a little. [*He kisses her.*]

BRIDE [*worried*]: No. I'd like to stretch out on my bed a little.

BRIDEGROOM: I'll keep you company.

BRIDE: Never! With all these people here? What would they say? Let me be quiet for a moment.

BRIDEGROOM: Whatever you say! But don't be like that tonight!

BRIDE [*at the door*]: I'll be better tonight.

BRIDEGROOM: That's what I want.

> *The* MOTHER *appears.*

MOTHER: Son.

BRIDEGROOM: Where've you been?

MOTHER: Out there—in all that noise. Are you happy?

BRIDEGROOM: Yes.

MOTHER: Where's your wife?

BRIDEGROOM: Resting a little. It's a bad day for brides!

MOTHER: A bad day? The only good one. To me it was like coming into my own.

The SERVANT *enters and goes toward the* BRIDE's *room.*

Like the breaking of new ground; the planting of new trees.
BRIDEGROOM: Are you going to leave?
MOTHER: Yes, I ought to be at home.
BRIDEGROOM: Alone.
MOTHER: Not alone. For my head is full of things: of men, and fights.
BRIDEGROOM: But now the fights are no longer fights.

The SERVANT *enters quickly; she disappears at the rear of the stage, running.*

MOTHER: While you live, you have to fight.
BRIDEGROOM: I'll always obey you!
MOTHER: Try to be loving with your wife, and if you see she's acting foolish or
    touchy, caress her in a way that will hurt her a little: a strong hug, a bite, and
    then a soft kiss. Not so she'll be angry, but just so she'll feel you're the man, the
    boss, the one who gives orders. I learned that from your father. And since you
    don't have him, I have to be the one to tell you about these strong defences.
BRIDEGROOM: I'll always do as you say.
FATHER [*entering*]: Where's my daughter?
BRIDEGROOM: She's inside.

The FATHER *goes to look for her.*

FIRST GIRL: Get the bride and groom! We're going to dance a round!
FIRST YOUTH [*to the* BRIDEGROOM]: You're going to lead it.
FATHER [*entering*]: She's not there.
BRIDEGROOM: No?
FATHER: She must have gone up to the railing.
BRIDEGROOM: I'll go see!

He leaves. A hubbub of excitement and guitars is heard.

FIRST GIRL: They've started it already! [*She leaves.*]
BRIDEGROOM [*entering*]: She isn't there.
MOTHER [*uneasily*]: Isn't she?
FATHER: But where could she have gone?
SERVANT [*entering*]: But where's the girl, where is she?
MOTHER [*seriously*]: That we don't know.

The BRIDEGROOM *leaves. Three* GUESTS *enter.*

FATHER [*dramatically*]: But, isn't she in the dance?
SERVANT: She's not in the dance.
FATHER [*with a start*]: There are a lot of people. Go look!
SERVANT: I've already looked.
FATHER [*tragically*]: Then where is she?
BRIDEGROOM [*entering*]: Nowhere. Not anywhere.
MOTHER [*to the* FATHER]: What does this mean? Where is your daughter?

LEONARDO'S WIFE *enters.*

LEONARDO'S WIFE: They've run away! They've run away! She and Leonardo. On the horse. With their arms around each other, they rode off like a shooting star!

FATHER: That's not true! Not my daughter!

MOTHER: Yes, your daughter! Spawn of a wicked mother, and he, he too. But now she's my son's wife!

BRIDEGROOM [*entering*]: Let's go after them! Who has a horse?

MOTHER: Who has a horse? Right away! Who has a horse? I'll give him all I have—my eyes, my tongue even . . .

VOICE: Here's one.

MOTHER [*to the* SON]: Go! After them!

He leaves with two young men.

No. Don't go. Those people kill quickly and well . . . but yes, run, and I'll follow!

FATHER: It couldn't be my daughter. Perhaps she's thrown herself in the well.

MOTHER: Decent women throw themselves in water; not that one! But now she's my son's wife. Two groups. There are two groups here.

They all enter.

My family and yours. Everyone set out from here. Shake the dust from your heels! We'll go help my son.

The people separate into two groups.

For he has his family: his cousins from the sea, and all who came from inland. Out of here! On all roads. The hour of blood has come again. Two groups! You with yours and I with mine. After them! After them!

CURTAIN

ACT THREE

SCENE I

A forest. It is night-time. Great moist tree trunks. A dark atmosphere. Two violins are heard. Three WOODCUTTERS *enter*.

FIRST WOODCUTTER: And have they found them?
SECOND WOODCUTTER: No. But they're looking for them everywhere.
THIRD WOODCUTTER: They'll find them.
SECOND WOODCUTTER: Sh-h-h!
THIRD WOODCUTTER: What?
SECOND WOODCUTTER: They seem to be coming closer on all the roads at once.
FIRST WOODCUTTER: When the moon comes out they'll see them.
SECOND WOODCUTTER: They ought to let them go.
FIRST WOODCUTTER: The world is wide. Everybody can live in it.
THIRD WOODCUTTER: But they'll kill them.
SECOND WOODCUTTER: You have to follow your passion. They did right to run away.
FIRST WOODCUTTER: They were deceiving themselves but at the last blood was stronger.
THIRD WOODCUTTER: Blood!
FIRST WOODCUTTER: You have to follow the path of your blood.
SECOND WOODCUTTER: But blood that sees the light of day is drunk up by the earth.
FIRST WOODCUTTER: What of it? Better dead with the blood drained away than alive with it rotting.
THIRD WOODCUTTER: Hush!
FIRST WOODCUTTER: What? Do you hear something?
THIRD WOODCUTTER: I hear the crickets, the frogs, the night's ambush.
FIRST WOODCUTTER: But not the horse.
THIRD WOODCUTTER: No.
FIRST WOODCUTTER: By now he must be loving her.
SECOND WOODCUTTER: Her body for him; his body for her.
THIRD WOODCUTTER: They'll find them and they'll kill them.
FIRST WOODCUTTER: But by then they'll have mingled their bloods. They'll be like two empty jars, like two dry arroyos.
SECOND WOODCUTTER: There are many clouds and it would be easy for the moon not to come out.
THIRD WOODCUTTER: The bridegroom will find them with or without the moon. I saw him set out. Like a raging star. His face the colour of ashes. He looked the fate of all his clan.
FIRST WOODCUTTER: His clan of dead men lying in the middle of the street.
SECOND WOODCUTTER: There you have it!

THIRD WOODCUTTER: You think they'll be able to break through the circle?
SECOND WOODCUTTER: It's hard to. There are knives and guns for ten leagues
'round.
THIRD WOODCUTTER: He's riding a good horse.
SECOND WOODCUTTER: But he's carrying a woman.
FIRST WOODCUTTER: We're close by now.
SECOND WOODCUTTER: A tree with forty branches. We'll soon cut it down.
THIRD WOODCUTTER: The moon's coming out now. Let's hurry.

From the left shines a brightness.

FIRST WOODCUTTER:

               O rising moon!
               Moon among the great leaves.

SECOND WOODCUTTER:

               Cover the blood with jasmines!

FIRST WOODCUTTER:

               O lonely moon!
               Moon among the great leaves.

SECOND WOODCUTTER:

               Silver on the bride's face.

THIRD WOODCUTTER:

               O evil moon!
               Leave for their love a branch in shadow.

FIRST WOODCUTTER:

               O sorrowing moon!
               Leave for their love a branch in shadow.

They go out. The MOON *appears through a shining brightness at the left. The*
MOON *is a young woodcutter with a white face. The stage takes on an intense*
blue radiance.

MOON:

               Round swan in the river
               and a cathedral's eye,
               false dawn on the leaves,
               they'll not escape; these things am I!
               Who is hiding? And who sobs
               in the thornbrakes of the valley?
               The moon sets a knife
               abandoned in the air
               which being a leaden threat
               yearns to be blood's pain.
               Let me in! I come freezing
               down to walls and windows!
               Open roofs, open breasts
               where I may warm myself!
               I'm cold! My ashes
               of somnolent metals
               seek the fire's crest
               on mountains and streets.

But the snow carries me
upon its mottled back
and pools soak me
in their water, hard and cold.
But this night there will be
red blood for my cheeks,
and for the reeds that cluster
at the wide feet of the wind.
Let there be neither shadow nor bower,
and then they can't get away!
O let me enter a breast
where I may get warm!
A heart for me!
Warm! That will spurt
over the mountains of my chest;
let me come in, oh let me!

[*To the branches.*]

I want no shadows. My rays
must get in everywhere,
even among the dark trunks I want
the whisper of gleaming lights,
so that this night there will be
sweet blood for my cheeks,
and for the needs that cluster
at the wide feet of the wind.
Who is hiding? Out, I say!
No! They will not get away!
I will light up the horse
with a fever bright as diamonds.

*He disappears among the trunks, and the stage goes back to its dark lighting.
An* OLD WOMAN *comes out completely covered by thin green cloth. She is
barefooted. Her face can barely be seen among the folds. This character does
not appear in the cast.*

BEGGAR WOMAN:

That moon's going away, just when they's near.
They won't get past here. The river's whisper
and the whispering tree trunks will muffle
the torn flight of their shrieks.
It has to be here, and soon. I'm worn out.
The coffins are ready, and white sheets
wait on the floor of the bedroom
for heavy bodies with torn throats.
Let not one bird awake, let the breeze,
gathering their moans in her skirt,
fly with them over black tree tops
or bury them in soft mud.

[*Impatiently.*]

Oh, that moon! That moon!

The MOON *appears. The intense blue light returns.*

MOON: They're coming. One band through the ravine and the other along the river. I'm going to light up the boulders. What do you need?

BEGGAR WOMAN: Nothing.

MOON: The wind blows hard now, with a double edge.

BEGGAR WOMAN: Light up the waistcoat and open the buttons; the knives will know the path after that.

MOON:
> But let them be a long time a-dying. So the blood
> will slide its delicate hissing between my fingers.
> Look how my ashen valleys already are waking
> in longing for this fountain of shuddering gushes!

BEGGAR WOMAN: Let's not let them get past the arroyo. Silence!

MOON: There they come!

He goes. The stage is left dark.

BEGGAR WOMAN: Quick! Lots of light! Do you hear me? They can't get away!

The BRIDEGROOM *and the* FIRST YOUTH *enter. The* BEGGAR WOMAN *sits down and covers herself with her cloak.*

BRIDEGROOM: This way.

FIRST YOUTH: You won't find them.

BRIDEGROOM [*angrily*]: Yes, I'll find them.

FIRST YOUTH: I think they've taken another path.

BRIDEGROOM: No. Just a moment ago I felt the galloping.

FIRST YOUTH: It could have been another horse.

BRIDEGROOM [*intensely*]: Listen to me. There's only one horse in the whole world, and this one's it. Can't you understand that? If you're going to follow me, follow me without talking.

FIRST YOUTH: It's only that I want to . . .

BRIDEGROOM: Be quiet. I'm sure of meeting them there. Do you see this arm? Well, it's not my arm. It's my brother's arm, and my father's, and that of all the dead ones in my family. And it has so much strength that it can pull this tree up by the roots, if it wants to. And let's move on, because here I feel the clenched teeth of all my people in me so that I can't breathe easily.

BEGGAR WOMAN [*whining*]: Ay-y-y!

FIRST YOUTH: Did you hear that?

BRIDEGROOM: You go that way and then circle back.

FIRST YOUTH: This is a hunt.

BRIDEGROOM: A hunt. The greatest hunt there is.

The YOUTH *goes off. The* BRIDEGROOM *goes rapidly to the left and stumbles over the* BEGGAR WOMAN, *Death.*

BEGGAR WOMAN: Ay-y-y!

BRIDEGROOM: What do you want?

BEGGAR WOMAN: I'm cold.

BRIDEGROOM: Which way are you going?

BEGGAR WOMAN [*always whining like a beggar*]: Over there, far away . . .
BRIDEGROOM: Where are you from?
BEGGAR WOMAN: Over there . . . very far away.
BRIDEGROOM: Have you seen a man and a woman running away on a horse?
BEGGAR WOMAN [*awakening*]: Wait a minute . . . [*She looks at him.*] Handsome
    young man. [*She rises.*] But you'd be much handsomer sleeping.
BRIDEGROOM: Tell me; answer me. Did you see them?
BEGGAR WOMAN: Wait a minute . . . What broad shoulders! How would you like
    to be laid out on them and not have to walk on the soles of your feet which are
    so small?
BRIDEGROOM [*shaking her*]: I asked you if you saw them! Have they passed
    through here?
BEGGAR WOMAN [*energetically*]: No. They haven't passed; but they're coming
    from the hill. Don't you hear them?
BRIDEGROOM: No.
BEGGAR WOMAN: Do you know the road?
BRIDEGROOM: I'll go, whatever it's like!
BEGGAR WOMAN: I'll go along with you. I know this country.
BRIDEGROOM [*impatiently*]: Well, let's go! Which way?
BEGGAR WOMAN [*dramatically*]: This way!

*They go rapidly out. Two violins, which represent the forest, are heard
distantly. The* WOODCUTTERS *return. They have their axes on their shoulders.
They move slowly among the tree trunks.*

FIRST WOODCUTTER:
                O rising death!
                Death among the great leaves.
SECOND WOODCUTTER:
                Don't open the gush of blood!
FIRST WOODCUTTER:
                O lonely death!
                Death among the dried leaves.
THIRD WOODCUTTER:
                Don't lay flowers over the wedding!
SECOND WOODCUTTER:
                O sad death!
                Leave for their love a green branch.
FIRST WOODCUTTER:
                O evil death!
                Leave for their love a branch of green!

They go out while they are talking. LEONARDO *and the* BRIDE *appear.*

LEONARDO:
                Hush!
BRIDE:
                From here I'll go on alone.
                You go now! I want you to turn back.
LEONARDO:
                Hush, I said!

BRIDE:

With your teeth, with your hands, anyway you can,
take from my clean throat
the metal of this chain,
and let me live forgotten
back there in my house in the ground.
And if you don't want to kill me
as you would kill a tiny snake,
set in my hands, a bride's hands,
the barrel of your shotgun.
Oh, what lamenting, what fire,
sweeps upward through my head!
What glass splinters are stuck in my tongue!

LEONARDO:

We've taken the step now; hush!
because they're close behind us,
and I must take you with me.

BRIDE:

Then it must be by force!

LEONARDO:

By force? Who was it first
went down the stairway?

BRIDE:

I went down it.

LEONARDO:

And who was it put
a new bridle on the horse?

BRIDE:

I myself did it. It's true.

LEONARDO:

And whose were the hands
strapped spurs to my boots?

BRIDE:

The same hands, these that are yours,
but which when they see you would like
to break the blue branches
and sunder the purl of your veins.
I love you! I love you! But leave me!
For if I were able to kill you
I'd wrap you 'round in a shroud
with the edges bordered in violets.
Oh, what lamenting, what fire,
sweeps upward through my head!

LEONARDO:

What glass splinters are stuck in my tongue!
Because I tried to forget you
and put a wall of stone
between your house and mine.
It's true. You remember?
And when I saw you in the distance
I threw sand in my eyes.

But I was riding a horse
and the horse went straight to your door.
And the silver pins of your wedding
turned my red blood black.
And in me our dream was choking
my flesh with its poisoned weeds.
Oh, it isn't my fault—
the fault is the earth's—
and this fragrance that you exhale
from your breasts and your braids.

BRIDE:

Oh, how untrue! I want
from you neither bed nor food,
yet there's not a minute each day
that I don't want to be with you,
because you drag me, and I come,
then you tell me to go back
and I follow you,
like chaff blown on the breeze.
I have left a good, honest man,
and all his people,
with the wedding feast half over
and wearing my bridal wreath.
But you are the one will be punished
and that I don't want to happen.
Leave me alone now! You run away!
There is no one who will defend you.

LEONARDO:

The birds of early morning
are calling among the trees.
The night is dying
on the stone's ridge.
Let's go to a hidden corner
where I may love you for ever,
for to me the people don't matter,
nor the venom they throw on us.

[*He embraces her strongly.*]

BRIDE:

And I'll sleep at your feet,
to watch over your dreams.
Naked, looking over the fields,
as though I were a bitch.
Because that's what I am! Oh, I look at you
and your beauty sears me.

LEONARDO:

Fire is stirred by fire.
The same tiny flame
will kill two wheat heads together.
Let's go!

BRIDE:

Where are you taking me?

LEONARDO:
Where they cannot come,
these men who surround us.
Where I can look at you!

BRIDE [*sarcastically*]:
Carry me with you from fair to fair,
a shame to clean women,
so that people will see me
with my wedding sheets
on the breeze like banners.

LEONARDO:
I, too, would want to leave you
if I thought as men should.
But wherever you go, I go.
You're the same. Take a step. Try.
Nails of moonlight have fused
my waist and your chains.

This whole scene is violent, full of great sensuality.

BRIDE:
Listen!

LEONARDO:
They're coming.

BRIDE:
Run!
It's fitting that I should die here,
with water over my feet,
with thorns upon my head.
And fitting the leaves should mourn me,
a woman lost and virgin.

LEONARDO:
Be quiet. Now they're appearing.

BRIDE:
Go now!

LEONARDO:
Quiet. Don't let them hear us.

The BRIDE *hesitates.*

BRIDE:
Both of us!

LEONARDO [*embracing her*]:
Any way you want!
If they separate us, it will be
because I am dead.

BRIDE:
And I dead too.

They go out in each other's arms.

The MOON *appears very slowly. The stage takes on a strong blue light. The two violins are heard. Suddenly two long, ear-splitting shrieks are heard, and the music of the two violins is cut short. At the second shriek the* BEGGAR WOMAN *appears and stands with her back to the audience. She opens her cape and stands in the centre of the stage like a great bird with immense wings. The* MOON *halts. The curtain comes down in absolute silence.*

SCENE 2

The Final Scene. A white dwelling with arches and thick walls. To the right and left, are white stairs. At the back, a great arch and a wall of the same colour. The floor also should be shining white. This simple dwelling should have the monumental feeling of a church. There should not be a single grey nor any shadow, not even what is necessary for perspective.

Two GIRLS *dressed in dark blue are winding a red skein.*

FIRST GIRL:

Wool, red wool,
what would you make?

SECOND GIRL:

Oh, jasmine for dresses,
fine wool like glass.
At four o'clock born,
at ten o'clock dead.
A thread from this wool yarn,
a chain 'round your feet
a knot that will tighten
the bitter white wreath.

LITTLE GIRL [*singing*]:
Were you at the wedding?

FIRST GIRL:
No.

LITTLE GIRL:

Well, neither was I!
What could have happened
'midst the shoots of the vineyards?
What could have happened
'neath the branch of the olive?
What really happened
that no one came back?
Were you at the wedding?

SECOND GIRL:
We told you once, no.

LITTLE GIRL [*leaving*]:
Well, neither was I!

SECOND GIRL:

Wool, red wool,
what would you sing?

FIRST GIRL:

Their wounds turning waxen.

>   balm-myrtle for pain.
>   Asleep in the morning,
>   and watching at night.
LITTLE GIRL [*in the doorway*]:
>   And then, the thread stumbled
>   on the flinty stones,
>   but mountains, blue mountains,
>   are letting it pass.
>   Running, running, running,
>   and finally to come
>   to stick in a knife blade,
>   to take back the bread.

[*She goes out.*]
SECOND GIRL:
>   Wool, red wool,
>   what would you tell?

FIRST GIRL:
>   The love is silent,
>   crimson the groom,
>   at the still shoreline
>   I saw them laid out.

[*She stops and looks at the skein.*]
LITTLE GIRL [*appearing in the doorway*]:
>   Running, running, running,
>   the thread runs to here.
>   All covered with clay
>   I feel them draw near.
>   Bodies stretched stiffly
>   in ivory sheets!

The WIFE *and* MOTHER-IN-LAW *of* LEONARDO *appear. They are anguished.*

FIRST GIRL: Are they coming yet?
MOTHER-IN-LAW [*harshly*]: We don't know.
SECOND GIRL: What can you tell us about the wedding?
FIRST GIRL: Yes, tell me.
MOTHER-IN-LAW [*curtly*]: Nothing.
LEONARDO'S WIFE: I want to go back and find out all about it.
MOTHER-IN-LAW [*sternly*]:
>   You, back to your house.
>   Brave and alone in your house.
>   To grow old and to weep.
>   But behind closed doors.
>   Never again. Neither dead nor alive.
>   We'll nail up our windows
>   and let rains and nights
>   fall on the bitter weeds.
LEONARDO'S WIFE: What could have happened?
MOTHER-IN-LAW:
>   It doesn't matter what.
>   Put a veil over your face.

Your children are yours,
that's all. On the bed
put a cross of ashes
where his pillow was.

They go out.

BEGGAR WOMAN [*at the door*]: A crust of bread, little girls.
LITTLE GIRL: Go away!

The GIRLS *huddle close together.*

BEGGAR WOMAN: Why?
LITTLE GIRL: Because you whine; go away!
FIRST GIRL: Child!
BEGGAR WOMAN:
              I might have asked for your eyes! A cloud
              of birds is following me. Will you have one?
LITTLE GIRL: I want to get away from here!
SECOND GIRL [*to the* BEGGAR WOMAN]: Don't mind her!
FIRST GIRL: Did you come by the road through the arroyo?
BEGGAR WOMAN: I came that way!
FIRST GIRL [*timidly*]: Can I ask you something?
BEGGAR WOMAN:
              I saw them: they'll be here soon: two torrents
              still at last, among the great boulders,
              two men at the horse's feet.
              Two dead men in the night's splendour.
        [*With pleasure.*]
              Dead, yes, dead.
FIRST GIRL: Hush, old woman, hush!
BEGGAR WOMAN:
              Crushed flowers for eyes, and their teeth
              two fistfuls of hard-frozen snow.
              Both of them fell, and the bride returns
              with bloodstains on her skirt and hair.
              And they come covered with two sheets
              carried on the shoulders of two tall boys.
              That's how it was; nothing more. What was
                 fitting.
              Over the golden flower, dirty sand.

She goes. The GIRLS *bow their heads and start going out rhythmically.*

FIRST GIRL:
              Dirty sand.
SECOND GIRL:
              Over the golden flower.
LITTLE GIRL:
              Over the golden flower
              they're bringing the dead from the arroyo.

Dark the one,
dark the other.
What shadowy nightingale flies and weeps
over the golden flower!

She goes. The stage is left empty. The MOTHER *and a* NEIGHBOUR WOMAN
appear. The NEIGHBOUR *is weeping.*

MOTHER: Hush.
NEIGHBOUR: I can't.
MOTHER: Hush, I said. [*At the door.*] Is there nobody here? [*She puts her hands
to her forehead.*] My son ought to answer me. But now my son is an armful of
shrivelled flowers. My son is a fading voice beyond the mountains now.
[*With rage, to the* NEIGHBOUR.] Will you shut up? I want no wailing in this
house. Your tears are only from your eyes, but when I'm alone mine will
come—from the soles of my feet, from my roots—burning more than blood.
NEIGHBOUR: You come to my house; don't you stay here.
MOTHER: I want to be here. Here. In peace. They're all dead now: and at
midnight I'll sleep, sleep without terror of guns or knives. Other mothers
will go to their windows, lashed by rain, to watch for their sons' faces. But not
I. And of my dreams I'll make a cold ivory dove that will carry camellias of
white frost to the graveyard. But no; not graveyard, not graveyard: the couch
of earth, the bed that shelters them and rocks them in the sky.

*A woman dressed in black enters, goes toward the right, and there kneels. To
the* NEIGHBOUR.

Take your hands from your face. We have terrible days ahead. I want to
see no one. The earth and I. My grief and I. And these four walls. Ay-y-y!
Ay-y-y! [*She sits down, overcome.*]
NEIGHBOUR: Take pity on yourself!
MOTHER [*pushing back her hair*]: I must be calm. [*She sits down.*] Because the
neighbour women will come and I don't want them to see me so poor. So
poor! A woman without even one son to hold to her lips.

The BRIDE *appears. She is without her wreath and wears a black shawl.*

NEIGHBOUR [*with rage, seeing the* BRIDE]: Where are you going?
BRIDE: I'm coming here.
MOTHER [*to the* NEIGHBOUR]: Who is it?
NEIGHBOUR: Don't you recognize her?
MOTHER: That's why I asked who it was. Because I don't want to recognize her,
so I won't sink my teeth in her throat. You snake! [*She moves wrathfully on
the* BRIDE, *then stops. To the* NEIGHBOUR.] Look at her! There she is, and she's
crying, while I stand here calmly and don't tear her eyes out. I don't under-
stand myself. Can it be I didn't love my son? But, where's his good name?
Where is it now? Where is it? [*She beats the* BRIDE *who drops to the floor.*]
NEIGHBOUR: For God's sake! [*She tries to separate them.*]
BRIDE [*to the* NEIGHBOUR]: Let her; I came here so she'd kill me and they'd take
me away with them. [*To the* MOTHER.] But not with her hands; with grappling
hooks, with a sickle—and with force—until they break on my bones, Let her! I

want her to know I'm clean, that I may be crazy, but that they can bury me without a single man ever having seen himself in the whiteness of my breasts.

MOTHER: Shut up, shut up; what do I care about that?

BRIDE: Because I ran away with the other one; I ran away! [*With anguish.*] You would have gone, too. I was a woman burning with desire, full of sores inside and out, and your son was a little bit of water from which I hoped for children, land, health; but the other one was a dark river, choked with brush, that brought near me the undertone of its rushes and its whispered song. And I went along with your son who was like a little boy of cold water—and the other sent against me hundreds of birds who got in my way and left white frost on my wounds, my wounds of a poor withered woman, of a girl caressed by fire. I didn't want to; remember that! I didn't want to. Your son was my destiny and I have not betrayed him, but the other one's arm dragged me along like the pull of the sea, like the head toss of a mule, and he would have dragged me always, always, always—even if I were an old woman and all your son's sons held me by the hair!

A NEIGHBOUR *enters.*

MOTHER: She is not to blame; nor am I! [*Sarcastically.*] Who is, then? It's a delicate, lazy, sleepless woman who throws away an orange blossom wreath and goes looking for a piece of bed warmed by another woman!

BRIDE: Be still! Be still! Take your revenge on me; here I am! See how soft my throat is; it would be less work for you than cutting a dahlia in your garden. But never that! Clean, clean as a new-born little girl. And strong enough to prove it to you. Light the fire. Let's stick our hands in; you, for your son, I, for my body. *You'll* draw yours out first.

Another NEIGHBOUR *enters.*

MOTHER: But what does your good name matter to me? What does your death matter to me? What does anything about anything matter to me? Bless̀ed be the wheat stalks, because my sons are under them: bless̀ed be the rain, because it wets the face of the dead. Bless̀ed be God, who stretches us out together to rest.

Another NEIGHBOUR *enters.*

BRIDE: Let me weep with you.

MOTHER: Weep. But at the door.

The GIRL *enters. The* BRIDE *stays at the door. The* MOTHER *is at the centre of the stage.*

LEONARDO'S WIFE [*entering and going to the left*]:
     He was a beautiful horseman,
     now he's a heap of snow.
     He rode to fairs and mountains
     and women's arms.
     Now, the night's dark moss
     crowns his forehead.

MOTHER:
> A sunflower to your mother,
> a mirror of the earth.
> Let them put on your breast
> the cross of bitter rosebay;
> and over you a sheet
> of shining silk;
> between your quiet hands
> let water form its lament.

WIFE:
> Ay-y-y, four gallant boys
> come with tired shoulders!

BRIDE:
> Ay-y-y, four gallant boys
> carry death on high!

MOTHER:
> Neighbours.

LITTLE GIRL [*at the door*]:
> They're bringing them now.

MOTHER:
> It's the same thing.
> Always the cross, the cross.

WOMEN:
> Sweet nails,
> cross adored,
> sweet name
> of Christ our Lord.

BRIDE: May the cross protect both the quick and the dead.

MOTHER:
> Neighbours: with a knife,
> with a little knife,
> on their appointed day, between two and three,
> these two men killed each other for love.
> With a knife,
> with a tiny knife
> that barely fits the hand,
> but that slides in clean
> through the astonished flesh
> and stops at the place
> where trembles, enmeshed,
> the dark root of a scream.

BRIDE:
> And this is a knife,
> a tiny knife
> that barely fits the hand;
> fish without scales, without river,
> so that on their appointed day, between two and
>   three,
> with this knife,
> two men are left stiff,
> with their lips turning yellow.

MOTHER:

And it barely fits the hand
but it slides in clean
through the astonished flesh
and stops there, at the place
where trembles enmeshed
the dark root of a scream.

The NEIGHBOURS, *kneeling on the floor, sob.*

CURTAIN

THE
GREAT GOD
BROWN
EUGENE
O'NEILL

THE GREAT GOD BROWN

First published in Great Britain in 1926 by
Jonathan Cape Limited
30 Bedford Square, London WC1

THE GREAT GOD BROWN

(1926)

CHARACTERS

WILLIAM A. BROWN
HIS FATHER (*a Contractor*)
HIS MOTHER
DION ANTHONY
HIS FATHER (*a Builder*)
HIS MOTHER
MARGARET
HER THREE SONS
CYBEL
TWO DRAUGHTSMEN (*in Brown's office*)
A STENOGRAPHER (*in Brown's office*)

PROLOGUE
The Pier of the Casino. Moonlight in middle June.
ACT ONE
Scene 1: Sitting-room, Margaret Anthony's apartment. Afternoon, seven years later.
Scene 2: Billy Brown's office. The same afternoon.
Scene 3: Cybel's parlour. That night.
ACT TWO
Scene 1: Cybel's parlour. Seven years later. Dusk.
Scene 2: Drafting-room, William A. Brown's office. That evening.
Scene 3: Library, William A. Brown's home. That night.
ACT THREE
Scene 1: Brown's office, a month later. Morning.
Scene 2: Library, Brown's home. That evening.
Scene 3: Sitting-room, Margaret's home. That night.
ACT FOUR
Scene 1: Brown's office, weeks later. Late afternoon.
Scene 2: Library, Brown's house, hours later. The same night.
EPILOGUE
The Pier of the Casino. Four years later.

PROLOGUE

SCENE: A cross-section of the pier of the Casino. In the rear, built out beyond the edge, is a rectangular space with benches on the three sides. A rail encloses the entire wharf at the back.

It is a moonlight night in mid-June. From the Casino comes the sound of the school quartet rendering 'Sweet Adeline' with many ultra-sentimental quavers. There is a faint echo of the ensuing hand-clapping—then nothing but the lapping of ripples against the piles and their swishing on the beach—then footsteps on the boards and BILLY BROWN walks along from right with his MOTHER and FATHER. The MOTHER is a dumpy woman of forty-five, overdressed in black lace and spangles. The FATHER is fifty or more, the type of bustling, genial, successful provincial business man, stout and hearty in his evening dress.

BILLY BROWN is a handsome, tall and athletic boy of nearly eighteen. He is blond and blue-eyed, with a likeable smile and a frank good-humoured face, its expression already indicating a disciplined restraint. His manner has the easy self-assurance of a normal intelligence. He is in evening dress.

They walk arm in arm, the MOTHER between.

MOTHER [*always addressing the* FATHER]: This Commencement dance is badly managed. Such singing! Such poor voices! Why doesn't Billy sing?

BILLY [*to her*]: Mine is a regular fog horn! [*He laughs.*]

MOTHER [*to the air*]: I had a pretty voice, when I was a girl. [*Then, to the* FATHER, *caustically.*] Did you see young Anthony strutting around the ballroom in dirty flannel trousers?

FATHER: He's just showing off.

MOTHER: Such impudence! He's as ignorant as his father.

FATHER: The old man's all right. My only kick against him is he's been too damned conservative to let me branch out.

MOTHER [*bitterly*]: He has kept you down to his level—out of pure jealousy.

FATHER: But he took me into partnership, don't forget—

MOTHER [*sharply*]: Because you were the brains! Because he was afraid of losing you! [*A pause.*]

BILLY [*admiringly*]: Dion came in his old clothes for a bet with me. He's a real sport. He wouldn't have been afraid to appear in his pyjamas! [*He grins with appreciation.*]

MOTHER: Isn't the moonlight clear!

> *She goes and sits on the centre bench.* BILLY *stands at the left corner, forward, his hand on the rail, like a prisoner at the bar, facing the judge. His* FATHER *stands in front of the bench on right. The* MOTHER *announces, with finality.*

After he's through college, Billy must study for a profession of some sort,

I'm determined on that! [*She turns to her husband, defiantly, as if expecting opposition.*]

FATHER [*eagerly and placatingly*]: Just what I've been thinking, my dear. Architecture! How's that? Billy a first-rate number-one architect! That's my proposition! What I've always wished I could have been myself. Only I never had the opportunity. But Billy—we'll make him a partner in the firm after. Anthony, Brown *and Son, architects* and builders—instead of *contractors* and builders!

MOTHER [*yearning for the realization of a dream*]: And we won't lay sidewalks—or dig sewers—ever again?

FATHER [*a bit ruffled*]: I and Anthony can build anything your pet can draw—even if it's a church. (*Then, selling his idea.*) It's a great chance for him! He'll design—expand us—make the firm famous.

MOTHER [*to the air—musingly*]: When you proposed, I thought your future promised success—my future—[*with a sigh*]—Well, I suppose we've been comfortable. Now, it's his future. How would Billy like to be an architect? [*She does not look at him.*]

BILLY [*to her*]: All right, Mother. [*Then sheepishly.*] I guess I've never bothered much about what I'd like to do after college—but architecture sounds all right to me, I guess.

MOTHER [*to the air—proudly*]: Billy used to draw houses when he was little.

FATHER [*jubilantly*]: Billy's got the stuff in him to win, if he'll only work hard enough.

BILLY [*dutifully*]: I'll work hard, Dad.

MOTHER: Billy can do anything!

BILLY [*embarrassed*]: I'll try, Mother. [*There is a pause.*]

MOTHER [*with a sudden shiver*]: The nights are so much colder than they used to be! Think of it, I once went moonlight bathing in June when I was a girl—but the moonlight was so warm and beautiful in those days, do you remember, Father?

FATHER [*puts his arm around her affectionately*]: You bet I do, Mother. [*He kisses her. The orchestra at the Casino strikes up a waltz.*] There's the music. Let's go back and watch the young folks dance.

They start off, leaving Billy standing there.

MOTHER [*suddenly calls back over her shoulder*]: I want to watch Billy dance.

BILLY [*dutifully*]: Yes, Mother!

He follows them. For a moment the faint sound of the music and the lapping of waves is heard. Then footsteps again and the three ANTHONYS *come in. First come the father and mother, who are not masked. The* FATHER *is a tall lean man of fifty-five or sixty, with a grim, defensive face, obstinate to the point of stupid weakness. The* MOTHER *is a thin, frail, faded woman, her manner perpetually nervous and distraught, but with a sweet and gentle face that had once been beautiful. The* FATHER *wears an ill-fitting black suit, like a mourner. The* MOTHER *wears a cheap, plain, black dress. Following them, as if he were a stranger, walking alone, is their son,* DION. *He is about the same height as young* BROWN, *but lean and wiry, without repose, continually in restless nervous movement. His face is masked. The mask is a fixed forcing of his own face—dark, spiritual, poetic, passionately supersensitive, helplessly unpro-*

tected in its childlike religious faith in life—into the expression of a mocking, reckless, defiant, gaily scoffing and sensual young Pan. He is dressed in a grey flannel shirt, open at the neck, rubber-soled shoes over bare feet, and soiled white flannel trousers. The FATHER *strides to the centre bench and sits down. The* MOTHER, *who has been holding to his arm, lets go and stands by the bench at the right. They both stare at* DION, *who, with a studied carelessness, takes his place at the rail, where young Brown had stood. They watch him, with queer, puzzled eyes.*

MOTHER [*suddenly—pleading*]: You simply must send him to college.

FATHER: I won't. I don't believe in it. Colleges turn out lazy loafers to sponge on their poor old fathers! Let him slave like I had to! That'll teach him the value of a dollar! College'll only make him a bigger fool than he is already! I never got above grammar school but I've made money and established a sound business. Let him make man out of himself like I made of myself!

DION [*mockingly—to the air*]: This Mr Anthony is my father, but he only imagines he is God the Father. [*They both stare at him.*]

FATHER [*with angry bewilderment*]: What—what—what's that?

MOTHER [*gently remonstrating to her son*]: Dion, dear! [*Then to her husband—tauntingly.*] Brown takes all the credit! He tells every one the success is all due to his energy—that you're only an old stick-in-the-mud!

FATHER [*stung, harshly*]: The damn fool! He knows better'n anyone if I hadn't held him down to common sense, with his crazy wild-cat notions, he'd have had us ruined long ago!

MOTHER: He's sending Billy to college—Mrs Brown just told me—going to have him study architecture afterwards, too, so's he can help expand your firm!

FATHER [*angrily*]: What's that? [*Suddenly turns on* DION *furiously.*] Then you can make up your mind to go too! And you'll learn to be a better architect than Brown's boy or I'll turn you out in the gutter without a penny! You hear?

DION [*mockingly—to the air*]: It's difficult to choose—but architecture sounds less laborious.

MOTHER [*fondly*]: You ought to make a wonderful architect, Dion. You've always painted pictures so well—

DION [*with a start—resentfully*]: Why must she lie? Is it my fault? She knows I only try to paint. [*Passionately.*] But I will, some day! [*Then quickly, mocking again.*] On to college! Well, it won't be home, anyway, will it? [*He laughs queerly and approaches them. His* FATHER *gets up defensively.* DION *bows to him.*] I thank Mr Anthony for this splendid opportunity to create myself—[*He kisses his* MOTHER, *who bows with a strange humility as if she were a servant being saluted by the young master—then adds lightly*]—in my mother's image, so she may feel her life comfortably concluded.

He sits in his FATHER's *place at centre and his mask stares with a frozen mockery before him. They stand on each side, looking dumbly at him.*

MOTHER [*at last, with a shiver*]: It's cold. June didn't use to be cold. I remember the June when I was carrying you, Dion—three months before you were born. [*She stares up at the sky.*] The moonlight was warm, then. I could feel the night wrapped around me like a grey velvet gown lined with warm sky and trimmed with silver leaves!

FATHER [*gruffly—but with a certain awe*]: My mother used to believe the full of the moon was the time to sow. She was terrible old-fashioned. [*With a grunt.*] I can feel it's bringing on my rheumatism. Let's go back indoors.

DION [*with intense bitterness*]: Hide! Be ashamed!

They both start and stare at him.

FATHER [*with bitter hopelessness. To his wife—indicating their son*]: Who is he? You bore him!

MOTHER [*proudly*]: He's my boy! He's Dion!

DION [*bitterly resentful*]: What else, indeed! The identical son. [*Then, mockingly.*] Are Mr Anthony and his wife going in to dance! The nights grow cold! The days are dimmer than they used to be! Let's play hide-and-seek! Seek the monkey in the moon!

He suddenly cuts a grotesque caper, like a harlequin, and darts off, laughing with forced abandon. They stare after him—then slowly follow. Again there is silence except for the sound of the lapping waves. Then MARGARET *comes in, followed by the humbly worshipping* BILLY BROWN. *She is almost seventeen, pretty and vivacious, blonde, with big romantic eyes, her figure lithe and strong, her facial expression intelligent but youthfully dreamy, especially now in the moonlight. She is in a simple white dress. On her entrance, her face is masked with an exact, almost transparent reproduction of her own features, but giving her the abstract quality of a Girl instead of the individual Margaret.*

MARGARET [*looking upward at the moon and singing in low tone as they enter*]: 'Ah, moon of my delight that knowest no wane!'

BILLY [*eagerly*]: I've got that record—John McCormack. It's a peach! Sing some more.

She looks upward in silence. He keeps standing respectfully behind her, glancing embarrassedly toward her averted face. He tries to make conversation.

I think the *Rubáiyát's* great stuff, don't you! I never could memorize poetry worth a darn. Dion can recite lots of Shelley's poems by heart.

MARGARET [*slowly takes off her mask—to the moon*]: Dion! [*A pause.*]

BILLY [*fidgeting*]: Margaret!

MARGARET [*to the moon*]: Dion is so wonderful!

BILLY [*blunderingly*]: I asked you to come out here because I wanted to tell you something.

MARGARET [*to the moon*]: Why did Dion look at me like that? It made me feel so crazy!

BILLY: I wanted to ask you something, too.

MARGARET: That one time he kissed me—I can't forget it! He was only joking—but I felt—and he saw and just laughed.

BILLY: Because that's the uncertain part. My end of it is a sure thing, and has been for a long time, and I guess everybody in town knows it—they're always kidding me—so it's a cinch you must know—how I feel about you.

MARGARET: Dion's so different from all the others. He can paint beautifully and write poetry and he plays and sings and dances so marvellously. But he's sad and shy, too, just like a baby sometimes, and he understands what I'm really like inside—and—and I'd love to run my fingers through his hair—and I love him! Yes, I love him! [*She stretches out her arms to the moon.*] Oh, Dion, I love you!

BILLY: I love you, Margaret.

MARGARET: I wonder if Dion—I saw him looking at me again to-night—Oh, I wonder . . .!

BILLY [*takes her hand and blurts out*]: Can't you love me? Won't you marry me—after college—

MARGARET: Where is Dion, now, I wonder?

BILLY [*shaking her hand in an agony of uncertainty*]: Margaret! Please answer me!

MARGARET [*her dream broken, puts on her mask and turns to him—matter-of-factly*]: It's getting chilly. Let's go back and dance, Billy.

BILLY [*desperately*]: I love you! [*He tries clumsily to kiss her.*]

MARGARET [*with an amused laugh*]: Like a brother! You can kiss me if you like. [*She kisses him.*] A big-brother kiss. It doesn't count.

He steps back crushed, with head bowed. She turns away and takes off her mask—to the moon.

I wish Dion would kiss me again!

BILLY [*painfully*]: I'm a poor boob. I ought to know better. I'll bet I know. You're in love with Dion. I've seen you look at him. Isn't that it?

MARGARET: Dion! I love the sound of it!

BILLY [*huskily*]: Well—he's always been my best friend—I'm glad it's him—and I guess I know how to lose—[*He takes her hand and shakes it*]—so here's wishing you all the success and happiness in the world, Margaret—and remember I'll always be your best friend! [*He gives her hand a final shake—swallows hard—then manfully.*] Let's go back in!

MARGARET [*to the moon—faintly annoyed*]: What is Billy Brown doing here? I'll go down to the end of the dock and wait. Dion is the moon and I'm the sea. I want to feel the moon kissing the sea. I want Dion to leave the sky to me. I want the tides of my blood to leave my heart and follow him! [*She whispers like a little girl.*] Dion! Margaret! Peggy! Peggy is Dion's girl—Peggy is Dion's little girl—[*She sings laughingly, elfishly.*] Dion is my Daddy-O! [*She is walking toward the end of the dock, off left.*]

BILLY [*who has turned away*]: I'm going. I'll tell Dion you're here.

MARGARET [*more and more strongly and assertively, until at the end she is a wife and a mother*]: And I'll be Mrs Dion—Dion's wife—and he'll be my Dion—my own Dion—my little boy—my baby! The moon is drowned in the tides of my heart, and peace sinks deep through the sea!

She disappears off left, her upturned unmasked face like that of a rapturous visionary. There is silence again, in which the dance music is heard. Then this stops and DION comes in. He walks quickly to the bench at centre, and throws himself on it, hiding his masked face in his hands. After a moment, he lifts his head, peers about, listens huntedly, then slowly takes off his mask. His real face is revealed in the bright moonlight, shrinking, shy and gentle, full of a deep sadness.

DION [*with a suffering bewilderment*]: Why am I afraid to dance, I who love
music and rhythm and grace and song and laughter? Why am I afraid to live,
I who love life and the beauty of flesh and the living colours of earth and sky
and sea? Why am I afraid of love, I who love love? Why am I afraid, I who am
not afraid? Why must I pretend to scorn in order to pity? Why must I hide
myself in self-contempt in order to understand? Why must I be so ashamed
of my strength, so proud of my weakness? Why must I live in a cage like a
criminal, defying and hating, I who love peace and friendship? [*Clasping his
hands above in supplication.*] Why was I born without a skin, O God, that I
must wear armour in order to touch or to be touched? [*A second's pause of
waiting silence—then he suddenly claps his mask over his face again, with a
gesture of despair, and his voice becomes bitter and sardonic.*] Or rather, Old
Graybeard, why the devil was I ever born at all?

    Steps are heard from the right. DION *stiffens and his mask stares straight
ahead.* BILLY *comes in from the right. He is shuffling along disconsolately.
When he sees* DION, *he stops abruptly and glowers resentfully—but at once the
'good loser' in him conquers this.*

BILLY [*embarrassedly*]: Hello, Dion. I've been looking all over for you. [*He sits
down on the bench at right, forcing a joking tone.*] What are you sitting here for,
you nut—trying to get more moon-struck? [*A pause—awkwardly.*] I just left
Margaret—
DION [*gives a start—immediately defensively mocking*]: Bless you, my children!
BILLY [*gruffly and slangily*]: I'm out of it—she gave me the gate. You're the
original white-haired boy. Go on in and win! We've been chums ever since
we were kids, haven't we?—and—I'm glad it's you, Dion. [*This huskily—he
fumbles for* DION'*s hand and gives it a shake.*]
DION [*letting his hand fall back—bitterly*]: Chums? Oh no, Billy Brown would
despise me!
BILLY: She's waiting for you now, down at the end of the dock.
DION: For me? Which? Who? Oh no, girls only allow themselves to look at what
is seen!
BILLY: She's in love with you.
DION [*moved—a pause—stammers*]: Miracle? I'm afraid! [*He chants flippantly.*] I
love, thou lovest, he loves, she loves! She loves, she loves—what?
BILLY: And I know damn well, underneath your nuttiness, you're gone on her.
DION [*moved*]: Underneath? I love love! I'd love to be loved! But I'm afraid!
[*Then aggressively.*] *Was* afraid! Not now! Now I can make love—to anyone!
Yes, I love Peggy! Why not? Who is she? Who am I? We love, you love, they
love, one loves! No one loves! All the world loves a lover, God loves us all and
we love Him! Love is a word—a shameless ragged ghost of a word—begging at
all doors for life at any price!
BILLY [*always as if he hadn't listened to what the other said*]: Say, let's you and me
room together at college—
DION: Billy wants to remain by her side!
BILLY: It's a bet, then! [*Forcing a grin.*] You can tell her I'll see that you behave!
[*Turns away.*] So long. Remember she's waiting. [*He goes.*]
DION [*dazedly, to himself*]: Waiting—waiting for me! [*He slowly removes his
mask. His face is torn and transfigured by joy. He stares at the sky raptly.*] O
God in the moon, did you hear? She loves me! I am not afraid! I am strong! I

can love! She protects me! Her arms are softly around me! She is warmly around me! She is my skin! She is my armour! Now I am born–I–the I!–one and indivisible–I who love Margaret! [*He glances at his mask triumphantly–in tones of deliverance.*] You are outgrown! I am beyond you! [*He stretches out his arms to the sky.*] O God, now I believe!

From the end of the wharf, her voice is heard.

MARGARET: Dion!
DION [*raptly*]: Margaret!
MARGARET [*nearer*]: Dion!
DION: Margaret!
MARGARET: Dion!

She comes running in, her mask in her hands. He springs toward her with outstretched arms, but she shrinks away with a frightened shriek and hastily puts on her mask. DION *starts back. She speaks coldly and angrily.*

Who are you? Why are you calling me? I don't know you!
DION [*heart-brokenly*]: I love you!
MARGARET [*freezingly*]: Is this a joke–or are you drunk?
DION [*with a final pleading whisper*]: Margaret!

But she only glares at him contemptuously. Then with a sudden gesture he claps his mask on and laughs wildly and bitterly.

Ha-ha-ha! That's one on you, Peg!
MARGARET [*with delight, pulling off her mask*]: Dion! How did you ever–Why, I never knew you!
DION [*puts his arm around her boldly*]: How? It's the moon–the crazy moon–the monkey in the moon–playing jokes on us! [*He kisses her with his masked face with a romantic actor's passion again and again.*] You love me! You know you do! Say it! Tell me! I want to hear! I want to feel! I want to know! I want to want! To want you as you want me!
MARGARET [*in ecstasy*]: Oh, Dion, I do! I do love you!
DION [*with ironic mastery–rhetorically*]: And I love you! Oh, madly, Oh, for ever and ever, amen! You are my evening star and all my Pleiades! Your eyes are blue pools in which gold dreams glide, your body is a young white birch leaning backward beneath the lips of spring. So! [*He has bent her back, his arms supporting her, his face above hers.*] So! [*He kisses her.*]

MARGARET [*with overpowering passionate languor*]: Oh, Dion! Dion! I love you!
DION [*with more and more mastery in his tone*]: I love, you love, we love! Come! Rest, Relax! Let go your clutch on the world! Dim and dimmer! Fading out in the past behind! Gone! Death! Now! Be born! Awake! Live! Dissolve into dew–into silence–into night–into earth–into space–into peace–into meaning–into joy–into God–into the Great God Pan!

While he has been speaking, the moon has passed gradually behind a black cloud, its light fading out. There is a moment of intense blackness and silence. then the light gradually comes on again. DION's *voice, at first in a whisper, then increasing in volume with the light, is heard.*

Wake up! Time to get up! Time to exist! Time for school! Time to learn!
Learn to pretend! Cover your nakedness! learn to lie! Learn to keep step! Join
the procession! Great Pan is dead! Be ashamed!

MARGARET [*with a sob*]: Oh, Dion, I am ashamed!

DION [*mockingly*]: Sssshh! Watch the monkey in the moon! See him dance! His
tail is a piece of string that was left when he broke loose from Jehovah and ran
away to join Charley Darwin's circus!

MARGARET: I know you must hate me now! [*She throws her arms around him and
hides her head on his shoulder.*]

DION [*deeply moved*]: Don't cry! Don't–! [*He suddenly tears off his mask–in a
passionate agony.*] Hate you? I love you with all my soul! Love me! Why can't
you love me, Margaret?

*He tries to kiss her but she jumps to her feet with a frightened cry, holding up
her mask before her face protectingly.*

MARGARET: Don't! Please! I don't know you. You frighten me!

DION [*puts on his mask again–quietly and bitterly*]: All's well. I'll never let you
see again. [*He puts his arm around her–gently mocking.*] By proxy, I love you.
There! Don't cry! Don't be afraid! Dion Anthony will marry you some day.
[*He kisses her.*] 'I take this woman–' [*Tenderly joking.*] Hello, woman! Do you
feel older by æons? Mrs Dion Anthony, shall we go in and may I have the
next dance?

MARGARET [*tenderly*]: You crazy child. [*Then, laughing with joy.*] Mrs Dion
Anthony! It sounds wonderful, doesn't it?

They go out as

THE CURTAIN FALLS

ACT ONE

SCENE I

SCENE: Seven years later.

The sitting-room of MRS DION ANTHONY's half of a two-family house in the residential quarter of the town—one of those one-design districts that daze the eye with multiplied ugliness. The four pieces of furniture shown are in keeping—an arm-chair at left, a table with a chair behind it at centre, a sofa at right. The same court-room effect of the arrangement of benches in Act One is held to here. The background is a backdrop on which the rear wall is painted with the intolerable lifeless realistic detail of the stereotyped paintings which usually adorn the sitting-rooms of such houses. It is late afternoon of a grey day in winter.

DION is sitting behind the table, staring before him. The mask hangs on his breast below his neck, giving the effect of two faces. His real face has aged greatly, grown more strained and tortured, but at the same time, in some queer way, more selfless and ascetic, more fixed in its resolute withdrawal from life. The mask, too, has changed. It is older, more defiant and mocking, its sneer more forced and bitter, its Pan quality becoming Mephistophelean. It has already begun to show the ravages of dissipation.

DION [*suddenly reaches out and takes up a copy of the New Testament which is on the table and, putting a finger in at random, opens and reads aloud the text at which it points*]: 'Come unto me all ye who are heavy laden and I will give you rest.' [*He stares before him in a sort of trance, his face lighted up from within but painfully confused—in an uncertain whisper.*] I will come—but where are you, Saviour? [*The noise of the outer door shutting is heard.* DION *starts and claps the mocking mask on his face again. He tosses the testament aside contemptuously.*] Blah! Fixation on old Mamma Christianity! You infant blubbering in the dark, you!

He laughs, with a bitter self-contempt. Footsteps approach. He picks up a newspaper and hides behind it hurriedly. MARGARET *enters. She is dressed in stylish, expensive clothes and a fur coat, which look as if they had been remodelled and seen service. She has grown mature and maternal, in spite of her youth. Her pretty face is still fresh and healthy but there is the beginning of a permanently worried, apprehensive expression about the nose and mouth—an uncomprehending hurt in her eyes.* DION *pretends to be engrossed in his paper. She bends down and kisses him.*

MARGARET [*with a forced gaiety*]: Good morning—at four in the afternoon! You were snoring when I left!

DION [*puts his arms around her with a negligent, accustomed gesture—mockingly*]:

The Ideal Husband!

MARGARET [*already preoccupied with another thought—comes and sits in chair on left*]: I was afraid the children would disturb you, so I took them over to Mrs Young's to play. [*A pause. He picks up the paper again. She asks anxiously.*] I suppose they'll be all right over there, don't you? [*He doesn't answer. She is more hurt than offended.*] I wish you'd try to take more interest in the children, Dion.

DION [*mockingly*]. Become a father—before breakfast? I'm in too delicate a condition. [*She turns away, hurt. Penitently he pats her hand—vaguely.*] All right. I'll try.

MARGARET [*squeezing his hand—with possessive tenderness*]: Play with them. You're a bigger kid than they are—underneath.

DION [*self-mockingly—flipping the Bible*]: Underneath—I'm becoming down-right infantile! 'Suffer these little ones!'

MARGARET [*keeping to her certainty*]: You're my oldest.

DION [*with mocking appreciation*]: She puts the Kingdom of Heaven in its place!

MARGARET [*withdrawing her hand*]: I was serious.

DION: So was I—about something or other. [*He laughs.*] This domestic diplomacy! We communicate in code—when neither has the other's key!

MARGARET [*frowns confusedly—then forcing a playful tone*]: I want to have a serious talk with you, young man! In spite of your promises, you've kept up the hard drinking and gambling you started the last year abroad.

DION: From the time I realized it wasn't in me to be an artist—except in living—and not even in that! [*He laughs bitterly.*]

MARGARET [*with conviction*]: But you *can* paint, Dion—beautifully!

DION [*with deep pain*]: No! [*He suddenly takes her hand and kisses it gratefully.*] I love Margaret! Her blindness surpasseth all understanding! [*Then bitterly*]—or is it pity?

MARGARET: We've only got about one hundred dollars left in the bank.

DION [*with dazed surprise*]. What? Is all the money from the sale of the house gone?

MARGARET [*wearily*]: Every day or so you've been cashing cheques. You've been drinking—you haven't counted—

DION [*irritably*]: I know! (*A pause—soberly.*) No more estate to fall back on, eh? Well, for five years it kept us living abroad in peace. It bought us a little happiness—of a kind—didn't it?—living and loving and having children—[*A slight pause—bitterly*]—thinking one was creating before one discovered one couldn't!

MARGARET [*this time with forced conviction*]: But you *can* paint—beautifully!

DION [*angrily*]: Shut up! [*A pause—then jeeringly.*] So my wife thinks it behoves me to settle down and support my family in the meagre style to which they'll have to become accustomed?

MARGARET [*shamefacedly*]: I didn't say—still—something's got to be done.

DION [*harshly*]: Will Mrs Anthony helpfully suggest what?

MARGARET: I met Billy Brown on the street. He said you'd have made a good architect, if you'd stuck to it.

DION: Flatterer! Instead of leaving college when my Old Man died? Instead of marrying Peggy and going abroad and being happy?

MARGARET [*as if she hadn't heard*]: He spoke of how well you used to draw.

DION: Billy was in love with Margaret at one time.

MARGARET: He wanted to know why you've never been in to see him.

DION: He's bound heaven-bent for success. It's the will of Mammon! Anthony and Brown, contractors and builders–death subtracts Anthony and I sell out–Billy graduates–Brown and Son, architects and builders–old man Brown perishes of paternal pride–and now we have William A. Brown, architect! Why his career itself already has an architectural design! One of God's mud pies!

MARGARET: He particularly told me to ask you to drop in.

DION [*springs to his feet–assertively*]: No! Pride! I have been alive!

MARGARET: Why don't you have a talk with him?

DION: Pride in my failure.

MARGARET: You were always such close friends.

DION [*more and more desperately*]: The pride which came after man's fall–by which he laughs as a creator at his self-defeats!

MARGARET: Not for my sake–but for your own–and, above all, for the children's!

DION [*with terrible despair*]: Pride! Pride without which the Gods are worms!

MARGARET [*after a pause, meekly and humbly*]: You don't want to? It would hurt you? All right, dear. Never mind. We'll manage somehow–you mustn't worry–you must start your beautiful painting again–and I can get that position in the library–it would be such fun for me working there! . . . [*She reaches out and takes his hand–tenderly.*] I love you, dear. I understand.

DION [*slumps down into his chair, crushed, his face averted from hers, as hers is from him, although their hands are still clasped–in a trembling, expiring voice*]: Pride is dying! [*As if he were suffocating, he pulls the mask from his resigned, pale, suffering face. He prays like a Saint in the desert, exorcizing a demon.*] Pride is dead! Blessed are the meek! Blessed are the poor in spirit!

MARGARET [*without looking at him–in a comforting motherly tone*]: My poor boy!

DION [*resentfully–clapping on his mask again and springing to his feet–derisively*]: Blessed are the meek for they shall inherit graves! Blessed are the poor in spirit for they are blind! [*Then with tortured bitterness.*] All right! Then I ask my wife to go and ask Billy Brown–that's more deadly than if I went myself! [*With wild mockery.*] Ask him if he can't find an opening for a talented young man who is only honest when he isn't sober–implore him, beg him in the name of old love, old friendship–to be a generous hero and save the woman and her children! [*He laughs with a sort of diabolical, ironical glee now, and starts to go out.*]

MARGARET [*meekly*]: Are you going up street, Dion?

DION: Yes.

MARGARET: Will you stop at the butcher's and ask them to send two pounds of pork chops?

DION: Yes.

MARGARET: And stop at Mrs Young's and tell the children to hurry right home?

DION: Yes.

MARGARET: Will you be back for dinner, Dion?

DION: No.

He goes, the outer door slams. MARGARET *sighs with a tired incomprehension and goes to the window and stares out.*

MARGARET [*worriedly*]: I hope they'll be careful, crossing the street.

CURTAIN

SCENE 2

SCENE: BILLY BROWN's office, at five in the afternoon. At centre, a fine mahogany desk with a swivel chair behind it. To the left of desk, an office armchair. To the right of desk, an office lounge. The background is a backdrop of an office wall, treated similarly to that of Scene I in its over-meticulous representation of detail.

BILLY BROWN is seated at the desk looking over a blue print by the light of a desk lamp. He has grown into a fine-looking, well-dressed, capable, college-bred American business man, boyish still and with the same engaging personality.

The telephone rings.

BROWN [*answering it*]. Yes? Who? [*This in surprise—then with eager pleasure.*] Ask her to come right in.

> *He gets up and goes to the door, expectant and curious.* MARGARET *enters. Her face is concealed behind the mask of the pretty young matron, still hardly a woman, who cultivates a naïvely innocent and bravely hopeful attitude toward things and acknowledges no wound to the world. She is dressed as in Scene I but with an added touch of effective primping here and there.*

MARGARET [*very gaily*]: Hello, Billy Brown!
BROWN [*awkwardly in her presence, shakes her hand*]: Come in. Sit down. This is a pleasant surprise, Margaret.

> *She sits down on the lounge. He sits in his chair behind the desk, as before.*

MARGARET [*looking around*]: What lovely offices! My, but Billy Brown is getting grand!
BROWN [*pleased*]: I've just moved in. The old place was too stuffy.
MARGARET: It looks so prosperous—but then, Billy is doing so wonderfully well, every one says.
BROWN [*modestly*]: Well, to be frank, it's been mostly luck. Things have come my way without my doing much about it. [*Then, with an abashed pride.*] Still—I have done a little something myself. [*He picks the plan from the desk.*] See this? It's my design for the New Municipal Building. It's just been accepted—provisionally—by the Committee.
MARGARET [*taking it—vaguely*]: Oh? [*She looks at it abstractedly. There is a pause. Suddenly.*] You mentioned the other day how well Dion used to draw—
BROWN [*a bit stiffly*]: Yes, he certainly did. [*He takes the drawing from her and at once becomes interested and squints at it frowningly*]: Did you notice that anything seemed lacking in this?
MARGARET [*indifferently*]: Not at all.
BROWN [*with a cheerful grin*]: The Committee want it made a little more American. It's too much of a conventional Greco-Roman tomb, they say. [*Laughs.*] They want an original touch of modern novelty stuck in to liven it

up and make it look different from other town halls. [*Putting the drawing back on his desk.*] And I've been figuring out how to give it to them, but my mind doesn't seem to run that way. Have you any suggestion?

MARGARET [*as if she hadn't heard*]: Dion certainly draws well, Billy Brown was saying?

BROWN [*trying not to show his annoyance*]: Why, yes—he did—and still can, I expect. [*A pause. He masters what he feels to be an unworthy pique and turns to her generously.*] Dion would have made a cracking good architect.

MARGARET [*proudly*]: I know. He could be anything he wanted to.

BROWN [*a pause—embarrassedly*]: Is he working at anything these days?

MARGARET [*defensively*]: Oh, yes! He's painting wonderfully! But he's just like a child, he's so impractical. He doesn't try to have an exhibition anywhere, or anything.

BROWN [*surprised*]: The one time I ran into him, I thought he told me he'd destroyed all his pictures—that he'd got sick of painting and completely given it up.

MARGARET [*quickly*]: He always tells people that. He doesn't want anyone even to look at his things, imagine! He keeps saying they're rotten—when they're really too beautiful! He's too modest for his own good, don't you think? But it is true he hasn't done so much lately since we've been back. You see the children take up such a lot of his time. He just worships them! I'm afraid he's becoming a hopeless family man, just the opposite of what anyone would expect who knew him in the old days.

BROWN [*painfully embarrassed by her loyalty and his knowledge of the facts*]: Yes, I know. [*He coughs self-consciously.*]

MARGARET [*aroused by something in his manner*]: But I suppose the gossips are telling the same silly stories about him they always did. [*She forces a laugh.*] Poor Dion! Give a dog a bad name! [*Her voice breaks a little in spite of herself.*]

BROWN [*hastily*]: I haven't heard any stories—[*he stops uncertainly, then decides to plunge in*]—except about money matters.

MARGARET [*forcing a laugh*]: Oh, perhaps they're true enough. Dion is such a generous fool with his money, like all artists.

BROWN [*with a certain doggedness*]: There's a rumour that you've applied for a position at the Library.

MARGARET [*forcing a gay tone*]: Yes, indeed! Won't it be fun! Maybe it'll improve my mind! And one of us has got to be practical, so why not me? [*She forces a gay, girlish laugh.*]

BROWN [*impulsively reaches out and takes her hand—awkwardly*]: Listen, Margaret. Let's be perfectly frank, will you? I'm such an old friend, and I want like the deuce to. . . . You know darn well I'd do anything in the world to help you—or Dion.

MARGARET [*withdrawing her hand, coldly*]: I'm afraid I—don't understand, Billy Brown.

BROWN [*acutely embarrassed*]: Well, I—I just meant—you know, if you needed—[*A pause, He looks questioningly at her averted face—then ventures on another tack, matter-of-factly.*] I've got a proposition to make to Dion—if I could ever get hold of him. It's this way: business has been piling up on me—a run of luck—but I'm short-handed. I need a crack chief draughtsman darn badly—or I'm liable to lose out. Do you think Dion would consider it—as a temporary stop-gap—until he felt in the painting mood again?

MARGARET [*striving to conceal her eagerness and relief—judicially*]: Yes—I really

do. He's such a good sport and Billy and he were such pals once. I know he'd
be only too tickled to help him out.

BROWN [*diffidently*]: I thought he might be sensitive about working for—I mean,
with me—when, if he hadn't sold out to dad he'd be my partner
now—[*earnestly*]—and, by jingo, I wish he was! [*Then, abruptly*.] Let's try to
nail him down right away, Margaret. Is he home now? [*He reaches for the
'phone.*]

MARGARET [*hurriedly*]: No, he—he went out for a long walk.

BROWN: Perhaps I can locate him later around town somewhere.

MARGARET [*with a note of pleading*]: Please don't trouble. It isn't necessary. I'm
sure when I talk to him—he's coming home to dinner—[*Getting up.*] Then it's
all settled, isn't it? Dion will be so glad to be able to help an old friend—he's so
terribly loyal, and he's always liked Billy Brown so much! [*Holding out her
hand.*] I really must go now!

BROWN [*shakes her hand*]: Good-bye Margaret. I hope you'll be dropping in on
us a lot when Dion gets here.

MARGARET: Yes. [*She goes.*]

BROWN [*sits at his desk again, looking ahead in a not unsatisfying melancholy
reverie. He mutters admiringly but pityingly*]: Poor Margaret! She's a game
sport, but it's pretty damn tough on her! [*Indignantly.*] By God, I'm going to
give Dion a good talking-to one of these days!

CURTAIN

SCENE 3

SCENE: CYBEL's parlour. An automatic, penny-in-the-slot player-piano is at
centre, rear. On its right is a dirty gilt second-hand sofa. At the left is a bald-
spotted crimson plush chair. The backdrop for the rear wall is cheap wall-paper
of a dull yellow-brown, resembling a blurred impression of a fallow field in
early spring. There is a cheap alarm clock on top of the piano. Beside it her
mask is lying.

DION is sprawled on his back, fast asleep on the sofa. His mask has fallen
down on his chest. His pale face is singularly pure, spiritual and sad.

The player-piano is groggily banging out a sentimental medley of
'Mother—Mammy' tunes.

CYBEL is seated on the stool in front of the piano. She is a strong, calm,
sensual, blonde girl of twenty or so, her complexion fresh and healthy, her
figure full-breasted and wide-hipped, her movements slow and solidly
languorous like an animal's, her large eyes dreamy with the reflected stirring of
profound instincts. She chews gum like a sacred cow forgetting time with an
eternal end. Her eyes are fixed, incuriously, on DION's pale face.

CYBEL [*as the tune runs out, glances at the clock, which indicates midnight, then
goes slowly over to DION and puts her hand gently on his forehead*]: Wake up!

DION [*stirs, sighs and murmurs dreamily*]. 'And He laid his hands on them and
healed them.' [*Then with a start he opens his eyes and, half sitting up, stares at
her bewilderedly.*] What—where—who are you? [*He reaches for his mask and
claps it on defensively.*]

CYBEL [*placidly*]: Only another female. You was camping on my steps, sound asleep. I didn't want to run any risk getting into more trouble with the cops pinching you there and blaming me, so I took you in to sleep it off.

DION [*mockingly*]: Blessed are the pitiful, Sister! I'm broke—but you will be rewarded in Heaven!

CYBEL [*calmly*]: I wasn't wasting my pity. Why should I? You were happy, weren't you?

DION [*approvingly*]: Excellent! You're not a moralist, I see.

CYBEL [*going on*]. And you look like a good boy, too—when you're asleep. Say, you better beat it home to bed or you'll be locked out.

DION [*mockingly*]: Now you're becoming maternal, Miss Earth. Is that the only answer—to pin my soul into every vacant diaper? [*She stares down at his mask, her face growing hard. He laughs.*] But please don't stop stroking my aching brow. Your hand is a cool mud poultice on the sting of thought!

CYBEL [*calmly*]: Stop acting. I hate ham fats. [*She looks at him as if waiting for him to remove his mask—then turns her back indifferently and goes to the piano.*] Well, if you simply got to be a regular devil like all the other visiting sports, I s'pose I got to play with you. [*She takes her mask and puts it on—then turns. The mask is the rouged and eye-blackened countenance of the hardened prostitute. In a coarse, harsh voice.*] Kindly state your dishonourable intentions, if any! I can't sit up all night keeping company! Let's have some music! [*She puts a plug in the machine. The same sentimental medley begins to play. The two masks stare at each other. She laughs.*] Shoot! I'm all set! It's your play, Kid Lucifer!

DION [*slowly removes his mask. She stops the music with a jerk. His face is gentle and sad—humbly*]: I'm sorry. It has always been such agony for me to be touched!

CYBEL [*taking off her mask—sympathetically as she comes back and sits down on her stool*]: Poor kid! I've never had one, but I can guess. They hug and kiss you and take you on their laps and pinch you and want to see you getting dressed and undressed—as if they owned you—I bet you I'd never let them treat one of mine that way!

DION [*turning to her*]: You're lost in blind alleys, too. [*Suddenly holding out his hand to her.*] But you're strong. Let's be friends.

CYBEL [*with a strange sternness, searches his face*]: And never nothing more?

DION [*with a strange smile*]. Let's say, never anything less!

She takes his hand. There is a ring at the outside door bell. They stare at each other. There is another ring.

CYBEL [*puts on her mask,* DION *does likewise. Mockingly*]: When you got to love to live it's hard to love living. I better join the A.F. of L. and soap-box for the eight-hour night! Got a nickel, baby? Play a tune.

She goes out. DION *puts a nickel in. The same sentimental tune starts.* CYBEL *returns, followed by* BILLY BROWN. *His face is rigidly composed, but his superior disgust for* DION *can be seen.* DION *jerks off the music and he and* BILLY *look at each other for a moment,* CYBEL *watching them both—then, bored, she yawns.*

He's hunting for you. Put out the lights when you go. I'm going to sleep.

[*She starts to go—then, as if reminded of something—to* DION]. Life's all right, if you let it alone. [*Then mechanically flashing a trade smile at* BILLY.] Now you know the way, Handsome, call again! [*She goes.*]

BROWN [*after an awkward pause*]: Hello, Dion! I've been looking all over town for you. This place was the very last chance. . . . [*another pause—embarrassedly.*] Let's take a walk.

DION [*mockingly*]: I've given up exercise. They claim it lengthens your life.

BROWN [*persuasively*]: Come on, Dion, be a good fellow. You're certainly not staying here—

DION: Billy would like to think me taken in *flagrante delicto*, eh?

BROWN: Don't be a damn fool! Listen to me! I've been looking you up for purely selfish reasons. I need your help.

DION [*astonished*]: What?

BROWN: I've a proposition to make that I hope you'll consider favourably out of old friendship. To be frank, Dion, I need you to lend me a hand down at the office.

DION [*with a harsh laugh*]: So it's the job, is it? Then my poor wife did a-begging go!

BROWN [*repelled—sharply*]: On the contrary, I had to beg her to beg you to take it! [*More angrily.*] Look here, Dion! I won't listen to you talk that way about Margaret! And you wouldn't if you weren't drunk! [*Suddenly shaking him.*] What in hell has come over you, anyway! You didn't use to be like this! What the devil are you going to do with yourself—sink into the gutter and drag Margaret with you? If you'd heard her defend you, lie about you, tell me how hard you were working, what beautiful things you were painting, how you stayed at home and idolized the children!—when every one knows you've been out every night sousing and gambling away the last of your estate. . . . [*He stops, ashamed, controlling himself.*]

DION [*wearily*]: She was lying about her husband, not me, you fool! But it's no use explaining. [*Then, in a sudden, excitable passion.*] What do you want? I agree to anything—except the humiliation of yelling secrets at the deaf!

BROWN [*trying a bullying tone—roughly*]: Bunk! Don't try to crawl out! There's no excuse and you know it. [*Then as* DION *doesn't reply—penitently.*] But I know I shouldn't talk this way, old man! It's only because we're such old pals—and I hate to see you wasting yourself—you who had more brains than any of us! But, damn it, I suppose you're too much of a rotten cynic to believe I mean what I've just said!

DION [*touched*]: I know Billy was always Dion Anthony's friend.

BROWN: You're damn right, I am—and I'd have proved it long ago if you'd only given me half a chance! After all, I couldn't keep chasing after you and be snubbed every time. A man has some pride!

DION [*bitterly mocking*]: Dead wrong! Never more! None whatever! It's unmoral! Blessed are the poor in spirit, Brother! When shall I report?

BROWN [*eagerly*]: Then you'll take the—you'll help me?

DION [*wearily bitter*]: I'll take the job. One must do something to pass away the time, while one is waiting—for one's next incarnation.

BROWN [*jokingly*]: I'd say it was a bit early to be worrying about that. [*Trying to get* DION *started.*] Come along, now. It's pretty late.

DION [*shakes his hand off his shoulder and walks away from him—after a pause*]: Is my father's chair still there?

BROWN [*turns away–embarrassed*]: I–I don't really remember, Dion–I'll look it up.

DION [*taking off his mask–slowly*]: I'd like to sit where he spun what I have spent. What aliens we were to each other! When he lay dead, his face looked so familiar that I wondered where I had met that man before. Only at the second of my conception. After that, we grew hostile with concealed shame. And my mother? I remember a sweet, strange girl, with affectionate, bewildered eyes as if God had locked her in a dark closet without any explanation. I was the sole doll our ogre, her husband, allowed her and she played mother and child with me for many years in that house until at last through two tears I watched her die with the shy pride of one who has lengthened her dress and put up her hair. And I felt like a forsaken toy and cried to be buried with her, because her hands alone had caressed without clawing. She lived long and aged greatly in the two days before they closed her coffin. The last time I looked, her purity had forgotten me, she was stainless and imperishable, and I knew my sobs were ugly and meaningless to her virginity; so I shrank away, back into life, with naked nerves jumping like fleas, and in due course of nature another girl called me her boy in the moon and married me and became three mothers in one person, while I got paint on my paws in an endeavour to see God! [*He laughs wildly–claps on his mask.*] But that Ancient Humorist had given me weak eyes, so now I'll have to foreswear my quest for Him and go in for the Omnipresent Successful Serious One, the Great God Mr Brown, instead! [*He makes him a sweeping, mocking bow.*]

BROWN [*repelled but cajolingly*]: Shut up, you nut! You're still drunk. Come on! Let's start! [*He grabs* DION *by the arm and switches off the light.*]

DION [*from the darkness–mockingly*]: I am thy shorn, bald, nude sheep! Lead on, Almighty Brown, thou Kindly Light!

CURTAIN

ACT TWO

SCENE I

SCENE: CYBEL's parlour—about sunset in spring seven years later. The arrangement of furniture is the same but the chair and sofa are new, bright-coloured, costly pieces. The old automatic piano at centre looks exactly the same. The cheap alarm clock is still on top of it. On either side of the clock, the masks of DION and CYBEL are lying. The background backdrop is brilliant, stunning wall-paper, on which crimson and purple flowers and fruits tumble over one another in a riotously profane lack of any apparent design.

Dion sits in the chair on left, CYBEL on the sofa. A card-table is between them. Both are playing solitaire. DION is now prematurely grey. His face is that of an ascetic, a martyr, furrowed by pain and self-torture, yet lighted from within by a spiritual calm and human kindliness.

CYBEL has grown stouter and more voluptuous, but her face is still unmarked and fresh, her calm more profound. She is like an unmoved idol of Mother Earth.

The piano is whining out its same old sentimental medley. They play their cards intently and contentedly. The music stops.

CYBEL [*musingly*]: I love those rotten old sob tunes. They make me wise to people. That's what's inside them—what makes them love and murder their neighbour—crying jags set to music!

DION [*compassionately*]: Every song is a hymn. They keep trying to find the Word in the Beginning.

CYBEL: They try to know too much. It makes them weak. I never puzzled over them myself. I gave them a Tart. They understood her and knew their parts and acted naturally. And on both sides we were able to keep our real virtue, if you get me. [*She plays her last card—indifferently*] I've made it again.

DION [*smiling*]: Your luck is uncanny. It never comes out for me.

CYBEL: You keep getting closer, but it knows you still want to win—a little bit—and it's wise all I care about is playing. [*She lays out another game.*] Speaking of my canned music, our Mr Brown hates that old box.

At the mention of BROWN, DION *trembles as if suddenly possessed, has a terrible struggle with himself, then while she continues to speak, gets up like an automaton and puts on his mask. The mask is now terribly ravaged. All of its Pan quality has changed into a diabolical Mephistophelean cruelty and irony.*

He doesn't mind the music inside. That gets him somehow. But he thinks the case looks shabby and he wants it junked. But I told him that just because he's been keeping me so long, he needn't start bossing like a husband or I'll—[*She looks up and sees the masked* DION *standing by the piano—calmly.*]

Hello! Getting jealous again?

DION [*jeeringly*]: Are you falling in love with your keeper, old Sacred Cow?

CYBEL [*without taking offence*]: Cut it! You've been asking me that for years. Be yourself! He's healthy and handsome—but he's too guilty. What makes you pretend you think love is so important, anyway? It's just one of a lot of things you do to keep life living.

DION [*in same tone*]: Then you've lied when you've said you loved me, have you, Old Filth?

CYBEL [*affectionately*]: You'll never grow up! We've been friends, haven't we, for seven years? I've never let myself want you nor you me. Yes, I love you. It takes all kinds of love to make a world! Ours is the living cream, I say, living rich and high! [*A pause. Coaxingly.*] Stop hiding. I know you.

DION [*taking off his mask, wearily comes and sits down at her feet and lays his head in her lap—with a grateful smile*]: You're strong. You always give. You've given my weakness strength to live.

CYBEL [*tenderly, stroking his hair maternally*]: You're not weak. You were born with ghosts in your eyes and you were brave enough to go looking into your own dark—and you got afraid. [*After a pause.*] I don't blame your being jealous of Mr Brown sometimes. I'm jealous of your wife, even though I know you do love her.

DION [*slowly*]: I love Margaret. I don't know who my wife is.

CYBEL [*after a pause—with a queer broken laugh*]: Oh, God, sometimes the truth hits me such a sock between the eyes I can see the stars!—and then I'm so damn sorry for the lot of you, every damn mother's son-of-a-gun of you, that I'd like to run out naked into the street and love the whole mob to death like I was bringing you all a new brand of dope that'd make you forget everything that ever was for good! [*Then, with a twisted smile.*] But they wouldn't see me, any more than they see each other. And they keep right on moving along and dying without my help anyway.

DION [*sadly*]: You've given me strength to die.

CYBEL: You may be important but your life's not. There's millions of it born every second. Life can cost too much even for a sucker to afford it—like everything else. And it's not sacred—only the you inside is. The rest is earth.

DION [*gets to his knees and with clasped hands looks up raptly and prays with an ascetic fervour*]: 'Into thy hands, O Lord,' . . . [*Then suddenly, with a look of horror.*] Nothing! To feel one's life blown out like the flame of a cheap match . . .! [*He claps on his mask and laughs harshly.*] To fall asleep and know you'll never, never be called to get on the job of existence again! 'Swift be thine approaching flight! Come soon—soon!' [*He quotes this last with a mocking longing.*]

CYBEL [*pats his head maternally*]. There, don't be scared. It's born in the blood. When the time comes, you'll find it's easy.

DION [*jumps to his feet and walks about excitedly*]: It won't be long. My wife dragged in a doctor the day before yesterday. He says my heart is gone—booze—He warned me, never another drop or—[*Mockingly.*] What say? Shall we have a drink?

CYBEL [*like an idol*]: Suit yourself. It's in the pantry. [*Then, as he hesitates.*] What set you off on this bat? You were raving on about some cathedral plans. . . .

DION [*wildly mocking*]: They've been accepted—Mr Brown's designs! My designs really! You don't need to be told that. He hands me one mathematically correct barn after another and I doctor them up with cute allurements so that fools will desire to buy, sell, breed, sleep, love, hate, curse and pray in them! I do this with devilish cleverness to their entire delight! Once I dreamed of painting wind on the sea and the skimming flight of cloud shadows over the tops of trees! Now . . . [*He laughs.*] But pride is a sin—even in a memory of the long deceased! Blessed are the poor in spirit! [*He subsides weakly on his chair, his hand pressed to his heart.*]

CYBEL [*like an idol*]: Go home and sleep. Your wife'll be worried.

DION: She knows—but she'll never admit to herself that her husband ever entered your door. [*Mocking.*] Aren't women loyal—to their vanity and their other things!

CYBEL: Brown is coming soon, don't forget.

DION: He knows too and can't admit. Perhaps he needs me here—unknown. What first aroused his passion to possess you exclusively, do you think? Because he knew you loved me and he felt himself cheated. He wanted what he thought was my love of the flesh! He feels I have no right to love. He'd like to steal it as he steals my ideas—complacently—righteously. Oh, the good Brown!

CYBEL: But you like him, too! You're brothers, I guess, somehow. Well, remember he's paying, he'll pay—in some way or other.

DION [*raises his head as if starting to remove the mask*]: I know. Poor Billy! God forgive me the evil I've done him!

CYBEL [*reaches out and takes his hand*]: Poor boy!

DION [*presses her convulsively—then with forced harshness*]: Well, homeward Christian Soldier! I'm off! By-bye, Mother Earth. [*He starts to go off right. She seems about to let him go.*]

CYBEL [*suddenly starts and calls with deep grief*]: Dion!

> He looks at her. A pause. He comes slowly back. She speaks strangely in a deep, far-off voice—and yet like a mother talking to her little son.

You mustn't forget to kiss me before you go, Dion. [*She removes his mask.*] Haven't I told you to take off your mask in the house? Look at me, Dion. I've—just—seen—something. I'm afraid you're going away a long, long way. I'm afraid I won't see you again for a long, long time. So it's good-bye, dear. [*She kisses him gently. He begins to sob. She hands him back his mask.*] Here you are. Don't get hurt. Remember, it's all a game, and after you're asleep I'll tuck you in.

DION [*in a choking, heart-broken cry*]. Mother! [*Then he claps on his mask with a terrible effort of will—mockingly.*] Go to the devil, you sentimental old pig! See you to-morrow! [*He goes, whistling, slamming the door.*]

CYBEL [*like an idol again*]. What's the good of bearing children? What's the use of giving birth to death?

> She sighs wearily, turns, puts a plug in the piano, which starts up its old sentimental tune. At the same moment BROWN enters quietly from the left. He is the ideal of the still youthful, good-looking, well-groomed, successful provincial American of forty. Just now, he is plainly perturbed. He is not able to see either CYBEL's face or her mask.

BROWN: Cybel!

She starts, jams off the music and reaches for her mask, but has no time to put it on.

Wasn't that Dion I just saw going out–after all your promises never to see him!

She turns like an idol, holding the mask behind her. He stares, bewildered–stammers.

I–I beg your pardon–I thought—

CYBEL [*in her strange voice*]: Cybel's gone out to dig in the earth and pray.

BROWN [*with more assurance*]: But–aren't those her clothes?

CYBEL: Cybel doesn't want people to see me naked. I'm her sister. Dion came to see me.

BROWN [*relieved*]: So that's what he's up to, is it? [*Then with a pitying sigh.*] Poor Margaret! [*Then with playful reproof.*] You really shouldn't encourage him. He's married and got three big sons.

CYBEL: And you haven't.

BROWN [*stung*]: No, I'm not married.

CYBEL: He and I were friends.

BROWN [*with a playful wink*]: Yes, I can imagine how the platonic must appeal to Dion's pure, innocent type! It's no good your kidding me about Dion. We've been friends since we were kids. I know him in and out. I've always stood up for him whatever he's done–so you can be perfectly frank. I only spoke as I did on account of Margaret–his wife–it's pretty tough on her.

CYBEL: You love his wife.

BROWN [*scandalized*]: What? What are you talking about? [*Then uncertainly.*] Don't be a fool! [*A pause–then as if impelled by an intense curiosity.*] So Dion is your lover, eh? That's very interesting. [*He pulls his chair closer to hers.*] Sit down. Let's talk. [*She continues to stand, the mask held behind her.*] Tell me–I've always been curious–what is it that makes Dion so attractive to women–especially certain types of women, if you'll pardon me? He always has been and yet I never could see exactly what they saw in him. Is it his looks–or because he's such a violent sensualist–or because he poses as artistic and temperamental–or because he's so wild–or just what is it?

CYBEL: He's alive!

BROWN [*suddenly takes one of her hands and kisses it–insinuatingly*]: Well, don't you think I'm alive, too? [*Eagerly.*] Listen. Would you consider giving up Dion–and letting me take care of you under a similar arrangement to the one I've made with Cybel? I like you, you can see that. I won't bother you much–I'm much too busy–you can do what you like–lead your own life–except for seeing him. [*He stops. A pause. She stares ahead unmoved as if she hadn't heard. He pleads.*] Well–what do you say? Please do!

CYBEL [*her voice very weary*]: Cybel asked me to tell you she'd be back next week, Mr Brown.

BROWN [*with queer agony*]: You mean you won't? Don't be so cruel! I love you!

She walks away. He clutches at her, pleadingly.

At least–I'll give you anything you ask!–please promise me you won't see Dion Anthony again!

CYBEL [*with deep grief*]. He will never see me again, I promise you. Good-bye!
BROWN [*jubilantly, kissing her hand—politely*]: Thank you! Thank you! I'm
exceedingly grateful. [*Tactfully*.] I won't disturb you any further. Please
forgive my intrusion, and remember me to Cybel when you write. [*He bows,
turns, and goes off left*.]

CURTAIN

SCENE 2

SCENE: The draughting-room in BROWN's office. DION's draughting table with a
high stool in front is at centre. Another stool is to the left of it. At the right is a
bench. It is in the evening of the same day. The black wall drop has windows
painted on it with a dim, street-lighted view of black houses across the way.

DION is sitting on the stool behind the table, reading aloud from the *Imitation
of Christ* by Thomas à Kempis to his mask, which is on the table before him.
His own face is gentler, more spiritual, more saintlike and ascetic than ever
before.

DION [*like a priest, offering up prayers for the dying*]: 'Quickly must thou be gone
from hence, see then how matters stand with thee. Ah, fool—learn now to die
to the world that thou mayst begin to live with Christ! Do now, beloved, do
now all thou canst because thou knowest not when thou shalt die; nor dost
thou know what shall befall thee after death. Keep thyself as a pilgrim, and a
stranger upon earth, to whom the affairs of this world do not—belong! Keep
thy heart free and raised upwards to God because thou hast not here a lasting
abode. "Because at what hour you know not the Son of Man will come!"'
Amen. [*He raises his hand over the mask as if he were blessing it, closes the book
and puts it back in his pocket. He raises the mask in his hands and stares at it with
a pitying tenderness*.] Peace, poor tortured one, brave pitiful pride of man,
the hour of our deliverance comes. To-morrow we may be with Him in
Paradise!

He kisses it on the lips and sets it down again. There is the noise of footsteps
climbing the stairs in the hallway. He grabs up the mask in a sudden panic and,
as a knock comes on the door, he claps it on and calls mockingly.

Come in, Mrs Anthony, come in!

Margaret enters. In one hand behind her, hidden from him, is the mask of the
brave face she puts on before the world to hide her suffering and
disillusionment, and which she has just taken off. Her own face is still sweet and
pretty, but lined, drawn and careworn for its years, sad, resigned, but a bit
querulous.

MARGARET [*wearily reproving*]: Thank goodness I've found you! Why haven't
you been home the last two days? It's bad enough your drinking again
without your staying away and worrying us to death!
DION [*bitterly*]: My ears knew her footsteps. One gets to recognize every-

thing–and to see nothing!

MARGARET: I finally sent the boys out looking for you and came myself. [*With tired solicitude.*] I suppose you haven't eaten a thing, as usual. Won't you come home and let me fry you a chop?

DION [*wonderingly*]: Can Margaret still love Dion Anthony? Is it possible she does?

MARGARET [*forcing a tired smile*]: I suppose so, Dion. I certainly oughtn't to, ought I?

DION [*in same tone*]: And I love Margaret! What haunted, haunting ghosts we are! We dimly remember so much it will take us so many million years to forget! [*He comes forward, putting one arm around her bowed shoulders, and they kiss.*]

MARGARET [*patting his hand affectionately*]: No, you certainly don't deserve it. When I stop to think of all you've made me go through in the years since we settled down here . . . ! I really don't believe I could ever have stood it if it weren't for the boys! [*Forcing a smile.*] But perhaps I would, I've always been such a big fool about you.

DION [*a bit mockingly*]: The boys! Three strong sons! Margaret can afford to be magnanimous!

MARGARET: If they didn't find you, they were coming to meet me here.

DION [*with sudden wildness–torturedly, sinking on his knees beside her*]: Margaret! Margaret! I'm lonely! I'm frightened! I'm going away! I've got to say good-bye!

MARGARET [*patting his hair*]: Poor boy! Poor Dion! Come home and sleep.

DION [*springs up frantically*]: No! I'm a man. I'm a lonely man! I can't go back! I have conceived myself! [*Then with desperate mockery.*] Look at me, Mrs Anthony! It's the last chance! To-morrow I'll have moved on to the next hell! Behold your man–the snivelling, cringing, life-denying Christian slave you have so nobly ignored in the father of your sons! Look! [*He tears the mask from his face, which is radiant with a great pure love for her and a great sympathy and tenderness.*] O woman–my love–that I have sinned against in my sick pride and cruelty–forgive my sins–forgive my solitude–forgive my sickness–forgive me! [*He kneels and kisses the hem of her dress.*]

MARGARET [*who has been staring at him with terror, raising her mask to ward off his face*]: Dion! Don't! I can't bear it! You're like a ghost. You're dead! Oh, my God! Help! Help!

She falls back fainting on the bench. He looks at her–then takes her hand which holds her mask and looks at that face–gently.

And now I am permitted to understand and love you, too!

He kisses the mask first–then kisses her face, murmuring.

And you, sweetheart! Blessed, thrice blessed are the meek!

There is a sound of heavy, hurrying footsteps on the stairs. He puts on his mask in haste. The three sons rush into the room. The ELDEST is about fourteen, the two others thirteen and twelve. They look healthy, normal, likeable boys, with much the same quality as BILLY BROWN's in Act One, Scene I. They stop short and stiffen all in a row, staring from the woman on the bench to their father, accusingly.

ELDEST: We heard some one yell. It sounded like Mother.

DION [*defensively*]: No. It was this lady—my wife.

ELDEST: But hasn't Mother come yet?

DION [*going to Margaret*]: Yes. Your Mother is here. [*He stands between them and puts her mask over* MARGARET's *face—then steps back.*] She has fainted. You'd better bring her to.

BOYS: Mother! [*They run to her side, kneel and rub her wrists. The* ELDEST *smooths back her hair.*]

DION [*watching them*]: At least I am leaving her well provided for. [*He addresses them directly.*] Tell your mother she'll get word from Mr Brown's house. I must pay him a farewell call. I am going. Good-bye.

They stop, staring at him fixedly, with eyes a mixture of bewilderment, distrust and hurt.

ELDEST [*awkwardly and shamefacedly*]: Honest, I think you ought to have . . .

SECOND: Yes, honest you ought . . .

YOUNGEST: Yes, honest . . .

DION [*in a friendly tone*]: I know. But I couldn't. That's for you who can. You must inherit the earth for her. Don't forget now, boys. Good-bye.

BOYS [*in the same awkward, self-conscious tone, one after another*]: Good-bye—good-bye—good-bye.

Dion goes.

CURTAIN

SCENE 3

SCENE: The library of WILLIAM BROWN's home—night of the same day. A backdrop of carefully painted, prosperous, bourgeois culture, bookcases filled with sets, etc. The heavy table at centre is expensive. The leather arm-chair at left of it and the couch at right are opulently comfortable. The reading lamp on the table is the only light.

BROWN sits in the chair at left reading an architectural periodical. His expression is composed and gravely receptive. In outline, his face suggests a Roman consul on an old coin. There is an incongruous distinction about it, the quality of unquestioning faith in the finality of its achievement.

There is a sudden loud thumping on the front door and the ringing of the bell. BROWN frowns and listens as a servant answers. DION's voice can be heard, raised mockingly.

DION: Tell him it's the devil come to conclude a bargain.

BROWN [*suppressing annoyance, calls out with forced good nature*]: Come on in, Dion.

Dion enters. He is in a wild state. His clothes are dishevelled, his masked face has a terrible deathlike intensity, its mocking irony becomes so cruelly malignant as to give him the appearance of a real demon, tortured into torturing others.

Sit down.

DION [*stands and sings*]: William Brown's soul lies mouldering in the crib, but his body goes marching on!

BROWN [*maintaining the same indulgent, big-brotherly tone, which he tries to hold throughout the scene*]: Not so loud, for Pete's sake! I don't mind—but I've got neighbours.

DION: Hate them! Fear thy neighbour as thyself! That's the leaden rule for the safe and sane. [*Then advancing to the table with a sort of deadly calm.*] Listen! One day when I was four years old, a boy sneaked up behind when I was drawing a picture in the sand he couldn't draw and hit me on the head with a stick and kicked out my picture and laughed when I cried. It wasn't what he'd done that made me cry, but him! I had loved and trusted him and suddenly the good God was disproved in his person and the evil and injustice of Man was born! Every one called me cry-baby, so I became silent for life and designed a mask of the Bad Boy Pan in which to live and rebel against that other boy's God and protect myself from His cruelty. And that other boy, secretly he felt ashamed but he couldn't acknowledge it; so from that day he instinctively developed into the good boy, the good friend, the good man, William Brown!

BROWN [*shamefacedly*]: I remember now. It was a dirty trick. [*Then with a trace of resentment.*] Sit down. You know where the booze is. Have a drink, if you like. But I guess you've had enough already.

DION [*looks at him fixedly for a moment—then strangely*]: Thanks be to Brown for reminding me. I must drink. [*He goes and gets a bottle of whisky and a glass.*]

BROWN [*with a good-humoured shrug*]: All right. It's your funeral.

DION [*returning and pouring out a big drink in the tumbler*]: And William Brown's! When I die, he goes to hell! Shöal! [*He drinks and stares malevolently. In spite of himself, BROWN is uneasy. A pause.*]

BROWN [*with forced casualness*]: You've been on this toot for a week now.

DION [*tauntingly*]: I've been celebrating the acceptance of *my* design for the cathedral.

BROWN [*humorously*]: You certainly helped me a lot on it.

DION [*with a harsh laugh*]: O perfect Brown! Never mind! I'll make him look in my mirror yet—and drown in it! [*He pours out another big drink.*]

BROWN [*rather tauntingly*]: Go easy. I don't want your corpse on my hands.

DION: But I do. [*He drinks.*] Brown will still need me—to reassure him he's alive! I've loved, lusted, won and lost, sung and wept! I've been life's lover! I've fulfilled her will and if she's through with me now it's only because I was too weak to dominate her in turn. It isn't enough to be her creature, you've got to create her or she requests you to destroy yourself.

BROWN [*good-naturedly*]: Nonsense. Go home and get some sleep.

DION [*as if he hadn't heard—bitingly*]: But to be neither creature nor creator! To exist only in her indifference! To be unloved by life! [*Brown stirs uneasily.*] To be merely a successful freak, the result of some snide neutralizing of life forces—a spineless cactus—a wild boar of the mountains altered into a packer's hog eating to become food—a Don Juan inspired to romance by a monkey's glands—and to have Life not even think you funny enough to see!

BROWN [*stung—angrily*]: Bosh!

DION: Consider Mr Brown. His parents bore him on earth as if they were thereby entering him in a baby parade with prizes for the fattest—and he's still being wheeled along in the procession, too fat now to learn to walk, let alone to dance or run, and he'll never live until his liberated dust quickens into earth!

BROWN [*gruffly*]: Rave on! [*Then with forced good-nature.*] Well, Dion, at any rate, I'm satisfied.

DION [*quickly and malevolently*]: No! Brown isn't satisfied! He's piled on layers of protective fat, but vaguely, deeply he feels at his heart the gnawing of a doubt! And I'm interested in that germ which wriggles like a question mark of insecurity in his blood, because it's part of the creative life Brown's stolen from me!

BROWN [*forcing a sour grin*]: Steal Germs? I thought you caught them.

DION [*as if he hadn't heard*]: It's mine—and I'm interested in seeing it thrive and breed and become multitudes and eat until Brown is consumed!

BROWN [*cannot restrain a shudder*]: Sometimes when you're drunk, you're positively evil; do you know it?

DION [*sombrely*]: When Pan was forbidden the light and warmth of the sun he grew sensitive and self-conscious and proud and revengeful—and became Prince of Darkness.

BROWN [*jocularly*]: You don't fit the rôle of Pan, Dion. It sounds to me like Bacchus, alias the Demon Rum, doing the talking.

> DION *recovers from his spasm with a start and stares at* BROWN *with terrible hatred. There is a pause. In spite of himself,* BROWN *squirms and adopts a placating tone.*

Go home. It's all well enough celebrating our design being accepted, but—

DION [*in steely voice*]: I've been the brains! I've been the design! I've designed even his success—drunk and laughing at him—laughing at his career! Not proud! Sick! Sick of myself and him! Designing and getting drunk? Saving my woman and children! [*He laughs.*] Ha! And this cathedral is my masterpiece! It will make Brown the most eminent architect in this state of God's Country. I put a lot into it—what was left of my life! It's one vivid blasphemy from pavement to the tips of its spires!—but so concealed that the fools will never know. They'll kneel and worship the ironic Silenus who tells them the best good is never to be born! [*He laughs triumphantly.*] Well, blasphemy is faith, isn't it? In self-preservation the devil must believe! But Mr Brown, the Great Brown, has no faith! He couldn't design a cathedral without it looking like the First Supernatural Bank! He only believes in the immortality of the moral belly! [*He laughs wildly—then sinks down in his chair, gasping, his hands pressed to his heart. Then suddenly becomes deadly calm and pronounces like a cruel malignant condemnation.*] From now on, Brown will never design anything. He will devote his life to renovating the house of my Cybel into a home for my Margaret!

BROWN [*springing to his feet, his face convulsed with strange agony*]: I've stood enough! How dare you . . . !

DION [*his voice like a probe*]: Why has no woman ever loved him? Why has he always been the Big Brother, the Friend? Isn't their trust—a contempt?

BROWN: You lie!

DION: Why has he never been able to love—since my Margaret? Why has he never married? Why has he tried to steal Cybel, as he once tried to steal Margaret? Isn't it out of revenge—and envy?

BROWN [*violently*]: Rot! I wanted Cybel, and I bought her!

DION: Brown bought her for me! She has loved me more than he will ever know!

BROWN: You lie! [*Then furiously.*] I'll throw her back on the street!

DION: To me! To her fellow-creature! Why hasn't Brown had children—he who loves children—he who loves *my* children—he who envies me *my* children?

BROWN [*brokenly*]: I'm not ashamed to envy you them!

DION: They like Brown, too—as a friend—as an equal—as Margaret has always liked him—

BROWN [*brokenly*]: And as I've liked her!

DION: How many million times Brown has thought how much better for her it would have been if she'd chosen him instead!

BROWN [*torturedly*]: You lie! [*Then with sudden frenzied defiance.*] All right! If you force me to say it, I do love Margaret! I always have loved her and you've always known I did!

DION [*with a terrible composure*]: No! That is merely the appearance, not the truth! Brown loves me! He loves me because I have always possessed the power he needed for love, because I am love!

BROWN [*frenziedly*]: You drunken fool! [*He leaps on* DION *and grabs him by the throat.*]

DION [*triumphantly, staring into his eyes*]: Ah! Now he looks into the mirror! Now he sees his face!

Brown lets go of him and staggers back to his chair, pale and trembling.

BROWN [*humbly*]: Stop, for God's sake! You're mad!

DION [*sinking in his chair, more and more weakly*]: I'm done. My heart, not Brown—[*Mockingly.*] My last will and testament! I leave Dion Anthony to William Brown—for him to love and obey—for him to become me—then my Margaret will love me—my children will love me—Mr and Mrs Brown and sons, happily ever after! [*Staggering to his full height and looking upward defiantly.*] Nothing more—but Man's last gesture—by which he conquers—to laugh! Ha—[*He begins, stops as if paralysed, and drops on his knees by Brown's chair, his mask falling off, his Christian Martyr's face at the point of death.*] Forgive me, Billy. Bury me, hide me, forget me for your own happiness! May Margaret love you! May you design the Temple of Man's Soul! Blessed are the meek and the poor in spirit! [*He kisses* BROWN's *feet—then more and more weakly and childishly.*] What was the prayer, Billy? I'm getting so sleepy. . . .

BROWN [*in a trancelike tone*]: 'Our Father who art in Heaven.'

DION [*drowsily*]: 'Our Father.' . . .

He dies. A pause. BROWN *remains in a stupor for a moment—then stirs himself, puts his hand on* DION's *breast.*

BROWN [*dully*]: He's dead—at last. [*He says this mechanically, but the last two words awaken him—wonderingly.*] At last? [*Then with triumph.*] At last! [*He stares at* DION's *real face contemptuously.*] So that's the poor weakling you really were! No wonder you hid! And I've always been afraid of you–yes, I'll confess it now, in awe of you! Paugh! [*He picks up the mask from the floor.*] No, not of you! Of this! Say what you like, it's strong if it is bad! And this is what Margaret loved, not you! Not you! This man!–this man who willed himself to me! [*Struck by an idea, he jumps to his feet.*] By God! [*He slowly starts to put the mask on. A knocking comes on the street door. He starts guiltily, laying the mask on the table. Then he picks it up again quickly, takes the dead body and carries it off left. He reappears immediately and goes to the front door as the knocking recommences–gruffly.*] Hello! Who's there?

MARGARET: It's Margaret, Billy. I'm looking for Dion.

BROWN [*uncertainly*]: Oh–all right–[*Unfastening door.*] Come in. Hello, Margaret. Hello, Boys! He's here. He's asleep. I–I was just dozing off too.

Margaret enters. She is wearing her mask. The three sons are with her.

MARGARET [*seeing the bottle, forcing a laugh*]: Has he been celebrating?

BROWN [*with strange glibness now*]: No. I was. He wasn't. He said he'd sworn off to-night–for ever–for your sake–and the kids!

MARGARET [*with amazed joy*]: Dion said that? [*Then hastily defensive.*] But of course he never does drink much. Where is he?

BROWN: Upstairs. I'll wake him. He felt bad. He took off his clothes to take a bath before he lay down. You just wait here.

She sits in the chair where DION had sat and stares straight before her. The SONS group around her, as if for a family photo. BROWN hurries out left.

MARGARET: It's late to keep you boys up. Aren't you sleepy?

BOYS: No, Mother.

MARGARET [*proudly*]: I'm glad to have three such strong boys to protect me.

ELDEST [*boastingly*]: We'd kill anyone that touched you, wouldn't we?

NEXT: You bet! We'd make him wish he hadn't!

YOUNGEST: You bet!

MARGARET: You're Mother's brave boys! [*She laughs fondly–then curiously.*] Do you like Mr Brown?

ELDEST: Sure thing! He's a regular fellow.

NEXT: He's all right!

YOUNGEST: Sure thing!

MARGARET [*half to herself*]: Your father claims he steals his ideas.

ELDEST [*with a sheepish grin*]: I'll bet father said that when he was–just talking.

NEXT: Mr Brown doesn't have to steal, does he?

YOUNGEST: I should say not! He's awful rich.

MARGARET: Do you love your father?

ELDEST [*scuffling–embarrassed*]: Why–of course—

NEXT [*ditto*]: Sure thing!

YOUNGEST: Sure I do.

MARGARET [*with a sigh*]: I think you'd better start on before–right now–before your father comes–He'll be very sick and nervous and he'll want to be quiet. So run along!

BOYS: All right.

They file out and close the front door as BROWN, dressed in DION's clothes and wearing his mask, appears at left.

MARGARET [*taking off her mask, gladly*]: Dion! [*She stares wonderingly at him and he at her; goes to him and puts an arm around him.*] Poor dear, do you feel sick? [*He nods.*] But you look [*squeezing his arms*]–why, you actually feel stronger and better already! Is it true what Billy told me–about your swearing off for ever? [*He nods. She exclaims intensely.*] Oh, if you'll only–and get well–we can still be so happy! Give Mother a kiss. [*They kiss. A shudder passes through both of them. She breaks away laughing with aroused desire.*] Why, Dion? Aren't you ashamed? You haven't kissed me like that for ages!

BROWN [*his voice imitating* DION's *and muffled by the mask*]: I've wanted to, Margaret!

MARGARET [*gaily and coquettishly now*]: Were you afraid I'd spurn you? Why, Dion, something has happened. It's like a miracle! Even your voice is changed! It actually sounds younger; do you know it? [*Then, solicitously.*] But you must be worn out. Let's go home. [*With an impulsive movement she flings her arms wide open, throwing her mask away from her as if suddenly no longer needing it.*] Oh, I'm beginning to feel so happy, Dion–so happy!

BROWN [*stifledly*]: Let's go home.

She puts her arm around him. They walk to the door.

CURTAIN

ACT THREE

SCENE I

SCENE: The draughting-room and private office of BROWN are both shown. The former is on the left, the latter on the right of a dividing wall at the centre. The arrangement of furniture in each room is the same as in previous scenes. It is ten in the morning of a day about a month later. The backdrop for both rooms is of plain wall with a few tacked-up designs and blue prints painted on it.

Two DRAUGHTSMEN, a middle-aged and a young man, both stoop-shouldered, are sitting on stools behind what was formerly DION's table. They are tracing plans. They talk as they work.

OLDER DRAUGHTSMAN: W. B. is late again.

YOUNGER DRAUGHTSMAN: Wonder what's got into him the last month?

A pause. They work silently.

OLDER DRAUGHTSMAN: Yes, ever since he fired Dion. . . .

YOUNGER DRAUGHTSMAN: Funny his firing him all of a sudden like that.

A pause. They work.

OLDER DRAUGHTSMAN: I haven't seen Dion around town since then. Have you?

YOUNGER DRAUGHTSMAN: No, not since Brown told us he'd sacked him. I suppose he's off drowning his sorrow!

OLDER DRAUGHTSMAN: I heard some one had seen him at home and he was sober and looking fine.

A pause. They work.

YOUNGER DRAUGHTSMAN: What got into Brown? They say he fired all his old servants that same day and only uses his house to sleep in.

OLDER DRAUGHTSMAN [*with a sneer*]: Artistic temperament, maybe—the real name of which is swelled head!

There is a noise of footsteps from the hall.

OLDER DRAUGHTSMAN [*warningly*]: Ssstt!

They bend over their table. MARGARET enters. She does not need to wear a mask now. Her face has regained the self-confident spirit of its youth, her eyes shine with happiness.

MARGARET [*heartily*]: Good morning! What a lovely day!

BOTH [*perfunctorily*]: Good morning, Mrs Anthony.

MARGARET [*looking around*]: You've been changing around in here, haven't you? Where is Dion?

They stare at her.

I forgot to tell him something important this morning and our phone's out of order. So if you'll tell him I'm here—

They don't move. A pause.

[*Margaret says stiffly.*] Oh, I realize Mr Brown has given strict orders Dion is not to be disturbed, but surely. . . . [*Sharply.*] Where is my husband, please?

OLDER DRAUGHTSMAN: We don't know.

MARGARET: You don't know?

YOUNGER DRAUGHTSMAN: We haven't seen him.

MARGARET: Why, he left home at eight-thirty!

OLDER DRAUGHTSMAN: To come here?

YOUNGER DRAUGHTSMAN: This morning?

MARGARET [*provoked*]: Why, of course, to come here–as he does every day!

They stare at her. A pause.

OLDER DRAUGHTSMAN [*evasively*]: We haven't seen him.

MARGARET [*with asperity*]: Where is Mr Brown?

YOUNGER DRAUGHTSMAN [*at a noise of footsteps from the hall–sulkily*]: Coming now.

BROWN *enters. He is now wearing a mask which is an exact likeness of his face as it was in the last scene–the self-assured success. When he sees* MARGARET, *he starts back apprehensively.*

BROWN [*immediately controlling himself–breezily*]: Hello, Margaret! This is a pleasant surprise! [*He holds out his hand.*]

MARGARET [*hardly taking it–reservedly*]: Good morning.

BROWN [*turning quickly to the* DRAUGHTSMEN]: I hope you explained to Mrs Anthony how busy Dion . . .

MARGARET [*interrupting him–stiffly*]: I certainly can't understand—

BROWN [*hastily*]: I'll explain. Come in here and be comfortable. [*He throws open the door and ushers her into his private office.*]

OLDER DRAUGHTSMAN: Dion must be putting over some bluff on her.

YOUNGER DRAUGHTSMAN: Pretending he's still here–and Brown's helping him. . . .

OLDER DRAUGHTSMAN: But why should Brown, after he . . .?

YOUNGER DRAUGHTSMAN: Well, I suppose—Search me.

They work.

BROWN: Have a chair, Margaret.

She sits on the chair stiffly. He sits behind the desk.

MARGARET [*coldly*]: I'd like some explanation. . . .

BROWN [*coaxingly*]: Now, don't get angry, Margaret! Dion is hard at work on his design for the new State Capitol, and I don't want him disturbed, not even by you! So be a good sport! It's for his own good, remember! I asked him to explain to you.

MARGARET [*relenting*]: He told me you'd agreed to ask me and the boys not to come here–but then, we hardly ever did.

BROWN: But you might! [*Then with confidential friendliness.*] This is for his sake, Margaret. I know Dion. He's got to be able to work without distractions. He's not the ordinary man; you appreciate that. And this design means his whole future! He's to get full credit for it, and as soon as it's accepted, I take him into partnership. It's all agreed. And after that I'm going to take a long vacation–go to Europe for a couple of years–and leave everything here in Dion's hands! Hasn't he told you all this?

MARGARET [*jubilant now*]: Yes–but I could hardly believe . . . [*Proudly.*] I'm sure he can do it. He's been like a new man lately, so full of ambition and energy! It's made me so happy! [*She stops in confusion.*]

BROWN [*deeply moved, takes her hand impulsively*]: And it has made me happy, too!

MARGARET [*confused–with an amused laugh*]: Why, Billy Brown! For a moment, I thought it was Dion, your voice sounded so much . . .!

BROWN [*with sudden desperation*]: Margaret, I've got to tell you! I can't go on like this any longer! I've got to confess . . .! There's something . . .!

MARGARET [*alarmed*]: Not–not about Dion?

BROWN [*harshly*]: To hell with Dion! To hell with Billy Brown! [*He tears off his mask and reveals a suffering face that is ravaged and haggard, his own face tortured and distorted by the demon of DION's mask.*] Think of me! I love you, Margaret! Leave him! I've always loved you! Come away with me! I'll sell out here! We'll go abroad and be happy!

MARGARET [*amazed*]: Billy Brown, do you realize what you're saying? [*With a shudder.*] Are you crazy? Your face–is terrible. You're sick! Shall I phone for a doctor?

BROWN [*turning away slowly and putting on his mask–dully*]: No. I've been on the verge–of a breakdown–for some time. I get spells. . . . I'm better now. [*He turns back to her.*] Forgive me! Forget what I said! But, for all our sakes, don't come here again.

MARGARET [*coldly*]: After this–I assure you . . .! [*Then looking at him with pained incredulity.*] Why, Billy–I simply won't believe–after all these years . . .!

BROWN: It will never happen again. Good-bye.

MARGARET: Good-bye. [*Then, wishing to leave on a pleasant change of subject–forcing a smile.*] Don't work Dion to death! He's never home for dinner any more.

She goes out past the DRAUGHTSMEN *and off right, rear.* BROWN *sits down at his desk, taking off the mask again. He stares at it with bitter, cynical amusement.*

BROWN: You're dead, William Brown, dead beyond hope of resurrection! It's the Dion you buried in your garden who killed you, not you him! It's

Margaret's husband who . . . [*He laughs harshly.*] Paradise by proxy! Love by mistaken identity! God! [*This is almost a prayer–then fiercely defiant.*] But it *is* paradise! I *do* love!

As he is speaking, a well-dressed, important, stout man enters the draughting-room. He is carrying a rolled-up plan in his hand. He nods condescendingly and goes directly to BROWN's *door, on which he raps sharply, and, without waiting for an answer, turns the knob.* BROWN *has just time to turn his head and get his mask on.*

MAN [*briskly*]: Ah, good morning! I came right in. Hope I didn't disturb . . .?
BROWN [*the successful architect now–urbanely*]: Not at all, sir. How are you? [*They shake hands.*] Sit down. Have a cigar. And now what can I do for you this morning?
MAN [*unrolling his plan*]: It's your plan. My wife and I have been going over it again. We like it–and we don't–and when a man plans to lay out half a million, why he wants everything exactly right, eh?

BROWN *nods.*

It's too cold, too spare, too like a tomb, if you'll pardon me, for a liveable home. Can't you liven it up, put in some decorations, make it fancier and warmer–you know what I mean. [*Looks at him a bit doubtfully.*] People tell me you had an assistant, Anthony, who was a real shark on these details but that you've fired him—
BROWN [*suavely*]: Gossip! He's still with me but, for reasons of his own, doesn't wish it known. Yes, I trained him and he's very ingenious. I'll turn this right over to him and instruct him to carry out your wishes.

CURTAIN

SCENE 2

SCENE: The same as Act Two, Scene 3–the library of BROWN's home about eight the same night. He can be heard feeling his way in through the dark. He switches on the reading lamp on the table. Directly under it on a sort of stand is the mask of DION, its empty eyes staring front.
BROWN takes off his own mask and lays it on the table before DION's. He flings himself down in the chair and stares without moving into the eyes of DION's mask. Finally, he begins to talk to it in a bitter, mocking tone.

BROWN: Listen! To-day was a narrow escape–for us! We can't avoid discovery much longer. We must get our plot to working! We've already made William Brown's will, leaving you his money and business. We must hustle off to Europe now–and murder him there! [*A bit tauntingly.*] Then you–the I in you–*I* will live with Margaret happily ever after. [*More tauntingly.*] She will have children by me! [*He seems to hear some mocking denial from the mask. He bends toward it.*] What? [*Then with a sneer.*] Anyway, that doesn't matter! Your children already love me more than they ever loved you! And Margaret loves me more! You think you've won, do you–that I've got to vanish into you in order to live? Not yet, my friend! Never! Wait! Gradually Margaret will love what is beneath–me! Little by little I'll teach her to know me, and then finally I'll reveal myself to her, and confess that I stole your place out of love for her, and she'll understand and forgive and love me! And you'll be forgotten! Ha [*Again he bends down to the mask as if listening–torturedly.*] What's that? She'll never believe? She'll never see? She'll never understand? You lie, devil! [*He reaches out his hands as if to take the mask by the throat, then shrinks back with a shudder of hopeless despair.*] God have mercy! Let me believe! Blessed are the merciful! Let me obtain mercy! [*He waits, his face upturned–pleadingly.*] Not yet? [*Despairingly.*] Never? [*A pause. Then, in a sudden panic of dread, he reaches out for the mask of* DION *like a dope fiend after a drug. As soon as he holds it, he seems to gain strength and is able to force a sad laugh.*] Now I am drinking your strength, Dion–strength to love in this world and die and sleep and become fertile earth, as you are becoming now in my garden–your weakness the strength of my flowers, your failure as an artist painting their petals with life! [*Then, with bravado.*] Come with me while Margaret's bridegroom dresses in your clothes, Mr Anthony! I need the devil when I'm in the dark! [*He goes off left, but can be heard talking.*] Your clothes begin to fit me better than my own! Hurry, Brother! It's time we were home. Our wife is waiting! [*He reappears, having changed his coat and trousers.*] Come with me and tell her again I love her! Come and hear her tell me how she loves you! [*He suddenly cannot help kissing the mask.*] I love you because she loves you! My kisses on your lips are for her! [*He puts the mask over his face and stands for a moment, seeming to grow tall and proud–then with a laugh of bold self-assurance.*] Out by the back way! I mustn't forget I'm a desperate criminal, pursued by God, and by myself! [*He goes out right, laughing with amused satisfaction.*]

CURTAIN

SCENE 3

SCENE: Is the same as Scene One of Act 1–the sitting-room of MARGARET's home. It is about half an hour after the last scene. MARGARET sits on the sofa, waiting with the anxious, impatient expectancy of one deeply in love. She is dressed with a careful, subtle extra touch to attract the eye. She looks young and happy. She is trying to read a book. The front door is heard opening and closing. She leaps up and runs back to throw her arms around BROWN as he enters from right, rear. She kisses him passionately.

MARGARET [*as he recoils with a sort of guilt–laughingly*]: Why, you hateful old thing, you! I really believe you were trying to avoid kissing me! Well, just for that, I'll never . . .
BROWN [*with fierce, defiant passion, kisses her again and again*]: Margaret!
MARGARET: Call me Peggy again. You used to when you really loved me. [*Softly.*] Remember the school commencement dance–you and I on the dock in the moonlight?
BROWN [*with pain*]: No. [*He takes his arms from around her.*]

MARGARET [*still holding him—with a laugh*]: Well, I like that! You old bear, you! Why not?

BROWN [*sadly*]: It was so long ago.

MARGARET [*a bit melancholy*]: You mean you don't want to be reminded that we're getting old?

BROWN: Yes. [*He kisses her gently.*] I'm tired. Let's sit down.

They sit on the sofa, his arm about her, her head on his shoulder.

MARGARET [*with a happy sigh*]: I don't mind remembering—now I'm happy. It's only when I'm unhappy that it hurts—and I've been so happy lately, dear—and so grateful to you!

He stirs uneasily. She goes on joyfully.

Everything's changed! I'd got pretty resigned to—and sad and hopeless, too—and then all at once you turn right around and everything is the same as when we were first married—much better even, for I was never sure of you then. You were always so strange and aloof and alone, it seemed I was never really touching you. But now I feel you've become quite human—like me—and I'm so happy, dear! [*She kisses him.*]

BROWN [*his voice trembling*]: Then I have made you happy—happier than ever before—no matter what happens?

She nods.

Then—that justifies everything! [*He forces a laugh.*]

MARGARET: Of course it does! I've always known that. But you—you wouldn't be—or you couldn't be—and I could never help you—and all the time I knew you were so lonely! I could always hear you calling to me that you were lost, but I couldn't find the path to you because I was lost, too! That's an awful way for a wife to feel! [*She laughs—joyfully.*] But now you're here! You're mine! You're my long-lost lover, and my husband, and my big boy, too!

BROWN [*with a trace of jealousy*]: Where are your other big boys to-night?

MARGARET: Out to a dance. They've all acquired girls, I'll have you know.

BROWN [*mockingly*]: Aren't you jealous?

MARGARET [*gaily*]: Of course! Terribly! But I'm diplomatic. I don't let them see. [*Changing the subject.*] Believe me, they've noticed the change in you! The eldest was saying to me to-day: 'It's great not to have Father so nervous, any more. Why, he's a regular sport when he gets started!' And the other two said very solemnly: 'You bet!' [*She laughs.*]

BROWN [*brokenly*]: I—I'm glad.

MARGARET: Dion! You're crying!

BROWN [*stung by the name, gets up—harshly*]: Nonsense! Did you ever know Dion to cry about anyone?

MARGARET [*sadly*]: You couldn't—then. You were too lonely. You had no one to cry to.

BROWN [*goes and takes a rolled-up plan from the table drawer—dully*]: I've got to do some work.

MARGARET [*disappointedly*]: What, has that old Billy Brown got you to work at home again, too?

BROWN [*ironically*]: It's for Dion's good, you know–and yours.

MARGARET [*making the best of it–cheerfully*]: All right, I won't be selfish. It really makes me proud for you to be so ambitious. Let me help.

She brings his drawing-board, which he puts on the table and pins his plan upon. She sits on sofa and picks up her book.

BROWN [*carefully casual*]: I hear you were in to see me to-day?

MARGARET: Yes, and Billy wouldn't hear of it! I was quite furious until he convinced me it was all for the best. When is he going to take you into partnership?

BROWN: Very soon now.

MARGARET: And will he really give you full charge when he goes abroad?

BROWN: Yes.

MARGARET [*practically*]: I'd pin him down if I could. Promises are all right, but–[*she hesitates*] I don't trust him.

BROWN [*with a start, sharply*]: What makes you say that?

MARGARET: Oh, something that happened to-day.

BROWN: What?

MARGARET: I don't mean I blame him, but–to be frank, I think the Great God Brown, as you call him, is getting a bit queer and it's time he took a vacation. Don't you?

BROWN [*his voice a bit excited–but guardedly*]: But why? What did he do?

MARGARET [*hesitatingly*]: Well–it's really too silly–he suddenly got awfully strange. His face scared me. It was like a corpse. Then he raved on some nonsense about he'd always loved me. He went on like a perfect fool! [*She looks at* BROWN, *who is staring at her. She becomes uneasy.*] Maybe I shouldn't tell you this. He simply wasn't responsible. Then he came to himself and was all right and begged my pardon and seemed dreadfully sorry, and I felt sorry for him. [*Then with a shudder.*] But honestly, Dion, it was just too disgusting for words to hear him! [*With kind, devastating contempt.*] Poor Billy!

BROWN [*with a show of tortured derision*]: Poor Billy! Poor Billy the Goat! [*With mocking frenzy.*] I'll kill him for you! I'll serve you his heart for breakfast!

MARGARET [*jumping up–frightenedly*]: Dion!

BROWN [*waving his pencil knife with grotesque flourishes*]: I tell you I'll murder this God-damned disgusting Great God Brown who stands like a fatted calf in the way of our health and wealth and happiness!

MARGARET [*bewilderedly, not knowing how much is pretending, puts an arm about him*]: Don't, dear! You're being horrid and strange again. It makes me afraid you haven't really changed, after all.

BROWN [*unheeding*]: And then my wife can be happy! Ha! [*He laughs. She begins to cry. He controls himself–pats her head–gently.*] All right, dear. Mr Brown is now safely in hell. Forget him!

MARGARET [*stops crying–but still worriedly*]: I should never have told you–but I never imagined you'd take it seriously. I've never thought of Billy Brown except as a friend, and lately not even that! He's just a stupid old fool!

BROWN: Ha-ha! Didn't I say he was in hell? They're torturing him! [*Then controlling himself again–exhaustedly.*] Please leave me alone now. I've got to work.

MARGARET: All right, dear. I'll go into the next room and anything you want, just call. [*She pats his face–cajolingly.*] Is it all forgotten?

BROWN: Will you be happy?
MARGARET: Yes.
BROWN: Then it's dead, I promise!

She kisses him and goes out. He stares ahead, then shakes off his thoughts and concentrates on his work—mockingly.

Our beautiful new Capitol calls you, Mr Dion! To work! We'll adroitly hide old Silenus on the cupola! Let him dance over their law-making with his eternal leer! [*He bends over his work.*]

CURTAIN

ACT FOUR

SCENE I

SCENE: Same as Scene One of Act 3–the draughting-room and BROWN's office.
It is dusk of a day about a month later.

The two DRAUGHTSMEN are bent over their table, working.

BROWN, at his desk, is working feverishly over a plan. He is wearing the mask
of DION. The mask of WILLIAM BROWN rests on the desk beside him. As he
works, he chuckles with malicious glee–finally flings down his pencil with a
flourish.

BROWN: Done! In the name of the Almighty Brown, amen, amen! Here's a
wondrous fair capitol! The design would do just as well for a Home for
Criminal Imbeciles! Yet to them, such is my art, it will appear to possess a
pure commonsense, a fat-bellied finality, as dignified as the suspenders of an
assemblyman! Only to me will that pompous façade reveal itself as the
wearily ironic grin of Pan as, his ears drowsy with the crumbling hum of past
and future civilizations, he half-listens to the laws passed by his fleas to
enslave him! Ha-ha-ha! [*He leaps grotesquely from behind his desk and cuts a
few goatish capers, laughing with lustful merriment.*] Long live Chief of Police
Brown! District Attorney Brown! Alderman Brown! Assemblyman Brown!
Mayor Brown! Congressman Brown! Governor Brown! Senator Brown!
President Brown! [*He chants.*] Oh, how many persons in one God make up
the good God Brown? Hahahaha!

The two DRAUGHTSMEN *in the next room have stopped work and are listening.*

YOUNGER DRAUGHTSMAN: Drunk as a fool!
OLDER DRAUGHTSMAN: At least Dion used to have the decency to stay away from
the office—
YOUNGER DRAUGHTSMAN: Funny how it's got hold of Brown so quick!
OLDER DRAUGHTSMAN: He was probably hitting it up on the Q.T. all the time.
BROWN [*has come back to his desk, laughing to himself and out of breath*]: Time to
become respectable again! [*He takes off the* DION *mask and reaches out for the*
WILLIAM BROWN *one—then stops, with a hand on each, staring down on the plan
with fascinated loathing. His real face is now sick, ghastly, tortured, hollow-
cheeked and feverish-eyed.*] Ugly! Hideous! Despicable! Why must the
demon in me pander to cheapness–then punish me with self-loathing and
life-hatred? Why am I not strong enough to perish–or blind enough to be
content? [*To heaven, bitterly but pleadingly.*] Give me the strength to destroy
this!–and myself!–and him!–and I will believe in Thee!

While he has been speaking there has been a noise from the stairs. The two

DRAUGHTSMEN *have bent over their work.* MARGARET *enters, closing the door behind her. At this sound,* BROWN *starts. He immediately senses who it is—with alarm.*

Margaret! [*He grabs up both masks and goes into room off right.*]

MARGARET [*she looks healthy and happy, but her face wears a worried, solicitous expression—pleasantly to the staring* DRAUGHTSMEN]: Good morning. Oh, you needn't look worried, it's Mr Brown I want to see, not my husband.

YOUNGER DRAUGHTSMAN [*hesitatingly*]: He's locked himself in—but maybe if you'll knock—

MARGARET [*knocks—somewhat embarrassedly*]: Mr Brown!

BROWN *enters his office, wearing the* WILLIAM BROWN *mask. He comes quickly to the other door and unlocks it.*

BROWN [*with a hectic cordiality*]: Come on, Margaret! Enter! This is delightful! Sit down! What can I do for you?

MARGARET [*taken aback—a bit stiffly.*]: Nothing much.

BROWN: Something about Dion, of course. Well, your darling pet is all right—never better!

MARGARET [*coldly*]: That's a matter of opinion. I think you're working him to death.

BROWN: Oh, no, not him. It's Brown who is to die. We've agreed on that.

MARGARET [*giving him a queer look*]: I'm serious.

BROWN: So am I. Deadly serious! Hahaha!

MARGARET [*checking her indignation*]: That's what I came to see you about. Really, Dion has acted so hectic and on edge lately I'm sure he's on the verge of a breakdown.

BROWN: Well, it certainly isn't drink. He hasn't had a drop. He doesn't need it! Haha! And I haven't either, although the gossips are beginning to say I'm soused all the time! It's because I've started to laugh! Hahaha! They can't believe in joy in this town except by the bottle! What funny little people! Hahaha! When you're the Great God Brown, eh, Margaret? Hahaha!

MARGARET [*getting up—uneasily*]: I'm afraid I—

BROWN: Don't be afraid, my dear! I won't make love to you again! Honour bright! I'm too near the grave for such folly! But it must have been funny for you when you came here the last time—watching a disgusting old fool like me, eh?—too funny for words! Hahaha! [*Then with a sudden movement he flourishes the design before her.*] Look! We've finished it! Dion has finished it! His fame is made!

MARGARET [*tartly*]: Really, Billy, I believe you are drunk!

BROWN: Nobody kisses me—so you can all believe the worst! Hahaha!

MARGARET [*chillingly*]: Then if Dion is through, why can't I see him?

BROWN [*crazily*]: See Dion? See Dion? Well, why not? It's an age of miracles. The streets are full of Lazaruses. Pray! I mean—wait a moment, if you please.

BROWN *disappears into the room off right. A moment later he reappears in the mask of* DION. *He holds out his arms and Margaret rushes into them. They kiss passionately. Finally he sits with her on the lounge.*

MARGARET: So you've finished it.

BROWN: Yes. The Committee is coming to see it soon. I've made all the changes they'll like, the fools!

MARGARET [*lovingly*]: And can we go on that second honeymoon, right away now?

BROWN: In a week or so, I hope—as soon as I've got Brown off to Europe.

MARGARET: Tell me—isn't he drinking hard?

BROWN [*laughing as Brown did*]: Haha! Soused to the ears all the time! Soused on life. He can't stand it! It's burning his insides out!

MARGARET [*alarmed*]: Dear! I'm worried about you. You sound as crazy as he did—when you laugh! You must rest!

BROWN [*controlling himself*]: I'll rest in peace—when he's gone!

MARGARET [*with a queer look*]: Why, Dion, that isn't your suit. It's just like—

BROWN: It's his! We're getting to be like twins. I'm inheriting his clothes already! [*Then calming himself as he sees how frightened she is.*] Don't be worried, dear. I'm just a trifle elated, now the job's done. I guess I'm a bit soused on life, too!

> The COMMITTEE, *three important-looking, average personages, come into the draughting-room.*

MARGARET [*forcing a smile*]: Well, don't let it burn *your* insides out!

BROWN: No danger! Mine were tempered in hell! Hahaha!

MARGARET [*kissing him, coaxingly*]: Come home, dear—please!

OLDER DRAUGHTSMAN [*knocks on the door*]: The Committee is here, Mr Brown.

BROWN [*hurriedly to Margaret*]: You receive them. Hand them the design. I'll get Brown. [*He raises his voice.*] Come right in, gentlemen.

> *He goes off right, as the* COMMITTEE *enter the office. When they see* MARGARET, *they stop in surprise.*

MARGARET [*embarrassedly*]: Good afternoon. Mr Brown will be right with you.

> *They bow.* MARGARET *holds out the design to them.*

This is my husband's design. He finished it to-day.

COMMITTEE: Ah! [*They crowd around to look at it—with enthusiasm.*] Perfect! Splendid! Couldn't be better! Exactly what we suggested.

MARGARET [*joyfully*]: Then you accept it? Mr Anthony will be so pleased!

MEMBER: Mr Anthony?

ANOTHER: Is he working here again?

THIRD: Did I understand you to say this was your husband's design?

MARGARET [*excitedly*]: Yes! Entirely his! He's worked like a dog—[*Appalled.*] You don't mean to say—Mr Brown never told you?

> *They shake their heads in solemn surprise.*

Oh, the contemptible cad! I hate him!

BROWN [*appearing at right—mockingly*]: Hate me, Margaret? Hate Brown? How superfluous! [*Oratorically.*] Gentlemen, I have been keeping a secret from you in order that you might be the more impressed when I revealed it. That design is entirely the inspiration of Mr Dion Anthony's genius. I had nothing to do with it.

MARGARET [*contritely*]: Oh, Billy! I'm sorry! Forgive me!

BROWN [*ignoring her, takes the plan from the* COMMITTEE *and begins unpinning it from the board—mockingly*]: I can see by your faces you have approved this. You are delighted, aren't you? And why not, my dear sirs? Look at it, and look at you! Hahaha! It'll immortalize you, my good men! You'll be as death-defying a joke as any in Joe Miller! [*Then with a sudden complete change of tone—angrily.*] You damn fools! Can't you see this is an insult—a terrible, blasphemous insult!—that this embittered failure Anthony is hurling in the teeth of our success—an insult to you, to me, to you, Margaret—and to Almighty God! [*In a frenzy of fury.*] And if you are weak and cowardly enough to stand for it, I'm not!

He tears the plan into four pieces. The COMMITTEE *stand aghast.* MARGARET *runs forward.*

MARGARET [*in a scream*]: You coward! Dion! Dion! [*She picks up the plan and hugs it to her bosom.*]

BROWN [*with a sudden goatish caper*]: I'll tell him you're here. [*He disappears, but reappears almost immediately in the mask of* DION. *He is imposing a terrible discipline on himself to avoid dancing and laughing. He speaks suavely.*] Everything is all right—all for the best—you mustn't get excited! A little paste, Margaret! A little paste, gentlemen! And all will be well. Life is imperfect, Brothers! Men have their faults, Sister! But with a few drops of glue much may be done! A little dab of pasty resignation here and there—and even broken hearts may be repaired to do yeoman service! [*He has edged toward the door. They are all staring at him with petrified bewilderment. He puts his finger to his lips.*] Ssssh! This is Daddy's bedtime secret for to-day: Man is born broken. He lives by mending. The grace of God is glue! [*With a quick prancing movement, he has opened the door, gone through, and closed it after him silently, shaking with suppressed laughter. He springs lightly to the side of the petrified* DRAUGHTSMEN—*in a whisper.*] They will find him in the little room. Mr William Brown is dead!

With light leaps he vanishes, his head thrown back, shaking with silent laughter. The sound of his feet leaping down the stairs, five at a time, can be heard. Then a pause of silence. The people in the two rooms stare. The YOUNGER DRAUGHTSMAN *is the first to recover.*

YOUNGER DRAUGHTSMAN [*rushing into the next room, shouts in terrified tones*]: Mr Brown is dead!

COMMITTEE: He murdered him!

They all run into the little room off right. MARGARET *remains, stunned with horror. They return in a moment, carrying the mask of* WILLIAM BROWN, *two on each side, as if they were carrying a body by the legs and shoulders. They solemnly lay him down on the couch and stand looking down at him.*

FIRST COMMITTEEMAN [*with a frightened awe*]: I can't believe he's gone.

SECOND COMMITTEEMAN [*in same tone*]: I can almost hear him talking. [*As if*

impelled, he clears his throat and addresses the mask importantly.] Mr Brown—
[*then stops short.*]

THIRD COMMITTEEMAN [*shrinking back*]: No. Dead, all right! [*Then suddenly,
hysterically angry and terrified.*] We must take steps at once to run Anthony to
earth!

MARGARET [*with a heart-broken cry*]: Dion's innocent!

YOUNGER DRAUGHTSMAN: I'll phone for the police, sir! [*He rushes to the phone.*]

CURTAIN

SCENE 2

SCENE: The same as Scene Two of Act 3–the library of WILLIAM BROWN's home.
The mask of DION stands on the table beneath the light, facing front.

On his knees beside the table, facing front, stripped naked except for a white
cloth around his loins, is BROWN. The clothes he has torn off in his agony are
scattered on the floor. His eyes, his arms, his whole body strain upward, his
muscles writhe with his lips as they pray silently in their agonized supplication.
Finally a voice seems torn out of him.

BROWN: Mercy, Compassionate Saviour of Man! Out of my depths I cry to you!
Mercy on thy poor clod, thy clot of unhallowed earth, thy clay, the Great
God Brown! Mercy, Saviour! [*He seems to wait for an answer–then leaping to
his feet he puts out one hand to touch the mask like a frightened child reaching out
for its nurse's hand–then with immediate mocking despair.*] Bah! I am sorry,
little children, but your kingdom is empty. God has become disgusted and
moved away to some far ecstatic star where life is a dancing flame! We must
die without him. [*Then–addressing the mask–harshly.*] Together, my
friend! You, too! Let Margaret suffer! Let the whole world suffer as I am
suffering!

*There is a sound of a door being pushed violently open, padding feet in slippers,
and* CYBEL, *wearing her mask, runs into the room. She stops short on seeing*
BROWN *and the mask, and stares from one to the other for a second in
confusion. She is dressed in a black kimono robe and wears slippers over her
bare feet. Her yellow hair hangs down in a great mane over her shoulders. She
has grown stouter, has more of the deep objective calm of an idol.*

BROWN [*staring at her–fascinated–with great peace as if her presence comforted
him*]: Cybel! I was coming to you! How did you know?

CYBEL [*takes off her mask and looks from* BROWN *to the* DION *mask, now with a
great understanding*]: So that's why you never came to me again! You are
Dion Brown!

BROWN [*bitterly*]: I am the remains of William Brown! [*He points to the mask of
DION.*] I am his murderer and his murdered!

CYBEL [*with a laugh of exasperated pity*]: Oh, why can't you ever learn to leave
yourselves alone and leave me alone.

BROWN [*boyishly and naïvely*]. I am Billy.

CYBEL [*immediately, with a motherly solicitude*]: Then run, Billy, run! They are hunting for some one! They came to my place, hunting for a murderer, Dion! They must find a victim! They've got to quiet their fears, to cast out their devils, or they'll never sleep soundly again! They've got to absolve themselves by finding a guilty one! They've got to kill some one now, to live! You're naked! You must be Satan! Run, Billy, run! They'll come here! I ran here to warn—some one! So run away if you want to live!

BROWN [*like a sulky child*]: I'm too tired. I don't want to.

CYBEL [*with motherly calm*]: All right, you needn't, Billy. Don't sulk. [*As a noise comes from outside.*] Anyway, it's too late. I hear them in the garden now.

BROWN [*listening, puts out his hand and takes the mask of* DION—*as he gains strength, mockingly*]: Thanks for this one last favour, Dion! Listen! Your avengers! Standing on your grave in the garden! Hahaha! [*He puts on the mask and springs to the left and makes a gesture as if flinging French windows open. Gaily mocking.*] Welcome, dumb worshippers! I am your great God Brown! I have been advised to run from you but it is my almighty whim to dance into escape over your prostrate souls!

Shouts from the garden and a volley of shots. BROWN *staggers back and falls on the floor by the couch, mortally wounded.*

CYBEL [*runs to his side, lifts him on to the couch and takes off the mask of* DION]. You can't take this to bed with you. You've got to go to sleep alone.

She places the mask of DION *back on its stand under the light and puts on her own, just as, after a banging of doors, crashing of glass, trampling of feet, a* SQUAD OF POLICE *with drawn revolvers, led by a grizzly, brutal-faced* CAPTAIN, *run into the room. They are followed by* MARGARET, *still distractedly clutching the pieces of the plan to her breast.*

CAPTAIN [*pointing to the mask of* DION—*triumphantly*]: Got him! He's dead!

MARGARET [*throws herself on her knees, takes the mask and kisses it—heartbrokenly*]: Dion! Dion! [*Her face hidden in her arms, the mask in her hands, above her bowed head, she remains, sobbing with deep, silent grief.*]

CAPTAIN [*noticing* CYBEL *and* BROWN—*startled*]: Hey! Look at this! What're you doin' here? Who's he?

CYBEL: You ought to know. You croaked him!

CAPTAIN [*with a defensive snarl—hastily*]: It was Anthony! I saw his mug! This feller's an accomplice, I bet yuh! Serves him right! Who is he? Friend o' yours! Crook! What's his name? Tell me or I'll fix yuh!

CYBEL: Billy.

CAPTAIN: Billy what?

CYBEL: I don't know. He's dying. [*Then suddenly.*] Leave me alone with him and maybe I'll get him to squeal it.

CAPTAIN: Yuh better! I got to have a clean report. I'll give yuh a couple o' minutes.

He motions to the POLICEMEN, *who follow him off left.* CYBEL *takes off her mask and sits down by* BROWN'S *head. He makes an effort to raise himself toward her and she helps him, throwing her kimono over his bare body, drawing his head on to her shoulder.*

BROWN [*snuggling against her—gratefully*]. The earth is warm.

CYBEL [*soothingly, looking before her like an idol*]: Ssshh! Go to sleep, Billy.

BROWN: Yes, Mother. [*Then explainingly.*] It was dark and I couldn't see where I was going and they all picked on me.

CYBEL: I know. You're tired.

BROWN: And when I wake up . . .?

CYBEL: The sun will be rising again.

BROWN: To judge the living and the dead! [*Frightenedly.*] I don't want justice. I want love.

CYBEL: There is only love.

BROWN: Thank you, Mother. [*Then feebly.*] I'm getting sleepy. What's the prayer you taught me—Our Father—?

CYBEL [*with calm exultance*]: Our Father Who Art!

BROWN [*taking her tone—exultantly*]: Who art! Who art! [*Suddenly—with ecstasy.*] I know! I have found Him! I hear Him speak! 'Blessed are they that weep, for they shall laugh!' Only he that has wept can laugh! The laughter of Heaven sows earth with a rain of tears, and out of Earth's transfigured birth-pain the laughter of Man returns to bless and play again in innumerable dancing gales of flame upon the knees of God! [*He dies.*]

CYBEL [*gets up and arranges his body on the couch. She bends down and kisses him gently—she straightens up and looks into space—with a profound pain*]: Always spring comes again bearing life! Always again! Always, always for ever again!—Spring again!—life again!—summer and autumn and death and peace again!—[*with agonized sorrow*]—but always, always, love and conception and birth and pain again—spring bearing the intolerable chalice of life again!—[*then with agonized exultance*]—bearing the glorious, blazing crown of life again! [*She stands like an idol of Earth, her eyes staring out over the world.*]

MARGARET [*lifting her head adoringly to the mask—triumphant tenderness mingled with her grief*]: My lover! My husband! My boy! [*She kisses the mask.*] Good-bye. Thank you for happiness! And you're not dead, sweetheart! You can never die till my heart dies! You will live for ever! You will sleep under my heart! I will feel you stirring in your sleep, for ever under my heart! [*She kisses the mask again. There is a pause.*]

CAPTAIN [*comes just into sight at left and speaks front without looking at them—gruffly*]: Well, what's his name?

CYBEL: Man!

CAPTAIN [*taking a grimy notebook and an inch-long pencil from his pocket*]: How d'yuh spell it?

CURTAIN

EPILOGUE

SCENE: Four years later.

The same spot on the same pier as in Prologue on another moonlight night in June. The sound of the waves and of distant dance music.

MARGARET and her THREE SONS appear from the right. The ELDEST is now eighteen. All are dressed in the height of correct school elegance. They are all tall, athletic, strong and handsome-looking. They loom up around the slight figure of their mother like protecting giants, giving her a strange aspect of lonely, detached, small femininity. She wears her mask of the proud, indulgent Mother. She has grown appreciably older. Her hair is now a beautiful grey. There is about her manner and voice the sad but contented feeling of one who knows her life-purpose well accomplished but is at the same time a bit empty and comfortless with the finality of it. She is wrapped in a grey cloak.

ELDEST: Doesn't Bee look beautiful to-night, Mother?

NEXT: Don't you think Mabel's the best dancer in there, Mother?

YOUNGEST: Aw, Alice has them both beat, hasn't she, Mother?

MARGARET [*with a sad little laugh*]: Each of you is right. [*Then, with strange finality.*] Good-bye, boys.

BOYS [*surprised*]: Good-bye.

MARGARET: It was here on a night just like this your father first–proposed to me. Did you ever know that?

BOYS [*embarrassedly*]: No.

MARGARET [*yearningly*]: But the nights now are so much colder than they used to be. Think of it, I went in for moonlight-bathing in June when I was a girl. It was so warm and beautiful in those days. I remember the Junes when I was carrying you boys–[*A pause. They fidget uneasily. She asks pleadingly.*] Promise me faithfully never to forget your father!

BOYS [*uncomfortably*]: Yes, Mother.

MARGARET [*forcing a joking tone*]: But you mustn't waste June on an old woman like me! Go in and dance. [*As they hesitate dutifully.*] Go on. I really want to be alone–with my Junes.

BOYS [*unable to conceal their eagerness*]: Yes, Mother. [*They go away.*]

MARGARET [*slowly removes her mask, laying it on the bench, and stares up at the moon with a wistful, resigned sweetness*]: So long ago! And yet I'm still the same Margaret. It's only our lives that grow old. We *are* where centuries only count as seconds and after a thousand lives our eyes begin to open–[*she looks around her with a rapt smile*]–and the moon rests in the sea! I want to feel the moon at peace in the sea! I want Dion to leave the sky for me! I want him to sleep in the tides of my heart! [*She slowly takes from under her cloak, from her bosom, as if from her heart, the mask of DION as it was at the last and holds it before her face.*] My lover! My husband! My boy! You can never die till my heart dies! You will live for ever! You are sleeping under my heart! I feel you stirring in your sleep, for ever under my heart. [*She kisses him on the lips with a timeless kiss.*]

CURTAIN

AN INSPECTOR CALLS

J. B. PRIESTLEY

AN INSPECTOR CALLS

First published in 1950 by William Heinemann
Limited

To Michael Macowan

AN INSPECTOR CALLS

CHARACTERS

ARTHUR BIRLING
SYBIL BIRLING
SHEILA BIRLING
ERIC BIRLING
GERALD CROFT
EDNA
INSPECTOR GOOLE

ACTS
All three Acts, which are continuous, take place in the dining-room of the Birlings' house in Brumley, an industrial city in the North Midlands. It is an evening in spring, 1912.

CAST
An Inspector Calls was first produced at The New Theatre in October 1946, with the following cast:

ARTHUR BIRLING	*Julien Mitchell*
GERALD CROFT	*Harry Andrews*
SHEILA BIRLING	*Margaret Leighton*
SYBIL BIRLING	*Marian Spencer*
EDNA	*Marjorie Dunkels*
ERIC BIRLING	*Alec Guinness*
INSPECTOR GOOLE	*Ralph Richardson*

produced by BASIL DEAN

ACT ONE

SCENE: The dining-room of the BIRLINGS' house in Brumley, an industrial city in the North Midlands. An evening in Spring, 1912.

It is the dining-room of a fairly large suburban house, belonging to a prosperous manufacturer; a solidly built square room, with good solid furniture of the period. There is only one door, which is up stage in the *left* wall. Up stage *centre*, set in an alcove, is a heavy sideboard with a silver tantalus, silver candlesticks, a silver champagne cooler and the various oddments of a dinner. The fireplace is in the *right* wall. Below the door is a desk with a chair in front of it. On the wall below the fireplace is a telephone. Slightly up stage of *centre* is a solid but not too large dining table, preferably oval, with a solid set of dining-room chairs round it. The table is laid with a white cloth and the closing stages of a dinner. Down stage of the fireplace is a leather armchair. A few imposing but tasteless pictures and large engravings decorate the walls, and there are light brackets above and below the fireplace and below the door. The former are lit, but the latter is not. The general effect is substantial and comfortable and old-fashioned, but not cosy and home-like.

When the CURTAIN *rises,* EDNA, *a neatly dressed parlourmaid is clearing the table of dessert plates and finger bowls, taking them to the sideboard.* ARTHUR BIRLING *is seated right of the table, and* MRS BIRLING *is left.* SHEILA BIRLING *and* GERALD CROFT *are seated above the table, right and left respectively.* ERIC BIRLING *sits below the table. All five are in evening dress, the men in tails and white ties.* ARTHUR BIRLING *is a heavy-looking, rather portentous man in his middle fifties, with fairly easy manners but rather provincial in his speech. His wife is about fifty, a rather cold woman and her husband's social superior.* SHEILA *is a pretty girl in her early twenties, very pleased with life and rather excited.* GERALD CROFT *is an attractive chap about thirty, rather too manly to be a dandy but very much the easy well-bred young man-about-town.* ERIC *is in his middle twenties, not quite at ease, half-shy, half-assertive. At the moment they have all had a good dinner, are celebrating a special occasion, and are pleased with themselves.*

BIRLING: Giving us the port, Edna?

EDNA *comes to* BIRLING'S *left with the decanter.*

That's right. [*He fills his glass and pushes it towards* SHEILA.] You ought to like this port Gerald. As a matter of fact, Finchley told me it's exactly the same port your father gets from him.

SHEILA *fills her glass and passes the port to* GERALD.

GERALD: Then it'll be all right. The governor prides himself on being a good judge of port. I don't pretend to know much about it. [*He fills his glass and then passes the decanter towards* MRS BIRLING.]

SHEILA [*gaily, possessively*]: I should jolly well think not, Gerald. I'd hate you to know all about port—like one of these purple-faced old men.

BIRLING: Here, I'm not a purple-faced old man.

SHEILA: No, not yet. But then, you don't know all about port—do you?

BIRLING [*noticing that* MRS BIRLING *has not taken any port*]: Now then, Sybil, you must take a little to-night. Special occasion, y'know, eh?

GERALD *starts to fill* MRS BIRLING's *glass.*

SHEILA: Yes, go on, Mummy. You must drink our health.

EDNA *picks up the tray, about to go.*

MRS BIRLING [*smiling*]: Very well, then. Just a little, thank you. [*She passes the decanter to* ERIC. *To* EDNA.] All right, Edna. I'll ring from the drawing room when we want coffee. Probably in about half-an-hour.

EDNA [*going*]: Yes, ma'am.

She goes out. They now have all the glasses filled. BIRLING *beams at them and clearly relaxes.*

BIRLING: Well, well—this is very nice. Good dinner too, Sybil. Tell cook from me.

GERALD [*politely*]: Absolutely first-class.

MRS BIRLING [*reproachfully*]: Arthur, you're not supposed to say such things—

BIRLING: Oh—come, come—I'm treating Gerald like one of the family. And I'm sure he won't object.

SHEILA [*with mock aggressiveness*]: Go on, Gerald—just you object.

GERALD [*smiling*]: Wouldn't dream of it. In fact, I insist upon being one of the family now. I've been trying long enough, haven't I? [*As* SHEILA *does not reply; with more insistence.*] Haven't I? You know I have.

MRS BIRLING [*smiling*]: Of course she does.

SHEILA [*half seriously, half playfully*]: Yes—except for all last summer, when you never came near me, and I wondered what had happened to you.

GERALD: And I've told you—I was awfully busy at the works all that time.

SHEILA [*in the same tone*]: Yes, that's what *you* say.

MRS BIRLING: Now, Sheila, don't tease him. When you're married you'll realise that men with important work to do sometimes have to spend nearly all their time and energy on their business. You'll have to get used to that, just as I had.

SHEILA: I don't believe I will. [*Half playful, half serious, to* GERALD.] So you be careful.

GERALD: Oh—I will, I will.

ERIC *suddenly guffaws. His parents look at him.*

SHEILA [*severely*]: Now—what's the joke?

ERIC: I don't know—really. Suddenly I felt I just had to laugh.

SHEILA: You're squiffy.

ERIC: I'm not.

MRS BIRLING: What an expression, Sheila! Really, the things you girls pick up these days!

ERIC: If you think that's the best she can do—

SHEILA: Don't be an ass, Eric.

MRS BIRLING: Now stop it, you two. Arthur, what about this famous toast of yours?

BIRLING: Yes, of course. [*He clears his throat.*] Well, Gerald, I know you agreed that we should only have this quiet little family party. It's a pity Sir George and–er–Lady Croft can't be with us, but they're abroad and so it can't be helped. As I told you, they sent me a very nice cable–couldn't be nicer. I'm not sorry that we're celebrating quietly like this—

MRS BIRLING: Much nicer really.

GERALD: I agree.

BIRLING: So do I, but it makes speech-making more difficult—

ERIC [*not too rudely*]: Well, don't do any. We'll drink their health and have done with it.

BIRLING: No we won't. It's one of the happiest nights of my life. And one day, I hope, Eric, when you've a daughter of your own, you'll understand why. Gerald, I'm going to tell you frankly without any pretences, that your engagement to Sheila means a tremendous lot to me. She'll make you happy. I'm sure you'll make her happy. You're just the kind of son-in-law I always wanted. Your father and I have been friendly rivals in business for some time now–though Crofts Limited are both older and bigger than Birling and Company–and now you've brought us together, and perhaps we may look forward to the time when Crofts and Birlings are no longer competing but are working together–for lower costs and higher prices.

GERALD: Hear, hear! And I think my father would agree to that.

MRS BIRLING: Now, Arthur, I don't think you ought to talk business on an occasion like this.

SHEILA: Neither do I. All wrong.

BIRLING: Quite so, I agree with you. I only mentioned it in passing. What I did want to say was–that Sheila's a lucky girl–and I think you're a pretty fortunate young man, too, Gerald.

GERALD: I know I am–this once anyhow.

BIRLING *raises his glass and rises.* MRS BIRLING *rises.*

BIRLING: So here's wishing the pair of you–the very best that life can bring. Gerald and Sheila!

MRS BIRLING [*raising her glass, smiling*]: Yes, Gerald. Yes, Sheila, darling. Our congratulations and very best wishes!

GERALD: Thank you. [*He rises.*]

MRS BIRLING *signals to* ERIC *to rise.*

ERIC [*rising; rather noisily*]: All the best! She's got a nasty temper sometimes–but she's not bad really. Good old Sheila!

They all sit.

SHEILA: Chump! I can't drink to this, can I? When do I drink?

GERALD: You can drink to me.

SHEILA [*rising; quiet and serious now*]: All right then. I drink to you, Gerald.

For a moment GERALD and SHEILA *look at each other.*

GERALD [*quietly*]: Thank you. And I drink to you–and hope I can make you as happy as you deserve to be.

SHEILA [*sitting; trying to be light and easy*]: You be careful–or I'll start weeping.

GERALD [*smiling*]: Well, perhaps this will help to stop it. [*He produces a ring case.*]

SHEILA [*excited*]: Oh–Gerald–you've got it–is it the one you wanted me to have?

GERALD [*giving the case to her*]: Yes–the very one.

SHEILA [*taking out the ring*]: Oh–it's wonderful! [*She rises and crosses behind* GERALD *to* MRS BIRLING.] Look–mummy–isn't it a beauty? [*She turns to* GERALD.] Oh–darling–[*She slips the ring on and kisses* GERALD *hastily, then crosses above him to* BIRLING.]

ERIC: Steady the Buffs!

SHEILA [*admiring the ring*]: I think it's perfect. Now I really feel engaged.

MRS BIRLING: So you ought, darling. It's a lovely ring. Be careful with it.

SHEILA: Careful! [*She sits.*] I'll never let it go out of my sight for an instant.

MRS BIRLING [*smiling*]: Well, it came just at the right moment. That was clever of you, Gerald. Now, Arthur, if you've no more to say, I think Sheila and I had better go into the drawing-room and leave you men–[*She is about to rise.*]

BIRLING [*rather heavily*]: I just want to say this. [*Noticing that* SHEILA *is still admiring her ring.*] Are you listening, Sheila? This concerns you too. And after all I don't often make speeches at you—

SHEILA: I'm sorry, Daddy. Actually I was listening.

She looks attentive, as they all do. BIRLING *holds them for a moment before continuing.*

BIRLING: I'm delighted about this engagement and I hope it won't be too long before you're married. And I want to say this. There's a good deal of silly talk about these days–*but*–and I speak as a hard-headed business man, who has to take risks and know what he's about–I say, you can ignore all this silly pessimistic talk. When you marry, you'll be marrying at a very good time. Yes, a very good time–and soon it'll be an even better time. Last month, just because the miners came out on strike, there's a lot of wild talk about possible labour trouble in the near future. Don't worry. We've passed the worst of it. We employers at last are coming together to see that our interests–and the interests of Capital–are properly protected. And we're in for a time of steadily increasing prosperity.

GERALD: I believe you're right, sir.

ERIC: But what about war?

BIRLING: Glad you mentioned it, Eric. I'm coming to that. Just because the Kaiser makes a speech or two, or a few German officers have too much to drink and begin talking nonsense, you'll hear some people say that war's inevitable. And to that I say–fiddlesticks! The Germans don't want war. Nobody wants war, except some half-civilised folks in the Balkans. And why? There's too much at stake these days. Everything to lose and nothing to gain by war.

ERIC: Yes, I know–but still—

BIRLING: Just let me finish, Eric. You've a lot to learn yet. And I'm talking as a hard-headed, practical man of business. And I say there isn't a chance of war. The world's developing so fast that it'll make war impossible. Look at the progress we're making. In a year or two we'll have aeroplanes that will be able to go anywhere. And look at the way the automobile's making headway–bigger and faster all the time. And then ships. Why, a friend of mine went over this new liner last week–the *Titanic*–she sails next week–forty-six thousand eight hundred tons–forty-six thousand eight hundred tons–New York in five days–and every luxury–and unsinkable, absolutely unsinkable. That's what you've got to keep your eye on, facts like that, progress like that–and not a few German officers talking nonsense and a few scaremongers here making a fuss about nothing. Now you three young people, just listen to this–and remember that I'm telling you now. In twenty or thirty years' time–let's say in 1940–you may be giving a little party like this–your son or daughter might be getting engaged–and I tell you, by that time you'll be living in a world that'll have forgotten all these Capital versus Labour agitations and all these silly little war scares. There'll be peace and prosperity and rapid progress everywhere–except of course in Russia, which will always be behindhand naturally.

MRS BIRLING *shows signs of interrupting.*

Yes, my dear–I know–I'm talking too much. But you youngsters just remember what I said. We can't let these Bernard Shaws and H. G. Wellses do all the talking. We hard-headed practical business men must say something sometimes. And we don't guess–we've had experience–and we *know*.

MRS BIRLING [*rising*]: Yes, of course, dear.

They all rise.

Well–don't keep Gerald in here too long. [*She turns to the door.*] Eric–I want you a minute.

GERALD *crosses above* MRS BIRLING *and opens the door.* MRS BIRLING *goes out followed by* SHEILA *and* ERIC. GERALD *shuts the door.*

BIRLING [*crossing below the table to the desk*]: Cigar? [*He takes one himself.*]

GERALD [*crossing to his chair*]: No, thanks. Can't really enjoy them. [*He takes a cigarette and lights it.*]

BIRLING [*moving to the left end of the table*]: Ah, you don't know what you're missing. I like a good cigar. [*Indicating the decanter.*] Help yourself. [*He lights his cigar.*]

GERALD *fills his glass and pushes the decanter towards* BIRLING, *and sits right above the table.*

Thanks. [*He sits left of the table. Confidentially.*] By the way, there's

something I'd like to mention–in strict confidence–while we're by
ourselves. I have an idea that your mother–Lady Croft–while she doesn't
object to my girl–feels you might have done better for yourself socially—

> GERALD, *rather embarrassed, begins to murmur some dissent, but* BIRLING
> *checks him.*

No, Gerald, that's all right. Don't blame her. She comes from an old county
family–landed people and so forth–and so it's only natural. But what I
wanted to say is–there's a fair chance that I might find my way into the next
Honours List. Just a knighthood, of course.
GERALD: Oh–I say–congratulations!
BIRLING: Thanks. But it's a bit too early for that. So don't say anything. But
  I've had a hint or two. You see, I was Lord Mayor here two years ago when
  Royalty visited us. And I've always been regarded as a sound useful party
  man. So–well–I gather there's a very good chance of a knighthood–so long
  as we behave ourselves, don't get into the police court or start a scandal–eh?
  [*He laughs complacently.*]
GERALD [*laughing*]: You seem to be a nice well-behaved family—
BIRLING: We think we are—
GERALD: So if that's the only obstacle, sir. I think you might as well accept my
  congratulations now.
BIRLING: No, no, I couldn't do that. And don't say anything yet.
GERALD: Not even to my mother? I know she'd be delighted.
BIRLING: Well, when she comes back, you might drop a hint to her. And you can
  promise her that we'll try to keep out of trouble during the next few months.

> *They both laugh.* ERIC *enters. He stands just inside the door.*

ERIC: What's the joke? Started telling stories?
BIRLING: No. Want another glass of port?
ERIC [*closing the door and moving below the table*]: Yes, please. [*He takes the
  decanter and helps himself.*] Mother says we mustn't stay too long. But I don't
  think it matters. I left 'em talking about clothes again. You'd think a girl had
  never had any clothes before she gets married. Women are potty about 'em.
  [*He moves to the chair right of the table and sits.*]
BIRLING: Yes, but you've got to remember, my boy, that clothes mean
  something quite different to a woman. Not just something to wear–and not
  only something to make 'em look prettier–but–well, a sort of sign or token of
  their self-respect.
GERALD: That's true.
ERIC [*eagerly*]: Yes, I remember— [*but he checks himself.*]
BIRLING: Well, what do you remember?
ERIC [*confused*]: Nothing.
BIRLING: Nothing?
GERALD [*amused*]: Sounds a bit fishy to me.
BIRLING [*taking it in the same manner*]: Yes, you don't know what some of these
  boys get up to nowadays. More money to spend and time to spare than I had
  when I was Eric's age. They worked us hard in those days and kept us short
  of cash. Though even then–we broke out and had a bit of fun sometimes.
GERALD: I'll bet you did.

BIRLING [*solemnly*]: But this is the point. I don't want to lecture you two young fellows again. But what so many of you don't seem to understand now, when things are so much easier, is that a man has to make his own way–has to look after himself–and his family too, of course, when he has one–and so long as he does that he won't come to much harm. But the way some of these cranks talk and write now, you'd think everybody has to look after everybody else, as if we were all mixed up together like bees in a hive–community and all that nonsense. But take my word for it, you youngsters–and I've learnt in the good hard school of experience–that a man has to mind his own business and look after himself and his own–and—

We hear the sharp ring of the front door bell. BIRLING *stops to listen.*

ERIC: Somebody at the front door.
BIRLING: Edna'll answer it. Well, have another glass of port, Gerald–and then we'll join the ladies. That'll stop me giving you good advice.
ERIC: Yes, you've piled it on a bit tonight, father.
BIRLING: Special occasion. And feeling contented, for once, I wanted you to have the benefit of my experience.

EDNA *enters.*

EDNA: Please, sir, an inspector's called.
BIRLING: An inspector? What kind of inspector?
EDNA: A police inspector. He says his name's Inspector Goole.
BIRLING: Don't know him. Does he want to see me?
EDNA: Yes, sir. He says it's important.
BIRLING: All right, Edna. Show him in here.

EDNA *goes out.*

I'm still on the Bench. [*As he rises and moves to the door and switches on the wall bracket over the desk.*] It may be something about a warrant.
GERALD [*lightly*]: Sure to be. Unless Eric's been up to something. [*Nodding confidentially to* BIRLING.] And that would be awkward, wouldn't it?
BIRLING [*humorously*]: Very. [*He moves in towards the table.*]
ERIC [*who is uneasy; sharply*]: Here, what do you mean?
GERALD [*lightly*]: Only something we were talking about when you were out. A joke really.
ERIC [*still uneasy*]: Well, I don't think it's very funny.
BIRLING [*staring at* ERIC; *sharply*]: What's the matter with *you*?
ERIC [*defiantly*]: Nothing. [*He helps himself to port.*]

EDNA *enters.*

EDNA [*announcing*]: Inspector Goole.

The INSPECTOR *enters. He need not be a big man but he creates at once an impression of massiveness, solidity, and purposefulness. He is a man in his fifties, dressed in a plain darkish suit of the period. He speaks carefully, weightily, and has a disconcerting habit of looking hard at the person he addresses before actually speaking.*

INSPECTOR: Mr Birling?
BIRLING: Yes, Sit down, Inspector.
INSPECTOR: Thank you, sir.

EDNA *takes the* INSPECTOR'*s hat and coat and goes out.*

BIRLING: Have a glass of port–or a little whisky.
INSPECTOR: No, thank you, Mr Birling. I'm on duty. [*He turns the desk chair a little away from the desk and sits.*]
BIRLING: You're new, aren't you?
INSPECTOR: Yes, sir. Only recently transferred.
BIRLING: I thought you must be. I was an alderman for years–and Lord Mayor two years ago–and I'm still on the Bench–so I know the Brumley police officers pretty well–and I thought I'd never seen you before. [*He sits left of the table.*]
INSPECTOR: Quite so.
BIRLING: Well, what can I do for you? Some trouble about a warrant?
INSPECTOR: No, Mr Birling.
BIRLING [*after a pause, with a touch of impatience*]: Well, what is it then?
INSPECTOR: I'd like some information, if you don't mind. Mr Birling. Two hours ago a young woman died in the Infirmary. She'd been taken there this afternoon because she'd swallowed a lot of strong disinfectant. Burnt her inside out, of course.
ERIC [*involuntarily*]: My God!
INSPECTOR: Yes, she was in great agony. They did everything they could for her at the Infirmary, but she died. Suicide of course.
BIRLING [*rather impatiently*]: Yes, yes. Horrible business. But I don't understand why you should come here, Inspector—
INSPECTOR [*cutting through, massively*]: I've been round to the room she had, and she'd left a letter there and a sort of diary. Like a lot of these young women who get into various kinds of trouble, she'd used more than one name. But her original name–her real name–was Eva Smith.
BIRLING [*thoughtfully*]: Eva Smith?
INSPECTOR: Do you remember her, Mr Birling?
BIRLING [*slowly*]: No–I seem to remember hearing that name–Eva Smith–somewhere. But it doesn't convey anything to me. And I don't see where I come into this.
INSPECTOR: She was employed in your works at one time.
BIRLING: Oh–that's it, is it? Well, we've several hundred young women there, y'know, and they keep changing.
INSPECTOR [*rising*]: This young woman, Eva Smith, was a bit out of the ordinary. I found a photograph of her in her lodgings. Perhaps you'd remember her from that. [*He takes a photograph about postcard size out of his pocket and moves towards* BIRLING]

GERALD *rises and moves above the table to look over* BIRLING'*s shoulder.* ERIC *rises and moves below the table to see the photograph. The* INSPECTOR *quickly moves above* BIRLING *and prevents both of them from seeing it. They are surprised and rather annoyed.* BIRLING *stares hard and with recognition at the photograph, which the* INSPECTOR *then takes from him and replaces in his pocket, as he moves down left centre.*

GERALD [*following the* INSPECTOR *down; showing annoyance*]: Any particular reason why I shouldn't see this girl's photograph, Inspector?

INSPECTOR [*moving to the desk*]: There might be.

ERIC: And the same applies to me, I suppose?

INSPECTOR: Yes.

GERALD: I can't imagine what it could be.

ERIC: Neither can I. [*He sits below the table.*]

BIRLING: And I must say, I agree with them, Inspector.

GERALD *breaks upstage.*

INSPECTOR: It's the way I like to go to work. [*He is watching* BIRLING.] One person and one line of enquiry at a time. Otherwise, there's a muddle.

BIRLING *notices the* INSPECTOR *watching him.*

[*He moves towards* BIRLING.] I think you remember Eva Smith now, don't you, Mr Birling?

BIRLING: Yes, I do. She was one of my employees and then I discharged her.

ERIC: Is that why she committed suicide? When was this, Father?

BIRLING: Just keep quiet, Eric, and don't get excited. This girl left us nearly two years ago. Let me see—it must have been in the early autumn of nineteen-ten.

INSPECTOR: Yes. End of September, nineteen-ten.

BIRLING: That's right.

GERALD [*moving centre above the table*]: Look here, sir. Wouldn't you rather I was out of this?

BIRLING: I don't mind your being here, Gerald. And I'm sure you've no objection, have you, Inspector? Perhaps I ought to explain first that this is Mr Gerald Croft—the son of Sir George Croft—you know, Crofts, Limited.

INSPECTOR: Mr Gerald Croft, eh?

BIRLING: Yes. Incidentally we've been modestly celebrating his engagement to my daughter Sheila.

INSPECTOR: I see. [*He crosses behind* BIRLING *to* GERALD.] Mr Croft is going to marry Miss Sheila Birling?

GERALD [*smiling*]: I hope so.

INSPECTOR [*gravely*]: Then I'd prefer you to stay.

GERALD [*surprised*]: Oh—all right. [*He sits right, above the table.*]

BIRLING [*somewhat impatiently*]: Look—there's nothing mysterious—or scandalous—about this business—at least not so far as I'm concerned. It's a perfectly straightforward case, and as it happened more than eighteen months ago—nearly two years ago—obviously it has nothing whatever to do with the wretched girl's suicide. Eh, Inspector?

INSPECTOR [*coming down to the table left of* GERALD]: No, sir. I can't agree with you there.

BIRLING: Why not?

INSPECTOR: Because what happened to her then may have determined what happened to her afterwards, and what happened to her afterwards may have driven her to suicide. A chain of events.

BIRLING: Oh well—put like that, there's something in what you say. Still, I can't accept any responsibility. If we were all responsible for everything that happened to everybody we'd had anything to do with, it would be very awkward, wouldn't it?

INSPECTOR: Very awkward.

BIRLING: We'd all be in an impossible position, wouldn't we?

ERIC: By jove, yes. And as you were saying, Dad, a man has to look after himself—

BIRLING [*rising and moving to the desk*]: Yes, well, we needn't go into all that.

INSPECTOR: Go into what?

BIRLING: Oh—just before you came—I'd been giving these young men a little good advice. Now—about this girl, Eva Smith. I remember her quite well now. She was a lively good-looking girl—country-bred, I fancy—and she'd been working in one of our machine shops for over a year. A good worker too. [*He sits at the desk.*] In fact, the foreman there told me he was ready to promote her into what we call a leading operator—head of a small group of girls. But after they came back from their holidays that August, they were all rather restless, and they suddenly decided to ask for more money. They were averaging about twenty-two and six, which was neither more nor less than is paid generally in our industry. They wanted the rates raised so that they could average about twenty-five shillings a week. I refused, of course.

INSPECTOR [*coming down left of the table to* BIRLING]: Why?

BIRLING [*surprised*]: Did you say 'Why?'

INSPECTOR: Yes. Why did you refuse?

BIRLING: Well, Inspector, I don't see that it's any concern of yours how I choose to run my business. Is it now?

INSPECTOR: It might be, you know.

BIRLING [*rising*]: I don't like that tone.

INSPECTOR: I'm sorry. But you asked me a question.

BIRLING [*crossing to the table*]: And you asked me a question before that, a quite unnecessary question too.

INSPECTOR: It's my duty to ask questions.

BIRLING [*turning to face the* INSPECTOR]: Well, it's my duty to keep labour costs down, and if I'd agreed to this demand for a new rate we'd have added about twelve per cent to our labour costs. Does that satisfy you? [*He sits left of the table.*] So I refused. Said I couldn't consider it. We were paying the usual rates and if they didn't like those rates, they could go and work somewhere else. It's a free country, I told them.

ERIC: It isn't if you can't go and work somewhere else.

INSPECTOR: Quite so.

BIRLING [*to* ERIC]: Look—just you keep out of this. You hadn't even started in the works when this happened. So they went on strike. That didn't last long, of course.

GERALD: Not if it was just after the holidays. They'd be all broke—if I know them.

BIRLING: Right, Gerald. They mostly were. And so was the strike, after a week or two. Pitiful affair. Well, we let them all come back—at the old rates—except the four or five ringleaders, who'd started the trouble. I went down myself and told them to clear out. And this girl, Eva Smith, was one of them. She'd had a lot to say—far too much—so she had to go.

GERALD: You couldn't have done anything else.

ERIC: He could. He could have kept her on instead of throwing her out. I call it tough luck.

BIRLING: Rubbish! If you don't come down sharply on some of these people, they'd soon be asking for the earth.

GERALD: I should say so!

INSPECTOR: They might. [*He crosses down stage to the fireplace.*] But after all it's better to ask for the earth than to take it.

BIRLING [*staring at the* INSPECTOR]: What did you say your name was, Inspector?

INSPECTOR: Goole. [*He keeps his back to them.*]

BIRLING: How do you get on with our Chief Constable, Colonel Roberts?

INSPECTOR: I don't see much of him.

BIRLING: Perhaps I ought to warn you that he's an old friend of mine, and that I see him fairly frequently. We play golf together sometimes up at the West Brumley.

INSPECTOR [*drily*]: I don't play golf.

BIRLING: I didn't suppose you did.

ERIC [*bursting out*]: Well, I think it's a dam' shame.

INSPECTOR [*turning to face them*]: No, I've never wanted to.

ERIC [*rising and crossing down left*]: No, I mean about this girl—Eva Smith. Why shouldn't they try for higher wages? We try for the highest possible prices. And I don't see why she should have been sacked just because she'd a bit more spirit than the others. You said yourself she was a good worker. I'd have let her stay.

BIRLING [*rather angrily*]: Unless you brighten your ideas, you'll never be in a position to let anybody stay or to tell anybody to go. It's about time you learnt to face a few responsibilities. That's something this public-school-and-Varsity life you've had doesn't seem to teach you.

ERIC [*crossing back to his chair and sitting: sulkily*]: Well, we don't need to tell the Inspector all about that, do we?

BIRLING: I don't see we need to tell the Inspector anything more. In fact, there's nothing I can tell him. I told the girl to clear out, and she went. That's the last I heard of her. Have you any ideas what happened to her after that? Get into trouble? Go on the streets?

INSPECTOR [*rather slowly*]: No, she didn't exactly go on the streets.

SHEILA *enters, overhearing these last words.*

SHEILA [*gaily*]: What's this about streets?

GERALD *rises and crosses to the door.*

[*She notices the* INSPECTOR.] Oh—sorry. I didn't know. Mummy sent me in to ask you why you didn't come along to the drawing-room.

BIRLING: We shall be along in a minute now. Just finishing.

INSPECTOR: I'm afraid not.

BIRLING [*abruptly*]: There's nothing else, y'know. I've just told you that.

SHEILA: What's all this about?

BIRLING [*rising and moving to* SHEILA]: Nothing to do with you, Sheila. Run along.

INSPECTOR: No, wait a minute, Miss Birling.

BIRLING [*angrily*]: Look here, Inspector, I consider this uncalled-for and officious. I've half a mind to report you. I've told you all I know—and it doesn't seem to me very important—and now there isn't the slightest reason why my daughter should be dragged into this unpleasant business.

SHEILA [*crossing* BIRLING *to left of the table*]: What business? What's happening?

INSPECTOR [*impressively*]: I'm a police inspector, Miss Birling. This afternoon a young woman drank some disinfectant, and died, after several hours of agony, tonight in the Infirmary.

SHEILA: Oh—how horrible! Was it an accident?

INSPECTOR: No. She wanted to end her life. She felt she couldn't go on any longer.

BIRLING [*coming down to the desk and sitting*]: Well, don't tell me that's because I discharged her from my employment nearly two years ago.

ERIC: That might have started it.

SHEILA: Did you, Dad?

BIRLING: Yes.

SHEILA *sits left of the table.*

The girl had been causing trouble in the works. I was quite justified.

GERALD: Yes, I think you were. [*He moves above the table.*] I know we'd have done the same thing. Don't look like that, Sheila.

SHEILA [*rather distressed*]: Sorry! It's just that I can't help thinking about this girl—destroying herself so horribly—and I've been so happy tonight. [*To the* INSPECTOR.] Oh I wish you hadn't told me. What was she like? Quite young?

INSPECTOR: Yes. [*He crosses slowly below the table towards left.*] Twenty-four.

SHEILA: Pretty?

INSPECTOR [*moving up left of* SHEILA]: She wasn't pretty when I saw her to-day but she had been pretty—very pretty. [*He continues above the table.*]

BIRLING: That's enough of that.

GERALD [*moving away right of the table*]: And I don't really see that this enquiry gets you anywhere, Inspector. It's what happened to her since she left Mr Birling's works that is important.

BIRLING: Obviously. I suggested that some time ago.

GERALD: And we can't help you there because we don't know.

He *sits right of the table.*

INSPECTOR [*slowly*]: Are you sure you don't know? [*He looks at* GERALD, *then at* ERIC, *then at* SHEILA. *Then he comes down to the table between the two chairs above it.*]

BIRLING [*rising*]: And are you suggesting now that one of them knows something about this girl?

INSPECTOR: Yes.

BIRLING: You didn't come here just to see me then?

INSPECTOR: No.

The *other four exchange bewildered and perturbed glances.* BIRLING *rises.*

BIRLING [*moving above* SHEILA'*s chair: with a marked change of tone*]: Well, of course, if I'd known that earlier, I wouldn't have called you officious and talked about reporting you. You understand that, don't you Inspector. I thought that—for some reason best known to yourself—you were making the most of this tiny bit of information I could give you. I'm sorry. This makes a difference. You're sure of your facts?

INSPECTOR: Some of them—yes.

BIRLING: I can't think they can be of any great consequence.

INSPECTOR: The girl's dead, though.

SHEILA: What do you mean by saying that? You talk as if we were responsible—

BIRLING [*cutting in*]: Just a minute, Sheila. Now, Inspector, perhaps you and I had better go and talk this over quietly in a corner—

SHEILA [*cutting in*]: Why should you? He's finished with you. He says it's one of us now.

BIRLING: Yes, and I'm trying to settle it sensibly for you.

GERALD: Well, there's nothing to settle as far as I'm concerned. I've never known an Eva Smith.

ERIC: Neither have I.

SHEILA: Was that her name? Eva Smith?

GERALD: Yes.

SHEILA: Never heard it before.

GERALD: So where are you now, Inspector?

INSPECTOR: Where I was before, Mr Croft. I told you—that like a lot of these young women, she'd used more than one name. She was still Eva Smith when Mr Birling sacked her—for wanting twenty-five shillings a week instead of twenty-two and six. But after that she stopped being Eva Smith. Perhaps she'd had enough of it.

ERIC: I can't blame her.

SHEILA [*to* BIRLING]: I think it was a mean thing to do. Perhaps that spoilt everything for her.

BIRLING: Rubbish! [*He comes down to the desk. To the* INSPECTOR.] Do you know what happened to this girl after she left my works? [*He sits.*]

INSPECTOR: Yes. She was out of work for the next two months. Both her parents were dead so that she'd no home to go back to. And she hadn't been able to save much out of what Birling and Company had paid her. So that after two months, with no work, no money coming in, and living in lodgings, with no relatives to help her, few friends, lonely, half-starved, she was feeling desperate.

SHEILA [*warmly*]: I should think so. It's a rotten shame.

INSPECTOR: There are a lot of young women living that sort of existence in every city and big town in this country, Miss Birling. If there weren't, the factories and warehouses wouldn't know where to look for cheap labour. Ask your father.

SHEILA: But these girls aren't cheap labour—they're *people*.

INSPECTOR [*moving round the table to* BIRLING, *drily*]: I'd had that notion myself from time to time. In fact, I've thought that it would do us all a bit of good if sometimes we tried to put ourselves in the place of these young women counting their pennies in their dingy little back bedrooms.

SHEILA: Yes, I expect it would. But what happened to her then?

INSPECTOR: She had what seemed to her a wonderful stroke of luck. She was taken on in a shop—and a good shop too—Milwards.

SHEILA: Milwards! We go there—in fact, I was there this afternoon—[*archly, to* GERALD]—for *your* benefit.

GERALD [*smiling*]: Good!

INSPECTOR: There was a good deal of influenza about at that time and Milwards suddenly found themselves short-handed. So that gave her her chance. And from what I can gather, she liked working there. It was a nice change from a factory. She enjoyed being among pretty clothes, I've no doubt. And now she felt she was making a good fresh start. You can imagine how she felt.

SHEILA: Yes, of course.

BIRLING: And then she got herself into trouble there, I suppose.

INSPECTOR [*moving to left of* SHEILA]: After about a couple of months, just when she felt she was settling down nicely, they told her she'd have to go.

BIRLING: Not doing her work properly?

INSPECTOR: There was nothing wrong with the way she was doing her work. They admitted that.

BIRLING: There must have been something wrong.

INSPECTOR: All she knew was—that a customer complained about her—and so she had to go.

SHEILA [*staring at him; agitatedly*]: When was this?

INSPECTOR [*impressively*]: At the end of January—last year.

SHEILA: What—what did this girl look like?

INSPECTOR: If you'll come over here, I'll show you. [*He moves to the door.*]

SHEILA *rises and moves to the* INSPECTOR. GERALD *rises and moves centre above the table. The* INSPECTOR *produces the photograph.* SHEILA *looks at it closely, recognises it with a little cry, gives a half-startled sob, and then opens the door and runs out. The* INSPECTOR *puts the photograph back into his pocket and stares speculatively after her. The other three stare in amazement for a moment.*

BIRLING [*rising*]: What's the matter with her?

GERALD *moves towards the* INSPECTOR.

ERIC [*rising and moving round the table to left; to the* INSPECTOR]: She recognised her from the photograph, didn't she?

INSPECTOR: Yes.

BIRLING [*angrily*]: Why the devil do you want to go upsetting the child like that?

INSPECTOR: I did nothing. She's upsetting herself. [*He comes down between* BIRLING *and* ERIC *and moves centre.*]

BIRLING: Well—why—why?

INSPECTOR [*crossing down right*]: I don't know—yet. That's something I have to find out.

BIRLING [*still angrily*]: Well—if you don't mind—I'll find out first.

GERALD [*moving to the door; to* BIRLING]: Shall I go to her?

BIRLING [*moving to the door*]: No, leave this to me. I must also have a word with my wife—tell her what's happening. [*He comes down left centre towards the* INSPECTOR.] We were having a nice little family celebration tonight. And a nasty mess you've made of it now, haven't you?

GERALD *moves above the table.*

INSPECTOR [*steadily*]: That's more or less what I was thinking earlier tonight, when I was in the Infirmary looking at what was left of Eva Smith. A nice little promising life there, I thought, and a nasty mess somebody's made of it. [*He crosses to the desk.*]

BIRLING *looks as if he is about to make some retort, then thinks better of it and goes out, closing the door sharply behind him.* GERALD *and* ERIC *exchange uneasy glances.* ERIC *sits below the table.*

GERALD [*coming down left of the table to the* INSPECTOR]: I'd like to have a look at that photograph now, Inspector.
INSPECTOR: All in good time.
GERALD: I don't see why—
INSPECTOR [*turning to him; cutting in massively*]: You heard what I said before, Mr Croft. One line of enquiry at a time. Otherwise we'll all be talking at once and won't know where we are.

GERALD *moves up to the sideboard.*

ERIC [*rising and moving left of the table; suddenly bursting out*]: Look here, I've had enough of this.
INSPECTOR [*drily*]: I dare say.
ERIC [*moving to the* INSPECTOR; *uneasily*]: I'm sorry—but you see—we were having a little party—and I've had a few drinks, including rather a lot of champagne—and I've got a headache—and as I'm only in the way here—I think I'd better turn in. [*He moves to the door.*]
INSPECTOR: And I think you'd better stay here.
ERIC: Why should I?
INSPECTOR: It might be less trouble. If you turn in, you might have to turn out again soon.
GERALD: Getting a bit heavy-handed, aren't you, Inspector?
INSPECTOR: Possibly. But if you're easy with me, I'm easy with you.
GERALD: After all, y'know, we're respectable citizens and not criminals.
INSPECTOR: Sometimes there isn't as much difference as you think. Often, if it was left to me, I wouldn't know where to draw the line.
GERALD: Fortunately, it isn't left to you, is it?
INSPECTOR: No, it isn't. But some things are left to me. Enquiries of this sort, for instance.

ERIC *crosses below the table to centre.* SHEILA *enters. She looks as if she has been crying.*

Well, Miss Birling?
SHEILA [*closing the door*]: You knew it was me all the time, didn't you?
INSPECTOR: I had an idea it might be—from something the girl herself wrote.
SHEILA: I've told my father—he didn't seem to think it amounted to much—but I felt rotten about it at the time and now I feel a lot worse. [*She moves to the left end of the table.*] Did it make much difference to her?
INSPECTOR: Yes, I'm afraid it did. It was the last really steady job she had. When she lost it—for no reason that she could discover—she decided she might as well try another kind of life. [*He moves to* SHEILA.]
SHEILA [*miserably*]: So I'm really responsible?

INSPECTOR: No, not entirely. A good deal happened to her after that. But you're partly to blame. Just as your father is.

SHEILA *sits left of the table.*

ERIC: But what did Sheila do?

SHEILA [*distressed*]: I went to the manager at Milwards and I told him that if they didn't get rid of that girl, I'd never go near the place again and I'd persuade mother to close our account with them.

INSPECTOR: And why did you do that?

SHEILA: Because I was in a furious temper.

INSPECTOR: And what had this girl done to make you lose your temper?

SHEILA: When I was looking at myself in the mirror I caught sight of her smiling at the assistant, and I was furious with her. I'd been in a bad temper anyhow.

INSPECTOR: And was it the girl's fault?

SHEILA: No, not really. It was my own fault. [*Suddenly to* GERALD.] All right, Gerald, you needn't look at me like that. At least, I'm trying to tell the truth. I expect you've done things you're ashamed of too.

GERALD [*surprised*]: Well, I never said I hadn't. [*He comes down to the table.*] I don't see why—

INSPECTOR [*cutting in*]: Never mind about that. You can settle that between you afterwards.

GERALD *sits left above the table.*

INSPECTOR [*to* SHEILA]: What happened?

SHEILA: I'd gone in to try something on. It was an idea of my own—mother had been against it, and so had the assistant—but I insisted. As soon as I tried it on, I knew they'd been right. It just didn't suit me at all. I looked silly in the thing. Well, this girl had brought the dress up from the workroom, and when the assistant—Miss Francis—had asked her something about it, this girl, to show us what she meant, had held the dress up, as if she was wearing it. And it just suited her. She was the right type for it, just as I was the wrong type. She was a very pretty girl too—with soft fine hair and big grey eyes—and that didn't make it any better. Well, when I tried the thing on and looked at myself and knew that it was all wrong, I caught sight of this girl smiling at Miss Francis—as if to say, 'Doesn't she look awful'—and I was absolutely furious. I was very rude to both of them, and then I went to the manager and told him that this girl had been very impertinent—and— [*She almost breaks down, but just controls herself.*] How could I know what would happen afterwards? If she'd been some miserable plain little creature, I don't suppose I'd have done it. But she was very pretty and looked as if she could take care of herself. I couldn't be sorry for her.

INSPECTOR: In fact, in a kind of way, you might be said to have been jealous of her.

SHEILA: Yes, I suppose so.

INSPECTOR: And so you used the power you had, as the daughter of a good customer and of a man well-known in the town, to punish the girl just because she made you feel like that.

SHEILA: Yes, but it didn't seem to be anything very terrible at the time. Don't you understand? And if I could help her now, I would—

INSPECTOR [*moving up stage to the sideboard; harshly*]: Yes, but you can't. It's too late. She's dead.

ERIC [*crossing to the fireplace*]: My God, it's a bit thick, when you come to think of it— [*He sits in the armchiar.*]

SHEILA [*stormily*]: Oh shut up, Eric. I know, I know. It's the only time I've ever done anything like that, and I'll never never do it again to anybody. I've noticed them giving me a sort of look sometimes at Milwards–I noticed it even this afternoon–and I suppose some of them remember. I feel now I can never go there again. Oh–why had this to happen?

INSPECTOR [*coming down right of the table, sternly*]: That's what I asked myself tonight when I was looking at that dead girl. And then I said to myself, 'Well, we'll try to understand why it had to happen.' And that's why I'm here, and why I'm not going until I know *all* that happened. [*He sits right of the table.*] Eva Smith lost her job with Birling and Company because the strike failed and they were determined not to have another one. At last she found another job–under what name I don't know–in a big shop, and had to leave there because you were annoyed with yourself and passed the annoyance on to her. Now she had to try something else. So first she changed her name to Daisy Renton—

GERALD [*startled*]: What?

INSPECTOR [*steadily*]: I said she changed her name to Daisy Renton.

GERALD *rises, moves up to the sideboard and pours himself out a whisky which he drinks.*

INSPECTOR [*rising and crossing below the table to centre*]: Where is your father, Miss Birling?

SHEILA: He went into the drawing-room, to tell my mother what was happening here. Eric, take the inspector along to the drawing-room.

ERIC *rises, crosses to the door and opens it. The* INSPECTOR *crosses to the door, looks from* SHEILA *to* GERALD, *then goes out with* ERIC. GERALD *comes down right of the table.*

Well, Gerald?

GERALD [*trying to smile*]: Well what, Sheila?

SHEILA: How did you come to know this girl–Eva Smith?

GERALD: I didn't.

SHEILA: Daisy Renton then–it's the same thing.

GERALD: Why should I have known her?

SHEILA: Oh don't be stupid. We haven't much time. You gave yourself away as soon as he mentioned her other name.

GERALD [*moving in to right of the table*]: All right. I knew her. Let's leave it at that.

SHEILA: We can't leave it at that.

GERALD: Now listen, darling—

SHEILA: No, that's no use. You not only knew her but you knew her very well. Otherwise, you wouldn't look so guilty about it. When did you first get to know her?

GERALD *does not reply. He sits right of the table.*

Was it after she left Milwards? When she changed her name, as he said, and began to lead a different sort of life? Were you seeing her last Spring and Summer, during that time when you hardly came near me and said you were so busy? Were you?

GERALD *does not reply, but looks at her.*

Yes, of course you were. [*She rises and comes slowly down left.*]
GERALD: I'm sorry, Sheila. But it was all over and done with last Summer. I hadn't set eyes on the girl for at least six months. I don't come into this suicide business.
SHEILA: I thought I didn't half-an-hour ago.
GERALD: You don't. Neither of us does. So—for God's sake—don't say anything to the Inspector.
SHEILA [*turning to him*]: About you and this girl?
GERALD: Yes. We can keep it from him.

SHEILA *laughs rather hysterically. She crosses to the chair below the table and kneels on it.*

SHEILA: Why—you fool—*he knows.* Of course he knows. And I hate to think how much he knows that we don't know yet. You'll see. You'll see. [*She looks at him almost in triumph.*]

GERALD *looks crushed. The door slowly opens and the* INSPECTOR *appears, looking steadily and searchingly at them.* GERALD *rises.*

The CURTAIN *falls.*

ACT TWO

SCENE: The same. The action is continuous.

When the CURTAIN *rises* GERALD *has just risen; the* INSPECTOR *is still at the door looking at* SHEILA *and* GERALD. *Then he comes forward a step, leaving the door open behind him.*

INSPECTOR [*to* GERALD]: Well?

SHEILA [*crossing to the fireplace; with an hysterical laugh, to* GERALD]: You see? What did I tell you?

INSPECTOR: What did you tell him? [*He closes the door.*]

GERALD [*moving below the table; with an effort*]: Inspector, I think Miss Birling ought to be excused any more of this questioning. She's had a long, exciting and tiring day—we were celebrating our engagement, you know—and now she's obviously had about as much as she can stand. You heard her.

SHEILA: He means that I'm getting hysterical now.

INSPECTOR: And are you?

SHEILA: Probably.

INSPECTOR: Well, I don't want to keep you here. [*He moves down left.*] I've no more questions to ask you.

SHEILA: No, but you haven't finished asking questions—have you?

INSPECTOR: No.

SHEILA [*to* GERALD]: You see? [*To the* INSPECTOR.] Then I'm staying.

GERALD: Why should you? It's bound to be unpleasant and disturbing.

INSPECTOR [*turning to* GERALD]: And you think young women ought to be protected against unpleasant and disturbing things?

GERALD: If possible—yes.

INSPECTOR [*moving up left of the table to the sideboard*]: Well, we know one young woman who wasn't, don't we?

GERALD: I suppose I asked for that.

SHEILA: Be careful you don't ask for any more, Gerald.

GERALD: I only meant to say to you—Why stay when you'll hate it?

SHEILA: It can't be any worse for me than it has been. And it might be better.

GERALD [*bitterly*]: I see.

SHEILA: What do you see?

GERALD: You've been through it—and now you want to see somebody else put through it.

SHEILA [*bitterly*]: So that's what you think I'm really like. I'm glad I realised it in time, Gerald.

GERALD [*moving away down left*]: No, no, I didn't mean—

SHEILA [*crossing to* GERALD; *cutting in*]: Yes, you did. And if you'd really loved me, you couldn't have said that. You listened to that nice story about me. I got that girl sacked from Milwards. And now you've made up your mind I must obviously be a selfish vindictive creature.

GERALD: I neither said that nor even suggested it.

SHEILA: Then why say I want to see somebody else put through it? That's not what I meant at all. [*She sits below the table.*]

GERALD: All right then, I'm sorry.

SHEILA: Yes, but you don't believe me. And this is just the wrong time not to believe me.

INSPECTOR [*coming down left of the table; massively taking charge*]: Allow me, Miss Birling. [*To* GERALD.] I can tell you why Miss Birling wants to stay on and why she says it might be better for her if she did. A girl died tonight. A pretty, lively sort of girl, who never did anybody any harm. But she died in misery and agony—hating life—

SHEILA [*distressed*]: Don't please—I know, I know—and I can't stop thinking about it—

INSPECTOR [*ignoring this*]: Now Miss Birling has just been made to understand what she did to this girl. She feels responsible. And if she leaves us now, and doesn't hear any more, then she'll feel she's entirely to blame, she'll be alone with her responsibility, the rest of tonight, all tomorrow, all the next night—

SHEILA [*eagerly*]: Yes, that's it. And I know I'm to blame—and I'm desperately sorry—but I can't believe—I won't believe—it's simply my fault that in the end she—she committed suicide. That would be too horrible—

INSPECTOR [*sternly to them both*]: You see, we have to share something. If there's nothing else, we'll have to share our guilt. [*He crosses to the fireplace.*]

GERALD *moves to* SHEILA.

SHEILA [*rising; staring at the* INSPECTOR]: Yes. That's true. You know. [*She goes closer to him, wonderingly.*] I don't understand about you.

INSPECTOR [*calmly*]: There's no reason why you should.

SHEILA: I don't know much about police inspectors—but the ones I have met weren't a bit like you.

INSPECTOR: And, in a way, it's a pity, isn't it?

SHEILA [*wonderingly*]: Yes, that's the strange part of it. [*She looks at him curiously, and talks almost to herself.*] I was just going to say something like that. They weren't but perhaps they ought to have been. As if—suddenly—there came a real one—at last. And that's absurd, isn't it?

INSPECTOR [*calmly*]: Is it? [*He regards her calmly.*]

SHEILA *stares at him wonderingly and dubiously.* MRS BIRLING *enters, briskly and self-confidently, quite out of key with the little scene which has just passed.* SHEILA *feels this at once.*

MRS BIRLING [*closing the door; smiling and social*]: Good-evening Inspector.

GERALD *moves up left of the table to the sideboard.*

INSPECTOR: Good-evening, madam.

MRS BIRLING [*in the same easy tone*]: I'm Mrs Birling, y'know. [*She comes down left centre.*] My husband has just explained why you're here, and while we'll be glad to tell you anything you want to know, I don't think we can help you much.

SHEILA [*crossing to* MRS BIRLING]: No, Mother—please!

MRS BIRLING [*affecting great surprise*]: What's the matter, Sheila?

SHEILA [*hesitantly*]: I know it sounds silly—

MRS BIRLING: What does?

SHEILA: You see, I feel you're beginning all wrong. And I'm afraid you'll say something or do something that you'll be sorry for afterwards.

MRS BIRLING: I don't know what you're talking about, Sheila.

SHEILA: We all started like that—so confident, so pleased with ourselves until he began asking us questions.

MRS BIRLING *looks from* SHEILA *to the* INSPECTOR *and crosses to him.*

MRS BIRLING: You seem to have made a great impression on this child, Inspector.

INSPECTOR [*coolly*]: We often do on the young ones. They're more impressionable.

He and MRS BIRLING *look at each other for a moment. Then* MRS BIRLING *turns to* SHEILA *again.*

MRS BIRLING: You're looking tired, dear. [*She moves centre below the table.*] I think you ought to go to bed—and forget about this absurd business. You'll feel better in the morning.

SHEILA: Mother, I couldn't possibly go. Nothing could be worse for me. We've settled all that. I'm staying here until I know why that girl killed herself.

MRS BIRLING [*sitting below the table*]: Nothing but morbid curiosity.

SHEILA: No it isn't.

MRS BIRLING: Please don't contradict me like that. And in any case I don't suppose for a moment that we can understand why the girl committed suicide. Girls of that class—

SHEILA [*cutting in; urgently*]: Mother, don't—please don't. For your own sake, as well as ours, you mustn't—

MRS BIRLING [*annoyed*]: Musn't—what? Really, Sheila!

SHEILA [*sitting left of the table; slowly, carefully now*]: You mustn't try to build up a kind of wall between us and that girl. If you do, then the Inspector will just break it down. And it'll be all the worse when he does.

MRS BIRLING: I don't understand you. [*To the* INSPECTOR.] Do you?

INSPECTOR: Yes. And she's right.

MRS BIRLING [*haughtily*]: I beg your pardon!

INSPECTOR [*crossing to* MRS BIRLING; *very plainly*]: I said, Yes—I do understand her. And she's right.

MRS BIRLING: That—I consider—is a trifle impertinent, Inspector.

SHEILA *gives a short hysterical laugh.*

Now, what is it, Sheila?

GERALD *comes down to the back of* SHEILA'*s chair.*

SHEILA: I don't know. Perhaps it's because *impertinent* is such a silly word. But, Mother, do stop before it's too late.

MRS BIRLING: If you mean that the Inspector will take offence—
INSPECTOR [*cutting in; calmly*]: No, no. I never take offence.
MRS BIRLING: I'm glad to hear it. Though I must add that it seems to me that we have more reason for taking offence.
INSPECTOR: Let's leave *offence* out of it, shall we?
GERALD: I think we'd better.
SHEILA: So do I.
MRS BIRLING [*rebuking them*]: *I'm* talking to the Inspector now, if you don't mind. [*To the* INSPECTOR, *rather grandly.*] I realise that you may have to conduct some sort of enquiry, but I must say that so far you seem to be conducting it in a rather peculiar and offensive manner. You know of course that my husband was Lord Mayor only two years ago and that he's still a magistrate—
GERALD [*cutting in; rather impatiently*]: Mrs Birling, the Inspector knows all that. And I don't think it's a very good idea to remind him—
SHEILA [*cutting in*]: It's crazy. Stop it, please, Mother.
INSPECTOR: They're right, y'know.
MRS BIRLING [*trying to crush him*]: Indeed!
INSPECTOR [*imperturbably*]: Yes. [*He crosses down left.*] Now what about Mr Birling?
MRS BIRLING: He's coming back in a moment. He's just talking to my son, Eric, who seems to be in an excitable silly mood.
INSPECTOR: What's the matter with him?
MRS BIRLING: Eric? Oh—I'm afraid he may have had rather too much to drink tonight. We were having a little celebration here—
INSPECTOR [*cutting in*]: Isn't he used to drinking?
MRS BIRLING: No, of course not. He's only a boy.
INSPECTOR: No, he's a young man. And some young men drink far too much.
SHEILA: And Eric's one of them.
MRS BIRLING [*very sharply*]: Sheila!
SHEILA [*rising and crossing below the table to the fireplace: urgently*]: I don't want to get poor Eric into trouble. He's probably in enough trouble already. But we really must stop these silly pretences. This isn't the time to pretend that Eric isn't used to drink. He's been steadily drinking too much for the last two years.
MRS BIRLING [*staggered*]: It isn't true. You know him, Gerald—and you're a man—you must know it isn't true.

    GERALD *hesitates.*

INSPECTOR: Well, Mr Croft?
GERALD [*apologetically to* MRS BIRLING]: I'm afraid it is, y'know. Actually I've never seen much of him outside this house—but—well, I have gathered that he does drink pretty hard.
MRS BIRLING [*rising and crossing to* SHEILA; *bitterly*]: And this is the time you choose to tell me.
SHEILA: Yes, of course it is. That's what I meant when I talked about building up a wall that's sure to be knocked flat. It makes it all the harder to bear.
MRS BIRLING: But it's you—and not the Inspector here—who's doing it—
SHEILA: Yes, but don't you see? *He hasn't started on you yet.*
MRS BIRLING [*after a pause; recovering herself*]: If necessary I shall be glad to

answer any questions the Inspector wishes to ask me. Though naturally I don't know anything about this girl.

INSPECTOR [*gravely*]: We'll see, Mrs Birling.

BIRLING *enters. He closes the door behind him.*

BIRLING [*rather hot, bothered*]: I've been trying to persuade Eric to go to bed, but he won't. [*To the* INSPECTOR.] Now he says you told him to stay up. Did you?

INSPECTOR: Yes, I did.

BIRLING: Why?

INSPECTOR: Because I shall want to talk to him, Mr Birling.

BIRLING [*crossing above the table to the fireplace*]: I don't see why you should, but if you must, then I suggest you do it now. Have him in and get it over, then let the lad go.

INSPECTOR: No, I can't do that yet. I'm sorry, but he'll have to wait.

BIRLING: Now look here, Inspector—

INSPECTOR [*moving centre below the table; cutting in; with authority*]: He must wait his turn.

SHEILA [*sitting in the armchair; to* MRS BIRLING]: You see?

MRS BIRLING: No, I don't. And please be quiet, Sheila.

BIRLING [*angrily*]: Inspector. I've told you before, I don't like your tone nor the way you're handling this enquiry. And I don't propose to give you much more rope.

INSPECTOR: You needn't give me any rope.

SHEILA [*rather wildly, with a laugh*]: No, he's giving us rope–so that we'll hang ourselves.

BIRLING [*to* MRS BIRLING]: What's the matter with that child?

MRS BIRLING: Over-excited. And she refuses to go. [*With sudden anger; to the* INSPECTOR.] Well, come along–what is it you want to know?

INSPECTOR [*moving slowly down left; coolly*]: At the end of January, last year, this girl Eva Smith had to leave Milwards, because Miss Birling compelled them to discharge her, and then she stopped being Eva Smith, looking for a job, and became Daisy Renton, with other ideas. [*Turning on* GERALD, *sharply.*] Mr Croft, when did you first get to know her?

There is an exclamation of surprise from BIRLING *and* MRS BIRLING.

GERALD: Where did you get the idea that I did know her?

SHEILA: It's not use, Gerald. You're wasting time.

INSPECTOR: As soon as I mentioned the name Daisy Renton, it was obvious you'd known her. You gave yourself away at once.

SHEILA [*rising and moving to the chair below the table; bitterly*]: Of course he did.

INSPECTOR: And anyhow I knew already. When and where did you first meet her?

GERALD: All right, if you must have it. [*He sits left of the table.*] I met her first, sometime in March last year, in the stalls bar at the Palace. I mean the Palace music hall here in Brumley—

SHEILA [*moving right round the table and above it*]: Well, we didn't think you meant Buckingham Palace.

GERALD [*to* SHEILA]: Thanks. You're going to be a great help, I can see. You've said your piece, and you're obviously going to hate this, so why on earth don't you leave us to it?

SHEILA: Nothing would induce me. I want to understand exactly what happens when a man says he's so busy at the works that he can hardly ever find time to come and see the girl he's supposed to be in love with. I wouldn't miss it for—

INSPECTOR [*with authority*]: Be quiet, please.

SHEILA *moves up to the sideboard.*

[*He crosses to the chair below the table and sits*]: Yes, Mr Croft—in the stalls bar at the Palace Variety Theatre . . .

GERALD: I happened to look in, one night, after a rather long dull day, and as the show wasn't very bright, I went down into the bar for a drink. It's a favourite haunt of women of the town—

MRS BIRLING: Women of the town?

INSPECTOR: Prostitutes.

MRS BIRLING: Yes—but here—in Brumley—

INSPECTOR: One of the worst cities in the country for prostitution.

BIRLING: Quite true. But I see no point in mentioning the subject—especially— [*Indicating* SHEILA.]

MRS BIRLING: It would be much better if Sheila didn't listen to this story at all.

SHEILA: But you're forgetting I'm supposed to be engaged to the hero of it. Go on, Gerald. [*She comes down to the back of* GERALD's *chair.*] You went down into the bar, which is a favourite haunt of women of the town.

GERALD: I'm glad I amuse you—

INSPECTOR [*sharply*]: Come along, Mr Croft. What happened?

GERALD: I didn't propose to stay long down there. I hate those hard-eyed, dough-faced women. But then I noticed a girl who looked quite different. She was very pretty—soft brown hair and big grey eyes— [*He breaks off.*] My God!

INSPECTOR: What's the matter?

GERALD [*distressed*]: Sorry—I—well, I've suddenly realised—taken it in properly—that she's dead—

INSPECTOR [*harshly*]: Yes, she's dead.

SHEILA: And probably between us we killed her.

MRS BIRLING [*sitting in the armchair; sharply*]: Sheila, don't talk nonsense.

INSPECTOR [*to* GERALD]: Go on.

GERALD: This girl was young and pretty and—well—quite out of place down there. And obviously she wasn't enjoying herself. Old Joe Meggarty, half-drunk and goggle-eyed, had wedged her into a corner with that obscene fat carcase of his—

MRS BIRLING [*cutting in*]: There's no need to be disgusting. And surely you don't mean Alderman Meggarty?

GERALD: Of course I do. He's a notorious womaniser as well as being one of the worst sots and rogues in Brumley.

INSPECTOR: Quite right.

MRS BIRLING [*staggered*]: Well, really! Alderman Meggarty! I must say, we *are* learning something tonight.

SHEILA [*coolly*]: Of course we are. But everybody knows about that horrible old

Meggarty. A girl I know had to see him at the Town Hall one afternoon and she only escaped with a torn blouse—

BIRLING [*shocked; sharply*]: Sheila!

INSPECTOR [*to* GERALD]: Go on.

GERALD: The girl saw me looking at her and then gave me a glance that was nothing less than a cry for help. So I went across and told Joe Meggarty some nonsense—that the manager had a message for him or something like that—got him out of the way—and then told the girl that if she didn't want any more of that sort of thing, she'd better let me take her out of there. She agreed at once. [*He rises and moves down left.*]

INSPECTOR: Where did you go?

GERALD: We went along to the County Hotel, which I knew would be quiet at that time of night, and we had a drink or two and talked.

INSPECTOR: Did she drink much at that time?

GERALD: No. She only had a port and lemonade—or some such concoction. [*He turns to the* INSPECTOR.] All she wanted was to talk—a little friendliness—and I gathered that Joe Meggarty's advances had left her rather shaken—as well they might—

INSPECTOR: She talked about herself?

GERALD: Yes. I asked her questions about herself. She told me her name was Daisy Renton, that she'd lost both parents, and that she came originally from somewhere outside Brumley. She also told me she'd had a job in one of the works here and had had to leave after a strike. She said something about the shop too but wouldn't say which it was, and she was deliberately vague about what happened. I couldn't get any exact details from her about her past life. [*He moves in to left of the table.*] She wanted to talk about herself—just because she felt I was interested and friendly—but at the same time she wanted to be Daisy Renton—and not Eva Smith. In fact, I heard that name for the first time tonight. What she did let slip—though she didn't mean to—was that she was desperately hard up and at that moment was actually hungry. I made the people at the County find some food for her.

INSPECTOR: And then you decided to keep her—as your mistress?

MRS BIRLING: What?

SHEILA [*coming down left*]: Of course, Mother. It was obvious from the start. Go on, Gerald. Don't mind Mother.

BIRLING *turns the chair from right of the table to the fire and sits.*

GERALD [*steadily*]: I discovered, not that night but two nights later, when we met again—not accidentally this time of course—that in fact she hadn't a penny and was going to be turned out of the miserable back-room she had. It happened that a friend of mine had gone off to Canada for six months and had let me have the key of a flat of his. So I insisted on Daisy moving into it and made her take some money to keep her going there. [*He sits left of the table. Carefully, to the* INSPECTOR.] I want you to understand that I didn't install her there so that I could make love to her. That came afterwards. I made her go there because I was sorry for her, and didn't like the idea of her going back to the Palace bar. I didn't ask for anything in return.

INSPECTOR: I see. [*He rises and moves right round the table up to the sideboard.*]

SHEILA [*to* GERALD]: Yes, but why are you saying that to him? You ought to be saying it to me.

GERALD: I suppose I ought, really. I'm sorry, Sheila. Somehow I— [*He hesitates.*]
SHEILA [*cutting in*]: I know. Somehow he makes you.
INSPECTOR [*to* GERALD]: But she became your mistress?
GERALD: Yes. I suppose It was inevitable.

SHEILA *moves to the desk.*

She was young and pretty and warm-hearted–and intensely grateful. I became at once the most important person in her life–you understand?
INSPECTOR: Yes. She was a woman. She was lonely. You'd been friendly and looked after her. And women want somebody to love. It's their weakness.
SHEILA: That's a nice thing to say.
INSPECTOR: The world being what it is–a battlefield rather than a home–this desire of women to love is a weakness. In another kind of world, it might be a source of strength. But not in the world we've made. [*To* GERALD.] Were you in love with her?
SHEILA: Just what I was going to ask.
BIRLING [*rising; angrily*]: I really must protest—
INSPECTOR [*turning on him sharply*]: Why should you do any protesting? It was you who turned the girl out in the first place.
BIRLING [*rather taken aback*]: Well, I only did what any employer might have done. And what I was going to say was that I protest against the way in which my daughter, a young unmarried girl, is being dragged into this—
INSPECTOR [*sharply*]: Your daughter isn't living on the moon. She's here in Brumley too. [*He comes down to the back of* GERALD*'s chair.*]
SHEILA: Yes, and it was I who had the girl turned out of her job at Milwards. *And* I'm supposed to be engaged to Gerald. And I'm not a child, don't forget. I've a right to know. [*She moves to* GERALD.] *Were* you in love with her, Gerald?
GERALD [*hesitantly*]: It's hard to say. I didn't feel about her as she felt about me.
SHEILA [*breaking away to centre below the table; with sharp sarcasm*]: Of course not. You were the wonderful Fairy Prince. You must have adored it, Gerald.
GERALD: All right–I did for a time. Almost any man would have done.
SHEILA [*turning to* GERALD]: That's probably about the best thing you've said tonight. At least it's honest. Did you go and see her every night? [*She sits below the table.*]
GERALD: No. I wasn't telling you a complete lie when I said I'd been very busy at the works all that time. We were very busy. But of course I did see a good deal of her.
MRS BIRLING [*rising*]: I don't think we want any further details of this disgusting affair—

The INSPECTOR *moves slowly down left.*

SHEILA [*cutting in*]: I do. And anyhow we haven't had any details yet.
GERALD [*rising*]: And you're not going to have any. [*To* MRS BIRLING.] You know, it wasn't disgusting.
MRS BIRLING: It was disgusting to me.
SHEILA: Yes, but after all, you didn't come into this, did you, Mother?
GERALD [*coming down to the* INSPECTOR]: Is there anything else you want to

know—that you ought to know?

INSPECTOR: Yes. When did this affair end?

GERALD: In the first week of September. I had to go away for several weeks then—on business—and by that time Daisy knew it was coming to an end. So I broke it off definitely before I went.

INSPECTOR: How did she take it?

GERALD: Better than I'd hoped. She was—very gallant—about it.

SHEILA [*with irony*]: That was nice for you.

GERALD: No it wasn't. [*He waits a moment; then in a low troubled tone.*] She told me she'd been happier than she'd ever been before—but that she knew it couldn't last—hadn't expected it to last. She didn't blame me at all. I wish to God she had now. Perhaps I'd feel better about it.

INSPECTOR: She had to move out of those rooms?

GERALD: Yes, we'd agreed about that. She'd saved a little money during the summer—she'd lived very economically on what I'd allowed her—and didn't want to take any more from me, but I insisted on a parting gift of enough money—though it wasn't so very much—to see her through to the end of the year.

INSPECTOR: Did she tell you what she proposed to do after you'd left her?

GERALD: No. She refused to talk about that. I got the idea, once or twice from what she said, that she thought of leaving Brumley. Whether she did or not—I don't know. Did she?

INSPECTOR [*moving up left of the table to the sideboard*]: Yes. She went away for about two months. To some seaside place.

GERALD: By herself?

INSPECTOR: Yes. I think she went away—to be alone, to be quiet, to remember all that had happened between you.

GERALD: How do you know that?

INSPECTOR: She kept a rough sort of diary. And she said there that she had to go away and be quiet and remember 'just to make it last longer.' She felt there'd never be anything as good again for her—so she had to make it last longer.

GERALD [*gravely*]: I see. Well, I never saw her again, and that's all I can tell you.

INSPECTOR: It's all I want to know from you.

GERALD: In that case—as I'm rather more—upset—by this business than I probably appear to be—and—well, I'd like to be alone for a little while—I'd be glad if you'd let me go.

INSPECTOR: Go where? Home?

GERALD: No. I'll just go out—walk about—for a while, if you don't mind. I'll come back. [*He turns to the door.*]

INSPECTOR: All right, Mr Croft.

SHEILA [*rising and crossing to* GERALD]: But just in case you forget—or decide not to come back, Gerald, I think you'd better take this with you. [*She hands him the ring.*]

GERALD: I see. Well, I was expecting this.

SHEILA: I don't dislike you as I did half-an-hour ago, Gerald. In fact, in some odd way, I rather respect you more than I've ever done before. I knew anyhow you were lying about those months last year when you hardly came near me. I knew there was something fishy about that time. And now at least you've been honest. And I believe what you told us about the way you helped her at first. Just out of pity. And it was my fault really that she was so desperate when you first met her. But this has made a difference. You and I

aren't the same people who sat down to dinner here. We'd have to start all
over again, getting to know each other—
BIRLING [*crossing towards* SHEILA, *below the table*]: Now, Sheila, I'm not
defending him. But you must understand that a lot of young men—
SHEILA: Don't interfere, please, Father. Gerald knows what I mean, and you
apparently don't.

> BIRLING *turns back to the fire.*

GERALD: Yes, I know what you mean. But I'm coming back—if I may.
SHEILA: All right. [*She sits left of the table.*]
MRS BIRLING [*moving centre below the table*]: Well, really, I don't know. I think
we've just about come to an end of this wretched business—
GERALD: I don't think so. Excuse me.

> *He goes out.* BIRLING *crosses up stage to the door to follow him but as he reaches
> the door the front door slams off stage.* MRS BIRLING *sits below the table.*

SHEILA [*to the* INSPECTOR]: You know, you never showed him that photograph
of her.
INSPECTOR: No, it wasn't necessary.
MRS BIRLING: You have a photograph of the girl?
INSPECTOR: Yes, I think you'd better look at it. [*He comes round right of the table
to* MRS BIRLING.]
MRS BIRLING: I don't see any particular reason why I should—
INSPECTOR: Probably not. But you'd better look at it.
MRS BIRLING: Very well.

> *The* INSPECTOR *produces the photograph and* MRS BIRLING *looks hard at it.*

INSPECTOR [*taking back the photograph*]: You recognise her?
MRS BIRLING: No. Why should I?
INSPECTOR: Of course she might have changed lately, but I can't believe she
could have changed so much.
MRS BIRLING: I don't understand you, Inspector.
INSPECTOR [*moving to the fireplace*]: You mean you don't choose to, Mrs Birling.
MRS BIRLING [*angrily*]: I meant what I said.
INSPECTOR: You're not telling me the truth.
MRS BIRLING [*rising*]: I beg your pardon!
BIRLING [*crossing to the table left of* MRS BIRLING; *angrily to the* INSPECTOR]: Look
here, I'm not going to have this, Inspector. You'll apologise at once.
INSPECTOR: Apologise for what—doing my duty?
BIRLING: No, for being so offensive about it. I'm a public man—
INSPECTOR [*massively*]: Public men, Mr Birling, have responsibilities as well as
privileges.
BIRLING: Possibly. But you weren't asked to come here to talk to me about my
responsibilities.
SHEILA: Let's hope not. Though I'm beginning to wonder.
MRS BIRLING: Does that mean anything, Sheila?
SHEILA [*rising*]: It means that we've no excuses now for putting on airs and that
if we've any sense we won't try. Father threw this girl out because she asked

for decent wages. I went and pushed her further out, right into the street, just because I was angry and she was pretty. Gerald set her up as his mistress and then dropped her when it suited him. And now you're pretending you don't recognise her from that photograph. I admit I don't know why you should, but I know jolly well you did in fact recognise her, from the way you looked. And if you're not telling the truth, why should the Inspector apologise? And can't you see, both of you, you're making it worse?

We hear the front door slam.

BIRLING: That was the door again.
MRS BIRLING: Gerald must have come back.
INSPECTOR: Unless your son has just gone out.
BIRLING: I'll see.

He turns to the door and goes out quickly. The INSPECTOR *turns to* MRS BIRLING.

INSPECTOR: Mrs Birling, you're a member—a prominent member—of the Brumley Women's Charity Organisation, aren't you?

MRS BIRLING *sits below the table. She does not reply.*

SHEILA: Go on, Mother. You might as well admit it. [*To the* INSPECTOR.] Yes, she is. Why? [*She sits left of the table.*]
INSPECTOR [*crossing down stage to the desk; calmly*]: It's an organisation to which women in distress can appeal for help in various forms. Isn't that so?
MRS BIRLING [*with dignity*]: Yes. We've done a great deal of useful work in helping deserving cases.
INSPECTOR: There was a meeting of the interviewing committee two weeks ago?
MRS BIRLING: I dare say there was.
INSPECTOR: You know very well there was, Mrs Birling. You were in the chair.
MRS BIRLING: And if I was, what business is it of yours?
INSPECTOR [*severely*]: Do you want me to tell you—in plain words?

BIRLING *enters. He is looking rather agitated. He closes the door.*

BIRLING: That must have been Eric.
MRS BIRLING [*alarmed*]: Have you been up to his room?
BIRLING: Yes. And I called out on both landings. It must have been Eric we heard go out then.
MRS BIRLING: Silly boy! Where can he have gone to?
BIRLING: I can't imagine. But he was in one of his excitable queer moods, and even though we don't need him here—
INSPECTOR [*cutting in, sharply*]: We do need him here. And if he's not back soon, I shall have to go and find him.

BIRLING *and* MRS BIRLING *exchange bewildered and rather frightened glances.*

SHEILA [*rising and crossing above the table to the fireplace*]: He's probably just gone to cool off. He'll be back soon.

INSPECTOR [*severely*]: I hope so.

MRS BIRLING: And why should you hope so?

INSPECTOR [*crossing to left of* MRS BIRLING]: I'll explain why when you've answered my questions, Mrs Birling.

BIRLING: Is there any reason why my wife should answer questions from you, Inspector?

INSPECTOR: Yes, a very good reason. You'll remember that Mr Croft told us–quite truthfully, I believe–that he hadn't spoken to or seen Eva Smith since last September. But Mrs Birling spoke to and saw her only two weeks ago.

SHEILA [*astonished*]: Mother!

BIRLING: Is this true?

MRS BIRLING [*after a pause*]: Yes, quite true.

SHEILA *sits in the armchair.*

INSPECTOR: She appealed to your organisation for help?

MRS BIRLING: Yes.

INSPECTOR: Not as Eva Smith?

MRS BIRLING: No. Nor as Daisy Renton.

INSPECTOR: As what then?

MRS BIRLING: First, she called herself Mrs Birling—

BIRLING [*astounded*]: *Mrs Birling!*

MRS BIRLING: Yes. I think it was simply a piece of gross impertinence–quite deliberate–and naturally that was one of the things that prejudiced me against her case.

BIRLING [*crossing up to the sideboard*]: And I should think so! Damned impudence! [*He pours himself a drink.*]

INSPECTOR: You admit being prejudiced against her case?

MRS BIRLING: Yes.

SHEILA: Mother, she's just died a horrible death–don't forget.

The INSPECTOR *moves up left, above the chair left of the table.*

MRS BIRLING: I'm very sorry. But I think she had only herself to blame.

INSPECTOR: Was it owing to your influence, as the most prominent member of the Committee, that help was refused the girl?

MRS BIRLING: Possibly.

INSPECTOR: Was it or was it not your influence?

BIRLING *moves down to the fireplace.*

MRS BIRLING [*rising and moving away to right; stung*]: Yes, it was. I didn't like her manner. She'd impertinently made use of our name, though she pretended afterwards it just happened to be the first she thought of. She had to admit, after I began questioning her, that she had no claim to the name, that she wasn't married, and that the story she told at first–about a husband who'd deserted her–was quite false. It didn't take me long to get the truth–or some of the truth–out of her.

INSPECTOR: Why did she ask for help?

MRS BIRLING [*moving up to the right end of the sideboard*]: You know very well why she asked for help.

INSPECTOR: No, I don't. I know why she *needed* help. But as I wasn't there, I don't know what she asked it for from your committee.

MRS BIRLING: I don't think we need discuss it.

INSPECTOR: You have no hope of *not* discussing it, Mrs Birling.

MRS BIRLING [*turning on the* INSPECTOR]: If you think you can bring any pressure to bear upon me, Inspector, you're quite mistaken. Unlike the other three, I did nothing I'm ashamed of or that won't bear investigation. The girl asked for assistance. We are asked to look carefully into the claims made upon us. I wasn't satisfied with this girl's claim—she seemed to me to be not a good case—and so I used my influence to have it refused. And in spite of what's happened to the girl since, I consider I did my duty. [*As she moves to the fireplace up stage of* MR BIRLING.] So if I prefer not to discuss it any further, you have no power to make me change my mind.

INSPECTOR: Yes I have.

MRS BIRLING [*turning to face the* INSPECTOR]: No you haven't. Simply because I've done nothing wrong—and you know it.

INSPECTOR [*very deliberately*]: I think you did something terribly wrong—and that you're going to spend the rest of your life regretting it. I wish you'd been with me tonight in the Infirmary. You'd have seen—

SHEILA [*bursting in*]: No, no, please! Not that again. I've imagined it enough already.

INSPECTOR [*very deliberately*]: Then the next time you imagine it, just remember that this girl was going to have a child.

SHEILA [*horrified*]: No! Oh—horrible—horrible! How could she have wanted to kill herself.

INSPECTOR: Because she'd been turned out and turned down too many times. This was the end.

SHEILA: Mother, you must have known.

INSPECTOR: It was because she was going to have a child that she went for assistance to your mother's committee.

BIRLING: Look here, this wasn't Gerald Croft—

INSPECTOR [*cutting in, sharply*]: No, no. Nothing to do with him.

SHEILA: Thank goodness for that! Though I don't know why I should care now.

INSPECTOR [*to* MRS BIRLING]: And you've nothing further to tell me, eh?

MRS BIRLING: I'll tell you what I told her. Go and look for the father of the child. It's his responsibility.

INSPECTOR: That doesn't make it any the less yours. She came to you for help, at a time when no woman could have needed it more. And you not only refused it yourself but saw to it that the others refused it too. She was here alone, almost penniless, desperate. She needed not only money but advice, sympathy, friendliness. You've had children. You must have known what she was feeling. And you slammed the door in her face.

SHEILA [*with feeling*]: Mother, I think it was cruel and vile.

BIRLING [*dubiously*]: I must say, Sybil, that when this comes out at the inquest, it isn't going to do us much good. The Press might easily take it up—

MRS BIRLING [*agitated now*]: Oh, stop it, both of you. And please remember before you start accusing me of anything again that it wasn't I who had her turned out of her employment—which probably began it all. [*She turns to the* INSPECTOR, *moves to the chair below the table and sits.*]

BIRLING *sits in the chair from right of the table.*

In the circumstances I think I was justified. The girl had begun by telling us a pack of lies. Afterwards, when I got at the truth, I discovered that she knew who the father was, she was quite certain about that, and so I told her it was her business to make him responsible. If he refused to marry her—and in my opinion he ought to be compelled to—then he must at least support her.

INSPECTOR: And what did she reply to that?

MRS BIRLING [*rising and crossing down left*]: Oh—a lot of silly nonsense.

INSPECTOR: What was it?

MRS BIRLING [*moving to the desk*]: Whatever it was, I know it made me finally lose all patience with her. She was giving herself ridiculous airs. She was claiming elaborate fine feelings and scruples that were simply absurd in a girl in her position.

INSPECTOR [*very sternly*]: Her position now is that she lies with a burnt-out inside on a slab.

BIRLING *rises and tries to protest.*

[*He turns on* BIRLING.] Don't stammer and yammer at me again, man. I'm losing all patience with you people. *What did she say?*

MRS BIRLING [*rather cowed*]: She said that the father was only a youngster—silly and wild and drinking too much. There couldn't be any question of marrying him—it would be wrong for them both. He had given her money but she didn't want to take any more money from him.

INSPECTOR: Why didn't she want to take any more money from him?

MRS BIRLING [*crossing to the fireplace*]: All a lot of nonsense—I didn't believe a word of it.

INSPECTOR: I'm not asking you if you believed it. I want to know what she said. Why didn't she want to take any more money from this boy?

MRS BIRLING: Oh—she had some fancy reason. As if a girl of that sort would ever refuse money!

INSPECTOR [*moving below the table towards* MRS BIRLING; *sternly*]: I warn you, you're making it worse for yourself. What reason did she give for not taking any more money?

MRS BIRLING: Her story was—that he'd said something one night, when he was drunk, that gave her the idea that it wasn't his money.

INSPECTOR: Where had he got it from then?

MRS BIRLING: He'd stolen it.

INSPECTOR [*turning and moving slowly left*]: So she'd come to you for assistance because she didn't want to take stolen money?

MRS BIRLING: That's the story she finally told, after I'd refused to believe her original story—that she was a married woman who'd been deserted by her husband. I didn't see any reason to believe that one story should be any truer than the other. Therefore, you're quite wrong to suppose I shall regret what I did.

She sits below the table.

INSPECTOR [*turning to* MRS BIRLING]: But if her story was true, if this boy had been giving her stolen money, then she came to you for help because she wanted to keep this youngster out of any more trouble—isn't that so?

MRS BIRLING: Possibly. But it sounded ridiculous to me. So I was perfectly justified in advising my committee not to allow her claim for assistance.

INSPECTOR: You're not even sorry now, when you know what happened to the girl?

MRS BIRLING: I'm sorry she should have come to such a horrible end. But I accept no blame for it at all.

INSPECTOR: Who is to blame then?

MRS BIRLING: First the girl herself.

SHEILA [*bitterly*]: For letting father and me have her chucked out of her jobs?

MRS BIRLING: Secondly, I blame the young man who was the father of the child she was going to have. If, as she said, he didn't belong to her class, and was some drunken young idler, then that's all the more reason why he shouldn't escape. He should be made an example of. If the girl's death is due to anybody, then it's due to him.

INSPECTOR: And if her story is true—that he was stealing money—

MRS BIRLING [*rather agitated now*]: There's no point in assuming that—

INSPECTOR: But supposing we do, what then?

MRS BIRLING: Then he'd be entirely responsible—because the girl wouldn't have come to us, and have been refused assistance, if it hadn't been for him—

INSPECTOR: So he's the chief culprit anyhow?

MRS BIRLING: Certainly. And he ought to be dealt with very severely—

SHEILA [*rising and crossing to* MRS BIRLING; *with sudden alarm*]: Mother—stop—stop.

BIRLING: Be quiet, Sheila!

SHEILA: But don't you see—

MRS BIRLING [*severely*]: You're behaving like a hysterical child tonight.

SHEILA *moves up right of the table.*

MRS BIRLING [*she turns to the* INSPECTOR]: And if you'd take some steps to find this young man and then make sure that he's compelled to confess in public his responsibility—instead of staying here asking quite unnecessary questions— then you really would be doing your duty.

INSPECTOR [*grimly*]: Don't worry, Mrs Birling. I shall do my duty! [*He looks at his watch.*]

MRS BIRLING [*triumphantly*]: I'm glad to hear it.

INSPECTOR: No hushing up, eh? Make an example of the young man, eh? Public confession of responsibility—um?

MRS BIRLING: Certainly. I consider it your duty. [*She rises.*] And now no doubt you'd like to say good-night.

INSPECTOR: Not yet. I'm waiting. [*He moves to the chair left of the table and sits.*]

MRS BIRLING: Waiting for what?

INSPECTOR: To do my duty.

SHEILA [*coming down right to* MRS BIRLING; *distressed*]: Now, Mother—don't you see? [*She turns to* BIRLING *and buries her face against his shoulder, crying.*]

MRS BIRLING *and* BIRLING *exchange frightened glances.*

BIRLING [*terrified now*]: Look, Inspector, you're not trying to tell us that—that my boy—is mixed up in this—?

INSPECTOR [*sternly*]: If he is, then we know what to do, don't we? Mrs Birling has just told us.

BIRLING [*crossing to* MRS BIRLING*; thunderstruck*]: My God! By—look here—

MRS BIRLING [*agitatedly*]: I don't believe it. I *won't* believe it . . . [*She sits below the table.*]

SHEILA [*moving below* MRS BIRLING *and kneeling*]: Mother—I begged and begged you to stop—

The INSPECTOR *holds up a hand. We hear the front door. The* INSPECTOR *rises and turns to face the door. They all wait, looking towards the door.* ERIC *enters, looking extremely pale and distressed. He meets their enquiring stares. There is a little cry from* MRS BIRLING *as—*

the CURTAIN *falls quickly.*

ACT THREE

SCENE: The same. The action is continuous.

When the CURTAIN *rises,* ERIC *is just entering. The others are staring at him.*

ERIC: You know, don't you?
INSPECTOR [*gravely*]: Yes we know. [*He moves up to the sideboard.*]

ERIC *shuts the door and comes further into the room.*

MRS BIRLING [*distressed*]: Eric, I can't believe it. There must be some mistake. You don't know what we've been saying.
SHEILA [*rising and crossing to the armchair*]: It's a good job for him he doesn't, isn't it?
ERIC: Why?
SHEILA: Because Mother's been busy blaming everything on the young man who got this girl into trouble, and saying he shouldn't escape and should be made an example of—
BIRLING: That's enough, Sheila.
ERIC [*bitterly*]: You haven't made it any easier for me, have you, Mother?
MRS BIRLING: But I didn't know it was *you*—I never dreamt. Besides, you're not that type—you don't get drunk—
SHEILA: Of course he does. I told you he did. [*She sits in the armchair.*]
ERIC: *You* told her. Why, you little sneak!
SHEILA: No, that's not fair, Eric. I could have told her months ago, but of course I didn't. I only told her tonight because I knew everything was coming out—it was simply bound to come out tonight—so I thought she might as well know in advance. Don't forget—I've already been through it.
MRS BIRLING: Sheila, I simply don't understand your attitude. [*She rises and crosses right to the chair from right of the table, in which she sits.*]
BIRLING: Neither do I. If you had any sense of loyalty—
INSPECTOR [*coming down right of the table; cutting in, smoothly*]: Just a minute, Mr Birling. There'll be plenty of time to adjust your family relationships when I've gone. But now I must hear what your son has to tell me. [*Sternly to the three of them.*] And I'll be obliged if you'll let us get on without any further interruptions. [*Turning to* ERIC.] Now then.
ERIC [*miserably*]: Could I have a drink first?
BIRLING [*explosively*]: No!
INSPECTOR [*firmly*]: Yes. [*As* BIRLING *looks like interrupting explosively.*] I know—he's your son and this is your house—but look at him. He needs a drink now just to see him through.
BIRLING [*to* ERIC]: All right. Go on.

ERIC *goes up to the sideboard and pours himself out a whisky. His whole manner of handling the decanter and then the drink shows his familiarity with quick heavy drinking. The others watch him narrowly.*

BIRLING [*bitterly*]: I understand a lot of things now I didn't understand before.

ERIC *comes down to the table, above the chair, left of it.*

INSPECTOR: Don't start on that. I want to get on. [*To* ERIC.] When did you first meet this girl?
ERIC: One night last November.
INSPECTOR: Where did you meet her?
ERIC: In the Palace bar. I'd been there an hour or so with two or three chaps. I was a bit squiffy. [*He sits left of the table.*]
INSPECTOR: What happened then?
ERIC: I began talking to her, and stood her a few drinks. I was rather far gone by the time we had to go.
INSPECTOR: Was she drunk too?
ERIC: She told me afterwards that she was a bit, chiefly because she'd not had much to eat that day.
INSPECTOR: Had she gone there–to solicit?
ERIC: No, she hadn't. She wasn't that sort really. But–well, I suppose she didn't know what to do. There was some woman who wanted her to go there. I never quite understood about that.
INSPECTOR: You went with her to her lodgings that night?
ERIC: Yes, I insisted–it seems. I'm not very clear about it, but afterwards she told me she didn't want me to go in but that–well, I was in that state when a chap easily turns nasty–and I threatened to make a row.
INSPECTOR: So she let you in?
ERIC: Yes. And that's when it happened. And I didn't even remember–that's the hellish thing. How stupid it all is!
MRS BIRLING [*rising; with a cry*]: Oh–Eric–how could you?
BIRLING [*sharply*]: Sheila, take your mother along to the drawing-room—
SHEILA [*protesting*]: But–I want to—
BIRLING [*very sharply*]: You heard what I said. [*Gentler.*] Go on, Sybil.

He leads MRS BIRLING *across to the door.* SHEILA *rises and follows, and takes* MRS BIRLING *out.* BIRLING *shuts the door.*

INSPECTOR: When did you meet her again?
ERIC [*rising and moving above the table to right*]: About a fortnight afterwards.
INSPECTOR: By appointment?
ERIC: No. And I couldn't remember her name or where she lived. It was all very vague. But I happened to see her again in the Palace bar.
INSPECTOR: More drinks?
ERIC: Yes, though that time I wasn't so bad.
INSPECTOR: But you took her home again?
ERIC [*coming down to the fireplace*]: Yes. And this time we talked a bit. She told me something about herself and I talked too. Told her my name and what I did.
INSPECTOR: And you made love again?

ERIC: Yes. I wasn't in love with her or anything–but I like her–she was pretty and a good sport—

BIRLING [*moving left centre; harshly*]: So you had to go to bed with her?

ERIC: Well, I'm old enough to be married, aren't I, and I'm not married, and I hate these fat old tarts round the town–the ones I see some of your respectable friends with—

BIRLING [*angrily*]: I don't want any of that talk from you—

INSPECTOR [*moving below the table to centre; very sharply*]: I don't want any of it from either of you. Settle it afterwards.

> BIRLING *sits left of the table.*

INSPECTOR [*to* ERIC]: Did you arrange to see each other after that?

ERIC: Yes. And the next time–or the time after that–she told me she thought she was going to have a baby.

INSPECTOR: And of course she was very worried about it?

ERIC: Yes, and so was I. I was in a hell of a state about it.

INSPECTOR: Did she suggest that you ought to marry her?

ERIC: No. She didn't want me to marry her. [*He comes down to the armchair.*] Said I didn't love her–and all that. In a way, she treated me–as if I were a kid. Though I was nearly as old as she was.

INSPECTOR: So what did you propose to do?

ERIC: Well, she hadn't a job–and didn't feel like trying again for one–and she'd no money left–so I insisted on giving her enough money to keep her going–until she refused to take any more—

INSPECTOR: How much did you give her altogether?

ERIC: I suppose–about fifty pounds all told.

BIRLING [*rising and crossing below the table to* ERIC]: Fifty pounds–on top of drinking and going round the town! Where did you get fifty pounds from?

> ERIC *does not reply.*

INSPECTOR [*moving to* ERIC]: That's my question too.

ERIC [*miserably*]: I got it–from the office—

BIRLING: *My* office?

> *The* INSPECTOR *moves up right of the table.*

ERIC [*sitting in the armchair*]: Yes.

INSPECTOR: You mean–you stole the money?

ERIC: Not really.

BIRLING [*angrily*]: What do you mean–*not really*?

> MRS BIRLING *and* SHEILA *enter.* ERIC *does not reply.*

SHEILA [*turning down to the desk*]: This isn't my fault.

MRS BIRLING [*to* BIRLING]: I'm sorry, Arthur, but I simply couldn't stay in there. I had to know what's happening.

BIRLING [*savagely*]: Well, I can tell you what's happening. He's admitted he was responsible for the girl's condition, and now he's telling us he supplied her with money he stole from the office.

MRS BIRLING [*shocked*]: Eric! You stole money? [*She comes below the table.*]
ERIC: No, not really. I intended to pay it back.
BIRLING: We've heard that story before. How could you have paid it back?
ERIC: I'd have managed somehow. I had to have some money—
BIRLING: I don't understand how you could take as much as that out of the office without somebody knowing.
ERIC: There were some small accounts to collect, and I asked for cash—
BIRLING: Gave the firm's receipt and then kept the money, eh?
ERIC: Yes.
BIRLING: You must give me a list of those accounts. I've got to cover this up as soon as I can. You damned fool—why didn't you come to me when you found yourself in this mess?

MRS BIRLING *sits below the table.*

ERIC: Because you're not the kind of father a chap could go to when he's in trouble—that's why.
BIRLING [*angrily*]: Don't talk to me like that. Your trouble is—you've been spoilt—
INSPECTOR [*coming down right of the table and crossing centre to left of* MRS BIRLING; *cutting in*]: And my trouble is—that I haven't much time. You'll be able to divide the responsibility between you when I've gone.

BIRLING *breaks to the fireplace.*

INSPECTOR [*to* ERIC]: Just one last question, that's all. The girl discovered that this money you were giving her was stolen, didn't she?
ERIC [*miserably*]: Yes. That was the worst of all. She wouldn't have any more, and she didn't want to see me again. [*In a sudden startled tone.*] Here, but how did you know that? Did she tell you?
INSPECTOR [*crossing up to the table right of* MRS BIRLING]: No. She told me nothing. I never spoke to her.
SHEILA: She told Mother.
MRS BIRLING [*alarmed*]: Sheila!
SHEILA: Well, he has to know.
ERIC [*rising and moving a step to left; to* MRS BIRLING]: She told you? Did she come here—but then she couldn't have done, she didn't even know I lived here. What happened?

MRS BIRLING, *distressed, shakes her head but does not reply.*

[*He crosses to* MRS BIRLING.] Come on, don't just look like that. Tell me—tell me—what happened?
INSPECTOR [*with calm authority*]: I'll tell you. She went to your mother's committee for help, after she'd done with you. Your mother refused that help.
ERIC [*nearly at breaking point*]: Then—you killed her. She came to you to protect me—and you turned her away—yes, and you killed her—and the child she'd have had too—my child—your own grandchild—you killed them both—damn you, damn you— [*He breaks away down right.*]
MRS BIRLING [*rising; very distressed now*]: No—Eric—please—I didn't know—I didn't understand—
ERIC [*crossing to* MRS BIRLING; *almost threatening her*]: You don't understand

anything. You never did. You never even tried—you—
SHEILA [*frightened*]: Eric, don't—don't—

BIRLING *comes down, catches* ERIC *by the arm and pushes him down right.*

BIRLING [*furious, intervening*]: Why, you hysterical young fool—get back—or
I'll—
INSPECTOR [*taking charge, masterfully*]: *Stop!*

They are suddenly quiet, staring at him.

And be quiet for a moment and listen to me. I don't need to know any more.
Neither do you. This girl killed herself—and died a horrible death. But each
of you helped to kill her. Remember that. Never forget it. [*He looks from one
to the other of them carefully.*] But then I don't think you ever will. Remember
what you did, Mrs Birling. You turned her away when she most needed help.
You refused her even the pitiable little bit of organised charity you had in
your power to grant her.

MRS BIRLING *moves away and sits left of the table.*

INSPECTOR [*to* ERIC]: Remember what you did—
ERIC [*sitting in the armchair; unhappily*]: My God—I'm not likely to forget.
INSPECTOR: Just used her for the end of a stupid drunken evening, as if she were
an animal, a thing, not a person. No, you won't forget. [*He looks at* SHEILA.]
SHEILA [*crossing to the* INSPECTOR; *bitterly*]: I know. I had her turned out of a
job. I started it.
INSPECTOR: You helped—but didn't start it.

SHEILA *sits below the table.*

INSPECTOR [*rather savagely to* BIRLING]: You started it. She wanted twenty-five
shillings a week instead of twenty-two and sixpence. You made her pay a
heavy price for that. And now she'll make you pay a heavier price still.
BIRLING [*unhappily*]: Look, Inspector—I'd give thousands—yes, thousands—
INSPECTOR: You're offering the money at the wrong time, Mr Birling.

BIRLING *sits in the chair from right of the table.*

[*He makes a move as if concluding the session. He surveys them sardonically.
Then he comes down centre.*] No, I don't think any of you will forget. Nor that
young man, Croft, though he at least had some affection for her and made her
happy for a time. [*He turns up stage to face them.*] Well, Eva Smith's gone.
You can't do her any more harm. And you can't do her any good now either.
You can't even say 'I'm sorry, Eva Smith.' [*He crosses to the door.*]
SHEILA [*crying quietly*]: That's the worst of it.
INSPECTOR [*turning at the door*]: But just remember this. One Eva Smith has
gone—but there are millions and millions and millions of Eva Smiths and
John Smiths still left with us, with their lives, their hopes and fears, their
suffering and chance of happiness, all intertwined with our lives, with what
we think and say and do. We don't live alone. We are members of one

body. We are responsible for each other. And I tell you that the time will soon come when, if men will not learn that lesson, then they will be taught it in fire and blood and anguish. Good-night.

He walks straight out, leaving them staring, subdued and wondering. SHEILA *is still quietly crying.* MRS BIRLING *has collapsed into a chair.* ERIC *is brooding desperately.* BIRLING, *the only active one, hears the front door slam, rises, moves hesitatingly towards the door, stops, and looks gloomily at the other three.*

BIRLING [*angrily to* ERIC]: You're the one I blame for this.

ERIC: I'll bet I am.

BIRLING [*angrily*]: Yes, and you don't realise yet all you've done. Most of this is bound to come out. There'll be a public scandal. [*He moves towards the sideboard.*]

ERIC: Well, I don't care now.

BIRLING [*stopping*]: You! You don't seem to care about anything. But I care. I was almost certain for a knighthood in the next honours list—

ERIC *rises and moves to the fire. He laughs rather hysterically, pointing at* BIRLING.

ERIC [*laughing*]: Oh—for God's sake! What does it matter now whether they give you a knighthood or not?

BIRLING [*stormily*]: It doesn't matter to you. Apparently nothing matters to you. But it may interest you to know that until every penny of that money you stole is repaid, you'll work for nothing. And there's going to be no more of this drinking round the town—and picking up women in the Palace bar—[*He moves to the sideboard and pours out a whisky.*]

MRS BIRLING [*coming to life*]: I should think not. Eric, I'm absolutely ashamed of you.

ERIC: Well, I don't blame you. But don't forget I'm ashamed of you as well—yes, both of you.

BIRLING [*coming down to the back of* MRS BIRLING'*s chair; angrily*]: Drop that. There's every excuse for what both your mother and I did—it turned out unfortunately, that's all—

SHEILA [*scornfully*]: *That's all.*

BIRLING: Well, what have you to say?

SHEILA: I don't know where to begin.

BIRLING: Then don't begin. Nobody wants you to.

SHEILA: I behaved badly, too. I know I did. I'm ashamed of myself. But now you're beginning all over again to pretend that nothing much has happened—

BIRLING: Nothing much has happened! Haven't I already said there'll be a public scandal—unless we're lucky—and who here will suffer from that more than I will?

SHEILA: But that's not what I'm talking about. I don't care about that. The point is, you don't seem to have learnt anything.

BIRLING: Didn't I? Well, you're quite wrong there. I learnt plenty tonight. And you don't want me to tell you what I've learnt, I hope. When I look back on tonight—when I think of what I was feeling when the five of us sat down to dinner at that table—

ERIC [*cutting in*]: Yes, and do you remember what you said to Gerald and me after dinner, when you were feeling so pleased with yourself? You told us that a man has to make his own way, look after himself and mind his own business, and that we weren't to take any notice of these cranks who tell us that everybody has to look after everybody else, as if we were all mixed up together. Do you remember? Yes—and then one of those cranks walked in—the Inspector. [*He laughs bitterly.*] I didn't notice you told him that it's every man for himself. [*He turns to the fire.*]

SHEILA [*sharply attentive*]: Is that when the Inspector came, just after father had said that? [*She rises and moves right of the table towards* ERIC.]

ERIC: Yes. What of it?

MRS BIRLING: Now what's the matter, Sheila?

SHEILA [*slowly*]: It's queer—very queer— [*She turns and looks at them reflectively.*]

MRS BIRLING [*with some excitement*]: I know what you're going to say. Because I've been wondering myself.

SHEILA: It doesn't much matter now, of course—but *was* he really a Police Inspector?

BIRLING: Well, if he wasn't, it matters a devil of a lot. Makes all the difference.

SHEILA: Well, it doesn't to me. And it oughtn't to you, either.

MRS BIRLING: Don't be childish, Sheila.

SHEILA [*flaring up*]: I'm not being. If you want to know, it's you two who are being childish—trying not to face the facts.

BIRLING: I won't have that sort of talk. Any more of that and you leave this room.

ERIC: That'll be terrible for her, won't it?

SHEILA: I'm going anyhow in a minute or two. But don't you see, if all that's come out tonight is true, then it doesn't much matter who it was who made us confess. And it *was* true, wasn't it? That's what's important—and not whether a man is a Police Inspector or not.

ERIC: He was our Police Inspector all right. [*He moves above the table.*]

SHEILA: That's what I mean, Eric. [*Turning to her parents.*] But if it's any comfort to you—and it isn't to me—I have an idea—and I had it all along vaguely—that there was something curious about him. He never seemed like an ordinary Police Inspector—

BIRLING [*rather excited*]: You're right. I felt it too. [*To* MRS BIRLING.] Didn't you?

MRS BIRLING: Well, I must say his manner was quite extraordinary. So—so rude—and assertive—

ERIC *sits right above the table.*

BIRLING [*crossing to the desk*]: Then look at the way he talked to me. Telling me to shut up—and so on. He must have known I was an ex-Lord Mayor and a magistrate and so forth. [*He turns.*] Besides—the way he talked—you remember. I mean, they don't *talk* like that. I've had dealings with dozens of them.

SHEILA [*slowly*]: You know, we hardly ever told him anything he didn't know. Did you notice that?

BIRLING [*sitting at the desk*]: That's nothing. He had a bit of information, left by the girl, and made a few smart guesses—but the fact remains that if we hadn't talked so much, he'd have had little to go on. [*He looks angrily at them.*] And really, when I come to think of it, why you all had to go letting everything come out like that, beats me.

SHEILA: It's all right talking like that now. But he made us confess. [*She moves up to the sideboard.*]

MRS BIRLING: He certainly didn't make me *confess*—as you call it. I told him quite plainly that I thought I had done no more than my duty.

SHEILA: Oh—Mother!

BIRLING: The fact is, you allowed yourselves to be bluffed. Yes—bluffed.

MRS BIRLING [*protesting*]: Now, really—Arthur.

BIRLING: No, not you, my dear. But these two. That fellow obviously didn't like us. He was prejudiced from the start. Probably a Socialist or some sort of crank—he talked like one. And then, instead of standing up to him, you let him bluff you into talking about your private affairs. You ought to have stood up to him.

ERIC [*rising and moving right of the table; sulkily*]: Well, I didn't notice you standing up to him.

BIRLING: No, because by that time you'd admitted you'd been taking money. What chance had I after that? I was a fool not to have insisted upon seeing him alone.

ERIC: That wouldn't have worked.

SHEILA: Of course it wouldn't.

MRS BIRLING: Really, from the way you children talk, you might be wanting to help him instead of us. [*She rises and comes down to* BIRLING.] Now just be quiet so that your father can decide what we ought to do. [*She looks expectantly at* BIRLING.]

BIRLING [*rising and moving below the table to centre; dubiously*]: Yes—well. We'll have to do something—and get to work quickly too.

> *There is a ring at the front door.* BIRLING *stops. They all look at each other in alarm.*

Now who's this? Had I better go?

MRS BIRLING: No. Edna'll go. I asked her to wait up to make us some tea.

SHEILA [*coming down to left of the table*]: It might be Gerald coming back.

> MRS BIRLING *sits at the desk.*

BIRLING [*sitting below the table; relieved*]: Yes, of course. I'd forgotten about him.

> EDNA *enters.*

EDNA: It's Mr Croft.

> GERALD *enters. He crosses below* SHEILA *to left centre.* EDNA *goes out.*

GERALD: I hope you don't mind my coming back?

MRS BIRLING: No, of course not, Gerald.

GERALD: I had a special reason for coming back. [*He moves centre.*] When did that Inspector go?

SHEILA [*coming down to left of* GERALD]: Only a few minutes ago. He put us all through it—

MRS BIRLING [*warningly*]: Sheila!

SHEILA: Gerald might as well know.

BIRLING [*hastily*]: Now–now–we needn't bother him with all that stuff.

SHEILA: All right. [*To* GERALD.] But we're all in it–up to the neck. It got worse after you left.

GERALD: How did he behave?

SHEILA: He was frightening.

BIRLING: If you ask me, he behaved in a very peculiar and suspicious manner.

MRS BIRLING: The rude way he spoke to Mr Birling and me–it was quite extraordinary! Why?

They all look enquiringly at GERALD.

BIRLING [*excitedly*]: You know something. What is it?

GERALD [*slowly*]: That man wasn't a police officer.

SHEILA *sits left of the table.*

BIRLING [*astounded*]: What?

MRS BIRLING: Are you certain?

GERALD: I'm almost certain. That's what I came back to tell you.

BIRLING [*excitedly*]: Good lad! You asked about him, eh?

GERALD: Yes. I met a police sergeant I know down the road. I asked him about the Inspector Goole and described the chap carefully to him. He swore there wasn't any Inspector Goole or anybody like him on the force here.

BIRLING [*excitedly*]: By jingo! A fake!

MRS BIRLING [*rising and moving to left of* SHEILA; *triumphantly*]: Didn't I tell you? Didn't I say I couldn't imagine a real police inspector talking like that to us?

GERALD: Well, you were right. There isn't any such Inspector. We've been had.

BIRLING [*rising*]: I'm going to make certain of this.

MRS BIRLING: What are you going to do?

BIRLING [*crossing to the telephone*]: Ring up the Chief Constable–Colonel Roberts.

MRS BIRLING [*coming below the table*]: Careful what you say, dear. [*She sits below the table.*]

BIRLING [*lifting the receiver*]: Of course. [*Into the telephone.*] Brumley eight-seven-five-two. [*To the others.*] I was going to do this anyhow.

ERIC *moves up to the sideboard and pours himself out a whisky.*

I've had my suspicions all along. [*Into the telephone.*] Colonel Roberts, please. Mr Arthur Birling here . . . Oh, Roberts–Birling here. Sorry to ring you up so late, but can you tell me if an Inspector Goole has joined your staff lately . . . Goole. G O O L E . . .

ERIC *comes down left of the table.*

. . . a new man . . . [*He describes the appearance of the actor playing the part of the Inspector.*] I see . . . yes . . . well, that settles it . . . No, just a little argument we were having here . . . Good-night. [*He puts down the telephone and looks at the others.*] There's no Inspector Goole on the police now. There's nobody who even looks like the man who came here. That man definitely wasn't a Police Inspector. As Gerald says—we've been had. [*He crosses to* MRS BIRLING.]

MRS BIRLING [*rising and crossing to the fire*]: I felt it all the time. He never talked like one. He never even looked like one.

BIRLING: This makes a difference, y'know. In fact, it makes *all* the difference.

SHEILA [*rising and moving to the desk; bitterly*]: I suppose we're all nice people now.

BIRLING: If you've nothing more sensible than that to say, Sheila, you'd better keep quiet.

ERIC: She's right, though.

BIRLING [*angrily*]: And you'd better keep quiet anyhow. If that *had* been a Police Inspector and he'd heard you confess—

MRS BIRLING [*warningly*]: Arthur—careful!

BIRLING [*hastily*]: Yes, yes.

SHEILA [*moving down left*]: You see, Gerald, you're not allowed to know the rest of our crimes and idiocies.

GERALD [*crossing to* SHEILA]: That's all right, I don't want to. [*He turns to* BIRLING.] What do you make of this business now? Was it a hoax.

BIRLING: Of course. Somebody put that fellow up to coming here and hoaxing us. There are people in this town who dislike me enough to do that. We ought to have seen through it from the first. In the ordinary way, I believe I would have done. But coming like that, bang on top of our little celebration, just when we were all feeling so pleased with ourselves, naturally it took me by surprise.

MRS BIRLING: I wish I'd been here when that man first arrived. I'd have asked *him* a few questions before I allowed him to ask us any.

GERALD *crosses to the armchair and sits.*

SHEILA [*moving in to the table left of the chair below it*]: It's all right saying that now.

MRS BIRLING: I was the only one of you who didn't give in to him. And now I say we must discuss this business quietly and sensibly and decide if there's anything to be done about it.

BIRLING [*with hearty approval*]: You're absolutely right, my dear. Already we've discovered one important fact—that that fellow was a fraud and we've been hoaxed—and that may not be the end of it by any means. [*He sits below the table.*]

GERALD: I'm sure it isn't.

ERIC *is moving restlessly down left.*

BIRLING [*keenly interested*]: You are, eh? Good! [*To* ERIC.] Eric, sit down.

ERIC [*sulkily*]: I'm all right.

BIRLING: All right? You're anything but all right. And you needn't stand there—as if—as if—

ERIC: As if—what?

BIRLING: As if you'd nothing to do with us. Just remember your own position, young man. If anybody's up to the neck in this business, you are, so you'd better take some interest in it.

ERIC: I do take some interest in it. I take too much, that's my trouble.

SHEILA: It's mine too.

BIRLING: Now listen, you two. If you're still feeling on edge, then the least you can do is to keep quiet. Leave this to us. I'll admit that fellow's antics rattled us a bit. But we've found him out—and all we have to do is to keep our heads. Now it's our turn.

SHEILA: Our turn to do—what?

MRS BIRLING [*sharply*]: To behave sensibly, Sheila—which is more than you're doing.

ERIC [*moving above the chair left of the table; bursting out*]: What's the use of talking about behaving sensibly. You're beginning to pretend now that nothing's really happened at all. And I can't see it like that. This girl's still dead, isn't she? Nobody's brought her to life, have they?

SHEILA [*eagerly*]: That's just what I feel, Eric. And it's what they don't seem to understand.

ERIC: Whoever that chap was, the fact remains that I did what I did. And mother did what she did. And the rest of you did what you did to her. It's all the same rotten story whether it's been told to a Police Inspector or to somebody else. According to you, I ought to feel a lot better—[*He crosses to* GERALD.] I stole some money, Gerald, you might as well know—

BIRLING *rises and tries to interrupt.*

I don't care, let him know. The money's not the important thing. It's what happened to the girl and what we all did to her that matters. And I still feel the same about it, and that's why I don't feel like sitting down and having a nice cosy talk. [*He moves up right of the table.*]

SHEILA: And Eric's absolutely right. And it's the best thing any one of us has said tonight and it makes me feel a bit less ashamed of us. You're just beginning to pretend all over again.

BIRLING: Look—for God's sake!

MRS BIRLING [*protesting*]: Arthur!

BIRLING: Well, my dear, they're so damned exasperating. [*He sits again.*] They just won't try to understand our position or to see the difference between a lot of stuff like this coming out in private and a downright public scandal.

ERIC [*crossing above the table to left; shouting*]: And I say the girl's dead and we all helped to kill her—and that's what matters—

BIRLING [*rising; shouting, threatening* ERIC]: And I say—either stop shouting or get out. [*He glares at him. In a quieter tone.*] Some fathers I know would have kicked you out of the house anyhow by this time. So hold your tongue if you want to stay here.

ERIC [*coming down left to the desk; quietly, bitterly*]: I don't give a damn now whether I stay here or not.

BIRLING [*crossing to* ERIC]: You'll stay here long enough to give me an account of that money you stole—yes, and to pay it back too.

SHEILA: But that won't bring Eva Smith back to life, will it?

ERIC: And it doesn't alter the fact that we all helped to kill her.

GERALD [*rising*]: But is it a fact?

ERIC: Of course it is. You don't know the whole story yet.

SHEILA: I suppose you're going to prove now you didn't spend last summer keeping this girl instead of seeing me, eh?

GERALD: I did keep a girl last summer. I've admitted it. And I'm sorry, Sheila.

SHEILA: Well, I must admit you came out of it better than the rest of us. The Inspector said that.

BIRLING [*moving up left of the table to the sideboard; angrily*]: He wasn't an Inspector.

SHEILA [*flaring up*]: Well, he inspected us all right. And don't let's start dodging and pretending now. Between us we drove that girl to commit suicide.

GERALD: Did we? [*He crosses to* SHEILA.] Who says so? Because I say—there's no more real evidence we did than there was that that chap was a Police Inspector.

SHEILA: Of course there is.

GERALD: No there isn't. Look at it. A man comes here pretending to be a police officer. It's a hoax of some kind. Now what does he do? Very artfully, working on bits of information he's picked up here and there, he bluffs us into confessing that we've all been mixed up in this girl's life in one way or another.

ERIC: And so we have.

GERALD [*crossing to* ERIC]: *But how do you know it's the same girl?*

BIRLING [*coming down to the fireplace; eagerly*]: Now wait a minute! Let's see how that would work. Now—[*He hesitates.*]—no, it wouldn't.

ERIC: We all admitted it.

GERALD: All right, you all admitted something to do with a girl. But how do you know it's the same girl? [*He looks round triumphantly at them.*]

As they puzzle this out, GERALD *turns to* BIRLING.

GERALD [*after a pause*]: Look here, Mr Birling. You sack a girl called Eva Smith. You've forgotten, but he shows you a photograph of her, and then you remember. Right?

BIRLING: Yes, that part's straightforward enough. But what then?

GERALD: Well, then he happens to know that Sheila once had a girl sacked from Milwards shop. He tells us that it's this same Eva Smith. And he shows her a photograph that she recognises.

SHEILA: Yes. The same photograph.

GERALD [*turning to* SHEILA]: How do you know it's the same photograph? Did you see the one your father looked at?

SHEILA: No, I didn't.

GERALD: And did your father see the one he showed you?

SHEILA: No, he didn't. And I see what you mean now.

GERALD: We've no proof it was the same photograph and therefore no proof it was the same girl. Now take me. I never saw a photograph, remember. He caught me out by suddenly announcing that this girl changed her name to Daisy Renton. I gave myself away at once because I'd known a Daisy Renton.

BIRLING [*eagerly*]: And there wasn't the slightest proof that this Daisy Renton was really Eva Smith. We've only his word for it, and we'd his word for it that he was a Police Inspector and we know now he was lying. So he could have been lying all the time.

GERALD: Of course he could. Probably was. Now what happened after I left?

MRS BIRLING: I was upset because Eric had left the house, and this man said that if Eric didn't come back, he'd have to go and find him. Well, that made me feel worse still. And his manner was so severe and he seemed so confident. Then quite suddenly he said Eva Smith had come to my committee for help only two weeks ago. And like a fool I said, yes she had.

SHEILA: But, Mother, don't forget that he showed you a photograph of the girl before that, and you obviously recognised it.

GERALD: Did anybody else see it?

MRS BIRLING: No, he showed it only to me.

GERALD: Then don't you see, there's still no proof it was really the same girl. He might have showed you the photograph of any girl who applied to the committee. And how do we know she was really Eva Smith or Daisy Renton?

BIRLING: Gerald's dead right. He could have used a different photograph each time and we'd be none the wiser. We may all have been recognising different girls.

GERALD: Exactly. [*He crosses to* ERIC.] Did he ask you to identify a photograph, Eric?

ERIC: No. He didn't need a photograph by the time he'd got round to me. But obviously it must have been the girl I knew who went round to see Mother.

GERALD: Why must it?

ERIC: She said she had to have help because she wouldn't take any more stolen money. And the girl I knew had told me that already.

GERALD: Even then, that may have been all nonsense.

ERIC: I don't see much nonsense about it when a girl goes and kills herself. You lot may be letting yourselves out nicely, but I can't. Nor can Mother. We did her in all right. [*He sits at the desk.*]

BIRLING [*coming forward a step; eagerly*]: Wait a minute, wait a minute. Don't be in such a hurry to put yourself into court. That interview with your mother could have been just as much a put-up job, like all the Police Inspector business. The whole damned thing can have been a piece of bluff.

ERIC [*angrily*]: How can it? The girl's dead, isn't she?

GERALD: What girl? There were probably four or five different girls.

ERIC [*rising*]: That doesn't matter to me. The one I knew is dead.

BIRLING: Is she? *How do we know she is?*

GERALD [*moving to left of* SHEILA]: That's right. You've got it. How do we know any girl killed herself today?

BIRLING [*looking at* ERIC: *triumphantly*]: Now answer that one.

ERIC *sits at the desk.*

Let's look at it from this fellow's point of view. We're having a little celebration here and feeling rather pleased with ourselves. Now he has to work a trick on us. Well, the first thing he has to do is to give us such a shock that after that he can bluff us all the time. So he starts right off. A girl has just died in the infirmary. She drank some strong disinfectant. Died in agony—

ERIC: All right, don't pile it on.

BIRLING [*triumphantly*]: There you are, you see. Just repeating it shakes you a bit. And that's what he had to do. Shake us at once—and then start questioning us—until we didn't know where we were. Oh—let's admit that. He took us in all right. He had the laugh of us.

ERIC: He could laugh his head off—if I knew it really was a hoax.

BIRLING: I'm convinced it is. No police enquiry. No one girl that all this happened to. No scandal—

SHEILA: And no suicide?

GERALD [*decisively*]: We can settle that at once.

SHEILA: How?

ERIC *rises*.

GERALD: By ringing up the infirmary. Either there's a dead girl there or there isn't.
BIRLING [*uneasily*]: It 'ud look a bit queer, wouldn't it—ringing up at this time of night—
GERALD [*crossing to the telephone*]: I don't mind doing it.
MRS BIRLING [*emphatically*]: And if there isn't—
GERALD: We'll see. [*He looks up the number.*]

BIRLING *moves to* MRS BIRLING. *They all watch tensely.*

Brumley eight-nine-eight-six . . . Is that the infirmary? This is Mr Gerald Croft—of Crofts Limited . . . Yes . . . we're rather worried about one of our employees. Have you had a girl brought in this afternoon who committed suicide by drinking disinfectant—or any suicide? Yes, I'll wait. [*He waits.*]

The others show their nervous tension. ERIC *rises and moves to* SHEILA. BIRLING *wipes his brow,* SHEILA *shivers,* ERIC *clasps and unclasps his hands.*

Yes? . . . You're certain of that . . . I see. Well, thank you very much . . . Good-night. [*He puts down the telephone and looks at them.*] No girl has died in there today. They haven't had a suicide for months.
BIRLING [*triumphantly*]: There you are! Proof positive. The whole story's just a lot of moonshine. Nothing but an elaborate sell! [*He produces a huge sigh of relief.*] Nobody likes to be sold as badly as that—but—for all that—[*He smiles at them all. He moves up to the sideboard.*] Gerald, have a drink.

SHEILA *sits below the table.*

GERALD [*smiling*]: Thanks, I think I could just do with one now. [*He moves up to the fireplace.*]
BIRLING [*pouring out two whiskies*]: So could I.
MRS BIRLING [*smiling*]: And I must say, Gerald, you've argued this very cleverly, and I'm most grateful. [*She sits in the chair from right of the table.*]
GERALD: Well, you see, while I was out of the house I'd time to cool off and think things out a little.

BIRLING *comes down to the fireplace and gives* GERALD *a drink.* GERALD *sits in the armchair.*

BIRLING: Yes, he didn't keep you on the run as he did the rest of us. I'll admit now he gave me a bit of a scare at the time. But I'd a special reason for not wanting any public scandal, just now. [*He raises his glass.*] Well, here's to us. Come on, Sheila, don't look like that. All over now.
SHEILA: The worst part is. But you're forgetting one thing I still can't forget. Everything we said had happened really had happened. If it didn't end tragically, then that's lucky for us. But it might have done.
BIRLING [*jovially*]: But the whole thing's different now. Come, come, you can

see that, can't you? [*He imitates the* INSPECTOR *in his final speech.*] You all helped to kill her. [*Pointing at* SHEILA *and* ERIC, *and laughing.*] And I wish you could have seen the look on your faces when he said that.

SHEILA *rises and moves towards the door.*

SHEILA [*tensely*]: I want to get out of this. It frightens me the way you talk.
BIRLING [*heartily*]: Nonsense! You'll have a good laugh over it yet. Look, you'd better ask Gerald for that ring you gave back to him, hadn't you? Then you'll feel better.
SHEILA [*passionately*]: You're pretending everything's just as it was before.
ERIC: I'm not!
SHEILA: No, but these others are.
BIRLING: Well, isn't it? We've been had, that's all.
SHEILA: So nothing really happened? So there's nothing to be sorry for, nothing to learn? We can all go on behaving just as we did?
MRS BIRLING: Well, why shouldn't we?
SHEILA: I tell you—whoever that Inspector was, it was anything but a joke. You knew it then. You began to learn something. And you've stopped now. You're ready to go on in the same old way.
BIRLING [*amused*]: And you're not, eh?
SHEILA: No, because I remember what he said, how he looked, and what he made me feel. 'Fire, blood and anguish!' And it frightens me the way you talk, and I can't listen to any more of it.
ERIC: I agree with Sheila, it frightens me too. [*He stands beside* SHEILA *at the door.*]
BIRLING: Well, go to bed then, and don't stand there being hysterical.
MRS BIRLING: They're over-tired. In the morning they'll be as amused as we are.
GERALD [*rising and crossing to* SHEILA]: Everything's all right now, Sheila. [*He holds up the ring.*] What about this ring?
SHEILA: No, not yet. It's too soon. I must think.
BIRLING [*pointing to* ERIC *and* SHEILA]: Now look at the pair of them—the famous younger generation who know it all. And they can't even take a joke—

The telephone rings sharply. There is a moment's complete silence. BIRLING *goes to answer it.*

Yes? . . . Mr Birling speaking . . . *What?*—Here?—

GERALD, SHEILA *and* ERIC *move in to left of the table.* MRS BIRLING *comes below the right end of the table.*

[*But obviously the other person has rung off. He puts the telephone down slowly and looks in a panic-stricken fashion at the others.*] That was the police. A girl has just died—on her way to the infirmary—after swallowing some disinfectant. And a Police Inspector is on his way here—to ask some—questions—

As they stare guiltily and dumbfounded—

the CURTAIN *falls.*

A STREETCAR NAMED DESIRE

TENNESSEE WILLIAMS

A STREETCAR
NAMED DESIRE

First published in England in 1949
Published in 1956 by
Martin Secker & Warburg Limited,
14 Carlisle Street, London W1

Acknowledgement
The lines from Hart Crane are reprinted from *Collected Poems of
Hart Crane* by permission of Liveright Publishing Corp. New York.

It's Only a Paper Moon, copyright 1933, by Harms, Inc. Used by
permission.

A STREETCAR
NAMED DESIRE

(1947)

And so it was I entered the broken world
To trace the visionary company of love, its voice
An instant in the wind [I know not whither hurled]
But not for long to hold each desperate choice.

'The Broken Tower' by Hart Crane

CHARACTERS

BLANCHE	A NEGRO WOMAN
STELLA	A DOCTOR
STANLEY	A NURSE
MITCH	A YOUNG COLLECTOR
EUNICE	A MEXICAN WOMAN
STEVE	A TAMALE VENDOR
PABLO	

CAST

The first London production of this play was at the
Aldwych Theatre on Wednesday, 12 October 1949,
with the following cast:

BLANCHE DUBOIS	*Vivien Leigh*
STELLA KOWALSKI	*Renee Asherson*
STANLEY KOWALSKI	*Bonar Colleano*
HAROLD MITCHELL	
(MITCH)	*Bernard Braden*
EUNICE HUBBEL	*Eileen Dale*
STEVE HUBBEL	*Lyn Evans*
PABLO GONZALES	*Theodore Bikel*
NEGRO WOMAN	*Bruce Howard*
A STRANGE MAN	
(DOCTOR)	*Sidney Monckton*
A STRANGE WOMAN	
(NURSE)	*Mona Lilian*
A YOUNG COLLECTOR	*John Forrest*
A MEXICAN WOMAN	*Eileen Way*

Directed by LAURENCE OLIVIER
Setting and lighting by JO MIELZINER
Costumes by BEATRICE DAWSON

SCENE ONE

The exterior of a two-storey corner building on a street in New Orleans which is named Elysian Fields and runs between the L & N tracks and the river. The section is poor but, unlike corresponding sections in other American cities, it has a raffish charm. The houses are mostly white frame, weathered grey, with rickety outside stairs and galleries and quaintly ornamented gables to the entrances of both. It is first dark of an evening early in May. The sky that shows around the dim white building is a peculiarly tender blue, almost turquoise, which invests the scene with a kind of lyricism and gracefully attenuates the atmosphere of decay. You can almost feel the warm breath of the brown river beyond the river warehouses with their faint redolences of bananas and coffee. A corresponding air is evoked by the music of Negro entertainers at a bar-room around the corner. In this part of New Orleans you are practically always just around the corner, or a few doors down the street, from a tinny piano being played with the infatuated fluency of brown fingers. This 'blue piano' expresses the spirit of the life which goes on here.

Two women, one white and one coloured, are taking the air on the steps of the building. The white woman is EUNICE, *who occupies the upstairs flat; the coloured woman a neighbour, for New Orleans is a cosmopolitan city where there is a relatively warm and easy intermingling of races in the old part of town.*
    Above the music of the 'blue piano' the voices of people on the street can be heard overlapping.

NEGRO WOMAN [*to* EUNICE]: . . . she says St Barnabas would send out his dog to lick her and when he did she'd feel an icy cold wave all up an' down her. Well, that night when—
A MAN [*to a* SAILOR]: You keep right on going and you'll find it. You'll hear them tapping on the shutters.
SAILOR [*to* NEGRO WOMAN *and* EUNICE]: Where's the Four Deuces?
VENDOR: Red hot! Red hots!
NEGRO WOMAN: Don't waste your money in that clip joint!
SAILOR: I've got a date there.
VENDOR: Re-e-ed h-o-o-t!
NEGRO WOMAN: Don't let them sell you a Blue Moon cocktail or you won't go out on your own feet!

Two men come round the corner, STANLEY KOWALSKI *and* MITCH. *They are about twenty-eight or thirty years old, roughly dressed in blue denim work clothes.* STANLEY *carries his bowling jacket and a red-stained package from a butcher's.*

STANLEY: [*to* MITCH]: Well, what did he say?

MITCH: He said he'd give us even money.
STANLEY: Naw! We gotta have odds!

They stop at the foot of the steps.

STANLEY [*bellowing*]: Hey, there! Stella, Baby!

STELLA *comes out on the first-floor landing, a gentle young woman, about twenty-five, and of a background obviously quite different from her husband's.*

STELLA [*mildly*]: Don't holler at me like that. Hi, Mitch.
STANLEY: Catch!
STELLA: What?
STANLEY: Meat!

He heaves the package at her. She cries out in protest but manages to catch it: then she laughs breathlessly. Her husband and his companion have already started back around the corner.

STELLA [*calling after him*]: Stanley! Where are you going?
STANLEY: Bowling!
STELLA: Can I come watch?
STANLEY: Come on. [*He goes out.*]
STELLA: Be over soon. [*To the white woman.*] Hello, Eunice. How are you?
EUNICE: I'm all right. Tell Steve to get him a poor boy's sandwich 'cause nothing's left here.

They all laugh; the COLOURED WOMAN *does not stop.* STELLA *goes out.*

COLOURED WOMAN: What was that package he th'ew at 'er? [*She rises from steps, laughing louder.*]
EUNICE: You hush, now!
NEGRO WOMAN: Catch *what*!

She continues to laugh. BLANCHE *comes around the corner, carrying a valise. She looks at a slip of paper, then at the building, then again at the slip and again at the building. Her expression is one of shocked disbelief. Her appearance is incongruous to this setting. She is daintily dressed in a white suit with a fluffy bodice, necklace and ear-rings of pearl, white gloves and hat, looking as if she were arriving at a summer tea or cocktail party in the garden district. She is about five years older than* STELLA. *Her delicate beauty must avoid a strong light. There is something about her uncertain manner, as well as her white clothes, that suggests a moth.*

EUNICE [*finally*]: What's the matter, honey? Are you lost?
BLANCHE [*with faintly hysterical humour*]: They told me to take a streetcar named Desire, and then transfer to one called Cemeteries and ride six blocks and get off at–Elysian Fields!
EUNICE: That's where you are now.
BLANCHE: At Elysian Fields?
EUNICE: This here is Elysian Fields.

BLANCHE: They mustn't have—understood—what number I wanted . . .
EUNICE: What number you lookin' for?

BLANCHE *wearily refers to the slip of paper.*

BLANCHE: Six thirty-two.
EUNICE: You don't have to look no further.
BLANCHE [*uncomprehendingly*]: I'm looking for my sister, Stella DuBois. I mean—Mrs Stanley Kowalski.
EUNICE: That's the party—You just did miss her, though.
BLANCHE: This—can this be—her home?
EUNICE: She's got the downstairs here and I got the up.
BLANCHE: Oh. She's—out?
EUNICE: You noticed that bowling alley around the corner?
BLANCHE: I'm—not sure I did.
EUNICE: Well, that's where she's at, watchin' her husband bowl.

There is a pause.

You want to leave your suitcase here an' go find her?
BLANCHE: No.
NEGRO WOMAN: I'll go tell her you come.
BLANCHE: Thanks.
NEGRO WOMAN: You welcome. [*She goes out.*]
EUNICE: She wasn't expecting you?
BLANCHE: No. No, not tonight.
EUNICE: Well, why don't you just go in and make yourself at home till they get back.
BLANCHE: How could I—do that?
EUNICE: We own this place so I can let you in.

She gets up and opens the downstairs door. A light goes on behind the blind, turning it light blue. BLANCHE *slowly follows her into the downstairs flat. The surrounding areas dim out as the interior is lighted. Two rooms can be seen, not too clearly defined. The one first entered is primarily a kitchen but contains a folding bed to be used by* BLANCHE. *The room beyond this is a bedroom. Off this room is a narrow door to a bathroom.*

EUNICE [*defensively, noticing* BLANCHE'*s look*]: It's sort of messed up right now but when it's clean it's real sweet.
BLANCHE: Is it?
EUNICE: Uh-huh, I think so. So you're Stella's sister?
BLANCHE: Yes. [*Wanting to get rid of her.*] Thanks for letting me in.
EUNICE: *Por nada,* as the Mexicans say, *por nada!* Stella spoke of you.
BLANCHE: Yes?
EUNICE: I think she said you taught school.
BLANCHE: Yes.
EUNICE: And you're from Mississippi, huh?
BLANCHE: Yes.
EUNICE: She showed me a picture of your home-place, the plantation.
BLANCHE: Belle Reve?

EUNICE: A great big place with white columns.
BLANCHE: Yes . . .
EUNICE: A place like that must be awful hard to keep up.
BLANCHE: If you will excuse me, I'm just about to drop.
EUNICE: Sure, honey. Why don't you set down?
BLANCHE: What I meant was I'd like to be left alone.
EUNICE [*offended*]: Aw. I'll make myself scarce, in that case.
BLANCHE: I didn't mean to be rude, but—
EUNICE: I'll drop by the bowling alley an' hustle her up. [*She goes out of the door.*]

BLANCHE *sits in a chair very stiffly with her shoulders slightly hunched and her legs pressed close together and her hands tightly clutching her purse as if she were quite cold. After a while the blind look goes out of her eyes and she begins to look slowly around. A cat screeches. She catches her breath with a startled gesture. Suddenly she notices something in a half-opened closet. She springs up and crosses to it, and removes a whisky bottle. She pours a half tumbler of whisky and tosses it down. She carefully replaces the bottle and washes out the tumbler at the sink. The she resumes her seat in front of the table.*

BLANCHE [*faintly to herself*]: I've got to keep hold of myself!

STELLA *comes quickly around the corner of the building and runs to the door of the downstairs flat.*

STELLA [*calling out joyfully*]: Blanche!

For a moment they stare at each other. Then BLANCHE *springs up and runs to her with a wild cry.*

BLANCHE: Stella, oh, Stella, Stella! Stella for Star!

She begins to speak with feverish vivacity as if she feared for either of them to stop and think. They catch each other in a spasmodic embrace.

Now, then, let me look at you. But don't you look at me, Stella, no, no, no, not till later, not till I've bathed and rested! And turn that over-light off! Turn that off! I won't be looked at in this merciless glare!

STELLA *laughs and complies.*

Come back here now! Oh, my baby! Stella! Stella for Star! [*She embraces her again.*] I thought you would never come back to this horrible place! What am I saying! I didn't mean to say that. I meant to be nice about it and say–Oh, what a convenient location and such–Ha-a-ha! Precious lamb! You haven't said a *word* to me.
STELLA: You haven't given me a chance to, honey! [*She laughs but her glance at* BLANCHE *is a little anxious.*]
BLANCHE: Well, now you talk. Open you pretty mouth and talk while I look around for some liquor! I know you must have some liquor on the place! Where could it be, I wonder? Oh, I spy, I spy! [*She rushes to the closet and*

removes the bottle; she is shaking all over and panting for breath as she tries to laugh. The bottle nearly slips from her grasp.]

STELLA [*noticing*]: Blanche, you sit down and let me pour the drinks. I don't know what we've got to mix with. Maybe a coke's in the icebox. Look'n see, honey, while I'm—

BLANCHE: No coke, honey, not with my nerves tonight! Where–where–where is—?

STELLA: Stanley? Bowling! He loves it. They're having a–found some soda!–tournament . . .

BLANCHE: Just water, baby, to chase it! Now don't get worried, your sister hasn't turned into a drunkard, she's just all shaken up and hot and tired and dirty! You sit down, now, and explain this place to me! What are you doing in a place like this?

STELLA: Now, Blanche—

BLANCHE: Oh, I'm not going to be hypocritical, I'm going to be honestly critical about it! Never, never, never in my worst dreams could I picture–Only Poe! Only Mr Edgar Allan Poe!–could do it justice! Out there I suppose is the ghoul-haunted woodland of Weir! [*She laughs.*]

STELLA: No, honey, those are the L & N tracks.

BLANCHE: No, now seriously, putting joking aside. Why didn't you tell me, why didn't you write me, honey, why didn't you let me know?

STELLA [*carefully, pouring herself a drink*]: Tell you what, Blanche?

BLANCHE: Why, that you had to live in these conditions!

STELLA: Aren't you being a little intense about it? It's not that bad at all! New Orleans isn't like other cities.

BLANCHE: This has got nothing to do with New Orleans. You might as well say–forgive me, blessed baby! [*She suddenly stops short.*] The subject is closed!

STELLA [*a little drily*]: Thanks.

During the pause, BLANCHE *stares at her. She smiles at* BLANCHE.

BLANCHE [*looking down at her glass, which shakes in her hand*]: You're all I've got in the world, and you're not glad to see me!

STELLA [*sincerely*]: Why, Blanche, you know that's not true.

BLANCHE: No?–I'd forgotten how quiet you were.

STELLA: You never did give me a chance to say much, Blanche. So I just got in the habit of being quiet around you.

BLANCHE [*vaguely*]: A good habit to get into . . . [*then abruptly*] You haven't asked me how I happened to get away from the school before the spring term ended.

STELLA: Well, I thought you'd volunteer that information–if you wanted to tell me.

BLANCHE: You thought I'd been fired?

STELLA: No, I–thought you might have–resigned. . . .

BLANCHE: I was so exhausted by all I'd been through my–nerves broke. [*Nervously tamping cigarette.*] I was on the verge of–lunacy, almost! So Mr Graves–Mr Graves is the high school superintendent–he suggested I take a leave of absence. I couldn't put all of those details into the wire. . . . [*She drinks quickly.*] Oh, this buzzes right through me and feels so *good*!

STELLA: Won't you have another?

BLANCHE: No, one's my limit.

STELLA: Sure?

BLANCHE: You haven't said a word about my appearance.

STELLA: You look just fine.

BLANCHE: God love you for a liar! Daylight never exposed so total a ruin! But you–you've put on some weight, yes, you're just as plump as a little partridge! And it's so becoming to you!

STELLA: Now, Blanche—

BLANCHE: Yes, it is, it is or I wouldn't say it! You just have to watch around the hips a little. Stand up.

STELLA: Not now.

BLANCHE: You hear me? I said stand up!

STELLA *complies reluctantly.*

You messy child, you, you've spilt something on that pretty white lace collar! About your hair–you ought to have it cut in a feather bob with your dainty features. Stella, you have a maid, don't you?

STELLA: No. With only two rooms it's—

BLANCHE: What? *Two* rooms, did you say?

STELLA: This one and—[*She is embarrassed.*]

BLANCHE: The other one? [*She laughs sharply. There is an embarrassed silence.*] How quiet you are, you're so peaceful. Look how you sit there with your little hands folded like a cherub in choir!

STELLA [*uncomfortably*]: I never had anything like your energy, Blanche.

BLANCHE: Well, I never had your beautiful self-control. I am going to take just one little tiny nip more, sort of to put the stopper on, so to speak. . . . Then put the bottle away so I won't be tempted. [*She rises.*] I want you to look at *my* figure! [*She turns around.*] You know I haven't put on one ounce in ten years, Stella? I weigh what I weighed the summer you left Belle Reve. The summer Dad died and you left us . . .

STELLA [*a little wearily*]: It's just incredible, Blanche, how well you're looking.

BLANCHE: You see I still have that awful vanity about my looks even now that my looks are slipping! [*She laughs nervously and glances at* STELLA *for reassurance.*]

STELLA [*dutifully*]: They haven't slipped one particle.

BLANCHE: After all I've been through? You think I believe that story? Blessed child! [*She touches her forehead shakily.*] Stella, there's–only two rooms?

STELLA: And a bathroom.

BLANCHE: Oh, you do have a bathroom! First door to the right at the top of the stairs?

They both laugh uncomfortably.

But, Stella, I don't see where you're going to put me!

STELLA: We're going to put you in here.

BLANCHE: What kind of bed's this–one of those collapsible things? [*She sits on it.*]

STELLA: Does it feel all right?

BLANCHE [*dubiously*]: Wonderful, honey. I don't like a bed that gives much. But there's no door between the two rooms, and Stanley–will it be decent?

STELLA: Stanley is Polish, you know.

BLANCHE: Oh, yes. They're something like Irish, aren't they?

STELLA: Well—

BLANCHE: Only not so–highbrow?

They both laugh again in the same way.

I brought some nice clothes to meet all your lovely friends in.

STELLA: I'm afraid you won't think they are lovely.

BLANCHE: What are they like?

STELLA: They're Stanley's friends.

BLANCHE: Polacks?

STELLA: They're a mixed lot, Blanche.

BLANCHE: Heterogeneous–types?

STELLA: Oh, yes. Yes, types is right!

BLANCHE: Well–anyhow–I brought nice clothes and I'll wear them. I guess you're hoping I'll say I'll put up at a hotel, but I'm not going to put up at a hotel. I want to be *near* you, got to be *with* somebody, I *can't* be *alone!* Because–as you must have noticed–I'm *not* very *well.* . . . [*Her voice drops and her look is frightened.*]

STELLA: You seem a little bit nervous or overwrought or something.

BLANCHE: Will Stanley like me, or will I be just a visiting in-law, Stella? I couldn't stand that.

STELLA: You'll get along fine together, if you'll just try not to–well–compare him with men that we went out with at home.

BLANCHE: Is he so–different?

STELLA: Yes. A different species.

BLANCHE: In what way; what's he like?

STELLA: Oh, you can't describe someone you're in love with! Here's a picture of him! [*She hands a photograph to* BLANCHE.]

BLANCHE: An officer?

STELLA: A Master Sergeant in the Engineers' Corps. Those are decorations!

BLANCHE: He had those on when you met him?

STELLA: I assure you I wasn't just blinded by all the brass.

BLANCHE: That's not what I—

STELLA: But of course there were things to adjust myself to later on.

BLANCHE: Such as his civilian background!

STELLA *laughs uncertainly.*

How did he take it when you said I was coming?

STELLA: Oh, Stanley doesn't know yet.

BLANCHE [*frightened*]: You–haven't told him?

STELLA: He's on the road a good deal.

BLANCHE: Oh. Travels?

STELLA: Yes.

BLANCHE: Good. I mean–isn't it?

STELLA [*half to herself*]: I can hardly stand it when he is away for a night. . . .

BLANCHE: Why, Stella?

STELLA: When he's away for a week I nearly go wild!

BLANCHE: Gracious!

STELLA: And when he comes back I cry on his lap like a baby. . . . [*She smiles to herself.*]
BLANCHE: I guess that is what I meant by being in love. . . .

STELLA *looks up with a radiant smile.*

Stella—
STELLA: What?
BLANCHE [*in an uneasy rush*]: I haven't asked you the things you probably thought I was going to ask. And so I'll expect you to be understanding about what *I* have to tell *you*.
STELLA: What, Blanche? [*Her face turns anxious.*]
BLANCHE: Well, Stella—you're going to reproach me, I know that you're bound to reproach me—but before you do—take into consideration—you left! I stayed and struggled! You came to New Orleans and looked out for yourself! *I* stayed at Belle Reve and tried to hold it together! I'm not meaning this in any reproachful way, but *all* the burden descended on *my* shoulders.
STELLA: The best I could do was make my own living, Blanche.

BLANCHE *begins to shake again with intensity.*

BLANCHE: I know, I know. But you are the one that abandoned Belle Reve, not I! I stayed and fought for it, bled for it, almost died for it!
STELLA: Stop this hysterical outburst and tell me what's happened? What do you mean fought and bled? What kind of—
BLANCHE: I knew you would, Stella. I knew you would take this attitude about it!
STELLA: About—what?—please!
BLANCHE [*slowly*]: The loss—the loss . . .
STELLA: Belle Reve? Lost, is it? No!
BLANCHE: Yes, Stella.

They stare at each other across the yellow-checked linoleum of the table. BLANCHE *slowly nods her head and* STELLA *looks slowly down at her hands folded on the table. The music of the 'blue piano' grows louder.* BLANCHE *touches her handkerchief to her forehead.*

STELLA: But how did it go? What happened?
BLANCHE [*springing up*]: You're a fine one to ask me how it went!
STELLA: Blanche!
BLANCHE: You're a fine one to sit there *accusing me* of it!
STELLA: *Blanche!*
BLANCHE: I, I, *I* took the blows in my face and my body! All of those deaths! The long parade to the graveyard! Father, mother! Margaret, that dreadful way! So big with it, it couldn't be put in a coffin! But had to be burned like rubbish! You just came home in time for the funerals, Stella. And funerals are pretty compared to deaths. Funerals are quiet, but deaths—not always. Sometimes their breathing is hoarse, and sometimes it rattles, and sometimes they even cry out to you, 'Don't let me go!' Even the old, sómetimes, say, 'Don't let me go.' As if you were able to stop them! But funerals are quiet, with pretty flowers. And, oh, what gorgeous boxes they

pack them away in! Unless you were there at the bed when they cried out, 'Hold me!' you'd never suspect there was the struggle for breath and bleeding. You didn't dream, but I saw! *Saw! Saw!* And now you sit there telling me with your eyes that I let the place go! How in hell do you think all that sickness and dying was paid for? Death is expensive, Miss Stella! And old Cousin Jessie's right after Margaret's, hers! Why, the Grim Reaper had put up his tent on our doorstep! . . . Stella. Belle Reve was his headquarters! Honey—that's how it slipped through my fingers! Which of them left us a fortune? Which of them left a cent of insurance even? Only poor Jessie—one hundred to pay for her coffin. That was all, Stella! And I with my pitiful salary at the school. Yes, accuse me! Sit there and stare at me, thinking I let the place go! *I* let the place go? Where were *you*. In bed with your—Polak!

STELLA [*springing*]: Blanche! You be still! That's enough! [*She starts out.*]

BLANCHE: Where are you going?

STELLA: I'm going into the bathroom to wash my face.

BLANCHE: Oh, Stella, Stella, you're crying!

STELLA: Does that surprise you? [*She goes into the bathroom.*]

Outside is the sound of men's voices. STANLEY, STEVE, *and* MITCH *cross to the foot of the steps.*

STEVE: And the old lady is on her way to Mass and she's late and there's a cop standin' in front of th' church an' she comes runnin' up an' says, 'Officer—is Mass out yet?' He looks her over and says, 'No, Lady, but y'r hat's on crooked!'

They give a hoarse bellow of laughter.

Playing poker tomorrow night?

STANLEY: Yeah—at Mitch's.

MITCH: Not at my place. My mother's still sick. [*He starts off.*]

STANLEY [*calling after him*]: All right, we'll play at my place . . . but you bring the beer.

EUNICE [*hollering down from above*]: Break it up down there! I made the spaghetti dish and ate it myself.

STEVE [*going upstairs*]: I told you and phoned you we was playing. [*To the men*] Jax beer!

EUNICE: You never phoned me once.

STEVE: I told you at breakfast—and phoned you at lunch . . .

EUNICE: Well, never mind about that. You just get yourself home here once in a while.

STEVE: You want it in the papers?

More laughter and shouts of parting come from the men. STANLEY *throws the screen door of the kitchen open and comes in. He is of medium height, about five feet eight or nine, and strongly, compactly built. Animal joy in his being is implicit in all his movements and attitudes. Since earliest manhood the centre of his life has been pleasure with women, the giving and taking of it, not with weak indulgence, dependently, but with the power and pride of a richly feathered male bird among hens. Branching out from this complete and satisfying centre are all the auxiliary channels of his life, such as his heartiness with men, his appreciation of rough humour, his love of good drink and food and games, his car, his radio, everything that is his, that bears his emblem of the gaudy seed-bearer. He sizes women up at a glance, with sexual classifications, crude images flashing into his mind and determining the way he smiles at them.*

BLANCHE [*drawing involuntarily back from his stare*]: You must be Stanley. I'm Blanche.
STANLEY: Stella's sister?
BLANCHE: Yes.
STANLEY: H'lo. Where's the little woman?
BLANCHE: In the bathroom.
STANLEY: Oh. Didn't know you were coming in town.
BLANCHE: I—uh—
STANLEY: Where you from, Blanche?
BLANCHE: Why, I—live in Laurel.

He has crossed to the closet and removed the whisky bottle.

STANLEY: In Laurel, huh? Oh, yeah, in Laurel, that's right. Not in my territory. Liquor goes fast in hot weather. [*He holds the bottle to the light to observe its depletion.*] Have a shot?
BLANCHE: No, I—rarely touch it.
STANLEY: Some people rarely touch it, but it touches them often.
BLANCHE: [*faintly*]: Ha-ha.
STANLEY: My clothes're stickin' to me. Do you mind if I make myself comfortable? [*He starts to remove his shirt.*]
BLANCHE: Please, please do.
STANLEY: Be comfortable is my motto.
BLANCHE: It's mine, too. It's hard to stay looking fresh. I haven't washed or even powdered my face and—here you are!
STANLEY: You know you can catch cold sitting around in damp things, especially when you been exercising hard like bowling is. You're a teacher, aren't you?
BLANCHE: Yes.
STANLEY: What do you teach, Blanche?
BLANCHE: English.
STANLEY: I never was a very good English student. How long you here for, Blanche?
BLANCHE: I—don't know yet.
STANLEY: You going to shack up here?
BLANCHE: I thought I would if it's not inconvenient for you all.
STANLEY: Good.
BLANCHE: Travelling wears me out.
STANLEY: Well, take it easy.

A cat screeches near the window. BLANCHE *springs up.*

BLANCHE: What's that?
STANLEY: Cats. . . . Hey, Stella!
STELLA [*faintly, from the bathroom*]: Yes, Stanley.

STANLEY: Haven't fallen in, have you?

He grins at BLANCHE. *She tries unsuccessfully to smile back. There is silence.*

I'm afraid I'll strike you as being the unrefined type. Stella's spoke of you a good deal. You were married once, weren't you?

The music of the polka rises up, faint in the distance.

BLANCHE: Yes. When I was quite young.
STANLEY: What happened?
BLANCHE: The boy—the boy died. [*She sinks back down.*] I'm afraid I'm—going to be sick!

Her head falls on her arms.

SCENE TWO

It is six o'clock the following evening. BLANCHE is bathing. STELLA is completing her toilette. BLANCHE's dress, a flowered print, is laid out on STELLA's bed.

STANLEY *enters the kitchen from outside, leaving the door open on the perpetual 'blue piano' around the corner.*

STANLEY: What's all this monkey doings?

STELLA: Oh, Stan! [*She jumps up and kisses him which he accepts with lordly composure.*] I'm taking Blanche to Galatoires' for supper and then to a show, because it's your poker night.

STANLEY: How about my supper, huh? I'm not going to no Galatoires' for supper!

STELLA: I put you a cold plate on ice.

STANLEY: Well, isn't that just dandy!

STELLA: I'm going to try to keep Blanche out till the party breaks up because I don't know how she would take it. So we'll go to one of the little places in the Quarter afterwards and you'd better give me some money.

STANLEY: Where is she?

STELLA: She's soaking in a hot tub to quiet her nerves. She's terribly upset.

STANLEY: Over what?

STELLA: She's been through such an ordeal.

STANLEY: Yeah?

STELLA: Stan, we've–lost Belle Reve!

STANLEY: The place in the country?

STELLA: Yes.

STANLEY: How?

STELLA [*vaguely*]: Oh, it had to be–sacrificed or something.

There is a pause while STANLEY *considers.* STELLA *is changing into her dress.*

When she comes in be sure to say something nice about her appearance. And, oh! Don't mention the baby. I haven't said anything yet, I'm waiting until she gets in a quieter condition.

STANLEY [*ominously*]: So?

STELLA: And try to understand her and be nice to her, Stan.

BLANCHE [*singing in the bathroom*]:
　　　　'From the land of the sky blue water,
　　　　They brought a captive maid!'

STELLA: She wasn't expecting to find us in such a small place. You see I'd tried to gloss things over a little in my letters.

STANLEY: So?

STELLA: And admire her dress and tell her she's looking wonderful. That's important with Blanche. Her little weakness!

STANLEY: Yeah. I get the idea. Now let's skip back a little to where you said the country place was disposed of.

STELLA: Oh!–yes . . .

STANLEY: How about that? Let's have a few more details on that subject.

STELLA: It's best not to talk much about it until she's calmed down.

STANLEY: So that's the deal, huh? Sister Blanche cannot be annoyed with business details right now!

STELLA: You saw how she was last night.

STANLEY: Uh-hum, I saw how she was. Now let's have a gander at the bill of sale.

STELLA: I haven't seen any.

STANLEY: She didn't show you no papers, no deed of sale or nothing like that, huh?

STELLA: It seems like it wasn't sold.

STANLEY: Well, what in hell was it then, give away? To charity?

STELLA: Shhh! She'll hear you.

STANLEY: I don't care if she hears me. Let's see the papers!

STELLA: There weren't any papers, she didn't show any papers, I don't care about papers.

STANLEY: Have you ever heard of the Napoleonic code?

STELLA: No, Stanley, I haven't heard of the Napoleonic code and if I have, I don't see what it—

STANLEY: Let me enlighten you on a point or two, baby.

STELLA: Yes?

STANLEY: In the state of Louisiana we have the Napoleonic code according to which what belongs to the wife belongs to the husband and vice versa. For instance, if I had a piece of property, or you had a piece of property—

STELLA: My head is swimming!

STANLEY: All right. I'll wait till she gets through soaking in a hot tub and then I'll inquire if *she* is acquainted with the Napoleonic code. It looks to me like you have been swindled, baby, and when you're swindled under the Napoleonic code I'm swindled *too*. And I don't like to be *swindled*.

STELLA: There's plenty of time to ask her questions later but if you do now she'll go to pieces again. I don't understand what happened to Belle Reve but you don't know how ridiculous you are being when you suggest that my sister or I or anyone of our family could have perpetrated a swindle on anyone else.

STANLEY: Then where's the money if the place was sold?

STELLA: Not sold–*lost, lost!*

He stalks into bedroom, and she follows him.

Stanley!

He pulls open the wardrobe trunk standing in the middle of room and jerks out an armful of dresses.

STANLEY: Open your eyes to this stuff! You think she got them out of a teacher's pay?

STELLA: Hush!

STANLEY: Look at these feathers and furs that she come here to preen herself in!

What's this here? A solid-gold dress, I believe! And this one! What is these here? Fox-pieces! [*He blows on them.*] Genuine fox fur-pieces, a half a mile long! Where are your fox-pieces, Stella? Bushy snow-white ones, no less! Where are your white fox-pieces?

STELLA: Those are inexpensive summer furs that Blanche has had a long time.

STANLEY: I got an acquaintance who deals in this sort of merchandise. I'll have him in here to appraise it. I'm willing to bet you there's thousands of dollars invested in this stuff here!

STELLA: Don't be such an idiot, Stanley!

He hurls the furs to the daybed. Then he jerks open a small drawer in the trunk and pulls up a fistful of costume jewellery.

STANLEY: And what have we here? The treasure chest of a pirate!

STELLA: Oh, Stanley!

STANLEY: Pearls! Ropes of them! What is this sister of yours, a deep-sea diver who brings up sunken treasures? Or is she the champion safe-cracker of all time! Bracelets of solid gold, too! Where are your pearls and gold bracelets?

STELLA: Shhh! Be still, Stanley!

STANLEY: And diamonds! A crown for an empress!

STELLA: A rhinestone tiara she wore to a costume ball.

STANLEY: What's rhinestone?

STELLA: Next door to glass.

STANLEY: Are you kidding? I have an acquaintance that works in a jewellery store. I'll have him in here to make an appraisal of this. Here's your plantation, or what was left of it, here!

STELLA: You have no idea how stupid and horrid you're being! Now close that trunk before she comes out of the bathroom!

He kicks the trunk partly closed and sits on the kitchen table.

STANLEY: The Kowalskis and the DuBois have different notions.

STELLA [*angrily*]: Indeed they have, thank heavens!–*I'm* going outside. [*She snatches up her white hat and gloves and crosses to the outside door.*] You come out with me while Blanche is getting dressed.

STANLEY: Since when do you give me orders?

STELLA: Are you going to stay here and insult her?

STANLEY: You're damn tootin' I'm going to stay here.

STELLA *goes out on the porch.* BLANCHE *comes out of the bathroom in a red satin robe.*

BLANCHE [*airily*]: Hello, Stanley! Here I am, all freshly bathed and scented, and feeling like a brand-new human being!

He lights a cigarette.

STANLEY: That's good.

BLANCHE [*drawing the curtains at the windows*]: Excuse me while I slip on my pretty new dress!!

STANLEY: Go right ahead, Blanche.

She closes the drapes between the rooms.

BLANCHE: I understand there's to be a little card party to which we ladies are cordially *not* invited.
STANLEY [*ominously*]: Yeah?

BLANCHE *throws off her robe and slips into a flowered print dress.*

BLANCHE: Where's Stella?
STANLEY: Out on the porch.
BLANCHE: I'm going to ask a favour of you in a moment.
STANLEY: What could that be, I wonder?
BLANCHE: Some buttons in back! You may enter!

He crosses through drapes with a smouldering look.

How do I look?
STANLEY: You look all right.
BLANCHE: Many thanks! Now the buttons!
STANLEY: I can't do nothing with them.
BLANCHE: You men with your big clumsy fingers. May I have a drag on your cig?
STANLEY: Have one for yourself.
BLANCHE: Why, thanks! . . . It looks like my trunk has exploded.
STANLEY: Me an' Stella were helping you unpack.
BLANCHE: Well, you certainly did a fast and thorough job of it!
STANLEY: It looks like you raided some stylish shops in Paris.
BLANCHE: Ha-ha! Yes—clothes are my passion!
STANLEY: What does it cost for a string of fur-pieces like that?
BLANCHE: Why, those were a tribute from an admirer of mine!
STANLEY: He must have had a lot of—admiration!
BLANCHE: Oh, in my youth I excited some admiration. But look at me now! [*She smiles at him radiantly.*] Would you think it possible that I was once considered to be—attractive?
STANLEY: Your looks are okay.
BLANCHE: I was fishing for a compliment, Stanley.
STANLEY: I don't go in for that stuff.
BLANCHE: What—stuff?
STANLEY: Compliments to women about their looks. I never met a woman that didn't know if she was good-looking or not without being told, and some of them give themselves credit for more than they've got. I once went out with a doll who said to me, 'I am the glamorous type, I am the glamorous type!' I said, 'So what?'
BLANCHE: And what did she say then?
STANLEY: She didn't say nothing. That shut her up like a clam.
BLANCHE: Did it end the romance?
STANLEY: It ended the conversation—that was all. Some men are took in by this Hollywood glamour stuff and some men are not.
BLANCHE: I'm sure you belong to the second category.
STANLEY: That's right.
BLANCHE: I cannot imagine any witch of a woman casting a spell over you.

STANLEY: That's—right.

BLANCHE: You're simple, straightforward and honest, a little bit on the primitive side I should think. To interest you a woman would have to—[*She pauses with an indefinite gesture.*]

STANLEY [*slowly*]: Lay . . . her cards on the table.

BLANCHE [*smiling*]: Yes—yes—cards on the table. . . . Well, life is too full of evasions and ambiguities, I think. I like an artist who paints in strong, bold colours, primary colours. I don't like pinks and creams and I never cared for wish-washy people. That was why, when you walked in here last night, I said to myself—'My sister has married a man!'—Of course that was all that I could tell about you.

STANLEY [*booming*]: Now let's cut the re-bop!

BLANCHE [*pressing hands to her ears*]: Ouuuuu!

STELLA [*calling from the steps*]: Stanley! You come out here and let Blanche finish dressing!

BLANCHE: I'm through dressing, honey.

STELLA: Well, you come out, then.

STANLEY: Your sister and I are having a little talk.

BLANCHE [*lightly*]: Honey, do me a favour. Run to the drugstore and get me a lemon-coke with plenty of chipped ice in it!—Will you do that for me, Sweetie?

STELLA [*uncertainly*]: Yes. [*She goes round the corner of the building.*]

BLANCHE: The poor thing was out there listening to us, and I have an idea she doesn't understand you as well as I do. . . . All right; now, Mr Kowalski, let us proceed without any more double-talk. I'm ready to answer all questions. I've nothing to hide. What is it?

STANLEY: There is such a thing in this State of Louisiana as the Napoleonic code, according to which whatever belongs to my wife is also mine—and vice versa.

BLANCHE: My, but you have an impressive judicial air!

> *She sprays herself with her atomizer; then playfully sprays him with it. He seizes the atomizer and slams it down on the dresser. She throws back her head and laughs.*

STANLEY: If I didn't know that you was my wife's sister I'd get ideas about you!

BLANCHE: Such as what?

STANLEY: Don't play so dumb. You know what!—Where's the papers?

BLANCHE: Papers?

STANLEY: Papers! That stuff people write on!

BLANCHE: Oh, papers, papers! Ha-ha! The first anniversary gift, all kinds of papers!

STANLEY: I'm talking of legal papers. Connected with the plantation.

BLANCHE: There *were* some papers.

STANLEY: You mean they're no longer existing?

BLANCHE: They probably are, somewhere.

STANLEY: But not in the trunk.

BLANCHE: Everything that I own is in that trunk.

STANLEY: Then why don't we have a look for them? [*He crosses to the trunk, shoves it roughly open, and begins to open compartments.*]

BLANCHE: What in the name of heaven are you thinking of! What's in the back of that little boy's mind of yours? That I am absconding with something, attempting some kind of treachery on my sister?—Let me do that! It will be faster and simpler. . . .[*She crosses to the trunk and takes out a box.*] I keep my papers mostly in this tin box. [*She opens it.*]

STANLEY: What's them underneath? [*He indicates another sheaf of paper.*]

BLANCHE: These are love-letters, yellowing with antiquity, all from one boy.

He snatches them up. She speaks fiercely.

Give those back to me!

STANLEY: I'll have a look at them first!

BLANCHE: The touch of your hands insults them!

STANLEY: Don't pull that stuff!

He rips off the ribbon and starts to examine them. BLANCHE *snatches them from him, and they cascade to the floor.*

BLANCHE: Now that you've touched them I'll burn them!

STANLEY [*staring, baffled*]: What in hell are they?

BLANCHE [*on the floor gathering them up*]: Poems a dead boy wrote. I hurt him the way that you would like to hurt me, but you can't! I'm not young and vulnerable any more. But my young husband was and I—never mind about that! Just give them back to me!

STANLEY: What do you mean by saying you'll have to burn them?

BLANCHE: I'm sorry, I must have lost my head for a moment. Everyone has something he won't let others touch because of their—intimate nature. . . . [*She now seems faint with exhaustion and she sits down with the strong box and puts on a pair of glasses and goes methodically through a large stack of papers.*] Ambler & Ambler. Hmmmmm. . . . Crabtree. . . . More Ambler & Ambler.

STANLEY: What is Ambler & Ambler?

BLANCHE: A firm that made loans on the place.

STANLEY: Then it *was* lost on a mortgage?

BLANCHE [*touching her forehead*]: That must've been what happened.

STANLEY: I don't want no ifs, ands, or buts! What's all the rest of them papers?

She hands him the entire box. He carries it to the table and starts to examine the papers.

BLANCHE [*picking up a large envelope containing more papers*]: There are thousands of papers, stretching back over hundreds of years, affecting Belle Reve as, piece by piece, our improvident grandfathers and father and uncles and brothers exchanged the land for their epic fornications—to put it plainly! [*She removes her glasses with an exhausted laugh.*] Till finally all that was left—and Stella can verify that!—was the house itself and about twenty acres of ground, including a graveyard, to which now all but Stella and I have retreated. [*She pours the contents of the envelope on the table.*] Here all of them are, all papers! I hereby endow you with them! Take them, peruse them—commit them to memory, even! I think it's wonderfully fitting that Belle Reve should finally be this bunch of old papers in your big, capable hands! . . . I wonder if Stella's come back with my lemon-coke. . . . [*She leans back and closes her eyes.*]

STANLEY: I have a lawyer acquaintance who will study these out.

BLANCHE: Present them to him with a box of aspirin tablets.

STANLEY [*becoming somewhat sheepish*]: You see, under the Napoleonic code—a man has to take an interest in his wife's affairs—especially now that she's going to have a baby.

BLANCHE opens her eyes. The 'blue piano' sounds louder.

BLANCHE: Stella? Stella going to have a baby? [*Dreamily.*] I didn't know she was going to have a baby!

She gets up and crosses to the outside door. Stella appears around the corner with a carton from the drug-store.
Stanley goes into the bedroom with the envelope and the box. The inner rooms fade to darkness and the outside wall of the house is visible. BLANCHE *meets* STELLA *at the foot of the steps to the sidewalk.*

Stella, Stella for Star! How lovely to have a baby!

She embraces her sister. STELLA *returns the embrace with a convulsive sob.* BLANCHE *speaks softly.*

Everything is all right; we thrashed it out. I feel a bit shaky, but I think I handled it nicely. I laughed and treated it all as a joke, called him a little boy and laughed—and flirted! Yes—I was flirting with your husband, Stella!

STEVE *and* PABLO *appear carrying a case of beer.*

In   The guests are gathering for the poker party.

The two men pass between them, and with a short, curious stare at BLANCHE, *they enter the house.*

STELLA I'm sorry he did that to you.
BLANCHE: He's just not the sort that goes for jasmine perfume! But maybe he's what we need to mix with our blood now that we've lost Belle Reve and have to go on without Belle Reve to protect us. . . . How pretty the sky is! I ought to go there on a rocket that never comes down.

A TAMALE VENDOR *calls out as he rounds the corner.*

VENDOR: Red hots! Red hots!

BLANCHE utters a sharp, frightened cry and shrinks away; then she laughs breathlessly again.

BLANCHE: Which way do we—go now—Stella?
VENDOR: Re-e-d ho-o-ot!
BLANCHE: The blind are—leading the blind!

They disappear around the corner, BLANCHE'S *desperate laughter ringing out once more.*
Then there is a bellowing laugh from the interior of the flat.
Then the 'blue piano' and the hot trumpet sound louder.

SCENE THREE

The Poker Night. There is a picture of Van Gogh's of a billiard-parlour at night. The kitchen now suggests that sort of lurid nocturnal brilliance, the raw colours of childhood's spectrum. Over the yellow linoleum of the kitchen table hangs an electric bulb with a vivid green glass shade. The poker players—STANLEY, STEVE, MITCH, and PABLO—wear coloured shirts, solid blues, a purple, a red-and-white check, a light green, and they are men at the peak of their physical manhood, as coarse and direct and powerful as the primary colours. There are vivid slices of watermelon on the table, whisky bottles, and glasses. The bedroom is relatively dim with only the light that spills between the portières and through the wide window on the street.

For a moment there is absorbed silence as a hand is dealt.

STEVE: Anything wild this deal?
PABLO: One-eyed jacks are wild.
STEVE: Give me two cards.
PABLO: You, Mitch?
MITCH: I'm out.
PABLO: One.
MITCH: Anyone want a shot?
STANLEY: Yeah. Me.
PABLO: Why don't somebody go to the Chinaman's and bring back a load of chop suey?
STANLEY: When I'm losing you want to eat! Ante up! Openers? Openers! Get off the table, Mitch. Nothing belongs on a poker table but cards, chips, and whisky. [*He lurches up and tosses some watermelon rinds to the floor.*]
MITCH: Kind of on your high horse, ain't you?
STANLEY: How many?
STEVE: Give me three.
STANLEY: One.
MITCH: I'm out again. I oughta go home pretty soon.
STANLEY: Shut up.
MITCH: I gotta sick mother. She don't go to sleep until I come in at night.
STANLEY: Then why don't you stay home with her?
MITCH: She says to go out, so I go, but I don't enjoy it. All the while I keep wondering how she is.
STANLEY: Aw, for God's sake, go home, then!
PABLO: What've you got?
STEVE: Spade flush.
MITCH: You all are married. But I'll be alone when she goes—I'm going to the bathroom.
STANLEY: Hurry back and we'll fix you a sugar-tit.

MITCH: Aw, lay off. [*He crosses through the bedroom into the bathroom.*]

STEVE [*dealing a hand*]: Seven card stud. [*Telling his joke as he deals.*] This ole nigger is out in back of his house sittin' down th'owing corn to the chickens when all at once he hears a loud cackle and this young hen comes lickety split around the side of the house with the rooster right behind her and gaining on her fast.

STANLEY [*impatient with the story*]: Deal!

STEVE: But when the rooster catches sight of the nigger th'owing the corn he puts on the brakes and lets the hen get away and starts pecking corn. And the old nigger says, 'Lord God, I hopes I never gits *that* hongry!'

> STEVE *and* PABLO *laugh. The sisters appear around the corner of the building.*

STELLA: The game is still going on.

BLANCHE: How do I look?

STELLA: Lovely, Blanche.

BLANCHE: I feel so hot and frazzled. Wait till I powder before you open the door. Do I look done in?

STELLA: Why no. You are as fresh as a daisy.

BLANCHE: One that's been picked a few days.

> STELLA *opens the door and they enter.*

STELLA: Well, well, well. I see you boys are still at it!

STANLEY: Where you been?

STELLA: Blanche and I took in a show. Blanche, this is Mr Gonzales and Mr Hubbel.

BLANCHE: Please don't get up.

STANLEY: Nobody's going to get up, so don't be worried.

STELLA: How much longer is this game going to continue?

STANLEY: Till we get ready to quit.

BLANCHE: Poker is so fascinating. Could I kibitz?

STANLEY: You could not. Why don't you women go up and sit with Eunice?

STELLA: Because it is nearly two-thirty.

> BLANCHE *crosses into the bedroom and partially closes the portières.*

Couldn't you call it quits after one more hand?

> *A chair scrapes.* STANLEY *gives a loud whack of his hand on her thigh.*

STELLA [*sharply*]: That's not fun, Stanley.

> *The men laugh.* STELLA *goes into the bedroom.*

STELLA: It makes me so mad when he does that in front of people.

BLANCHE: I think I will bathe.

STELLA: Again.

BLANCHE: My nerves are in knots. Is the bathroom occupied?

STELLA: I don't know.

BLANCHE *knocks.* MITCH *opens the door and comes out, still wiping his hands on a towel.*

BLANCHE: Oh!–good evening.
MITCH: Hello. [*He stares at her.*]
STELLA: Blanche, this is Harold Mitchell. My sister, Blanche DuBois.
MITCH [*with awkward courtesy*]: How do you do, Miss DuBois.
STELLA: How is your mother now, Mitch?
MITCH: About the same, thanks. She appreciated your sending over that custard.–Excuse me, please.

He crosses slowly back into the kitchen, glancing back at BLANCHE *and coughing a little shyly. He realizes he still has the towel in his hands and with an embarrassed laugh hands it to* STELLA. BLANCHE *looks after him with a certain interest.*

BLANCHE: That one seems–superior to the others.
STELLA: Yes, he is.
BLANCHE: I thought he had a sort of sensitive look.
STELLA: His mother is sick.
BLANCHE: Is he married?
STELLA: No.
BLANCHE: Is he a wolf?
STELLA: Why, Blanche!

BLANCHE *laughs.*

I don't think he would be.
BLANCHE: What does–what does he do? [*She is unbuttoning her blouse.*]
STELLA: He's on the precision bench in the spare parts department. At the plant Stanley travels for.
BLANCHE: Is that something much?
STELLA: No. Stanley's the only one of his crowd that's likely to get anywhere.
BLANCHE: What makes you think Stanley will?
STELLA: Look at him.
BLANCHE: I've looked at him.
STELLA: Then you should know.
BLANCHE: I'm sorry, but I haven't noticed the stamp of genius even on Stanley's forehead. [*She takes off the blouse and stands in her pink silk brassière and white skirt in the light through the portières. The game has continued in undertones.*]
STELLA: It isn't on his forehead and it isn't genius.
BLANCHE: Oh. Well, what is it, and where? I would like to know.
STELLA: It's a drive that he has. You're standing in the light, Blanche!
BLANCHE: Oh, am I!

She moves out of the yellow streak of light. STELLA *has removed her dress and put on a light blue satin kimono.*

STELLA [*with girlish laughter*]: You ought to see their wives.

BLANCHE [*laughingly*]: I can imagine. Big, beefy things, I suppose.
STELLA: You know that one upstairs? [*More laughter.*] One time [*laughing*] the plaster—[*laughing*] cracked—
STANLEY: You hens cut out that conversation in there!
STELLA: You can't hear us.
STANLEY: Well, you can hear me and I said to hush up!
STELLA: This is my house and I'll talk as much as I want to!
BLANCHE: Stella, don't start a row.
STELLA: He's half drunk!—I'll be out in a minute.

She goes into the bathroom. BLANCHE *rises and crosses leisurely to a small white radio and turns it on.*

STANLEY: Awright, Mitch, you in?
MITCH: What? Oh!–No, I'm out!

BLANCHE *moves back into the streak of light. She raises her arms and stretches, as she moves indolently back to the chair. Rhumba music comes over the radio.* MITCH *rises at the table.*

STANLEY: Who turned that on in there?
BLANCHE: I did. Do you mind?
STANLEY: Turn it off!
STEVE: Aw, let the girls have their music.
PABLO: Sure, that's good, leave it on!
STEVE: Sounds like Xavier Cugat!

STANLEY *jumps up and, crossing to the radio, turns it off. He stops short at sight of* BLANCHE *in the chair. She returns his look without flinching. Then he sits again at the poker table.*
Two of the men have started arguing hotly.

I didn't hear you name it.
PABLO: Didn't I name it, Mitch?
MITCH: I wasn't listenin'.
PABLO: What were you doing, then?
STANLEY: He was looking through them drapes. [*He jumps up and jerks roughly at curtains to close them.*] Now deal the hand over again and let's play cards or quit. Some people get ants when they win.

MITCH *rises as* STANLEY *returns to his seat.*

STANLEY [*yelling*]: Sit down!
MITCH: I'm going to the 'head'. Deal me out.
PABLO: Sure he's got ants now. Seven five-dollar bills in his pants pocket folded up tight as spitballs.
STEVE: Tomorrow you'll see him at the cashier's window getting them changed into quarters.
STANLEY: And when he goes home he'll deposit them one by one in a piggy bank his mother gave him for Christmas. [*Dealing.*] This game is Spit in the Ocean.

MITCH *laughs uncomfortably and continues through the portières. He stops just inside.*

BLANCHE [*softly*]: Hello! The Little Boys' Room is busy right now.
MITCH: We've—been drinking beer.
BLANCHE: I hate beer.
MITCH: It's—a hot weather drink.
BLANCHE: Oh, I don't think so; it always makes me warmer. Have you got any cigs? [*She has slipped on the dark red satin wrapper.*]
MITCH: Sure.
BLANCHE: What kind are they?
MITCH: Luckies.
BLANCHE: Oh, good. What a pretty case. Silver?
MITCH: Yes. Yes; read the inscription.
BLANCHE: Oh, is there an inscription? I can't make it out.

He strikes a match and moves closer.

Oh! [*reading with feigned difficulty*]
             'And if God choose,
        I shall but love thee better—after death!'
Why, that's from my favourite sonnet by Mrs Browning!
MITCH: You know it?
BLANCHE: Certainly I do!
MITCH: There's a story connected with that inscription.
BLANCHE: It sounds like a romance.
MITCH: A pretty sad one.
BLANCHE: Oh?
MITCH: The girl's dead now.
BLANCHE [*in a tone of deep sympathy*]: Oh!
MITCH: She knew she was dying when she give me this. A very strange girl, very sweet—very!
BLANCHE: She must have been fond of you. Sick people have such deep, sincere attachments.
MITCH: That's right, they certainly do.
BLANCHE: Sorrow makes for sincerity, I think.
MITCH: It sure brings it out in people.
BLANCHE: The little there is belongs to people who have experienced some sorrow.
MITCH: I believe you are right about that.
BLANCHE: I'm positive that I am. Show me a person who hasn't known any sorrow and I'll show you a shuperficial—Listen to me! My tongue is a little—thick! You boys are responsible for it. The show let out at eleven and we couldn't come home on account of the poker game so we had to go somewhere and drink. I'm not accustomed to having more than one drink. Two is the limit—and *three!* [*She laughs.*] Tonight I had three.
STANLEY: Mitch!
MITCH: Deal me out. I'm talking to Miss—
BLANCHE: DuBois.
MITCH: Miss DuBois?
BLANCHE: It's a French name. It means woods and Blanche means white, so the

two together mean white woods. Like an orchard in spring! You can remember it by that.

MITCH: You're French?

BLANCHE: We are French by extraction. Our first American ancestors were French Huguenots.

MITCH: You are Stella's sister, are you not?

BLANCHE: Yes, Stella is my precious little sister. I call her little in spite of the fact she's somewhat older than I. Just slightly. Less than a year. Will you do something for me?

MITCH: Sure. What?

BLANCHE: I bought this adorable little coloured paper lantern at a Chinese shop on Bourbon. Put it over the light bulb! Will you, please?

MITCH: Be glad to.

BLANCHE: I can't stand a naked light bulb, any more than I can a rude remark or a vulgar action.

MITCH [*adjusting the lantern*]: I guess we strike you as being a pretty rough bunch.

BLANCHE: I'm very adaptable–to circumstances.

MITCH: Well, that's a good thing to be. You are visiting Stanley and Stella?

BLANCHE: Stella hasn't been so well lately, and I came down to help her for a while. She's very run down.

MITCH: You're not—?

BLANCHE: Married? No, no. I'm an old maid schoolteacher!

MITCH: You may teach school but you're certainly not an old maid.

BLANCHE: Thank you, sir! I appreciate your gallantry!

MITCH: So you are in the teaching profession?

BLANCHE: Yes. Ah, yes . . .

MITCH: Grade school or high school or—

STANLEY [*bellowing*]: *Mitch!*

MITCH: *Coming!*

BLANCHE: Gracious, what lung-power! . . . I teach high school. In Laurel.

MITCH: What do you teach? What subject?

BLANCHE: Guess!

MITCH: I bet you teach art or music?

BLANCHE *laughs delicately*.

Of course I could be wrong. You might teach arithmetic.

BLANCHE: Never arithmetic, sir; never arithmetic! [*with a laugh*] I don't even know my multiplication tables! No, I have the misfortune of being an English instructor. I attempt to instil a bunch of bobby-soxers and drug-store Romeos with reverence for Hawthorne and Whitman and Poe!

MITCH: I guess that some of them are more interested in other things.

BLANCHE: How very right you are! Their literary heritage is not what most of them treasure above all else! But they're sweet things! And in the spring, it's touching to notice them making their first discovery of love! As if nobody had ever known it before!

The bathroom door opens and STELLA *comes out*. BLANCHE *continues talking to* MITCH.

Oh! Have you finished? Wait–I'll turn on the radio.

She turns the knobs on the radio and it begins to play 'Wien Wien, nur du allein'. She waltzes to the music with romantic gestures. MITCH *is delighted and moves in awkward imitation like a dancing bear.*

STANLEY *stalks fiercely through the portières into the bedroom. He crosses to the small white radio and snatches it off the table. With a shouted oath, he tosses the instrument out of the window.*

STELLA: *Drunk—drunk—animal thing, you!* [*She rushes through to the poker table.*] All of you—please go home! If any of you have one spark of decency in you—
BLANCHE [*wildly*]: Stella, watch out, he's—

STANLEY *charges after* STELLA.

MEN [*feebly*]: Take it easy, Stanley. Easy, fellow.—Let's all—
STELLA: You lay your hands on me and I'll—

She backs out of sight. He advances and disappears. There is the sound of a blow. STELLA *cries out.* BLANCHE *screams and runs into the kitchen. The men rush forward and there is grappling and cursing. Something is overturned with a crash.*

BLANCHE [*shrilly*]: My sister is going to have a baby!
MITCH: This is terrible.
BLANCHE: Lunacy, absolute lunacy!
MITCH: Get him in here, men.

STANLEY *is forced, pinioned by the two men, into the bedroom. He nearly throws them off. Then all at once he subsides and is limp in their grasp. They speak quietly and lovingly to him and he leans his face on one of their shoulders.*

STELLA [*in a high, unnatural voice, out of sight*]: I want to go away, I want to go away!
MITCH: Poker shouldn't be played in a house with women.

BLANCHE *rushes into the bedroom.*

BLANCHE: I want my sister's clothes! We'll go to that woman's upstairs!
MITCH: Where is the clothes?
BLANCHE [*opening the closet*]: I've got them! [*She rushes through to* STELLA.] Stella, Stella, precious! Dear, dear little sister, don't be afraid! [*With her arms around* STELLA, BLANCHE *guides her to the outside door and upstairs.*]
STANLEY [*dully*]: What's the matter; what's happened?
MITCH: You just blew your top, Stan.
PABLO: He's okay now.
STEVE: Sure, my boy's okay!
MITCH: Put him on the bed and get a wet towel.
PABLO: I think coffee would do him a world of good, now.
STANLEY [*thickly*]: I want water.
MITCH: Put him under the shower!

The men talk quietly as they lead him to the bathroom.

STANLEY: Let go of me, you sons of bitches!

Sounds of blows are heard. The water goes on full tilt.

STEVE: Let's get quick out of here!

They rush to the poker table and sweep up their winnings on their way out.

MITCH [*sadly but firmly*]: Poker should not be played in a house with women.

The door closes on them and the place is still. The Negro entertainers in the bar around the corner play 'Paper Doll' slow and blue. After a moment STANLEY *comes out of the bathroom dripping water and still in his clinging wet polka dot drawers.*

STANLEY: Stella! [*There is a pause.*] My baby doll's left me! [*He breaks into sobs. Then he goes to the phone and dials, still shuddering with sobs.*] Eunice? I want my baby! [*He waits a moment; then he hangs up and dials again.*] Eunice! I'll keep on ringin' until I talk with my baby!

An indistinguishable shrill voice is heard. He hurls phone to floor. Dissonant brass and piano sounds as the rooms dim out to darkness and the outer walls appear in the night light. The 'blue piano' plays for a brief interval.
   Finally, STANLEY *stumbles half-dressed out to the porch and down the wooden steps to the pavement before the building. There he throws back his head like a baying hound and bellows his wife's name:*

Stella! Stella, sweetheart! Stella! Stell-*lahhhhh!*
EUNICE [*calling down from the door of her upper apartment*]: Quit that howling out there an' go back to bed!
STANLEY: I want my baby down here. Stella, Stella!
EUNICE: She ain't comin' down so you quit! Or you'll git th' law on you!
STANLEY: Stella!
EUNICE: You can't beat a woman an' then call 'er back! She won't come! And her goin' t' have a baby! . . . You stinker! You whelp of a Polack, you! I hope they do haul you in and turn the fire hose on you, same as the last time!
STANLEY [*humbly*]: Eunice, I want my girl to come down with me!
EUNICE: Hah! [*She slams her door.*]
STANLEY [*with heaven-splitting violence*]: *STELLL-AHHHHH!*

The low-tone clarinet moans. The door upstairs opens again. STELLA *slips down the rickety stairs in her robe. Her eyes are glistening with tears and her hair loose about her throat and shoulders. They stare at each other. Then they come together with low, animal moans. He falls on his knees on the steps and presses his face to her belly, curving a little with maternity. Her eyes go blind with tenderness as she catches his head and raises him level with her. He snatches the screen door open and lifts her off her feet and bears her into the dark flat.*

BLANCHE *comes out on the upper landing in her robe and slips fearfully down the steps.*

BLANCHE: Where is my little sister? Stella? Stella? [*She stops before the dark entrance of her sister's flat. Then catches her breath as if struck. She rushes down to the walk before the house. She looks right and left as if for sanctuary.*]

The music fades away. MITCH *appears from around the corner.*

MITCH: Miss DuBois?
BLANCHE: Oh!
MITCH: All quiet on the Potomac now?
BLANCHE: She ran downstairs and went back in there with him.
MITCH: Sure she did.
BLANCHE: I'm terrified!
MITCH: Ho-ho! There's nothing to be scared of. They're crazy about each other.
BLANCHE: I'm not used to such—
MITCH: Naw, it's a shame this had to happen when you just got here. But don't take it serious.
BLANCHE: Violence! Is so—
MITCH: Set down on the steps and have a cigarette with me.
BLANCHE: I'm not properly dressed.
MITCH: That don't make no difference in the Quarter.
BLANCHE: Such a pretty silver case.
MITCH: I showed you the inscription, didn't I?
BLANCHE: Yes. [*During the pause, she looks up at the sky.*] There's so much—so much confusion in the world. . . .

He coughs diffidently.

Thank you for being so kind! I need kindness now.

SCENE FOUR

It is early the following morning. There is a confusion of street cries like a choral chant.

> STELLA *is lying down in the bedroom. Her face is serene in the early morning sunlight. One hand rests on her belly, rounding slightly with new maternity. From the other dangles a book of coloured comics. Her eyes and lips have that almost narcotized tranquillity that is in the faces of Eastern idols.*
> *The table is sloppy with remains of breakfast and the debris of the preceding night, and* STANLEY's *gaudy pyjamas lie across the threshold of the bathroom. The outside door is slightly ajar on a sky of summer brilliance.*
> BLANCHE *appears at this door. She has spent a sleepless night and her appearance entirely contrasts with* STELLA's. *She presses her knuckles nervously to her lips as she looks through the door, before entering.*

BLANCHE: Stella?
STELLA [*stirring lazily*]: Hmmh?

> BLANCHE *utters a moaning cry and runs into the bedroom, throwing herself down beside* STELLA *in a rush of hysterical tenderness.*

BLANCHE: Baby, my baby sister!
STELLA [*drawing away from her*]: Blanche, what is the matter with you?

> BLANCHE *straightens up slowly and stands beside the bed looking down at her sister with knuckles pressed to her lips.*

BLANCHE: He's left?
STELLA: Stan? Yes.
BLANCHE: Will he be back?
STELLA: He's gone to get the car greased. Why?
BLANCHE: Why! I've been half crazy, Stella! When I found out you'd been insane enough to come back in here after what happened—I started to rush in after you!
STELLA: I'm glad you didn't.
BLANCHE: What were you thinking of?

> STELLA *makes an indefinite gesture.*

Answer me! What? What?
STELLA: Please, Blanche! Sit down and stop yelling.
BLANCHE: All right, Stella. I will repeat the question quietly now. How could you come back in this place last night? Why, you must have slept with him!

STELLA *gets up in a calm and leisurely way.*

STELLA: Blanche, I'd forgotten how excitable you are. You're making much too much fuss about this.

BLANCHE: Am I?

STELLA: Yes, you are, Blanche. I know how it must have seemed to you and I'm awful sorry it had to happen, but it wasn't anything as serious as you seem to take it. In the first place, when men are drinking and playing poker anything can happen. It's always a powder-keg. He didn't know what he was doing. . . . He was as good as a lamb when I came back and he's really very, very ashamed of himself.

BLANCHE: And that—that makes it all right?

STELLA: No, it isn't all right for anybody to make such a terrible row, but—people do sometimes. Stanley's always smashed things. Why, on our wedding night—soon as we came in here—he snatched off one of my slippers and rushed about the place smashing the light-bulbs with it.

BLANCHE: He did—*what?*

STELLA: He smashed all the light-bulbs with the heel of my slipper! [*She laughs.*]

BLANCHE: And you—you *let* him? Didn't *run*, didn't *scream?*

STELLA: I was—sort of—thrilled by it. [*She waits for a moment.*] Eunice and you had breakfast?

BLANCHE: Do you suppose I wanted any breakfast?

STELLA: There's some coffee left on the stove.

BLANCHE: You're so—matter of fact about it, Stella.

STELLA: What other can I be? He's taken the radio to get it fixed. It didn't land on the pavement so only one tube was smashed.

BLANCHE: And you are standing there smiling!

STELLA: What do you want me to do?

BLANCHE: Pull yourself together and face the facts.

STELLA: What are they, in your opinion?

BLANCHE: In my opinion? You're married to a madman!

STELLA: No!

BLANCHE: Yes, you are, your fix is worse than mine is! Only you're not being sensible about it. I'm going to *do* something. Get hold of myself and make myself a new life!

STELLA: Yes?

BLANCHE: But you've given in. And that isn't right, you're not old! You can get out.

STELLA [*slowly and emphatically*]: I'm not in anything I want to get out of.

BLANCHE [*incredulously*]: What—Stella?

STELLA: I said I am not in anything that I have a desire to get out of. Look at the mess in this room! And those empty bottles! They went through two cases last night! He promised this morning that he was going to quit having these poker parties, but you know how long such a promise is going to keep. Oh, well, it's his pleasure, like mine is movies and bridge. People have got to tolerate each other's habits, I guess.

BLANCHE: I don't understand you.

STELLA *turns toward her.*

I don't understand your indifference. Is this a Chinese philosophy you've—cultivated?

STELLA: Is what—what?

BLANCHE: This—shuffling about and mumbling—'One tube smashed—beer-bottles—mess in the kitchen'—as if nothing out of the ordinary has happened!

STELLA *laughs uncertainly and, picking up the broom, twirls it in her hands.*

Are you deliberately shaking that thing in my face?

STELLA: No.

BLANCHE: Stop it. Let go of that broom. I won't have you cleaning up for him!

STELLA: Then who's going to do it? Are you?

BLANCHE: I? I!

STELLA: No, I didn't think so.

BLANCHE: Oh, let me think, if only my mind would function! We've got to get hold of some money, that's the way out!

STELLA: I guess that money is always nice to get hold of.

BLANCHE: Listen to me. I have an idea of some kind. [*Shakily she twists a cigarette into her holder.*] Do you remember Shep Huntleigh?

STELLA *shakes her head.*

Of course you remember Shep Huntleigh. I went out with him at college and wore his pin for a while. Well—

STELLA: Well?

BLANCHE: I ran into him last winter. You know I went to Miami during the Christmas holidays?

STELLA: No.

BLANCHE: Well, I did. I took the trip as an investment, thinking I'd meet someone with a million dollars.

STELLA: Did you?

BLANCHE: Yes. I ran into Shep Huntleigh—I ran into him on Biscayne Boulevard, on Christmas Eve, about dusk . . . getting into his car—Cadillac convertible; must have been a block long!

STELLA: I should think it would have been—inconvenient in traffic!

BLANCHE: You've heard of oil-wells?

STELLA: Yes—remotely.

BLANCHE: He has them, all over Texas. Texas is literally spouting gold in his pockets.

STELLA: My, my.

BLANCHE: Y'know how indifferent I am to money. I think of money in terms of what it does for you. But he could do it, he could certainly do it!

STELLA: Do what, Blanche?

BLANCHE: Why—set us up in a—shop!

STELLA: What kind of a shop?

BLANCHE: Oh, a—shop of some kind! He could do it with half what his wife throws away at the races.

STELLA: He's married?

BLANCHE: Honey, would I be here if the man weren't married?

STELLA *laughs a little.* BLANCHE *suddenly springs up and crosses to phone. She speaks shrilly.*

How do I get Western Union? Operator! Western Union!
STELLA: That's a dial phone, honey.
BLANCHE: I can't dial, I'm too—
STELLA: Just dial O.
BLANCHE: O?
STELLA: Yes, 'O' for Operator!

BLANCHE *considers a moment; then she puts the phone down.*

BLANCHE: Give me a pencil. Where is a slip of paper? I've got to write it down first—the message, I mean. . . . [*She goes to the dressing-table, and grabs up a sheet of Kleenex and an eyebrow pencil for writing equipment.*] Let me see now . . . [*She bites the pencil.*] 'Darling Shep. Sister and I in desperate situation.'
STELLA: I beg your pardon!
BLANCHE: 'Sister and I in desperate situation. Will explain details later. Would you be interested in—?' [*She bites the pencil again.*] 'Would you be—interested—in . . .' [*She smashes the pencil on the table and springs up.*] You never get anywhere with direct appeals!
STELLA [*with a laugh*]: Don't be so ridiculous, darling!
BLANCHE: But I'll think of something, I've *got* to think of—*some*thing! Don't, don't laugh at me, Stella! Please, please don't—I—I want you to look at the contents of my purse! Here's what's in it! [*She snatches her purse open.*] Sixty-five measly cents in coin of the realm!
STELLA [*crossing to bureau*]: Stanley doesn't give me a regular allowance, he likes to pay bills himself, but—this morning he gave me ten dollars to smooth things over. You take five of it, Blanche, and I'll keep the rest.
BLANCHE: Oh, no. No, Stella.
STELLA [*insisting*]: I know how it helps your morale just having a little pocket-money on you.
BLANCHE: No, thank you—I'll take to the streets!
STELLA: Talk sense! How did you happen to get so low on funds?
BLANCHE: Money just goes—it goes places. [*She rubs her forehead.*] Sometime today I've got to get hold of a bromo!
STELLA: I'll fix you one now.
BLANCHE: Not yet—I've got to keep thinking!
STELLA: I wish you'd just let things go, at least for a—while . . .
BLANCHE: Stella, I can't live with him! You can, he's your husband. But how could I stay here with him, after last night, with just those curtains between us?
STELLA: Blanche, you saw him at his worst last night.
BLANCHE: On the contrary, I saw him at his best! What such a man has to offer is animal force and he gave a wonderful exhibition of that! But the only way to live with such a man is to—go to bed with him! And that's your job—not mine!
STELLA: After you've rested a little, you'll see it's going to work out. You don't have to worry about anything while you're here. I mean—expenses . . .
BLANCHE: I have to plan for us both, to get us both—out!
STELLA: You take it for granted that I am in something that I want to get out of.
BLANCHE: I take it for granted that you still have sufficient memory of Belle Reve to find this place and these poker players impossible to live with.

STELLA: Well, you're taking entirely too much for granted.

BLANCHE: I can't believe you're in earnest.

STELLA: No?

BLANCHE: I understand how it happened—a little. You saw him in uniform, an officer, not here but—

STELLA: I'm not sure it would have made any difference where I saw him.

BLANCHE: Now don't say it was one of those mysterious electric things between people! If you do I'll laugh in your face.

STELLA: I am not going to say anything more at all about it!

BLANCHE: All right, then, don't!

STELLA: But there are things that happen between a man and a woman in the dark—that sort of make everything else seem—unimportant. [*Pause.*]

BLANCHE: What you are talking about is brutal desire—just—Desire!—the name of that rattle-trap street-car that bangs through the Quarter, up one old narrow street and down another . . .

STELLA: Haven't you ever ridden on that street-car?

BLANCHE: It brought me here—Where I'm not wanted and where I'm ashamed to be . . .

STELLA: Then don't you think your superior attitude is a bit out of place?

BLANCHE: I am not being or feeling at all superior, Stella. Believe me I'm not! It's just this. This is how I look at it. A man like that is someone to go out with—once—twice—three times when the devil is in you. But live with! Have a child by?

STELLA: I have told you I love him.

BLANCHE: Then I *tremble* for you! I just—*tremble* for you. . . .

STELLA: I can't help your trembling if you insist on trembling!

There is a pause.

BLANCHE: May I—speak—*plainly?*

STELLA: Yes, do. Go ahead. As plainly as you want to.

Outside a train approaches. They are silent till the noise subsides. They are both in the bedroom.

Under cover of the train's noise STANLEY *enters from outside. He stands unseen by the women, holding some packages in his arms, and overhears their following conversation. He wears an undershirt and grease-stained seersucker pants.*

BLANCHE: Well—if you'll forgive me—he's *common!*

STELLA: Why, yes, I suppose he is.

BLANCHE: Suppose! You can't have forgotten that much of our bringing up, Stella, that you just *suppose* that any part of a gentleman's in his nature! *Not one particle, no!* Oh, if he was just—*ordinary!* Just *plain*—but good and wholesome, but—*no.* There's something downright—*bestial*—about him! You're hating me saying this, aren't you?

STELLA [*coldly*]: Go on and say it all, Blanche.

BLANCHE: He acts like an animal, has an animal's habits! Eats like one, moves like one, talks like one! There's even something—sub-human—something not quite to the stage of humanity yet! Yes, something—ape-like about him, like one of those pictures I've seen in—anthropological studies! Thousands and thousands of years have passed him right by, and there he is–Stanley Kowalski– survivor of the Stone Age! Bearing the raw meat home from the kill in the jungle! And you–*you* here–*waiting* for him! Maybe he'll strike you or maybe grunt and kiss you! That is, if kisses have been discovered yet! Night falls and the other apes gather! There in the front of the cave, all grunting like him, and swilling and gnawing and hulking! His poker night!–you call it–this party of apes! Somebody growls–some creature snatches at something–the fight is on! *God!* Maybe we are a long way from being made in God's image, but Stella–my sister–there has been *some* progress since then! Such things as art– as poetry and music–such kinds of new light have come into the world since then! In some kinds of people some tenderer feelings have had some little beginning! That we have got to make *grow!* And *cling* to, and hold as our flag! In this dark march toward whatever it is we're approaching. . . . *Don't–don't hang back with the brutes!*

Another train passes outside. STANLEY *hesitates, licking his lips. Then suddenly he turns stealthily about and withdraws through the front door. The women are still unaware of his presence. When the train has passed he calls through the closed front door.*

STANLEY: Hey! Hey! Stella!
STELLA [*who has listened gravely to* BLANCHE]: Stanley!
BLANCHE: Stell, I—

But STELLA *has gone to the front door.* STANLEY *enters casually with his packages.*

STANLEY: Hiyuh, Stella, Blanche back?
STELLA: Yes, she's back.
STANLEY: Hiyuh, Blanche. [*He grins at her.*]
STELLA: You must've got under the car.
STANLEY: Them darn mechanics at Fritz's don't know their can from third base!

STELLA *has embraced him with both arms, fiercely, and full in the view of* BLANCHE. *He laughs and clasps her head to him. Over her head he grins through the curtains at* BLANCHE.
As the lights fade away, with a lingering brightness on their embrace, the music of the 'blue piano' and trumpet and drums is heard.

SCENE FIVE

BLANCHE *is seated in the bedroom fanning herself with a palm leaf as she reads over a just completed letter. Suddenly she bursts into a peal of laughter.* STELLA *is dressing in the bedroom.*

STELLA: What are you laughing at, honey?
BLANCHE: Myself, myself, for being such a liar! I'm writing a letter to Shep. [*She picks up the letter.*] 'Darling Shep. I am spending the summer on the wing, making flying visits here and there. And who knows, perhaps I shall take a sudden notion to *swoop* down on *Dallas!* How would you feel about that? Ha-ha! [*She laughs nervously and brightly, touching her throat as if actually talking to* SHEP.] Forewarned is forearmed, as they say!'—How does that sound?
STELLA: Uh-huh . . .
BLANCHE [*going on nervously*]: 'Most of my sister's friends go north in the summer but some have homes on the Gulf and there has been a continued round of entertainments, teas, cocktails, and luncheons—'

A disturbance is heard upstairs at the HUBBELS' *apartment.*

STELLA [*crossing to the door*]: Eunice seems to be having some trouble with Steve.

EUNICE'S *voice shouts in terrible wrath.*

EUNICE: I heard about you and that blonde!
STEVE: That's a damn lie!
EUNICE: You ain't pulling the wool over my eyes! I wouldn't mind if you'd stay down at the Four Deuces, but you always going up.
STEVE: Who ever seen me up?
EUNICE: I seen you chasing her 'round the balcony—I'm gonna call the vice squad!
STEVE: Don't you throw that at me!
EUNICE [*shrieking*]: You hit me! I'm gonna call the police!

A clatter of aluminium striking a wall is heard, followed by a man's angry roar, shouts, and overturned furniture. There is a crash; then a relative hush.

BLANCHE [*brightly*]: Did he *kill* her?

EUNICE *appears on the steps in daemonic disorder.*

STELLA: No! She's coming downstairs.

EUNICE: Call the police, I'm going to call the police! [*She rushes around the corner.*]

STELLA [*returning from the door*]: Some of your sister's friends have stayed in the city.

They laugh lightly. STANLEY *comes around the corner in his green and scarlet silk bowling shirt. He trots up the steps and bangs into the kitchen.* BLANCHE *registers his entrance with nervous gestures.*

STANLEY: What's a matter with Eun-uss?

STELLA: She and Steve had a row. Has she got the police?

STANLEY: Naw. She's gettin' a drink.

STELLA: That's much more practical!

STEVE *comes down nursing a bruise on his forehead and looks in the door.*

STEVE: *She here?*

STANLEY: Naw, naw. At the Four Deuces.

STEVE: That hunk! [*He looks around the corner a bit timidly, then turns with affected boldness and runs after her.*]

BLANCHE: I must jot that down in my notebook. Ha-ha! I'm compiling a notebook of quaint little words and phrases I've picked up here.

STANLEY: You won't pick up nothing here you ain't heard before.

BLANCHE: Can I count on that?

STANLEY: You can count on it up to five hundred.

BLANCHE: That's a mighty high number.

He jerks open the bureau drawer, slams it shut, and throws shoes in a corner. At each noise BLANCHE *winces slightly. Finally she speaks.*

What sign were you born under?

STANLEY [*while he is dressing*]: Sign?

BLANCHE: Astrological sign. I bet you were born under Aries. Aries people are forceful and dynamic. They dote on noise! They love to bang things around! You must have had lots of banging around in the army, and now that you're out, you make up for it by treating inanimate objects with such a fury!

STELLA *has been going in and out of closet during this scene. Now she pops her head out of the closet.*

STELLA: Stanley was born just five minutes after Christmas.

BLANCHE: Capricorn–the Goat!

STANLEY: What sign were *you* born under?

BLANCHE: Oh, my birthday's next month, the fifteenth of September, that's under Virgo.

STANLEY: What's Virgo?

BLANCHE: Virgo is the Virgin.

STANLEY [*contemptuously*]: Hah! [*He advances a little as he knots his tie.*] Say, do you happen to know somebody named Shaw?

Her face expresses a faint shock. She reaches for the cologne bottle and dampens her handkerchief as she answers carefully.

BLANCHE: Why, everybody knows somebody named Shaw!
STANLEY: Well, this somebody named Shaw is under the impression he met you in Laurel, but I figure he must have got you mixed up with some other party because this other party is someone he met at a hotel called the Flamingo.

> BLANCHE *laughs breathlessly as she touches the cologne-dampened handkerchief to her temples.*

BLANCHE: I'm afraid he does seem to have me mixed up with this 'other party'. The Hotel Flamingo is not the sort of establishment I would dare to be seen in!
STANLEY: You know of it?
BLANCHE: Yes, I've seen it and smelled it.
STANLEY: You must've got pretty close if you could smell it.
BLANCHE: The odour of cheap perfume is penetrating.
STANLEY: That stuff you use is expensive?
BLANCHE: Twenty-five dollars an ounce! I'm nearly out. That's just a hint if you want to remember my birthday! [*She speaks lightly but her voice has a note of fear.*]
STANLEY: Shaw must've got you mixed up. He goes in and out of Laurel all the time, so he can check on it and clear up any mistake.

> *He turns away and crosses to the portières.* BLANCHE *closes her eyes as if faint. Her hand trembles as she lifts the handkerchief again to her forehead.*
> STEVE *and* EUNICE *come around the corner.* STEVE's *arm is around* EUNICE's *shoulder and she is sobbing luxuriously and he is cooing love-words. there is a murmur of thunder as they go slowly upstairs in a tight embrace.*

STANLEY [*to* STELLA]: I'll wait for you at the Four Deuces!
STELLA: Hey! Don't I rate one kiss?
STANLEY: Not in front of your sister.

> *He goes out.* BLANCHE *rises from her chair. She seems faint; looks about her with an expression of almost panic.*

BLANCHE: Stella! What have you heard about me?
STELLA: Huh?
BLANCHE: What have people been telling you about me?
STELLA: Telling?
BLANCHE: You haven't heard any–unkind–gossip about me?
STELLA: Why, no, Blanche, of course not!
BLANCHE: Honey, there was–a good deal of talk in Laurel.
STELLA: About *you*, Blanche?
BLANCHE: I wasn't so good the last two years or so, after Belle Reve had started to slip through my fingers.
STELLA: All of us do things we—
BLANCHE: I never was hard or self-sufficient enough. When people are soft–soft people have got to court the favour of hard ones, Stella. Have got to be seductive–put on soft colours, the colours of butterfly wings, and

glow—make a little—temporary magic just in order to pay for—one night's shelter! That's why I've been—not so awf'ly good lately. I've run for protection, Stella, from under one leaky roof to another leaky roof—because it was storm—all storm, and I was—caught in the centre. . . . People don't see you—*men* don't—don't even admit your existence unless they are making love to you. And you've got to have your existence admitted by someone, if you're going to have someone's protection. And so the soft people have got to—shimmer and glow—put a—paper lantern over the light. . . . But I'm scared now—awf'ly scared. I don't know how much longer I can turn the trick. It isn't enough to be soft. You've got to be soft *and attractive*. And I—I'm fading now!

The afternoon has faded to dusk. STELLA *goes into the bedroom and turns on the light under the paper lantern. She holds a bottled soft drink in her hand.*

Have you been listening to me?
STELLA: I don't listen to you when you are being morbid! [*She advances with the bottled coke.*]
BLANCHE [*with abrupt change to gaiety*]: Is that coke for me?
STELLA: Not for anyone else!
BLANCHE: Why, you precious thing, you! Is it just coke?
STELLA [*turning*]: You mean you want a shot in it!
BLANCHE: Well, honey, a shot never does a coke any harm! Let me? You mustn't wait on me!
STELLA: I like to wait on you, Blanche. It makes it seem more like home. [*She goes into the kitchen, finds a glass, and pours a shot of whisky into it.*]
BLANCHE: I have to admit I love to be waited on. . . .

She rushes into the bedroom. STELLA *goes to her with the glass.* BLANCHE *suddenly clutches* STELLA'S *free hand with a moaning sound and presses the hand to her lips.* STELLA *is embarrassed by her show of emotion.* BLANCHE *speaks in a choked voice.*

You're—you're—so *good* to me! And I—
STELLA: Blanche.
BLANCHE: I know, I won't! You hate me to talk sentimental. But honey, *believe* I feel things more than I *tell* you! I *won't* stay long! I won't, I *promise* I—
STELLA: Blanche!
BLANCHE [*hysterically*]: I won't, I promise, *I'll* go! Go *soon!* I will *really!* I *won't* hang around until he—throws me out. . . .
STELLA: Now will you stop talking foolish?
BLANCHE: Yes, honey. Watch how you pour—that fizzy stuff foams over!

BLANCHE *laughs shrilly and grabs the glass, but her hand shakes so it almost slips from her grasp.* STELLA *pours the coke into the glass. It foams over and spills.* BLANCHE *gives a piercing cry.*

STELLA [*shocked by the cry*]: Heavens!
BLANCHE: Right on my pretty white skirt!
STELLA: Oh. . . . Use my hanky. Blot gently.
BLANCHE [*slowly recovering*]: I know—gently—gently . . .

STELLA: Did it stain?

BLANCHE: Not a bit. Ha-ha! Isn't that lucky? [*She sits down shakily, taking a grateful drink. She holds the glass in both hands and continues to laugh a little.*]

STELLA: Why did you scream like that?

BLANCHE: I don't know why I screamed! [*Continuing nervously.*] Mitch—Mitch is coming at seven. I guess I am just feeling nervous about our relations. [*She begins to talk rapidly and breathlessly.*] He hasn't gotten a thing but a good-night kiss, that's all I have given him, Stella. I want his respect. And men don't want anything they get too easy. But on the other hand men lose interest quickly. Especially when the girl is over—thirty. They think a girl over thirty ought to—the vulgar term is—'put out'. . . . And I—I'm not 'putting out'. Of course he—he doesn't know—I mean I haven't informed him—of my real age!

STELLA: Why are you sensitive about your age?

BLANCHE: Because of hard knocks my vanity's been given. What I mean is—he thinks I'm sort of—prim and proper, you know! [*She laughs out sharply.*] I want to *deceive* him enough to make him—want me. . . .

STELLA: Blanche, do you want *him?*

BLANCHE: I want to *rest!* I want to breathe quietly again! Yes—I *want* Mitch . . . *very badly!* Just think! If it happens! I can leave here and not be anyone's problem. . . .

STANLEY *comes round the corner with a drink under his belt.*

STANLEY [*bawling*]: Hey, Steve! Hey, Eunice! Hey, Stella!

There are joyous calls from above. Trumpet and drums are heard from around the corner.

STELLA [*kissing* BLANCHE *impulsively*]: It *will* happen!

BLANCHE [*doubtfully*]: It will?

STELLA: It *will!* [*She goes across into the kitchen, looking back at* BLANCHE.] It will, honey, *it will*. . . . But don't take another drink! [*Her voice catches as she goes out of the door to meet her husband.*]

BLANCHE *sinks faintly back in her chair with her drink.* EUNICE *shrieks with laughter and runs down the steps.* STEVE *bounds after her with goat-like screeches and chases her around corner.* STANLEY *and* STELLA *twine arms as they follow, laughing. Dusk settles deeper. The music from the Four Deuces is slow and blue.*

BLANCHE: Ah, me, ah, me, ah, me . . .

Her eyes fall shut and the palm leaf drops from her fingers. She slaps her hand on the chair arm a couple of times; then she raises herself wearily to her feet and picks up the hand mirror. There is a little glimmer of lightning about the building. The NEGRO WOMAN, *cackling hysterically, swaying drunkenly, comes around the corner from the Four Deuces. At the same time, a* YOUNG MAN *enters from the opposite direction. The* NEGRO WOMAN *snaps her fingers before his belt.*

NEGRO WOMAN: Hey! Sugar!

She says something indistinguishable. The YOUNG MAN *shakes his head violently and edges hastily up the steps. He rings the bell.* BLANCHE *puts down the mirror. The* NEGRO WOMAN *has wandered down the street.*

BLANCHE: Come in.

The YOUNG MAN *appears through the portières. She regards him with interest.*

Well, well! What can I do for *you?*
YOUNG MAN: I'm collecting for the *Evening Star.*
BLANCHE: I didn't know that stars took up collections.
YOUNG MAN: It's the paper.
BLANCHE: I know, I was joking—feebly! Will you—have a drink?
YOUNG MAN: No, ma'am. No, thank you. I can't drink on the job.
BLANCHE: Oh, well, now, let's see. . . . No, I don't have a dime! I'm not the lady of the house. I'm her sister from Mississippi. I'm one of those poor relations you've heard about.
YOUNG MAN: That's all right. I'll drop by later.

He starts to go out. She approaches a little.

BLANCHE: Hey!

He turns back shyly. She puts a cigarette in a long holder.

Could you give me a light?

She crosses toward him. They meet at the door between the two rooms.

YOUNG MAN: Sure. [*He takes out a lighter.*] This doesn't always work.
BLANCHE: It's temperamental? [*It flares.*] Ah! Thank you.
YOUNG MAN: Thank *you!* [*He starts away again.*]
BLANCHE: Hey!

He turns again, still more uncertainly. She goes close to him.

What time is it?
YOUNG MAN: Fifteen of seven.
BLANCHE: So late? Don't you just love these long rainy afternoons in New Orleans when an hour isn't just an hour—but a little bit of Eternity dropped in your hands—and who knows what to do with it?
YOUNG MAN: Yes, ma'am.

In the ensuing pause, the 'blue piano' is heard. It continues through the rest of this scene and the opening of the next. The YOUNG MAN *clears his throat and looks glancingly at the door.*

BLANCHE: You—uh—didn't get wet in the shower?
YOUNG MAN: No, ma'am. I stepped inside.

BLANCHE: In a drug-store? And had a soda?
YOUNG MAN: Uhhuh.
BLANCHE: Chocolate?
YOUNG MAN: No, ma'am. Cherry.
BLANCHE: Mmmm!
YOUNG MAN: A cherry soda!
BLANCHE: You make my mouth water.
YOUNG MAN: Well, I'd better be—
BLANCHE: Young man! Young, young, young, young–man! Has anyone ever told you that you look like a young prince out of the Arabian Nights?
YOUNG MAN: No, ma'am.

The YOUNG MAN *laughs uncomfortably and stands like a bashful kid.* BLANCHE *speaks softly to him.*

BLANCHE: Well, you do, honey lamb. Come here! Come on over here like I told you! I want to kiss you–just once–softly and sweetly on your mouth. [*Without waiting for him to accept, she crosses quickly to him and presses her lips to his.*] Run along now! It would be nice to keep you, but I've got to be good and keep my hands off children. Adios!
YOUNG MAN: Huh?

He stares at her a moment. She opens the door for him and blows a kiss to him as he goes down the steps with a dazed look. She stands there a little dreamily after he has disappeared. Then MITCH *appears around the corner with a bunch of roses.*

BLANCHE: Look who's coming! My Rosenkavalier! Bow to me first! Now present them.

He does so. She curtsies low.

Ahhh! Merciiii!

SCENE SIX

It is about two a.m. the same night. The outer wall of the building is visible.
BLANCHE *and* MITCH *come in. The utter exhaustion which only a neurasthenic personality can know is evident in* BLANCHE'S *voice and manner.* MITCH *is stolid but depressed. They have probably been out to the amusement park on Lake Pontchartrain, for* MITCH *is bearing, upside down, a plaster statuette of Mae West, the sort of prize won at shooting-galleries and carnival games of chance.*

BLANCHE [*stopping lifelessly at the steps*]: Well–

MITCH *laughs uneasily.*

Well . . .
MITCH: I guess it must be pretty late–and you're tired.
BLANCHE: Even the hot tamale man has deserted the street, and he hangs on till the end.

MITCH *laughs uneasily again.*

How will you get home?
MITCH: I'll walk over to Bourbon and catch an owl-car.
BLANCHE [*laughing grimly*]: Is that streetcar named Desire still grinding along the tracks at this hour?
MITCH [*heavily*]: I'm afraid you haven't gotten much fun out of this evening, Blanche.
BLANCHE: I spoiled it for *you*.
MITCH: No, you didn't, but I felt all the time that I wasn't giving you much–entertainment.
BLANCHE: I simply couldn't rise to the occasion. That was all. I don't think I've ever tried so hard to be gay and made such a dismal mess of it. I get ten points for trying!–I *did* try.
MITCH: Why did you try if you didn't feel like it, Blanche?
BLANCHE: I was just obeying the law of nature.
MITCH: Which law is that?
BLANCHE: The one that says the lady must entertain the gentleman–or no dice! See if you can locate my door-key in this purse. When I'm so tired my fingers are all thumbs!
MITCH [*rooting in her purse*]: This it?
BLANCHE: No, honey, that's the key to my trunk which I must soon be packing.
MITCH: You mean you are leaving here soon?
BLANCHE: I've outstayed my welcome.
MITCH: This it?

The music fades away.

BLANCHE: Eureka! Honey, you open the door while I take a last look at the sky.

She leans on the porch rail. He opens the door and stands awkwardly behind her.

I'm looking for the Pleiades, the Seven Sisters, but these girls are not out tonight. Oh, yes they are, there they are! God bless them! All in a bunch going home from their little bridge party. . . . Y' get the door open? Good boy! I guess you—want to go now . . .

He shuffles and coughs a little.

MITCH: Can I—uh—kiss you—good-night?
BLANCHE: Why do you always ask me if you may?
MITCH: I don't know whether you want me to or not.
BLANCHE: Why should you be so doubtful?
MITCH: That night when we parked by the lake and I kissed you, you—
BLANCHE: Honey, it wasn't the kiss I objected to. I liked the kiss very much. It was the other little—familiarity—that I—felt obliged to—discourage. . . . I didn't resent it! Not a bit in the world! In fact, I was somewhat flattered that you—desired me! But, honey, you know as well as I do that a single girl, a girl alone in the world, has got to keep a firm hold on her emotions or she'll be lost!
MITCH [*solemnly*]: Lost?
BLANCHE: I guess you are used to girls that like to be lost. The kind that get lost immediately, on the first date!
MITCH: I like you to be exactly the way that you are, because in all my—experience—I have never known anyone like you.

BLANCHE *looks at him gravely; then she bursts into laughter and then claps a hand to her mouth.*

Are you laughing at me?
BLANCHE: No, honey. The lord and lady of the house have not yet returned, so come in. We'll have a night-cap. Let's leave the lights off. Shall we?
MITCH: You just—do what you want to.

BLANCHE *precedes him into the kitchen. The outer wall of the building disappears and the interiors of the two rooms can be dimly seen.*

BLANCHE [*remaining in the first room*]: The other room's more comfortable—go on in. This crashing around in the dark is my search for some liquor.
MITCH: You want a drink?
BLANCHE: I want *you* to have a drink! You have been so anxious and solemn all evening, and so have I; we have both been anxious and solemn and now for these few last remaining moments of our lives together—I want to create—*joie de vivre!* I'm lighting a candle.
MITCH: That's good.
BLANCHE: We are going to be very Bohemian. We are going to pretend that we

are sitting in a little artists' café on the Left Bank in Paris! [*She lights a candle stub and puts it in a bottle.*] *Je suis la Dame aux Camellias! Vous êtes–Armand!* Understand French?

MITCH [*heavily*]: Naw. Naw, I—

BLANCHE: *Voulez-vous couchez avec moi ce soir? Vous ne comprenez pas? Ah, quel dommage!*–I mean it's a damned good thing. . . . I've found some liquor! Just enough for two shots without any dividends, honey . . .

MITCH [*heavily*]: That's–good.

She enters the bedroom with the drinks and the candle.

BLANCHE: Sit down! Why don't you take off your coat and loosen your collar?

MITCH: I better leave it on.

BLANCHE: No. I want you to be comfortable.

MITCH: I am ashamed of the way I perspire. My shirt is sticking to me.

BLANCHE: Perspiration is healthy. If people didn't perspire they would die in five minutes. [*She takes his coat from him.*] This is a nice coat. What kind of material is it?

MITCH: They call that stuff alpaca.

BLANCHE: Oh. Alpaca.

MITCH: It's very light-weight alpaca.

BLANCHE: Oh. Light-weight alpaca.

MITCH: I don't like to wear a wash-coat even in summer because I sweat through it.

BLANCHE: Oh.

MITCH: And it don't look neat on me. A man with a heavy build has got to be careful of what he puts on him so he don't look too clumsy.

BLANCHE: You are not too heavy.

MITCH: You don't think I am?

BLANCHE: You are not the delicate type. You have a massive bone-structure and a very imposing physique.

MITCH: Thank you. Last Christmas I was given a membership to the New Orleans Athletic Club.

BLANCHE: Oh, good.

MITCH: It was the finest present I ever was given. I work out there with the weights and I swim and I keep myself fit. When I started there, I was getting soft in the belly but now my belly is hard. It is so hard that now a man can punch me in the belly and it don't hurt me. Punch me! Go on! See? [*She pokes lightly at him.*]

BLANCHE: Gracious. [*Her hand touches her chest.*]

MITCH: Guess how much I weigh, Blanche?

BLANCHE: Oh, I'd say in the vicinity of–one hundred and eighty?

MITCH: Guess again.

BLANCHE: Not that much?

MITCH: No. More.

BLANCHE: Well, you're a tall man and you can carry a good deal of weight without looking awkward.

MITCH: I weigh two hundred and seven pounds and I'm six feet one and a half inches tall in my bare feet–without shoes on. And that is what I weigh stripped.

BLANCHE: Oh, my goodness, me! It's awe-inspiring.

MITCH [*embarrassed*]: My weight is not a very interesting subject to talk about. [*He hesitates for a moment.*] What's yours?
BLANCHE: My weight?
MITCH: Yes.
BLANCHE: Guess!
MITCH: Let me lift you.
BLANCHE: Samson! Go on, lift me.

He comes behind her and puts his hands on her waist and raises her lightly off the ground.

Well?
MITCH: You are light as a feather.
BLANCHE: Ha-ha!

He lowers her but keeps his hands on her waist. BLANCHE *speaks with an affectation of demureness.*

You may release me now.
MITCH: Huh?
BLANCHE [*gaily*]: I said unhand me, sir.

He fumblingly embraces her. Her voice sounds gently reproving.

Now, Mitch. Just because Stanley and Stella aren't at home is no reason why you shouldn't behave like a gentleman.
MITCH: Just give me a slap whenever I step out of bounds.
BLANCHE: That won't be necessary. You're a natural gentleman, one of the very few that are left in the world. I don't want you to think that I am severe and old maid school-teacherish or anything like that. It's just—well—
MITCH: Huh?
BLANCHE: I guess it is just that I have—old-fashioned ideals!

She rolls her eyes, knowing he cannot see her face. MITCH *goes to the front door. There is a considerable silence between them.* BLANCHE *sighs and* MITCH *coughs self-consciously.*

MITCH [*finally*]: Where's Stanley and Stella tonight?
BLANCHE: They have gone out. With Mr and Mrs Hubbel upstairs.
MITCH: Where did they go?
BLANCHE: I think they were planning to go to a midnight preview of Loew's State.
MITCH: We should all go out together some night.
BLANCHE: No. That wouldn't be a good plan.
MITCH: Why not?
BLANCHE: You are an old friend of Stanley's?
MITCH: We was together in the Two-forty-first.
BLANCHE: I guess he talks to you frankly?
MITCH: Sure.
BLANCHE: Has he talked to you about me?
MITCH: Oh—not very much.

BLANCHE: The way you say that, I suspect that he has.

MITCH: No, he hasn't said much.

BLANCHE: But what he *has* said. What would you say his attitude toward me was?

MITCH: Why do you want to ask that?

BLANCHE: Well—

MITCH: Don't you get along with him?

BLANCHE: What do you think?

MITCH: I don't think he understands you.

BLANCHE: That is putting it mildly. If it weren't for Stella about to have a baby, I wouldn't be able to endure things here.

MITCH: He isn't–nice to you?

BLANCHE: He is insufferably rude. Goes out of his way to offend me.

MITCH: In what way, Blanche?

BLANCHE: Why, in every conceivable way.

MITCH: I'm surprised to hear that.

BLANCHE: Are you?

MITCH: Well, I–don't see how anybody could be rude to you.

BLANCHE: It's really a pretty frightful situation. You see, there's no privacy here. There's just these portières between the two rooms at night. He stalks through the rooms in his underwear at night. And I have to ask him to close the bathroom door. That sort of commonness isn't necessary. You probably wonder why I don't move out. Well, I'll tell you frankly. A teacher's salary is barely sufficient for her living-expenses. I didn't save a penny last year and so I had to come here for the summer. That's why I have to put up with my sister's husband. And he has to put up with me, apparently so much against his wishes. . . . Surely he must have told you how much he hates me!

MITCH: I don't think he hates you.

BLANCHE: He hates me. Or why would he insult me? Of course there is such a thing as the hostility of–perhaps in some perverse kind of way he–No! To think of it makes me . . . [*She makes a gesture of revulsion. Then she finishes her drink. A pause follows.*]

MITCH: Blanche—

BLANCHE: Yes, honey?

MITCH: Can I ask you a question?

BLANCHE: Yes. What?

MITCH: How old are you?

She makes a nervous gesture.

BLANCHE: Why do you want to know?

MITCH: I talked to my mother about you and she said, 'How old is Blanche?' And I wasn't able to tell her.

There is another pause.

BLANCHE: You talked to your mother about me?

MITCH: Yes.

BLANCHE: Why?

MITCH: I told my mother how nice you were, and I liked you.

BLANCHE: Were you sincere about that?

MITCH: You know I was.
BLANCHE: Why did your mother want to know my age?
MITCH: Mother is sick.
BLANCHE: I'm sorry to hear it. Badly?
MITCH: She won't live long. Maybe just a few months.
BLANCHE: Oh.
MITCH: She worries because I'm not settled.
BLANCHE: Oh.
MITCH: She wants me to be settled down before she—[*His voice is hoarse and he clears his throat twice, shuffling nervously around with his hands in and out of his pockets.*]
BLANCHE: You love her very much, don't you?
MITCH: Yes.
BLANCHE: I think you have a great capacity for devotion. You will be lonely when she passes on, won't you?

MITCH *clears his throat and nods.*

I understand what that is.
MITCH: To be lonely?
BLANCHE: I loved someone, too, and the person I loved I lost.
MITCH: Dead?

She crosses to the window and sits on the sill, looking out. She pours herself another drink.

A man?
BLANCHE: He was a boy, just a boy, when I was a very young girl. When I was sixteen, I made the discovery—love. All and once and much, much too completely. It was like you suddenly turned a blinding light on something that had always been half in shadow, that's how it struck the world for me. But I was unlucky. Deluded. There was something different about the boy, a nervousness, a softness and tenderness which wasn't like a man's, although he wasn't the least bit effeminate-looking—still—that thing was there.... He came to me for help. I didn't know that. I didn't find out anything till after our marriage when we'd run away and come back and all I knew was I'd failed him in some mysterious way and wasn't able to give the help he needed but couldn't speak of! He was in the quicksands and clutching at me—but I wasn't holding him out, I was slipping in with him! I didn't know that. I didn't know anything except I loved him unendurably but without being able to help him or help myself. Then I found out. In the worst of all possible ways. By coming suddenly into a room that I thought was empty—which wasn't empty, but had two people in it ...

A locomotive is heard approaching outside. She claps her hands to her ears and crouches over. The headlight of the locomotive glares into the room as it thunders past. As the noise recedes she straightens slowly and continues speaking.

Afterwards we pretended that nothing had been discovered. Yes, the three of us drove out to Moon Lake Casino, very drunk and laughing all the way.

Polka music sounds, in a minor key faint with distance.

We danced the Varsouviana! Suddenly in the middle of the dance the boy I had married broke away from me and ran out of the casino. A few moments later—a shot!

The polka stops abruptly. BLANCHE *rises stiffly. Then the polka resumes in a major key.*

I ran out—all did—all ran and gathered about the terrible thing at the edge of the lake! I couldn't get near for the crowding. Then somebody caught my arm. 'Don't go any closer! Come back! You don't want to see!' See? See what! Then I heard voices say—Allan! Allan! The Grey boy! He'd stuck the revolver into his mouth, and fired—so that the back of his head had been—blown away!

She sways and covers her face.

It was because—on the dance-floor—unable to stop myself—I'd suddenly said—'I know! I know! You disgust me . . .' And then the searchlight which had been turned on the world was turned off again and never for one moment since has there been any light that's stronger than this—kitchen—candle. . . .

MITCH *gets up awkwardly and moves towards her a little. The polka music increases.* MITCH *stands beside her.*

MITCH [*drawing her slowly into his arms*]: You need somebody. And I need somebody, too. Could it be—you and me, Blanche?

She stares at him vacantly for a moment. Then with a soft cry huddles in his embrace. She makes a sobbing effort to speak but the words won't come. He kisses her forehead and her eyes and finally her lips. The polka tune fades out. Her breath is drawn and released in long, grateful sobs.

BLANCHE: Sometimes—there's God—so quickly!

SCENE SEVEN

It is late afternoon in mid-September. The portières are open and a table is set for a birthday supper, with cake and flowers.

STELLA *is completing the decorations as* STANLEY *comes in.*

STANLEY: What's all this stuff for?
STELLA: Honey, it's Blanche's birthday.
STANLEY: She here?
STELLA: In the bathroom.
STANLEY [*mimicking*]: 'Washing out some things'?
STELLA: I reckon so.
STANLEY: How long she been in there?
STELLA: All afternoon.
STANLEY [*mimicking*]: 'Soaking in a hot tub'?
STELLA: Yes.
STANLEY: Temperature 100 on the nose, and she soaks herself in a hot tub.
STELLA: She says it cools her off for the evening.
STANLEY: And you run out an' get her cokes, I suppose? And serve 'em to Her Majesty in the tub?

[STELLA *shrugs.*]

Set down here a minute.
STELLA: Stanley, I've got things to do.
STANLEY: Set down! I've got th' dope on your big sister, Stella.
STELLA: Stanley, stop picking on Blanche.
STANLEY: That girl calls *me* common!
STELLA: Lately you have been doing all you can think of to rub her the wrong way, Stanley, and Blanche is sensitive and you've got to realize that Blanche and I grew up under very different circumstances than you did.
STANLEY: So I been told. And told and told and told! You know she's been feeding us a pack of lies here?
STELLA: No, I don't, and—
STANLEY: Well, she has, however. But now the cat's out of the bag! I found out some things!
STELLA: What—things?
STANLEY: Things I already suspected. But now I got proof from the most reliable sources—which I have checked on!

BLANCHE *is singing in the bathroom a saccharine popular ballad which is used contrapuntally with* STANLEY's *speech.*

STELLA [*to* STANLEY]: Lower your voice!

STANLEY: Some canary-bird, huh!

STELLA: Now please tell me quietly what you think you've found out about my sister.

STANLEY: Lie Number One: All this squeamishness she puts on! You should just know the line she's been feeding to Mitch. He thought she had never been more than kissed by a fellow! But Sister Blanche is no lily! Ha-ha! Some lily she is!

STELLA: What have you heard and who from?

STANLEY: Our supply-man down at the plant has been going through Laurel for years and he knows all about her and everybody else in the town of Laurel knows all about her. She is as famous in Laurel as if she was the President of the United States, only she is not respected by any party! This supply-man stops at a hotel called the Flamingo.

BLANCHE [*singing blithely*]:
'Say, it's only a paper moon, Sailing over a cardboard sea–But it wouldn't be make-believe If you believed in me!'

STELLA: What about the–Flamingo?

STANLEY: She stayed there, too.

STELLA: My sister lived at Belle Reve.

STANLEY: This is after the home-place had slipped through her lily-white fingers! She moved to the Flamingo! A second-class hotel which has the advantage of not interfering in the private social life of the personalities there! The Flamingo is used to all kinds of goings-on. But even the management of the Flamingo was impressed by Dame Blanche! In fact they were so impressed by Dame Blanche that they requested her to turn in her room-key– for permanently! This happened a couple of weeks before she showed here.

BLANCHE [*singing*]:
'It's a Barnum and Bailey world, Just as phony as it can be–But it wouldn't be make-believe If you believed in me!'

STELLA: What–contemptible–lies!

STANLEY: Sure, I can see how you would be upset by this. She pulled the wool over your eyes as much as Mitch's!

STELLA: It's pure invention! There's not a word of truth in it and if I were a man and this creature had dared to invent such things in my presence—

BLANCHE [*singing*]:
                    'Without your love,
                    It's a honky-tonk parade!
                    Without your love,
                    It's a melody played In a penny arcade. . . .'

STANLEY: Honey, I told you I thoroughly checked on these stories! Now wait till I finish. The trouble with Dame Blanche was that she couldn't put on her act any more in Laurel! They got wised up after two or three dates with her and then they quit, and she goes on to another, the same old lines, same old act, same old hooey! But the town was too small for this to go on for ever! And as time went by she became a town character. Regarded as not just different but downright loco–nuts.

STELLA *draws back.*

And for the last year or two she has been washed up like poison. That's why she's here this summer, visiting royalty, putting on all this act—because she's practically told by the mayor to get out of town! Yes, did you know there was an army camp near Laurel and your sister's was one of the places called 'Out-of-Bounds'?

BLANCHE:

'It's only a paper moon, Just as phony as it can be—But it wouldn't be make-believe If you believed in me!'

STANLEY: Well, so much for her being such a refined and particular type of girl. Which brings us to Lie Number Two.

STELLA: I don't want to hear any more!

STANLEY: She's not going back to teach school! In fact I am willing to bet you that she never had no idea of returning to Laurel! She didn't resign temporarily from the high school because of her nerves! No, siree, Bob! She didn't. They kicked her out of that high school before the spring term ended—and I hate to tell you the reason that step was taken! A seventeen-year-old boy—she'd gotten mixed up with!

BLANCHE:

'It's a Barnum and Bailey world, Just as phony as it can be—'

In the bathroom the water goes on loud, little breathless cries and peals of laughter are heard as if a child were frolicking in the tub.

STELLA: This is making me—sick!

STANLEY: The boy's dad learned about it and got in touch with the high school superintendent. Boy, oh, boy, I'd like to have been in that office when Dame Blanche was called on the carpet! I'd like to have seen her trying to squirm out of that one! But they had her on the hook good and proper that time and she knew that the jig was all up! They told her she better move on to some fresh territory. Yep, it was practickly a town ordinance passed against her!

The bathroom door is opened and BLANCHE *thrusts her head out holding a towel about her hair.*

BLANCHE: Stella!

STELLA [*faintly*]: Yes, Blanche?

BLANCHE: Give me another bath-towel to dry my hair with. I've just washed it.

STELLA: Yes, Blanche. [*She crosses in a dazed way from the kitchen to the bathroom door with a towel.*]

BLANCHE: What's the matter, honey?

STELLA: Matter? Why?

BLANCHE: You have such a strange expression on your face!

STELLA: Oh—[*She tries to laugh.*] I guess I'm a little tired!

BLANCHE: Why don't you bathe, too, soon as I get out?

STANLEY [*calling from the kitchen*]: How soon is that going to be?

BLANCHE: Not so terribly long! Possess your soul in patience!

STANLEY: It's not my soul I'm worried about!

BLANCHE *slams the door.* STANLEY *laughs harshly.* STELLA *comes slowly back into the kitchen.*

Well, what do you think of it?

STELLA: I don't believe all of those stories and I think your supply-man was mean and rotten to tell them. It's possible that some of the things he said are partly true. There are things about my sister I don't approve of—things that caused sorrow at home. She was always—flighty!

STANLEY: Flighty is some word for it!

STELLA: But when she was young, very young, she had an experience that—killed her illusions!

STANLEY: What experience was that?

STELLA: I mean her marriage, when she was—almost a child! She married a boy who wrote poetry. . . . He was extremely good-looking. I think Blanche didn't just love him but worshipped the ground he walked on! Adored him and thought him almost too fine to be human! But then she found out—

STANLEY: What?

STELLA: This beautiful and talented young man was a degenerate. Didn't your supply-man give you that information?

STANLEY: All we discussed was recent history. That must have been a pretty long time ago.

STELLA: Yes, it was—a pretty long time ago. . . .

> STANLEY *comes up and takes her by the shoulders rather gently. She gently withdraws from him. Automatically she starts sticking little pink candles in the birthday cake.*

STANLEY: How many candles you putting in that cake?

STELLA: I'll stop at twenty-five.

STANLEY: Is company expected?

STELLA: We asked Mitch to come over for cake and ice-cream.

> STANLEY *looks a little uncomfortable. He lights a cigarette from the one he has just finished.*

STANLEY: I wouldn't be expecting Mitch over tonight.

> STELLA *pauses in her occupation with candles and looks slowly around at* STANLEY.

STELLA: *Why?*

STANLEY: Mitch is a buddy of mine. We were in the same outfit together—Two-forty-first Engineers. We work in the same plant and now on the same bowling team. You think I could face him if—

STELLA: Stanley Kowalski, did you—did you repeat what that—?

STANLEY: You're goddam right I told him! I'd have that on my conscience the rest of my life if I knew all that stuff and let my best friend get caught!

STELLA: Is Mitch through with her?

STANLEY: Wouldn't you be if—?

STELLA: I said, *Is Mitch through with her?*

> BLANCHE's *voice is lifted again, serenely as a bell. She sings 'But it wouldn't be make-believe If you believed in me.'*

STANLEY: No, I don't think he's necessarily through with her—just wised up!

STELLA: Stanley, she thought Mitch was–going to–going to marry her. I was hoping so, too.

STANLEY: Well, he's not going to marry her. Maybe he *was*, but he's not going to jump in a tank with a school of sharks–now! [*He rises*]: Blanche! Oh, Blanche! Can I please get in my bathroom? [*There is a pause.*]

BLANCHE: Yes, indeed, sir! Can you wait one second while I dry?

STANLEY: Having waited one hour I guess one second ought to pass in a hurry.

STELLA: And she hasn't got her job? Well, what will she do!

STANLEY: She's not stayin' here after Tuesday. You know that, don't you? Just to make sure I bought her ticket myself. A bus-ticket!

STELLA: In the first place, Blanche wouldn't go on a bus.

STANLEY: She'll go on a bus and like it.

STELLA: No, she won't, no, she won't, Stanley!

STANLEY: *She'll go!* Period. P.S. She'll go *Tuesday*!

STELLA [*slowly*]: What'll–she–do? What on earth will she–*do!*

STANLEY: Her future is mapped out for her.

STELLA: What do you mean?

BLANCHE *sings*.

STANLEY: Hey, canary bird! Toots! Get *OUT* of the *BATHROOM!* Must I speak more plainly?

The bathroom door flies open and BLANCHE *emerges with a gay peal of laughter, but as* STANLEY *crosses past her, a frightened look appears in her face, almost a look of panic. He doesn't look at her but slams the bathroom door shut as he goes in.*

BLANCHE [*snatching up a hair-brush*]: Oh, I feel so good after my long, hot bath, I feel so good and cool and–rested!

STELLA [*sadly and doubtfully from the kitchen*]: Do you, Blanche?

BLANCHE [*brushing her hair vigorously*]: Yes, I do, so refreshed. [*She tinkles her highball glass.*] A hot bath and a long, cold drink always gives me a brand-new outlook on life! [*She looks through the portières at* STELLA, *standing between them, and slowly stops brushing.*] Something has happened!–What is it?

STELLA [*turning quickly away*]: Why, nothing has happened, Blanche.

BLANCHE: You're lying! Something has!

She stares fearfully at STELLA, *who pretends to be busy at the table. The distant piano goes into a hectic breakdown.*

· SCENE EIGHT

Three-quarters of an hour later. The view through the big windows is fading gradually into a still-golden dusk. A torch of sunlight blazes on the side of a big water-tank or oil-drum across the empty lot toward the business district which is now pierced by pin-points of lighted windows or windows reflecting the sunset.

The three people are completing a dismal birthday supper. STANLEY *looks sullen.* STELLA *is embarrassed and sad.* BLANCHE *has a tight, artificial smile on her drawn face. There is a fourth place at the table which is left vacant.*

BLANCHE [*suddenly*]: Stanley, tell us a joke, tell us a funny story to make us all laugh. I don't know what's the matter, we're all so solemn. Is it because I've been stood up by my beau?

STELLA *laughs feebly.*

It's the first time in my entire experience with men, and I've had a good deal of all sorts, that I've actually been stood up by anybody! Ha-ha! I don't know how to take it. . . . Tell us a funny little story, Stanley! Something to help us out.
STANLEY: I didn't think you liked my stories, Blanche.
BLANCHE: I like them when they're amusing but not indecent.
STANLEY: I don't know any refined enough for your taste.
BLANCHE: Then let me tell one.
STELLA: Yes, you tell one, Blanche. You used to know lots of good stories.

The music fades.

BLANCHE: Let me see, now. . . . I must run through my repertoire! Oh, yes—I love parrot stories! Do you all like parrot stories? Well, this one's about the old maid and the parrot. This old maid, she had a parrot that cursed a blue streak and knew more vulgar expressions than Mr Kowalski!
STANLEY: Huh.
BLANCHE: And the only way to hush the parrot up was to put the cover back on its cage so it would think it was night and go back to sleep. Well, one morning the old maid had just uncovered the parrot for the day—when who should she see coming up the front walk but the preacher! Well, she rushed back to the parrot and slipped the cover back on the cage and then she let in the preacher. And the parrot was perfectly still, just as quiet as a mouse, but just as she was asking the preacher how much sugar he wanted in his coffee—the parrot broke the silence with a loud—(*she whistles*)—and said—'God *damn*, but that was a short day!'

She throws back her head and laughs. STELLA *also makes an ineffectual effort to seem amused.* STANLEY *pays no attention to the story but reaches way over the table to spear his fork into the remaining chop which he eats with his fingers.*

Apparently Mr Kowalski was not amused.

STELLA: Mr Kowalski is too busy making a pig of himself to think of anything else!

STANLEY: That's right, baby.

STELLA: Your face and your fingers are disgustingly greasy. Go and wash up and then help me clear the table.

He hurls a plate to the floor.

STANLEY: That's how I'll clear the table! [*He seizes her arm.*] Don't ever talk that way to me! 'Pig–Polack–disgusting–vulgar–greasy!'–them kind of words have been on your tongue and your sister's too much around here! What do you two think you are? A pair of queens? Remember what Huey Long said– 'Every Man is a King!' And I am the king around here, so don't forget it! [*He hurls a cup and saucer to the floor*]. My place is cleared! You want me to clear your places?

STELLA *begins to cry weakly.* STANLEY *stalks out on the porch and lights a cigarette. The Negro entertainers around the corner are heard.*

BLANCHE: What happened while I was bathing? What did he tell you, Stella?

STELLA: Nothing, nothing, nothing!

BLANCHE: I think he told you something about Mitch and me! You know why Mitch didn't come but you won't tell me!

STELLA *shakes her head helplessly.*

I'm going to call him!

STELLA: I wouldn't call him, Blanche.

BLANCHE: I am, I'm going to call him on the phone.

STELLA [*miserably*]: I wish you wouldn't.

BLANCHE: I intend to be given some explanation from someone!

She rushes to the phone in the bedroom. STELLA *goes out on the porch and stares reproachfully at her husband. He grunts and turns away from her.*

STELLA: I hope you're pleased with your doings. I never had so much trouble swallowing food in my life, looking at the girl's face and the empty chair. [*She cries quietly.*]

BLANCHE [*at the phone*]: Hello, Mr Mitchell, please. . . . Oh. . . . I would like to leave a number if I may. Magnolia 9047. And say it's important to call. . . . Yes, very important. . . . Thank you. [*She remains by the phone with a lost, frightened look.*]

STANLEY *turns slowly back towards his wife and takes her clumsily in his arms.*

STANLEY: Stell, it's gonna be all right after she goes and after you've had the baby. It's gonna be all right again between you and me the way that it was. You remember that way that it was? Them nights we had together? God, honey, it's gonna be sweet when we can make noise in the night the way that we used to and get the coloured lights going with nobody's sister behind the curtains to hear us!

Their upstairs neighbours are heard in bellowing laughter at something. STANLEY *chuckles.*

Steve an' Eunice . . .

STELLA: Come on back in. [*She returns to the kitchen and starts lighting the candles on the white cake.*] Blanche?

BLANCHE: Yes. [*She returns from the bedroom to the table in the kitchen.*] Oh, those pretty, pretty little candles! Oh, don't burn them, Stella.

STELLA: I certainly will.

STANLEY *comes back in.*

BLANCHE: You ought to save them for baby's birthdays. Oh, I hope candles are going to glow in his life and I hope that his eyes are going to be like candles, like two blue candles lighted in a white cake!

STANLEY [*sitting down*]: What poetry!

BLANCHE: His Auntie knows candles aren't safe, that candles burn out in little boys' and girls' eyes, or wind blows them out and after that happens, electric light bulbs go on and you see too plainly . . . [*She pauses reflectively for a moment.*] I shouldn't have called him.

STELLA: There's lots of things could have happened.

BLANCHE: There's no excuse for it, Stella. I don't have to put up with insults. I won't be taken for granted.

STANLEY: Goddamn, it's hot in here with the steam from the bathroom.

BLANCHE: I've said I was sorry three times.

The piano fades out.

I take hot baths for my nerves. Hydro-therapy, they call it. You healthy Polack, without a nerve in your body, of course you don't know what anxiety feels like!

STANLEY: I am not a Polack. People from Poland are Poles, not Polacks. But what I am is a one hundred per cent American, born and raised in the greatest country on earth and proud as hell of it, so don't ever call me a Polack.

The phone rings. BLANCHE *rises expectantly.*

BLANCHE: Oh, that's for me, I'm sure.

STANLEY: *I'm* not sure. Keep your seat. [*He crosses leisurely to phone.*] H'lo. Aw, yeh, hello, Mac.

He leans against wall, staring insultingly in at BLANCHE. *She sinks back in her chair with a frightened look.* STELLA *leans over and touches her shoulder.*

BLANCHE: Oh, keep your hands off me, Stella. What is the matter with you?

Why do you look at me with that pitying look?

STANLEY [*bawling*]: QUIET IN THERE!–We've got a noisy woman on the place.–Go on, Mac. At Rileys? No, I don't wanta bowl at Riley's. I had a little trouble with Riley last week. I'm the team-captain, ain't I? All right, then, we're not gonna bowl at Riley's, we're gonna bowl at the West Side or the Gala! All right, Mac. See you!

> *He hangs up and returns to the table.* BLANCHE *fiercely controls herself, drinking quietly from her tumbler of water. He doesn't look at her but reaches in a pocket. Then he speaks slowly and with false amiability.*

Sister Blanche, I've got a little birthday remembrance for you.

BLANCHE: Oh, have you, Stanley? I wasn't expecting any, I–I don't know why Stella wants to observe my birthday! I'd much rather forget it–when you– reach twenty-seven! Well–age is a subject that you'd prefer to–ignore!

STANLEY: Twenty-seven!

BLANCHE [*quickly*]: What is it? Is it for *me*?

> *He is holding a little envelope towards her.*

STANLEY: Yes, I hope you like it!

BLANCHE: Why, why–Why, it's a—

STANLEY: Ticket! Back to Laurel! On the Greyhound! Tuesday!

> *The Varsouviana music steals in softly and continues playing.* STELLA *rises abruptly and turns her back.* BLANCHE *tries to smile. Then she tries to laugh. Then she gives both up and springs from the table and runs into the next room. She clutches her throat and then runs into the bathroom. Coughing, gagging sounds are heard.*

Well!

STELLA: You didn't need to do that.

STANLEY: Don't forget all that I took off her.

STELLA: You needn't have been so cruel to someone alone as she is.

STANLEY: Delicate piece she is.

STELLA: She is. She was. You didn't know Blanche as a girl. Nobody, nobody, was tender and trusting as she was. But people like you abused her, and forced her to change.

> *He crosses into the bedroom, ripping off his shirt, and changes into a brilliant silk bowling shirt. She follows him.*

Do you think you're going bowling now?

STANLEY: Sure.

STELLA: You're not going bowling. [*She catches hold of his shirt.*] Why did you do this to her?

STANLEY: I done nothing to no one. Let go of my shirt. You've torn it.

STELLA: I want to know why. Tell me why.

STANLEY: When we first met, me and you, you thought I was common. How right you was, baby. I was common as dirt. You showed me the snapshot of the place with the columns. I pulled you down off them columns and how you loved it, having them coloured lights going! And wasn't we happy together, wasn't it all okay till she showed here?

STELLA *makes a slight movement. Her look goes suddenly inward as if some interior voice had called her name. She begins a slow, shuffling progress from the bedroom to the kitchen, leaning and resting on the back of the chair and then on the edge of a table with a blind look and listening expression.* STANLEY, *finishing with his shirt, is unaware of her reaction.*

And wasn't we happy together? Wasn't it all okay? Till she showed here. Hoity-toity, describing me as an ape. [*He suddenly notices the change in* STELLA.] Hey, what is it, Stell? [*He crosses to her.*]
STELLA [*quietly*]: Take me to the hospital.

He is with her now, supporting her with his arm, murmuring indistinguishably as they go outside. The 'Varsouviana' is heard, its music rising with sinister rapidity as the bathroom door opens slightly. BLANCHE *comes out twisting a wash-cloth. She begins to whisper the words as the light fades slowly.*

BLANCHE: *El pan de mais, el pan de mais,*
      El pan de mais sin sal.
      El pan de mais, el pan de mais,
      El pan de mais sin sal . . .

SCENE NINE

A while later that evening. BLANCHE is seated in a tense hunched position in a bedroom chair that she has re-covered with diagonal green and white stripes. She has on her scarlet satin robe. On the table beside chair is a bottle of liquor and a glass. The rapid, feverish polka tune, the 'Varsouviana', is heard. The music is in her mind; she is drinking to escape it and the sense of disaster closing in on her, and she seems to whisper the words of the song. An electric fan is turning back and forth across her.

> MITCH *comes around the corner in work clothes: blue denim shirt and pants. He is unshaven. He climbs the steps to the door and rings.* BLANCHE *is startled.*

BLANCHE: Who is it, please?
MITCH [*hoarsely*]: Me. Mitch.

> *The polka tune stops.*

BLANCHE: Mitch!–Just a minute. [*She rushes about frantically, hiding the bottle in a closet, crouching at the mirror and dabbing her face with cologne and powder. She is so excited that her breath is audible as she dashes about. At last she rushes to the door in the kitchen and lets him in.*] Mitch!–Y'know, I really shouldn't let you in after the treatment I have received from you this evening! So utterly uncavalier! But hello, beautiful!

> *She offers him her lips. He ignores it and pushes past her into the flat. She looks fearfully after him as he stalks into the bedroom.*

My, my, what a cold shoulder! And a face like a thundercloud! And such uncouth apparel! Why, you haven't even shaved! The unforgivable insult to a lady! But I forgive you. I forgive you because it's such a relief to see you. You've stopped that polka tune that I had caught in my head. Have you ever had anything caught in your head? Some words, a piece of music? That goes relentlessly on and on in your head? No, of course you haven't, you dumb angel-puss, you'd never get anything awful caught in your head!

> *He stares at her while she follows him while she talks. It is obvious that he has had a few drinks on the way over.*

MITCH: Do we have to have that fan on?
BLANCHE: No!
MITCH: I don't like fans.
BLANCHE: Then let's turn it off, honey. I'm not partial to them!

She presses the switch and the fan nods slowly off. She clears her throat uneasily as MITCH *plumps himself down on the bed in the bedroom and lights a cigarette.*

I don't know what there is to drink. I–haven't investigated.

MITCH: I don't want Stan's liquor.

BLANCHE: It isn't Stan's. Everything here isn't Stan's. Some things on the premises are actually mine! How is your mother? Isn't your mother well?

MITCH: Why?

BLANCHE: Something's the matter tonight, but never mind. I won't cross-examine the witness. I'll just—[*She touches her forehead vaguely. The polka tune starts up again.*]—pretend I don't notice anything different about you! That–music again . . .

MITCH: What music?

BLANCHE: The 'Varsouviana'? The polka tune they were playing when Allan–Wait!

A distant revolver shot is heard, BLANCHE *seems relieved.*

There now, the shot! It always stops after that.

The polka music dies out again.

Yes, now it's stopped.

MITCH: Are you boxed out of your mind?

BLANCHE: I'll go and see what I can find in the way of—[*She crosses into the closet, pretending to search for the bottle.*] Oh, by the way, excuse me for not being dressed. But I'd practically given you up! Had you forgotten your invitation to supper?

MITCH: I wasn't going to see you any more.

BLANCHE: Wait a minute. I can't hear what you're saying and you talk so little that when you do say something, I don't want to miss a single syllable of it. . . . What am I looking around here for? Oh, yes–liquor! We've had so much excitement around here this evening that I *am* boxed out of my mind!

She pretends suddenly to find the bottle. He draws his foot up on the bed and stares at her contemptuously.

Here's something. Southern Comfort! What is that I wonder?

MITCH: If you don't know, it must belong to Stan.

BLANCHE: Take your foot off the bed. It has a light cover on it. Of course you boys don't notice things like that. I've done so much with this place since I've been here.

MITCH: I bet you have.

BLANCHE: You saw it before I came. Well, look at it now! This room is almost–dainty! I want to keep it that way. I wonder if this stuff ought to be mixed with something? Ummm, it's sweet, so sweet! It's terribly, terribly sweet! Why, it's a *liqueur*, I believe! Yes, that's what it *is*, a liqueur!

MITCH *grunts.*

I'm afraid you won't like it, but try it, and maybe you will.

MITCH: I told you already I don't want none of his liquor and I mean it. You ought to lay off his liquor. He says you been lapping it up all summer like a wild-cat!

BLANCHE: What a fantastic statement! Fantastic of him to say it, fantastic of you to repeat it! I won't descend to the level of such cheap accusations to answer them, even!

MITCH: Huh.

BLANCHE: What's in your mind? I see something in your eyes!

MITCH [*getting up*]: It's dark in here.

BLANCHE: I like it dark. The dark is comforting to me.

MITCH: I don't think I ever seen you in the light.

BLANCHE *laughs breathlessly*.

That's a fact!

BLANCHE: Is it?

MITCH: I've never seen you in the afternoon.

BLANCHE: Whose fault is that?

MITCH: You never want to go out in the afternoon.

BLANCHE: Why, Mitch, you're at the plant in the afternoon!

MITCH: Not Sunday afternoon. I've asked you to go out with me sometimes on Sundays but you always make an excuse. You never want to go out till after six and then it's always some place that's not lighted much.

BLANCHE: There is some obscure meaning in this but I fail to catch it.

MITCH: What it means is I've never had a real good look at you, Blanche.

BLANCHE: What are you leading up to?

MITCH: Let's turn the light on here.

BLANCHE [*fearfully*]: Light? Which light? What for?

MITCH: This one with the paper thing on it.

He tears the paper lantern off the light bulb. She utters a frightened gasp.

BLANCHE: What did you do that for?

MITCH: So I can take a look at you good and plain!

BLANCHE: Of course you don't really mean to be insulting!

MITCH: No, just realistic.

BLANCHE: I don't want realism.

MITCH: Naw, I guess not.

BLANCHE: I'll tell you what I want. Magic!

MITCH *laughs*.

Yes, yes, magic! I try to give that to people. I misrepresent things to them. I don't tell the truth. I tell what *ought* to be truth. And if that is sinful, then let me be damned for it!—*Don't turn the light on!*

MITCH *crosses to the switch. He turns the light on and stares at her. She cries out and covers her face. He turns the light off again.*

MITCH [*slowly and bitterly*]: I don't mind you being older than what I thought.

But all the rest of it—God! That pitch about your ideals being so old-fashioned and all the malarkey that you've dished out all summer. Oh, I knew you weren't sixteen any more. But I was a fool enough to believe you was straight.

BLANCHE: Who told you I wasn't—'straight'? My loving brother-in-law. And you believed him.

MITCH: I called him a liar at first. And then I checked on the story. First I asked our supply-man who travels through Laurel. And then I talked directly over long-distance to this merchant.

BLANCHE: Who is the merchant?

MITCH: Kiefaber.

BLANCHE: The merchant Kiefaber of Laurel! I know the man. He whistled at me. I put him in his place. So now for revenge he makes up stories about me.

MITCH: Three people, Kiefaber, Stanley, and Shaw, swore to them!

BLANCHE: Rub-a-dub-dub, three men in a tub! And such a filthy tub!

MITCH: Didn't you stay at a hotel called The Flamingo?

BLANCHE: Flamingo? No! Tarantula was the name of it! I stayed at a hotel called The Tarantula Arms!

MITCH [*stupidly*]: Tarantula?

BLANCHE: Yes, a big spider! That's where I brought my victims. [*She pours herself another drink.*] Yes, I had many intimacies with strangers. After the death of Allan—intimacies with strangers was all I seemed able to fill my empty heart with. . . . I think it was panic, just panic, that drove me from one to another, hunting for some protection—here and there, in the most—unlikely places—even, at last, in a seventeen-year-old boy but—somebody wrote the superintendent about it—'This woman is morally unfit for her position!' [*She throws back her head with convulsive, sobbing laughter. Then she repeats the statement, gasps, and drinks.*] True? Yes, I suppose—unfit somehow—anyway. . . . So I came here. There was nowhere else I could go. I was played out. You know what played out is? My youth was suddenly gone up the water-spout, and—I met you. You said you needed somebody. Well, I needed somebody, too. I thanked God for you, because you seemed to be gentle—a cleft in the rock of the world that I could hide in! The poor man's Paradise—is a little peace. . . . But I guess I was asking, hoping—too much! Kiefaber, Stanley, and Shaw have tied an old tin can to the tail of the kite.

There is a pause. MITCH *stares at her dumbly.*

MITCH: You lied to me, Blanche.

BLANCHE: Don't say I lied to you.

MITCH: Lies, lies, inside and out, all lies.

BLANCHE: Never inside, I didn't lie in my heart. . . .

A Vendor comes around the corner. She is a blind MEXICAN WOMAN *in a dark shawl, carrying bunches of those gaudy tin flowers that lower-class Mexicans display at funerals and other festive occasions. She is calling barely audibly. Her figure is only faintly visible outside the building.*

MEXICAN WOMAN: *Flores. Flores. Flores para los muertos. Flores. Flores.*

BLANCHE: What? Oh! Somebody outside. . . . I—lived in a house where dying

old women remembered their dead men . . .
MEXICAN WOMAN: *Flores. Flores para los muertos* . . .

The polka tune fades in.

BLANCHE [*as if to herself*]: Crumble and fade and—regrets—recriminations . . .
'If you'd done this, it wouldn't've cost me that!'
MEXICAN WOMAN: *Corones para los muertos. Corones* . . .
BLANCHE: Legacies! Huh . . . And other things such as blood-stained pillow-
slips—'Her linen needs changing'—'Yes, Mother. But couldn't we get a
coloured girl to do it?' No, we couldn't of course. Everything gone but the—
MEXICAN WOMAN: *Flores.*
BLANCHE: Death—I used to sit here and she used to sit over there and death was
as close as you are. . . . We didn't dare even admit we had ever heard of it!
MEXICAN WOMAN: *Flores para los muertos, flores—flores.* . .
BLANCHE: The opposite is desire. So do you wonder? How could you possibly
wonder! Not far from Belle Reve, before we had lost Belle Reve, was a camp
where they trained young soldiers. On Saturday nights they would go in
town to get drunk—
MEXICAN WOMAN [*softly*]: *Corones* . . .
BLANCHE:—and on the way back they would stagger on to my lawn and
call—'Blanche! Blanche!'—The deaf old lady remaining suspected nothing.
But sometimes I slipped outside to answer their calls. . . . Later the paddy-
wagon would gather them up like daisies . . . the long way home . . .

The MEXICAN WOMAN *turns slowly and drifts back off with her soft mournful
cries.* BLANCHE *goes to the dresser and leans forward on it. After a moment,*
MITCH *rises and follows her purposefully. The polka music fades away. He
places his hands on her waist and tries to turn her about.*

What do you want?
MITCH [*fumbling to embrace her*]: What I been missing all summer.
BLANCHE: Then marry me, Mitch!
MITCH: I don't think I want to marry you any more.
BLANCHE: No?
MITCH [*dropping his hands from her waist*]: You're not clean enough to bring in
the house with my mother.
BLANCHE: Go away, then. [*He stares at here.*] Get out of here quick before I start
screaming fire! [*Her throat is tightening with hysteria.*] Get out of here quick
before I start screaming fire.

*He still remains staring. She suddenly rushes to the big window with its pale
blue square of the soft summer light and cries wildly.*

Fire! Fire! Fire!

With a startled gasp, MITCH *turns and goes out of the outer door, clatters
awkwardly down the steps and around the corner of the building.* BLANCHE
*staggers back from the window and falls to her knees. The distant piano is slow
and blue.*

SCENE TEN

It is a few hours later that night. BLANCHE has been drinking fairly steadily since MITCH left. She has dragged her wardrobe trunk into the centre of the bedroom. It hangs open with flowery dresses thrown across it. As the drinking and packing went on, a mood of hysterical exhilaration came into her and she has decked herself out in a somewhat soiled and crumpled white satin evening gown and a pair of scuffed silver slippers with brilliants set in their heels.

Now she is placing the rhinestone tiara on her head before the mirror of the dressing-table and murmuring excitedly as if to a group of spectral admirers.

BLANCHE: How about taking a swim, a moonlight swim at the old rock-quarry? If anyone's sober enough to drive a car! Ha-Ha! Best way in the world to stop your head buzzing! Only you've got to be careful to dive where the deep pool is—if you hit a rock you don't come up till tomorrow. . . .

Tremblingly she lifts the hand mirror for a closer inspection. She catches her breath and slams the mirror face down with such violence that the glass cracks. She moans a little and attempts to rise.
    STANLEY *appears around the corner of the building. He still has on the vivid green silk bowling shirt. As he rounds the corner the honky-tonk music is heard. It continues softly throughout the scene.*
    He enters the kitchen, slamming the door. As he peers in at BLANCHE, *he gives a low whistle. He has had a few drinks on the way and has brought some quart beer bottles home with him.*

How is my sister?
STANLEY: She is doing okay.
BLANCHE: And how is the baby?
STANLEY [*grinning amiably*]: The baby won't come before morning so they told me to go home and get a little shut-eye.
BLANCHE: Does that mean we are to be alone in here?
STANLEY: Yep. Just me and you, Blanche. Unless you got somebody hid under the bed. What've you got on those fine feathers for?
BLANCHE: Oh, that's right. You left before my wire came.
STANLEY: You got a wire?
BLANCHE: I received a telegram from an old admirer of mine.
STANLEY: Anything good?
BLANCHE: I think so. An invitation.
STANLEY: What to? A fireman's ball?
BLANCHE [*throwing back her head*]: A cruise of the Caribbean on a yacht!
STANLEY: Well, well. What do you know?
BLANCHE: I have never been so surprised in my life.

STANLEY: I guess not.

BLANCHE: It came like a bolt from the blue!

STANLEY: Who did you say it was from?

BLANCHE: An old beau of mine.

STANLEY: The one that give you the white fox-pieces!

BLANCHE: Mr Shep Huntleigh. I wore his ATO pin my last year at college. I hadn't seen him again until last Christmas. I ran in to him on Biscayne Boulevard. Then—just now—this wire—inviting me on a cruise of the Caribbean! The problem is clothes. I tore into my trunk to see what I have that's suitable for the tropics!

STANLEY: And come up with that—gorgeous—diamond—tiara?

BLANCHE: This old relic! Ha-ha! It's only rhinestones.

STANLEY: Gosh. I thought it was Tiffany diamonds. [*He unbuttons his shirt.*]

BLANCHE: Well, anyhow, I shall be entertained in style.

STANLEY: Uh-huh. It goes to show, you never know what is coming.

BLANCHE: Just when I thought my luck had begun to fail me—

STANLEY: Into the picture pops this Miami millionaire.

BLANCHE: This man is not from Miami. This man is from Dallas.

STANLEY: This man is from Dallas?

BLANCHE: Yes, this man is from Dallas where gold spouts out of the ground!

STANLEY: Well, just so he's from somewhere! [*He starts removing his shirt.*]

BLANCHE: Close the curtains before you undress any further.

STANLEY [*amiably*]: This is all I'm going to undress right now. [*He rips the sack off a quart beer-bottle.*] Seen a bottle-opener?

She moves slowly towards the dresser, where she stands with her hands knotted together.

I used to have a cousin who could open a beer-bottle with his teeth. [*Pounding the bottle cap on the corner of table.*] That was his only accomplishment, all he could do—he was just a human bottle-opener. And then one time, at a wedding party, he broke his front teeth off! After that he was so ashamed of himself he used t' sneak out of the house when company came . . . [*The bottle cap pops off and a geyser of foam shoots up.* STANLEY *laughs happily, holding up the bottle over his head.*] Ha-ha! Rain from heaven! [*He extends the bottle towards her.*] Shall we bury the hatchet and make it a loving-cup? Huh?

BLANCHE: No, thank you.

STANLEY: Well, it's a red-letter night for us both. You having an oil-millionaire and me having a baby. [*He goes to the bureau in the bedroom and crouches to remove something from the bottom drawer.*]

BLANCHE [*drawing back*]: What are you doing in here?

STANLEY: Here's something I always break out on special occasions like this! The silk pyjamas I wore on my wedding night!

BLANCHE: Oh.

STANLEY: When the telephone rings and they say, 'You've got a son!' I'll tear this off and wave it like a flag! [*He shakes out a brilliant pyjama coat.*] I guess we are both entitled to put on the dog. [*He goes back to the kitchen with the coat over his arm.*]

BLANCHE: When I think of how divine it is going to be to have such a thing as privacy once more—I could weep with joy!

STANLEY: This millionaire from Dallas is not going to interfere with your privacy any?

BLANCHE: It won't be the sort of thing you have in mind. This man is a gentleman and he respects me. [*Improvising feverishly.*] What he wants is my companionship. Having great wealth sometimes makes people lonely!

STANLEY: I wouldn't know about that.

BLANCHE: A cultivated woman, a woman of intelligence and breeding, can enrich a man's life—immeasurably! I have those things to offer, and this doesn't take them away. Physical beauty is passing. A transitory possession. But beauty of the mind and richness of the spirit and tenderness of the heart—and I have all of those things—aren't taken away, but grow! Increase with the years! How strange that I should be called a destitute woman! When I have all of these treasures locked in my heart. [*A choked sob comes from her.*] I think of myself as a very, very rich woman! But I have been foolish—casting my pearls before swine!

STANLEY: Swine, huh?

BLANCHE: Yes, swine! Swine! And I'm thinking not only of you but of your friend, Mr Mitchell. He came to see me tonight. He dared to come here in his work-clothes! And to repeat slander to me, vicious stories that he had gotten from you! I gave him his walking papers . . .

STANLEY: You did, huh?

BLANCHE: But then he came back. He returned with a box of roses to beg my forgiveness! He implored my forgiveness. But some things are not forgivable. Deliberate cruelty is not forgivable. It is the one unforgivable thing in my opinion and it is the one thing of which I have never, never been guilty. And so I told him, I said to him, Thank you, but it was foolish of me to think that we could ever adapt ourselves to each other. Our ways of life are too different. Our attitudes and our backgrounds are incompatible. We have to be realistic about such things. So farewell, my friend! And let there be no hard feelings . . .

STANLEY: Was this before or after the telegram came from the Texas oil millionaire?

BLANCHE: What telegram? No! No, after! As a matter of fact, the wire came just as—

STANLEY: As a matter of fact there wasn't no wire at all!

BLANCHE: Oh, oh!

STANLEY: There isn't no millionaire! And Mitch didn't come back with roses 'cause I know where he is—

BLANCHE: Oh!

STANLEY: There isn't a goddam thing but imagination!

BLANCHE: Oh!

STANLEY: And lies and conceit and tricks!

BLANCHE: Oh!

STANLEY: And look at yourself! Take a look at yourself in that worn-out Mardi Gras outfit, rented for fifty cents from some rag-picker! And with the crazy crown on! What queen do you think you are!

BLANCHE: Oh—God . . .

STANLEY: I've been on to you from the start! Not once did you pull any wool over this boy's eyes! You come in here and sprinkle the place with powder and spray perfume and cover the light-bulb with a paper lantern, and lo and behold the place has turned into Egypt and you are the Queen of the Nile!

Sitting on your throne and swilling down my liquor! I say–*Ha–Ha!* Do you hear me? *Ha–ha–ha!* [*He walks into the bedroom.*]
BLANCHE: Don't come in here!

Lurid reflections appear on the walls around BLANCHE. *The shadows are of a grotesque and menacing form. She catches her breath, crosses to the phone, and jiggles the hook.* STANLEY *goes into the bathroom and closes the door.*

Operator, operator! Give me long-distance, please. . . . I want to get in touch with Mr Shep Huntleigh of Dallas. He's so well known he doesn't require any address. Just ask anybody who–Wait!–No, I couldn't find it right now. . . . Please understand, I–No! No, wait! . . . One moment! Someone is–Nothing! Hold on, please! [*She sets the phone down and crosses warily into the kitchen.*]

The night is filled with inhuman voices like cries in a jungle.
The shadows and lurid reflections move sinuously as flames along the wall spaces.
Through the back wall of the rooms, which have become transparent, can be seen the sidewalk. A prostitute has rolled a drunkard. He pursues her along the walk, overtakes her, and there is a struggle. A policeman's whistle breaks it up. The figures disappear.
Some moments later the NEGRO WOMAN *appears around the corner with a sequined bag which the prostitute had dropped on the walk. She is rooting excitedly through it.*

Operator! Operator! Never mind long-distance. Get Western Union. There isn't time to be–Western–Western Union. [*She waits anxiously.*] Western Union? Yes! I–want to–Take down this message! 'In desperate, desperate circumstances! Help me! Caught in a trap. Caught in–' *Oh!*

The bathroom door is thrown open and STANLEY *comes out in the brilliant silk pyjamas. He grins at her as he knots the tasselled sash about his waist. She gasps and backs away from the phone. He stares at her for a count of ten. Then a clicking becomes audible from the telephone, steady and rasping.*

STANLEY: You left th' phone off th' hook.

He crosses to it deliberately and sets it back on the hook. After he has replaced it, he stares at her again, his mouth slowly curving into a grin, as he waits between BLANCHE *and the outer door.*
The barely audible 'blue piano' begins to drum up louder. The sound of it turns into the roar of an approaching locomotive. BLANCHE *crouches, pressing her fists to her ears until it has gone by.*

BLANCHE [*finally straightening*]: Let me–let me get by you!
STANLEY: Get by me? Sure. Go ahead. [*He moves back a pace in the doorway.*]
BLANCHE: You–you stand over there! [*She indicates a further position.*]
STANLEY [*grinning*]: You got plenty of room to walk by me now.
BLANCHE: Not with you there! But I've got to get out somehow!
STANLEY: You think I'll interfere with you? Ha-ha!

The 'blue piano' goes softly. She turns confusedly and makes a faint gesture. The inhuman jungle voices rise up. He takes a step towards her, biting his tongue which protrudes between his lips.

STANLEY [*softly*]: Come to think of it—maybe you wouldn't be bad to—interfere with . . .

BLANCHE *moves backward through the door into the bedroom.*

BLANCHE: Stay back! Don't you come towards me another step or I'll—
STANLEY: What?
BLANCHE: Some awful thing will happen! It will!
STANLEY: What are you putting on now?

They are now both inside the bedroom.

BLANCHE: I warn you, don't, I'm in danger!

He takes another step. She smashes a bottle on the table and faces him, clutching the broken top.

STANLEY: What did you do that for?
BLANCHE: So I could twist the broken end in your face!
STANLEY: I bet you would do that!
BLANCHE: I would: I will if you—
STANLEY: Oh! So you want some rough-house! All right, let's have some rough-house!

He springs towards her, overturning the table. She cries out and strikes at him with the bottle top but he catches her wrist.

Tiger—tiger! Drop the bottle-top! Drop it! We've had this date with each other from the beginning!

She moans. The bottle-top falls. She sinks to her knees. He picks up her inert figure and carries her to the bed. The hot trumpet and drums from the Four Deuces sound loudly.

SCENE ELEVEN

It is some weeks later. STELLA is packing BLANCHE's things. Sound of water can be heard running in the bathroom.

The portières are partly open on the poker players—STANLEY, STEVE, MITCH, and PABLO—who sit around the table in the kitchen. The atmosphere of the kitchen is now the same raw, lurid one of the disastrous poker night.

The building is framed by the sky of turquoise. STELLA has been crying as she arranges the flowery dresses in the open trunk.

> EUNICE *comes down the steps from her flat above and enters the kitchen. There is another burst from the poker table.*

STANLEY: Drew to an inside straight and made it, by God.
PABLO: *Maldita sea tu suerto!*
STANLEY: Put it in English, greaseball.
PABLO: I am cursing your goddam luck.
STANLEY [*prodigiously elated*]: You know what luck is? Luck is believing you're lucky. Take at Salerno. I believed I was lucky. I figured that 4 out of 5 would not come through but I would . . . and I did. I put that down as a rule. To hold front position in this rat-race you've got to believe you are lucky.
MITCH: You . . . you . . . you . . . Brag . . . brag . . .bull . . .bull.

> STELLA *goes into the bedroom and starts folding a dress.*

STANLEY: What's the matter with him?
EUNICE [*walking past the table*]: I always did say that men are callous things with no feelings, but this does beat anything. Making pigs of yourselves. [*She comes through the portières into the bedroom.*]
STANLEY: What's the matter with her?
STELLA: How is my baby?
EUNICE: Sleeping like a little angel. Brought you some grapes. [*She puts them on a stool and lowers her voice.*] Blanche?
STELLA: Bathing.
EUNICE: How is she?
STELLA: She wouldn't eat anything but asked for a drink.
EUNICE: What did you tell her?
STELLA: I—just told her that—we'd made arrangements for her to rest in the country. She's got it mixed in her mind with Shep Huntleigh.

> BLANCHE *opens the bathroom door slightly.*

BLANCHE: Stella.
STELLA: Yes, Blanche?

BLANCHE: If anyone calls while I'm bathing take the number and tell them I'll call right back.

STELLA: Yes.

BLANCHE: That cool yellow silk—the bouclé. See if it's crushed. If it's not too crushed I'll wear it and on the lapel that silver and turquoise pin in the shape of a seahorse. You will find them in the heart-shaped box I keep my accessories in. And Stella . . . Try and locate a bunch of artificial violets in that box, too, to pin with the seahorse on the lapel of the jacket.

She closes the door. STELLA *turns to* EUNICE.

STELLA: I don't know if I did the right thing.

EUNICE: What else could you do?

STELLA: I couldn't believe her story and go on living with Stanley.

EUNICE: Don't ever believe it. Life has got to go on. No matter what happens, you've got to keep on going.

The bathroom door opens a little.

BLANCHE [*looking out*]: Is the coast clear?

STELLA: Yes, Blanche. [*To* EUNICE.] Tell her how well she's looking.

BLANCHE: Please close the curtains before I come out.

STELLA: They're closed.

STANLEY: —How many for you.

PABLO: Two.—

STEVE:—Three.

BLANCHE *appears in the amber light of the door. She has a tragic radiance in her red satin robe following the sculptural lines of her body. The 'Varsouviana' rises audibly as* BLANCHE *enters the bedroom.*

BLANCHE [*with faintly hysterical vivacity*]: I have just washed my hair.

STELLA: Did you?

BLANCHE: I'm not sure I got the soap out.

EUNICE: Such fine hair!

BLANCHE [*accepting the compliment*]: It's a problem. Didn't I get a call?

STELLA: Who from, Blanche?

BLANCHE: Shep Huntleigh . . .

STELLA: Why, not yet, honey!

BLANCHE: How strange! I—

At the sound of BLANCHE's *voice* MITCH's *arm supporting his cards has sagged and his gaze is dissolved into space.* STANLEY *slaps him on the shoulder.*

STANLEY: Hey, Mitch, come to!

The sound of this new voice shocks BLANCHE. *She makes a shocked gesture, forming his name with her lips.* STELLA *nods and looks quickly away.* BLANCHE *stands quite still for some moments—the silver-backed mirror in her hand and a look of sorrowful perplexity as though all human experience shows on her face.* BLANCHE *finally speaks with sudden hysteria.*

BLANCHE: What's going on here?

She turns from STELLA *to* EUNICE *and back to* STELLA. *Her rising voice penetrates the concentration of the game.* MITCH *ducks his head lower but* STANLEY *shoves back his chair as if about to rise.* STEVE *places a restraining hand on his arm.*

BLANCHE [*continuing*]: What's happened here? I want an explanation of what's happened here.
STELLA [*agonizingly*]: Hush! Hush!
EUNICE: Hush! Hush! Honey.
STELLA: Please, Blanche.
BLANCHE: Why are you looking at me like that? Is something wrong with me?
EUNICE: You look wonderful, Blanche. Don't she look wonderful?
STELLA: Yes.
EUNICE: I understand you are going on a trip.
STELLA: Yes, Blanche *is*. She's going on vacation.
EUNICE: I'm green with envy.
BLANCHE: Help me, help me get dressed!
STELLA [*handing her dress*]: Is this what you—
BLANCHE: Yes, it will do! I'm anxious to get out of here–this place is a trap!
EUNICE: What a pretty blue jacket.
STELLA: It's lilac coloured.
BLANCHE: You're both mistaken. It's Della Robbia blue. The blue of the robe in the old Madonna pictures. Are these grapes washed?

She fingers the bunch of grapes which EUNICE *has brought in.*

EUNICE: Huh?
BLANCHE: Washed, I said. Are they washed?
EUNICE: They're from the French Market.
BLANCHE: That doesn't mean they've been washed.

The cathedral bells chime.

Those cathedral bells–they're the only clean thing in the Quarter. Well, I'm going now. I'm ready to go.
EUNICE [*whispering*]: She's going to walk out before they get here.
STELLA: Wait, Blanche.
BLANCHE: I don't want to pass in front of those men.
EUNICE: Then wait'll the game breaks up.
STELLA: Sit down and . . .

BLANCHE *turns weakly, hesitantly about. She lets them push her into a chair.*

BLANCHE: I can smell the sea air. The rest of my time I'm going to spend on the sea. And when I die, I'm going to die on the sea. You know what I shall die of? [*She plucks a grape.*] I shall die of eating an unwashed grape one day out on the ocean. I will die–with my hand in the hand of some nice-looking ship's doctor, a very young one with a small blond moustache and a big silver watch. 'Poor lady,' they'll say, 'the quinine did her no good. That unwashed grape has transported her soul to heaven.' [*The cathedral chimes are heard.*] And I'll be buried at sea sewn up in a clean white sack and dropped overboard—at noon—in the blaze of summer—and into an ocean as blue as [*chimes again*] my first lover's eyes!

A DOCTOR *and a* MATRON *have appeared around the corner of the building and climbed the steps to the porch. The gravity of their profession is exaggerated—the unmistakable aura of the state institution with its cynical detachment. The* DOCTOR *rings the doorbell. The murmur of the game is interrupted.*

EUNICE [*whispering to* STELLA]: That must be them.

STELLA *presses her fist to her lips.*

BLANCHE [*rising slowly*]: What is it?
EUNICE [*affectedly casual*]: Excuse me while I see who's at the door.
STELLA: Yes.

EUNICE *goes into the kitchen.*

BLANCHE [*tensely*]: I wonder if it's for me.

A whispered colloquy takes place at the door.

EUNICE [*returning, brightly*]: Someone is calling for Blanche.
BLANCHE: It *is* for me, then! [*She looks fearfully from one to the other and then to the portières. The 'Varsouviana' faintly plays.*] Is it the gentleman I was expecting from Dallas?
EUNICE: I think it is, Blanche.
BLANCHE: I'm not quite ready.
STELLA: Ask him to wait outside.
BLANCHE: I . . .

EUNICE *goes back to the portières. Drums sound very softly.*

STELLA: Everything packed?
BLANCHE: My silver toilet articles are still out.
STELLA: Ah!
EUNICE [*returning*]: They're waiting in front of the house.
BLANCHE: They! Who's 'they'?
EUNICE: There's a lady with him.
BLANCHE: I cannot imagine who this 'lady' could be! How is she dressed?
EUNICE: Just—just a sort of a—plain-tailored outfit.
BLANCHE: Possibly she's—[*Her voice dies out nervously.*]
STELLA: Shall we go, Blanche?
BLANCHE: Must we go through that room?
STELLA: I will go with you.
BLANCHE: How do I look?
STELLA: Lovely.

EUNICE [*echoing*]: Lovely.

> BLANCHE *moves fearfully to the portières.* EUNICE *draws them open for her.* BLANCHE *goes into the kitchen.*

BLANCHE [*to the men*]: Please don't get up. I'm only passing through.

> *She crosses quickly to outside door.* STELLA *and* EUNICE *follow. The poker players stand awkwardly at the table—all except* MITCH, *who remains seated, looking at the table.* BLANCHE *steps out on a small porch at the side of the door. She stops short and catches her breath.*

DOCTOR: How do you do?

BLANCHE: You are not the gentleman I was expecting. [*She suddenly gasps and starts back up the steps. She stops by* STELLA, *who stands just outside the door, and speaks in a frightened whisper.*] That man isn't Shep Huntleigh.

> *The 'Varsouviana' is playing distantly.* STELLA *stares back at* BLANCHE. EUNICE *is holding* STELLA's *arm. There is a moment of silence—no sound but that of* STANLEY *steadily shuffling the cards.*
>
> BLANCHE *catches her breath again and slips back into the flat. She enters the flat with a peculiar smile, her eyes wide and brilliant. As soon as her sister goes past her,* STELLA *closes her eyes and clenches her hands.* EUNICE *throws her arms comfortingly about her. Then she starts up to her flat.* BLANCHE *stops just inside the door.* MITCH *keeps staring down at his hands on the table, but the other men look at her curiously. At last she starts around the table towards the bedroom. As she does,* STANLEY *suddenly pushes back his chair and rises as if to block her way. The* MATRON *follows her into the flat.*

STANLEY: Did you forget something?

BLANCHE [*shrilly*]: Yes! Yes, I forgot something! [*She rushes past him into the bedroom. Lurid reflections appear on the walls in odd, sinuous shapes. The 'Varsouviana' is filtered into weird distortion, accompanied by the cries and noises of the jungle.* BLANCHE *seizes the back of a chair as if to defend herself.*]

STANLEY: Doc, you better go in.

DOCTOR [*motioning to the* MATRON]: Nurse, bring her out.

> *The* MATRON *advances on one side,* STANLEY *on the other. Divested of all the softer properties of womanhood, the* MATRON *is a peculiarly sinister figure in her severe dress. Her voice is bold and toneless as a fire-bell.*

MATRON: Hello, Blanche.

> *The greeting is echoed and re-echoed by other mysterious voices behind the walls, as if reverberated through a canyon of rock.*

STANLEY: She says that she forgot something.

> *The echo sounds in threatening whispers.*

MATRON: That's all right.

STANLEY: What did you forget, Blanche?

BLANCHE: I–I—

MATRON: It don't matter. We can pick it up later.

STANLEY: Sure. We can send it along with the trunk.

BLANCHE [*retreating in panic*]: I don't know you–I don't know you. I want to be–left alone–please!

MATRON: Now, Blanche!

ECHOES [*rising and falling*]: Now, Blanche–now, Blanche–now, Blanche!

STANLEY: You left nothing here but spilt talcum and old empty perfume bottles–unless it's the paper lantern you want to take with you. You want the lantern?

> *He crosses to dressing-table and seizes the paper lantern, tearing it off the light bulb, and extends it towards her. She cries out as if the lantern was herself. The* MATRON *steps boldly towards her. She screams and tries to break past the* MATRON. *All the men spring to their feet.* STELLA *runs out to the porch, with* EUNICE *following to comfort her, simultaneously with the confused voices of the men in the kitchen.* STELLA *rushes into* EUNICE'*s embrace on the porch.*

STELLA: Oh, my God, Eunice, help me! Don't let them do that to her, don't let them hurt her! Oh, God, oh, please God, don't hurt her! What are they doing to her? What are they doing? [*She tries to break from* EUNICE'*s arms.*]

EUNICE: No, honey, no, no, honey. Stay here. Don't go back in there. Stay with me and don't look.

STELLA: What have I done to my sister? Oh, God, what have I done to my sister?

EUNICE: You done the right thing, the only thing you could do. She couldn't stay here; there wasn't no other place for her to go.

> *While* STELLA *and* EUNICE *are speaking on the porch the voices of the men in the kitchen overlap them.*

STANLEY [*running in from the bedroom*]: Hey! Hey! Doctor! Doctor, you better go in!

DOCTOR: Too bad, too bad. I always like to avoid it.

PABLO: This is a very bad thing.

STEVE: This is no way to do it. She should've been told.

PABLO: *Madre de Dios! Cosa mala, muy, muy mala!*

> MITCH *has started towards the bedroom.* STANLEY *crosses to block him.*

MITCH [*wildly*]: You! You done this, all o' your God damn interfering with things you—

STANLEY: Quit the blubber! [*He pushes him aside.*]

MITCH: I'll kill you! [*He lunges and strikes at* STANLEY.]

STANLEY: Hold this bone-headed cry-baby!

STEVE [*grasping* MITCH]: Stop it, Mitch.

PABLO: Yeah, yeah, take it easy!

> MITCH *collapses at the table, sobbing. During the preceding scenes, the* MATRON *catches hold of* BLANCHE'*s arm and prevents her flight.* BLANCHE

turns wildly and scratches at the MATRON. *The heavy woman pinions her arms.* BLANCHE *cries out hoarsely and slips to her knees.*

MATRON: These fingernails have to be trimmed.

The DOCTOR *comes into the room and she looks at him.*

Jacket, Doctor?
DOCTOR: Not unless necessary.

He takes off his hat and now becomes personalized. The inhuman quality goes. His voice is gentle and reassuring as he crosses to BLANCHE *and crouches in front of her. As he speaks her name, her terror subsides a little. The lurid reflections fade from the walls, the inhuman cries and noises die out and her own hoarse crying is calmed.*

Miss DuBois.

She turns her face to him and stares at him with desperate pleading. He smiles; then he speaks to the MATRON.

It won't be necessary.
BLANCHE [*faintly*]: Ask her to let go of me.
DOCTOR [*to the* MATRON]: Let go.

The MATRON *releases her.* BLANCHE *extends her hands towards the* DOCTOR. *He draws her up gently and supports her with his arm and leads her through the portières.*

BLANCHE [*holding tight to his arm*]: Whoever you are—I have always depended on the kindness of strangers.

The poker players stand back as BLANCHE *and the* DOCTOR *cross the kitchen to the front door. She allows him to lead her as if she were blind. As they go out on the porch,* STELLA *cries out her sister's name from where she is crouched a few steps upon the stairs.*

STELLA: Blanche! Blanche, Blanche!

BLANCHE *walks on without turning, followed by the* DOCTOR *and the* MATRON. *They go around the corner of the building.*
EUNICE *descends to* STELLA *and places the child in her arms. It is wrapped in a pale blue blanket.* STELLA *accepts the child, sobbingly.* EUNICE *continues downstairs and enters the kitchen where the men except for* STANLEY, *are returning silently to their places about the table.* STANLEY *has gone out on the porch and stands at the foot of the steps looking at* STELLA.

STANLEY [*a bit uncertainly*]: Stella?

She sobs with inhuman abandon. There is something luxurious in her complete surrender to crying now that her sister is gone.

STANLEY [*voluptuously, soothingly*]: Now, honey. Now, love. Now, now love. [*He kneels beside her and his fingers find the opening of her blouse.*] Now, now, love. Now, love. . . .

The luxurious sobbing, the sensual murmur fade away under the swelling music of the 'blue piano' and the muted trumpet.

STEVE: This game is seven-card stud.

CURTAIN

DEATH
OF A
SALESMAN
ARTHUR
MILLER

DEATH OF A SALESMAN

First published in England in 1958
Published in 1967 by Martin Secker & Warburg
Limited,
14 Carlisle Street, London W1

Copyright © 1949 by Arthur Miller

DEATH OF A SALESMAN

(1949)

Certain private conversations
in Two Acts and a requiem

CHARACTERS

WILLY LOMAN
LINDA
BIFF
HAPPY
BERNARD
THE WOMAN
CHARLEY
UNCLE BEN
HOWARD WAGNER
JENNY
STANLEY
MISS FORSYTHE
LETTA

The action takes place in Willy Loman's house and yard and in various places he visits in the New York and Boston of today.

ACT ONE

A melody is heard, played upon a flute. It is small and fine, telling of grass and trees and the horizon. The curtain rises.

Before us is the Salesman's house. We are aware of towering, angular shapes behind it, surrounding it on all sides. Only the blue light of the sky falls upon the house and forestage; the surrounding area shows an angry glow of orange. As more light appears, we see a solid vault of apartment houses around the small, fragile-seeming home. An air of the dream clings to the place, a dream rising out of reality. The kitchen at center seems actual enough, for there is a kitchen table with three chairs, and a refrigerator. But no other fixtures are seen. At the back of the kitchen there is a draped entrance, which leads to the living-room. To the right of the kitchen, on a level raised two feet, is a bedroom furnished only with a brass bedstead and a straight chair. On a shelf over the bed a silver athletic trophy stands. A window opens onto the apartment house at the side.

Behind the kitchen, on a level raised six and a half feet, is the boys' bedroom, at present barely visible. Two beds are dimly seen, and at the back of the room a dormer window. (This bedroom is above the unseen living-room.) At the left a stairway curves up to it from the kitchen.

The entire setting is wholly or, in some places, partially transparent. The roof-line of the house is one-dimensional; under and over it we see the apartment buildings. Before the house lies an apron, curving beyond the forestage into the orchestra. This forward area serves as the back yard as well as the locale of all WILLY's imaginings and of his city scenes. Whenever the action is in the present the actors observe the imaginary wall-lines, entering the house only through its door at the left. But in the scenes of the past these boundaries are broken, and characters enter or leave a room by stepping 'through' a wall onto the forestage.

From the right, WILLY LOMAN, the Salesman, enters, carrying two large sample cases. The flute plays on. He hears but is not aware of it. He is past sixty years of age, dressed quietly. Even as he crosses the stage to the doorway of the house, his exhaustion is apparent. He unlocks the door, comes into the kitchen, and thankfully lets his burden down, feeling the soreness of his palms. A word-sigh escapes his lips—it might be 'Oh, boy, oh, boy.' He closes the door, then carries his cases out into the living-room, through the draped kitchen doorway.

LINDA, his wife, has stirred in her bed at the right. She gets out and puts on a robe, listening. Most often jovial, she has developed an iron repression of her exceptions to WILLY's behaviour—she more than loves him, she admires him, as though his mercurial nature, his temper, his massive dreams and little cruelties, served her only as sharp reminders of the turbulent longings within him, longings which she shares but lacks the temperament to utter and follow to their end.

LINDA [*hearing* WILLY *outside the bedroom, calls with some trepidation*]: Willy!

WILLY: It's all right. I came back.

LINDA: Why? What happened? [*Slight pause.*] Did something happen, Willy?

WILLY: No, nothing happened.

LINDA: You didn't smash the car, did you?

WILLY [*with casual irritation*]: I said nothing happened. Didn't you hear me?

LINDA: Don't you feel well?

WILLY: I'm tired to the death.

The flute has faded away. He sits on the bed beside her, a little numb.

I couldn't make it. I just couldn't make it, Linda.

LINDA [*very carefully, delicately*]: Where were you all day? You look terrible.

WILLY: I got as far as a little above Yonkers. I stopped for a cup of coffee. Maybe it was the coffee.

LINDA: What?

WILLY [*after a pause*]: I suddenly couldn't drive any more. The car kept going off onto the shoulder, y'know?

LINDA [*helpfully*]: Oh. Maybe it was the steering again. I don't think Angelo knows the Studebaker.

WILLY: No, it's me, it's me. Suddenly I realize I'm goin' sixty miles an hour and I don't remember the last five minutes. I'm—I can't seem to—keep my mind to it.

LINDA: Maybe it's your glasses. You never went for your new glasses.

WILLY: No, I see everything. I came back ten miles an hour. It took me nearly four hours from Yonkers.

LINDA [*resigned*]: Well, you'll just have to take a rest, Willy, you can't continue this way.

WILLY: I just got back from Florida.

LINDA: But you didn't rest your mind. Your mind is overactive, and the mind is what counts, dear.

WILLY: I'll start out in the morning. Maybe I'll feel better in the morning.

She is taking off his shoes.

These goddam arch supports are killing me.

LINDA: Take an aspirin. Should I get you an aspirin? It'll soothe you.

WILLY [*with wonder*]: I was driving along, you understand? And I was fine. I was even observing the scenery. You can imagine, me looking at scenery, on the road every week of my life. But it's so beautiful up there, Linda, the trees are so thick, and the sun is warm. I opened the windshield and just let the warm air bathe over me. And then all of a sudden I'm goin' off the road! I'm tellin' ya, I absolutely forgot I was driving. If I'd've gone the other way over the white line I might've killed somebody. So I went on again—and five minutes later I'm dreamin' again, and I nearly—[*He presses two fingers against his eyes.*] I have such thoughts, I have such strange thoughts.

LINDA: Willy, dear. Talk to them again. There's no reason why you can't work in New York.

WILLY: They don't need me in New York. I'm the New England man. I'm vital in New England.

LINDA: But you're sixty years old. They can't expect you to keep traveling every week.

WILLY: I'll have to send a wire to Portland. I'm supposed to see Brown and Morrison tomorrow morning at ten o'clock to show the line. Goddammit, I could sell them! [*He starts putting on his jacket.*]

LINDA [*taking the jacket from him*]: Why don't you go down to the place tomorrow and tell Howard you've simply got to work in New York? You're too accommodating, dear.

WILLY: If old man Wagner was alive I'd a been in charge of New York now! That man was a prince, he was a masterful man. But that boy of his, that Howard, he don't appreciate. When I went north the first time, the Wagner Company didn't know where New England was!

LINDA: Why don't you tell those things to Howard, dear?

WILLY [*encouraged*]: I will, I definitely will. Is there any cheese?

LINDA: I'll make you a sandwich.

WILLY: No, go to sleep. I'll take some milk. I'll be up right away. The boys in?

LINDA: They're sleeping. Happy took Biff on a date tonight.

WILLY [*interested*]: That so?

LINDA: It was so nice to see them shaving together, one behind the other, in the bathroom. And going out together. You notice? The whole house smells of shaving lotion.

WILLY: Figure it out. Work a lifetime to pay off a house. You finally own it, and there's nobody to live in it.

LINDA: Well, dear, life is a casting off. It's always that way.

WILLY: No, no, some people—some people accomplish something. Did Biff say anything after I went this morning?

LINDA: You shouldn't have criticized him, Willy, especially after he just got off the train. You mustn't lose your temper with him.

WILLY: When the hell did I lose my temper? I simply asked him if he was making any money. Is that a criticism?

LINDA: But, dear, how could he make any money?

WILLY [*worried and angered*]: There's such an undercurrent in him. He became a moody man. Did he apologize when I left this morning?

LINDA: He was crestfallen, Willy. You know how he admires you. I think if he finds himself, then you'll both be happier and not fight any more.

WILLY: How can he find himself on a farm? Is that a life? A farmhand? In the beginning, when he was young, I thought, well, a young man, it's good for him to tramp around, take a lot of different jobs. But it's more than ten years now and he has yet to make thirty-five dollars a week!

LINDA: He's finding himself, Willy.

WILLY: Not finding yourself at the age of thirty-four is a disgrace!

LINDA: Shh!

WILLY: The trouble is he's lazy, goddammit!

LINDA: Willy, please!

WILLY: Biff is a lazy bum!

LINDA: They're sleeping. Get something to eat. Go on down.

WILLY: Why did he come home? I would like to know what brought him home.

LINDA: I don't know. I think he's still lost, Willy. I think he's very lost.

WILLY: Biff Loman is lost. In the greatest country in the world a young man with such—personal attractiveness, gets lost. And such a hard worker. There's one thing about Biff—he's not lazy.

LINDA: Never.

WILLY [*with pity and resolve*]: I'll see him in the morning; I'll have a nice talk with him. I'll get him a job selling. He could be big in no time. My God! Remember how they used to follow him around in high school? When he smiled at one of them their faces lit up. When he walked down the street . . . [*He loses himself in reminiscences.*]

LINDA [*trying to bring him out of it*]: Willy, dear, I got a new kind of American-type cheese today. It's whipped.

WILLY: Why do you get American when I like Swiss?

LINDA: I just thought you'd like a change—

WILLY: I don't want a change! I want Swiss cheese. Why am I always being contradicted?

LINDA [*with a covering laugh*]: I thought it would be a surprise.

WILLY: Why don't you open a window in here, for God's sake?

LINDA [*with infinite patience*]: They're all open, dear.

WILLY: The way they boxed us in here. Bricks and windows, windows and bricks.

LINDA: We should've bought the land next door.

WILLY: The street is lined with cars. There's not a breath of fresh air in the neighborhood. The grass don't grow any more, you can't raise a carrot in the back yard. They should've had a law against apartment houses. Remember those two beautiful elm trees out there? When I and Biff hung the swing between them?

LINDA: Yeah, like being a million miles from the city.

WILLY: They should've arrested the builder for cutting those down. They massacred the neighborhood. [*Lost.*] More and more I think of those days, Linda. This time of year it was lilac and wisteria. And then the peonies would come out, and the daffodils. What fragrance in this room!

LINDA: Well, after all, people had to move somewhere.

WILLY: No, there's more people now.

LINDA: I don't think there's more people. I think—

WILLY: There's more people! That's what ruining this country! Population is getting out of control. The competition is maddening! Smell the stink from that apartment house! And another one on the other side . . . How can they whip cheese?

On WILLY's *last line,* BIFF *and* HAPPY *raise themselves up in their beds, listening.*

LINDA: Go down, try it. And be quiet.

WILLY [*turning to* LINDA, *guiltily*]: You're not worried about me, are you sweetheart?

BIFF: What's the matter?

HAPPY: Listen!

LINDA: You've got too much on the ball to worry about.

WILLY: You're my foundation and my support, Linda.

LINDA: Just try to relax, dear. You make mountains out of mole-hills.

WILLY: I won't fight with him any more. If he wants to go back to Texas, let him go.

LINDA: He'll find his way.

WILLY: Sure. Certain men just don't get started till later in life. Like Thomas

Edison, I think. Or B. F. Goodrich. One of them was deaf. [*He starts for the bedroom doorway.*] I'll put my money on Biff.

LINDA: And Willy—if it's warm Sunday we'll drive in the country. And we'll open the windshield, and take lunch.

WILLY: No, the windshields don't open on the new cars.

LINDA: But you opened it today.

WILLY: Me? I didn't. [*He stops.*] Now isn't that peculiar! Isn't that a remarkable—[*He breaks off in amazement and fright as the flute is heard distantly.*]

LINDA: What, darling?

WILLY: That is the most remarkable thing.

LINDA: What, dear?

WILLY: I was thinking of the Chevvy. [*Slight pause.*] Nineteen twenty-eight . . . when I had that red Chevvy—[*Breaks off.*] That funny? I coulda sworn I was driving that Chevvy today.

LINDA: Well, that's nothing. Something must've reminded you.

WILLY: Remarkable. Ts. Remember those days? The way Biff used to simonize that car? The dealer refused to believe there was eighty thousand miles on it. [*He shakes his head.*] Heh! [*To* LINDA.] Close you eyes, I'll be right up. [*He walks out of the bedroom.*]

HAPPY [*to* BIFF]: Jesus, maybe he smashed up the car again!

LINDA [*calling after* WILLY]: Be careful on the stairs, dear! The cheese is on the middle shelf! [*She turns, goes over to the bed, takes his jacket, and goes out of the bedroom.*]

Light has risen on the boys' room. Unseen, WILLY *is heard talking to himself, 'Eighty thousand miles,' and a little laugh.* BIFF *gets out of bed, comes downstage a bit, and stands attentively.* BIFF *is two years older than his brother* HAPPY, *well built, but in these days bears a worn air and seems less self-assured. He has succeeded less, and his dreams are stronger and less acceptable than* HAPPY's. HAPPY *is tall, powerfully made. Sexuality is like a visible color on him, or a scent that many women have discovered. He, like his brother, is lost, but in a different way, for he has never allowed himself to turn his face toward defeat and is thus more confused and hard-skinned, although seemingly more content.*

HAPPY [*getting out of bed*]: He's going to get his license taken away if he keeps that up. I'm getting nervous about him, y'know, Biff?

BIFF: His eyes are going.

HAPPY: No, I've driven with him. He sees all right. He just doesn't keep his mind on it. I drove into the city with him last week. He stops at a green light and then it turns red and he goes. [*He laughs.*]

BIFF: Maybe he's color-blind.

HAPPY: Pop? Why he's got the finest eye for color in the business. You know that.

BIFF [*sitting down on his bed*]: I'm going to sleep.

HAPPY: You're not still sour on Dad, are you, Biff?

BIFF: He's all right, I guess.

WILLY [*underneath them, in the living-room*]: Yes, sir, eighty thousand miles—eighty-two thousand!

BIFF: You smoking?

HAPPY [*holding out a pack of cigarettes*]: Want one?

BIFF [*taking a cigarette*]: I can never sleep when I smell it.

WILLY: What a simonizing job, heh!

HAPPY [*with deep sentiment*]: Funny, Biff, y'know? Us sleeping in here again? The old beds. [*He pats his bed affectionately.*] All the talk that went across those two beds, huh? Our whole lives.

BIFF: Yeah. Lotta dreams and plans.

HAPPY [*with a deep and masculine laugh*]: About five hundred women would like to know what was said in this room.

They share a soft laugh.

BIFF: Remember that big Betsy something—what the hell was her name—over on Bushwick Avenue?

HAPPY [*combing his hair*]: With the collie dog!

BIFF: That's the one. I got you in there, remember?

HAPPY: Yeah, that was my first time—I think. Boy, there was a pig!

They laugh, almost crudely.

You taught me everything I know about women. Don't forget that.

BIFF: I bet you forgot how bashful you used to be. Especially with girls.

HAPPY: Oh, I still am, Biff.

BIFF: Oh, go on.

HAPPY: I just control it, that's all. I think I got less bashful and you got more so. What happened, Biff? Where's the old humor, the old confidence?

He shakes BIFF's *knee.* BIFF *gets up and moves restlessly about the room.*

What's the matter?

BIFF: Why does Dad mock me all the time?

HAPPY: He's not mocking you, he—

BIFF: Everything I say there's a twist of mockery on his face. I can't get near him.

HAPPY: He just wants you to make good, that's all. I wanted to talk to you about Dad for a long time, Biff. Something's—happening to him. He—talks to himself.

BIFF: I noticed that this morning. But he always mumbled.

HAPPY: But not so noticeable. It got so embarrassing I sent him to Florida. And you know something? Most of the time he's talking to you.

BIFF: What's he say about me?

HAPPY: I can't make it out.

BIFF: What's he say about me?

HAPPY: I think the fact that you're not settled, that you're still kind of up in the air . . .

BIFF: There's one or two other things depressing him, Happy.

HAPPY: What do you mean?

BIFF: Never mind. Just don't lay it all to me.

HAPPY: But I think if you just got started—I mean—is there any future for you out there?

BIFF: I tell ya, Hap, I don't know what the future is. I don't know—what

I'm supposed to want.

HAPPY: What do you mean?

BIFF: Well, I spent six or seven years after high school trying to work myself up. Shipping clerk, salesman, business of one kind or another. And it's a measly manner of existence. To get on that subway on the hot mornings in summer. To devote your whole life to keeping stock, or making phone calls, or selling or buying. To suffer fifty weeks of the year for the sake of a two-week vacation, when all you really desire is to be outdoors, with your shirt off. And always to have to get ahead of the next fella. And still—that's how you build a future.

HAPPY: Well, you really enjoy it on a farm? Are you content out there?

BIFF [*with rising agitation*]: Hap, I've had twenty or thirty different kinds of jobs since I left home before the war, and it always turns out the same. I just realized it lately. In Nebraska when I herded cattle, and the Dakotas, and Arizona, and now in Texas. It's why I came home now, I guess, because I realized it. This farm I work on, it's spring there now, see? And they've got about fifteen new colts. There's nothing more inspiring or—beautiful than the sight of a mare and a new colt. And it's cool there now, see? Texas is cool now, and it's spring. And whenever spring comes to where I am, I suddenly get the feeling, my God, I'm not gettin' anywhere! What the hell am I doing, playing around with horses, twenty-eight dollars a week! I'm thirty-four years old, I oughta be makin' my future. That's when I come running home. And now, I get here, and I don't know what to do with myself. [*After a pause.*] I've always made a point of not wasting my life, and everytime I come back here I know that all I've done is to waste my life.

HAPPY: You're a poet, you know that, Biff? You're a—you're an idealist!

BIFF: No, I'm mixed up very bad. Maybe I oughta get married. Maybe I oughta get stuck into something. Maybe that's my trouble. I'm like a boy. I'm not married, I'm not in business, I just—I'm like a boy. Are you content, Hap? You're a success, aren't you? Are you content?

HAPPY: Hell, no!

BIFF: Why? You're making money, aren't you?

HAPPY [*moving about with energy, expressiveness*]: All I can do now is wait for the merchandise manager to die. And suppose I get to be merchandise manager? He's a good friend of mine, and he just built a terrific estate on Long Island. And he lived there about two months and sold it, and now he's building another one. He can't enjoy it once it's finished. And I know that's just what I would do. I don't know what the hell I'm workin' for. Sometimes I sit in my apartment—all alone. And I think of the rent I'm paying. And it's crazy. But then, it's what I always wanted. My own apartment, a car, and plenty of women. And still goddammit, I'm lonely.

BIFF [*with enthusiasm*]: Listen, why don't you come out West with me?

HAPPY: You and I, heh?

BIFF: Sure, maybe we could buy a ranch. Raise cattle, use our muscles. Men built like we are should be working out in the open.

HAPPY [*avidly*]: The Loman Brothers, heh?

BIFF [*with vast affection*]: Sure, we'd be known all over the counties!

HAPPY [*enthralled*]: That's what I dream about, Biff. Sometimes I want to just rip my clothes off in the middle of the store and outbox that goddam merchandise manager. I mean I can outbox, outrun, and outlift anybody in that store, and I have to take orders from those common, petty sons-of-bitches till I can't stand it any more.

BIFF: I'm tellin' you, kid, if you were with me I'd be happy out there.

HAPPY [*enthused*]: See, Biff, everybody around me is so false that I'm constantly lowering my ideals . . .

BIFF: Baby, together we'd stand up for one another, we'd have someone to trust.

HAPPY: If I were around you—

BIFF: Hap, the trouble is we weren't brought up to grub for money. I don't know how to do it.

HAPPY: Neither can I!

BIFF: Then let's go!

HAPPY: The only thing is–what can you make out there?

BIFF: But look at your friend. Builds an estate and then hasn't the peace of mind to live in it.

HAPPY: Yeah, but when he walks into the store the waves part in front of him. That's fifty-two thousand dollars a year coming through the revolving door, and I got more in my pinky finger than he's got in his head.

BIFF: Yeah, but you just said—

HAPPY: I gotta show some of those pompous, self-important executives over there that Hap Loman can make the grade. I want to walk into the store the way he walks in. Then I'll go with you, Biff. We'll be together yet, I swear. But take those two we had tonight. Now weren't they gorgeous creatures?

BIFF: Yeah, yeah, most gorgeous I've had in years.

HAPPY: I get that any time I want, Biff. Whenever I feel disgusted. The only trouble is, it gets like bowling or something. I just keep knockin' them over and it doesn't mean anything. You still run around a lot?

BIFF: Naa. I'd like to find a girl–steady, somebody with substance.

HAPPY: That's what I long for.

BIFF: Go on! You'd never come home.

HAPPY: I would! Somebody with character, with resistance! Like Mom, y'know? You're gonna call me a bastard when I tell you this. That girl Charlotte I was with tonight is engaged to be married in five weeks. [*He tries on his new hat.*]

BIFF: No kiddin'!

HAPPY: Sure, the guy's in line for the vice-presidency of the store. I don't know what gets into me, maybe I just have an overdeveloped sense of competition or something, but I went and ruined her, and furthermore I can't get rid of her. And he's the third executive I've done that to. Isn't that a crummy characteristic? And to top it all, I go to their weddings! [*Indignantly, but laughing.*] Like I'm not supposed to take bribes. Manufacturers offer me a hundred-dollar bill now and then to throw an order their way. You know how honest I am, but it's like this girl, see. I hate myself for it. Because I don't want the girl, and, still, I take it and–I love it!

BIFF: Let's go to sleep.

HAPPY: I guess we didn't settle anything, heh?

BIFF: I just got one idea that I think I'm going to try.

HAPPY: What's that?

BIFF: Remember Bill Oliver?

HAPPY: Sure, Oliver is very big now. You want to work for him again?

BIFF: No, but when I quit he said something to me. He put his arm on my shoulder, and he said, 'Biff, if you ever need anything, come to me.'

HAPPY: I remember that. That sounds good.

BIFF: I think I'll go to see him. If I could get ten thousand or even seven or eight thousand dollars I could buy a beautiful ranch.

HAPPY: I bet he'd back you. 'Cause he thought highly of you, Biff. I mean, they all do. You're well liked, Biff. That's why I say to come back here, and we both have the apartment. And I'm tellin' you, Biff, any babe you want . . .

BIFF: No, with a ranch I could do the work I like and still be something. I just wonder though. I wonder if Oliver still thinks I stole that carton of basketballs.

HAPPY: Oh, he probably forgot that long ago. It's almost ten years. You're too sensitive. Anyway, he didn't really fire you.

BIFF: Well, I think he was going to. I think that's why I quit. I was never sure whether he knew or not. I know he thought the world of me, though. I was the only one he'd let lock up the place.

WILLY [*below*]: You gonna wash the engine, Biff?

HAPPY: Shh!

BIFF *looks at* HAPPY, *who is gazing down, listening.* WILLY *is mumbling in the parlor.*

You hear that?

They listen. WILLY *laughs warmly.*

BIFF [*growing angry*]: Doesn't he know Mom can hear that?

WILLY: Don't get your sweater dirty, Biff!

A look of pain crosses Biff's face.

HAPPY: Isn't that terrible? Don't leave again, will you? You'll find a job here. You gotta stick around. I don't know what to do about him, it's getting embarrassing.

WILLY: What a simonizing job!

BIFF: Mom's hearing that!

WILLY: No kiddin', Biff, you got a date? Wonderful!

HAPPY: Go on to sleep. But talk to him in the morning, will you?

BIFF [*reluctantly getting into bed*]: With her in the house. Brother!

HAPPY [*getting into bed*]: I wish you'd have a good talk with him.

The light on their room begins to fade.

BIFF [*to himself in bed*]: That selfish, stupid . . .

HAPPY: Sh . . . Sleep, Biff.

Their light is out. Well before they have finished speaking, WILLY's *form is dimly seen below in the darkened kitchen. He opens the refrigerator, searches in there, and takes out a bottle of milk. The apartment houses are fading out, and the entire house and surroundings become covered with leaves. Music insinuates itself as the leaves appear.*

WILLY: Just wanna be careful with those girls, Biff, that's all. Don't make any promises. No promises of any kind. Because a girl, y'know, they always believe what you tell 'em, and you're very young, Biff, you're too young to be talking seriously to girls.

> *Light rises on the kitchen.* WILLY, *talking, shuts the refrigerator door and comes downstage to the kitchen table. He pours milk into a glass. He is totally immersed in himself, smiling faintly.*

Too young entirely, Biff. You want to watch your schooling first. Then when you're all set, there'll be plenty of girls for a boy like you. [*He smiles broadly at a kitchen chair.*] That so? The girls pay for you? [*He laughs.*] Boy, you must really be makin' a hit. [WILLY *is gradually addressing—physically—a point offstage, speaking through the wall of the kitchen, and his voice has been rising in volume to that of a normal conversation.*] I been wondering why you polish the car so careful. Ha! Don't leave the hubcaps, boys. Get the chamois to the hubcaps. Happy, use newspaper on the windows, it's the easiest thing. Show him how to do it, Biff! You see, Happy? Pad it up, use it like a pad. That's it, that's it, good work. You're doin' all right, Hap. [*He pauses, then nods in approbation for a few seconds, then looks upward.*] Biff, first thing we gotta do when we get time is clip that big branch over the house. Afraid it's gonna fall in a storm and hit the roof. Tell you what. We get a rope and sling her around, and then we climb up there with a couple of saws and take her down. Soon as you finish the car, boys, I wanna see ya. I got a surprise for you, boys.

BIFF [*offstage*]: Whatta ya got, Dad?

WILLY: No, you finish first. Never leave a job till you're finished—remember that. [*Looking toward the 'big trees'.*] Biff, up in Albany I saw a beautiful hammock. I think I'll buy it next trip, and we'll hang it right between those two elms. Wouldn't that be something? Just swingin' there under those branches. Boy, that would be . . .

> YOUNG BIFF *and* YOUNG HAPPY *appear from the direction* WILLY *was addressing.* HAPPY *carries rags and a pail of water.* BIFF, *wearing a sweater with a block 'S', carries a football.*

BIFF [*pointing in the direction of the car offstage*]: How's that, Pop, professional?

WILLY: Terrific. Terrific job, boys. Good work, Biff.

HAPPY: Where's the surprise, Pop?

WILLY: In the back seat of the car.

HAPPY: Boy! [*He runs off.*]

BIFF: What is it, Dad? Tell me, what'd you buy?

WILLY [*laughing, cuffs him*]: Never mind, something I want you to have.

BIFF [*turns and starts off*]: What is it, Hap?

HAPPY [*offstage*]: It's a punching bag!

BIFF: Oh, Pop!

WILLY: It's got Gene Tunney's signature on it!

> HAPPY *runs onstage with a punching bag.*

BIFF: Gee, how'd you know we wanted a punching bag?

WILLY: Well, it's the finest thing for the timing.

HAPPY [*lies down on his back and pedals with his feet*]: I'm losing weight, you notice, Pop?

WILLY [*to* HAPPY]: Jumping rope is good too.

BIFF: Did you see the new football I got?

WILLY [*examining the ball*]: Where'd you get a new ball?

BIFF: The coach told me to practice my passing.

WILLY: That so? And he gave you the ball, heh?

BIFF: Well, I borrowed it from the locker room. [*He laughs confidentially.*]

WILLY [*laughing with him at the theft*]: I want you to return that.

HAPPY: I told you he wouldn't like it!

BIFF [*angrily*]: Well, I'm bringing it back!

WILLY [*stopping the incipient argument, to* HAPPY]: Sure, he's gotta practice with a regulation ball, doesn't he? [*To* BIFF.] Coach'll probably congratulate you on your initiative!

BIFF: Oh, he keeps congratulating my initiative all the time, Pop.

WILLY: That's because he likes you. If somebody else took that ball there'd be an uproar. So what's the report, boys, what's the report?

BIFF: Where'd you go this time, Dad? Gee we were lonesome for you.

WILLY [*pleased, puts an arm around each boy and they come down to the apron*]: Lonesome, heh?

BIFF: Missed you every minute.

WILLY: Don't say? Tell you a secret, boys. Don't breathe it to a soul. Someday I'll have my own business, and I'll never have to leave home any more.

HAPPY: Like Uncle Charley, heh?

WILLY: Bigger than Uncle Charley! Because Charley is not–liked. He's liked, but he's not–well liked.

BIFF: Where'd you go this time, Dad?

WILLY: Well, I got on the road, and I went north to Providence. Met the Mayor.

BIFF: The Mayor of Providence!

WILLY: He was sitting in the hotel lobby.

BIFF: What'd he say?

WILLY: He said, 'Morning!' And I said, 'You got a fine city here, Mayor.' And then he had coffee with me. And then I went to Waterbury. Waterbury is a fine city. Big clock city, the famous Waterbury clock. Sold a nice bill there. And then Boston–Boston is the cradle of the Revolution. A fine city. And a couple of other towns in Mass., and on to Portland and Bangor and straight home!

BIFF: Gee, I'd love to go with you sometime, Dad.

WILLY: Soon as summer comes.

HAPPY: Promise?

WILLY: You and Hap and I, and I'll show you all the towns. America is full of beautiful towns and fine, upstanding people. And they know me, boys, they know me up and down New England. The finest people. And when I bring you fellas up, there'll be open sesame for all of us, 'cause one thing, boys: I have friends. I can park my car in any street in New England, and the cops protect it like their own. This summer, heh?

BIFF and HAPPY [*together*]: Yeah! You bet!

WILLY: We'll take our bathing suits.

HAPPY: We'll carry your bags, Pop!

WILLY: Oh, won't that be something! Me comin' into the Boston stores with you boys carryin' my bags. What a sensation!

BIFF *is prancing around, practicing passing the ball.*

You nervous, Biff, about the game?

BIFF: Not if you're gonna be there.

WILLY: What do they say about you in school, now that they made you captain?

HAPPY: There's a crowd of girls behind him everytime the classes change.

BIFF [*taking* WILLY*'s hand*]: This Saturday, Pop, this Saturday—just for you, I'm going to break through for a touchdown.

HAPPY: You're supposed to pass.

BIFF: I'm takin' one play for Pop. You watch me, Pop, and when I take off my helmet, that means I'm breakin' out. Then you watch me crash through that line!

WILLY [*kisses* BIFF]: Oh, wait'll I tell this in Boston!

BERNARD *enters in knickers. He is younger than* BIFF, *earnest and loyal, a worried boy.*

BERNARD: Biff, where are you? You're supposed to study with me today.

WILLY: Hey, looka Bernard. What're you lookin' so anemic about, Bernard?

BERNARD: He's gotta study, Uncle Willy. He's got Regents next week.

HAPPY [*tauntingly, spinning* BERNARD *around*]: Let's box, Bernard!

BERNARD: Biff! [*He gets away from* HAPPY.] Listen, Biff, I heard Mr Birnbaum say that if you don't start studyin' math he's gonna flunk you, and you won't graduate. I heard him!

WILLY: You better study with him, Biff. Go ahead now.

BERNARD: I heard him!

BIFF: Oh, Pop, you didn't see my sneakers! [*He holds up a foot for* WILLY *to look at.*]

WILLY: Hey, that's a beautiful job of printing!

BERNARD [*wiping his glasses*]: Just because he printed University of Virginia on his sneakers doesn't mean they've got to graduate him, Uncle Willy!

WILLY [*angrily*]: What're you talking about? With scholarships to three universities they're gonna flunk him?

BERNARD: But I heard Mr Birnbaum say—

WILLY: Don't be a pest, Bernard! [*To his boys.*] What an anemic!

BERNARD: Okay, I'm waiting for you in my house, Biff.

BERNARD *goes off. The* LOMANS *laugh.*

WILLY: Bernard is not well liked, is he?

BIFF: He's liked, but he's not well liked.

HAPPY: That's right, Pop.

WILLY: That's just what I mean. Bernard can get the best marks in school, y'understand, but when he gets out in the business world, y'understand, you are going to be five times ahead of him. That's why I thank Almighty God you're both built like Adonises. Because the man who makes an appearance in the business world, the man who creates personal interest, is the man who gets ahead. Be liked and you will never want. You take me, for instance. I never have to wait in line to see a buyer. 'Willy Loman is here!' That's all they have to know, and I go right through.

BIFF: Did you knock them dead, Pop?

WILLY: Knocked 'em cold in Providence, slaughtered 'em in Boston.

HAPPY [*on his back, pedaling again*]: I'm losing weight, you notice, Pop?

LINDA *enters, as of old, a ribbon in her hair, carrying a basket of washing.*

LINDA [*with youthful energy*]: Hello, dear!

WILLY: Sweetheart!

LINDA: How'd the Chevvy run?

WILLY: Chevrolet, Linda, is the greatest car ever built. [*To the boys.*] Since when do you let your mother carry wash up the stairs?

BIFF: Grab hold there, boy!

HAPPY: Where to, Mom?

LINDA: Hang them up on the line. And you better go down to your friends, Biff. The cellar is full of boys. They don't know what to do with themselves.

BIFF: Ah, when Pop comes home they can wait!

WILLY [*laughs appreciatively*]: You better go down and tell them what to do, Biff.

BIFF: I think I'll have them sweep out the furnace room.

WILLY: Good work, Biff.

BIFF [*goes through wall-line of kitchen to doorway at back and calls down*]: Fellas! Everybody sweep out the furnace room! I'll be right down!

VOICES: All right! Okay, Biff.

BIFF: George and Sam and Frank, come out back! We're hangin' up the wash! Come on, Hap, on the double! [*He and* HAPPY *carry out the basket.*]

LINDA: The way they obey him!

WILLY: Well, that's training, the training. I'm tellin' you, I was sellin' thousands and thousands, but I had to come home.

LINDA: Oh, the whole block'll be at that game. Did you sell anything?

WILLY: I did five hundred gross in Providence and seven hundred gross in Boston.

LINDA: No! Wait a minute, I've got a pencil. [*She pulls pencil and paper out of her apron pocket.*] That makes your commission . . . Two hundred—my God! Two hundred and twelve dollars!

WILLY: Well, I didn't figure it yet, but . . .

LINDA: How much did you do?

WILLY: Well, I—I did—about a hundred and eighty gross in Providence. Well, no—it came to—roughly two hundred gross on the whole trip.

LINDA [*without hesitation*]: Two hundred gross. That's . . . [*She figures.*]

WILLY: The trouble was that three of the stores were half closed for inventory in Boston. Otherwise I woulda broke records.

LINDA: Well, it makes seventy dollars and some pennies. That's very good.

WILLY: What do we owe?

LINDA: Well, on the first there's sixteen dollars on the refrigerator—

WILLY: Why sixteen?

LINDA: Well, the fan belt broke, so it was a dollar eighty.

WILLY: But it's brand new.

LINDA: Well, the man said that's the way it is. Till they work themselves in, y'know.

They move through the wall-line into the kitchen.

WILLY: I hope we didn't get stuck on that machine.

LINDA: They got the biggest ads of any of them!

WILLY: I know, it's a fine machine. What else?

LINDA: Well, there's nine-sixty for the washing machine. And for the vacuum cleaner there's three and a half due on the fifteenth. Then the roof, you got twenty-one dollars remaining.

WILLY: It don't leak, does it?

LINDA: No, they did a wonderful job. Then you owe Frank for the carburetor.

WILLY: I'm not going to pay that man! That goddam Chevrolet, they ought to prohibit the manufacture of that car!

LINDA: Well, you owe him three and a half. And odds and ends, comes to around a hundred and twenty dollars by the fifteenth.

WILLY: A hundred and twenty dollars! My God, if business don't pick up I don't know what I'm gonna do!

LINDA: Well, next week you'll do better.

WILLY: Oh, I'll knock 'em dead next week. I'll go to Hartford. I'm very well liked in Hartford. You know, the trouble is, Linda, people don't seem to take to me.

They move onto the forestage.

LINDA: Oh, don't be foolish.

WILLY: I know it when I walk in. They seem to laugh at me.

LINDA: Why? Why would they laugh at you? Don't talk that way, Willy.

WILLY *moves to the edge of the stage.* LINDA *goes into the kitchen and starts to darn stockings.*

WILLY: I don't know the reason for it, but they just pass me by. I'm not noticed.

LINDA: But you're doing wonderful, dear. You're making seventy to a hundred dollars a week.

WILLY: But I gotta be at it ten, twelve hours a day. Other men—I don't know—they do it easier. I don't know why—I can't stop myself—I talk too much. A man oughta come in with a few words. One thing about Charley. He's a man of few words, and they respect him.

LINDA: You don't talk too much, you're just lively.

WILLY [*smiling*]: Well, I figure, what the hell, life is short, a couple of jokes. [*To himself.*] I joke too much! [*The smile goes.*]

LINDA: Why? You're—

WILLY: I'm fat. I'm very—foolish to look at, Linda. I didn't tell you, but Christmas time I happened to be calling on F. H. Stewarts, and a salesman I know, as I was going in to see the buyer I heard him say something about—walrus. And I—I cracked him right across the face. I won't take that. I simply will not take that. But they do laugh at me. I know that.

LINDA: Darling . . .

WILLY: I gotta overcome it. I know I gotta overcome it. I'm not dressing to advantage, maybe.

LINDA: Willy, darling, you're the handsomest man in the world—

WILLY: Oh, no, Linda.

LINDA: To me you are. [*Slight pause.*] The handsomest.

From the darkness is heard the laughter of a woman. WILLY *doesn't turn to it, but it continues through* LINDA's *lines.*

And the boys, Willy. Few men are idolized by their children the way you are.

Music is heard as behind a scrim, to the left of the house, THE WOMAN, *dimly seen, is dressing.*

WILLY [*with great feeling*]: You're the best there is, Linda, you're a pal, you know that? On the road—on the road I want to grab you sometimes and just kiss the life outa you.

The laughter is loud now, and he moves into a brightening area at the left, where THE WOMAN *has come from behind the scrim and is standing, putting on her hat, looking into a 'mirror' and laughing.*

'Cause I get so lonely—especially when business is bad and there's nobody to talk to. I get the feeling that I'll never sell anything again, that I won't make a living for you, or a business, a business for the boys.

He talks through THE WOMAN's *subsiding laughter.* THE WOMAN *primps at the 'mirror.'*

There's so much I want to make for—
THE WOMAN: Me? You didn't make me, Willy. I picked you.
WILLY [*pleased*]: You picked me?
THE WOMAN [*who is quite proper-looking, Willy's age*]: I did. I've been sitting at that desk watching all the salesmen go by, day in, day out. But you've got such a sense of humor, and we do have such a good time together, don't we?
WILLY: Sure, sure. [*He takes her in his arms.*] Why do you have to go now?
THE WOMAN: It's two o'clock . . .
WILLY: No, come on in! [*He pulls her.*]
THE WOMAN: . . . my sisters'll be scandalized. When'll you be back?
WILLY: Oh, two weeks about. Will you come up again?
THE WOMAN: Sure thing. You do make me laugh. It's good for me. [*She squeezes his arm, kisses him.*] And I think you're a wonderful man.
WILLY: You picked me, heh?
THE WOMAN: Sure. Because you're so sweet. And such a kidder.
WILLY: Well, I'll see you next time I'm in Boston.
THE WOMAN: I'll put you right through to the buyers.
WILLY [*slapping her bottom*]: Right. Well, bottoms up!
THE WOMAN [*slaps him gently and laughs*]: You just kill me, Willy.

He suddenly grabs her and kisses her roughly.

You kill me. And thanks for the stockings. I love a lot of stockings. Well, good night.
WILLY: Good night. And keep your pores open!
THE WOMAN: Oh, Willy!

THE WOMAN *bursts out laughing, and* LINDA'*s laughter blends in.* THE WOMAN *disappears into the dark. Now the area at the kitchen table brightens.* LINDA *is sitting where she was at the kitchen table, but now is mending a pair of her silk stockings.*

LINDA: You are, Willy. The handsomest man. You've got no reason to feel that—

WILLY [*coming out of* THE WOMAN'*s dimming area and going over to* LINDA]: I'll make it all up to you, Linda, I'll—

LINDA: There's nothing to make up, dear. You're doing fine, better than—

WILLY [*noticing her mending*]: What's that?

LINDA: Just mending my stockings. They're so expensive—

WILLY [*angrily, taking them from her*]: I won't have you mending stockings in this house! Now throw them out!

LINDA *puts the stockings in her pocket.*

BERNARD [*entering on the run*]: Where is he? If he doesn't study!

WILLY [*moving to the forestage, with great agitation*]: You'll give him the answers!

BERNARD: I do, but I can't on a Regents! That's a state exam! They're liable to arrest me!

WILLY: Where is he? I'll whip him, I'll whip him!

LINDA: And he'd better give back that football, Willy, it's not nice.

WILLY: Biff! Where is he? Why is he taking everything?

LINDA: He's too rough with the girls, Willy. All the mothers are afraid of him!

WILLY: I'll whip him!

BERNARD: He's driving the car without a license!

THE WOMAN'*s laugh is heard.*

WILLY: Shut up!

LINDA: All the mothers—

WILLY: Shut up!

BERNARD [*backing quietly away and out*]: Mr Birnbaum says he's stuck up.

WILLY: Get outa here!

BERNARD: If he doesn't buckle down he'll flunk math! [*He goes off.*]

LINDA: He's right, Willy, you've gotta—

WILLY [*exploding at her*]: There's nothing the matter with him! You want him to be a worm like Bernard? He's got spirit, personality . . .

As he speaks, LINDA, *almost in tears, exits into the living-room.* WILLY *is alone in the kitchen, wilting and staring. The leaves are gone. It is night again, and the apartment houses look down from behind.*

Loaded with it. Loaded! What is he stealing? He's giving it back, isn't he? Why is he stealing? What did I tell him? I never in my life told him anything but decent things.

HAPPY *in pajamas has come down the stairs;* WILLY *suddenly becomes aware of* HAPPY'*s presence.*

HAPPY: Let's go now, come on.

WILLY [*sitting down at the kitchen table*]: Huh! Why did she have to wax the floors herself? Everytime she waxes the floors she keels over. She knows that!

HAPPY: Shh! Take it easy. What brought you back tonight?

WILLY: I got an awful scare. Nearly hit a kid in Yonkers. God! Why didn't I go to Alaska with my brother Ben that time! Ben! That man was a genius, that man was success incarnate! What a mistake! He begged me to go.

HAPPY: Well, there's no use in—

WILLY: You guys! There was a man started with the clothes on his back and ended up with diamond mines!

HAPPY: Boy, someday I'd like to know how he did it.

WILLY: What's the mystery? The man knew what he wanted and went out and got it! Walked into a jungle, and comes out, the age of twenty-one, and he's rich! The world is an oyster, but you don't crack it open on a mattress!

HAPPY: Pop, I told you I'm gonna retire you for life.

WILLY: You'll retire me for life on seventy goddam dollars a week? And your women and your car and your apartment, and you'll retire me for life! Christ's sake, I couldn't get past Yonkers today! Where are you guys, where are you? The woods are burning! I can't drive a car!

CHARLEY *has appeared in the doorway. He is a large man, slow of speech, laconic, immovable. In all he says, despite what he says, there is pity, and, now, trepidation. He has a robe over pajamas, slippers on his feet. He enters the kitchen.*

CHARLEY: Everything all right?

HAPPY: Yeah, Charley, everything's . . .

WILLY: What's the matter?

CHARLEY: I heard some noise. I thought something happened. Can't we do something about the walls? You sneeze in here, and in my house hats blow off.

HAPPY: Let's go to bed, Dad. Come on.

CHARLEY *signals to* HAPPY *to go.*

WILLY: You go ahead, I'm not tired at the moment.

HAPPY [*to* WILLY]: Take it easy, huh? [*He exits.*]

WILLY: What're you doin' up?

CHARLEY [*sitting down at the kitchen table opposite* WILLY]: Couldn't sleep good. I had a heartburn.

WILLY: Well, you don't know how to eat.

CHARLEY: I eat with my mouth'

WILLY: No, you're ignorant. You gotta know about vitamins and things like that.

CHARLEY: Come on, let's shoot. Tire you out a little.

WILLY [*hesitantly*]: All right. You got cards?

CHARLEY [*taking a deck from his pocket*]: Yeah, I got them. Someplace. What is it with those vitamins?

WILLY [*dealing*]: They build up your bones. Chemistry.

CHARLEY: Yeah, but there's no bones in a heartburn.

WILLY: What are you talkin' about? Do you know the first thing about it?

CHARLEY: Don't get insulted.
WILLY: Don't talk about something you don't know anything about.

They are playing. Pause.

CHARLEY: What're you doin' home?
WILLY: A little trouble with the car.
CHARLEY: Oh. [*Pause.*] I'd like to take a trip to California.
WILLY: Don't say.
CHARLEY: You want a job?
WILLY: I got a job, I told you that. [*After a slight pause.*] What the hell are you offering me a job for?
CHARLEY: Don't get insulted.
WILLY: Don't insult me.
CHARLEY: I don't see no sense in it. You don't have to go on this way.
WILLY: I got a good job. [*Slight pause.*] Why do you keep comin' in here for?
CHARLEY: You want me to go?
WILLY [*after a pause, withering*]: I can't understand it. He's going back to Texas again. What the hell is that?
CHARLEY: Let him go.
WILLY: I got nothin' to give him, Charley, I'm clean, I'm clean.
CHARLEY: He won't starve. None a them starve. Forget about him.
WILLY: Then what have I got to remember?
CHARLEY: You take it too hard. To hell with it. When a deposit bottle is broken you don't get your nickel back.
WILLY: That's easy enough for you to say.
CHARLEY: That ain't easy for me to say.
WILLY: Did you see the ceiling I put up in the living-room?
CHARLEY: Yeah, that's a piece of work. To put up a ceiling is a mystery to me. How do you do it?
WILLY: What's the difference?
CHARLEY: Well, talk about it.
WILLY: You gonna put up a ceiling?
CHARLEY: How could I put up a ceiling?
WILLY: Then what the hell are you bothering me for?
CHARLEY: You're insulted again.
WILLY: A man who can't handle tools is not a man. You're disgusting.
CHARLEY: Don't call me disgusting, Willy.

UNCLE BEN, *carrying a valise and an umbrella, enters the forestage from around the right corner of the house. He is a stolid man, in his sixties, with a mustache and an authoritative air. He is utterly certain of his destiny, and there is an aura of far places about him. He enters exactly as* WILLY *speaks.*

WILLY: I'm getting awfully tired, Ben.

BEN's *music is heard.* BEN *looks around at everything.*

CHARLEY: Good, keep playing; you'll sleep better. Did you call me Ben?

BEN *looks at his watch.*

WILLY: That's funny. For a second there you reminded me of my brother Ben.

BEN: I only have a few minutes.

He strolls, inspecting the place. WILLY *and* CHARLEY *continue playing.*

CHARLEY: You never heard from him again, heh? Since that time?

WILLY: Didn't Linda tell you? Couple of weeks ago we got a letter from his wife in Africa. He died.

CHARLEY: That so.

BEN [*chuckling*]: So this is Brooklyn, eh?

CHARLEY: Maybe you're in for some of his money.

WILLY: Naa, he had seven sons. There's just one opportunity I had with that man . . .

BEN: I must make a train, William. There are several properties I'm looking at in Alaska.

WILLY: Sure, sure! If I'd gone with him to Alaska that time, everything would've been totally different.

CHARLEY: Go on, you'd froze to death up there.

WILLY: What're you talking about?

BEN: Opportunity is tremendous in Alaska, William. Surprised you're not up there.

WILLY: Sure, tremendous.

CHARLEY: Heh?

WILLY: There was the only man I ever met who knew the answers.

CHARLEY: Who?

BEN: How are you all?

WILLY [*taking a pot, smiling*]: Fine, fine.

CHARLEY: Pretty sharp tonight.

BEN: Is Mother living with you?

WILLY: No, she died a long time ago.

CHARLEY: Who?

BEN: That's too bad. Fine specimen of a lady, Mother.

WILLY [*to* CHARLEY]: Hey?

BEN: I'd hoped to see the old girl.

CHARLEY: Who died?

BEN: Heard anything from Father, have you?

WILLY [*unnerved*]: What do you mean, who died?

CHARLEY [*taking a pot*]: What're you talkin' about?

BEN [*looking at his watch*]: William, it's half-past eight!

WILLY [*as though to dispel his confusion he angrily stops* CHARLEY*'s hand*]: That's my build!

CHARLEY: I put the ace—

WILLY: If you don't know how to play the game I'm not gonna throw my money away on you!

CHARLEY [*rising*]: It was my ace, for God's sake!

WILLY: I'm through, I'm through!

BEN: When did Mother die?

WILLY: Long ago. Since the beginning you never knew how to play cards.

CHARLEY [*picks up the cards and goes to the door*]: All right! Next time I'll bring a deck with five aces.

WILLY: I don't play that kind of game!

CHARLEY [*turning to him*]: You ought to be ashamed of yourself!

WILLY: Yeah?

CHARLEY: Yeah! [*He goes out.*]

WILLY [*slamming the door after him*]: Ignoramus!

BEN [*as* WILLY *comes toward him through the wall-line of the kitchen*]: So you're William.

WILLY [*shaking* BEN'*s hand*]: Ben! I've been waiting for your so long! What's the answer? How did you do it?

BEN: Oh, there's a story in that.

LINDA *enters the forestage, as of old, carrying the wash basket.*

LINDA: Is this Ben?

BEN [*gallantly*]: How do you do, my dear.

LINDA: Where've you been all these years? Willy's always wondered why you—

WILLY [*pulling* BEN *away from her impatiently*]: Where is Dad? Didn't you follow him? How did you get started?

BEN: Well, I don't know how much you remember.

WILLY: Well, I was just a baby, of course, only three or four years old—

BEN: Three years and eleven months.

WILLY: What a memory, Ben!

BEN: I have many enterprises, William, and I have never kept books.

WILLY: I remember I was sitting under the wagon in—was it Nebraska?

BEN: It was South Dakota, and I gave you a bunch of wild flowers.

WILLY: I remember you walking away down some open road.

BEN [*laughing*]: I was going to find Father in Alaska.

WILLY: Where is he?

BEN: At that age I had a very faulty view of geography, William. I discovered after a few days that I was heading due south, so instead of Alaska, I ended up in Africa.

LINDA: Africa!

WILLY: The Gold Coast!

BEN: Principally diamond mines.

LINDA: Diamond mines!

BEN: Yes, my dear. But I've only a few minutes—

WILLY: No! Boys! Boys!

Young BIFF *and* HAPPY *appear.*

Listen to this. This is your Uncle Ben, a great man! Tell my boys, Ben!

BEN: Why, boys, when I was seventeen I walked into the jungle, and when I was twenty-one I walked out. [*He laughs.*] And by God I was rich.

WILLY [*to the boys*]: You see what I been talking about? The greatest things can happen!

BEN [*glancing at his watch*]: I have an appointment in Ketchikan Tuesday week.

WILLY: No, Ben! Please tell about Dad. I want my boys to hear. I want them to know the kind of stock they spring from. All I remember is a man with a big beard, and I was in Mamma's lap, sitting around a fire, and some kind of high music.

BEN: His flute. He played the flute.

WILLY: Sure, the flute, that's right!

New music is heard, a high, rollicking tune.

BEN: Father was a very great and a very wild-hearted man. We would start in Boston, and he'd toss the whole family into the wagon, and then he'd drive the team right across the country; through Ohio, and Indiana, Michigan, Illinois, and all the Western states. And we'd stop in the towns and sell the flutes that he'd made on the way. Great inventor, Father. With one gadget he made more in a week than a man like you could make in a lifetime.

WILLY: That's just the way I'm bringing them up, Ben—rugged, well liked, all-around.

BEN: Yeah? [*To* BIFF.] Hit that, boy—hard as you can. [*He pounds his stomach.*]

BIFF: Oh, no, sir!

BEN [*taking boxing stance*]: Come on, get to me! [*He laughs.*]

WILLY: Go to it, Biff! Go ahead, show him!

BIFF: Okay! [*He cocks his fists and starts in.*]

LINDA [*to* WILLY]: Why must he fight, dear?

BEN [*sparring with* BIFF]: Good boy! Good boy!

WILLY: How's that, Ben, heh?

HAPPY: Give him the left, Biff!

LINDA: Why are you fighting?

BEN: Good boy! [*Suddenly comes in, trips* BIFF, *and stands over him, the point of his umbrella poised over* BIFF's *eye.*]

LINDA: Look out, Biff!

BIFF: Gee!

BEN [*patting* BIFF's *knee*]: Never fight fair with a stranger, boy. You'll never get out of the jungle that way. [*Taking* LINDA's *hand and bowing.*] It was an honor and a pleasure to meet you, Linda.

LINDA [*withdrawing her hand coldly, frightened*]: Have a nice—trip.

BEN [*to* WILLY]: And good luck with your—what do you do?

WILLY: Selling.

BEN: Yes. Well . . . [*He raises his hand in farewell to all.*]

WILLY: No, Ben, I don't want you to think . . . [*He takes* BEN's *arm to show him.*] It's Brooklyn, I know, but we hunt too.

BEN: Really, now.

WILLY: Oh, sure, there's snakes and rabbits and—that's why I moved out here. Why, Biff can fell any one of these trees in no time! Boys! Go right over to where they're building the apartment house and get some sand. We're gonna rebuild the entire front stoop right now! Watch this, Ben!

BIFF: Yes, sir! On the double, Hap!

HAPPY [*as he and* BIFF *run off*]: I lost weight, Pop, you notice?

CHARLEY enters in knickers, even before the boys are gone.

CHARLEY: Listen, if they steal any more from that building the watchman'll put the cops on them!

LINDA [*to* WILLY]: Don't let Biff . . .

BEN *laughs lustily.*

WILLY: You shoulda seen the lumber they brought home last week. At least a dozen six-by-tens worth all kinds a money.

CHARLEY: Listen, if that watchman—

WILLY: I gave them hell, understand. But I got a couple of fearless characters there.

CHARLEY: Willy, the jails are full of fearless characters.

BEN [*clapping* WILLY *on the back, with a laugh at* CHARLEY]: And the stock exchange, friend!

WILLY [*joining in* BEN's *laughter*]: Where are the rest of your pants?

CHARLEY: My wife bought them.

WILLY: Now all you need is a golf club and you can go upstairs and go to sleep. [*To* BEN.] Great athlete! Between him and his son Bernard they can't hammer a nail!

BERNARD [*rushing in*]: The watchman's chasing Biff!

WILLY [*angrily*]: Shut up! He's not stealing anything!

LINDA [*alarmed, hurrying off left*]: Where is he? Biff, dear! [*She exits.*]

WILLY [*moving toward the left, away from* BEN]: There's nothing wrong. What's the matter with you?

BEN: Nervy boy. Good!

WILLY [*laughing*]: Oh, nerves of iron, that Biff!

CHARLEY: Don't know what it is. My New England man comes back and he's bleedin', they murdered him up there.

WILLY: It's contacts, Charley, I got important contacts!

CHARLEY [*sarcastically*]: Glad to hear it, Willy. Come in later, we'll shoot a little casino. I'll take some of your Portland money. [*He laughs at* WILLY *and exits.*]

WILLY [*turning to* BEN]: Business is bad, it's murderous. But not for me, of course.

BEN: I'll stop by on my way back to Africa.

WILLY [*longingly*]: Can't you stay a few days? You're just what I need, Ben, because I–I have a fine position here, but I–well, Dad left when I was such a baby and I never had a chance to talk to him and I still feel–kind of temporary about myself.

BEN: I'll be late for my train.

They are at opposite ends of the stage.

WILLY: Ben, my boys–can't we talk? They'd go into the jaws of hell for me, see, but I—

BEN: William, you're being first-rate with your boys. Outstanding, manly chaps!

WILLY [*hanging on to his words*]: Oh, Ben, that's good to hear! Because sometimes I'm afraid that I'm not teaching them the right kind of–Ben, how should I teach them?

BEN [*giving great weight to each word, and with a certain vicious audacity*]: William, when I walked into the jungle, I was seventeen. When I walked out I was twenty-one. And, by God, I was rich!

He goes off into darkness around the right corner of the house.

WILLY: . . . was rich! That's just the spirit I want to imbue them with! To walk into a jungle! I was right! I was right! I was right!

> BEN *is gone, but* WILLY *is still speaking to him as* LINDA, *in nightgown and robe, enters the kitchen, glances around for* WILLY, *then goes to the door of the house, looks out and sees him. Comes down to his left. He looks at her.*

LINDA: Willy, dear? Willy?
WILLY: I was right!
LINDA: Did you have some cheese?

> *He can't answer.*

It's very late, darling. Come to bed, heh?
WILLY [*looking straight up*]: Gotta break your neck to see a star in this yard.
LINDA: You coming in?
WILLY: Whatever happened to that diamond watch fob? Remember? When Ben came from Africa that time? Didn't he give me a watch fob with a diamond in it?
LINDA: You pawned it, dear. Twelve, thirteen years ago. For Biff's radio correspondence course.
WILLY: Gee, that was a beautiful thing. I'll take a walk.
LINDA: But you're in your slippers.
WILLY [*starting to go around the house at the left*]: I was right! I was! [*Half to* LINDA, *as he goes, shaking his head.*] What a man! There was a man worth talking to. I was right!
LINDA [*calling after* WILLY]: But in your slippers, Willy!

> WILLY *is almost gone when* BIFF, *in his pajamas, comes down the stairs and enters the kitchen.*

BIFF: What is he doing out there?
LINDA: Sh!
BIFF: God Almighty, Mom, how long has he been doing this?
LINDA: Don't, he'll hear you.
BIFF: What the hell is the matter with him?
LINDA: It'll pass by morning.
BIFF: Shouldn't we do anything?
LINDA: Oh, my dear, you should do a lot of things, but there's nothing to do, so go to sleep.

> HAPPY *comes down the stairs and sits on the steps.*

HAPPY: I never heard him so loud, Mom.
LINDA: Well, come around more often; you'll hear him. [*She sits down at the table and mends the lining of* WILLY's *jacket.*]
BIFF: Why didn't you ever write me about this, Mom?
LINDA: How would I write to you? For over three months you had no address.
BIFF: I was on the move. But you know I thought of you all the time. You know that, don't you, pal?
LINDA: I know, dear, I know. But he likes to have a letter. Just to know that there's still a possibility for better things.

BIFF: He's not like this all the time, is he?

LINDA: It's when you come home he's always the worst.

BIFF: When I come home?

LINDA: When you write you're coming, he's all smiles, and talks about the future, and—he's just wonderful. And then the closer you seem to come, the more shaky he gets, and then, by the time you get here, he's arguing, and he seems angry at you. I think it's just that maybe he can't bring himself to—to open up to you. Why are you so hateful to each other? Why is that?

BIFF [*evasively*]: I'm not hateful, Mom.

LINDA: But you no sooner come in the door than you're fighting!

BIFF: I don't know why. I mean to change. I'm tryin', Mom, you understand?

LINDA: Are you home to stay now?

BIFF: I don't know. I want to look around, see what's doin'.

LINDA: Biff, you can't look around all your life, can you?

BIFF: I just can't take hold, Mom. I can't take hold of some kind of a life.

LINDA: Biff, a man is not a bird, to come and go with the spring-time.

BIFF: Your hair . . . [*He touches her hair*]. Your hair got so gray.

LINDA: Oh, it's been gray since you were in high school. I just stopped dyeing it, that's all.

BIFF: Dye it again, will ya? I don't want my pal looking old. [*He smiles.*]

LINDA: You're such a boy! You think you can go away for a year and . . . You've got to get it into your head now that one day you'll knock on this door and there'll be strange people here—

BIFF: What are you talking about? You're not even sixty, Mom.

LINDA: But what about your father?

BIFF [*lamely*]: Well, I meant him too.

HAPPY: He admires Pop.

LINDA: Biff, dear, if you don't have any feeling for him, then you can't have any feeling for me.

BIFF: Sure I can, Mom.

LINDA: No. You can't just come to see me, because I love him. [*With a threat, but only a threat, of tears.*] He's the dearest man in the world to me, and I won't have anyone making him feel unwanted and low and blue. You've got to make up your mind now, darling, there's no leeway any more. Either he's your father and you pay him that respect, or else you're not to come here. I know he's not easy to get along with—nobody knows that better than me—but . . .

WILLY [*from the left, with a laugh*]: Hey, hey, Biffo!

BIFF [*starting to go out after* WILLY]: What the hell is the matter with him?

HAPPY *stops him.*

LINDA: Don't—don't go near him!

BIFF: Stop making excuses for him! He always, always wiped the floor with you. Never had an ounce of respect for you.

HAPPY: He's always had respect for—

BIFF: What the hell do you know about it?

HAPPY [*surlily*]: Just don't call him crazy!

BIFF: He's got no character—Charley wouldn't do this. Not in his own house—spewing out that vomit from his mind.

HAPPY: Charley never had to cope with what he's got to.

BIFF: People are worse off than Willy Loman. Believe me, I've seen them!

LINDA: Then make Charley your father, Biff. You can't do that, can you? I don't say he's a great man. Willy Loman never made a lot of money. His name was never in the paper. He's not the finest character that ever lived. But he's a human being, and a terrible thing is happening to him. So attention must be paid. He's not to be allowed to fall into his grave like an old dog. Attention, attention must be finally paid to such a person. You called him crazy—

BIFF: I didn't mean—

LINDA: No, a lot of people think he's lost his–balance. But you don't have to be very smart to know what his trouble is. The man is exhausted.

HAPPY: Sure!

LINDA: A small man can be just as exhausted as a great man. He works for a company thirty-six years this March, opens up unheard-of territories to their trademark, and now in his old age they take his salary away.

HAPPY [*indignantly*]: I didn't know that, Mom.

LINDA: You never asked, my dear! Now that you get your spending money someplace else you don't trouble your mind with him.

HAPPY: But I gave you money last—

LINDA: Christmas time, fifty dollars! To fix the hot water it cost ninety-seven fifty! For five weeks he's been on straight commission, like a beginner, an unknown!

BIFF: Those ungrateful bastards!

LINDA: Are they any worse than his sons? When he brought them business, when he was young, they were glad to see him. But now his old friends, the old buyers that loved him so and always found some order to hand him in a pinch–they're all dead, retired. He used to be able to make six, seven calls a day in Boston. Now he takes his valises out of the car and puts them back and takes them out again and he's exhausted. Instead of walking he talks now. He drives seven hundred miles, and when he gets there no one knows him any more, no one welcomes him. And what goes through a man's mind, driving seven hundred miles home without having earned a cent? Why shouldn't he talk to himself? Why? When he has to go to Charley and borrow fifty dollars a week and pretend to me that it's his pay? How long can that go on? How long? You see what I'm sitting here and waiting for? And you tell me he has no character? The man who never worked a day but for your benefit? When does he get the medal for that? Is this his reward–to turn around at the age of sixty-three and find his sons, who he loved better than his life, one a philandering bum—

HAPPY: Mom!

LINDA: That's all you are, my baby! [*To* BIFF]: And you! What happened to the love you had for him? You were such pals! How you used to talk to him on the phone every night! How lonely he was till he could come home to you!

BIFF: All right, Mom. I'll live here in my room, and I'll get a job. I'll keep away from him, that's all.

LINDA: No, Biff. You can't stay here and fight all the time.

BIFF: He threw me out of this house, remember that.

LINDA: Why did he do that? I never knew why.

BIFF: Because I know he's a fake and he doesn't like anybody around who knows!

LINDA: Why a fake? In what way? What do you mean?

BIFF: Just don't lay it all at my feet. It's between me and him–that's all I have to say. I'll chip in from now on. He'll settle for half my pay check. He'll be all right. I'm going to bed. [*He starts for the stairs.*]

LINDA: He won't be all right.

BIFF [*turning on the stairs, furiously*]: I hate this city and I'll stay here. Now what do you want?

LINDA: He's dying, Biff.

HAPPY *turns quickly to her, shocked.*

BIFF [*after a pause*]: Why is he dying?

LINDA: He's been trying to kill himself.

BIFF [*with great horror*]: How?

LINDA: I live from day to day.

BIFF: What're you talking about?

LINDA: Remember I wrote you that he smashed up the car again? In February?

BIFF: Well?

LINDA: The insurance inspector came. He said that they have evidence. That all these accidents in the last year–weren't–weren't–accidents.

HAPPY: How can they tell that? That's a lie.

LINDA: It seems there's a woman . . . [*She takes a breath as*]

  ⎰ BIFF [*sharply but contained*]: What woman?
  ⎱ LINDA [*simultaneously*]: . . . and this woman . . .

LINDA: What?

BIFF: Nothing. Go ahead.

LINDA: What did you say?

BIFF: Nothing. I just said what woman?

HAPPY: What about her?

LINDA: Well, it seems she was walking down the road and saw his car. She says that he wasn't driving fast at all, and that he didn't skid. She says he came to that little bridge, and then deliberately smashed into the railing, and it was only the shallowness of the water that saved him.

BIFF: Oh, no, he probably just fell asleep again.

LINDA: I don't think he fell asleep.

BIFF: Why not?

LINDA: Last month . . . [*With great difficulty.*] Oh, boys, it's so hard to say a thing like this! He's just a big stupid man to you, but I tell you there's more good in him than in many other people. [*She chokes, wipes her eyes.*] I was looking for a fuse. The lights blew out, and I went down the cellar. And behind the fuse box–it happened to fall out–was a length of rubber pipe–just short.

HAPPY: No kidding?

LINDA: There's a little attachment on the end of it. I knew right away. And sure enough, on the bottom of the water heater there's a new little nipple on the gas pipe.

HAPPY [*angrily*]: That–jerk.

BIFF: Did you have it taken off?

LINDA: I'm–I'm ashamed to. How can I mention it to him? Every day I go down and take away that little rubber pipe. But, when he comes home, I put it back where it was. How can I insult him that way? I don't know what to do. I live from day to day, boys. I tell you, I know every thought in his mind. It sounds so old-fashioned and silly, but I tell you he put his whole life into you and you've turned your backs on him. [*She is bent over in the chair, weeping, her face in her hands.*] Biff, I swear to God! Biff, his life is in your hands!

HAPPY [*to* BIFF]: How do you like that damned fool!

BIFF [*kissing her*]: All right, pal, all right. It's all settled now. I've been remiss. I know that, Mom. But now I'll stay, and I swear to you, I'll apply myself. [*Kneeling in front of her, in a fever of self-reproach.*] It's just—you see, Mom, I don't fit in business. Not that I won't try. I'll try, and I'll make good.

HAPPY: Sure you will. The trouble with you in business was you never tried to please people.

BIFF: I know, I—

HAPPY: Like when you worked for Harrison's. Bob Harrison said you were tops, and then you go and do some damn fool thing like whistling whole songs in the elevator like a comedian.

BIFF [*against* HAPPY]: So what? I like to whistle sometimes.

HAPPY: You don't raise a guy to a responsible job who whistles in the elevator!

LINDA: Well, don't argue about it now.

HAPPY: Like when you'd go off and swim in the middle of the day instead of taking the line around.

BIFF [*his resentment rising*]: Well, don't you run off? You take off sometimes, don't you? On a nice summer day?

HAPPY: Yeah, but I cover myself!

LINDA: Boys!

HAPPY: If I'm going to take a fade the boss can call any number where I'm supposed to be and they'll swear to him that I just left. I'll tell you something that I hate to say, Biff, but in the business world some of them think you're crazy.

BIFF [*angered*]: Screw the business world!

HAPPY: All right, screw it! Great, but cover yourself!

LINDA: Hap, Hap!

BIFF: I don't care what they think! They've laughed at Dad for years, and you know why? Because we don't belong in this nuthouse of a city! We should be mixing cement on some open plain, or—or carpenters. A carpenter is allowed to whistle!

WILLY *walks in from the entrance of the house, at left.*

WILLY: Even you grandfather was better than a carpenter.

Pause. They watch him.

You never grew up. Bernard does not whistle in the elevator, I assure you.

BIFF [*as though to laugh* WILLY *out of it*]: Yeah, but you do, Pop.

WILLY: I never in my life whistled in an elevator! And who in the business world thinks I'm crazy?

BIFF: I didn't mean it like that, Pop. Now don't make a whole thing out of it, will ya?

WILLY: Go back to the West! Be a carpenter, a cowboy, enjoy yourself!

LINDA: Willy, he was just saying—

WILLY: I heard what he said!

HAPPY [*trying to quiet* WILLY]: Hey, Pop, come on now . . .

WILLY [*continuing over* HAPPY's *line*]: They laugh at me, heh? Go to Filene's, go to the Hub, go to Slattery's, Boston. Call out the name Willy Loman and see what happens! Big shot!

BIFF: All right, Pop.

WILLY: Big!

BIFF: All right!

WILLY: Why do you always insult me?

BIFF: I didn't say a word. [*To* LINDA.] Did I say a word?

LINDA: He didn't say anything, Willy.

WILLY [*going to the doorway of the living-room*]: All right, good night, good night.

LINDA: Willy, dear, he just decided . . .

WILLY [*to* BIFF]: If you get tired hanging around tomorrow, paint the ceiling I put up in the living-room.

BIFF: I'm leaving early tomorrow.

HAPPY: He's going to see Bill Oliver, Pop.

WILLY [*interestedly*]: Oliver? For what?

BIFF [*with reserve, but trying, trying*]: He always said he'd stake me. I'd like to go into business, so maybe I can take him up on it.

LINDA: Isn't that wonderful?

WILLY: Don't interrupt. What's wonderful about it? There's fifty men in the City of New York who'd stake him. [*To* BIFF.] Sporting goods?

BIFF: I guess so. I know something about it and—

WILLY: He knows something about it! You know sporting goods better than Spalding, for God's sake! How much is he giving you?

BIFF: I don't know, I didn't even see him yet, but—

WILLY: Then what're you talkin' about?

BIFF [*getting angry*]: Well, all I said was I'm gonna see him, that's all!

WILLY [*turning away*]: Ah, you're counting your chickens again.

BIFF [*starting left for the stairs*]: Oh, Jesus, I'm going to sleep!

WILLY [*calling after him*]: Don't curse in this house!

BIFF [*turning*]: Since when did you get so clean?

HAPPY [*trying to stop them*]: Wait a . . .

WILLY: Don't use that language to me! I won't have it!

HAPPY [*grabbing* BIFF, *shouts*]: Wait a minute! I got an idea. I got a feasible idea. Come here, Biff, let's talk this over now, let's talk some sense here. When I was down in Florida last time, I thought of a great idea to sell sporting goods. It just came back to me. You and I, Biff—we have a line, the Loman Line. We train a couple of weeks, and put on a couple of exhibitions, see?

WILLY: That's an idea!

HAPPY: Wait! We form two basketball teams, see? Two water-polo teams. We play each other. It's a million dollars' worth of publicity. Two brothers, see? The Loman Brothers. Displays in the Royal Palms—all the hotels. And banners over the ring and the basketball court: 'Loman Brothers.' Baby, we could sell sporting goods!

WILLY: That is a one-million-dollar idea!

LINDA: Marvelous!

BIFF: I'm in great shape as far as that's concerned.

HAPPY: And the beauty of it is, Biff, it wouldn't be like a business. We'd be out playin' ball again . . .

BIFF [*enthused*]: Yeah, that's . . .

WILLY: Million-dollar . . .

HAPPY: And you wouldn't get fed up with it, Biff. It'd be the family again. There'd be the old honor, and comradeship, and if you wanted to go off for a swim or somethin'—well, you'd do it! Without some smart cooky gettin' up ahead of you!

WILLY: Lick the world! You guys together could absolutely lick the civilized world.

BIFF: I'll see Oliver tomorrow. Hap, if we could work that out . . .

LINDA: Maybe things are beginning to—

WILLY [*wildly enthused to* LINDA]: Stop interrupting! [*To* BIFF.] But don't wear sport jacket and slacks when you see Oliver.

BIFF: No, I'll—

WILLY: A business suit, and talk as little as possible, and don't crack any jokes.

BIFF: He did like me. Always liked me.

LINDA: He loved you!

WILLY [*to* LINDA]: Will you stop! [*To* BIFF.] Walk in very serious. You are not applying for a boy's job. Money is to pass. Be quiet, fine, and serious. Everybody likes a kidder, but nobody lends him money.

HAPPY: I'll try to get some myself, Biff. I'm sure I can.

WILLY: I see great things for you kids, I think your troubles are over. But remember, start big and you'll end big. Ask for fifteen. How much you gonna ask for?

BIFF: Gee, I don't know—

WILLY: And don't say 'Gee.' 'Gee' is a boy's word. A man walking in for fifteen thousand dollars does not say 'Gee!'

BIFF: Ten, I think, would be top though.

WILLY: Don't be so modest. You always started too low. Walk in with a big laugh. Don't look worried. Start off with a couple of your good stories to lighten things up. It's not what you say, it's how you say it—because personality always wins the day.

LINDA: Oliver always thought the highest of him—

WILLY: Will you let me talk?

BIFF: Don't yell at her, Pop, will ya?

WILLY [*angrily*]: I was talking, wasn't I?

BIFF: I don't like you yelling at her all the time, and I'm tellin' you, that's all.

WILLY: What're you, takin' over this house?

LINDA: Willy—

WILLY [*turning on her*]: Don't take his side all the time, goddammit!

BIFF [*furiously*]: Stop yelling at her!

WILLY [*suddenly pulling on his cheek, beaten down, guilt ridden*]: Give my best to Bill Oliver—he may remember me. [*He exits through the living-room doorway.*]

LINDA [*her voice subdued*]: What'd you have to start that for?

BIFF *turns away.*

You see how sweet he was as soon as you talked hopefully? [*She goes over to* BIFF.] Come up and say good night to him. Don't let him go to bed that way.

HAPPY: Come on, Biff, let's buck him up.

LINDA: Please, dear. Just say good night. It takes so little to make him happy. Come. [*She goes through the living-room doorway, calling upstairs from within the living-room.*] Your pajamas are hanging in the bathroom, Willy!

HAPPY [*looking toward where* LINDA *went out*]: What a woman! They broke the mold when they made her. You know that, Biff?

BIFF: He's off salary. My God, working on commission!

HAPPY: Well, let's face it: he's no hot-shot selling man. Except that sometimes, you have to admit, he's a sweet personality.

BIFF [*deciding*]: Lend me ten bucks, will ya? I want to buy some new ties.

HAPPY: I'll take you to a place I know. Beautiful stuff. Wear one of my striped shirts tomorrow.

BIFF: She got gray. Mom got awful old. Gee, I'm gonna go in to Oliver tomorrow and knock him for a—

HAPPY: Come on up. Tell that to Dad. Let's give him a whirl. Come on.

BIFF [*steamed up*]: You know, with ten thousand bucks, boy!

HAPPY [*as they go into the living-room*]: That's the talk, Biff, that's the first time I've heard the old confidence out of you! [*From within the living-room, fading off.*] You're gonna live with me, kid, and any babe you want just say the word . . .

> *The last lines are hardly heard. They are mounting the stairs to their parents' bedroom.*

LINDA [*entering her bedroom and addressing* WILLY, *who is in the bathroom. She is straightening the bed for him*]: Can you do anything about the shower? It drips.

WILLY [*from the bathroom*]: All of a sudden everything falls to pieces! Goddam plumbing, oughta be sued, those people. I hardly finished putting it in and the thing . . . [*His words rumble off.*]

LINDA: I'm just wondering if Oliver will remember him. You think he might?

WILLY [*coming out of the bathroom in his pajamas*]: Remember him? What's the matter with you, you crazy? If he'd've stayed with Oliver he'd be on top by now! Wait'll Oliver gets a look at him. You don't know the average caliber any more. The average young man today— [*he is getting into bed*]— is got a caliber of zero. Greatest thing in the world for him was to bum around.

> BIFF *and* HAPPY *enter the bedroom. Slight pause.*

WILLY [*stops short, looking at* BIFF]: Glad to hear it, boy.

HAPPY: He wanted to say good night to you, sport.

WILLY [*to* BIFF]: Yeah. Knock him dead, boy. What'd you want to tell me?

BIFF: Just take it easy, Pop. Good night. [*He turns to go.*]

WILLY [*unable to resist*]: And if anything falls off the desk while you're talking to him—like a package or something—don't you pick it up. They have office boys for that.

LINDA: I'll make a big breakfast—

WILLY: Will you let me finish? [*To* BIFF.] Tell him you were in the business in the West. Not farm work.

BIFF: All right, Dad.

LINDA: I think everything—

WILLY [*going right through her speech*]: And don't undersell yourself. No less than fifteen thousand dollars.

BIFF [*unable to bear him*]: Okay. Good night, Mom. [*He starts moving.*]

WILLY: Because you got a greatness in you, Biff, remember that. You got all kinds a greatness . . .

He lies back, exhausted. BIFF *walks out.*

LINDA [*calling after* BIFF]: Sleep well, darling!
HAPPY: I'm gonna get married, Mom. I wanted to tell you.
LINDA: Go to sleep, dear.
HAPPY [*going*]: I just wanted to tell you.
WILLY: Keep up the good work.

HAPPY *exits.*

God . . . remember that Ebbets Field game? The championship of the city?
LINDA: Just rest. Should I sing to you?
WILLY: Yeah. Sing to me.

LINDA *hums a soft lullaby.*

When that team came out—he was the tallest, remember?
LINDA: Oh, yes. And in gold.

BIFF *enters the darkened kitchen, takes a cigarette, and leaves the house. He comes downstage into a golden pool of light. He smokes, staring at the night.*

WILLY: Like a young god. Hercules—something like that. And the sun, the sun all around him. Remember how he waved to me? Right up from the field, with the representatives of three colleges standing by? And the buyers I brought, and the cheers when he came out—Loman, Loman, Loman! God Almighty, he'll be great yet. A star like that, magnificent, can never really fade away!

The light on WILLY *is fading. The gas heater begins to glow through the kitchen wall, near the stairs, a blue flame beneath red coils.*

LINDA [*timidly*]: Willy dear, what has he got against you?
WILLY: I'm so tired. Don't talk any more.

BIFF *slowly returns to the kitchen. He stops, stares toward the heater.*

LINDA: Will you ask Howard to let you work in New York?
WILLY: First thing in the morning. Everything'll be all right.

BIFF *reaches behind the heater and draws out a length of rubber tubing. He is horrified and turns his head toward* WILLY's *room, still dimly lit, from which the strains of* LINDA's *desperate but monotonous humming rise.*

WILLY [*staring through the window into the moonlight*]: Gee, look at the moon moving between the buildings!

BIFF *wraps the tubing around his hand and quickly goes up the stairs.*

CURTAIN

ACT TWO

Music is heard, gay and bright. The curtain rises as the music fades away. WILLY, *in shirt sleeves, is sitting at the kitchen table, sipping coffee, his hat in his lap.* LINDA *is filling his cup when she can.*

WILLY: Wonderful coffee. Meal in itself.

LINDA: Can I make you some eggs?

WILLY: No. Take a breath.

LINDA: You look so rested, dear.

WILLY: I slept like a dead one. First time in months. Imagine, sleeping till ten on a Tuesday morning. Boys left nice and early, heh?

LINDA: They were out of here by eight o'clock.

WILLY: Good work!

LINDA: It was so thrilling to see them leaving together. I can't get over the shaving lotion in this house!

WILLY [*smiling*]: Mmm—

LINDA: Biff was very changed this morning. His whole attitude seemed to be hopeful. He couldn't wait to get downtown to see Oliver.

WILLY: He's heading for a change. There's no question, there simply are certain men that take longer to get—solidified. How did he dress?

LINDA: His blue suit. He's so handsome in that suit. He could be a—anything in that suit!

WILLY *gets up from the table.* LINDA *holds his jacket for him.*

WILLY: There's no question, no question at all. Gee, on the way home tonight I'd like to buy some seeds.

LINDA [*laughing*]: That'd be wonderful. But not enough sun gets back there. Nothing'll grow any more.

WILLY: You wait, kid, before it's all over we're gonna get a little place out in the country, and I'll raise some vegetables, a couple of chickens . . .

LINDA: You'll do it yet, dear.

WILLY *walks out of his jacket.* LINDA *follows him.*

WILLY: And they'll get married, and come for a weekend. I'd build a little guest house. 'Cause I got so many fine tools, all I'd need would be a little lumber and some peace of mind.

LINDA [*joyfully*]: I sewed the lining . . .

WILLY: I could build two guest houses, so they'd both come. Did he decide how much he's going to ask Oliver for?

LINDA [*getting him into the jacket*]: He didn't mention it, but I imagine ten or fifteen thousand. You going to talk to Howard today?

WILLY: Yeah. I'll put it to him straight and simple. He'll just have to take me off the road.

LINDA: And Willy, don't forget to ask for a little advance, because we've got the insurance premium. It's the grace period now.

WILLY: That's a hundred . . .?

LINDA: A hundred and eight, sixty-eight. Because we're a little short again.

WILLY: Why are we short?

LINDA: Well, you had the motor job on the car . . .

WILLY: That goddam Studebaker!

LINDA: And you got one more payment on the refrigerator . . .

WILLY: But it just broke again!

LINDA: Well, it's old, dear.

WILLY: I told you we should've bought a well-advertised machine. Charley bought a General Electric and it's twenty years old and it's still good, that son-of-a-bitch.

LINDA: But, Willy—

WILLY: Whoever heard of a Hastings refrigerator? Once in my life I would like to own something outright before it's broken! I'm always in a race with the junkyard! I just finished paying for the car and it's on its last legs. The refrigerator consumes belts like a goddam maniac. They time those things. They time them so when you finally paid for them, they're used up.

LINDA [*buttoning up his jacket as he unbuttons it*]: All told, about two hundred dollars would carry us, dear. But that includes the last payment on the mortgage. After this payment, Willy, the house belongs to us.

WILLY: It's twenty-five years!

LINDA: Biff was nine years old when we bought it.

WILLY: Well, that's a great thing. To weather a twenty-five year mortgage is—

LINDA: It's an accomplishment.

WILLY: All the cement, the lumber, the reconstruction I put in this house! There ain't a crack to be found in it any more.

LINDA: Well, it served its purpose.

WILLY: What purpose? Some stranger'll come along, move in, and that's that. If only Biff would take this house, and raise a family . . . [*He starts to go.*] Good-by, I'm late.

LINDA [*suddenly remembering*]: Oh, I forgot! You're supposed to meet them for dinner.

WILLY: Me?

LINDA: At Frank's Chop House on Forty-eighth near Sixth Avenue.

WILLY: Is that so! How about you?

LINDA: No, just the three of you. They're gonna blow you to a big meal!

WILLY: Don't say! Who thought of that?

LINDA: Biff came to me this morning, Willy, and he said, 'Tell Dad, we want to blow him to a big meal.' Be there six o'clock. You and your two boys are going to have dinner.

WILLY: Gee whiz! That's really somethin'. I'm gonna knock Howard for a loop, kid. I'll get an advance, and I'll come home with a New York job. Goddammit, now I'm gonna do it!

LINDA: Oh, that's the spirit, Willy!

WILLY: I will never get behind a wheel the rest of my life!

LINDA: It's changing, Willy, I can feel it changing!

WILLY: Beyond a question. G'by, I'm late. [*He starts to go again.*]
LINDA [*calling after him as she runs to the kitchen table for a handkerchief*]: You got your glasses?
WILLY [*feels for them, then comes back in*]: Yeah, yeah, got my glasses.
LINDA [*giving him the handkerchief*]: And a handkerchief.
WILLY: Yeah, handkerchief.
LINDA: And your saccharine?
WILLY: Yeah, my saccharine.
LINDA: Be careful on the subway stairs.

She kisses him, and a silk stocking is seen hanging from her hand. WILLY *notices it.*

WILLY: Will you stop mending stockings? At least while I'm in the house. It gets me nervous. I can't tell you. Please.

LINDA *hides the stocking in her hand as she follows* WILLY *across the forestage in front of the house.*

LINDA: Remember, Frank's Chop House.
WILLY [*passing the apron*]: Maybe beets would grow out there.
LINDA [*laughing*]: But you tried so many times.
WILLY: Yeah. Well, don't work hard today. [*He disappears around the right corner of the house.*]
LINDA: Be careful!

As WILLY *vanishes,* LINDA *waves to him. Suddenly the phone rings. She runs across the stage and into the kitchen and lifts it.*

Hello? Oh, Biff! I'm so glad you called, I just ... Yes, sure, I just told him. Yes, he'll be there for dinner at six o'clock, I didn't forget. Listen, I was just dying to tell you. You know that little rubber pipe I told you about? That he connected to the gas heater? I finally decided to go down the cellar this morning and take it away and destroy it. But it's gone! Imagine? He took it away himself, it isn't there! [*She listens.*] When? Oh, then you took it. Oh–nothing, it's just that I'd hoped he'd taken it away himself. Oh, I'm not worried, darling, because this morning he left in such high spirits, it was like the old days! I'm not afraid any more. Did Mr Oliver see you? ... Well, you wait there then. And make a nice impression on him, darling. Just don't perspire too much before you see him. And have a nice time with Dad. He may have big news too! ... That's right, a New York job. And be sweet to him tonight dear. Be loving to him. Because he's only a little boat looking for a harbor. [*She is trembling with sorrow and joy.*] Oh, that's wonderful, Biff, you'll save his life. Thanks, darling. Just put your arm around him when he comes into the restaurant. Give him a smile. That's the boy ... Good-by, dear. ... You got your comb? ... That's fine. Good-by, Biff dear.

In the middle of her speech, HOWARD WAGNER, *thirty-six, wheels on a small typewriter table on which is a wire-recording machine and proceeds to plug it in. This is on the left forestage. Light slowly fades on* LINDA *as it rises on* HOWARD. HOWARD *is intent on threading the machine and only glances over his shoulder as* WILLY *appears.*

WILLY: Pst! Pst!
HOWARD: Hello, Willy, come in.
WILLY: Like to have a little talk with you, Howard.
HOWARD: Sorry to keep you waiting. I'll be with you in a minute.
WILLY: What's that, Howard?
HOWARD: Didn't you ever see one of these? Wire recorder.
WILLY: Oh. Can we talk a minute?
HOWARD: Records things. Just got delivery yesterday. Been driving me crazy, the most terrific machine I ever saw in my life. I was up all night with it.
WILLY: What do you do with it?
HOWARD: I bought it for dictation, but you can do anything with it. Listen to this. I had it home last night. Listen to what I picked up. The first one is my daughter. Get this. [*He flicks the switch and 'Roll out the Barrel' is heard being whistled.*] Listen to that kid whistle.
WILLY: That is lifelike, isn't it?
HOWARD: Seven years old. Get that tone.
WILLY: Ts, ts. Like to ask a little favor if you . . .

The whistling breaks off, and the voice of HOWARD's DAUGHTER *is heard.*

HIS DAUGHTER: 'Now you, Daddy.'
HOWARD: She's crazy for me!

Again the same song is whistled.

That's me! Ha! [*He winks.*]
WILLY: You're very good!

The whistling breaks off again. The machine runs silent for a moment.

HOWARD: Sh! Get this now, this is my son.
HIS SON: 'The capital of Alabama is Montgomery; the capital of Arizona is Phoenix; the capital of Arkansas is Little Rock; the capital of California is Sacramento . . .' [*and on, and on.*]
HOWARD [*holding up five fingers*]: Five years old, Willy!
WILLY: He'll make an announcer some day!
HIS SON [*continuing*]: 'The capital . . .'
HOWARD: Get that—alphabetical order!

The machine breaks off suddenly.

Wait a minute. The maid kicked the plug out.
WILLY: It certainly is a—
HOWARD: Sh, for God's sake!
HIS SON: 'It's nine o'clock, Bulova watch time. So I have to go to sleep.'
WILLY: That really is—
HOWARD: Wait a minute! The next is my wife.

They wait.

HOWARD'S VOICE: 'Go on, say something.' [*Pause.*] 'Well, you gonna talk?'

HIS WIFE: 'I can't think of anything.'

HOWARD'S VOICE: 'Well, talk—it's turning.'

HIS WIFE [*shyly, beaten*]: 'Hello.'

Silence.

'Oh, Howard, I can't talk into this . . .'

HOWARD [*snapping the machine off*]: That was my wife.

WILLY: That is a wonderful machine. Can we—

HOWARD: I tell you, Willy, I'm gonna take my camera, and my bandsaw, and all my hobbies, and out they go. This is the most fascinating relaxation I ever found.

WILLY: I think I'll get one myself.

HOWARD: Sure, they're only a hundred and a half. You can't do without it. Supposing you wanna hear Jack Benny, see? But you can't be at home at that hour. So you tell the maid to turn the radio on when Jack Benny comes on, and this automatically goes on with the radio . . .

WILLY: And when you come home you . . .

HOWARD: You can come home twelve o'clock, one o'clock, any time you like, and you get yourself a Coke and sit yourself down, throw the switch, and there's Jack Benny's program in the middle of the night!

WILLY: I'm definitely going to get one. Because lots of time I'm on the road, and I think to myself, what I must be missing on the radio!

HOWARD: Don't you have a radio in the car?

WILLY: Well, yeah, but who ever thinks of turning it on?

HOWARD: Say, aren't you supposed to be in Boston?

WILLY: That's what I want to talk to you about, Howard. You got a minute? [*He draws a chair in from the wing.*]

HOWARD: What happened? What're you doing here?

WILLY: Well . . .

HOWARD: You didn't crack me up again, did you?

WILLY: Oh, no. No . . .

HOWARD: Geez, you had me worried there for a minute. What's the trouble?

WILLY: Well, tell you the truth, Howard. I've come to the decision that I'd rather not travel any more.

HOWARD: Not travel! Well, what'll you do?

WILLY: Remember, Christmas time, when you had the party here? You said you'd try to think of some spot for me here in town.

HOWARD: With us?

WILLY: Well, sure.

HOWARD: Oh, yeah, yeah. I remember. Well, I couldn't think of anything for you, Willy.

WILLY: I tell ya, Howard. The kids are all grown up, y'know. I don't need much any more. If I could take home—well, sixty-five dollars a week, I could swing it.

HOWARD: Yeah, but Willy, see I—

WILLY: I tell ya why, Howard. Speaking frankly and between the two of us, y'know—I'm just a little tired.

HOWARD: Oh, I could understand that, Willy. But you're a road man, Willy, and we do a road business. We've only got a half-dozen salesmen on the floor here.

WILLY: God knows, Howard, I never asked a favor of any man. But I was with the firm when your father used to carry you in here in his arms.

HOWARD: I know that, Willy, but—

WILLY: Your father came to me the day you were born and asked me what I thought of the name of Howard, may he rest in peace.

HOWARD: I appreciate that, Willy, but there just is no spot here for you. If I had a spot I'd slam you right in, but I just don't have a single solitary spot.

He looks for his lighter. WILLY *has picked it up and gives it to him. Pause.*

WILLY [*with increasing anger*]: Howard, all I need to set my table is fifty dollars a week.

HOWARD: But where am I going to put you, kid?

WILLY: Look, it isn't a question of whether I can sell merchandise, is it?

HOWARD: No, but it's a business, kid, and everybody's gotta pull his own weight.

WILLY [*desperately*]: Just let me tell you a story, Howard—

HOWARD: 'Cause you gotta admit, business is business.

WILLY: [*angrily*]: Business is definitely business, but just listen for a minute. You don't understand this. When I was a boy—eighteen, nineteen—I was already on the road. And there was a question in my mind as to whether selling had a future for me. Because in those days I had a yearning to go to Alaska. See, there were three gold strikes in one month in Alaska, and I felt like going out. Just for the ride, you might say.

HOWARD [*barely interested*]: Don't say.

WILLY: Oh, yeah, my father lived many years in Alaska. He was an adventurous man. We've got quite a little streak of self-reliance in our family. I thought I'd go out with my older brother and try to locate him, and maybe settle in the North with the old man. And I was almost decided to go, when I met a salesman in the Parker House. His name was Dave Singleman. And he was eighty-four years old, and he'd drummed merchandise in thirty-one states. And old Dave, he'd go up to his room, y'understand, put on his green velvet slippers—I'll never forget—and pick up his phone and call the buyers, and without ever leaving his room, at the age of eighty-four, he made his living. And when I saw that, I realized that selling was the greatest career a man could want. 'Cause what could be more satisfying than to be able to go, at the age of eighty-four, into twenty or thirty different cities, and pick up a phone, and be remembered and loved and helped by so many different people? Do you know? when he died—and by the way he died the death of a salesman, in his green velvet slippers in the smoker of the New York, New Haven and Hartford, going into Boston—when he died, hundreds of salesmen and buyers were at his funeral. Things were sad on a lotta trains for months after that.

He stands up. HOWARD *has not looked at him.*

In those days there was personality in it, Howard. There was respect, and comradeship, and gratitude in it. Today, it's all cut and dried, and there's no chance for bringing friendship to bear—or personality. You see what I mean?

They don't know me any more.

HOWARD [*moving away, toward the right*]: That's just the thing, Willy.

WILLY: If I had forty dollars a week–that's all I'd need. Forty dollars, Howard.

HOWARD: Kid, I can't take blood from a stone, I—

WILLY [*desperation is on him now*]: Howard, the year Al Smith was nominated, your father came to me and—

HOWARD [*starting to go off*]: I've got to see some people, kid.

WILLY [*stopping him*]: I'm talking about your father! There were promises made across this desk! You mustn't tell me you've got people to see–I put thirty-four years into this firm, Howard, and now I can't pay my insurance! You can't eat the orange and throw the peel away–a man is not a piece of fruit! [*After a pause.*] Now pay attention. Your father–in 1928 I had a big year. I averaged a hundred and seventy dollars a week in commissions.

HOWARD [*impatiently*]: Now, Willy, you never averaged—

WILLY [*banging his hand on the desk*]: I averaged a hundred and seventy dollars a week in the year of 1928! And your father came to me–or rather, I was in the office here–it was right over this desk–and he put his hand on my shoulder—

HOWARD [*getting up*]: You'll have to excuse me, Willy, I gotta see some people. Pull yourself together. [*Going out.*] I'll be back in a little while.

On HOWARD's exit, *the light on his chair grows very bright and strange.*

WILLY: Pull myself together! What the hell did I say to him? My God, I was yelling at him! How could I! [WILLY *breaks off, staring at the light, which occupies the chair, animating it. He approaches this chair, standing across the desk from it.*] Frank, Frank, don't you remember what you told me that time? How you put your hand on my shoulder, and Frank . . . [*He leans on the desk and as he speaks the dead man's name he accidentally switches on the recorder, and instantly*]

HOWARD'S SON: '. . . of New York is Albany. The capital of Ohio is Cincinnati, the capital of Rhode Island is . . .' [*The recitation continues.*]

WILLY [*leaping away with fright, shouting*]: Ha! Howard! Howard! Howard!

HOWARD [*rushing in*]: What happened?

WILLY [*pointing at the machine, which continues nasally, childishly, with the capital cities*]: Shut it off! Shut it off!

HOWARD [*pulling the plug out*]: Look, Willy . . .

WILLY [*pressing his hands to his eyes*]: I gotta get myself some coffee. I'll get some coffee . . .

WILLY *starts to walk out.* HOWARD *stops him.*

HOWARD [*rolling up the cord*]: Willy, look . . .

WILLY: I'll go to Boston.

HOWARD: Willy, you can't go to Boston for us.

WILLY: Why can't I go?

HOWARD: I don't want you to represent us. I've been meaning to tell you for a long time now.

WILLY: Howard, are you firing me?

HOWARD: I think you need a good long rest, Willy.

WILLY: Howard—

HOWARD: And when you feel better, come back, and we'll see if we can work something out.

WILLY: But I gotta earn money, Howard. I'm in no position to—

HOWARD: Where are your sons? Why don't your sons give you a hand?

WILLY: They're working on a very big deal.

HOWARD: This is no time for false pride, Willy. You go to your sons and you tell them that you're tired. You've got two great boys, haven't you?

WILLY: Oh, no question, no question, but in the meantime . . .

HOWARD: Then that's that, heh?

WILLY: All right, I'll go to Boston tomorrow.

HOWARD: No, no.

WILLY: I can't throw myself on my sons. I'm not a cripple!

HOWARD: Look, kid, I'm busy this morning.

WILLY [*grasping* HOWARD's *arm*]: Howard, you've got to let me go to Boston!

HOWARD [*hard, keeping himself under control*]: I've got a line of people to see this morning. Sit down, take five minutes, and pull yourself together, and then go home, will ya? I need the office, Willy. [*He starts to go, turns, remembering the recorder, starts to push off the table holding the recorder.*] Oh, yeah. Whenever you can this week, stop by and drop off the samples. You'll feel better, Willy, and then come back and we'll talk. Pull yourself together, kid, there's people outside.

> HOWARD *exits, pushing the table off left.* WILLY *stares into space, exhausted. Now the music is heard*—BEN's *music—first distantly, then closer, closer. As* WILLY *speaks,* BEN *enters from the right. He carries valise and umbrella.*

WILLY: Oh, Ben, how did you do it? What is the answer? Did you wind up the Alaska deal already?

BEN: Doesn't take much time if you know what you're doing. Just a short business trip. Boarding ship in an hour. Wanted to say good-by.

WILLY: Ben, I've got to talk to you.

BEN [*glancing at his watch*]: Haven't the time, William.

WILLY [*crossing the apron to* BEN]: Ben, nothing's working out. I don't know what to do.

BEN: Now, look here, William. I've bought timberland in Alaska and I need a man to look after things for me.

WILLY: God, timberland! Me and my boys in those grand outdoors!

BEN: You've a new continent at your doorstep, William. Get out of these cities, they're full of talk and time payments and courts of law. Screw on your fists and you can fight for a fortune up there.

WILLY: Yes, yes! Linda, Linda!

> LINDA *enters as of old, with the wash.*

LINDA: Oh, you're back?

BEN: I haven't much time.

WILLY: No, wait! Linda, he's got a proposition for me in Alaska.

LINDA: But you've got—[*To* BEN.] He's got a beautiful job here.

WILLY: But in Alaska, kid, I could—

LINDA: You're doing well enough, Willy!

BEN [*to* LINDA]: Enough for what, my dear?

LINDA [*frightened of* BEN *and angry at him*]: Don't say those things to him!

Enough to be happy right here, right now. [*To* WILLY, *while* BEN *laughs.*] Why must everybody conquer the world? You're well liked, and the boys love you, and someday– [*to* BEN]–why, old man Wagner told him just the other day that if he keeps it up he'll be a member of the firm, didn't he, Willy?

WILLY: Sure, sure. I am building something with this firm, Ben, and if a man is building something he must be on the right track, mustn't he?

BEN: What are you building? Lay your hand on it. Where is it?

WILLY [*hesistantly*]: That's true, Linda, there's nothing.

LINDA: Why? [*To* BEN.] There's a man eighty-four years old—

WILLY: That's right, Ben, that's right. When I look at that man I say, what is there to worry about?

BEN: Bah!

WILLY: It's true, Ben. All he has to do is go into any city, pick up the phone, and he's making his living and you know why?

BEN [*picking up his valise*]: I've got to go.

WILLY [*holding* BEN *back*]: Look at this boy!

BIFF, *in his high school sweater, enters carrying suitcase.* HAPPY *carries* BIFF'*s shoulder guards, gold helmet, and football pants.*

Without a penny to his name, three great universities are begging for him, and from there the sky's the limit, because it's not what you do, Ben. It's who you know and the smile on your face! It's contacts, Ben, contacts! The whole wealth of Alaska passes over the lunch table at the Commodore Hotel, and that's the wonder, the wonder of this country, that a man can end with diamonds here on the basis on being liked! [*He turns to* BIFF.] And that's why when you get out on that field today it's important. Because thousands of people will be rooting for you and loving you. [*To* BEN, *who has again begun to leave.*] And Ben! when he walks into a business office his name will sound out like a bell and all the doors will open to him! I've seen it, Ben, I've seen it a thousand times! You can't feel it with your hand like timber, but it's there!

BEN: Good-by, William.

WILLY: Ben, am I right? Don't you think I'm right? I value your advice.

BEN: There's a new continent at your doorstep, William. You could walk out rich. Rich! [*He is gone.*]

WILLY: We'll do it here, Ben! You hear me? We're gonna do it here!

Young BERNARD *rushes in. The gay music of the Boys is heard.*

BERNARD: Oh, gee, I was afraid you left already!

WILLY: Why? What time is it?

BERNARD: It's half-past one!

WILLY: Well, come on, everybody! Ebbets Field next stop! Where's the pennants? [*He rushes through the wall-line of the kitchen and out into the living-room.*]

LINDA [*to* BIFF]: Did you pack fresh underwear?

BIFF [*who has been limbering up*]: I want to go!

BERNARD: Biff, I'm carrying your helmet, ain't I?

HAPPY: No, I'm carrying the helmet.

BERNARD: Oh, Biff, you promised me.

HAPPY: I'm carrying the helmet.

BERNARD: How am I going to get in the locker room?

LINDA: Let him carry the shoulder guards. [*She puts her coat and hat on in the kitchen.*]

BERNARD: Can I, Biff? 'Cause I told everybody I'm going to be in the locker room.

HAPPY: In Ebbets Field it's the clubhouse.

BERNARD: I meant the clubhouse. Biff!

HAPPY: Biff!

BIFF [*grandly, after a slight pause*]: Let him carry the shoulder guards.

HAPPY [*as he gives* BERNARD *the shoulder guards*]: Stay close to us now.

WILLY *rushes in with the pennants.*

WILLY [*handing them out*]: Everybody wave them when Biff comes out on the field.

HAPPY *and* BERNARD *run off.*

You set now, boy?

The music has died away.

BIFF: Ready to go, Pop. Every muscle is ready.

WILLY [*at the edge of the apron*]: You realize what this means?

BIFF: That's right, Pop.

WILLY [*feeling* BIFF'*s muscles*]: You're comin' home this afternoon captain of the All-Scholastic Championship Team of the City of New York.

BIFF: I got it, Pop. And remember, pal, when I take off my helmet, that touchdown is for you.

WILLY: Let's go! [*He is starting out, with his arm around* BIFF, *when* CHARLEY *enters, as of old, in knickers.*] I got no room for you, Charley.

CHARLEY: Room? For what?

WILLY: In the car.

CHARLEY: You goin' for a ride? I wanted to shoot some casino.

WILLY [*furiously*]: Casino! [*Incredulously.*] Don't you realize what today is?

LINDA: Oh, he knows, Willy. He's just kidding you.

WILLY: That's nothing to kid about!

CHARLEY: No, Linda, what's goin' on?

LINDA: He's playing in Ebbets Field.

CHARLEY: Baseball in this weather?

WILLY: Don't talk to him. Come on, come on! [*He is pushing them out.*]

CHARLEY: Wait a minute, didn't you hear the news?

WILLY: What?

CHARLEY: Don't you listen to the radio? Ebbets Field just blew up.

WILLY: You go to hell!

CHARLEY *laughs. Pushing them out.*

Come on, come on! We're late.

CHARLEY [*as they go*]: Knock a homer, Biff, knock a homer!

WILLY [*the last to leave, turning to* CHARLEY]: I don't think that was funny,

Charley. This is the greatest day of his life.

CHARLEY: Willy, when are you going to grow up?

WILLY: Yeah, heh? When this game is over, Charley, you'll be laughing out of the other side of your face. They'll be calling him another Red Grange. Twenty-five thousand a year.

CHARLEY [*kidding*]: Is that so?

WILLY: Yeah, that's so.

CHARLEY: Well, then, I'm sorry, Willy. But tell me something.

WILLY: What?

CHARLEY: Who is Red Grange?

WILLY: Put up your hands. Goddam you, put up your hands!

CHARLEY, *chuckling, shakes his head and walks away, around the left corner of the stage.* WILLY *follows him. The music rises to a mocking frenzy.*

Who the hell do you think you are, better than everybody else? You don't know everything, you big, ignorant, stupid . . . Put up your hands!

Light rises, on the right side of the forestage, on a small table in the reception room of CHARLEY's *office. Traffic sounds are heard.* BERNARD, *now mature, sits whistling to himself. A pair of tennis rackets and an overnight bag are on the floor beside him.*

WILLY [*offstage*]: What are you walking away for? Don't walk away! If you're going to say something say it to my face! I know you laugh at me behind my back. You'll laugh out of the other side of your goddam face after this game. Touchdown! Touchdown! Eighty thousand people! Touchdown! Right between the goal posts.

BERNARD *is a quiet, earnest, but self-assured young man.* WILLY's *voice is coming from right upstage now.* BERNARD *lowers his feet off the table and listens.* JENNY, *his father's secretary, enters.*

JENNY [*distressed*]: Say, Bernard, will you go out in the hall?

BERNARD: What is that noise? Who is it?

JENNY: Mr Loman. He just got off the elevator.

BERNARD [*getting up*]: Who's he arguing with?

JENNY: Nobody. There's nobody with him. I can't deal with him any more, and your father gets all upset everytime he comes. I've got a lot of typing to do, and your father's waiting to sign it. Will you see him?

WILLY [*entering*]: Touchdown! Touch—[*He sees* JENNY.] Jenny, Jenny, good to see you. How're ya? Workin'? Or still honest?

JENNY: Fine. How've you been feeling?

WILLY: Not much any more, Jenny. Ha, ha! [*He is surprised to see the rackets.*]

BERNARD: Hello, Uncle Willy.

WILLY [*almost shocked*]: Bernard! Well, look who's here! [*He comes quickly, guiltily, to* BERNARD *and warmly shakes his hand.*]

BERNARD: How are you? Good to see you.

WILLY: What are you doing here?

BERNARD: Oh, just stopped by to see Pop. Get off my feet till my train leaves. I'm going to Washington in a few minutes.

WILLY: Is he in?

BERNARD: Yes, he's in his office with the accountant. Sit down.

WILLY [*sitting down*]: What're you going to do in Washington?

BERNARD: Oh, just a case I've got there, Willy.

WILLY: That so? [*Indicating the rackets.*] You going to play tennis there?

BERNARD: I'm staying with a friend who's got a court.

WILLY: Don't say. His own tennis court. Must be fine people, I bet.

BERNARD: They are, very nice. Dad tells me Biff's in town.

WILLY [*with a big smile*]: Yeah, Biff's in. Working on a very big deal, Bernard.

BERNARD: What's Biff doing?

WILLY: Well, he's been doing very big things in the West. But he decided to establish himself here. Very big. We're having dinner. Did I hear your wife had a boy?

BERNARD: That's right. Our second.

WILLY: Two boys! What do you know!

BERNARD: What kind of a deal has Biff got?

WILLY: Well, Bill Oliver—very big sporting-goods man—he wants Biff very badly. Called him in from the West. Long distance, carte blanche, special deliveries. Your friends have their own private tennis court?

BERNARD: You still with the old firm, Willy?

WILLY [*after a pause*]: I'm—I'm overjoyed to see how you made the grade, Bernard, overjoyed. It's an encouraging thing to see a young man really—really— Looks very good for Biff—very—[*He breaks off, then.*] Bernard—[*He is so full of emotion, he breaks off again.*]

BERNARD: What is it, Willy?

WILLY [*small and alone*]: What—what's the secret?

BERNARD: What secret?

WILLY: How—how did you? Why didn't he ever catch on?

BERNARD: I wouldn't know that, Willy.

WILLY [*confidentially, desperately*]: You were his friend, his boyhood friend. There's something I don't understand about it. His life ended after that Ebbets Field game. From the age of seventeen nothing good ever happened to him.

BERNARD: He never trained himself for anything.

WILLY: But he did, he did. After high school he took so many correspondence courses. Radio mechanics; television; God knows what, and never made the slightest mark.

BERNARD [*taking off his glasses*]: Willy, do you want to talk candidly?

WILLY [*rising, faces* BERNARD]: I regard you as a very brilliant man, Bernard. I value your advice.

BERNARD: Oh, the hell with the advice, Willy. I couldn't advise you. There's just one thing I've always wanted to ask you. When he was supposed to graduate, and the math teacher flunked him—

WILLY: Oh, that son-of-a-bitch ruined his life.

BERNARD: Yeah, but, Willy, all he had to do was go to summer school and make up that subject.

WILLY: That's right, that's right.

BERNARD: Did you tell him not to go to summer school?

WILLY: Me? I begged him to go. I ordered him to go!

BERNARD: Then why wouldn't he go?

WILLY: Why? Why! Bernard, that question has been trailing me like a ghost for the last fifteen years. He flunked the subject, and laid down and died like a hammer hit him!

BERNARD: Take it easy, kid.

WILLY: Let me talk to you—I got nobody to talk to. Bernard, Bernard, was it my fault? Y'see? It keeps going around in my mind, maybe I did something to him. I got nothing to give him.

BERNARD: Don't take it so hard.

WILLY: Why did he lay down? What is the story there? You were his friend!

BERNARD: Willy, I remember, it was June, and our grades came out. And he'd flunked math.

WILLY: That son-of-a-bitch!

BERNARD: No, it wasn't right then. Biff just got very angry, I remember, and he was ready to enroll in summer school.

WILLY [*surprised*]: He was?

BERNARD: He wasn't beaten by it all. But then, Willy, he disappeared from the block for almost a month. And I got the idea that he'd gone up to New England to see you. Did he have a talk with you then?

WILLY *stares in silence.*

Willy?

WILLY [*with a strong edge of resentment in his voice*]: Yeah, he came to Boston. What about it?

BERNARD: Well, just that when he came back—I'll never forget this, it always mystifies me. Because I'd thought so well of Biff, even though he'd always taken advantage of me. I loved him, Willy, y'know? And he came back after that month and took his sneakers—remember those sneakers with 'University of Virginia' printed on them? He was so proud of those, wore them every day. And he took them down in the cellar, and burned them up in the furnace. We had a fist fight. It lasted at least half an hour. Just the two of us, punching each other down the cellar, and crying right through it. I've often thought of how strange it was that I knew he'd given up his life. What happened in Boston, Willy?

WILLY *looks at him as at an intruder.*

I just bring it up because you asked me.

WILLY [*angrily*]: Nothing. What do you mean, 'What happened?' What's that got to do with anything?

BERNARD: Well, don't get sore.

WILLY: What are you trying to do, blame it on me? If a boy lays down is that my fault?

BERNARD: Now, Willy, don't get—

WILLY: Well, don't—don't talk to me that way! What does that mean, 'What happened?'

CHARLEY *enters. He is in his vest, and he carries a bottle of bourbon.*

CHARLEY: Hey, you're going to miss that train. [*He waves the bottle.*]

BERNARD: Yeah, I'm going. [*He takes the bottle.*] Thanks, Pop. [*He picks up his rackets and bag.*] Good-by, Willy, and don't worry about it. You know, 'If at

first you don't succeed . . .'
WILLY: Yes, I believe in that.
BERNARD: But sometimes, Willy, it's better for a man just to walk away.
WILLY: Walk away?
BERNARD: That's right.
WILLY: But if you can't walk away?
BERNARD [*after a slight pause*]: I guess that's when it's tough. [*Extending his hand.*] Good-by, Willy.
WILLY [*shaking* BERNARD's *hand*]: Good-by, boy.
CHARLEY [*an arm on* BERNARD's *shoulder*]: How do you like this kid? Gonna argue a case in front of the Supreme Court.
BERNARD [*protesting*]: Pop!
WILLY [*genuinely shocked, pained, and happy*]: No! The Supreme Court!
BERNARD: I gotta run. 'By, Dad!
CHARLEY: Knock 'em dead, Bernard!

BERNARD *goes off.*

WILLY [*as* CHARLEY *takes out his wallet*]: The Supreme Court! And he didn't even mention it!
CHARLEY [*counting out money on the desk*]: He don't have to—he's gonna do it.
WILLY: And you never told him what to do, did you? You never took any interest in him.
CHARLEY: My salvation is that I never took any interest in anything. There's some money—fifty dollars. I got an accountant inside.
WILLY: Charley, look . . . [*With difficulty.*] I got my insurance to pay. If you can manage it—I need a hundred and ten dollars.

CHARLEY *doesn't reply for a moment; merely stops moving.*

I'd draw it from my bank but Linda would know, and I . . .
CHARLEY: Sit down, Willy.
WILLY [*moving toward the chair*]: I'm keeping an account of everything, remember. I'll pay every penny back. [*He sits.*]
CHARLEY: Now listen to me, Willy.
WILLY: I want you to know I appreciate . . .
CHARLEY [*sitting down on the table*]: Willy, what're you doin'? What the hell is goin' on in your head?
WILLY: Why? I'm simply . . .
CHARLEY: I offered you a job. You can make fifty dollars a week. And I won't send you on the road.
WILLY: I've got a job.
CHARLEY: Without pay? What kind of a job is a job without pay? [*He rises.*] Now, look, kid, enough is enough. I'm no genius but I know when I'm being insulted.
WILLY: Insulted!
CHARLEY: Why don't you want to work for me?
WILLY: What's the matter with you? I've got a job.
CHARLEY: Then what're you walkin' in here every week for?
WILLY [*getting up*]: Well, if you don't want me to walk in here—
CHARLEY: I am offering you a job.

WILLY: I don't want your goddam job!

CHARLEY: When the hell are you going to grow up?

WILLY [*furiously*]: You big ignoramus, if you say that to me again I'll rap you one! I don't care how big you are!

He's ready to fight. Pause.

CHARLEY [*kindly, going to him*]: How much do you need, Willy?

WILLY: Charley, I'm strapped, I'm strapped. I don't know what to do. I was just fired.

CHARLEY: Howard fired you?

WILLY: That snotnose. Imagine that? I named him. I named him Howard.

CHARLEY: Willy, when're you gonna realize that them things don't mean anything? You named him Howard, but you can't sell that. The only thing you got in this world is what you can sell. And the funny thing is that you're a salesman, and you don't know that.

WILLY: I've always tried to think otherwise, I guess. I always felt that if a man was impressive, and well liked, that nothing—

CHARLEY: Why must everybody like you? Who liked J.P. Morgan? Was he impressive? In a Turkish bath he'd look like a butcher. But with his pockets on he was very well liked. Now listen, Willy, I know you don't like me, and nobody can say I'm in love with you, but I'll give you a job because—just for the hell of it, put it that way. Now what do you say?

WILLY: I—I just can't work for you, Charley.

CHARLEY: What're you, jealous of me?

WILLY: I can't work for you, that's all, don't ask me why.

CHARLEY [*angered, takes out more bills*]: You been jealous of me all your life, you damned fool! Here, pay your insurance. [*He puts the money in* WILLY's *hand.*]

WILLY: I'm keeping strict accounts.

CHARLEY: I've got some work to do. Take care of yourself. And pay your insurance.

WILLY [*moving to the right*]: Funny, y'know? After all the highways, and the trains, and the appointments, and the years, you end up worth more dead than alive.

CHARLEY: Willy, nobody's worth nothin' dead. [*After a slight pause.*] Did you hear what I said?

WILLY *stands still, dreaming.*

Willy!

WILLY: Apologize to Bernard for me when you see him. I didn't mean to argue with him. He's a fine boy. They're all fine boys, and they'll end up big—all of them. Someday they'll all play tennis together. Wish me luck, Charley. He saw Bill Oliver today.

CHARLEY: Good luck.

WILLY [*on the verge of tears*]: Charley, you're the only friend I got. Isn't that a remarkable thing? [*He goes out.*]

CHARLEY: Jesus!

CHARLEY *stares after him a moment and follows. All light blacks out. Suddenly raucous music is heard, and a red glow rises behind the screen at right.* STANLEY, *a young waiter, appears, carrying a table, followed by* HAPPY, *who is carrying two chairs.*

STANLEY [*putting the table down*]: That's all right, Mr Loman, I can handle it myself. [*He turns and takes the chairs from* HAPPY *and places them at the table.*]
HAPPY [*glancing around*]: Oh, this is better.
STANLEY: Sure, in the front there you're in the middle of all kinds a noise. Whenever you got a party, Mr Loman, you just tell me and I'll put you back here. Y'know, there's a lotta people they don't like it private, because when they go out they like to see a lotta action around them because they're sick and tired to stay in the house by theirself. But I know you, you ain't from Hackensack. You know what I mean?
HAPPY [*sitting down*]: So how's it coming, Stanley?
STANLEY: Ah, it's a dog's life. I only wish during the war they'd a took me in the Army. I coulda been dead by now.
HAPPY: My brother's back, Stanley.
STANLEY: Oh, he come back, heh? From the Far West.
HAPPY: Yeah, big cattle man, my brother, so treat him right. And my father's coming too.
STANLEY: Oh, your father too!
HAPPY: You got a couple of nice lobsters?
STANLEY: Hundred per cent, big.
HAPPY: I want them with the claws.
STANLEY: Don't worry, I don't give you no mice.

HAPPY *laughs.*

How about some wine? It'll put a head on the meal.
HAPPY: No. You remember, Stanley, that recipe I brought you from overseas? With the champagne in it?
STANLEY: Oh, yeah, sure. I still got it tacked up yet in the kitchen. But that'll have to cost a buck apiece anyways.
HAPPY: That's all right.
STANLEY: What'd you, hit a number or somethin'?
HAPPY: No, it's a little celebration. My brother is—I think he pulled off a big deal today. I think we're going into business together.
STANLEY: Great! That's the best for you. Because a family business, you know what I mean?—that's the best.
HAPPY: That's what I think.
STANLEY: 'Cause what's the difference? Somebody steals? It's in the family. Know what I mean? [*Sotto voce.*] Like this bartender here. The boss is goin' crazy what kinda leak he's got in the cash register. You put it in but it don't come out.
HAPPY [*raising his head*]: Sh!
STANLEY: What?
HAPPY: You notice I wasn't lookin' right or left, was I?
STANLEY: No.
HAPPY: And my eyes are closed.
STANLEY: So what's the—?
HAPPY: Strudel's comin'.
STANLEY [*catching on, looks around*]: Ah, no, there's no—

He breaks off as a furred, lavishly dressed girl enters and sits at the next table. Both follow her with their eyes.

Geez, how'd ya know?

HAPPY: I got radar or something. [*Staring directly at her profile.*] Oooooooo . . . Stanley.

STANLEY: I think that's for you, Mr Loman.

HAPPY: Look at that mouth. Oh, God. And the binoculars.

STANLEY: Geez, you got a life, Mr Loman.

HAPPY: Wait on her.

STANLEY [*going to the girl's table*]: Would you like a menu, ma'am?

GIRL: I'm expecting someone, but I'd like a—

HAPPY: Why don't you bring her—excuse me, miss, do you mind? I sell champagne, and I'd like you to try my brand. Bring her a champagne, Stanley.

GIRL: That's awfully nice of you.

HAPPY: Don't mention it. It's all company money. [*He laughs.*]

GIRL: That's a charming product to be selling, isn't it?

HAPPY: Oh, gets to be like everything else. Selling is selling, y'know.

GIRL: I suppose.

HAPPY: You don't happen to sell, do you?

GIRL: No, I don't sell.

HAPPY: Would you object to a compliment from a stranger? You ought to be on a magazine cover.

GIRL [*looking at him a little archly*]: I have been.

STANLEY *comes in with a glass of champagne.*

HAPPY: What'd I say before, Stanley? You see? She's a cover girl.

STANLEY: Oh, I could see, I could see.

HAPPY [*to the* GIRL]: What magazine?

GIRL: Oh, a lot of them. [*She takes the drink.*] Thank you.

HAPPY: You know what they say in France, don't you? 'Champagne is the drink of the complexion'–Hya, Biff!

BIFF *has entered and sits with* HAPPY.

BIFF: Hello, kid. Sorry I'm late.

HAPPY: I just got here. Uh, Miss—?

GIRL: Forsythe.

HAPPY: Miss Forsythe, this is my brother.

BIFF: Is Dad here?

HAPPY: His name is Biff. You might've heard of him. Great football player.

GIRL: Really? What team?

HAPPY: Are you familiar with football?

GIRL: No, I'm afraid I'm not.

HAPPY: Biff is quarterback with the New York Giants.

GIRL: Well, that is nice, isn't it? [*She drinks.*]

HAPPY: Good health.

GIRL: I'm happy to meet you.

HAPPY: That's my name. Hap. It's really Harold, but at West Point they called me Happy.

GIRL [*now really impressed*]: Oh, I see. How do you do? [*She turns her profile.*]

BIFF: Isn't Dad coming?

HAPPY: You want her?

BIFF: Oh, I could never make that.

HAPPY: I remember the time that idea would never come into your head. Where's the old confidence, Biff?

BIFF: I just saw Oliver—

HAPPY: Wait a minute. I've got to see that old confidence again. Do you want her? She's on call.

BIFF: Oh, no. [*He turns to look at the* GIRL.]

HAPPY: I'm telling you. [*Watch this. Turning to the* GIRL.] Honey? [*She turns to him.*] Are you busy?

GIRL: Well, I am . . . but I could make a phone call.

HAPPY: Do that, will you, honey? And see if you can get a friend. We'll be here for a while. Biff is one of the greatest football players in the country.

GIRL [*standing up*]: Well, I'm certainly happy to meet you.

HAPPY: Come back soon.

GIRL: I'll try.

HAPPY: Don't try, honey, try hard.

The GIRL *exits.* STANLEY *follows, shaking his head in bewildered admiration.*

Isn't that a shame now? A beautiful girl like that? That's why I can't get married. There's not a good woman in a thousand. New York is loaded with them, kid!

BIFF: Hap, look—

HAPPY: I told you she was on call!

BIFF [*strangely unnerved*]: Cut it out, will ya? I want to say something to you.

HAPPY: Did you see Oliver?

BIFF: I saw him all right. Now look, I want to tell Dad a couple of things and I want you to help me.

HAPPY: What? Is he going to back you?

BIFF: Are you crazy? You're out of your goddam head, you know that?

HAPPY: Why? What happened?

BIFF [*breathlessly*]: I did a terrible thing today, Hap. It's been the strangest day I ever went through. I'm all numb, I swear.

HAPPY: You mean he wouldn't see you?

BIFF: Well, I waited six hours for him, see? All day. Kept sending my name in. Even tried to date his secretary so she'd get me to him, but no soap.

HAPPY: Because you're not showin' the old confidence, Biff. He remembered you, didn't he?

BIFF [*stopping* HAPPY *with a gesture*]: Finally, about five o'clock, he comes out. Didn't remember who I was or anything. I felt like such an idiot, Hap.

HAPPY: Did you tell him my Florida idea?

BIFF: He walked away. I saw him for one minute. I got so mad I could've torn the walls down! How the hell did I ever get the idea I was a salesman there? I even believed myself that I'd been a salesman for him! And then he gave me one look and–I realized what a ridiculous lie my whole life has been! We've been talking in a dream for fifteen years. I was a shipping clerk.

HAPPY: What'd you do?

BIFF [*with great tension and wonder*]: Well, he left, see. And the secretary went out. I was alone in the waiting-room. I don't know what came over me, Hap. The next thing I know I'm in his office—paneled walls, everything. I can't explain it. I–Hap, I took his fountain pen.

HAPPY: Geez, did he catch you?

BIFF: I ran out. I ran down all eleven flights. I ran and ran and ran.

HAPPY: That was an awful dumb—what'd you do that for?

BIFF [*agonized*]: I don't know, I just–wanted to take something, I don't know. You gotta help me, Hap, I'm gonna tell Pop.

HAPPY: You crazy? What for?

BIFF: Hap, he's got to understand that I'm not the man somebody lends that kind of money to. He thinks I've been spiting him all these years and it's eating him up.

HAPPY: That's just it. You tell him something nice.

BIFF: I can't.

HAPPY: Say you got a lunch date with Oliver tomorrow.

BIFF: So what do I do tomorrow?

HAPPY: You leave the house tomorrow and come back at night and say Oliver is thinking it over. And he thinks it over for a couple of weeks, and gradually it fades away and nobody's the worse.

BIFF: But it'll go on forever!

HAPPY: Dad is never so happy as when he's looking forward to something!

WILLY *enters.*

Hello, scout!

WILLY: Gee, I haven't been here in years!

STANLEY *has followed* WILLY *in and sets a chair for him.* STANLEY *starts off but* HAPPY *stops him.*

HAPPY: Stanley!

STANLEY *stands by, waiting for an order.*

BIFF [*going to* WILLY *with guilt, as to an invalid*]: Sit down, Pop. You want a drink?

WILLY: Sure, I don't mind.

BIFF: Let's get a load on.

WILLY: You look worried.

BIFF: N-no. [*To* STANLEY.] Scotch all around. Make it doubles.

STANLEY: Doubles, right. [*He goes.*]

WILLY: You had a couple already, didn't you?

BIFF: Just a couple, yeah.

WILLY: Well, what happened, boy? [*Nodding affirmatively, with a smile.*] Everything go all right?

BIFF [*takes a breath, then reaches out and grasps* WILLY's *hand*]: Pal . . . [*He is smiling bravely, and* WILLY *is smiling too.*] I had an experience today.

HAPPY: Terrific, Pop.

WILLY: That so? What happened?

BIFF [*high, slightly alcoholic, above the earth*]: I'm going to tell you everything from first to last. It's been a strange day. [*Silence. He looks around, composes himself as best he can, but his breath keeps breaking the rhythm of his voice.*] I had to wait quite a while for him, and—

WILLY: Oliver?

BIFF: Yeah, Oliver. All day, as a matter of cold fact. And a lot of—instances—facts, Pop, facts about my life came back to me. Who was it, Pop? Who ever said I was a salesman with Oliver?

WILLY: Well, you were.

BIFF: No, Dad, I was a shipping clerk.

WILLY: But you were practically—

BIFF [*with determination*]: Dad, I don't know who said it first, but I was never a salesman for Bill Oliver.

WILLY: What're you talking about?

BIFF: Let's hold on to the facts tonight, Pop. We're not going to get anywhere bullin' around. I was a shipping clerk.

WILLY [*angrily*]: All right, now listen to me—

BIFF: Why don't you let me finish?

WILLY: I'm not interested in stories about the past or any crap of that kind because the woods are burning, boys, you understand? There's a big blaze going on all around. I was fired today.

BIFF [*shocked*]: How could you be?

WILLY: I was fired, and I'm looking for a little good news to tell your mother, because the woman has waited and the woman has suffered. The gist of it is that I haven't got a story left in my head, Biff. So don't give me a lecture about facts and aspects. I am not interested. Now what've you got to say to me?

STANLEY *enters with three drinks. They wait until he leaves.*

Did you see Oliver?

BIFF: Jesus, Dad!

WILLY: You mean you didn't go up there?

HAPPY: Sure he went up there.

BIFF: I did. I—saw him. How could they fire you?

WILLY [*on the edge of his chair*]: What kind of a welcome did he give you?

BIFF: He won't even let you work on commission?

WILLY: I'm out! [*Driving.*] So tell me, he gave you a warm welcome?

HAPPY: Sure, Pop, sure!

BIFF [*driven*]: Well, it was kind of—

WILLY: I was wondering if he'd remember you. [*To* HAPPY.] Imagine, man doesn't see him for ten, twelve years and gives him that kind of a welcome!

HAPPY: Damn right!

BIFF [*trying to return to the offensive*]: Pop, look—

WILLY: You know why he remembered you, don't you? Because you impressed him in those days.

BIFF: Let's talk quietly and get this down to the facts, huh?

WILLY [*as though* BIFF *had been interrupting*]: Well, what happened? It's great news, Biff. Did he take you into his office or'd you talk in the waiting-room?

BIFF: Well, he came in, see, and—

WILLY [*with a big smile*]: What'd he say? Betcha he threw his arm around you.

BIFF: Well, he kinda—

WILLY: He's a fine man. [*To* HAPPY.] Very hard man to see, y'know.

HAPPY [*agreeing*]: Oh, I know.

WILLY [*to* BIFF]: Is that where you had the drinks?

BIFF: Yeah, he gave me a couple of–no, no!

HAPPY [*cutting in*]: He told him my Florida idea.

WILLY: Don't interrupt. [*To* BIFF.] How'd he react to the Florida idea?

BIFF: Dad, will you give me a minute to explain?

WILLY: I've been waiting for you to explain since I sat down here! What happened? He took you into his office and what?

BIFF: Well–I talked. And–and he listened, see.

WILLY: Famous for the way he listenes, y'know. What was his answer?

BIFF: His answer was—[*He breaks off, suddenly angry.*] Dad, you're not letting me tell you what I want to tell you!

WILLY [*accusing, angered*]: You didn't see him, did you?

BIFF: I did see him!

WILLY: What'd you insult him or something? You insulted him, didn't you?

BIFF: Listen, will you let me out of it, will you just let me out of it!

HAPPY: What the hell!

WILLY: Tell me what happened!

BIFF [*to* HAPPY]: I can't talk to him!

> *A single trumpet note jars the ear. The light of green leaves stains the house, which holds the air of night and a dream.* YOUNG BERNARD *enters and knocks on the door of the house.*

YOUNG BERNARD [*frantically*]: Mrs Loman, Mrs Loman!

HAPPY: Tell him what happened!

BIFF [*to* HAPPY]: Shut up and leave me alone!

WILLY: No, no! You had to go and flunk math!

BIFF: What math? What're you talking about?

YOUNG BERNARD: Mrs Loman, Mrs Loman!

> LINDA *appears in the house, as of old.*

WILLY [*wildly*]: Math, math, math!

BIFF: Take it easy, Pop!

YOUNG BERNARD: Mrs Loman!

WILLY [*furiously*]: If you hadn't flunked you'd've been set by now!

BIFF: Now, look, I'm gonna tell you what happened, and you're going to listen to me.

YOUNG BERNARD: Mrs Loman!

BIFF: I waited six hours—

HAPPY: What the hell are you saying?

BIFF: I kept sending in my name but he wouldn't see me. So finally he . . . [*He continues unheard as light fades low on the restaurant.*]

YOUNG BERNARD: Biff flunked math!

LINDA: No!

YOUNG BERNARD: Birnbaum flunked him! They won't graduate him!

LINDA: But they have to. He's gotta go to the university. Where is he? Biff! Biff!

YOUNG BERNARD: No, he left. He went to Grand Central.

LINDA: Grand— You mean he went to Boston!
YOUNG BERNARD: Is Uncle Willy in Boston?
LINDA: Oh, maybe Willy can talk to the teacher. Oh, the poor, poor boy!

Light on house area snaps out.

BIFF [*at the table, now audible, holding up a gold fountain pen*]: . . . so I'm washed up with Oliver, you understand? Are you listening to me?
WILLY [*at a loss*]: Yeah, sure. If you hadn't flunked—
BIFF: Flunked what? What're you talking about?
WILLY: Don't blame everything on me! I didn't flunk math–you did! What pen?
HAPPY: That was awful dumb, Biff, a pen like that is worth—
WILLY [*seeing the pen for the first time*]: You took Oliver's pen?
BIFF [*weakening*]: Dad, I just explained it to you.
WILLY: You stole Bill Oliver's fountain pen!
BIFF: I didn't exactly steal it! That's just what I've been explaining to you!
HAPPY: He had it in his hand and just then Oliver walked in, so he got nervous and stuck it in his pocket!
WILLY: My God, Biff!
BIFF: I never intended to do it, Dad!
OPERATOR'S VOICE: Standish Arms, good evening!
WILLY [*shouting*]: I'm not in my room!
BIFF [*frightened*]: Dad, what's the matter?

He and HAPPY *stand up.*

OPERATOR: Ringing Mr Loman for you!
WILLY: I'm not there, stop it!
BIFF [*horrified, gets down on one knee before* WILLY]: Dad, I'll make good, I'll make good.

WILLY *tries to get to his feet.* BIFF *holds him down.*

Sit down now.
WILLY: No, you're no good, you're no good for anything.
BIFF: I am, Dad, I'll find something else, you understand? Now don't worry about anything. [*He holds up* WILLY'*s face.*] Talk to me, Dad.
OPERATOR: Mr Loman does not answer. Shall I page him?
WILLY [*attempting to stand, as though to rush and silence the* OPERATOR]: No, no, no!
HAPPY: He'll strike something, Pop.
WILLY: No, no . . .
BIFF [*desperately, standing over* WILLY]: Pop, listen! Listen to me! I'm telling you something good. Oliver talked to his partner about the Florida idea. You listening? He–he talked to his partner, and he came to me . . . I'm going to be all right, your hear? Dad, listen to me, he said it was just a question of the amount!
WILLY: Then you . . . got it?
HAPPY: He's gonna be terrific, Pop!
WILLY [*trying to stand*]: Then you got it, haven't you? You got it! You got it!

BIFF [*agonized, holds* WILLY *down*]: No, no. Look, Pop. I'm supposed to have lunch with them tomorrow. I'm just telling you this so you'll know I can still make an impression, Pop. And I'll make good somewhere, but I can't go tomorrow, see?

WILLY: Why not? You simply—

BIFF: But the pen, Pop!

WILLY: You give it to him and tell him it was an oversight!

HAPPY: Sure, have lunch tomorrow!

BIFF: I can't say that—

WILLY: You were doing a crossword puzzle and accidentally used his pen!

BIFF: Listen, kid, I took those balls years ago, now I walk in with his fountain pen? That clinches it, don't you see? I can't face him like that! I'll try elsewhere.

PAGE'S VOICE: Paging Mr Loman!

WILLY: Don't you want to be anything?

BIFF: Pop, how can I go back?

WILLY: You don't want to be anything, is that what's behind it?

BIFF [*now angry at* WILLY *for not crediting his sympathy*]: Don't take it that way! You think it was easy walking into that office after what I'd done to him? A team of horses couldn't have dragged me back to Bill Oliver!

WILLY: Then why'd you go?

BIFF: Why did I go? Why did I go! Look at you! Look at what's become of you!

Off left, THE WOMAN *laughs.*

WILLY: Biff, you're going to go to that lunch tomorrow, or—

BIFF: I can't go. I've got no appointment!

HAPPY: Biff, for . . . !

WILLY: Are you spiting me?

BIFF: Don't take it that way! Goddammit!

WILLY [*strikes* BIFF *and falters away from the table*]: You rotten little louse! Are you spiting me?

THE WOMAN: Someone's at the door, Willy!

BIFF: I'm no good, can't you see what I am?

HAPPY [*separating them*]: Hey, you're in a restaurant! Now cut it out, both of you?

The girls enter.

Hello, girls, sit down.

THE WOMAN *laughs, off left.*

MISS FORSYTHE: I guess we might as well. This is Letta.

THE WOMAN: Willy, are you going to wake up?

BIFF [*ignoring* WILLY]: How're ya, miss, sit down. What do you drink?

MISS FORSYTHE: Letta might not be able to stay long.

LETTA: I gotta get up very early tomorrow. I got jury duty. I'm so excited! Were you fellows ever on a jury?

BIFF: No, but I been in front of them!

The girls laugh.

This is my father.
LETTA: Isn't he cute? Sit down with us, Pop.
HAPPY: Sit him down, Biff!
BIFF [*going to him*]: Come on, slugger, drink us under the table. To hell with it! Come on, sit down, pal.

On BIFF's *last insistence,* WILLY *is about to sit.*

THE WOMAN [*now urgently*]: Willy, are you going to answer the door!

THE WOMAN's *call pulls* WILLY *back. He starts right, befuddled.*

BIFF: Hey, where are you going?
WILLY: Open the door.
BIFF: The door?
WILLY: The washroom . . . the door . . . where's the door?
BIFF [*leading* WILLY *to the left*]: Just go straight down.

WILLY *moves left.*

THE WOMAN: Willy, Willy, are you going to get up, get up, get up, get up?

WILLY *exits left.*

LETTA: I think it's sweet you bring your daddy along.
MISS FORSYTHE: Oh, he isn't really your father!
BIFF [*at left, turning to her resentfully*]: Miss Forsythe, you've just seen a prince walk by. A fine, troubled prince. A hardworking, unappreciated prince. A pal, you understand? A good companion. Always for his boys.
LETTA: That's so sweet.
HAPPY: Well, girls, what's the program? We're wasting time. Come on, Biff. Gather round. Where would you like to go?
BIFF: Why don't you do something for him?
HAPPY: Me!
BIFF: Don't you give a damn for him, Hap?
HAPPY: What're you talking about? I'm the one who—
BIFF: I sense it, you don't give a good goddam about him. [*He takes the rolled-up hose from his pocket and puts it on the table in front of* HAPPY.] Look what I found in the cellar, for Christ's sake. How can you bear to let it go on?
HAPPY: Me? Who goes away? Who runs off and—
BIFF: Yeah, but he doesn't mean anything to you. You could help him–I can't! Don't you understand what I'm talking about? He's going to kill himself, don't you know that?
HAPPY: Don't I know it! Me!
BIFF: Hap, help him! Jesus . . . help him . . . Help me, help me, I can't bear to look at his face! [*Ready to weep, he hurries out, up right.*]
HAPPY [*starting after him*]: Where are you going?
MISS FORSYTHE: What's he so mad about?
HAPPY: Come on, girls, we'll catch up with him.

MISS FORSYTHE [*as* HAPPY *pushes her out*]: Say, I don't like that temper of his!

HAPPY: He's just a little overstrung, he'll be all right!

WILLY [*off left, as* THE WOMAN *laughs*]: Don't answer! Don't answer!

LETTA: Don't you want to tell your father—

HAPPY: No, that's not my father. He's just a guy. Come on, we'll catch Biff, and, honey, we're going to paint this town! Stanley, where's the check! Hey, Stanley!

They exit. STANLEY *looks toward left.*

STANLEY [*calling to* HAPPY *indignantly*]: Mr Loman! Mr Loman!

STANLEY *picks up a chair and follows them off. Knocking is heard off left.* THE WOMAN *enters, laughing.* WILLY *follows her. She is in a black slip; he is buttoning his shirt. Raw, sensuous music accompanies their speech.*

WILLY: Will you stop laughing? Will you stop?

THE WOMAN: Aren't you going to answer the door? He'll wake the whole hotel.

WILLY: I'm not expecting anybody.

THE WOMAN: Whyn't you have another drink, honey, and stop being so damn self-centered?

WILLY: I'm so lonely.

THE WOMAN: You know you ruined me, Willy? From now on, whenever you come to the office, I'll see that you go right through to the buyers. No waiting at my desk any more, Willy. You ruined me.

WILLY: That's nice of you to say that.

THE WOMAN: Gee, you are self-centered! Why so sad? You are the saddest, self-centeredest soul I ever did see-saw.

She laughs. He kisses her.

Come on inside, drummer boy. It's silly to be dressing in the middle of the night.

As knocking is heard.

Aren't you going to answer the door?

WILLY: They're knocking on the wrong door.

THE WOMAN: But I felt the knocking. And he heard us talking in here. Maybe the hotel's on fire!

WILLY [*his terror rising*]: It's a mistake.

THE WOMAN: Then tell him to go away!

WILLY: There's nobody there.

THE WOMAN: It's getting on my nerves, Willy. There's somebody standing out there and it's getting on my nerves!

WILLY [*pushing her away from him*]: All right, stay in the bathroom here, and don't come out. I think there's a law in Massachusetts about it, so don't come out. It may be that new room clerk. He looked very mean. So don't come out. It's a mistake, there's no fire.

The knocking is heard again. He takes a few steps away from her, and she vanishes into the wing. The light follows him, and now he is facing young BIFF, *who carries a suitcase.* BIFF *steps toward him. The music is gone.*

BIFF: Why didn't you answer?

WILLY: Biff! What are you doing in Boston?

BIFF: Why didn't you answer? I've been knocking for five minutes, I called you on the phone—

WILLY: I just heard you. I was in the bathroom and had the door shut. Did anything happen home?

BIFF: Dad–I let you down.

WILLY: What do you mean?

BIFF: Dad . . .

WILLY: Biffo, what's this about? [*Putting his arm around* BIFF.] Come on, let's go downstairs and get you a malted.

BIFF: Dad, I flunked math.

WILLY: Not for the term?

BIFF: The term. I haven't got enough credits to graduate.

WILLY: You mean to say Bernard wouldn't give you the answers?

BIFF: He did, he tried, but I only got a sixty-one.

WILLY: And they wouldn't give you four points?

BIFF: Birnbaum refused absolutely. I begged him, Pop, but he won't give me those points. You gotta talk to him before they close the school. Because if he saw the kind of man you are, and you just talked to him in your way, I'm sure he'd come through for me. The class came right before practice, see, and I didn't go enough. Would you talk to him? He'd like you, Pop. You know the way you could talk.

WILLY: You're on. We'll drive right back.

BIFF: Oh, Dad, good work! I'm sure he'll change it for you!

WILLY: Go downstairs and tell the clerk I'm checkin' out. Go right down.

BIFF: Yes, sir! See, the reason he hates me, Pop–one day he was late for class so I got up at the blackboard and imitated him. I crossed my eyes and talked with a lithp.

WILLY [*laughing*]: You did? The kids like it?

BIFF: They nearly died laughing!

WILLY: Yeah? What'd you do?

BIFF: The thquare root of thixthy twee is . . .

WILLY *bursts out laughing;* BIFF *joins him.*

And in the middle of it he walked in!

WILLY *laughs and* THE WOMAN *joins in offstage.*

WILLY [*without hesitation*]: Hurry downstairs and—

BIFF: Somebody in there?

WILLY: No, that was next door.

THE WOMAN *laughs offstage.*

BIFF: Somebody got in your bathroom!

WILLY: No, it's the next room, there's a party—
THE WOMAN [*enters, laughing. She lisps this*]: Can I come in? There's something
in the bathtub, Willy, and it's moving!

WILLY *looks at* BIFF, *who is staring open-mouthed and horrified at* THE
WOMAN.

WILLY: Ah–you better go back to your room. They must be finished painting
by now. They're painting her room so I let her take a shower here. Go back,
go back . . . [*He pushes her.*]
THE WOMAN [*resisting*]: But I've got to get dressed, Willy, I can't—
WILLY: Get out of here! Go back, go back . . . [*Suddenly striving for the
ordinary*]: This is Miss Francis, Biff, she's a buyer. They're painting her
room. Go back, Miss Francis, go back . . .
THE WOMAN: But my clothes, I can't go out naked in the hall!
WILLY [*pushing her offstage*]: Get outa here! Go back, go back!

BIFF *slowly sits down on his suitcase as the argument continues offstage.*

THE WOMAN: Where's my stockings? You promised me stockings, Willy!
WILLY: I have no stockings here!
THE WOMAN: You had two boxes of size nine sheers for me, and I want them!
WILLY: Here, for God's sake, will you get outa here!
THE WOMAN [*enters holding a box of stockings*]: I just hope there's nobody in the
hall. That's all I hope. [*To* BIFF.] Are you football or baseball?
BIFF: Football.
THE WOMAN [*angry, humiliated*]: That's me too. G'night. [*She snatches her
clothes from* WILLY, *and walks out.*]
WILLY [*after a pause*]: Well, better get going. I want to get to the school first
thing in the morning. Get my suits out of the closet. I'll get my valise.

BIFF *doesn't move.*

What's the matter?

BIFF *remains motionless, tears falling.*

She's a buyer. Buys for J. H. Simmons. She lives down the hall–they're
painting. You don't imagine—[*He breaks off. After a pause.*] Now listen, pal,
she's just a buyer. She sees merchandise in her room and they have to keep it
looking just so . . . [*Pause. Assuming command.*] All right, get my suits.

BIFF *doesn't move.*

Now stop crying and do as I say. I gave you an order! Is that what you do
when I give an order? How dare you cry! [*Putting his arm around* BIFF.] Now
look, Biff, when you grow up you'll understand about these things. You
mustn't–you mustn't overemphasize a thing like this. I'll see Birnbaum first
thing in the morning.
BIFF: Never mind.
WILLY [*getting down beside* BIFF]: Never mind! He's going to give you those

points. I'll see to it.

BIFF: He wouldn't listen to you.

WILLY: He certainly will listen to me. You need those points for the U. of Virginia.

BIFF: I'm not going there.

WILLY: Heh? If I can't get him to change that mark you'll make it up in summer school. You've got all summer to—

BIFF [*his weeping breaking from him*]: Dad . . .

WILLY [*infected by it*]: Oh, my boy . . .

BIFF: Dad . . .

WILLY: She's nothing to me, Biff. I was lonely, I was terribly lonely.

BIFF: You–you gave her Mama's stockings! [*His tears break through and he rises to go.*]

WILLY [*grabbing for* BIFF]: I gave you an order!

BIFF: Don't touch me, you–liar!

WILLY: Apologize for that!

BIFF: You fake! You phony little fake! You fake!

Overcome, he turns quickly and weeping fully goes out with his suitcase. WILLY *is left on the floor on his knees.*

WILLY: I gave you an order! Biff, come back here or I'll beat you! Come back here! I'll whip you!

STANLEY *comes quickly in from the right and stands in front of* WILLY.

WILLY [*shouts at* STANLEY]: I gave you an order . . .

STANLEY: Hey, let's pick it up, pick it up, Mr Loman. [*He helps* WILLY *to his feet.*] Your boys left with the chippies. They said they'll see you home.

A second waiter watches some distance away.

WILLY: But we were supposed to have dinner together.

Music is heard, WILLY's *theme.*

STANLEY: Can you make it?

WILLY: I'll–sure, I can make it. [*Suddenly concerned about his clothes.*] Do I–I look all right?

STANLEY: Sure, you look all right. [*He flicks a speck off* WILLY's *lapel.*]

WILLY: Here–here's a dollar.

STANLEY: Oh, your son paid me. It's all right.

WILLY [*putting it in* STANLEY's *hand*]: No, take it. You're a good boy.

STANLEY: Oh, no, you don't have to . . .

WILLY: Here–here's some more, I don't need it any more. [*After a slight pause.*] Tell me–is there a seed store in the neighborhood?

STANLEY: Seeds? You mean like to plant?

As WILLY *turns,* STANLEY *slips the money back into his jacket pocket.*

WILLY: Yes. Carrots, peas . . .

STANLEY: Well, there's hardware stores on Sixth Avenue, but it may be too late now.

WILLY [*anxiously*]: Oh, I'd better hurry. I've got to get some seeds. [*He starts off to the right.*] I've got to get some seeds, right away. Nothing's planted. I don't have a thing in the ground.

> WILLY *hurries out as the light goes down.* STANLEY *moves over to the right after him, watches him off. The other waiter has been staring at* WILLY.

STANLEY [*to the waiter*]: Well, whatta you looking at?

> *The waiter picks up the chairs and moves off right.* STANLEY *takes the table and follows him. The light fades on this area. There is a long pause, the sound of the flute coming over. The light gradually rises on the kitchen, which is empty.* HAPPY *appears at the door of the house, followed by* BIFF. HAPPY *is carrying a large bunch of long-stemmed roses. He enters the kitchen, looks around for* LINDA. *Not seeing her, he turns to* BIFF, *who is just outside the house door, and makes a gesture with his hands, indicating 'Not here, I guess.' He looks into the living-room and freezes. Inside,* LINDA, *unseen, is seated,* WILLY's *coat on her lap. She rises ominously and quietly and moves toward* HAPPY, *who backs up into the kitchen, afraid.*

HAPPY: Hey, what're you doing up?

> LINDA *says nothing but moves toward him implacably.*

Where's Pop?

> *He keeps backing to the right, and now* LINDA *is in full view in the doorway to the living-room.*

Is he sleeping?

LINDA: Where were you?

HAPPY [*trying to laugh it off*]: We met two girls, Mom, very fine types. Here, we brought you some flowers. [*Offering them to her.*] Put them in your room, Ma.

> *She knocks them to the floor at* BIFF's *feet. He has now come inside and closed the door behind him. She stares at* BIFF, *silent.*

Now what'd you do that for? Mom, I want you to have some flowers—

LINDA [*cutting* HAPPY *off, violently to* BIFF]: Don't you care whether he lives or dies?

HAPPY [*going to the stairs*]: Come upstairs, Biff.

BIFF [*with a flare of disgust, to* HAPPY]: Go away from me! [*To* LINDA.] What do you mean, lives or dies? Nobody's dying around here, pal.

LINDA: Get out of my sight! Get out of here!

BIFF: I wanna see the boss.

LINDA: You're not going near him!

BIFF: Where is he?

He moves into the living-room and LINDA *follows.*

LINDA [*shouting after* BIFF]: You invite him for dinner. He looks forward to it all day—

BIFF *appears in his parents' bedroom, looks around, and exits*

—and then you desert him there. There's no stranger you'd do that to!
HAPPY: Why? He had a swell time with us. Listen, when I—

LINDA *comes back into the kitchen*

—desert him I hope I don't outlive the day!
LINDA: Get out of here!
HAPPY: Now look, Mom . . .
LINDA: Did you have to go to women tonight? You and your lousy rotten whores!

BIFF *re-enters the kitchen.*

HAPPY: Mom, all we did was follow Biff around trying to cheer him up! [*To* BIFF.] Boy, what a night you gave me!
LINDA: Get out of here, both of you, and don't come back! I don't want you tormenting him any more. Go on now, get your things together! [*To* BIFF.] You can sleep in his apartment. [*She starts to pick up the flowers and stops herself.*] Pick up this stuff, I'm not your maid any more. Pick it up, you bum, you!

HAPPY *turns his back to her in refusal.* BIFF *slowly moves over and gets down on his knees, picking up the flowers.*

You're a pair of animals! Not one, not another living soul would have had the cruelty to walk out on that man in a restaurant!
BIFF [*not looking at her*]: Is that what he said?
LINDA: He didn't have to say anything. He was so humiliated he nearly limped when he came in.
HAPPY: But, Mom, he had a great time with us—
BIFF [*cutting him off violently*]: Shut up!

Without another word, HAPPY *goes upstairs.*

LINDA: You! You didn't even go in to see if he was all right!
BIFF [*still on the floor in front of* LINDA, *the flowers in his hand; with self-loathing*]: No. Didn't. Didn't do a damned thing. How do you like that, heh? Left him babbling in a toilet.
LINDA: You louse. You . . .
BIFF: Now you hit it on the nose! [*He gets up, throws the flowers in the wastebasket.*] The scum of the earth, and you're looking at him!
LINDA: Get out of here!
BIFF: I gotta talk to the boss, Mom. Where is he?
LINDA: You're not going near him. Get out of this house!

BIFF [*with absolute assurance, determination*]: No. We're gonna have an abrupt conversation, him and me.
LINDA: You're not talking to him!

> *Hammering is heard from outside the house, off right.* BIFF *turns toward the noise.*

LINDA [*suddenly pleading*]: Will you please leave him alone?
BIFF: What's he doing out there?
LINDA: He's planting the garden!
BIFF [*quietly*]: Now? Oh, my God!

> BIFF *moves outside,* LINDA *following. The light dies down on them and comes up on the center of the apron as* WILLY *walks into it. He is carrying a flashlight, a hoe, and a handful of seed packets. He raps the top of the hoe sharply to fix it firmly, and then moves to the left, measuring off the distance with his foot. He holds the flashlight to look at the seed packets, reading off the instructions. He is in the blue of night.*

WILLY: Carrots . . . quarter-inch apart. Rows . . . one-foot rows. [*He measures it off.*] One foot. [*He puts down a package and measures off.*] Beets. [*He puts down another package and measures again.*] Lettuce. [*He reads the package, puts it down.*] One foot—

> *He breaks off as Ben appears at the right and moves slowly down to him.*

What a proposition, ts, ts. Terrific, terrific. 'Cause she's suffered. Ben, the woman has suffered. You understand me? A man can't go out the way he came in, Ben, a man has got to add up to something. You can't, you can't—

> *Ben moves toward him as though to interrupt.*

You gotta consider, now. Don't answer so quick. Remember, it's a guaranteed twenty-thousand-dollar proposition. Now look, Ben, I want you to go through the ins and outs of this thing with me. I've got nobody to talk to, Ben, and the woman has suffered, you hear me?
BEN [*standing still, considering*]: What's the proposition?
WILLY: It's twenty thousand dollars on the barrelhead. Guaranteed, gilt-edged, you understand?
BEN: You don't want to make a fool of yourself. They might not honor the policy.
WILLY: How can they dare refuse? Didn't I work like a coolie to meet every premium on the nose? And now they don't pay off! Impossible!
BEN: It's called a cowardly thing, William.
WILLY: Why? Does it take more guts to stand here the rest of my life ringing up a zero?
BEN [*yielding*]: That's a point, William. [*He moves, thinking, turns.*] And twenty thousand—that *is* something one can feel with the hand, it is there.
WILLY [*now assured, with rising power*]: Oh, Ben, that's the whole beauty of it! I see it like a diamond, shining in the dark, hard and rough, that I can pick up

and touch in my hand. Not like–like an appointment! This would not be another damned-fool appointment, Ben, and it changes all the aspects. Because he thinks I'm nothing, see, and so he spites me. But the funeral–[*Straightening up.*] Ben, that funeral will be massive! They'll come from Maine, Massachusetts, Vermont, New Hampshire! All the old-timers with the strange license plates–that boy will be thunder-struck, Ben, because he never realized–I am known! Rhode Island, New York, New Jersey–I am known, Ben, and he'll see it with his eyes once and for all. He'll see what I am, Ben! He's in for a shock, that boy!

BEN [*coming down to the edge of the garden*]: He'll call you a coward.

WILLY [*suddenly fearful*]: No, that would be terrible.

BEN: Yes. And a damned fool.

WILLY: No, no, he mustn't, I won't have that! [*He is broken and desperate.*]

BEN: He'll hate you, William.

The gay music of the boys is heard.

WILLY: Oh, Ben, how do we get back to all the great times? Used to be so full of light, and comradeship, the sleigh-riding in winter, and the ruddiness on his cheeks. And always some kind of good news coming up, always something nice coming up ahead. And never even let me carry the valises in the house, and simonizing, simonizing that little red car! Why, why can't I give him something and not have him hate me?

BEN: Let me think about it. [*He glances at his watch.*] I still have a little time. Remarkable proposition, but you've got to be sure you're not making a fool of yourself.

BEN *drifts off upstage and goes out of sight.* BIFF *comes down from the left.*

WILLY [*suddenly conscious of* BIFF, *turns and looks up at him, then begins picking up the packages of seeds in confusion*]: Where the hell is that seed? [*Indignantly.*] You can't see nothing out here! They boxed in the whole goddam neighborhood!

BIFF: There are people all around here. Don't you realize that?

WILLY: I'm busy. Don't bother me.

BIFF [*taking the hoe from* WILLY]: I'm saying good-by to you, Pop.

WILLY *looks at him, silent, unable to move.*

I'm not coming back any more.

WILLY: You're not going to see Oliver tomorrow?

BIFF: I've got no appointment, Dad.

WILLY: He put his arm around you, and you've got no appointment?

BIFF: Pop, get this now, will you? Everytime I've left it's been a fight that sent me out of here. Today I realized something about myself and I tried to explain it to you and I–I think I'm just not smart enough to make any sense out of it for you. To hell with whose fault it is or anything like that. [*He takes* WILLY's *arm.*] Let's just wrap it up, heh? Come on in, we'll tell Mom. [*He gently tries to pull* WILLY *to left.*]

WILLY [*frozen, immobile, with guilt in his voice*]: No, I don't want to see her.

BIFF: Come on!

He pulls again, and WILLY *tries to pull away.*

WILLY [*highly nervous*]: No, no, I don't want to see her.
BIFF [*tries to look into* WILLY'*s face, as if to find the answer there*]: Why don't you want to see her?
WILLY [*more harshly now*]: Don't bother me, will you?
BIFF: What do you mean, you don't want to see her? You don't want them calling you yellow, do you? This isn't your fault; it's me, I'm a bum. Now come inside!

WILLY *strains to get away.*

Did you hear what I said to you?

WILLY *pulls away and quickly goes by himself into the house.* BIFF *follows.*

LINDA [*to* WILLY]: Did you plant, dear?
BIFF [*at the door, to* LINDA]: All right, we had it out. I'm going and I'm not writing any more.
LINDA [*going to* WILLY *in the kitchen*]: I think that's the best way, dear. 'Cause there's no use drawing it out, you'll just never get along.

WILLY *doesn't respond.*

BIFF: People ask where I am and what I'm doing, you don't know, and you don't care. That way it'll be off your mind and you can start brightening up again. All right? That clears it, doesn't it?

WILLY *is silent, and* BIFF *goes to him.*

You gonna wish me luck, scout? [*He extends his hand.*] What do you say?
LINDA: Shake his hand, Willy.
WILLY [*turning to her, seething with hurt*]: There's no necessity to mention the pen at all, y'know.
BIFF [*gently*]: I've got no appointment, Dad.
WILLY [*erupting fiercely*]: He put his arm around . . . ?
BIFF: Dad, you're never going to see what I am, so what's the use of arguing? If I strike oil I'll send you a check. Meantime forget I'm alive.
WILLY [*to* LINDA]: Spite, see?
BIFF: Shake hands, Dad.
WILLY: Not my hand.
BIFF: I was hoping not to go this way.
WILLY: Well, this is the way you're going. Good-by.

BIFF *looks at him a moment, then turns sharply and goes to the stairs.*

WILLY [*stops him with*]: May you rot in hell if you leave this house!

BIFF [*turning*]: Exactly what is it that you want from me?

WILLY: I want you to know, on the train, in the mountains, in the valleys, wherever you go, that you cut down your life for spite!

BIFF: No, no.

WILLY: Spite, spite, is the word of your undoing! And when you're down and out, remember what did it. When you're rotting somewhere beside the railroad tracks, remember, and don't you dare blame it on me!

BIFF: I'm not blaming it on you!

WILLY: I won't take the rap for this, you hear?

HAPPY *comes down the stairs and stands on the bottom step, watching.*

BIFF: That's just what I'm telling you!

WILLY [*sinking into a chair at the table, with full accusation*]: You're trying to put a knife in me—don't think I don't know what you're doing!

BIFF: All right, phony! Then let's lay it on the line. [*He whips the rubber tube out of his pocket and puts it on the table.*]

HAPPY: You crazy—

LINDA: Biff!

She moves to grab the hose, but BIFF *holds it down with his hand.*

BIFF: Leave it there! Don't move it!

WILLY [*not looking at it*]: What is that?

BIFF: You know goddam well what that is.

WILLY [*caged, wanting to escape*]: I never saw that.

BIFF: You saw it. The mice didn't bring it into the cellar! What is this supposed to do, make a hero out of you? This supposed to make me sorry for you?

WILLY: Never heard of it.

BIFF: There'll be no pity for you, you hear it? No pity!

WILLY [*to* LINDA]: You hear the spite!

BIFF: No, you're going to hear the truth—what you are and what I am!

LINDA: Stop it!

WILLY: Spite!

HAPPY [*coming down toward* BIFF]: You cut it now!

BIFF [*to* HAPPY]: The man don't know who we are! The man is gonna know! [*To* WILLY.] We never told the truth for ten minutes in this house!

HAPPY: We always told the truth!

BIFF [*turning on him*]: You big blow, are you the assistant buyer? You're one of the two assistants to the assistant, aren't you?

HAPPY: Well, I'm practically—

BIFF: You're practically full of it! We all are! And I'm through with it. [*To* WILLY.] Now hear this, Willy, this is me.

WILLY: I know you!

BIFF: You know why I had no address for three months? I stole a suit in Kansas City and I was in jail.

To LINDA, *who is sobbing.*

Stop crying. I'm through with it.

LINDA *turns away from them, her hands covering her face.*

WILLY: I suppose that's my fault!

BIFF: I stole myself out of every good job since high school!

WILLY: And whose fault is that?

BIFF: And I never got anywhere because you blew me so full of hot air I could never stand taking orders from anybody! That's whose fault it is!

WILLY: I hear that!

LINDA: Don't, Biff!

BIFF: It's goddam time you heard that! I had to be boss big shot in two weeks, and I'm through with it!

WILLY: Then hang yourself! For spite, hang yourself!

BIFF: No! Nobody's hanging himself, Willy! I ran down eleven flights with a pen in my hand today. And suddenly I stopped, you hear me? And in the middle of that office building, do you hear this? I stopped in the middle of that building and I saw—the sky. I saw the things that I love in this world. The work and the food and time to sit and smoke. And I looked at the pen and said to myself, what the hell am I grabbing this for? Why am I trying to become what I don't want to be? What am I doing in an office, making a contemptuous, begging fool of myself, when all I want is out there, waiting for me the minute I say I know who I am! Why can't I say that, Willy?

He tries to make WILLY *face him, but* WILLY *pulls away and moves to the left.*

WILLY [*with hatred, threateningly*]: The door of your life is wide open!

BIFF: Pop! I'm a dime a dozen, and so are you!

WILLY [*turning on him now in an uncontrolled outburst*]: I am not a dime a dozen! I am Willy Loman, and you are Biff Loman!

BIFF *starts for* WILLY, *but is blocked by* HAPPY. *In his fury,* BIFF *seems on the verge of attacking his father.*

BIFF: I am not a leader of men, Willy, and neither are you. You were never anything but a hard-working drummer who landed in the ash can like all the rest of them! I'm one dollar an hour, Willy! I tried seven states and couldn't raise it. A buck an hour! Do you gather my meaning? I'm not bringing home any prizes any more, and you're going to stop waiting for me to bring them home!

WILLY [*directly to* BIFF]: You vengeful, spiteful mut!

BIFF *breaks from* HAPPY. WILLY, *in fright, starts up the stairs.* BIFF *grabs him.*

BIFF [*at the peak of his fury*]: Pop, I'm nothing! I'm nothing, Pop. Can't you understand that? There's no spite in it any more. I'm just what I am, that's all.

BIFF'*s fury has spent itself, and he breaks down, sobbing, holding on to* WILLY, *who dumbly fumbles for* BIFF'*s face.*

WILLY [*astonished*]: What're you doing? What're you doing? [*To* LINDA.] Why is he crying?

BIFF [*crying, broken*]: Will you let me go, for Christ's sake? Will you take that phony dream and burn it before something happens? [*Struggling to contain himself, he pulls away and moves to the stairs.*] I'll go in the morning. Put him—put him to bed. [*Exhausted,* BIFF *moves up the stairs to his room.*]

WILLY [*after a long pause, astonished, elevated*]: Isn't that—isn't that remarkable? Biff—he likes me!

LINDA: He loves you, Willy!

HAPPY [*deeply moved*]: Always did, Pop.

WILLY: Oh, Biff! [*Staring wildly.*] He cried! Cried to me. [*He is choking with his love, and now cries out his promise.*] That boy—that boy is going to be magnificent!

BEN *appears in the light just outside the kitchen.*

BEN: Yes, outstanding, with twenty thousand behind him.

LINDA [*sensing the racing of his mind, fearfully, carefully*]: Now come to bed, Willy. It's all settled now.

WILLY [*finding it difficult not to rush out of the house*]: Yes, we'll sleep. Come on. Go to sleep, Hap.

BEN: And it does take a great kind of a man to crack the jungle.

In accents of dread, BEN's *idyllic music starts up.*

HAPPY [*his arm around* LINDA]: I'm getting married, Pop, don't forget it. I'm changing everything. I'm gonna run that department before the year is up. You'll see, Mom. [*He kisses her.*]

BEN: The jungle is dark but full of diamonds, Willy.

WILLY *turns, moves, listening to* BEN.

LINDA: Be good. You're both good boys, just act that way, that's all.

HAPPY: 'Night, Pop. [*He goes upstairs.*]

LINDA [*to* WILLY]: Come, dear.

BEN [*with greater force*]: One must go in to fetch a diamond out.

WILLY [*to* LINDA, *as he moves slowly along the edge of the kitchen, toward the door*]: I just want to get settled down, Linda. Let me sit alone for a little.

LINDA [*almost uttering her fear*]: I want you upstairs.

WILLY [*taking her in his arms*]: In a few minutes, Linda. I couldn't sleep right now. Go on, you look awful tired. [*He kisses her.*]

BEN: Not like an appointment at all. A diamond is rough and hard to the touch.

WILLY: Go on now. I'll be right up.

LINDA: I think this is the only way, Willy.

WILLY: Sure, it's the best thing.

BEN: Best thing!

WILLY: The only way. Everything is gonna be—go on, kid, get to bed. You look so tired.

LINDA: Come right up.

WILLY: Two minutes.

LINDA *goes into the living-room, then reappears in her bedroom.* WILLY *moves just outside the kitchen door.*

Loves me. [*Wonderingly.*] Always loved me. Isn't that a remarkable thing? Ben, he'll worship me for it!

BEN [*with promise*]: It's dark there, but full of diamonds.

WILLY: Can you imagine that magnificence with twenty thousand dollars in his pocket?

LINDA [*calling from her room*]: Willy! Come up!

WILLY [*calling into the kitchen*]: Yes! Yes. Coming! It's very smart, you realize that, don't you, sweetheart? Even Ben sees it. I gotta go, baby. 'By! 'By! [*Going over to Ben, almost dancing.*] Imagine? When the mail comes he'll be ahead of Bernard again!

BEN: A perfect proposition all around.

WILLY: Did you see how he cried to me? Oh, if I could kiss him, Ben!

BEN: Time, William, time!

WILLY: Oh, Ben, I always knew one way or another we were gonna make it, Biff and I!

BEN [*looking at his watch*]: The boat. We'll be late. [*He moves slowly off into the darkness.*]

WILLY [*elegiacally, turning to the house*]: Now when you kick off, boy, I want a seventy-yard boot, and get right down the field under the ball, and when you hit, hit low and hit hard, because it's important, boy. [*He swings around and faces the audience.*] There's all kinds of important people in the stands, and the first thing you know . . . [*Suddenly realizing he is alone.*] Ben! Ben, where do I . . . ? [*He makes a sudden movement of search.*] Ben, how do I . . . ?

LINDA [*calling*]: Willy, you coming up?

WILLY [*uttering a gasp of fear, whirling about as if to quiet her*]: Sh! [*He turns around as if to find his way; sounds, faces, voices, seem to be swarming in upon him and he flicks at them, crying.*] Sh! Sh! [*Suddenly music, faint and high, stops him. It rises in intensity, almost to an unbearable scream. He goes up and down on his toes, and rushes off around the house.*] Shhh!

LINDA: Willy?

There is no answer. LINDA *waits.* BIFF *gets up off his bed. He is still in his clothes.* HAPPY *sits up.* BIFF *stands listening.*

LINDA [*with real fear*]: Willy, answer me! Willy!

There is the sound of a car starting and moving away at full speed.

No!

BIFF [*rushing down the stairs*]: Pop!

As the car speeds off, the music crashes down in a frenzy of sound, which becomes the soft pulsation of a single cello string. BIFF *slowly returns to his bedroom. He and* HAPPY *gravely don their jackets.* LINDA *slowly walks out of her room. The music has developed into a dead march. The leaves of day are appearing over everything.* CHARLEY *and* BERNARD, *somberly dressed, appear and knock on the kitchen door.* BIFF *and* HAPPY *slowly descend the stairs to the kitchen as* CHARLEY *and* BERNARD *enter. All stop a moment when* LINDA, *in clothes of mourning, bearing a little bunch of roses, comes through the draped doorway into the kitchen. She goes to* CHARLEY *and takes his arm. Now all move toward the audience, through the wall-line of the kitchen. At the limit of the apron,* LINDA *lays down the flowers, kneels, and sits back on her heels. All stare down at the grave.*

REQUIEM

CHARLEY: It's getting dark, Linda.

LINDA *doesn't react. She stares at the grave.*

BIFF: How about it, Mom? Better get some rest, heh? They'll be closing the gate soon.

LINDA *makes no move. Pause.*

HAPPY [*deeply angered*]: He had no right to do that. There was no necessity for it. We would've helped him.
CHARLEY [*grunting*]: Hmmm.
BIFF: Come along, Mom.
LINDA: Why didn't anybody come?
CHARLEY: It was a very nice funeral.
LINDA: But where are all the people he knew? Maybe they blame him.
CHARLEY: Naa. It's a rough world, Linda. They wouldn't blame him.
LINDA: I can't understand it. At this time especially. First time in thirty-five years we were just about free and clear. He only needed a little salary. He was even finished with the dentist.
CHARLEY: No man only needs a little salary.
LINDA: I can't understand it.
BIFF: There were a lot of nice days. When he'd come home from a trip; or on Sundays, making the stoop; finishing the cellar; putting on the new porch; when he built the extra bathroom; and put up the garage. You know something, Charley, there's more of him in that front stoop than in all the sales he ever made.
CHARLEY: Yeah. He was a happy man with a batch of cement.
LINDA: He was so wonderful with his hands.
BIFF: He had the wrong dreams. All, all, wrong.
HAPPY [*almost ready to fight* BIFF]: Don't say that!
BIFF: He never knew who he was.
CHARLEY [*stopping* HAPPY's *movement and reply. To* BIFF]: Nobody dast blame this man. You don't understand: Willy was a salesman. And for a salesman, there is no rock bottom to the life. He don't put a bolt to a nut, he don't tell you the law or give you medicine. He's a man way out there in the blue, riding on a smile and a shoeshine. And when they start not smiling back–that's an earthquake. And then you get yourself a couple of spots on your hat, and you're finished. Nobody dast blame this man. A salesman is got to dream, boy. It comes with the territory.
BIFF: Charley, the man didn't know who he was.
HAPPY [*infuriated*]: Don't say that!

BIFF: Why don't you come with me, Happy?

HAPPY: I'm not licked that easily. I'm staying right in this city, and I'm gonna beat this racket! [*He looks at* BIFF, *his chin set.*] The Loman Brothers!

BIFF: I know who I am, kid.

HAPPY: All right, boy. I'm gonna show you and everybody else that Willy Loman did not die in vain. He had a good dream. It's the only dream you can have—to come out number-one man. He fought it out here, and this is where I'm gonna win it for him.

BIFF [*with a hopeless glance at* HAPPY, *bends toward his mother*]: Let's go, Mom.

LINDA: I'll be with you in a minute. Go on, Charley.

He hesitates.

I want to, just for a minute. I never had a chance to say good-by.

CHARLEY *moves away, followed by* HAPPY. BIFF *remains a slight distance up and left of* LINDA. *She sits there, summoning herself. The flute begins, not far away, playing behind her speech.*

Forgive me, dear. I can't cry. I don't know what it is, but I can't cry. I don't understand it. Why did you ever do that? Help me, Willy, I can't cry. It seems to me that you're just on another trip. I keep expecting you. Willy, dear, I can't cry. Why did you do it? I search and search and I search, and I can't understand it, Willy. I made the last payment on the house today. Today, dear. And there'll be nobody home. [*A sob rises in her throat.*] We're free and clear. [*Sobbing more fully, released.*] We're free.

BIFF *comes slowly toward her.*

We're free . . . We're free . . .

BIFF *lifts her to her feet and moves out up right with her in his arms.* LINDA *sobs quietly.* BERNARD *and* CHARLEY *come together and follow them, followed by* HAPPY. *Only the music of the flute is left on the darkening stage as over the house the hard towers of the apartment buildings rise into sharp focus.*

CURTAIN

A MAN
FOR ALL
SEASONS
ROBERT
BOLT

A MAN FOR
ALL SEASONS

First published by Heinemann Educational Books
1960

A MAN FOR ALL SEASONS

(1960)

A Play of Sir Thomas More

CAST

A Man For All Seasons was first presented in London at the Globe Theatre on 1 July 1960 by H. M. Tennent Ltd, with the following cast:

THE COMMON MAN	*Leo McKern*
THOMAS MORE	*Paul Scofield*
RICHARD RICH	*John Bown*
THE DUKE	*Alexander Gauge*
ALICE MORE	*Wynne Clark*
MARGARET MORE	*Pat Keen*
THE CARDINAL	*Willoughby Goddard*
THOMAS CROMWELL	*Andrew Keir*
THE AMBASSADOR	*Geoffrey Dunn*
HIS ATTENDANT	*Brian Harrison*
WILLIAM ROPER	*John Carson*
THE KING	*Richard Leech*
A WOMAN	*Beryl Andrews*
THE ARCHBISHOP	*William Roderick*

Directed by NOËL WILLMAN
Scenery and costumes by MOTLEY

SIR THOMAS MORE
More is a man of an angel's wit and singular learning; I know not his fellow. For where is the man of that gentleness, lowliness, and affability? And as time requireth a man of marvellous mirth and pastimes; and sometimes of as sad gravity: a man for all seasons.
Robert Whittinton

A person of the greatest virtue this Kingdom ever produced.
Jonathan Swift

ACT ONE

When the curtain rises, the set is in darkness but for a single spot which descends vertically upon the COMMON MAN, *who stands in front of a big property basket.*

COMMON MAN: It is perverse! To start a play made up of Kings and Cardinals in speaking costumes and intellectuals with embroidered mouths, with me.

If a King, or a Cardinal had done the prologue he'd have had the right materials. And an intellectual would have shown enough majestic meanings, coloured propositions, and closely woven liturgical stuff to dress the House of Lords! But this!

Is this a costume? Does this say anything? It barely covers one man's nakedness! A bit of black material to reduce Old Adam to the Common Man.

Oh, if they'd let me come on naked, I could have shown you something of my own. Which would have told you without words—! . . . Something I've forgotten . . . Old Adam's muffled up. [*Backing towards basket.*] Well, for a proposition of my own, I need a costume. [*Takes out and puts on the coat and hat of* STEWARD.] Matthew! The Household Steward of Sir Thomas More!

Lights come up swiftly on set. He takes from the basket five silver goblets, one large than the others, and a jug with a lid, with which he furnishes the table. A burst of conversational merriment off; he pauses and indicates head of stairs.

There's company to dinner. [*Finishes business at table.*] All right! A Common Man! A Sixteenth-Century Butler! [*He drinks from the jug.*] All right – the Six—[*Breaks off, agreeably surprised by the quality of the liquor, regards the jug respectfully and drinks again.*] The Sixteenth Century is the Century of the Common Man. [*Puts down the jug.*] Like all the other centuries. [*Crossing right.*] And that's my proposition.

During the last part of the speech, voices off. Now, enter, at head of stairs, SIR THOMAS MORE.

STEWARD: That's Sir Thomas More.
MORE: The wine please, Matthew?
STEWARD: It's there, Sir Thomas.
MORE [*looking into jug*]: Is it good?
STEWARD: Bless you, sir! *I* don't know.
MORE [*mildly*]: Bless you too, Matthew.

Enter RICH *at head of stairs.*

RICH [*enthusiastically pursuing an argument*]: But every man has his price!

STEWARD [*contemptuous*]: Master Richard Rich.

RICH: But yes! In money too.

MORE [*gentle impatience*]: No no no.

RICH: Or pleasure. Titles, women, bricks-and-mortar, there's always something.

MORE: Childish.

RICH: Well, in suffering, certainly.

MORE [*interested*]: Buy a man with suffering?

RICH: Impose suffering, and offer him – escape.

MORE: Oh. For a moment I thought you were being profound. [*Gives cup to* RICH.]

RICH [*to* STEWARD]: Good evening, Matthew.

STEWARD [*snubbing*]: 'Evening, sir.

RICH: No, not a bit profound; it then becomes a purely practical question of how to make him suffer sufficiently.

MORE: Mm. . . . [*Takes him by the arm and walks with him.*] And . . . who recommended you to read Signor Machiavelli?

RICH *breaks away laughing; a fraction too long.* MORE *smiles.*

No, who? [*More laughter.*] . . . Mm?

RICH: Master Cromwell.

MORE: Oh. . . . [*Back to the wine jug and cups.*] He's a very able man.

RICH: And so he is!

MORE: Yes, I say he is. He's very able.

RICH: And he will do something for me, he says.

MORE: I didn't know you knew him.

RICH: Pardon me, Sir Thomas, but how much do you know about me?

MORE: Whatever you've let me know.

RICH: I've let you know everything!

MORE: Richard, you should go back to Cambridge; you're deteriorating.

RICH: Well, I'm not used! . . . D'you know how much I have to show for seven months' work—

MORE: —Work?

RICH: —Work! Waiting's work when you wait as I wait, hard! . . . For seven months, that's two hundred days, I have to show: the acquaintance of the Cardinal's outer doorman, the indifference of the Cardinal's inner doorman, and the Cardinal's chamberlain's hand in my chest! . . . Oh–also one half of a Good Morning delivered at fifty paces by the Duke of Norfolk. Doubtless he mistook me for someone.

MORE: He was very affable at dinner.

RICH: Oh, everyone's affable *here*. . . .

MORE *is pleased.*

Also of course, the friendship of Sir Thomas More. Or should I say acquaintance?

MORE: Say friendship.

RICH: Well, there! 'A friend of Sir Thomas and still no office? There must be something wrong with him.'

MORE: I thought we said friendship. . . . [*Considers; then*] The Dean of St Paul's offers you a post; with a house, a servant and fifty pounds a year.

RICH: What? What post?

MORE: At the new school.

RICH [*bitterly disappointed*]: A teacher!

MORE: A man should go where he won't be tempted. Look, Richard, see this. [*Hands a silver cup.*] Look. . . . Look. . . .

RICH: Beautiful.

MORE: Italian. . . . Do you want it?

RICH: Why—?

MORE: No joke; keep it; or sell it.

RICH: Well I—Thank you of course—Thank you! Thank you! But—?

MORE: You'll sell it, won't you?

RICH: Yes, I think so. Yes, I will.

MORE: And buy, what?

RICH [*sudden ferocity*]: Some decent clothes!

MORE [*with sympathy*]: Ah.

RICH: I want a gown like yours.

MORE: You'll get several gowns for that I should think. It was sent to me a little while ago by some woman. Now she's put a lawsuit into the Court of Requests. It's a bribe, Richard.

RICH: Oh. . . . [*Chagrined.*] So you give it away of course.

MORE: Yes!

RICH: To me?

MORE: Well, I'm not going to keep it, and you need it. Of course – if you feel it's contaminated . . .

RICH: No no. I'll risk it. (*Both smile.*)

MORE: But, Richard, in office they offer you all sorts of things. I was once offered a whole village, with a mill, and a manor house, and heaven knows what else–a coat of arms I shouldn't be surprised. Why not be a teacher? You'd be a fine teacher. Perhaps, a great one.

RICH: And if I was who would know it?

MORE: You, your pupils, your friends, God. Not a bad public, that. . . . Oh, and a *quiet* life.

RICH [*laughing*]; *You* say that!

MORE: Richard, I was commanded into office; it was inflicted on me. . . .

RICH *regards him.*

Can't you believe that?

RICH: It's hard.

MORE [*grimly*]: Be a teacher.

Enter at head of stairs NORFOLK.

STEWARD [*to audience*]: The Duke of Norfolk. A lord.

NORFOLK: I tell you he stooped from the clouds! [*Breaks off, irritable.*] Alice!

Enter instantly at head of stairs ALICE.

ALICE [*irritable*]: Here!

STEWARD [*to audience*]: Lady Alice. My master's wife.

NORFOLK: I tell you he stooped—
ALICE: —He didn't—
NORFOLK: —Goddammit he did—
ALICE: —Couldn't—
NORFOLK: —He *does*—
ALICE: Not possible—
NORFOLK: —But *often*—
ALICE: —Never.
NORFOLK: Well, damn my soul! [*Takes wine.*] Thank you, Thomas.
MORE [*to* MARGARET, *having appeared on gallery*]: Come down, Meg.
STEWARD [*to audience, soapy*]: Lady Margaret, my master's daughter, lovely;
   really lovely.
ALICE [*glances suspiciously at* STEWARD]: Matthew, get about your business.

   Exit STEWARD.

We'll settle this, my lord, we'll put it to Thomas. Thomas, no falcon could
stoop from a cloud, could it?
MORE: I don't know, my dear; it sounds unlikely. I have seen falcons do some
   very splendid things.
ALICE: But how could he stoop from a cloud? He couldn't see where he was
   going.
NORFOLK: You see, Alice—you're ignorant of the subject; a real falcon don't *care*
   where he's going! Anyway, I'm talking to Meg. [*A sportsman's story.*] 'Twas
   the very first cast of the day, Meg; the sun was behind us. And from side to
   side of the valley like the roof of a tent, was solid mist—
ALICE: Oh, mist.
NORFOLK: Well, mist is cloud isn't it?
ALICE: No.
RICH: The opinion of Aristotle is that mists are an exhalation of the earth
   whereas clouds—
NORFOLK: He stooped five hundred feet! Like *that*! Like an Act of God isn't he,
   Thomas?
MORE: He's tremendous.
NORFOLK [*to* ALICE]: Tremendous.
MARGARET: Did he kill the heron?
NORFOLK: Oh, the *heron* was *clever*. [*Very discreditable evidently.*] It was a royal
   stoop though. [*Sly.*] If you could ride, Alice, I'd show you.
ALICE [*hotly*]: I can ride, my lord!
MORE: No, no, you'll make yourself ill.
ALICE: And I'll bet—twenty-five—no thirty shillings I see no falcon stoop from
   no cloud!
NORFOLK: Done.
MORE: Alice—you can't ride with *them*.
ALICE: God's body, Thomas, remember who you are. Am I a City Wife?
MORE: No indeed, you've just lost thirty shillings I think; there *are* such birds.
   And the heron got home to his chicks, Meg, so everything was satisfac-
   tory.
MARGARET [*smiling*]: Yes.
MORE: What was that of Aristotle's, Richard?
RICHARD: Nothing, Sir Thomas—'twas out of place.

NORFOLK [*to* RICH]: I've never found much use in Aristotle myself, not practically. Great philosopher of course. Wonderful mind.

RICH: Exactly, Your Grace!

NORFOLK [*suspicious*]: Eh?

MORE: Master Rich is newly converted to the doctrines of Machiavelli.

RICH: Oh *no* . . .!

NORFOLK: Oh, the Italian. Nasty book, from what I hear.

MARGARET: Very practical, Your Grace.

NORFOLK: You read it? Amazing girl, Thomas, but where are you going to find a husband for her?

MORE [MORE *and* MEG *exchange a glance*]: Where indeed?

RICH: The doctrines of Machiavelli have been largely mistaken I think; indeed properly apprehended he has no doctrine. Master Cromwell has the sense of it I think when he says—

NORFOLK: You know Cromwell?

RICH: . . . Slightly, Your Grace. . . .

NORFOLK: The Cardinal's Secretary.

Exclamations of shock from MORE, MARGARET *and* ALICE.

It's a fact.

MORE: When, Howard?

NORFOLK: Two, three days.

They move about uneasily.

ALICE: A *farrier's* son?

NORFOLK: Well, the Cardinal's a butcher's son, isn't he?

ALICE: It'll be up quick and down quick with Master Cromwell.

NORFOLK *grunts.*

MORE [*quietly*]: Did you know this?

RICH: No!

MARGARET: Do you *like* Master Cromwell, Master Rich?

ALICE: He's the only man in London if he does!

RICH: I think I do, Lady Alice!

MORE [*pleased*]: Good. . . . Well, you don't need *my* help now.

RICH: Sir Thomas, if only you knew how much, much rather I'd yours than his!

Enter STEWARD *at head of stairs. Descends and gives letter to* MORE *who opens it and reads.*

MORE: Talk of the Cardinal's Secretary and the Cardinal appears. He wants me. Now.

ALICE: At this time of the night?

MORE [*mildly*]: The King's business.

ALICE: The Queen's business.

NORFOLK: More than likely, Alice, more than likely.

MORE [*cuts in sharply*]: What's the time?

STEWARD: Eleven o'clock, sir.
MORE: Is there a boat?
STEWARD: Waiting, sir.
MORE [*to* ALICE *and* MARGARET]: Go to bed. You'll excuse me, Your Grace? Richard? [*Kisses wife and daughter.*] Now you'll go to bed. . . .

The MORE *family, as a matter of routine, put their hands together and:*

MORE ⎫ Dear Lord give us rest tonight, or if we must be wakeful,
ALICE ⎬ cheerful. Careful only for our soul's salvation. For Christ's sake.
MARGARET ⎭ Amen.
MORE: And Bless our Lord the King.
ALICE ⎫
MARGARET ⎬ And Bless our Lord the King.
ALL: Amen ⎭

And then immediately a brisk leave-taking, MORE *moving off below, the others mounting the stairs.*

MORE: Howard, are *you* at Richmond?
NORFOLK: No, down the river.
MORE: Then good night! [*Sees* RICH *disconsolate.*] Oh, Your Grace, here's a young man desperate for employment. Something in the clerical line.
NORFOLK: Well, if you recommend him.
MORE: No, I don't recommend him; but I point him out. [*Moving off.*] He's at the New Inn. You could take him there.
NORFOLK [*to* RICH *mounting stairs*]: All right, come on.
RICH: My Lord.
NORFOLK: We'll hawk at Hounslow, Alice.
ALICE: Wherever you like.

ALICE *and* MARGARET *follow* NORFOLK.

RICH [*at foot of stairs*]: Sir Thomas! . . .

MORE *turns.*

Thank you.
MORE: Be a teacher. [*Moving off again.*] Oh— The ground's hard at Hounslow, Alice!
NORFOLK: Eh? [*Delighted roar.*] That's where the Cardinal crushed his bum!
MORE ⎫
NORFOLK ⎬ Good night! Good night!
ALICE ⎪
RICH ⎭

They process off along the gallery.

MORE [*softly*]: Margaret!
MARGARET: Yes?
MORE: Go to bed.

MARGARET *exits above,* MORE *exits below. After a moment* RICH *walks swiftly back down stage, picks up the goblet and is going off with it.*

STEWARD: Eh!
RICH: What—! Oh. . . . It's a gift, Matthew. Sir Thomas gave it to me.

STEWARD *takes it and regards it silently.*

He gave it to me.
STEWARD [*returns it*]: Very nice present, sir.
RICH [*backing away with it*]: Yes. Good night, Matthew.
STEWARD: Sir Thomas has taken quite a fancy to you, sir.
RICH: Er, here—[*Gives money and goes.*]
STEWARD: Thank you, sir. . . . [*To audience.*] That one'll come to nothing. [*Begins packing props into basket, Pauses with cup in hand.*] My master Thomas More would give anything to anyone. Some say that's good and some say that's bad, but I say he can't help it—and that's bad . . . because some day someone's going to ask him for something that he wants to keep; and he'll be out of practice. [*Puts cloth with papers, ink, etc., on table.*] There must be something that he wants to keep. That's only Common Sense.

Enter WOLSEY. *He sits at table and immediately commences writing, watched by* COMMON MAN *who then exits. Enter* MORE.

WOLSEY [*writing*]: It's half-past one. Where've you been?

Bell strikes one.

MORE: One o'clock, Your Grace. I've been on the river.

WOLSEY *writes in silence, while* MORE *waits standing.*

WOLSEY [*still writing, pushes paper across table*]: Since you seemed so violently opposed to the Latin dispatch, I thought you'd like to look it over.
MORE [*touched*]: Thank you, Your Grace.
WOLSEY: Before it goes.
MORE [*smiles*]: Your Grace is very kind. [*Takes and reads.*] Thank you.
WOLSEY: Well, what d'you think of it? [*He is still writing.*]
MORE: It seems very well phrased, Your Grace.
WOLSEY [*permits himself a chuckle*]: The devil it does! [*Sits back.*] And apart from the style, Sir Thomas?
MORE: I think the Council should be told before that goes to Italy.
WOLSEY: Would you tell the Council? Yes, I believe you would. You're a constant regret to me, Thomas. If you could just see facts flat on, without that moral squint; with just a little common sense, you could have been a statesman.
MORE [*little pause*]: Oh, Your Grace flatters me.
WOLSEY: Don't frivel. . . . Thomas, are you going to help me?
MORE [*hesitates, looks away*]: If Your Grace will be specific.
WOLSEY: Ach, you're a plodder! Take you altogether, Thomas, your scholarship, your experience, what are you?

A single trumpet calls, distant, frosty and clear. WOLSEY *gets up and goes and looks from window.*

Come here.

MORE *joins him.*

The King.
MORE: Yes.
WOLSEY: Where has he been? D'you know?
MORE: I, Your Grace?
WOLSEY: Oh, spare me your discretion. He's been to play in the muck again.
MORE [*coldly*]: Indeed.
WOLSEY: Indeed! Indeed! Are you going to oppose me?

Trumpet again. WOLSEY *visibly relaxes.*

He's gone in. . . . [*Leaves window.*] All right, we'll plod. The King wants a son; what are you going to do about it?
MORE [*dry murmur*]: I'm very sure the King needs no advice from me on what to do about it.
WOLSEY [*from behind grips his shoulder fiercely*]: Thomas, we're alone. I give you my word. There's no one here.
MORE: I didn't suppose there was, Your Grace.
WOLSEY: Oh.

Goes to table, sits, signs MORE *to sit.* MORE *unsuspectingly obeys. Then, deliberately loud.*

Do you favour a change of dynasty, Sir Thomas? D'you think two Tudors is sufficient?
MORE [*starting up in horrified alarm*]:—For God's sake, Your Grace—!
WOLSEY: Then the King needs a son; I repeat what are you going to do about it?
MORE [*steadily*]: I pray for it daily.
WOLSEY [*snatches up candle and holds to* MORE's *face. Softly*]: God's death, he means it. . . . That thing out there's at least fertile, Thomas.
MORE: But she's not his wife.
WOLSEY: No, Catherine's his wife and she's as barren as brick. Are you going to pray for a miracle?
MORE: There *are* precedents.
WOLSEY: Yes. All right. Good. Pray. Pray by all means. But in addition to Prayer there is Effort. My effort's to secure a divorce. Have I your support or have I not?
MORE [*sits*]: A dispensation was given so that the King might marry Queen Catherine, for state reasons. Now we are to ask the Pope to—dispense with his dispensation, also for state reasons?
WOLSEY:—I don't *like* plodding, Thomas, don't make me plod longer than I have to— Well?
MORE: Then clearly all we have to do is approach His Holiness and ask him.

The pace becomes rapid.

WOLSEY:—I think we might influence His Holiness' answer—
MORE:—Like this?—[*The dispatch.*]
WOLSEY:—Like that and in other ways—
MORE:—I've already expressed my opinion on this—
WOLSEY:—Then, good night! Oh, your conscience is your own affair; but you're a statesman! Do you *remember* the Yorkist Wars?
MORE: Very clearly.
WOLSEY: Let him die without an heir and we'll have them back again. Let him die without an heir and this 'peace' you think so much of will go out like that! [*Extinguishes candle.*] Very well, then England needs an heir; certain measures, perhaps regrettable, perhaps not—[*pompous*] there is much in the Church that *needs* reformation, Thomas—

MORE *smiles.*

All right, regrettable! But necessary, to get us an heir! Now explain how you as Councillor of England can obstruct those measures for the sake of your own, private, conscience.
MORE: Well . . . I believe, when statesmen forsake their own private conscience for the sake of their public duties . . . they lead their country by a short route to chaos. [*During this speech he relights the candle with another.*] And we shall have my prayers to fall back on.
WOLSEY: You'd like that, wouldn't you? To govern the country by prayers?
MORE: Yes, I should.
WOLSEY: I'd like to be there when you try. Who *will* deal with all this—paper, after me? You? Fisher? Suffolk?
MORE: Fisher for me.
WOLSEY: Aye, but for the King. What about my Secretary, Master Cromwell?
MORE: Cromwell!
WOLSEY: You'd rather do it yourself?
MORE: Me rather than Cromwell.
WOLSEY: Then come down to earth. . . . And until then, allow for an enemy, here!
MORE: As Your Grace pleases.
WOLSEY: As God wills!
MORE: Perhaps, Your Grace. [*Mounting stairs.*]
WOLSEY: More! You should have been a cleric!
MORE [*amused, looking down from gallery*]: Like yourself, Your Grace?

Exit MORE. WOLSEY *is left staring, then exits through the lower arches with candle, taking most of the light from the stage as he does so. But the whole rear of the stage now patterns with webbed reflections thrown from brightly moonlit water, so that the structure is thrown into black relief, while a strip of light descends along the front of the stage, which is to be the acting area for the next scene.*

An oar and a bundle of clothing are lowered into this area from above. Enter COMMON MAN; *he unties the bundle and dons the coat and hat of* BOAT-MAN.

MORE [*off*]: Boat! [*Approaching.*] Boat!
BOATMAN [*donning coat and hat*]: Here, sir!
MORE [*off*]: A boatman please!
BOATMAN: Boat here, sir! [*He seizes the oar.*]

Enter MORE.

MORE [*peering*]: Boatman?
BOATMAN: Yes, sir. [*To audience, indicating oar.*] A boatman.
MORE: Take me home.
BOATMAN [*pleasantly*]: I was just going home myself, sir.
MORE: Then find me another boat.
BOATMAN: Bless you, sir–that's all right! [*Comfortably.*] I expect you'll make it worth my while, sir.

CROMWELL *steps from behind arch, left.*

CROMWELL: Boatman, have you a licence?
BOATMAN: Eh? Bless you, sir, yes; I've got a licence.
CROMWELL: Then you know that the fares are fixed— [*Turns to* MORE. *Exaggerated pleasure.*] Why, it's Sir Thomas!
MORE: Good morning, Master Cromwell. You work very late.
CROMWELL: I'm on my way to the Cardinal. [*He expects an answer.*]
MORE: Ah.
CROMWELL: You have just left him I think.
MORE: Yes, I have.
CROMWELL: You left him . . . in his laughing mood, I hope?
MORE: On the whole I would say, not. No, not laughing.
CROMWELL: Oh, I'm sorry. [*Backing to exit.*] I am one of your *multitudinous* admirers, Sir Thomas. A penny ha'penny to Chelsea, Boatman.

Exit CROMWELL.

BOATMAN: The coming man they say, sir.
MORE: Do they? Well, where's your boat?
BOATMAN: Just along the wharf, sir.

They are going, when enter CHAPUYS *and* ATTENDANT *from archway, Right.*

CHAPUYS: Sir Thomas More!
MORE: Signor Chapuys? You're up very late, Your Excellency.
CHAPUYS [*significantly*]: So is the Cardinal, Sir Thomas.
MORE [*closing up*]: He sleeps very little.
CHAPUYS: You have just left him, I think.
MORE: You are correctly informed. As always.
CHAPUYS: I will not ask you the subject of your conversation. . . . [*He waits.*]
MORE: No, of course not.
CHAPUYS: Sir Thomas, I will be plain with you . . . plain, that is, so far as the diplomatic decencies permit. [*Loudly.*] My master Charles, the King of Spain! [*Pulls* MORE *aside, discreet.*] My master Charles, the King of Spain, feels himself concerned in anything concerning his blood relation! He would

feel himself insulted by any insult offered to his father's sister! I refer of course to Queen Catherine. [*Regards* MORE, *keenly.*] The King of Spain would feel himself insulted by any insult offered to Queen Catherine.

MORE: His feeling would be natural.

CHAPUYS [*consciously sly*]: Sir Thomas, may I ask if you and the Cardinal parted, how shall I say, amicably?

MORE: Amicably. . . . Yes.

CHAPUYS [*a shade indignant*]: In agreement?

MORE: Amicably.

CHAPUYS [*warmly*]: Say no more, Sir Thomas; I understand.

MORE [*a shade worried*]: I hope you do, Your Excellency.

CHAPUYS: You are a good man.

MORE: I don't see how you deduce that from what I've told you.

CHAPUYS [*holds up hand*]: A nod is as good as a wink to a blind horse. I understand. You are a good man. [*Turns to exit.*] Dominus vobiscum.

Exit CHAPUYS. MORE *looks after him. Then:*

MORE [*abstracted*]: . . . spiritu tuo . . .

BOATMAN [*mournful; he is squatting on the ground*]: People seem to think boats stay afloat on their own, sir, but they don't; they cost money.

MORE *is abstractedly gazing over the audience.*

Take anchor rope, sir, you may not believe me for a little skiff like mine, but it's a penny a fathom.

MORE *is still abstracted.*

And with a young wife, sir, as you know. . . .

MORE [*abstracted*]: I'll pay what I always pay you. . . . The river looks very black tonight. They say it's silting up, is that so?

BOATMAN [*joining him*]: Not in the middle, sir. There's a channel there getting deeper all the time.

MORE: How is your wife?

BOATMAN: She's losing her shape, sir, losing it fast.

MORE: Well, so are we all.

BOATMAN: Oh yes, sir; it's common.

MORE [*going*]: Well, take me home.

Exit MORE.

BOATMAN: That I will, sir! [*Crossing to basket and pulling it out.*] From Richmond to Chelsea, downstream, a penny halfpenny . . . coat, hat . . . coat, hat [*goes for table-cloth*] from Chelsea to Richmond, upstream, a penny halfpenny. Whoever makes the regulations doesn't row a boat. Cloth. . . . [*Puts cloth in basket, takes out slippers.*] Home again.

Lighting changes to MORE's *house interior.*
Enter MORE *on stairs. Sits wearily. Takes off hat, half takes off coat, but is too tired. It chimes three.* STEWARD *kneels to put on his slippers for him.*

MORE: Ah, Matthew. . . . Thank you. Is Lady Alice in bed?
STEWARD: Yes, sir.
MORE: Lady Margaret?
STEWARD: No, sir, Master Roper's here.
MORE [*surprised*]: At this hour? . . . Who let him in?
STEWARD: He's a hard man to keep out, sir.
MORE: Where are they?

Enter MARGARET *and* ROPER.

MARGARET: Here, Father.
MORE [*regarding them, resignedly*]: Good morning, William. It's a little early for breakfast.
ROPER [*solidly*]: I haven't come for breakfast, sir.

MORE *looks at him and sighs.*

MARGARET: Will wants to marry me, Father.
MORE: Well, he can't marry you.
ROPER: Sir Thomas, I'm to be called to the Bar.
MORE [*warmly*]: Oh, congratulations, Roper!
ROPER: My family may not be at the palace, sir, but in the City—
MORE: The Ropers were advocates when the Mores were selling pewter; there's nothing wrong with your family. There's nothing wrong with your fortune—there's nothing wrong with you—[*sourly*] except you need a clock—
ROPER: I can buy a clock, sir.
MORE: Roper, the answer's 'no'. [*Firmly.*] And will be 'no' so long as you're a heretic.
ROPER [*firing*]: That's a word I don't like, Sir Thomas!
MORE: It's not a likeable word. [*Coming to life.*] It's not a likeable thing!

MARGARET *is alarmed, and from behind* MORE *tries to silence* ROPER.

ROPER: The Church is heretical! Doctor Luther's proved that to my satisfaction!
MORE: Luther's an excommunicate.
ROPER: From a heretic Church! Church? It's a shop— Forgiveness by the florin! Joblots now in Germany! . . . Mmm, and divorces.
MORE [*expressionless*]: Divorces?
ROPER: Oh, half England's buzzing with that.
MORE: 'Half England.' The Inns of Court may be buzzing, England doesn't buzz so easily.
ROPER: It will. And is that a Church? Is that a Cardinal? Is that a Pope? Or Antichrist!

MORE *looks up angrily.* MARGARET *signals frantically.*

Look, what I know I'll say!
MARGARET: You've no sense of the *place*!
MORE [*rueful*]: He's no sense of the time.
ROPER: I—

But MORE *gently holds up his hand and he stops.*

MORE: Listen, Roper. Two years ago you were a passionate Churchman; now you're a passionate–Lutheran. We must just pray, that when your head's finished turning your face is to the front again.
ROPER: Don't lengthen your prayers with *me*, sir!
MORE: Oh, one more or less. . . . Is your horse here?
ROPER: No, I walked.
MORE: Well, take a horse from the stables and get back home.

ROPER *hesitates.*

Go along.
ROPER: May I come again?

MORE *indicates* MARGARET.

MARGARET: Yes. Soon.
ROPER: Good night, sir.

Exit ROPER.

MARGARET: Is that final, Father?
MORE: As long as he's a heretic, Meg, that absolute. [*Warmly.*] Nice boy. . . . Terribly strong principles though. I told you to go to bed.
MARGARET: Yes, why?
MORE [*lightly*]: Because I intended you to *go* to bed. You're very pensive?
MARGARET: You're very gay. Did he talk about the divorce?
MORE: Mm? You know I think we've been on the wrong track with Will— It's no good arguing with a Roper—
MARGARET: Father, did he?
MORE: *Old* Roper was just the same. Now let him think he's going *with* the current and he'll turn round and start swimming in the opposite direction. What we want is a really substantial attack on the Church.
MARGARET: We're going to get it, aren't we?
MORE: Margaret, I'll not have you talk treason. . . . And I'll not have you repeat lawyer's gossip. I'm a lawyer myself and I know what it's worth.
ALICE [*off. Indignant and excited*]: Thomas—!
MORE: Now look what you've done.

Enter ALICE *at head of stairs in nightgown.*

ALICE: Young Roper! I've just seen young Roper! On *my* horse.
MORE: He'll bring it back, dear. He's been to see Margaret.
ALICE: Oh–why you don't beat that girl!
MORE: No no, she's full of education–and it's a delicate commodity.
ALICE: Mm! And more's the pity!
MORE: Yes, but it's there now and think what it cost. [*He sneezes.*]
ALICE [*pouncing*]: Ah! Margaret–hot water.

Exit MARGARET.

MORE: I'm sorry you were awakened, chick.

ALICE: I wasn't sleeping very deeply. Thomas—what did Wolsey want?

MORE [*innocent*]: Young Roper asked for Margaret.

ALICE: What! Impudence!

MORE: Yes, wasn't it?

ALICE: Old fox! What did he want, Thomas?

MORE: He wanted me to read a dispatch.

ALICE: Was that all?

MORE: A Latin dispatch.

ALICE: Oh! Won't you talk about it?

MORE [*gently*]: No.

Enter MARGARET *with cup which she takes to* MORE.

ALICE: Norfolk was speaking for you as Chancellor before he left.

MORE: He's a dangerous friend then. Wolsey's Chancellor, God help him. We don't want another.

MARGARET *takes cup to him; he sniffs it.*

I don't want this.

ALICE: Drink it. Great men get colds in the head just the same as commoners.

MORE: That's dangerous, levelling talk, Alice. Beware of the Tower. [*Rises.*] I will, I'll drink it in bed.

All move to stairs and ascend, talking.

MARGARET: Would you want to be Chancellor?

MORE: No.

MARGARET: That's what I said. But Norfolk said if Wolsey fell—

MORE [*no longer flippant*]: If Wolsey fell, the splash would swamp a few small boats like ours. There will be no new Chancellors while Wolsey lives.

Exit above.
  The light is dimmed there and a bright spot descends below. Into this bright circle from the wings is thrown the great red robe and the Cardinal's hat. The COMMON MAN *enters from the opposite wing and roughly piles them into his basket. He then takes from his pocket a pair of spectacles and from the basket a book. He reads:*

COMMON MAN [*reading*]: 'Whether we follow tradition in ascribing Wolsey's death to a broken heart, or accept Professor Larcomb's less feeling diagnosis of pulmonary pneumonia, its effective cause was the King's displeasure. He died at Leicester on 29 November 1530 while on his way to the Tower under charge of High Treason.

'England's next Lord Chancellor was Sir Thomas More, a scholar and, by popular repute, a saint. His scholarship is supported by his writings; saintliness is a quality less easy to establish. But from his wilful indifference to realities which were obvious to quite ordinary contemporaries, it seems all too probable that he had it.'

Exit COMMON MAN. *As he goes, lights come up and a screen is lowered depicting Hampton Court.* CROMWELL *is sitting halfway up the stairs. Enter* RICH, *crossing.*

CROMWELL: Rich! [RICH *stops, sees him, and smiles willingly.*] What brings you to Hampton?

RICH: I came with the Duke last night, Master Cromwell. They're hunting again.

CROMWELL: It's a kingly pastime, Master Rich. [*Both smile.*] I'm glad you found employment. You're the Duke's Secretary are you not?

RICH [*flustered*]: My work *is* mostly secretarial.

CROMWELL [*as one making an effort of memory*]: Or is it his librarian you are?

RICH: I do look after His Grace's library, yes.

CROMWELL: Oh. Well, that's something. And I don't suppose you're bothered much by His Grace—in the library?

RICH *smiles uncertainly.*

It's odd how differently men's fortunes flow. My late master died in disgrace, and here I am in the King's own service. There you are in a *comparative* backwater—yet the new Lord Chancellor's an old friend of yours. [*He looks at him directly.*]

RICH [*uncertainly*]: He isn't really my *friend.* . . .

CROMWELL: Oh, I thought he was. [*Gets up, prepares to go.*]

RICH:—In a sense he is.

CROMWELL [*reproachful*]: Well, I always understood he set you up in life.

RICH: Master Cromwell—what *is* it that you do for the King?

Enter CHAPUYS.

CHAPUYS [*roguish*]: Yes, *I* should like to know that, Master Cromwell.

CROMWELL: Ah, Signor Chapuys. You've met His Excellency, Rich? [*Indicates* CHAPUYS.] The Spanish Ambassador. [*Indicates* RICH.] The Duke of Norfolk's librarian.

CHAPUYS: But how should we introduce *you*, Master Cromwell, if we had the happiness?

CROMWELL: Oh sly! Do you notice how sly he is, Rich? [*Walks away.*] Well, I suppose you would call me [*suddenly turns*] 'The King's Ear'. . . . [*Deprecating shrug.*] It's a useful organ, the ear. But in fact it's even simpler than that. When the King wants something done, I do it.

CHAPUYS: Ah. [*Mock interest.*] But then why these Justices, Chancellors, Admirals?

CROMWELL: Oh, *they* are the constitution. Our ancient, English constitution. I merely do things.

CHAPUYS: For example, Master Cromwell. . . .

CROMWELL [*admiring*]: Oho—beware these professional diplomats. Well now, for example; next week at Deptford we are launching the *Great Harry*—one thousand tons, four masts, sixty-six guns, an overall length of one hundred and seventy-five feet, it's expected to be very effective—all this you probably know. However you may not know that the King himself will guide her down the river; yes, the King himself will be her pilot. He will have assistance of course but he himself will be her pilot. He will have a pilot's whistle upon which he will blow, and he will wear in every respect a common pilot's uniform. Except for the material, which will be cloth of gold. These innocent fancies require more preparation than you might suppose and someone has to do it. [*He spreads his hands.*] Meanwhile, I do prepare myself for, higher things. I stock my mind.

CHAPUYS: Alas, Master Cromwell, don't we all? This ship for instance–it has fifty-six guns by the way, not sixty-six and only forty of them heavy— After the launching I understand, the King will take his barge to Chelsea.

> CROMWELL's *face darkens during this speech.*

CROMWELL [*sharply*]: Yes—
CHAPUYS:—To—
CROMWELL ⎱
CHAPUYS   ⎰ [*together*]: Sir Thomas More's.
CHAPUYS [*sweetly*]: Will you be there?
CROMWELL: Oh no–they'll talk about the divorce.

> *It is* CHAPUYS' *turn to be shocked:* RICH *draws away uneasily.*

The King will ask him for an answer.
CHAPUYS [*ruffled*]: He has given his answer!
CROMWELL: The King will ask him for another.
CHAPUYS: Sir Thomas is a good son of the Church!
CROMWELL: Sir Thomas is a man.

> *Enter* STEWARD. *Both* CROMWELL *and* CHAPUYS *look towards him sharply, then back at one another.*

CHAPUYS [*innocently*]: Isn't that his Steward now?
CROMWELL: I believe it is. Well, good day, Your Excellency.
CHAPUYS [*eager*]. Good day, Master Cromwell. [*He expects him to go.*]
CROMWELL [*standing firm*]: Good day.

> *And* CHAPUYS *has to go.*
> CROMWELL *walks side stage, with furtive and urgent beckonings to* STEWARD *to follow.* RICH *follows but hangs off. Meanwhile* CHAPUYS *and his* ATTENDANT *have gone behind screen, beneath which their legs protrude clearly.*

STEWARD [*conspiratorial*]: Sir, Sir Thomas doesn't talk about it. [*He waits but* CROMWELL *remains stony.*] He doesn't talk about it, to his wife, sir. [*He waits again.*]
CROMWELL: This is worth nothing.
STEWARD [*significant*]: But he doesn't talk about it to Lady Margaret–that's his daughter, sir.
CROMWELL: So?
STEWARD: So he's worried, sir . . .

> CROMWELL *is interested*

Frightened. . . .

CROMWELL *takes out a coin but pauses suspiciously.*

Sir, he goes *white* when it's mentioned!
CROMWELL [*hands coin*]: All right.
STEWARD [*looks at coin; reproachful*]: Oh, sir—!
CROMWELL [*waves him away*]: Are you coming in my direction, Rich?
RICH [*still hanging off*]: No no.
CROMWELL: I think you should, you know.
RICH: *I* can't tell you anything!

Exit RICH *and* CROMWELL *left and right.* CHAPUYS *and* ATTENDANT *come from behind screen.*

CHAPUYS [*beckons* STEWARD]: Well?
STEWARD: Sir Thomas rises at six, sir, and prays for an hour and a half.
CHAPUYS: Yes?
STEWARD: During Lent, sir, he lived entirely on bread and water.
CHAPUYS: Yes?
STEWARD: He goes to confession twice a week, sir. Parish priest. Dominican.
CHAPUYS: Ah. He is a true son of the Church.
STEWARD [*soapy*]: That he is, sir.
CHAPUYS: What did Master Cromwell want?
STEWARD: Same as you, sir.
CHAPUYS: No man can serve two masters, Steward.
STEWARD: No, indeed, sir; I serve one. [*He pulls to the front an enormous cross until then hanging at his back on a length of string—a caricature of the ebony cross worn by* CHAPUYS.]
CHAPUYS: Good, simple man. Here. [*Gives coin. Going.*] Peace be with you.
STEWARD: And with you, sir.
CHAPUYS: Our Lord watch you.
STEWARD: You too, sir.

Exit CHAPUYS.

That's a very religious man.

Enter RICH.

RICH: What does Signor Chapuys want, Matthew?
STEWARD: I've no idea, sir.
RICH [*gives coin*]: What did you tell him?
STEWARD: I told him that Sir Thomas says his prayers and goes to confession.
RICH: Why that?
STEWARD: That's what he wanted to know, sir. I mean I could have told him any number of things about Sir Thomas—that he has rheumatism, prefers red wine to white, is easily sea-sick, fond of kippers, afraid of drowning. But that's what he wanted to know, sir.
RICH: What did he say?
STEWARD: He said that Sir Thomas is a good churchman, sir.

RICH [*going*]: Well, that's true, isn't it?

STEWARD: I'm just telling you what he said, sir. Master Cromwell went that way, sir.

RICH [*furious*]: Did I ask you which way Master Cromwell went?

Exit RICH *opposite.*

STEWARD [*to audience, thoughtfully*]: The great thing's not to get out of your depth. . . . What I can tell them's common knowledge! But now they've given money for it and everyone wants value for his money. They'll make a secret of it now to prove they've not been bilked. . . . They'll make it a secret by making it dangerous. . . . Mm. . . . Oh, when I can't touch the bottom I'll go deaf blind and dumb. [*Holds out coins.*] And that's more than I *earn* in a fortnight!

On this; a fanfare of trumpets; plainsong; the rear of the stage becomes a source of glittering blue light; Hampton Court is hoisted out of sight, and other screens are lowered one after the other, each masking the rest, bearing respectively sunflowers, hollyhocks, roses, magnolias. When the fanfare ceases the plainsong goes on quietly, and the screens throw long shadows like the shadows of trees, and NORFOLK, ALICE, MARGARET, *erupt on to the stage.*

ALICE [*distressed*]: No sign of him, my lord!

NORFOLK: God's body, Alice, he must be found!

ALICE [*to* MEG]: He *must* be in the house!

MARGARET: He's *not* in the house, Mother!

ALICE: Then he must be here in the garden!

They 'search' among the screens.

NORFOLK: He takes things too far, Alice.

ALICE: Do I not know it?

NORFOLK: It will end badly for him!

ALICE: I know that too!

They 'notice' the STEWARD.

MARGARET ⎫		Matthew! Where's my father?
ALICE ⎬	[*together*]:	Where is Sir Thomas?
NORFOLK ⎭		Where's your master?

Fanfare, shorter but nearer.

NORFOLK [*despairing*]: Oh my God.

ALICE: Oh Jesus!

STEWARD: My lady—the King?

NORFOLK: Yes, fool! [*Threatening.*] And if the King arrives and the Chancellor's not here—

STEWARD: Sir, my lady, it's not *my* fault!

NORFOLK [*quietly displeased*]: Lady Alice, Thomas'll get no good of it. This is not how Wolsey made himself great.

ALICE [*stiffly*]: Thomas has his own way of doing things, my lord!
NORFOLK [*testy*]: Yes yes, Thomas is unique; but where *is* Thomas?

> STEWARD *swings onstage small gothic door. Plainsong. All run to the door.*
> NORFOLK *opens it.*

ALICE: Thomas!
STEWARD: Sir!
MARGARET: Father!
NORFOLK [*indignant*]: My Lord Chancellor!

> *Enter* MORE *through the doorway. He blinks in the light. He is wearing a*
> *cassock. Shuts door behind him.*

What sort of fooling is this? Does the King visit you every day.
MORE: No, but I go to Vespers most days.
NORFOLK: He's here!
MORE: But isn't this visit *meant* to be a surprise?
NORFOLK [*grimly*]: For you, yes, not for him.
MARGARET: Father. . . . [*Indicates cassock.*]
NORFOLK: Yes–d'you propose to meet the King disguised as a parish clerk.

> *They fall upon him and drag the cassock over his head.*

A parish clerk, my lord Chancellor! You dishonour the King and his office!
MORE [*appearing momentarily in the folds of the cassock*]: The service of God is
not a dishonour to any office.

> *The cassock is pulled off.*

Believe me, my friend, I do not belittle the honour His Majesty is doing me.
[*Briskly.*] Well! That's a lovely dress, Alice; so's that, Margaret. [*Looks at*
NORFOLK.] I'm a dowdy bird, aren't I? [*Looks at* ALICE.] Calm yourself, Alice,
we're all ready now. [*He turns about and we see that his gown is caught up*
behind him revealing his spindly legs in long hose laced up at the thighs.]
ALICE: Thomas!

> MARGARET *laughs.*

MORE: What's the matter?

> *Turns round again and his women folk pursue him to pull down the gown while*
> NORFOLK *throws his hands in the air. Expostulation, explanation,*
> *exclamation, overlapping in a babble.*

NORFOLK:—By God you can be hare-brained—!
MARGARET:—Be still—!
ALICE:—Oh, Thomas! Thomas!—
NORFOLK:—What whim possessed you—
MORE:—'Twas not a whim—!
ALICE:—Your second best stockings—!

MARGARET:—Father, be still—!
NORFOLK:—Oh, enough's enough—!
MORE:—Haven't you done—!

HENRY, *in a cloth of gold, runs out of the sunlight half-way down the steps, and blows a blast on his pilot's whistle. All kneel. In the silence he descends slowly to their level, blowing softly . . .*

MORE: Your Majesty does my house more honour than I fear my household can bear.
HENRY: No ceremony, Thomas! No ceremony! [*They rise.*] A passing fancy–I happened to be on the river. [*Holds out shoe, proudly.*] Look, mud.
MORE: We do it in better style, Your Grace, when we come by the road.
HENRY: Oh, the road! There's the road for me, Thomas, the river; *my* river. . . . By heaven what an evening! I fear we come upon you unexpectedly, Lady Alice.
ALICE [*shocked*]: Oh no, Your Grace–[*remembering*] that is yes, but we are ready for you–ready to entertain Your Grace that is.
MORE: This is my daughter Margaret, sir. She has not had the honour to meet Your Grace. [*She curtseys low.*]
HENRY [*looks her over, then*]: Why, Margaret, they told me you were a scholar.

MARGARET *is confused.*

MORE: Answer, Margaret.
MARGARET: Among women I pass for one Your Grace. NORFOLK *and* ALICE *exchange approving glances.*
HENRY: Antiquone modo Latine loqueris, an Oxoniensi?
[Is your Latin the old Latin, or Oxford Latin?]
MARGARET: Quem me docuit pater, Domine.
[My father's Latin, Sire.]
HENRY: Bene. Optimus est. Graecamne linguam quoque te docuit?
[Good. That is the best. And has he taught you Greek too?]
MARGARET: Graecam me docuit non pater meus sed mei patris amicus, Johannes Coletus, Sancti Pauli Decanus. In litteris Graecis tamen, non minus quam Latinis, ars magistri minuitur discipuli stultitia.
[Not my father, Sire, but my father's friend, John Colet, Dean of St Paul's. But it is with the Greek as it is with the Latin; the skill of the master is lost in the pupil's lack of it.]

Her Latin is better than his; he is not altogether pleased.

HENRY: Ho!

He walks away from her, talking; she begins to rise from her curtsey, MORE *gently presses her down again before the King turns.*

Take care, Thomas: 'There is no end to the making of books and too much reading is a weariness of the flesh.' [*Back to* MARGARET.] Can you dance, too?
MARGARET: Not well, Your Grace.
HENRY: Well, *I* dance superlatively! [*Plants his leg before her face.*] That's a

dancer's *leg*, Margaret!

She has the wit to look straight up and smile at him. All good humour he pulls her to her feet; sees NORFOLK *grinning the grin of a comrade.*

Hey, Norfolk? [*Indicates* NORFOLK's *leg with much distaste.*] Now *that's* a wrestler's leg. But I can throw him. [*Seizes* NORFOLK.] Shall I show them, Howard?

NORFOLK *is alarmed for his dignity. To* MARGARET.

Shall I?

MARGARET [*looking at* NORFOLK, *gently*]: No, Your Grace.
HENRY [*releases* NORFOLK, *seriously*]: You are gentle. [*To* MORE, *approving.*] That's good. [*To* MARGARET.] You shall read to me.

MARGARET *is about to demur.*

No no, you shall read to me. Lady Alice, the river's given me an appetite.
ALICE: If Your Grace would share a very simple supper.
HENRY: It would please me to. [*Preparing to lead off, sees* MARGARET *again.*] I'm something of a scholar too; did you know?
MARGARET: All the world knows Your Grace's Book, asserting the seven sacraments of the Church.
HENRY: Ah yes. Between ourselves, your father had a hand in that; eh, Thomas?
MORE: Here and there, Your Grace. In a minor capacity.
HENRY [*looking at him*]: He seeks to shame me with his modesty. . . . [*Turns to* ALICE.] On second thoughts we'll follow, Lady Alice, Thomas and I will follow.

He waves them off. They bow, withdraw, prepare for second bow.

Wait! [*Raises whistle to lips; then:*] Margaret, are you fond of music?
MARGARET: Yes, Your Grace.
HENRY [*beckons her to him; holds out whistle*]: Blow.

She is uncertain.

Blow.

She does.

Louder!

She does and at once music without, stately and oversweet. Expressions of pleasure all round.

I brought them with me, Lady Alice; take them in!

Exit all but MORE *and* HENRY. *The music continues receding.*

Listen to this, Thomas. [*He walks about, the auditor, beating time.*] Do you know it?

MORE: No, Your Grace, I—

HENRY: Sh! [MORE *is silent;* HENRY *goes on with his listening.*] . . . I launched a ship today, Thomas.

MORE: Yes, Your Grace, I—

HENRY: *Listen*, man, *listen.* . . . [*A silence.*] . . . The *Great Harry* . . . I steered her, Thomas, under sail.

MORE: You have many accomplishments, Your Grace.

HENRY [*holds up a finger for silence.* . . . *A silence*]: A great experience.

MORE *keeps silent.*

. . . A great experience, Thomas.

MORE: Yes, Your Grace.

The music is growing fainter.

HENRY: I am a fool.

MORE: How so, Your Grace?

A silence, during which the music fades to silence.

HENRY: . . . What else but a fool to live in a Court, in a licentious mob—when I have friends, with gardens.

MORE: Your Grace—

HENRY: No courtship, no ceremony, Thomas. Be seated. You *are* my friend are you not?

MORE *sits.*

MORE: Your Majesty.

HENRY: And thank God I have a friend for my Chancellor. [*Laughing.*] Readier to be friends I trust than he was to be Chancellor.

MORE: My own knowledge of my poor abilities—

HENRY: I will judge of your abilities, Thomas. . . . Did you know that Wolsey named you for Chancellor?

MORE: Wolsey!

HENRY: Aye; before he died. Wolsey named you and Wolsey was no fool.

MORE: He was a statesman of incomparable ability, Your Grace.

HENRY: Was he? Was he so? [*Rises.*] Then why did he fail me? Be seated—it was villainy then! Yes villainy. I was right to break him; he was all pride, Thomas; a proud man; pride right through. And he failed me!

MORE *opens his mouth.*

He failed me in the one thing that mattered! The one thing that matters, Thomas, then or now. And why? He wanted to be Pope! Yes, he wanted to be the Bishop of Rome. I'll tell you something. Thomas, and you can check this for yourself—it was never merry in England while we had Cardinals amongst us. [*He nods significantly at* MORE *who lowers his eyes.*] But look now—[*walking away*]–I shall forget the feel of that . . . great tiller under my hands . . . I took her down to Dogget's Bank, went about and brought her up in Tilbury Roads. A man could sail clean round the world in that ship.

MORE [*affectionate admiration*]: Some men could, Your Grace.

HENRY [*off-hand*]: Touching this matter of my divorce, Thomas; have you thought of it since we last talked?

MORE: Of little else.

HENRY: Then you see your way clear to me?

MORE: That you should put away Queen Catherine, sire? Oh, alas [*thumps table in distress*], as I think of it I see so clearly that I can *not* come with Your Grace that my endeavour is not to think of it at all.

HENRY: Then you have not thought enough! . . . [*With real appeal.*] Great God, Thomas, why do you hold out against me in the desire of my heart–the very wick of my heart?—

MORE [*draws up sleeve, baring his arm*]: There is my right arm. [*A practical proposition.*] Take your dagger and saw it from my shoulder, and I will laugh and be thankful, if by that means I can come with Your Grace with a clear conscience.

HENRY [*uncomfortably pulls at the sleeve*]: I know it, Thomas, I know. . . .

MORE [*rises, formally*]: I crave pardon if I offend.

HENRY [*suspiciously*]: Speak then.

MORE: When I took the Great Seal your Majesty promised not to pursue me on this matter.

HENRY: Ha! So I break my word, Master More! No, no, I'm joking . . . I joke roughly . . . [*Wanders away.*] I often think I'm a rough fellow. . . . Yes, a rough young fellow. [*Shakes his head indulgently.*] Be seated. . . . That's a magnolia. We have one like it at Hampton–not so red as that though. Ha–I'm in an excellent frame of mind. [*Glances at the magnolia.*] Beautiful. [*Reasonable, pleasant.*] You must consider, Thomas, that I stand in peril of my soul. It was no marriage; she was my brother's widow. Leviticus: 'Thou shalt not uncover the nakedness of thy brother's wife.' Leviticus, Chapter 18, Verse 16.

MORE: Yes, Your Grace. But Deuteronomy—

HENRY [*triumphant*]: Deuteronomy's ambiguous!

MORE [*bursting out*]: Your Grace, I'm not fit to meddle in these matters–to me it seems a matter for the Holy See—

HENRY [*reproving*]: Thomas, Thomas, does a man need a Pope to tell him when he's sinned? It was a sin, Thomas; I admit it; I repent. And God has punished me; I have no son. . . . Son after son she's borne me, Thomas, all dead at birth, or dead within the month; I never saw the hand of God so clear in anything. . . . I have a daughter, she's a good child, a well-set child— But I have no son. [*Flares up.*] It is my bounden *duty* to put away the Queen and all the Popes back to St Peter shall not come between me and my duty! How is it that you cannot see? Everyone else does.

MORE [*eagerly*]: Then why does Your Grace need my poor support?

HENRY: Because you are honest. What's more to the purpose, you're known to be honest. . . . There are those like Norfolk who follow me because I wear the crown, and there are those like Master Cromwell who follow me because they are jackals with sharp teeth and I am their lion, and there is a mass that follows me because it follows anything that moves–and there is you.

MORE: I am sick to think how much I must displease Your Grace.

HENRY: No, Thomas, I respect your sincerity. Respect? Oh, man it's water in the desert. . . . How did you like our music? That air they played, it had a certain—well, tell me what you thought of it.

MORE [*relieved at this turn; smiling*]: Could it have been Your Grace's own?

HENRY [*smiles back*]: Discovered! Now I'll never know your true opinion. And that's irksome, Thomas, for we artists, though we love praise, yet we love truth better.

MORE [*mildly*]: Then I will tell Your Grace truly what I thought of it.

HENRY [*a little disconcerted*]: Speak then.

MORE: To me it seemed—delightful.

HENRY: Thomas—I chose the right man for Chancellor.

MORE: I must in fairness add that my taste in music is reputedly deplorable.

HENRY: Your taste in music is excellent. It exactly coincides with my own. Ah music! Music! Send them back without me, Thomas; I will live here in Chelsea and make music.

MORE: My house is at Your Grace's disposal.

HENRY: Thomas, you understand me; we will stay here together and make music.

MORE: Will Your Grace honour my roof at dinner?

HENRY [*has walked away, blowing moodily on his whistle*]: Mm? Yes; I expect I'll bellow for you. . . .

MORE: My wife will be more—

HENRY: Yes, yes. [*He turns, his face set.*] Touching this other business, mark you, Thomas, I'll have no opposition.

MORE [*sadly*]: Your Grace?

HENRY: No opposition I say! No opposition! Your conscience is your own affair; but you are my Chancellor! There, you have my word—I'll leave you out of it. But I don't take it kindly, Thomas, and I'll have no opposition! I see how it will be; the Bishops will oppose me. The full-fed, hypocritical, 'Princes of the *Church*'! Ha! As for the Pope—Am I to burn in Hell because the Bishop of Rome with the Emperor's knife to his throat, mouths me Deuteronomy? Hypocrites! They're all hypocrites! Mind they do not take you in, Thomas! Lie low if you will, but I'll brook no opposition—no words, no signs, no letters, no pamphlets—mind that, Thomas—no writings against me!

MORE: Your Grace is unjust. I am Your Grace's loyal minister. If I cannot serve Your Grace in this great matter of the Queen—

HENRY: I have no Queen! Catherine is not my wife and no priest can make her so, and they that say she is my wife are not only liars . . . but Traitors! Mind it, Thomas!

MORE: Am I a babbler, Your Grace? [*But his voice is unsteady.*]

HENRY: You are stubborn. . . . [*Wooingly.*] If you could come with me, you are the man I would soonest raise—yes, with my own hand.

MORE [*covers his face*]: Oh, Your Grace overwhelms me!

A complicated chiming of little bells is heard.

HENRY: What's that?

MORE: Eight o'clock, Your Grace.

HENRY [*uneasily eyeing* MORE]: Oh, lift yourself up, man—have I not promised?

MORE *braces.*

Shall we eat?

MORE: If Your Grace pleases. [*Recovering.*] What will Your Grace sing for us?

They approach the stairs.

HENRY: Eight o'clock you said? Thomas, the tide will be changing. I was forgetting the tide. I'd better go.

MORE [*gravely*]: I'm sorry, Your Grace.

HENRY: I must catch the tide or I'll not get back to Richmond till. . . . No, don't come. Tell Norfolk.

He has his foot on the bottom stair when enter ALICE *and* STEWARD *above.*

Oh, Lady Alice, I must go.

ALICE *descends, her face serious.*

I want to catch the tide. To tell the truth, Lady Alice, I have forgotten in your haven here how time flows past outside. Affairs call me to court and so I give you my thanks and say Good night. [*He mounts.*]

MORE ⎱
ALICE ⎰ [*bowing*]: Good night, Your Grace.

Exit HENRY, *above.*

ALICE: What's this? You crossed him.

MORE: Somewhat.

ALICE: Why?

MORE [*apologetic*]: I couldn't find the other way.

ALICE [*angrily*]: You're too nice altogether, Thomas!

MORE: Woman, mind your house.

ALICE: I *am* minding my house!

MORE [*takes in her anxiety*]: Well, Alice. What would you *want* me to do?

ALICE: Be ruled! If you won't rule him, be ruled!

MORE [*quietly*]: I neither could nor would rule my King. [*Pleasantly.*] But there's a little . . . little, area . . . where I must rule myself. It's very little—less to him than a tennis court.

Her face is still full of foreboding: he sighs.

Look; it was eight o'clock. At eight o'clock, Lady Anne likes to dance.

ALICE [*relieved*]: Oh?

MORE: I think so.

ALICE [*irritation*]: And *you* stand between them!

MORE: I? What stands between them is a sacrament of the Church. I'm less important than you think, Alice.

ALICE [*appealing*]: Thomas, stay friends with him.

MORE: Whatever can be done by smiling, you may rely on me to do.

ALICE: You don't know *how* to flatter.

MORE: I flatter very well! My recipe's beginning to be widely copied. It's the basic syrup with just a soupçon of discreet impudence. . . .

ALICE [*still uneasy*]: I wish he'd eaten here. . . .
MORE: Yes—we shall be living on that 'simple supper' of yours for a fortnight.

She won't laugh.

Alice. . . .

She won't turn.

Alice. . . .

She turns.

Set your mind at rest—this [*tapping himself*] is not the stuff of which martyrs are made.

Enter above, quickly, ROPER.

ROPER: Sir Thomas!
MORE [*winces*]: Oh, no . . .!
ALICE: Will Roper, what d'you want?

Enter after ROPER, MARGARET.

MARGARET: William, I told you not to!
ROPER: I'm not easily 'told', Meg.
MARGARET: I *asked* you not to.
ROPER: Meg, I'm full to here! [*Indicates throat.*]
MARGARET: It's not convenient!
ROPER: Must everything be made convenient? I'm not a convenient man, Meg—I've got an inconvenient conscience!

MARGARET *gestures helplessly to* MORE.

MORE [*laughs*]: Joshua's trumpet. One note on that brass conscience of yours and my daughter's walls are down.
ROPER [*descending*]: You raised her, sir.
MORE [*a bit puzzled*]: How long have you been here? Are you in the King's party?
ROPER: No, sir, I am *not* in the King's party! [*Advancing.*] It's of that I wish to speak to you. My spirit is perturbed.
MORE [*suppressing a grin*]: Is it, Will? Why?
ROPER: I've been offered a seat in the next Parliament.

MORE *looks up sharply.*

Ought I to take it?
MORE: No . . . Well that depends. With your views on Church Reformation I should have thought you could do yourself a lot of good in the next Parliament.
ROPER: My views on the Church—I must confess— Since last we met my views

have somewhat modified.

MORE *and* MARGARET *exchange a smile.*

I modify nothing concerning the *body* of the Church—the money-changers in the temple must be scourged from thence—with a scourge of fire if that is needed! . . . But an attack on the Church herself! No, I see behind that an attack on God—

MORE:—Roper—

ROPER: The Devil's work!

MORE:—Roper—!

ROPER: To be done by the Devil's ministers!

MORE: For heaven's sake remember my office!

ROPER: Oh, if you stand on your office—

MORE: I don't stand on it, but there are certain things I may not hear!

ROPER: Sophistication. It is what I was told. The Court has corrupted you, Sir Thomas; you are not the man you were; you have learnt to study your 'convenience'; you have learnt to flatter!

MORE: There, Alice; you see? I have a reputation for it.

ALICE: God's Body, young man, if I was the Chancellor I'd have you whipped!

Enter STEWARD.

STEWARD: Master Rich is here, Sir Thomas.

RICH *follows him closely.*

RICH: Good evening, sir.

MORE: Ah, Richard?

RICH: Good evening, Lady Alice.

ALICE *nods, noncommittal.*

Lady Margaret.

MARGARET [*quite friendly but very clear*]: Good evening, Master Rich.

A pause.

MORE: Do you know—? [*indicates* ROPER.] William Roper, the younger.

RICH: By reputation, of course.

ROPER: Good evening, Master . . .

RICH: Rich.

ROPER: Oh. [*Recollecting something.*] Oh.

RICH [*quick and hostile*]: You have heard of me?

ROPER [*shortly*]: Yes.

RICH [*excitedly*]: In what connection? I don't know what you can have heard— [*Looks about: hotly.*] I sense that I'm not welcome here! [*He has jumped the gun; they are startled.*]

MORE [*gently*]: Why, Richard, have you done something that should make you not welcome?

RICH: Why, do you suspect me of it?

MORE: I shall begin to.

RICH [*draws closer to him and speaks hurriedly*]: Cromwell is asking questions. About you. About you particularly.

> MORE *is unmoved.*

He is continually collecting information about you!

MORE: I know it.

> STEWARD *begins to slide out.*

Stay a minute, Matthew.

RICH [*pointing*]: *That's* one of his sources!

MORE: Of course; that's one of my servants.

RICH [*hurried, low voice again*]: Signor Chapuys, the Imperial Ambassador—

MORE:—Collects information too. That's one of his functions. [*He looks at* RICH *very gravely.*]

RICH [*voice cracking*]: You look at me as though I were an enemy!

MORE [*puts out a hand to steady him*]: Why, Richard, you're shaking.

RICH: I'm adrift. Help me.

MORE: How?

RICH: Employ me.

MORE: No.

RICH [*desperately*]: Employ me!

MORE: No!

RICH [*moves swiftly to exit; turns there*]: I would be steadfast!

MORE: Richard, you couldn't answer for yourself even so far as tonight.

> *Exit* RICH. *All watch him; the others turn to* MORE, *their faces alert.*

ROPER: Arrest him.

ALICE: Yes!

MORE: For what?

ALICE: He's dangerous!

ROPER: For libel; he's a spy.

ALICE: He is! Arrest him!

MARGARET: Father, that man's bad.

MORE: There is no law against that.

ROPER: There is! God's law!

MORE: Then God can arrest him.

ROPER: Sophistication upon sophistication!

MORE: No, sheer simplicity. The law, Roper, the law. I know what's legal not what's right. And I'll stick to what's legal.

ROPER: Then you set Man's law above God's!

MORE: No, far below; but let me draw your attention to a fact—I'm *not* God. The currents and eddies of right and wrong, which you find such plain-sailing, I can't navigate, I'm no voyager. But in the thickets of the law, oh there I'm a forester. I doubt if there's a man alive who could follow me there, thank God. . . . [*He says this to himself.*]

ALICE [*exasperated, pointing after* RICH]: While you talk, he's gone!

MORE: And go he should if he was the devil himself until he broke the law!

ROPER: So now you'd give the Devil benefit of law!

MORE: Yes. What would you do? Cut a great road through the law to get after the Devil?

ROPER: I'd cut down every law in England to do that!

MORE [*roused and excited*]: Oh? [*Advances on* ROPER.] And when the last law was down, and the Devil turned round on you—where would you hide, Roper, the laws all being flat? [*Leaves him.*] This country's planted thick with laws from coast to coast—Man's laws, not God's—and if you cut them down—and you're just the man to do it—d'you really think you could stand upright in the winds that would blow then? [*Quietly.*] Yes, I'd give the Devil benefit of law, for my own safety's sake.

ROPER: I have long suspected this; this is the golden calf; the law's your god.

MORE [*wearily*]: Oh, Roper, you're a fool, God's my god.... [*Rather bitter.*] But I find him rather too [*very bitter*] subtle . . . I don't know where he is nor what he wants.

ROPER: My god wants service, to the end and unremitting; nothing else!

MORE [*dry*]: Are you sure that's God?—He sounds like Moloch. But indeed it may be God—And whoever hunts for me, Roper, God or Devil, will find me hiding in the thickets of the law! And I'll hide my daughter with me! Not hoist her up the mainmast of your seagoing principles! They put about too nimbly!

Exit MORE. *They all look after him.* MARGARET *touches* ROPER*'s hand.*

MARGARET: Oh, that was harsh.

ROPER [*turning to her, serious*]: What's happened here?

ALICE [*still with her back to them, her voice strained*]: He can't abide a fool, that's all! Be off!

ROPER [*to* MARGARET]: Hide you. Hide you from what?

ALICE [*turning, near to tears*]: He said nothing about hiding me you noticed! I've got too fat to hide I suppose!

MARGARET: You know he meant us both.

ROPER: But from what?

ALICE: I don't know. I don't know if he knows. He's not said one simple, direct word to me since this divorce came up. It's not God who's gone subtle! It's him!

Enter MORE, *a little sheepish. Goes to* ROPER.

MORE [*kindly*]: Roper, that was harsh: your principles are—[*can't resist sending him up*] excellent—the very best quality.

ROPER *bridles. Contrite.*

No truly now, your principles are fine. [*Indicating stairs, to all.*] Look, we must make a start on all that food.

MARGARET: Father, can't you be plain with us?

MORE [*looks quickly from daughter to wife. Takes* ALICE*'s hand*]: I stand on the wrong side of no statute, and no common law. [*Takes* MEG*'s hand too.*] I have not disobeyed my sovereign. I truly believe no man in England is safer than myself. And I want my supper. [*He starts them up the stairs and goes to*

ROPER.] We shall need your assistance, Will. There's an excellent Burgundy—if your principles permit.

ROPER: They don't, sir.

MORE: Well, have some water in it.

ROPER: Just the water, sir.

MORE: My poor boy.

ALICE [*stopping at head of stairs, as one who will be answered*]: Why does Cromwell collect information about you?

MORE: I'm a prominent figure. Someone somewhere's collecting information about Cromwell. Now no more shirking; we must make a start. [*Shepherding* ROPER *up the stairs.*] There's a stuffed swan if you please.

>   ALICE *and* MARGARET *exit above.*

Will, I'd trust *you* with my life. But not your principles. [*They mount the stairs.*] You see, we speak of being anchored to our principles. But if the weather turns nasty you up with an anchor and let it down where there's less wind, and the fishing's better. And 'look' we say 'I'm anchored!' [*Laughing, inviting* ROPER *to laugh with him.*] 'To my principles!'

>   *Exit above,* MORE *and* ROPER. *Enter* COMMON MAN *pulling basket. From it he takes an Inn Sign which he hangs on to the alcove. He inspects it.*

COMMON MAN: 'The Loyal Subject' . . . [*to audience*] a pub [*takes from basket and puts on jacket, cap and napkin*]. A publican. [*Places two stools at the table, and mugs and a candle which he lights.*] Oh, he's a deep one that Sir Thomas More. . . . Deep. . . . It takes a lot of education to get a man as deep as that. . . . [*Straight to audience.*] And a deep nature to begin with too. [*Deadpan.*] The likes of me can hardly be *expected* to follow the processes of a man like that. . . . [*Sly.*] Can we? [*Inspects pub.*] Right, ready. [*Goes right.*] Ready, sir!

>   *Enter* CROMWELL, *carrying bottle. Goes to alcove.*

CROMWELL: Is this a *good* place for a conspiracy, innkeeper?

PUBLICAN [*woodenly*]: You asked for a private room, sir.

CROMWELL [*looking round*]: Yes, I want one without too many little dark corners.

PUBLICAN: I don't understand you, sir. Just the four corners as you see.

CROMWELL [*sardonic*]: You don't understand me.

PUBLICAN: That's right, sir.

CROMWELL: Do you know who I am?

PUBLICAN [*promptly*]: No, sir.

CROMWELL: Don't be too tactful, innkeeper.

PUBLICAN: I don't understand, sir.

CROMWELL: When the likes of you *are* too tactful, the likes of me begin to wonder who's the fool.

PUBLICAN: I just don't understand you, sir.

CROMWELL [*puts back his head and laughs silently*]: The master statesman of us all. 'I don't understand.' [*Looks at* PUBLICAN *almost with hatred.*] All right. Get out.

>   *Throws coin. Exit* PUBLICAN. CROMWELL *goes to exit opposite. Calling.*

Come on.

Enter RICH. *He glances at bottle in* CROMWELL*'s hand and remains cautiously by the exit.*

Yes, it may be that I am a little intoxicated. [*Leaves* RICH *standing.*] But not with alcohol, with success! And who has a strong head for success? None of us gets enough of it. Except Kings. And they're born drunk.
RICH: Success? What success.
CROMWELL: Guess.
RICH: Collector of Revenues for York.
CROMWELL [*amused*]: You do keep your ear to the ground don't you? No. Better than that.
RICH: High Constable.
CROMWELL: Better than that.
RICH: Better than High Constable?
CROMWELL: Much better. Sir Thomas Paget is–retiring.
RICH: Secretary to the Council!
CROMWELL: 'Tis astonishing, isn't it?
RICH [*hastily*]: Oh no–I mean–one sees, it's logical.
CROMWELL: No ceremony, no courtship. Be seated.

RICH *sits.*

As His Majesty would say.

RICH *laughs nervously and involuntarily glances round.*

Yes; see how I trust you.
RICH: Oh, I would never repeat or report a thing like that—
CROMWELL [*pouring wine*]: What kind of thing would you repeat or report?
RICH: Well, nothing said in friendship–may I say 'friendship'?
CROMWELL: If you like. D'you believe that–that you would never repeat or report anything etcetera?
RICH: Why yes!
CROMWELL: No, but seriously.
RICH: Yes!
CROMWELL [*puts down bottle. Not sinister, but rather as a kindly teacher with a promising pupil*]: Rich; seriously.
RICH [*pauses, then bitterly*]: It would depend what I was offered.
CROMWELL: Don't say it just to please me.
RICH: It's true. It would depend what I was offered.
CROMWELL [*patting his arm*]: Everyone knows it; not many people can say it.
RICH: There are *some* things one wouldn't do for anything. Surely.
CROMWELL: Mm–that idea's like these lifelines they have on the embankment: comforting, but you don't expect to have to use them. [*Briskly.*] Well, congratulations!
RICH [*suspicious*]: On what?
CROMWELL: I think you'd make a good Collector of Revenues for York Diocese.
RICH [*gripping on to himself*]: Is it in your gift?
CROMWELL: Effectively.

RICH [*conscious cynicism*]: What do I have to do for it?

CROMWELL: Nothing. [*He lectures, pacing pedantically up and down.*] It isn't like that, Rich. There are no rules. With rewards and penalties—so much wickedness purchases so much worldly prospering—[*He breaks off and stops, suddenly struck.*] Are you sure you're not religious?

RICH: Almost sure.

CROMWELL: Get sure. [*Resumes pacing.*] No, it's not like that, it's much more a matter of convenience, administrative convenience. The normal aim of administration is to keep steady this factor of convenience—and Sir Thomas would agree. Now normally when a man wants to change his woman, you let him if it's convenient and prevent him if it's not—normally indeed it's of so little importance that you leave it to the priests. But the constant factor is this element of convenience.

RICH: Whose convenience?

CROMWELL *stops.*

CROMWELL: Oh ours. But everybody's too. [*Sets off again.*] However, in the present instance the man who wants to change his woman is our Sovereign Lord, Harry, by the Grace of God, the Eighth of that name. Which is a quaint way of saying that if he wants to change his woman he will. So *that* becomes the constant factor. And our job as administrators is to make it as convenient as we can. I say 'our' job, on the assumption that you'll take this post at York I've offered you?

RICH: Yes . . . yes, yes. [*But he seems gloomy.*]

CROMWELL [*sits. Sharply*]: It's a bad sign when people are depressed by their own good fortune.

RICH [*defensive*]: I'm not depressed!

CROMWELL: You look depressed.

RICH [*hastily buffooning*]: I'm lamenting. I've lost my innocence.

CROMWELL: You lost that some time ago. If you've only just noticed, it can't have been very important to you.

RICH [*much struck*]: That's true! Why that's true, it can't!

CROMWELL: We experience a sense of release do we, Master Rich? An unfamiliar freshness in the head, as of open air?

RICH [*takes wine*]: Collector of Revenues isn't bad!

CROMWELL: Not bad for a start. [*He watches* RICH *drink.*] Now our present Lord Chancellor—*there's* an innocent man.

RICH [*puts down glass. Indulgently.*] The odd thing is—he *is*.

CROMWELL [*looks at him with dislike*]: Yes, I say he is. [*The light tone again.*] The trouble is, his innocence is tangled in this proposition that you can't change your woman without a divorce, and can't have a divorce unless the Pope says so. And although his present Holiness is—judged even by the most liberal standards—a strikingly corrupt old person, yet he still has this word 'Pope' attached to him. And from this quite meaningless circumstance I fear some degree of . . .

RICH [*pleased, waving his cup*]: Administrative inconvenience.

CROMWELL [*nodding as to a pupil word perfect*]: Just so. [*Dead-pan.*] This goblet that he gave you, how much was it worth?

RICH *puts down cup, looks down.*

CROMWELL [*quite gently*]: Come along. Rich, he gave you a silver goblet. How much did you get for it?

RICH: Fifty shillings.

CROMWELL: Could you take me to the shop?

RICH: Yes.

CROMWELL: Where did he get it?

No reply.

It was a gift from a litigant, a woman, wasn't it?

RICH: Yes.

CROMWELL: Which court? Chancery? [*Restrains* RICH *from filling his glass.*] No, don't get drunk. In which court was this litigant's case?

RICH: Court of Requests.

CROMWELL [*grunts, his face abstracted. Becoming aware of* RICH'*s regard he smiles*]: There, that wasn't too painful was it?

RICH [*laughing a little and a little rueful*]: No!

CROMWELL [*spreading his hands*]: That's all there is. And you'll find it easier next time.

RICH [*looks up briefly, unhappily*]: What application do they have, these titbits of information you collect?

CROMWELL: None at all, usually.

RICH [*stubbornly, not looking up*]: But sometimes.

CROMWELL: Well, there *are* those men, you know—'upright', 'steadfast', men who want themselves to be the constant factor in the situation. Which of course they can't be. The situation rolls forward in any case.

RICH [*the same*]: So what happens?

CROMWELL [*not liking his tone, coldly*]: If they've any sense they get out of its way.

RICH: What if they haven't any sense?

CROMWELL [*the same*]: What none at all? Well, then they're only for for Heaven. But Sir Thomas has plenty of sense; he could be frightened.

RICH [*looks up, his face nasty*]: Don't forget he's an innocent, Master Cromwell.

CROMWELL: I think we'll finish there for tonight. [*Rising.*] After all, he *is* the Lord Chancellor. [*Going.*]

RICH: You wouldn't find him easy to frighten! [*Calls after him.*] You've mistaken your man this time! He doesn't know how to be frightened!

CROMWELL [*returning.* RICH *rises at his approach*]: Doesn't know how to be frightened? Why, then he never put his hand in a candle. . . . Did he? [*And seizing* RICH *by the wrist he holds his hand in the candle flame.*]

RICH [*screeches and darts back, hugging his hand in his armpit, regarding* CROMWELL *with horror*]: You enjoyed that!

CROMWELL'*s downturned face is amazed.*

RICH [*triumphantly*]: You enjoyed it!

CURTAIN

ACT TWO

The scene is as for start of Act One. When the curtain rises the stage is in darkness save for a spot, front stage, in which stands the COMMON MAN. *He carries the book, a place marked by his finger, and wears his spectacles.*

COMMON MAN: The interval started early in the year 1530 and it's now the middle of May 1532. [*Explanatory.*] Two years. During that time a lot of water's flowed under the bridge and among the things that have come floating along on it is . . . [*Reads.*] 'The Church of England, that finest flower of our Island genius for compromise; that system, peculiar to these shores, which deflects the torrents of religious passion down the canals of moderation.' That's very well put. [*Returns to book, approvingly.*] 'Typically, this great effect was achieved not by bloodshed but by simple Act of Parliament. Only an unhappy few were found to set themselves against the current of their times, and in so doing to court disaster. For we are dealing with an age less fastidious than our own. Imprisonment without trial, and even examination under torture, were common practice.'

Lights rise to show MORE, *seated, and* ROPER, *standing. Exit* COMMON MAN. ROPER *is dressed in black and wears a cross. He commences to walk up and down, watched by* MORE. *A pause.*

MORE: Must you wear those clothes, Will?

ROPER: Yes, I must.

MORE: Why?

ROPER: The time has come for decent men to declare their allegiance!

MORE: And what allegiance are those designed to express?

ROPER: My allegiance to the Church.

MORE: Well, you *look* like a Spaniard.

ROPER: All credit to Spain then!

MORE: You wouldn't last six months in Spain. You'd have been burned alive in Spain, during your heretic period.

ROPER: I suppose you have the right to remind me of it. [*Points accusingly.*] That chain of office that *you* wear is a degradation.

MORE [*glances down at it*]: I've told you. If the bishops in Convocation submitted this morning, I'll take it off. . . . It's no degradation. Great men have worn this.

ROPER: When d'you expect to hear from Canterbury?

MORE: About now. The Archbishop promised me an immediate message.

ROPER [*recommences pacing*]: I don't see what difference Convocation can make. The Church is already a wing of the Palace is it not? The King is already its 'Supreme head'! Is he not?

MORE: No.

ROPER [*is startled*]: You are denying the Act of Supremacy!

MORE: No, I'm not; the Act states that the King—

ROPER:—is Supreme Head of the Church in England.

MORE: Supreme Head of the Church in England— [*Underlining the words.*] ' so far as the law of God allows.' How far the law of God does allow it remains a matter of opinion, since the Act doesn't state it.

ROPER: A legal quibble.

MORE: Call it what you like, it's there, thank God.

ROPER: Very well: in your opinion how far does the law of God allow this?

MORE: I'll keep my opinion to myself, Will.

ROPER: Yes? I'll tell you mine—!

MORE: Don't! If your opinion's what I think it is, it's High Treason, Roper!

Enter MARGARET *above, unseen.*

Will, you remember you've a wife now! And may have children!

MARGARET: Why must he remember that?

ROPER: To keep myself 'discreet'.

MARGARET [*smiling*]: Then I'd rather you forgot it.

MORE [*unsmiling*]: You are either idiots, or children.

Enter CHAPUYS, *above.*

CHAPUYS: Or saints, my lord! [*Very sonorous.*]

MARGARET: Oh, Father, Signor Chapuys has come to see you.

MORE [*rising*]: Your Excellency.

CHAPUYS [*strikes pose with* MARGARET *and* ROPER]: Or saints, my lord; or saints.

MORE [*grins maliciously at* ROPER]: That's it of course—saints! Roper—turn your head a bit—yes, I think I do detect, a faint radiance. [*Reproachful.*] You should have told us, Will.

CHAPUYS: Come come, my lord; you too at this time are not free from some suspicion of saintliness.

MORE [*quietly*]: I don't like the sound of that. Your Excellency. What do you require of *me*? What, Your Excellency?

CHAPUYS [*awkward beneath his sudden keen regard*]: May I not come simply, to pay my respects to the English Socrates—as I see your angelic friend Erasmus calls you.

MORE [*wrinkles nose*]: Yes, I'll think of something presently to call Erasmus. [*Checks.*] Socrates! I've no taste for hemlock, Your Excellency, if that's what you require.

CHAPUYS [*display of horror*]: Heaven forbid!

MORE [*dryly*]: Amen.

CHAPUYS [*spreads hands*]: Must I require anything? [*Sonorous.*] After all, we are brothers in Christ, you and I!

MORE: A characteristic we share with the rest of humanity. You live in Cheapside, Signor? To make contact with a brother in Christ you have only to open your window and empty a chamberpot. There was no need to come to Chelsea.

CHAPUYS *titters nervously.*

MORE [*coldly*]: William. The Imperial Ambassador is here on business. Would you mind?

ROPER *and* MARGARET *going.*

CHAPUYS [*rising, unreal protestations*]: Oh no! I protest!
MORE: He is clearly here on business.
CHAPUYS [*the same*]: No; but really, I protest!

It is no more than token: when ROPER *and* MARGARET *reach head of stairs he calls:*

Dominus vobiscum filii mei!
ROPER [*pompous*]: Et cum spiritu tuo, excellencis!

Exit ROPER *and* MARGARET.

CHAPUYS [*approaching* MORE, *thrillingly*]: And how much longer shall we hear that holy language in these shores?
MORE [*alert, poker-faced*]: 'Tisn't 'holy', Your Excellency; just old.

CHAPUYS *sits with the air of one coming to brass tacks.*

CHAPUYS: My Lord, I cannot believe you will allow yourself to be associated with the recent actions of King Henry! In respect of Queen Catherine.
MORE: Subjects are associated with the actions of Kings willy-nilly.
CHAPUYS: The Lord Chancellor is not an ordinary subject. He bears responsibility [*he lets the word sink in:* MORE *shifts*] for what is done.
MORE [*agitation begins to show through*]: Have you considered that what has been done badly, might have been done worse, with a different Chancellor?
CHAPUYS [*mounting confidence, as* MORE's *attention is caught*]: Believe me, Sir Thomas, your influence in these policies has been much searched for, and where it has been found it has been praised—*but* . . . There comes a point, does there not? . . .
MORE: Yes. [*Agitated.*] There does come such a point.
CHAPUYS: When the sufferings of one unfortunate lady swell to an open attack on the religion of an entire country that point has been passed. Beyond that point, Sir Thomas, one is not merely 'compromised', one is in truth corrupted.
MORE [*stares at him*]: What do you want?
CHAPUYS: Rumour has it that if the Church in Convocation has submitted to the King, you will resign.
MORE [*looks down and regains composure*]: I see. [*Suave.*] Supposing rumour to be right. Would you approve of that?
CHAPUYS:Approve, applaud, admire.
MORE [*still looking down*]: Why?
CHAPUYS: Because it would show one man—and that man known to be temperate—unable to go further with this wickedness.
MORE [*the same*]: And that man known to be Chancellor of England too.
CHAPUYS: Believe me, my lord, such a signal would be seen—
MORE [*the same*]: 'Signal'?

CHAPUYS: Yes, my lord; it would be seen and understood.
MORE [*the same, and now positively silky*]: By whom?
CHAPUYS: By half of your fellow countrymen!

Now MORE *looks up sharply.*

Sir Thomas, I have just returned from Yorkshire and Northumberland,
where I have made a tour.
MORE [*softly*]: Have you indeed?
CHAPUYS: Things are very different there, my lord. There they are ready.
MORE: For what?
CHAPUYS: Resistance!

Enter ROPER, *above, excited.*

ROPER: Sir Thomas—!

MORE *looks up angrily.*

Excuse me, sir— [*Indicates off.*] His Grace the Duke of Norfolk—

MORE *and* CHAPUYS *rise.* ROPER *excitedly descends.*

It's all over, sir, they've—

Enter NORFOLK *above,* ALICE *and* MARGARET, *below.*

NORFOLK: One moment, Roper, I'll do this! Thomas—[*Sees* CHAPUYS.] Oh. [*He
stares at* CHAPUYS, *hostile.*]
CHAPUYS: I was on the point of leaving, Your Grace. Just a personal call. I have
been trying . . . er to borrow a book–but without success–you're sure you
have no copy, my lord? Then I'll leave you. [*Bowing.*] Gentlemen, ladies.
[*Going, up stairs. Stops unseen as* ROPER *speaks.*]
ROPER: Sir Thomas—
NORFOLK: I'll do it, Roper! Convocation's knuckled under, Thomas. They're to
pay a fine of a hundred thousand pounds. And . . . we've severed the
connection with Rome.
MORE [*smiling bitterly*]: 'The connection with Rome' is nice. [*Bitter.*] 'The
connection with Rome.' Did *anyone* resist?
NORFOLK: Bishop Fisher.
MORE: Lovely man.

NORFOLK *shrugs.*

ROPER [*looking at* MORE:] Your Grace, this is quite certain is it?
NORFOLK: Yes.

MORE *puts his hand to his chain.* CHAPUYS *exit. All turn.*

Funny company, Thomas?
MORE: It's quite unintentional. He doesn't mean to be funny. [*Fumbles with*

chain.] Help me with this.

NORFOLK: Not I.

ROPER [*takes a step forward. Then, subdued*]: Shall I, sir?

MORE: No thank you, Will. Alice?

ALICE: Hell's fire—God's blood and body *no*! Sun and moon, Master More, you're taken for a wise man! Is this wisdom—to betray your ability, abandon practice, forget your station and your duty to your kin and behave like a printed book!

MORE [*listens gravely: then*]: Margaret, will you?

MARGARET: If you want.

MORE: There's my clever girl.

She takes it from his neck.

NORFOLK: Well, Thomas, Why? Make me understand—because I'll tell you now, from where I stand, this looks like cowardice!

MORE [*excited and angry*]: All right I will—this isn't 'Reformation'; this is war against the Church! . . . [*Indignant.*] Our King, Norfolk, has declared war on the Pope—because the Pope will not declare that our Queen is not his wife.

NORFOLK: And is she?

MORE [*cunning*]: I'll answer that question for one person only, the King. Aye, and that in private too.

NORFOLK [*contemptuous*]: Man, you're cautious.

MORE: Yes, cautious. I'm not one of your hawks.

NORFOLK [*walks away and turns*]: All right—we're at war with the Pope! The Pope's a Prince, isn't he?

MORE: He is.

NORFOLK: And a bad one?

MORE: Bad enough. But the theory is that he's also the Vicar of God, the descendant of St Peter, our only link with Christ.

NORFOLK [*sneer*]: A tenuous link.

MORE: Oh, tenuous indeed.

NORFOLK [*to the others*]: Does this make sense?

No reply; they look at MORE.

You'll forfeit all you've got—which includes the respect of your country—for a theory?

MORE [*hotly*]: The Apostolic Succession of the Pope is— [*Stops: interested.*] . . . Why, it's a theory yes; you can't see it; can't touch it; it's a theory. [*To* NORFOLK, *very rapid but calm.*] But what matters to me is not whether it's true or not but that I believe it to be true, or rather not that I *believe* it, but that *I* believe it . . . I trust I make myself obscure?

NORFOLK: Perfectly.

MORE: That's good. Obscurity's what I have need of now.

NORFOLK: Man, you're sick. This isn't Spain you know.

MORE [*looks at him; takes him aside: lowered voice*]: Have I your word, that what we say here is between us and has no existence beyond these walls?

NORFOLK [*impatient*]: Very well.

MORE [*almost whispering*]: And if the King should command you to repeat what I have said?

NORFOLK: I should keep my word to you!

MORE: Then what has become of your oath of obedience to the King?

NORFOLK [*indignant*]: You lay traps for me!

MORE [*now grown calm*]: No, I show you the times.

NORFOLK: Why do you insult me with these lawyer's tricks?

MORE: Because I am afraid.

NORFOLK: And here's your answer. The King accepts your resignation very sadly; he is mindful of your goodness and past loyalty and in any matter concerning your honour and welfare he will be your good lord. So much for your fear.

MORE [*flatly*]: You will convey my humble gratitude.

NORFOLK: I will. Good day, Alice [*Going.*] I'd rather deal with you than your husband.

MORE [*complete change of tone; briskly professional*]: Oh, Howard! [*Goes to him.*] Signor Chapuys tells me he's just made a 'tour' of the North Country. He thinks we shall have trouble there. So do I.

NORFOLK [*stolid*]: Yes? What kind of trouble?

MORE: The Church—the old Church, not the new Church—is, very strong up there. I'm serious, Howard, keep an eye on the Border, this next year; and bear in mind the Old Alliance.

NORFOLK [*looks at him*]: We will. We do. . . . As for the Dago, Thomas, it'll perhaps relieve your mind to know that one of Secretary Cromwell's agents made the tour with him.

MORE: Oh. [*Flash of jealousy.*] Of course if Master Cromwell has matters in hand—

NORFOLK:—He has.

MORE: Yes, I can imagine.

NORFOLK: But thanks for the information. [*Going.*] It's good to know you still have . . . some vestige of patriotism.

MORE [*anger*]: That's a remarkably stupid observation, Norfolk!

Exit NORFOLK.

ALICE: So there's an end of you. What will you do now—sit by the fire and make goslings in the ash?

MORE: Not at all, Alice, I expect I'll write a bit. [*He woos them with unhappy cheerfulness.*] I'll write, I'll read, I'll think. I think I'll learn to fish! I'll play with my grandchildren—when son Roper's done his duty. [*Eager.*] Alice, shall I teach you to read?

ALICE: No, by God!

MORE: . . . Son Roper, *you're* pleased with me I hope?

ROPER [*goes to him: moved*]: Sir, you've made a noble gesture.

MORE [*blankly*]: A gesture? [*Eager.*] It wasn't possible to continue, Will. I was not *able* to continue. I would have if I could! I make no gesture! [*Apprehensive, looks after* NORFOLK.] My God, I hope it's understood I make no gesture! [*Turns back to them.*]—Alice, you don't think I would do this to you for a gesture! *That's* a gesture! [*Thumbs his nose.*] *That's* a gesture! [*Jerks up two fingers.*] I'm no street acrobat to make gestures! I'm practical!

ROPER: You belittle yourself, sir, this was not practical; [*resonant*] this was moral!

MORE: Oh now I understand you, Will. Morality's *not* practical. Morality's a gesture. A complicated gesture learned from books—that's what you say, Alice, isn't it? . . . And you, Meg?

MARGARET: It *is*, for most of us, Father.

MORE: Oh no, if you're going to plead humility—! Oh, you're cruel. I have a cruel family.

ALICE: Yes, you can fit the cap on anyone you want, I know that well enough. If there's cruelty in this house, I know where to look for it.

MARGARET: No, Mother—!

ALICE: Oh, you'd walk on the bottom of the sea and think yourself a crab if he suggested it! [*To* ROPER.] And you! You'd dance him to the Tower— You'd dance him to the block! Like David with a harp! Scattering hymn-books in his path! [*To* MORE.] Poor silly man, d'you think they'll *leave* you here to learn to fish?

MORE [*straight at her*]: If we govern our tongues they will! . . . Look, I have a word to say about that. I have made no statement. I've resigned, that's *all*. On the King's Supremacy, the King's divorce which he'll now grant himself, the marriage he'll then make—have you heard me make a statement?

ALICE: No—and if I'm to lose my rank and fall to housekeeping I want to know the reason; so make a statement now.

MORE: No—

ALICE *exhibits indignation.*

—Alice, it's a point of law! Accept it from me, Alice, that in silence is my safety under the law, but my silence must be absolute, it must extend to you.

ALICE: In short you don't trust us!

MORE [*impatient*]: Look—[*advances on her*] I'm the Lord Chief Justice, I'm Cromwell, I'm the King's Head Jailer—and I take your hand [*does so*] and I clamp it on the Bible, on the Blessed Cross [*clamps her hand on his closed fist*] and I say: 'Woman, has your husband made a statement on these matters?' Now—on peril of your soul remember—what's your answer?

ALICE: No.

MORE: And so it must remain. [*He looks round on their grave faces.*] Oh, it's only a life-line, we shan't have to use it but it's comforting to have. No, no, when they find I'm silent they'll ask nothing better than to leave me silent; you'll see.

Enter STEWARD.

STEWARD: Sir, the household's in the kitchen. They want to know what's happened.

MORE: Oh. Yes. We must speak to them. Alice, they'll mostly have to go, my dear. [*To* STEWARD.] But not before we've found them places.

ALICE: We can't find places for them all!

MORE: Yes, we can; yes, we can. Tell them so.

ALICE: God's death it comes on us quickly . . .

Exit ALICE, MARGARET *and* ROPER.

MORE: What about you, Matthew? It'll be a smaller household now, and for you I'm afraid, a smaller wage. Will you stay?

STEWARD: Don't see how I could then, sir.

MORE: You're a single man.

STEWARD [*awkward*]: Well, yes, sir, but I mean I've got my own—

MORE [*quickly*]: Quite right, why should you? . . . I shall miss you, Matthew.

STEWARD [*man to man jocosity*]: No-o-o. You never had much time for *me*, sir. You see through *me*, sir, I know that. [*He almost winks.*]

MORE [*gently insists*]: I shall miss you, Matthew; I shall miss you.

Exit MORE. STEWARD *snatches off hat and hurls it to the floor.*

STEWARD: Now, damn me isn't that them all over! [*He broods, face downturned.*] Miss—? . . . He— . . . Miss—? . . . *Miss* me? . . . What's *in* me for *him* to miss . . .? [*Suddenly he cries out like one who sees a danger at his very feet.*] Wo-AH! [*Chuckling.*] We-e-eyup! [*To audience.*] I nearly fell for it. [*Walks away.*] 'Matthew, will you kindly take a cut in your wages?' 'No, Sir Thomas, I will not.' That's it and [*fiercely*] that's all of it! [*Falls to thought again. Resentfully.*] All right so he's down on his luck! I'm sorry. I don't mind saying that: I'm sorry! Bad luck! If I'd any good luck to spare he could have some. I wish we could *all* have good luck, *all* the time! I wish we had wings! I wish rainwater was beer! But it isn't! . . . And what with not having wings but walking–on two flat feet; and good luck and bad luck being just exactly even stevens; and rain being water–don't you complicate the job by putting things in me for me to miss! [*He takes off* STEWARD's *coat, picks up his hat: draws the curtain to alcove. Chuckling.*] I did you know. I nearly fell for it.

Exit COMMON MAN. NORFOLK *and* CROMWELL *enter to alcove.*

NORFOLK: But he makes no noise, Mr Secretary; he's silent, why not leave him silent?

CROMWELL [*patiently*]: Not being a man of letters, Your Grace, you perhaps don't realise the extent of his reputation. This 'silence' of his is bellowing up and down Europe! Now may I recapitulate: He reported the Ambassador's conversation to you, informed on the Ambassador's tour of the North-country, warned against a possible rebellion there.

NORFOLK: He did!

CROMWELL: We may say then, that he showed himself hostile to the hopes of Spain.

NORFOLK: That's what I *say*!

CROMWELL [*patiently*]: Bear with me, Your Grace. Now if he opposes Spain, he supports us. Well, surely that follows? [*Sarcastically.*] Or do you see some third alternative?

NORFOLK: No, no, that's the line-up all right. And I may say Thomas More—

CROMWELL: Thomas More will line up on the right side.

NORFOLK: Yes! Crank he may be, traitor he is not.

CROMWELL [*spreading his hands*]: And with a little pressure, he can be got to say so. And that's all we need–a brief declaration of his loyalty to the present administration.

NORFOLK: I still say let sleeping dogs lie.

CROMWELL [*heavily*]: The King does not agree with you.

NORFOLK [*glances at him; flickers, but then rallies*]: What kind of 'pressure' d'you think you can bring to bear?

CROMWELL: I have evidence that Sir Thomas, during the period of his judicature, accepted bribes.

NORFOLK [*incredulous*]: What! Goddammit he was the only judge since Cato who *didn't* accept bribes! When was there last a Chancellor whose possessions after three years in office totalled one hundred pounds and a gold chain.

CROMWELL [*rings hand-bell and calls*]: Richard! It is, as you imply, common practice, but a practice may be common and remain an offence; this offence could send a man to the Tower.

NORFOLK [*contemptuous*]: I don't believe it.

Enter RICH *and* A WOMAN. *He motions her to remain, and approaches the table, where* CROMWELL *indicates a seat. He has acquired self-importance.*

CROMWELL: Ah, Richard. You know His Grace of course.

RICH [*respectful affability*]: Indeed yes, we're *old* friends.

NORFOLK [*savage snub*]: Used to look after my books or something, didn't you?

CROMWELL [*clicks his fingers at* WOMAN]: Come here. This woman's name is Catherine Anger; she comes from Lincoln. And she put a case in the Court of Requests in— [*Consults paper.*]

WOMAN: A property case, it was.

CROMWELL: Be quiet. A property case in the Court of Requests in April 1526.

WOMAN: And got a wicked false judgement!

CROMWELL: And got an impeccably correct judgement from our friend Sir Thomas.

WOMAN: No, sir, it was not!

CROMWELL: We're not concerned with the judgement but the gift you gave the judge. Tell this gentleman about that. The judgement for what it's worth was the right one.

WOMAN: No, sir!

CROMWELL looks at her: she hastily addresses NORFOLK.

I sent him a cup, sir; an Italian silver cup I bought in Lincoln for a hundred shillings.

NORFOLK: Did Sir Thomas accept this cup?

WOMAN: I sent it.

CROMWELL: He did accept it, we can corroborate that. You can go.

She opens her mouth.

Go!

Exit WOMAN.

NORFOLK [*scornful*]: Is that your witness?

CROMWELL: No; by an odd coincidence this cup later came into the hands of Master Rich here.

NORFOLK: How?

RICH: He gave it to me.

NORFOLK [*brutal*]: Can you corroborate that?

CROMWELL: I have a fellow outside who can; he was More's steward at that time. Shall I call him?

NORFOLK: Don't bother, I know him. When did Thomas give you this thing?

RICH: I don't exactly remember.

NORFOLK: Well, make an effort. Wait! I can tell you! I can tell you—it was that Spring—it was that night we were there together. You had a cup with you when we left; was that it?

RICH *looks to* CROMWELL *for guidance but gets none.*

RICH: It may have been.

NORFOLK: Did he often give you cups?

RICH: I don't suppose so. Your Grace.

NORFOLK: That was it then. [*New realisation.*] And it was April! The April of 26. The very month that cow first put her case before him! [*Triumphant.*] In other words the moment he knew it was a bribe, he got rid of it.

CROMWELL [*nodding judicially*]: The facts will bear that interpretation I suppose.

NORFOLK: Oh, this is a horse that won't run, Master Secretary.

CROMWELL: Just a trial canter, Your Grace. We'll find something better.

NORFOLK [*between bullying and plea*]: Look here, Cromwell, I want no part of this.

CROMWELL: You have no choice.

NORFOLK: What's that you say?

CROMWELL: The King particularly wishes you to be active in the matter.

NORFOLK [*winded*]: He has not told me that.

CROMWELL [*politely*]: Indeed? He told me.

NORFOLK: But *why*?

CROMWELL: We feel that, since you are known to have been a friend of More's, your participation will show that there is nothing in the nature of a 'persecution', but only the strict processes of law. As indeed you've just demonstrated. I'll tell the King of your loyalty to your friend. If you like, I'll tell him that you 'want no part of it', too.

NORFOLK [*furious*]: Are you threatening me, Cromwell?

CROMWELL: My *dear* Norfolk. . . . This isn't Spain.

NORFOLK *stares, turns abruptly and exits.* CROMWELL *turns a look of glacial coldness upon* RICH.

RICH: I'm sorry, Secretary, I'd forgotten he was there that night.

CROMWELL [*scrutinises him dispassionately, then*]: You must try to remember these things.

RICH: Secretary, I'm sincerely—!

CROMWELL [*dismisses the topic with a wave and turns to look after* NORFOLK]: Not such a fool as he looks, the Duke.

RICH [*Civil Service simper*]: That would hardly be possible, Secretary.

CROMWELL [*straightening papers, briskly*]: Sir Thomas is going to be a slippery fish, Richard; we need a net with a finer mesh.

RICH: Yes, Secretary?

CROMWELL: We'll weave one for him shall we, you and I?

RICH [*uncertain*]: I'm only anxious to do what is correct, Secretary.

CROMWELL [*smiling at him*]: Yes, Richard, I know. [*Straight-faced.*] You're absolutely right, it must be done by law. It's just a matter of finding the right law. Or making one. Bring my papers, will you?

Exit CROMWELL. *Enter* STEWARD.

STEWARD: Could we have a word now, sir?
RICH: We don't require you after all, Matthew.
STEWARD: No, sir, but about . . .
RICH: Oh yes. . . . Well, I begin to need a steward, certainly; my household is expanding. . . . [*Sharply.*] But as I remember, Matthew, your attitude to me was sometimes–disrespectful! [*The last word is shrill.*]
STEWARD [*with humble dignity*]: Oh. Oh, I must contradict you there, sir; that's your imagination. In those days, sir, you still had your way to make. And a gentleman in that position often imagines these things. Then when he's risen to his proper level, sir, he stops thinking about it. [*As one offering tangible proof.*] Well–I don't think you find people 'disrespectful' nowadays, do you, sir?
RICH: There may be something in that. Bring my papers. [*Going, turns at exit and anxiously scans* STEWARD*'s face for signs of impudence.*] I'll permit no breath of insolence!
STEWARD [*the very idea is shocking*]: I should hope not, sir.

Exit RICH.

Oh, I can manage this one! He's just my size!

Lighting changes so that the set looks drab and chilly.

Sir Thomas More's again gone down a bit.

Exit COMMON MAN.
    Enter, side, CHAPUYS *and* ATTENDANT, *cloaked. Above,* ALICE, *wearing big coarse apron over her dress.*

ALICE: My husband is coming down, Your Excellency.
CHAPUYS: Thank you, madam.
ALICE: And I beg you to be gone before he does!
CHAPUYS [*patiently*]: Madam, I have a Royal Commission to perform.
ALICE: Aye. You said so. [*Exit* ALICE.]
CHAPUYS: For sheer barbarity, commend me to a good-hearted Englishwoman of a certain class. . . . [*Wraps cloak about him.*]
ATTENDANT: It's very cold, Excellency.
CHAPUYS: I remember when these rooms were warm enough.
ATTENDANT [*looking about*]: 'Thus it is to incur the enmity of a Prince.'
CHAPUYS: A heretic Prince. [*Looking about.*] Yes, Sir Thomas is a good man.
ATTENDANT: Yes, Excellency, I like Sir Thomas very much.
CHAPUYS: Carefully, carefully.
ATTENDANT: It's uncomfortable dealing with him, isn't it?
CHAPUYS: Goodness presents its own difficulties. Attend and learn now.
ATTENDANT: Excellency?

CHAPUYS: Well?

ATTENDANT: Excellency, is he really *for* us?

CHAPUYS [*testy*]: He's opposed to Cromwell. He's shown that, I think?

ATTENDANT: Yes, Excellency, but—

CHAPUYS: If he's opposed to Cromwell, he's for us. There's no third alternative.

ATTENDANT: I suppose not, Excellency.

CHAPUYS: I wish your mother had chosen some other career for you; you've no political sense whatever. Sh!

Enter MORE. *His clothes match the atmosphere of the room and he moves rather more deliberately than before.*

MORE [*descending*]: Is this another 'personal' visit, Chapuys, or is it official?

CHAPUYS: It falls between the two, Sir Thomas.

MORE [*reaching the bottom of stairs*]. Official then.

CHAPUYS: No, I have a personal letter for you.

MORE: From whom?

CHAPUYS: From King Charles!

MORE *puts hands behind back.*

You will take it?

MORE: I will not lay a finger on it.

CHAPUYS: It is in no way an affair of State. It expresses my master's admiration for the stand which you and Bishop Fisher of Rochester have taken over the so-called divorce of Queen Catherine.

MORE: I have taken no stand!

CHAPUYS: But your views, Sir Thomas, are well known—

MORE: My views are much guessed at. [*Irritably.*] Oh come, sir, could you undertake to convince [*grimly*] King Harry that this letter is 'in no way an affair of State'?

CHAPUYS: My dear Sir Thomas, I have taken extreme precautions. I came here very much incognito. [*Self-indulgent chuckle.*] Very nearly in disguise.

MORE: You misunderstood me. It is not a matter of your precautions but my duty; which would be to take this letter immediately to the King.

CHAPUYS [*flabbergasted*]: But, Sir Thomas, your views—

MORE: —Are well known you say. It seems my loyalty is less so.

Enter MARGARET *bearing before her a huge bundle of bracken.*

MARGARET: Look, Father! [*Dumps it.*] Will's getting more.

MORE: Oh, well done! [*Not whimsy; they're cold and their interest in fuel is serious.*] Is it dry? [*Feels it expertly.*] Oh it is. [*Sees* CHAPUYS *staring; laughs.*] It's bracken, Your Excellency. We burn it.

Enter ALICE.

Alice, look at this. [*The bracken.*]

ALICE [*eyeing* CHAPUYS]: Aye.

MORE [*crossing to* CHAPUYS]: May I—? [*Takes letter to* ALICE *and* MARGARET.] This is a letter from King Charles; I want you to see it's not been opened. I have declined it. You see the seal has not been broken? [*Returning it to* CHAPUYS.] I wish I could ask you to stay, Your Excellency—the bracken fire is a luxury.

CHAPUYS [*cold smile*]: One I must forego. [*Aside to* ATTENDANT.] Come. [*Crosses to exit, pauses.*] May I say I am sure my master's admiration will not be diminished. [*Bows.*]

MORE: I am gratified. [*Bows, women curtsey.*]

CHAPUYS [*aside to* ATTENDANT]: The man's utterly unreliable!

Exit CHAPUYS *and* ATTENDANT.

ALICE [*after a little silence kicks the bracken*]: 'Luxury!' [*She sits wearily on the bundle.*]

MORE: Well, it's a luxury while it lasts. . . . There's not much sport in it for you, is there? . . .

She neither answers nor looks at him from the depths of her fatigue. After a moment's hesitation he braces himself.

Alice, the money from the Bishops. I wish—oh heaven how I wish I could take it! But I can't.

ALICE [*as one who has ceased to expect anything*]: I didn't think you would.

MORE [*reproachful*]: Alice, there *are* reasons.

ALICE: We couldn't come so deep into your confidence as to *know* these reasons why a man in poverty can't take four thousand pounds?

MORE [*gently but very firm*]: Alice, this isn't poverty.

ALICE: D'you know what we shall eat tonight?

MORE [*trying for a smile*]: Yes, parsnips.

ALICE: Yes, parsnips and stinking mutton! [*Straight at him.*] For a knight's lady!

MORE [*pleading*]: But at the worst, we could be beggars, and still keep company, and be merry together!

ALICE [*bitterly*]: Merry!

MORE [*sternly*]: Aye, merry!

MARGARET [*her arm about her mother's waist*]: *I* think you should take that money.

MORE: Oh, don't you see? [*Sits by them.*] If I'm paid by the Church for my writings—

ALICE: —This had nothing to do with your writings! This was charity pure and simple! Collected from the clergy high and low!

MORE: It would *appear* as payment.

ALICE: You're not a man who deals in appearances!

MORE [*fervent*]: Oh, am I not though. . . . [*Calmly.*] If the King takes this matter any further, with me or with the Church, it will be very bad, if I even appear to have been in the pay of the Church.

ALICE [*sharply*]: Bad?

MORE: If you will have it, dangerous. [*He gets up.*]

MARGARET: But you don't write against the King.

MORE: I write! And that's enough in times like these!

ALICE: You said there *was* no danger!

MORE: I don't think there is! And I don't want there to be!

Enter ROPER *carrying sickle.*

ROPER [*steadily*]: There's a gentleman here from Hampton Court. You are to go before Secretary Cromwell. To answer certain charges.

ALICE *and* MARGARET, *appalled, turn to* MORE.

MORE [*after a silence, rubs his nose*]: Well, that's all right. We expected that. [*Not very convincing.*] When?
ROPER: Now.

ALICE *exhibits distress.*

MORE: That means nothing, Alice; that's just technique. . . . Well, I suppose 'now' means now.

Lighting change commences, darkness gathering on the others, leaving MORE *isolated in the light, out of which he answers them in the shadows.*

MARGARET: Can I come with you?
MORE: Why? No. I'll be back for dinner. I'll bring Cromwell to dinner, shall I? It'd serve him right.
MARGARET: Oh, Father, don't be witty!
MORE: Why not? Wit's what's in question.
ROPER [*quietly*]: While we are witty, the Devil may enter us unawares.
MORE: He's not the Devil, son Roper, he's a lawyer! And my case is watertight!
ALICE: They say he's a very nimble lawyer.
MORE: What, Cromwell? Pooh, he's a pragmatist—and that's the only resemblance he has to the Devil, son Roper; a pragmatist, the merest plumber.

Exit ALICE, MARGARET, ROPER, *in darkness.*
Lights come up. Enter CROMWELL, *bustling, carrying file of papers.*

CROMWELL: I'm sorry to invite you here at such short notice, Sir Thomas; good of you to come. [*Draws back curtain from alcove, revealing* RICH *seated at table, with writing materials.*] Will you take a seat? I think you know Master Rich?
MORE: Indeed yes, we're old friends. That's a nice gown you have, Richard.
CROMWELL: Master Rich will make a record of our conversation.
MORE: Good of you to tell me, Master Secretary.
CROMWELL [*laughs appreciatively. Then*]: Believe me, Sir Thomas—no, that's asking too much—but let me tell you all the same, you have no more sincere admirer than myself.

RICH *begins to scribble.*

Not yet, Rich, not yet. [*Invites* MORE *to join him in laughing at* RICH.]
MORE: If I might hear the charges?
CROMWELL: Charges?
MORE: I understand there are certain charges.

CROMWELL: Some ambiguities of behaviour I should like to clarify–hardly 'charges'.

MORE: Make a note of that will you, Master Rich? There are no charges.

CROMWELL [*laughing and shaking head*]. Sir Thomas, Sir Thomas. . . . You know it amazes me that you, who were once so effective *in* the world, and are now so *much* retired from it, should be opposing yourself to the whole movement of the times? [*He ends on a note of interrogation.*]

MORE [*nods*]: It amazes me too.

CROMWELL [*picks up and drops paper. Sadly*]: The King is not pleased with you.

MORE: I am grieved.

CROMWELL: Yet do you know that even now, if you could bring yourself to agree with the Universities, the Bishops, and the Parliament of this realm, there is no honour which the King would be likely to deny you?

MORE [*stonily*]: I am well acquainted with His Grace's generosity.

CROMWELL [*coldly*]: Very well. [*Consults paper.*] You have heard of the so-called 'Holy Maid of Kent'–who was executed for prophesying against the King?

MORE: Yes; I knew the poor woman.

CROMWELL [*quick*]: You sympathise with her?

MORE: She was ignorant and misguided; she was a bit mad I think. And she has paid for her folly. Naturally I sympathise with her.

CROMWELL [*grunts*]: You admit meeting her. You met her–and yet you did not warn His Majesty of her treason. How was that?

MORE: She spoke no treason. Our conversation was not political.

CROMWELL: My dear More, the woman was notorious! Do you expect me to believe that?

MORE: Happily there were witnesses.

CROMWELL: You wrote a letter to her?

MORE: Yes, I wrote advising her to abstain from meddling with the affairs of Princes and the State. I have a copy of this letter–also witnessed.

CROMWELL: You have been cautious.

MORE: I like to keep my affairs regular.

CROMWELL: Sir Thomas, there is a more serious charge—

MORE: Charge?

CROMWELL: For want of a better word. In the May of 1521 the King published a book [*he permits himself a little smile*], a theological work. It was called *A Defence of the Seven Sacraments*.

MORE: Yes. [*Bitterly.*] For which he was named 'Defender of the Faith', by His Holiness the Pope.

CROMWELL: —By the Bishop of Rome. Or do you insist on 'Pope'?

MORE: No, 'Bishop of Rome' if you like. It doesn't alter his authority.

CROMWELL: Thank you, you come to the point very readily; what *is* that authority? As regards the Church in other parts of Europe; [*approaching*] for example, the Church of England. What exactly *is* the Bishop of Rome's authority?

MORE: You will find it very ably set out and defended, Master Secretary, in the King's book.

CROMWELL: The book published under the King's name would be more accurate. You wrote that book.

MORE: —I wrote no part of it.

CROMWELL: —I do not mean you actually held the pen.

MORE: —I merely answered to the best of my ability certain questions on canon law which His Majesty put to me. As I was bound to do.

CROMWELL: —Do you deny that you *instigated* it?

MORE: —It was from first to last the King's own project. This is trivial, Master Cromwell.

CROMWELL: I should not think so if I were in your place.

MORE: Only two people know the truth of the matter. Myself and the King. And, whatever he may have said to you, he will not give evidence to support this accusation.

CROMWELL: Why not?

MORE: Because evidence is given on oath, and he will not perjure himself. If you don't know that, you don't yet know him.

CROMWELL *looks at him viciously.*

CROMWELL [*goes apart, formally*]: Sir Thomas More, is there anything you wish to say to me concerning the King's marriage with Queen Anne?

MORE [*very still*]: I understood I was not to be asked that again.

CROMWELL: Evidently you understood wrongly. These charges—

MORE [*anger breaking through*]: They are terrors for children, Mr Secretary, not for me!

CROMWELL: Then know that the King commands me to charge you in his name with great ingratitude! And to tell you that there never was nor never could be so villainous a servant nor so traitorous a subject as yourself!

MORE: So I am brought here at last.

CROMWELL: Brought? You brought yourself to where you stand now.

MORE: Yes. Still, in another sense I was brought.

CROMWELL [*indifferent*]: Oh yes. [*Official.*] You may go home now. For the present.

Exit MORE.

I don't like him so well as I did. There's a man who raises the gale and won't come out of harbour.

Scene change commences here, i.e., rear of stage becoming water patterned.

RICH [*covert jeer*]: Do you still think you can frighten him?

CROMWELL: No, he's misusing his intelligence.

RICH: What will you do now, then?

CROMWELL [*as to an importunate child*]: Oh, be quiet, Rich. . . . We'll do whatever's necessary. The King's a man of conscience and he wants either Sir Thomas More to bless his marriage or Sir Thomas More destroyed. Either will do.

RICH [*shakily*]: They seem odd alternatives, Secretary.

CROMWELL: Do they? That's because you're not a man of conscience. If the King destroys a man, that's proof to the King that it must have been a bad man, the kind of man a man of conscience *ought* to destroy—and of course a bad man's blessing's not worth having. So either will do.

RICH [*subdued*]: I see.

CROMWELL: Oh, there's no going back, Rich. I find we've made ourselves the keepers of this conscience. And it's ravenous.

Exit CROMWELL *and* RICH.
Enter MORE.

MORE [*calling*]: Boat! . . . Boat! . . . [*To himself.*] Oh, come along, it's not as bad as that. . . . [*Calls.*] Boat!

Enter NORFOLK. *He stops.*

MORE [*pleased*]: Howard! . . . I can't get home. They won't bring me a boat.
NORFOLK: Do you blame them?
MORE: Is it as bad as that?
NORFOLK: It's every bit as bad as that!
MORE [*gravely*]: Then it's good of you to be seen with me.
NORFOLK [*looking back, off*]: I followed you.
MORE [*surprised*]: Were *you* followed?
NORFOLK: Probably. [*Facing him.*] So listen to what I have to say: You're behaving like a fool. You're behaving like a crank. You're not behaving like a gentleman—All right, that means nothing to you; but what about your friends?
MORE: What about them?
NORFOLK: Goddammit, you're dangerous to know!
MORE: Then don't know me.
NORFOLK: There's something further. . . . You must have realised by now there's a . . . policy, with regards to you.

MORE *nods.*

The King is using me in it.
MORE: That's clever. That's Cromwell. . . . You're between the upper and the nether millstones then.
NORFOLK: I am!
MORE: Howard, you must cease to know me.
NORFOLK: I do know you! I wish I didn't but I do!
MORE: I mean as a friend.
NORFOLK: You *are* my friend!
MORE: I can't relieve you of your obedience to the King, Howard. You must relieve yourself of our friendship. No one's safe now, and you have a son.
NORFOLK: You might as well advise a man to change the colour of his hair! I'm fond of you, and there it is! You're fond of me, and there it is!
MORE: What's to be done then?
NORFOLK [*with deep appeal*]: Give in.
MORE [*gently*]: I can't give in, Howard–[*smile*] you might as well advise a man to change the colour of his eyes. I can't. Our friendship's more mutable than *that.*
NORFOLK: Oh, that's immutable is it? The one fixed point in a world of changing friendships is that Thomas More will not give in!
MORE [*urgent to explain*]: To me it *has* to be, for that's myself! Affection goes as deep in me as you I think, but only God is love right through, Howard; and *that's* my *self.*

NORFOLK: And who are you? Goddammit, man, it's disproportionate! *We're* supposed to be the arrogant ones, the proud, splenetic ones—and we've all given in! Why must you stand out? [*Quiet and quick.*] You'll break my heart.

MORE [*moved*]: We'll do it now, Howard: part, as friends, and meet as strangers. [*He attempts to take* NORFOLK'*s hand.*]

NORFOLK [*throwing it off*]: Daft, Thomas! Why d'you want to take your friendship from me? For friendship's sake! You say we'll meet as strangers and every word you've said confirms our friendship!

MORE [*takes a last affectionate look at him*]: Oh, that can be remedied. [*Walks away, turns: in a tone of deliberate insult.*] Norfolk, you're a fool.

NORFOLK [*starts: then smiles and folds his arms*]: *You* can't place a quarrel; you haven't the style.

MORE: Hear me out. You and your class have 'given in'—as you rightly call it—because the religion of this country means nothing to you one way or the other.

NORFOLK: Well, that's a foolish saying for a start; the nobility of England has always been—

MORE: The nobility of England, my lord, would have snored through the Sermon on the Mount. But you'll labour like Thomas Aquinas over a rat-dog's pedigree. Now what's the name of those distorted creatures you're all breeding at the moment?

NORFOLK [*steadily, but roused towards anger by* MORE'*s tone*]: An artificial quarrel's not a quarrel.

MORE: Don't deceive yourself, my lord, we've had a quarrel since the day we met, our friendship was but sloth.

NORFOLK: You can be cruel when you've a mind to be; but I've always known that.

MORE: What's the name of those dogs? Marsh mastiffs? Bog beagles?

NORFOLK: Water spaniels!

MORE: And what would you do with a water spaniel that was afraid of water? You'd hang it! Well, as a spaniel is to water, so is a man to his own self. I will not give in because I oppose it—*I* do—not my pride, not my spleen, nor any other of my appetites but *I* do—*I*!

He goes up to him and feels him up and down like an animal. MARGARET'*s voice is heard, well off, calling her father.* MORE'*s attention is irresistibly caught by this; but he turns back determinedly to* NORFOLK.

Is there no single sinew in the midst of this that serves no appetite of Norfolk's but is, just, Norfolk? There is! Give *that* some exercise, my lord!

MARGARET [*off, nearer*]: Father?

NORFOLK [*breathing hard*]: Thomas. . . .

MORE: Because as you stand, you'll go before your Maker in a very ill condition!

Enter MARGARET, *below; she stops, amazed at them.*

NORFOLK: Now steady, Thomas. . . .

MORE: And he'll have to think that somewhere back along your pedigree—a bitch got over the wall!

NORFOLK *lashes out at him; he ducks and winces. Exit* NORFOLK.

MARGARET: Father! [*As he straightens up.*] Father, what was that?
MORE: That was Norfolk. [*Looks after him wistfully.*]

Enter ROPER.

ROPER [*excited, almost gleeful*]: Do you know, sir? Have you heard?

MORE *still looking off, unanswering.*

ROPER [*to* MARGARET]: Have you told him?
MARGARET [*gently*]: We've been looking for you, Father.

MORE *the same.*

ROPER: There's to be a new Act through Parliament, sir!
MORE [*half-turning, half attending*]: Act?
ROPER: Yes, sir—about the Marriage!
MORE [*indifferent*]: Oh. [*Turning back again.*]

ROPER *and* MARGARET *look at one another.*

MARGARET [*puts hand on his arm*]: Father, by this Act, they're going to administer an oath.
MORE [*instantaneous attention*]: An oath! [*Looks from one to other.*] On what compulsion?
ROPER: It's expected to be treason!
MORE [*very still*]: What is the oath?
ROPER [*puzzled*]: It's about the Marriage, sir.
MORE: But what is the wording?
ROPER: We don't need to know the [*contemptuous*] wording—we know what it will mean!
MORE: It will mean what the words say! An oath is *made* of words! It may be possible to take it. Or avoid it. Have we a copy of the Bill? [*To* MARGARET.]
MARGARET: There's one coming out from the City.
MORE: Then let's get home and look at it. Oh, I've no boat. [*He looks off again after* NORFOLK.]
MARGARET [*gently*]: What happened, Father?
MORE: I spoke, slightingly, of water spaniels. Let's get home. [*He turns and sees* ROPER *excited and truculent.*] Now listen, Will. And, Meg, you know I know you well, you listen too. God made the *angels* to show him splendour—as he made animals for innocence and plants for their simplicity. But Man he made to serve him wittily, in the tangle of his mind! If he suffers us to fall to such a case that there is no escaping, then we may stand to our tackle as best we can, and yes, Will, then we may clamour like champions . . . if we have the spittle for it. And no doubt it delights God to see splendour where he only looked for complexity. But it's God's part, not our own, to bring ourselves to that extremity! Our natural business lies in escaping—so let's get home and study this Bill.

Exit MORE, ROPER *and* MARGARET.
Enter COMMON MAN, *dragging basket. The rear of the stage remains water-*

lit in moonlight. Iron grills now descend to cover all the apertures. Also, a rack, which remains suspended, and a cage which is lowered to the floor. While this takes place the COMMON MAN *arranges three chairs behind a table. Then he turns and watches the completion of the transformation.*

COMMON MAN [*aggrieved*]: Now look! . . . I don't suppose anyone enjoyed it any more than he did. Well, not much more. [*Takes from basket and dons coat and hat.*] Jailer! [*Shrugs.*] It's a job. The pay scale being what it is they have to take a rather common type of man into the prison service. But it's a job like any other job. Bit nearer the knuckle than most perhaps.

Enter right, CROMWELL, NORFOLK, CRANMER, *who sit, and* RICH, *who stands behind them. Enter left,* MORE, *who enters the cage and lies down.*

They'd let him out if they could but for various reasons they can't. [*Twirling keys.*] I'd let him out if I could but I can't. Not without taking up residence in there myself. And he's in there already, so what'd be the point? You know the old adage? 'Better a live rat than a dead lion,' and that's about it.
[*An envelope descends swiftly before him. He opens it and reads*]: 'With reference to the old adage: Thomas Cromwell was found guilty of High Treason and executed on 28 July 1540. Norfolk was found guilty of High Treason and should have been executed on 27 January 1547 but on the night of 26 January, the King died of syphilis and wasn't able to sign the warrant. Thomas Cranmer.' [*Jerking thumb.*] That's the other one–'was burned alive on 21 March 1556.' [*He is about to conclude but sees a postscript.*] Oh. 'Richard Rich became a Knight and Solicitor-General, a Baron and Lord Chancellor, and died in his bed.' So did I. And so, I hope [*pushing off basket*] will all of you.

He goes to MORE *and rouses him. Heavy bell strikes one.*

MORE [*rousing*]: What, again?
JAILER: Sorry, sir.
MORE [*flops back*]: What time is it?
JAILER: Just struck one, sir.
MORE: Oh, this is iniquitous!
JAILER [*anxious*]: Sir.
MORE [*sitting up*]: All right. [*Putting on slippers.*] Who's there?
JAILER: The Secretary, the Duke, and the Archbishop.
MORE: I'm flattered. [*Stands. Claps hand to hip*]. Ooh!

Preceded by JAILER *limps across stage right: he has aged and is pale, but his manner though wary, is relaxed: while that of the Commission is bored, tense, and jumpy.*

NORFOLK [*looks at him*]: A chair for the prisoner. [*While* JAILER *brings a chair and* MORE *sits in it,* NORFOLK *rattles off*]: This is the Seventh Commission to enquire into the case of Sir Thomas More, appointed by His Majesty's Council. Have you anything to say?
MORE: No. [*To* JAILER.] Thank you.
NORFOLK [*sitting back*]: Mr Secretary.

CROMWELL: Sir Thomas–[*breaks off*]–do the witnesses attend?
RICH: Mr Secretary.
JAILER: Sir.
CROMWELL [*to* JAILER]: Nearer! [*He advances a bit.*] Come where you can hear!

JAILER *takes up stance by* RICH

CROMWELL [*to* MORE]: Sir Thomas, you have seen this document before?
MORE: Many times.
CROMWELL: It is the Act of Succession. These are the names of those who have sworn to it.
MORE: I have, as you say, seen it before.
CROMWELL: Will you swear to it?
MORE: No.
NORFOLK: Thomas, we must know plainly—
CROMWELL [*throws down document*]: Your Grace, *please!*
NORFOLK: Master Cromwell!

They regard one another in hatred.

CROMWELL: I beg Your Grace's pardon. [*Sighing, rests head in hands.*]
NORFOLK: Thomas, we must know plainly whether you recognise the offspring of Queen Anne as heirs to His Majesty.
MORE: The King in Parliament tells me that they are. Of course I recognise them.
NORFOLK: Will you swear that you do?
MORE: Yes.
NORFOLK: Then why won't you swear to the Act?
CROMWELL [*impatient*]: Because there is more than that *in* the Act.
NORFOLK: Is that it?
MORE [*after a pause*]: Yes.
NORFOLK: Then we must find out what it is in the Act that he objects to!
CROMWELL: Brilliant.

NORFOLK *rounds on him.*

CRANMER [*hastily*]: Your Grace—May I try?
NORFOLK: Certainly. I've no pretension to be an expert, in Police work.

During next speech CROMWELL straightens up and folds arms resignedly.

CRANMER [*clears throat fussily*]: Sir Thomas, it states in the preamble that the King's former marriage, to the Lady Catherine, was unlawful, she being previously his brother's wife and the–er– 'Pope' having no authority to sanction it. [*Gently.*] Is that what you deny? [*No reply.*] Is that what you dispute? [*No reply.*] Is that what you are not sure of? [*No reply.*]
NORFOLK: Thomas, you insult the King and His Council in the person of the Lord Archbishop!
MORE: I insult no one. I will not take the oath. I will not tell you why I will not.
NORFOLK: Then your reasons must be treasonable!
MORE: Not 'must be'; may be.

NORFOLK: It's a fair assumption!

MORE: The law requires more than an assumption; the law requires a fact.

CROMWELL *looks at him and away again.*

CRANMER: I cannot judge your legal standing in the case; but until I know the *ground* of your objections, I can only guess your spiritual standing too.

MORE [*is for a second furiously affronted; then humour overtakes him*]: If you're willing to guess at that, Your Grace, it should be a small matter to guess my objections.

CROMWELL [*quickly*]: You do have objections to the Act?

NORFOLK [*happily*]: Well, we know *that*, Cromwell!

MORE: You don't, my lord. You may *suppose* I have objections. All you *know* is that I will not swear to it. From sheer delight to give you trouble it might be.

NORFOLK: Is it material why you won't?

MORE: It's most material. For refusing to swear my goods are forfeit and I am condemned to life imprisonment. You cannot lawfully harm me further. But if you were right in supposing I had reasons for refusing and right again in supposing my reasons to be treasonable, the law would let you cut my head off.

NORFOLK [*he has followed with some difficulty*]: Oh yes.

CROMWELL [*admiring murmur*]: Oh, well done, Sir Thomas. I've been trying to make that clear to His Grace for some time.

NORFOLK [*hardly responds to the insult; his face is gloomy and disgusted*]: Oh, confound all this. . . . [*With real dignity.*] I'm not a scholar, as Master Cromwell never tires of pointing out, and frankly I don't know whether the marriage was lawful or not. But damn it, Thomas, look at those names. . . . You know those men! Can't you do what I did, and come with us, for fellowship?

MORE [*moved*]: And when we stand before God, and you are sent to Paradise for doing according to your conscience, and I am damned for not doing according to mine, will you come with me, for fellowship?

CRANMER: So those of us whose names are there are damned, Sir Thomas?

MORE: I don't know, Your Grace. I have no window to look into another man's conscience. I condemn no one.

CRANMER: Then the matter is capable of question?

MORE: Certainly.

CRANMER: But that you owe obedience to your King is not capable of question. So weigh a doubt against a certainty—and sign.

MORE: Some men think the Earth is round, others think it flat; it is a matter capable of question. But if it is flat, will the King's command make it round? And if it is round, will the King's command flatten it? No, I will not sign.

CROMWELL [*leaping up, with ceremonial indignation*]: Then you have more regard to your own doubt than you have to his command!

MORE: For myself, I have no doubt.

CROMWELL: No doubt of what?

MORE: No doubt of my grounds for refusing this oath. Grounds I will tell to the King alone, and which you, Mr Secretary, will not trick out of me.

NORFOLK: Thomas—

MORE: Oh, gentlemen, can't I go to bed?

CROMWELL: You don't seem to appreciate the seriousness of your position.

MORE: I defy anyone to live in that cell for a year and not appreciate the
  seriousness of his position.
CROMWELL: Yet the State has harsher punishments.
MORE: You threaten like a dockside bully.
CROMWELL: How should I threaten?
MORE: Like a Minister of State, with justice!
CROMWELL: Oh, justice is what you're threatened with.
MORE: Then I'm not threatened.
NORFOLK: Master Secretary, I think the prisoner may retire as he requests.
  Unless you, my lord—?
CRANMER [*pettish*]: No, I see no purpose in prolonging the interview.
NORFOLK: Then good night, Thomas.
MORE [*hesitates*]: Might I have one or two more books?
CROMWELL: You have books?
MORE: Yes.
CROMWELL: I didn't know; you shouldn't have.
MORE [*turns to go: pauses. Desperately*]: May I see my family?
CROMWELL: No!

> MORE *returns to cell.*

Jailer!
JAILER: Sir!
CROMWELL: Have you ever heard the prisoner speak of the King's divorce, or
  the King's Supremacy of the Church, or the King's marriage?
JAILER: No, sir, not a word.
CROMWELL: If he does, you will of course report it to the Lieutenant.
JAILER: Of course, sir.
CROMWELL: You will swear an oath to that effect.
JAILER [*cheerfully*]: Certainly, sir!
CROMWELL: Archbishop?
CRANMER [*laying cross of vestment on table*]: Place your left hand on this and raise
  your right hand–take your hat off–Now say after me: I swear by my
  immortal soul–[JAILER *overlapping, repeats the oath with him*] that I will
  report truly anything said by Sir Thomas More against the King, the
  Council or the State of the Realm. So help me God. Amen.
JAILER [*overlapping*]: So help me God. Amen.
CROMWELL: And there's fifty guineas in it if you do.
JAILER [*looks at him gravely*]: Yes, sir. [*And goes.*]
CRANMER [*hastily*]: That's not to tempt you into perjury, my man!
JAILER: No sir! [*At exit pauses; to audience.*] Fifty guineas isn't tempting; fifty
  guineas is alarming. If he'd left it at swearing. . . . But fifty—That's serious
  money. If it's worth that much now it's worth my neck presently. [*Decision.*]
  I want no part of it. They can sort it out between them. I feel my deafness
  coming on.

> *Exit* JAILER. *The Commission rises.*

CROMWELL: Rich!
RICH: Secretary?
CROMWELL: Tomorrow morning, remove the prisoner's books.

NORFOLK: Is that necessary?

CROMWELL [*suppressed exasperation*]: Norfolk. With regards this case, the King is becoming impatient.

NORFOLK: Aye, with you.

CROMWELL: With all of us. [*He walks over to the rack.*] You know the King's impatience, how commodious it is!

> NORFOLK *and* CRANMER *exit.* CROMWELL *is brooding over the instrument of torture.*

RICH: Secretary!

CROMWELL [*abstracted*]: Yes . . .?

RICH: Sir Redvers Llewellyn has retired.

CROMWELL [*not listening*]: Mm . . .?

RICH [*goes to other end of rack and faces him. Some indignation*]: The Attorney-General for Wales. His post is vacant. You said I might approach you.

CROMWELL [*contemptuous impatience*]: Oh, not *now*. . . . [*Broods.*] He must submit, the alternatives are bad. While More's alive the King's conscience breaks into fresh stinking flowers every time he gets from bed. And if I bring about More's death–I plant my own, I think. There's no other good solution! He must submit! [*He whirls the windlass of the rack, producing a startling clatter from the ratchet. They look at each other. He turns it again slowly, shakes his head and lets go.*] No; the King will not permit it. [*Walks away.*] We have to find some gentler way.

> *The scene change commences as he says this and exit* RICH *and* CROMWELL. *From night it becomes morning, cold grey light from off the grey water. And enter* JAILER *and* MARGARET.

JAILER: Wake up, Sir Thomas! Your family's here!

MORE [*starting up. A great cry*]: Margaret! What's this? You can visit me? [*Thrusts arms through cage.*] Meg. Meg. [*She goes to him. Then horrified.*] For God's sake, Meg, they've not put *you* in here?

JAILER [*reassuring*]: No-o-o, sir. Just a visit; a short one.

MORE [*excited*]: Jailer, jailer, let me out of this.

JAILER [*stolid*]: Yes, sir. I'm allowed to let you out.

MORE: Thank you. [*Goes to door of cage, gabbling while* JAILER *unlocks it.*] Thank you, thank you.

> *Comes out. He and she regard each other; then she drops into a curtsey.*

MARGARET: Good morning, Father.

MORE [*ecstatic, wraps her to him*]: Oh, good morning— Good morning.

> *Enter* ALICE, *supported by* WILL. *She, like* MORE, *has aged and is poorly dressed.*

Good morning, Alice. Good morning, Will.

> ROPER *is staring at the rack in horror.* ALICE *approaches* MORE *and peers at him technically.*

ALICE [*almost accusatory*]: Husband, how do you do?

MORE [*smiling over* MARGARET]: As well as need be, Alice. Very happy now. Will?

ROPER: This is an awful place!

MORE: Except it's keeping me from you, my dears, it's not so bad. Remarkably like any other place.

ALICE [*looks up critically*]: It drips!

MORE: Yes. Too near the river.

ALICE *goes apart and sits, her face bitter.*

MARGARET [*disengages from him, takes basket from her mother*]: We've brought you some things. [*Shows him. There is constraint between them.*] Some cheese. . . .

MORE: Cheese.

MARGARET: And a custard. . . .

MORE: A custard!

MARGARET: And, these other things. . . . [*She doesn't look at him.*]

ROPER: And a bottle of wine. [*Offering it.*]

MORE: Oh. [*Mischievous.*] Is it good, son Roper?

ROPER: I don't know, sir.

MORE [*looks at them, puzzled*]. Well.

ROPER: Sir, come out! Swear to the Act! Take the oath and come out!

MORE: Is this why they let you come?

ROPER: Yes . . . Meg's under oath to persuade you.

MORE [*coldly*]: That was silly, Meg. How did you come to do that?

MARGARET: I wanted to!

MORE: You want me to swear to the Act of Succession?

MARGARET: 'God more regards the thoughts of the heart than the words of the mouth' or so you've always told me.

MORE: Yes.

MARGARET: Then say the words of the oath and in your heart think otherwise.

MORE: What is an oath then but words we say to God?

MARGARET: That's very neat.

MORE: Do you mean it isn't true?

MARGARET: No, it's true.

MORE: Then it's a poor argument to call it 'neat', Meg. When a man takes an oath, Meg, he's holding his own self in his own hands. Like water [*cups hands*] and if he opens his fingers *then*–he needn't hope to find himself again. Some men aren't capable of this, but I'd be loathe to think your father one of them.

MARGARET: So should I. . . .

MORE: Then—

MARGARET: There's something else I've been thinking.

MORE: Oh, Meg!

MARGARET: In any state that was half good, you would be raised up high, not here, for what you've done already.

MORE: All right.

MARGARET: It's not your fault the State's three-quarters bad.

MORE: No.

MARGARET: Then if you elect to suffer for it, you elect yourself a hero.

MORE: That's very neat. But look now . . . if we lived in a State where virtue was profitable, common sense would make us good, and greed would make us saintly. And we'd live like animals or angels in the happy land that *needs* no heroes. But since in fact we see that avarice, anger, envy, pride, sloth, lust and stupidity commonly profit far beyond humility, chastity, fortitude, justice and thought, and have to choose, to be human at all . . . why then perhaps we *must* stand fast a little–even at the risk of being heroes.

MARGARET [*emotional*]: But in reason! Haven't you done as much as God can reasonably *want*?

MORE: Well . . . finally . . . it isn't a matter of reason; finally it's a matter of love.

ALICE [*hostile*]: You're content then, to be shut up here with mice and rats when you might be home with us!

MORE [*flinching*]: Content? If they'd open a crack that wide [*between finger and thumb*] I'd be through it. [*To* MARGARET.] Well, has Eve run out of apples?

MARGARET: I've not yet told you what the house is like, without you.

MORE: Don't, Meg.

MARGARET: What we do in the evenings, now that you're not there.

MORE: Meg, have done!

MARGARET: We sit in the dark because we've no candles. And we've no talk because we're wondering what they're doing to you here.

MORE: The King's more merciful than you. He doesn't use the rack.

Enter JAILER.

JAILER: Two minutes to go, sir. I thought you'd like to know.

MORE: Two minutes!

JAILER: Till seven o'clock, sir. Sorry. Two minutes.

Exit JAILER.

MORE: Jailer—! [*Seizes* ROPER *by the arm*.] Will–go to him, talk to him, keep him occupied— [*Propelling him after* JAILER.]

ROPER: How, sir?

MORE: Anyhow! –Have you got any money?

ROPER [*eager*]: Yes!

MORE: No, don't try and bribe him! Let him play for it; he's got a pair of dice. And talk to him, you understand! And take this [*the wine*]–and mind you share it–do it properly, Will!

ROPER *nods vigorously and exits.*

Now listen, you must leave the country. All of you must leave the country.

MARGARET: And leave you here?

MORE: It makes no difference, Meg; they won't let you see me again. [*Breathlessly, a prepared speech under pressure.*] You must all go on the same day, but not on the same boat; different boats from different ports—

MARGARET: After the trial, then.

MORE: There'll be no trial, they have no case. Do this for me I beseech you?

MARGARET: Yes.

MORE: Alice? [*She turns her back.*] Alice, I command it!

ALICE [*harshly*]: Right!

MORE [*looks into basket*]: Oh, this is splendid; I know who packed this.

ALICE [*harshly*]: I packed it.

MORE: Yes. [*Eats a morsel.*] You still make superlative custard, Alice.

ALICE: Do I?

MORE: That's a nice dress you have on.

ALICE: It's my cooking dress.

MORE: It's very nice anyway. Nice colour.

ALICE [*turns. Quietly*]: By God, you think very little of me. [*Mounting bitterness.*] I know I'm a fool. But I'm no such fool as at this time to be lamenting for my dresses! Or to relish complimenting on my custard!

MORE [*regarding her with frozen attention. He nods once or twice*]: I am well rebuked. [*Holds out his hands.*] Al—!

ALICE: No! [*She remains where she is, glaring at him.*]

MORE [*he is in great fear of her*]: I am faint when I think of the worst that they may do to me. But worse than that would be to go, with you not understanding why I go.

ALICE: I don't!

MORE [*just hanging on to his self-possession*]: Alice, if you can tell me that you understand, I think I can make a good death, if I have to.

ALICE: Your death's no 'good' to me!

MORE: Alice, you must tell me that you understand!

ALICE: I don't! [*She throws it straight at his head.*] I don't believe this had to happen.

MORE [*his face is drawn*]: If you say that, Alice, I don't see how I'm to face it.

ALICE: It's the truth!

MORE [*gasping*]: You're an honest woman.

ALICE: Much good may it do me! I'll tell you what I'm afraid of; that when you've gone, I shall hate you for it.

MORE [*turns from her: his face working*]: Well, you mustn't, Alice that's all.

Swiftly she crosses the stage to him; he turns and they clasp each other fiercely.

You mustn't, you—

ALICE [*covers his mouth with her hand*]: S-s-sh. . . . As for understanding, I understand you're the best man that I ever met or am likely to; and if you go—well God knows why I suppose—though as God's my witness God's kept deadly quiet about it! And if anyone wants my opinion of the King and his Council they've only to ask for it!

MORE: Why, it's a lion I married! A lion! A lion! [*He breaks away from her his face shining.*] Get them to take half this to Bishop Fisher—they've got him in the upper gallery—

ALICE: It's for you, not Bishop Fisher!

MORE: Now do as I ask— [*Breaks off a piece of the custard and eats it.*] Oh, it's good, it's very, very good.

He puts his face in his hands; ALICE *and* MARGARET *comfort him;* ROPER *and* JAILER *erupt on to the stage above, wrangling fiercely.*

JAILER: It's no good, sir! I know what you're up to! And it can't be done!

ROPER: Another minute, man!

JAILER [*to* MORE *descending*]: Sorry, sir, time's up!

ROPER [*gripping his shoulder from behind*]: For pity's sake—!
JAILER [*shaking him off*]: Now don't do that, sir! Sir Thomas, the ladies will have to go now!
MORE: You said seven o'clock!
JAILER: It's seven now. You must understand my position, sir.
MORE: But one more minute!
MARGARET: Only a little while—give us a little while!
JAILER [*reproving*]: Now, Miss, you don't want to get me into trouble.
ALICE: Do as you're told. Be off at once!

The first stroke of seven is heard on a heavy, deliberate bell, which continues, reducing what follows to a babble.

JAILER [*taking* MARGARET *firmly by the upper arm*]: Now come along, Miss; you'll get your father into trouble as well as me.

ROPER *descends and grabs him.*

Are you obstructing me, sir?

MARGARET *embraces* MORE, *and dashes up the stairs and exits, followed by* ROPER. *Taking* ALICE *gingerly by the arm.*

Now, my lady, no trouble!
ALICE [*throwing him off as she rises*]: Don't put your muddy hand on me!
JAILER: Am I to call the guard then? Then come on!

ALICE, *facing him, puts foot on bottom stair and so retreats before him, backwards.*

MORE: For God's sake, man, we're saying good-bye!
JAILER: You don't know what you're asking, sir. You don't know how you're watched.
ALICE: Filthy, stinking, gutter-bred turnkey!
JAILER: Call me what you like, ma'am; you've got to go.
ALICE: I'll see you suffer for this!
JAILER: You're doing your husband no good!
MORE: Alice, good-bye, my love!

On this, the last stroke of the seven sounds. ALICE *raises her hand, turns, and with considerable dignity, exits.* JAILER *stops at head of stairs and addresses* MORE, *who, still crouching, turns from him, facing audience.*

JAILER [*reasonably*]: You understand my position, sir, there's nothing I can do; I'm a plain simple man and just want to keep out of trouble.
MORE [*cries out passionately*]: Oh, Sweet Jesus! These plain, simple, men!

Immediately: (*1*) *Music, portentous and heraldic.*
　　　　　　 (*2*) *Bars, rack and cage flown swiftly upwards.*
　　　　　　 (*3*) *Lighting change from cold grey to warm yellow, re-creating a warm interior.*

(*4*) *Several narrow panels, scarlet and bearing the monogram*
'HR VIII' *in gold are lowered. Also an enormous Royal*
Coat-of-Arms which hangs above the table stage right.
(*5*) *The* JAILER, *doffing costume comes down the stairs and:*
(*A*) *Places a chair for the Accused, helps* MORE *to it, and gives him a scroll*
which he studies.
(*B*) *Fetches from the wings his prop basket, and produces:* (*I*) *A large hour-*
glass and papers which he places on table, stage right. (*II*) *Twelve*
folding stools which he arranges in two rows of six each. While he is
still doing this, and just before the panels and Coat-of-Arms have
finished their descent, enter CROMWELL. *He ringingly addresses the*
audience (while the COMMON MAN *is still bustling about his chores) as*
soon as the music ends, which it does at this point, on a fanfare.

CROMWELL [*indicating descending props*]:

> What Englishman can behold without Awe
> The Canvas and the Rigging of the Law!

Brief fanfare.

> Forbidden here the galley-master's whip—
> Hearts of Oak, in the Law's Great Ship!

Brief fanfare.

CROMWELL [*to* COMMON MAN *who is tiptoeing discreetly off stage*]: Where are you
going?
COMMON MAN: I've finished here, sir.

Above the two rows of stools the COMMON MAN *has suspended from two wires,*
supported by two pairs of sticks, two rows of hats for the presumed occupants.
Seven are plain grey hats, four are those worn by the STEWARD, BOATMAN,
INNKEEPER *and* JAILER. *And the last is another of the plain grey ones. The*
basket remains on stage, clearly visible.

CROMWELL: You're the Foreman of the Jury.
COMMON MAN: Oh no, sir.
CROMWELL: You are John Dauncey. A general dealer?
COMMON MAN [*gloomy*]: Yes, sir?
CROMWELL [*resuming his rhetorical stance*]: Foreman of the Jury. Does the cap
fit?

COMMON MAN *puts on the grey hat. It fits.*

COMMON MAN: Yes, sir.
CROMWELL [*resuming rhetorical stance*]:

> So, now we'll apply the good, plain sailor's art,
> And fix these quicksands on the Law's plain chart!

Renewed, more prolonged fanfare, during which enter CRANMER *and*
NORFOLK, *who stand behind the table stage right. On their entry* MORE *and*
FOREMAN *rise. So soon as fanfare is finished* NORFOLK *speaks.*

NORFOLK [*takes refuge behind a rigorously official manner*]: Sir Thomas More,
you are called before us here at the Hall of Westminster to answer charge of
High Treason. Nevertheless, and though you have heinously offended the
King's Majesty, we hope if you will even now forthink and repent of your
obstinate opinions, you may still taste his gracious pardon.
MORE: My lords, I thank you. Howbeit I make my petition to Almighty God
that he will keep me in this, my honest mind to the last hour that I shall live.
. . . As for the matters you may charge me with, I fear, from my present
weakness, that neither my wit nor my memory will serve to make sufficient
answers. . . . I should be glad to sit down.
NORFOLK: Be seated. Master Secretary Cromwell, have you the charge?
CROMWELL: I have, my lord.
NORFOLK: Then read the charge.
CROMWELL [*approaching* MORE, *behind him, with papers; informally*]: It is the
same charge, Sir Thomas, that was brought against Bishop Fisher. . . . [*As
one who catches himself up punctiliously.*] The *late* Bishop Fisher I should
have said.
MORE [*tonelessly*]: 'Late'?
CROMWELL: Bishop Fisher was executed this morning.

MORE'*s face expresses violent shock, then grief; he turns his head away from*
CROMWELL *who is observing him clinically.*

NORFOLK: Master Secretary, read the charge!
CROMWELL [*formal*]: That you did conspire traitorously and maliciously to
deny and deprive our liege lord Henry of his undoubted certain title,
Supreme Head of the Church in England.
MORE [*surprise, shock, and indignation*]: But I have never denied this title!
CROMWELL: You refused the oath tendered to you at the Tower and
elsewhere—
MORE [*the same*]: Silence is not denial. And for my silence I am punished with
imprisonment. Why have I been called again? [*At this point he is sensing that
the trial has been in some way rigged.*]
NORFOLK: On a charge of High Treason, Sir Thomas.
CROMWELL: For which the punishment is *not* imprisonment.
MORE: Death . . . comes for us all, my lords. Yes, even for Kings he comes, to
whom amidst all their Royalty and brute strength he will neither kneel nor
make them any reverence nor pleasantly desire them to come forth, but
roughly grasp them by the very breast and rattle them until they be stark
dead! So causing their bodies to be buried in a pit and sending *them* to a
judgement . . . whereof at their death their success is uncertain.
CROMWELL: Treason enough here!
NORFOLK: The death of Kings is not in question, Sir Thomas.
MORE: Nor mine, I trust, until I'm proven guilty.
NORFOLK [*leaning forward urgently*]: Your life lies in your own hand, Thomas,
as it always has.
MORE [*absorbs this*]: For our own deaths, my lord, yours and mine, dare we for

shame desire to enter the Kingdom with ease, when Our Lord Himself entered with so much pain? [*And now he faces* CROMWELL *his eyes sparkling with suspicion.*]

CROMWELL: Now, Sir Thomas, you stand upon your silence.

MORE: I do.

CROMWELL: But, Gentlemen of the Jury, there are many kinds of silence. Consider first the silence of a man when he is dead. Let us say we go into the room where he is lying; and let us say it is in the dead of night—there's nothing like darkness for sharpening the ear; and we listen. What do we hear? Silence. What does it betoken, this silence? Nothing. This is silence, pure and simple. But consider another case. Suppose I were to draw a dagger from my sleeve and make to kill the prisoner with it, and suppose their lordships there, instead of crying out for me to stop or crying out for help to stop me, maintained their silence. That *would* betoken! It would betoken a willingness that I should do it, and under the law they would be guilty with me. So silence can, according to circumstances, speak. Consider now, the circumstances of the prisoner's silence. The oath was put to good and faithful subjects up and down the country and they had declared His Grace's Title to be just and good. And when it came to the prisoner he refused. He calls this silence. Yet is there a man in this court, is there a man in this country, who does not *know* Sir Thomas More's opinion of this title? Of course not! But how can that be? Because this silence betokened—nay this silence *was*—not silence at all, but most eloquent denial.

MORE [*with some of his academic's impatience for a shoddy line of reasoning*]: Not so, Mr Secretary, the maxim is 'qui tacet consentire'. [*Turns to* COMMON MAN.] The maxim of the law is: [*very carefully*] 'Silence Gives Consent'. If therefore, you wish to construe what my silence 'betokened', you must construe that I consented, not that I denied.

CROMWELL: Is that what the world in fact construes from it? Do you pretend that is what you *wish* the world to construe from it?

MORE: The world must construe according to its wits. This Court must construe according to the law.

CROMWELL: I put it to the Court that the prisoner is perverting the law—making smoky what should be a clear light to discover to the Court his own wrongdoing! [CROMWELL's *official indignation is slipping into genuine anger and* MORE *responds.*]

MORE: The law is not a 'light' for you or any man to see by; the law is not an instrument of any kind. [*To the* FOREMAN.] The law is a causeway upon which so long as he keeps to it a citizen may walk safely. [*Earnestly addressing him.*] In matters of conscience—

CROMWELL [*bitterly smiling*]: The conscience, the conscience . . .

MORE [*turning*]: The word is not familiar to you?

CROMWELL: By God, too familiar! I am very used to hear it in the mouths of criminals!

MORE: I am used to hear bad men misuse the name of God, yet God exists. [*Turning back.*] In matters of conscience, the loyal subject is more bounden to be loyal *to* his conscience than to any other thing.

CROMWELL [*breathing hard: straight at* MORE]:—And so provide a noble motive for his frivolous self-conceit!

MORE [*earnestly*]: It is not so, Master Cromwell—very and pure necessity for respect of my own soul.

CROMWELL: —Your own self you mean!

MORE: Yes, a man's soul is his self!

CROMWELL [*thrusts his face into* MORE'*s. They hate each other and each other's standpoint*]: A miserable thing, whatever you call it, that lives like a bat in a Sunday School! A shrill incessant pedagogue about its own salvation—but nothing to say of your place in the State! Under the King! In a great native country!

MORE [*not untouched*]: Can I help my King by giving him lies when he asks for truth? Will you help England by populating her with liars?

CROMWELL [*backs away. His face stiff with malevolence*]: My lords, I wish to call [*raises voice*] Sir Richard Rich!

Enter RICH. *He is now splendidly official, in dress and bearing; even* NORFOLK *is a bit impressed.*

Sir Richard [*indicating* CRANMER].

CRANMER [*proffering Bible*]: I do solemnly swear . . .

RICH: I do solemnly swear that the evidence I shall give before the Court shall be the truth, the whole truth, and nothing but the truth.

CRANMER [*discreetly*]: So help me God, Sir Richard.

RICH: So help me God.

NORFOLK: Take your stand there, Sir Richard.

CROMWELL: Now, Rich, on 12 March, you were at the Tower?

RICH: I was.

CROMWELL: With what purpose?

RICH: I was sent to carry away the prisoner's books.

CROMWELL: Did you talk with the prisoner?

RICH: Yes.

CROMWELL: Did you talk about the King's Supremacy of the Church?

RICH: Yes.

CROMWELL: What did you say?

RICH: I said to him: 'Supposing there was an Act of Parliament to say that I, Richard Rich, were to be King, would not you, Master More, take me for King?' 'That I would,' he said, 'for then you would be King.'

CROMWELL: Yes?

RICH: Then he said—

NORFOLK [*sharply*]: The prisoner?

RICH: Yes, my lord. 'But I will put you a higher case,' he said. 'How if there were an Act of Parliament to say that God should not be God?'

MORE: This is true, and then you said—

NORFOLK: Silence! Continue.

RICH: I said 'Ah, but I will put you a middle case. Parliament has made our King Head of the Church. Why will you not accept him?'

NORFOLK [*strung up*]: Well?

RICH: Then he said Parliament had no power to do it.

NORFOLK: Repeat the prisoner's words!

RICH: He said 'Parliament has not the competence.' Or words to that effect.

CROMWELL: He denied the title?

RICH: He did.

All look to MORE *but he looks to* RICH.

MORE: In good faith, Rich, I am sorrier for your perjury than my peril.

NORFOLK: Do you deny this?

MORE: Yes! My lords, if I were a man who heeded not the taking of an oath, you know well I need not to be here. Now I will take an oath! If what Master Rich has said is true, then I pray I may never see God in the face! Which I would not say were it otherwise for anything on earth.

CROMWELL [*to* FOREMAN, *calmly, technical*]: That is not evidence.

MORE: Is it probable—is it probable—that after so long a silence, on this, the very point so urgently sought of me, I should open my mind to such a man as that?

CROMWELL [*to* RICH]: Do you wish to modify your testimony?

RICH: No, Secretary.

MORE: There were two other men! Southwell and Palmer!

CROMWELL: Unhappily, Sir Richard Southwell and Master Palmer are both in Ireland on the King's business.

MORE *gestures helplessly.*

It has no bearing. I have their deposition here in which the Court will see they state that being busy with the prisoner's books they did not hear what was said. [*Hands deposition to* FOREMAN *who examines it with much seriousness.*]

MORE: If I had really said this is it not obvious he would instantly have called these men to witness?

CROMWELL: Sir Richard, have you anything to add?

RICH: Nothing, Mr Secretary.

NORFOLK: Sir Thomas?

MORE [*looking at* FOREMAN]: To what purpose? I am a dead man. [*To* CROMWELL.] You have your desire of me. What you have hunted me for is not my actions, but the thoughts of my heart. It is a long road you have opened. For first men will disclaim their hearts and presently they will have no hearts. God help the people whose Statesmen walk your road.

NORFOLK: Then the witness may withdraw.

RICH *crosses stage, watched by* MORE.

MORE: I *have* one question to ask the witness.

RICH *stops.*

That's a chain of office you are wearing.

Reluctantly RICH *faces him.*

May I see it?

NORFOLK *motions him to approach.* MORE *examines the medallion.*

The red dragon. [*To* CROMWELL.] What's this?

CROMWELL: Sir Richard is appointed Attorney-General for Wales.

MORE [*looking into* RICH's *face: with pain and amusement*]: For Wales? Why

Richard, it profits a man nothing to give his soul for the whole world. . . . But for Wales—!

Exit RICH, *stiff faced, but infrangibly dignified.*
CROMWELL: Now I must ask the Court's indulgence! I have a message for the prisoner from the King: [*urgent*] Sir Thomas, I am empowered to tell you that even now—
MORE: No no. It cannot be.
CROMWELL: The case rests!

NORFOLK *is staring at* MORE.

My lord!
NORFOLK: The Jury will retire and consider the evidence.
CROMWELL: Considering the evidence it shouldn't be necessary for them to retire. [*Standing over* FOREMAN.] Is it necessary?

FOREMAN *shakes his head.*

NORFOLK: Then is the prisoner guilty or not guilty?
FOREMAN: Guilty, my lord!
NORFOLK [*leaping to his feet; all rise save* MORE]: Prisoner at the bar, you have been found guilty of High Treason. The sentence of the Court—
MORE: My lord!

NORFOLK *breaks off.* MORE *has a sly smile. From this point to end of play his manner is of one who has fulfilled all his obligations and will now consult no interests but his own.*

My lord, when *I* was practising the law, the manner was to ask the prisoner *before* pronouncing sentence, if he had anything to say.
NORFOLK [*flummoxed*]: Have you anything to say?
MORE: Yes. [*He rises: all others sit.*] To avoid this I have taken every path my winding wits would find. Now that the court has determined to condemn me, God knoweth how, I will discharge my mind . . . concerning my indictment and the King's title. The indictment is grounded in an Act of Parliament which is directly repugnant to the Law of God. The King in Parliament cannot bestow the Supremacy of the Church because it is a Spiritual Supremacy! And more to this the immunity of the Church is promised both in Magna Carta and the King's own Coronation Oath!
CROMWELL: Now we plainly see that you *are* malicious!
MORE: Not so, Mr Secretary! [*He pauses, and launches, very quietly, ruminatively, into his final stock-taking.*] I am the King's true subject, and pray for him and all the realm . . . I do none harm, I say none harm, I think none harm. And if this be not enough to keep a man alive, in good faith I long not to live . . . I have, since I came into prison, been several times in such a case that I thought to die within the hour, and I thank Our Lord I was never sorry for it, but rather sorry when it passed. And therefore, my poor body is at the King's pleasure. Would God my death might do him some good. . . . [*With a great flash of scorn and anger.*] Nevertheless, it is not for the

Supremacy that you have sought my blood—but because I would not bend to the marriage!

Immediately scene change commences, while NORFOLK *reads the sentence.*

NORFOLK: Prisoner at the bar, you have been found guilty on the charge of High Treason. The sentence of the Court is that you shall be taken from this Court to the Tower, thence to the place of execution, and there your head shall be stricken from your body, and may God have mercy on your soul!

The scene change is as follows:
(I) *The trappings of justice are flown upwards.*
(II) *The lights are dimmed save for three areas: spots, left and right front, and the arch at the head of the stairs which begins to show blue sky.*
(III) *Through this arch—where the axe and the block are silhouetted against a light of steadily increasing brilliance—comes the murmuration of a large crowd, formalised almost into a chant and mounting, so that* NORFOLK *has to shout the end of his speech.*
In addition to the noise of the crowd and the flying machinery there is stage activity: FOREMAN *doffs cap, and as* COMMON MAN *removes the prisoner's chair and then goes to the spot, left.*
CRANMER *also goes to spot, left.*
MORE *goes to spot, right.*
WOMAN *enters, up right, and goes to spot, left.*
NORFOLK *remains where he is.*
*When these movements are complete—they are made naturally, technically—*CROMWELL *goes and stands in the light streaming down the stairs. He beckons the* COMMON MAN *who leaves spot, left, and joins him.* CROMWELL *points to the head of the stairs.* COMMON MAN *shakes his head and indicates in mime that he has no costume. He drags basket into the light and again indicates that there is no costume in it.* CROMWELL *takes a small black mask from his sleeve and offers it to him. The* COMMON MAN *puts it on, thus, in his black tights, becoming the traditional headsman. He ascends the stairs, straddles his legs and picks up the axe, silhouetted against the bright sky. At once the crowd falls silent.*
Exit CROMWELL, *dragging basket.*
NORFOLK *joins* MORE *in spot, right.*

NORFOLK: I can come no further, Thomas. [*Proffering goblet.*] Here, drink this.
MORE: My master had easel and gall, not wine, given him to drink. Let me be going.
MARGARET: Father! [*She runs to him in the spot from right and flings herself upon him.*] Father! Father, Father, Father, Father!
MORE: Have patience, Margaret, and trouble not thyself. Death comes for us all; even at our birth [*he holds her head and looks down at it for a moment in recollection*]—even at our birth, death does but stand aside a little. It is the law of nature, and the will of God. [*He disengages from her. Dispassionately.*] You have long known the secrets of my heart.
WOMAN: Sir Thomas! [*He stops.*] Remember me, Sir Thomas? When you were Chancellor, you gave a false judgement against me. Remember that now.
MORE: Woman, you see how I am occupied. [*With sudden decision goes to her in*

spot, left. Crisply.] I remember your matter well, and if I had to give sentence now I assure you I should not alter it. You have no injury; so go your ways; and content yourself; and trouble me not! [*He walks swiftly to the stairs. Then stops, realising that* CRANMER, *carrying his Bible, has followed him. Quite kindly.*] I beseech Your Grace, go back.

Offended, CRANMER *does so. The lighting is now complete, i.e., darkness save for three areas of light, the one at head of stairs now dazzlingly brilliant. When* MORE *gets to head of stairs by the* HEADSMAN *there is a single shout from the crowd. He turns to* HEADSMAN.

Friend, be not afraid of your office. You send me to God.
CRANMER [*envious rather than waspish*]: You're very sure of that, Sir Thomas.
MORE [*takes off his hat, revealing the grey disordered hair*]: He will not refuse one who is so blithe to go to him. [*Kneeling.*]

Immediately, harsh roar of kettledrums and total blackout at head of stairs. While the drums roar, WOMAN *backs into* CRANMER *and exit together,* NORFOLK *assists* MARGARET *from the stage, which is now 'occupied' only by the two spots left and right front. The drums cease.*

HEADSMAN [*from the darkness:*] Behold–the head–of a traitor!

Enter into spots left and right, CROMWELL *and* CHAPUYS. *They stop on seeing one another, arrested in postures of frozen hostility while the light spreads plainly over the stage, which is empty save for themselves.*
    Then simultaneously they stalk forward, crossing mid-stage with heads high and averted. But as they approach their exits they pause, hesitate, and slowly turn. Thoughtfully they stroll back towards one another. CROMWELL *raises his head and essays a smile.* CHAPUYS *responds. They link arms and approach the stairs. As they go we hear that they are chuckling. There is nothing sinister or malignant in the sound; rather it is the self-mocking, self-indulgent, rather rueful laughter of men who know what the world is and how to be comfortable in it. As they go,* THE CURTAIN FALLS.

ALTERNATIVE ENDING

In the London production of this play at the Globe Theatre the play ended as follows:

Instead of the CROMWELL *and* CHAPUYS *entrance after the* HEADSMAN's *line* 'Behold—the head—of a traitor!', *the* COMMON MAN *came to the centre stage, having taken off his mask as the executioner, and said:*

'I'm breathing. . . . Are you breathing too? . . . It's nice isn't it? It isn't difficult to keep alive friends . . . just don't make trouble—or if you must make trouble, make the sort of trouble that's expected. Well, I don't need to tell you that. Good night. If we should bump into one another, recognise me.' [*Exits.*]

CURTAIN

WHO'S AFRAID OF VIRGINIA WOOLF?

EDWARD ALBEE

WHO'S AFRAID OF VIRGINIA WOOLF?

First published in the U.S.A. 1962
Published in Great Britain by Jonathan Cape Limited 1964

WHO'S AFRAID OF VIRGINIA WOOLF?

(1962)

For Richard Barr and
Clinton Wilder

CHARACTERS

MARTHA (*a large, boisterous Woman, 52, looking somewhat younger. Ample, but not fleshy*)
GEORGE (*her Husband, 46. Thin; hair going grey*)
HONEY (*26, a petite blonde Girl, rather plain*)
NICK (*30, her Husband. Bland, well-put-together, good-looking*)

The scene is the living-room of a house on the campus of a small New England college.

Who's Afraid of Virginia Woolf? was first performed at the Billy Rose Theater, New York City, on 13 October 1962 with the following cast:

MARTHA	*Uta Hagen*
GEORGE	*Arthur Hill*
NICK	*George Grizzard*
HONEY	*Melinda Dillon*

Directed by ALAN SCHNEIDER

ACT ONE

FUN AND GAMES

Set in darkness. Crash against front door. MARTHA'*s laughter heard. Front door opens, lights are switched on.* MARTHA *enters followed by* GEORGE.

MARTHA: Je*sus* . . .
GEORGE: . . . Shhhhhhh. . . .
MARTHA: . . . H. Christ . . .
GEORGE: For God's sake, Martha, it's two o'clock in the . . .
MARTHA: Oh, George!
GEORGE: Well, I'm *sorry*, but . . .
MARTHA: What a cluck! What a cluck you are.
GEORGE: It's late, you know? Late.
MARTHA [*looks about the room. Imitates Bette Davis*]: What a dump. Hey, what's that from? 'What a dump!'
GEORGE: How would I know what . . .
MARTHA: Aw, come on! What's it from? *You* know . . .
GEORGE: . . . Martha . . .
MARTHA: WHAT'S IT FROM, FOR CHRIST'S SAKE?
GEORGE [*wearily*]: What's what from?
MARTHA: I just told you; I just did it. 'What a dump!' Hunh? What's that from?
GEORGE: I haven't the faintest idea what . . .
MARTHA: Dumbbell! It's from some goddamn Bette Davis picture . . . some goddamn Warner Brothers epic. . . .
GEORGE: *I* can't remember all the pictures that . . .
MARTHA: Nobody's asking you to remember every single goddamn Warner Brothers epic . . . just one! One single little epic! Bette Davis gets peritonitis in the end . . . she's got this big black fright wig she wears all through the picture and she gets peritonitis, and she's married to Joseph Cotten or something. . . .
GEORGE: . . . Some*body* . . .
MARTHA: . . . some*body* . . . and she wants to go to Chicago all the time, 'cause she's in love with that actor with the scar. . . . But she gets sick, and she sits down in front of her dressing-table. . . .
GEORGE: What actor? What scar?
MARTHA: *I* can't remember his name, for God's sake. What's the name of the *picture*? I want to know what the name of the *picture* is. She sits down in front of her dressing-table . . . and she's got this peritonitis . . . and she tries to put her lipstick on, but she can't . . . and she gets it all over her face . . . but she decides to go to Chicago anyway, and . . .
GEORGE: *Chicago!* It's called *Chicago*.
MARTHA: Hunh? What . . . what is?
GEORGE: The picture . . . it's called *Chicago*. . . .
MARTHA: Good grief! Don't you know *anything*? *Chicago* was a thirties musical,

starring little Miss Alice *Faye*. Don't you know *anything*?

GEORGE: Well, that was probably before my *time*, but . . .

MARTHA: Can it! Just cut that out! This picture . . . Bette Davis comes home from a hard day at the grocery store. . . .

GEORGE: She works in a grocery store?

MARTHA: She's a housewife; she buys things . . . and she comes home with the groceries, and she walks into the modest living-room of the modest cottage modest Joseph Cotten has set her up in. . . .

GEORGE: Are they married?

MARTHA [*impatiently*]: Yes. They're married. To each other. Cluck! And she comes in, and she looks around, and she puts her groceries down, and she says, 'What a dump!'

GEORGE [*pause*]: Oh.

MARTHA [*pause*]: She's discontent.

GEORGE [*pause*]: Oh.

MARTHA [*pause*]: Well, what's the name of the picture?

GEORGE: I really don't know, Martha. . . .

MARTHA: Well, think!

GEORGE: I'm tired, dear . . . it's late . . . and besides . . .

MARTHA: I don't know what you're so tired about . . . you haven't *done* anything all day; you didn't have any classes, or anything. . . .

GEORGE: Well, I'm tired. . . . If your father didn't set up these goddamn Saturday night orgies all the time. . . .

MARTHA: Well, that's too bad about you, George. . . .

GEORGE [*grumbling*]: Well, that's how it is, anyway.

MARTHA: You didn't *do* anything; you never *do* anything; you never *mix*. You just sit around and *talk*.

GEORGE: What do you want me to do? Do you want me to act like you? Do you want me to go around all night *braying* at everybody, the way you do?

MARTHA [*braying*]: I DON'T BRAY!

GEORGE [*softly*]: All right . . . you don't bray.

MARTHA [*hurt*]: I do not *bray*.

GEORGE: All right. I said you didn't bray.

MARTHA [*pouting*]: Make me a drink.

GEORGE: What?

MARTHA [*still softly*]: I said, make me a drink.

GEORGE [*moving to the portable bar*]: Well, I don't suppose a nightcap'd kill either one of us. . . .

MARTHA: A nightcap! Are you kidding? We've got guests.

GEORGE [*disbelieving*]: We've got what?

MARTHA: Guests. GUESTS.

GEORGE: GUESTS!

MARTHA: Yes . . . guests . . . people. . . . We've got guests coming over.

GEORGE: When?

MARTHA: NOW!

GEORGE: Good Lord, Martha . . . do you know what time it . . . *Who*'s coming over?

MARTHA: What's-their-name.

GEORGE: Who?

MARTHA: WHAT'S-THEIR-NAME!

GEORGE: Who what's-their-name?

MARTHA: I don't know what their name is, George. . . . You met them tonight . . . they're new . . . he's in the math department, or something. . . .

GEORGE: Who . . . who are these people?

MARTHA: You met them tonight, George.

GEORGE: I don't remember meeting anyone tonight. . . .

MARTHA: Well you did. . . . Will you give me my drink, please. . . . He's in the math department . . . about thirty, blond, and . . .

GEORGE: . . . and good-looking. . . .

MARTHA: Yes . . . and good-looking. . . .

GEORGE: It figures.

MARTHA: . . . and his wife's a mousey little type, without any hips, or anything.

GEORGE [*vaguely*]: Oh.

MARTHA: You remember them now?

GEORGE: Yes, I guess so, Martha. . . . But why in God's name are they coming over here now?

MARTHA [*in a so-there voice*]: Because Daddy said we should be nice to them, that's why.

GEORGE [*defeated*]: Oh, Lord.

MARTHA: May I have my drink, please? Daddy said we should be nice to them. Thank you.

GEORGE: But why now? It's after two o'clock in the morning, and . . .

MARTHA: Because Daddy said we should be nice to them!

GEORGE: Yes. But I'm sure your father didn't mean we were supposed to stay up all *night* with these people. I mean, we could have them over some Sunday or something. . . .

MARTHA: Well, never mind. . . . Besides, it *is* Sunday. Very early Sunday.

GEORGE: I mean . . . it's ridiculous. . . .

MARTHA: Well, it's *done!*

GEORGE [*resigned and exasperated*]: All right. Well . . . where are they? If we've got guests, where are they?

MARTHA: They'll be here soon.

GEORGE: What did they do . . . go home and get some sleep first, or something?

MARTHA: They'll *be* here!

GEORGE: I wish you'd *tell* me about something sometime. . . . I wish you'd stop *springing* things on me all the time.

MARTHA: I don't *spring* things on you all the time.

GEORGE: Yes, you do . . . you really do . . . you're always *springing* things on me.

MARTHA [*friendly-patronizing*]: Oh, George!

GEORGE: Always.

MARTHA: Poor Georgie-Porgie, put-upon pie! [*As he sulks.*] Awwwwww . . . what are you doing? Are you sulking? Hunh? Let me see . . . are you sulking? Is that what you're doing?

GEORGE [*very quietly*]: Never mind, Martha. . . .

MARTHA: AWWWWWWWWWW!

GEORGE: Just don't bother yourself. . . .

MARTHA: AWWWWWWWWWW! [*No reaction.*] Hey! [*No reaction.*] HEY!

GEORGE *looks at her, put-upon.*

Hey. [*She sings.*]

Who's afraid of Virginia Woolf,
Virginia Woolf,
Virginia Woolf . . .

Ha, ha, ha, HA! [*No reaction.*] What's the matter . . . didn't you think that was
funny? Hunh? [*Defiantly.*] I thought it was a scream . . . a real scream. You
didn't like it, hunh?

GEORGE: It was all right, Martha. . . .

MARTHA: You laughed your head off when you heard it at the party.

GEORGE: I smiled. I didn't laugh my head off . . . I smiled, you know? . . . it was
all right.

MARTHA [*gazing into her drink*]: You laughed your goddamn head off.

GEORGE: It was all right. . . .

MARTHA [*ugly*]: It was a scream!

GEORGE [*patiently*]: It was very funny; yes.

MARTHA [*after a moment's consideration*]: You make me puke!

GEORGE: What?

MARTHA: Uh . . . you make me puke!

GEORGE [*thinks about it . . . then . . .*]: That wasn't a very nice thing to say,
Martha.

MARTHA: That wasn't *what*?

GEORGE: . . . a very nice thing to say.

MARTHA: I like your anger. I think that's what I like about you most . . . your
anger. You're such a . . . such a simp! You don't even have the . . . the
what? . . .

GEORGE: . . . guts? . . .

MARTHA: PHRASEMAKER! [*Pause . . . then they both laugh.*] Hey, put some more
ice in my drink, will you? You never put any ice in my drink. Why is that,
hunh?

GEORGE [*takes her drink*]: I always put ice in your drink. You eat it, that's all. It's
that habit you have . . . chewing your ice cubes . . . like a cocker spaniel.
You'll crack your big teeth.

MARTHA: THEY'RE MY BIG TEETH!

GEORGE: Some of them . . . some of them.

MARTHA: I've got more teeth than you've got.

GEORGE: Two more.

MARTHA: Well, two more's a lot more.

GEORGE: I suppose it is. I suppose it's pretty remarkable . . . considering how
old you are.

MARTHA: YOU CUT THAT OUT! [*Pause.*] You're not so young yourself.

GEORGE [*with boyish pleasure . . . a chant*]: I'm six years younger than you
are. . . . I always have been and I always will be.

MARTHA [*glumly*]: Well . . . you're going bald.

GEORGE: So are you. [*Pause . . . they both laugh.*] Hello, honey.

MARTHA: Hello. C'mon over here and give your Mommy a big sloppy kiss.

GEORGE: . . . oh, now . . .

MARTHA: I WANT A BIG SLOPPY KISS!

GEORGE [*preoccupied*]: I don't *want* to kiss you, Martha. Where *are* these people?
Where are these *people* you invited over?

MARTHA: They stayed on to talk to Daddy. . . . They'll be here. . . . *Why* don't
you want to kiss me?

GEORGE [*too matter-of-fact*]: Well, dear, if I kissed you I'd get all excited . . . I'd get beside myself, and I'd take you, by force, right here on the living-room rug, and then our little guests would walk in, and . . . well, just think what your father would say about *that*.

MARTHA: You pig!

GEORGE [*haughtily*]: Oink! Oink!

MARTHA: Ha, ha, ha, HA! Make me another drink . . . lover.

GEORGE [*taking her glass*]: My God, you can swill it down, can't you?

MARTHA [*imitating a child*]: I'm firsty.

GEORGE: Jesus!

MARTHA [*swinging around*]: Look, sweetheart, I can drink you under any goddamn table you want . . . so don't worry about me!

GEORGE: Martha, I gave you the prize years ago. . . . There isn't an abomination award going that you . . .

MARTHA: I swear . . . if you existed I'd divorce you. . . .

GEORGE: Well, just stay on your feet, that's all. . . . These people are your guests, you know, and . . .

MARTHA: I can't even see you . . . I haven't been able to see you for years. . . .

GEORGE: . . . if you pass out, or throw up, or something . . .

MARTHA: . . . I mean, you're a blank, a cipher. . . .

GEORGE: . . . and try to keep your clothes on, too. There aren't many more sickening sights than you with a couple of drinks in you and your skirt up over your head, you know. . . .

MARTHA: . . . a zero. . . .

GEORGE: . . . your *heads*, I should say. . . .

The front door-bell chimes.

MARTHA: Party! Party!

GEORGE [*murderously*]: I'm really looking forward to this, Martha. . . .

MARTHA [*same*]: Go answer the door.

GEORGE [*not moving*]: You answer it.

MARTHA: Get to that door, you.

He does not move.

I'll fix you, you . . .

GEORGE [*fake-spits*]: . . . to you. . . .

Door chime again.

MARTHA [*shouting . . . to the door*]: C'MON IN! [*To* GEORGE, *between her teeth.*] I said, get over there!

GEORGE [*moves a little towards the door, smiling slightly*]: All right, love . . . whatever love wants. [*Stops.*] Just don't start on the bit, that's all.

MARTHA: The bit? The bit? What kind of language is that? What are you talking about?

GEORGE: The bit. Just don't start in on the bit.

MARTHA: You imitating one of your students, for God's sake? What are you trying to do? WHAT BIT?

GEORGE: Just don't start in on the bit about the kid, that's all.

MARTHA: What do you take me for?

GEORGE: Much too much.

MARTHA [*really angered*]: Yeah? Well, I'll start in on the kid if I want to.

GEORGE: Just leave the kid out of this.

MARTHA [*threatening*]: He's mine as much as he is yours. I'll talk about him if I want to.

GEORGE: I'd advise against it, Martha.

MARTHA: Well, good for you. [*Knock.*] C'mon in. Get over there and open the door!

GEORGE: You've been advised.

MARTHA: Yeah . . . sure. Get over there!

GEORGE [*moving towards the door*]: All right, love . . . whatever love wants. Isn't it nice the way some people have manners, though, even in this day and age? Isn't it nice that some people won't just come breaking into other people's houses even if they *do* hear some sub-human monster yowling at 'em from inside . . .?

MARTHA: SCREW YOU!

Simultaneously with MARTHA's *last remark,* GEORGE *flings open the front door.* HONEY *and* NICK *are framed in the entrance. There is a brief silence, then . . .*

GEORGE [*ostensibly a pleased recognition of* HONEY *and* NICK, *but really satisfaction at having* MARTHA's *explosion overheard*]: Ahhhhhhhhh!

MARTHA [*a little too loud . . . to cover*]: HI! Hi, there . . . c'mon in!

HONEY *and* NICK [*ad lib*]: Hello, here we are . . . hi . . . [*etc.*]

GEORGE [*very matter-of-factly*]: You must be our little guests.

MARTHA: Ha, ha, ha, HA! Just ignore old sour-puss over there. C'mon in, kids . . . give your coats and stuff to sour-puss.

NICK [*without expression*]: Well, now, perhaps we shouldn't have come. . . .

HONEY: Yes . . . it *is* late, and . . .

MARTHA: Late! Are you kidding? Throw your stuff down anywhere and c'mon in.

GEORGE [*vaguely . . . walking away*]: Anywhere . . . furniture, floor . . . doesn't make any difference around this place.

NICK [*to* HONEY]: I told you we shouldn't have come.

MARTHA [*stentorian*]: I said c'mon in! Now c'mon!

HONEY [*giggling a little as she and* NICK *advance*]: Oh, dear.

GEORGE [*imitating* HONEY's *giggle*]: Hee, hee, hee, hee.

MARTHA [*swinging on* GEORGE]: Look, muckmouth . . . you cut that out!

GEORGE [*innocence and hurt*]: Martha! [*To* HONEY *and* NICK.] Martha's a devil with language; she really is.

MARTHA: Hey, *kids* . . . sit down.

HONEY [*as she sits*]: Oh, isn't this lovely!

NICK [*perfunctorily*]: Yes indeed . . . very handsome.

MARTHA: Well, thanks.

NICK [*indicating the abstract painting*]: Who . . . who did the . . .?

MARTHA: That? Oh, that's by . . .

GEORGE: . . . some Greek with a moustache Martha attacked one night in . . .

HONEY [*to save the situation*]: Oh, ho, ho, ho, HO.

NICK: It's got a . . . a . . .
GEORGE: A quiet intensity?
NICK: Well, no . . . a . . .
GEORGE: Oh. [*Pause.*] Well, then, a certain noisy relaxed quality, maybe?
NICK [*knows what* GEORGE *is doing, but stays grimly, coolly polite*]: No. What I
meant was . . .
GEORGE: How about . . . uh . . . a quietly noisy relaxed intensity.
HONEY: Dear! You're being joshed.
NICK [*cold*]: I'm aware of that.

A brief, awkward silence.

GEORGE [*truly*]: I *am* sorry.

NICK *nods condescending forgiveness.*

GEORGE: What it is, actually, is it's a pictorial representation of the order of
Martha's mind.
MARTHA: Ha, ha, ha, HA! Make the kids a drink, George. What do you want,
kids? What do you want to drink, hunh?
NICK: Honey? What would you like?
HONEY: I don't know, dear . . . A little brandy, maybe. 'Never mix–never
worry.' [*She giggles.*]
GEORGE: Brandy? Just brandy? Simple; simple. [*Moves to the portable bar.*]
What about you . . . uh . . .
NICK: Bourbon on the rocks, if you don't mind.
GEORGE [*as he makes the drinks*]: Mind? No, I don't mind. I don't think I mind.
Martha? Rubbing alcohol for you?
MARTHA: Sure. 'Never mix–never worry.'
GEORGE: Martha's tastes in liquor have come down . . . simplified over the
years . . . crystallized. Back when I was courting Martha–well, I don't
know if that's exactly the right word for it–but back when I was courting
Martha . . .
MARTHA [*cheerfully*]: Screw, sweetie!
GEORGE [*returning with* HONEY'*s and* NICK'*s drinks*]: At any rate, back when I was
courting Martha, she'd order the damnedest things! You wouldn't believe it!
We'd go into a bar . . . you know, a *bar* . . . a whisky, beer, and bourbon
bar . . . and what she'd do would be, she'd screw up her face, think real hard,
and come up with . . . brandy Alexanders, creme de cacao frappes, gimlets,
flaming punch-bowls . . . seven-layer liqueur things.
MARTHA: They were good . . . I liked them.
GEORGE: Real lady-like little drinkies.
MARTHA: Hey, where's my rubbing alcohol?
GEORGE [*returning to the portable bar*]: But the years have brought to Martha a
sense of essentials . . . the knowledge that cream is for coffee, lime juice for
pies . . . and alcohol [*Brings* MARTHA *her drink.*] pure and simple . . . here you
are, angel . . . for the pure and simple. [*Raises his glass.*] For the mind's blind
eye, the heart's ease, and the liver's craw. Down the hatch, all.
MARTHA [*to them all*]: Cheers, dears. [*They all drink.*] You have a poetic nature,
George . . . a Dylan Thomas-y quality that gets me right where I live.
GEORGE: Vulgar girl! With guests here!

MARTHA: Ha, ha, ha, HA! [*To* HONEY *and* NICK.] Hey; hey! [*Sings, conducts with her drink in her hand.* HONEY *joins in towards the end.*]

> Who's afraid of Virginia Woolf,
> Virginia Woolf,
> Virginia Woolf,
> Who's afraid of Virginia Woolf . . .

MARTHA *and* HONEY *laugh;* NICK *smiles.*

HONEY: Oh, wasn't that funny? That was so funny. . . .
NICK [*snapping to*]: Yes . . . yes, it was.
MARTHA: I thought I'd bust a gut; I really did. . . . I really thought I'd bust a gut laughing. George didn't like it. . . . George didn't think it was funny at all.
GEORGE: Lord, Martha, do we have to go through this again?
MARTHA: I'm trying to shame you into a sense of humour, angel, that's all.
GEORGE [*over-patiently, to* HONEY *and* NICK]: Martha didn't think I laughed loud enough. Martha thinks that unless . . . as she demurely puts it . . . that unless you 'bust a gut' you aren't amused. You know? Unless you carry on like a hyena you aren't having any fun.
HONEY: Well, I certainly had fun . . . it was a *wonderful* party.
NICK [*attempting enthusiasm*]: Yes . . . it certainly was.
HONEY [*to* MARTHA]: And your father! Oh! He is so marvellous!
NICK [*as above*]: Yes . . . yes, he is.
HONEY: Oh, I tell you.
MARTHA [*genuinely proud*]: He's quite a guy, isn't he? Quite a guy.
GEORGE [*at* NICK]: And you'd better believe it!
HONEY [*admonishing* GEORGE]: Ohhhhhhhhh! He's a wonderful man.
GEORGE: I'm not trying to tear him down. He's a God, we all know that.
MARTHA: You lay off my father!
GEORGE: Yes, love. [*To* NICK.] All I mean is . . . when you've had as many of these faculty parties as I have . . .
NICK [*killing the attempted rapport*]: I rather appreciated it. I mean, aside from enjoying it, I appreciated it. You know, when you're new at a place. . . .

GEORGE *eyes him suspiciously.*

Meeting everyone, getting introduced around . . . getting to know some of the men. . . . When I was teaching in Kansas . . .
HONEY: You won't believe it, but we had to make our way all by *ourselves* . . . isn't that right, dear?
NICK: Yes, it is. . . . We . . .
HONEY: . . . We had to make our own way. . . . I had to go up to wives . . . in the library, or at the supermarket . . . and say, 'Hello, I'm new here . . . you must be Mrs So-and-so, Doctor So-and-so's wife.' It really wasn't very nice at all.
MARTHA: Well, *Daddy* knows how to run things.
NICK [*not enough enthusiasm*]: He's a remarkable man.
MARTHA: You bet your sweet life.
GEORGE [*to* NICK . . . *a confidence, but not whispered*]: Let me tell you a secret, baby. There are easier things in the world, if you happen to be teaching at a university, there are easier things than being married to the daughter of the

president of that university. There are easier things in this world.

MARTHA [*loud . . . to no one in particular*]: It *should* be an extraordinary opportunity . . . for *some* men it would be the chance of a lifetime!

GEORGE [*to* NICK . . . *a solemn wink*]: There are, believe me, easier things in this world.

NICK: Well, I can understand how it might make for some . . . awkwardness, perhaps . . . conceivably, but . . .

MARTHA: *Some* men would give their right arm for the chance!

GEORGE [*quietly*]: Alas, Martha, in reality it works out that the sacrifice is usually of a somewhat more private portion of the anatomy.

MARTHA [*a snarl of dismissal and contempt*]: NYYYAAAHHHH!

HONEY [*rising quickly*]: I wonder if you could show me where the . . . [*Her voice trails off.*]

GEORGE [*to* MARTHA, *indicating* HONEY]: Martha . . .

NICK [*to* HONEY]: Are you all right?

HONEY: Of course, dear. I want to . . . put some powder on my nose.

GEORGE [*as* MARTHA *is not getting up*]: Martha, won't you show her where we keep the . . . euphemism?

MARTHA: Huh? What? Oh! Sure! [*Rises.*] I'm sorry, c'mon. I want to show you the house.

HONEY: I think I'd like to . . .

MARTHA: . . . wash up? Sure . . . c'mon with me. [*Takes* HONEY *by the arm. To the men.*] You two do some men talk for a while.

HONEY [*to* NICK]: We'll be back, dear.

MARTHA [*to* GEORGE]: Honestly, George, you burn me up!

GEORGE [*happily*]: All right.

MARTHA: You really do, George.

GEORGE: O.K. Martha . . . O.K. Just . . . trot along.

MARTHA: You really do.

GEORGE: Just don't shoot your mouth off . . . about . . . you-know-what.

MARTHA [*surprisingly vehement*]: I'll talk about any goddamn thing I want to, George!

GEORGE: O.K. O.K. Vanish.

MARTHA: Any goddamn thing I want to! [*Practically dragging* HONEY *out with her.*] C'mon. . . .

GEORGE: Vanish. [*The women have gone.*] So? What'll it be?

NICK: Oh, I don't know . . . I'll stick to bourbon, I guess.

GEORGE [*takes* NICK's *glass, goes to portable bar*]: That what you were drinking over at Parnassus?

NICK: Over at . . . ?

GEORGE: Parnassus.

NICK: I don't understand. . . .

GEORGE: Skip it. [*Hands him his drink.*] One bourbon.

NICK: Thanks.

GEORGE: It's just a private joke between li'l ol' Martha and me. [*They sit.*] So? [*Pause.*] So . . . you're in the math department, eh?

NICK: No . . . uh, no.

GEORGE: Martha said you were. I think that's what she said. [*Not too friendly.*] What made you decide to be a teacher?

NICK: Oh . . . well, the same things that . . . uh . . . motivated you, I imagine.

GEORGE: What were they?

NICK [*formal*]: Pardon?

GEORGE: I said, what were they? What were the things that motivated me?

NICK [*laughing uneasily*]: Well . . . I'm sure I don't know.

GEORGE: You just finished saying that the things that motivated you were the same things that motivated me.

NICK [*with a little pique*]: I said I *imagined* they were.

GEORGE [*off hand*]: Did you? [*Pause.*] Well. . . . [*Pause.*] You like it here?

NICK [*looking about the room*]: Yes . . . it's . . . it's fine.

GEORGE: I mean the University.

NICK: Oh. . . . I thought you meant . . .

GEORGE: Yes . . . I can see you did. [*Pause.*] I meant the University.

NICK: Well, I . . . I like it . . . fine.

As GEORGE *just stares at him.*

Just fine. [*Same.*] You . . . you've been here quite a long time, haven't you?

GEORGE [*absently, as if he had not heard*]: What? Oh . . . yes. Ever since I married . . . uh, What's-her-name . . . uh, Martha. Even before that. [*Pause.*] For ever. [*To himself.*] Dashed hopes, and good intentions. Good, better, best, bested. [*Back to* NICK.] How do you like that for a declension, young man? Eh?

NICK: Sir, I'm sorry if we . . .

GEORGE [*with an edge in his voice*]: You didn't answer my question.

NICK: Sir?

GEORGE: Don't you condescend to me! [*Toying with him.*] I asked you how you liked that for a declension: Good; better, best, bested. Hm? Well?

NICK [*with some distaste*]: I really don't know what to say.

GEORGE [*feigned incredulousness*]: You really don't know what to *say*?

NICK [*snapping it out*]: All right . . . what so you want me to say? Do you want me to say it's funny, so you can contradict me and say it's sad? Or do you want me to say it's sad so you can turn around and say no, it's funny. You can play that damn little game any way you want to, you know!

GEORGE [*feigned awe*]: Very good! Very good!

NICK [*even angrier than before*]: And when my wife comes back, I think we'll just . . .

GEORGE [*sincere*]: Now, now . . . calm down, my boy. Just . . . calm . . . down. [*Pause.*] All right? [*Pause.*] You want another drink? Here, give me your glass.

NICK: I still have one. I *do* think that when my wife comes downstairs . . .

GEORGE: Here . . . I'll freshen it. Give me your glass. [*Takes it.*]

NICK: What I mean is . . . you two . . . you and your wife . . . seem to be having *some* sort of a . . .

GEORGE: Martha and I are having . . . nothing. Martha and I are merely . . . exercising . . . that's all . . . we're merely walking what's left of our wits. Don't pay any attention to it.

NICK [*undecided*]: Still . . .

GEORGE [*an abrupt change of pace*]: Well, now . . . let's sit down and talk, hunh?

NICK [*cool again*]: It's just that I don't like to . . . become involved . . . [*An afterthought.*] uh . . . in other people's affairs.

GEORGE [*comforting a child*]: Well, you'll get over that . . . small college and all. Musical beds is the faculty sport around here.

NICK: Sir?

GEORGE: I said, musical beds is the faculty . . . Never mind. I wish you wouldn't go 'Sir' like that . . . not with the question-mark at the end of it. You know? Sir? I know it's meant to be a sign of respect for your [*Winces.*] elders . . . but . . . uh . . . the way you do it. . . . Uh . . . Sir? . . . Madam?

NICK [*with a small, noncommittal smile*]: No disrespect intended.

GEORGE: How old *are* you?

NICK: Twenty-eight.

GEORGE: I'm forty-something. [*Waits for reaction . . . gets none.*] Aren't you surprised? I mean . . . don't I look older? Doesn't this . . . *grey* quality suggest the fifties? Don't I sort of fade into backgrounds . . . get lost in the cigarette smoke? Hunh?

NICK [*looking around for an ashtray*]: I think you look . . . fine.

GEORGE: I've always been lean . . . I haven't put on five pounds since I was your age. I don't have a paunch, either. . . . What I've got . . . I've got this little distension just below the belt . . . but it's hard. . . . It's not soft flesh. I use the handball courts. How much do *you* weigh?

NICK: I . . .

GEORGE: Hundred and fifty-five, sixty . . . something like that? Do you play handball?

NICK: Well, yes . . . no . . . I mean, not very well.

GEORGE: Well, then . . . we shall play some time. Martha is a hundred and eight . . . years *old*. She weighs somewhat more than that. How old is *your* wife?

NICK [*a little bewildered*]: She's twenty-six.

GEORGE: Martha is a remarkable woman. I would imagine she weighs around a hundred and ten.

NICK: Your . . . wife . . . weighs . . .?

GEORGE: No, no, my boy. Yours! *Your* wife. My wife is Martha.

NICK: Yes . . . I know.

GEORGE: If you were married to Martha you would know what it means. [*Pause.*] But then, if I were married to your wife I would know what that means, too . . . wouldn't I?

NICK [*after a pause*]: Yes.

GEORGE: Martha says you're in the Math Department, or something.

NICK [*as if for the hundredth time*]: No . . . I'm not.

GEORGE: Martha is seldom mistaken . . . maybe you *should* be in the Math Department, or something.

NICK: I'm a biologist. I'm in the Biology Department.

GEORGE [*after a pause*]: Oh. [*Then, as if remembering something.*] OH!

NICK: Sir?

GEORGE: You're the one! You're the one's going to make all that trouble . . . making everyone the same, rearranging the chromozones, or whatever it is. Isn't that right?

NICK [*with that small smile*]: Not exactly: chromo*somes.*

GEORGE: I'm very mistrustful. Do you believe . . . [*Shifting in his chair.*] . . . do you believe that people learn nothing from history? Not that there is nothing to learn, mind you, but that people learn nothing? I am in the History Department.

NICK: Well . . .

GEORGE: I am a Doctor. A.B. . . . M.A. . . . PH.D. . . . ABMAPHID! Abmaphid has been variously described as a wasting disease of the frontal lobes, and as a wonder drug. It is actually both. I'm really very mistrustful. Biology, hunh?

NICK *does not answer . . . nods . . . looks.*

I read somewhere that science fiction is really not fiction at all . . . that you people are rearranging my genes, so that everyone will be like everyone else. Now, I won't have that! It would be a . . . shame. I mean . . . look at me! Is it really such a good idea . . . if everyone was forty-something and looked fifty-five? You didn't answer my question about history.

NICK: This genetic business you're talking about . . .

GEORGE: Oh, that. [*Dismisses it with a wave of his hand.*] That's very upsetting . . . very . . . disappointing. But history is a great deal more . . . disappointing. I am in the History Department.

NICK: Yes . . . you told me.

GEORGE: I know I told you . . . I shall probably tell you several more times. Martha tells me often, that I am *in* the History Department . . . as opposed to *being* the History Department . . . in the sense of *running* the History Department. I do not run the History Department.

NICK: Well, I don't run the Biology Department.

GEORGE: You're twenty-one!

NICK: Twenty-eight.

GEORGE: Twenty-eight! Perhaps when you're forty-something and look fifty-five, you will run the History Department. . . .

NICK: . . . Biology. . . .

GEORGE: . . . The Biology Department, I *did* run the History Department, for four years, during the war, but that was because everybody was away. Then . . . everybody came back . . . because nobody got killed. That's New England for you. Isn't that amazing? Not one single man in this whole place got his head shot off. That's pretty irrational. [*Broods.*] Your wife *doesn't* have any hips . . . has she . . . does she?

NICK: What?

GEORGE: I don't mean to suggest that I'm hip-happy. . . . I'm not one of those thirty-six, twenty-two, seventy-eight men. No-siree . . . not me. Everything in proportion. I was implying that your wife is . . . slim-hipped.

NICK: Yes . . . she is.

GEORGE [*looking at the ceiling*]: What are they *doing* up there? I assume that's where they are.

NICK [*false heartiness*]: You know women.

GEORGE [*gives* NICK *a long stare, of feigned incredulity . . . then his attention moves*]: Not one son-of-a-bitch got killed. Of course, nobody bombed Washington. No . . . that's not fair. You have any kids?

NICK: Uh . . . no . . . not yet. [*Pause.*] You?

GEORGE [*a kind of challenge*]: That's for me to know and you to find out.

NICK: Indeed?

GEORGE: No kids, hunh?

NICK: Not yet.

GEORGE: People do . . . uh . . . have kids. That's what I meant about history. You people are going to make them in test tubes, aren't you? You biologists. Babies. Then the rest of us . . . them as wants to . . . can screw to their heart's content. What will happen to the tax deduction? Has anyone figured that out yet?

NICK, *who can think of nothing better to do, laughs mildly.*

But you *are* going to have kids . . . anyway. In spite of history.

NICK [*hedging*]: Yes . . . certainly. We . . . want to wait . . . a little . . . until we're settled.

GEORGE: And this . . . [*With a handsweep taking in not only the room, the house, but the whole countryside.*] . . . this is your heart's content—Illyria . . . Penguin Island . . . Gomorrah. . . . You think you're going to be happy here in New Carthage, eh?

NICK [*a little defensively*]: I hope we'll stay here.

GEORGE: And every definition has its boundaries, eh? Well, it isn't a bad college, I guess. I mean . . . it'll do. It isn't M.I.T. . . . it isn't U.C.L.A. . . . it isn't the Sorbonne . . . or Moscow U. either, for that matter.

NICK: I don't mean . . . for ever.

GEORGE: Well, don't you let that get bandied about. The old man wouldn't like it. Martha's father expects loyalty and devotion out of his . . . staff. I was going to use another word. Martha's father expects his . . . staff . . . to cling to the walls of this place, like the ivy . . . to come here and grow old . . . to fall in the line of service. One man, a professor of Latin and Elocution, actually fell in the cafeteria line, one lunch. He was buried, as many of us have been, and as many more of us will be, under the shrubbery around the chapel. It is said . . . and I have no reason to doubt it . . . that we make excellent fertilizer. But the old man is not going to be buried under the shrubbery . . . the old man is not going to die. Martha's father has the staying power of one of those Micronesian tortoises. There are rumours . . . which you must not breathe in front of Martha, for she foams at the mouth . . . that the old man, her father, is over two hundred years old. There is probably an irony involved in this, but I am not drunk enough to figure out what it is. How many kids you going to have?

NICK: I . . . I don't know. . . . My wife is . . .

GEORGE: Slim-hipped. [*Rises.*] Have a drink.

NICK: Yes.

GEORGE: MARTHA! [*No answer.*] DAMN IT! [*To* NICK.] You asked me if I knew women. . . . Well, one of the things I do *not* know about them is what they talk about while the men are talking. [*Vaguely.*] I must find out some time.

MARTHA'S VOICE: WHADD'YA WANT?

GEORGE [*to* NICK]: Isn't that a wonderful sound? What I mean is . . . what do you think they really *talk* about . . . or don't you care?

NICK: Themselves, I would imagine.

MARTHA'S VOICE: GEORGE?

GEORGE [*to* NICK]: Do you find women . . . puzzling?

NICK: Well . . . yes and no.

GEORGE [*with a knowing nod*]: Unh-hunh.

Moves towards the hall, almost bumps into HONEY, *re-entering.*

Oh! Well, here's one of you, at least.

HONEY *moves towards* NICK. GEORGE *goes to the hall.*

HONEY [*to* GEORGE]: She'll be right down. [*To* NICK.] You must see this house, dear . . . this is such a wonderful old house.

NICK: Yes, I . . .

GEORGE: MARTHA!

MARTHA'S VOICE: FOR CHRIST'S SAKE, HANG ON A MINUTE, WILL YOU?

HONEY [*to* GEORGE]: She'll be right down . . . she's changing.

GEORGE [*incredulous*]: She's *what?* She's changing?

HONEY: Yes.

GEORGE: Her clothes?

HONEY: Her dress.

GEORGE [*suspicious*]: Why?

HONEY [*with a nervous little laugh*]: Why, I imagine she wants to be . . . comfortable.

GEORGE [*with a threatening look towards the hall*]: Oh she does, does she?

HONEY: Well, heavens, I should think . . .

GEORGE: YOU DON'T KNOW!

NICK [*as* HONEY *starts*]: You feel all right?

HONEY [*reassuring, but with the echo of a whine. A long-practised tone*]: Oh, yes, dear . . . perfectly fine.

GEORGE [*fuming . . . to himself*]: So she wants to be comfortable, does she? Well, we'll see about that.

HONEY [*to* GEORGE, *brightly*]: I didn't know until just a minute ago that you had a *son*.

GEORGE [*wheeling, as if struck from behind*]: WHAT?

HONEY: A son! I hadn't known.

NICK: You to know and me to find out. Well, he must be quite a big . . .

HONEY: Twenty-one . . . twenty-one tomorrow . . . tomorrow's his birthday.

NICK [*a victorious smile*]: Well!

GEORGE [*to* HONEY]: She told you about him?

HONEY [*flustered*]: Well, *yes.* Well, I mean . . .

GEORGE [*nailing it down*]: She told you about him.

HONEY [*a nervous giggle*]: Yes.

GEORGE [*strangely*]: You say she's changing?

HONEY: Yes. . . .

GEORGE: And she mentioned . . .?

HONEY [*cheerful, but a little puzzled*]: . . . your son's birthday . . . yes.

GEORGE [*more or less to himself*]: O.K., Martha . . . O.K.

NICK: You look pale, Honey. Do you want a . . .?

HONEY: Yes, dear . . . a little more brandy, maybe. Just a drop.

GEORGE: O.K., Martha.

NICK: May I use the . . . uh . . . bar?

GEORGE: Hm? Oh, yes . . . yes . . . by all means. Drink away . . . you'll need it as the years go on. [*For* MARTHA, *as if she were in the room.*] You goddamn destructive . . .

HONEY [*to cover*]: What time is it, dear?

NICK: Two-thirty.

HONEY: Oh, it's so late . . . we *should* be getting home.

GEORGE [*nastily, but he is so preoccupied he hardly notices his own tone*]: For what? You keeping the babysitter up, or something?

NICK [*almost a warning*]: I told you we didn't have children.

GEORGE: Hm? [*Realizing.*] Oh, I'm sorry. I wasn't even listening ... or thinking ... [*With a flick of his hand.*] ... whichever one applies.

NICK [*softly, to* HONEY]: We'll go in a little while.

GEORGE [*driving*]: Oh no, now ... you mustn't. Martha is changing ... and Martha is not changing for *me*. Martha hasn't changed for *me* in years. If Martha is changing, it means we'll be here for ... days. You are being accorded an honour, and you must not forget that Martha is the daughter of our beloved boss. She is his ... right ball, you might say.

NICK: You might not understand this ... but I wish you wouldn't talk that way in front of my wife.

HONEY: Oh, now ...

GEORGE [*incredulous*]: Really? Well, you're quite right. ... We'll leave that sort of talk to Martha.

MARTHA [*entering*]: What sort of talk? [*She has changed her clothes, and she looks, now, more comfortable and ... and this is most important ... most voluptuous.*]

GEORGE: There you are, my pet.

NICK [*impressed; rising*]: Well, now ...

GEORGE: Why, Martha ... your Sunday chapel dress!

HONEY [*slightly disapproving*]: Oh, that's most attractive.

MARTHA [*showing off*]: You like it? Good! [*To* GEORGE.] What the hell do you mean screaming up the stairs at me like that?

GEORGE: We got lonely, darling ... we got lonely for the soft purr of your little voice.

MARTHA [*deciding not to rise to it*]: Oh. Well, then, you just trot over to the barie-poo ...

GEORGE [*taking the tone from her*]: ... and make your little mommy a gweat big dwink.

MARTHA [*giggles*]: That's right. [*To* NICK.] Well, did you two have a nice little talk? You men solve the problems of the world, as usual?

NICK: Well, no, we ...

GEORGE [*quickly*]: What we did, actually, if you really want to know, what we did actually is try to figure out what you two were talking about.

HONEY *giggles,* MARTHA *laughs.*

MARTHA [*to* HONEY]: Aren't they something? Aren't these ... [*Cheerfully disdainful.*] ... men the absolute end? [*To* GEORGE.] Why didn't you sneak upstairs and listen in?

GEORGE: Oh, I wouldn't have *listened*, Martha ... I would have *peeked*.

HONEY *giggles,* MARTHA *laughs.*

NICK [*to* GEORGE, *with false heartiness*]: It's a conspiracy.

GEORGE: And now we'll never know. Shucks!

MARTHA [*to* NICK, *as* HONEY *beams*]: Hey, you must be quite a boy, getting your Masters when you were ... what ... twelve? You hear that, George?

NICK: Twelve and a half, actually. No, nineteen really. [*To* HONEY.] Honey, you needn't have mentioned that. It ...

HONEY: Ohhhh ... I'm *proud* of you. ...

GEORGE [*seriously, if sadly*]: That's very ... impressive.

MARTHA [*aggressively*]: You're damned right!

GEORGE [*between his teeth*]: I said I was impressed, Martha. I'm beside myself with jealousy. What do you want me to do, throw up? [*To* NICK.] That really is very impressive. [*To* HONEY.] You should be right proud.

HONEY [*coy*]: Oh, he's a pretty nice fella.

GEORGE [*to* NICK]: I wouldn't be surprised if you *did* take over the History Department one of these days.

NICK: The Biology Department.

GEORGE: The *Biology* Department . . . of course. I seem preoccupied with history. Oh! What a remark. [*He strikes a pose, his hand over his heart, his head raised, his voice stentorian.*] 'I am preoccupied with history.'

MARTHA [*as* HONEY *and* NICK *chuckle*]: Ha, ha, ha, HA!

GEORGE [*with some disgust*]: I think I'll make *myself* a drink.

MARTHA: George is not preoccupied with *history*. . . . George is preoccupied with the *History Department*. George is preoccupied with the History Department because . . .

GEORGE: . . . because he is *not* the History Department, but is only *in* the History Department. We know, Martha . . . we went all through it while you were upstairs . . . getting up. There's no need to go through it again.

MARTHA: That's right, baby . . . keep it clean. [*To the others.*] George is bogged down in the History Department. He's an old bog in the History Department, that's what George is. A bog. . . . A fen. . . . A.G.D. swamp. Ha, ha, ha, HA! A SWAMP! Hey, swamp! Hey SWAMPY!

GEORGE [*with a great effort he controls himself . . . then, as if she had said nothing more than 'George, dear' . . .*]: Yes, Martha? Can I get you something?

MARTHA [*amused at his game*]: Well . . . uh . . . sure, you can light my cigarette, if you're of a mind to.

GEORGE [*considers, then moves off*]: No . . . there are limits. I mean, man can put up with only so much without he descends a rung or two on the old evolutionary ladder . . . [*Now a quick aside to* NICK.] . . . which is up your line . . . [*Then back to* MARTHA.] . . . sinks, Martha, and it's a funny ladder . . . you can't reverse yourself . . . start back up once you're descending.

MARTHA *blows him an arrogant kiss.*

Now . . . I'll hold your hand when it's dark and you're afraid of the bogey man, and I'll tote your gin bottles out after midnight, so no one'll see . . . but I will not light your cigarette. And that, as they say, is that.

Brief silence.

MARTHA [*under her breath*]: Jesus! [*Then, immediately, to* NICK.] Hey, you played football, hunh?

HONEY [*as* NICK *seems sunk in thought*]: Dear . . .

NICK: Oh! Oh, yes . . . I was a . . . quarterback . . . but I was much more . . . adept . . . at boxing, really.

MARTHA [*with great enthusiasm*]: BOXING! You hear that, George?

GEORGE [*resignedly*]: Yes, Martha.

MARTHA [*to* NICK, *with peculiar intensity and enthusiasm*]: You musta been pretty good at it . . . I mean, you don't look like you got hit in the face at all.

HONEY [*proudly*]: He was intercollegiate state middleweight champion.

NICK [*embarrassed*]: Honey . . .

HONEY: Well, you were.

MARTHA: You look like you still got a pretty good body *now*, too . . . is that right? Have you?

GEORGE [*intensely*]: Martha . . . decency forbids . . .

MARTHA [*to* GEORGE . . . *still staring at* NICK, *though*]: SHUT UP! [*Now, back to* NICK.] Well, have, you? Have you kept your body?

NICK [*unselfconscious . . . almost encouraging her*]: It's still pretty good. I work out.

MARTHA [*with a half-smile*]: Do you!

NICK: Yeah.

HONEY: Oh, yes . . . he has a very . . . firm body.

MARTHA [*still with that smile . . . a private communication with* NICK]: Have you! Oh, I think that's very nice.

NICK [*narcissistic, but not directly for* MARTHA]: Well, you never know . . . [*Shrugs.*] . . . you know . . . once you have it . . .

MARTHA: . . . you never know when it's going to come in handy.

NICK: I was going to say . . . why give it up until you have to.

MARTHA: I couldn't agree with you more.

They both smile, and there is a rapport of some unformed sort established.

I couldn't agree with you more.

GEORGE: Martha, your obscenity is more than . . .

MARTHA: George, here, doesn't cotton much to body talk . . . do you, sweetheart? [*No reply.*] George isn't too happy when we get to muscle. You know . . . flat bellies, pectorals. . . .

GEORGE [*to* HONEY]: Would you like to take a walk around the garden?

HONEY [*chiding*]: Oh, now. . . .

GEORGE [*incredulous*]: You're amused? [*Shrugs.*] All right.

MARTHA: Paunchy over there isn't too happy when the conversation moves to muscle. How much do you weigh?

NICK: A hundred and fifty-five, a hundred and . . .

MARTHA: Still at the old middleweight limit, eh? That's pretty good. [*Swings around.*] Hey George, tell 'em about the boxing match *we* had.

GEORGE [*slamming his drink down, moving towards the hall*]: Christ!

MARTHA: George! Tell 'em about it!

GEORGE [*with a sick look on his face*]: You tell them, Martha. You're good at it. [*Exits.*]

HONEY: Is he . . . all right?

MARTHA [*laughs*]: Him? Oh, sure. George and I had this boxing match . . . Oh, Lord, twenty years ago . . . a couple of years after we were married.

NICK: A boxing match? The two of you?

HONEY: Really?

MARTHA: Yup . . . the two of us . . . really.

HONEY [*with a little shivery giggle of anticipation*]: I can't imagine it.

MARTHA: Well, like I say, it was twenty years ago, and it wasn't in a ring, or anything like that, you know what I mean. It was wartime, and Daddy was on this physical fitness kick . . . Daddy's always admired physical fitness . . . says a man is only part brain . . . he has a body, too, and it's his responsibility to keep both of them up . . . you know?

NICK: Unh-hunh.
MARTHA: Says the brain can't work unless the body's working, too.
NICK: Well, that's not exactly so. . . .
MARTHA: Well, maybe that *isn't* what he says . . . something like it. *But* . . . it was wartime, and Daddy got the idea all the men should learn how to box . . . self-defence. I suppose the idea was if the Germans landed on the coast, or something, the whole faculty'd go out and punch 'em to death. . . . I don't know.
NICK: It was probably more the principle of the thing.
MARTHA: No kidding. Anyway, so Daddy had a couple of us over one Sunday and we went out in the back, and Daddy put on the gloves himself. Daddy's a strong man. . . . Well, *you* know.
NICK: Yes . . . yes.
MARTHA: And he asked George to box with him. Aaaaannnnd . . . George didn't *want* to . . . probably something about not wanting to bloody-up his meal ticket. . . .
NICK: Unh-hunh.
MARTHA: . . . Anyway, George said he didn't want to, and Daddy was saying. 'Come on, young man . . . what sort of son-in-law *are* you?' . . . and stuff like that.
NICK: Yeah.
MARTHA: So, while this was going on . . . I don't know why I *did* it . . . I got into a pair of gloves myself . . . you know, I didn't lace 'em up, or anything . . . and I snuck up behind George, just kidding, and I yelled 'Hey, George!' and at the same time I let go sort of a roundhouse right . . . just kidding, you know?
NICK: Unh-hunh.
MARTHA: . . . and George wheeled around real quick, and he caught it right in the jaw . . . POW!

NICK *laughs.*

I hadn't meant it . . . honestly. Anyway . . . POW! Right in the jaw . . . and he was off balance . . . he must have been . . . and he stumbled back a few steps, and then, CRASH, he landed . . . flat . . . in a huckleberry bush!

NICK *laughs.* HONEY *goes tsk, tsk, tsk, tsk, and shakes her head.*

It was awful, really. It was funny, but it was awful. [*She thinks, gives a muffled laugh in rueful contemplation of the incident.*] I think it's coloured our whole life. Really I do! It's an excuse, anyway.

GEORGE *enters now, his hands behind his back. No one sees him.*

It's what he uses for being bogged down, anyway . . . why he hasn't *gone* anywhere.

GEORGE *advances.* HONEY *sees him.*

MARTHA: And it was an *accident* . . . a real, goddamn accident!

GEORGE *takes from behind his back a short-barrelled shotgun, and calmly aims it at the back of* MARTHA*'s head.* HONEY *screams . . . rises.* NICK *rises, and, simultaneously,* MARTHA *turns her head to face* GEORGE. GEORGE *pulls the trigger.*

GEORGE: POW!!!

Pop! From the barrel of the gun blossoms a large red and yellow Chinese parasol. HONEY *screams again, this time less, and mostly from relief and confusion.*

You're dead! Pow! You're dead!
NICK [*laughing*]: Good Lord.

HONEY *is beside herself.* MARTHA *laughs too . . . almost breaks down, her great laugh booming.* GEORGE *joins in the general laughter and confusion. It dies, eventually.*

HONEY: Oh! My goodness!
MARTHA [*joyously*]: Where'd you get that, you bastard?
NICK [*his hand out for the gun*]: Let me see that, will you?

GEORGE *hands him the gun.*

HONEY: I've never been so frightened in my life! Never!
GEORGE [*a trifle abstracted*]: Oh, I've had it awhile. Did you like that?
MARTHA [*giggling*]: You bastard.
HONEY [*wanting attention*]: I've *never* been so frightened . . . never.
NICK: This is quite a gadget.
GEORGE [*leaning over* MARTHA]: You liked that, did you?
MARTHA: Yeah . . . that was pretty good. [*Softer.*] C'mon . . . give me a kiss.
GEORGE [*indicating* NICK *and* HONEY]: Later, sweetie.

But MARTHA *will not be dissuaded. They kiss,* GEORGE *standing, leaning over* MARTHA*'s chair. She takes his hand, places it on her stage-side breast. He breaks away.*

Oh-ho! That's what you're after, is it? What are we going to have . . . blue games for the guests? Hunh? Hunh?
MARTHA [*angry-hurt*]: You . . . prick!
GEORGE [*a Pyrrhic victory*]: Everything in its place, Martha . . . everything in its own good time.
MARTHA [*an unspoken epithet*]: You . . .
GEORGE [*over to* NICK, *who still has the gun*]: Here, let me show you . . . it goes back in, like this. [*Closes the parasol, reinserts it in the gun.*]
NICK: That's damn clever.
GEORGE [*puts the gun down*]: Drinks now! Drinks for all! [*Takes* NICK*'s glass without question . . . goes to* MARTHA.]
MARTHA [*still angry-hurt*]: I'm not finished.
HONEY [*as* GEORGE *puts out his hand for her glass*]: Oh, I think I need *something.*

He takes her glass, moves back to the portable bar.

NICK: Is that Japanese?

GEORGE: Probably.

HONEY [*to* MARTHA]: I was never so frightened in my life. Weren't you frightened? Just for a second?

MARTHA [*smothering her rage at* GEORGE]: I don't remember.

HONEY: Ohhhh, now . . . I bet you were.

GEORGE: Did you really think I was going to kill you, Martha?

MARTHA [*dripping contempt*]: You? . . . Kill me? . . . That's a laugh.

GEORGE: Well, now, I might . . . some day.

MARTHA: Fat chance.

NICK [*as* GEORGE *hands him his drink*]: Where's the john?

GEORGE: Through the hall there . . . and down to your left.

HONEY: Don't you come back with any guns, or anything, now.

NICK [*laughs*]: Oh, no.

MARTHA: You don't need any props, do you, baby?

NICK: Unh-unh.

MARTHA [*suggestive*]: I'll bet not. No fake Jap gun for you, eh?

NICK [*smiles at* MARTHA. *Then, to* GEORGE, *indicating a side table near the hall*]: May I leave my drink here?

GEORGE [*as* NICK *exits without waiting for a reply*]: Yeah . . . sure . . . why not? We've got half-filled glasses everywhere in the house, wherever Martha forgets she's left them . . . in the linen closet, on the edge of the bathtub . . . I even found one in the freezer, once.

MARTHA [*amused in spite of herself*]: You did not!

GEORGE: *Yes* I did.

MARTHA [*ibid.*]: You did *not*!

GEORGE [*giving* HONEY *her brandy*]: Yes I *did*. [*To* HONEY.] Brandy doesn't give you a hangover?

HONEY: I never mix. And then, I don't drink very much, either.

GEORGE [*grimaces behind her back*]: Oh . . . that's good. Your . . . your husband was telling me all about the . . . chromosomes.

MARTHA [*ugly*]: The what?

GEORGE: The chromosomes, Martha . . . the genes, or whatever they are [*To* HONEY.] You've got quite a . . . terrifying husband.

HONEY [*as if she's being joshed*]: Ohhhhhhhhh. . . .

GEORGE: No, really. He's quite terrifying, with his chromosomes, and all.

MARTHA: He's in the Math Department.

GEORGE: No, Martha . . . he's a biologist.

MARTHA [*her voice rising*]: He's in the *Math* Department!

HONEY [*timidly*]: Uh . . . biology.

MARTHA [*unconvinced*]: Are *you* sure?

HONEY [*with a little giggle*]: Well, I ought to. [*Then as an afterthought.*] Be.

MARTHA [*grumpy*]: I suppose *so*. I don't know who said he was in the Math Department.

GEORGE: You did, Martha.

MARTHA [*by way of irritable explanation*]: Well, I can't be expected to remember *everything*. I meet fifteen new teachers and their goddamn wives . . . present company outlawed, of course . . .

HONEY *nods, smiles sillily.*

. . . and I'm supposed to remember *everything*. [*Pause.*] So? He's a biologist. Good for him. Biology's even better. It's less . . . abstruse.

GEORGE: Abstract.

MARTHA: ABSTRUSE! In the sense of recondite. [*Sticks her tongue out at* GEORGE.] Don't you tell me words. Biology's even better. It's . . . right at the *meat* of things.

> NICK *re-enters.*

You're right at the meat of things, baby.

NICK [*taking his drink from the side table*]: Oh?

HONEY [*with that giggle*]: They thought you were in the Math Department.

NICK: Well, maybe I ought to be.

MARTHA: You stay right where you are . . . you stay right at the . . . *meat* of things.

GEORGE: You're obsessed with that phrase, Martha. . . . It's ugly.

MARTHA [*ignoring* GEORGE . . . *to* NICK]: You stay right there. [*Laughs.*] Hell you can take over the History Department just as easy from there as anywhere else. God knows, *some*body's going to take over the History Department, *some* day, and it ain't going to be Georgie-boy, there . . . that's for sure. Are ya, swampy . . . are ya, Hunh?

GEORGE: In my mind, Martha, you are buried in cement, right up to your neck.

> MARTHA *giggles.*

No . . . right up to your nose . . . that's much quieter.

MARTHA [*to* NICK]: Georgie-boy, here, says you're terrifying. Why are you terrifying?

NICK [*with a small smile*]: I didn't know I was.

HONEY [*a little thickly*]: It's because of your chromosomes, dear.

NICK: Oh, the chromosome business. . . .

MARTHA [*to* NICK]: What's all this about chromosomes?

NICK: Well, chromosomes are . . .

MARTHA: I know what chromosomes are, sweetie, I love 'em.

NICK: Oh. . . . Well, then.

GEORGE: Martha eats them . . . for breakfast . . . she sprinkles them on her cereal. [*To* MARTHA, *now.*] It's very simple, Martha, this young man is working on a system whereby chromosomes can be altered . . . well not all by himself—he probably has one or two co-conspirators—the genetic make-up of a sperm cell changed, reordered . . . *to* order, actually . . . for hair and eye colour, stature, potency . . . I imagine . . . hairiness, features, health . . . and *mind*. Most important . . . Mind. All imbalances will be corrected, sifted out . . . propensity for various diseases will be gone, longevity assured. We will have a race of men . . . test-tube-bred . . . incubator-born . . . superb and sublime.

MARTHA [*impressed*]: Hunh!

HONEY: How exciting!

GEORGE: *But!* Everyone will tend to be rather the same. . . . Alike. Everyone . . . and I'm sure I'm not wrong here . . . will tend to look like this young man here.

MARTHA: *That's* not a bad idea.

NICK [*impatient*]: All right, now. . . .

GEORGE: It will, on the surface of it, be all rather pretty . . . quite jolly. But of course there will be a dank side to it, too. A certain amount of regulation will be necessary . . . uh . . . for the experiment to succeed. A certain number of sperm tubes will have to be cut.

MARTHA: Hunh! . . .

GEORGE: Millions upon millions of them . . . millions of tiny little slicing operations that will leave just the smallest scar, on the underside of the scrotum [MARTHA *laughs*.] but which will assure the sterility of the imperfect . . . the ugly, the stupid . . . the . . . unfit.

NICK [*grimly*]: Now look . . .!

GEORGE: . . . with this, we will have, in time, a race of glorious men.

MARTHA: Hunh!

GEORGE: I suspect we will not have much music, much painting, but we will have a civilization of men, smooth, blond, and right at the middleweight limit.

MARTHA: Awww. . . .

GEORGE: . . . a race of scientists and mathematicians, each dedicated to and working for the greater glory of the super-civilization.

MARTHA: Goody.

GEORGE: There will be a certain . . . loss of liberty, I imagine, as a result of this experiment . . . but diversity will no longer be the goal. Cultures and races will eventually vanish . . . the ants will take over the world.

NICK: Are you finished?

GEORGE [*ignoring him*]: And I, naturally, am rather opposed to all this. History, which is my field . . . history, of which I am one of the most famous bogs . . .

MARTHA: Ha, ha, HA!

GEORGE: . . . will lose its glorious variety and unpredictability. I, and with me the . . . the surprise, the multiplexity, the sea-changing rhythm of . . . history, will be eliminated. There will be order and constancy . . . and I am unalterably opposed to it. I will not give up Berlin!

MARTHA: You'll give up Berlin, sweetheart. You going to defend it with your paunch?

HONEY: I don't see what Berlin has to *do* with anything.

GEORGE: There is a saloon in West Berlin where the barstools are five feet high. And the earth . . . the floor . . . is . . . so . . . far . . . below you. I will not give up things like that. No . . . I won't. I will fight you, young man . . . one hand on my scrotum, to be sure . . . but with my free hand I will battle you to the death.

MARTHA [*mocking, laughing*]: Bravo!

NICK [*to* GEORGE]: That's right. And I am going to be the wave of the future.

MARTHA: You bet you are, baby.

HONEY [*quite drunk–to* NICK]: I don't see why you want to do all those things, dear. You never told me.

NICK [*angry*]: Oh for God's sake!

HONEY [*shocked*]: OH!

GEORGE: The most profound indication of a social malignancy . . . no sense of humour. None of the monoliths could take a joke. Read history. I know something about history.

NICK [*to* GEORGE, *trying to make light of it all*]: You . . . you don't know much about science, do you?

GEORGE: I know something about history. I know when I'm being threatened.

MARTHA [*salaciously—to* NICK]: So, everyone's going to look like you, eh?

NICK: Oh, sure. I'm going to be a personal screwing machine!

MARTHA: Isn't that nice.

HONEY [*her hands over her ears*]: Dear, you mustn't . . . you mustn't . . . you mustn't.

NICK [*impatiently*]: I'm sorry, Honey.

HONEY: Such language. It's . . .

NICK: I'm *sorry*. All right?

HONEY [*pouting*]: Well . . . all right. [*Suddenly she giggles insanely, subsides. To* GEORGE.] . . . When is your son? [*Giggles again.*]

GEORGE: What?

NICK [*distastefully*]: Something about your son.

GEORGE: SON!

HONEY: When is . . . where is your son . . . coming home? [*Giggles.*]

GEORGE: Ohhhh. [*Too formal.*] Martha? When is our son coming home?

MARTHA: Never mind.

GEORGE: No, no . . . I want to know . . . you brought it out into the open. When is he coming home, Martha?

MARTHA: I said never mind. I'm sorry I brought it up.

GEORGE: Him up . . . not it. You brought *him* up. Well, more or less. When's the little bugger going to appear, hunh? I mean isn't tomorrow meant to be his birthday, or something?

MARTHA: I don't want to talk about it!

GEORGE [*falsely innocent*]: But Martha . . .

MARTHA: I DON'T WANT TO TALK ABOUT IT!

GEORGE: I'll bet you don't. [*To* HONEY *and* NICK.] Martha does not want to talk about it . . . him. Martha is sorry she brought it up . . . him.

HONEY [*idiotically*]: When's the little bugger coming home? [*Giggles.*]

GEORGE: Yes, Martha . . . since you had the bad taste to bring the matter up in the first place . . . when *is* the little bugger coming home?

NICK: Honey, do you think you . . .?

MARTHA: George talks disparagingly about the little bugger because . . . well, because he has problems.

GEORGE: The little bugger has problems? What problems has the little bugger got?

MARTHA: Not the little bugger . . . stop calling him that! You! You've got problems.

GEORGE [*feigned disdain*]: I've never heard of anything more ridiculous in my life.

HONEY: Neither have I!

NICK: Honey . . .

MARTHA: George's biggest problem about the little . . . ha, ha, ha HA! . . . about our son, about our great big son, is that deep down in the private-most pit of his gut, he's not completely sure it's his own kid.

GEORGE [*deeply serious*]: My God, you're a wicked woman.

MARTHA: And I've told you a million times, baby . . . I wouldn't conceive with anyone but you . . . you know that, baby.

GEORGE: A deeply wicked person.

HONEY [*deep in drunken grief*]: My, my, my, my. Oh, my.

NICK: I'm not sure that this is a subject for . . .

GEORGE: Martha's lying. I want you to know that, right now. Martha's lying.

MARTHA *laughs.*

There are very few things in this world that I *am* sure of . . . national boundaries, the level of the ocean, political allegiances, practical morality . . . none of these would I stake my stick on any more . . . but the one thing in this whole sinking world that I am sure of is my partnership, my chromoso-mological partnership in the . . . creation of our . . . blond-eyed, blue-haired . . . son.

HONEY: Oh, I'm so glad!

MARTHA: That was a very pretty speech, George.

GEORGE: Thank you, Martha.

MARTHA: You rose to the occasion . . . good. Real good.

HONEY: Well . . . real well.

NICK: Honey . . .

GEORGE: Martha knows . . . she knows better.

MARTHA [*proudly*]: I know better. I been to college like everybody else.

GEORGE: Martha been to college. Martha been to a convent when she were a little twig of a thing, too.

MARTHA: And I was an atheist. [*Uncertainly.*] I still am.

GEORGE: Not an atheist, Martha . . . a pagan. [*To* HONEY *and* NICK.] Martha is the only true pagan on the eastern seaboard.

MARTHA *laughs.*

HONEY: Oh, that's nice. Isn't that nice, dear?

NICK [*humouring her*]: Yes . . . wonderful.

GEORGE: And Martha paints blue circles around her things.

NICK: You do?

MARTHA [*defensively, for the joke's sake*]: Sometimes. [*Beckoning.*] You wanna see?

GEORGE [*admonishing*]: Tut, tut, tut.

MARTHA: Tut, tut yourself . . . you old floozie!

HONEY: He's not a floozie . . . he can't be a floozie . . . you're a floozie. [*Giggles.*]

MARTHA [*shaking a finger at* HONEY]: Now you watch yourself!

HONEY [*cheerfully*]: All right. I'd like a nipper of brandy, please.

NICK: Honey, I think you've had enough, now . . .

GEORGE: Nonsense! Everybody's ready, I think. [*Takes glasses, etc.*]

HONEY [*echoing* GEORGE]: Nonsense.

NICK [*shrugging*]: O.K.

MARTHA [*to* GEORGE]: Our son does *not* have blue hair . . . or blue eyes, for that matter. He has green eyes . . . like me.

GEORGE: He has blue eyes, Martha.

MARTHA [*determined*]: Green.

GEORGE [*patronizing*]: Blue, Martha.

MARTHA [*ugly*]: GREEN! [*To* HONEY *and* NICK.] He has the loveliest green eyes . . . they aren't all flaked with brown and grey, you know . . . hazel . . . they're real green . . . deep, pure green eyes . . . like mine.

NICK [*peers*]: Your eyes are . . . brown, aren't they?

MARTHA: Green! [*A little too fast.*] Well, in some lights they *look* brown, but they're green. Not green like his . . . more hazel. George has watery blue eyes . . . milky blue.

GEORGE: Make up your mind, Martha.

MARTHA: I was giving you the benefit of the doubt. [*Now back to the others.*] Daddy has green eyes, too.

GEORGE: He does not! Your father has tiny red eyes . . . like a white mouse. In fact, he *is* a white mouse.

MARTHA: You wouldn't dare say a thing like that if he was here! You're a coward!

GEORGE [*to* HONEY *and* NICK]: You know . . . that great shock of white hair, and those little beady red eyes . . . a great big white mouse.

MARTHA: George hates Daddy . . . not for anything Daddy's done to him, but for his own . . .

GEORGE [*nodding . . . finishing it for her*]: . . . inadequacies.

MARTHA [*cheerfully*]: That's right. You hit it . . . right on the snout. [*Seeing* GEORGE *exiting.*] Where do you think *you're* going?

GEORGE: We need some more booze, angel.

MARTHA: Oh. [*Pause.*] So, go.

GEORGE [*exiting*]: Thank you.

MARTHA [*seeing that* GEORGE *has gone*]: He's a good bartender . . . a good bar nurse. The S.O.B., he hates my father. You know that?

NICK [*trying to make light of it*]: Oh, come on.

MARTHA [*offended*]: You think I'm kidding? You think I'm joking? I never joke . . . I don't have a sense of humour. [*Almost pouting.*] I have a fine sense of the ridiculous, but no sense of humour. [*Affirmatively.*] I have no sense of humour!

HONEY [*happily*]: I haven't, either.

NICK [*half-heartedly*]: Yes, you have, Honey . . . a quiet one.

HONEY [*proudly*]: Thank you.

MARTHA: You want to know *why* the S.O.B. hates my father? You want me to tell you? All right. . . . I will now tell you why the S.O.B. hates my father.

HONEY [*swinging to some sort of attention*]: Oh, good!

MARTHA [*sternly, to* HONEY]: *Some* people feed on the calamities of others.

HONEY [*offended*]: They do not!

NICK: Honey. . . .

MARTHA: All right! Shut up! Both of you! [*Pause.*] All right, now. Mommy died early, see, and I sort of grew up with Daddy. [*Pause–thinks.*] . . . I went away to school, and stuff, but I more or less grew up with him. Jesus, I admired that guy! I worshipped him . . . I absolutely worshipped him. I still do. And he was pretty fond of me, too . . . you know? We had a real . . . rapport going . . . a real rapport.

NICK: Yeah, yeah.

MARTHA: And Daddy built this college . . . I mean, he built it up from what it was . . . it's his whole life. He *is* the college.

NICK: Unh-hunh.

MARTHA: The college is him. You know what the endowment was when he took over, and what it is *now*? You look it up some time.

NICK: I know . . . I read about it. . . .

MARTHA: Shut up and listen . . . [*As an afterthought.*] . . . cutie. So after I got done with college and stuff, I came back here and sort of . . . sat around, for a while. I wasn't married, or anything. Wellllll, I'd *been* married . . . sort of . . . for a week, my sophomore year at Miss Muff's Academy for Young Ladies . . . college. A kind of junior Lady Chatterley arrangement, as it turned out . . . the marriage. [NICK *laughs*.] He mowed the lawn at Miss Muff's, sitting up there, all naked, on a big power mower, mowing away. But Daddy and Miss Muff got together and put an end to that . . . real quick . . . annulled . . . which is a laugh . . . because theoretically you can't get an annulment if there's entrance. Ha! Anyway, so I was revirginized, finished at Miss Muff's . . . where they had one less gardener's boy, and a real shame, that was . . . and I came back here and sort of sat around for a while. I was hostess for Daddy and I took care of him . . . and it was . . . nice. It was very nice.

NICK: Yes . . . yes.

MARTHA: What do you mean, yes, yes? How would you know?

NICK *shrugs helplessly*.

Lover.

NICK *smiles a little*.

And I got the idea, about then, that I'd marry into the college . . . which didn't seem to be quite as stupid as it turned out. I mean, Daddy had a sense of history . . . of . . . continuation. . . . Why don't you come over here and sit by me?

NICK [*indicating* HONEY, *who is barely with it*]: I . . . don't think I . . . should. . . . I . . .

MARTHA: Suit yourself. A sense of continuation . . . history . . . and he'd always had it in the back of his mind to . . . *groom* someone to take over . . . some time, when he quit. A succession . . . you know what I mean?

NICK: Yes, I do.

MARTHA: Which is natural enough. When you've made something, you want to pass it on, to somebody. So, I was sort of on the lookout, for . . . prospects with the new men. An heir-apparent. [*Laughs*.] It wasn't *Daddy's* idea that I had to necessarily marry the guy. I mean, I wasn't the albatross . . . you didn't have to take me to get the prize, or anything like that. It was something *I* had in the back of *my* mind. And a lot of the new men were married . . . naturally.

NICK: Sure.

MARTHA [*with a strange smile*]: Like you, baby.

HONEY [*a mindless echo*]: Like you, baby.

MARTHA [*ironically*]: But then George came along . . . along come George.

GEORGE [*re-entering, with liquor*]: And along came George, bearing hooch. What are you doing now, Martha?

MARTHA [*unfazed*]: I'm telling a story. Sit down . . . you'll learn something.

GEORGE [*stays standing. Puts the liquor on the portable bar*]: All rightie.

HONEY: You've come back!

GEORGE: That's right.

HONEY: Dear! He's come back!

NICK: Yes, I see . . . I see.

MARTHA: Where was I?

HONEY: I'm *so* glad.

NICK: Shhhhh.

HONEY [*imitating him*]: Shhhhh.

MARTHA: Oh yeah. And along came George. That's right. WHO was young . . .
intelligent . . . and . . . bushy-tailed, and . . . sort of cute . . . if you can
imagine it . . .

GEORGE: . . . and younger than you. . . .

MARTHA: . . . and younger than me. . . .

GEORGE: . . . by six years. . . .

MARTHA: . . . by six years. . . . It doesn't bother me, George. . . . And along he
came, bright-eyed, into the History Department. And you know what I did,
dumb cluck that I am? You know what I did? I fell for him.

HONEY [*dreamy*]: Oh, that's nice.

GEORGE: Yes, she did. You should have seen it. She'd sit outside of my room, on
the lawn, at night, and she'd howl and claw at the turf . . . I couldn't work.

MARTHA [*laughs, really amused*]: I actually fell for him . . . it . . . that, there.

GEORGE: Martha's a Romantic at heart.

MARTHA: That I am. So, I actually fell for him. And the match seemed . . .
practical, too. You know, Daddy was looking for someone to . . .

GEORGE: Just a minute, Martha. . . .

MARTHA: . . . take over, some time, when he was ready to . . .

GEORGE [*stony*]: Just a minute, Martha.

MARTHA: . . . retire, and so I thought . . .

GEORGE: STOP IT, MARTHA!

MARTHA [*irritated*]: Whadda you want?

GEORGE [*too patiently*]: I'd thought you were telling the story of our courtship,
Martha . . . I didn't know you were going to start in on the other business.

MARTHA [*so-thereish*]: Well, I am!

GEORGE: I wouldn't, if I were you.

MARTHA: Oh . . . you wouldn't? Well, you're not!

GEORGE: Now, you've already sprung a leak about you-know-what. . . .

MARTHA [*a duck*]: What? What?

GEORGE: . . . about the apple of our eye . . . the sprout . . . the little bugger . . .
[*Spits it out.*] . . . our *son* . . . and if you start on this other business, I warn
you, Martha, it's going to make me angry.

MARTHA [*laughing at him*]: Oh, it is, is it?

GEORGE: I warn you.

MARTHA [*incredulous*]: You *what*?

GEORGE [*very quietly*]: I warn you.

NICK: Do you really think we have to go through . . . ?

MARTHA: I stand warned! [*Pause . . . then, to* HONEY *and* NICK.] So, anyway, I
married the S.O.B., and I had it all planned out. . . . He was the groom . . . he
was going to be groomed. He'd take over some day . . . first, he'd take over the
History Department, and then, when Daddy retired, he'd take over the
college . . . you know? That's the way it was supposed to be. [*To* GEORGE, *who
is at the portable bar with his back to her.*] You getting angry, baby? Hunh?
[*Now back.*] That's the way it was *supposed* to be. Very simple. And Daddy
seemed to think it was a pretty good idea, too. For a while. Until he watched
for a couple of years! [*To* GEORGE *again.*] You getting angrier? [*Now back.*]
Until he watched for a couple of years and started thinking maybe it wasn't
such a good idea after all . . . that maybe Georgie-boy didn't have the *stuff* . . .
that he didn't have it in him!

GEORGE [*still with his back to them all*]: Stop it, Martha.

MARTHA [*viciously triumphant*]: The hell I will! You see, George didn't have much . . . push . . . he wasn't particularly aggressive. In fact he was sort of a . . . [*Spits the word at* GEORGE's *back.*] . . . a FLOP! A great . . . big . . . fat . . . FLOP!

> CRASH! *Immediately after* FLOP! GEORGE *breaks a bottle against the portable bar and stands there, still with his back to them all, holding the remains of the bottle by the neck. There is a silence, with everyone frozen. Then . . .*

GEORGE [*almost crying*]: I said stop, Martha.

MARTHA [*after considering what course to take*]: I hope that was an empty bottle, George. You don't want to waste good liquor . . . not on your salary.

> GEORGE *drops the broken bottle on the floor, not moving.*

Not on an Associate Professor's salary. [*To* NICK *and* HONEY.] I mean, he'd be . . . no good . . . at trustees' dinners, fund raising. He didn't have any . . . personality, you know what I mean? Which was disappointing to Daddy, as you can imagine. So, here I am, stuck with this flop. . . .

GEORGE [*turning around*]: . . . don't go on, Martha. . . .

MARTHA: . . . this BOG in the History Department. . . .

GEORGE: . . . don't, Martha, don't. . . .

MARTHA [*her voice rising to match his*]: . . . who's married to the President's daughter, who's expected to *be* somebody, not just some nobody, some bookworm, somebody who's so damn . . . contemplative, he can't make anything out of himself, somebody without the *guts* to make anybody proud of him . . . ALL RIGHT, GEORGE!	GEORGE [*under her, then covering, to drown her*]: I said, don't. All right . . . all right: [*Sings.*] Who's afraid of Virginia Woolf, Virginia Woolf, Virginia Woolf, Who's afraid of Virginia Woolf, early in the morning.

GEORGE *and* HONEY [*who joins him drunkenly*]:
> Who's afraid of Virginia Woolf,
> Virginia Woolf,
> Virginia Woolf . . . [*etc.*]

MARTHA: STOP IT!

> *A brief silence.*

HONEY [*rising, moving towards the hall*]: I'm going to be sick . . . I'm going to be sick . . . I'm going to vomit. [*Exits.*]

NICK [*going after her*]: Oh, for God's sake! [*Exits.*]

MARTHA [*going after them, looks back at* GEORGE *contemptuously*]: Jesus! [*Exits.*]

> GEORGE *is alone on stage.*

CURTAIN

ACT TWO

WALPURGISNACHT

GEORGE, *by himself:* NICK *re-enters.*

NICK [*after a silence*]: I . . . guess . . . she's all right. [*No answer.*] She . . . really shouldn't drink. [*No answer.*] She's . . . frail. [*No answer.*] Uh . . . slim-hipped, as you'd have it. [GEORGE *smiles vaguely.*] I'm really very sorry.

GEORGE [*quietly*]: Where's my little yum yum? Where's Martha?

NICK: She's making coffee . . . in the kitchen. She . . . gets sick quite easily.

GEORGE [*preoccupied*]: Martha? Oh no, Martha hasn't been sick a day in her life, unless you count the time she spends in the rest home. . . .

NICK [*he, too, quietly*]: No, no; *my* wife . . . *my* wife gets sick quite easily. Your wife is Martha.

GEORGE [*with some rue*]: Oh, yes . . . I know.

NICK [*a statement of fact*]: She doesn't really spend any time in a rest home.

GEORGE: Your wife?

NICK: No. Yours.

GEORGE: Oh! Mine. [*Pause.*] No, no, she doesn't . . . *I* would; I mean if I were . . . her . . . she . . . *I* would. But I'm not . . . and so I don't. [*Pause.*] I'd like to, though. It gets pretty bouncy around here sometimes.

NICK [*coolly*]: Yes . . . I'm sure.

GEORGE: Well, you saw an example of it.

NICK: I try not to . . .

GEORGE: Get involved. Um? Isn't that right?

NICK: Yes . . . that's right.

GEORGE: I'd imagine not.

NICK: I find it . . . embarrassing.

GEORGE [*sarcastic*]: Oh, you do, hunh?

NICK: Yes. Really. Quite.

GEORGE [*mimicking him*]: Yes. Really. Quite. [*Then aloud, but to himself.*] IT'S DISGUSTING!

NICK: Now look! I didn't have anything . . .

GEORGE: DISGUSTING! [*Quietly, but with great intensity.*] Do you think I like having that . . . whatever-it-is . . . ridiculing me, tearing me down, in front of . . . [*Waves his hand in a gesture of contemptuous dismissal.*] YOU? Do you think I *care* for it?

NICK [*cold–unfriendly*]: Well, no . . . I don't imagine you care for it at all.

GEORGE: Oh, you don't imagine it, hunh?

NICK [*antagonistic*]: No . . . I don't. I don't imagine you do!

GEORGE [*withering*]: Your sympathy disarms me . . . your . . . your compassion makes me weep! Large, salty, unscientific tears!

NICK [*with great disdain*]: I just don't see why you feel you have to subject *other* people to it.

GEORGE: *I?*

NICK: If you and your . . . wife . . . want to go at each other, like a couple of . . .
GEORGE: *I!* Why *I* want to!
NICK: . . . animals, I don't see why you don't do it when there aren't any . . .
GEORGE [*laughing through his anger*]: Why, you smug, self-righteous little . . .
NICK [*a genuine threat*]: CAN . . . IT . . . MISTER!

Silence.

Just . . . watch it!
GEORGE: . . . scientist.
NICK: I've never hit an older man.
GEORGE [*considers it*]: Oh. [*Pause.*] You just hit younger men . . . and children . . . women . . . birds. [*Sees that* NICK *is not amused.*] Well, you're quite right, of course. It isn't the prettiest spectacle . . . seeing a couple of middle-age types hacking away at each other, all red in the face and winded, missing half the time.
NICK: Oh, you two don't miss . . . you two are pretty good. Impressive.
GEORGE: And impressive things impress you, don't they? You're . . . easily impressed . . . sort of a . . . pragmatic idealism.
NICK [*a tight smile*]: No, it's that sometimes I can admire things that I don't admire. Now, flagellation isn't my idea of good times, but . . .
GEORGE: . . . but you can admire a good flagellator . . . a real pro.
NICK: Unh-hunh . . . yeah.
GEORGE: Your wife throws up a lot, eh?
NICK: I didn't say that. . . . I said she gets sick quite easily.
GEORGE: Oh. I thought by sick you meant . . .
NICK: Well, it's true . . . She . . . she does throw up a lot. Once she starts . . . there's practically no stopping her. . . . I mean, she'll go right on . . . for hours. Not all the time, but . . . regularly.
GEORGE: You can tell time by her, hunh?
NICK: Just about.
GEORGE: Drink?
NICK: Sure. [*With no emotion, except the faintest distaste, as* GEORGE *takes his glass to the bar.*] I married her because she was pregnant.
GEORGE [*pause*]: Oh? [*Pause.*] But you said you didn't have any children . . . When I asked you, you said . . .
NICK: She wasn't . . . really. It was a hysterical pregnancy. She blew up, and then she went down.
GEORGE: And while she was up, you married her.
NICK: And then she went down.

They both laugh, and are a little surprised that they do.

GEORGE: Uh . . . Bourbon *is* right.
NICK: Uh . . . yes, Bourbon.
GEORGE [*at the bar, still*]: When I was sixteen and going to prep school, during the Punic Wars, a bunch of us used to go into New York on the first day of vacations, before we fanned out to our homes, and in the evening this bunch of us used to go to this gin mill owned by the gangster-father of one of us—for this was during the Great Experiment, or Prohibition, as it is more frequently called, and it was a bad time for the liquor lobby, but a fine time

for the crooks and the cops—and we would go to this gin mill, and we could drink with the grown-ups and listen to the jazz. And one time, in the bunch of us, there was this boy who was fifteen, and he had killed his mother with a shotgun some years before—accidentally, completely accidentally, without even an unconscious motivation, I have no doubt, no doubt at all—and this one evening this boy went with us, and we ordered our drinks, and when it came his turn he said, I'll have bergin . . . give me some bergin, please . . . bergin and water. Well, we all laughed . . . he was blond and he had the face of a cherub, and we all laughed, and his cheeks went red and the colour rose in his neck, and the assistant crook who had taken our order told people at the next table what the boy had said, and then they laughed, and then more people were told and the laughter grew, and more people and more laughter, and no one was laughing more than us, and none of us more than the boy who had shot his mother. And soon, everyone in the gin mill knew what the laughter was about, and everyone started ordering bergin, and laughing when they ordered it. And soon, of course, the laughter became less general, but it did not subside, entirely, for a very long time, for always at this table or that someone would order bergin and a new area of laughter would rise. We drank free that night, and we were bought champagne by the management, by the gangster-father of one of us. And, of course, we suffered the next day, each of us, alone, on his train, away from New York, each of us with a grown-up's hangover . . . but it was the grandest day of my . . . youth. [*Hands* NICK *a drink on the word.*]

NICK [*very quietly*]: Thank you. What . . . what happened to the boy . . . the boy who had shot his mother?

GEORGE: I won't tell you.

NICK: All right.

GEORGE: The following summer, on a country road, with his learner's permit in his pocket and his father on the front seat to his right, he swerved the car, to avoid a porcupine, and drove straight into a large tree.

NICK [*faintly pleading*]: No.

GEORGE: He was not killed, of course. And in the hospital, when he was conscious and out of danger, and when they told him that his father *was* dead, he began to laugh, I have been told, and his laughter grew and he would not stop, and it was not until after they jammed a needle in his arm, not until after that, until his consciousness slipped away from him, that his laughter subsided . . . stopped. And when he was recovered from his injuries enough so that he could be moved without damage should he struggle, he was put in an asylum. That was thirty years ago.

NICK: Is he . . . still there?

GEORGE: Oh, yes. And I'm told that for these thirty years he has . . . not . . . uttered . . . one . . . sound.

A rather long silence: five seconds, please.

MARTHA! [*Pause.*] MARTHA!

NICK: I told you . . . she's making coffee.

GEORGE: For your hysterical wife, who goes up and down.

NICK: Went. Up and down.

GEORGE: Went. No more?

NICK: No more. Nothing.

GEORGE [_after a sympathetic pause_]: The saddest thing about men. . . . Well, no, one of the saddest things about men is the way they age . . . some of them. Do you know what it is with insane people? Do you? . . . the quiet ones?

NICK: No.

GEORGE: They don't change . . . they don't grow old.

NICK: They must.

GEORGE: Well, eventually, probably, yes. But they don't . . . in the usual sense. They maintain a . . . a firm-skinned serenity . . . the . . . the under-use of everything leaves them . . . quite whole.

NICK: Are you recommending it?

GEORGE: No. Some things are sad, though. [_Imitates a pep-talker._] But ya jest gotta buck up an' face 'em, 'at's all. Buck up! [_Pause._] Martha doesn't have hysterical pregnancies.

NICK: My wife had _one_.

GEORGE: Yes. Martha doesn't have pregnancies at all.

NICK: Well, no . . . I don't imagine so . . . now. Do you have any other kids? Do you have any daughters, or anything?

GEORGE [_as if it's a great joke_]: Do we have any _what_?

NICK: Do you have any . . . I mean, do you have only one . . . kid . . . uh . . . your son?

GEORGE [_with a private knowledge_]: Oh no . . . just one . . . one boy . . . our son.

NICK: Well . . . [_Shrugs._] . . . that's nice.

GEORGE: Oh ho, ho. Yes, well, he's a . . . comfort, a bean bag.

NICK: A what?

GEORGE: A bean bag. Bean bag. You wouldn't understand [_Over-distinct._] Bean . . . bag.

NICK: I _heard_ you . . . I didn't say I was deaf . . . I said I didn't understand.

GEORGE: You didn't say that at all.

NICK: I meant I was _implying_ I didn't understand. [_Under his breath._] For Christ's sake!

GEORGE: You're getting testy.

NICK [_testy_]: I'm sorry.

GEORGE: All I said was, our son . . . the apple of our three eyes, Martha being a Cyclops . . . our son is a bean bag, and you get testy.

NICK: I'm sorry! It's late, I'm tired, I've been drinking since nine o'clock, my wife is vomiting, there's been a lot of screaming going on around here. . . .

GEORGE: And so you're testy. Naturally. Don't . . . worry about it. Anybody who comes here ends up getting . . . testy. It's expected . . . don't be upset.

NICK [_testy_]: I'm not upset!

GEORGE: You're testy.

NICK: Yes.

GEORGE: I'd like to set you straight about something . . . while the little ladies are out of the room . . . I'd like to set you straight about what Martha said.

NICK: I don't . . . make judgements, so there's no need, really, unless you . . .

GEORGE: Well, I want to. I know you don't like to become involved . . . I know you like to . . . preserve your scientific detachment in the face of–for lack of a better word–Life . . . and all . . . but still, I want to tell you.

NICK [_a tight, formal smile_]: I'm a . . . guest. You go right ahead.

GEORGE [_mocking appreciation_]: Oh . . . well, thanks. Now! That makes me feel all warm and runny inside.

NICK: Well, if you're going to . . .

MARTHA'S VOICE: HEY!

NICK: . . . if you're going to start that kind of stuff again . . .

GEORGE: Hark! Forest sounds.

NICK: Hm?

GEORGE: Animal noises.

MARTHA [*sticking her head in*]: Hey!

NICK: Oh!

GEORGE: Well, here's nursie.

MARTHA [*to* NICK]: We're sitting up . . . we're having coffee, and we'll be back in.

NICK [*not rising*]: Oh . . . is there anything I should do?

MARTHA: Nayh. You just stay here and listen to George's side of things. Bore yourself to death.

GEORGE: Monstre!

MARTHA: Cochon!

GEORGE: Bête!

MARTHA: Canaille!

GEORGE: Putain!

MARTHA [*with a gesture of contemptuous dismissal*]: Yaaaahhhh! You two types amuse yourselves . . . we'll be in. [*As she goes.*] You clean up the mess you made, George?

GEORGE [MARTHA *goes.* GEORGE *speaks to the empty hallway*]: No, Martha, I did not clean up the mess I made. I've been trying for years to clean up the mess I made.

NICK: Have you?

GEORGE: Hm?

NICK: *Have* you been trying for years?

GEORGE [*after a long pause . . . looking at him*]: Accommodation, malleability, adjustment . . . those do seem to be in the order of things, don't they?

NICK: Don't try to put me in the same class with you!

GEORGE [*pause*]: Oh. [*Pause.*] No, of course not. Things are simpler with you . . . you marry a woman because she's all blown up . . . while I, in my clumsy, old-fashioned way . . .

NICK: There was more to it than that!

GEORGE: Sure! I'll bet she has money, too!

NICK [*looks hurt. Then, determined, after a pause*]: Yes.

GEORGE: Yes? [*Joyfully.*] YES! You mean I was right? I hit it?

NICK: Well, you see . . .

GEORGE: My God, what archery! First try, too. How about that!

NICK: You see . . .

GEORGE: There were other things.

NICK: Yes.

GEORGE: To compensate.

NICK: Yes.

GEORGE: There always are. [*Sees that* NICK *is reacting badly.*] No, I'm sure there are. I didn't mean to be . . . flip. There are *always* compensating factors . . . as in the case of Martha and myself. . . . Now, on the surface of it . . .

NICK: We sort of grew up together, you know . . .

GEORGE: . . . it looks to be a kind of knock-about, drag-out affair, on the *surface* of it . . .

NICK: We knew each other from, oh God, I don't know, when we were *six*, or something . . .

GEORGE: . . . but somewhere back there, at the beginning of it, right when I first came to New Carthage, back then . . .

NICK [*with some irritation*]: I'm *sorry*.

GEORGE: Hm? Oh. No, no . . . *I'm* sorry.

NICK: No . . . it's . . . it's all right.

GEORGE: No . . . you go ahead.

NICK: No . . . please.

GEORGE: I insist. . . . You're a guest. You go first.

NICK: Well, it seems a little silly . . . now.

GEORGE: Nonsense! [*Pause.*] But if you were six, she must have been four, or something.

NICK: Maybe I was eight . . . she was six. We . . . we used to play . . . doctor.

GEORGE: That's a good healthy heterosexual beginning.

NICK [*laughing*]: Yup.

GEORGE: The scientist even then, eh?

NICK [*laughs*]: Yeah. And it was . . . always taken for granted . . . you know . . . by our families, and by us, too, I guess. And . . . so, we did.

GEORGE [*pause*]: Did what?

NICK: We got married.

GEORGE: When you were eight?

NICK: No. No, of course not. Much later.

GEORGE: I wondered.

NICK: I wouldn't say there was any . . . particular *passion* between us, even at the beginning . . . of our marriage, I mean.

GEORGE: Well, certainly no surprise, no earth-shaking discoveries, after Doctor, and all.

NICK [*uncertainly*]: No. . . .

GEORGE: Everything's all pretty much the same, anyway . . . in *spite* of what they say about Chinese women.

NICK: What is that?

GEORGE: Let me freshen you up. [*Takes* NICK's *glass.*]

NICK: Oh, thanks. After a while you don't get any drunker, do you?

GEORGE: Well, you *do* . . . but it's different . . . everything slows down. . . . you get sodden. . . . unless you can up-chuck . . . like your wife . . . then you can sort of start all over again.

NICK: Everybody drinks a lot here in the East. [*Thinks about it.*] Everybody drinks a lot in the middle-west, too.

GEORGE: We drink a great deal in this country, and I suspect we'll be drinking a great deal more, too . . . if we survive. We should be Arabs or Italians . . . the Arabs don't drink, and the Italians don't get drunk much, except on religious holidays. We should live on Crete, or something.

NICK [*sarcastically . . . as if killing a joke*]: And that, of course, would make us cretins.

GEORGE [*mild surprise*]: So it would. [*Hands* NICK *his drink.*] Tell me about your wife's money.

NICK [*suddenly suspicious*]: Why?

GEORGE: Well . . . don't then.

NICK: What do you want to know about my wife's money for? [*Ugly.*] Hunh?

GEORGE: Well, I thought it would be nice.

NICK: No you didn't.

GEORGE [*still deceptively bland*]: All right. . . . I want to know about your wife's money because . . . well, because I'm fascinated by the methodology . . . by the pragmatic accommodation by which you wave-of-the-future boys are going to take over.

NICK: You're starting in again.

GEORGE: Am I? No I'm not. Look . . . Martha has money too. I mean, her father's been robbing this place blind for years, and . . .

NICK: No, he hasn't. He has not.

GEORGE: He hasn't?

NICK: No.

GEORGE [*shrugs*]: Very well. . . . Martha's father has *not* been robbing this place blind for years, and Martha does not have any money. O.K.?

NICK: We were talking about *my* wife's money . . . not yours.

GEORGE: O.K. . . . talk.

NICK: No. [*Pause.*] My father-in-law . . . was a man of the Lord, and he was very rich.

GEORGE: What faith?

NICK: He . . . my father-in-law . . . was called by God when he was six, or something, and he started preaching, and he baptized people, and he saved them, and he travelled around a lot, and he became pretty famous . . . not like some of them, but he became pretty famous . . . and when he died he had a lot of money.

GEORGE: God's money.

NICK: No . . . his own.

GEORGE: What happened to God's money?

NICK: He spent God's money . . . and he saved his own. He built hospitals, and he sent off Mercy ships, and he brought the outhouses indoors, and he brought the people outdoors, into the sun, and he built three churches, or whatever they were, and two of them burned down . . . and he ended up pretty rich.

GEORGE [*after considering it*]: Well, I think that's very nice.

NICK: Yes. [*Pause. Giggles a little.*] And so, my wife's got some money.

GEORGE: But not God's money.

NICK: No. Her own.

GEORGE: Well, I think that's very nice.

NICK *giggles a little.*

Martha's got money because Martha's father's second wife . . . not Martha's mother, but after Martha's mother died . . . was a very old lady with warts who was very rich.

NICK: She was a witch.

GEORGE: She was a *good* witch, and she married the white mouse . . .

NICK *begins to giggle.*

. . . with the tiny red eyes . . . and he must have nibbled her warts, or something like that, because she went up in a puff of smoke almost immediately. POUF!

NICK: POUF!

GEORGE: POUF! And all that was left, aside from some wart medicine, was a big fat will. . . . A peach pie, with some for the township of New Carthage, some for the college, some for Martha's daddy, and just this much for Martha.

NICK [*quite beside himself*]: Maybe . . . maybe my father-in-law and the witch with the warts should have gotten together, because he was a mouse, too.

GEORGE [*urging* NICK *on*]: He was?

NICK [*breaking down*]: Sure . . . he was a church mouse!

> *They both laugh a great deal, but it is sad laughter . . . eventually they subside, fall silent.*

Your wife never mentioned a stepmother.

GEORGE [*considers it*]: Well . . . maybe it isn't true.

NICK [*narrowing his eyes*]: And maybe it is.

GEORGE: Might be . . . might not. Well, I think your story's a lot nicer . . . about your pumped-up little wife, and your father-in-law who was a priest. . . .

NICK: He was not a priest . . . he was a man of God.

GEORGE: Yes.

NICK: And my wife wasn't pumped up . . . she blew up.

GEORGE: Yes, yes.

NICK [*giggling*]: Get things straight.

GEORGE: I'm sorry . . . I will. I'm sorry.

NICK: O.K.

GEORGE: You realize, of course, that I've been drawing you out on this stuff, not because I'm interested in your terrible lifehood, but only because your represent a direct and pertinent threat to my lifehood, and I want to get the goods on you.

NICK [*still amused*]: Sure . . . sure.

GEORGE: I mean . . . I've warned you . . . you stand warned.

NICK: I stand warned. [*Laughs.*] It's you sneaky types worry me the most, you know. You ineffectual sons of bitches . . . you're the worst.

GEORGE: Yes . . . we are. Sneaky. An elbow in your steely-blue eye . . . a knee in your solid gold groin . . . we're the worst.

NICK: Yup.

GEORGE: Well, I'm glad you don't believe me. . . . I know you've got history on your side, and all. . . .

NICK: Unh-unh. *You've* got history on *your* side. . . . I've got biology on mine. History, biology.

GEORGE: I know the difference.

NICK: You don't act it.

GEORGE: No? I thought we'd decided that you'd take over the History Department first, before you took over the whole works. You know . . . a step at a time.

NICK [*stretching . . . luxuriating . . . playing the game*]: Nyaah . . . what I thought I'd do is . . . I'd sort of insinuate myself generally, play around for a while, find all the weak spots, shore 'em up, but with my own name plate on 'em . . . become sort of a fact, and then turn into a . . . a what . . .?

GEORGE: An inevitability.

NICK: Exactly. . . . An inevitability. You know. . . . Take over a few courses from the older men, start some special groups for myself . . . plough a few pertinent wives. . . .

GEORGE: Now that's it! You can take over all the courses you want to, and get as much of the young elite together in the gymnasium as you like, but until you start ploughing pertinent wives, you really aren't working. The way to a man's heart is through his wife's belly, and don't you forget it.

NICK [*playing along*]: Yeah. . . . I know.

GEORGE: And the women around here are no better than puntas—you know, South American ladies of the night. You know what they do in South America . . . in Rio? The Puntas? Do you know? They hiss . . . like geese. . . . They stand around in the street and they hiss at you . . . like a bunch of geese.

NICK: Gangle.

GEORGE: Hm?

NICK: Gangle . . . gangle of geese . . . not bunch . . . gangle.

GEORGE: Well, if you're going to get all cute about it, all ornithological, it's gaggle . . . not gangle, *gaggle.*

NICK: Gaggle? Not Gangle?

GEORGE: Yes, gaggle.

NICK [*crestfallen*]: Oh.

GEORGE: Oh. Yes. . . . Well they stand around on the street and they hiss at you, like a bunch of geese. All the faculty wives, downtown in New Carthage, in front of the A&P, hissing away like a bunch of geese. That's the way to power—plough 'em all!

NICK [*still playing along*]: I'll bet you're right.

GEORGE: Well, I am.

NICK: And I'll bet your wife's the biggest goose in the gangle, isn't she . . .? Her father president, and all.

GEORGE: You bet your historical inevitability she is!

NICK: Yessirree. [*Rubs his hands together.*] Well now, I'd just better get her off in a corner and mount her like a goddamn dog, eh?

GEORGE: Why, you'd certainly better.

NICK [*looks at* GEORGE *a minute, his expression a little sick*]: You know, I almost think you're serious.

GEORGE [*toasting him*]: No, baby . . . *you* almost think you're serious, and it scares the hell out of you.

NICK [*exploding in disbelief*]: ME!

GEORGE [*quietly*]: Yes . . . you.

NICK: You're kidding!

GEORGE [*like a father*]: I wish I were. . . . I'll give you some good advice if you want me to. . . .

NICK: Good advice! From you? Oh boy! [*Starts to laugh.*]

GEORGE: You haven't learned yet. . . . Take it wherever you can get it. . . . Listen to me, now.

NICK: Come off it!

GEORGE: I'm giving you good advice, now.

NICK: Good God . . .!

GEORGE: There's quicksand here, and you'll be dragged down, just as . . .

NICK: Oh boy . . .!

GEORGE: . . . before you know it . . . sucked down. . . .

NICK *laughs derisively.*

You disgust me on principle, and you're a smug son of a bitch personally, but I'm trying to give you a survival kit. DO YOU HEAR ME?

NICK [*still laughing*]: I hear you. You come in loud.

GEORGE: ALL RIGHT!

NICK: Hey, Honey.

GEORGE [*silence. Then quietly*]: All right . . . O.K. You want to play it by ear, right? Everything's going to work out anyway, because the time-table's history, right?

NICK: Right . . . right. You just tend to your knitting, grandma. . . . I'll be O.K.

GEORGE [*after a silence*]: I've tried to . . . tried to reach you . . . to . . .

NICK [*contemptuously*]: . . . make contact?

GEORGE: Yes.

NICK [*still*]: . . . communicate?

GEORGE: Yes. Exactly.

NICK: Aw . . . that *is* touching . . . that is . . . downright moving . . . that's what it is. [*With sudden vehemence.*] UP YOURS!

GEORGE [*brief pause*]: Hm?

NICK [*threatening*]: You heard me!

GEORGE [*at* NICK, *not to him*]: You take the trouble to construct a civilization . . . to . . . to build a society, based on the principles of . . . of principle . . . you endeavour to make communicable sense out of natural order, morality out of the unnatural disorder of man's mind . . . you make government and art, and realize that they are, must be, both the same . . . you bring things to the saddest of all points . . . to the point where there *is* something to lose . . . then all at once, through all the music, through all the sensible sounds of men building, attempting, comes the *Dies Irae*. And what is it? What does the trumpet sound? Up yours. I suppose there's justice to it, after all the years. . . . Up yours.

NICK [*brief pause . . . then applauding*]: Ha! ha! Bravo! Ha, ha! [*Laughs on.*]

And MARTHA *re-enters, leading* HONEY, *who is wan but smiling bravely.*

HONEY [*grandly*]: Thank you . . . thank you.

MARTHA: Here we are, a little shaky, but on our feet.

GEORGE: Goodie.

NICK: What? Oh . . . OH! Hi, Honey . . . you better?

HONEY: A little bit, dear. . . . I'd better sit down, though.

NICK: Sure . . . c'mon . . . you sit by me.

HONEY: Thank you, dear.

GEORGE [*beneath his breath*]: Touching . . . touching.

MARTHA [*to* GEORGE]: Well? Aren't you going to apologize?

GEORGE [*squinting*]: For what, Martha?

MARTHA: For making the little lady throw up, what else?

GEORGE: I did not make her throw up.

MARTHA: You most certainly did!

GEORGE: I did not!

HONEY [*papal gesture*]: No, now . . . no.

MARTHA [*to* GEORGE]: Well, who do you think did . . . Sexy over there? You think he made his *own* little wife sick?

GEORGE [*helpfully*]: Well, you make *me* sick.

MARTHA: THAT'S DIFFERENT!

HONEY: No, now. I . . . I throw up . . . I mean, I get sick . . . occasionally, all by myself . . . without any reason.

GEORGE: Is that a fact?

NICK: You're . . . you're delicate, Honey.

HONEY [*proudly*]: I've always done it.

GEORGE: Like Big Ben.

NICK [*a warning*]: Watch it!

HONEY: And the doctors say there's nothing wrong with me . . . organically. You know?

NICK: Of course there isn't.

HONEY: Why, just before we got married, I developed . . . appendicitis . . . or everybody *thought* it was appendicitis . . . but it turned out to be . . . it was a . . . [*Laughs briefly.*] . . . false alarm.

GEORGE *and* NICK *exchange glances.*

MARTHA [*to* GEORGE]: Get me a drink.

GEORGE *moves to the bar.*

George makes everybody sick. . . . When our son was just a little boy, he used to . . .

GEORGE: Don't, Martha. . . .

MARTHA: . . . he used to throw up all the time, because of George. . . .

GEORGE: I said, don't!

MARTHA: it got so bad that whenever George came into the room he'd start right in retching, and . . .

GEORGE: . . . the real reason [*Spits out the words.*] our son . . . used to throw up all the time, wife and lover, was nothing more complicated than that he couldn't stand you fiddling at him all the time, breaking into his bedroom with your kimono flying, fiddling at him all the time, with your liquor breath on him, and your hands all over his . . .

MARTHA: YEAH? An I suppose that's why he ran away from home twice in one month, too. [*Now to the guests.*] Twice in one month! Six times in one year!

GEORGE [*also to the guests*]: Our son ran away from home all the time because Martha here used to corner him.

MARTHA [*braying*]: I NEVER CORNERED THE SON OF A BITCH IN MY LIFE!

GEORGE [*handing* MARTHA *her drink*]: He used to run up to me when I'd get home, and he'd say, 'Mama's always coming at me.' That's what he'd say.

MARTHA: Liar!

GEORGE [*shrugging*]: Well, that's the way it was . . . you were always coming at him. I thought it was very embarrassing.

NICK: If you thought it was so embarrassing, what are you talking about it for?

HONEY [*admonishing*]: Dear . . .!

MARTHA: Yeah! [*To* NICK.] Thanks, sweetheart.

GEORGE [*to them all*]: I didn't want to talk about him at all . . . I would have been perfectly happy not to discuss the whole subject. . . . I never want to talk about it.

MARTHA: Yes you do.

GEORGE: When we're alone, maybe.

MARTHA: We're alone!

GEORGE: Uh . . . no, love . . . we've got guests.

MARTHA [*with a covetous look at* NICK]: We sure have.

HONEY: Could I have a little brandy? I think I'd like a little brandy.

NICK: Do you think you should?

HONEY: Oh, yes . . . yes, dear.

GEORGE [*moving to the bar again*]: Sure! Fill 'er up!

NICK: Honey, I don't think you . . .

HONEY [*petulance creeping in*]: It will steady me, *dear*. I feel a little unsteady.

GEORGE: Hell, you can't walk steady on half a bottle . . . got to do it right.

HONEY: Yes. [*To* MARTHA.] I love brandy . . . I really do.

MARTHA [*somewhat abstracted*]: Good for you.

NICK [*giving up*]: Well, if you think it's a good idea . . .

HONEY [*really testy*]: I know what's best for me, dear.

NICK [*not even pleasant*]: Yes . . . I'm sure you do.

HONEY [GEORGE *hands her a brandy*]: Oh, goodie! Thank you. [*To* NICK.] Of course I do, dear.

GEORGE [*pensively*]: I used to drink brandy.

MARTHA [*privately*]: You used to drink bergin, too.

GEORGE [*sharp*]: Shut up, Martha!

MARTHA [*her hand over her mouth in a little girl gesture*]: Oooooops.

NICK [*something having clicked, vaguely*]: Hm?

GEORGE [*burying it*]: Nothing . . . nothing.

MARTHA [*she, too*]: You two men have it out while we were gone? George tell you his side of things? He bring you to tears, hunh?

NICK: Well . . . no. . . .

GEORGE: No, what we did, actually, was . . . we sort of danced around.

MARTHA: Oh, yeah? Cute!

HONEY: Oh, I love dancing.

NICK: He didn't mean that, Honey.

HONEY: Well, I didn't think he did! Two grown men dancing . . . heavens!

MARTHA: You mean he didn't start in on how he would have amounted to something if it hadn't been for Daddy? How his high moral sense wouldn't even let him *try* to better himself? No?

NICK [*qualified*]: No. . . .

MARTHA: And he didn't run on about how he tried to publish a goddamn book, and Daddy wouldn't let him.

NICK: A book? No.

GEORGE: Please, Martha. . . .

NICK [*egging her on*]: A book? What book?

GEORGE [*pleading*]: Please. Just a book.

MARTHA [*mock incredulity*]: Just a book!

GEORGE: *Please*, Martha!

MARTHA [*almost disappointed*]: Well, I guess you didn't get the whole sad story. What's the matter with you, George? You given up?

GEORGE [*calm . . . serious*]: No . . . no. It's just I've got to figure out some new way to fight you, Martha. Guerilla Tactics, maybe . . . internal subversion . . . I don't know. Something.

MARTHA: Well, you figure it out, and you let me know when you do.

GEORGE [*cheery*]: All right, love.

HONEY: Why don't we dance? I'd love some dancing.

NICK: Honey. . . .

HONEY: I would! I'd love some dancing.

NICK: Honey . . .

HONEY: I *want* some! I want some dancing!

GEORGE: All right . . .! For heaven's sake . . . we'll have some dancing.

HONEY [*all sweetness again*] [*To* MARTHA]: Oh, I'm so glad . . . I just love dancing. Don't you?

MARTHA [*with a glance at* NICK]: Yeah . . . yeah, that's not a bad idea.

NICK [*genuinely nervous*]: Gee.

GEORGE: Gee.

HONEY: I dance like the wind.

MARTHA [*without comment*]: Yeah?

GEORGE [*picking a record*]: Martha had her daguerrotype in the paper once . . . oh, 'bout twenty-five years ago. . . . Seems she took second prize in one o' them seven-day dancin' contest things . . . biceps all bulging, holding up her partner.

MARTHA: Will you put a record on and shut up?

GEORGE: Certainly, love [*To all.*] How are we going to work this? Mixed doubles?

MARTHA: Well, you certainly don't think I'm going to dance with *you*, do you?

GEORGE [*considers it*]: Noooooo . . . not with him around . . . that's for sure. And not with twinkle-toes here, either.

HONEY: I'll dance with anyone . . . I'll dance by myself.

NICK: Honey. . . .

HONEY: I dance like the wind.

GEORGE: All right, kiddies . . . choose up and hit the sack.

Music starts. . . . Second movement, Beethoven's 7th Symphony.

HONEY [*up, dancing by herself*]: De, de de *da* da, da-da de, da *da*-da de da . . . wonderful . . .!

NICK: Honey. . . .

MARTHA: All right, George . . . cut that out!

HONEY: Dum de de da da, da-da de, dum de *da* da da. . . . Wheeeee . . .!

MARTHA: Cut it out, George!

GEORGE [*pretending not to hear*]: What, Martha? What?

NICK: Honey. . . .

MARTHA [*as* GEORGE *turns up the volume*]: CUT IT OUT, GEORGE!

GEORGE: WHAT?

MARTHA [*gets up, moves quickly, threateningly, to* GEORGE]: All right, you son of a bitch. . . .

GEORGE [*record off, at once. Quietly*]: What did you say, love?

MARTHA: You son of a . . .

HONEY [*in an arrested posture*]: You stopped! Why did you stop?

NICK: Honey. . . .

HONEY [*to* NICK, *snapping*]: Stop that!

GEORGE: I thought it was fitting, Martha.

MARTHA: Oh you did, hunh?

HONEY: You're always *at* me when I'm having a good time.

NICK [*trying to remain civil*]: I'm sorry, Honey.

HONEY: Just . . . leave me alone!

GEORGE: Well, why don't *you* choose, Martha? [*Moves away from the phonograph . . . leaves it to* MARTHA.] Martha's going to run things . . . the little lady's going to lead the band.

HONEY: I like to dance and you don't want me to.

NICK: *I* like you to dance.
HONEY: Just . . . leave me alone. [*She sits . . . takes a drink.*]
GEORGE: Martha's going to put on some rhythm she understands . . . Sacre du Printemps, maybe. [*Moves . . . sits by* HONEY.] Hi, sexy.
HONEY [*a little giggle-scream*]: Ooooooohhhhh!
GEORGE [*laughs mockingly*]: Ha, ha, ha, ha, ha. Choose it, Martha . . . do your stuff!
MARTHA [*concentrating on the machine*]: You're damn right!
GEORGE [*to* HONEY]: You want to dance with me, angel-tits?
NICK: What did you call my wife?
GEORGE [*derisively*]: Oh boy!
HONEY [*petulantly*]: No! If I can't do my interpretive dance, I don't want to dance with anyone. I'll just sit here and . . . [*Shrugs . . . drinks.*]
MARTHA [*Record on . . . a jazzy slow pop tune*]: O.K. stuff, let's go. [*Grabs* NICK.]
NICK: Hm? Oh . . . hi.
MARTHA: Hi. [*They dance, close together, slowly.*]
HONEY [*pouting*]: We'll just sit here and watch.
GEORGE: That's *right*!
MARTHA [*to* NICK]: Hey, you *are* strong, aren't you?
NICK: Unh-hunh.
MARTHA: I like that.
NICK: Unh-hunh.
HONEY: They're dancing like they've danced before.
GEORGE: It's a familiar dance . . . they both know it. . . .
MARTHA: Don't be shy.
NICK: I'm . . . not. . . .
GEORGE [*to* HONEY]: it's a very old ritual, monkey-nipples . . . old as they come.
HONEY: I . . . I don't know what you mean.

> NICK *and* MARTHA *move apart now, and dance on either side of where* GEORGE *and* HONEY *are sitting; they face each other, and while their feet move but little, their bodies undulate congruently. . . . It is as if they were pressed together.*

MARTHA: I like the way you move.
NICK: I like the way you move, too.
GEORGE [*to* HONEY]: They like the way they move.
HONEY [*not entirely with it*]: That's nice.
MARTHA [*to* NICK]: I'm surprised George didn't give you his side of things.
GEORGE [*to* HONEY]: Aren't they cute?
NICK: Well, he didn't.
MARTHA: That surprises me. [*Perhaps* MARTHA's *statements are more or less in time to the music.*]
NICK: Does it?
MARTHA: Yeah . . . he usually does . . . when he gets the chance.
NICK: Well, what do you know.
MARTHA: It's really a very sad story.
GEORGE: You have ugly talents, Martha.
NICK: Is it?
MARTHA: It would make you weep.
GEORGE: Hideous gifts.

NICK: Is that so?
GEORGE: Don't encourage her.
MARTHA: Encourage me.
NICK: Go on.

They may undulate towards each other and then move back.

GEORGE: I warn you . . . don't encourage her.
MARTHA: He warns you . . . don't encourage me.
NICK: I heard him . . . tell me more.
MARTHA [*consciously making rhymed speech*]:

> Well, Georgie-boy had lots of big ambitions
> In spite of something funny in his past. . . .

GEORGE [*quietly warning*]: Martha . . .

MARTHA: Which Georgie-boy here turned into a novel. . . .
> His first attempt and also his last. . . .

Hey! I rhymed! I rhymed!
GEORGE: I warn you, Martha.
NICK: Yeah . . . you rhymed. Go on, go on.
MARTHA: But Daddy took a look at Georgie's novel . . .
GEORGE: You're looking for a punch in the mouth. . . . You know that, Martha.
MARTHA: Do tell! . . . and he was very shocked by what he read.
NICK: He was?
MARTHA: Yes . . . he was. . . . A novel all about a naughty boy-child . . .
GEORGE [*rising*]: I will not tolerate this!
NICK [*offhand, to* GEORGE]: Oh, can it.
MARTHA: . . . ha, ha!

> naughty boychild
> who . . . uh . . . who killed his mother and his father dead.

GEORGE: STOP IT, MARTHA!
MARTHA: And Daddy said . . . Look here, I will not let you publish such a thing. . . .
GEORGE [*rushes to phonograph . . . rips the record off*]: That's it! The dancing's over. That's it. Go on now!
NICK: What do you think you're doing, hunh?
HONEY [*happily*]: Violence! Violence!
MARTHA [*loud: a pronouncement*]: And Daddy said . . . Look here, kid, you don't think for a second I'm going to let you publish this crap, do you? Not on your life, baby . . . not while you're teaching here. . . . You publish that goddamn book and you're out . . . on your ass!
GEORGE: DESIST! DESIST!
MARTHA: Ha, ha, ha, HA!
NICK [*laughing*]: De . . . sist!
HONEY: Oh, violence . . . violence!
MARTHA: Why, the idea! A teacher at a respected, conservative institution like

this, in a town like New Carthage, publishing a book like that? If you respect your position here, young man, young . . . whippersnapper, you'll just withdraw that manuscript. . . .

GEORGE: I will not be made mock of!

NICK: He will not be made mock of, for Christ's sake. [*Laughs.*]

HONEY *joins in the laughter, not knowing exactly why.*

GEORGE: I will not!

All three are laughing at him.

GEORGE [*infuriated*]: THE GAME IS OVER!

MARTHA [*pushing on*]: Imagine such a thing! A book about a boy who murders his mother and kills his father, and pretends it's all an accident!

HONEY [*beside herself with glee*]: An accident!

NICK [*remembering something related*]: Hey . . . wait a minute . . .

MARTHA [*her own voice now*]: And you want to know the clincher? You want to know what big brave Georgie said to Daddy?

GEORGE: NO! NO! NO! NO!

NICK: Wait a minute now. . . .

MARTHA: Georgie said . . . but Daddy . . . I mean . . . ha, ha, ha, ha . . . but *Sir*, it isn't a *novel* at all . . . [*Other voice.*] Not a novel? [*Mimicking* GEORGE'*s voice.*] No, sir . . . it isn't a novel at all. . . .

GEORGE [*advancing on her*]: You will not say this!

NICK [*sensing the danger*]: Hey.

MARTHA: The hell I won't. Keep away from me, you bastard! [*Backs off a little . . . uses* GEORGE'*s voice again.*] No, Sir, this isn't a novel at all . . . this is the truth . . . this really happened. . . . TO ME!

GEORGE [*on her*]: I'LL KILL YOU!

Grabs her by the throat. They struggle.

NICK: HEY! [*Comes between them.*]

HONEY [*wildly*]: VIOLENCE! VIOLENCE!

GEORGE, MARTHA, *and* NICK *struggle . . . yells, etc.*

MARTHA: IT HAPPENED! TO ME! TO ME!

GEORGE: YOU SATANIC BITCH!

NICK: STOP THAT! STOP THAT!

HONEY: VIOLENCE! VIOLENCE!

The other three struggle. GEORGE'*s hands are on* MARTHA'*s throat.* NICK *grabs him, tears him from* MARTHA, *throws him on the floor.* GEORGE, *on the floor;* NICK *over him;* MARTHA *to one side, her hand on her throat.*

NICK: That's enough now!

HONEY [*disappointment in her voice*]: Oh . . . oh . . . oh . . .

GEORGE *drags himself into a chair. He is hurt, but it is more a profound humiliation than a physical injury.*

GEORGE [*they watch him . . . a pause . . .*]: All right . . . all right . . . very quiet now . . . we will all be . . . very quiet.

MARTHA [*softly, with a slow shaking of her head*]: Murderer. Mur . . . der . . . er.

NICK [*softly to* MARTHA]: O.K. now . . . that's enough.

A brief silence. They all move around a little, self-consciously, like wrestlers flexing after a fall.

GEORGE [*composure seemingly recovered, but there is a great nervous intensity*]: Well! That's one game. What shall we do now, hunh?

MARTHA *and* NICK *laugh nervously.*

Oh come on . . . let's think of something else. We've played Humiliate the Host . . . we've gone through that one . . . what shall we do now?

NICK: Aw . . . look. . . .

GEORGE: AW LOOK! [*Whines it.*] Awww . . . looooook. [*Alert.*] I mean, come on! We must know other games, college-type types like us . . . that can't be the . . . limit of our vocabulary, can it?

NICK: I think maybe . . .

GEORGE: Let's see now . . . what else can we do? There are other games. How about . . . how about . . . Hump the Hostess? HUNH? How about that? How about Hump the Hostess? [*To* NICK.] You wanna play that one? You wanna play Hump the Hostess? HUNH? HUNH?

NICK [*a little frightened*]: Calm down, now.

MARTHA *giggles quietly.*

GEORGE: Or is that for later . . . mount her like a goddamn dog?

HONEY [*wildly toasting everybody*]: Hump the Hostess!

NICK [*to* HONEY . . . *sharply*]: Just shut up . . . will you?

HONEY *does, her glass in mid-air.*

GEORGE: You don't wanna play that now, hunh? You wanna save that game till later? Well, what'll we play now? We gotta play a game.

MARTHA [*quietly*]: Portrait of a man drowning.

GEORGE [*affirmatively, but to none of them*]: I am not drowning.

HONEY [*to* NICK, *tearfully indignant*]: You told me to shut up!

NICK [*impatiently*]: I'm sorry.

HONEY [*between her teeth*]: No you're not.

NICK [*to* HONEY, *even more impatiently*]: I'm sorry.

GEORGE [*claps his hands together, once, loud*]: I've got it! I'll tell you what game we'll play. We're done with Humiliate the Host . . . this round, anyway . . . we're done with that . . . and we don't want to play Hump the Hostess, yet . . . not yet . . . so I know what we'll play. . . . We'll play a round of Get the Guests. How about that? How about a little game of Get the Guests?

MARTHA [*turning away, a little disgusted*]: Jesus, George.

GEORGE: Book dropper! Child mentioner!

HONEY: I don't like these games.

NICK: Yeah. . . . I think maybe we've had enough of games, now. . . .

GEORGE: Oh, no . . . oh, no . . . we haven't. We've had only one game. . . . Now we're going to have another. You can't fly on one game.

NICK: I think maybe . . .

GEORGE [*with great authority*]: SILENCE! [*It is respected.*] Now, how are we going to play Get the Guests?

MARTHA: For God's sake, George. . . .

GEORGE: You be quiet!

MARTHA *shrugs.*

I wonder. . . . I wonder. [*Puzzles . . . then . . .*] O.K.! Well . . . Martha . . . in her indiscreet way . . . well, not really indiscreet, because Martha is naïve, at heart . . . anyway, Martha told you all about my first novel. True or false? Hunh? I mean, true or false that there ever was such a thing. HA! But, Martha told you about it . . . my first novel, my . . . memory book . . . which I'd sort of preferred she hadn't, but hell, that's blood under the bridge. BUT! what she didn't do . . . what Martha didn't tell you about is she didn't tell us all about my *second* novel.

MARTHA *looks at him with puzzled curiosity.*

No, you didn't know about that, did you, Martha? About my second novel, true or false. True or false?

MARTHA [*sincerely*]: No.

GEORGE: No. [*He starts quietly but as he goes on his tone becomes harsher, his voice louder.*] Well, it's an allegory, really—probably—but it can be read as straight, cosy prose . . . and it's all about a nice young couple who come out of the middle-west. It's a bucolic you see. AND, this nice young couple comes out of the middle-west, and he's blond and about thirty, and he's a scientist, a teacher, a scientist . . . and his mouse is a wifey little type who gargles brandy all the time . . . and . . .

NICK: Just a minute here. . . .

GEORGE: . . . and they got to know each other when they was only teensie little types, and they used to get under the vanity table and poke around, and . . .

NICK: I said JUST A MINUTE!

GEORGE: This is my game! You played yours . . . you people. This is my game!

HONEY [*dreamy*]: I want to hear the story. I love stories.

MARTHA: George, for heaven's sake. . . .

GEORGE: AND! And Mousie's father was a holy man, see, and he ran sort of a travelling clip joint, based on Christ and all those girls, and he took the faithful . . . that's all . . . just took 'em. . . .

HONEY [*puzzling*]: This is familiar. . . .

NICK [*voice shaking a little*]: No kidding!

GEORGE: . . . and he died eventually, Mousie's pa, and they pried him open, and all sorts of money fell out. . . . Jesus money, Mary money. . . . LOOT!

HONEY [*dreamy, puzzling*]: I've heard this story before.

NICK [*with quiet intensity . . . to waken her*]: Honey. . . .

GEORGE: But that's in the backwash, in the early part of the book. Anyway,

Blondie and his frau out of the plain states came. [*Chuckles.*]

MARTHA: Very funny, George. . . .

GEORGE: . . . thank you . . . and settled in a town just like nouveau Carthage here. . . .

NICK [*threatening*]: I don't think you'd better go on, mister. . . .

GEORGE: Do you not!

NICK [*less certainly*]: No. I . . . I don't think you'd better.

HONEY: I love familiar stories . . . they're the best.

GEORGE: How right you are. But Blondie was in disguise, really, all got up as a teacher, 'cause his baggage ticket had bigger things writ on it . . . H.I. HI! Historical inevitability.

NICK: There's no need for you to go any further, now. . . .

HONEY [*puzzling to make sense out of what she is hearing*]: Let them go on.

GEORGE: We shall. And he had this baggage with him, and part of this baggage was in the form of his mouse. . . .

NICK: We don't have to listen to this!

HONEY: Why not?

GEORGE: Your bride has a point. And one of the things nobody could understand about Blondie was his baggage . . . his mouse, I mean, here he was, pan-Kansas swimming champeen, or something, and he had this mouse, of whom he was solicitous to a point that faileth human understanding . . . given that she was sort of a simp, in the long run. . . .

NICK: This isn't fair of you. . . .

GEORGE: Perhaps not. Like, as I said, his mouse, she tooted brandy immodestly and spent half of her time in the upchuck. . . .

HONEY [*focusing*]: I know these people. . . .

GEORGE: Do you! . . . But she was a money baggage amongst other things . . . Godly money ripped from the golden teeth of the unfaithful, a pragmatic extension of the big dream . . . and she was put up with. . . .

HONEY [*some terror*]: I don't like this story. . . .

NICK [*surprisingly pleading*]: Please . . . please don't.

MARTHA: Maybe you better stop, George. . . .

GEORGE: . . . and she was put up with. . . . STOP? Ha-ha.

NICK: Please . . . please don't.

GEORGE: Beg, baby.

MARTHA: George. . . .

GEORGE: . . . and . . . oh, we get a flashback here, to How They Got Married.

NICK: NO!

GEORGE [*triumphant*]: YES!

NICK [*almost whining*]: Why?

GEORGE: How They Got Married. Well, how they got married is this. . . . The Mouse got all puffed up one day, and she went over to Blondie's house, and she stuck out her puff, and she said . . . look at me.

HONEY [*white . . . on her feet*]: I . . . don't . . . like this.

NICK [*to* GEORGE]: Stop it!

GEORGE: Look at me . . . I'm all puffed up. Oh my goodness, said Blondie. . . .

HONEY [*as from a distance*]: . . . and so they were married . . .

GEORGE: . . . and so they were married. . . .

HONEY: . . . and then . . .

GEORGE: . . . and then . . .

HONEY [*hysteria*]: WHAT? . . . and then, WHAT?

NICK: NO! No!

GEORGE [*as if to a baby*]: . . . and then the puff went *away* . . . like magic . . . pouf!

NICK [*almost sick*]: Jesus God. . . .

HONEY: . . . the puff went away. . . .

GEORGE [*softly*]: . . . pouf.

NICK: Honey . . . I didn't mean to . . . honestly, I didn't mean to . . .

HONEY: You . . . you told them. . . .

NICK: Honey . . . I didn't mean to. . . .

HONEY [*with outlandish horror*]: You . . . told them! You told them! OOOOHHHH! Oh, no, no, no, no! You couldn't have told them . . . oh, noooo!

NICK: Honey, I didn't mean to. . . .

HONEY [*grabbing at her belly*]: Ohhhhh . . . nooooo.

NICK: Honey . . . baby . . . I'm sorry . . . I didn't mean to. . . .

GEORGE [*abruptly and with some disgust*]: And that's how you play Get the Guests.

HONEY: I'm going to . . . I'm going to be . . . sick. . . .

GEORGE: Naturally!

NICK: Honey. . . .

HONEY [*hysterical*]: Leave me alone . . . I'm going . . . to . . . be . . . sick. [*She runs out of the room.*]

MARTHA [*shaking her head, watching* HONEY*'s retreating form*]: God Almighty.

GEORGE [*shrugging*]: The patterns of history.

NICK [*quietly shaking*]: You shouldn't have done that . . . you shouldn't have done that at all.

GEORGE [*calmly*]: I hate hypocrisy.

NICK: That was cruel . . . and vicious . . .

GEORGE: . . . she'll get over it. . . .

NICK: . . . and damaging . . .!

GEORGE: . . . she'll recover. . . .

NICK: DAMAGING!! TO ME!!

GEORGE [*with wonder*]: To you!

NICK: TO ME!!

GEORGE: To you!!

NICK: YES!!

GEORGE: Oh beautiful . . . beautiful. By God, you gotta have a swine to show you where the truffles are. [*So calmly.*] Well, you just rearrange your alliances, boy. You just pick up the pieces where you can . . . you just look around and make the best of things . . . you scramble back up on your feet.

MARTHA [*quietly, to* NICK]: Go look after your wife.

GEORGE: Yeah . . . go pick up the pieces and plan some new strategy.

NICK [*to* GEORGE, *as he moves towards the hall*]: You're going to regret this.

GEORGE: Probably. I regret everything.

NICK: I mean, I'm going to make you regret this.

GEORGE [*softly*]: No doubt. Acute embarrassment, eh?

NICK: I'll play the charades like you've got 'em set up. . . . I'll play in your language. . . . I'll be what you say I am.

GEORGE: You are already . . . you just don't know it.

NICK [*shaking within*]: No . . . no. Not really. But I'll *be* it, mister. . . . I'll show you something come to life you'll wish you hadn't set up.

GEORGE: Go clean up the mess.

NICK [*quietly . . . intensely*]: You just wait, mister.

He exits. Pause. GEORGE *smiles at* MARTHA.

MARTHA: Very good, George.
GEORGE: Thank you, Martha.
MARTHA: Really good.
GEORGE: I'm glad you liked it.
MARTHA: I mean . . . You did a good job . . . you really fixed it.
GEORGE: Unh-hunh.
MARTHA: It's the most . . . life you've shown in a long time.
GEORGE: You bring out the best in me, baby.
MARTHA: Yeah . . . pigmy hunting!
GEORGE: PIGMY!
MARTHA: You're really a bastard.
GEORGE: I? I?
MARTHA: Yeah . . . you.
GEORGE: Baby, if quarterback there is a pigmy, you've certainly changed your style. What are you after now . . . giants?
MARTHA: You make me sick.
GEORGE: It's perfectly all right for you. . . . I mean, you can make your own rules . . . you can go around like a hopped-up Arab, slashing away at everything in sight, scarring up half the world if you want to. But somebody else try it . . . no sir!
MARTHA: You miserable . . .
GEORGE [*mocking*]: Why baby, I did it all for you. I thought you'd like it, sweetheart . . . it's sort of to your taste . . . blood, carnage and all. Why, I thought you'd get all excited . . . sort of heave and pant and come running at me, your melons bobbling.
MARTHA: You've really screwed up, George.
GEORGE [*spitting it out*]: Oh, for God's sake, Martha!
MARTHA: I mean it . . . you really have.
GEORGE [*barely contained anger now*]: You can sit there in that chair of yours, you can sit there with the gin running out of your mouth, and you can humiliate me, you can tear me apart . . . ALL NIGHT . . . and that's perfectly all right . . . that's O.K. . . .
MARTHA: YOU CAN STAND IT!
GEORGE: I CANNOT STAND IT!
MARTHA: YOU CAN STAND IT! YOU MARRIED ME FOR IT!!

A silence.

GEORGE [*quietly*]: That is a desperately sick lie.
MARTHA: DON'T YOU KNOW IT, EVEN YET?
GEORGE [*shaking his head*]: Oh . . . Martha.
MARTHA: My arm has gotten tired whipping you.
GEORGE [*stares at her in disbelief*]: You're mad.
MARTHA: For twenty-three years!
GEORGE: You're deluded . . . Martha, you're deluded.
MARTHA: IT'S NOT WHAT I'VE WANTED!.
GEORGE: I thought at least you were . . . on to yourself. I didn't know. I . . . didn't know.
MARTHA [*anger taking over*]: I'm on to myself.

GEORGE [*as if she were some sort of bug*]: No . . . no . . . you're . . . sick.

MARTHA [*rises—screams*]: I'LL SHOW YOU WHO'S SICK!

GEORGE: All right, Martha . . . you're going too far.

MARTHA [*screams again*]: I'LL SHOW YOU WHO'S SICK. I'LL SHOW YOU.

GEORGE [*he shakes her*]: Stop it! [*Pushes her back in her chair.*] Now, stop it!

MARTHA [*calmer*]: I'll show you who's sick. [*Calmer.*] Boy, you're really having a field day, hunh? Well, I'm going to finish you . . . before I'm through with you. . . .

GEORGE: . . . you and the quarterback . . . you both gonna finish me . . .?

MARTHA: . . . before I'm through with you you'll wish you'd died in that automobile, you bastard.

GEORGE [*emphasizing with his forefinger*]: And you'll wish you'd never mentioned our son!

MARTHA [*dripping contempt*]: You . . .

GEORGE: Now, I said I warned you.

MARTHA: I'm impressed.

GEORGE: I warned you not to go too far.

MARTHA: I'm just beginning.

GEORGE [*calmly, matter-of-factly*]: I'm numbed enough . . . and I don't mean by liquor, though maybe that's been part of the process—a gradual, over-the-years going to sleep of the brain cells—I'm numbed enough, now, to be able to take you when we're alone. I don't listen to you . . . or when I *do* listen to you, I sift everything, I bring everything down to reflex response, so I don't really *hear* you, which is the only way to manage it. But you've taken a new tack, Martha, over the past couple of centuries—or however long it's been I've lived in this house with you—that makes it just too much . . . too much. I don't mind your dirty underthings in public . . . well, I *do* mind, but I've reconciled myself to that . . . but you've moved bag and baggage into your own fantasy world now, and you've started playing variations on your own distortions, and, as a result . . .

MARTHA: Nuts!

GEORGE: Yes . . . you have.

MARTHA: Nuts!

GEORGE: Well, you can go on like that as long as you want to. And, when you're done . . .

MARTHA: Have you ever listened to your sentences, George? Have you ever listened to the way you talk? You're so frigging . . . convoluted . . . that's what you are. You talk like you were writing one of your stupid papers.

GEORGE: Actually, I'm rather worried about you. About your mind.

MARTHA: Don't you worry about my mind, sweetheart!

GEORGE: I think I'll have you committed.

MARTHA: YOU WHAT?

GEORGE [*quietly . . . distinctly*]: I think I'll have you committed.

MARTHA [*breaks into long laughter*]: Oh baby, aren't you something!

GEORGE: I've got to find some way to really get at you.

MARTHA: You've got at me, George . . . you don't have to do anything. Twenty-three years of you has been quite enough.

GEORGE: Will you go quietly, then?

MARTHA: You know what's happened, George? You want to know what's *really happened*? [*Snaps her fingers.*] It's snapped, finally. Not me . . . *it*. The whole arrangement. You can go along . . . forever, and everything's . . .

manageable. You make all sorts of excuses to yourself . . . *you* know . . . this is life . . . maybe tomorrow *you'll* be dead . . . all sorts of excuses. But then, one day, one night, something happens . . . and SNAP! It breaks. And you just don't give a damn any more. I've tried with you, baby . . . really, I've tried.

GEORGE: Come off it, Martha.

MARTHA: I've tried . . . I've really tried.

GEORGE [*with some awe*]: You're a monster . . . you *are*.

MARTHA: I'm loud, and I'm vulgar, and I wear the pants in this house because somebody's got to, but I am *not* a monster. I am *not*.

GEORGE: You're a spoiled, self-indulgent, wilful, dirty-minded, liquor-ridden . . .

MARTHA: SNAP! It went snap. Look, I'm not going to try to get through to you any more. . . . I'm not going to try. There was a second back there, maybe, there was a second, just a second, when I could have gotten through to you, when maybe we could have cut through all this crap. But that's past, and now I'm not going to try.

GEORGE: Once a month, Martha! I've gotten used to it . . . once a month and we get misunderstood Martha, the good-hearted girl underneath the barnacles, the little Miss that the touch of kindness'd bring to bloom again. And I've believed it more times than I want to remember, because I don't want to think I'm that much of a sucker. I don't believe you . . . I just don't believe you. There is no moment . . . there is no moment any more when we could . . . come together.

MARTHA [*armed again*]: Well, maybe you're right, baby. You can't come together with nothing, and you're nothing! SNAP! it went snap tonight at Daddy's party. [*Dripping contempt, but there is fury and loss under it.*] I sat there at Daddy's party, and I watched you . . . I watched you sitting there, and I watched the younger men around you, the men who were going to go somewhere. And I sat there and I watched you, and *you* weren't *there*! And it snapped! It finally snapped! And I'm going to howl it out, and I'm not going to give a damn what I do, and I'm going to make the damned biggest explosion you ever heard.

GEORGE [*very pointedly*]: You try it and I'll beat you at your own game.

MARTHA [*hopefully*]: Is that a threat, George? Hunh?

GEORGE: That's a threat, Martha.

MARTHA [*fake-spits at him*]: You're going to get it, baby.

GEORGE: Be careful, Martha . . . I'll rip you to pieces.

MARTHA: You aren't man enough . . . you haven't got the guts.

GEORGE: Total war?

MARTHA: Total.

Silence. They both seem relieved . . . elated. NICK *re-enters.*

NICK [*brushing his hands off*]: Well . . . she's . . . resting.

GEORGE [*quietly amused at* NICK's *calm, off-hand manner*]: Oh?

MARTHA: Yeah? She all right?

NICK: I think so . . . now. I'm . . . terribly sorry. . . .

MARTHA: Forget about it.

GEORGE: Happens all the time around here.

NICK: She'll be all right.

MARTHA: She lying down? You put her upstairs? On a bed?

NICK [*making himself a drink*]: Well, no, actually. Uh . . . may I? She's . . . in the bathroom . . . on the bathroom floor . . . she's lying there.

GEORGE [*considers it*]: Well . . . that's not very nice.

NICK: She likes it. She says it's . . . cool.

GEORGE: Still, I don't think. . . .

MARTHA [*overruling him*]: If she wants to lie on the bathroom floor, let her. [*To* NICK, *seriously.*] Maybe she'd be more comfortable in the tub?

NICK [*he, too, seriously*]: No, she says she likes the floor . . . she took up the mat, and she's lying on the tiles. She . . . she lies on the floor a lot . . . she really does.

MARTHA [*pause*]: Oh.

NICK: She . . . she gets lots of headaches and things, and she always lies on the floor. [*To* GEORGE.] Is there . . . ice?

GEORGE: What?

NICK: Ice. Is there ice?

GEORGE [*as if the word were unfamiliar to him*]: Ice?

NICK: Ice. Yes.

MARTHA: Ice.

GEORGE [*as if he suddenly understood*]: Ice!

MARTHA: Attaboy.

GEORGE [*without moving*]: Oh, yes . . . I'll get some.

MARTHA: Well, go. [*Mugging . . . to* NICK.] Besides, we want to be alone.

GEORGE [*moving to take the bucket*]: I wouldn't be surprised, Martha . . . I wouldn't be surprised.

MARTHA [*as if insulted*]: Oh, you wouldn't, hunh?

GEORGE: Not a bit, Martha.

MARTHA [*violent*]: NO?

GEORGE [*he too*]: NO! [*Quietly again.*] You'll try anything, Martha. [*Picks up the ice bucket.*]

NICK [*to cover*]: Actually, she's very . . . frail, and . . .

GEORGE: . . . slim-hipped.

NICK [*remembering*]: Yes . . . exactly.

GEORGE [*at the hallway . . . not kindly*]: That why you don't have any kids? [*He exits.*]

NICK [*to* GEORGE's *retreating form*]: Well, I don't know that that's . . . [*Trails off.*] . . . if that has anything to do with any . . . thing.

MARTHA: Well, if it does, who cares? Hunh?

NICK: Pardon?

MARTHA *blows him a kiss.*

NICK [*still concerned with* GEORGE's *remark*]: I . . . what? . . . I'm sorry.

MARTHA: I said . . . [*Blows him another kiss.*]

NICK [*uncomfortable*]: Oh . . . yes.

MARTHA: Hey . . . hand me a cigarette . . . lover.

NICK *fishes in his pocket.*

That's a good boy.

He gives her one.

Unh . . . thanks.

He lights it for her. As he does, she slips her hand between his legs, somewhere between the knee and the crotch, bringing her hand around to the outside of his leg.

Ummmmmmmmm.

He seems uncertain, but does not move. She smiles, moves her hand a little.

Now, for being such a good boy, you can give me a kiss. C'mon.
NICK [*nervously*]: Look . . . I don't think we should. . . .
MARTHA: C'mon, baby . . . a friendly kiss.
NICK [*still uncertain*]: Well. . . .
MARTHA: . . . you won't get hurt, little boy. . . .
NICK: . . . not so little. . . .
MARTHA: I'll bet you're not. C'mon. . . .
NICK [*weakening*]: But what if he should come back in, and . . . or . . .?
MARTHA [*all the while her hand is moving up and down his leg*]: George? Don't worry about him. Besides, who could object to a friendly little kiss? It's all in the faculty.

They both laugh, quietly . . . NICK *a little nervously.*

We're a close-knit family here . . . Daddy always says so. . . . Daddy wants us to get to know each other . . . that's what he had the party for tonight. So c'mon . . . let's get to know each other a little bit.
NICK: It isn't that I don't want to . . . believe me. . . .
MARTHA: You're a scientist, aren't you? C'mon . . . make an experiment . . . make a little experiment. Experiment on old Martha.
NICK [*giving in*]: . . . not very old. . . .
MARTHA: That's right, not very old, but lots of good experience . . . lots of it.
NICK: I'll . . . I'll bet.
MARTHA [*as they draw slowly closer*]: It'll be a nice change for you, too.
NICK: Yes it would.
MARTHA: And you could go back to your little wife all refreshed.
NICK [*closer . . . almost whispering*]: She wouldn't know the difference.
MARTHA: Well, nobody else's going to know, either.

They come together. What might have been a joke rapidly becomes serious, with MARTHA *urging it in that direction. There is no frenetic quality, but rather a slow, continually involving intertwining. Perhaps* MARTHA *is still more or less in her chair, and* NICK *is sort of beside and on the chair.*

GEORGE *enters . . . stops . . . watches a moment . . . smiles . . . laughs silently, nods his head, turns, exits, without being noticed.*

NICK, *who has already had his hand on* MARTHA's *breast, now puts his hand inside her dress.*

MARTHA [*slowing him down*]: Hey . . . hey. Take it easy, boy. Down, baby. Don't rush it, hunh?

NICK [*his eyes still closed*]: Oh, c'mon, now. . . .

MARTHA [*pushing him away*]: Unh-hunh. Later, baby . . . later.

NICK: I told you . . . I'm a biologist.

MARTHA [*soothing him*]: I know. I can tell. Later, hunh?

> GEORGE *is heard off-stage, singing 'Who's afraid of Virginia Woolf?'* MARTHA
> *and* NICK *go apart,* NICK *wiping his mouth,* MARTHA *checking her clothes.*
> *Safely later,* GEORGE *re-enters with the ice bucket.*

GEORGE: . . . of Virginia Woolf,
                    Virginia Woolf,
                    Virginia . . .

. . . ah! Here we are . . . ice for the lamps of China, Manchuria thrown in. [*To*
NICK.] You better watch those yellow bastards, my love . . . they aren't
amused. Why don't you come on over to our side, and we'll blow the hell out
of 'em. Then we can split up the money between us and be on Easy Street.
What d'ya say?

NICK [*not at all sure what is being talked about*]: Well . . . sure. Hey! Ice!

GEORGE [*with hideously false enthusiasm*]: Right! [*Now to* MARTHA, *purring.*]
Hello, Martha . . . my dove. . . . You look . . . radiant.

MARTHA [*off-hand*]: Thank you.

GEORGE [*very cheerful*]: Well now, let me see. I've got the ice . . .

MARTHA: . . . gotten. . . .

GEORGE: *Got*, Martha. Got is perfectly correct . . . it's just a little . . . archaic,
like you.

MARTHA [*suspicious*]: What are you so cheerful about?

GEORGE [*ignoring the remark*]: Let's see now . . . I've got the ice. Can I make
someone a drink? Martha, can I make you a drink?

MARTHA [*bravura*]: Yeah, why not?

GEORGE [*taking her glass*]: Indeed . . . why not? [*Examines the glass.*] Martha!
You've been nibbling away at the glass.

MARTHA: I have not!

GEORGE [*to* NICK, *who is at the bar*]: I see you're making your own, which is
fine . . . fine. I'll just hootch up Martha, here, and then we'll be all set.

MARTHA [*suspicious*]: All set for what?

GEORGE [*pause . . . considers*]: Why, I don't know. We're having a party, aren't
we? [*To* NICK *who has moved from the bar.*] I passed your wife in the hall. I
mean, I passed the john and I looked in on her. Peaceful . . . so peaceful.
Sound asleep . . . and she's actually . . . sucking her thumb.

MARTHA: Awwwwww!

GEORGE: Rolled up like a foetus, sucking away.

NICK [*a little uncomfortably*]: I suppose she's all right.

GEORGE [*expansively*]: Of course she is! [*Hands* MARTHA *her drink.*] There you
are.

MARTHA [*still on her guard*]: Thanks.

GEORGE: And now one for me. It's my turn.

MARTHA: Never, baby . . . it's never your turn.

GEORGE [*too cheerful*]: Oh, now, I wouldn't say that, Martha.

MARTHA: You moving on the principle the worm turns? Well, the worm part's
O.K. . . . 'cause that fits you fine, but the turning part . . . unh-unh! You're in

a straight line, buddy-boy, and it doesn't lead anywhere ... [*A vague afterthought.*] ... except maybe the grave.

GEORGE [*chuckles, takes his drink*]: Well, you just hold that thought, Martha ... hug it close ... run your hands over it. Me, I'm going to sit down ... if you'll excuse me. ... I'm going to sit down over there and read a book. [*He moves to a chair facing away from the centre of the room, but not too far from the front door.*]

MARTHA: You're gonna do *what*?

GEORGE [*quietly, distinctly*]: I am going to read a book. Read. Read. Read? You've heard of it? [*Picks up a book.*]

MARTHA [*standing*]: Whaddya mean you're gonna read? What's the matter with you?

GEORGE too clamly]: There's nothing the matter with me, Martha. ... I'm going to read a book. That's all.

MARTHA [*oddly furious*]: We've got company!

GEORGE [*over-patiently*]: I know, my dear ... [*Looks at his watch.*] ... but ... it's after four o'clock, and I always read around this time. Now, you ... [*Dismisses her with a little wave.*] ... go about your business. ... I'll sit here very quietly. ...

MARTHA: You read in the afternoon! You read at four o'clock in the afternoon ... you don't read at four o'clock in the morning! Nobody reads at four o'clock in the morning!

GEORGE [*absorbing himself in his book*]: Now, now, now.

MARTHA [*incredulously, to* NICK]: He's going to read a book. ... The son of a bitch is going to read a book!

NICK [*smiling a little*]: So it would seem.

Moves to MARTHA, *puts his arm around her waist.* GEORGE *cannot see this, of course.*

MARTHA [*getting an idea*]: Well, we can amuse oursleves, can't we?

NICK: I imagine so.

MARTHA: We're going to amuse ourselves, George.

GEORGE [*not looking up*]: Unh-hunh. That's nice.

MARTHA You might not like it.

GEORGE [*never looking up*]: No, no, now ... you go right ahead ... you entertain your guests.

MARTHA: I'm going to entertain myself, too.

GEORGE: Good ... good.

MARTHA: Ha, ha. You're a riot, George.

GEORGE: Unh-hunh.

MARTHA: Well, I'm a riot, too, George.

GEORGE: Yes you are, Martha.

NICK *takes* MARTHA'*s hand, pulls her to him. They stop for a moment, then kiss, not briefly.*

MARTHA [*after*]: You know what I'm doing, George?

GEORGE: No, Martha ... what are you doing?

MARTHA: I'm entertaining. I'm entertaining one of the guests. I'm necking with one of the guests.

GEORGE [*seemingly relaxed and preoccupied, never looking*]: Oh, that's nice. Which one?

MARTHA [*livid*]: Oh, by God, you're funny. [*Breaks away from* NICK . . . *moves into* GEORGE's *side-line of vision by herself. Her balance is none too good, and she bumps into or brushes against the door chimes by the door. They chime.*]

GEORGE: Someone at the door, Martha.

MARTHA: Never mind that. I said I was necking with one of the guests.

GEORGE: Good . . . good. You go right on.

MARTHA [*pauses . . . not knowing quite what to do*]: Good?

GEORGE: Yes, good . . . good for you.

MARTHA [*her eyes narrowing, her voice becoming hard*]: Oh, I see what you're up to, you lousy little . . .

GEORGE: I'm up to page a hundred and . . .

MARTHA: Cut it! Just cut it out! [*She hits against the door chimes again; they chime.*] Goddamn bongs.

GEORGE: They're chimes, Martha. Why don't you go back to your necking and stop bothering me? I want to read.

MARTHA: Why, you miserable. . . . I'll show *you.*

GEORGE [*swings around to face her . . . says, with great loathing*]: No . . . show him, Martha . . . he hasn't seen it. *Maybe* he hasn't seen it. [*Turn to* NICK.] You haven't seen it yet, have you?

NICK [*turning away, a look of disgust on his face*]: I . . . I have no respect for you.

GEORGE: And none for yourself, either. . . . [*Indicating* MARTHA.] I don't know what the younger generation's coming to.

NICK: You don't . . . you don't even . . .

GEORGE: Care? You're quite right. . . . I couldn't care less. So, you just take this bag of laundry here, throw her over your shoulder, and . . .

NICK: You're disgusting.

GEORGE [*incredulous*]: Because *you're* going to hump Martha, *I'm* disgusting? [*He breaks down in ridiculing laughter.*]

MARTHA [*to* GEORGE]: You Mother! [*To* NICK.] Go wait for me, hunh? Go wait for me in the kitchen. [*But* NICK *does not move.* MARTHA *goes to him, puts her arms around him.*] C'mon, baby . . . please. Wait for me . . . in the kitchen . . . be a good baby,

NICK *takes her kiss, glares at* GEORGE . . . *who has turned his back again . . . and exits.*

MARTHA [*swings around to* GEORGE]: Now you listen to me. . . .

GEORGE: I'd rather read, Martha, if you don't mind. . . .

MARTHA [*her anger has her close to tears, her frustration to fury*]: Well, I do mind. Now, you pay attention to me! You come off this kick you're on, or I swear to God I'll do it. I swear to God I'll follow that guy into the kitchen, and then I'll take him upstairs, and . . .

GEORGE [*swinging around to her again . . . loud . . . loathing*]: SO WHAT, MARTHA?

MARTHA [*considers him for a moment . . . then, nodding her head, backing off slowly*]: O.K. . . . O.K. . . . You asked for it . . . and you're going to get it.

GEORGE [*softly, sadly*]: Lord, Martha, if you want the boy that much . . . have him . . . but do it honestly, will you? Don't cover it over with all this . . . all this . . . footwork.

MARTHA [*hopeless*]: I'll make you sorry you made me want to marry you. [*At the hallway.*] I'll make you regret the day you ever decided to come to this college. I'll make you sorry you ever let yourself down. [*She exits.*]

> *Silence.* GEORGE *sits still, staring straight ahead. Listening . . . but there is no sound. Outwardly calm, he returns to his book, reads a moment, then looks up . . . considers. . . .*

GEORGE: 'And the west, encumbered by crippling alliances, and burdened with a morality too rigid to accommodate itself to the swing of events, must . . . eventually . . . fall.'

> *He laughs, briefly, ruefully . . . rises, with the book in his hand. He stands still . . . then, quickly, he gathers all the fury he has been containing within himself . . . he shakes . . . he looks at the book in his hand and, with a cry that is part growl, part howl, he hurls it at the chimes. They crash against one another, ringing wildly. A brief pause, then* HONEY *enters.*

HONEY [*the worse for wear, half asleep, still sick, weak, still staggering a little . . . vaguely, in something of a dream world*]: Bell. Ringing. I've been hearing bells.

GEORGE: Jesus!

HONEY: I couldn't sleep . . . for the bells. Ding-ding, bong . . . it woke me up. What time is it?

GEORGE [*quietly beside himself*]: Don't bother me.

HONEY [*confused and frightened*]: I was asleep, and the bells started . . . they BOOMED! Poe-bells . . . they were Poe-bells . . . Bing-bing-bong-BOOM!

GEORGE: BOOM!

HONEY: I was asleep, and I was dreaming of . . . something . . . and I heard the
' sounds coming, and I didn't know what it was.

GEORGE [*never quite to her*]: It was the sound of bodies. . . .

HONEY: And I didn't want to wake up, but the sound kept coming. . . .

GEORGE: . . . go back to sleep. . . .

HONEY: . . . and it FRIGHTENED ME!

GEORGE [*quietly . . . to* MARTHA, *as if she were in the room*]: I'm going to get you . . . Martha.

HONEY: And it was so . . . cold. The wind was . . . the wind was so cold! And I was lying somewhere, and the covers kept slipping away from me, and I didn't want them to . . .

GEORGE: Somehow, Martha.

HONEY: . . . and there was someone there . . .!

GEORGE: There was no one there.

HONEY [*frightened*]: And I didn't want someone there. . . . I was . . . naked . . .!

GEORGE: You don't know what's going on, do you?

HONEY [*still with her dream*]: I DON'T WANT ANY . . . NO . . .!

GEORGE: You don't know what's been going on around here while you been having your snoozette, do you.

HONEY: NO! . . . I DON'T WANT ANY . . . I DON'T WANT THEM. . . . GO 'WAY. . . . [*Begins to cry.*] I DON'T WANT . . . ANY . . . CHILDREN. . . . I . . . don't . . . want . . . any . . . children. I'm afraid! I don't want to be hurt. . . . PLEASE!

GEORGE [*nodding his head . . . speaks with compassion*]: I should have known.

HONEY [*snapping awake from her reverie*]: What! What?

GEORGE: I should have known . . . the whole business . . . the headaches . . . the whining . . . the . . .

HONEY [*terrified*]: What are you talking about?

GEORGE [*ugly again*]: Does *he* know that? Does that . . . stud you're married to know about that, hunh?

HONEY: About what? Stay away from me!

GEORGE: Don't worry, baby . . . I wouldn't. . . . Oh, my God, that *would* be a joke, wouldn't it! But don't worry, baby. HEY! How you do it? Hunh? How do you make your secret little murders stud-boy doesn't know about, hunh? Pills? PILLS? You got a secret supply of pills? Or what? Apple jelly? WILL POWER?

HONEY: I feel sick.

GEORGE: You going to throw up again? You going to lie down on the cold tiles, your knees pulled up under your chin, your thumb stuck in your mouth . . .?

HONEY [*panicked*]: Where is he?

GEORGE: Where's who? There's nobody here, baby.

HONEY: I want my husband! I want a drink!

GEORGE: Well, you just crawl over to the bar and make yourself one.

From off-stage comes the sound of MARTHA's *laughter and the crashing of dishes.*

GEORGE [*yelling*]: That's right! Go at it!

HONEY: I want . . . something. . . .

GEORGE: You know what's going on in there, little Miss? Hunh? You hear all that? You know what's going on in there?

HONEY: I don't want to know anything!

GEORGE: There are a couple of people in there. . . .

MARTHA's *laughter again.*

. . . they are in there, in the kitchen. . . . Right there, with the onion skins and the coffee grounds . . . sort of . . . sort of a . . . sort of a dry run for the wave of the future.

HONEY [*beside herself*]: I . . . don't . . . understand . . . you. . . .

GEORGE [*a hideous elation*]: It's very simple. . . . When people can't abide things as they are, when they can't abide the present, they do one of two things . . . either they . . . either they turn to a contemplation of the past, as I have done, or they set about to . . . alter the future. And when you want to change something . . . you BANG! BANG! BANG! BANG!

HONEY: Stop it!

GEORGE: And you, you simpering bitch . . . you don't want *children*?

HONEY: You leave me . . . alone. Who . . . WHO RANG?

GEORGE: What?

HONEY: What were the bells? Who rang?

GEORGE: You don't want to know, do you? You don't want to listen to it, hunh?

HONEY [*shivering*]: I don't want to listen to you. . . . I want to know who rang.

GEORGE: Your husband is . . . and you want to know who *rang*?

HONEY: Who rang? Someone rang!

GEORGE [*his jaw drops open . . . he is whirling with an idea*]: . . . Someone . . .

HONEY: RANG!

GEORGE: . . . someone . . . rang . . . yes . . . yessss. . . .

HONEY: The . . . bells . . . rang. . . .

GEORGE [*his mind racing ahead*]: The bells rang . . . and it was someone . . .

HONEY: Somebody. . . .

GEORGE [*he is home, now*]: . . . somebody rang . . . it was somebody . . . with . . . I'VE GOT IT! I'VE GOT IT, MARTHA . . .! Somebody with a message . . . and the message was . . . our son . . . OUR SON! [*Almost whispered.*] It was a message . . . the bells rang and it was a message, and it was about . . . our son . . . and the message . . . was . . . and the message was . . . our . . . son . . . is . . . DEAD!

HONEY [*almost sick*]: Oh . . . no.

GEORGE [*cementing it in his mind*]: Our son is . . . dead. . . . And . . . Martha doesn't know. . . . I haven't told . . . Martha.

HONEY: No . . . no . . . no.

GEORGE [*slowly, deliberately*]: Our son is dead, and Martha doesn't know.

HONEY: Oh. God in heaven . . . no.

GEORGE [*to* HONEY . . . *slowly, deliberately, dispassionately*]: And you're not going to tell her.

HONEY [*in tears*]: Your son is dead.

GEORGE: I'll tell her myself . . . in good time. I'll tell her myself.

HONEY [*so faintly*]: I'm going to be sick.

GEORGE [*turning away from her . . . he, too, softly*]: Are you? That's nice.

MARTHA's *laugh is heard again.*

Oh, listen to that.

HONEY: I'm going to die.

GEORGE [*quite by himself now*]: Good . . . good . . . you go right ahead. [*Very softly, so* MARTHA *could not possibly hear.*] Martha? Martha? I have some . . . terrible news for you. [*There is a strange half-smile on his lips.*] It's about our . . . son. He's dead. Can you hear me, Martha? Our boy is dead. [*He begins to laugh, very softly . . . it is mixed with crying.*]

CURTAIN

ACT THREE

THE EXORCISM

MARTHA *enters, talking to herself.*

MARTHA: Hey, hey. . . . Where is everybody . . .? [*It is evident she is not bothered.*] So? Drop me; pluck me like a goddamn . . . whatever-it-is . . . creeping vine, and throw me over your shoulder like an old shoe . . . George? [*Looks about her.*] George? [*Silence.*] George! What are you doing: Hiding, or something? [*Silence.*] GEORGE!! [*Silence.*] Oh, fa Chri . . . [*Goes to the bar, makes herself a drink and amuses herself with the following performance.*] Deserted! Abandoned! Left out in the cold like an old pussy-cat. HA! Can I get you a drink, Martha? Why, thank you, George; that's very kind of you. No, Martha, no; why I'd do anything for you. Would you, George? Why, I'd do anything for you, too. Would you, Martha? Why, certainly, George. Martha, I've misjudged you. And I've misjudged you, too, George. WHERE IS EVERYBODY!!! Hump the Hostess! [*Laughs greatly at this, falls into a chair; calms down, looks defeated, says, softly.*] Fat chance. [*Even softer.*] Fat chance. [*Baby-talk now.*] Daddy? Daddy? Martha is abandon-ed. Left to her own vices at . . . [*Peers at a clock.*] . . . something o'clock in the old A.M. Daddy White-Mouse; do you really have red eyes? Do you? Let me see. Ohhhhh! You do! You do! Daddy, you have red eyes . . . because you cry all the time, don't you, Daddy. Yes; you do. You cry alllll the time. I'LL GIVE ALL YOU BASTARDS FIVE TO COME OUT FROM WHERE YOU'RE HIDING!! [*Pause.*] I cry all the time too, Daddy. I cry alllll the time; but deep inside, so no one can see me. I cry all the time. And Georgie cries all the time, too. We both cry all the time, and then, what we do, we cry, and we take our tears, and we put 'em in the ice box, in the goddamn ice trays [*Begins to laugh.*] until they're all frozen [*Laughs even more*] and then . . . we put them . . . in our . . . drinks. [*More laughter, which is something else, too. After sobering silence.*] Up the drain, down the spout, dead, gone and forgotten. . . . Up the spout, not down the spout; *Up* the spout: THE POKER NIGHT. Up the spout. . . . [*Sadly.*] I've got windshield wipers on my eyes, because I married you . . . baby! . . . Martha, you'll be a songwriter yet. [*Jiggles the ice in her glass.*] CLINK! [*Does it again.*] CLINK! [*Giggles, repeats it several times.*] CLINK! . . . CLINK! . . . CLINK! . . . CLINK!

NICK *enters while* MARTHA *is clinking; he stands in the hall entrance and watches her; finally he comes in.*

NICK: My God, you've gone crazy too.
MARTHA: Clink?
NICK: I said, you've gone crazy too.
MARTHA [*considers it*]: Probably . . . probably.
NICK: You've all gone crazy: I come downstairs, and what happens. . . .
MARTHA: What happens?

NICK: . . . my wife's gone into the can with a liquor bottle, and she winks at me . . . winks at me! . . .

MARTHA [*sadly*]: She's never wunk at you; what a shame. . . .

NICK: She is lying down on the floor again, the tiles, all curled up, and she starts peeling the label off the liquor bottle, the brandy bottle. . . .

MARTHA: . . . we'll never get the deposit back that way. . . .

NICK: . . . and I ask her what she's doing, and she goes: shhhhhh!, nobody knows I'm here; and I come back in here, and you're sitting there going Clink!, for God's sake. Clink!

MARTHA: CLINK!

NICK: You've all gone crazy.

MARTHA: Yes. Sad but true.

NICK: Where is your husband?

MARTHA: He is vanish-ed. Pouf!

NICK: You're all crazy: nuts.

MARTHA [*affects a brogue*]: Awww, 'tis the refuge we take when the unreality of the world weighs too heavy on our tiny heads. [*Normal voice again.*] Relax; sink into it; you're no better than anybody else.

NICK [*wearily*]: I think I am.

MARTHA [*her glass to her mouth*]: You're certainly a flop in some departments.

NICK [*wincing*]: I beg your pardon . . .?

MARTHA [*unnecessarily loud*]: I said, you're certainly a flop in some . . .

NICK [*he, too, too loud*]: I'm sorry you're disappointed.

MARTHA [*braying*]: I didn't say I was disappointed! Stupid!

NICK: You should try me some time when we haven't been drinking for ten hours, and maybe . . .

MARTHA [*still braying*]: I wasn't talking about your potential; I was talking about your goddamn performance.

NICK [*softly*]: Oh.

MARTHA [*she softer, too*]: Your potential's fine. It's dandy. [*Wiggles her eyebrows.*] Absolutely dandy. I haven't seen such a dandy potential in a long time. Oh, but baby, you sure are a flop.

NICK [*snapping it out*]: Everybody's a flop to you! Your husband's a flop, *I'm* a flop. . . .

MARTHA [*dismissing him*]: You're all flops. I am the Earth Mother, and you're all flops. [*More or less to herself.*] I disgust me. I pass my life in crummy, totally pointless infidelities . . . [*Laughs ruefully.*] *would*-be infidelities. Hump the Hostess? That's a laugh. A bunch of boozed-up . . . impotent lunk-heads. Martha makes goo-goo eyes, and the lunk-heads grin, and roll their beautiful, beautiful eyes back, and grin some more, and Martha licks her chops, and the lunk-heads slap over to the bar to pick up a little courage, *and* they pick up a little courage, and they bounce back over to old Martha, who does a little dance for them, which heats them all up . . . mentally . . . and so they slap over to the bar again, and pick up a little more courage, and their wives and sweethearts stick their noses up in the air . . . right through the ceiling, sometimes . . . which sends the lunk-heads back to the soda fountain again where they fuel up some more, while Martha-poo sits there with her dress up over her head . . . suffocating–you don't know how *stuffy* it is with your dress up over your head–suffocating! waiting for the lunk-heads; so, *finally* they get their courage up . . . but that's all, baby! Oh my, there is sometimes some very nice potential, but, oh my! My, my, my. [*Brightly.*] But that's how it is in a civilized society. [*To herself again.*] All the gorgeous lunk-heads. Poor babies. [*To* NICK, *now; earnestly.*] There is only one man in my life who has ever . . . made me happy. Do you know that? One!

NICK: The . . . the what-do-you-call-it? . . . uh . . . the lawn mower, or something?

MARTHA: No; I'd forgotten him. But when I think about him and me it's almost like being a voyeur. Hunh. No; I didn't mean him; I meant George, of course. [*No response from* NICK.] Uh . . . George; my husband.

NICK [*disbelieving*]: You're kidding.

MARTHA: Am I?

NICK: You must be. Him?

MARTHA: Him.

NICK [*as if in on a joke*]: Sure; sure.

MARTHA: You don't believe it.

NICK [*mocking*]: Why, of course I do.

MARTHA: You always deal in appearances?

NICK [*derisively*]: Oh, for God's sake. . . .

MARTHA: . . . George who is out somewhere there in the dark. . . . George who is good to me, and whom I revile; who understands me, and whom I push off; who can make me laugh, and I choke it back in my throat; who can hold me, at night, so that it's warm, and whom I will bite so there's blood; who keeps learning the games we play as quickly as I can change the rules; who can make me happy and I do not wish to be happy, and yes I do wish to be happy. George and Martha: sad, sad, sad.

NICK [*echoing, still not believing*]: Sad.

MARTHA: . . . whom I will not forgive for having come to rest; for having seen me and having said: yes; this will do; who has made the hideous, the hurting, the insulting mistake of loving me and must be punished for it. George and Martha: sad, sad, sad.

NICK [*puzzled*]: Sad.

MARTHA: . . . who tolerates, which is intolerable; who is kind, which is cruel; who understands, which is beyond comprehension. . . .

NICK: George and Martha: sad, sad, sad.

MARTHA: Some day . . . hah! some *night* . . . some stupid, liquor-ridden night . . . I will go too far . . . and I'll either break the man's back . . . or push him off for good . . . which is what I deserve.

NICK: I don't think he's got a vertebra intact.

MARTHA [*laughing at him*]: You don't, huh? You don't think so. Oh, little boy, you got yourself hunched over that microphone of yours. . . .

NICK: Microscope. . . .

MARTHA: . . . yes . . . and you don't see anything, do you? You see everything but the goddamn mind; you see all the little specs and crap, but you don't see what goes on, do you?

NICK: I know when a man's had his back broken; I can see that.

MARTHA: Can you!

NICK: You're damn right.

MARTHA: Oh . . . you know so little. And you're going to take over the world, hunh?

NICK: All right, now. . . .

MARTHA: You think a man's got his back broken 'cause he makes like a clown and walks bent, hunh? Is that *really* all you know?

NICK: I said, all *right*!

MARTHA: Ohhhh! The stallion's mad, hunh. The gelding's all upset. Ha, ha, ha, HA!

NICK [*softly; wounded*]: You . . . you swing wild, don't you.

MARTHA [*triumphant*]: HAH!

NICK: Just . . . anywhere.

MARTHA: HAH! I'm a gattling gun. Hahahahahahahahaha!

NICK [*in wonder*]: Aimless . . . butchery. Pointless.

MARTHA: Aw! You poor little bastard.

NICK: Hit out at everything.

The door chimes chime.

MARTHA: Go answer the door.

NICK [*amazed*]: What did you say?

MARTHA: I said, go answer the door. What are you, deaf?

NICK [*trying to get it straight*]: You . . . want me . . . to go answer the door?

MARTHA: That's right, lunk-head; answer the door. There must be something you can do well; or, are you too drunk to do that, too? Can't you get the latch up, either?

NICK: Look, there's no need . . .

Door chimes again.

MARTHA [*shouting*]: Answer it! [*Softer.*] You can be houseboy around here for a while. You can start off being houseboy right now.

NICK: Look, lady, I'm no flunky to you.

MARTHA [*cheerfully*]: Sure you are! You're ambitious, aren't you, boy? You didn't chase me around the kitchen and up the goddamn stairs out of mad, driven passion, did you now? You were thinking a little bit about your career, weren't you? Well, you can just houseboy your way up the ladder for a while.

NICK: There's no limit to you, is there?

Door chimes again.

MARTHA [*calmly, surely*]: No, baby; none. Go answer the door.

NICK hesitates.

Look, boy; once you stick your nose in it, you're not going to pull out just whenever you feel like it. You're in for a while. Now, git!

NICK: Aimless . . . wanton . . . pointless. . . .

MARTHA: Now, now, now; just do what you're told; show old Martha there's something you *can* do. Hunh? Atta boy.

NICK [*considers, gives in, moves towards the door. Chimes again*]: I'm coming, for Christ's sake!

MARTHA [*claps her hands*]: Ha, HA! Wonderful; marvellous. [*Sings.*] 'Just a gigolo, everywhere I go, people always say . . .'

NICK: STOP THAT!

MARTHA [*giggles*]: Sorry, baby; go on now; open the little door.

NICK [*with great rue*]: Christ. [*He flings open the door, and a hand thrusts into the opening a great bunch of snapdragons; they stay there for a moment.* NICK *strains his eyes to see who is behind them.*]

MARTHA: Oh, how lovely!

GEORGE [*appearing in the doorway, the snapdragons covering his face; speaks in a hideously cracked falsetto*]: Flores; flores para los muertos. Flores.

MARTHA: Ha, ha, ha, HA!

GEORGE [*a step into the room; lowers the flowers; sees* NICK; *his face becomes gleeful; he opens his arms*]: Sonny! You've come home for your birthday! At last!

NICK [*backing off*]: Stay away from me.

MARTHA: Ha, ha, ha, HA! That's the houseboy, for God's sake.

GEORGE: Really? That's not our own little sonny-Jim? Our own little all-American something-or-other?

MARTHA [*giggling*]: Well, I certainly hope not; he's been acting awful funny, if he is.

GEORGE [*almost manic*]: Ohhhh! I'll bet! Chippie-chippie-chippie, hunh? [*Affecting embarrassment.*] I . . . I brungya dese flowers, Mart's, 'cause I . . . wull, 'cause you'se . . . awwwwww hell. Gee.

MARTHA: Pansies! Rosemary! Violence! My wedding bouquet!

NICK [*starting to move away*]: Well, if you two kids don't mind, I think I'll just . . .

MARTHA: Ach! You just stay where you are. Make my hubby a drink.

NICK: I don't think I will.

GEORGE: No, Martha, no; that would be too much; he's your houseboy, baby, not mine.

NICK: I'm nobody's houseboy. . . .

GEORGE *and* MARTHA: . . . Now! [*Sing.*] I'm nobody's houseboy now. . . . [*Both laugh.*]

NICK: Vicious . . .

GEORGE [*finishing it for him*]: . . . children. Hunh? That right? Vicious children, with their oh-so-sad games, hop-scotching their way through life, etcetera, etcetera. Is that it?

NICK: Something like it.

GEORGE: Screw, baby.

MARTHA: Him can't. Him too fulla booze.

GEORGE: Weally? [*Handing the snapdragons to* NICK.] Here; dump these in some gin. [*Nick takes them, looks at them, drops them on the floor at his feet.*]

MARTHA [*sham dismay*]: Awwwwwww.

GEORGE: What a terrible thing to do . . . to Martha's snapdragons.

MARTHA: Is that what they are?

GEORGE: Yup. And here I went out into the moonlight to pick 'em for Martha tonight, and for our sonny-boy tomorrow, for his birfday.

MARTHA [*passing on information*]: There is no moon now. I saw it go down from the bedroom.

GEORGE [*feigned glee*]: From the bedroom! [*Normal tone.*] Well, there was a moon.

MARTHA [*too patient; laughing a little*]: There couldn't have been a moon.

GEORGE: Well, there was. There is.

MARTHA: There is no moon; the moon went down.

GEORGE: There is a moon; the moon is up.

MARTHA [*straining to keep civil*]: I'm afraid you're mistaken.

GEORGE [*too cheerful*]: No; no.

MARTHA [*between her teeth*]: There is no goddamn moon.

GEORGE: My dear Martha . . . I did not pick snapdragons in the stony dark. I did not go stumbling around Daddy's greenhouse in the pitch.

MARTHA: Yes . . . you did. You would.

GEORGE: Martha, I do not pick flowers in the blink. I have never robbed a hothouse without there is a light from heaven.

MARTHA [*with finality*]: There is no moon; the moon went down.

GEORGE [*with great logic*]: That may very well be, Chastity; the moon may very well have gone down . . . but it came back up.

MARTHA: The moon does *not* come back up; when the moon has gone down it stays down.

GEORGE [*getting a little ugly*]: You don't know anything. IF the moon went down, then it came back up.

MARTHA: BULL!

GEORGE: Ignorance! Such . . . ignorance.

MARTHA: Watch who you're calling ignorant!

GEORGE: Once . . . once, when I was sailing past Majorca, drinking on deck with a correspondent who was talking about Roosevelt, the moon went down, thought about it for a little . . . considered it, you know what I mean? . . . and then, POP, came up again. Just like that.

MARTHA: That is not true! That is such a lie!

GEORGE: You must not call everything a lie, Martha. [*To* NICK.] Must she?

NICK: Hell, I don't know when you people are lying, or what.

MARTHA: You're damned right!

GEORGE: You're not supposed to.

MARTHA: Right!

GEORGE: At any rate, I was sailing past Majorca. . . .

MARTHA: You never sailed past Majorca. . . .

GEORGE: Martha. . . .

MARTHA: You were never in the goddamn Mediterranean at all . . . ever. . . .

GEORGE: I certainly was! My Mommy and Daddy took me there as a college graduation present.

MARTHA: Nuts!

NICK: Was this after you killed them?

> GEORGE *and* MARTHA *swing around and look at him; there is a brief, ugly pause.*

GEORGE [*defiantly*]: Maybe.

MARTHA: Yeah; maybe not, too.

NICK: Jesus!

> GEORGE *swoops down, picks up the bunch of snapdragons, shakes them like a feather duster in* NICK's *face, and moves away a little.*

GEORGE: HAH!

NICK: Damn you.

GEORGE [*to* NICK]: Truth and illusion. Who knows the difference, eh, toots? Eh?

MARTHA: You were never in the Mediterranean . . . truth or illusion . . . either way.

GEORGE: If I wasn't in the Mediterranean, how did I get to the Aegean? Hunh?

MARTHA: OVERLAND!

NICK: Yeah!

GEORGE: Don't you side with her, houseboy.

NICK: I am not a houseboy.

GEORGE: Look! I know the game! You don't make it in the sack, you're a houseboy.

NICK: I AM NOT A HOUSEBOY!

GEORGE: No? Well then, you must have made it in the sack. Yes? [*He is breathing a little heavy; behaving a little manic.*] Yes? Someone's lying around here; somebody isn't playing the game straight. Yes? come on; come on; who's lying? Martha? Come on!

NICK [*after a pause; to* MARTHA, *quietly with intense pleading*]: Tell him I'm not a houseboy.

MARTHA [*after a pause, quietly, lowering her head*]: No; you're not a houseboy.

GEORGE [*with great, sad relief*]: So be it.

MARTHA [*pleading*]: Truth and illusion, George; you don't know the difference.

GEORGE: No; but we must carry on as though we did.

MARTHA: Amen.

GEORGE [*flourishing the flowers*]: SNAP WENT THE DRAGONS!!

　　NICK *and* MARTHA *laugh weakly.*

Hunh? Here we go round the mulberry bush, Hunh?

NICK [*tenderly, to* MARTHA]: Thank you.

MARTHA: Skip it.

GEORGE [*loud*]: I said, here we go round the mulberry bush!

MARTHA [*impatiently*]: Yeah, yeah; we know; snap go the dragons.

GEORGE [*taking a snapdragon, throwing it, spear-like, stem-first at* MARTHA]: SNAP!

MARTHA: Don't, George.

GEORGE [*throws another*]: SNAP!

NICK: Don't do that.

GEORGE: Shut up, stud.

NICK: I'm not a stud!

GEORGE [*throws one at* NICK]: SNAP! Then you're a houseboy. Which is it? Which are you? Hunh? Make up your mind. Either way . . . [*Throws another at him.*] SNAP! . . . *you disgust me.*

MARTHA: Does it matter to you, George!?

GEORGE [*throws one at her*]: SNAP! No, actually, it doesn't. Either way . . . I've had it.

MARTHA: Stop throwing those goddamn things at me!

GEORGE: Either way. [*Throws another at her.*] SNAP!

NICK [*to* MARTHA]: Do you want me to . . . do something to him?

MARTHA: You leave him alone!

GEORGE: If you're a houseboy, baby, you can pick up after me; if you're a stud, you can go protect your plough. Either way. Either way. . . . Everything.

NICK: Oh for God's . . .

MARTHA [*a little afraid*]: Truth or illusion, George. Doesn't it matter to you . . . at all?

GEORGE [*without throwing anything*]: SNAP! [*Silence.*] You got your answer, baby?

MARTHA [*sadly*]: Got it.

GEORGE: You just gird your blue-veined loins, girl. [*Sees* NICK *moving towards the hall.*] Now; we got one more game to play. And it's called bringing up baby.

NICK [*more-or-less under his breath*]: Oh, for Lord's sake. . . .

MARTHA: George. . . .

GEORGE: I don't want any fuss. [*To* NICK.] You don't want any scandal around here, do you, big boy? You don't want to wreck things, do you? Hunh? You want to keep to your time-table, don't you? Then sit! [NICK *sits.*] [*To* MARTHA.] And you, pretty Miss, you like fun and games, don't you? You're a sport from way back, aren't you?

MARTHA [*quietly, giving in*]: All right, George, all right.

GEORGE [*seeing them both cowed; purrs*]: Goooooooood; gooooood. [*Looks about him.*] But, we're not all here. [*Snaps his fingers a couple of times at* NICK.] You; you . . . uh . . . you; your little wifelet isn't here.

NICK: Look; she's had a rough night, now; she's in the can, and she's . . .

GEORGE: Well, we can't play without everyone here. Now that's a fact. We gotta have your little wife. [*Hog-calls towards the hall.*] SOOOWWWIIIEEE!! SOOOWWWIIIEEE!!

NICK [*as* MARTHA *giggles nervously*]: Cut that!

GEORGE [*swinging around, facing him*]: Then get your butt out of that chair and bring the little dip back in here.

As NICK *does not move.*

Now be a good puppy. Fetch, good puppy, go fetch.

NICK *rises, opens his mouth to say something, thinks better of it, exits.*

One more game.

MARTHA [*after* NICK *goes*]: I don't like what's going to happen.

GEORGE [*surprisingly tender*]: Do you know what it is?

MARTHA [*pathetic*]: No. But I don't like it.

GEORGE: Maybe you will, Martha.

MARTHA: No.

GEORGE: Oh, it's a real fun game, Martha.

MARTHA [*pleading*]: No more games.

GEORGE [*quietly triumphant*]: One more, Martha. One more game, and then beddie-bye. Everybody pack up his tools and baggage and stuff and go home. And you and me, well, we gonna climb them well-worn stairs.

MARTHA [*almost in tears*]: No, George; no.

GEORGE [*soothing*]: Yes, baby.

MARTHA: No, George; please?

GEORGE: It'll all be done with before you know it.

MARTHA: No, George.

GEORGE: No climb stairs with Georgie?

MARTHA [*a sleepy child*]: No more games . . . please. It's games I don't want. No more games.

GEORGE: Aw, sure you do, Martha . . . original game-girl and all, 'course you do.

MARTHA: Ugly games . . . ugly. And now this new one?

GEORGE [*stroking her hair*]: You'll love it, baby.

MARTHA: No George.

GEORGE: You'll have a ball.

MARTHA [*tenderly; moves to touch him*]: Please, George, no more games; I . . .

GEORGE [*slapping her moving hand with vehemence*]: Don't you touch me! You keep your paws clean for the undergraduates!

MARTHA [*a cry of alarm, but faint.*]

GEORGE [*grabbing her hair, pulling her head back*]: Now, you listen to me, Martha; you have had quite an evening . . . quite a night for yourself, and you can't just cut it off whenever you've got enough blood in your mouth. We are going on, and I'm going to have at you, and it's going to make your performance tonight look like an Easter pageant. Now I want you to get yourself a little alert. [*Slaps her lightly with his free hand.*] I want a little life in you, baby. [*Again.*]

MARTHA [*struggling*]: Stop it!

GEORGE [*again*]: Pull yourself together! [*Again.*] I want you on your feet and slugging, sweetheart, because I'm going to knock you around, and I want you up for it.

> *Again; he pulls away, releases her; she rises.*

MARTHA: All right, George. What do you want, George?

GEORGE: An equal battle, baby; that's all.

MARTHA: You'll get it!

GEORGE: I want you mad.

MARTHA: I'M MAD!!

GEORGE: Get madder!

MARTHA: DON'T WORRY ABOUT IT!

GEORGE: Good for you, girl; now, we're going to play this one to the death.

MARTHA: Yours!

GEORGE: You'd be surprised. Now, here come the tots; you be ready for this.

MARTHA [*she paces, actually looks a bit like a fighter*]: I'm ready for you.

> NICK *and* HONEY *re-enter;* NICK *supporting* HONEY, *who still retains her brandy bottle and glass.*

NICK [*unhappily*]: Here we are.

HONEY [*cheerfully*]: Hip, hop. Hip, hop.

NICK: You a bunny, Honey? [*She laughs greatly, sits.*]

HONEY: I'm a bunny, Honey.

GEORGE [*to* HONEY]: Well, now; how's the bunny?

HONEY: Bunny funny! [*She laughs again.*]

NICK [*under his breath*]: Jesus.

GEORGE: Bunny funny? Good for bunny!

MARTHA: Come on, George!

GEORGE [*to* MARTHA]: Honey funny bunny!

> HONEY *screams with laughter.*

NICK: Jesus God. . . .

GEORGE [*slaps his hands together, once*]: All right! Here we go! Last game! All sit.

NICK *sits.*

Sit down, Martha. This is a civilized game.

MARTHA [*cocks her fist, doesn't swing. Sits*]: Just get on with it.

HONEY [*to* GEORGE]: I've decided I don't remember anything. [*To* NICK.] Hello, Dear.

GEORGE: Hunh? What?

MARTHA: It's almost dawn, for God's sake. . . .

HONEY [*ibid.*]: I don't remember anything, and you don't remember anything, either. Hello, Dear.

GEORGE: You what?

HONEY [*ibid. An edge creeping into her voice*]: You heard me, nothing. Hello, Dear.

GEORGE [*to* HONEY, *referring to* NICK]: You do know that's your husband, there, don't you?

HONEY [*with great dignity*]: Well, I certainly know *that.*

GEORGE [*close to* HONEY'*s ear*]: It's just some things you can't remember . . . hunh?

HONEY [*a great laugh to cover; then quietly, intensely to* GEORGE]: *Don't* remember; not *can't.* [*At* NICK, *cheerfully.*] Hello, Dear.

GEORGE [*to* NICK]: Well, speak to your little wifelet, your little bunny, for God's sake.

NICK [*softly, embarrassed*]: Hello, Honey.

GEORGE: Awww, that was nice. I think we've been having a . . . a real good evening . . . all things considered. . . . We've sat around, and got to know each other, and had fun and games . . . curl-up-on-the-floor, for example. . . .

HONEY: . . . the tiles. . . .

GEORGE: . . . the tiles. . . . Snap the Dragon.

HONEY: . . . peel the label. . . .

GEORGE: . . . peel the . . . what?

MARTHA: Label. Peel the label.

HONEY [*apologetically, holding up her brandy bottle*]: I peel labels.

GEORGE: We all peel labels, sweetie; and when you get through the skin, all three layers, through the muscle, slosh aside the organs [*An aside to* NICK.] them which is still sloshable—[*Back to* HONEY.] and get down to bone . . . you know what you do then?

HONEY [*terribly interested*]: No!

GEORGE: When you get down to bone, you haven't got all the way, yet. There's something inside the bone . . . the marrow . . . and that's what you gotta get at. [*A strange smile at* MARTHA.]

HONEY: Oh! I see.

GEORGE: The marrow. But bones are pretty resilient, especially in the young. Now, take our son . . .

HONEY [*strangely*]: Who?

GEORGE: Our son . . . Martha's and my little joy!

NICK [*moving towards the bar*]: Do you mind if I . . .?

GEORGE: No, no; you go right ahead.

MARTHA: George. . . .

GEORGE [*too kindly*]: Yes, Martha?

MARTHA: Just what are you doing?

GEORGE: Why love, I was talking about our son.

MARTHA: Don't.

GEORGE: Isn't Martha something? Here we are, on the eve of our boy's home-coming, the eve of his twenty-first birfday, the eve of his majority . . . and Martha says don't talk about him.

MARTHA: Just . . . don't.

GEORGE: But I want to, Martha! It's very important we talk about him. Now bunny and the . . . well, whichever he is . . . here don't know much about junior, and I think they should.

MARTHA: Just . . . don't.

GEORGE [*snapping his fingers at* NICK]: You. Hey, you! You want to play bringing up baby, don't you!

NICK [*hardly civil*]: Were you snapping at me?

GEORGE: That's right. [*Instructing him.*] *You* want to hear about our bouncy boy.

NICK [*pause; then, shortly*]: Yeah; sure.

GEORGE [*to* HONEY]: And you, my dear? You want to hear about him, too, don't you.

HONEY [*pretending not to understand*]: Whom?

GEORGE: Martha's and my son.

HONEY [*nervously*]: Oh, you have a child?

MARTHA *and* NICK *laugh uncomfortably.*

GEORGE: Oh, indeed; do we ever! Do you want to talk about him Martha, or shall I? Hunh?

MARTHA [*a smile that is a sneer*]: Don't, George.

GEORGE: All rightie. Well, now; let's see. He's a nice kid, really, in spite of his home life; I mean, most kids'd grow up neurotic, what with Martha here carrying on the way she does: sleeping till four in the P.M., climbing all over the poor bastard, trying to break the bathroom door down to wash him in the tub when he's sixteen, dragging strangers into the house at all hours. . . .

MARTHA [*rising*]: O.K. YOU!

GEORGE [*mock concern*]: Martha!

MARTHA: That's enough!

GEORGE: Well, do you want to take over?

HONEY [*to* NICK]: Why would anybody want to wash somebody who's sixteen years old?

NICK [*slamming his drink down*]: Oh, for Christ's sake, Honey!

HONEY [*stage whisper*]: Well, why?

GEORGE: Because it's her baby-poo.

MARTHA: ALL RIGHT!! [*By rote; a kind of almost-tearful recitation.*] Our son. You want our son? You'll have it.

GEORGE: You want a drink, Martha?

MARTHA [*pathetically*]: Yes.

NICK [*to* MARTHA *kindly*]: We don't have to hear about it . . . if you don't want to.

GEORGE: Who says so? You in a position to set the rules around here?

NICK [*pause; tight-lipped*]: No.

GEORGE: Good boy; you'll go far. All right, Martha; your recitation, please.

MARTHA [*from far away*]: What, George?

GEORGE [*prompting*]: 'Our son . . .'

MARTHA: All right. Our son. Our son was born in a September night, a night not unlike tonight, though tomorrow, and twenty . . . one . . . years ago.

GEORGE [*beginning of quiet asides*]: You see? I told you.

MARTHA: It was an easy birth. . . .

GEORGE: Oh, Martha; no. You laboured . . . how you laboured.

MARTHA: It was an easy birth . . . once it had been . . . accepted, relaxed into.

GEORGE: Ah . . . yes. Better.

MARTHA: It was an easy birth, once it had been accepted, and I was young.

GEORGE: And I was younger. . . . [*Laughs quietly to himself.*]

MARTHA: And I was young, and he was a healthy child, a red, bawling child, with slippery firm limbs . . .

GEORGE: . . . Martha thinks she saw him at delivery. . . .

MARTHA: . . . with slippery, firm limbs, and a full head of black, fine, fine hair which, oh, later, later, became blond as the sun, our son.

GEORGE: He was a healthy child.

MARTHA: And I had wanted a child . . . oh, I had wanted a child.

GEORGE [*prodding her*]: A son? A daughter?

MARTHA: A child! [*Quieter.*] A child. And I had my child.

GEORGE: Our child.

MARTHA [*with great sadness*]: Our child. And we raised him . . . [*Laughs, briefly, bitterly.*] yes, we did; we raised him . . .

GEORGE: With teddy bears and an antique bassinet from Austria . . . and *no nurse.*

MARTHA: . . . with teddy bears and transparent floating goldfish, and a pale blue bed with cane at the headboard when he was older, cane which he wore through . . . finally . . . with his little hands . . . in his . . . sleep. . . .

GEORGE: . . . nightmares. . . .

MARTHA: . . . *sleep.* . . . He was a restless child. . . .

GEORGE: . . . [*Soft chuckle, head-shaking of disbelief.*] . . . Oh Lord. . . .

MARTHA: . . . sleep . . . and a croup tent . . . a pale green croup tent, and the shining kettle hissing in the one light of the room that time he was sick . . . those four days . . . and animal crackers, and the bow and arrow he kept under his bed. . . .

GEORGE: . . . the arrows with rubber cups at their tip . . .

MARTHA: . . . at their tip, which he kept beneath his bed. . . .

GEORGE: Why? Why, Martha?

MARTHA: . . . for fear . . . for fear of . . .

GEORGE: For fear. Just that: for fear.

MARTHA [*vaguely waving him off; going on*]: . . . and . . . and sandwiches on Sunday night, and Saturdays . . . [*Pleased recollection.*] . . . and Saturdays the banana boat, the whole peeled banana, scooped out on top, with green grapes for the crew, a double line of green grapes, and along the sides, stuck to the boat with toothpicks, orange slices. . . . SHIELDS.

GEORGE: And for the oar?

MARTHA [*uncertainly*]: A . . . carrot?

GEORGE: Or a swizzle stick, whatever was easier.

MARTHA: No. A carrot. And his eyes were green . . . green with . . . if you peered so deep into them . . . so deep . . . bronze . . . bronze parentheses around the irises . . . such green eyes!

GEORGE: . . . blue, green, brown. . . .

MARTHA: . . . and he loved the sun! . . . He was tan before and after everyone . . . and in the sun his hair . . . became . . . fleece.

GEORGE [*echoeing her*]: . . . fleece. . . .

MARTHA: . . . beautiful, beautiful boy.

GEORGE: Absolve, Domine, animas omnium fidelium defunctorum ab omni vinculo delictorum.

MARTHA: . . . and school . . . and summer camp . . . and sledding . . . and swimming. . . .

GEORGE: Et gratia tua illis succurrente, mereantur evadere judicium ultionis.

MARTHA [*laughing, to herself*]: . . . and how he broke his arm . . . how funny it was . . . oh, no, it hurt him! . . . but, oh, it was funny . . . in a field, his very first cow, the first he'd ever seen . . . and he went into the field, to the cow, where the cow was grazing, head down, busy . . . and he moo'd at it! [*Laughs ibid.*] He moo'd at it . . . and the beast, oh, surprised, swung its head up and moo'd at him, all three years of him, and he ran, startled, and he stumbled . . . fell . . . and broke his poor arm. [*Laughs ibid.*] Poor lamb.

GEORGE: Et lucis aeternae beatitudine perfrui.

MARTHA: George cried! Helpless . . . George . . . cried. I carried the poor lamb. George snuffling beside me, I carried the child, having fashioned a sling . . . and across the great fields.

GEORGE: In Paradisum deducant te Angeli.

MARTHA: And as he grew . . . and as he grew . . . oh! so wise! . . . he walked evenly between us . . . [*She spreads her hands.*] . . . a hand out to each of us for what we could offer by way of support, affection, teaching, even love . . . and these hands, still, to hold us off a bit, for mutual protection, to protect us all from George's . . . weakness . . . and my . . . necessary greater strength . . . to protect himself . . . and *us*.

GEORGE: In memoria aeterna erit justus: ab auditione mala non timebit.

MARTHA: So wise; so wise.

NICK [*to* GEORGE]: What is this? What are you doing?

GEORGE: Shhhhh.

HONEY: Shhhhh.

NICK [*shrugging*]: O.K.

MARTHA: So beautiful; so wise.

GEORGE [*laughs quietly*]: All truth being relative.

MARTHA: It was true! Beautiful; wise; perfect.

GEORGE: There's a real mother talking.

HONEY [*suddenly; almost tearfully*]: I want a child.

NICK: Honey. . . .

HONEY [*more forcefully*]: I want a child!

GEORGE: On principle?

HONEY [*in tears*]: I want a child. I want a baby.

MARTHA [*waiting out the interruption, not really paying it any mind*]: Of course, this state, this perfection . . . couldn't last. Not with George . . . not with George around.

GEORGE [*to the others*]: There; you see? I knew she'd shift.

HONEY: Be still!

GEORGE [*mock awe*]: Sorry . . . mother.

NICK: Can't you be still?

GEORGE [*making a sign at* NICK]: Dominus vobiscum.

MARTHA: Not with George around. A drowning man takes down those nearest.

George tried, but, oh, God, how I fought him. God, how I fought him.

GEORGE [*a satisfied laugh*]: Ahhhhhhh.

MARTHA: Lesser states can't stand those above them. Weakness, imperfection cries out against strength, goodness and innocence. And George tried.

GEORGE: How did I try, Martha? How did I try?

MARTHA: How did you . . . what? . . . No! No . . . he grew . . . our son grew . . . up; he is grown up; he is away at school, college. He is fine, everything is fine.

GEORGE [*mocking*]: Oh, come on, Martha!

MARTHA: No. That's all.

GEORGE: Just a minute! You can't cut a story off like that, sweetheart. You started to say something . . . now you say it!

MARTHA: No!

GEORGE: Well, I will.

MARTHA: No!

GEORGE: You see, Martha, here, stops just when the going gets good . . . just when things start getting a little rough. Now, Martha, here, is a misunderstood little girl; she really is. Not only does she have a husband who is a bog . . . a younger-than-she-is bog albeit . . . not only does she have a husband who is a bog, she has as well a tiny problem with spirituous liquors—like she can't get enough. . . .

MARTHA [*without energy*]: No more, George.

GEORGE: . . . and on top of all that, poor weighed-down girl, PLUS a father who really doesn't give a damn whether she lives or dies, who couldn't care less *what* happens to his only daughter . . . on top of all that she has a *son*. She has a son who fought her every inch of the way, who didn't want to be turned into a weapon against his father, who didn't want to be used as a goddamn club whenever Martha didn't get things like she wanted them!

MARTHA [*rising to it*]: Lies! Lies!!

GEORGE: Lies? All right. A son who would *not* disown his father, who came to him for advice, for information, for love that wasn't mixed with sickness—and you know what I mean, Martha!—who could not tolerate the slashing, braying residue that called itself his MOTHER. MOTHER? HAH!!

MARTHA [*cold*]: All right, you. A son who was so ashamed of his father he asked me if it—possibly—wasn't true, as he had heard, from some cruel boys, maybe, that he was not our child; who could not tolerate the shabby failure his father had become. . . .

GEORGE: Lies!

MARTHA: Lies? Who would not bring his girl friends to the house . . .

GEORGE: . . . in shame of his mother. . . .

MARTHA: . . . of his father! Who writes letters only to me!

GEORGE: Oh, so you think! To me! At my office!

MARTHA: Liar!

GEORGE: I have a stack of them!

MARTHA: YOU HAVE NO LETTERS!

GEORGE: And you have?

MARTHA: He has no letters. A son . . . a son who spends his summers away . . . away from his family . . . ON ANY PRETEXT . . . because he can't stand the shadow of a man flickering around the edges of a house. . . .

GEORGE: . . . who spends his summers away . . . and he does! . . . who spends his summers away because there isn't room for him in a house full of empty bottles, lies, strange men, and a harridan who . . .

MARTHA: Liar!!

GEORGE: Liar?

MARTHA: . . . A son who I have raised as best I can against . . . vicious odds, against the corruption of weakness and petty revenges. . . .

GEORGE: . . . A son who is, deep in his gut, sorry to have been born. . . .

BOTH TOGETHER.

MARTHA: I have tried, oh God I have tried; the one thing . . . the one thing I've tried to carry pure and unscathed through the sewer of this marriage; through the sick nights, and the pathetic, stupid days, through the derision and the laughter . . . *God*, the laughter, through one failure after another, one failure compounding another failure, each attempt more sickening, more numbing than the one before; the one thing, the one *person* I have tried to protect, to raise above the mire of this vile, crushing marriage; the one light in all this hopeless . . . *dark*ness . . . our SON.

GEORGE: Libera me, Domine, de morte aeterna, in die illa tremenda: Quando caeli movendi sunt et terra: Dum veneris judicare saeculum per ignem. Tremens factus sum ego, et timeo, dum discussio venerit, atque ventura ira. Quando caeli movendi sunt et terra. Dies illa, dies irae, calamitatis et miseriae; dies magna et amara valde. Dum veneris judicare saeculum per ignem. Requiem aeternam dona eis, Domine: et lux perpetua luceat eis. Libera me Domine de morte aeterna in die illa tremenda: quando caeli movendi sunt et terra; Dum veneris judicare saeculum per ignem.

End together.

HONEY [*her hands to her ears*]: STOP IT!! STOP IT!!

GEORGE [*with a hand sign*]: Kyrie, eleison. Christe, eleison. Kyrie, eleison.

HONEY: JUST STOP IT!!

GEORGE: Why, baby? Don't you like it?

HONEY [*quite hysterical*]: You . . . can't . . . do . . . this!

GEORGE [*triumphant*]: Who says!

HONEY: I! Say!

GEORGE: Tell us why, baby.

HONEY: No!

NICK: is this game over?

HONEY: Yes! Yes, it is.

GEORGE: Ho-ho! Not by a long shot. [*To* MARTHA.] We got a little surprise for you, baby. It's about sunny-Jim.

MARTHA: No more, George.

GEORGE: YES!

NICK: Leave her be!

GEORGE: I'M RUNNING THIS SHOW! [*To* MARTHA.] Sweetheart, I'm afraid I've got some bad news for you . . . for us, of course. Some rather sad news.

HONEY *begins weeping, head in hands.*

MARTHA [*afraid, suspicious*]: What is this?

GEORGE [*oh, so patiently*]: Well, Martha, while you were out of the room, while the ... two of you were out of the room ... I mean, I don't know where, hell, you both must have been somewhere [*Little laugh.*]. ... While you were out of the room, for a while ... well, Missey and I were sittin' here havin' a little talk, you know: a chaw and a talk ... and the doorbell rang. ...

HONEY [*head still in hands*]: Chimed.

GEORGE: Chimed ... and ... well, it's hard to tell you, Martha. ...

MARTHA [*a strange throaty voice*]: Tell me.

HONEY: Please ... don't.

MARTHA: Tell me.

GEORGE: ... and ... what it was ... it was good old Western Union, some little boy about seventy.

MARTHA [*involved*]: Crazy Billy?

GEORGE: Yes, Martha, that's right ... crazy Billy ... and he had a telegram, and it was for us, and I have to tell you about it.

MARTHA [*as if from a distance*]: Why didn't they phone it? Why did they bring it; why didn't they telephone it?

GEORGE: Some telegrams you have to deliver, Martha; some telegrams you can't phone.

MARTHA [*rising*]: What do you mean?

GEORGE: Martha. ... I can hardly bring myself to say it ...

HONEY: Don't.

GEORGE [*to* HONEY]: Do you want to do it?

HONEY [*defending herself against an attack of bees*]: No no no no no.

GEORGE [*sighing heavily*]: All right. Well, Martha ... I'm afraid our boy isn't coming home for his birthday.

MARTHA: Of course he is.

GEORGE: No, Martha.

MARTHA: Of course he is. I say he is!

GEORGE: He ... can't.

MARTHA: He is! I say so!

GEORGE: Martha ... [*Long pause.*] ... our son is ... dead.

Silence.

He was ... killed ... late in the afternoon ...

Silence.

[*A tiny chuckle*] on a country road, with his learner's permit in his pocket, he swerved, to avoid a porcupine, and drove straight into a ...

MARTHA [*rigid fury*]: YOU ... CAN'T ... DO ... THAT!

GEORGE: ... large tree.

MARTHA: YOU CANNOT DO THAT!

NICK [*softly*]: Oh my God.

HONEY *is weeping louder.*

GEORGE [*quietly, dispassionately*]: I thought you should know.

NICK: Oh my God; no.

MARTHA [*quivering with rage and loss*]: NO! NO! YOU CANNOT DO THAT! YOU CAN'T DECIDE THAT FOR YOURSELF! I WILL NOT LET YOU DO THAT!

GEORGE: We'll have to leave around noon, I suppose . . .

MARTHA: I WILL NOT LET YOU DECIDE THESE THINGS!

GEORGE: . . . because there are matters of identification, naturally, and arrangements to be made. . . .

MARTHA [*leaping at* GEORGE, *but ineffectual*]: YOU CAN'T DO THIS!

NICK *rises, grabs hold of* MARTHA, *pins her arms behind her back.*

I WON'T LET YOU DO THIS, GET YOUR HANDS OFF ME!

GEORGE [*as* NICK *holds on; right in* MARTHA's *face*]: You don't seem to understand, Martha; I haven't done anything. Now, pull yourself together. Our son is DEAD! Can you get that into your head?

MARTHA: YOU CAN'T DECIDE THESE THINGS.

NICK: Lady, please.

MARTHA: LET ME GO!

GEORGE: Now listen, Martha; listen carefully. We got a telegram; there was a car accident, and he's dead. POUF! Just like that! Now, how do you like it?

MARTHA [*a howl which weakens into a moan*]: NOOOOOOOoooooo.

GEORGE [*to* NICK]: Let her go. [MARTHA *slumps to the floor in a sitting position.*] She'll be all right now.

MARTHA [*pathetic*]: No; no, he is *not* dead; he is not *dead.*

GEORGE: He is dead. Kyrie, eleison. Christe, eleison. Kyrie, eleison.

MARTHA: You can*not.* You may not decide these things.

NICK [*leaning over her; tenderly*]: He hasn't decided anything, lady. It's not his doing. He doesn't have the power. . . .

GEORGE: That's right, Martha; I'm not a God. I don't have the power over life and death, do I?

MARTHA: YOU CAN'T KILL HIM! YOU CAN'T HAVE HIM DIE!

HONEY: Lady . . . please. . . .

MARTHA: YOU CAN'T!

GEORGE: There was a telegram, Martha.

MARTHA [*up; facing him*]: Show it to me! Show me the telegram!

GEORGE [*long pause; then, with a straight face*]: I ate it.

MARTHA [*a pause; then with the greatest disbelief possible, tinged with hysteria*]: What did you just say to me?

GEORGE [*barely able to stop exploding with laughter*]: I . . . ate . . . it.

MARTHA *stares at him for a long moment, then spits in his face.*

GEORGE [*with a smile*]: Good for you, Martha.

NICK [*to* GEORGE]: Do you think that's the way to treat her at a time like this? Making an ugly goddamn joke like that? Hunh?

GEORGE [*snapping his fingers at* HONEY]: Did I eat the telegram or did I not?

HONEY [*terrified*]: Yes; yes, you ate it. I watched . . . I watched you . . . you . . . you ate it all down.

GEORGE [*prompting*]: . . . like a good boy.

HONEY: . . . like a . . . g-g-g-good . . . boy. Yes.

MARTHA [*to* GEORGE, *coldly*]: You're not going to get away with this.

GEORGE [*with disgust*]: YOU KNOW THE RULES, MARTHA! FOR CHRIST'S SAKE, YOU KNOW THE RULES!

MARTHA: NO!

NICK [*with the beginnings of a knowledge he cannot face*]: What are you two talking about?

GEORGE: I can kill him, Martha, if I want to.

MARTHA: HE IS OUR CHILD!

GEORGE: Oh yes, and you bore him, and it was a good delivery. . . .

MARTHA: HE IS OUR CHILD!

GEORGE: AND I HAVE KILLED HIM!

MARTHA: NO!

GEORGE: YES!

Long silence.

NICK [*very quietly*]: I think I understand this.

GEORGE [*ibid.*]: Do you?

NICK [*ibid.*]: Jesus Christ, I think I understand this.

GEORGE [*ibid.*]: Good for you, buster.

NICK [*violently*]: JESUS CHRIST I THINK I UNDERSTAND THIS!

MARTHA [*great sadness and loss*]: You have no right . . . you have no right at all. . . .

GEORGE [*tenderly*]: I have the right, Martha. We never spoke of it; that's all. I could kill him any time I wanted to.

MARTHA: But why? Why?

GEORGE: You broke our rule, baby. You mentioned him . . . you mentioned him to someone else.

MARTHA [*tearfully*]: I did *not*. I never did.

GEORGE: Yes, you did.

MARTHA: Who? WHO?!

HONEY [*crying*]: To me. You mentioned him to me.

MARTHA [*crying*]: I FORGET! Sometimes . . . sometimes when it's night, when it's late, and . . . and everybody else is . . . talking . . . I forget and I . . . want to mention him . . . but I . . . HOLD ON . . . I hold on . . . but I've wanted to . . . so often . . . oh, George, you've *pushed* it . . . there was no need . . . there was no need for *this*. I *men*tioned him . . . all right . . . but you didn't have to push it over the EDGE. You didn't have to . . . kill him.

GEORGE: Requiescat in pace.

HONEY: Amen.

MARTHA: You didn't have to have him die, George.

GEORGE: Requiem aeternam dona eis, Domine.

HONEY: Et lux perpetua luceat eis.

MARTHA: That wasn't . . . needed.

A long silence.

GEORGE [*softly*]: It will be dawn soon. I think the party's over.

NICK [*to* GEORGE; *quietly*]: You couldn't have . . . any?

GEORGE: *We* couldn't.

MARTHA [*a hint of communion in this*]: *We* couldn't.

GEORGE [*to* NICK *and* HONEY]: Home to bed, children; it's way past your bedtime.

NICK [*his hand out to* HONEY]: Honey?

HONEY [*rising, moving to him*]: Yes.

MARTHA *is sitting on the floor by a chair now.*

GEORGE: You two go now.
NICK: Yes.
HONEY: Yes.
NICK: I'd like to . . .
GEORGE: Good night.
NICK [*pause*]: Good night.

> NICK *and* HONEY *exit;* GEORGE *closes the door after them; looks around the room; sighs, picks up a glass or two, takes them to the bar.*
> *This whole last section very softly, very slowly.*

GEORGE: Do you want anything, Martha?
MARTHA [*still looking away*]: No . . . nothing.
GEORGE: All right. [*Pause.*] Time for bed.
MARTHA: Yes.
GEORGE: Are you tired?
MARTHA: Yes.
GEORGE: I am.
MARTHA: Yes.
GEORGE: Sunday tomorrow; all day.
MARTHA: Yes.

> *A long silence between them.*

Did you . . . did you . . . have to?
GEORGE [*pause*]: Yes.
MARTHA: It was . . .? You had to?
GEORGE [*pause*]: Yes.
MARTHA: I don't know.
GEORGE: It was . . . time.
MARTHA: Was it?
GEORGE: Yes.
MARTHA [*pause*]: I'm cold.
GEORGE: It's late.
MARTHA: Yes.
GEORGE [*long silence*]: It will be better.
MARTHA [*long silence*]: I don't . . . know.
GEORGE: It will be . . . maybe.
MARTHA: I'm . . . not . . . sure.
GEORGE: No.
MARTHA: Just . . . us?
GEORGE: Yes.
MARTHA: I don't suppose, maybe, we could . . .
GEORGE: No, Martha.
MARTHA: Yes. No.
GEORGE: Are you all right?
MARTHA: Yes. No.
GEORGE [*puts his hand gently on her shoulder; she puts her head back and he sings to her, very softly*]:

Who's afraid of Virginia Woolf
Virginia Woolf
Virginia Woolf,

MARTHA: I . . . am . . . George. . . .
GEORGE: Who's afraid of Virginia Woolf. . . .
MARTHA: I . . . am . . . George . . . I . . . am. . . .

GEORGE *nods, slowly.*
Silence; tableau.

CURTAIN